KREGEL EXEGETICAL LIBRARY

A COMMENTARY ON
JEREMIAH

MICHAEL B. SHEPHERD

KREGEL ACADEMIC

A Commentary on Jeremiah

© 2023 by Michael B. Shepherd

Published by Kregel Academic, an imprint of Kregel Publications, 2450 Oak Industrial Dr. NE, Grand Rapids, MI 49505-6020.

The English translations of the original Greek or Hebrew texts of the Bible are the author's own.

The Hebrew font used in this book is NewJerusalemU and the Greek font is GraecaU; both are available from www.linguisticsoftware.com/lgku.htm, +1-425-775-1130.

ISBN 978-0-8254-4608-5

Printed in Colombia
23 24 25 26 27 / 5 4 3 2 1

CONTENTS

COMMON ABBREVIATIONS

ANET	*Ancient Near Eastern Texts Relating to the Old Testament*
Aq.	*Aquila*
BDB	*The Brown-Driver-Briggs Hebrew and English Lexicon*
BHS	*Biblia Hebraica Stuttgartensia*
Codex L	*The Leningrad Codex*
DCH	*Dictionary of Classical Hebrew*
GKC	*Gesenius' Hebrew Grammar*
HALOT	*The Hebrew and Aramaic Lexicon of the Old Testament*
LXX	*Septuagint*
MT	*Masoretic Text*
NETS	*New English Translation of the Septuagint*
SP	*Samaritan Pentateuch*
Symm.	*Symmachus*
Syr.	*Syriac Peshitta*
Tg. Jon.	*Targum Jonathan*

COMMON ABBREVIATIONS

Theod.   *Theodotion*

TLOT   *Theological Lexicon of the Old Testament*

Vulg.   *Latin Vulgate*[1]

---

1.   Abbreviations in footnotes can be found in the Bibliography. See also the second edition of *The SBL Handbook of Style*.

INTRODUCTION

Given the plethora of commentaries on biblical books, the publication of a new commentary requires some justification. The present commentary on the book of Jeremiah makes an original contribution to the field in its combination of three features. First, the base text of this commentary is the Hebrew source text behind the Old Greek of Jeremiah. Most commentaries on Jeremiah primarily follow the traditional Hebrew text (the Masoretic Text),[1] yet the growing consensus among textual critics is that the Hebrew source of Greek Jeremiah is the earlier edition.[2] Second, the object of study in the present commentary is the literature that bears the name of the prophet Jeremiah. It is not an account of the life and times of the prophet. It is not an examination of the oral preaching of Jeremiah. It is also not a reconstruction of the literary prehistory of the book. Rather, it is an analysis and exposition of the composition of the book in its final form. Third,

---

1.   Georg Walser's commentary is an exception (*Jeremiah: A Commentary Based on Ieremias in Codex Vaticanus* [Leiden: Brill, 2012]), but it is based on the Greek text, not the Hebrew source text.

2.   See Emanuel Tov, *Textual Criticism of the Hebrew Bible*, 3rd ed. (Minneapolis: Fortress, 2012), 286–94. See also Hermann-Josef Stipp, *Das masoretische und alexandrische Sondergut des Jeremiasbuches*, OBO 136 (Fribourg: Universitätsverlag, 1994). Furthermore, it is this earlier edition that serves as the basis for Ezekiel's interpretation of Jeremiah's enemy from the north (Ezek. 38:14–17) and the interpretation of Jeremiah's prophecy of seventy years in Daniel 9 (see Michael B. Shepherd, *Daniel in the Context of the Hebrew Bible*, StBibLit 123 [New York: Lang, 2009], 39–44, 95–99).

this commentary works with the conviction that the book of Jeremiah was built to last. That is, the eschatological shaping of the book gives it ongoing relevance for future generations of readers. Thus, the task of the commentator is not to "update" the book with contemporary application but to reorient the reader to the perennially relevant concerns of the biblical author. The book itself is fashioned to self-interpret and to self-apply. The interpreter needs only to learn how to follow the clues to its composition.

THE TEXT OF JEREMIAH

The Old Greek translation of Jeremiah is about one-sixth or one-seventh shorter than the Masoretic Text (MT), which is the basis of most modern English translations.[3] The longest continuous passages absent from the Greek are Jeremiah 33:14–26 and 39:4–13. The Old Greek is also in a different arrangement, most notably in the placement of the section on the nations (Jer. 46–51) directly after Jeremiah 25:13 in the following order: 49:34–39; 46:2–28; 50–51; 47; 49:7–22, 1–5, 28–33, 23–27; 48. In the nineteenth century, biblical scholars were divided on the question of whether the major differences in length and arrangement between the Old Greek and the MT were due to the presence of a different Hebrew source text or to the work of the translator.[4] With the discovery of the Dead Sea Scrolls in the twentieth century, it is now generally recognized that the Old Greek of Jeremiah was based on a Hebrew text that differed considerably from the one found in the MT.[5] Furthermore, the literal translation technique of Greek Jeremiah

---

3. An English translation of the Greek may be found in Albert Pietersma and Benjamin G. Wright, eds., *A New English Translation of the Septuagint* (Oxford: Oxford University Press, 2007). The standard critical edition of the Greek text is Joseph Ziegler, ed., *Jeremias, Baruch, Threni, Epistula Jeremiae*, 3rd ed., Septuaginta XV (Göttingen: Vandenhoeck & Ruprecht, 2006).

4. See C. F. Keil, *The Prophecies of Jeremiah*, trans. David Patrick and James Kennedy, Keil & Delitzsch Commentary on the Old Testament 8 (Edinburgh: T&T Clark, 1866–1891; repr., Peabody, MA: Hendrickson, 2001), 21. The problem was noted in the early church by Jerome who argued that the Greek text was "sporadically unreliable, having been corrupted by copyists" (Dean O. Wenthe, ed., *Jeremiah, Lamentations*, ACCS XII [Downers Grove, IL: InterVarsity, 2008], xxiii).

5. But see Georg Fischer, *Jeremiah Studies: From Text and Contexts to Theology*, FAT 139 (Tübingen: Mohr Siebeck, 2020), 41–59. See also Sven Soderlund, *The Greek Text of Jeremiah: A Revised Hypothesis* (Sheffield: JSOT, 1985).

has suggested all along that it would have been highly unlikely for the translator to deviate substantially from his source text.[6]

The book of Jeremiah is thus extant in two distinct editions, which stood in their final forms at the beginning of two separate processes of transmission. The earlier, shorter edition is represented by the Old Greek and by Hebrew fragments of Jeremiah from Qumran that agree with the Old Greek in shortness and arrangement (4QJer[b, d]).[7] The later, longer edition is represented by proto-MT

---

6. "In general, if a certain book is rendered literally, it is not to be assumed that the translator omitted large sections that were found in his *Vorlage*. An alternative explanation of the brevity of the LXX is that the translator worked from a shorter *Hebrew* text. By the same token, if a translation unit is free or even paraphrastic, exegetical omissions (even long ones) may be expected" (Emanuel Tov, *The Text-Critical Use of the Septuagint in Biblical Research*, 3rd ed. [Winona Lake, IN: Eisenbrauns, 2015], 19). Of course, it is possible that the translator may have omitted some text by accident. It is also important to allow for occasional paraphrase or interpretive renderings (or even inner-Greek corruption), but for the most part the major differences in Jeremiah appear to be due to the presence of a different Hebrew source text (see Tov, *Textual Criticism*, 115–27). Along with this comes an important caveat: "even if a retroverted variant bears all the marks of a well-supported reading, *such a reading may never have existed anywhere but in the translator's mind*" (Tov, *Text-Critical Use*, 98). Nevertheless, it is irresponsible to ignore the evidence of the LXX altogether simply because of the presence of this difficulty. As an aside, the present commentary works under the assumption that Greek Jeremiah is the product of a single translator, not two or more. Even the tendency to replace one standard word equivalent with another after LXX chapter 29 can be explained according to the translator's desire to vary his equivalents based on context (see Andrew G. Shead, "The Text of Jeremiah (MT and LXX)," in *The Book of Jeremiah: Composition, Reception, and Interpretation*, eds. Jack R. Lundbom, Craig A. Evans, and Bradford A. Anderson, VTSup 178 [Leiden: Brill, 2018], 261–63). It has been suggested that the books of Jeremiah, Ezekiel, and the Twelve were originally rendered into Greek by the same translator (see Emanuel Tov, "The Septuagint," in *Outside the Bible: Ancient Jewish Writings Related to Scripture*, vol. 1, eds. Louis H. Feldman, James L. Kugel, and Lawrence H. Schiffman [Philadelphia: Jewish Publication Society, 2013], 3).

7. The tendency of ancient scribes was to add text, not to subtract text. Therefore, the shorter text is generally considered the earlier text unless other factors are involved (e.g., *homoioteleuton, homoioarchton*). The Greek and 4QJer[b] do not contain Jer. 10:6–8, 10. In both witnesses the verses in chapter 10 occur in the order 1–5a, 9, 5b, 11–12. The Greek and

13

witnesses from the Dead Sea Scrolls, any early versions based on the proto-MT (the Syriac Peshitta, *Targum Jonathan*, and the Latin Vulgate), and the MT itself.[8] These are not merely two stages in the same literary development of the book, as if the Hebrew text attested by the Old Greek and 4QJer[b, d] were a preliminary form of the composition that continued to mature into the final expression found in the MT. Rather, the first edition was a recognizable final form of the book that stood at the beginning of its own process of transmission, which continued (primarily through the Old Greek translation tradition) beyond the making of the second edition.[9] The second edition

---

4QJer[d] both have the shorter readings in Jer. 43:4–6 (LXX 50:4–6). These Hebrew fragments from Qumran are not to be equated with the *Vorlage* of the Old Greek (i.e., they sometimes agree with the MT against the LXX or have nonaligned readings), but they are very similar to it in significant ways. The Dead Sea Scrolls can be viewed in English in Martin Abegg Jr., Peter Flint, and Eugene Ulrich, *The Dead Sea Scrolls Bible* (San Francisco: Harper San Francisco, 1999). Hebrew transcription is available in Eugene Ulrich, ed., *The Biblical Qumran Scrolls: Transcriptions and Textual Variants* (Leiden: Brill, 2010). 4QJer[a] generally agrees with the MT, although it also has agreements with the LXX against the MT and possesses some nonaligned readings. It has Jeremiah 7:30–8:3 added by a second hand (originally omitted by scribal oversight). 2QJer and 4QJer[c] are generally closer to the MT than to the LXX, although they sometimes agree with the LXX against the MT and sometimes have nonaligned readings. DSS F.Jer 1 (Manuscript Schøyen 4612/9) and DSS F.Jer 2 (Manuscript Museum of the Bible SCR.003172) have readings in Jeremiah 3:15, 19 and Jeremiah 23:8 respectively that agree with the LXX against the MT. The nonaligned readings from the Qumran fragments are probably not enough to posit entire literary stages before, between, or after the two editions represented by the LXX and the MT. By the time of the Dead Sea Scrolls, it is probably better to think of scribal adjustment of Hebrew manuscripts based on knowledge of the two existing Hebrew editions and other factors. For a full discussion of the Qumran witnesses, see Armin Lange, "Texts of Jeremiah in the Qumran Library," in *The Book of Jeremiah: Composition, Reception, and Interpretation*, eds. Jack R. Lundbom, Craig A. Evans, and Bradford A. Anderson, VTSup 178 (Leiden: Brill, 2018), 280–302.

8. The proto-MT is the consonantal framework of the MT prior to the addition of vowel pointing, accents, and marginal notes.

9. Following the events of the first century AD, the Jewish Old Greek translation of Jeremiah was preserved in the Christian community. Rabbinic Judaism adopted the proto-MT as its standard text. The Qumran community responsible for 4QJer[b, d] did not survive the first century. Given

represents a punctuation in the transmission process of the first edition that produced a systematic and comprehensive layer of revision, creating the head of a completely separate stream of transmission known as the history of the MT.[10]

It is important to note that the second edition of the book is not simply a collection of disparate textual variants to the first edition. It is the product of consistent editing across the whole. Emanuel Tov has provided a helpful list of editorial (addition of headings, repetition of sections, addition of new verses and sections, addition of new details, free rewriting), exegetical (clarification, homogenizing additions, contextual clarifications, amplified formulas), and other aspects (peculiar words and expressions, resumptive repetition; tendencies: the guilt of the nation, the centrality of God, actualization, priestly subjects, fulfillment of prophecy) that define the nature of the added layer of the

---

the tradition of the origin of the Septuagint in Alexandria, Egypt (*Letter of Aristeas*), it has been suggested that the Hebrew form of Jeremiah behind its Greek translation had its beginnings in Egypt (see Jer. 43–44), while the MT form is linked to Babylon and Palestine. It must be said, however, that both forms are attested from the same time and place among the Dead Sea Scrolls.

10. John Van Seters has objected to the use of terms such as "edition" and "editor" to describe the biblical literature and those who produced it as anachronistic (*The Edited Bible: The Curious History of the "Editor" in Biblical Criticism* [Winona Lake, IN: Eisenbrauns, 2006]). Van Seters rightly insists that the biblical compositions are the products of authors/composers. Nevertheless, as Joel Baden has noted in his review of Van Seters (*JNES* 68, no. 2 [2009]: 129–31), it is one thing to object to the use of certain terms, but it is quite another to object to the ideas attached to them. With regard to Jeremiah, Van Seters prefers William McKane's proposal of a "rolling corpus" as advocated in his two-volume commentary in the International Critical Commentary series. According to McKane, the MT does not represent a systematic revision of the LXX *Vorlage*. Rather, it is the result of many small-scale scribal additions and adjustments accrued over time in the process of transmission. The problem with this view is that there is very little extant textual evidence for the supposed intermediary stages of development between the LXX *Vorlage* and the MT. The consistency with which the same kinds of additions and adjustments are made throughout MT Jeremiah argues against a rolling corpus (see J. Gerald Janzen, *Studies in the Text of Jeremiah*, HSM 6 [Cambridge, MA: Harvard University Press, 1973]). McKane's analysis at the microlevel is brilliant, but his lack of conception of the book as a whole does not position him very well to see that two different versions of the same book with two very distinct messages have been produced.

second edition.[11] The material found in this layer should not inform the textual critic's establishment of the text of the first edition. Of course, textual variants in the second edition found outside the added layer may contribute to an understanding of the text of the first edition.[12]

It is often said that the major changes from the first edition of Jeremiah to the second do not substantially affect the book's theological message.[13] This is not quite correct. The changes affect the reading of the book in at least two very important ways. In the first edition, the mysterious enemy from the north (Jer. 1:13–15; LXX 25:1–13; et al.) is never identified with a historical enemy. This leaves open the possibility of an eschatological enemy, which is the way Ezekiel reads the prophecy (Ezek. 38:14–17; cf. LXX Num. 24:7; Rev. 20:8). In the

---

11. Emanuel Tov, *The Greek and Hebrew Bible: Collected Essays on the Septuagint* (Atlanta: SBL, 2006), 365–83. It has been observed that the first edition contains similar features (e.g., headings [Jer. 46:2, 13; 49:28, 34]). This might suggest to some that the two extant versions of the book represent two moments in one larger stream of tradition with still earlier, shorter versions prior to the extant versions and with incrementally larger versions between the extant versions (see, e.g., Justus Theodore Ghormley, "Scribal Revision: A Post-Qumran Perspective on the Formation of Jeremiah," *Textus* 27 [2018]: 161–86). This is all very hypothetical. There is no a priori reason why the original final form of the book must lack editorial/authorial and exegetical features. The situation is not unlike the transmission history of the book of Psalms. Greek tradition has additional psalm superscriptions compared to what is found in Hebrew witnesses. Thus, scholars typically presuppose a trajectory that goes back to a time when none of the psalms had a superscription. Nevertheless, there is no textual witness to the book of Psalms that completely lacks superscriptions. A purely text-critical approach would evaluate the merits of each reading on a case-by-case basis. Regarding Jeremiah, the task is to explain the extant texts, not texts that do not exist.

12. "But again, texts and their variants have a rich life, and individual variants can and do cross the boundaries between variant editions. Thus those who say simply that texts exhibiting different editions should not be used to correct individual variants in the other begin with a good premise but are also likely to be mistaken as often as they are correct" (Eugene Ulrich, *The Dead Sea Scrolls and the Origins of the Bible* [Grand Rapids: Eerdmans, 1999], 110).

13. E.g., "Apart from the certainly remarkable different positioning of the oracles to the nations, however, the LXX version does not present any notable differences in content by comparison with the Hebrew" (Rolf Rendtorff, *The Canonical Hebrew Bible: A Theology of the Old Testament*, trans. David E. Orton [Leiden: Deo, 2005], 203).

second edition, the enemy from the north is identified with Babylon (e.g., MT Jer. 25:1–13).[14] This becomes an internal problem for the MT in Jeremiah 50:3 where it is anticipated that the enemy from the north will come against Babylon.[15] Second, in the first edition of the book, Jeremiah's prophecy of seventy years (Jer. 25:11; 29:10) is understood in two different ways. In Jeremiah 29:10, Jeremiah is writing to the exiles in Babylon and encouraging them to submit to Babylonian authority, to accept God's just judgment, and to await restoration at the end of a literal period of seventy years. This is the way Daniel understands the prophecy in Daniel 9:1–19. In the Hebrew text behind the Old Greek of Jeremiah 25:1–13 (see Jer. 25:11), there is no reference to Babylon in the prophecy of seventy years, leaving open the possibility that the number seventy is symbolic of a complete, indefinite period (cf. Gen. 4:24; Matt. 18:22). This is the way Gabriel interprets the prophecy in Daniel 9:24–27 ("seventy sevens"). Thus, the historical return from Babylon prefigures an eschatological restoration. On the other hand, the MT (i.e., the second edition) of Jeremiah 25:11 limits the prophecy to a historical fulfillment when it identifies the enemy from the north as Babylon. To summarize, the first edition of Jeremiah (Old Greek, 4QJer[b, d]) is not only the earlier, shorter edition but also the open-ended, potentially eschatological edition read by Ezekiel and Daniel.[16] The second edition of the book

---

14. The tendency of ancient scribes was to add historical information to help their readers, but where the original intent was to leave the text open ended, the addition of historical information obscured the meaning. One such example of this occurs in Numbers 24:7. Where the Hebrew text behind the LXX refers to an unidentified, eschatological enemy named "Gog" (see the Samaritan Pentateuch; cf. Ezek. 38–39; Rev. 20:8), the MT refers to the historical Amalekite king "Agag" in 1 Samuel 15.

15. This is usually thought to be the Medes (Jer. 51:11, 28; cf. Isa. 13:17; Dan. 5:28), but the Medes are never explicitly identified as the enemy from the north. Both Babylon and Media are to the east in relation to Israel. This problem is typically resolved by explaining that a nation from the east like Babylon would attack the land of Israel from the north (see Ezek. 21:25 [Eng., 21:20]; 26:7), although it is also important to note that the coalition of kings led by Chedorlaomer in Genesis 14 entered from the south and departed northward.

16. This feature of the first edition's content can also be seen in the placement and arrangement of the nations section after Jeremiah 25:13. The first (Jer. 49:34–39) and last (Jer. 48) units conclude with the phrase "at the end of the days" (Jer. 49:39; 48:47), framing the nations oracles as images of eschatological events. The absence of Jeremiah 48:45–47 in the

(MT) is not only the later, longer, and rearranged edition but also the historicized edition.[17]

A biblical doctrine of inspiration (2 Tim. 3:14–17; 2 Pet. 1:19–21), not to mention the exigencies of making a translation and commentary, requires a careful text-critical decision about which edition of Jeremiah is God-breathed and superintended by the Spirit. The present commentary follows the original edition of the book attested by the Old Greek and 4QJer[b, d] while keeping a close eye on the MT and other witnesses for additional help with the text and its early history of interpretation. A full presentation of the Hebrew *Vorlage* (source text) of Greek Jeremiah based on Joseph's Ziegler's critical edition in the Göttingen Septuagint series is available for the first time at the end of this volume.[18]

THE MAKING OF THE BOOK OF JEREMIAH

Bernhard Duhm and Sigmund Mowinckel articulated the position of classic historical-critical scholarship by identifying the presence of three basic strata in the book of Jeremiah: (1) the authentic words of Jeremiah found largely in the poetry of Jeremiah 1:1–25:13; (2) the historical-biographical material of Baruch found mostly in the prose of Jeremiah 26–45; and (3) the "sermonic" prose of the book's Deuteronomistic redaction (parts of Jer. 7:1–8:3; 11; 14; 18; 21; 25; 26; 32; 34; 40; 44).[19] According to John Bright, the so-called confessions of

---

Old Greek is due to *homoioteleuton* (Jer. 48:44b, 47a). Such framing has influenced the frequent allusion to Jeremiah 50–51 in Revelation 17–18. See commentary for further details.

17. This feature of the second edition's content can be seen in its placement and arrangement of the nations section at the end of the book (Jer. 46–51) prior to the appendix in Jeremiah 52. The arrangement follows the list of nations in Jeremiah 25:15–26 to whom the cup of judgment passes, culminating with Babylon. Thus, the book concludes in Jeremiah 50–51 with the main historical interest of this edition—Babylon.

18. See also Louis Stulman's backtranslation of the prose sections of Greek Jeremiah, *The Other Text of Jeremiah: A Reconstruction of the Hebrew Text Underlying the Greek Version of the Prose Sections of Jeremiah with English Translation* (Lanham, MD: University Press of America, 1986).

19. Bernhard Duhm, *Das Buch Jeremia*, KHC 11 (Tübingen: Mohr Siebeck, 1901); Sigmund Mowinckel, *Zur Komposition des Buches Jeremia* (Kristiana: Dybwad, 1914). See Otto Eissfeldt, *The Old Testament: An Introduction*, trans. Peter R. Ackroyd (New York: Harper and Row, 1965), 348–65. See also William L. Holladay, *Jeremiah 2: A Commentary on the Book of the Prophet Jeremiah Chapters 26–52*, Hermeneia (Minneapolis: Fortress, 1989), 10–95. There was also a D source, which consisted of Jeremiah 30–31.

Jeremiah located in Jeremiah 11–20 are "as close an approximation as is possible of the prophet's *ipsissima verba*,"[20] while the Deuteronomic prose discourses are the prophet's preaching "as it was remembered, understood, and repeated in the circle of his followers."[21] For Bright, the contrast between the Jeremiah of the poetry and the Jeremiah of the prose has been greatly exaggerated, and he suggests the unlikelihood of a major distortion of his message during the lifetime of his associates.

The above modern critical analysis in its various manifestations has unfortunately not led to a better understanding of the book in its entirety. In fact, the book's lack of storyline and chronological arrangement has left many interpreters with the impression that it is little more than a disorganized anthology of reminiscences that provides a rather imperfect window into the past. To say the least, there is certainly a void when it comes to explanation of how the book has been able to function coherently as Scripture down through the ages in the context of the Hebrew canon.[22] Form-critical analysis has provided a helpful way to categorize prophetic oracles at the microlevel, but the goal of such analysis has traditionally been the *Sitz im Leben* ("setting in life").[23] The "new" form criticism seeks rather to investigate the prophetic literature as the primary object of study in its own right—the *Sitz im Text* ("setting in the text").[24] This paves the way for analysis of

---

20. John Bright, *Jeremiah*, AB (Garden City, NY: Doubleday, 1965), lxix.
21. Bright, *Jeremiah*, lxxii. Cf. Isa. 8:16. Leslie Allen compares this to the making of the NT Gospels: "Each Gospel possesses its own interpretive framework; its contents are nuanced differently, addressing the particular needs of the Christian community for which it was written. Each is a product of a later generation than the time of the scenes it narrates. Each Gospel shapes the Jesus tradition in its own way ('the Gospel according to . . .'), as it takes over and develops earlier oral and written records. Inspiration lies in the Gospels at the book level, despite the red type used in some Bibles to highlight words attributed to Jesus" (*Jeremiah: A Commentary*, OTL [Louisville: Westminster John Knox, 2008], 7).
22. Biblical scholars have now largely abandoned the classic critical view of the book in favor of various redactional theories or more holistic approaches.
23. See Claus Westermann, *Basic Forms of Prophetic Speech*, trans. Hugh Clayton White (Philadelphia: Westminster, 1967; repr., Louisville: Westminster John Knox, 1991).
24. See Michael H. Floyd, "New Form Criticism and Beyond: The Historicity of Prophetic Literature Revisited," in *The Book of the Twelve and the New Form Criticism*, eds. Mark J. Boda, Michael H. Floyd, and Colin M. Toffelmire (Atlanta: SBL, 2015), 17–36.

compositional strategy at the macrolevel and recognition of the hermeneutical features of the prophetic books that have exerted such a powerful influence on readers both ancient and modern and enabled the texts to remain relevant to the present and the future.[25] The prophetic books are composite yet unified.[26] Techniques employed to unify the prophetic compositions include, for example, the use of programmatic passages (e.g., Isa. 2:1–5; Jer. 1:10; Hos. 3:4–5), macrostructural framing (e.g., Isa. 1:1–2:5; 65–66),[27] seam work (e.g., the Book of the Twelve),[28] parallels (e.g., Jer. 7 and 26; 39 and 52), and repetition (e.g., the recognition formula in Ezekiel).

The way the book of Jeremiah presents itself is the way it is intended to be read. This must be respected even if the critic reconstructs a different reality. Thus, if the book presents itself as the product of Jeremiah and Baruch reading the Torah through the lens of Deuteronomy (see Deut. 1:5) in conversation with the larger context of the canon, then this meaning must be recognized as the book's intended design. For the present commentary, no distinction is made between the book's presentation and reality. On the surface, the first edition of the book attested by

---

25. Those responsible for this literature "redefined prophecy in terms of the records of past revelations rather than oracles currently being spoken, and they reshaped the prophetic tradition by delimiting the prophets and oracles that make up the prophetic canon. In the way that they integrated interpretive commentary with the oracle collections that provided the raw material for the prophetic books, they also modeled and thus defined the right way of interpreting this canon" (Floyd, "New Form Criticism and Beyond," 30). According to Karel van der Toorn, these "scribes" (e.g., Baruch) were the "new prophets" (see LXX Prov. 29:18) (*Scribal Culture and the Making of the Hebrew Bible* [Cambridge, MA: Harvard University Press, 2007], 107, 169, 173–204). See Joseph Blenkinsopp, *Prophecy and Canon: A Contribution to the Study of Jewish Origins* (Notre Dame, IN: University of Notre Dame Press, 1977), 128–29. See also Allen, *Jeremiah*, 14–18.

26. "In my view, Jeremiah is the work of 'one mind,' intended exactly in this way with all its complexity and 'irregularities'" (Fischer, *Jeremiah Studies*, 12). For this view of authorship and composition, see S. R. Driver, *An Introduction to the Literature of the Old Testament* (New York: Charles Scribner's Sons, 1891), xi; Jeffrey H. Tigay, *The Evolution of the Gilgamesh Epic* (Philadelphia: University of Pennsylvania Press, 1982; repr., Wauconda, IL: Bolchazy-Carducci, 2002), 42.

27. See Brevard S. Childs, *Isaiah: A Commentary*, OTL (Louisville: Westminster John Knox, 2000), 542–47.

28. See Michael B. Shepherd, *A Commentary on the Book of the Twelve: The Minor Prophets*, KEL (Grand Rapids: Kregel Academic, 2018), 23–36.

the Old Greek follows the basic judgment (Jer. 1:1–25:13)–nations (Jer. 49:34–39; 46:2–28; 50–51; 47; 49:7–22, 1–5, 28–33, 23–27; 48)–restoration (Jer. 30–33) pattern known to readers of other prophetic books.[29] The opening of the book (Jer. 1:1–2:13) introduces the prophet (Jer. 1:4–9), the program (Jer. 1:10), and the major themes to be developed (divine faithfulness, the enemy from the north, idolatry, opposition, divine presence [Jer. 1:11–19]) and sets them firmly within the context of the biblical narrative (Jer. 2:2–13). The book's appended conclusion (Jer. 52) not only complements the account of the Babylonian invasion in Jeremiah 39 but also points the reader forward in a manner not unlike its parallel at the end of the book of Kings (2 Kgs. 25). The broad division of the book into poetry (Jer. 1–25) and prose (Jer. 26–45) sets up a mutual relationship between Jeremiah's words, which interpret the events, and the narratives that provide a context for his words. Thus, for example, Jeremiah's speech at the temple gate in chapter 7 receives its counterpart in the narrative of the response to the speech in chapter 26. The narrative of the fulfillment of Jeremiah's historical prophecies in chapters 34–44 serves as a down payment on the fulfillment of Jeremiah's eschatological prophecies (e.g., Jer. 30–31).

Beyond this it is necessary to look within the book for signals and specific clues to its composition. The opening superscription (Jer. 1:1–3) marks the entire book as "The word of God that came to Jeremiah" (MT: "The words of Jeremiah . . . to whom the word of the LORD came"; cf. MT Jer. 51:64b) and indicates the span of the prophet's ministry. The next major macrostructural marker occurs in Jeremiah 25:13: "all that is written in this book." This closing note clearly delineates the "book" (*sēfer*) of Jeremiah.[30] Immediately following the conclusion to Jeremiah's book is the heading to the nations section: "That which Jeremiah prophesied concerning the nations."[31] According to the

---

29. E.g., Isaiah: judgment (Isa. 1–12), nations (Isa. 13–23), and restoration (Isa. 40–66); Ezekiel: judgment (Ezek. 4–24), nations (Ezek. 25–32), and restoration (Ezek. 34–39); Zephaniah: judgment (Zeph. 1:1–2:3), nations (Zeph. 2:4–15); and restoration (Zeph. 3:9–20).

30. See commentary for discussion of whether this refers to what precedes or to what follows. The term *sēfer* in biblical Hebrew means "document" and can refer to a smaller document such as a letter or a deed (e.g., Jer. 29:1; 32:10–15), but it can also refer to a larger literary work on a "scroll" (*megillah*). It does not refer to a bound codex or book.

31. The MT takes this relative clause with what precedes rather than as a heading for what follows. It then adds the material in Jeremiah 25:14 and continues with the passage about the cup of judgment in Jeremiah 25:15–26.

Vorlage of the Old Greek, this introduces a collection of oracles that begins with Elam (Jer. 49:34–39; 46:2–28; 50–51; 47; 49:7–22, 1–5, 28–33, 23–27; 48).[32] The material in Jeremiah 25:15–29:32 between the nations corpus and the book in Jeremiah 30–33 does not have a formal introduction or conclusion. Its boundaries are marked by the clearly delineated sections that precede and follow.

The next "book" (*sēfer*) is the one Jeremiah is instructed by the LORD to write or to have written in Jeremiah 30:2: "Write for yourself all the words that I have spoken to you in a book." This book is known as the Book of Comfort (or Consolation) because it contains the highest concentration of words of restoration. It is possible that this book only consisted of the poetic material in Jeremiah 30–31 at one time, but it now features the prose material in Jeremiah 32–33 as well. It is also possible that the message of hope once had a life of its own and only applied to the immediate return from Babylon in the latter part of the sixth century BC, but now within the larger context of the composition of Jeremiah these words of future deliverance are thoroughly eschatological.[33] The final section of substantial size then appears in chapters 34–44. This section is primarily prose and divided into subunits by its use of the heading, "The word that came to Jeremiah from the LORD" (Jer. 34:1, 8; 35:1; 40:1; 44:1; cf. MT 36:1b; see also Jer. 34:12; 35:12; 36:27; 37:6; 39:15; 42:7; 43:8).[34]

The very brief chapter 45 is the word or message that Jeremiah spoke to his scribe Baruch. It is thus a scribal colophon that concludes the main body of the book. The use of colophons to conclude sections (e.g., Lev. 7:37–38) and books (e.g., Eccl. 12:9–14; Rom. 16:22) is well attested in biblical literature.[35] This may also be compared to the presence

---

32. Within the nations section there is a reference to a "book" (*sēfer*) in which Jeremiah wrote or had written all the calamity that would come to Babylon, namely, all the words written in Jeremiah 50–51 (Jer. 51:60). Seraiah was to take this book to Babylon and read it publicly (Jer. 51:61–62). Upon completion of this reading, he was to bind a stone to it and cast it in the Euphrates as a sign that Babylon would sink and not rise (Jer. 51:63–64).

33. "The promises have thus been loosened from their original historical moorings and given a fully eschatological function. Both Israel and Judah—and every successive generation of God's people—live from this same promise of divine faithfulness" (Brevard S. Childs, *Introduction to the Old Testament as Scripture* [Philadelphia: Fortress, 1979], 351).

34. This heading also occurs earlier in the book (Jer. 7:1; 11:1; 18:1; 21:1; 30:1; 32:1).

35. See Michael Fishbane, *Biblical Interpretation in Ancient Israel* (Oxford: Clarendon, 1985), 27–32.

of introductory and concluding notices in later codices from the scribes who produced them. For instance, the oldest complete manuscript of the Hebrew Bible is the Leningrad Codex (c. AD 1008). This manuscript begins with a colophon from its scribe, Samuel ben Jacob, and includes information about the manuscript such as its date and city of origin (Cairo). The scribe's name also appears in two of the carpet pages (ff. 474r and 479r) toward the end of the manuscript between the Masoretic lists and again at the very end with an appended poem written by the scribe (f. 491r). For the book of Jeremiah, the presence of a scribal colophon in chapter 45 means that the following final chapter, Jeremiah 52, is rightly labeled an appendix, even though it is now an integral part of the book's composition. Even the MT, which rearranges the nations corpus and moves it from its original location after Jeremiah 25:13 to its position between chapters 45 and 52 (MT Jer. 46–51), thus obliterating the role of chapter 45 as a scribal colophon, still recognizes the need to set chapter 52 apart and adds at the end of Jer. 51:64: "up to here are the words of Jeremiah" (> Old Greek; cf. MT Jer. 1:1). This raises the question of who appended chapter 52—Jeremiah himself, Baruch, or someone else. Given the intriguing relationship between this chapter and 2 Kings 25 (see also 2 Chr. 36), it is possible that its inclusion is owed to someone like Ezra (Ezra 7:6, 10), who fitted Jeremiah's book to the larger context of the received biblical canon.[36]

Perhaps more than any other biblical book, the book of Jeremiah bears witness to its own process of composition. This is nowhere more the case than in the story of Jeremiah 36. According to this story, Jeremiah receives divine instruction in the fourth year of Jehoiakim

---

36. Comparable to this are the added conclusions to the Pentateuch (Deut. 34:5–12) and the Prophets (Mal. 3:22–24 [Eng., 4:4–6]) divisions of the canon (see Blenkinsopp, *Prophecy and Canon*, 85–89, 120–23; John H. Sailhamer, *Introduction to Old Testament Theology: A Canonical Approach* [Grand Rapids: Zondervan, 1995], 239–52). The death account of Moses is traditionally not attributed to Moses but to Joshua (*b. B. Bat.* 14b), yet the perspective is that of someone like Ezra in the postexilic period looking back over the history of Israel's prophets ("And never again did a prophet arise in Israel like Moses" [Deut. 34:10a; see Deut. 18:15, 18]). The last three verses of Malachi are appended to the book and do not form part of the six disputations that constitute the book's main body. They look back to the Torah of Moses and anticipate the coming of a prophet like Elijah who will prepare the way of the LORD (see Mal. 3:1). It is noteworthy then that both texts are followed at the beginning of the canonical divisions (as in Luke 24:44) that come after them by unique texts identical to one another (Josh. 1:8; Ps. 1:2).

to take a scroll and write in it all the words that the LORD has spoken to him since the days of Josiah in the hope that the people will hear of the impending calamity and repent (Jer. 36:1–3). Jeremiah then summons his scribe Baruch, who writes the words at Jeremiah's dictation (Jer. 36:4). Jeremiah is not allowed to enter the temple (see Jer. 7; 26), so he instructs Baruch to give the public reading of the scroll (Jer. 36:5–7). When Baruch reads the scroll, Micaiah reports it to the officials (Jer. 36:9–13), who then request Baruch to read the scroll to them (Jer. 36:14–15). When they hear the content of the scroll, they advise Baruch and Jeremiah to go into hiding before it is read to the king (Jer. 36:16–19). The officials initially report the words of the scroll to the king, while the scroll itself remains in safekeeping (Jer. 36:20), but the king sends Jehudi to take the scroll, and Jehudi reads the scroll before the king and his officials (Jer. 36:21). As Jehudi reads three or four columns of text at a time, the scroll is torn with a scribe's knife and thrown into the fire until it is destroyed in its entirety, despite the objection of some (Jer. 36:22–23, 25). Jehoiakim does not respond to the reading with the tearing of his clothes in the manner of the response of his father Josiah to the reading of the Torah (Jer. 36:24; cf. 2 Kgs. 22:11), but he does order the arrest of Baruch and Jeremiah, who are in hiding (Jer. 36:26). Jeremiah then receives instruction to have the scroll rewritten (Jer. 36:27–28); when the scroll is rewritten, many words are added to the original (Jer. 36:32).

The story is remarkable here for at least three reasons: the content of the scroll, the making of the scroll, and the remaking of the scroll. It is generally agreed that the content of the original scroll consisted of material from Jeremiah 1:1–25:13 to some extent. This is because the message of judgment most closely matches that section (Jer. 36:3, 29–31; cf. Jer. 20:4–5; 22:18–19; 25:5). Within the final form of the book of Jeremiah, the scroll of the book in Jeremiah 36:2, 4 is the "book" of Jeremiah in 25:13b, if indeed 25:13b refers to what precedes. The account of the making of the scroll is clearly outlined: (1) Jeremiah collects words received from the LORD over the course of his prophetic ministry; (2) Jeremiah dictates these words to his scribe Baruch; and (3) Baruch gives these words their textual form. It is difficult to overstate the role of Baruch in this. He not only textualizes the prophecy, but he also "performs" the text in its public reading. In the remaking of the scroll, the added words are not to be thought of as a mere expansion of an earlier version of Jeremiah 1:1–25:13, nor are they a reference to the making of the second edition of the book. Within the final form of the book of Jeremiah, this speaks of the growth of the book beyond the boundaries of

Jeremiah 1:1–25:13.[37] The scribal colophon in Jeremiah 45 likely stood at the end of Jeremiah 1:1–25:13 at one time (see Jer. 25:1; 36:1; 45:1).[38] As the nations section, the Book of Comfort, and the material in Jeremiah 34–44 were added, the colophon would move to occupy the final position until the addition of the appendix in chapter 52.

JEREMIAH IN THE CONTEXT OF THE CANON

The book of Jeremiah was not created in a literary vacuum. It was created in the context of an emerging canon as a work that not only cited other biblical literature but also was itself cited among the biblical books.[39] This was the way the book of Jeremiah was received and understood by those who gave the biblical books their final shape. They composed and arranged the books in light of one another in order to form a coherent and unified body of literature.[40] Thus, the Prophets received Moses, but they also transmitted Moses (e.g., 2 Kgs. 17:13;

---

37. "The book of Jeremiah is like an old English country house, originally built and then added to in the Regency period, augmented with Victorian wings, and generally refurbished throughout the Edwardian years. It grew over a long period of time" (Allen, *Jeremiah*, 11).

38. See Holladay, *Jeremiah 2*, 308–9.

39. Holladay, *Jeremiah*, 35–95; Benjamin D. Sommer, *A Prophet Reads Scripture: Allusion in Isaiah 40–66* (Stanford, CA: Stanford University Press, 1998), 61–66. See also Christopher R. Seitz, *The Goodly Fellowship of the Prophets: The Achievement of Association in Canon Formation* (Grand Rapids: Baker, 2009).

40. "The reception of the authoritative tradition by its hearers gave shape to the same writings through a historical and theological process of selecting, collecting, and ordering. The formation of the canon was not a late extrinsic validation of a corpus of writings, but involved a series of decisions deeply affecting the shape of the books" (Childs, *Introduction to the Old Testament as Scripture*, 59). "The reuse and reapplication of previous writings within biblical tradition argues for an implicit understanding of canonicity; also . . . the editors of the biblical canon have intentionally inserted specific indications of reshaped existing literary junctures in order to interpret the various parts of the biblical canon in light of the whole" (Stephen B. Chapman, *The Law and the Prophets: A Study in Old Testament Canon Formation*, FAT 27 [Tübingen: Mohr Siebeck, 2000], 105). See also the helpful discussion in Julius Steinberg and Timothy J. Stone, "The Historical Formation of the Writings in Antiquity," in *The Shape of the Writings*, eds. Julius Steinberg and Timothy J. Stone (Winona Lake, IN: Eisenbrauns, 2015), 4–35.

Jer. 26:4–5; Dan. 9:10; Ezra 9:10–11).[41] Likewise, the Prophets show an awareness of one another (e.g., Ezek. 38:17; Zech. 1:4–6; 7:7, 12), and the Writings are in dialogue with both Moses and the Prophets (e.g., Ps. 1; Dan. 9:2; Neh. 8–9; Chr.). It is precisely in this way that the Hebrew Bible is built to interpret itself and to maintain its relevance.[42]

Jeremiah falls within the Prophets division of the Hebrew Bible (see Dan. 9:2), which is the second of three divisions known as the Tanakh (see Zech. 7:12): [T]orah (Gen.–Deut.), [N]eviim (Former Prophets [*b. Sotah* 48b]: Josh.-Judg.-Sam.-Kgs.; Latter Prophets: Isa.-Jer.-Ezek.-Twelve [Hos.–Mal.]), and [K]etuvim or Writings (Ps.-Job-Prov.; the Megilloth: Ruth-Song-Eccl.-Lam.-Est.; Dan.-Ez./Neh.-Chr.). All direct witnesses to the Hebrew Bible attest to this basic threefold

---

41. Transmission of Moses was originally entrusted to the priests (Deut. 31:9), but their failure to uphold this responsibility is evident in the story of 2 Kings 22. "The prophets were aware of the meaning of the Pentateuch through their own reading and study of it. As a result of that, they helped to preserve it by producing a new 'prophetic edition' of the Pentateuch based on their understanding of Mosaic law. This is the 'canonical Pentateuch' in our Bible today. Further evidence of the 'prophetic update of the Penta-teuch' is found in some early texts and versions" (John H. Sailhamer, *The Meaning of the Pentateuch: Revelation, Composition, and Interpretation* [Downers Grove, IL: InterVarsity, 2009], 14). "The act of quotation sets in motion a hermeneutical dynamic by which the quoted and the quoting text mutually interpret each other" (Richard L. Schultz, *The Search for Quotation: Verbal Parallels in the Prophets*, JSOTSupp 180 [Sheffield: Sheffield Academic, 1999], 198).

42. "The Bible, despite its textual heterogeneity, can be read as a self-glossing book. One learns to study it by following the ways in which one portion of the text illumines another. The generations of scribes who shaped and reshaped the Scriptures appear to have designed them to be studied in just this way. Thus Brevard S. Childs speaks of 'the interpretive structure which the biblical text has received from those who formed and used it as sacred scripture' . . . ; rather it means that the parts are made to relate to one another reflexively, with later texts, for example, throwing light on the earlier, even as they themselves always stand in the light of what precedes and follows them" (Gerald Bruns, "Midrash and Allegory," in *The Literary Guide to the Bible*, eds. Frank Kermode and Robert Alter [Cambridge, MA: Belknap, 1987], 626–27). "Also, within the canon, in the final versions of the prophetic books, material that is not contemporary again becomes con-temporary material in a higher sense for all later generations who wish to orient themselves toward the Bible" (Odil Hannes Steck, *The Prophetic Books and Their Theological Witness*, trans. James D. Nogalski [St. Louis: Chalice, 2000], 186).

shape (e.g., Prol. Sir.; 4QMMT; Luke 24:44; Philo *Contempl.* 1f., 25; *b. B. Bat.* 14b–15a; Codex B19ᵃ), although there is some variation in the order of books within the Latter Prophets and particularly in the Writings.[43] The Writings division need not concern the present discussion. It is enough to say that there is good evidence for Psalms at the beginning (4QMMT; Luke 24:44; *Contempl.* 1f., 25) and Chronicles at the end (Matt. 23:35; *b. B. Bat.* 14b).[44] As for the Latter Prophets, there

---

43. With the exception of Jerome who follows the tripartite structure of the Hebrew canon, early Christian authors who provide lists of canonical books do not require a specific order of books (see E. Earle Ellis, "The Old Testament Canon in the Early Church," in *Mikra: Text, Translation, Reading, and Interpretation of the Hebrew Bible in Ancient Judaism and Early Christianity*, eds. Martin Jan Mulder and Harry Sysling [Philadelphia: Fortress, 1988; repr., Peabody, MA: Hendrickson, 2004], 653–90). They seem more concerned to indicate what books are in the canon than to argue for a particular arrangement. The great fourth- and fifth-century codices of the Greek Bible (Vaticanus, Sinaiticus, and Alexandrinus), which vary in their presentation, do not make claims either explicitly or implicitly about what books are to be included or in what order they are to appear. They are best understood "more as service books than as a defined and normative canon of scripture" (Ellis, "Old Testament Canon," 678). The earliest reference to Greek translation speaks of translation of the threefold shape of the Hebrew Bible (Prol. Sir.). Thus, inclusion of apocryphal books says very little about the extent of the canon ("there is no evidence whatever that any of the Apocrypha ever had a place in any of the three divisions of the canon" [Roger T. Beckwith, "Formation of the Hebrew Bible," in *Mikra*, 83–84]). Likewise, separation of the Former and Latter Prophets in Vaticanus and its placement of the Latter Prophets at the end of the "Old Testament" in the order of The Book of the Twelve, Isaiah, Jeremiah-Baruch-Lamentations-Epistle of Jeremiah, Ezekiel, and Daniel-Susanna-Bel and the Dragon are of little consequence as a historical witness to the shaping of the Hebrew Bible. Even later translation traditions within Christianity that follow the placement of the Latter Prophets at the end do not follow the extent and order of these books in Vaticanus. The placement of the Latter Prophets in these traditions appears due to what was received rather than to conscious reflection on composition at the canonical level. On the other hand, Hebrew tradition presses readers to follow internal clues to composition beyond the book level.

44. See Hendrik J. Koorevar, "Chronicles as the Intended Conclusion to the Old Testament Canon" and Georg Steins, "Torah-Binding and Canon Closure: On the Origin and Canonical Function of the Book of Chronicles," in *Shape of the Writings*, 207–35, 237–80. For the Psalms-Job sequence, see Will Kynes, "Reading Job Following the Psalms," in *Shape of the Writings*, 131–45. Job then provides an important canonical context

are two competing orders within Hebrew tradition.[45] The oldest and most common is the order found in Sirach 48–49, the Aleppo Codex, the Cairo Codex, and the Leningrad Codex among others: Isaiah, Jeremiah, Ezekiel, and the Twelve.[46] This puts the Prophets in the chronological order of the prophets with whom the books are associated (with the Book of the Twelve on the end spanning from preexilic to postexilic prophecy). The other order is somewhat anomalous and is found in the Babylonian Talmud: Jeremiah, Ezekiel, Isaiah, and the Twelve (*b. B. Bat.* 14b). The rationale given for this order is driven by the connection with the preceding book of Kings, which the Talmud believes to be written by Jeremiah (*b. B. Bat.* 15a): "Since the end of the book of Kings is about the destruction, and Jeremiah is wholly devoted to destruction, and Ezekiel starts off with destruction but ends up with consolation, while Isaiah is wholly consolation, we locate destruction adjacent to destruction, consolation to consolation."[47]

This commentary will keep a close eye on the intertextual relationships that the book of Jeremiah has with other books in the biblical canon.[48] Jeremiah's use of the language and theology of Deuteronomy

---

for reading Proverbs (see Tremper Longman III, *Proverbs*, BCOT [Grand Rapids: Baker, 2006], 61–63). For the Megilloth and Daniel-Ezra/Nehemiah-Chronicles, see Steinberg and Stone, "The Historical Formation of the Writings in Antiquity," 49–51; Shepherd, *Daniel in the Context of the Hebrew Bible*, 1–7, 59–61, 67–68; John H. Sailhamer, "Biblical Theology and the Composition of the Hebrew Bible," in *Biblical Theology: Retrospect and Prospect*, ed. Scott J. Hafemann (Downers Grove, IL: InterVarsity, 2002), 25–37.

45. The placement of Lamentations after Jeremiah, and Daniel after Ezekiel (e.g., Vaticanus), is not a feature of Hebrew tradition. Both Lamentations and Daniel are among the Writings.

46. Isaiah has a strong textual link to the Former Prophets (2 Kgs. 18–20; Isa. 36–39).

47. Jacob Neusner, *The Babylonian Talmud: A Translation and Commentary*, vol. 15, Tractate *Baba Batra* (Peabody, MA: Hendrickson, 2005), 54. While the characterization of these three books is somewhat simplistic, the effort to explain the arrangement of the books shows an interest in the establishment of canonical order and its meaning. Note that there is no explanation for the placement of the Twelve.

48. The term "citation" will be used somewhat broadly as a catchall to describe many of these connections. Terminology in the field of analysis of textual dependence and inner-biblical exegesis (e.g., allusion, echo) is not standardized, and everyone seems to have their own pet definitions. Furthermore, demonstration of citation does not constitute proof. Study of literature deals in probabilities. Therefore, while it is important to establish

is well known and need not be rehearsed here in full,[49] but suffice it to say that the relationship between the two is not unlike that between Deuteronomy and the Former Prophets (the so-called Deuteronomistic History).[50] That is, Deuteronomy presents itself as Moses' own exposition of the Torah built into the composition of the Pentateuch (Deut. 1:5). It provides commentary on the laws (e.g., Deut. 5 [Exod. 20]; 12–26; 28 [Lev. 26]), narratives (e.g., Deut. 2–3 [Num. 13–14; 20–21]; 9 [Exod. 32]), and poetry (e.g., Deut. 33 [Gen. 49]) of Genesis through Numbers. What better way then for the Former Prophets and Jeremiah to relate to the book of Moses than through its own explanation of itself? The Former Prophets offer a Deuteronomistic narrative context for the prophecies in Jeremiah punctuated and interpreted by the speeches of its major characters and the reflections of its narrator (Josh. 1:8; 24; Judg. 2; 1 Sam. 12; 1 Kgs. 8; 2 Kgs. 17; see also 1 Sam. 2:1–10; 2 Sam 1:17–27; 7; 22:1–23:7). Also, the Deuteronomistic material in Jeremiah is not merely a redactional layer to be peeled back for separate examination but an integral part of the fabric of the book's final composition.

Jeremiah's relationship to other members of the Latter Prophets and to the Writings is extensive and will bear itself out in the course of the following commentary, but a few comments are in order here to set the stage. The book of Jeremiah shares with the books of Isaiah, Ezekiel, and the Twelve the concern not merely to document the past but to look forward to the future and final work of God in Christ.[51] This comes primarily in the depiction of what lies beyond Babylonian exile in the eschaton for the people of God (Isa. 40–66; Jer. 30–33; Ezek. 34–39; Joel 3:1–5 [Eng., 2:28–32]; Amos 9:11–15; Zech.). Such an eschatological and messianic outlook makes possible the reading of the new covenant passage (Jer. 31:31–34) in Hebrews 8, which does not see the fulfillment of Jeremiah's prophecy in the postexilic period but in the formation of a people fitted for the last days. Likewise, while there is plenty to say about Psalms-Job-Proverbs, the Megilloth (especially Lam.), and Ezra/Nehemiah-Chronicles in relation to Jeremiah, it is primarily the book of Daniel among the Writings that highlights

---

criteria (e.g., verbal links, grammar/syntax, sequence, context, expansion, etc.), there will always be room for doubt. See Michael B. Shepherd, *The Text in the Middle*, StBibLit 162 (New York: Lang, 2014), 1–6, 107–9.

49. See Holladay, *Jeremiah 2*, 53–64.

50. See Martin Noth, *The Deuteronomistic History*, JSOTSupp 15 (Sheffield: JSOT, 1981).

51. For citation of Jeremiah in the composition of the Twelve, see Shepherd, *Commentary on the Book of the Twelve*, 23–36.

the eschatological and messianic value of Jeremiah and forms a bridge between it and the NT book of Revelation (Dan. 9). Its vision of the last days, the Messiah, and the defeat of a final enemy would not be possible without its reading of Jeremiah's book.

AUTHORSHIP AND DATE

The above discussion of text, composition, and canon should make it evident that matters of authorship and date with regard to the book of Jeremiah are anything but simple and straightforward. Therefore, the following treatment seeks only to present the biblical witness to these issues. First and foremost, it must be said in accordance with the superscription (Jer. 1:1–3) that the entire composition is "The word of God that came to Jeremiah" (MT: "The words of Jeremiah . . . to whom the word of the LORD came"). This means that Jeremiah's words are God's words. Jeremiah's interpretations of things are not merely his own (2 Pet. 1:20). The given span of Jeremiah's prophetic ministry is c. 627–587 BC, but the book indicates that he functioned in his role as prophet even beyond this time period (Jer. 40–44). Jeremiah was a young man in 627 (Jer. 1:6), so he presumably could have lived into the second half of the sixth century. There is no account of Jeremiah's death in the book, but the LORD says through Zechariah in 520 BC that "the former prophets" (i.e., preexilic prophets) like Jeremiah and Ezekiel do not live forever, yet the words that the LORD spoke through them, which are now vindicated, remain in the texts that bear their names (Zech. 1:1, 4–6).[52]

Two other names must be mentioned in connection with the composition of Jeremiah: Baruch and Ezra. The book itself testifies to the central role of Baruch in its making (Jer. 36; 45; see also Jer. 32:12, 13, 16; 43:3, 6).[53] It is Baruch who gives textual expression to God's words, which have come through Jeremiah (2 Tim. 3:15–17; 2 Pet. 1:19–21). This relationship between prophet and scribe is one that must not be overlooked, especially given the importance of the written text of Scripture. Jeremiah's priestly background (Jer. 1:1) would presumably have provided him with access to written texts and scribal training,[54] but he nevertheless entrusted the writing of his

---

52. Tradition also assigns Kings and Lamentations to Jeremiah (*b. B. Bat.* 15a). See the superscription to LXX Lamentations.

53. See also Yuval Goren and Eran Arie, "The Authenticity of the Bullae of Berekhyahu Son of Neriyahu the Scribe," *BASOR* 372 (2014): 147–58.

54. See William M. Schniedewind, *How the Bible Became a Book: The Textualization of Ancient Israel* (Cambridge: Cambridge University Press, 2004),

words to Baruch.[55] Of course, Baruch's years overlapped Jeremiah's, but it is not clear if Baruch was significantly older or younger than Jeremiah.

As for Ezra, his name comes into play in both biblical and postbiblical tradition (Ezra 7:6, 10; 9:10–11; Neh. 8–9; *m. Avot.* 1:1; *b. B. Bat.* 15a; *b. Sanh.* 21b) as one who along with his associates (the Men of the Great Assembly) had a hand in shaping the received biblical texts into the form known to Jesus and the NT authors (Luke 24:44; 2 Tim. 3:15–17; 2 Pet. 1:19–21).[56] Among other things, the lack of direct attribution of the appendix in Jeremiah 52 (2 Kgs 25) to either Jeremiah (see again MT Jer. 51:64b) or Baruch (Jer. 45) suggests a link to this work.[57] The hermeneutical gain from this is the fact that those responsible for the present form of the biblical texts had the vantage point to view all the literature simultaneously. This makes possible the reading of the Hebrew Bible as a single book made of many books.

THE MESSAGE OF JEREMIAH

The message of the book of Jeremiah is concisely stated in the programmatic text of Jeremiah 1:10: "See, I have appointed you this day over the nations and over the kingdoms to pluck up and to tear down and to destroy [MT adds: and to throw down], and to build and to plant." The language of this text is distributed throughout the entire composition (Jer. 12:14–17; 18:7–10; 24:6; 31:27–28, 40; 32:41; 42:10; 45:4). It is a message of judgment and restoration, not

---

165–94; Christopher A. Rollston, *Writing and Literacy in the World of Ancient Israel: Epigraphic Evidence from the Iron Age* (Atlanta: SBL, 2010), 132–34.

55. This is analogous to the apostle Paul who had the requisite training (Acts 22:3), yet he dictated his letter to the Romans to his amanuensis Tertius (Rom. 16:22).

56. A comparison with the language of Ecclesiastes 12:12 suggests that Ezra's activity involved studying, "making" or "composing," and teaching the Torah (Ezra 7:10), but his exposition in Nehemiah extends beyond the boundaries of the Pentateuch into the Former Prophets (Neh. 9:23–31), and his prayer in Ezra 9:10–11 shows his general indebtedness to the prophets. The Talmud attributes several books of the Prophets and the Writings to Ezra (Ezra/Nehemiah, Chronicles) and the Men of the Great Assembly (Ezekiel, the Twelve, Daniel, Esther).

57. The Talmud attributes to Jeremiah the book of Kings, which contains the parallel to Jeremiah 52 in 2 Kings 25. Thus, Ezra may have used Jeremiah's own work, which was not part of the book of Jeremiah as produced by the prophet, to connect the book of Jeremiah to the Former Prophets (Joshua–Kings).

only the historical judgment at the hands of the Babylonians and the subsequent return but also the prefigured eschatological judgment of all worldly opposition to God and his people and the final restoration of the lost blessing of life and dominion in the land of the covenant. It is a message of the consequences of a broken covenant relationship (Jer. 11:9–14) and the hope of a new covenant (Jer. 31:31–34). It is a message of a failed monarchy (Jer. 21:1–23:4) and the hope of a messianic king (Jer. 23:5–6). This message is not for one nation only but for all nations (Jer. 1:5, 10; 3:17; 4:2). Likewise, the book is not for one audience but for all who read it.

THE "BOOK" OF JEREMIAH
(Jer. 1:1–25:13)

JEREMIAH 1:1–2:13

1:1 The word of God that came to Jeremiah [MT: The words of Jeremiah] the son of Hilkiah from the priests who were in Anathoth in the land of Benjamin 1:2 to whom the word of God [MT: the word of the LORD] came in the days of Josiah the son of Amon [LXX: Amos; cf. Isa. 1:1] the king of Judah in the thirteenth year of his reign.[1] 1:3 And it came in the days of Jehoiakim the son of Josiah the king of Judah until [MT adds: the completion of] the eleventh year of Zedekiah the son of Josiah the king of Judah, until the exile of Jerusalem in the fifth month.

The superscription designates the book in its entirety, not merely its individual parts, as the revelatory word of God. The composition of the book is not a record of revelation but the revelation itself. In other words, the poetics of the literary work is the means of communication. The syntax of 1:1 ("The word of God that came to") is comparable to other prophetic superscriptions (Hos. 1:1; Joel 1:1; Mic. 1:1; Zeph. 1:1). The MT ("The words of Jeremiah") presents the book as a collection of the words of the prophet to whom the word of the LORD came (cf. Deut.

---

1. Or, "that which was the word of God to him" (cf. MT Jer. 14:1; 46:1; 47:1; 49:34; see GKC §138e). The use of this construction as a heading occurs in the *Vorlage* of Greek Jeremiah in LXX 25:14 (= MT 25:13b2) (see also LXX 26:13; 49:19 [MT 42:19; 46:13]), but the text of 1:2 differs from the examples of headings that begin with a relative. It cannot stand alone as a heading. The use of the pronoun "him" requires the presence of 1:1 to provide the antecedent ("Jeremiah").

1:1, 3; Amos 1:1; see also Jer. 36:10).[2] Jeremiah's name is variously understood to be a combination of a prefixed form of רום ("rise"), רמה ("cast"), or רמה ("slacken") and the divine name (Yah[weh]), but there is little indication that the prophet's name has exegetical significance within the book (see BDB, 941; *HALOT* 1:440). This Jeremiah is said to be the son of Hilkiah (see also Bar. 1:1) whom *Targum Jonathan* appears to identify with the Hilkiah in 2 Kings 22:8, the high priest who discovered the book of the Torah during the temple repairs in the eighteenth year of Josiah's reign, but this connection is dubious at best. English translations often give the impression that Jeremiah was "one of the priests" in Anathoth (e.g., ESV, NET), but there is no evidence that Jeremiah ever functioned in a priestly role. It is perhaps preferable to say that he, like Moses before him and like Ezekiel and Zechariah after him (Ezek. 1:3; Zech. 1:1; Neh 12:16), came "from" a priestly family (BDB, 579; see 1 Kgs. 2:26; 1 Chr. 6:45) but was called to be a prophet (see also Exod. 7:1). Jeremiah's place of origin, Anathoth in the land of Benjamin (Josh. 21:18), plays an important role later in the book (Jer. 11:21, 23; 32:7–9).

The syntactical relationship of 1:2 to 1:1 is comparable to what the reader can find in 1 Kings 18:31: "according to the number of the tribes of the sons of Jacob to whom the word of the LORD came" (see GKC §155). The *Vorlage* of the Greek text in 1:2 uses the phrase "the word of God," while the MT revises this to the more frequent phrase "the word of the LORD."[3] Verse 1 indicates the content of the book ("The word of God that came to Jeremiah"), while verse 2 indicates when this content came to the prophet. It came to him beginning in the thirteenth year of Josiah's reign (c. 627 BC; cf. Jer. 3:6; 25:3).[4] This is usually understood to be the first year of Jeremiah's prophetic ministry, but William Holladay argues

---

2. It might appear on the surface that the LXX ("The word of God") is secondary, changing the MT ("The words of Jeremiah") to a more standard form, but the secondary addition of "up to here are the words of Jeremiah" in MT Jeremiah 51:64b, which does not occur in the LXX, suggests that the phrase in MT 1:1 is the later reading designed to create bookends with the addition in Jeremiah 51:64b.

3. The Greek translation uses ῥῆμα and λόγος interchangeably for דבר in 1:1 and 1:2. This is apparently for stylistic variation.

4. It is important to note that Jeremiah did not dictate to Baruch the words he received in the days of Josiah until the fourth year of Jehoiakim (c. 605 BC; see Jer. 36:1–2; 45:1).

that this is actually the date of the prophet's birth.[5] He does not find any oracles in the book datable to this early period, and he considers the lack of reference to Josiah's reform in 622 BC (2 Kgs. 22–23) to be an insurmountable problem for the common view. For Holladay, Jeremiah was set apart in the womb as a prophet in the year 627 (Jer. 1:5).[6] In response to this, it must be admitted that the dating of oracles is not an exact science. The book itself does not provide the kind of consistent date formulae that the reader finds in the book of Ezekiel (but see Jer. 3:6; 25:3; 36:2). As for Josiah's reform, there is a reference to the discovery of the book of the Torah in the MT of Jeremiah 15:16 (cf. 2 Kgs. 22:8; but not in LXX Jer. 15:16), and Jeremiah's lament over Josiah's death (2 Chr. 35:25) strongly suggests that he was sympathetic to the king's program. At the very least, the influence of Deuteronomy on both Josiah and Jeremiah is evident. Jeremiah's appeal to the Torah is an implicit appeal to Josiah's reform. The reality was that a major gap existed between the official reforms of the king and the life of the people, making way for their ready apostasy in the wake of the king's death (thus necessitating Jeremiah's ministry).[7] It is reasonable to ask why it would be any less of a problem that there is no explicit reference to Josiah's reform even if Jeremiah's prophetic ministry began at a later time.[8] Finally, the

---

5. William L. Holladay, *Jeremiah 2: A Commentary on the Book of the Prophet Jeremiah Chapters 26–52*, Hermeneia (Minneapolis: Fortress, 1989), 25–26.
6. Holladay also points out other perceived issues with the traditional view: (1) the enemy from the north in 1:15 could not be Babylon in 627 (which is not a problem in Greek Jeremiah because the enemy remains unidentified); (2) Jeremiah's call to celibacy (Jer. 16:1–4), which is not dated, would have had to occur when Jeremiah was at least thirty-eight years old according to Holladay (which is not a problem unless it is arbitrarily assumed to have come earlier); and (3) Jeremiah 15:16, which in the MT (but not in the LXX) references Hilkiah's discovery of the book of the Torah (2 Kgs. 22:8), could not predate Jeremiah 1:9 (which is not a problem since 15:16 need not be read as a reference to an event prior to the prophet's call).
7. This is analogous to the resurfacing of the problem of cohabitation with foreign women in the postexilic community despite the official position of the leadership (Ezra 9–10; Neh. 13:23–27). While critics have suggested rethinking the date and arrangement of the material, the book of Ezra/Nehemiah itself presents this as a recurring problem of human nature.
8. This is comparable to the debate over the date of the apostle Paul's epistle to the Galatians. Conservative scholarship generally dates the letter earlier than 1 and 2 Thessalonians in part because it does not explicitly appeal to the "decree" of the Jerusalem Council (Acts 15), but Paul does not appeal to this decree in any of his letters that postdate the Council. His

setting apart of Jeremiah in the womb (Jer. 1:5) is not the same thing as the word of God coming to Jeremiah (Jer. 1:2). In all other prophetic superscriptions where the word of the LORD is said to have come to an individual, it is a clear marker of the prophet's actual ministry. Nowhere does the text indicate that the word of God came to Jeremiah in the womb (see Jer. 25:3).

The word of God continued to come to Jeremiah in the days of King Jehoiakim the son of Josiah (c. 609–598 BC) until the eleventh year of Zedekiah (c. 587 BC), which was the year of Jerusalem's exile to Babylon in the fifth month (Jer. 1:3; see 2 Kgs. 25:8; Jer. 39:2; 52:12). The word of the LORD came to Jeremiah after the eleventh year of Zedekiah (Jer. 40:1; 42:7; 43:8; 44:1), but the span from 627 (Jer. 1:2) to 587 (Jer. 1:3) marked a forty-year ministry that culminated with the fulfillment of Jeremiah's prophecy of Babylonian invasion.[9] The relationship of the dates in 1:2–3 to "The word of God that came to Jeremiah" in 1:1 is an important one, indicating that the word is not merely a particular word that came to the prophet (e.g., Jer. 1:4, 11, 13) but the full breadth of what the reader finds in the book as a whole (cf. Isa. 1:1; Hos. 1:1; Amos 1:1; Mic. 1:1; Zeph. 1:1).

1:4 And the word of the LORD came to him [MT: to me, saying], 1:5 "Before I formed [see GKC §71] you in the belly I knew [NET: chose] you, and before you went forth from womb I set you apart. A prophet to the nations [LXX catenae: nation] I appointed [lit., gave; BDB, 680] you."[10] 1:6 And I said, "Ah [LXX: The one who is; see LXX Exod. 3:14], LORD GOD! Look, I do not know speaking [Tg. Jon.: prophesying], for a youth [LXX: too young] am I."[11] 1:7 And the LORD said to me, "Do not say, 'A

---

appeal is to his own apostolic authority (Gal. 1:1, 11–12). Likewise, Jeremiah does not base his ministry on Josiah's reform. This is not necessarily because he was too young at the time of the event or because he disagreed with it, but because his own calling as a prophet and reception of the Torah provided the basis for his ministry. He could have easily appealed to the reform at any time later in his ministry, but he did not, so the lack of such an appeal in his supposedly early ministry is not necessarily an indication that a ministry beginning in the year 627 did not exist.

9. Jeremiah's forty-year ministry began in the land of Israel and ended in Egypt (Jer. 43–44). Moses' forty-year ministry began in Egypt and ended on the verge of entry into the Promised Land.

10. *Tg. Jon.*: "A prophet giving a cup of curse to the peoples to drink I appointed you." Cf. Jeremiah 25:15–26.

11. *Tg. Jon.* adds: "and from my beginning [some witnesses: and because of my service in the Temple] I have been prophesying distress and exile concerning this people." Cf. 1 Samuel 2:11, 18; 3:1.

youth am I.' For [Luther: sondern] to [or, against] all that [Tg. Jon.: to every place that; NET: to whomever] I send you, you will go; and all that I command you, you will speak [Tg. Jon.: prophesy]. 1:8 Do not be afraid from before [i.e., because of] them [BDB, 818], for with you am I to rescue you," the prophetic utterance of the LORD. *1:9 And the* LORD *extended his hand to me [to me > MT] and touched [MT: caused to touch] my mouth.*[12] *And the* LORD *said to me, "Look, I have put [lit., given] my words in your mouth. 1:10 See, I have appointed you this day over the nations and over the kingdoms to pluck up and to tear down and to destroy [MT adds: and to throw down], and [and > MT; Tg. Jon.: and over the house of Israel] to build and to plant."*

This unit is the account of Jeremiah's call as a prophet (cf. Isa. 6; Ezek. 1–3). It is fronted in the composition of the book not only to establish the legitimacy of Jeremiah's prophetic voice for the reader but also to introduce material that will prove to be programmatic for the book as a whole. The difference between the LXX and the MT of 1:4 is perspective. The *Vorlage* of Greek Jeremiah maintains the third-person perspective of 1:1–3 ("to him"). On the other hand, the MT introduces the first-person perspective ("to me") in anticipation of 1:6, 7a, 9a and the formulae in 1:11, 13 and MT 2:1 (> LXX).

The LORD says to Jeremiah, "Before I formed you in the belly I knew you" (Jer. 1:5a; cf. Gen. 2:7; Isa. 44:24; 49:1; Jer. 10:16; Pss. 22:10–11 [Eng., 22:9–10]; 119:73; 139:13; Job 10:11; 31:15). The parallel to this is: "and before you went forth from womb I set you apart" (cf. Gen. 17:19; 25:23; Exod. 2:2; Judg. 13:3–5; 1 Sam. 1:11; Sir. 49:7; Luke 1; Gal. 1:15).[13] The combination of בטרם ("before") and the prefixed conjugation at the beginning of both parts of this line is a common construction in biblical Hebrew (see GKC §107c). Parts A and B of the parallelism are not synonymous. Rather, part B advances the thought of part A.[14] Thus, part A refers to a time before the formation of Jeremiah in his mother's belly. Part B refers to a time before Jeremiah's birth from the womb. Likewise, the suffixed verbs "knew" and "set apart" are not synonymous. The Hebrew verb ידע ("know") does not mean "consecrate," nor is it the same as בחר ("choose"). Here it indicates a special relationship

---

12. *Tg. Jon.*: "And the Lord sent the words of his prophecy and arranged in my mouth."
13. Jeremiah later wishes he had never been born (Jer. 20:14–18).
14. See James L. Kugel, *The Idea of Biblical Poetry: Parallelism and Its History* (New Haven, CT: Yale University Press, 1981; repr., Baltimore: The Johns Hopkins University Press, 1998), 1–58.

with the LORD that serves as the basis for Jeremiah's consecration (cf. Amos 3:2; see *TLOT* 2:515–16).[15]

The final clause in 1:5b ("A prophet to the nations I appointed you") stands outside the parallelism and functions to comment on the foreknowledge and consecration of Jeremiah in 1:5a (cf. Jer. 6:27a). It explains that Jeremiah was set apart specifically for an appointment as a "prophet" (נביא ["called one"]; *TLOT* 2:697). It will become apparent in the following verses what the role of a prophet involves, but at this point the only qualifier given is that Jeremiah has been appointed a prophet "to the nations" (cf. Isa. 49:6; MT Ezek. 2:3a). Despite some witnesses to the LXX that have the singular in their rendering ("nation"), and despite the efforts of some commentators to make this refer only to Israel,[16] it is clear from the content of the book that Jeremiah's message of judgment and restoration is not only for Judah and Jerusalem but also for the nations (e.g., Jer. 1:10; 3:17; 4:2; 12:14–17; 16:19; 25:15–26; 36:2; 46–51).[17] Abraham and his seed were intended to be the means of restoring the lost blessing to all the nations (Gen. 12:3; 22:18; Jer. 4:2).

Jeremiah's instinct is to resist what he was born to do (Jer. 1:6).[18] The expression, "Ah, Lord GOD (אהה אדני יהוה)," occurs elsewhere to indicate an alarmed response (Jer. 4:10; 14:13; 32:17; see also Josh. 7:7; Judg. 6:22; Ezek. 4:14; 9:8; 11:13; 21:5).[19] The Greek translation Ὁ Ὤν ("The one who is") does not reflect a different Hebrew source text. It is a misreading of the interjection אהה as if it were אהיה (see Exod. 3:14). Jeremiah points out (הנה) that he does not know speaking. This does not mean that Jeremiah does not know how to speak in general. Rather, in light of his call to be a prophet (Jer. 1:5), he replies that

---

15. Theodoret of Cyr: "God's choice of Jeremiah was not without basis: knowledge preceded it. Notice it says that God had knowledge and then he consecrated, for he knows everything before it happens" (Dean O. Wenthe, ed., *Jeremiah, Lamentations*, ACCS XII [Downers Grove, IL: InterVarsity, 2008], 2).

16. Rashi: "To Israel, who behave like the nations" (A. J. Rosenberg, trans., *Mikraoth Gedoloth: Jeremiah Volume One* [Brooklyn: Judaica, 1985], 4).

17. See John Calvin, *Commentaries on the Book of the Prophet Jeremiah and the Lamentations*, vol. 1, trans. John Owen, Calvin's Commentaries IX (Grand Rapids: Baker, 2005), 37.

18. Calvin attributes this to the prophet's humility (Calvin, *Commentaries on the Book of the Prophet Jeremiah and the Lamentations*, 1:38; see James 3:1)

19. The word pair אדני יהוה may be the *qere* or reading tradition ("Lord") written into the text with the unspoken divine name Yahweh. This combination frequently occurs in MT Ezekiel, where the LXX simply translates "Lord," reflecting the *Vorlage* יהוה.

he does not know how to prophesy (see *Tg. Jon.*). This is remarkably similar to Moses' resistance to his call (Exod. 3:11 [cf. 2 Sam. 7:18]; 4:10, 13) where he claims, "Not a man of words am I," and, "Heavy of mouth and heavy of tongue am I" (Exod. 4:10). At first glance this looks like an appeal to lack of eloquence or to a speech impediment of some kind, but the context suggests that Moses feels not up to the task of prophetic speech. When the compromise is made to employ the help of Aaron (Exod. 4:14–17), the result is that Aaron becomes Moses' prophetic mouthpiece (Exod. 7:1–2). Jeremiah explains his objection by saying that he is "too young" (see LXX) to prophesy (cf. Zech. 2:8 [Eng., 2:4]). This explanation has a point of contact with Gideon's resistance to his divine call (Judg. 6:15). The Hebrew word נער ("youth") can refer to someone as young as an infant (Exod. 2:6), a young boy (1 Sam. 2:11) or a teenager (Gen. 37:2), or to a young man (2 Sam. 18:5).

The LORD rebukes Jeremiah's objection (Jer. 1:7a; cf. 1 Tim. 4:12). Jeremiah will indeed go wherever or to whomever the LORD sends him and will prophesy whatever the LORD commands him (Jer. 1:7b; cf. Exod. 3:10; 7:2; Deut. 18:18; Acts 26:17). In other words, Jeremiah does not really have a choice in the matter (see Jer. 20:9; Amos 3:8). The conjunction כי at the beginning of 1:7b can be rendered "For" (explanatory) or "But" (adversative). The preposition על can be "to" or "against," but "against" suggests that Jeremiah's message is entirely negative, which is not the case according to 1:10. It is not clear whether כל אשר ("all that") means "wherever" or "whomever," and it may very well be intentionally ambiguous (cf. Jer. 45:5b). The LORD then exposes the real reason for Jeremiah's resistance: fear (Jer. 1:8a, 17).[20] When the LORD says, "Do not fear from before them" (cf. Ezek. 2:6; 3:9), it is not immediately evident who the referent of the pronoun "them" might be. This matter will be resolved in 1:18. The reason why Jeremiah need not fear is that the LORD himself is with him to rescue him (Jer. 1:8b; cf. Jer. 1:17, 19; 15:20–21; 20:11, 13; see also Gen. 26:3, 24; 31:3; Deut. 31:8; Acts 18:9–10; etc.). This is another connection that Jeremiah has with Moses and Gideon (Exod. 3:12; Judg. 6:16). His abilities do not matter. Only the LORD's presence matters. This is true not only for Jeremiah in the book but also for the faithful remnant of the people of God represented by Jeremiah throughout (see Jer. 23:4; 30:10–11 [MT]; 42:11; 46:27–28).

Verse 9a narrates how the LORD extended his hand to Jeremiah and "touched" (*qal* stem) his mouth. This is purely an anthropomorphism in the *Vorlage* of Greek Jeremiah. On the other hand, the MT has

---

20. Calvin, *Jeremiah*, 1:41.

the *hiphil* stem: "he caused to touch." The text does not indicate what person or thing the LORD may have caused to touch Jeremiah's mouth, but the link to the call of Isaiah in Isaiah 6:7 provides a clue: "And he [the seraph (Isa. 6:6)] touched [*hiphil*] my mouth (with it [the hot coal (Isa. 6:6)]) and said, 'Look, this [the hot coal] has touched [*qal*] your lips. And your iniquity is removed; and as for your sin, it is covered.'" This text does not describe Isaiah's salvation experience but the purification of his "unclean" lips in preparation for his prophetic ministry (Isa. 6:5). According to *Targum Jonathan* for Jeremiah 1:9a, the text speaks of the deposit and arrangement of prophetic words in Jeremiah's mouth. Thus, the LORD says in Jeremiah 1:9b, "Look, I have put my words in your mouth" (cf. Isa. 51:16; 59:21; Jer. 5:14).[21] This may be seen to go hand in hand with Jeremiah's reception of the words of the Torah in MT Jeremiah 15:16 (cf. Josh. 1:8; Ezek. 2:8–3:3; Rev. 10:8–11). The wording of 1:9b is a rather deliberate reference to the prophet like Moses: "A prophet will I raise up for them from the midst of their brothers like you [i.e., Moses], and I will put my words in his mouth, and he will speak to them all that I command him" (Deut. 18:18; cf. Deut. 18:15).[22] From the perspective of someone like Ezra living in the postexilic period and looking back over the history of Israel's prophets, this prophet had yet to come (Deut. 34:10; see Luke 9:35; Acts 3:22; 7:37).[23] But because Moses was the prophet par excellence, the legitimacy of subsequent prophets could be determined not only by the test in Deuteronomy 18:20–22 but also by comparison with Moses himself.

As noted in the Introduction ("The Message of Jeremiah"), the text of Jeremiah 1:10 is programmatic for the entire book (Jer. 12:14–17; 18:7–10; 24:6; 31:27–28, 40; 32:41; 42:10; 45:4; see also Ps. 28:5; Job 12:14); and as commented on 1:5, Jeremiah has been appointed a prophet to nations and kingdoms in the plural, not to a singular nation (cf. Rev. 10:11). This does not mean that Jeremiah himself will travel to various nations and deliver messages to them. It does mean that God's plan for his people will play out on an international stage. The words

---

21. This does not need to be a "prophetic perfect" (NET: "I most assuredly will give you the words you are to speak for me"). Rather, it represents the moment of Jeremiah's call and preparation for his task.

22. For other links to Deuteronomy 18:15–22 throughout the book of Jeremiah, see Jeremiah 14:14; 20:9; 23:32; 26:16; 28:9; 35:13; 44:16.

23. Deuteronomy 34:10 does not interpret Deuteronomy 18:15, 18 to mean that there would be a succession of prophets like Moses but that there would be one prophet in particular like Moses (cf. John 1:21; 6:14; 7:40). Jeremiah was in a sense a prophet like Moses, but not *the* prophet like Moses.

of judgment directed toward the nations in Jeremiah 46–51 are primarily words of encouragement for the faithful remnant of Judah and Jerusalem, but there is also salvation for the nations (Jer. 3:17; 4:2; 12:14–17; 16:19; 46:26b [MT]; 48:47; 49:6 [MT], 39). Within the context of the book, *Targum Jonathan* is most certainly not correct to divide 1:10 between judgment for the nations alone and restoration for Israel alone. There will be judgment for both and deliverance for both. As it goes for the believing remnant of Israel, so it will go for the believing remnant of Gentiles. This judgment and the subsequent restoration are first of all historical in that they refer to Babylonian exile and the following return therefrom (cf. Deut. 29:27 [Eng., 29:28]), but this historical realization also serves within the book to prefigure the defeat of a final enemy and the eschatological deliverance of the people of God (e.g., Jer. 31:27–28, 40; 32:41).

Of course, Jeremiah is not to destroy and to rebuild nations physically with his own hands. Rather, he is the messenger of the effective word of God, which the LORD himself is sure to accomplish (Isa. 55:10–11; Jer. 1:12). What is it exactly about these nations that will be destroyed and rebuilt? The language of this verse suggests that this is more than mere destruction for destruction's sake. The roots of the first three infinitives in 1:10 ("to pluck up and to tear down and to destroy" [לנתש ולנתוץ ולהאביד]) can be used for the destruction of Asherah poles (Mic. 5:13); Baal altars (Exod. 34:13; Deut. 7:5; 12:3; Judg. 2:2; 6:30–32; 2 Kgs. 23:12), high places (2 Kgs. 23:8, 15), pillars (2 Kgs. 10:27), and temples (2 Kgs. 10:27; 11:18); and idols (Ezek. 30:13; see also Deut. 12:2).[24] The MT adds a fourth infinitive ("to throw down" [להרוס]) whose root appears elsewhere in the book (Jer. 24:6; 31:28, 40; 42:10; 45:4; cf. Jer. 18:7). It can also be used for the destruction of altars (Judg. 6:25; 1 Kgs. 18:30; 19:10, 14). On the other hand, the final two infinitives ("to build and to plant" [לבנות ולנטוע]) can be used for the building of legitimate places of worship (1 Kgs. 6:1–2) and the establishment of the people of God in the land of the covenant (Exod. 15:17; Ezek. 36:36; Amos 9:15; Ps. 44:3 [Eng., 44:2]; see also Isa. 28:23–29; Eccl. 3:3). Thus, it seems likely that God seeks to destroy the alternative worship that led to the broken covenant relationship and to establish true worship among his people in a new covenant relationship. It is this fundamental distinction between genuine faith and lack thereof that will separate two different groups of humanity in the eschaton.

---

24. See also נתץ in Jeremiah 33:4.

1:11 And the word of the LORD came to me, saying, "What do you see [MT adds: Jeremiah]?" And I said, "A branch from an almond tree [Tg. Jon.: A king hastening to do harm; Vulg., Luther: a vigilant twig; MT adds: I see]." 1:12 And the LORD said to me, "You have done well to see [or, You have seen well (GKC §114n²)], for I am watching over my words to do them [MT: over my word to do it]." 1:13 And the word of the LORD came to me a second time [cf. Jer. 13:3], saying, "What do you see [Cairo Genizah adds: Jeremiah]?" And I said, "A blown pot [or, A boiling pot (BDB, 656); LXX: A cauldron burning from below; MT adds: I see], and its face is from the north [lit., from before northward (see GKC §90e); Luther 1912: from midnight]."²⁵ 1:14 And the LORD said to me, "From [the] north the evil [or, calamity] will be opened [i.e., let loose; LXX: ignited] upon / against all the inhabitants of the land. 1:15 For look, I am about to summon [lit., I am calling to; see GKC §116p] all (the) kingdoms of (the) north [LXX adds: of the land / earth; MT: all the families of the kingdoms of the north; see GKC §130a]," the prophetic utterance of the LORD, "and they will come and put each his throne at the entrance of the gates of Jerusalem and against all its surrounding walls and against all the cities of Judah. 1:16 And I will speak with them judgment [LXX: with judgment; MT: my judgments with them] concerning all their evil, because [LXX: how] they forsook me and sent sacrifices up in smoke to other gods and prostrated themselves to the works of their hands [or, worshiped the works of their hands]. 1:17 And as for you, you will gird up your loins and rise up and speak [MT adds: to them] all that I command you. Do not be afraid from before them [or, because of them; cf. 1:8a; MT: Do not be dismayed from before them] and do not be dismayed before them [MT: lest I cause you to be dismayed before them],²⁶ for with you am I to rescue you," the prophetic utterance of the LORD [cf. 1:8b; for with you am I to rescue you," the prophetic utterance of the LORD > MT].²⁷ 1:18 "Look [MT: And as for me, look], I have made [or, appointed; lit., given] you today as a fortified city [see BDB, 512 (cf. Syr., Tg. Jon.); MT adds: and as an iron pillar] and as a fortified [fortified > MT] bronze wall

---

25. *Tg. Jon.* 1:13b: "And I said, 'A king who is hot like a pot I see and the arrangement of his armies, which are advancing and coming from the north.'" Luther's "from midnight" appears to be based on the etymology of צָפוֹן as the "hidden" or "dark" region of the world (see BDB, 860).

26. *Tg. Jon.*: "Do not withhold from reproving them lest I break you before them."

27. See Georg A. Walser, *Jeremiah: A Commentary Based on Ieremias in Codex Vaticanus* (Leiden: Brill, 2012), 202.

[Tg. Jon. adds: to give a cup of curse to drink (cf. 1:5)] against all the kings of Judah and against its officials and against the people of the land [MT: against all the land, against the kings of Judah, against its officials, against its priests (Syr. adds: and against their prophets), and against the people of the land]. 1:19 And they will fight against you [Tg. Jon. adds: to destroy the words of your prophecy], but they will not prevail against you, for with you am I to rescue you," the prophetic utterance of the LORD.

This unit introduces the major subthemes of the program of 1:10 to be developed over the course of the book: divine faithfulness and providence (Jer. 1:11–12; cf. Isa. 40:8; 55:10–11), the enemy from the north (Jer. 1:13–15; 3:12, 18; 4:6; 6:1, 22; 10:22; 13:20; 15:12; 16:15; 23:8; 25:9, 26; 31:8; 46:6, 10, 20, 24; 47:2; 50:3, 9, 41, 48), idolatry (Jer. 1:16; 2:9–13; 5:19; 7:6, 16–20, 30–31; 9:12–13 [Eng., 9:13–14]; 10:11; 11:10–13; 16:11; 19:4; 22:9; 25:6; 35:15; 44), opposition (Jer. 1:17–18; 2:8; 4:9; 5:31; 6:13–15, 27; 8:8, 10–12; 11:18–12:6; 15:20; 17:18; 20:1–8; 23:9–40; 26; 28; 36–38; 42–43), and divine presence (Jer. 1:8, 17, 19; 15:20–21; 20:11; 30:11 [MT]; 46:28). It begins with two messages from the LORD (Jer. 1:11–12, 13–14) that follow the question-and-answer pattern of other prophetic visions (Jer. 24:1–3; Amos 7:7–9; 8:1–3; Zech. 4:2; 5:2). These also involve wordplays in the original language that usually do not surface in translation (cf. Amos 8:1–3).

Now that the book as a whole has been introduced as "The word of God that came to Jeremiah" (Jer. 1:1–3), and now that "the word of the LORD" has come to Jeremiah to inform him (and the reader) that he has been appointed a prophet to deliver God's "words" of judgment and restoration to the nations (Jer. 1:4–9), it is only fitting that the first "word of the LORD" in 1:11–12 highlights the fact that God faithfully and providentially oversees the effectiveness of his "word" so that it accomplishes the purpose for which it is sent (see Jer. 31:28; cf. Isa. 40:8; 55:10–11; Dan. 9:12–14; Neh. 9:8b). This breeds confidence not only in the prophet but also in the reader. The LORD asks Jeremiah what he sees, to which Jeremiah responds that he sees a branch from an "almond tree" (*shāqēd*). The LORD then says that Jeremiah has seen well. The reason why Jeremiah has seen well is that he has correctly identified what he has seen using the key word *shāqēd* ("almond tree") that will form a wordplay with *shōqēd* ("watching"): "for I am watching [*shōqēd*] over my words to do them." The relationship between "almond tree" and "watching" is hardly intelligible in translation, but in Hebrew it makes a memorable impression. There is likely no significance to the almond tree apart from this simple play on words.[28] BDB notes the etymology of *shāqēd* ("almond tree"): "so called from its early *waking* out of winter's sleep" (1052).[29] This may very well be part of the influence for *Targum Jonathan's* rendering, "A king hastening to do harm," which perhaps understands the branch to be a ruler's rod (cf. Num. 17:23) and anticipates prematurely the imagery of 1:13–15, but the text of 1:11–12 gives no indication that the branch of the almond tree represents a king. Furthermore, the text gives no reason to think that the use of *shāqēd* ("almond tree") indicates that the LORD is hastening to accomplish his word as early as possible like the early bloom of the almond tree. Rather, the sense of the text is quite to the contrary. Unlike the almond tree, which passively awaits early spring, the LORD actively accomplishes his word according to his own predetermined time (cf. Hab. 2:3).

The second word of the LORD that comes to Jeremiah in 1:13–14 also features a vision and a wordplay (cf. Jer. 33:1). Jeremiah sees a "blown" (*nafûaḥ* [נפוח]) pot facing from the north. The LORD then informs him that the evil or calamity will be "opened" (*tippāṯaḥ* [תפתח]) or unleashed against all the inhabitants of the land (i.e., the land of Judah and Jerusalem).[30] Much like the image of the almond tree branch, the primary function of the blown pot is to create a memorable play on the key word of the message. The blown pot is ordinarily understood to be a pot full of water heated to a boiling point by fanned flames of fire (cf. Ezek. 21:36; 22:20; Sir. 43:4).[31] Holladay, however, argues that the pot is empty and being heated in order to remove baked-on food remains (cf. Ezek. 24:11).[32] The pot is also often assumed to be tipped or even on its side,[33] but this is a misunderstanding of what is meant by its face being from the north. Holladay rightly notes that a pot has no "front,"

---

28. See William McKane, *A Critical and Exegetical Commentary on Jeremiah*, vol. 1, *Introduction and Commentary on Jeremiah I–XXV*, ICC (London: Bloomsbury T&T Clark, 1986), 15.

29. See William L. Holladay, *Jeremiah 1: A Commentary on the Book of the Prophet Jeremiah Chapters 1–25*, Hermeneia (Philadelphia: Fortress, 1986), 37.

30. There is no reason to alter תפתח ("opened") to a word from the root נפח ("blow") (see the *BHS* apparatus).

31. See also Job 41:12, 23 (Eng., 41:20, 31). Johannes Lindblom suggests that the pot itself is blown by the wind ("Der Kessel in Jeremiah 1:13f," *ZAW* 68 [1956]: 223–24).

32. Holladay, *Jeremiah 1*, 39. It should be noted that the example of the empty pot in Ezekiel 24:11 is only valid in the MT. The pot is not empty in the LXX.

33. Holladay, *Jeremiah 1*, 39; McKane, *Jeremiah I–XXV*, 17–18.

but the front here is simply the side of the pot that faces the direction in which the pot moves from north to south from the perspective of someone in the land of Judah (cf. Hab. 1:9).[34] The pot does not represent Judah (cf. Ezek. 11:1–13; 24:1–14),[35] but according to 1:14–16 it represents the calamity that will be brought against Judah by means of the enemy from the north (*Tg. Jon.* 1:13b: And I said, "A king who is hot like a pot I see and the arrangement of his armies, which are advancing and coming from the north").[36]

Who is this enemy from the north? Those who argue for the Scythians contend that the enemy must have been a present historical force circa 627 BC (see Jer. 1:2). The most obvious problem with this view is that such an identification is never made in the book of Jeremiah or in the Hebrew canon. The most common view is that Babylon is the enemy from the north (i.e., the enemy from the east that would most likely attack from the north). This identification is made only in MT Jeremiah 25:9, 26, and there are several difficulties that make it very implausible. First, the *Vorlage* of Greek Jeremiah does not identify the enemy from the north with Babylon anywhere in the book. Second, both editions of the book do not even identify Babylon as the historical enemy of Judah until Jeremiah 20:4. Third, the enemy from the north comes against Babylon in Jeremiah 50:3.[37] The most plausible view is that the enemy from the north is the eschatological enemy Gog from the land of Magog (Num. 24:7 [LXX, SP]; Ezek. 38–39; Dan. 9:2, 24–27; Rev. 20:8) and his horde of nations (Ezek. 38:1–9; cf. Jer. 1:15).[38] This identification is made explicit in Ezekiel 38:14–17. After Gog is said to be an enemy who comes from the "north" (Ezek. 38:15) in "the last days" (Ezek. 38:16), the text of verse 17 says, "Thus says the LORD [LXX adds: to Gog], 'Are you the one of whom I spoke in former days by the hand of my servants the prophets [e.g., Jeremiah (cf. Zech. 1:4)] who prophesied in those days, years, to bring you upon

---

34. See Keil, *Jeremiah*, 29.
35. Contra Redak (Rosenberg, trans., *Mikraoth Gedoloth: Jeremiah Volume One*, 6); Calvin, *Jeremiah*, 1:1, 53; Holladay, *Jeremiah 1*, 39. Holladay admits that this reading is possible only if 1:16 is ignored as a later reinterpretation.
36. See Keil, *Jeremiah*, 29.
37. This is usually thought to be the Medes (Jer. 51:11, 28), but the Medes are never explicitly identified as the enemy from the north in the manner that MT Jeremiah 25:9, 26 identifies Babylon as such.
38. McKane cites Weiser, who argues that Jeremiah did not have a particular historical enemy in mind (*Jeremiah I–XXV*, 19–20).

them?'" The following verse answers this question in the affirmative (Ezek. 38:18). Thus, while Babylon is clearly the historical enemy in Jeremiah, the historical enemy serves to prefigure the eschatological enemy from the north.

Verse 15 explains that the Lord is imminently summoning all the kingdoms of the north (cf. Jer. 25:9).[39] In other words, the enemy is an instrument in the Lord's hand (cf. Ezek. 38:4; Hab. 1:6). This is often understood to mean the subjugated kingdoms within the Babylonian empire (see Jer. 34:1; 52:32; Ezek. 23:34; 26:7), but the text itself gives no clear indication of this. Of course, the Babylonian invasion will prove to be somewhat analogous to what this envisions, but the text of verse 15 speaks of a united horde of nations willingly following their leader (cf. Jer. 50:9, 41; Ezek. 38:1–9). Each king will come and set his throne at the entrance of the gates of Jerusalem. This is commonly compared to Jeremiah 39:3, where Nebuchadnezzar's officers come and sit or dwell in the Middle Gate (cf. Jer. 43:8–13; 49:38), in which case the setting up of thrones would be what happens in the wake of victory in preparation for judgment (see Jer. 1:16; 39:5 [MT]; cf. Dan. 7:9–14).[40] The present text of verse 15, however, speaks of multiple kings of multiple kingdoms setting up multiple thrones at the entrance of multiple gates; and the following phrases ("against all its surrounding walls and against all the cities of Judah") suggest an attack rather than a victory (cf. Ezek. 38–39; Joel 4 [Eng., Joel 3]; Zech. 12; 14; Luke 21:20; Rev. 20:7–10). Thus, the setting up of thrones is a metaphor for the assertion of authority over a people with the encampment of hostile armies. This is comparable to the text of Jeremiah 6:3, which speaks of the enemy from the north coming against Jerusalem under the metaphor of shepherds (i.e., kings) and their flocks (i.e., armies) pitching their tents (i.e., encamping) all around it.

When 1:16a says that the Lord will speak with them judgment concerning all their evil, it is evident from 1:16b that this is not judgment

---

39. Cf. the imminence of the Day of the Lord (e.g., Joel 1:15; 2:1; Obad. 15; Zeph. 1:14).

40. "Such a judicial situation as is here described is depicted in the reliefs of Nineveh showing the Assyrian siege of Lachish: an enthroned Sennacherib is seen receiving Judahite captives, bowed low in obeisance at the feet of their Assyrian overlord. But this scene is part of a relief, other scenes of which show the siege of the city; so that the additional phrases at the end of v 15, implying siege or at least military activity, are the verbal equivalent of the 'montage,' on the relief, of the sequence of events which take place, one after the other" (Holladay, *Jeremiah 1*, 41). McKane, on the other hand, does not consider this to be a judgment scene at all (*Jeremiah I–XXV*, 18).

of the enemy in 1:15 but judgment of those who have forsaken the LORD. It is true that the language of 1:16a is analogous to that of the account of King Zedekiah's capture in MT Jeremiah 39:5 in which Nebuchadnezzar speaks judgments with him (see also Jer. 52:9), but the present context is not about the judgment that the enemy speaks with Judah and Jerusalem. It is about the judgment that the LORD pronounces and executes by means of the enemy (cf. Jer. 4:12). The reason given for the judgment (and the description of their "evil") in 1:16b is repeated throughout the book:[41] "they forsook me and sent sacrifices up in smoke to other gods and prostrated themselves to the works of their hands" (Jer. 2:13; 5:19; 9:12–13 [Eng., 9:13–14]; 11:10–13; 16:11; 19:4; 22:9; 44:3, 5, 8, 15; cf. 2 Kgs. 22:17; Jer. 25:6). These are parallel expressions for the worship of idols. There are no "other gods," only idols made by human hands (Ps. 96:5). An idol can be an image of the one true God forbidden as an object of worship (e.g., Exod. 32; Deut. 9), or it can be a representation of an imaginary, false god as an object of worship (see Isa. 44:9–20; see also the metaphorical use of the terms "idolater" and "idolatry" in Eph. 5:5; Col. 3:5). This action of abandoning the LORD and worshiping idols—the prohibition of which is foundational to the covenant relationship (Exod. 20:2–6; Deut. 5:6–10; 13)—constitutes the fracture of the covenant (see Jer. 11:10) and the rejection of the fundamental instruction of the Torah. If this has been true of Israel throughout its history (Deut. 9:24; Jer. 7:25–26; 32:30) in spite of the fact that the nation has had a privileged role in God's plan (Amos 3:1–2), then it is certainly true of the Gentiles (see Jer. 2:11). Idolatry has been the basic problem common to all of fallen humanity from the beginning (Gen. 3:5; Rom. 1:23, 25),[42] and thus divine judgment has been due not only historically for Israel's breaking of the Sinai covenant but also eschatologically for all the unredeemed who do not participate in the new covenant (Jer. 31:31–34; see Isa. 66:24; Dan. 12:2).

The fronted pronoun at the beginning of 1:17a marks a shift in the discourse: "And as for you" (וְאַתָּה). The LORD instructs Jeremiah to gird up his loins (i.e., to prepare himself; cf. 1 Kgs. 18:46; 2 Kgs. 4:29; 9:1; Job 38:3; 40:7; 1 Pet. 1:13) and to rise up and speak all that he is commanded (cf. Jer. 1:7). The text of 1:17b differs considerably between the *Vorlage* of Greek Jeremiah ("Do not be afraid from before them [or,

---

41. Note how the judgment of their "evil" (רָעָה) is the unleashing of the "evil" or "calamity" (רָעָה) from the north (Jer. 1:14; cf. Jer. 11:17). This is the *lex talionis* ("law of retaliation"; see Exod. 21:23b–25; Lev. 24:20; Obad. 15; see also Jer. 6:19; 11:11; 19:3–4, 15; 35:17; 36:3, 31).

42. All other sins are symptomatic of this problem (see, e.g., Jer. 5:7–8).

because of them] and do not be dismayed before them, for with you am I to rescue you," the prophetic utterance of the Lord) and the MT ("Do not be dismayed from before them [or, because of them] lest I cause you to be dismayed before them"). The *Vorlage* of Greek Jeremiah uncharacteristically has the longer text here and echoes the wording of 1:8 (see also Jer. 17:18; 23:4; 30:10–11 [MT]; 42:11; 46:27–28; cf. Deut. 1:21; 31:8; Josh. 1:9; Ezek. 2:6; 3:9). In contrast to the encouraging words of the Greek text and its Hebrew source, the MT version issues a threat to the prophet (cf. Jer. 49:37).

For the Lord's part (MT: ואני ["And as for me"]), he has presently appointed Jeremiah as a prophet (cf. Jer. 1:5, 10) to be like a "fortified city" and a "fortified bronze wall" (MT adds "iron pillar" between these two) against his own people (Jer. 1:18a; cf. Jer. 6:27; 15:20; Ezek. 3:8; *4 Bar.* 1:2). This does not mean that Jeremiah will be like one well-protected inside a city wall. Rather, he must be the city wall itself, which absorbs the blows of its opposition.[43] This opposition consists of the kings of Judah, the officials, and the general populace (Jer. 1:18b). The MT adds the priests to this list, and the Syriac adds the prophets (cf. Jer. 32:32; see also Jer. 2:8; 5:31; 6:13). In other words, much like other true prophets (e.g., Isa. 6:9–10; Ezek. 2:3–5), Jeremiah will face opposition from every segment of society throughout the course of his ministry.[44] They will fight against him, but they will not prevail, precisely because of the Lord's active presence with him to rescue him (Jer. 1:19; cf. Jer. 1:8, 17). This means not only that they will reject his words but also that they will threaten his life (e.g., Jer. 11:18–23). Nevertheless, the Lord will preserve him to fulfill his calling (cf. Jer. 45:5).

2:2 And he said,[45] *"Thus says the Lord, 'I remember [MT adds: you (or, for you)] the covenant loyalty of your youth and [and > MT] the love of your betrothal [LXX: completion], your walking after the Holy One of Israel [MT: your walking after me in the wilderness, in a land not sown],' the prophetic utterance of the Lord [> MT].*[46] *2:3 'Israel was holy*

---

43. See Randall C. Bailey, "Jeremiah: Fortified City, Bronze Walls, and Iron Pillar Against the Whole Land," *HS* 57 (2016): 117–38. Bailey also argues for the militant character of Jeremiah's prophetic ministry.

44. See Jeremiah 2:8; 4:9; 5:31; 6:13–15, 27; 8:8, 10–12; 11:18–12:6; 15:20; 17:18; 20:1–8; 23:9–40; 26; 28; 36–38; 42–43.

45. MT: 2:1: "And the word of the Lord came to me, saying, 'Go and proclaim in the ears of Jerusalem, saying . . .'"

46. *Tg. Jon.*: "I remember you [or, for you], the goodness of former days, the love of your forefathers who believed in my word and went after my two

[or, set apart] to the LORD, *the first fruits of his produce. All who ate [Tg. Jon.: plundered] him would be guilty; calamity would come to them,' the prophetic utterance of the* LORD.

2:4 Hear the word of the LORD, *O house of Jacob and all the families of the house of Israel. 2:5 Thus says the* LORD, *'What injustice did your forefathers find in me that they became distant from me and went after what was empty [Tg. Jon.: idols] and became empty? 2:6 And they did not say / think, "Where is the* LORD *who brought us up from the land of Egypt, who walked us through the wilderness in a land of desert and pit, in a dry and barren land [MT: in a dry land and deep darkness (or, shadow of death)], in a land through which no one passes and where humanity does not dwell?" 2:7 And I brought you to the fertile land [LXX: Carmel] to eat its fruit and its goodness. And you came and defiled my land, and my inheritance you made into an abomination [Tg. Jon.: the worship of idols]. 2:8 The priests, they have not said, "Where is the* LORD?" *And those who have handled the Torah [Tg. Jon.: taught the Torah], they have not acknowledged me. And the shepherds [Tg. Jon.: kings], they have transgressed against me. And the prophets [Tg. Jon.: false prophets], they have prophesied by Baal, and after those that could not benefit have they gone [Vulg.: and they followed idols]. 2:9 Therefore, still will I contend with you,' the prophetic utterance of the* LORD, *'and with the sons of [the sons of > pc Mss, Vulg.] your sons will I contend. 2:10 For cross over to the isles of Kittim [or, the coasts of Cyprus] and see, and to Kedar [Tg. Jon.: the province of the Arabs] send and consider carefully; and see if it has happened like this.*[47] *2:11 Do nations exchange their gods [MT: Does a nation exchange gods], and they are non-gods [or, even though they are non-gods]? And my people, it exchanges its glory*[48] *for those that*

---

    messengers Moses and Aaron in the wilderness for forty years without provisions in a land not sown."

47. *Tg. Jon.:* "and see the peoples who go into exile [or, wander] from city to city and from province to province carrying their idols and bringing them with them. And in the place where they dwell they pitch their tents, and they set up their idols and worship them. Where is the people or tongue that does like you, O house of Israel?"

48. In Masoretic tradition, "its glory" (כבודו) is one of the *Tiqqune sopherim* ("corrections of scribes"). It is considered a euphemistic scribal correction for "my glory" (כבודי) (cf. Hos. 4:7; Ps. 106:20). See Ernst Würthwein, *The Text of the Old Testament: An Introduction to the Biblia Hebraica*, trans. Erroll F. Rhodes, 2nd ed. (Grand Rapids: Eerdmans, 1994), 17–18. See McKane, *Jeremiah I–XXV*, 34.

do not benefit [MT: for that which does not benefit]. 2:12 Be appalled, O sky, concerning this, and bristle very greatly [MT: and bristle, be very desolate],' the prophetic utterance of the LORD.[49] *2:13 'For there are two evils that my people have committed: (1) me have they forsaken [or, it is I whom they have forsaken], the fountain of living water [or, fresh, running water], (2) to cut out [or, by cutting out] for themselves broken cisterns [MT: cisterns, broken cisterns; Tg. Jon.: idols that are like broken pits] that cannot hold the water.'"*

It is customary in modern commentary to separate 2:1–3 from 2:4–13. This is not without reason. The MT makes a break between verses 3 and 4 by starting a new, "opened" (פתוחא) paragraph flush right in the Hebrew text of verse 4. Verse 4 itself (cf. 7:2) and the beginning of verse 5 (cf. 2:2) constitute new introductory formulae. Furthermore, the LORD addresses the people in 2:2 using second feminine singular pronouns, while in 2:5, 7, 9, 10 he addresses them with second masculine plural pronouns and imperatives. The use of second feminine singular pronouns resumes in 2:14. Nevertheless, there is also good reason to believe that 2:2–13 is now intended to be read as a unit that sets Jeremiah's prophecy firmly within the larger context of the biblical narrative.[50] This is the textual world of the Bible that serves as the primary frame of reference for the biblical authors (cf. Jer. 32:16–25). The reference to the wilderness experience in 2:2–3 thus establishes a necessary antecedent for 2:6–8.

The Hebrew text behind Greek Jeremiah begins this section very simply, "And he said," continuing from the introductory material in chapter 1. On the other hand, the MT expands with a word of the LORD formula (1:1 And the word of the LORD came to me saying, 2:1 "Go and proclaim in the ears of Jerusalem, saying . . ."; cf. Jer. 1:4, 11, 13).[51]

---

49. *Tg. Jon.*: "Mourn, O sky, concerning this, concerning the land of Israel, which is about to be ruined, and concerning the sanctuary, which is about to be desolate, and because my people have committed evil deeds very much so, says the Lord."

50. Cf. Deuteronomy 6:20–25; 26:5–9; 32; Joshua 24:1–15; Judges 2:1–5; 6:7–10; 10:11–15; 1 Samuel 12:6–17; Isaiah 63:7–14; Ezekiel 16; 20; Amos 2:6–16; Micah 6:1–8; Psalms 78; 105; 106; 135; 136; Nehemiah 9; Acts 7; 13:13–41; Hebrews 11. See Michael B. Shepherd, *The Textual World of the Bible*, StBibLit 156 (New York: Lang, 2013).

51. "The contents of 2–6 did not originate as speeches, and we are not to think of them as oral communications which were subsequently reduced to writing. Rather they originated with Jeremiah as written compositions and were thereafter 'published' in order to be read. Hence the superscription

This is comparable to what happens in 7:1–2 where the *Vorlage* of the Greek text has a brief introduction upon which the MT expands considerably. The text of 2:2 continues with a standard introduction to prophetic discourse, "Thus says the Lord" (153 occurrences in Jeremiah, substantially more than any other biblical book).

When the Lord says, "I remember," it calls to mind for the audience something that will eventually be set against the current situation. The MT adds to this לְךָ, which can be the object of the verb ("I remember you") or the equivalent of a dative of advantage ("I remember for you"). This then requires the following phrases in 2:2 to be understood adverbially. These phrases are the object of the verb in the *Vorlage* of Greek Jeremiah: "I remember the covenant loyalty of your youth and the love of your betrothal, your walking after the Holy One of Israel." The Hebrew text here employs the second feminine singular pronominal suffixes ("your") to refer to the present generation of Israel, which consists of Judah and Jerusalem, as if it were also the wilderness generation of Israel. Solidarity between past and present generations of the people of God and the ability to speak of these generations interchangeably as if every subsequent generation had experienced the entirety of the biblical story are common features of the Bible's literature (e.g., Deut. 26:5–9; Josh. 24:5–8; Hos. 12:5b [Eng., 12:4b]; Rom. 4:22–25; 15:4; 1 Cor. 9:10; 10:11).[52] Thus, the testimony of the individual believer is not merely the story of his or her personal journey but also (and more importantly) the biblical story of all the people of God (see Deut. 26:5–9).[53]

    (so Duhm) must be declared entirely inappropriate in respect of the material which it purports to introduce" (McKane, *Jeremiah I–XXV*, 26).

52. "The striking contemporization of past tradition ('you') aligns with Hos 13:4–5; other prophets also used this convention in relation to the exodus and wilderness (see Amos 2:10; Mic 6:4). The present generation was the current heir of such traditions and could spiritually identify with their forebears' encounter with God as a once-for-all experience. Time was bridged in a community whose religious heritage had been kept alive in worship down the centuries. The NT took up this concept of historical solidarity via a sacramental theology, for instance in Eph 2:5, 'God made us alive together with Christ'" (Leslie C. Allen, *Jeremiah: A Commentary*, OTL [Louisville: Westminster John Knox, 2008], 35).

53. "Typology does not make scriptural contents into metaphors for extrascriptural realities, but the other way around. It does not suggest, as if often said in our day, that believers find their stories in the Bible, but rather that they make the story of the Bible their story" (George A. Lindbeck, *The Nature of Doctrine: Religion and Theology in a Postliberal Age* [Philadelphia:

The LORD remembers the "covenant loyalty" (חסד) of Israel's youth (cf. Jer. 3:4). This term is often parallel to "faithfulness" (אמונה) (BDB, 339). Commentators have historically been divided as to whether the construct relationship in the Hebrew text approximates a subjective genitive (the covenant loyalty that young Israel had toward the LORD) or an objective genitive (the covenant loyalty that the LORD had toward young Israel). Keil argues that the walking after the LORD in 2:2b is decisive, assuming that this means Israel faithfully followed the LORD (cf. Isa. 1:21).[54] According to this view, 2:2 sets up a contrast between the fidelity of the wilderness generation and the lack thereof in subsequent generations (Jer. 2:5–8), but the biblical witness is unanimous that there was never a time when Israel was faithful (see Deut. 9:24; 31:27; 1 Sam. 8:8; 2 Kgs. 21:15; Isa. 43:27; 48:8; Jer. 2:20; 3:25; 7:25–26; 22:21; 32:30; Ezek. 2:3b; 20; 23:3; Amos 5:25–27; Mal. 3:7; Ezra 9:7; see also Gen. 6:5; 8:21).[55] Passages that speak of an ideal early period do not mention Israel's loyalty to the covenant relationship but the LORD's faithfulness and provision (Exod. 16–17; Deut. 32:10; Isa. 5:1–7; Jer. 2:6; Ezek. 16:1–14, 60; Hos. 2:16–17; [Eng., 2:14–15]; 9:10; 11:1; 13:4–6), implying great potential for Israel in light of such divine fidelity. According to this view, 2:2 sets up the subsequent rejection of the LORD by Israel (Jer. 2:5–8) as incongruous with his demonstrated covenant loyalty.

The LORD's covenant loyalty is paralleled by the phrase "the love (אהבה) of your betrothal" (cf. Jer. 31:2–3). This is not merely a feeling that the LORD had for Israel but a voluntary devotion and commitment to the covenant relationship established with the patriarchs (Gen.

Westminster, 1984], 118). "Midrashic exegesis is the way into that world; it does not seek to view present-day reality through biblical spectacles, neither to find referents of biblical prophecy in present-day happenings, nor to find referents to the daily life of the soul in biblical allegory. Instead it simply overwhelms the present; the Bible's time is important, while the present is not; and so it invites the reader to cross over into the enterable world of Scripture" (James Kugel, "Two Introductions to Midrash," in *Midrash and Literature*, ed. Geoffrey H. Hartman and Sanford Budick [New Haven: Yale University Press, 1986], 90; quoted in Daniel Boyarin, *Intertextuality and the Reading of Midrash* [Bloomington: Indiana University Press, 1990], 129). See also Erich Auerbach, *Mimesis: The Representation of Reality in Western Literature*, trans. Willard R. Trask, 50th anniv. ed. (Princeton: Princeton University Press, 2003), 14–15; Hans Frei, *The Eclipse of Biblical Narrative: A Study in Eighteenth and Nineteenth Century Hermeneutics* (New Haven, CT: Yale University Press, 1974), 152–53.

54. Keil, *Jeremiah*, 34–35. See also *Tg. Jon.*

55. See Calvin, *Jeremiah*, 1:69–70; Walser, *Jeremiah*, 203.

15:18; Exod. 2:24; Deut. 7:7–8).[56] Given the marriage metaphor with the LORD as the husband and Israel as the bride,[57] the use of second feminine singular pronouns in 2:2 now seems appropriate. This is a metaphor that Jeremiah appears to have on loan from Hosea (see Hos. 1–3; see also Ezek. 16). It is also one that will recur in Jeremiah's book (e.g., Jer. 3). The LORD's covenant loyalty and love made possible Israel's "walking after" him by means of the exodus (Jer. 2:2b, 6). The *Vorlage* of Greek Jeremiah, "your walking after the Holy One of Israel," is rightly interpreted by the MT, "your walking after me in the wilderness, in a land not sown" (cf. Jer. 31:27; Hos. 2:25 [Eng., 2:23]; Zech. 10:9).[58] There is no distinction in the text between pre-Sinai wilderness (Exod. 16–17) and post-Sinai (Num. 11–20).[59]

Verse 3 is an exegesis of the priestly law in Leviticus 22:14–16:[60] "And a man, when he eats what is holy [or, set apart] inadvertently, he will add its fifth to it and give to the priest that which is holy. And they will not profane the holy things of the sons of Israel that they offer to the LORD and cause them to bear punishment for guilt when they eat their holy things, for I am the LORD who makes them holy." Israel was holy or set apart to the LORD (Exod. 19:6; Deut. 7:6; Isa. 6:13; Ezra 9:2), the first fruits of his produce (cf. 2 Thess. 2:13; Jas. 1:18). According to the law, the

---

56. See Michael B. Shepherd, *Textuality and the Bible* (Eugene, OR: Wipf & Stock, 2016), 94–102.

57. McKane contends that the word translated "betrothal" refers instead to the first days of a marriage (*Jeremiah I–XXV*, 27–28). But see also Hosea 2:21–22 (Eng., 2:19–20).

58. McKane (*Jeremiah I–XXV*, 27) suggests that the Greek translator paraphrased "after me" (אחרי) as "after the Holy One of Israel," which is a favorite title for the LORD in the book of Isaiah (e.g., Isa. 1:4; 12:6; see also Jer. 50:29b; 51:5b). But if the translator would have done anything with אחרי in his source text, it is more likely that he would have interpreted the *yodh* suffix as an abbreviation for the divine name: אחר יהוה ("after the LORD") (cf. MT and LXX Jer. 6:11 and 25:37 [LXX 32:23]). It seems rather that the translator had אַחֲרֵי meaning "after" followed by the phrase "the Holy One of Israel." Those responsible for the MT read אַחֲרַי as "after me" followed by "the Holy One of Israel" in apposition. This was due to the expectation that the LORD would refer to himself in the first person rather than the third. The seemingly superfluous appositional explanation of "me" was then replaced by what was thought to be a more helpful guide for the reader—an explanation of where Israel walked after the LORD.

59. Contra Keil, *Jeremiah*, 35.

60. See Michael Fishbane, *Biblical Interpretation in Ancient Israel* (Oxford: Clarendon, 1985), 300–304.

first fruits were to be devoted to the LORD (e.g., Exod. 23:19; 34:26; Lev. 2:12; 23:10; Prov. 3:9; see *Tg. Jon.* Jer. 2:3; see also Ezek. 48:14). Thus, anyone who tried to "eat" Israel would be counted guilty and suffer the consequences (cf. Jer. 5:17; 10:25; 30:16; 50:7, 17–18; 51:34).

The following subunit in Jeremiah 2:4–13 begins with a call to the house of Jacob and all the families of the house of Israel to hear the word of the LORD (Jer. 2:4; cf. Jer. 5:20; Amos 3:1; LXX Mic. 6:1a). Again, Judah and Jerusalem of Jeremiah's day are addressed in this section as if they were all Israel from the beginning of their story. Verse 5 then opens with the formula, "Thus says the LORD." What follows has several points of contact with Micah 6:1–5, which is commonly known as an example of a prophetic lawsuit (ריב). In Micah 6:3, the LORD says, "My people, what have I done to you [LXX adds: or how have I grieved you] and how have I wearied you? Answer me [or, Testify against me]." These words are echoed in Jeremiah 2:5, "What injustice did your forefathers find in me that they became distant from me and went after what was empty and became empty" (cf. 1 Sam. 12:21; Jer. 2:31; Ezek. 11:15; 44:10)? The questions have a striking rhetorical effect, but they also invite a response, and the LORD himself makes a case in defense of his justice (Deut. 32:4; Ps. 92:16 [Eng., 92:15]), contending that the people's abandonment of him has been unwarranted. The language of going after "what was empty" (ההבל) is generally recognized to be a play on "the Baal" (הבעל), the Canaanite storm/fertility god (see Deut. 32:21; Judg. 2:11–13; 1 Kgs. 16:13b, 26b, 31–32; 18:21; 2 Kgs. 17:15–16; Jer. 2:8b, 11, 13, 23; 10:15; 16:19; 51:18; 23:16; LXX Hos. 5:11; see also *Tg. Jon.* Jer. 2:5b; 1 Cor. 8:4). To become empty like the empty idols/gods was not only to become blind and deaf to the prophet's message (Isa. 6:9–10; Jer. 5:21; Ezek. 12:2; Hab. 2:18; Pss. 115:4–8; 135:15–18) but also to be subject to destruction (Lev. 26:30; Deut. 7:26; Jer. 7:19; 8:19b; 10:3, 14–15; 11:17; 51:17–18; Hos. 9:10; Ps. 78:33; see also Rom. 1:21).

The forefathers did not say, "Where is the LORD who brought us up from the land of Egypt" (Jer. 2:6a; cf. Jer. 5:24; Mic. 6:4)? In other words, they did not reject the LORD and choose Baal because the LORD failed them in some way. Rather, they rejected the LORD because they forgot what he had done for them (see Deut. 8:14–16; Pss. 78:11; 106:7). The exodus was the central act of deliverance in Israel's history, yet there appeared to be no memory of it. The nature of the question in 2:6a is not to ask about the LORD's perceived absence (e.g., Jer. 2:28) but to call on him to deliver in the present as he once did in the past (e.g., 2 Kgs. 2:14; Isa. 63:11; Jer. 2:8). He is the one who led them through the wilderness, a deserted and pit-filled place, a dry and barren place without people (Jer. 2:6b; cf. Mic. 6:5a; see also Deut. 2:7; 29:4 [Eng., 29:5]; Jer. 4:25, 29;

51:43; Hos. 2:16–17 [Eng., 2:14–15]; Amos 2:10; Ps. 106:9; Neh. 9:21).[61] The forefathers, however, did not remember this. Verse 7a then switches to the second masculine plural pronoun "you," treating the forefathers and the present generation interchangeably as in 2:2 (see Exod. 20:5b): "And I brought you to the fertile land [LXX: Carmel] to eat its fruit and its goodness" (cf. Mic. 6:5b; see also Neh. 9:36).[62] הכרמל can be a reference to Mt. Carmel on the Mediterranean coast (so LXX) or simply a reference to a good, fruitful land. In either case it is a way to refer to the entire land as the opposite of the wilderness (see Jer. 4:26; 50:19). The Lord was faithful to bring the people into the land of the covenant (Josh. 21:43–45), but they "defiled" the land and made the Lord's inheritance into an "abomination" (*Tg. Jon.*: "the worship of idols"; Jer. 2:7b; cf. Jer. 16:18). This refers specifically to the violation of the terms of the covenant (Jer. 7:9; 11:10) and the adoption of Canaanite religious practices (e.g., Jer. 7:17–19, 30–31) that made the land religiously unclean and unfit for worship (see Lev. 18:19–30; Num. 35:34; Deut. 24:4; Jer. 3:1; Ezek. 36:17). The land of the covenant was the Lord's inheritance (Lev. 25:23), which he granted to whomever he pleased (cf. Dan. 4:14 [Eng., 4:17]; Jer. 27:5–6). Israel was also the Lord's portion and inheritance (e.g., Deut. 32:9; Jer. 10:16 [MT]), so it is somewhat ironic that the land and the people are here at odds with each other.

Verse 8 of chapter 2 delineates four different groups within Israelite society who have failed in their responsibilities throughout the people's history.[63] Each group is fronted in the Hebrew syntax for the purpose of topicalization.[64] First, the priestly leadership has neglected to ask the same question from verse 6a ("Where is the Lord?") within the mediating role of its cultic duties (see, e.g., Exod. 32; Deut. 9),[65] thus setting

---

61. For the MT's צלמות, see the helpful discussion in James Barr, *Comparative Philology and the Text of the Old Testament* (Oxford: Oxford University Press, 1968; repr., Winona Lake, IN: Eisenbrauns, 1987), 375–80.
62. LXX Nehemiah 9:36–37 has a shorter text than the MT. This is likely due to scribal or translator oversight wherein the scribe or translator accidentally skipped from פריה ("its fruit") to מרבה and thus omitted the intervening text.
63. See Holladay, *Jeremiah 1*, 88–89.
64. See Adina Moshavi, *Word Order in the Biblical Hebrew Finite Clause: A Syntactic and Pragmatic Analysis of Preposing*, LSAWS 4 (Winona Lake, IN: Eisenbrauns, 2010), 160–61.
65. According to Redak, the priests should have asked the people, "Where is the Lord, that you worship other deities?" (Rosenberg, trans., *Mikraoth Gedoloth: Jeremiah Volume One*, 11).

itself in opposition to the LORD and any true prophet who speaks on his behalf (Jer. 1:18b; 2:26; 5:31; 6:13; Ezek. 22:26; Zeph. 3:4b). Second, the scribes who have handled the text of the Torah have not acknowledged the LORD (cf. Jer. 8:8; 18:18; Hos. 4:6, 9).[66] These scribes may very well have been of priestly stock, which gave them access to texts and scribal training, but they failed in their responsibility to copy, transmit, and teach faithfully the Torah that had been entrusted to them (Deut. 17:11; 31:9; 33:10; Mal. 2:4–7; 2 Chr. 17:7–9).[67] They may have "known" of the LORD and claimed to worship him, but they did not acknowledge him in their thoughts and actions (Jer. 2:23, 35; cf. Jer. 4:22; 9:2b, 5 [Eng., 9:3b, 6]; Hos. 2:4–15 [Eng., 2:2–13]; Prov. 3:5–6). Third, the shepherds are the kings who have transgressed against the LORD (Jer. 1:18b; 21:1–23:4; cf. Ezek. 34). Within the book of Jeremiah, the failure of the sons of Josiah in particular sets up the hope of the messianic shepherd who is yet to come (Jer. 3:15; 23:5–6). And fourth, the false prophets have prophesied by Baal.[68] These prophets told the people what they wanted to hear (Jer. 5:31; 6:14) and opposed the true prophecy of those like Jeremiah (Jer. 28; cf. 1 Kgs. 22). They not only prophesied in Baal's name but also prophesied in the LORD's name falsely (Jer. 23:9–40). Contrary to popular opinion, it was not the worship of Baal that benefited the people but the worship of the LORD (cf. 1 Sam. 12:21; Jer. 2:11, 13; Hos. 2:10 [Eng., 2:8]; Hab. 2:18–20).[69]

The conjunction לכן ("Therefore") at the beginning of 2:9 normally introduces an announcement of judgment inferred after a formal accusation in prophetic discourse (e.g., Jer. 5:14; Mic. 2:3; 3:6, 12), but here

---

66. See Holladay, *Jeremiah 1*, 89; McKane, *Jeremiah I–XXV*, 32. Given the extensive references to the five books of Moses (Gen.–Deut.) throughout the book of Jeremiah, his use of "Torah" is likely a reference to the whole Pentateuch.

67. This resulted not only in the textual corruption and misuse of the Torah but also in the forgetting of the Torah that led to the need for its rediscovery (2 Kgs. 22). Faithful transmission of the Torah came by the prophets (2 Kgs. 17:13; Dan. 9:10; Ezra 9:10–11).

68. The Old Greek text uses the feminine article with the name of the male deity Baal. This reflects the common replacement of בעל ("Baal") with בשת ("shame") (e.g., MT Jer. 11:13). The Greek word for "shame" is feminine (ἡ αἰσχύνη). Change from the use of the feminine to the use of the masculine is one indicator of revision in Greek tradition. See Siegfried Kreuzer, *The Bible in Greek: Translation, Transmission, and Theology of the Septuagint*, SCS 63 (Atlanta: SBL, 2015), 22–23, 236–38.

69. The foreign god Baal is comparable to a foreign nation that cannot provide any aid, only shame (see Isa. 30:5, 6).

it introduces the LORD's statement that he will continue to "contend" (cf. Mic. 6:2; see also Jer. 25:31; 50:34; 51:36; Hos. 4:1; 12:3 [Eng., 12:2]) with the present and future generations due to the correlation with the past generations just outlined (see Exod. 20:5; Jer. 31:29). Verses 10–13 then explain further why the people's failure is so egregious. According to 2:10, if the people were to cross over to Cyprus or send to Kedar, they would find that their unwarranted abandonment of the LORD for the worship of Baal is an unprecedented kind of action among the religions of the world (cf. Deut. 4:32; Jer. 18:13; Amos 6:2). The island of Cyprus in the Mediterranean and Kedar in the Arabian region are not two destinations but are like two points on a compass representing the west (Cyprus) and the east (Kedar). The rhetorical question in 2:11a expects a negative answer. Foreign nations do not exchange their false gods. They hold on to them and faithfully worship them, even though they are "non-gods" that cannot possibly benefit them in any way (see Deut. 32:17, 21; Isa. 44:9; Jer. 2:8b; 5:7; Hos. 8:6; Hab. 2:18; Ps. 96:5; see also GKC §152a[1]). This is contrary to the expectation that such gods would be forsaken eventually (Jer. 16:19–21). On the other hand, the expectation is even greater that worshipers of the one true God who benefits his followers would remain devoted to him, but this is ironically not the case with the chosen people of God. Without reason they have exchanged "their glory" who delivered them from Egypt and brought them into the land. They have exchanged him for gods/idols that bring them no such benefit (Jer. 2:11b; cf. Deut. 32:17, 21; Hab. 2:16; Rom. 1:25). The expression "their glory" refers to the glory of the LORD (cf. Hos. 4:7; Ps. 106:20; see Exod. 40:34; 1 Kgs. 8:11; Isa. 6:3–4; Ezek. 43:5; but see also Ps. 3:4 [Eng., 3:3]).[70] Their shame is Baal (Jer. 3:24; 11:13).

Verse 12 calls upon the sky to be appalled and to bristle very greatly at the situation just described in verse 11. This type of address to inanimate things is a figure of speech known as apostrophe.[71] It is thus not necessarily an address to the heavenly assembly of angels (see 1 Kgs. 22:19–23; Isa. 6:1–8; Job 1:6; 2:1; Dan. 4:14 [Eng., 4:17]), although such an understanding of the text is not out of the question.[72] The Hebrew imperative translated "be appalled" can also be rendered "be desolated." This understanding of the text is reflected in the MT of

---

70. See John Bright, *Jeremiah*, AB (Garden City, NY: Doubleday, 1965), 15; J. A. Thompson, *The Book of Jeremiah*, NICOT (Grand Rapids: Eerdmans, 1980), 170.
71. See E. W. Bullinger, *Figures of Speech Used in the Bible* (London: Eyre and Spottiswoode, 1898; repr., Grand Rapids: Baker, 1968), 905.
72. See Holladay, *Jeremiah 1*, 91.

2:12b, which has חרבו ("be desolate") instead of הרבה ("greatly"). Given the water imagery of 2:13, it is possible that those responsible for the MT understood verse 12 to be a command that would bring into effect the covenant curse of a drought ("Be desolated, O sky, because of this, and bristle, be very desolate") in order to set up the contrast in verse 13 between what the LORD provides and what the false gods lack (see Deut. 28:23–24; Jer. 3:3; 14:1–6).[73] On the other hand, the imperative "bristle" is the odd man out in the MT. It seems better to follow the Hebrew source of Greek Jeremiah in which the imperatives "be appalled" and "bristle" invite the all-seeing eyes of the sky to bear witness to the actions of the people (cf. Mic. 6:1–2; see Deut. 4:26; 30:19; 31:28; 32:1; Isa. 1:2; see also Ezek. 27:35; 32:10). The testimony of creation against Israel matches that of the creator.

Verse 13 concludes this section with an explanation of why the sky should be appalled. God's people have committed two evils. The first is that they have forsaken the LORD, the fountain of living water (cf. Jer. 1:16; 16:10–13; 17:13; *1 En.* 96:6). The fronting of the pronoun "me" in the Hebrew text is significant, as if to say, "Me of all options have they forsaken." But in what sense is the LORD a source of living water? On the one hand, he is the one who provides the rain and the fresh, running water necessary for life (Gen. 26:19; Lev. 14:5–6; Deut. 28:12; Ezek. 47:8–12; Zech. 14:8; Rev. 22:1). On the other hand, he is the source of spiritual life symbolized by water (Ezek. 36:25–27; Ps. 36:10 [Eng., 36:9]; John 3:5; 4:7–15; 7:37–39; Rev. 7:17; 21:6; 22:17; see also Isa. 12:3).[74] The second evil of God's people is given as the purpose of the first (or perhaps the means by which the first was accomplished): "to cut out [or, by cutting out] for themselves broken cisterns that cannot hold the water" (cf. Jer. 14:3). These broken cisterns represent the false gods and idols by which the people became empty not only physically but also spiritually (see *Tg. Jon.*; see also Jer. 1:5; 3:3, 24). The irony is that they preferred these waterless containers to the fountain of living

---

73. Holladay, *Jeremiah 1*, 91.

74. Redak: "Scripture compares God, Who lavishes good upon Israel when they hold onto His Torah, to a spring of living waters, which flow endlessly" (Rosenberg, trans., *Mikraoth Gedoloth: Jeremiah Volume One*, 13). Cf. Psalm 1; Baruch 3:12; 4:1. See also Michael Fishbane, "The Well of Living Water: A Biblical Motif and Its Ancient Transformations," in *"Sha'arei Talmon": Studies in the Bible, Qumran, and the Ancient Near East Presented to Shemaryahu Talmon*, eds. Michael Fishbane and Emanuel Tov (Winona Lake, IN: Eisenbrauns, 1992), 3–16.

water.[75] This text is like a mirror held up to humanity, which has from the very beginning fallen prey to the temptation of empty promises despite the blessings of God (Gen. 2:16–17; 3:1–7). The LORD offers free "water" and "food" that satisfy, while the worship of idols comes at a great price and does not satisfy (Isa. 55:1–2).[76]

APPLICATION OF JEREMIAH 1:1–2:13

Application sections in the present commentary are not intended to provide supplementary guidance on what to do with the biblical text. Rather, they are designed to exegete the author's own application for his future readership. In other words, the application is part of the meaning of the text and not a separate entity. Because the text is put together in such a way that the eschatological message of the book survives any supposedly original audience, the book remains relevant for the modern interpreter, not requiring any sort of artificial update. When urged to be content with the revealed message of the biblical text, readers are often tempted to ask instead about things that it does not address. It is suggested here that readers should resist this temptation.[77] The biblical text is sufficient because it reveals all that

---

75. As the Canaanite storm/fertility god, Baal would have been expected to produce rainfall, but this proved to be an empty hope (see 1 Kgs. 18; cf. Jer. 5:24; 10:13).

76. "It would seem that Our Lord finds our desires not too strong, but too weak. We are half-hearted creatures, fooling about with drink and sex and ambition when infinite joy is offered us, like an ignorant child who wants to go on making mud pies in a slum because he cannot imagine what is meant by the offer of a holiday at the sea. We are far too easily pleased" (C. S. Lewis, *The Weight of Glory: And Other Addresses* [New York: HarperOne, 2000], 26).

77. Willingness to resist this temptation and to submit to the concerns of the biblical text results in a transformation of the kinds of questions asked by the reader from reader-centered questions to text-centered questions. This calls to mind the words of the old hymn by H. H. Lemmel, "Turn your eyes upon Jesus / Look full in His wonderful face / And the things of earth will grow strangely dim / In the light of His glory and grace" (Tom Fettke, ed., *The Hymnal for Worship and Celebration* [Waco, TX: Word, 1986], 335). Given that the Jesus upon whom readers turn their eyes is the biblical Jesus, the words could also be, "Turn your eyes upon Scripture, look full in its wonderful text, and the things of earth will grow strangely dim in the light of its glory and grace." By the work of the Spirit, preoccupation with the words of Scripture rearranges the priorities of the reader and bears fruit in the believer (Pss. 1; 19).

is important for life with God and others, not because it addresses all that its readers deem to be important. That is, it is not a blemish on the biblical text for it not to speak to things that distract its readers from what really matters. How can readers know what is important? Whatever is in the text is important.

The first item from the text of Jeremiah that the reader must receive and embrace is the claim that the book as a whole is the word of God that came to the prophet (Jer. 1:1–3). This claim is supported by the presentation of Jeremiah as a genuine prophet like Moses (Jer. 1:4–10). The book is not simply another piece of world literature designed to entertain or to inform. It aims to subject its readers to its will. The reader does not have the option of a neutral response, keeping the book at arm's length as a mere object of study. There is only belief and unbelief, both with very real consequences.[78] This is because the textual world of Jeremiah is the real world. It is an integral part of a biblical world that shapes and defines the world for its readers.

The second point of application is reorientation to the program of the book (Jer. 1:10) and its subthemes (Jer. 1:11–19). This reorientation of the reader is bolstered by the context of the textual world of the Bible provided in Jeremiah 2:1–13. The program, its subthemes, and the Bible's representation of reality are the important issues to the author. Therefore, they should be the important issues to the reader. It is not the reader's place to evaluate the relative importance of the word of God. The reader's role is to accept what is revealed (see Deut. 29:28; 1 Cor. 4:6). As noted in the commentary, the program of judgment and restoration set forth in 1:10 refers not merely to a documentary of past events for those with historical interests but also to the manner in which past events prefigure the future and final work of God in Christ. The subthemes of God watching over his word, the enemy from the north, idolatry, opposition, and divine presence (Jer. 1:11–19) serve the purpose of the program not only for Jeremiah and his contemporaries

---

78. It is recommended here that readers should take a faith stance toward the book of Jeremiah not in order to read dogma into the text but because the book itself requires it. In other words, the reader who reads the book without faith does not read it according to the author's intention. Of course, it is possible to discover a great deal about the text's meaning on the strength of exegetical skills alone, but such skills need to be combined with a conscious dependence upon God in the hermeneutical process in order to overcome the presuppositional baggage carried by every reader (Ps. 119:18) and in order to receive what is written (1 Cor. 2:6–16). On the other hand, a reader who has faith but no exegetical skills reads in vain.

but also for the faithful remnant of the people of God throughout the ages. This solidarity among past, present, and future generations of God's people is affirmed in Jeremiah 2:1–13 where the biblical story is the testimony of all. It is evident from this story that the biblical God is the only one who satisfies, despite the people's failure to acknowledge him. Rightful recognition of the LORD requires a new covenant relationship (Jer. 31:31–34).

JEREMIAH 2:14–37

2:14 "'Is it a servant that Israel is? Is it a homeborn slave that he is? Why has he become plunder? 2:15 Over him young lions [Tg. Jon.: kings] roar and [and > MT] give [Syr., Tg. Jon.: raise] their voice. They make [MT: And they make] his land into a desolation [or, object of horror]. And [And > MT] as for his cities, they are torn down so that there is no inhabitant.[1] 2:16 Also the sons of Noph [or, Memphis] and Tahpanhes, they know you and mock you. Is not this what your forsaking me has done to you?' 2:17 the prophetic utterance of the LORD your God.[2] 2:18 'And now what do you have to do with the road to Egypt [lit., And now what to you and to the road of Egypt; MT: And now what to you with reference to the road to Egypt; see BDB, 553] to drink the water of (the) Gihon [MT: Shihor; = the Nile; see Gen. 2:13; Sir. 24:27]?[3] And what do you have to do with the road to Assyria [lit., And what to you and to the road of Assyria; MT: And what to you with reference to the road to Assyria] to drink the water of (the) River [i.e., the Euphrates]?[4] 2:19 Your evil will discipline you; and your apostasy, it will reprove you. And know and see that bitter to you [MT: And know and see that evil and bitter] is your forsaking me,' the prophetic utterance of the LORD your God [MT: is your forsaking the LORD your God]. 'And I do not delight in you,' the prophetic utterance of the LORD your

---

1. The Hebrew source of Greek Jeremiah and a few MT manuscripts have נתצו ("they are torn down"). A few MT manuscripts have נתצה ("each is torn down"). See GKC §44m, 145k. The *kethiv* in the Leningrad Codex is נצתה ("each is ruined" [from נצה] or "each is burned" [from יצת]). The *qere* in the Leningrad Codex is נצתו ("they are burned"). Cf. Jeremiah 4:7, 26; 9:9, 11 (Eng., 9:10, 12).
2. Leningrad Codex: "Also the sons of Noph [or, Memphis] and Tahpanhes, they graze/tend [Syr.: crush] you on top of the head [*Tg. Jon.*: they slay your warriors and plunder your possessions]. Is not this what your forsaking the LORD your God at the time of walking you on the path does to you?"
3. *Tg. Jon.*: "And now what to you to be joined to Pharaoh the king of Egypt to cast your males into the river [see Exod. 1:22]?" The Shihor is a branch of the Nile (BDB, 1009). The Latin Vulgate (*aquam turbidam*) apparently reads שְׁחוֹר ("blackness") instead of שִׁחוֹר (Shihor) (see Lam. 4:8; cf. Ezek. 32:2). The usual word for the Nile is יאר or יאור.
4. *Tg. Jon.*: "And what to you to make a covenant with the Assyrian to take you into exile beyond the other side of the Euphrates [see 2 Kings 17]?" For "(the) River" as the Euphrates (פרת), see BDB, 625.

God [MT: 'And not fear of me to you,' the prophetic utterance of the Lord GOD of hosts]."[5]

If verses 4–13 of chapter 2 demonstrate Israel's unwarranted and foolish abandonment of the LORD who has been faithful from the beginning (Jer. 2:2), then verses 14–19 indicate Israel's change in status from that of a protected people (Jer. 2:3) to that of a vulnerable one as a result of such abandonment. At first glance the two parallel questions in 2:14a would seem to require a negative answer (see GKC §150h). Ever since redemption from Egyptian bondage (Deut. 5:15), Israel (i.e., Judah and Jerusalem) has supposedly been no one's "servant" or "slave" (עבד) by purchase, captivity, or any other means, nor has Israel been anyone's "homeborn slave" (יליד בית) (see Gen. 14:14; 17:12, 13, 23, 27; Lev. 22:11; cf. John 8:33). Israel is the servant of the LORD (Isa. 41:8), the LORD's firstborn son (Exod. 4:22) and special possession (Exod. 19:5), and the bride of the LORD (Jer. 2:2) set apart as the protected first fruits (Jer. 2:3). Why then has Israel become plunder (Jer. 2:14b; cf. Num. 14:3; Ezek. 34:28)?[6] It is because of the broken covenant relationship. Israel is now at the mercy of its enemies as anticipated in the curse of Deuteronomy 28:47–48: "Because you did not serve the LORD your God with joy and with goodness of heart from an abundance of all, you will serve your enemies whom the LORD will send against you."

It is over Israel, the human plunder subjected to servitude, that the lions roar and give their voice (Jer. 2:15a; cf. Jer. 25:30; Amos 1:2). The lions are the kings (see *Tg. Jon.*; Gen. 49:9; Num. 24:9; Isa. 5:29; Jer. 4:7; 5:6; 50:17; 51:38; Ezek. 19:1–9; 32:2; Nah. 2:12–14 [Eng., 2:11–13]) of Israel's enemies who have captured their "prey" (Isa. 31:4; Amos 3:4). These are not necessarily limited to the Assyrian kings, nor is it necessary to see this as a reference to a particular historical moment. The Hebrew verbs here are gnomic, not referring to the past, present, or future. The difficulty created by the MT's *yqtl-qtl* sequence does not exist in the Hebrew source of Greek Jeremiah, which has a standard *yqtl-wqtl* sequence.[7] Of course, Assyria had taken the

---

5. *Tg. Jon.*: "I brought upon you sufferings, but you did not withhold your evil. And because you did not turn to the Torah, repayment will be exacted from you. And know and see that evil and bitterness I will bring upon you, O Jerusalem, because you forsook the worship of the Lord your God and you did not set the fear of me before your eyes, says the Lord God of hosts."
6. For the form of the questions in the Hebrew text, see Jeremiah 8:19, 22.
7. Holladay attempts to resolve the difficulty in the MT with references to Isaiah 5:6 and Kugel's discussion of the verb in Hebrew parallelism in *The*

northern kingdom of Israel into captivity and subsequently threatened the southern kingdom of Judah (2 Kgs. 17–18), but there was also a new "Assyria" on the horizon—Babylon (see Isa. 52:3–6). The "lions" make Israel's land into a desolate place whose cities are torn down (or burned; see note to translation above) without inhabitant (Jer. 2:15b; cf. Isa. 1:7; 6:11; Jer. 4:7, 26; 9:9, 11 [Eng., 9:10, 12]).[8]

Verse 16 adds Egypt to the lions of verse 15. Egypt as a whole is represented by the former capital Memphis (Hebrew: "Noph" or "Moph" [Hos. 9:6]) and Tahpanhes or Daphne (see Jer. 43:7–9; 44:1). According to the Leningrad Codex, the Egyptians "graze" (from רעה) Israel on the top of the head, which presumably refers to the shaving of the head in sorrow and disgrace (cf. Isa. 3:17; Jer. 47:5; 48:37) and/or the plundering of possessions (see *Tg. Jon.*).[9] It is also possible to read this text to mean that the Egyptians "tend" or "shepherd" Israel as their head or leader. According to the Syriac, however, the Egyptians "crush" (from רעע) Israel on the top of the head, which could refer to the defeat and death of the Judean king (cf. ראש [BDB, 911]). Both the Leningrad Codex and the Syriac appear to have in view Pharaoh Necho's defeat of Josiah and his subsequent dealings with Jehoahaz and Eliakim/Jehoiakim (2 Kgs. 23:28–35; Jer. 46:2). On the other hand, a few Masoretic manuscripts and the Hebrew source of Greek Jeremiah have ידעוך ("they know you") rather than ירעוך ("they graze/tend/crush you"). Furthermore, the Hebrew source of Greek Jeremiah has וקלסוך ("and they mock you") rather than קדקד ("top of the head"). This need not change the reference to Pharaoh Necho, but it does give a different sense. It is Israel's forsaking of the LORD as noted in Jeremiah 2:13 that has brought about this reversal of fortune (LXX 2:16; MT 2:17; see GKC §114a). MT 2:17 adds that this is specifically the forsaking of

---

Idea of Biblical Poetry, 17–19 (*Jeremiah 1*, 94), but the verb sequence in Isaiah 5:6 is *qtl-yqtl*, not *yqtl-qtl* as in MT Jeremiah 2:15a. Furthermore, Kugel's discussion is about *qtl-yqtl* sequences (not *yqtl-qtl*) and how they relate to his understanding of parallelism ("A is so, and what's more, B").

8. Again, the strange *wyyqtl*-x+*qtl* sequence in the MT does not appear in the Hebrew source of Greek Jeremiah, which has *yqtl*-x+*qtl*. The use of *wyyqtl* in Hebrew parallelism is somewhat rare unless there is a specific reason for it such as the imitation of prose. The "x + *qtl*" construction in the second half of 2:15b fronts the subject of the clause ("his cities") in order to make a clarifying comment about the desolation of the land.

9. This Hebrew verb in the sense "graze" would ordinarily not be transitive.

the LORD when he led the people on the path in the wilderness (see Jer. 2:6, 19; see also Jer. 6:16).[10]

The use of נאם יהוה אלהיך ("the prophetic utterance of the LORD your God") in the Hebrew source of Greek Jeremiah 2:17 concludes the thought of 2:14–17 (cf. LXX Jer. 1:8, 17, 19; 2:2, 3, 12, 19). The occurrence of ועתה ("And now") at the beginning of 2:18 introduces a logical inference in the form of two rhetorical questions (BDB, 774). Given the fact that Israel has essentially become enslaved to the kings of nations like Egypt and Assyria, why would the nation seek help from them rather than the LORD?[11] But this is ironically what Israel had done historically and would continue to do (see 2 Kgs. 16; Isa. 7; 30:1–5; 31:1–3; 36:6; Jer. 42; Ezek. 17:15; 29:16; Hos. 5:13; 7:11; 8:9; 2 Chr. 28).[12] Such misplaced trust will only bring shame in the end (Jer. 2:36; 43–44; 46:2–12; Ezek. 30:5). The irrational nature of Israel's seeking of "water" (i.e., foreign aid and alliance) from harmful enemies like Egypt and Assyria is comparable to that of their abandonment of the LORD, the fountain of living water, in favor of worthless idols, the broken cisterns (Jer. 2:13; cf. LXX Hos. 14:9 [Eng., 14:8]). The Hebrew source of Greek Jeremiah and the MT of 2:18 give slightly different senses in their syntax, but both express the general idea that Israel has no business going to Egypt for Nile water or to Assyria for Euphrates water (cf. Lam. 5:6). The language of this verse is reminiscent of Isaiah 8:5–8 (see *Lam. Rab.* 19:1), which says that because the people have rejected the gently flowing water of Shiloah, the Lord is bringing against them the mighty and abundant water of the river (i.e., the Euphrates), namely, the king of Assyria. Holladay notes well the irony of this allusion: "there, for Isaiah, the waters of the Great River (= the Euphrates) and the king of Assyria will flood Judah; here, by contrast, Judah goes off to the Great River to drink."[13]

The language of discipline (cf. Prov. 1:2, 7; 19:18; 29:17; 31:1; Jer. 2:30) and reproof (Prov. 1:23; 3:11; 5:12; 6:23; 9:7–8; 10:17; 12:1; 13:18; 15:5, 10, 12, 32; 19:25; 24:25; 25:12) in 2:19 calls to mind the

---

10. The MT refers to the LORD in the third person in verses 17 and 19 where the Hebrew source of Greek Jeremiah (vv. 16 and 19) refers to him in the first person.

11. *Targum Jonathan* brings out the sense of this nicely. Why would Israel want to return to Pharaoh who ordered their males to be cast into the Nile? Why would they make an agreement with Assyria who took the northern kingdom into exile beyond the Euphrates?

12. See also the comparison between Egypt and Assyria in Ezekiel 31.

13. Holladay, *Jeremiah 1*, 96.

wisdom literature. Normally God is the one who does the disciplining in Jeremiah (Jer. 10:24; 30:11 [MT]; 31:18; 46:28), but here it is Israel's evil and its acts of apostasy that do the job (see Jer. 3:6–8, 11–12, 14–22; 5:6; 8:5; 14:7; 31:22). Of course, the LORD is the one who will bring the punishment for Israel's evil, but the people's sin will testify against them (cf. Isa. 3:9; 59:12; Jer. 5:25; 14:7; Ezek. 23:48–49; Hos. 5:5; 7:10). The consequences of their forsaking the LORD will be bitter (Jer. 4:18). According to the Hebrew source of Greek Jeremiah 2:19a, the verse initially appears to end with נאם יהוה אלהיך ("the prophetic utterance of the LORD your God"), but then it continues, "And I do not delight in you" (followed by נאם יהוה אלהיך) (cf. Hos. 8:8; Mal. 2:17). On the other hand, the MT appears to be the result of reading עזבך אתי ("your forsaking me") as an abbreviation for עזבך את יהוה אלהיך ("your forsaking the LORD your God") and thus does not have נאם יהוה אלהיך at the end of 2:19a. The text of MT 2:19b then says, "And not fear of me to you" (i.e., "And you have no fear of me"; cf. Hos. 3:5), which is followed by the MT's own concluding formula ("the prophetic utterance of the Lord GOD of hosts").

2:20 "'For from of old you broke [MT: I broke; see GKC §44h¹] your yoke [Vulg.: my yoke], you tore off [MT: I tore off; see GKC §44h¹] your bonds [Vulg.: my bonds]. And you said, "I will not serve, but I will go upon every high hill and under every flourishing tree. There I will bend over in my fornication."¹⁴ 2:21 But as for me, I planted you a choice vine, all of it true seed. How you have turned yourself into bitterness, O foreign grapevine [MT: How you have turned yourself to me the turned aside of the grapevine, foreign]! 2:22 Even if you wash with natron and increase for yourself alkali, you are stained by your iniquities [MT: iniquity] before me,' the prophetic utterance of the LORD [MT: Lord GOD]. 2:23 'How can you say, "I am not defiled, and after the Baal [MT: after the Baals] I have not gone"? See your ways [MT: way] in the valley [LXX: in the common burial place (lit., in the place full of men)] and [and > MT] acknowledge what you have done. In the evening, her voice, it howls [MT: a swift female camel twisting her ways/paths (i.e., running here and there); Syr.: You have*

---

14. MT: "And you said, 'I will not serve [*qere*: I will not transgress].' For upon every high hill and under every flourishing tree you bend over fornicating [*Tg. Jon.*: you worship idols]." Syr.: "And you said, 'I will never again worship other gods.' But look, upon every high hill and under every thick tree you wander and fornicate."

raised your voice, you have perverted your ways].[15] 2:24 As for her ways /
paths, she increases to wilderness waters [MT: a wild donkey taught in
the wilderness; Tg. Jon.: Like a wild donkey that lives in the wilderness].
In the desire of her soul, she snuffs up wind [or, pants for air; LXX: she is
carried by the wind]. She is handed over [MT: In her time of copulation;
Syr., Tg. Jon.: Like the jackal], who will turn her back [Tg. Jon.: thus the
congregation of Israel has rebelled and wandered from the Torah]? All
those who seek her, they will not grow faint. When she is humbled [MT: In
her month; Syr.: In her ways], they will find her.[16] 2:25 Withhold your foot
from roughness [LXX: from a rough way; MT: from bareness[17]] and your
throat from thirst.[18] And she said [MT: And you said], "I despair [LXX:
I will act like a man;[19] MT: It is hopeless / useless.[20] No]." For she loved
strangers, and after them she would go [MT: "For I love strangers, and
after them I will go"]. 2:26 Like a thief's shame when he is found, so are
the sons of Israel [MT: the house of Israel] put to shame, they and [and >
MT] their kings and [and > Codex L] their officials and [and > mlt Mss]
their priests and their prophets. 2:27 To the wood they said [MT: They say
to the wood], "You are my father," and to the stone, "You are the one who
gave birth to me [MT qere: to us]," and [MT: for] they turned to me neck /
nape and not their [their > MT] face. But in the time of their calamity
they will say, "Rise up and deliver us." 2:28 And where are your gods that
you made for yourself? If they rise up and deliver you in the time of your
calamity [i.e., They certainly will not rise up and deliver you in the time
of your calamity; see GKC §149b; MT: Let them rise up, if they will deliver
you in the time of your calamity].[21] For the number of your cities are your
gods, O Judah, and the number of the streets of Jerusalem they sacrifice
to the Baal [and the number of the streets of Jerusalem they sacrifice to
the Baal > MT].'"

---

15. The last word of MT 2:23 (דרכיה ["her ways/paths"]) is the first word of
LXX 2:24.

16. *Tg. Jon.* 2:24b: "All those who seek my Torah will not be abandoned. In its
time they will find it."

17. The masculine form of יחף ("bareness") requires it to be a substantive
rather than an adjective, in which case it would need to be feminine in
order to agree with the feminine noun רגל ("foot").

18. *Tg. Jon.* 2:25a: "Withhold your foot from being joined to the peoples and
your mouth from worshiping the idols."

19. The translator mistakenly thought נואש to be from the root איש or אנש. Cf.
the Syriac. See also Jeremiah 18:12.

20. *Tg. Jon.*: "I have turned from the worship of you."

21. See Walser, *Jeremiah*, 213.

The conjunction כִּי ("For") at the beginning of 2:20 introduces an explanation of the preceding material. The MT of 2:20 appears to have the first two verbs as first common singular: "For from of old I broke your yoke, I tore off your bonds." This would presumably refer to the LORD's deliverance of Israel from Egyptian bondage and from oppression at the hands of foreign enemies throughout their history (e.g., Judg. 3–16; cf. Jer. 27:2; 28:2, 4, 10–14; 30:8; Nah. 1:13; Lam. 3:27). This would also make the remainder of the verse into a quote of the people's responsive vow ("I will not serve [other gods]"; or, MT *qere*: "I will not transgress") followed by an indication that this was a promise rendered empty by the practice of idolatry at alternative worship sites (cf. Judg. 10:15–16). The Greek text of 2:20, however, translates the first two verbs as if they were second feminine singular forms in the Hebrew text: "For from of old you broke your yoke, you tore off your bonds." Thus, either the forms that appear in the MT were read like Aramaic second feminine singular verbs, or the Greek translator had a Hebrew text with the normal second feminine singular suffix (cf. Jer. 2:33). In this case, Israel has since long ago broken the bonds of the covenant relationship with the LORD like an animal rebels against its owner (cf. Deut. 32:15; Isa. 1:3; Jer. 5:5; Ezek. 20:37; Hos. 10:11; 11:4; Ps. 2:3).[22] The Hebrew source of Greek Jeremiah for the latter part of the verse is then Israel's statement of defiance. It is not that Israel would have said this out loud. Rather, it is that the people effectively said this with their religious actions. Israel as a nation was to be the servant of the LORD (Isa. 41:8), but the people chose to serve other gods and thus became the servant of other nations (Jer. 2:14–19; cf. Rom. 6:16). The language of 2:20b refers to idolatrous worship sites designed as alternatives to the temple in Jerusalem (see Deut. 12:2; 1 Kgs. 14:23; 2 Kgs. 17:10; Isa. 57:5, 7; Jer. 3:6, 13; MT 17:2; Ezek. 6:13; 20:28; Hos. 4:13).[23] It was at these locations that Israel would assume the position to fornicate like a prostitute or an adulterous woman (see Jer. 3; Ezek. 16; Hos. 1–3). This does not necessarily refer to sexual acts performed as part of the Canaanite fertility cult (cf. Hos. 4:11–14) but to the spiritual harlotry of Israel the bride (Jer. 2:2) abandoning her husband the LORD in favor of another "man" (i.e., Baal; see Exod. 34:15–16).

Verse 21 switches metaphors from animal (2:20) to vine. As noted in 2:7, the LORD was faithful to bring Israel into the land of the covenant.

---

22. This confirms the earlier reading of Jeremiah 2:2. It was not Israel who was loyal in her youth but the LORD.

23. See Geoffrey H. Parke-Taylor, *The Formation of the Book of Jeremiah: Doublets and Recurring Phrases* (Atlanta: SBL, 2000), 284.

He "planted" the people in the land like a choice vine with reliable seed (cf. Exod. 15:17; Isa. 5:1–7; 27:2–6; Jer. 5:10; 6:9; 11:16–17; 12:10; Ezek. 15; 19:10–14; Hos. 10:1; Ps. 80:9 [Eng., 80:8]; Matt. 21:33–46; John 15:1–17), but this vine did not produce the expected good grapes, only bitter ones, so that Israel became a foreign grapevine to the Lord (cf. Deut. 32:32). This speaks not only of the people's failure to produce spiritual fruit in accordance with the covenant but also of the bitterness generated by their idol worship. The exclamatory אֵיךְ ("How!") at the beginning of 2:21b is not so much an interrogative as it is an introduction to a lament over what has happened (cf. 2 Sam. 1:19; Jer. 9:18 [Eng., 9:19]; Mic. 2:4). Verse 22 then switches the metaphor again to that of a grape-stained or blood-stained garment (cf. Isa. 1:15–20; Jer. 2:34; Mal. 3:2; Ps. 51:4, 9 [Eng., 51:2, 7]; Job 9:30).[24] Israel is the garment, and their iniquities make the stain. Even if they were to wash with natron and increase the use of alkali, the stain would remain. This gives the impression that the impending judgment is inevitable and cannot be averted. Rabbinic interpretation has long noted that this appears to be at odds with Jeremiah 4:14 where the Lord calls on the people to wash their heart from evil, suggesting that 4:14 is prior to the sealing of the judgment decree and that 2:22 is after,[25] but there seems to be a fundamental difference between the washing of the garment and the washing of the heart. Attempts to change the external appearance will not suffice. There must be an internal change of the heart (see Jer. 4:4; 31:33).

The question in 2:23a presupposes that Israel has continued to claim allegiance to the Lord even while persisting in Baal worship (cf. Jer. 2:35; 16:10; Hos. 8:2; see also Jer. 8:8; 48:14). Given the practice described in 2:20, how can the people insist that they are not religiously defiled by their idolatry (cf. Ezek. 20:30, 31, 43; 23:7, 13, 30; Hos. 5:3; 6:10)? The claim not to follow after the Baal flatly contradicts the divine accusation in 2:5b, 8b, 11b.[26] It is as if the people have so confused Baal and the Lord that they do not know when they are worshiping one or the other, or they worship one as if he were the other

---

24. The verb כבס is used for the washing of garments. The verb רחץ is used for the washing of the body.

25. See Jacob Neusner, *Jeremiah in Talmud and Midrash: A Source Book,* Studies in Judaism (Lanham, MD: University Press of America, 2006), 15, 292, 311, 314.

26. The MT uses the plural "the Baals" to refer to multiple local manifestations such as Baal of Peor (Num. 25:3; see also Hos. 2:15, 19 [Eng., 2:13, 17]; 11:2).

(see Hos. 2:18 [Eng., 2:16]). The LORD is their true "Baal" ("husband/ master"; see Jer 3:14; 31:32). They do not recognize that Baal worship destroys (Jer. 3:24), while it is the worship of the LORD that benefits them (Jer. 2:13). They wrongly credit Baal with what the LORD provides (Hos. 2:10 [Eng., 2:8]). Thus, the LORD calls on them to "acknowledge" (cf. Jer. 3:13) their "ways" or religious practices in "the valley," that is, the Valley of Ben Hinnom where they practiced child sacrifice to Baal and to Molech, the god of the Ammonites (1 Kgs. 11:7; 2 Kgs. 23:10; Jer. 7:31; 19:5; 32:35). The Greek translation calls this "the place full of men" (i.e., the cemetery).

The text of 2:23b differs considerably between the Hebrew source of Greek Jeremiah and the MT. The Greek has, "In the evening, her voice, it howls," reflecting בערב קלה היליל. This apparently continues the description of Israel's religious rites in the valley (cf. Jer. 3:9, 21; 9:18 [Eng., 9:19]; 25:34). The MT, however, has, "a swift female camel twisting her ways/paths" (בכרה קלה משרכת דרכיה), which envisions Israel running here and there to other gods and not to the LORD. The MT then switches at the beginning of 2:24 to the image of "a wild donkey taught in the wilderness" (פרה למד מדבר) (cf. Jer. 3:2; Hos. 4:16; 8:9; 10:11). The Hebrew text uses masculine forms here, but the remainder of the verse presupposes that this is a female donkey that picks up the scent of a male and pursues him during her time of copulation in such a way that she is easily available to any who seek her (cf. Jer. 14:6). This is a picture of Israel in her lust for idols (cf. Hos. 4:12b; 5:4; see also Hos. 12:2 [Eng., 12:1]).[27] The Greek text at the beginning of 2:24 reflects דרכיה פרצה למי מדבר ("As for her ways/paths, she increases to wilderness waters"). Israel goes looking for water in the wilderness where there is none, forsaking the fountain of living water (the LORD) in favor of broken cisterns (idols) (Jer. 2:13). In her desire (cf. 1 Sam. 23:20) she longs for her lover (Baal), and she is "handed over" (נתנה instead of MT תאנתה ["in her time of copulation"]) to it irrevocably ("who will turn her back?"). She is easy prey to those who seek her, and they will not grow faint in doing so. In other words, Israel is easily susceptible to idol worship. When she is "humbled" (בענתה instead of MT בחדשה ["in her month"]), they will find her.

The imperative in the MT of 2:25a has been variously understood to command either (1) prevention of bare feet and thirst due to hasty (and thus unshod and waterless) departure into the wilderness in pursuit of idols and/or foreign aid, or (2) prevention of bare feet and thirst due to

---

27. The comparison to a wild donkey may also be a way to say that what was intended for Ishmael (Gen. 16:12) has now become true for Israel.

wandering in the wilderness (resulting in worn out footwear and lack of water) in pursuit of the same. The language of bare feet and thirst, however, could also suggest that the text commands prevention of exile as a consequence of idol worship (see 2 Sam. 15:30; Isa. 20:2–4; 41:17; Hos. 2:5 [Eng., 2:3]). The Hebrew source of Greek Jeremiah commands Israel to withhold her foot "from roughness" (מרכס) (see Isa. 40:4 where this is the terrain to be leveled for return from exile). McKane rightly comments on the nature of the imperative here, "The summons in v. 25 is not so much an authentic call to penitence as a device for underlining Israel's total inability to respond, and so a way of summing up the finality of her despair."[28] The Hebrew source of Greek Jeremiah of 2:25b features a brief quote from Israel ("I despair") followed by an explanation ("For she loved strangers, and after them she would go"). According to this text, Israel's pursuit of strange gods (cf. Deut. 32:16) and foreigners (cf. Isa. 1:7; Hos. 7:9, 11) ends in despair (cf. Isa. 57:10; see Jer. 2:5b, 8b, 11b, 13, 18, 23), although another possible sense is that the LORD's imperative is hopeless or of no use because Israel insists on the pursuit of strangers (cf. Jer. 18:12). The MT, on the other hand, can be read in at least two ways, and both require the entirety of 2:25b to be a quote from Israel: (1) "It is hopeless/useless. No. For I love strangers, and after them I will go"; (2) "It is hopeless/useless. No, for I love strangers, and after them I will go" (cf. Gen. 18:15). In the first option, the LORD's imperative is hopeless/useless, and Israel responds to it in the negative and explains that she loves strangers. In the second, Israel denies that her pursuit of idols is hopeless/useless and then explains that she loves strangers.[29]

In verse 26 the LORD compares the manner in which Israel is put to shame to that of a thief whose seemingly hidden actions are brought to light when the thief is caught (see Exod. 22:1–2 [Eng., 22:2–3]; Prov. 6:30–31). Holladay suggests that the *hiphil* of בוש in this verse should be rendered "act shamefully" as would normally be the case: "Like the shame of a thief when he's caught, so the children of Israel have behaved shamefully."[30] This may very well be right, but the *hiphil* of בוש occurs several times in Jeremiah with what appears to be the sense "be put to shame" (Jer. 6:15; 8:9, 12; 46:24; 48:1, 20; 50:2; see BDB, 102). The point is not that the people of Israel now feel ashamed of their actions. Rather, it is that they are now publicly disgraced yet still defiant.[31] It will become

---

28. McKane, *Jeremiah I–XXV*, 47.
29. Again, this would be an admission in action, not in word (see Jer. 2:20, 23).
30. Holladay, *Jeremiah 1*, 54, 103.
31. See McKane, *Jeremiah I–XXV*, 48. But see Jeremiah 2:36b.

apparent that Israel is not ashamed of its actions at all (Jer. 3:3b; 6:15; 8:12; but see Jer. 9:18 [Eng., 9:19]).[32] This applies not only to the general populace but also to its leaders—kings, officials, priests, and prophets (see Jer. 1:15; 2:8; 4:9; 5:31; 23:30; 32:32).

The LORD then accuses the people of addressing the wood as their father and the stone as the one who gave them birth (i.e., their mother) (Jer. 2:27a; cf. Jer. 3:9; Ezek. 20:32; see also Deut. 28:36, 64; 29:16 [Eng., 29:17]; 2 Kgs. 19:18; Isa. 37:19; *Jub.* 22:18).[33] It has been suggested that the confusion of grammatical gender with natural gender in the Hebrew text is intended to reflect the confusion in Israel's brand of worship.[34] The "wood" (עֵץ), which is grammatically masculine, presumably refers to the Asherah pole that represents the female Canaanite deity, yet the people call this their father. The "stone" (אֶבֶן), which is grammatically feminine, presumably refers to a pillar that represents the male Canaanite deity, yet the people call this their mother. It is likely, however, that the writer's use of these terms is not quite so precious. For instance, the word עֵץ ("wood") does not necessarily refer to an Asherah pole in this sort of context (e.g., Isa. 44:19b; Hos. 4:12; see also Jer. 2:20b). The accusation seems not to be so much about confusion over which Canaanite deity is father or mother as it is about confusion over who is Israel's true father and giver of life. The LORD is Israel's father and creator (Deut. 32:6, 18; Isa. 63:16; 64:7; Jer. 3:4, 19; 31:9, 20; Mal. 1:6; 2:10). He is the one who comforts his people like a mother (Isa. 66:13), but the people have turned the back of the neck to him in rebellion (see Exod. 32:9; Jer. 7:24, 26; 18:17 [MT]; 32:33; 2 Chr. 29:6). They have not faced him in submission. Furthermore, they unwittingly admit the error of their ways when, in time of trouble, they call not to the idols that they worship but to the LORD who has delivered them in the past (Jer. 2:27b; cf. Neh. 9:27; Ps. 78:34).

In times of trouble the LORD will no longer respond to the cries for salvation (see Jer. 11:11).[35] He will ask, "And where are your gods that you made for yourself" (Jer. 2:28a)? If such gods are worthy of worship, then they should be the ones upon whom the people call for help. Of course,

---

32. See Redak's comments in Rosenberg, trans., *Mikraoth Gedoloth: Jeremiah Volume One*, 19.

33. The *qal* of יָלַד can mean "to father/beget," but normally the *hiphil* stem would be used for this sense (see BDB, 408–9).

34. See Thompson, *The Book of Jeremiah*, 180; Holladay, *Jeremiah 1*, 103–4.

35. The people have not responded when the LORD has called to them (Jer. 7:13, 25–27). Thus, he will not respond when they call to him (but see MT Jer. 29:12).

the question is not designed to concede the existence of these so-called gods but to highlight the ridiculousness and hypocrisy of Israel's ways and the very fact that non-gods are by definition not able to deliver (see Isa. 46:7; Jer. 11:12). The question, "Where are your gods?" is a rhetorical way to say, "Your gods are not here" (cf. Deut. 32:37; Isa. 36:19; Joel 2:17; Mic. 7:10; Pss. 42:4, 11 [Eng., 42:3, 10]; 79:10; 115:2). The second half of 2:28a in the Hebrew source of Greek Jeremiah begins with אם ("If"), which often introduces an oath whose self-imprecation (e.g., "The Lord do so unto me") is elided: ". . . if they rise up and deliver you in the time of your calamity" (= "They certainly will not rise up and deliver you in the time of your calamity"). It is also possible that אם simply introduces a question, which in this case assumes a negative response: "Will they rise up and deliver you in the time of your calamity?" In the MT, however, אם follows the verb יקומו ("Let them rise up"): "Let them rise up, if they will deliver you in the time of your calamity" (cf. Deut. 32:38; Isa. 57:13). Again, the אם could also introduce a question: "Let them rise up. Will they deliver you in the time of your calamity?"[36] According to Jeremiah 2:28b, the sheer number of Judah's gods/idols is an implicit argument from the people that their cries for deliverance should be directed to those gods/idols. They have as many gods as they do cities. This does not necessarily mean that each city has its own god, although it may refer to the manifestations of Baal worship in each location. Rather, it is a way to highlight the great abundance of Judah's idolatry. Ironically, as the LORD's blessings increased, so the people's idolatry increased (Hos. 4:7; 10:1). The Hebrew source of Greek Jeremiah 2:28b has the longer text ("and the number of the streets of Jerusalem they sacrifice to the Baal" [i.e., the number of sacrifices to Baal is as many as the number of streets in Jerusalem]), which is not in the MT. This text does appear

---

36. In a reflection on the cycle of apostasy narrated in the book of Judges, the LORD notes his many deliverances of his people in response to their outcries and how they have forsaken him to serve other gods (Judg. 10:11–13). Therefore, he says, the people should cry out to those gods and see if they will deliver them (Judg. 10:14). It is this notion that moves the people to confess their sin and remove their foreign gods (at least temporarily) in order to serve the LORD (Judg. 10:15–16). It should be noted that the LORD's response to this in Judges 10:16b is somewhat ambiguous. Was he impatient with the trouble caused for the people of Israel by their oppressors, or was he impatient with the trouble caused by Israel in their worship of other gods? In the former case, the sense would seem to be that the LORD relented and delivered Israel again. In the latter, the idea would be that the LORD was unmoved by Israel's actions in verses 15 and 16. See Daniel I. Block, *Judges, Ruth*, NAC 6 (Nashville: Broadman & Holman, 1999), 348–49.

in a slightly different form in the MT and the LXX of Jeremiah 11:13. It is possible that 2:28 is the source for 11:13, in which case 11:13 and the Hebrew source of Greek Jeremiah 2:28 have preserved the original longer text of 2:28. McKane, however, considers the short text of MT 2:28 to be original, and he deems the longer text of LXX 2:28 and MT/LXX 11:13 to be an expansion.[37]

2:29 "Why do you speak to me [MT: Why do you complain to me; Syr.: Why do you contend with me (cf. Vulg.)]? All of you, you have transgressed; and all of you, you have committed a crime against me,' the prophetic utterance of the LORD.[38] 2:30 'For nothing [or, In vain] I struck your sons [or, children; NET: people]. As for discipline, you [MT: they] did not accept (it). A sword [MT: Your sword] devoured your prophets like a destroying lion, and you did not fear [and you did not fear > MT].' 2:31 Hear the word of the LORD. Thus says the LORD [MT: O generation, you, see the word of the LORD], 'Is it a wilderness that I have been to Israel, or a land of deep darkness [or, darkness of Yah (cf. Song 8:6: flame of Yah);[39] LXX: a dried land]? Why do my people say, "We will not be ruled [MT: We have wandered; Syr.: We have descended], and we will not come again to you"? 2:32 Does a bride [MT: virgin] forget her ornament, or a virgin [MT: bride] her sashes? But my people, they have forgotten me days without number. 2:33 How good you make your ways [MT: way] to seek love [Tg. Jon.: to be joined to the peoples]! Not so [or, Not right; MT: Therefore], indeed you, you have acted wickedly to defile your ways [MT: even the evil women[40] you have taught your ways (see

---

37. McKane, *Jeremiah I–XXV*, 47.
38. For 2:29b, the MT simply has, "'All of you, you have transgressed against me [Syr.: you have deceived me],' the prophetic utterance of the LORD." The Hebrew source of Greek Jeremiah appears to have had a double version, or it may have been the result of dittography. Note that the phrase "against me" (בי) is not in the first clause. It is likely that the verb in both clauses was the same (פשע), but the translator consciously chose to use two different Greek words within the same semantic field for stylistic purposes. On the other hand, the shorter text of the MT may be the result of haplography.
39. It has been suggested that the theophoric element "Yah[weh]" (LORD) gives the noun "darkness" a superlative or elative sense. This would be similar to the use of "El" or "Elohim" ("God") for the same purpose (Gen. 30:8; Exod. 9:28; 1 Sam. 14:25; Jon. 3:3; Pss. 36:7; 80:11 [Eng., 36:6; 80:10]).
40. The *piel* of למד ("teach") normally has a double object: to teach someone something (BDB, 540). This makes it very unlikely that הרעות in the MT means "the evil deeds" (Jer. 3:5b) rather than "the evil women."

GKC §44h)]. 2:34 Also on the palms of your hands bloodshed of inno-cent lives is found [MT: Also on your skirts are found blood of lives of innocent poor people].[41] *Not in a place dug [or, in the act of breaking in] did I find them [or, did you find them],*[42] *but by every oak [MT: but by all these; ESV: Yet in spite of all these things]. 2:35 And you said, "I am innocent. Only let his anger be turned from me [MT: Surely his anger has turned from me]." Look, I am about to enter into judgment with you because you said, "I have not sinned." 2:36 What / Why do you despise greatly [or, How you despise greatly! MT: Why do you go about greatly (or, How you go about greatly!); see GKC §68h] to repeat [MT: to change] your ways [MT: way]? Also of Egypt you will be ashamed just as you were ashamed of Assyria. 2:37 For [> MT] also / moreover from this you will go out, and your hands will be on your head [or, with your hands on your head; Tg. Jon.: and the shame of your guilt on your head]. For the* Lord *has rejected the object of your confidence, and you will not prosper through it [MT: to them; Syr.: through them].'"*

The somewhat ambiguous Hebrew source of Greek Jeremiah 2:29a ("Why do you speak to me?") is interpreted in the MT to mean, "Why do you complain to me?" (cf. Judg. 21:22; Jer. 12:1; Job 33:13). It is the Lord who has a point of contention with Israel (Jer. 2:9), but the people of Israel act as if they have a legal case against the Lord (Jer. 2:5; cf. Hos. 4:4). The context suggests that Israel's complaint is not only about the Lord's accusations, which they deny (Jer. 2:23, 35), but also about his punishments and the perception that it would be better to serve other gods and to seek help from other nations (Jer. 2:11, 18, 20, 25, 27, 30–31, 35–37). But the people of Israel in their entirety, not the Lord, are the ones who have transgressed; and it is against the Lord in par-ticular that they have committed their crime (Jer. 2:29b; cf. Isa. 1:2).

The expression לשוא ("For nothing") at the beginning of 2:30a is normally understood to introduce the thought that the Lord's disci-pline of his people has been in vain, and its usage in Jeremiah supports this (Jer. 4:30; 6:29; 46:11; but see Jer. 18:15). Rabbinic interpreta-tion, however, has understood this expression to refer to the taking

---

41. There is a difficulty with the lack of agreement between verb (pl.) and subject (sg.) in the MT.

42. The form מצאתים can be interpreted as first common singular or as second feminine singular. The LXX translator understood it to be first common singular.

of oaths or vows in vain (see Deut. 5:11, 20).[43] That is, the LORD has disciplined Israel for empty or false oaths/vows. It is also possible that it refers to idolatry (see Jer. 18:15), but neither of these latter two options fits well with the immediate context of 2:30a, which contains the parallel thought, "As for discipline, you did not accept it." When the LORD says, "For nothing I struck your sons," it is not to distinguish between the older generation and the younger generation, although the use of the third person in the parallel clause of the MT certainly gives this impression ("As for discipline, they did not accept it"). "Your sons" is another way to say "your people" (i.e., "the sons of your people" [Lev. 19:18]; cf. "the sons of Judah" [Joel 4:6 (Eng., 3:6)], "the sons of Israel" [Exod. 13:18]). The Hebrew source of Greek Jeremiah accordingly has the second person in the parallel clause. Despite the LORD's instruction and discipline, Israel has not been receptive (Jer. 5:3; 7:28; cf. Amos 4:6–11; Zeph. 3:2; Prov. 1:3, 7), demonstrating the need for an internal change of the heart (Jer. 31:33). According to the MT of 2:30b, the people's sword ("Your sword") devoured their own prophets ("your prophets"; i.e., the prophets sent to them by the LORD) like a destroying lion (cf. 1 Kgs. 18:4, 13; 19:10; Jer. 4:7; 5:6; 26:23; Neh. 9:26; Matt. 23:34–35), but the Hebrew source of Greek Jeremiah has "A sword" instead of "Your sword," which leaves open the possibility that this is the LORD's sword that devoured the false prophets (see Jer. 12:12; 28:15–17). The final clause of the Hebrew source of Greek Jeremiah ("and you did not fear"), which does not appear in the MT, seems to confirm this latter reading. Just as the people did not accept the LORD's discipline when he struck them, so they did not fear him when he devoured their false prophets.

The Hebrew source of Greek Jeremiah 2:31 and the MT feature two very different reintroductions to the word of the LORD by the prophet (cf. Jer. 2:1–2): (1) Hebrew source of Greek Jeremiah, "Hear the word of the LORD. Thus says the LORD" (cf. Jer. 10:1; 17:20); (2) MT, "O generation, you, see the word of the LORD" (cf. Deut. 32:5; Jer. 23:18; Ps. 24:6). The LORD asks if he has been a wilderness to Israel or a land of deep darkness (Jer. 2:31a). Do the people really have a case against the LORD that they should now follow other gods and seek other nations (see again Jer. 2:5)? In the judgment of the northern kingdom of Israel, the LORD turned the land into a wilderness (Hos. 2:5b [Eng., 2:3b]; cf. Jer. 4:23–29), but this was due to the people's failure, not the LORD's. The LORD had been faithful from the beginning to lead the people through

___

43. See Neusner, *Jeremiah in Talmud and Midrash*, 69, 85, 86, 88, 98, 206, 277, 315.

the wilderness and into the land of the covenant where he proved to be a fountain of living water rather than a dry source (Jer. 2:2–3, 6–7, 13). Why then do the people say with their actions, "We will not be ruled [from רדה],[44] and we will not come again to you" (cf. Jer. 2:20, 25, 27; 5:31)? Such a response to the Lord's provision is inexplicable apart from the depravity of the human heart (see MT Jer. 17:9).

The word order of 2:32 differs slightly between the Hebrew source of Greek Jeremiah and the MT. In the Hebrew source of Greek Jeremiah, "bride" is first and then "virgin." In the MT, it is the opposite arrangement, but the sense of the verse remains the same. Thompson notes that the text takes the literary form of a "disputation," which consists of a rhetorical question and an indictment.[45] A bride does not forget her ornament (Gen. 24:22; Ezek. 16:11), nor a virgin her sashes (Isa. 3:20; 49:18), yet the Lord's people, his bride (Jer. 2:2), they have forgotten their husband (Jer. 3:14; MT 31:32; cf. Jer. 18:15) and their glory (Jer. 2:11) for days without number (see Jer. 3:21). This is essentially an argument from the lesser to the greater. What Israel should be expected to know she does not know (Isa. 1:3; Jer. 8:7). On the other hand, according to Isaiah 49:15, even if the unthinkable were to happen and a woman were to forget her nursing infant, the Lord would not forget his people (see also Isa. 49:24–25; Ps. 27:10).

Israel has not improved her ways to do the will of the Lord (Jer. 7:3, 5), but how well she has done to seek the love of other gods and other nations (Jer. 2:33a; cf. Jer. 2:18, 23; Mic. 7:3)! The people are like foolish children with wisdom only to do evil. They lack understanding to do good (Jer. 4:22) and are unable to change their ways (Jer. 13:23). The text of 2:33b then differs considerably between the Hebrew source of Greek Jeremiah and the MT. The Greek text reflects the following consonantal text and vocalization: לֹא־כֵן גַּם אַתְּ הֲרֵעוֹת לְטַמֵּא אֶת־דְּרָכָיִךְ ("Not so [or, Not right], indeed you, you have acted wickedly to defile your ways") (cf. Jer. 7:23). The sense of לֹא־כֵן here is either a negation ("Not so") of 2:33a (i.e., 2:33a is sarcasm, not a commendation) or an indication that Israel's pursuit of lovers is "Not right" (cf. Jer. 23:10b). On the other hand, the MT reads, לָכֵן גַּם אֶת־הָרָעוֹת לִמַּדְתִּי [לִמַּדְתְּ] אֶת־דְּרָכָיִךְ ("Therefore, even the evil women you have taught your ways"). According to this text, Israel has done so well in seeking foreign love that she has become a teacher, so to speak, of prostitutes and promiscuous women. That is, she could teach others a thing or two about how to be unfaithful (see again Jer. 2:10–13).

---

44. MT: "We have wandered" (from רוד; cf. Hos. 12:1b [Eng., 11:12b]).
45. Thompson, *The Book of Jeremiah*, 184. Cf. Jer. 3:1–5; 8:14–15; 13:23; 44:15–25; Mal. 2:10–11; Job 15:2–6; 22:2–11.

According to the Hebrew source of Greek Jeremiah 2:34a, the Lord says that the bloodshed of innocent lives has been found "on the palms of your hands" (בכפיך) (cf. Isa. 1:15; see Deut. 27:25; Jer. 19:4; 22:17; 26:15; Sir. 34:21–22). According to the MT, the Lord says that the blood of the lives of innocent "poor people" (אביונים) is found "on your skirts" (בכנפיך) (cf. Jer. 2:22).[46] The differences between the Greek and the MT are even more marked in 2:34b, even though the Greek does not follow a different consonantal text. The Greek interprets מחתרת to be "a place dug"; it also interprets the verb as a first-person form ("did I find them"); and it assumes vocalization of אלה as אֵלָה ("oak"): "Not in a place dug did I find them, but by every oak." This would mean that Israel was not even ashamed enough to do their worship of other gods in hiding. They did it openly at the alternative worship sites (Jer. 2:20, 27). It is not clear then what the precise relationship of this to 2:34a might be, although there seems to be a connection between the taking of innocent lives and the worship of other gods (see Jer. 3:24). The MT, however, is normally interpreted to mean that the people of Israel ("you") did not find their victims "in the act of breaking in" (במחתרת), which would have warranted homicide (Exod. 22:1 [Eng., 22:2]): "Not in the act of breaking in did you find them."[47] In other words, the bloodshed of 2:34a was not justifiable, which is somewhat redundant given the designation of the victims as "innocent." The last part of the MT—"but by all these (אֵלֶּה)"—is difficult. It is typically either rendered as an introduction to the following verse (ESV: "Yet in spite of all these things") or emended.[48]

Israel is guilty of the bloodshed of "innocent" lives (Jer. 2:34a), yet she insists that she is "innocent" (Jer. 2:35a; cf. Jer. 2:23). This claim is followed in the Hebrew source of Greek Jeremiah by an expression of desire to have the Lord's anger removed accordingly ("Only let his anger be turned from me"). The same claim is followed in the MT by a declaration that the Lord's anger has already been removed ("Surely his anger has turned from me"). It is sufficiently clear from the remainder of the book that this is either a false hope or a false assumption

---

46. According to Keil, the "poor" are not necessarily the financially strapped but the "pious" who are oppressed by the powerful (*Jeremiah, Lamentations*, 48; see Pss. 40:18 [Eng., 40:17]; 72:13; 86:1–2).

47. *Leviticus Rabbah* 10:3 interprets the verb as first person and the clause as a rhetorical question: "Did I not find them breaking in?" This is with reference to the golden calf incident in Exodus 32 where the Israelites acted like a thief in the absence of Moses.

48. See Holladay, *Jeremiah 1*, 110.

(see Jer. 4:8; 23:20; 30:24; cf. Isa. 5:25b; 9:11b, 16b, 20b [Eng., 9:12b, 17b, 21b]; 10:4b). In the end, it is not Israel who has a case against the LORD (Jer. 2:29). It is the LORD who has a case against Israel (Jer. 2:9). Therefore, he is about to enter into judgment with her for her refusal to acknowledge her sin (Jer. 2:35b; cf. Isa. 66:16; Jer. 25:31; Ezek. 17:20; 20:35–36; 38:22; Joel 4:2 [Eng., 3:2]).

The LXX and the MT interpret the consonantal text of 2:36a differently. The LXX interprets it to say, "What/Why do you despise (תֵּזְלִי from זלל) greatly [or, How you despise greatly!] to repeat (לִשְׁנוֹת) your ways (דרכיך)?" This would be similar to Jeremiah 2:5. What has the LORD done wrong that Israel should despise him so much and repeat her sinful ways (see Jer. 2:18, 23, 33; see also Jer. 15:19; Lam. 1:8)? The MT interprets the text to say, "Why do you go about (תֵּזְלִי from אזל) greatly [or, How you go about greatly!] to change (לְשַׁנּוֹת) your way (דרכך)?" According to this reading, Israel has gone about not only after other gods but also to foreign nations, deviating from the path of following the LORD (see Jer. 2:2, 5, 8b, 18, 23, 33). Israel will be ashamed of Egypt just as she was of Assyria (Jer. 2:36b; cf. Jer. 2:18, 26; 22:22). Commentators differ on whether this is a reference to dealings with Egypt during Jehoiakim's reign (see 2 Kgs. 23:29–24:7) or to an undocumented appeal to the Egyptians during the reign of Josiah. The text is not so specific, nor does it note the nature of Israel's dependence upon Egypt as voluntary or as under compulsion. The focus is on the disappointment that will come as a result of such dependence. Just as the Assyrians proved to be more trouble than help when Ahaz appealed to them (2 Chr. 28:16–21), so the Egyptians will fail them and fall to the very Babylonians from whom Israel would seek refuge (2 Kgs. 24:7; Jer. 42–44; 46 [= LXX 49–51; 26]). The people of Israel will depart from Egypt with their hands on their head in an outward demonstration of grief and shame (Jer. 2:37a; cf. 2 Sam. 13:19). This is because the LORD has rejected Egypt as an object of Israel's trust (Jer. 2:37b). Therefore, due to Israel's failure to confess her sin (Jer. 2:35), she will not find success by means of her misplaced trust (Jer. 2:37b; cf. Prov. 28:13).

JEREMIAH 3:1–4:4

3:1 "'[MT (> Ms) and Tg. Jon. add: Saying; Vulg.: It is commonly said; Luther: And he said] If a man sends his wife away [GKC §159w], and she goes from him and becomes another man's [Luther: and takes another man], will she indeed return to him again [MT: will he return to her again; Tg. Jon.: is it possible that he could return to her again]? Will not that woman [MT: land] surely be polluted [Tg. Jon.: become guilty; Vulg.: Will not that woman be polluted and defiled; GKC §112p]? And you, you have fornicated with many shepherds [cf. Syr.; MT: companions; Tg. Jon.: you have gone astray and been joined to many peoples], and you return to me [Tg. Jon.: and return from now on to the worship of me;[1] GKC §113ee]?' the prophetic utterance of the LORD. *3:2 'Lift up straight ahead [cf. Vulg.] your eyes [MT: Lift up your eyes upon bare places; Syr., Tg. Jon.: Lift up your eyes upon the paths] and see. Where have you not been ravished [MT qere: been lain with; Tg. Jon.: been joined to worship idols; Vulg.: been prostrated]?[2] By the [the > MT] ways have you sat for them like a raven [cf. Syr.; MT: like an Arab; Vulg.: like a bandit] in the wilderness. And you polluted (the) land with your acts of fornication [pc Mss, Syr.: with your fornication; Tg. Jon.: with your idol] and your evil deeds [Codex L, Syr., Tg. Jon.: your evil].[3] 3:3 And you had many shepherds as a snare [LXX: stumbling block] to you [MT: And copious showers were withheld; and as for latter spring rain, it was not]. A prostitute's forehead [LXX: A prostitute's face; MT: And a forehead of a fornicating woman; Tg. Jon.: boldness like a streetwalking woman] is what you had. You refused to be ashamed at all [at all > MT; LXX: You acted shamefully to all; Syr.: And you did not want to be hindered; Tg. Jon.: refusing to submit]. 3:4 Was it not "dwelling place" that you called me, and "father" and the "friend / chief" of your youth [MT: Is it not from now that you call to me, "My father, the friend / chief of my youth are you"[4] (see GKC §44h)]? 3:5 "Will he keep (anger) indefinitely? Will he maintain (it) forever [cf. Tg. Jon.; GKC §117g, 150h]?"[5] Look, you*

---

1. The Targum makes this clause imperative rather than interrogative (cf. Syr., Vulg., KJV, ASV).
2. Luther: "Lift up your eyes to the heights and see how you do whoredom everywhere."
3. The NET translates the last two words in the Hebrew text of this verse as an example of hendiadys: "wicked prostitution."
4. *Tg. Jon.*: "My Lord, you are my redeemer who is from of old [cf. Hos. 11:1]."
5. The NET renders 3:5a as a continuation of the LORD's discourse from 3:4: "Surely, it [i.e., youth/maidenhood] will not remain forever, nor will it be maintained to victory?"

spoke [GKC §44h], and you did the evil things, and you prevailed [GKC §69r, 145t; Tg. Jon.: and you multiplied; NET: That is what you say, but you continually do all the evil that you can].'"

Jeremiah 3:1–5 continues the LORD's discourse from chapter 2 (see Jer. 2:1–2, 31).[6] The MT's addition of לאמר ("Saying") at the beginning of this passage has given rise to a wide variety of explanations (Vulg.: "It is commonly said"; Luther: "And he said"),[7] but perhaps the most convincing of these is the suggestion of Michael Fishbane that לאמר here is a citation formula that introduces the following reference to Deuteronomy 24:1–4.[8] Fishbane notes that the entirety of Jeremiah 3:1 follows the same pattern found in Haggai 2:11–13 where this formula introduces a reference to biblical law (Lev. 6:20; 7:19; Num. 19:22): "As in Hag. 2:12–13, the Jeremiah sequence is initial condition + secondary complication + ritual question. And, finally, like Haggai's queries, Jeremiah's legal question is also followed by an answer, in v. 1b."[9]

The exegesis of Deuteronomy 24:1–4 in Jeremiah 3:1 continues the use of the marriage metaphor for the covenant relationship (see Jer. 2:2, 5, 11) and is likely filtered through Hosea's reading of the same

---

6. Rudolph (*BHS*) sets 3:1–5 as poetry (cf. 3:12–13, 19–25; 4:1–4), but this is doubtful given the lack of sustained parallelism. Such formatting is driven by a foreign conception of meter.

7. Rashi: "I have to say that you are no longer fit for me, for so is the way of one who sends away his wife and she goes away"; Kara: "So did the Lord command me to say"; Redak and Keil connect it to 2:37 (Rosenberg, trans., *Mikraoth Gedoloth: Jeremiah Volume One*, 23–24; Keil, *Jeremiah*, 51). Calvin: "Suppose a case" (*Jeremiah*, 1:152). Thompson: "(The word of Yahweh came to me) as follows" (*The Book of Jeremiah*, 187; cf. Bright, *Jeremiah*, 19). Holladay considers it to be a continuation of 2:9 (*Jeremiah 1*, 112).

8. Fishbane, *Biblical Interpretation in Ancient Israel*, 307. Cf. Psalm 105:11. Several passages in the rabbinic literature provide exegesis of Genesis 2:16 wherein the infinitive לאמר is said to be an intertextual reference to Jeremiah 3:1 (Neusner, *Jeremiah in Talmud and Midrash*, 106–7, 156, 204, 350–51). This obviously presupposes an approach to the Hebrew Bible that views it as one book, but for the present discussion it is worth noting that an understanding of the infinitive as a citation formula apparently underlies the exegesis.

9. Both Haggai and Jeremiah introduce their initial condition with הן in the Aramaic sense ("if") rather than the Hebrew sense ("look"). See also Jeremiah 2:10.

biblical case law (Hos. 1–3; see also Ezek. 16).[10] In this metaphor, the LORD is the faithful husband (Jer. 2:2–3; 3:14; 31:32; Hos. 1:2; 3:1), and Israel is the unfaithful wife (Jer. 2:5, 11; 3:8, 20; Hos. 1:2; 3:1). Israel has committed adultery with another "man," Baal, and has become his wife. She has acted like a prostitute with many lovers—the Baals (MT Jer. 2:23; Hos. 2:15, 19 [Eng., 2:13, 17]) and the foreign nations (Jer. 2:18, 36–37). The reference to Deuteronomy's divorce law presupposes a broken covenant relationship (Jer. 11:10), suggesting that any future restoration will not take place according to the terms of the old Sinai covenant but in the context of a new covenant relationship (Jer. 3:12–4:4; 31:31–34; Ezek. 16:59–63; Hos. 2:16–25 [Eng., 2:14–23]; 3:5).

The conditional clause in 3:1a ("If a man sends his wife away, and she goes from him and becomes another man's") is an abbreviated version of the lengthy condition in Deuteronomy 24:1–3: "When a man (אִישׁ) takes a woman (אשה) and marries her, if (אם) she does not find favor in his eyes because he has found in her nakedness of a thing, and he writes for her a document of divorce and puts (it) in her hand and sends her away (ושלחה) from his house, and she goes forth from his house, and she goes and becomes another man's (והלכה והיתה לאיש אחר), and the latter man rejects her and writes for her a document of divorce and puts (it) in her hand and sends her away from his house, or if the latter man who took her as his wife dies . . .". According to the law, which was added because of transgression (Exod. 19:16b; Matt. 19:8; Gal. 3:19),[11] the basis for the divorce is the discovery of "nakedness of a thing" (ערות דבר), which may be a general expression for indecency (see Deut. 23:15b; cf. Gen. 3:8–10), but in the present context it has traditionally been understood to refer to sexual immorality (Matt. 19:9; see also *b. Git.* 90a).[12] As an analogy for God's covenant relationship with

---

10. It is not that marriage is a covenant. Rather, certain aspects of marriage are suitable for illustration of the covenant relationship. Biblical marriage is a union (see Gen. 2:24; Matt. 19:4–6; Eph. 5:21–33). The two passages often cited as proof texts for marriage as a covenant (Mal. 2:14; Prov. 2:17) are in fact about the covenant relationship between God and his people. See the discussion in Michael B. Shepherd, *A Commentary on the Book of the Twelve: The Minor Prophets*, KEL (Grand Rapids: Kregel Academic, 2018), 490–94.

11. See John H. Sailhamer, *The Pentateuch as Narrative: A Biblical-Theological Commentary* (Grand Rapids: Zondervan, 1992), 47–57. The law allows for divorce under certain conditions but does not require it.

12. This naturally raises the question of the relationship of this law to passages that treat adultery as a capital offense (Deut. 22:20–22). Why would an adulterous wife facing the death penalty be issued a divorce document

his people, the sexual immorality in this law represents the people's (i.e., the bride's) idolatry and dependence upon foreign aid. The condition of the law goes on to say that the divorced wife not only becomes another man's wife but also is subsequently rejected by him (or he dies), which represents Israel becoming Baal's (and the nations') "wife" only to find that relationship disappointing (Jer. 2:13, 36–37).

The apodosis in Deuteronomy 24:4 then reads as follows: "the former husband who sent her away will not be able to return to take her (לשוב לקחתה [i.e., to take her again]) to be his wife after she has been defiled (הטמאה), for it is an abomination before the LORD, and

---

and allowed to marry another man? *Sifre* to Deuteronomy (270:4) suggests that the law encompasses the betrothal period (Deut. 22:23–28; Matt. 1:19) and the case of a wife merely accused of unfaithfulness (Deut. 22:13–19), but biblical law already has a method for dealing with suspicion of adultery (Num. 5:11–28), which curiously does not issue the death penalty for a wife found guilty but results in the loss of any pregnancy from the adulterous relationship. These examples illustrate the fact that the presentation of laws in the Pentateuch is neither systematic nor comprehensive for the reader's use but representative of what was delivered to Moses at Sinai for ancient Israel (see John H. Sailhamer, *Introduction to Old Testament Theology: A Canonical Approach* [Grand Rapids: Zondervan, 1995], 255–60). Calvin argues on the basis of Isaiah 50:1 that God did not divorce his people: "For if any one then departed from his wife, the law compelled him to take some blame on himself; for what was the bill of divorcement? It was a testimony to the wife's chastity; for if any one was found guilty of adultery, there was no need of divorcement, as it was a capital crime" (*Jeremiah*, 1:153). Calvin goes on to say that Israel has "fornicated" (i.e., committed idolatry) and that God stands ready to pardon and receive her precisely because there has been no divorce. Thus, the point in Jeremiah 3:1 is that Israel would be in real trouble if in fact a divorce had occurred, but since there has been no such divorce, the possibility of a return remains. The problem with this explanation is twofold. First, the denial in Isaiah 50:1 is not a denial of divorce (i.e., the broken covenant; see Jer. 3:8). Rather, it presupposes the divorce. What the LORD denies is the accusation that he ever divorced or sold his people because of a debt he owed (see also Isa. 52:3). He divorced and sold them because of their iniquities and transgressions. Second, to characterize Jeremiah 3:1 merely as good news that there is still an opportunity to return is to miss the force of the argument. It is necessary to acknowledge the condemnation of Israel under the old covenant law in order to appreciate the following grace of the new covenant hope. Any call to repentance under the old covenant only serves to illustrate that Israel is unable to repent without an internal transformation of the heart (Isa. 6:9–10; Jer. 4:4).

you will not make guilty of sin (תחטיא) the land that the LORD your God is giving to you for an inheritance." Jeremiah 3:1 has a rhetorical question in place of this apodosis, which carries more force because it requires the reader to call to mind the answer from the law, but the question differs between the Hebrew source of Greek Jeremiah and the MT. According to the Hebrew source of Greek Jeremiah, the divorced wife is the subject of the verb: "will she indeed return to him again?"[13] This agrees with Hosea 2:9 (see also, Jer. 3:1b; cf. Zech. 1:3; Mal. 3:7; 2 Chr. 30:6). The MT, however, has the husband as the subject: "will he return to her again?" This agrees with Deuteronomy 24:4 (see also Hos. 3:1; cf. Jer. 31:18; Lam. 5:21). Of course, the answer to both questions is "no" according to the law. The husband cannot take back the wife, nor can she return to him, because she is "defiled" (an abomination before the LORD), and such an action would result in the guilt of the inherited land (Deut. 24:4; cf. Lev. 18:25, 28; 19:29; Hos. 4:2–3; Amos 4:6–11).[14] The Hebrew source of Greek Jeremiah of Jeremiah 3:1 is probably correct then to ask first whether the wife rather than the land (MT) is "polluted" ("Will not that woman [MT: land] surely be polluted?") before noting the pollution of the land itself (Jer. 3:2b).[15]

The LORD then makes the application to Israel in 3:1b: "And you, you have fornicated with many shepherds." The MT reads רֵעִים ("companions") instead of רֹעִים ("shepherds") (see Hos. 3:1). Thus, Israel has not merely been unfaithful with one lover. She has been with "other gods" in the plural (Jer. 1:16b; 2:28). She has worshiped Baal in his various local manifestations at multiple worship sites (Jer. 2:20, 23; Hos. 4:13).[16] She has appealed to multiple foreign nations (Jer. 2:18, 36–37; see *Tg. Jon.* Jer. 3:1b). If the law in Deuteronomy 24:1–4 applies to a woman divorced for her infidelity and remarried to one man, how much more does it apply to Israel who has been with many? Therefore, the final clause of Jeremiah 3:1b is undoubtedly a question—"and you return to me?" (so LXX)—rather than a command (Syr., *Tg. Jon.*, Vulg.), although the use of the infinitive absolute in the Hebrew text

---

13. Note how שוב is now not merely an adverb—"to return to take her" (לשוב לקחתה [i.e., to take her again])—but the main verb with its own adverb עוד ("again"). This sets up the central role of this verb in what follows (Jer. 3:3b, 7, 12, 14, 22; 4:1).

14. No further explanation of the status of the woman or the land is offered in Deuteronomy 24:4.

15. See McKane, *Jeremiah I–XXV*, 58–59. Contra Holladay, *Jeremiah 1*, 113.

16. See also the reference to "Molech," the god of the Ammonites in MT Jeremiah 32:35 (cf. 1 Kgs. 11:5, 7; Jer. 49:1, 3).

has created some ambiguity in the history of interpretation. According to the terms of the law just cited, there is no way that Israel can return to the LORD (cf. Jer. 5:7; Ps. 73:27). Given the reference to the law, it is most unlikely that the LORD would now command Israel to return to him contrary to his own instruction. Subsequent calls for repentance presuppose a later new covenant context (Jer. 3:12, 14, 22; 4:1) in which the people have a new heart (Jer. 4:4; 31:31–34), or they serve to highlight Israel's inability to turn to the LORD in the context of the old covenant (Jer. 26:3; 36:3). Condemnation under the old covenant must come before restoration in the new covenant (Deut. 29–30).

In Jeremiah 3:2a, the LORD calls upon Israel to see and acknowledge her ways (cf. Jer. 2:23; 3:13). According to the Hebrew source of Greek Jeremiah, the text says, "Lift up straight ahead (על מישרים) your eyes and see." The text of the MT says, "Lift up your eyes upon bare places (על שפים) and see." These bare places are presumably the alternative places of worship (Jer. 2:20; see Num. 22:41; 23:2; Jer. 3:21; 7:29; Ezek. 16:25). Where has Israel not been ravished? The answer is "nowhere" (see Jer. 2:28; cf. Prov. 7:12). The MT commonly gives שכב ("to lie with") as the *qere* for the *kethiv* שגל ("to ravish") (Deut. 28:30; Isa. 13:16; Zech. 14:2), but the reader must not lose sight of the fact that Israel has been taken again and again, used and abused by her "lovers" (i.e., the idols [see *Tg. Jon.*] and the foreign nations [Jer. 2:18, 20, 23, 28, 36–37; 3:24]; Ezek. 16:36–43). Israel has sat by the paths for them like a whore (Gen. 38:14; Ezek. 16:15–35). The LXX and Syriac compare her to a "raven" (ערב) in the wilderness (1 Kgs. 17:4, 6), which calls to mind the image of an unclean bird feeding on dead flesh (Gen. 8:7; Lev. 11:15; Deut. 14:14). The MT, on the other hand, compares her to an "Arab" (ערבי) in the wilderness. It is not clear then whether this is an image of a bandit as in the Latin Vulgate (cf. Prov. 7:10–22) or that of a trader peddling goods (cf. Gen. 37:25–28, 36). Both would suit well the description of Israel as a prostitute. By these evil acts of fornication (i.e., idolatry [*Tg. Jon.*]) Israel "polluted" the land (Jer. 3:2b; cf. Num. 35:33; Deut. 24:4; Isa. 24:5; Jer. 2:7; 3:1a, 9; Mic. 4:11; Hag. 2:14–17; Ps. 106:38–39).[17]

The difference between the Hebrew source of Greek Jeremiah and the MT of 3:3a is substantial. The Hebrew source of Greek Jeremiah

---

17. Keil suggests that the evil here "refers to the moral enormities bound up with idolatry, e.g., the shedding of innocent blood, 2:30, 35. The shedding of blood is represented as defilement of the land in Num. 35:33" (*Jeremiah*, 52). When the land is defiled, it is unfit as a sanctuary and must reject those responsible for the defilement (Lev. 18:24–30).

reads, "And you had many shepherds (רעים רבים) as a snare (למוקש) to you." This refers back to the "shepherds" mentioned in the Hebrew source of Greek Jeremiah 3:1b. The MT, however, reads, "And copious showers (רבבים) were withheld; and as for latter spring rain (מלקוש), it was not." This refers to the covenant curse of lack of rainfall (Lev. 26:19; Deut. 28:24; Jer. 14:1–6; Amos 4:7). When coupled with "latter spring rain" (מלקוש), the term "copious showers" (רבבים) may refer to "early fall rain" (יורה) (see Jer. 5:24). The text of 3:3b speaks to Israel's stubbornness and boldness. She had the brazen countenance of a harlot (cf. Isa. 48:4; Jer. 2:27; Ezek. 3:7; Prov. 7:3) and refused to be humbled (cf. Jer. 2:26, 36; 5:3; 6:15; 8:12).

According to the Hebrew source of Greek Jeremiah 3:4, the LORD asks Israel if she has not called him by three titles in the past, expecting a positive answer for the sake of argument: "dwelling place" (מענה), "father," and "friend/chief" of her youth.[18] This text and the text of 3:5a are a setup for the accusation in 3:5b. Israel has said one thing and done another. Her actions have contradicted her words (Jer. 3:10). Israel has in the past referred to her husband the LORD as home, a refuge, a "dwelling place" (Deut. 33:27; Zeph. 3:7; Pss. 71:3; 90:1; 91:9), but she has wandered far from him (Jer. 2:20). She has called him "father" (Deut. 32:6), but now she refers to wooden idols as such (Jer. 2:27; 3:19).[19] The LORD was the "friend/chief" of her youth (i.e., her faithful husband [Jer. 2:2; Prov. 2:17; cf. Mic. 7:5]), but she forsook him without cause (Jer. 2:5). According to the MT, the LORD asks if it is not "from now" (מעתה) that Israel calls to him, "My father, the friend/chief of my youth are you."[20] While both Rashi and Calvin take this to mean that Israel now has an opportunity to repent,[21] it is more likely that the

---

18. McKane argues that אלוף ("friend/chief") means "teacher" (*Jeremiah I–XXV*, 61).

19. The term "father" seems to be an odd choice for a husband (see Holladay, *Jeremiah 1*, 115), and this may very well be a mixture of metaphors (cf. Jer. 3:19–20). On the other hand, Boaz addresses Ruth as "my daughter" in response to her proposal (Ruth 3:11).

20. Redak interprets the *kethiv* קראתי as a true first common singular ("I called") rather than as a long form of the second feminine singular ("you called"): "Whenever I called out to you through my prophet, 'My son,' your practice was to say to me, 'My father, you were the teacher of my youth.' But your deeds did not match your professions" (quoted in McKane, *Jeremiah I–XXV*, 60–61).

21. See Rosenberg, trans., *Mikraoth Gedoloth: Jeremiah Volume One*, 25; Calvin, *Jeremiah*, 1:160.

sense of the text is that Israel only calls on the Lord as father now that she finds herself in trouble (cf. Jer. 2:27–28). In other words, she is disingenuous in what she says (Jer. 3:10; 5:2).[22] Will she or should she now call on the Lord in such a manner and expect deliverance? The very thought that she does so serves as an indictment against her, given her record of infidelity.

The two questions in 3:5a about whether the Lord will continue to be angry indefinitely do not form part of the Lord's discourse (cf. Lev. 19:18; Isa. 57:16; Jer. 3:12; Amos 1:11b; Nah. 1:2; Ps. 103:9), as if the Lord were referring to himself in the third person and suggesting that his mercy is on the horizon. These rhetorical questions are a quote of the people's thought, which assumes that the Lord's anger will soon pass and that all will go back to normal. They presume upon the Lord's mercy. But the Lord points out in 3:5b that despite what the people say, their evil actions testify against them (Jer. 2:23; cf. Tit. 1:16). They may claim that the Lord is their father (Jer. 3:4), but it is a wooden idol that they call their father (Jer. 2:27). They may expect the Lord's judgment to pass (Jer. 3:5a), but they offer no expression of genuine repentance (see Jer. 3:22b–25). It is true that the Lord does not hold on to his anger forever (Isa. 57:16; Ps. 103:9), but this does not apply to his enemies (Nah. 1:2), and it does not reverse the consequences of the broken covenant relationship. The Lord remains faithful to judge according to the terms of the old covenant. The hope of averting his wrath comes with the new covenant (Jer. 3:12). Modern English translations typically render the latter part of 3:5b to say that Israel did all the evil that she could (e.g., ESV, NET, NIV, NLT, NRSV, TEV), which is difficult to imagine. Does anyone ever fully maximize their potential to sin?[23] Rather, the sense of the text seems to be that Israel has insisted on doing evil and has prevailed (see BDB, 408; NASB). Despite the efforts of the Lord to instruct, warn, and discipline through the prophets, the people have persisted in their sin (cf. Jer. 2:30).

3:6 And the Lord said to me in the days of Josiah the king, "Have you seen what apostate one [Tg. Jon.: those who keep themselves from returning to my worship], Israel [see GKC §132b; LXX: the settlement of Israel (cf. Syr.)], has done? They went [MT: She goes; Syr.: She went; Tg.

---

22. See Keil, *Jeremiah*, 52.
23. The doctrine of total depravity does not teach that human beings are as bad as they could be. Rather, it teaches that every part of the human being is affected by sin (see Wayne Grudem, *Systematic Theology: An Introduction to Biblical Doctrine* [Grand Rapids: Zondervan, 1994], 496–98).

Jon.: They go] upon every high mountain and under every flourishing tree and fornicated [MT: and you fornicated (see GKC §75ii); Syr.: and she fornicated; Tg. Jon.: and they worship the idols] there. 3:7 And I thought after she did all these things that to me she would return [LXX: And I said after she did all these things, 'To me return'], but she did not return. And treacherous one [GKC §84ᵃk], her sister, Judah, saw [LXX: And the faithless Judah saw her faithlessness]. 3:8 And I saw [Ms, LXXᴹˢˢ, Syr.: And she saw] that because apostate one, Israel, committed adultery [LXX: that concerning all that she was caught in which the settlement of Israel committed adultery], I sent her away [Tg. Jon.: I exiled them] and gave to her a document of divorce [MT: gave her document of divorce to her], but treacherous one, Judah [MT adds: her sister], did not fear, and she went and fornicated also she. 3:9 And so, her fornication amounted to nothing at all²⁴ [MT: And it would be, because of the frivolity (or, sound) of her fornication, she polluted the land (or, she was polluted with the land)], and she committed adultery with wood and stone [MT: stone and wood]. 3:10 And also/even in all this [LXX: in all these things] treacherous one [MT adds: her sister], Judah, did not return to me with all her heart but in deception [MT adds: the prophetic utterance of the LORD]."

3:11 And the LORD said to me, "Israel has justified itself [MT: Apostate one, Israel, has justified herself] more than treacherous one [Syr. adds: its sister], Judah. 3:12 Go and proclaim [LXX: read; Tg. Jon.: prophesy] all these words northward and say, 'Return [or, Return hither] apostate one, Israel,' the prophetic utterance of the LORD. 'And I will not cause my face to fall [or, look displeased (BDB, 658)] at you [LXX: And I will not set my face against you; Tg. Jon.: When you return, I will not send my anger against you]. For loyal [LXX: merciful; Syr.: good] am I,' the prophetic utterance of the LORD. 'And I will not keep anger [LXX adds: against you] forever [Tg. Jon.: Your debts will not be kept forever]. 3:13 Only acknowledge your iniquity [LXX: injustice; Syr.: sins], that it was against the LORD your God that you transgressed [or, committed a crime; LXX: lived ungodly] and scattered your ways to strangers [Tg. Jon.: perverted your ways by associating with the peoples, the worshipers of idols] under every flourishing tree and that it was my voice that you [LXX sg., MT pl.] did not obey,' the prophetic utterance of the LORD."

Divine discourse is reintroduced in Jeremiah 3:6 and set "in the days of Josiah the king" (cf. Jer. 1:2; 25:3; 36:2). The inherent ambiguity

---

24. Cf. Jeremiah 13:7b, 10b.

in the phrase "in the days of Josiah the king" requires the reader to be cautious about locating the discourse more specifically either before or after Josiah's reforms (2 Kgs. 23). It is clear from the following context that practices supposedly eradicated by the reforms continue to persist (see, e.g., Jer. 3:9), but it is also evident that some measure of "return" has occurred, albeit disingenuously and not wholeheartedly (Jer. 3:10). This could refer either to the reforms of Hezekiah (2 Kgs. 18:4), which did not last (2 Kgs. 21), or to the reforms of Josiah, which were embraced by the king and his followers but not by the general populace.

The rhetorical question in 3:6 expects a positive answer (cf. Jer. 33:24): "Have you seen what apostate one, Israel, has done?" This refers to the apostasy or rebellion of the northern kingdom of Israel, which led to its downfall and exile to Assyria in 722 BC (2 Kgs. 17). Of course, Jeremiah was not an eyewitness to this apostasy, but the LORD is asking him to consider what was common knowledge. The term "apostate one" (משבה) comes from the root שוב ("return") and fits nicely within a context that consistently ponders the idea of Israel/Judah "returning" to the LORD after having "turned" from him (Jer. 3:1, 7, 10, 12, 14, 22; 4:1; cf. Jer. 8:5; 31:22). The Greek and Syriac translations, however, render this same term as if it were from the root ישב ("dwell")— "the settlement of Israel"—which has very little to do with the context. The LORD then makes explicit what it is that he has in mind: "They went upon every high mountain and under every flourishing tree and fornicated there" (cf. Isa. 30:25; 57:7). This refers to the same practice of alternative worship of which Judah was accused in Jeremiah 2:20. The reference to fornication continues the metaphor for idolatry and dependence upon foreign nations from 3:1b.

The LORD thought that Israel would return to him after dabbling in apostasy (cf. Hos. 2:9 [Eng., 2:7]), but she did not (Jer. 3:7a). The LXX renders this as if it were a self-quote of the LORD's command to Israel: "And I said after she did all these things, 'To me return.'" Rashi also understands the Hebrew text this way and interprets it to be a reference to the message of the LORD to Israel through the prophets Amos and Hosea.[25] The question of whether Israel (or Judah) could return to the LORD in the context of the old covenant after apostasy has already been addressed in 3:1 with reference to the divorce law in Deuteronomy 24:1–4. It is only in the hope of a new covenant relationship that a return will be possible (Jer. 3:12, 14, 18, 22; 4:1–4), but the LORD thought that Israel would at least attempt a return after finding foreign gods

---

25. Rosenberg, trans., *Mikraoth Gedoloth: Jeremiah Volume One*, 26.

and foreign nations to be unsatisfactory.[26] Israel's "treacherous" or "unfaithful" (בגודה) sister Judah saw this persistent apostasy (Jer. 3:7b; cf. Jer. 3:20, 5:11; 9:1 [Eng., 9:2]).[27] Such a negative designation for Judah already anticipates the fact that Judah not only witnessed Israel's apostasy but also adopted it. The extended metaphor of the two harlot sisters Ohola (Israel) and Oholiba (Judah) in Ezekiel 23 indicates that Judah exceeded Israel's apostasy (Ezek. 23:11; cf. Ezek. 16:46–47).

Witnesses vary on whether the verb at the beginning of Jeremiah 3:8a is first common singular ("And I saw") or third feminine singular ("And she saw"). According to the former ("And I saw"), the trajectory of what was seen extends through Jeremiah 3:8b.[28] That is, the LORD saw that Judah did not fear when he divorced Israel for her infidelity. According to the latter ("And she saw"), the trajectory extends only through 3:8a. That is, Judah saw that the LORD divorced Israel for her infidelity, but she did not fear. It is possible that there was a change from first person to third person based on limiting the trajectory of what was seen to 3:8a, in which case a first-person verb would appear odd, indicating only that the LORD witnessed his own action.

According to 3:8a, the LORD sent apostate Israel away and gave a document of divorce to her (i.e., sent her into exile and gave notice of the broken covenant) because she committed adultery (cf. Deut. 24:1–4; Jer. 3:1). The LXX describes this in terms of being "caught" in the act of adultery: "that concerning all that she was caught in which the settlement of Israel committed adultery" (cf. Deut. 22:22). Because of the similarity between this Greek text and that of John 8:3–4, McKane wonders whether such additional language in the Greek translation of Jeremiah 3:8a might be a Christian gloss.[29] Commentators have historically struggled to reconcile the text of Jeremiah 3:8a with Isaiah

---

26. This is not a denial of divine foreknowledge. It is a way of saying that Israel should have been expected to behave in a certain manner; thus, her failure to do so was all the more egregious (cf. Jer. 3:19; Zeph. 3:6–7).

27. The LXX ("And the faithless Judah saw her faithlessness") does not translate "her sister," but this does not necessarily indicate the presence of a different Hebrew source text. It is possible that the translator understood "her sister" to be the object that Judah saw rather than a designator for Judah. In other words, unfaithful Judah saw her sister Israel. The translator then decided to make explicit what it was that Judah saw in her sister ("her faithlessness"). On the other hand, the Syriac translation includes a similar object for the verb "saw" but also includes "his sister" as a designator for Judah: "And his sister Judah saw his lie."

28. See Keil, *Jeremiah*, 55–56.

29. McKane, *Jeremiah I–XXV*, 65.

50:1, either by limiting the divorce in 3:8a to the northern kingdom of Israel (Redak; but see Jer. 3:1) or by treating the divorce in 3:8a as something altogether different from the kind of divorce referenced in Deuteronomy 24:1–4; Isaiah 50:1; Jeremiah 3:1 (Calvin). Such attempts work under the assumption that the Lord denies giving his people a document of divorce in Isaiah 50:1, but Isaiah 50:1 is not a denial of divorce. It is a denial that the Lord was compelled to divorce and sell his people because of a debt owed. He did sell and divorce his people (Judah), but it was because of their iniquities and transgressions. When he divorced Israel, it struck no fear in the heart of unfaithful Judah (Jer. 3:8b). The people in the south went and fornicated as well. Even later in the book, when the Lord appeals to Judah through Jeremiah to learn from what happened to Israel (Jer. 7:12–15), there is no change. Thus, Judah would go into exile for the same reasons as Israel did (2 Kgs. 17:7–23; Jer. 25:4–7).

"And so" (καὶ ἐγένετο = ויהי; cf. MT והיה), Judah's fornication amounted to nothing at all (Jer. 3:9a). Her devotion to idols and her appeals to the nations resulted in emptiness (Jer. 2:5, 13; 3:24). The Greek εἰς οὐθέν may be a rendering of מקל, but elsewhere in Jeremiah this phrase translates לכל (Jer. 13:7, 10).[30] The MT's מקל זנותה is often understood to mean "because of the frivolity of her fornication" (see *Masora parva*; BDB, 887). That is, Judah behaved the way she did because she did not take seriously the consequences of her actions. Another possibility is that the phrase means "because of the sound of her fornication" (cf. Jer. 3:21).[31] The MT also has added text here: וַתֶּחֱנַף אֶת הָאָרֶץ (cf. Jer. 3:1a, 2b). The verb is either an unusual *qal* transitive ("and she polluted the land") or the usual *qal* intransitive ("and she was polluted with the land"). Many commentators vocalize the verb as *hiphil* (וַתַּחֲנֵף), which is the more common transitive stem for this root (see *BHS* apparatus). Judah committed adultery with wood and stone (i.e., with wood idols and stone idols; cf. Jer. 2:27; 3:8). The MT has the order "stone and wood" (cf. Lev. 14:45; Ezek. 26:12; 1 Chr. 22:15; 2 Chr. 2:13).

The *Masora parva* at the beginning of Jeremiah 3:10 notes that וגם stands at the beginning of six verses in Jeremiah (Jer. 3:10; 5:18; 13:26; 26:20; 36:25; 40:11). The Greek translation renders each of these simply with καί. In all the aforementioned things (cf. Sir. 48:15; MT: "in

---

30. The supposed Hebrew source text ויהי לכל זנותה is somewhat elliptical.
31. See Neusner, *Jeremiah in Talmud and Midrash*, 68; Keil, *Jeremiah*, 56; McKane, *Jeremiah I–XXV*, 66.

all this" [cf. Ps. 78:32]),[32] unfaithful Judah, like apostate Israel (Jer. 3:7), did not return to the LORD wholeheartedly. The LORD required full devotion of the whole self (Deut. 6:5), but Judah only returned in "deception" (שקר).[33] This means that there was some measure of outward repentance in an attempt to gain the LORD's favor in times of trouble, but inwardly there was no intent to change (see Jer. 2:27; 5:2; Ps. 78:34–37; Neh. 9:27–28). There was an inconsistency between the people's words and their actions that revealed the inauthentic nature of their return (Jer. 3:4–5). Their heart could not be trusted (Prov. 26:24–25). The LORD had not yet given them a heart/mind to know him and to return to him in a new covenant relationship (Deut. 4:30; 28:69 [Eng., 29:1]; 29:3 [Eng., 29:4]; 30:2, 6; Jer. 4:4; 31:31–34; Ezek. 11:19–20), yet they were held accountable for their voluntary actions.

After a brief pause between 3:10 and 3:11, which the Leningrad Codex marks by setting the start of 3:11 flush right, the LORD's discourse is reintroduced. The conclusion drawn from the comparison between Israel and Judah in 3:6–10 is that Israel has justified itself (MT: "herself") more than Judah (Jer. 3:11). The point is clearly not that Israel is righteous or without sin but that she appears more righteous when compared with Judah (see the use of similar language in Gen. 38:26; Hab. 1:13). Why is this so? Rashi suggests, "She has been cleared and she has freed herself from an unfavorable verdict, for she had no one to learn from."[34] Judah, on the other hand, should have learned from the lesson of Israel. This may explain the use of the terms "apostate" for Israel and "treacherous/unfaithful" for Judah. Israel was apostate/rebellious/turning away from the beginning (1 Kgs. 12:25–33). Judah,

---

32. "While כל זאת does not occur a second time in the book of Jeremiah, its renderings in the Greek translations of 1 Sam. 22:15; Isa. 5:25; 9:11, 16, 20; 10:4; Hos. 7:10; Ps. 78:32; Job 1:22; 2:10; Neh. 10:1 correspond to the πᾶσι τούτοις of Jer-LXX 3:10. That Jer-LXX 3:10 employs the plural form τούτοις instead of the singular form זאת should hence be regarded as a matter of translation technique only" (Armin Lange, "The Book of Jeremiah in the Hebrew and Greek Texts of Ben Sira," in *Making the Biblical Text: Textual Studies in the Hebrew and Greek Bible*, ed. Innocent Himbaza [Göttingen: Vandenhoeck & Ruprecht, 2015], 141).

33. This term plays a key role throughout the book of Jeremiah, occurring more than thirty times—more than any other biblical book (Jer. 3:10, 23; 5:2, 31; 6:13; 7:4, 8, 9; 8:8, 10; 9:2, 4 [Eng., 9:3, 5]; 10:14; 13:25; 14:14; 16:19; 20:6; 23:14, 25, 26, 32; 27:10, 14–16; 28:15; 29:9, 21, 23, 31; 37:14; 40:16; 43:2; 51:17).

34. Rosenberg, trans., *Mikraoth Gedoloth: Jeremiah Volume One*, 28.

however, was entrusted with the temple and the Davidic monarchy yet proved to be unfaithful or unreliable. With greater responsibility comes greater judgment (cf. Amos 3:1–2). But the prophet Ezekiel goes beyond what Rashi suggests, saying that it was not merely a matter of failing to learn from Israel's mistakes. Judah actually became more corrupt in her lust and surpassed her sister in her acts of fornication (Ezek. 16:46–47, 51–52; 23:11; see also Jer. 23:13–14).

The first part of Jeremiah 3:12 may be translated, "Go and proclaim all these words northward and say," or, "Go and read all these words northward and say" (see LXX; Jer. 36:6; 51:61; BDB, 895). A command to proclaim implies simple oral delivery of a message, but a command to read presupposes the presence of a written text. It is highly unlikely that Jeremiah was to travel northward and then to Assyria in the east to locate a group of scattered descendants of the exiles of the northern kingdom of Israel in order to address them. Rather, the words of 3:12–13 were to be spoken "northward,"[35] but they were heard by Judah and subsequently read by the readership of the book of Jeremiah. Thus, following the vindication of Israel vis-à-vis Judah in 3:11, the words of restoration directed to the north would have provoked Judah to jealousy (cf. Deut. 32:21; Rom. 11:11). Furthermore, the inclusion of the north and the nations in the following message of restoration for Judah helps the reader understand the overall conception of the people of God in the book of Jeremiah (Jer. 3:17–18).

The command for apostate Israel to return is a play on words in the Hebrew text that essentially summons Israel to turn back from the direction to which she formerly turned (Jer. 3:12; cf. Hos. 14:2 [Eng., 14:1]). This is not a call to return from exile. It is a call to repentance, to turn back to the LORD (cf. Jer. 3:1, 7, 14, 22; 4:1). Only when Israel repents will there be a return from exile and a restoration of fortunes (Deut. 30:1–10), but how can Israel (or Judah) repent?[36] According to the terms of the old covenant, neither Israel nor Judah could return to the LORD (Jer. 3:1). Indeed, both Israel and Judah had shown the inability to return (Jer. 3:7, 10; 13:23). Thus, the call to repent presupposes a new covenant relationship in which the circumcised heart makes obedience possible (Deut. 28:69 [Eng., 29:1]; 30:6; Jer. 4:4; 31:31–34; Ezek. 11:19–20). Such is the eschatological hope of Jeremiah 3:14–18; 4:1–4.[37]

---

35. See Neusner, *Jeremiah in Talmud and Midrash*, 366–67.

36. Neusner, *Jeremiah in Talmud and Midrash*, 191–92.

37. The eschatological nature of this is clear, at the very least, from the fact that there never was a historical return of the northern kingdom of Israel from Assyria.

The Lord assures Israel that genuine repentance will not be met with displeasure ("I will not cause my face to fall at you" [cf. Gen. 4:5; Num. 6:24–26]; LXX: "I will not set my face against you" [cf. Lev. 20:6; Jer. 44:1]). He explains that this is because he, as opposed to Israel and Judah, is "loyal" (חסיד) to the covenant (cf. Ps. 145:17). He was faithful to judge his people according to the terms of the old covenant, which relied upon human fidelity, and he will be faithful to the terms of the new covenant, which depends upon divine faithfulness. He will not hold on to his anger forever (cf. Isa. 57:16; Pss. 30:6 [Eng., 30:5]; 103:9). Of course, it was precisely upon this feature of the Lord's character that Judah presumed (Jer. 3:5), but the appeasement of his anger is not for the enemies of God (Nah. 1:2), whether from the nations or from Israel/Judah. It is for the authentic repentance of the new covenant people of God. The Lord is slow to anger and abundant in covenant loyalty, but he will not leave the guilty unpunished (Exod. 34:6–7).[38]

Israel must acknowledge her iniquity (Jer. 3:13; cf. Jer. 2:23a; 3:25a). The conjunction כי after the first clause of verse 13 does not introduce the reason why Israel must confess but the content of what must be acknowledged. It was not against just anyone that Israel transgressed and scattered her ways to the strange gods under every flourishing tree (Deut. 32:16; Jer. 2:20, 25; 3:6). It was against the Lord her God. It was the Lord's voice that she did not obey (cf. Jer. 3:25b). The expression "scattered your ways" does not mean "spread your legs" (contra Rashi), although such a meaning would be suitable to the metaphor of a prostitute or adulterous wife.[39] Rather, the "ways" of Israel here are the same brand of idolatrous ways spoken of Judah in 2:23, 33; 3:2, 21.[40]

3:14 "Return, apostate sons," the prophetic utterance of the Lord. "For I, I am lord / husband over you [Syr., Tg. Jon.: I am pleased with you], and I will take you [Tg. Jon. adds: as if you were a remnant] one from a city and two from a family [see GKC §134s] and bring you to Zion.

---

38. Origen: "Note the kindness and severity of God. For he is not kind without being severe or severe without being kind. For if he were only kind and not severe, we would not think much of his kindness. If he were severe and not kind, perhaps we would also despair in our sins. But God is both a kind and a severe God—for we who repent need his kindness, but those of us who persist in sins need his severity" (Wenthe, ed., *Jeremiah, Lamentations*, 34).

39. See McKane, *I–XXV*, 70–71.

40. See also Jeremiah 2:18, 36; Holladay, *Jeremiah 1*, 119.

3:15 And I will give to you shepherds according to my heart [Tg. Jon.: stewards who do my will], and they will tend you, tending and having insight [LXX: shepherding with skill; MT: with knowledge and insight]. 3:16 And it will be, when [LXX: if] you are fruitful and multiply [cf. Syr.; MT: you multiply and are fruitful] in the land in those days," the prophetic utterance of the LORD, "they will never again say, 'The ark of the covenant of the Holy One of Israel [MT: The ark of the covenant of the LORD].' It [MT: And it] will not come to mind. They [MT: And they] will not remember it [LXX: It will not be named], and they will not miss it [LXX: nor will it be considered; Tg. Jon.: and they will not move it], and it will never again be made [Tg. Jon.: and they will never again wage war with it (see 1 Sam. 4)]. 3:17 In those days and [In those days and > MT] at that time, they will call Jerusalem the throne of the LORD [Tg. Jon.: the place of the house of the dwelling of the Lord]. And all the nations will be collected to it [MT adds: to the name of the LORD, to Jerusalem],[41] and they will never again go after the stubbornness [LXX: thoughts (cf. Syr., Tg. Jon., Luther)] of their evil heart. 3:18 In those days, the house of Judah will go in addition to the house of Israel, and they will come together from the land of the north and from all the lands [and from all the lands > MT] to the land that I caused their fathers [Codex L: your fathers] to inherit."

The call to return in 3:14 ("Return, apostate sons") is identical to the one in 3:22, but it is not the same as the one in 3:12 ("Return, apostate one, Israel"). It is a plural imperative rather than a singular one, and it is addressed to apostate sons (cf. Isa. 57:17) rather than the apostate one, Israel. Commentators differ on whether this command is directed to the northern kingdom of Israel (e.g., Keil) or to the southern kingdom of Judah (e.g., McKane), but the context envisions an eschatological collection of a repentant people of God from all the nations, Judah, and the northern kingdom of Israel (Jer. 3:17–18) in messianic times (Jer. 3:15). Again, as in 3:12 (cf. Jer. 3:1, 7, 22; 4:1), the call to return is not merely a call to come back from exile but to return to the LORD in repentance in order that he might take the members of the faithful remnant and bring them to Zion, the new Jerusalem (Isa. 65:18), for full participation in the messianic kingdom and the new creation in the last days (Isa. 11:1–10; 65:17–25).

The LORD explains that he in particular (note the fronted pronoun "I") is the "lord" or "husband" (בַּעַל) of those who have turned away and should now return (cf. Isa. 54:5; MT Jer. 31:32). This is undoubtedly a

---

41. Syr.: "And all the peoples will wait for the name of the Lord." Cf. *Tg. Jon.*

continuation of the marriage metaphor from 3:1–10 and a play on the name of "Baal" (בעל). The people had followed after Baal as if he were their lord or husband (Jer. 2:5, 8, 23), but they must acknowledge the LORD as their true lord/husband (see Hos. 2:18 [Eng., 2:16]). This is not only for the covenant people of Israel and Judah but also for the nations who turn to the LORD (see Jer. 12:16). The LORD will then take "one from a city and two from a family [or, clan (see BDB, 1046–47)]" to bring them to Zion (see Jer. 31:6). There is no indication that this means only representatives of the remnant will go to Zion. Rather, it reveals that the membership of the true remnant itself will be relatively small in comparison to those who do not repent—only one from an entire city or two from a full tribal division. Nevertheless, this remnant will be blessed and multiplied (Jer. 3:16; cf. Exod. 1:5, 7; see also Isa. 10:22; Hos. 2:1 [Eng., 1:10]).

The LORD says that he will give his people "shepherds" who are according to his heart (Jer. 3:15a). This is not a reference to pastors of the church (contra Calvin). These are kings (cf. Jer. 2:8) who, like David, will have minds in accordance with the LORD's mind and will thus do his will and be pleasing to him (see 1 Sam. 13:14; 16:7; cf. 1 Sam. 2:35). Several kings of the southern kingdom of Judah were said to be like David (e.g., 1 Kgs. 15:11; 22:43; 2 Kgs. 18:3; 22:2), but the last kings of Judah after Josiah did not live up to his standard of righteousness (Jer. 21:1–23:4). The northern kingdom of Israel only had kings who followed in the sins of Jeroboam (1 Kgs. 12:25–33). The Messiah will be the new and better "David" who will reign over a reunited kingdom of Israel and Judah and shepherd the people in accordance with the LORD's will (Jer. 23:5–6; 30:9; Ezek. 34:23; 37:24; Hos. 3:5). He will be a light to the nations (Isa. 42:6; 49:6), and to him will belong obedience from multiple peoples (Gen. 49:10; Isa. 11:10). Passages like Jeremiah 3:15 that speak of a plurality of future shepherds (e.g., Isa. 32:1; Jer. 23:4; Mic. 5:4–5 [Eng., 5:5–6]; cf. Isa. 1:26) refer to the saints to whom the lost blessing of life and dominion in the land will be restored (Gen. 1:26–28) and who will reign with Christ (Dan. 7:13–14, 27; Rev. 5:10; 20:6; 22:5).[42]

The Hebrew source of Greek Jeremiah 3:15b says that the shepherds will tend the people, "tending (רעה) and having insight" (see DSS F.Jer 1; LXX: "shepherding with skill"). The MT says that they will tend the people "with knowledge (דֵּעָה) and insight." Confusion between the letters ר and ד was common in textual transmission, making it difficult to

---

42. See Shepherd, *Commentary on the Book of the Twelve*, 266. See also Redak's comments in Rosenberg, trans., *Mikraoth Gedoloth: Jeremiah Volume One*, 29.

come to a firm decision on which reading to follow in many cases. David was known for his "insight" (1 Sam. 18:14), and the Davidic Messiah will also have this quality (Jer. 23:5; see also Isa. 11:2; 52:13). Such insight comes from the reading of the Torah (Deut. 4:6; 17:19; 29:8 [Eng., 29:9]; Josh. 1:8), which will be taught to the nations in the last days (Isa. 2:1–5; Mic. 4:1–5; cf. Deut. 31:9–13; Neh. 8–9). What people will the shepherds tend if the people are the shepherds? That is, over whom will the saints reign if the saints are also the members of the kingdom? The answer seems to be that Christ will reign supreme over the people, and the people will self-govern insofar as governance is entrusted to them.

Verse 16 looks forward to a time ("in those days" [cf. Jer. 31:29]) when the people "are fruitful and multiply" (MT: "multiply and are fruitful" [cf. Ezek. 36:11]) in the land (cf. Jer. 23:3). This language comes from the original words of blessing to mankind in Genesis 1:28: "And God blessed them, and God said to them, 'Be fruitful and multiply and fill the land and subdue it. Rule over the fish of the sea and over the flying creatures of the sky and over every living creature that creeps on the land'" (see Ps. 8:4–9 [Eng., 8:3–8]; Heb. 2:5–9). What was lost from the garden of Eden will be restored through Abraham and his seed (Gen. 3:15; 12:1–3; 22:18; 27:29; 49:8–12; Num. 24:7–9; Jer. 4:2; Ps. 72:17; Gal. 3:16, 29) and through David and his seed (2 Sam. 7:8–17; Isa. 9:5–6 [Eng., 9:6–7; 11:1–10; Jer. 23:5–6; Zech. 6:12–13; Dan. 7:13–14, 27).[43] In those days, they will never again say (cf. Jer. 7:32; 16:14; 23:7; 31:23, 29), "The ark of the covenant of the Holy One of Israel" (cf. LXX Jer. 2:2b; MT: "The ark of the covenant of the Lord"). It will not come to mind (cf. Isa. 65:17b). The people will not remember it, nor will they miss it. This phrase had apparently become something like an empty mantra, not unlike the phrase "the temple of the Lord" referenced in Jeremiah 7:4. The last clause of 3:16 ("and it will never again be made") apparently anticipates that the ark will not be remade after it is lost or destroyed (see 2 Macc. 2:1–18; *2 Bar.* 6:7–10; *m. Sheqal.* 6:1–2).[44] *Targum Jonathan* takes this last clause to mean that "they will never again wage war with it" (as in 1 Sam. 4).

What is meant by the absence of the phrase, "The ark of the covenant of the Holy One of Israel"? Calvin suggests that Judah's exclusive claim to the ark and the temple in Jerusalem will no longer be a source of division between Israel and Judah, since God will be present with

---

43. See Michael B. Shepherd, *The Text in the Middle*, StBibLit 162 (New York: Lang, 2014), 21–24, 122–29.
44. Note the appearance of the ark in the vision of Revelation 11:19.

them all.[45] Keil sees the answer to this question in 3:17a.[46] The ark of the covenant will no longer be the throne of the LORD. Jerusalem will be. It is also important to note that the ark of the covenant represents the words of the covenant placed therein (Exod. 25:16; Deut. 4:13; 1 Kgs. 8:9). It is clear from the book of Jeremiah that the old covenant from Sinai is broken and no longer in effect except for the negative consequences of breaking it (Jer. 11:10). It is also said in the book of Jeremiah that the law of the old covenant was added secondarily because of transgression (Jer. 7:21–23; 11:8; Gal. 3:19) and was not an original feature of the covenant with the patriarchs. Thus, the absence of the phrase "the ark of the covenant" also suggests the absence of the old covenant and the presence of the new (Jer. 31:31–34).

At the time referenced in 3:16, they will call Jerusalem the throne of the LORD (Jer. 3:17a; cf. Jer. 14:21; 17:12; Ezek. 43:7; see Ps. 122:1–5). This means that the ark of the covenant will no longer be the LORD's throne (see Exod. 25:22; 1 Sam. 4:4; 2 Sam. 6:2; 1 Kgs. 8:6; 2 Kgs. 19:15; Isa. 37:16; Pss. 80:2 [Eng., 80:1]; 99:1; 1 Chr. 13:6) nor his footstool (Pss. 99:5; 132:7–8; Lam. 2:1; 1 Chr. 28:2). How is this conception of the LORD's throne to be reconciled with Isaiah 66:1a ("The sky is my throne, and the land is my footstool")?[47] Both texts speak of a new Jerusalem in the messianic kingdom and the new creation where the sanctuary is no longer a temporary structure such as the tabernacle or the temple but the new and better garden of Eden (Isa. 51:3; 65:17–25 [cf. Isa. 11:1–10]; Ezek. 36:35) where the glory of the LORD fills all the land (Isa. 6:3; 11:9; Hab. 2:14 [cf. Exod. 40:35; 1 Kgs. 8:11; Ezek. 43:5]). The LORD's presence will be there (Ezek. 48:35; Rev. 21:1, 3, 22 [cf. Gen. 9:27; Exod. 29:45–46; Zech. 2:15 (Eng., 2:11); John 1:18]), and he will be king on his throne (Exod. 15:18; Zeph. 3:14–15; Zech. 2:14 [Eng., 2:10]; 9:9–10; Ps. 99:1–2).[48]

All the nations will be "collected" (like the water in Gen. 1:9) to Jerusalem, the city of David, in the last days.[49] This is what the Prophets

---

45. Calvin, *Jeremiah*, 1:183.

46. Keil, *Jeremiah*, 60.

47. See also Isaiah 60:13; Psalms 11:4; 110:1; Acts 7:47–50.

48. This includes the idea of God in the flesh as the messianic king (Isa. 7:14; 9:5–6 [Eng., 9:6–7]; 10:21; Jer. 23:5–6). See Shepherd, *Commentary on the Book of the Twelve*, 373–74, 405–6, 444–46.

49. See Neusner, *Jeremiah in Talmud and Midrash*, 104, 140–41, 185, 216. Cf. Isaiah 49:20; Zechariah 2:8 (Eng., 2:4); 10:10. Rudolph (*BHS* apparatus) questions whether the phrase "all the nations" (כל הגוים) should be changed to "from all the nations" (מכל הגוים), indicating not a collection of Gentiles

envision elsewhere (Isa. 2:1–5; 66:18–24; Jer. 16:19; Mic. 4:1–5; Zech. 2:15 [Eng., 2:11]; 8:20–23). The believing remnant of Gentiles will join the believing remnant of Israel and Judah to form the new covenant people of God (Jer. 31:31–34).[50] The message of restoration for Israel and Judah is also the message of restoration for the nations. This is because Abraham and his descendants were never meant to be the only people of God with a future exclusive to them. Rather, they were to be the means of restoring the lost blessing to all the nations (Gen. 12:3), primarily through the coming of the Messiah (Gen. 27:29; 49:8, 10; see also Gen. 22:18; Jer. 4:2; Ps. 72:17; Gal. 3:16). The MT adds the specification in 3:17a that the nations will be collected "to the name of the LORD, to Jerusalem." This is a reference to the fact that the city of Jerusalem bears the LORD's name (Deut. 12:5; Ezek. 48:35), and it is in his name that the people will come (Mic. 4:5). Those who go to Jerusalem in this manner in the last days "will never again go after the stubbornness of their evil heart" (Jer. 3:17b; cf. 1QS 1:6). This refers to going stubbornly after the "gods" of the nations contrary to the LORD's will (Deut. 29:15–20 [Eng., 29:16–21]; Jer. 2:5, 8, 23; 7:24–31; 9:13 [Eng., 9:14]; 11:6–13; 13:10; 16:11–12; 18:11–17; 23:16–29). Thus, while this language normally applies to Israel and Judah, its use here obviously presupposes that the nations have the same problem. They too will turn from false gods and idols to the true God (1 Thess. 1:9).

In those days, the house of Judah will go "in addition to" (עַל) the house of Israel (Jer. 3:18a). There is no prioritization of one over the other here. The text simply speaks of a reunited kingdom of Israel and Judah, a "return" so to speak to an ideal version of the golden age of Israel under David and Solomon (see Isa. 11:11–16; Jer. 50:4; Ezek. 37:15–28; Hos. 2:2 (Eng., 1:11); Zech. 8:13; 9:13; 10:6; see also Isa. 1:26; Jer. 33:7, 11; Zech. 12:7). They will come together from the land of the "north" and from all the lands ("and from all the lands" >

---

but a collection of dispersed Israelites and Judeans among the nations. This is because the term for "stubbornness" of heart in 3:17b applies elsewhere only to Israel and Judah (Deut. 29:18 [Eng., 29:19]; Ps. 81:13 [Eng., 81:12]; Jer. 7:24; 9:13 [Eng., 9:14]; 11:8; 13:10; 16:12; 18:12; 23:17). There is no textual evidence for the change. It appears that language customarily applied to Israel and Judah is being applied to the nations as well. Jeremiah is, after all, a prophet to the nations (Jer. 1:5, 10). The phrase "all the nations" does not mean "all the tribes" of Israel (contra Calvin).

50. This is not meant to pass over what happens at Pentecost (Joel 3:1–5 [Eng., 2:28–32]; Acts 2) and in church history. Rather, it looks to the fruit of Jewish-Gentile conversion in the final state of things.

MT) to the land that the LORD caused their forefathers to inherit (Jer. 3:18b; see Jer. 16:14–21; 23:5–8). This cannot refer to the historical return of Israel from Assyria and of Judah from Babylon. There never was a marked return of Israel from Assyria, and there never was a reunified kingdom of Israel and Judah in the period following Judah's return from Babylon in the latter part of the sixth century BC. This text refers to deliverance from the eschatological enemy from the north (see commentary on Jer. 1:14; see also Jer. 25:8–13; Ezek. 38–39; Dan 9:24–27). The new covenant people of God consisting of believers from Israel, Judah, and the nations will come to the land of the Abrahamic covenant (Gen. 15:18),[51] which was originally the land of blessing for all humanity (Gen. 2:11–14). This will happen because of the work of the LORD in blessing Abraham and his seed to restore what was lost to mankind in general. Thus, Abraham is the father of all who believe (Gen. 15:6; 17:4–5; Rom. 4).

3:19 And as for me, I said, "Amen, LORD." For [you said], "I would set you among the sons [Vaticanus: nations][52] and give to you a land of desire, an inheritance of a God of hosts of nations [LXX: an inheritance of God Almighty of nations]. And I thought, '"Father" is what you [LXX: pl.] would call me, and from after me you [LXX: pl.] would not return."[53] 3:20 But as a wife acts treacherously from her companion [see GKC §161b; BDB, 93], so the house of Israel has acted treacherously against me [MT: so you (m. pl.) have acted treacherously against me, O house of

---

51. See Deuteronomy 1:38; 3:28; 12:10; 19:3; 31:7; Joshua 1:6; Jeremiah 12:14.
52. See Isac Leo Seeligmann, *The Septuagint Version of Isaiah and Cognate Studies*, eds. Robert Hanhart and Hermann Spieckermann, FAT 40 (Tübingen: Mohr Siebeck, 2004), 75.
53. MT: "And as for me, I thought, 'How I would set you [f. sg.] among the sons and give to you [f. sg.] a land of desire, an inheritance of beauty of beauties [Syr.: the army of the armies] of nations!' And I thought, '"My father" is what you [*kethiv*: m. pl.; *qere*: f. sg.] would call me [Tg. Jon.: "My lord/master" you would pray before me], and from after me you [*kethiv*: m. pl.; *qere*: f. sg.] would not return.'" The verse could also be rendered as a series of questions that expect a negative answer: (1) Hebrew source of Greek Jeremiah: "And as for me, I said, 'Amen, LORD.' For [you said], 'Would I set you among the sons and give to you a land of desire, an inheritance of a God of hosts of nations?' And I thought, 'Is "Father" what you would call me, and from after me would you not return?'"; (2) MT: "And as for me, I thought, 'How would I set you among the sons and give to you a land of desire, an inheritance of beauty of hosts of nations?' And I thought, 'Is "My father" is what you would call me, and from after me would you not return?'"

Israel]," the prophetic utterance of the Lord. *3:21 A voice upon lips [MT: A sound upon bare places (Syr., Tg. Jon.: paths)] is heard, weeping and supplication [cf. Syr., Tg. Jon.; MT: weeping of supplication] of the sons of Israel [Syr.: the house of Israel]. For they have perverted their ways [MT: their way], they have forgotten the* Lord *[Tg. Jon.: the worship of the Lord] their holy one [MT: their God]. 3:22 "Return, apostate sons, and [cf. Syr.; and > MT] I will heal your fractures [MT: your apostasies; Tg. Jon.: I will forgive you when you return]." [Syr. adds: And they said,] "Look, we are yours [cf. Syr.; MT: Look we, we have come to you], for you are the* Lord *our God. 3:23 Surely for deception are the hills and a crowd / roar [LXX, Syr.: power] of mountains [mlt Mss: Surely for deception from hills a crowd / roar of mountains; Tg. Jon.: Then for deception we have worshiped upon the high places, and not for profit have we trembled on the mountains]. But in the* Lord *our God is the salvation of Israel. 3:24 And as for the shame [Tg. Jon.: shame of sins], it has consumed the product of the toil of our fathers from our youth, their sheep and their cattle and [and > Codex L] their sons and their daughters. 3:25 Let us lie down in our shame, and let our humiliation cover us, for it is against our God [MT: the* Lord *our God] that we have sinned, we and our fathers from our youth to this day. And we have not obeyed the voice of the* Lord *our God."*

The unit in Jeremiah 3:19–25 is not a continuation of 3:14–18, although there are some points of contact between the two (e.g., Jer. 3:14a, 22a). Rather, these last verses of chapter 3 pick up where 3:1–5 and 3:6–13 left off. The text features the voice of the Lord (Jer. 3:19–20, 22a), the voice of the prophet (Jer. 3:21), and what would ideally be the voice of the people (Jer. 3:22b–25). The Hebrew source of Greek Jeremiah begins verse 19 with the voice of the prophet: "And as for me, I said, 'Amen, Lord.' For . . ." The last three words of this text—"'Amen, Lord.' For" (אמן יהוה כי)—could be an exegesis of what appears in the MT as איך ("How!"), each letter representing one of the three words (see Rudolph, *BHS* apparatus; see also LXX Jer. 15:11). On the other hand, the MT could be an abbreviation of the three words reflected by the Greek translation.[54] The Hebrew text of DSS F.Jer 1 has the reading אמן יהוה כי. According to the Hebrew source of Greek Jeremiah, the prophet affirms the Lord's words, but what words does he affirm? It is natural to assume an affirmation of 3:1–18, but the following causal

---

54. For other examples of abbreviation, see Fishbane, *Biblical Interpretation in Ancient Israel,* 63–64; Emanuel Tov, *Textual Criticism of the Hebrew Bible,* 3rd ed. (Minneapolis: Fortress, 2012), 238–39.

conjunction suggests that what the prophet affirms may be found in the explanation of his affirmation. In contrast to the LXX *Vorlage*, the MT begins verse 19 with the LORD's own introduction of what he thought.

The contrast between what the LORD thought would happen (Jer. 3:19) and what actually happened (Jer. 3:20) is not unlike what the reader finds in 3:7 (cf. Isa. 63:8; Zeph. 3:6–7), only there the referenced thought occurred after the people's apostasy rather than prior to it. This is not an example of a failed prediction. It is instead an expression of the LORD's desire. The LORD thought that he would put his "bride" (represented in 3:19 by the second feminine singular pronominal suffixes; cf. Jer. 2:2) among the "sons." This appears to be more than an unusual mixture of metaphors. The point is not that there were other sons among whom the people would be counted. Rather, the wife would be given the status of a son in order to become the heir of the desirable land of the covenant (cf. Zech. 7:14; Ps. 106:24).[55] The LXX describes this land as "an inheritance of God Almighty of nations,"[56] which reflects נחלת אלהי צבאות גוים ("an inheritance of a God of hosts of nations") wherein צבאות is understood to be from the root צבא. The MT (נחלת צבי צבאות גוים) is usually taken to mean "an inheritance of beauty of beauties of nations," in which case צבאות would be the plural of צבי. According to the MT, the land of the covenant is the most beautiful of all the nations (cf. Ezek. 20:6, 15; Lam. 2:15; Dan. 8:9; 11:16, 41, 45; see also Isa. 13:19). Given all that the LORD did for his people to ensure their inheritance (e.g., Jer. 2:2–3), it was reasonable to expect that they would call him "father" (MT: "my father"; see Deut. 32:6; Isa. 63:16; 64:7; Jer. 3:4; Mal. 2:10) and not return from following after him (Jer. 3:19b; cf. Jer. 2:2b), but they called a wooden idol father (Jer. 2:27a), and went after Baal (Jer. 2:5b, 8b, 23a). Thus, they became "apostate," that is, those who returned from following after him (Jer. 3:6, 14, 22).

At the beginning of 3:20, both the Hebrew source of Greek Jeremiah (אך כבגד), which has an infinitive construct, and the MT (אכן בגדה), which has a finite verb, introduce a contrast ("But") with what the LORD desired (3:19) in which a comparison is made between an unfaithful wife who has departed from her husband and the house of Israel. Neither אך nor אכן should be understood as asseverative ("Surely") in this context. The Hebrew source of Greek Jeremiah keeps

---

55. See Holladay, *Jeremiah 1*, 122. McKane, however, sees the sons here as the other nations among whom the LORD would give his people a superior position (*Jeremiah I–XXV*, 78–79; see Deut. 32:8–9).

56. See Deuteronomy 4:21; 15:4; 19:10; 20:16; 21:28; 24:4; 25:19; 26:1; Jeremiah 12:14.

this comparison in the third person ("so the house of Israel has acted treacherously against me"), while the MT uses the second person ("so you have acted treacherously against me, O house of Israel"). The metaphor of the unfaithful wife has already been employed in the citation of the divorce law in 3:1. Israel was the "apostate" one who fornicated and committed spiritual adultery, and Judah was the "treacherous" or "unfaithful" (בגודה) one who followed Israel's example and even went beyond it (Jer. 3:6–11; see also Hos. 5:7; 6:7).

The Greek text at the start of 3:21 reflects קול על שפתים ("A voice upon lips"), while the MT has קול על שפיים ("A sound upon bare places") (cf. Jer. 7:29). This voice or sound is further said to be the "weeping and supplication [MT: weeping of supplication] of the sons of Israel" (cf. Jer. 31:9; Pss. 28:2, 6; 31:23 [Eng., 31:22]; 86:6; 116:1; 130:2; 140:7 [Eng., 140:6]). According to Holladay, this is comparable to Rachel's weeping for her children in Jeremiah 31:15: "By this understanding, then, it is not that the Israelites are weeping to Yahweh, but rather that Yahweh is weeping for his lost children, the Israelites" (cf. Jer. 9:9 [Eng., 9:10]).[57] On the other hand, if the MT is correct in its association of this voice or sound with the "bare places" (cf. Jer. 3:2; 7:29), then the voice/sound is likely that of Israel's spiritual fornication at the alternative places of worship (see Jer. 2:20, 23; 3:6, 9, 23).[58] Thus, it is not merely the sound of Israel's suffering (Calvin), although it may be related to that (Jer. 9:18 [Eng., 9:19]), and it is certainly not the sound of Israel's repentance. Rather, it is Israel's voice directed to Baal. This is because the people have "perverted their way(s)" (Jer. 3:21b; see Jer. 2:23, 33; 3:2, 13). They have "forgotten" the LORD (cf. Jer. 2:32; Ps. 78:7) their "holy one" (MT: "their God"; cf. LXX Jer. 2:2b).

The text of 3:22a repeats the call to repentance ("Return, apostate sons") from 3:14 (see Jer. 8:4; 31:18b, 21b, 22), adding that the LORD will "heal" their "fractures" (cf. Isa. 30:26; Jer. 6:14; 8:11; see also Jer. 8:21; 10:19; 14:17; 30:12; MT: "apostasies" [cf. Hos. 14:5 (Eng., 14:4); see also Isa. 57:18–19]). What follows in 3:22b–25 is not the actual voice of the people, nor is it an expression of disingenuous repentance. It is what the LORD would like to hear from the people (cf. Jer. 14:7–9, 19–22; Hos. 6:1–3; 14:2–4 [Eng., 14:1–3]; see also Isa. 63:15–64:11 [Eng., 64:12]). According to Rashi, it is the prayer of confession that the prophet teaches the people to say.[59] The opening declaration of this confession in 3:22b differs between the Hebrew source of Greek Jeremiah and the

---

57. Holladay, *Jeremiah 1*, 123.

58. See McKane, *Jeremiah I–XXV*, 80. See also Ezekiel 8:14; Malachi 2:13.

59. Rosenberg, trans., *Mikraoth Gedoloth: Jeremiah Volume One*, 32.

MT. The Hebrew source of Greek Jeremiah (cf. Syr.) has הנה אנחנו לך ("Look, we are yours") (cf. Exod. 32:26). The MT has הננו אתנו לך ("Look we, we have come to you"). The people had said that they would not come again to the LORD (Jer. 2:31b), but the confession in 3:22b–25 envisions the new covenant reality of the future. The explanation, "for you are the LORD our God," also occurs in the prayer for restoration found within the Book of Comfort (Jer. 31:18b).

3:23a and 3:23b feature the two main uses of אכן, the first asseverative ("Surely") and the second contrastive ("But"; cf. Jer. 3:20). The difficulties of 3:23a are well documented, and the text reads differently depending upon whether it is the Hebrew source of Greek Jeremiah ("Surely for deception are the hills and a crowd/roar of mountains") or the MT (mlt Mss: "Surely for deception from hills a crowd/roar of mountains"). The Leningrad Codex (*BHS*) has the added difficulty of המון ("crowd/roar") in the absolute state rather than the construct state. There is fortunately general agreement, however, that this refers to the "deception" (שקר)[60] of false worship on the high places (see *Tg. Jon.*) where the sound of religious ritual can be heard (cf. Jer. 2:20, 23; 3:2, 6, 9, 21; 7:29; 17:2–3 [MT]; Ezek. 23:42), but the ideal voice of the people confesses that in the LORD, their one true God, is the salvation of Israel (Jer. 3:23b).

The Hebrew text has הבשת ("the shame") fronted in the syntax of 3:24a. This is a term for Baal (see Jer. 11:13b [MT]; Hos. 9:10). בשת or *bosheth* ("shame") and בעל or *baal* ("lord") are used interchangeably in the names Ishbosheth (2 Sam. 2:8; LXX[Ms]: Εισβααλ) and Eshbaal (1 Chr. 8:33), and in the names Mephibosheth (2 Sam. 4:4; LXX[L]: Μεμφιβααλ) and Meribaal (1 Chr. 8:34). What does it mean then that Baal or the worship of Baal has "consumed the product of the toil of our fathers from our youth, their sheep and their cattle and their sons and their daughters" (cf. Jer. 5:17, 23–25; 44:7; Hos. 7:9; 8:7)?[61] On the one hand, it means that Baal worship has not benefited the people in the manner anticipated (Jer. 2:8b, 11b, 13b).[62] It has been deceptive (Jer. 3:23a). On the other hand, it also means that the people have experienced the curses for their breaking of the covenant (Lev. 26; Deut. 28) even from their "youth" as a nation (Jer. 2:2, 5; 3:4; 31:19b; see also Jer. 20:5).

---

60. See commentary on Jeremiah 3:10b for a list of texts in Jeremiah where this term occurs.

61. Note how the confession acknowledges the sin of Baal worship according to the instruction in Jeremiah 2:23.

62. According to Hosea 2:10 (Eng., 2:8), Israel tried to give credit to Baal for the LORD's blessings.

Furthermore, the people have wasted the resources of their livestock in the multiplication of animal sacrifices as part of their Baal worship (Jer. 11:13 [MT]; Hos. 10:1; see also Hos. 2:13–15 [Eng., 2:11–13]; 5:7). They have lost their children in the unconscionable practice of child sacrifice to Baal (Jer. 7:31; 19:5).

The LXX renders the first two verbs of 3:25 with aorist forms (NETS: "We lay down in our shame, and our dishonor covered us"), but this does not seem to be the sense of the prefixed verbal forms in the Hebrew source text: "Let us lie down in our shame, and let our humiliation cover us." This is an expression of a desire to accept the rightful consequences of past actions, to lie down in shame (cf. 2 Sam. 12:16; 13:31; 1 Kgs. 21:4) and to be covered in humiliation (cf. Pss. 35:26; 69:8 [Eng., 69:7]; 109:29; Mic. 7:10; Obad. 10).[63] In contrast to 2:35, the ideal voice of the people admits that this is because they and their fathers have sinned against their God since their youth (see Jer. 2:2; 3:4, 13a, 24; 7:25; 8:14; 14:7, 20; 22:21; 32:30; Ezek. 2:3; cf. Gen. 8:21). They have disobeyed the voice of the LORD their God (Jer. 3:25b; cf. Jer. 3:13b; 11:7–8 [MT]).

4:1 "If Israel returns," the prophetic utterance of the LORD, "(if) to me he returns, if he removes his detestable idols from his mouth and from before me does not wander [LXX: and from before me acts reverently], 4:2 and (if) he swears, 'As the LORD lives [or, By the life of the LORD] . . . ,' in faithfulness [or, truth], in justice and in righteousness, then 'nations will be blessed in him [LXX: nations will bless in him; Vulg.: nations will bless him],' and they will praise God in Jerusalem."[64] 4:3 For thus says the LORD to the men of Judah and to the inhabitants of [the inhabitants of > Codex L] Jerusalem, "Plow for yourselves unplowed ground [LXX: Renew for yourselves new things; Syr.: Light for yourselves a lamp; Tg. Jon.: Do for yourselves good deeds] and do not sow among thorns [Tg. Jon.: and do not seek deliverance in sins]. 4:4 Be circumcised [or, Circumcise yourselves] to your God [MT: to the LORD; Tg. Jon.: Return to the worship of the Lord] and remove the foreskin [Codex L: foreskins; Tg. Jon.: wickedness]

---

63. See Keil, *Jeremiah*, 64.

64. MT Jeremiah 4:1–2: "If you return, O Israel," the prophetic utterance of the LORD, "(if) to me you return [*Tg. Jon.*: your repentance will be accepted before your decree is sealed], and if you remove your detestable idols from before me [Cairo Genizah: from before you] and do not wander, and (if) you swear, 'As the LORD lives . . . ,' in faithfulness [or, truth], in justice and in righteousness, then 'nations will be blessed in him [*Tg. Jon.*: in Israel],' and in him they will boast."

of your heart / mind, O men of Judah and inhabitants of Jerusalem, lest like a fire my wrath go forth and burn and there be no one to extinguish [Tg. Jon.: no mercy] because of the evil of your deeds."

The above translation assumes that 4:1–2a is a series of protases ("if" clauses) followed by the apodoses ("then" clauses) in 4:2b (cf. NEB, NJV).[65] Most translations render the second clause of 4:1a as an apodosis. Some render the second clause of 4:1b as an apodosis and/or 4:2a as an apodosis. Holladay argues for the protasis-apodosis relationship in 4:1a—"If you turn (at all), Israel, oracle of Yahweh, (then) to me you should turn"—suggesting that "Israel is capable of turning to evil from Yahweh, or from evil to Yahweh."[66] The reality, however, is that Israel has already turned to evil. The question is whether Israel can or will turn to the LORD, the only other option (cf. Jer. 8:4). Thus, the second clause of 4:1a is simply part B of the parallelism, which completes the thought of part A by adding "to me."[67] If in reply it is said that not all the clauses in 4:1–2a are marked conditions, it should be noted that the apodoses are also not marked (see GKC §159). The only reason why there is general agreement on the apodoses in 4:2b is the fact that there is nothing to follow them that could function as such.

The Greek translation of 4:1–2a has third-person verbs rather than the second-person verbs of the MT. McKane thinks that the translator had the same Hebrew verbal forms that appear in the MT, but he rendered the second masculine singular prefixed forms in 4:1 as if they were the identical third feminine singular forms.[68] According to McKane, this was done under the influence of the third masculine singular pronominal suffixes in 4:2b, which he assumes the translator believed to refer to Israel. This does not explain the translation of the verb at the beginning of 4:2a as third person, nor does it explain the mixture of third-feminine verbs in 4:1 with third masculine singular suffixes on the forms שקוציו (rather than MT's שקוציך) and מפיו presumably behind the Greek translation, which uses third masculine singular pronouns. It seems more likely that the translator had a *Vorlage* with third masculine singular verbal forms in 4:1–2a. This would fit with the masculine gender of "Israel."[69]

---

65. See also Keil, *Jeremiah*, 65; Thompson, *Book of Jeremiah*, 211.

66. Holladay, *Jeremiah 1*, 61, 127.

67. See Kugel, *Idea of Biblical Poetry*, 54.

68. McKane, *Jeremiah I–XXV*, 84.

69. The subsequent change to second-person forms in the MT may be explained as a development from an initial change to third feminine singular

The language of the first condition in 4:1a (i.e., if Israel "returns" to the LORD) hearkens back to Jeremiah 3:1b, 7, 12, 14, 22 (see also Jer. 5:3; 15:19). Thus, "Israel" is not limited to the northern kingdom of Israel here but includes the southern kingdom of Judah and all those from the nations who might follow the example of the faithful remnant of Israel/Judah in repentance (Jer. 3:17–18; 4:2b). Israel's repentance is a condition for the blessing in 4:2b (cf. Jer. 15:19; Zech. 1:3; 2 Mal. 3:7; Chr. 30:6; Tob. 13:6), but there is also indication within the book that Israel is incapable of such repentance (Jer. 3:7; 5:3; 13:23) and in need of divine initiation (Jer. 31:18; cf. Lam. 5:21; see also Deut. 30:1–7).[70] The second condition ("if he removes his detestable idols from his mouth") reads differently in the MT ("if you remove your detestable idols from before me") (Jer. 4:1b). According to the Hebrew source of Greek Jeremiah, Israel must remove his "detestable idols" (see BDB, 1055) from his mouth either in the sense of the removal of unclean food dedicated to idols and eaten like a fellowship offering (cf. Zech. 9:7) or in the sense of the removal of oaths spoken in the name of other gods (or in the name of the LORD disingenuously) (Jer. 4:2a; 5:2). The MT, however, speaks of the removal of idols "from before" the LORD. This alludes to the prohibition in Exodus 20:3 and Deuteronomy 5:7 ("You must not have other gods before me").[71] There are to be no idols in the LORD's presence (see also Deut. 32:39). The Hebrew source of Greek Jeremiah 4:1b puts the phrase "from before me" with the third condition: "and from before me does not wander" (LXX: "and from before me acts reverently"). Holladay compares this wandering to Cain's wandering in Genesis 4:14 and then contrasts it with being like Abraham (see Jer. 4:2b; cf. Gen. 22:18).[72] Historically, neither Israel nor Judah repented, and thus each were cast "from before" the LORD to live in exile (Jer. 7:15).

The fourth and final condition appears in 4:2a: "and (if) he swears [MT: you swear], 'As the LORD lives [or, By the life of the LORD] . . . ,'

---

verbal forms based on the metaphor of Israel as the LORD's bride. These forms were then read as second masculine singular with "Israel" as a vocative, resulting in the use of a second masculine singular pronominal suffix on שקוציך. What would have been the third feminine singular form ונשבעה at the beginning of 4:2a was read as ונשבעת. The phrase מפיו dropped out due to haplography (cf. מפני).

70. See Shepherd, *Text in the Middle*, 96–99.

71. Some take the phrase "before me" to me either "in preference to me" or "in addition to me" (see BDB, 818). Cf. LXX: "except me."

72. Holladay, *Jeremiah 1*, 127.

in faithfulness [or, truth], in justice and in righteousness." According to *HALOT* 2:1397, to "swear" or "to bind oneself by oath" (*niphal* of שבע) is "to make a statement, to give a pledge, under oath, invoking God, a commitment to do good." In many cases, it "simply means a solemn, irrevocable promise, whatever circumstances may arise, to undertake to do something, or not to do it." The law stipulated that the LORD's name was not to be taken in vain (Exod. 20:7; Deut. 5:11) by swearing falsely (Lev. 19:12; Jer. 7:9; Hos. 4:2; Zech. 5:4; Ps. 24:4), specifically with regard to false testimony against a neighbor (Exod. 20:16; Deut. 5:20; 19:16–19).[73] The Jeremiah context seems to have in view usage of the standard introductory oath formula (חי יהוה) in which the name of Yahweh is invoked disingenuously (see Jer. 5:2; cf. Isa. 48:1; Hos. 4:15) in a futile effort to veil swearing by non-gods (see Jer. 5:7; 12:16; 44:17, 25, 26; cf. Amos 8:14; Zeph. 1:5; see also Hos. 2:18 [Eng., 2:16]). What the LORD requires is swearing in his name "genuinely" (באמת) (see Deut. 6:13; 10:20; Jer. 16:14–15; 23:7–8; Ps. 63:12 [Eng., 63:11]; cf. Jer. 49:13; see also Josh. 24:14; Isa. 10:20), to which the two coordinated phrases, "in justice" and "in righteousness" are placed in apposition in Jeremiah 4:2a (cf. Isa. 1:27; Jer. 22:2, 15; Hos. 2:21 [Eng., 2:19]; Zech. 8:8). Bullinger considers this an instance of *hendiatris* ("three for one") in which three words are used, but one thing is meant.[74] The people are to be both truthful and faithful in their covenant relationship with the LORD, behaving justly and rightly toward God and toward one another (see Zech. 7:8–10; 8:16–17).

The two apodoses in 4:2b are introduced by *waw* apodosis: "then 'nations will be blessed in him [*Tg. Jon.*: in Israel; LXX: nations will bless in him; Vulg.: nations will bless him],' and they will praise God in Jerusalem [MT: and in him they will boast]." The first clause is a citation from one or more of the following texts:[75] (1) "all the families of the earth will be blessed [*niphal*] in you [i.e., Abram]" (Gen. 12:3b); (2) "all the nations of the earth will be blessed [*niphal*] in him [i.e., Abraham]" (Gen. 18:18b); (3) "all the nations of the earth will be blessed [*hithpael*] in your seed" (Gen. 22:18a); (4) "all the nations of the earth will be blessed [*hithpael*] in your seed" (Gen. 26:4b); and (5) "all the families of the earth will be blessed [*niphal*] in you [i.e.,

---

73. See also the prohibitions against swearing in Matthew 5:33–37; 23:16–22; James 5:12.

74. Bullinger, *Figures of Speech*, 673. See also Holladay, *Jeremiah 1*, 128.

75. Heinrich Ewald: "a learned quotation from a book" (quoted [unfavorably] in Keil, *Jeremiah*, 65).

Jacob]" (Gen. 28:14b).[76] The texts of Genesis 22:18a and 26:4b employ the *hithpael* stem as in Jeremiah 4:2b. The immediate contexts of Genesis 22:18a and 26:4b also feature the *niphal* of שבע ("swear") as in Jeremiah 4:2a (see Gen. 22:16; 26:3; see also Heb. 6:13–20; 7:20–22). The text of Genesis 18:18b uses the phrase "in him" (rather than "in you" or "in your seed") as in Jeremiah 4:2b. The context of Genesis 18:18b also mentions "righteousness" and "justice" as in Jeremiah 4:2a (see Gen. 18:19).

Both the *niphal* and the *hithpael* stems in the above-cited Genesis passages are often understood to be reflexive ("will bless themselves") and thus interchangeable. The *hithpael* in Jeremiah 4:2b is typically assigned a similar meaning. That is, it is assumed that these texts speak of the use of Israel's name in a blessing formula: "such will be their well-being that nations will use the formulae, 'May you be blessed like Israel' or 'May you be renowned like Israel.'"[77] There are two unresolved problems with this interpretation. The first is that none of the passages makes explicit reference to such a formula. It is not too much to expect at least one example of the sort of formula provided in Genesis 48:20: "By you Israel will bless [LXX and Syr. have passive forms] saying, 'May God make you like Ephraim and like Manasseh'" (cf. Jer. 29:22). The second problem is that the LXX consistently renders the Genesis passages with passive forms rather than active forms with reflexive pronouns (Gen. 12:3b; 18:18b; 22:18a; 26:4b; 28:14b; see also Ps. 72:17; cf. Jer. 4:2b),[78] and this influences the citations in the Greek New Testament (Acts 3:25; Gal. 3:8). This evidence suggests that it is at least equally plausible to understand these texts to mean that the nations are blessed "in" (positionally) and/or "by means of" Abraham/Jacob and Abraham's seed. It is also worth noting that the *niphal* stem is consistently used when the text speaks of the families or nations being blessed in a patriarch—Abram/Abraham or Jacob (Gen. 12:3b; 18:18b; 28:14b). The *hithpael* stem (perhaps iterative) occurs when the text speaks of

---

76. The addition of "and in your seed" at the end of Genesis 28:14b appears to be secondary (see *BHS* apparatus). The same secondary addition occurs in the Syriac version of Genesis 12:3b.

77. McKane, *Jeremiah I–XXV*, 86.

78. The LXX of Jeremiah 4:2 ("nations will bless in him") is the anomaly in this group. It is neither passive nor reflexive. The object of "bless" (themselves? others?) is not explicit.

the nations being blessed in Abraham's seed (Gen. 22:18a; 26:4b; Jer. 4:2b; Ps. 72:17).[79]

The final exegetical issue with regard to the citation ("nations will be blessed in him") is the antecedent or referent of the third masculine singular pronominal suffix "him." *Targum Jonathan*, which follows the MT, states explicitly that the antecedent is "Israel," but this cannot be the case in the MT, which refers to Israel using second masculine singular forms throughout Jeremiah 4:1–2a. It is possible that the pronoun "him" refers to Israel in the LXX and its *Vorlage*, but it remains to be seen if this is the correct interpretation of the Genesis passages on which the citation is based. The Latin Vulgate ("nations will bless [or, praise] him") seems to presuppose that the LORD is the antecedent, which would anticipate the following clause in the LXX and its *Vorlage*: "and they will praise God in Jerusalem" (cf. MT: "and in him they will boast" [see Isa. 45:25; Jer. 9:23 (Eng., 9:24); Ps. 63:12 (Eng., 63:11); Rom. 5:11]). But a third-person pronominal reference to the LORD in 4:2b would be sudden and unexpected. A first common singular pronominal suffix would be more appropriate to the context.

John Sailhamer has demonstrated that the "seed" of Abraham in Genesis 22:18a and 26:4b is part of a larger development in the composition of the Pentateuch that begins with the "seed" of the woman in Genesis 3:15 and works its way through the narrative into the poetic seams of Genesis 49 and Numbers 24 where the reader finds the hope of a messianic king from the tribe of Judah who will appear in the last days.[80] Thus, while Eve, Abraham, and eventually David all have a plurality of descendants, the text also focuses the reader's attention on one particular member of their offspring (cf. 2 Sam. 7:13; Zech. 6:12–13). The narrative traces the seed of Genesis 3:15 through the story of the flood and to the remaining family of Noah and his three sons. From there the text shows the seventy nations from the three sons of Noah (Gen. 10) and follows two lines of Shem (Gen. 10:21–32 and 11:10–26). The first line of Shem ends in the story of the Tower of Babylon (Gen. 11:1–9). The second ends with the story of Abram/ Abraham (Gen. 11:27–25:11) to whom the LORD says, "I will bless those

---

79. The *hithpael* of ברך is most likely reflexive in Deuteronomy 29:18 (Eng., 29:19). The usage in Isaiah 65:16 could be either passive or reflexive. See Benjamin J. Noonan, "Abraham, Blessing, and the Nations," *HS* 51 (2010): 73–93.

80. John H. Sailhamer, *The Meaning of the Pentateuch: Revelation, Composition, and Interpretation* (Downers Grove, IL: InterVarsity, 2009), 473–510. See also Shepherd, *Text in the Middle*, 21–24.

who bless you, and anyone who treats you lightly will I curse," and, "To your seed I will give this land" (Gen. 12:3a, 7a). This language resurfaces in Isaac's words of blessing, which were intended for Esau but directed to Jacob disguised as Esau: "May peoples serve you, and may nations bow down to you. Be lord to your brothers, and may the sons of your mother bow down to you. May each one who curses you be cursed, and may each one who blesses you be blessed" (Gen. 27:29). Not only does this scenario play itself out in the life of Joseph to whom his brothers bow down (Gen. 37:5–11; 42:6, 9), but also the story of Joseph serves to prefigure the coming king from the tribe of Judah in Jacob's blessing: "Judah, as for you, your brothers will praise you. Your hand will be at the neck of your enemies. The sons of your father will bow down to you. Judah is a lion's cub. From prey, my son, you have gone up. He bows down, he lies down like a lion, and like a lioness who will arouse him? . . . to him will belong obedience of peoples" (Gen. 49:8–9, 10b; see also Gen. 49:1, 10a, 11–12, 22–26). Balaam's third oracle then picks up the language of all three texts (i.e., Gen. 12:3a; 27:29b; 49:9b): "He bows down, he lies down like a lion, and like a lioness who will arouse him? Each one who blesses you is blessed, and each one who curses you is cursed" (Num. 24:9). This text speaks of a messianic king who will rise like a star in the last days to crush the head of the enemy (Num. 24:7 [LXX, SP], 14, 17; cf. Gen 3:15) and whom God will bring like a lion "out of Egypt" in a new act of deliverance (Num. 24:8; see Deut. 28:68; Hos. 8:13; 9:3; 11:1, 5, 11; Matt. 2:15) just as he brought Israel out of Egypt like a lion in the original exodus (Num. 23:22, 24).

The larger compositional strategy of the Pentateuch strongly suggests that the "seed" in the text(s) cited in Jeremiah 4:2b is not Israel. Rather, the referent of the pronoun "him" in Jeremiah 4:2b is the messianic king in whom all the nations will be blessed. That is, by means of the work accomplished by this king, all those who are "in him" by faith will experience the full restoration of the lost blessing of life and dominion in the land of the new creation and the new garden of Eden and will reign with him forever in his kingdom. It is worth noting then that the desired justice and righteousness of Jeremiah 4:2a are the very hallmarks of the Davidic Messiah and his kingdom in the composition of the book of Jeremiah (Jer. 23:5–8; cf. Isa. 9:5–6 [Eng., 9:6–7]; 11:3–5).[81] Psalm 72:17b, which also cites Genesis 22:18 and 26:4b, likewise

---

81. The suffering of the Messiah as an acceptable substitutionary sacrifice (Isa. 52:13–53:12) makes justification by faith in his work possible (Isa. 53:1, 11; 60:21) and enables the bearing of the fruit of righteousness (Isa. 61:1–3). The premature death of the righteous king Josiah serves to

has this ideal king in view: "And they will be blessed in him, all nations will call him blessed." He will bring justice and righteousness to the world (Ps. 72:1–16).[82] Paul thus has ample exegetical warrant and intertextual precedent to insist that Christ is the seed of Abraham (Gal. 3:16) and that the Jewish-Gentile people of God are the seed of Abraham by faith in the person and work of Christ and by their new spiritual position and status in him (Gal. 3:26–29; cf. Rom. 4). It is one of the special concerns of the book of Jeremiah to highlight the inclusion of the nations in God's plan (see Jer. 1:5; 3:17; 4:2b; 12:14–17; 16:19; 46:26b [MT]; 48:47b; 49:6 [MT], 39).

The conjunction כִּי ("For") at the beginning of Jeremiah 4:3 introduces verses 3 and 4 as an explanation of Jeremiah 4:1–2. The metaphorical illustration of repentance and heart transformation in 4:3b–4a parses the nature of the return required by the LORD in 4:1–2a. The warning of judgment for lack of change found in 4:4b balances the hopeful consequence of true repentance in 4:2b. Jeremiah's reintroduction of the LORD's discourse in 4:3a addresses the words to "the men of Judah and to the inhabitants of [the inhabitants of > Codex L] Jerusalem" (cf. Isa. 5:3; Jer. 4:4a). This is Jeremiah's immediate audience, but it is evident from the context that the words ultimately apply to the northern kingdom of Israel and the nations as well (Jer. 3:14–18). Moreover, the textual form of Jeremiah enables future generations of readers to access the message.[83] The imperative, "Plow for yourselves unplowed ground [LXX: Renew for yourselves new things],"[84] bears a relationship to Hosea 10:12–13 (see also Prov. 11:18; 22:8; Gal. 6:7–9), although McKane suggests that it is not as direct as some have thought: "If the seed is צדקה, the crop will be חסד; if it is רשע, the crop will be עולה. In Jer 4.3, on the other hand, there is no antithesis of good and bad seed, but only of well-prepared and ill-prepared soil: the seed which is sown on thorns produces nothing, but the fault is not

---

prefigure the suffering Messiah in the book of Jeremiah (Jer. 22:10, 15; see Zech. 12:9–13:1).

82. Psalm 72 concludes book two of the Psalter (Pss. 42–72). Each of the first four books concludes with a doxology (Pss. 41:14 [Eng., 41:13]; 72:18–19; 89:53 [Eng., 89:52]; 106:48) and a messianic psalm (Pss. 40–41 [see Heb. 10:5–10; John 13:18]; 72; 89; 110 [near the beginning of book five]).

83. The prophets and their "original" audiences are long gone, but their words remain relevant in the texts that bear their names (Zech. 1:4–6).

84. The Syriac ("Light for yourselves a lamp") apparently misreads ניר ("unplowed ground") as if it were נר ("lamp").

in the seed."[85] *Targum Jonathan* interprets the plowing to mean, "Do for yourselves good deeds," but a more precise understanding of this in context would recognize that the plowing requires a change in the pollution of the land described in Jeremiah 3:1–2 (cf. Lev. 19:29). The parallel clause, "and do not sow among thorns" (*Tg. Jon.*: "and do not seek deliverance in sins"), not only echoes the effects of the original fall of humanity (Gen. 3:18; cf. Isa. 5:6; 7:23–25) but also anticipates the seed among the thorns in Jesus' parable of the sower (Matt. 13:7, 22; see also Jer. 12:13).

The first imperative in Jeremiah 4:4a, which is in the *niphal* stem, can be rendered as passive ("Be circumcised to your God [MT: to the Lord]") or reflexive ("Circumcise yourselves to your God [MT: to the Lord]").[86] The reflexive option would seem to work best with the following imperative ("and remove the foreskin of your heart"), indicating what the people ("the men of Judah and the inhabitants of Jerusalem") are responsible to do for themselves, but the matter is not so simple. Just as the "return" of the people (Jer. 4:1; Zech. 1:3; Mal. 3:7) requires the Lord to turn them (Jer. 31:18; Lam. 5:21), and just as the people's making of a new heart and a new spirit for themselves (Ezek. 18:31) requires the Lord to give them a new heart and a new spirit (Ezek. 11:19–20; 36:26), so the imperative to circumcise their own hearts (Deut. 10:16) requires the Lord to perform the circumcision for them (Deut. 30:6; see also 4Q434, 504). Thus, the people are held responsible, yet they are at the same time dependent upon the Lord. The physical sign of the covenant with Abraham, which marked the male organ as the bearer of the seed (Gen. 17:9–14, 23–27), is metaphorically the spiritual sign of the new covenant, which marks the presence of a new heart/mind that is receptive to the will of God (Deut. 28:69; 29:3 [Eng., 29:1, 4]; 30:6; Jer. 31:31, 33; Rom. 2:28–29; Col. 2:11; see also Lev. 26:41; Jer. 9:24–25 [Eng., 9:25–26]).[87] The imperative to remove the foreskin of the heart, which the Greek text of Codex Vaticanus interprets to be the circumcision

---

85. McKane, *Jeremiah I–XXV*, 87.
86. Cf. "consecrate yourselves to the Lord" (e.g., Exod. 32:29; see also Exod. 28:41). See also Jeremiah 4:14.
87. Tertullian: "Just as the physical circumcision, which was temporary, was made to be a 'sign' in a rebellious people, so spiritual circumcision has been given for salvation to an obedient people" (Wenthe, ed., *Jeremiah, Lamentations*, 41). There is a sense of continuity with the Abrahamic covenant, which was unconditional and based on faith (Gen. 15:6) rather than works. Both the Abrahamic covenant and the new covenant contribute to the restoration of the lost blessing to all the nations in their own unique way.

of hard-heartedness, calls for the preparation and change of heart necessary to make it soft and malleable. This is not unlike the image of the uncircumcised ear (Jer. 6:10), which requires a kind of circumcision to make it ready to hear and obey.

The prophet's audience (i.e., the readership) must have their hearts circumcised lest the wrath of the Lord's final judgment go forth like a fire that burns and is not extinguished due to the evil of their deeds (Jer. 4:4b; cf. Jer. 7:20; 21:12; Amos 5:6; see also Deut. 28:20; Isa. 1:16; Jer. 11:16; 26:3; Ps. 89:47 [Eng., 89:46]). This is not merely the judgment that manifested itself in the burning of Jerusalem and the temple (Jer. 39:8; 52:13) but also the fiery judgment of the last days (e.g., Isa. 66:15–17, 24). Thus, the simile "like a fire" becomes a reality, the literal fire of the Lord's wrath in judgment. The necessity and severity of this judgment make the provision of spiritual circumcision appear all the more gracious and merciful.

APPLICATION OF JEREMIAH 2:14–4:4

The central problem that the Lord addresses through the prophet Jeremiah in this section is idolatry and misplaced trust, a development of the theme introduced in Jeremiah 1:16; 2:5, 8, 11, 13. The primary metaphor for this problem is spiritual fornication, which illustrates the broken covenant relationship between God and his people. This problem is not unique to ancient Israel and Judah. Worship of "other gods" is something that Israel and Judah have always shared with all nations. What makes the failure of Israel and Judah so egregious is the fact that they had been the recipients of a special covenant relationship with the Lord (Amos 3:1–2). Access to special revelation through Moses and the prophets gave them a greater responsibility. Thus, given such a privileged position, their seemingly inexplicable inability to live up to the standards of the old covenant speaks to the fact that fallen humanity in general is unable to do so.

The text's concern with idolatry is a concern with the main problem of human sin. In other words, the prophet is not dealing with symptoms of a larger issue. Idolatry is the larger issue. Idolatry takes several forms in the biblical literature. First of all, humanity has from the very beginning attempted to become "like God" (Gen. 3:5, 22) in a way that is contrary to design (Gen. 1:26–28). The most common form of idolatry in the Bible is the conscious worship of an image made either to represent the one true God (e.g., Exod. 32) or to represent false, nonexistent gods such as Baal. Very often illegitimate worship in the Bible is a mixture of the two (syncretism). Because this kind of worship seems foreign to many Christians living in the Western world, the application of biblical texts about idolatry tends to turn very quickly to metaphorical idolatry (e.g., greed), which is only mentioned in two cognate texts in Paul's epistles (Eph. 5:5; Col. 3:5), but the reality is that false religion manifests itself in a wide variety of ways in the unbelieving world around Christians everywhere.[88]

As noted in the above exposition, the hope of the new covenant gospel in Jeremiah 3:14–18 and 4:1–4 is for everyone. For unbelieving readers, the application is to repent and to have their hearts circumcised to the Lord. For believing readers, the application is to hold fast to the hope of the new covenant and to speak the truth of the gospel into an unbelieving world mired in idolatry and worship of false gods, being careful to warn of the judgment to come. This is the message of Christ and his kingdom for all the nations. It is applicable to every age because it ultimately looks forward to the final state of affairs in the last days.

---

88. It should be noted that both literal and metaphorical idolatry in the Bible are said to be the activities of unbelievers. The text of Jeremiah 2:14–4:4 should not be used to address Christians as if they were unbelieving Israelites living in the context of the broken Sinai covenant as unregenerate and unredeemed people without the power of the Spirit to obey.

JEREMIAH 4:5–31

4:5 *"Declare in Judah and in Jerusalem, cause to hear [or, make procla-
mation], and say, 'Blast in the land a shofar [MT: Blast a shofar in the
land] and [and > MT] proclaim fully [GKC §120h], say [MT: and say],
"Gather together, and let us enter [or, that we may enter] the fortified
cities."' 4:6 Lift up, flee to Zion [MT: Lift up a banner—To Zion]. Seek
refuge [LXX: hasten], do not stay. For calamity is what I am bringing
from (the) north, and great breaking. 4:7 A lion [Syr., Tg. Jon.: king]
went up from its thicket, a destroyer [MT: and a destroyer] of nations, he
set out and [and > MT] went forth from his place to make the land [MT:
your land] into a desolation [or, an object of horror]; and as for cities,
they will fall in ruins so that there is no inhabitant." 4:8 Concerning
this, gird on sackcloth and [and > MT] mourn and wail, for the anger
[MT: the burning of the anger] of the* Lord *has not turned from us.*

4:9 *"In that day," the prophetic utterance of the* Lord, *"the heart of the
king will perish, and the heart of the leaders, and the priests will be appalled, and as for the prophets, they will be astonished." 4:10 And I said
[LXX^A: And they said], "Ah, Lord* God, *surely you have completely deceived [Tg. Jon.: the false prophets are leading astray] this people and
Jerusalem, saying, 'Peace [or, Well-being] is what will be,' and look, a
sword has reached up to their life." 4:11 "At that time, they will say [MT:
it will be said] to this people and to Jerusalem, 'A spirit of distortion
[MT: a glowing hot wind from bare places] in the wilderness, the way
of the daughter of my people [or, my daughter-my people] not to cleanse
[MT: not to scatter] and not to purify [LXX: nor to what is holy]. 4:12 A
full spirit [MT: a wind too full for these] will come to me [or, for me].*[1]
*Now, also/indeed I, I will speak judgments with them.' 4:13 Look, like
a cloud [MT: clouds; Tg. Jon.: like a cloud that goes up and covers the
land] he [Tg. Jon.: a king with his armies] goes up, and like a whirlwind are his chariots. His horses are swifter than eagles." "Woe to us,
for we are destroyed." 4:14 "Wash from evil your heart, O Jerusalem,
in order that you may be saved. How long will the thoughts of your
trouble lodge [GKC §145k] within you? 4:15 For a declaring voice from
Dan will come [MT: For a voice declares from Dan], and trouble will be
heard from Mount [or, the hill country of] Ephraim [MT: and causes to*

---

1. *Tg. Jon.*: "Because they went astray after the false prophets who prophesied to them in a spirit of deception, thus armies of peoples, swifter than
   these, like the wind will come upon them."

hear (or, proclaims) trouble from Mount Ephraim].[2] *4:16 Remind the nations, 'Look, they have come [they have come > MT].' Cause to hear [or, Make proclamation] in Jerusalem, 'Foes [MT: watchmen/block-aders (or, besiegers)] are coming from a distant land [MT: the distant land].' And they gave to/against the cities of Judah their voice. 4:17 Like keepers/guards of a field are they against her all around, for it is against me that she has been rebellious [LXX: for me she has neglected; Syr.: for to me she has been bitter]," the prophetic utterance of the* Lord. *4:18 "Your ways [Codex L: Your way] and your deeds, they have done these things to you. This is your evil/calamity [f. sg.]. Indeed [LXX: because], it is bitter [m. sg.]. Indeed [LXX: because], it reaches [m. sg.] up to your heart."*

Jeremiah 4:5–8 picks up where 4:4b left off—with the threat of judgment. The Lord summons the heralds to declare in Judah and Jerusalem (see Jer. 4:3a, 4a) and to make proclamation to those re-sponsible for sounding the warning of an attack (Jer. 4:5a; cf. Jer. 5:20; 46:14). The blast of the shofar would provide such a warning (see Num. 10:1–10; Jer. 4:19; 6:1; Hos. 5:8; Amos 3:6), even in the Day of the Lord (Joel 2:1, 15; Zeph. 1:16; see Joel 4 [Eng., 3]; Zech. 12:1–6; 14; Ezek. 38–39). This blast is to be accompanied by a call to proclaim fully,[3] "Gather together, and let us enter the fortified cities" (Jer. 4:5b; cf. Lev. 26:25; Jer. 8:14; 35:11). These cities, which would seem to be logical choices for refuge and defense, would ultimately prove to be insuffi-cient (Jer. 5:17b).

The Hebrew source of Greek Jeremiah at the beginning of 4:6a says, "Lift up, flee (נֻסוּ or נֻס) to Zion." According to this reading, the instruction is to heed the warning of the shofar blast and to flee to one of the fortified cities, Zion (cf. Josh. 10:20). The MT, however, has, "Lift up a banner (נֵס)—To Zion." According to this reading, a standard or a flag is to be raised as a signal to go to Zion in response to the blast of the shofar (cf. Isa. 13:2; Jer. 4:21; 50:2). The people must seek refuge. They cannot simply stay where they are. The reason for this is that

---

2. *Tg. Jon.:* "For the voice of the prophets prophesying to them that they will go into exile because they worshiped the calves that were at Dan; and those proclaiming bad news, murderers, will come upon them because they submitted themselves to the image that Micah set up on the moun-tain of the house of Ephraim." See Judges 17; 1 Kings 12:28–29.

3. It has been suggested that מלאו in this context means "mobilize" (cf. Job 16:10). See D. Winton Thomas, *"Ml'w in Jeremiah 4:5: A Military Term,"* *JJS* 3 (1952): 47–52.

the LORD himself is bringing calamity from the north (Jer. 4:6b; 6:1, 19; cf. Huldah's prophecy in 2 Kgs. 22:16). This threat from the north has already been introduced in Jeremiah 1:13–15, and, as noted in the commentary on that passage, the Hebrew text behind Greek Jeremiah never identifies the enemy from the north as a historical one. The MT, which does not even mention Babylon until Jeremiah 20:4, eventually identifies Babylon as the enemy from the north in Jeremiah 25:9 (but see Jer. 50:3). Thus, while Babylon was in fact the historical enemy in Jeremiah's day, the Hebrew text represented by Greek Jeremiah employs the historical situation as a storehouse of imagery to describe and depict an eschatological foe from the north.[4] The "great breaking" mentioned in Jeremiah 4:6b (cf. Jer. 6:1) is not only for Judah and Jerusalem but also for other nations (Jer. 48:3), including Babylon (Jer. 50:3, 22; 51:54), in the Day of the LORD (Zeph. 1:7, 10). Ezekiel draws upon this passage in Jeremiah to describe Gog as the enemy from the north that will appear in the last days (Jer. 4:13; Ezek. 38:14–17; see LXX, SP Num. 24:7; Rev. 20:8).

In verse 7, the LORD envisions the enemy from the north as a lion going up from its thicket. The Syriac and *Targum Jonathan* interpret this lion to be a king (cf. Jer. 2:15a; 5:6; see also *b. Meg.* 11a).[5] This lion is a "destroyer" of nations who goes forth from his place to make the land into a desolation (cf. Jer. 2:30b). The verbal forms in the Hebrew source of Greek Jeremiah 4:7a (*qatal-qatal-wayyiqtol*) suggest imitation of biblical narrative style. On the other hand, the MT has three *qatal* forms. Neither of these should be taken to mean that the advance or the attack of the enemy is already under way. Rather, such a depiction of the enemy is for rhetorical effect.[6] The cities will fall in ruins without inhabitant as a result of the attack (Jer. 4:7b; cf. Isa. 6:11; Jer. 2:15b; 4:26; 9:9, 11 [Eng., 9:10, 12]). Concerning this situation, says Jeremiah, the people should gird on sackcloth and mourn and wail (Jer. 4:8a; cf. Jer. 6:26; Joel 1:13; Mic. 1:8; Lam. 2:10), because the LORD's anger has not turned away from them (Jer. 4:8b; cf. Jer.

---

4. "But it may be that in this passage Jeremiah, with his eschatological visions of doom, was not concerned with the identity of those he saw in his visions because they were not purely historical in character" (Thompson, *Book of Jeremiah*, 221).

5. See Neusner, *Jeremiah in Talmud and Midrash*, 143, 219.

6. McKane makes a similar comment about 4:15–17: "The prophet envisages how the end will come about (vv. 15–17), for this is surely an imaginative construction of events or a vision of the end rather than a description of an invasion which is already in progress" (*Jeremiah I–XXV*, 99).

2:35; 4:26; 23:20).[7] It is not immediately clear whether this is a call for repentance (cf. Jon. 3:5; Neh. 9:1; see also Jer. 4:14) or simply an indication that there is nothing left to do but to mourn the inevitable consequences of their actions (see Jer. 4:9).

The use of the phrase "in that day" at the beginning of Jeremiah 4:9 reinforces the understanding that 4:5–8 anticipates something that is yet to come rather than an event that is already underway. The LORD says that the hearts of the king and the leaders will perish (cf. Isa. 7:2, 6), the priests will be appalled (cf. Jer. 2:12), and the (false) prophets will be astonished (cf. Hab. 1:5). This refers to the same groups noted in Jeremiah 1:18b; 2:8, 26 who stood in opposition to Jeremiah. These groups did not believe that there would be grave consequences for their actions, otherwise they would have changed their ways. Therefore, they will be disheartened and surprised at the unexpected outcome.

Calvin notes three different interpretations of Jeremiah's response in 4:10.[8] The first is that the prophet speaks here on behalf of the people (cf. LXX[A]: "And they said"). The second is that Jeremiah means to say that the LORD has allowed the false prophets to deceive the people (cf. *Tg. Jon.*: "the false prophets are leading astray"; see also Jer. 14:13). The third, which is Calvin's own view, is that Jeremiah is taunting or mocking the false prophets whose promises of peace have proven to be untrue (Jer. 6:14; 8:11; 28:9).[9] In other words, when Jeremiah addresses the LORD, he is really addressing the false prophets who claim to represent the LORD. Commentators typically do not explore the option that Jeremiah actually means what he says here. The LORD is clear, however, in Ezekiel 14:9–11 that when a false prophet is deceived, he has been deceived by the LORD as an act of judgment against that prophet and the people (cf. 1 Kgs. 22:20–22). Jeremiah himself later claims that he has been deceived by the LORD (Jer. 20:7). Thus, it is at least plausible that the deception of which Jeremiah speaks in 4:10 is part of the divine judgment. The message of false security sent through the so-called prophets is now contradicted by the image of the sword coming to the point of taking the very life of the people (cf. Jer. 4:18b).[10]

In verses 11 and 12 of Jeremiah 4, the LORD quotes what the true prophets will say on his behalf to the people at the time of judgment envisioned in verse 9. The difference between the Hebrew source of

---

7. See Isaiah 5:25; 9:11, 16, 20 [Eng., 9:12, 17, 21]; 10:4.

8. Calvin, *Jeremiah*, 1:213.

9. Note the play on "Jerusalem" and *shalom* ("peace" or "well-being"). Cf. Psalm 122:6.

10. NET: "a sword is already at our throats."

Greek Jeremiah and the MT is based on different understandings of the word רוח, which can mean "spirit" or "wind." According to the Hebrew source of Greek Jeremiah, a "spirit of distortion" (רוח עועים [cf. Isa. 19:14]) or a "spirit of wandering" in the wilderness is the way of the people, not "to cleanse" (לְזַכּוֹת) and not to purify (Jer. 4:11). That is, the people are like the wilderness generation in Numbers—rebellious, idolatrous, and wandering in the wilderness, awaiting their demise. A "full spirit" (רוח מלא) will come to or for the LORD (Jer. 4:12a).[11] The MT, however, speaks of a "glowing hot wind from bare places" (רוח צח שפיים) in the wilderness as the way of the people, not "to scatter" (לִזְרוֹת) and not to purify (cf. Jer. 13:24). This wind, which is figurative for the invading army (see *Tg. Jon.* Jer. 4:12), is only harmful and not useful for necessary tasks such as winnowing (cf. Jer. 15:7).[12] It is a "wind too full for these" (רוח מלא מאלה). Jeremiah 4:12b ("Now, also/indeed I, I will speak judgments with them") hearkens back to Jeremiah 1:16a ("And I will speak with them judgment [MT: my judgments with them] concerning all their evil"), which is part of the vision of the enemy from the north (Jer. 1:13–15).

The LORD goes on to depict the enemy in 4:13 "like a cloud" that goes up and covers the land (see *Tg. Jon.*). This is precisely the image that the LORD uses to describe the final enemy Gog when he appears in the last days (Ezek. 38:9, 16). This enemy's chariots are "like a whirlwind" (cf. Isa. 5:28b). His horses appear to be "swifter than eagles" (cf. Deut. 28:49; Jer. 6:23; 8:16; Hab. 1:8; Lam. 4:19; see also 2 Sam. 1:23). Jeremiah thus exclaims on behalf of the people, "Woe to us, for we are destroyed" (cf. Jer. 9:18 [Eng., 9:19]; Mic. 2:4), but the LORD commands the people of Jerusalem to wash their heart from evil in order that they may be saved (Jer. 4:14a; cf. Isa. 1:16; Ps. 51:4, 9 [Eng., 51:2, 7]). This was not really a possibility under the old covenant (Deut. 29:3 [Eng., 29:4]; Jer. 2:22; 5:23–24; see also the Hebrew source of Greek Jer. 4:11b), but it would become a reality in the new covenant with the circumcision of the heart (Deut. 30:6; Jer. 4:4a; 31:33). The salvation in view here is not merely physical deliverance from a historical enemy. It is both physical

---

11. The meaning of this is not entirely clear. It perhaps speaks of the new covenant people of God filled by the Spirit in contrast to the wandering spirit of the old covenant people (cf. Exod. 31:3; Mic. 3:8; Eph. 5:18).

12. "The scorching wind which blows in from the desert has no beneficent aspect or social usefulness. It is not a wind which can be put to constructive tasks; it cannot be harnessed to the processes of agriculture. The wind is not the friend of man and society, but a hostile, destructive force" (McKane, *Jeremiah I–XXV*, 97).

and spiritual deliverance in the Day of the LORD (cf. Joel 3:5 [Eng., 2:32]; Rom. 10:13; see again Jer. 4:5 and Joel 2:1, 15). The LORD laments, "How long will the thoughts of your trouble lodge within you" (Jer. 4:14b; cf. Isa. 6:11; 55:7–8; 59:7; Jer. 6:19; Prov. 6:18)? The once faithful city of Jerusalem where righteousness "lodged" has now become a harlot (Isa. 1:21; cf. Jer. 3). This will last until the city of righteousness, the faithful city, is restored as the new Jerusalem (Isa. 1:26; 65:18).

The LORD explains in 4:15 that a report will come from Dan in the far north (cf. Jer. 8:16), and he says that trouble or sorrow will be heard from Mount Ephraim. This imagines the progression of the enemy's advance from its entry into the land in the north to its approach toward the border of Judah and Jerusalem in the hill country of Ephraim. Reports of calamity are coming to the people of Judah and Jerusalem from various points along the enemy's path as he comes closer and closer, creating a sense of tension and suspense. The "trouble" (אָוֶן) brought by this enemy is the judgment for the people's "thoughts of trouble" (Jer. 4:14b). *Targum Jonathan*, however, understands "trouble" here to be the idolatry of the people (see BDB, 20). According to this understanding, the voice in 4:15a is that of the prophets prophesying that the people will go into exile because they worshiped Jeroboam's golden calf at Dan (1 Kgs. 12:28–29). Murderers will come upon them because they submitted themselves to the image that Micah set up in Ephraim (Jer. 4:15b; see Judg. 17; 18:30–31). The Targum apparently understands Judah and Jerusalem to have participated in the same kind of idolatrous activity as the northern kingdom (Jer. 3:6–11).

It is not immediately clear who is being addressed (the prophets? the people?) by the LORD with the plural imperative at the beginning of verse 16, "Remind the nations" (cf. Jer. 6:18–19), but the more difficult problem for most commentators is the presence of "the nations" where "Judah" or "Jerusalem" might be expected.[13] Keil, responding to Hitzig's remark that such concern for the nations would have been unnatural for a Jew like Jeremiah, comments that the prophet is not so narrow-minded: "The charge is but a rhetorical form, conveying the idea that there is no doubt about the matter to be published, and that it concerned not Jerusalem alone, but the nations too."[14] Jeremiah was called to be a prophet to the nations (Jer. 1:5b). His message is for the nations (Jer. 1:10). Believers from the nations will be part of the people of God just like believers from Israel (Jer. 3:17; 4:2; 12:14–17; 16:19; 46:26b [MT]; 48:47; 49:6 [MT], 39). Unbelievers from the nations will

---

13. The *BHS* apparatus proposes either "Warn Benjamin" or "Declare in Judah."
14. Keil, *Jeremiah*, 72.

be judged just like unbelievers from Israel (Jer. 4:6b; 48:3; 50:3, 22; 51:54). Here in 4:16 the reminder is that the members of the enemy's army have come (but see MT). Again, the point is not to say that this has transpired in Jeremiah's day but to give a sense of the imminence of the event. The proclamation in Jerusalem is that "foes" (צרים) are coming from a distant land (cf. Jer. 5:15).[15] The final clause in 4:16b ("And they gave to/against the cities of Judah their voice") is often taken to be a continuation of what is to be proclaimed in Jerusalem (e.g., GKC §111w), but the use of the *wayyiqtol* form may argue against this. The above translation understands this to be a "narration" of sorts.[16] It either speaks of the voice of those making proclamation to the cities of Judah or the voice of the foes against the cities of Jerusalem.

The foes in 4:16 are compared to keepers of a field in 4:17a. The role of such guards would normally be to keep unwanted animals from the crop of the field. McKane thus explains well the use of the simile here: "The figure is applied in reverse, for the circle of steel around Judah will prevent anyone from getting out and effecting an escape."[17] This is because the city of Jerusalem has rebelled against (LXX: "neglected") the Lord in particular (Jer. 4:17b; cf. Lam. 1:18, 20). The Syriac version interprets מרתה to be from the root מרר ("to be bitter") rather than the root מרה ("to be rebellious"). This is perhaps in anticipation of the use of the word מר ("bitter") in 4:18b. According to the Lord's words in 4:18a, the people's ways and deeds—that is, their idolatry and misplaced trust outlined in the first three chapters—have done these things to them (cf. Jer. 7:3, 5–6).[18] "This" (זאת), referring to the preceding context, is the calamity that their evil has brought upon them (Jer. 4:18b; cf. Jer. 1:14, 16; 4:6, 8). The latter part of 4:18 is usually understood to say that the "calamity" (f. sg.) is "bitter" (m. sg.) and that the "calamity" (f. sg.) "reaches" (m. sg.) the heart (cf. Jer.

---

15. The MT has נצרים, variously understood to mean "watchmen," "blockaders," or "besiegers" (cf. Isa. 1:8b). Redak takes this to mean "Nezarites" from the last two syllables of Nebuchadnezzar's name (Rosenberg, trans., *Mikraoth Gedoloth: Jeremiah Volume One*, 39).

16. Another option is that the *wayyiqtol* indicates the purpose of the preceding clause. That is, foes are coming from a distant land in order to give their voice against the cities of Judah.

17. McKane, *Jeremiah I–XXV*, 101.

18. See Neusner, *Jeremiah in Talmud and Midrash*, 226. It is inconsequential whether עשו is interpreted as an infinitive absolute (עָשׂוֹ) or as a finite verb (עָשׂוּ) since the infinitive absolute often stands in the place of a finite verb (GKC §113y).

2:19; 4:10b), but the lack of agreement in grammatical gender suggests that a different interpretation may be necessary. It may be that the general situation described in 4:5–18 is what is bitter and reaching the heart (i.e., threatening life). It is also possible that the enemy from the north is the one who is bitter and reaching the heart. The term "bitter" (מר) is likely a play on the word "rebellious" (מרתה) in 4:17b. Because Jerusalem has been rebellious, the consequence will be bitter.[19]

4:19 My bowels, in my bowels I writhe [Syr., Tg. Jon.: My bowels, my bowels feel pain for me], and in the walls [LXX: senses] of my heart [MT: My bowels, my bowels! I writhe (qere: I wait) in the walls of my heart (pc Mss: I cause the walls of my heart to writhe)]![20] Upset for me is my self [> MT], upset for me is my heart. I cannot be silent. For a sound of a shofar I have heard [lit., my self has heard],[21] a shout of war. 4:20 And destruction upon [or, in addition to] breaking [MT: Breaking upon breaking] is announced [Syr.: comes; Tg. Jon.: meets], for all the land is destroyed. Suddenly the tent is destroyed [MT: Suddenly my tents (Tg. Jon.: my land) are destroyed], my curtains [Tg. Jon.: my city] are torn apart [MT: in a moment my curtains]. 4:21 How long will I see one fleeing [MT: a banner], hearing [MT: will I hear] a sound of a shofar? 4:22 "For the leaders of my people [MT: For my people are foolish], me they do not acknowledge. Foolish sons [or, children] are they, and they do not understand. They are wise to do evil, but they do not know how to do good."

---

19. There is an interesting parallel to this in the Mekilta's interpretation of Exodus 15:22–27. According to the MT, the people were unable to drink the water because it was "bitter" (מָרִים), but the same consonantal text can be read to say that they were unable to drink the water because the people themselves were "rebellious" (מֹרִים). Daniel Boyarin summarizes the account according to the Mekilta: "They went three days in the desert and they did not find water = Torah (as in the Isaiah verse), and they came to Mara, but they could not drink water (study Torah) in Mara, because they were rebellious. Moses prayed and God taught him a word of Torah, which is a 'tree of life,' and the bitter waters (rebellious, Torah-less people) became sweet" (Daniel Boyarin, *Intertextuality and the Reading of Midrash* [Bloomington: Indiana University Press, 1990], 66).
20. See GKC §108g.
21. נפשי can substitute for the personal pronoun (BDB, 660). Thus, it can work with either the *kethiv* ("I have heard") or the *qere* ("you have heard, O my self") of the MT (see *BHS* apparatus). See also GKC §44h, which says the *kethiv* is an archaic form of the second feminine singular. The LXX reflects a finite verb (cf. Syr., *Tg. Jon.*) rather than the participle suggested by Rudolph ("my self has heard" = "I have heard").

4:23 I see the land, and look, uninhabitable [LXX: nothing; Tg. Jon.: deserted and empty];[22] and to the sky, and its light is not. 4:24 I see the mountains, and [MT: and look] they are quaking; and all the hills, they shake. 4:25 I see, and look, there are no people; and as for all the flying creatures of the sky, they have fled [LXX: are terrified]. 4:26 I see, and look, the fertile land [LXX: Carmel; Tg. Jon.: the land of Israel, which was planted like Carmel] is a wilderness [MT: the wilderness]; and as for all the cities [MT: its cities], they are burned [MT: torn down] from before [or, because of] the LORD, and from before [or, because of] the burning of his anger they are desolated [they are desolated > MT].

4:27 Thus says the LORD [MT: For thus says the LORD], "A desolation is what the whole of the land will be, but a complete destruction I will not make. 4:28 Concerning this, the land will mourn [LXX: let the land mourn], and the sky will be dark [LXX: let the sky be dark] from above. Therefore [MT: For], I speak, and I do not relent; I have planned, and I will not turn back from it [MT: I have spoken, I have planned, and I have not relented; and I will not turn back from it]." 4:29 From a sound of a horseman [or, horse] and of a bent bow [Codex L: an archer; nonn Mss: archers] all the land [MT: all the city] is fleeing. They enter the caves and hide [the caves and hide > MT] in the thickets, and in/among the rocks they go up. Every city [MT: All the city] is forsaken, [MT adds: and] there is no one living in them. 4:30 And as for you [MT: And you are destroyed; see GKC §32h], what will you do? Though you dress in scarlet and [MT: though you] put on golden jewelry, though you make your eyes large with makeup [lit., tear your eyes with antimony (black powder)], it is for nothing that you make yourself beautiful. Those who lust for you [MT: Those who lust] reject you; what's more, it is your life that they seek. 4:31 For a sound like a woman in labor I hear, your distress [LXX: your groaning; MT: distress] like a woman giving birth to her first child. It is the voice of Daughter Zion. She gasps for breath and spreads her palms, "Woe to me for my life is faint for those slain [MT: those who slay]."

---

22. The one-word translation οὐθέν ("nothing") in the Old Greek does not necessarily reflect the single word בהו in its *Vorlage* instead of the MT's תהו ובהו (contra Rudolph, *BHS* apparatus), despite the fact that Aquila and Origen both add a noun and a conjunction prior to this Greek noun in their translations (cf. Symm.). The translator may have understood the two coordinated words in his Hebrew source to communicate a single idea. Furthermore, it is unlikely that בהו would have appeared by itself since it never appears independently of תהו elsewhere (see Gen. 1:2; Isa. 34:11). Only תהו appears by itself (Deut. 32:10; Isa. 45:18).

Thompson considers 4:19–21 to be one of Jeremiah's confessions,[23] but this designation is best reserved for material found in chapters 11–20. The passage is nevertheless a deep expression of the prophet's emotional response to the vision of the enemy from the north (Jer. 4:5–18).[24] This is evident from the description of the manner in which Jeremiah has been affected physically in the core of his being by the trauma. He writhes in his bowels and in the "walls" of his heart (Jer. 4:19a; cf. Jer. 10:19; 23:9; 31:20b; Lam. 1:20; 2:11; see also Isa. 21:3–4). He is very upset and cannot remain silent. The reason for this state of being is given clearly in 4:19b—the sound of the shofar commanded in 4:5 and a shout of war. Reports of one act of destruction (or, "breaking") after another are coming in the vision (Jer. 4:20a; cf. Jer. 4:6b, 15; Job 1:13–22; Lam. 3:48), for the whole of the land is destroyed. "Suddenly the tent is destroyed [MT: Suddenly my tents are destroyed], my curtains are torn apart [MT: in a moment my curtains]" (Jer. 4:20b; cf. Jer. 10:20). According to *Targum Jonathan*, which follows the MT, this is a reference to the land (Judah) and the city (Jerusalem),[25] but the singular and definite הָאֹהֶל ("the tent") of the Hebrew source of Greek Jeremiah strongly suggests another possibility. The tent and curtains are those of the tabernacle (cf. Exod. 26:1–14), which stands here for the temple (cf. 1 Kgs. 8:4).[26]

The prophet laments in 4:21 (cf. Isa. 6:11a; Jer. 4:14b; Ps. 6:4 [Eng., 6:3]), "How long will I see one fleeing (נָס), hearing a sound of a shofar?" This is a reference back to 4:5 (the blast of the shofar) and 4:6 ("flee" [נֻסוּ or נֻסִי]). The MT ("How long will I see a banner [נֵס]?") is also a reference back to its own version of 4:6 ("Lift up a banner [נֵס]"). The Lord responds in 4:22 to Jeremiah's lament as if the question were "Why?" instead of "How long?" According to the MT, the explanation is that the

---

23. Thompson, *Book of Jeremiah*, 227.

24. "The prophet certainly is expressing his personal feelings regarding the nearing catastrophe, but in doing so he lends words to the grief which all the godly will feel" (Keil, *Jeremiah*, 73).

25. "It is thought that the Prophet here compares strongly fortified cities to tents and curtains, in order to expose the foolish confidence with which the Jews were proudly filled, thinking that their cities were a sufficient protection from enemies" (Calvin, *Jeremiah*, 1:231). McKane considers the tents and the curtains to be the homes of the people (*Jeremiah I–XXV*, 105). Cf. Isaiah 54:2; Jeremiah 30:18; 49:29; Lamentations 2:4.

26. See F. Kenro Kumaki, "A New Look at Jer 4,19–22 and 10,19–21," *Annual of the Japanese Biblical Institute* 8 (1982): 113–22; Holladay, *Jeremiah 1*, 162. See also "Oholibah" ("my tent is in her") as a name for Jerusalem in Ezekiel 23.

people are "foolish" (אֱוִיל); they do not acknowledge the LORD (cf. Isa. 1:3; 5:13; Jer. 9:2b, 5 [Eng., 9:3b, 6]; Hos. 2:10 [Eng., 2:8]; 4:6). According to the Hebrew source of Greek Jeremiah, it is that the "leaders" (אֵילִי) of the people do not acknowledge the LORD (cf. Jer. 2:8). The people/ leaders are foolish children without understanding (cf. Deut. 32:6; Isa. 27:11; Jer. 5:21; Hos. 13:13). They are only "wise" to do evil (cf. Gen. 3:6; Mic. 2:1; 7:3), but they do not know how to do what is good (cf. Isa. 1:16–17; Jer. 13:23). Thus, they lack the wisdom of the Torah (Deut. 4:6; Jer. 8:8–9).

In Jeremiah 4:23–26, the prophet provides a vision of what he sees or has seen regarding the condition of the land of the covenant in the wake of the enemy invasion. The repetition of רָאִיתִי ("I see") at the beginning of each verse is a figure of speech known as *anaphora*, which draws special attention to what the prophet says.[27] This passage depicts the judgment of the land as a return to the state of the land in Genesis 1:2 prior to its preparation for habitation.[28] It envisions the eschaton or the "end" (*Endzeit*) as the "beginning" (*Urzeit*)—a reversal of the created order (cf. Zeph. 1:2–3).[29] The text is not merely a prophetic vision of the state of the land following Babylonian exile (e.g., Isa. 64:9) but a picture of the devastation to be brought by the future and final enemy from the north in the Day of the LORD (Zeph. 1:2–3, 7, 14–16).[30] It is from this condition that the land will be in need of a final restoration or re-creation (cf. Gen. 8, where the land is cleared of water again after the flood in order to be prepared for habitation; see also Isa. 65:17–18; 2 Pet. 3; Rev. 21–22).

Genesis 1:1–2 provides the background for the narrative that begins in Genesis 1:3.[31] The whole world ("the sky and the land") was created by God in the beginning (Gen. 1:1); but as for "the land" (הָאָרֶץ), it was "uninhabitable" (תֹהוּ וָבֹהוּ) (Gen. 1:2). This land eventually becomes identified in Genesis 2 as the Garden of Eden, which has the same boundaries as the land of the covenant with Abram (Gen. 2:10–14; 15:18).[32] The traditional English translation of the phrase תֹהוּ וָבֹהוּ as

---

27. See Bullinger, *Figures of Speech*, 199, 201.

28. See Neusner, *Jeremiah in Talmud and Midrash*, 186; Rosenberg, trans., *Mikraoth Gedoloth: Jeremiah Volume One*, 41.

29. See McKane, *Jeremiah I–XXV*, 106.

30. See Bright, *Jeremiah*, 32–33; Victor Eppstein, "The Day of Yahweh in Jer 4:23–28," *JBL* 87 (1968): 93–97; Holladay, *Jeremiah 1*, 164.

31. See Alviero Niccacci, *Syntax of the Verb in Classical Hebrew Prose*, trans. W. G. E. Watson, JSOTSup 86 (Sheffield: JSOT, 1990), 37–38.

32. See John H. Sailhamer, *Genesis Unbound* (Sisters, OR: Multnomah, 1996).

"formless and void" comes from the ancient Greek rendering of Genesis 1:2 ("invisible and unformed"), which was influenced by Greek philosophical concepts about the formation of the world out of chaos.[33] The Hebrew term תהו refers to an uninhabited wilderness (Deut. 32:10; Isa. 45:18), and the combination תהו ובהו refers to a place uninhabitable for human life (cf. Isa. 34:11). Thus, *Targum Neofiti* explains the phrase in Genesis 1:2 to mean that there were no humans, animals, or plants there. This is because the land was covered with water—a water wilderness—and needed to be cleared for habitation (i.e., made "good" [טוב]). The text of Genesis 1:2 also indicates that it was dark ("nighttime"), setting the stage for the summoning of the "light" (אור) in Genesis 1:3 (cf. Gen. 1:14–19, which gives the purpose for the various light sources). The Prophets employ this to depict salvation in terms of a morning sunrise breaking through the darkness of night (e.g., Isa. 9:1 [Eng., 9:2]; 60:1–3, 19–20; Mic. 7:8–9).

Jeremiah sees "the land" (הארץ) in 4:23, and the reader is able to see ("look") through the prophet's eyes that it is "uninhabitable" (תהו ובהו) and without the "light" (אור) of the luminaries in the sky. Darkness as a metaphor for judgment is typical of prophetic descriptions of the Day of the LORD (Joel 2:2; Amos 5:18–20; 8:9). The prophet Joel depicts the sun turning to darkness and the moon into blood (Joel 3:4 [Eng., 2:31]). According to Jeremiah's vision, even the mountains and the hills, which are normally stable in the landscape, are shaking and easily moved in this time of judgment (Jer. 4:24; Nah. 1:5). There are no people in this uninhabitable place (Jer. 4:25a; cf. Gen. 2:5b; Jer. 2:6; 9:10 [Eng., 9:11]; 49:18, 33; 50:3, 40; Zeph. 1:3), and the flying creatures of the sky have all fled (Jer. 4:25b; cf. Gen. 1:20–23; Jer. 9:9 [Eng., 9:10]; Zeph. 1:3). Jeremiah sees the once fertile land (*Tg. Jon.*: "the land of Israel, which was planted like Carmel") as a "wilderness" (Jer. 4:26a; see Jer. 2:7; cf. Jer. 23:10). All the cities are "burned" (נצתו; MT: "torn down" [נתצו]; cf. Jer. 1:10; 2:15; 4:7; 9:9, 11 [Eng., 9:10, 12]; Nah. 1:6b) before or because of the LORD, and before or because of "the burning of his anger" they are desolated (Jer. 4:26b; cf. Jer. 4:8b; Nah. 1:6a). The MT does not have the final verb נשמו ("they are desolated").[34]

The prophetic word from the LORD, which begins in 4:27, offers a commentary on the vision in 4:23–26. The whole of the land will be a desolation (Jer. 4:27a; cf. Exod. 23:29), but the LORD will not make

---

33. "As the Platonic influences on the translation of Gen 1–2 demonstrate, the translators of the Septuagint were familiar with Plato" (Kreuzer, *Bible in Greek*, 20).

34. Cf. the parallelism in Judges 5:5; Psalm 68:9 (Eng., 68:8).

a complete destruction of it (Jer. 4:27b). This second clause is often thought to be out of sorts with 4:28b. Thus, it is either interpreted to be a question expecting the answer yes ("And will I not make a complete destruction?") or emended (Rudolph, *BHS* apparatus: "And a complete destruction of it [לָהּ] I will make"; cf. Zeph. 1:18),[35] but neither reading fits very well with the use of this expression elsewhere (see Lev. 26:44; Jer. 5:10, 18; 30:11b [MT]; 46:28b; Ezek. 9:8; 11:13; Amos 9:8; Neh. 9:31), which suggests that 4:27a and 4:28b are being qualified in order to indicate that there will be room for a remnant and a restoration (see Jer. 6:8; cf. Isa. 1:7; 6:13; 65:8; Ezek. 6:8; Ezra 9:14). Concerning this (i.e., the desolation), the land will mourn, and the sky will be dark as in 4:23 (Jer. 4:28a; see also Jer. 2:12). The text of 4:28a1 is a citation of Hosea 4:3, which includes the inhabitants, the wild animals, the flying creatures of the sky, and the fish of the sea in the mourning, languishing, and gathering for judgment (cf. Jer. 4:25–26; 12:4). The Hebrew source of Greek Jeremiah of 4:28b ("Therefore, I speak, and I do not relent; I have planned, and I will not turn back from it") suggests that the LORD does not relent in general and therefore will not do so in the present situation (cf. Num. 23:19; 1 Sam. 15:29, 35). The MT ("For I have spoken, I have planned, and I have not relented; and I will not turn back from it") appears to speak only of the current situation (cf. Jer. 18:8, 10; Amos 7:3, 6). Thus, God does not relent in a deceptive and unreliable way like human beings do (Num. 23:19), but he does relent when he has made provision for such action in the meeting of certain conditions (e.g., Jon. 3). In this particular case, no such provision has been made (see Zech. 8:14). The people's relationship with the LORD is in disrepair, and the consequences are inevitable, not only historically for Judah, which had every advantage of the special revelation of God, but also eschatologically for fallen humanity, which has inherently rejected what the heavens declare (Ps. 19:1–7 [Eng., 19:1–6]; Rom. 1:18–32).

Jeremiah 4:29a explains why the inhabitants of the land flee, leaving the land in the state seen in 4:23–26: "From a sound of a horseman [or, horse] and of a bent bow [Codex L: an archer; nonn Mss: archers] all the land [MT: all the city] is fleeing." The Greek ἐντεταμένου τόξου ("of a bent bow") reflects דרכת קשת ("bent of bow"), which is an example of an epexegetical "genitive" (GKC §128x; cf. Isa. 21:15; Jer. 50:14, 29). MT witnesses either have the singular "an archer" (רמה קשת) or the

---

35. Calvin seems to think that this clause means God will not bring the destruction to an end prematurely: "The real meaning then is—that God would to the end carry on his work of desolation" (*Jeremiah*, 1:241).

plural "archers" (רמי קשת) (cf. Ps. 78:9). The people "enter the caves and hide [the caves and hide > MT] in the thickets, and in/among the rocks they go up" (cf. Judg. 6:2; 1 Sam. 13:6; Isa. 2:19, 21; Rev. 6:15). McKane explains well the shorter text of the MT (see also the *BHS* apparatus): "If the assumption is made that Sept. derives from a Hebrew text which is superior to MT, the shorter text is explained as a consequence of scribal mishap: the omission of במערות ויחבאו is due to *homoioteleuton* (Volz, Rudolph); the scribe confused באו with the ending of ויחבאו which consists of the same consonants and so במערות ויחבאו was omitted."[36] According to the Hebrew source of Greek Jeremiah 4:29b, "Every city (כל עיר) is forsaken, there is no one living in them" (cf. Isa. 6:11; Jer. 22:6b; 44:2; 51:43). The MT's "All the city" (כל העיר), which is presumably intended to be a reference to Jerusalem (see also MT Jer. 4:29a), does not work well as an antecedent for the later plural pronoun "them."

The Lord then returns in 4:30 to the metaphor of the unfaithful wife seeking other lovers (cf. Jer. 2:1–13; 3). In light of her impending destruction, what will she do? It will do no good to dress in scarlet and put on gold jewelry. It will do no good to put on makeup and appear beautiful (cf. Hos. 2:15 [Eng., 2:13]). The imagery here, which is reminiscent of Jezebel's unsuccessful attempt to seduce Jehu when he sought her life (2 Kgs. 9:30; cf. Ezek. 23:40; see also Ezek. 16:11–15), depicts the people's efforts to attract the aid of foreign nations such as Egypt and Assyria (Jer. 2:18, 33); but just as the idols, which the people prefer, prove to be a disappointment (Jer. 2:13), so the foreign nations in whom they put their trust fail them (Jer. 2:36). Those who lust for her do not care for her (Jer. 30:14; Lam. 1:2; cf. Ezek. 23:5, 7, 9, 11, 12, 16, 20). Rather, they reject her. They use and abuse her, seeking to take her very life. This is what she chooses in place of her faithful husband, the Lord, who has delivered her and provided for her. Her appeals to lovers are in vain, for the Lord hears a sound like a woman in labor (Jer. 4:31a; cf. Jer. 6:24). It is the sound of Daughter Zion in distress, like a woman giving birth to her first child, which is particularly difficult because of the lack of experience and the unexpected nature of the pain (cf. 1 Thess. 5:3). This suffering, however, will not result in the joy of childbirth (cf. Isa. 37:3). Rather, it will end in death. She gasps for breath and spreads her palms and says (cf. Isa. 1:15; Ezra 9:5), "Woe to me for my life is faint for those slain [MT: those who slay]." Just as creation turns to un-creation (Jer. 4:23–26), so childbirth turns to death. Zion is faint because she does not hope in the Lord (Isa. 40:31).

---

36. McKane, *Jeremiah I–XXV*, 110.

JEREMIAH 5

5:1 "Go about in the streets of Jerusalem and see and know, and seek in its squares whether you can find a person, whether there is anyone doing justice and [and > MT] seeking faithfulness, that I may forgive it," the prophetic utterance of the Lord *[the prophetic utterance of the* Lord *> MT]. 5:2 "[MT adds: And if,] 'As the* Lord *lives [or, By the life of the* Lord*] . . . ,' they say, therefore [mlt Mss, Syr.: surely/but] falsely they swear [LXX: are they not swearing falsely?]." 5:3 O* Lord, *your eyes, are they not to faithfulness [Tg. Jon.: O* Lord, *is it not revealed before you to do good to those who do faithfulness]? You strike them [Tg. Jon.: As for the wicked, you punish them], and they do not writhe [or, and they are not sick]. You destroy them, and [and > MT] they refuse to receive discipline. They make their faces harder than rock, and [and > MT] they refuse to return. 5:4 And as for me, I thought, "Surely/But they are poor. They are foolish [LXX: Therefore, they are unable],*[1] *for they do not know the way of the* Lord *and [and > MT] the justice/judgment [i.e., ordinance] of God [MT: their God]. 5:5 I will go [MT adds: for myself] to the nobles [lit., the great ones] and speak with them [MT: and speak them]. Surely [or, For] they, they know the way of the* Lord *and [and > MT] the justice/judgment [i.e., ordinance] of God [MT: their God]." And look [MT: Also they], together they have broken yoke, they have torn off bonds. 5:6 Therefore, a lion strikes them from a forest [Tg. Jon.: a king with his armies comes up against them like a lion from a forest and slays them], and furthermore a wolf up to house [LXX: the houses; MT: a wolf of desert plains; Aq., Syr., Tg. Jon., Vulg.: a wolf of evening] destroys them. And [And > MT] a leopard watches over their cities, anyone who goes out from them is torn apart [LXX: all who go out from them are hunted]. For their transgressions are many, their apostasies are numerous [LXX: because they multiplied their impieties and were strong in their apostasies]. 5:7 "How [BDB, 32] can I forgive you?*[2] *Your sons [or, children], they forsook me and swore by non-gods [GKC §152a*[1]*], and I satisfied them [pc Mss: and I caused them to swear (but see BDB, 989)], and they committed adultery; and it was in a house of fornication/harlotry that they would stay [Codex L: assemble themselves (or, cut themselves); Syr.: fight]. 5:8 Lustful horses [or, Horses showing (large) testicles; MT kethiv: Well-fed, lustful horses; MT qere: Sexually*

---

1. Syr.: "Because they are poor they have turned aside."
2. According to *Targum Jonathan*, the Lord instructs the prophet to say this to the congregation of Israel.

aroused,[3] lustful horses] are they, each to the wife of his neighbor they neigh. 5:9 Concerning these things will I not visit/punish [nonn Mss add: them; or, Upon these will I not visit (i.e., Will I not punish these)]?" the prophetic utterance of the Lord, *"And on a nation such as this will I [see BDB, 660] not avenge myself?"*

The plural imperatives in 5:1 appear not to be directed to any group in particular (cf. Isa. 40:1–2). There is no evidence whatsoever that they are addressed to the heavenly court. Rather, the thought seems to be that any group could "go about" (cf. Amos 8:12; Dan. 12:4) in the streets of Jerusalem and see and know for themselves that there is no one who does what the Lord requires (cf. Jer. 2:10). If they were to seek in the city squares and find someone doing justice and seeking faithfulness (cf. Deut. 32:4; Jer. 7:5; 9:23 [Eng., 9:24]; 22:15; 23:5), then the Lord would forgive Jerusalem. The reality is that no such person can be found (cf. 1 Kgs. 8:46; Isa. 59:4; Jer. 8:6; 15:1–4; Ezek. 22:30; Pss. 14:1–3; 53:2–4 [Eng., 53:1–3]; 143:2; Prov. 20:6; Eccl. 7:20),[4] and thus the Lord cannot forgive the city (Jer. 5:7; cf. Jer. 31:34). This is reminiscent of the exchange between Abraham and the Lord in Genesis 18:23–33 (see also Num. 16:22). Abraham, hoping for the sake of his nephew Lot that the city of Sodom might be spared, initially asks if the Lord would spare the city for the sake of fifty righteous and then works his way down to ten. It remains unknown if he could have lowered the number even further, but it is apparent from the following story that ten righteous people were not found in the city to avert the disaster. Lot and his family were simply removed (see 2 Pet. 2:7). The Lord only requires one righteous person in Jerusalem to avoid judgment, but such a one cannot be found. The implicit comparison to Sodom speaks to the depths to which Jerusalem has fallen (cf. Gen. 19 and Judg. 19; Isa. 1:10; Ezek. 16:48; Rev. 11:8).

The text of 5:2 translates differently depending on whether לכן ("therefore"), as in the Hebrew source of Greek Jeremiah and Codex L, or אכן ("surely/but"), as in a multitude of Masoretic manuscripts and the Syriac, is read at the beginning of 5:2b: (1) "'As the Lord lives [or, By the life of the Lord] . . . ,' they say, therefore (לכן) falsely they swear." (2) "And

---

3. BDB, 402: *"furnished with weights*, i.e., testicles."
4. This naturally raises the question of the status of Jeremiah, Baruch, and the faithful remnant. Jeremiah was not from the city of Jerusalem (Jer. 1:1). It is not clear if Baruch and the others were elsewhere at the time. It is also possible that what is said here simply applies in general to the overwhelming majority of the city.

if, 'As the LORD lives [or, By the life of the LORD] . . . ,' they say, surely/
but (אכן) falsely they swear." According to the first reading, a conclusion
or inference about swearing falsely in the LORD's name (Exod. 20:7; Lev.
19:12; Deut. 5:11; Hos. 4:2; Zech. 5:4; Ps. 24:4) can be made from the
mere use of the oath formula (cf. Jer. 16:14–15; 23:7–8). According to the
second, if there is use of the oath formula, it is surely a false one (cf. Jer.
3:10). This is because the people do not swear faithfully, with justice and
righteousness, as the LORD requires (Jer. 4:2; see also Deut. 10:20; Jer.
49:13). Rather, they use the LORD's name disingenuously and swear by
non-gods such as Baal (Jer. 5:7; 12:16; Hos. 4:15; Amos 8:14; Zeph. 1:5).

Jeremiah responds in 5:3, "O LORD, your eyes, are they not to faithfulness [*Tg. Jon.*: O LORD, is it not revealed before you to do good to
those who do faithfulness]?" That is, the prophet reiterates with a rhetorical question that the LORD looks with favor on those who swear in
his name in faithfulness or genuinely (Jer. 4:2; 5:1–2; cf. Jer. 32:19;
Zech. 4:10; Ps. 33:18; Prov. 15:3; 2 Chr. 16:9),[5] but such faithfulness is
not found (see Jer. 7:28). The LORD strikes the people, but they do not
"writhe" (cf. Jer. 2:30). By placing the accent on the first syllable of חלו,
the Masoretes indicate that they understand the verb to come from חול/
חיל ("writhe"; see Jer. 4:31; 5:22). If the stress were to fall on the last
syllable, it would be from חלה ("be sick"; see Isa. 1:5). The point seems
to be that despite the experience of writhing or sickness (Isa. 1:5; Jer.
4:31), the people do not recognize and receive it as the LORD's correction
(cf. Prov. 17:10; 22:15; 23:35). The LORD destroys them, but they refuse
to accept the discipline. The people make their faces harder than rock,
which indicates their obstinacy (cf. Jer. 3:3b; Ezek. 3:7–8), and refuse to
return (cf. Jer. 3:7). This latter comment recalls the repetition in Amos
4:6b, 8b, 9b, 10b, 11b: "but you have not returned to me." Despite the
covenant curses of famine, drought, and plague, the northern kingdom
of Israel did not repent (cf. Rev. 9:21; 16:9, 11).

Jeremiah then reflects on the people's refusal to accept discipline
and repent: "And as for me, I thought, 'Surely/But they are poor. They
are foolish,[6] for they do not know the way of the LORD and [and > MT]
the justice/judgment [i.e., ordinance] of God [MT: their God]'" (Jer. 5:4).
The "poor" (דלים) are the non-elite who would eventually be left in the
land after the Babylonian invasion (Jer. 39:10; 40:7; 52:16). They are
"foolish" in the sense that they have acted sinfully out of ignorance

---

5. Some understand אמונה, which normally means "faithfulness," to mean
   "faith" in this context (cf. Hab. 2:4; see Rosenberg, trans., *Mikraoth Gedoloth:
   Jeremiah Volume One*, 45; Neusner, *Jeremiah in Talmud and Midrash*, 47).
6. LXX: Therefore, they are unable [= ללא יכלו?].

(cf. Num. 12:11). They do not know "the way of the LORD" or "the justice/judgment of God" (i.e., "ordinance"; see Gen. 18:19; 2 Kgs. 17:26; Jer. 6:16; 8:7). Redak paraphrases the prophet's words, "When I reproved the people and they did not respond, I thought that 'they are but poor,' and the poorer class is usually devoid of wisdom. They are not as learned and erudite as the wealthier classes since they devote their time to tilling the soil and dressing the vines, and they do not engage in the study of the Torah and religious ethics."[7] Thus, Jeremiah assumed that there was a logical reason (poverty) for the people's refusal to turn, and he initially gave the elite classes the benefit of the doubt, but when he investigated "the great ones," he found that the situation was not any different (Jer. 5:5). He thought that he could go to the nobles or upper classes (e.g., Jer. 2:8) and speak with them, assuming that they would surely know "the way of the LORD" and "the justice/judgment of God," but he points out that they too have collectively broken the yoke and torn off their bonds. This refers to their rebellion against the LORD's authority (see Jer. 2:20; 28; Ps. 2:3).

"Therefore," says the prophet, a lion comes out of the forest to strike them (Jer. 5:6a). What's more, a wolf comes out of the wild up to their very houses to destroy them.[8] A leopard watches over their cities to tear apart anyone who goes out from them. Keil understands this to be the covenant curse of Leviticus 26:22, according to which literal wild animals come against the people (2 Kgs. 2:24; 17:25; Ezek. 5:17; 14:15).[9] Others interpret the different animals to represent different enemy nations in the manner of Daniel 7 (cf. Jer. 2:15).[10] *Targum Jonathan,* however, has the most contextually appropriate rendering. It sees one king (the lion) coming with his armies (cf. Jer. 4:7). This king has a horde of nations (wolves) with him (cf. Jer. 1:15; Ezek. 38) whose officers are as strong as leopards. The reason for this attack is stated in Jeremiah 5:6b: "their transgressions are many, their apostasies are numerous" (cf. Jer. 13:22; 30:14; Amos 5:12).

---

7. Rosenberg, trans., *Mikraoth Gedoloth: Jeremiah Volume One*, 45. Cf. John 7:49.

8. The translation "a wolf up to house" reflects זאב עד בית (cf. LXX). The MT has "a wolf of desert plains" (זאב ערבות). Aquila, the Syriac, *Targum Jonathan*, and the Latin Vulgate all have "a wolf of evening" (= זאב ערב). See Habakkuk 1:8; Zephaniah 3:3.

9. Keil, *Jeremiah*, 78. See Isaiah 11:6–8 and 65:25 for the opposite of this. See also Hosea 5:14 where the LORD says he is like a lion to the people.

10. See Neusner, *Jeremiah in Talmud and Midrash*, 143; Rosenberg, trans., *Mikraoth Gedoloth: Jeremiah Volume One*, 46.

The LORD asks in 5:7, "How can I forgive you?"[11] This is addressed to the people through the prophet using the second feminine singular pronoun (cf. Jer. 2:2). If there were someone doing justice and seeking faithfulness, then the LORD could forgive (Jer. 5:1), but such is not the case. Only in the new covenant relationship will the LORD be able to forgive (Jer. 31:34). He adds, "Your sons, they forsook me" (cf. Jer. 1:16). This "x + *qatal*" clause sets up the following narrative sequence of three *wayyiqtol* clauses. The first is: "and [they] swore by non-gods" (cf. Deut. 32:17, 21; Jer. 2:5, 11, 13; 5:2; 12:16; 16:20; Hos. 8:6; Ps. 96:5). The second involves a textual variant: "and I satisfied (וָאַשְׂבִּעַ) them" (cf. Deut. 32:15; Jer. 2:7; Hos. 13:6; Neh. 9:25–26). A few Masoretic manuscripts read: "and I caused them to swear" (וָאַשְׁבִּעַ). According to the first reading, the LORD satisfied the people, but they did not appreciate it. According to the second, the LORD brought the people into a covenant relationship by oath, but they broke it. The first option is more likely due to the fact that the grammatical subject of the *hiphil* of שבע is elsewhere always human (see BDB, 989). The third *wayyiqtol* clause says: "and they committed adultery." That is, they committed spiritual adultery with other gods (see Jer. 3:1, 8, 9; 9:1 [Eng., 9:2]; Hos. 3:1). The final clause of 5:7 is not part of the *wayyiqtol* sequence. It is a comment in the form of an "x + *yiqtol*" clause. According to the Hebrew source of Greek Jeremiah and a few Masoretic manuscripts, it says: "and it was in a house of fornication/harlotry [cf. Josh. 6:22] that they would stay (יתגוררו)" (cf. 1 Kgs. 17:20). This house would not be a literal brothel but something more like a pagan temple or worship site where spiritual fornication would occur.[12] The reading in Codex L could be interpreted in a similar manner to mean that they would "assemble themselves" (יתגודדו) in a house of fornication, but it could also mean that they "cut themselves" (יתגודדו) in the manner of pagan religious rituals (see Deut. 14:1; 1 Kgs. 18:28; Jer. 16:6; Hos. 7:14; Zech. 13:6).

The idolatry mentioned in 5:7 is the core human sin problem. All other sins are symptoms of it. Thus, the spiritual adultery of 5:7 manifests itself in the literal adultery of 5:8 (see Exod. 20:17; Deut. 5:18; Jer. 7:9; 29:23).[13] The men become like animals, lustful horses (cf. *Pss. Sol.* 8:10; see also Jer. 8:6), each neighing to the wife of his neighbor (cf. Jer. 13:27; Ezek. 33:25–26).[14] The syntax of the following rhetorical

---

11. 4Q182 interprets this passage to be about the last days.

12. It is not necessary to conclude from this that fertility cults involving sexual relations with temple prostitutes are in view (but see Hos. 4:14).

13. See Calvin, *Jeremiah*, 1:270–71; Bright, *Jeremiah*, 39.

14. See Wenthe, ed., *Jeremiah, Lamentations*, 50–51.

question in 5:9a can be taken in two different ways: (1) "Concerning these things will I not visit/punish?" or (2) "Upon these will I not visit [or, Will I not punish these]?"[15] The text of 5:29 is identical to 5:9. The text of 9:8 [Eng., 9:9] in the MT (but not in the Hebrew source of Greek Jeremiah) follows the first option and adds בם ("them") as the object of the verb "visit/punish." The second option follows the syntactical combination of פקד plus על in other passages such as Exodus 20:5 (see BDB, 823). The parallel in 5:9b also seems to favor the second option: "And on a nation such as this will I not avenge myself?"[16]

5:10 "Go up in her rows [LXX: battlements; Syr.: walls; Tg. Jon.: cities] and destroy, but a complete destruction do not make. Leave her tendrils [LXX: supports; Tg. Jon.: fortresses], for to the Lord *they belong [MT: Remove her tendrils, for not to the* Lord *do they belong]. 5:11 For the house of Israel and the house of Judah [Syr.: For the sons of Israel and the sons of Judah] have surely acted treacherously [or, unfaithfully] against me [MT adds: the prophetic utterance of the* Lord*]." 5:12 They acted deceptively against[17] the* Lord *[or, They denied the* Lord*] and said, "It is not so [or, Not he/that; Tg. Jon.: Not from before him does good come upon us], [MT adds: and] calamity will not come upon us, and sword and famine we will not see. 5:13 Our prophets [Tg. Jon.: The prophets of falsehood], they have become wind [MT: The prophets, they will become wind], and the word of the* Lord *is not in them [Tg. Jon.: and their false prophecy will not be established; for Codex L, see GKC §52o, 138i]. Thus will it be for them [MT: Thus will it be done to them; > LXX^A]." 5:14 Therefore, thus says the* Lord *of hosts [MT: the* Lord *God of hosts], "Because you [pl.] spoke this word, look, I am putting my words in your [sg.] mouth as fire and this people as wood, and it will consume them. 5:15 Look, I am about to bring upon you a nation from far away, O house of Israel," the prophetic utterance of the* Lord*, "[MT adds: a perennial nation it is, a nation from long ago it is] a nation whose language you will not hear [MT: a nation whose language you will not know, and you will not hear what it speaks]. 5:16 [MT adds: His quiver (Syr.: throat) is like an opened grave] All of them are mighty men, and they will devour your harvest 5:17 and your bread/food,[18] and they will*

---

15. See Holladay, *Jeremiah 1*, 182.
16. Cf. Nahum 1:2.
17. BDB, 471: "seem to acknowledge, but not really do so."
18. The Göttingen Septuagint, which is followed here, and *BHS* divide these verses differently. The MT according to *BHS* has the following division: "His quiver is like an opened grave, all of them are mighty men, and he

devour your sons and your daughters, and they will devour your sheep and your cattle, and they will devour your grapevine and your fig tree and your olive tree [and your olive tree > MT], and they will beat down[19] *your fortified cities in which you have trusted with the sword.*[20] *5:18 And it will be [MT: And also/indeed] in those days," the prophetic utterance of the* LORD *your God [your God > MT], "I will not make you [MT: with you] a complete destruction. 5:19 And it will be when you [pl.] say, 'Why has the* LORD *our God done to us all these things?' you [sg.] will say to them, 'Just as you served/worshiped foreign gods in your land [MT: Just as you forsook me and served/worshiped foreign gods in your land], so you will serve strangers/foreigners [Tg. Jon. adds: the worshipers of idols] in a land that does not belong to you.'"*

Similar expressions in 5:10 ("but a complete destruction do not make") and 5:18 ("I will not make you a complete destruction") help to mark the boundaries of the unit in 5:10–19. Bullinger considers 5:10 to be an example of the figure of speech known as *apostrophe* in which "the speaker turns away from the real auditory whom he is addressing, and speaks to an imaginary one."[21] In this case, the imaginary audience is the enemy who will fulfill the prophecy. The initial instruction to "go up in her rows and destroy" is variously understood by the early versions. The pronoun "her" likely refers to the city of Jerusalem, but "rows" has been rendered "battlements" (LXX), "walls" (Syr.), and "cities" (*Tg. Jon.*). Nevertheless, the reference to tendrils in 5:10b (cf. Isa. 18:5; Jer. 48:32) strongly suggests that the rows are rows of a vineyard. Thus, the city of Jerusalem is here compared to a vineyard as in Jeremiah 2:21; 12:10 (cf. Isa. 5:1–7; Ezek. 15:1–8; see also Jer. 6:9). The command to destroy this vineyard is mitigated: "but a complete destruction do not make" (cf. Isa. 65:8). As in 4:27 (see comments there), efforts to remove the negation (Rudolph) or alter the sense of "complete destruction" (Calvin) do not find much support from the use of this expression elsewhere (see also Jer. 5:18; but see Zeph. 1:18). The "tendrils" (LXX: supports; *Tg. Jon.*: fortresses) are to be left, for they

---

will devour your harvest and your bread/food." Rahlfs' edition and the NETS simply have "All are strong" for 5:16 and then continue with 5:17 ("and they will devour . . .").

19. The Syriac interprets this verb as if it were from רוש ("to be poor") rather than רשש ("to beat down").

20. Where the MT has third masculine singular *yiqtol* forms in this verse, the Greek text reflects a Hebrew source with third common plural *weqatal* forms.

21. Bullinger, *Figures of Speech*, 901.

belong to the LORD. On the other hand, the MT of 5:10b communicates the opposite meaning: "Remove her tendrils, for not to the LORD do they belong." This forms a parallel with the first half of 5:10a. The Hebrew source of Greek Jeremiah, however, forms a parallel with the mitigation. According to the Hebrew source of Greek Jeremiah, a remnant will be left to rebuild because they are the LORD's people. The reason given for the judgment is the treachery of both the house of Israel and the house of Judah (Jer. 5:11; see Jer. 3:6–13), which suggests that the destruction in view is eschatological, involving all the unfaithful, rather than historical, dealing with the north (Assyrian invasion) and the south (Babylonian invasion) separately.

The shift to third-person reference to the LORD in 5:12 suggests that Jeremiah is the speaker. He echoes the LORD's statement in 5:11 about the people's treachery: "They acted deceptively against the LORD." That is, they only pretended to acknowledge him, and in doing so they effectively denied him. This was evident in their words: "It is not so [lit., Not he/that], calamity will not come upon us, and sword and famine we will not see" (cf. Jer. 14:13; 23:17; Mic. 3:11). These words do not express a philosophical denial of the LORD's existence but a practical denial. In other words, the people spoke and acted as if the LORD did not exist (cf. Pss. 14:1; 53:2). They denied the message of judgment from the LORD's true prophet, Jeremiah (e.g., Jer. 11:22; cf. Deut. 32:24–25), and embraced the message of well-being from the false prophets (Jer. 6:14; 8:11), indicating that they did not believe that there would be consequences for their behavior (see Zeph. 1:12; Mal. 2:17).

If 5:13 is a continuation of what the people said, then the prophets of whom they spoke (Greek: "Our prophets"; MT: "The prophets") must have been the prophets like Jeremiah who announced judgment. According to the people, such prophets "have become wind" (MT: "will become wind"), "and the word of the LORD is not in them." To say that the message of the prophets is nothing more than empty "wind" (רוח) is a contradiction of the claim of the true prophets to have the "Spirit" (רוח) (Mic. 3:8; cf. Hos. 9:7). To say that the word of the LORD is not in them denies that someone like Jeremiah is a prophet like Moses in whose mouth the LORD has put his words (Deut. 18:18; Jer. 1:9b; 5:14b). The final clause of 5:13 ("Thus will it be for them" [MT: "Thus will it be done to them"]), which is not in Codex Alexandrinus, would then be a prediction that the so-called windbag prophets will amount to nothing more than the empty content of their prophecy. On the other hand, if 5:13 is not a continuation of what the people said, then the verse must be a comment from Jeremiah about the false prophets of well-being (*Tg. Jon.*: "The prophets of falsehood") (see Jer. 5:31). They are the ones who have become wind (cf. Mic.

2:11), and the word of the Lord is not in them (*Tg. Jon.*: "and their false prophecy will not be established") (see Jer. 23:30–32). They will come to naught (see Jer. 28:15–17; cf. Deut. 18:20).

Verse 14 draws an inference or conclusion ("Therefore") from the words of the people in verses 12 and 13 (or simply verse 12, depending on the interpretation of verse 13). Jeremiah introduces the Lord's discourse with the typical formula ("thus says the Lord") and identifies the Lord as the God of hosts or armies,[22] which is appropriate for the following announcement in 5:15–17. Because the people spoke the previously cited words, the Lord points out that he is putting his words in Jeremiah's mouth (cf. Jer. 1:9). These words will be like fire (cf. Jer. 6:29; 20:9; 23:29; Rev. 11:5), and the people will be like wood. This fire will consume them (cf. Hos. 6:5). That is, the words of judgment will be effective (Jer. 1:11–12) and destructive (Jer. 1:10a; cf. Jer. 39:8) by means of the announced enemy nation that will consume or devour them (Jer. 5:17).

The Lord indicates in 5:15 that he is about to bring upon the people of Israel (cf. Jer. 5:11) "a nation from far away" (see Deut. 28:49; cf. Jer. 4:16) The language does not necessarily mean that the nation must come in the near future. Rather, it gives a sense of imminence (see GKC §116p), the feeling that the nation could come at any moment. The nation here is the same as the enemy from the north in Jeremiah 1:13–15; 4:6. The MT adds a description of this nation that does not appear in the Hebrew source of Greek Jeremiah: "a perennial nation it is, a nation from long ago it is" (cf. Isa. 23:7). It is possible that the scribe responsible for the Hebrew source of Greek Jeremiah or the Greek translator himself accidentally skipped from גוי ("nation") at the beginning of this description to גוי at the beginning of "a nation whose language you will not hear," omitting the intervening text (homoio-archton), but this would have required skipping the two instances of גוי in "a perennial nation it is, a nation from long ago it is." The addition in the MT bears the marks of a scribal comment. It is not part of the original text, but it does provide a helpful interpretation of the original text. The nation in view here is not merely the historical Babylon of the latter part of the seventh century BC and the first half of the sixth century BC. It is a nation from long ago that has always been around and will always be around until the last days. It is the "Babylon" that represents worldly opposition to God and his people from the story of the Tower of Babylon in Genesis 11:1–9 to the depiction of the final enemy

---

22. This is explicit in the MT, but it is implied in the Hebrew source of Greek Jeremiah since Lord (Yahweh) cannot be in the construct state. Thus, "Lord of hosts" is always short for "Lord God of hosts."

in Revelation 17–18.[23] This nation will also be one whose language the people will not hear (i.e., understand; cf. Isa. 28:11).[24] The Hebrew source of Greek Jeremiah again has the shorter text here ("a nation whose language you will not hear"), but this is not an abridgement of the MT ("a nation whose language you will not know, and you will not hear what it speaks" [cf. Jer. 9:15 (Eng., 9:16)]). The Hebrew source of Greek Jeremiah is in fact a citation from Deuteronomy 28:49b, which the MT has expanded.

Verses 16 and 17 continue the description of the enemy nation, and once again the Hebrew source of Greek Jeremiah has a substantially shorter text than the MT. The MT adds at the beginning of 5:16, "His quiver is like an opened grave," which apparently speaks of the deaths from the arrows shot from the enemy's bow. The Syriac ("His throat is like an opened grave") interprets this clause according to the closest parallel in Psalm 5:10 (Eng., 5:9): "an opened grave is their throat." The Hebrew source of Greek Jeremiah, however, simply begins with the following clause, "All of them are mighty men," and continues into 5:17 with the list of all that these warriors will "devour" (אכל; cf. Jer. 5:14b).[25] This list includes the people's harvest, their food, their sons and daughters, their sheep and cattle, their grapevines and fig trees, and their olive trees ("and your olive tree" > MT).[26] There was a time when Israel was "set apart to the LORD, the firstfruits of his produce" (Jer. 2:3). All who tried to "eat" or "devour" (אכל) him would be guilty, but Israel's preference for Baal has since led to the consumption (אכל) of the product of their toil—sheep, cattle, sons, and daughters (Jer. 3:24; 5:23–25). The coming enemy will be the end result of this. The warriors will use the "sword" (i.e., weaponry) to beat down the people's fortified cities in which they have trusted (see Jer. 4:5b) in fulfillment of the covenant curse found in Deuteronomy 28:52 (see also Luke 21:21).

In the days of judgment anticipated in 5:10–17,[27] the LORD will not make a "complete destruction" of the people (Jer. 5:18; see

---

23. See Rashi in Rosenberg, trans., *Mikraoth Gedoloth: Jeremiah Volume One*, 49; Sailhamer, *Pentateuch as Narrative*, 132–39.

24. "The unintelligibility of the language which the invaders speak increases the terror of their aspect and invests them with an appearance of inhumanity" (McKane, *Jeremiah I–XXV*, 124).

25. Note the prayer for retribution for such devouring in Jeremiah 10:25.

26. This language comes from Deuteronomy 28:51, 53. It is a reversal of the ideal articulated in 1 Kings 5:5 (Eng., 4:25) (see also Mic. 4:4; Zech. 3:10).

27. For the eschatological use of the phrase "In those days," see Jeremiah 3:16, 18; 31:29; 33:15, 16 [MT]; 50:4, 20.

commentary on Jer. 4:27; 5:10; see also Jer. 9:15 [Eng., 9:16]; MT 30:11; 46:28). When the people say, "Why has the Lord our God done to us all these things?" Jeremiah is to say to them, "Just as you served/worshiped foreign gods in your land,[28] so you will serve strangers/foreigners in a land that does not belong to you" (Jer. 5:19; cf. Jer. 8:19b; 9:11–12 [Eng., 9:12–13]; 13:22). This text has several points of contact with Deuteronomy 29:23–27 (Eng., 29:24–28). There it is anticipated that the nations will ask why the Lord has destroyed the land in the manner described in Deuteronomy 29:21–22 (Eng., 29:22–23). The response will be that it is because the people forsook the covenant of the Lord and served or worshiped other gods, and the Lord subsequently exiled them to another land (see also 1 Kgs. 9:8–9; Jer. 22:8–9; 2 Chr. 7:21–22). Likewise, Jeremiah 16:10–13 anticipates that the people will ask the prophet why the Lord speaks words of judgment against them, to which he will respond that it is because their forefathers forsook the Lord and went after other gods, and the present generation has become worse in this than its ancestors. The comparative construction ("Just as . . . so . . .") in Jeremiah 5:19b sets up the *lex talionis* (Exod. 21:23–25; Lev. 24:20). The people served foreign gods in their own land, so their punishment will fit their crime. They will serve strangers in a foreign land. It is possible that "strangers" here means "foreign gods" (Deut. 32:12, 16; Jer. 2:25; 16:13), in which case the punishment is to give the people what they apparently want. If they want to worship foreign gods, then they can go into exile in a foreign land to do so. Most, however, understand "strangers" to be the foreign people (*Tg. Jon.*: "worshipers of idols") whom they must serve in exile as a consequence of their devotion to foreign gods in the land of the covenant (cf. *Tg. Jon.* Jer. 16:13; see also Jer. 30:8).

5:20 "Declare this [LXX: these things] in the house of Jacob, and cause it to be heard [or, and make proclamation of it; LXX: and let it be heard] in Judah [MT adds: saying]: 5:21 Hear this [LXX: these things], O people foolish and without mind, who have eyes but do not see, who have ears but do not hear. 5:22 Am I the one whom you do not fear?" the prophetic utterance of the Lord, "Is it before me that you do not writhe, I who made sand a border for the sea, an everlasting statute, and it does not cross over it, and it tosses but does not prevail [MT: and they toss and do not

---

28. For the MT ("Just as you forsook me and served/worshiped foreign gods in your land"), see Jeremiah 1:16; 2:13; 5:7. See also Huldah's prophecy (2 Kgs. 22:17) in response to Josiah's inquiry about the recently discovered book of the Torah.

prevail], and its waves roar, but it does not cross over it [MT: but they do not cross over it]? 5:23 But to this people belongs a stubborn and rebellious heart / mind. They turned aside and walked away. 5:24 And they have not said / thought in their heart / mind, 'Let us fear the LORD our God who gives to us rain, early [i.e., autumn] rain and latter [i.e., spring] rain,[29] in its time, satisfaction of statute of harvest, and he kept for us [MT: weeks of statutes of harvest he keeps for us; Syr.: and produce of summer for winter he keeps for us].' 5:25 Your iniquities, they have turned away these things; and your sins, they have withheld the good from you. 5:26 For found among my people are wicked ones, and snares [MT: he watches like crouching of fowlers; LXX[OL], Aq., Symm., Theod.: like a fowler's net; Vulg.: like fowlers; BHS: they put together a net like fowlers] are what they set up to destroy men [MT: they set up destruction], and they capture [MT: men they capture]. 5:27 Like a basket [or, cage] full of birds [or, flying creatures], so their houses are full of deceit. Therefore, they have become great and gained riches. 5:28 [MT adds: They have grown fat, they are smooth / shiny.] Also, they transgress judgment [MT: Also, they transgress in matters of evil (or, with evil words)]. They do not plead an orphan's cause [MT: With judgment they do not plead an orphan's cause so that they might succeed], and a widow's legal right [MT: and a legal right of needy people] they do not vindicate. 5:29 Concerning these things will I not visit / punish [Cairo Geniza, nonn Mss add: them; or, Upon these will I not visit (i.e., Will I not punish these)]?" the prophetic utterance of the LORD, "On [pc Mss: And on] a nation such as this will I [see BDB, 660] not avenge myself? 5:30 An appalling and horrible thing has occurred in the land: 5:31 the prophets, they prophesy in / with / by deception; and the priests, they rule [Tg. Jon.: help] according to their hands [i.e., at their guidance / direction; or, by their sides (see BDB, 391); LXX: they seized (some witnesses, Vulg.: clapped / applauded) with their hands; Syr.: they take / hold their hands]; and my people, they prefer thus. And what will you [pl.] do at its end?"

The LORD is presumably the speaker in 5:20, but it is not immediately evident to whom he addresses the plural imperatives (cf. Jer. 5:1). Perhaps these are directed to Jeremiah and his associates. The

---

29. Redak: "According to the 'keri,' 'the early rain and the latter rain' is an elaboration of 'Who gives rain.' According to the 'kethib,' however, the verse reads: 'Who gives rain, and the early rain and the latter rain.' The explanation is that God gives rain for the gardens, for the cattle, for drinking, and for the grain He gives the early rain and the latter rain, each in its time" (Rosenberg, trans., *Mikraoth Gedoloth: Jeremiah Volume One*, 52).

following message begins with a call for the people to hear (Jer. 5:21), but it is more of a one-way conversation about the people between the LORD and the prophet. The imperatives in 5:20 are similar to the ones in 4:5 and 46:14 (see also Jer. 2:4), which are commands to warn of invasion, but in 5:20 they are commands to declare the reason for the threat of invasion. McKane has noted that the description of the people in 5:21 as "foolish" (סכל) and "without mind" (אין לב) has affiliations with the wisdom literature, Proverbs and Ecclesiastes in particular (see also Hos. 7:11).[30] Thus, apart from Jeremiah 4:22 and 5:21, the other occurrences of סכל are all in Ecclesiastes (Eccl. 2:19; 7:17; 10:3, 14). McKane also compares the phrase אין לב to חסר לב ("lacking mind") in Proverbs 6:32; 7:7; 9:4, 16; 10:13; 11:12; 12:11; 15:21. The people do not yet have a "heart" or "mind" to know/acknowledge, eyes to see, and ears to hear (Deut. 29:3 [Eng., 29:4]; cf. Isa. 6:9–10; 42:20; Ezek. 12:2; Mark 8:18). They are in need of the new covenant circumcision of the heart (Deut. 30:6; Jer. 4:4; 9:25 [Eng., 9:26]; 31:31, 33; Ezek. 11:19–20; Rom. 2:28–29). They have become like the empty idols that they worship (see Jer. 2:5b), possessing hearts/minds without understanding, eyes without sight, and ears without hearing (see Deut. 4:28; Isa. 44:18; Pss. 115:5–8; 135:15–18). They are like dumb, unresponsive objects headed for destruction (Isa. 1:31; Jer. 10:14–15).

The foolish, blind, and deaf nature of the people is illustrated in 5:22–23 by the contrast with the ocean (cf. Isa. 1:3; Jer. 2:32; 8:7). The absurdity of not fearing the LORD is highlighted at the beginning of 5:22 by the fronting in the Hebrew syntax: "Am I the one whom you do not fear?" the prophetic utterance of the LORD, "Is it before me that you do not writhe [cf. Jer. 5:3]?" Of all the available options, why would it be the LORD whom the people choose not to worship? He is the creator of the world (see Jer. 10:11–12; 51:15)! The LORD's description of himself as the one "who made sand (חול) a border for the sea" creates a wordplay with the verb in the previous question, "Is it before me that you do not writhe (תחילו)?" This border is an everlasting "statute" or limit over which the sea does not cross (see Gen. 1:9–10; Ps. 104:5–9; 148:6; Job 38:10–11; Prov. 8:29; *1 En.* 69:18; 80:1–8; 101:6–7).[31] The sea may toss, but it does not prevail.[32] Its waves may roar (see Jer. 31:35

---

30. McKane, *Jeremiah I–XXV*, 129.

31. See also Neusner, *Jeremiah in Talmud and Midrash*, 30, 147, 343.

32. The MT has plural forms here ("and they toss and do not prevail"). This apparently assumes that the waves in the immediately following clause are the subject. The singular forms of the Hebrew source of Greek Jeremiah

[LXX 31:36]), but it does not cross over the boundary set for it.[33] In contrast to the "obedience" of the raging ocean to the Lord's limitation, the people of Judah have a "stubborn and rebellious heart/mind" (Jer. 5:23a; cf. Jer. 4:14; 6:28; 7:24; 13:10; Ezek. 2:6). They have behaved like a disobedient son to whom stoning is due according to the law (Deut. 21:18, 20). "They turned aside and walked away" (Jer. 5:23b).[34] That is, they turned aside from the Lord and his will and went after other so-called gods like Baal (Jer. 2:5b, 8b).[35]

The text of 5:24 provides an answer to the question posed at the beginning of 5:22 ("Am I the one whom you do not fear?"). The ocean respects the Lord's "statute" (i.e., limit), but the people of Judah have not "said" or "thought" (cf. Jer. 2:6) in their "stubborn and rebellious heart" (Jer. 5:23), "Let us fear the Lord our God who gives to us rain, early [i.e., autumn] rain and latter [i.e., spring] rain, in its time, satisfaction of statute of harvest, and he kept for us" (cf. Deut. 11:14; Jer. 10:13; 14:22; Joel 2:23; Ps. 147:8; Acts 14:17). The gift of appropriately seasonal rains and the resulting harvest has been attributed to Baal (Hos. 2:10 [Eng., 2:8]). The MT has שְׁבֻעוֹת חֻקּוֹת ("weeks of statutes") rather than שִׂבְעַת חֻקַּת ("satisfaction of statute") reflected by the Greek. This is usually understood to be a reference to the seven weeks between Passover (barley harvest) and the Feast of Weeks (wheat harvest) (see Lev. 23:10–17; Deut. 16:9–12).[36] Either way, the failure to recognize and acknowledge this statute stands in sharp contrast to the sea's honoring of its own God-given "statute" (cf. Isa. 1:3). The people's iniquities have turned the blessings of 5:24 away from them (Jer. 5:25a; see Deut. 28:24 [covenant curse]; Isa. 59:2a; Jer. 3:3, 24; 5:17; 14:4). Their

---

    and the Syriac, which have the already introduced "sea" as their subject, are more appropriate to the context.

33. Again, the MT, in contrast to the Hebrew source of Greek Jeremiah and the Syriac, has a plural verb ("but they do not cross over it") as if the waves were the subject, but the issue at hand is not whether the waves in particular cross the boundary but whether the sea in general crosses it.

34. The "*qatal . . . wayyiqtol*" sequence suggests that this is a brief narrative of Judah's story.

35. It is possible that the description of the Lord's control of the sea here is designed to show his superiority to Yam, the god of the sea in Canaanite mythology (cf. Exod. 12:12; Num. 33:4), but there is little indication in the Hebrew Bible that the people of Judah ever worshiped Yam.

36. "*Kara* renders שְׁבֻעֹת, as oaths. This alludes to God's oath to Noah that 'seeding and harvest, heat and cold, summer and winter, and day and night shall not cease' (Gen. 8:22)" (Rosenberg, trans., *Mikraoth Gedoloth: Jeremiah Volume One*, 52).

sins have withheld from them the good that the LORD has for them (Jer. 5:25b; see Isa. 59:2b; Jer. 2:19; 12:4). There is a separation between the LORD and his people because of their iniquities and sins (Isa. 59:2).

The text of 5:26 provides the explanation for the verdict in 5:25. "For found among my people are wicked ones" (Jer. 5:26a). This reminds the reader of the initial search in 5:1 to see if there might be anyone "found" in Jerusalem who does justice and seeks faithfulness in order that the LORD may forgive the city. No such person has been found (Jer. 5:7). Instead, there are "wicked ones" found among the people. The fact that they are "among the people" in this context suggests that they are a distinct group among a people generally lacking in justice and faithfulness. The following verses will make clear that the "wicked ones" here are specifically the leaders who have abused their position and failed in their responsibility to orphans and widows (Jer. 5:27–28; see also Jer. 5:31). The remainder of 5:26 features differences between the Hebrew source of Greek Jeremiah and the MT. The MT has ישור כשך יקושים הציבו משחית אנשים ילכדו ("he [i.e., each one of the wicked ones] watches like crouching of fowlers, they set up destruction, men they capture"). The reference to "fowlers" seems to anticipate 5:27. The Hebrew source of Greek Jeremiah has ומוקשים הציבו השחית אנשים ולכדו ("and snares are what they set up to destroy men, and they capture"). McKane, however, back-translates the Greek text differently: יקושים הציבו לשחת אנשים וילכדו.[37] But the Hebrew word for "snares" is מוקשים, not יקושים, which means "fowlers." Also, it is more likely that the *hiphil* infinitive is the regular form השחית (cf. the MT's משחית) rather than a shortened form (לשחת) with a *lamedh* prefix that takes the place of the *he* prefix (see GKC §53q). Finally, it is quite possible that the verb at the end of the verse should be *wayyiqtol* (וילכדו) as McKane has it, but the above reconstruction (ולכדו) understands it to be a simple *waw* plus *qatal* (not *weqatal*) so that the two coordinated clauses in 5:26b both have *qatal* forms. In both the Hebrew source of Greek Jeremiah and the MT, the wicked leaders are destructive (cf. Mic. 3). They trap their own people and capture them like prisoners of war (cf. Jer. 6:11b).

5:27 compares the houses of the wicked leaders to baskets or cages full of birds. Given the context of 5:26, the reader might expect that this means the birds are the people captured by the wicked leaders (cf. Ezek. 13:20), but it is clear that the houses are full of "deceit" rather than people (cf. Gen. 27:35; Hos. 12:1, 8 [Eng., 11:12; 12:7]). That is, their houses are full of wealth gained by deceiving the people (cf. Amos 3:10; Zeph. 1:9; Sir. 11:29–34; see also Jer. 17:11). Therefore, they have

---

37. McKane, *Jeremiah I–XXV*, 133.

become great and rich at the people's expense. This is apparently what 5:26 means by its reference to trapping and capturing people. The MT adds at the beginning of 5:28, "They have grown fat, they are smooth/shiny" (cf. Deut. 32:15; MT Ezek. 34:16b). This understands the birds in the cage to be the wicked leaders fattened for slaughter by their own greed. In an ironic twist, the very ones who seek to trap and capture others are caught in their own web of lies (cf. Prov. 1:17–19).

The Hebrew source of Greek Jeremiah of 5:28 has a considerably shorter text than the MT. The MT's addition at the beginning of the verse ("They have grown fat, they are smooth/shiny") has already been noted. On the other hand, the Hebrew source of Greek Jeremiah begins, "Also, they transgress judgment."[38] This speaks of the leadership's failure to contend for the helpless in legal matters. The MT has, "Also, they transgress in matters of evil [or, with evil words]." Bright translates, "Nay more, they wink at evil."[39] According to the Hebrew source of Greek Jeremiah, this manifests itself in dealings with orphans (the fatherless) and widows (the husbandless): "They do not plead an orphan's cause, and a widow's (אלמנה) legal right they do not vindicate" (cf. Isa. 1:17, 23; Jer. 7:5–6; see BDB, 450). According to the MT, the text says, "With judgment they do not plead an orphan's cause so that they might succeed,[40] and a legal right of needy people (אביונים) they do not vindicate" (cf. Jer. 22:16). Thus, the conclusion in 5:29, "Concerning these things will I not visit/punish [Cairo Geniza, nonn Mss add: them; or, Upon these will I not visit (i.e., Will I not punish these)]?" the prophetic utterance of the LORD, "On [pc Mss: And on] a nation such as this will I [see BDB, 660] not avenge myself" (see comments on Jer. 5:9; see also Jer. 6:6; 9:8 [Eng., 9:9])?[41]

The LORD announces in 5:30 that an "appalling and horrible" thing has occurred in the land (cf. Jer. 2:12; 18:13; 23:14; Hos. 6:10) and then

---

38. There is a contrast here between the way the leaders "transgress" (עבר) judgment and the way the sea does not "cross over" (עבר) the statute or limit set for it (Jer. 5:22).

39. "Perhaps it is best to take the verb in the sense of 'overlook, excuse'" (Bright, *Jeremiah*, 40). See Amos 7:8; 8:2; Micah 7:18; Proverbs 19:11.

40. This is usually understood to mean "so that orphans might win their case." It is possible that the leaders are the subject of this verb, which would mean that they deliberately fail in their duty in order to prosper at the expense of orphans.

41. As in 5:9, the judgment is not only for the core problem of idolatry (Jer. 5:7) but also for the symptoms of this core problem such as adultery (Jer. 5:8) and social injustice (Jer. 5:26–28; cf. Jer. 7:5–11).

explains this in 5:31 as the work of the false prophets and the priests (see Isa. 28:7; Jer. 23:11). As for the prophets, they prophesy בשקר ("in/with/by deception"; cf. Jer. 6:13; 20:6; 23:25; 27:15; 29:9). On analogy with Jeremiah 2:8b, this would appear to mean that they prophesy by Baal (a false god) (cf. Jer. 23:13–14). On the other hand, it could mean that they prophesy falsely in support of the unjust practices outlined in 5:26–28.[42] But these two options are not mutually exclusive. As noted in the commentary on Jeremiah 5:7–9, idolatry is the central problem from which all other sins stem. As for the priests, they "rule according to their hands." This is variously interpreted in the early versions as noted in the translation above.[43] The phrase "according to their hands" could mean that the priests rule at their own guidance or direction without acknowledgment of the LORD (cf. Jer. 2:8a). It could also mean that they rule at the guidance of the false prophets (cf. 1 Chr. 25:2, 3, 6; 2 Chr. 23:18). The same phrase can be translated "by their sides" (BDB, 391), in which case it would mean that the priests come alongside the false prophets and work in conjunction with them. Unfortunately, this is the preference of the people (cf. Jer. 14:10; Amos 4:5). The people like the professional prophets for hire to tell them what they want to hear (Jer. 6:14; 8:11; Mic. 2:11; 3:11). The concluding question—"And what will you [pl.] do at its end?"—suggests a final consequence or judgment that the people and their leaders will not be able to avoid (cf. Deut. 32:20; Isa. 10:3; Jer. 5:9, 29; 9:8 [Eng., 9:9]; 12:4 [MT]; 23:20; 30:24; Hos. 9:5).

---

42. See Bright, *Jeremiah*, 41; McKane, *Jeremiah I–XXV*, 136.

43. Rudolph (in the *BHS* apparatus) notes the proposed emendation יוֹרוּ or הוֹרוּ ("they teach") in place of יְרְדוּ ("they rule"). Holladay suggests that ירדו is from רדה ("scrape") and translates, "they deconsecrate themselves."

JEREMIAH 6

6:1 Seek refuge [LXX: Strengthen; Tg. Jon.: Go into exile (cf. Syr.)], O sons of Benjamin, from the midst of Jerusalem; and in Tekoa blast a shofar, and over Beth Hakkerem lift up a signal. For calamity peers from (the) north, and great breaking. 6:2 And as for your height, it is destroyed [MT: The lovely (or, The pasture) and the delicate I destroy (Syr.: you are like; Vulg.: I liken)], O Daughter Zion. 6:3 To her will come shepherds and their flocks [Tg. Jon.: kings and their armies], and [and > MT] they will pitch tents against her around, and [and > MT] they will tend each with his hand [or, graze each his portion; Tg. Jon.: help one another]. 6:4 "Consecrate against her war. Arise and let us go up [or, that we may go up] at noon. Woe to us, for the day has turned, for evening shadows are stretched out. 6:5 Arise and let us go up [or, that we may go up] at night and destroy her citadels [LXX: foundations]." 6:6 For thus says the LORD [MT adds: of hosts], "Cut down her trees [or, counsel; see GKC §91e], pour out against Jerusalem a mound [LXX: a force; Syr.: lie in wait against Jerusalem for an ambush]. Alas, city of deception [MT: She is the city (f.) to be punished (m.)], all oppression is in her midst [NETS: there is nothing but oppression within her; MT: all of it is oppression in her midst]. 6:7 As a cistern [qere: well] keeps water [MT: her/its water] cool/fresh [Syr.: collects its water], so she keeps her evil cool/fresh [Syr.: collects her evil]. Violence and destruction[1] will be heard [or, are heard] in her, before her continually. With sickness and wound [MT: Before me continually are sickness and wound] 6:8 you must be disciplined [MT: Be disciplined], O Jerusalem, lest I [lit., my self] be alienated from you, lest I make you a desolation [or, object of horror], an uninhabitable land [Tg. Jon.: like the land of Sodom, which is uninhabited]."

This unit (Jer. 6:1–8) runs parallel to Jeremiah 4:5–8 and has affinities with Amos 3:9–11. The text features three speakers: Jeremiah (Jer. 6:1–3), the enemy (Jer. 6:4–5), and the LORD (Jer. 6:6–8). The prophet summons the sons of Benjamin to "seek refuge" from the midst of Jerusalem (Jer. 6:1a). This may be compared to the call to Judah and Jerusalem to be gathered to the fortified cities (Jer. 4:5). Now the people must seek refuge even from such a fortified city, which is subject to invasion (cf. Jer. 5:17b; Luke 21:21). The call goes out to the sons of

---

1. I.e., sounds or reports of violence and destruction. The use of a singular verb with a compound subject here in the Hebrew text suggests that the subject is an example of hendiadys. See Holladay, *Jeremiah 1*, 208.

Benjamin in particular because the city of Jerusalem was located in Benjamin's territory (Josh. 18:11–28). The LXX translates העזו with "strengthen," as if the imperative were from עזז ("be strong") rather than עוז ("seek refuge"). *Targum Jonathan* renders, "Go into exile" (cf. Syr.), as if to say refuge must be sought in submission to the authority of the enemy (cf. Jer. 29:4–7; 38:2, 17–18). Jeremiah also commands a shofar to be blasted in nearby Tekoa to the south (cf. Jer. 4:5a; 51:27a; Hos. 5:8) and a signal (perhaps a smoke signal [see Judg. 20:38, 40; cf. Jer. 4:6a; 51:27a]) to be lifted up over Beth Hakkerem (Neh. 3:14), whose location is uncertain. The place name "Tekoa" is likely chosen for the wordplay that it forms with the imperative "blast" (ובתקוע תקעו) (cf. Ezek. 7:14).[2] The reason for such alarm is that "calamity peers from (the) north, and great breaking" (Jer. 6:1b; cf. Jer. 1:13–15; 4:6b; Ps. 85:12 [Eng., 85:11]). As noted in the commentary on Jeremiah 4:5–8, this enemy from the north is not a historical enemy such as Babylon, although Babylon certainly prefigures the eschatological foe. Rather, the language of these verses speaks of the great Day of the LORD (see Isa. 13:2, 6, 9; Joel 1:13, 15; 2:1, 15; Zeph. 1:7, 10).

The Greek translation of Jeremiah 6:2 cannot be based on the Hebrew text of the MT. Usage suggests the following Hebrew *Vorlage*: וקומתך נדמתה בת ציון ("And as for your height, it is destroyed, O Daughter Zion") (cf. Jer. 52:21, 22; Ezek. 19:11). The MT is open to several different interpretations: הנוה והמעננה דמיתי בת ציון ("The lovely [or, The pasture] and the delicate I destroy, O Daughter Zion").[3] This rendering understands Jerusalem to be a pampered city now vulnerable to destruction (cf. Jer. 25:37; Hos. 4:5–6). It is possible, however, that the verb דמיתי is an archaic second feminine singular form (see GKC §44h) that means "you are like" (see Syr.):[4] "The lovely and the delicate you are like, O Daughter Zion." It is also possible that the verb should be re-vocalized as a *piel*, which could yield "I liken" (see Vulg.) and make "Daughter Zion" an object rather than a vocative: "To the lovely and the delicate I liken Daughter Zion." It is to Daughter Zion that shepherds and their flocks will come (Jer. 6:3a). *Targum Jonathan* rightly

---

2.   Note also the cognate object in "lift up a signal" (שאו משאת). The warning in the south is usually taken as an indication that the enemy is advancing from the north, although it has been suggested that the enemy is moving "northward" to Jerusalem, having conquered other cities of Judah to the south (cf. Jer. 34:7; see McKane, *Jeremiah I–XXV*, 139–40).

3.   Note that this translation requires a shift of speaker from Jeremiah to the LORD.

4.   דמה ("be like") and דמה ("destroy") are homonyms.

interprets the shepherds and their flocks here to be kings and their armies (cf. Jer. 2:8; 3:15; 23:1–4; 51:23; see also LXX Jer. 6:18).[5] These will come and "pitch" (ותקעו)[6] their tents (i.e., encamp) against the city of Jerusalem all around (Jer. 6:3b; cf. Jer. 1:15; 4:17; Zech. 12:3b; 14:2). Each king will tend to the area assigned to his authority (cf. Num. 2:17; 2 Sam. 19:44 [Eng., 19:43]; 2 Kgs. 11:7).

Verses 4 and 5 of Jeremiah 6 are the words of the enemy. The call to consecrate war against Daughter Zion is a summons to holy war (cf. Jer. 22:7; 51:27, 28; Mic. 3:5; Joel 4:9 [Eng., 3:9]), a consciously religious act set apart by the offering of a sacrifice (see BDB, 873). The enemy plans to go up "at noon" (cf. 1 Kgs. 20:16; Jer. 15:8; Zeph. 2:4). Holladay considers this to be the great confidence of the enemy, going up in the heat of the day when half the day has already passed.[7] Ordinarily an army would start fresh at daybreak and take as much advantage of the daylight as possible (cf. Josh. 10:12–14), but the expression "at noon" may not mean anything more here than "in clear daylight."[8] "Woe to us," the enemy says, "for the day has turned [cf. Ps. 90:9], for evening shadows are stretched out." This is usually understood to be an expression of the enemy's disappointment that it is already too late to go up in clear daylight. Holladay, however, thinks that the expression "Woe to us" is too strong for disappointment.[9] He attributes it to the voice of the people of Jerusalem. Yet the contrast between what the enemy says in 6:4a ("Arise and let us go up at noon") and what he says in 6:5 ("Arise and let us go up at night and destroy her citadels") suggests a change in tactic based on the time rather than an indication that the enemy could go up at either time or both. An attack at night would certainly not be typical, but it would also not be impossible for such a formidable foe (cf. Judg. 7:9, 15).

---

5. Holladay thinks that "To her will come" here is the idiom for sexual relations (e.g., 2 Sam. 16:21) (*Jeremiah 1*, 206). Jerome suggests that רעים ("shepherds") could be vocalized as רֵעִים ("lovers") (see McKane, *Jeremiah I–XXV*, 140).

6. The MT has simple *qatal* forms in Jeremiah 6:3b, while the Greek text reflects the use of *weqatal* forms, which are better suited to the context ("it is the choice of the most contextually appropriate reading that is the main task of the textual critic" [Tov, *Textual Criticism*, 281]). The verb ותקעו ("and pitch") maintains the wordplay with ובתקוע תקעו ("and in Tekoa blast") in Jeremiah 6:1a.

7. Holladay, *Jeremiah 1*, 206–7.

8. Keil, *Jeremiah*, 86.

9. Holladay, *Jeremiah 1*, 206.

Verse 6 introduces the Lord's discourse ("For thus says the Lord") as the explanation for the words of the enemy in verses 4 and 5. That is, the Lord himself is commanding the attack. Thus, the MT appropriately adds that the Lord is the Lord of hosts or armies. The commands to cut down Jerusalem's trees and pour out against her a mound are in preparation for the siege (see Deut. 20:19–20).[10] The reading עֵצָה in the Leningrad Codex is usually taken as the equivalent of עֵצָהּ ("her trees") (cf. pc Mss), but עֵצָה normally means "counsel." Thus, McKane suggests that the idiom "cut counsel" (i.e., "finalize the plans") could be related to the more familiar idiom "cut a covenant" (i.e., "make a covenant"): "The time for strategic discussion is over and the attack must be launched: 'Build a ramp from which to attack Jerusalem.'"[11] The Hebrew source of Greek Jeremiah then has הוי עיר השקר ("Alas, city of deception") (see Jer. 3:10, 23; 5:2, 31; cf. Jer. 22:13; Nah. 3:1). The MT has היא העיר הפקד ("She is the city [f.] to be punished [m.]) (cf. Jer. 5:9, 29; 9:8 [Eng., 9:9]). This latter reading is problematic due to the incongruence of grammatical gender. The final clause of verse 6 ("all oppression is in her midst"; cf. MT: "all of it is oppression in her midst") is typically taken in the sense "there is nothing but oppression within her" (NETS) (cf. Jer. 22:17).

The Leningrad Codex marks Jeremiah 6:7 as "the middle of the Scripture" (חצי המקרא). *BHS* marks בור as possessing "the middle of the Scripture in letters" (חצי המקרא באותיות) but does not indicate which of the letters this is (cf. Lev. 11:42 where the middle letter of the Torah is an enlarged *waw*). This word also differs between the *kethiv* (בּוֹר "cistern" [m.]) and *qere* (בָּיִר = בְּאֵר "well" [f.]). Since most of the occurrences of באר ("well" [f.]) are in the Pentateuch, it is likely that the correct reading in Jeremiah 6:7 is the more widely occurring בור ("cistern" [m.]), perhaps with the more appropriate meaning "well" in this context (see BDB, 92).[12] This is a problem for the MT ("As a cistern/well [m.] keeps its [f.] water cool/fresh"), thus necessitating a feminine noun in the *qere* to maintain agreement between pronoun and antecedent. It is not a problem, however, for the Hebrew source

---

10. Another possibility is that the trees here are the cedars out of which the royal palace in Jerusalem was made (see Jer. 22:6–7). The cedars were so abundant in this project that the palace was known as "the forest of Lebanon" (1 Kgs. 7:2).

11. McKane, *Jeremiah I–XXV*, 142.

12. See Yoel Elitzur, "The Interface Between Language and Realia in the Pre-exilic Books of the Bible," *HS* 59 (2018): 133–35. See also Keil, *Jeremiah*, 87; Holladay, *Jeremiah 1*, 203.

behind Greek Jeremiah ("As a cistern/well keeps water cool/fresh").
The LORD makes a comparison here between a well keeping water cool
and Jerusalem keeping its evil fresh.[13] The following clause indicates
that sounds or reports of "violence and destruction" will be heard or
are heard in Jerusalem. The choice of verb tense in translation here
depends upon whether "violence and destruction" describes what the
enemy will bring to Jerusalem or the current activity of Jerusalem
itself (cf. Jer. 20:8; Amos 3:10; Hab. 1:3). The following text of the
Hebrew source behind Greek Jeremiah ("before her continually. With
sickness and wound") suggests the former, while the following text of
the MT ("Before me continually are sickness and wound") suggests the
latter. In the Hebrew source behind Greek Jeremiah, the phrase "With
sickness and wound" (cf. Isa. 1:5–6; Jer. 10:19; 30:12, 15) at the end
of 6:7 leads into 6:8 (cf. Syr.): "With sickness and wound you must be
disciplined." This text features a finite verb (cf. Jer. 31:18), whereas
the MT begins verse 8 with an imperative ("Be disciplined" [cf. Ps.
2:10]). Despite the impending attack of the enemy, the disaster could
be avoided, if only Jerusalem would accept the LORD's discipline: "lest I
be alienated from you [cf. Ezek. 23:18], lest I make you a desolation, an
uninhabitable land [cf. Jer. 4:4b, 7, 28; 10:22; 22:6b]" (see Jer. 7:3, 5–7;
17:24–27; 18:7–12; 26:3; 36:3; but see also Jer. 7:13–15, 16; 11:14; 14:11
where the judgment seems unavoidable).[14] Of course, Jerusalem would
not accept such discipline at all. Only in the new covenant would there
be a change of heart (Jer. 31:18, 31–34).

*6:9 For [> MT] thus says the LORD [MT adds: of hosts], "Glean, glean
[MT: Gleaning they will glean] like a grapevine the remnant of Israel.
Turn back [MT adds: your hand] like a grape gatherer to his [his > MT]
basket(s) [or, branches (BDB, 700)]." 6:10 To whom can I speak and*

---

13. "The form הקיר indicates a derivation from קור ["dig"], whereas הקרה
points to קרר ["be cold"]. It is unlikely that the one is to be derived differently from the other; we have to conclude either that הקיר is double *ayin*
with the form of *ayin waw* (GK 67w) or that הקרה is *ayin waw* with the
form of double *ayin*. Both forms should be derived from קרר as they are in
Sept. (ψύχει, twice) and Vulg. (*frigidam fecit*, twice)" (McKane, *Jeremiah
I–XXV*, 142–43).

14. While it is true that there was a historical enemy (Babylon) to be avoided,
it is also true that there is an ever-imminent final enemy from whom the
people must take refuge and a final judgment at which only the righteous by faith will be vindicated (Ezek. 38–39; Nah. 1:7; Hab. 2:4; Eccl.
12:13–14).

admonish/warn [LXX: testify] that they might listen? Look, uncircumcised is their ear, and they are not able to pay attention. Look, the word of the LORD *has become to them a reproach. They [mlt Mss, LXX^A, Old Latin, Syr., Vulg., Luther: And they] do not delight in it. 6:11 And I am full of [LXX: And I filled; Syr.: And you (f. sg.) are full of] the fury of the* LORD *[LXX: my fury],*[15] *and I am weary [LXX: and I held back; Syr.: and you (f. sg.) are weary], yet I have not finished them [MT: I am weary of holding it; Syr.: measure (f. sg. impv.)]. "I will pour out [MT: Pour out; Syr.: and pour out; Tg. Jon.: and I am not able to pour out] upon children in the street [LXX: outside] and upon an assembly of young men together. For both man and woman will be captured, old with one full of days. 6:12 And their houses will be turned over to others, fields and their [their > MT] wives together. For I will stretch out my hand against the inhabitants of this [this > MT] land," the prophetic utterance of the* LORD. *6:13 "For from their least to their greatest, each one makes unjust gain. From priest to prophet [LXX: false prophet; MT: And from prophet (Syr.: false prophet; Tg. Jon.: scribe) to priest], each one practices deception. 6:14 And they healed the breaking/fracture of my people [mlt Mss, LXX^O, Symm., Syr., Vulg.: the breaking of the daughter of my people (cf. Jer. 8:11)] lightly [or, superficially; LXX: despising; Tg. Jon.: with their false words] saying [LXX: and saying], 'Peace, peace,' and where is peace [MT: and there is no peace]?*[16] *6:15 They are put to shame, for they forsook (me) [or, Are they ashamed that they forsook (me)?].*[17] *Also [or, Indeed], they are certainly not ashamed, and they do not know to be ashamed [MT: to exhibit shame; Syr.: to hinder themselves].*[18] *Therefore, they will fall in their falling [MT: they will fall among the fallen]. At the time of their visitation [MT: At the time that I visit them] they will stumble," says the* LORD.

6:16 Thus says the LORD, *"Stand upon roads [or, crossroads] and see [GKC §110f], and ask for the ancient paths of the* LORD *[of the* LORD *>*

---

15. The Greek text reflects י חמת, which is an abbreviation for חמת יהוה (= MT). The translator mistook the *yodh* for a first common singular pronominal suffix.

16. Given the healing metaphor, it is likely that the sense of שלום here is "health" rather than "peace," yet the metaphor itself refers to the false message of well-being and security.

17. MT: "They are put to shame, for an abomination is what they committed [or, Are they ashamed that an abomination is what they committed?]."

18. The "גם . . . גם" construction in the MT may have the sense of "Both . . . and": "Both they are certainly not ashamed, and they do not know to exhibit shame" (see GKC §162b), but compare Jeremiah 8:12.

MT], and see [> MT] what [MT: where] is the good way [MT: the way of good] and walk in it, and find rest [LXX: purification] for your [2mp] self." And they said, "We will not walk." 6:17 "[MT adds: And (see GKC §112dd)] I raised over you [pc Mss: over them] watchmen [Tg. Jon.: teachers; Rashi, Redak: prophets], 'Pay attention to (the) sound of (the) shofar [Tg. Jon.: Receive the words of the prophets].'" And they said, "We will not pay attention." 6:18 "Therefore, the nations heard [MT: Therefore, hear, O nations], and those who shepherd their flocks [MT: and know, O congregation (BHS: and know knowledge), what is in/ against them (Tg. Jon.: their sins; Vulg.: what I will do with them)]. 6:19 Hear, O land [Tg. Jon.: land of Israel]. Look, I am about to bring to/upon this people calamity [MT: I am about to bring calamity to/ upon this people], the fruit of their apostasy. For to my words [Tg. Jon.: the words of my servants the prophets] they have not paid attention, and my instruction [or, my Torah; LXX: my law] they have rejected [MT: and as for my instruction, they rejected it (see GKC §111h, 143d)]. 6:20 Why to me frankincense from Sheba do you bring [MT: Why to me does frankincense from Sheba come], and cinnamon [MT: and good/sweet cane] from a distant land? Your burnt offerings are not for acceptance [BDB, 953], and your sacrifices are not pleasing to me." 6:21 Therefore, thus says the LORD, *"Look, I am about to give to this people a stumbling block [LXX: weakness; MT: stumbling blocks], and they will stumble over it [LXX: and they will be weak with it; MT: and they will stumble over them]. Fathers and sons together, a neighbor and his friend, they will perish [qere has weqatal form rather than yiqtol]."*

There are two subunits in this section (Jer. 6:9–15 and 6:16–21) marked off by כה אמר יהוה ("Thus says the LORD"). The Hebrew source of Greek Jeremiah begins 6:9 with the causal conjunction כי, which introduces the reason for the warning of desolation in 6:8. This conjunction is lacking in the MT (cf. Jer. 6:6). The Hebrew source of Greek Jeremiah begins the LORD's discourse in 6:9 with two plural imperatives ("Glean, glean"), while the MT has an infinitive absolute plus a third person plural finite verb of the same root ("Gleaning they will glean"). It is highly unlikely then that an individual such as Jeremiah is being tasked with the gleaning here. It is also improbable, given the context of 6:8, that the gleaning is a positive image for rescue.[19] Rather, the enemy kings and their armies (Jer. 6:3) are to "glean" like a grapevine the remnant of Israel (cf. Isa. 17:4–6; 24:13;

---

19. See Holladay, *Jeremiah 1*, 213.

Jer. 2:3, 21; 5:10; 6:6; 8:13; 12:10; Mic. 7:1).[20] The remnant of Israel here is not the faithful remnant of the people of God. It is simply what is left of Israel to be judged in order to make the land an uninhabited desolation (Jer. 6:8b; cf. Jer. 15:9b). There is still hope for the faithful remnant that the destruction will not be complete (Jer. 4:27; 5:10, 18). The singular imperative, "Turn back [MT adds: your hand]," is either directed to the enemy in general or to each enemy soldier in particular (Jer. 6:9b; cf. Isa. 1:25; Ezek. 38:12; Amos 1:8; Zech. 13:7). The command is to turn back like a grape gatherer either to his baskets or his branches (see BDB, 700). Thus, the image is either that of a grape gatherer going back and forth collecting grapes from the vine into his baskets or that of a grape gatherer going over the branches repeatedly until all that is left is gone. Either way, it speaks of the desolation and depopulation of the land.

The prophet Jeremiah asks, "To whom can I speak and admonish/warn [LXX: testify] that they might listen" (Jer. 6:10a; cf. 2 Kgs. 17:13–14; Jer. 25:4–7; 26:5)? This is a rhetorical affirmation of the LORD's words of judgment. There is no one willing to heed the warning given by the LORD through Jeremiah (Jer. 1:17–19; 2:8; 5:1, 31). He points out ("Look") that this is because the ear of the people is "uncircumcised," which is to say that their ear is covered so that they are unable to listen and obey (see Deut. 29:3 [Eng., 29:4]; Jer. 5:21; Acts 7:51; cf. Exod. 6:30; Deut. 10:16; 30:6; Jer. 4:4; 9:25 [Eng., 9:26]).[21] The prophetic word of the LORD has in fact become a "reproach" to them (Jer. 6:10b; cf. Isa. 28:13). This is explained to mean that the people take no delight in it (cf. Ps. 1:2). That is, it is something that they find offensive and reject. In Jeremiah 20:8b, Jeremiah expresses that the word of the LORD has become a reproach to him, but it is for a different reason. It is not because he takes no delight in the word itself (see MT Jer. 15:16). Rather, it is because he has become the object of the people's reproach as the bearer of the offensive and rejected message.

Because of the reproach from the people that Jeremiah must bear for his ministry, he has become sympathetic to the LORD's message of judgment against them. He says that he is "full of the fury of the LORD" (Jer. 6:11a1; cf. Jer. 15:17; Mic. 3:8). The LXX has, "I filled my fury," as if the LORD were the speaker, but this is the result of a mistake on the part of the translator who misread the abbreviation

---

20. See also the use of the homonym עלל ("act severely") in Lamentations 1:12, 22; 2:20.
21. See Neusner, *Jeremiah in Talmud in Midrash*, 113.

חמתי (= חמת יהוה ["the wrath of the LORD"]) as חמתי ("my wrath").[22] According to the Hebrew source of Greek Jeremiah, the prophet then says, "and I am weary, yet I have not finished them (ונלאיתי ולא כליתים)," which may be a mitigation of 6:9 (cf. Jer. 4:27; 5:10, 18). The LXX ("and I held back and did not finish them") certainly gives the sense that the LORD is the speaker here (cf. Jer. 15:6b), but this is largely due to its treatment of the first clause of the verse. The sense of the Hebrew text is that the prophet is full of the fury of the LORD to the point of weariness, but he has not declared the complete end of the people. The MT, however, has, "I am weary of holding it (נלאיתי הכיל)." This is comparable to the prophet's words in Jeremiah 20:9 (see also Jer. 15:6b).[23] The remainder of what follows in 6:11 is the LORD's discourse: "I will pour out upon children in the street and upon an assembly of young men together. For both man and woman will be captured, old with one full of days." It is possible to interpret the MT's imperative ("Pour out") to be the prophet's prayer,[24] but by the end of 6:12 it is clear that the LORD has been the speaker. Thus, translations of the MT typically have the LORD giving Jeremiah the command to pour out the fury of which he is full. This is presumably a command to speak the words of judgment. On the other hand, the Hebrew source of Greek Jeremiah has a first-person verb ("I will pour out") (cf. Jer. 14:16b; Ezek. 7:8–9; 14:19; 20:8, 13, 21, 22; 30:15; 36:18; LXX 39:29). This outpouring of divine fury is indiscriminate, affecting young and old, male and female (cf. Deut. 28:50; 32:25; see also the reversal of this in Jer. 31:13; Joel 3:1–2 [Eng., 2:28–29]; Zech. 8:4–5).[25]

The text of Jeremiah 6:12–15 has a parallel in MT 8:10–12 but not in the LXX, which only has the first part of 8:10. The houses of those mentioned in 6:11 will be turned over to others, "fields and their [their > MT] wives together" (Jer. 6:12a; cf. Jer. 8:10a: "Therefore, I will give their wives to others, and [and > MT] their

---

22. The Syriac takes the first-person verb מלאתי ("I am full") as the archaic second feminine singular ("you are full"), as if the speech were addressed to the city of Jerusalem (see GKC §44h; see also the Syriac of the following verb).

23. The Syriac has, "and you [fs] are weary, measure [fs] and pour out [fs] . . .", again directed to the city of Jerusalem.

24. *Targum Jonathan* seems to have Jeremiah as the speaker here but gives the text a contrary sense: "and I am not able to pour out."

25. Keil interprets the verb "will be captured" not to mean "will be taken captive" but to mean "will be overtaken by the wrath" (cf. Jer. 8:9) (*Jeremiah, Lamentations*, 88).

fields to dispossessors"; see also Deut. 28:30; Jer. 32:15). The text of 6:12b has no parallel in 8:10: "For I will stretch out my hand against the inhabitants of this [this > MT] land," the prophetic utterance of the Lord (cf. Jer. 15:6b). This judgment is due to the widespread nature of the people's corruption: "For from their least to their greatest, each one makes unjust gain" (Jer. 6:13a; cf. Jer. 16:6; 31:34; Hab. 2:9). Everyone from priest to prophet (MT: "from prophet to priest") practices deception (see Jer. 2:8; 5:31; cf. Hos. 7:1). According to the LXX and Syriac, "prophet" here means "false prophet." *Targum Jonathan* renders "prophet" with the term "scribe," which reflects the understanding of the prophet as an exegete who reads and interprets Scripture (see, e.g., MT and LXX Prov. 29:18).[26] Within the book of Jeremiah, Baruch is an example of a scribal prophet, giving textual form to Jeremiah's prophecy (Jer. 36). Scribes who mishandle texts are false prophets (Jer. 2:8; 8:8).

Those mentioned in 6:13, particularly the false prophets and the priests who have forgotten the Lord (Jer. 2:8), have "healed" the breaking or fracture of the Lord's people only in a superficial way (Jer. 6:14; cf. Jer. 8:11; Job 13:4). The great "breaking" is the impending doom (Jer. 4:6), but the message of well-being ("Peace, peace") only gives the people a false sense of security and does not alert them to the problems that need to be addressed in order to avoid disaster (see Deut. 29:18 [Eng., 29:19]; Jer. 4:10; 23:17; 28; Mic. 3:5; Lam. 2:14; 1 Thess. 5:3; cf. Isa. 57:19), which is unfortunately the way the people like it (Isa. 30:10; Jer. 5:31; Mic. 2:11).[27] The reality is that there is no peace (Jer. 16:5; 30:5; Ezek. 13:10, 16). The MT states this flatly: "and there is no peace (ואין שלום)." The Hebrew source of Greek Jeremiah puts it in the form of a rhetorical question: "and where is peace (ואיה שלום)?" This should be a source of great shame for the responsible parties, but it is not (Jer. 6:15a; 8:12; cf. Jer. 2:26). Both the Hebrew source of Greek Jeremiah ("They are put to shame, for they forsook [me]"; or, "Are they ashamed that they forsook [me]?") and the MT ("They are put to shame, for an abomination is what they committed"; or, "Are they ashamed that an abomination is what they committed?") can be rendered either as a statement ("They are put to shame") of the Lord putting them to shame in judgment for their deeds or as a rhetorical question ("Are they ashamed?") that expects a

---

26. Karel van der Toorn, *Scribal Culture and the Making of the Hebrew Bible* (Cambridge, MA: Harvard University Press, 2007), 107. See also *b. Megillah* 14b.
27. See Bullinger, *Figures of Speech*, 189, 196.

negative answer.[28] The text of 6:15b states emphatically that they are not ashamed at all (cf. Jer. 3:3b; 9:18 [Eng., 9:19]). They do not even know to be ashamed (MT: "to exhibit shame" [NET: "how to blush"]; Syr.: "to hinder themselves" [from כלא]) (cf. Zeph. 3:5). Therefore (cf. Jer. 6:18, 21), "they will fall in their falling" (MT: "they will fall among the fallen"). "At the time of their visitation they will stumble" (cf. Jer. 6:21; 8:12; 11:23; 23:12; 46:21; 48:44; 50:27; MT: "At the time that I visit them they will stumble"). That is, in the day of their judgment they will not stand with the righteous (Ps. 1:5).

The second subunit (Jer. 6:16–21) begins with a series of plural imperatives: "Thus says the LORD, 'Stand upon roads and see, and ask for the ancient paths of the LORD [MT: the ancient paths], and see [> MT] what [MT: where] is the good way [MT: the way of good] and walk in it, and find rest [LXX: purification] for your [2mp] self'" (Jer. 6:16a; cf. Deut. 4:32; 32:7; Ps. 139:24; Job 8:8; see also Jer. 31:2b). Redak considers the roads here to be the road of good and the road of evil (see Jer. 18:15; Job 22:15; see also Deut. 11:26–28; 30:15–16).[29] The task is to identify and select the good road. He compares this to 1 Kings 18:21, where Elijah challenges the people to choose between the LORD and Baal. The ancient paths of the LORD are likely the traditional teachings of the Torah passed down from generation to generation (cf. Ps. 78:1–8) and transmitted by true prophets like Jeremiah but rejected by the people and their false prophets (see Jer. 6:19b). In the Torah, the people can find rest for themselves,[30] but Jeremiah comments: "And they said, 'We will not walk'" (Jer. 6:16b; cf. Isa. 28:12; 30:15; Jer. 5:4). The LORD adds that he raised up "watchmen" (i.e., prophets [see Ezek.

---

28. Both the forsaking of the LORD (LXX) and the abomination (MT) refer to the practice of idolatry (Jer. 2:7, 13), which goes hand in hand with social injustice (Jer. 5:26–31; 6:13; 7:5–6) and failure to heed the LORD's voice (Jer. 3:13, 25; 6:14).
29. Rosenberg, trans., *Mikraoth Gedoloth: Jeremiah Volume One*, 59–60.
30. Note the rendering of Genesis 2:15b in *Targum Neofiti*: "And he gave him rest in the Garden of Eden to worship in the Torah and keep its statutes." For a discussion of the exegesis of this verse, see Shepherd, *Textual World of the Bible*, 97–98. In Matthew 11:28–30, Jesus invites all who labor and are burdened to come to him so that he may give them rest. Those who take up his yoke and learn from him will find rest for themselves. His yoke is easy compared to that of the Pharisees (see Matt. 23:4; Acts 15:10; *b. Sanh.* 94b). This citation of Jeremiah 6:16a suggests that Jesus is the one of whom the Torah speaks (Matt. 5:17–18; John 5:39, 46–47).

3:17; Hab. 2:1])[31] who warned the people to pay attention to the sound of the shofar (Jer. 6:17a; *Tg. Jon.*: "Receive the words of the prophets"; cf. Jer. 4:5; 6:1; Amos 3:6–8). Jeremiah comments again, "And they said, 'We will not pay attention'" (Jer. 6:17b).

The consequence, an announcement of judgment, for the people's failure to walk the good road and pay attention to the prophets is introduced in 6:18 with the conjunction לכן ("Therefore") (cf. Jer. 6:15b, 21). The verb שמעו can be interpreted either as the third common plural suffixed conjugation (LXX: "the nations heard") or as the masculine plural imperative (MT: "hear, O nations"). As the fate of the people plays out on an international stage, the nations bear witness to the LORD's judgment (cf. Mic. 1:2). The remainder of 6:18 differs substantially between the Hebrew source of Greek Jeremiah and the MT. The Hebrew source of Greek Jeremiah has והרעים את עדריהם ("and those who shepherd their flocks").[32] This refers to the kings of the nations and their armies (see *Tg. Jon.* Jer. 6:3). The MT has ודעי עדה את אשר בם ("and know, O congregation, what is in/against them"). The "congregation" here is the congregation of nations summoned to hear and know. The object clause "what is in/against them" either refers to the sins counted against the people (*Tg. Jon.*) or to what the LORD is about to do with them because of their sins (Vulg.). It is possible that the object marker את indicates a scribal comment here (cf. Hag. 2:5).[33]

The summons at the beginning of 6:19a ("Hear, O land") is not directed to the land of Israel (contra *Tg. Jon.*) but to the inhabited earth and should be read in conjunction with the reference to the nations in 6:18. Another possibility is that the call is to the all-hearing ears of creation to bear witness to the LORD's judgment (see, e.g., Deut. 32:1; Isa. 1:2; Mic. 6:1–2). The LORD indicates that he is about to bring "calamity" upon the people, which refers to the coming of the enemy from the north (cf. Jer. 4:6). According to the Hebrew source of Greek Jeremiah, this is "the fruit of their apostasy" (פרי משובתם) (cf. Jer. 17:10: "the fruit of their deeds"; see also Jer. 2:19; 3:6, 8, 11, 12, 22; 5:6; 8:5; 14:7; Hos.

---

31. As in Jeremiah 6:13b, *Targum Jonathan* understands the prophets to be scribes and teachers of the Torah.

32. Emanuel Tov reconstructs this as ורעי עדרם but considers it the translator's "attempt to 'rescue' the sense of the verse within the options provided by the consonantal framework of his *Vorlage*" (*The Text-Critical Use of the Septuagint in Biblical Research*, 3rd ed. [Winona Lake, IN: Eisenbrauns, 2015], 184, 186). In other words, it is a pseudo-variant that only existed in the mind of the translator.

33. See Fishbane, *Biblical Interpretation in Ancient Israel*, 48–51.

14:5 [Eng., 14:4]). According to the MT, it is "the fruit of their thoughts" (פרי מחשבותם) (see Isa. 55:7; Jer. 4:14).[34] This is because the people have not paid attention to the LORD's words (*Tg. Jon.*: "the words of my servants the prophets") and have rejected his written Torah (cf. Isa. 5:24b; Jer. 2:8; 8:8–9). This combination also occurs in Zechariah 7:12a: "And as for their heart, they made it too hard to hear the Torah and the words that the LORD of hosts sent by his Spirit by the hand of the former prophets."[35]

The LORD questions the effort to bring to him frankincense from Sheba (see 1 Kgs. 10:1, 10; Ezek. 27:22) and "cinnamon" (LXX = קנמון) or "sweet cane" (MT emended: קנה טוב) from a distant land (Jer. 6:20a). Frankincense was an ingredient required for the incense in Exodus 30:34–38 (see also Jer. 41:5). Both cinnamon and cane were ingredients for the anointing oil (Exod. 30:23). The LORD goes on to say that burnt offerings do not make the worshipers who bring them acceptable to him (Jer. 6:20b; cf. Lev. 1:3; Jer. 14:12). The sacrifices are not pleasing to him (cf. Hos. 9:4). This text anticipates Jeremiah's temple gate speech in 7:1–15 in which the LORD calls into question the legitimacy of the cult in light of the syncretistic nature of the people's worship and their neglect of social justice and the moral will of God. It also anticipates Jeremiah 7:21–23, where the LORD commands the people to add their burnt offerings to their sacrifices and eat meat in violation of the law. He does because he did not command them concerning matters of burnt offering and sacrifice when he brought them out of Egypt. Rather, he simply called them to obey his voice and thus be his people (Exod. 19:4–6). The text of Jeremiah 6:20 also stands in a long line of passages that contrast the offerings and sacrifices with what the LORD truly requires of his people (e.g., 1 Sam. 15:22; Isa. 1:10–17; Hos. 6:6; Amos 5:21–24; Mic. 6:6–8; Ps. 40:7–9 [Eng., 40:6–8]; Prov. 21:3).[36] Of

---

34. "Jeremiah says that if someone intends to commit a sin, it is credited to him as though he had done so. But the Talmud says that that is so only if the intention bears fruit" (Neusner, *Jeremiah in Talmud and Midrash*, 331). See also Matthew 5:28; James 1:15.

35. This is different from statements about the Torah coming by means of the prophets (e.g., 2 Kgs. 17:13). It seems to imply an emergent canon of Moses and the Prophets (see Michael B. Shepherd, *Textuality and the Bible* [Eugene, OR: Wipf & Stock, 2016], 28–32). For example, Jeremiah is already part of a larger prophetic corpus in Daniel 9:2.

36. For a discussion of the interrelationship of these texts, see Shepherd, *Text in the Middle*, 120–22.

course, such offerings and sacrifices are acceptable from those whose hearts are right (Ps. 51:18–21 [Eng., 51:16–19]).

Jeremiah 6:21 serves as a concluding announcement of judgment introduced by לָכֵן ("Therefore") (cf. Jer. 6:15b, 18). The LORD points to the imminence of his giving a "stumbling block" to the people over which they will stumble (Jer. 6:21a; cf. Isa. 8:14–15; Jer. 6:15b). Holladay wonders whether this is a violation of the prohibition not to put a stumbling block in front of a blind person (Lev. 19:14), given the fact that the people of Judah and Jerusalem are in a sense "blind" (Jer. 5:21).[37] Since the covenant is broken (Jer. 11:10), it is possible that the law no longer applies (see, e.g., Jer. 7:21), but it is more likely that the judgment in Jeremiah 6:21 and the law in Leviticus 19:14 are not analogous. The law speaks of mean-spirited behavior toward those who are literally blind. The judgment in Jeremiah 6:21 applies to those who are willfully blind in a metaphorical sense, having become like the idols they worship (see Jer. 5:21; John 9:39, 41). "Fathers and sons together, a neighbor and his friend, they will perish" (Jer. 6:21b; cf. Mal. 3:24 [Eng., 4:6]).

6:22 Thus says the LORD, "Look, a people coming from (the) north, and nations [MT: a great nation] are aroused from earth's remote parts. 6:23 Bow and javelin / spear will they grasp. He is [nonn Mss: They are] cruel [LXX: bold], and he does not have compassion [MT: and they do not have compassion]. His sound [MT: Their sound] like the sea roars. Upon horses and chariots [MT: And upon horses will they ride] he is arranged like fire [Codex L: like a man][38] for battle [pc Mss: like a man of battle = warrior] against you, Daughter Zion." 6:24 "We have heard the report about them [MT: him]. Our hands have gone slack. Distress, it has gripped us, writhing [or, anguish] like that of a woman in labor. 6:25 Do not go out [MT kethiv: 2fs; MT qere: 2mp] into the field [or, country], and on the roads [MT: road] do not go [MT kethiv: 2fs; MT qere: 2mp]. For a sword of the enemies sojourns around [MT: For a sword of an enemy (or, For an enemy has a sword), terror from around]." 6:26 O daughter of my people [or, O my daughter—my people], gird on sackcloth and roll [LXX: sprinkle] in ashes. Mourning for an only child [LXX: for a

---

37. Holladay, *Jeremiah 1*, 223.

38. Rudolph (*BHS* apparatus): "every man" (כָּל אִישׁ). J. A. Emerton ("A Problem in the Hebrew Text of Jeremiah vi. 23 and l. 42," *JTS* NS 23 [1972]: 106–13): "each" (אִישׁ). The singular עָרוּךְ ("arranged") has prompted these conjectural emendations in order to provide a singular subject, but there is no textual evidence for them. The subject is likely the grammatically singular עַם ("people") from 6:22.

beloved] make for yourself, bitter wailing. For suddenly the destruc-tion [LXX: misery/hardship; MT: the destroyer; Tg. Jon.: plunderers] will come upon/against us [so Ziegler; Rahlfs: upon/against you]. 6:27 "A tester/assayer [or, tower; Tg. Jon.: chosen one] have I given/ appointed you among peoples of fortification [LXX: tested peoples; MT: my people, a fortification]. And you will know [LXX adds: me], and I will test their way [LXX: when I test their way; MT: and you will test their way]." 6:28 All of them are stubborn [LXX: disobedient; Codex L: turning aside ones of stubborn ones; mlt Mss: leaders of stubborn ones], slanderers [lit., goers of slander; LXX: going crookedly], bronze and iron [Tg. Jon.: as bronze mixed with iron], all of them act corruptly [LXX: are corrupted].[39] *6:29 Bellows blow [or, burn; LXX: failed].*[40] *By fire [MT kethiv: By their fire]*[41] *lead is consumed [LXX: failed].*[42] *For nothing he refines continually [NETS: in vain does a silversmith coin silver]. Their evil is not removed [LXX: Their evil did not melt; MT: And evil people are not removed]. 6:30 "Rejected silver" call them [MT: they call them], for the LORD has rejected them.*

This final section of Jeremiah 6 continues the theme of the enemy from the north (Jer. 1:13–15; 4:6, 13; 5:15; 6:1, 22). According to the Hebrew source of Greek Jeremiah, the LORD envisions a people from the north and a horde of nations roused from the remote parts of earth (Jer. 6:22; cf. Jer. 1:15; 25:9 [MT]; see also Jer. 25:32). The MT, however, has "a people" and "a great nation" (cf. Jer. 5:15; 50:3). The parallel text in Jeremiah 50:41 has singular forms in both the LXX and the MT but adds "many kings." It is important to note that the enemy from the north in Jeremiah 50:41–43, which is parallel to Jeremiah 6:22–24, is not Babylon but an enemy who comes against Babylon (Jer. 50:3). Thus, if the reader accepts the MT's identification of the enemy from the north with Babylon in Jeremiah 25:9, then he or she must posit a change of referent in Jeremiah 50–51. On the other hand, the Hebrew source text of Greek Jeremiah never makes the identification with

---

39. For the syntactical construction of this last clause in the Hebrew text, see Robert D. Holmstedt and Andrew R. Jones, "The Pronoun in Tripartite Verbless Clauses in Biblical Hebrew: Resumption for Left-dislocation or Pronominal Copula?" *JSS* 59 (2014): 53–89.

40. *Targum Jonathan* compares this to the voice of the prophets who urge the people in vain to return to the Torah.

41. NETS reads the phrase "from/by fire" with what precedes: "Bellows failed from a fire."

42. Bright (*Jeremiah*, 47, 49): "But the lead comes whole from the fire."

Babylon, which allows for the enemy from the north to be the same eschatological enemy in both 6:22–24 and 50:41–43 (see Ezek. 38–39).

According to 6:23, the members of the enemy army will grasp bow and javelin/spear. The enemy is cruel and without compassion (cf. Isa. 47:6). The MT and LXX of 50:42 (LXX 27:42) have the same variation between singular and plural forms as they do here. The sound of the enemy roars like the sea (cf. Isa. 5:30; 17:12). The remainder of the verse then differs considerably between the Hebrew source of Greek Jeremiah and the MT. The Hebrew source of Greek Jeremiah has, "Upon horses and chariots (על סוסים ורכב) he is arranged like fire (ערוך כאש) for battle against you, Daughter Zion" (cf. Jer. 4:13; 8:16; Hab. 1:8). The Leningrad Codex has, "And upon horses will they ride (ועל סוסים ירכבו), arranged like a man (כאיש) for battle [pc Mss: like a man of battle (כאיש מלחמה)] against you, Daughter Zion." Variation between אש ("fire") and איש ("man") occurs elsewhere (e.g., Ezek. 8:2). Carolyn Sharp thinks that the Hebrew source of Greek 6:23 and 50:42 (LXX 27:42) is due to scribal error,[43] but it is unlikely that the same unintentional error occurred in both places. It is quite possible that the unusual image of fire arranged for battle was intentionally changed in both places to the more expected image of a man arranged for battle (cf. Exod. 15:3; 1 Sam. 17:33; Isa. 3:2; 42:13; Jer. 46:3; Joel 2:5).

The text of 6:24–25 switches to the voice of the people. They have heard the report about the enemy from the north (Jer. 6:24a; cf. Josh. 2:10–11). Their hands have gone slack—an indication of their despair (cf. Isa. 13:7; Jer. 50:43a; Ezek. 7:17). Just as the enemy soldiers "grasp" (*hiphil* of חזק) their bows and javelins (Jer. 6:23a), so distress has "gripped" (*hiphil* of חזק) the people (Jer. 6:24b), "writhing like that of a woman in labor" (cf. Isa. 13:8; Jer. 4:31; 22:23; 49:24; 50:43b; Hos. 13:13; Mic. 4:9). When combined with the instructions in 4:5 and 6:1, the prohibitions in 6:25a ("Do not go out into the field, and on the roads do not go")[44] seem to give no option.[45] On the one hand, the people are

---

43. Carolyn J. Sharp, "'Take Another Scroll and Write': A Study of the LXX and the MT of Jeremiah's Oracles Against Egypt and Babylon," *VT* 47 (1997): 503.

44. The Hebrew source of Greek Jeremiah and the MT *qere* have second masculine plural forms addressed to the people from the people (or perhaps from Jeremiah or the LORD to the people). The MT *kethiv* has second feminine singular forms addressed either to the city (f.) of Jerusalem or to the land (f.) of Judah.

45. "'Don't go out to the field'—to do one's work of cultivation, of course; but what alternative is there? Huddle in the village? What contradictory

to get out of Jerusalem (Jer. 6:1); on the other hand, they cannot go into the fields or on the roads (Jer. 6:25a). According to the Hebrew source of Greek Jeremiah, this is because "a sword of their enemies sojourns around" (חרב לאיבים גרה מסביב) (Jer. 6:25b). According to the MT, it is because "a sword of an enemy [or, an enemy has a sword], terror from around" (חרב לאיב מגור מסביב) (cf. Jer. 20:3, 10; 46:5; 49:29).

Jeremiah appears to be the speaker in 6:26 according the final phrase of the MT and Ziegler's Greek text ("upon/against us"). Rahlfs' Greek text ("upon/against you") seems to have the LORD as the speaker.[46] The text is a call to the "daughter of my people" (or, "my daughter-my people"; cf. Jer. 4:11) to gird on sackcloth (cf. Jer. 4:8; Est. 4:1) and roll in ashes (cf. Jer. 25:34; Ezek. 27:30; Mic. 1:10). In context, this is not a call to repentance (as in Jon. 3:5, 8). It is a call to express outwardly their mourning over the now inevitable judgment. The people are to mourn as for the loss of an only child (cf. Amos 8:10; Zech. 12:10), the irreplaceable loss of the only heir—cause for "bitter wailing" indeed. The language here anticipates that of the description of Rachel's bitter weeping for her children in Jeremiah 31:15, which is the context out of which the hope of eschatological restoration comes (Jer. 31:16–40; see also Matt. 2:16–18). The reason for such mourning is stated succinctly in 6:26b: "For suddenly the destruction [MT: the destroyer] will come upon/against us" (cf. Jer. 4:20b).

The LORD addresses the prophet in 6:27 and says that he has given or appointed him as a בחון "among peoples of fortification" (בְּעַמִּי מִבְצָר; LXX: "tested peoples") (cf. Jer. 1:5b: "A prophet to the nations I appointed you"; see also Jer. 6:17 where the prophets are watchmen on watchtowers [cf. Hab. 2:1]). This Hebrew word can mean "tester" (i.e., "metal assayer") or "tower."[47] The context of 6:28–30 seems to favor the

---

orders we have heard! 'Flee to the walled cities!' (4:5)—but the enemy will destroy those cities (5:17). 'Get out of Jerusalem!' (6:1)—but then refugees will have nowhere to turn but thickets and caves (4:29). It does not appear that Yahweh as provided any escape for folk who want to stay alive. 'Don't even go out for a walk!' (One notes in passing the chiasmus of the two cola, in which the predicates are sandwiched by the two verbs.) It was learned in 5:6 that everyone who 'goes out' from the cities will be torn by the lion (that is, the enemy), and in 4:7 that the destroyed of nations has 'gone out' from his own place" (Holladay, *Jeremiah 1*, 225).

46. Due to itacism, ἡμῶν ("us") and ὑμῶν ("you") were commonly confused in transmission of Greek texts.

47. *Targum Jonathan* translates it as "chosen one" as if it were from the root בחר ("choose") rather than the root בחן ("test").

sense "tester." On the other hand, the imagery of Jeremiah 1:18 ("Look [MT: And as for me, look], I have made [or, appointed; lit., given] you today as a fortified city [לְעִיר מִבְצָר]") and the MT's version of 6:27a ("A tower have I given/appointed you among my people, a fortification [בְעַמִּי מִבְצָר]") seem to favor the sense "tower." Whereas the Hebrew source of Greek Jeremiah 6:27a has the prophet against the resistant fortified peoples, the MT has the word מבצר ("fortification") as a gloss for בחון ("tower"). Jeremiah is a tower among the LORD's people, that is, a fortification that absorbs the people's opposition.[48] Nevertheless, the second half of the verse does use the verbal root בחן ("test"): "And you will know [LXX adds: me], and I will test their way [LXX: when I test their way; MT: and you will test their way]" (Jer. 6:27b). This is either an explication of בחון in the sense "tester" or a play on בחון in the sense "tower." It is not clear what is meant by "you will know." Without an object it appears to mean that the prophet will know what the people really are when he tests them. The LXX supplies the object "me," which may suggest the sense "you will acknowledge me." According to the Hebrew source of Greek Jeremiah, it is the LORD who will test the way of life of the people ("and I will test [וּבָחַנְתִּי] their way"; cf. Isa. 48:9–11; Jer. 9:6 [Eng., 9:7]; 11:20; 17:10; 20:12; Zech. 13:9; Prov. 17:3), presumably through the prophet. According to the MT, however, it is the prophet who will test the way of the people ("and you will test [וּבָחַנְתָּ] their way").

Jeremiah reports in 6:28 that the people are all "stubborn" (סוֹרְרִים). The Leningrad Codex has "turning aside ones of stubborn ones" (סָרֵי סוֹרְרִים), which is often taken as a superlative construction (i.e., "rebels of rebels" or "arch rebels"; see GKC §133i), but the two words are from different roots (סור ["turn aside"] and סרר ["be stubborn"]) and together likely refer to those who stubbornly turn aside from the will of God (cf. Jer. 2:21; 5:23; 17:5b, 13b). Other Masoretic manuscripts have the homophonic "leaders of stubborn ones" (שָׂרֵי סוֹרְרִים), which could also yield the sense "stubborn leaders" (cf. Isa. 1:23; Hos. 9:15b) or refer to those who lead the way in stubbornness (cf. Jer. 2:33). The people are "slanderers" (cf. Lev. 19:16; Jer. 9:3b [Eng., 9:4b]; Ezek. 22:9; Prov. 11:13; 20:19). They are "bronze and iron" (cf.

---

48. The term מִבְצָר is common in the Hebrew Bible and is intelligible here. Nevertheless, several suggestions have been made that require revocalization: מִבְצָר "without gold" (see Keil, *Jeremiah*, 93–94; cf. Job 22:24); מְבַצֵּר "gold assayer" (*HALOT* 1:148); מִבֹּצֵר "rather than a grape-gatherer" (Holladay, *Jeremiah 1*, 228; cf. Jer. 6:9).

Jer. 1:18; 15:12; Ezek. 22:18, 20).[49] Rudolph (*BHS* apparatus) indicates that this latter description is probably to be deleted, yet there is no textual evidence for its deletion. It either speaks of the stubborn, hardened people as those with iron necks and bronze foreheads refusing to turn (see Isa. 48:4; cf. Jer. 3:3b; Ezek. 3:7), or it speaks of the people as the less valuable metal (bronze and iron = hard, stubborn, disobedient, unfaithful) compared to gold and silver (= obedient, faithful; see Isa. 60:17). BDB suggests that it is figurative of worthless people, the mere dross or slag of silver (BDB, 639). All of these people act corruptly (cf. Deut. 31:29; Isa. 1:4). They have been tested and found lacking.

The bellows in 6:29 represent Jeremiah's prophetic ministry (see *Tg. Jon.*; BDB, 656).[50] The verb נחר is either the *qal* stem of the root נחר ("blow"; cf. Job 39:20) or the *niphal* stem of the root חרר ("burn" or "be scorched"). According to the former, the bellows fan the fire, and by this fire the lead is consumed (or, Bright: "But the lead comes whole from the fire").[51] According to the latter, the bellows are scorched by the fire. The instrument has been overused in an effort to achieve the desired result, and it has consequently been burned by the very fire it was used to fan (cf. Jer. 20:9). According to Holladay, "What is not clear is whether Jrm is describing the extraction of silver from crude lead or the refining of impure silver by the use of lead as a flux."[52] Holladay and other commentators settle on the latter option (cf. Isa. 1:22; Ezek. 22:17–22).[53] In vain the refiner continues his work (cf. Isa. 48:9–11; 49:4a; Jer. 9:6 [Eng., 9:7]; Zech. 13:9). According to the Hebrew source of Greek Jeremiah, "Their evil is not removed" (רעתם לא נתקה). That is, the impurities of the people have not been extracted due to the failure of the refining process. The MT says, "And evil people are not removed" (ורעים לא נתקו). The people are thus called "rejected silver," for the LORD has rejected them (Jer. 6:30; cf. 1 Sam. 15:23; Jer. 7:29b). Just as they have rejected the Torah (Jer. 6:19b), so the LORD has rejected them.

---

49. *Targum Jonathan* has "as bronze mixed with iron" (cf. Dan. 2:43).

50. Calvin thinks that this refers to the punishments and judgments by which God had chastised his people without benefit (*Jeremiah*, 1:358). Cf. Isaiah 48:9–11. See also Jeremiah 5:14.

51. Normally אכל rather than תמם would be used for fire's consumption of something.

52. Holladay, *Jeremiah 1*, 232.

53. See Rashi; Keil, *Jeremiah*, 94; Thompson, *Book of Jeremiah*, 266–67; McKane, *Jeremiah I–XXV*, 157.

APPLICATION OF JEREMIAH 4:5–6:30

The lengthy section from Jeremiah 4:5 through 6:30 is largely devoted to development of the theme of the enemy from the north introduced in Jeremiah 1:13–15 (Jer. 4:6, 13; 5:15; 6:1, 22). The applicability of this section depends for the most part on which text of Jeremiah the reader is following and on what decision the interpreter has made regarding the identity of the enemy from the north. As noted in the Introduction, the Hebrew source behind Greek Jeremiah does not make an explicit identification of the enemy from the north with any historical foe, leaving open the possibility that the enemy is an eschatological one (see Ezek. 38:14–17; Dan. 9:1–2, 24–27). The ongoing relevance of this understanding of the text is self-evident. On the other hand, the MT identifies the enemy from the north with Babylon (Jer. 25:9). While there are some internal problems with this understanding of the enemy (e.g., Jer. 50:3), there is also the issue of whether it limits the applicability of the book to the time of Jeremiah. Such an identification essentially renders the book a documentary of past prophecy long since fulfilled without any real significance for future generations of readers apart from that supplied by means of artificial updates not tied to the author's intention.

The eschatological prophecy of the Hebrew source behind Greek Jeremiah continues to speak directly to modern readers about their future. Unfortunately, not everyone appreciates how applicable biblical prophecy is to daily life. The apostle Peter, however, reminds his Christian readers of the importance of what the prophets (OT) and apostles (NT) say about the last days (2 Pet. 3:2). He asks what sort of lives of holiness and godliness Christians should lead in light of the revelation of things to come (2 Pet. 3:11). In other words, knowledge of the final judgment of the wicked and the vindication of those who are righteous by faith in Christ should transform the way believers think and conduct themselves today. The prophets themselves are models of this, awaiting events that they would not necessarily see in their lifetime (Isa. 8:16–18; Hab. 3:17–19; Dan. 12:13).

The book of Jeremiah thus transcends any particular historical moment. Readers must be careful not to allow their familiarity with the book and its story of the past to breed contempt and complacency. They must come to the text afresh with an appreciation for the uniqueness of what has been entrusted to them in the book. It is important for readers to ask themselves whether they genuinely act as though they believe that the book of Jeremiah is in fact the revelatory word of God given in a specific form and sequence by design (Jer. 1:1–3). If the book were suddenly to appear as such today for the first time (cf. Josiah's discovery of the book of Torah in 2 Kgs. 22–23), would readers do as they so often do now and set their own agenda for the book, making it address personal concerns and the hot topics and trends of contemporary culture?[54]

Alternatively, would they approach the book on its own terms? Would they mine it for what it is and for all that it is worth, setting aside other issues and aligning themselves with matters of importance to the biblical author? While prophecy of the last days may not be what is immediately on the minds of readers, it is imperative to acknowledge that it is a central concern of the author; and if readers accept the book as the word of God, then they are obliged to do the hard work of reorienting themselves to this concern.

---

54. We often assume that whatever is important to us must also be important to God and thus must be addressed by the biblical authors, but this is not necessarily the case. If we fail to recognize this, we run the risk of making the biblical authors address things that they do not intend to address.

JEREMIAH 7:1–8:3

7:2 Hear the word of the L*ORD*, *all Judah [LXX: Judea].*[1] *7:3 Thus says the* L*ORD* *[MT adds: of hosts] the God of Israel, "Improve your ways and your deeds, and I will settle you [Vulg., Luther: and I will dwell with you] in this place. 7:4 Do not trust [see GKC §119s] in the words of deception [Tg. Jon.: the words of the false prophets], for they will not benefit you at all [for they will not benefit you at all > MT], saying, 'The temple of the* L*ORD*, *the temple of the* L*ORD* *it is [MT: The temple of the* L*ORD*, *the temple of the* L*ORD*, *the temple of the* L*ORD* *are they (Syr.: are you)].'*[2] *7:5 For if you do indeed improve your ways and your deeds and practice justice [MT: if (Syr.: and if) you practice justice] with one another 7:6 and do not oppress [Syr.: and do not take advantage of and do not oppress] a resident foreigner or [or > MT] an orphan or a widow and do not pour out innocent blood and do not go after other gods to your own harm, 7:7 then I will settle you [pc Mss, Vulg., Luther: then I will dwell with you] in this place, in the land that I gave to your forefathers from everlasting to everlasting. 7:8 Look, you are trusting [LXX: If you trust] in the words of deception [Tg. Jon.: in the words of the false prophets] so as not to benefit 7:9 and murdering and committing adultery and stealing and swearing falsely and sending sacrifices up in smoke to Baal*[3] *and going after other gods that you do not know 7:10 to your own harm [to your own harm > MT] and you come and stand before me in the house upon which my name is called and say, 'We are rescued [Syr.: Rescue us],' in order to do all these abominations [NETS: 'We have kept away from doing all these abominations'].*[4] *7:11 A den / cave of violent people [LXX: robbers], is that what my house [MT: this house] upon which my name is called there [there > MT] is*

---

1. MT 7:1–2: "The word that came to Jeremiah from the L*ORD*, saying, 'Stand in the gate of the house of the L*ORD* and proclaim [*Tg. Jon.*: prophesy] there this word and say, "Hear the word of the L*ORD*, all Judah, those who enter these gates to worship the L*ORD*."'"

2. *Tg. Jon.*: "Before the temple of the Lord you are worshiping; before the temple of the Lord you are sacrificing; before the temple of the Lord you are bowing. Three times during the year you are appearing before him."

3. The Greek uses the feminine τῇ Βααλ for τῇ αἰσχύνῃ ("shame") (see MT Jer. 11:13).

4. MT: "Will you steal, murder, and commit adultery and swear falsely and send sacrifices up in smoke to Baal and go after other gods that you do not know and then come and stand before me in this house upon which my name is called and say, 'We are rescued,' in order to do all these abominations?"

in your eyes?[5] *Indeed / Also I, look, I have seen," the prophetic utterance of the* LORD. *7:12 "For / Indeed go to my place [Tg. Jon.: the place of my sanctuary] that was in Shiloh where I caused my name [Tg. Jon.: my dwelling presence] to dwell formerly and see what I did to it because of the evil of my people Israel. 7:13 And now, because you have done all these things [MT adds: the prophetic utterance of the* LORD], *and I spoke to you [Tg. Jon.: and I sent to you; MT adds: rising early and speaking (i.e., urgently speaking)], and you did not listen to me [to me > MT], and I called you [Tg. Jon.: and they prophesied to you], and you did not answer [Tg. Jon.: turn], 7:14 I will do to the house upon which my name is called, in which you are trusting, and to the place that I gave to you and to your forefathers just as I did to Shiloh, 7:15 and I will cast [Tg. Jon.: exile] you from before me just as I cast [Tg. Jon.: exiled] your relatives, all the seed of Ephraim."*

This is Jeremiah's speech at the temple gate. The response to this speech is in Jeremiah 26. The speech itself has three main sections (cf. Jer. 11:1–17; 17:19–27; 34:8–22): opening proclamation (Jer. 7:1–7), accusation (Jer. 7:8–12), and announcement of judgment (Jer. 7:13–15). The shorter introduction to the speech in the Hebrew source behind Greek Jeremiah 7:2 is generally considered more original (cf. Jer. 2:1–2): "Hear the word of the LORD, all Judah" (cf. Jer. 2:4; 17:20; 19:3; 21:11; 22:2, 29; 29:20; 31:10; 34:4; 42:15; 44:24, 26). The text added around this in the longer introduction of the MT (Jer. 7:1–2) is a mosaic of introductory material from elsewhere in the book: "The word that came to Jeremiah from the LORD saying" (cf. Jer. 11:1; 18:1; 30:1); "Stand in the gate of the house of the LORD and proclaim there this word and say" (cf. Jer. 17:19; 26:2); "those who enter these gates" (cf. Jer. 17:20b; 22:2b); "to worship the LORD" (cf. Jer. 26:2). The text of Jeremiah 26:1 sets this event in the "beginning" of the kingdom of Jehoiakim who reigned from 609 to 598 BC (cf. MT Jer. 27:1; 28:1).[6] According to Jeremiah 26:2, Jeremiah was not to withhold a word of all that the LORD commanded him to speak to the people.[7]

---

5. The Syriac begins this verse with the conjunction "lest" and apparently does not understand 7:11a to be a question but a negative purpose clause.
6. Calvin infers from the address to "all Judah" that this must have taken place on a feast day when the majority of the inhabitants would have been present (*Jeremiah*, 1:362).
7. It has been suggested that the speech in Jeremiah 7 is an example of "Entry Torah" (cf. Pss. 15 and 24), which would instruct the worshiper in how to be fit for temple worship (see Gerhard von Rad, *Old Testament*

Jeremiah introduces the Lord's discourse in 7:3 with a formula common to the book as a whole: "Thus says the Lord [MT adds: of hosts] the God of Israel" (see comment on Jer. 2:2). The relationship between the next two clauses seems to be that of a protasis and an apodosis ("if . . . then") not unlike what is explicit in the more extended version of this in 7:5–7. "Improve your ways and your deeds," says the Lord, "and I will settle you [Vulg., Luther: and I will dwell with you] in this place." The language of the first part of this is easy to locate elsewhere (see Jer. 4:18; 7:5; 17:10; 18:11; 23:22; 25:5; 26:13; 32:19). The difficulty of the second part lies both in the vocalization of ואשכנה אתכם as either וַאֲשַׁכְּנָה אֶתְכֶם ("and I will settle you") or וְאֶשְׁכְּנָה אִתְּכֶם ("and I will dwell with you") and in the identification of the referent of "this place" (the land or the temple). On the one hand, both the LXX and the MT favor the first option ("and I will settle you"), in which case "this place" refers to the land of the covenant as in verse 7 (cf. Jer. 14:13 [MT], 15; 24:5–6). This is an unusual use of the *piel* of this root (only in Num. 14:30; Jer. 7:3, 7), but the idea that obedience to the covenant stipulations leads to blessing in the land and avoids exile is well established (e.g., Lev. 26; Deut. 28). On the other hand, the Latin Vulgate and Luther's German translation take the second option ("and I will dwell with you"), in which case "this place" refers to the temple (cf. Jer. 7:12 where "my place" refers to the sanctuary at Shiloh; see also LXX Jer. 14:13).[8] The Lord brought the people out of Egypt in order to dwell among his people in a sanctuary, initially the tabernacle (Exod. 25:8; 29:43–46; cf. *Tg. Neof.* Gen. 9:27; Lev. 26:11–12; Num. 35:34; Ezek. 37:27; Zech. 2:14 [Eng., 2:10]; 8:3; Rev. 21:3). He said that he would choose a place "to establish" (לשכן) his name there (Deut. 12:5, 11; 14:23; 16:2, 6, 11; 26:2), and this became identified with Solomon's temple in Jerusalem (1 Kgs. 6:12–13; 8:12–13, 29–30, 35; Jer. 7:10; Neh. 1:9; see also Ezek. 43:7, 9).[9] Failure to heed the Lord's instruction, however, would result

---

Theology, vol. 1, *The Theology of Israel's Historical Traditions*, trans. D. M. G. Stalker [San Francisco: HarperSanFrancisco, 1962; repr., Louisville: Westminster John Knox, 2001], 377–78). See the discussion in McKane, *Jeremiah I–XXV*, 159–60.

8. See the discussion in Abraham Geiger, *Urschrift und Uebersetzungen der Bibel in ihrer Abhängigkeit von der inner Entwickelung des Judenthums* (Breslau: Hainauer, 1857), 320–23. See also the repeated use of "the place," "this place," and "that place" to describe Bethel in Genesis 28:11, 16, 17, 19 (cf. Isa. 66:1; see also John 11:48).

9. The tabernacle and the temple were temporary reminders of the unbroken fellowship with the Lord that humanity enjoyed in the garden of Eden.

in the loss of this special divine presence among the people (2 Kgs. 23:27; Ezek. 11:22–23). Thus, given the fact that both interpretations of Jeremiah 7:3 work equally well in context, it does not seem prudent simply to choose one or the other. This is perhaps a case of intentional ambiguity or double entendre.

In Jeremiah 7:4, the LORD instructs the people through the prophet not to trust in "the words of deception" (cf. Jer. 5:17b). *Targum Jonathan* interprets these words to be those of the false prophets encouraging the people to rest in the security of their temple worship (cf. Jer. 5:12; 27:10; Mic. 3:11).[10] Such words will not benefit the people at all (> MT; cf. Jer. 2:8b, 11b; 7:8). The MT has these words in the form of a threefold repetition of the phrase "the temple of the LORD" (cf. MT Isa. 6:3; MT Jer. 22:29; MT Ezek. 21:32 [Eng., 21:27]), which *Targum Jonathan* refers to the worshiping, sacrificing, and bowing before the temple.[11] The Hebrew source behind Greek Jeremiah only has the phrase twice (cf. 1QIsaᵃ 6:3; LXX Jer. 22:29; LXX Ezek. 21:32).[12] Its repetition is apparently a kind of mantra designed to bolster confidence in the mere presence of the temple structure and its sacrificial system to the neglect of the covenant relationship with the LORD and its moral code (cf. Jer. 3:16).[13] The pronoun המה ("they") at the end of the verse in the MT may have "the words of deception" as its antecedent. It has also been suggested that it refers to the halls of the entire temple complex (cf. 2 Chr. 8:11).[14] The proposal in the *BHS* apparatus is that המה is an

---

They also pointed to the hope of a new sanctuary in the eschaton (Ezek. 40–48; Rev. 21:22).

10. It is also possible that the words were about Baal worship in the temple (see Jer. 2:8b; 5:31; 7:9).

11. The Targum also notes that the people appear before the LORD three times a year (see Exod. 23:14–19). Both Redak and Calvin understand the threefold repetition to refer to the three parts of the temple: the court, the temple, and the Holy of Holies (Rosenberg, trans., *Mikraoth Gedoloth: Jeremiah Volume One*, 65; Calvin, *Jeremiah*, 1:364). The Talmud (*b. Nazir 32b*) interprets it to refer to the destruction of the first and second sanctuaries (see Neusner, *Jeremiah in Talmud and Midrash*, 319).

12. "According to Sutcliffe היכל יהוה המה was originally a marginal note on דברי שקר and so the twofold היכל יהוה of Sept. preserves the original text" (McKane, *Jeremiah I–XXV*, 160–61).

13. "These are solemn and powerful words; they have a spell-like character and they rivet themselves in the minds of those who recite them or hear them recited. The false doctrine is reinforced by a liturgy" (McKane, *Jeremiah I–XXV*, 161; see also Holladay, *Jeremiah 1*, 242).

14. Keil, *Jeremiah*, 97.

abbreviation for הַמָּקוֹם הַזֶּה ("this place"; cf. Jer. 7:3b, 6a, 7a, 12a). On the other hand, the Syriac reflects the second masculine plural pronoun אַתֶּם ("you"), which has been attributed by some to early Christian influence (cf. 1 Cor. 3:16–17).[15]

כִּי אִם ("For if") at the beginning of Jeremiah 7:5 introduces a series of protases that runs through 7:6.[16] The apodosis comes in 7:7. This is essentially an expanded version of what the reader finds in 7:3. It explains why the instruction in 7:4 not to trust in the words of deception should be heeded. The text of 7:5 adds an infinitive absolute to the exhortation of 7:3 to improve ways and deeds and includes the further condition to practice justice with one another (cf. Jer. 5:1). The kind of justice envisioned here is parsed in the Hebrew text of 7:6 by fronting three different groups in their respective clauses. First, resident foreigners, orphans (the fatherless), and widows (the husbandless) are not to be oppressed (cf. Exod. 22:20–23 [Eng., 22:21–24]; Lev. 19:33–34; Deut. 10:18; 14:29; 16:11, 14; 24:19–21; Isa. 1:17, 23; Jer. 5:28; Zech. 7:10; Mal. 3:5; Ps. 146:9). These are put for all the disadvantaged and defenseless who should be protected rather than abused by those in positions of power.[17] Second, innocent blood is not to be shed (cf. Prov. 6:17). According to Keil, "Shedding innocent blood refers in part to judicial murders (condemnation of innocent persons), in part to violent attacks made by the kings on prophets and godly men, such as we hear of in Manasseh's case, 2 Kings 21:16."[18] And third, other gods are not to be pursued to the detriment of the people (cf. Jer. 1:16; 2:5, 8, 11, 13; 7:9–10 [LXX]; 25:6; 35:15). Thus, the people are to love God and love their neighbor (Lev. 19:18; Deut. 6:5; Matt. 22:34–40). If they do, then the LORD will settle the people in the land of the covenant given to their forefathers (Jer. 7:7; cf. Gen. 12:7; 13:15; 15:18;

---

15. See Gillian Greenberg, "Jeremiah in the Peshitta," in *The Book of Jeremiah: Composition, Reception, and Interpretation*, eds. Jack R. Lundbom, Craig A. Evans, and Bradford A. Anderson (Leiden: Brill, 2018), 354–56. See also Wenthe, ed., *Jeremiah, Lamentations*, 64–65.

16. The use of the negation אַל in the second clause of MT 7:6, which would indicate a prohibition rather than a protasis (cf. Jer. 22:3), should be corrected to לֹא. This error in the MT also affected the first clause in some witnesses (see *BHS* apparatus).

17. See Bullinger, *Figures of Speech*, 629.

18. Keil, *Jeremiah*, 97. See 2 Kings 21:16; 24:4; Jeremiah 2:34; 19:4; 22:3, 17; 26:15; Sirach 34:21–22. See also 2 Chronicles 24:20–22 and Matthew 5:21–26.

Num. 14:30; Deut. 12:1–5; Jer. 25:25).[19] According to the terms of the Sinai covenant, the people cannot stay in the land if they are idolaters and breakers of the covenant relationship (Lev. 26; Deut. 28), but the offer of life and blessing in the land through obedience to the law is only hypothetical (Lev. 18:5; Ezek. 20:11, 13, 21, 25; Rom. 7). No one is able to keep the law (Ps. 143:2; Rom. 3:20; Gal. 3:11–12). The law only serves the expose the people's sin (Rom. 5:20).[20] It does not solve the problem. Therefore, the judgment is still imminent and inevitable (Jer. 4:5–6:30; 7:13–15) despite the occasional indication that things would be different if the people would only obey (e.g., Jer. 6:8; 17:24–27; 26:3; 36:3). Only with circumcised hearts in the new covenant relationship by faith in the person and work of Christ will the people be counted righteous and live righteously (Gen. 15:6; 26:5; Deut. 30:6; Isa. 53:11; 61:3b; Jer. 4:1–4; 31:31–34).

Just as the prohibition not to trust in the words of deception in 7:4 immediately follows the implied protasis-apodosis of 7:3, so the accusation of trust in the words of deception in 7:8 immediately follows the explicit protases-apodosis of 7:5–7: "Look, you are trusting [LXX: If you trust] in the words of deception [Tg. Jon.: the words of the false prophets] so as not to benefit." The MT has הנה ("Look") at the beginning of 7:8 (cf. Jer. 17:15), while the Hebrew source behind Greek Jeremiah has הן, which the Greek translator interpreted as the Aramaic word for "If" (cf. Jer. 2:10b; 3:1),[21] but this interpretation cannot be correct since the following context has no clear apodosis. The word הן in Hebrew normally means "Look." Verse 8 concludes with "so as not to benefit" (לבלתי הועיל) (cf. Isa. 44:10), which, given the use of the *hiphil* of this root elsewhere (e.g., Jer. 2:8b, 11b; LXX 7:4a; 23:32b), probably speaks of how the words of deception that encourage a false sense of security in idolatrous temple worship do not benefit the people in the manner expected by them.

Jeremiah 7:9 highlights the people's failure to keep the Decalogue with several representative examples (cf. Hos. 4:2; Zech. 5:4; Mal. 3:5;

---

19. This verse has the same vocalization issues as 7:3 ("then I will settle you [pc Mss, Vulg., Luther: then I will dwell with you]"), but the *piel* ("I will settle you") is more appropriate here because "this place" in this context is "the land that I gave to your forefathers from everlasting to everlasting."
20. "And sacrifices, what was their design? To shew the people that they deserved eternal death, and also that they were to flee to God for mercy, there being no other expiation but the blood of Christ" (Calvin, *Jeremiah*, 1:369).
21. See Walser, *Jeremiah*, 241.

Matt. 19:18; Mark 10:19; Luke 18:20; Rom. 13:9).[22] The Decalogue, which is placed at the beginning of the giving of the law in Exodus 20:1–17 (cf. Exod. 34:10–26) and at the beginning of the exposition of the law in Deuteronomy 5:6–21 (see Deut. 1:5; 4:44), represents the covenant in its entirety (Deut. 4:13). The Hebrew source behind Greek Jeremiah presents these as a continuation of 7:8 in the following order: murdering, committing adultery, stealing, swearing falsely, burning incense/sacrifices to Baal, and going after other gods.[23] The list of wrongdoing then continues in 7:10. The MT, however, starts 7:9 with an interrogative ה and has a slightly different order: "Will you steal, murder, and commit adultery and swear falsely and burn incense/sacrifices to Baal and go after other gods that you do not know?" The text of 7:10 then describes what the people presume to do after they commit the wrongs of 7:9. It appears that the order of the first four items in the Hebrew source behind Greek Jeremiah 7:9 is a secondary adjustment of the order found in the MT. This adjustment was made to align the text with the order in MT Exodus 20:13–16 and Deuteronomy 5:17–20 (but not LXX). רצח is specifically "murdering" rather than "killing" in general, as is commonly recognized. נאף ("committing adultery") is the act whereby a man has sexual relations with another man's wife (e.g., 2 Sam. 11; Jer. 5:8). It does not refer to acts of fornication or sexual immorality in general. The term has also been used to describe Judah's unfaithfulness to her husband Yahweh in her relationship with Baal (Jer. 3:9; 5:7; cf. Hos. 3:1). גנב is usually interpreted to be "stealing" more broadly, but the Covenant Code initially understands it to be "kidnapping" (Exod. 21:16). "Swearing falsely" (השבע לשקר) is likely a combination of Exodus 20:7 ("Do not take the name of the LORD your God in vain") and Exodus 20:16 ("Do not testify against your neighbor as a false witness") (cf. Deut. 5:11, 20), referring to the taking of the LORD's name as part of an oath to support false testimony in a court of law (Lev. 19:11–12; Deut. 10:20; 19:18; Ps. 24:4). Going after other gods not known (see Deut. 11:28; 13:3, 7, 14; 29:25 [Eng., 29:26]; 32:17; Jer. 19:4; 44:3; see also Amos 3:2) refers to Exodus 20:3–6 (Deut. 5:7–10), which is illustrated in the golden calf episode (Exod. 32; Deut. 9) as the making and worship of an image/idol intended to represent the LORD, the God who brought the people out of Egypt (Exod. 32:4; Neh. 9:18).[24]

---

22. See Gary D. Martin, *Multiple Originals: New Approaches to Hebrew Bible Textual Criticism* (Atlanta: SBL, 2010), 205–48.

23. Jeremiah 17:21–27 adds the breaking of the Sabbath law.

24. Jewish tradition counts the prologue in Exodus 20:2 as the first of the "ten words." The text of Exodus 20:3–6 constitutes the second. Protestant

The specific manifestation of this in Jeremiah's context is the sending of sacrifices up in smoke to Baal (cf. Jer. 1:16; 2:5, 8, 11, 13; 11:13; 18:15). Baal was not only a non-god or false god but also a replacement for Yahweh represented by golden calf idols (see 1 Kgs. 12:28; Hos. 2:10 [Eng., 2:8]; 8:4–5; 13:1–2).

The phrase "to your own harm" in the Hebrew source behind Greek Jeremiah at the beginning of 7:10 is a continuation of 7:9 (cf. Jer. 7:6b; 25:6b). The MT does not have this phrase. The people come and stand before the LORD (cf. Gen. 18:22; 1 Kgs. 17:1) represented by the ark of the covenant (Exod. 16:33–34; Jer. 3:16) and act as if there is nothing amiss in the manner of their worship (cf. Isa. 1:11–15) in the house upon which the LORD's name is called (see 1 Kgs. 8:43; Jer. 7:11, 14, 30; 14:9; 15:16; 25:29; 32:34; 34:15). The syntax of what the people say when they come into the temple can be understood in more than one way. According to the KJV, the remainder of the verse is the quote of the people, "We are delivered to do these abominations."[25] Of course, the idea with this rendering is not that the people are actually saying that they are rescued by the LORD for the purpose of doing what they think are abominable acts such as idolatry. On the contrary, the people think that their worship is perfectly acceptable, but their behavior "speaks" the words of 7:10b (cf. Jer. 2:20). On the other hand, the placement of the disjunctive accent *athnach* in the MT suggests that the quote of the people stops short of the purpose clause: "'We are rescued [Syr.: Rescue us],' in order to do all these abominations." That is, the people express their sense of security in the temple, but the LORD can see that this only serves to free them to do what is contrary to his will.

The word for "den" or "cave" is fronted in the Hebrew text of 7:11a: "A den/cave of violent people [LXX: robbers], is that what my house [MT: this house] upon which my name is called there [there > MT] is

---

tradition separates the prohibition of "other gods" in Exodus 20:3 from the prohibition of images/idols in Exodus 20:4–6 and counts these as the first two of the ten words. Samaritan tradition counts Exodus 20:3–6 as the first of the ten words, which leaves room at the end of the words for an additional one about the building of the altar on Mount Gerizim (see SP Deut. 27:4).

25. The LXX also interprets the remainder of the verse to be the quote of the people, but it gives a very different sense: "We have kept away from doing all these abominations" (NET). It is not clear, however, that the translator had a different source text from that found in the MT. The verb "rescued" has been read in the sense "kept away from," and "in order to do" has been read as "doing." The suggestion in the *BHS* apparatus that "in order to do" should be read as "in order to change" has no attestation in the textual witnesses.

in your eyes?" This is a rhetorical question. The temple has become something like a hideout for criminals (cf. 1 Sam. 22:1; 24:4; Zeph. 1:9; see also Ezek. 7:22; 18:10; Rom. 2:22). The people think that they can live in the manner outlined in 7:9 and then take refuge in the rituals of temple worship (see Rom. 6:1). This text is coupled with Isaiah 56:7 in Mark's account of Jesus' cleansing of the temple: "My house will be called a house of prayer for all the nations, but you have made it a den of robbers" (Mark 11:17; cf. Matt. 21:13; Luke 19:46).[26] This is essentially what the temple is in the eyes of the people according to their own actions, and such disregard for the temple has not escaped the notice of the LORD ("Indeed/Also I, look, I have seen") (Jer. 7:11b). Therefore, it will not escape his judgment (see 1 Sam. 16:7; Isa. 29:15; see also Rashi).

The function of כִּי at the beginning of 7:12 is not immediately clear. If it is causal ("For"), then it must introduce an explanation of the judgment implied by the final words of 7:11. It may also be asseverative ("Indeed"), but the precise relationship of this to the foregoing is not evident. The people are instructed to go to the LORD's "place" (*Tg. Jon.*: "the place of my sanctuary") that was once in Shiloh where he caused his name to dwell formerly. This was the location of the tabernacle and the ark of the covenant in the days of Eli and Samuel (1 Sam. 1–3). The people can now go there and witness the remaining evidence of divine judgment due to the evil of "Israel,"[27] but the biblical account in 1 Samuel 4 describes the loss of the ark of the covenant to the Philistines rather than the destruction of Shiloh and the exile of its people, although it is usually assumed from the archaeological evidence that the Philistines did destroy Shiloh in close temporal proximity to this event. At the very least, the people can see that the tabernacle and the ark of the covenant, which gave Shiloh a false sense of security as they persisted in idolatry (1 Sam. 4:3; 7:3), are no longer there.

---

26. John's account of temple cleansing comes toward the beginning of his Gospel (John 2:13–22) rather than toward the end as in the Synoptic Gospels. This may be deliberate rearrangement for literary and theological purposes that override concern for chronological presentation (cf. Luke 4:16–30), but differences in details suggest that John's account describes a separate event from the one in the Synoptics, an event that occurred earlier in Jesus' earthly ministry. One very important difference in detail is the lack of citation from Isaiah and Jeremiah. The citation in John's account is from Psalm 69:10 (Eng., 69:9) (John 2:17).

27. It is not clear if this is "Israel" as it was known formerly or the northern kingdom of Israel (see Jer. 7:15).

Verse 13 begins the announcement of judgment with וְעַתָּה ("And now"; cf. לָכֵן [Jer. 7:20]). Because the people have done all the things outlined in Jeremiah 7:8–11 and have not responded well to the LORD who has spoken to them through the prophets (cf. Jer. 7:25–27; 11:7 [MT]; 25:4; 26:5; 29:19 [MT]; 35:15, 17; 44:4; see also Isa. 65:12; 66:4), the LORD will do to the current object of the people's trust (Solomon's temple) and to the land what he did to Israel's former object of trust— the tabernacle and the ark of the covenant at Shiloh (Jer. 7:14; 26:6; cf. 1 Kgs. 9:6–9; Ezek. 24:21). And he will "cast" (i.e., exile) them from before him just as he did their relatives, "all the seed of Ephraim" (Jer. 7:15; cf. Jer. 52:3). In what way is the fate of Shiloh in the hands of the Philistines (1 Sam. 4) analogous to what happens to Judah in the hands of the Babylonians (Jer. 39; 52)? Both are examples of divine judgment. In both cases, the ark of the covenant is lost (see Jer. 3:16). Shiloh ceases to be the location of the tabernacle (1 Sam. 21:1; 1 Chr. 16:39). Likewise, the temple in Jerusalem is destroyed. There is no account in the biblical narrative of the devastation of Shiloh that is analogous to what happens to Jerusalem and the cities of Judah, al- though the destruction of Shiloh apparently did occur. There is also no account nor extrabiblical evidence of an exile of the people of Shiloh to Philistia comparable to the Babylonian exile. Thus, the comparison is made to the Assyrian destruction and exile of the northern kingdom of Israel ("all the seed of Ephraim"), renewing the analogy between Israel and Judah from Jeremiah 3:6–11 where it was clear that Judah had not learned any lessons from Israel's downfall (see 2 Kgs. 17:13–23). "Ephraim," the tribe named after the preferred son of Joseph (Gen. 48), is commonly used by Hosea and Isaiah for the northern kingdom of Israel due to the size of its territory and its status in the north (BDB, 68). Shiloh was located in the territory of Ephraim. Thus, the story of its demise in 1 Samuel 4 became a foreshadow of the fate of the northern kingdom in general (see Judg. 18:30–31; Ps. 78:60–67).

7:16 "And as for you, do not pray on behalf of this people, and do not lift up on their behalf a cry [NETS: and do not request to petition (τοῦ δεη- θῆναι) about them; Brenton: and intercede not for them to be pitied (τοῦ ἐλεηθῆναι)] or a prayer [LXX: and do not pray/vow], and do not entreat me on their behalf [on their behalf > MT], for I am not listening [MT: for I am not hearing you].[28] *7:17 Do you not see what they are doing in the cities of Judah and in the streets of Jerusalem? 7:18 Their sons [MT: The sons] gather wood, and their fathers [MT: and the fathers] kindle the*

---

28. For the Greek variation in this verse, see Walser, *Jeremiah*, 243.

fire, and their women/wives [MT: and the women/wives] knead dough to make sacrificial cakes [Tg. Jon.: tunics] for the host of the sky [MT: the work of the sky; Tg. Jon.: the star(s) of the sky (= Venus); Vulg.: the queen of the sky], and they pour out drink offerings to other gods in order to provoke me. 7:19 Is it I whom they are provoking?" the prophetic utterance of the Lord. "(Are they) not (provoking) themselves for the sake of the shame of their faces?" 7:20 Therefore, thus says the Lord [MT: Lord God], "My anger and my wrath are being poured out to/on this place and [and > MT] on the humans and on the animals and on all the trees of the field and on the fruit of the ground, and it will burn and not be extinguished [pc Mss: and there will be no one extinguishing]."

7:21 Thus says the Lord [MT adds: of hosts, the God of Israel], "As for your burnt offerings, add them to your sacrifices and eat meat. 7:22 For I did not speak with your forefathers and I did not command them when I brought [MT kethiv: when bringing] them out of the land of Egypt concerning matters of burnt offering and sacrifice. 7:23 But this word is what I commanded them, saying, 'Obey my voice, and I will become your God; and as for you, you will become my people, and you will walk in all my ways [MT: the way] that I command you in order that it may go well for you.' 7:24 And they did not listen to me [to me > MT], and they did not incline their ear, and they walked/went [MT adds: in counsels] in the stubbornness of their evil heart/mind, and they were [pc Mss: and they walked/went] backward and not forward [Tg. Jon.: and they turned against the worship of me neck/back and did not put the fear of me before them]. 7:25 From the day that their [MT: your] forefathers came out of the land of Egypt and [and > MT] to this day, I sent to you [Ms, Syr.: them] all my servants the prophets daily [cf. Syr.] and [and > MT] urgently sending [lit., rising early and sending]. 7:26 But they did not listen to me, and they did not incline their ear, and they hardened/stiffened their neck more than their forefathers [MT: and they hardened/stiffened their neck, they acted evilly more than their forefathers]." 7:28 "And you will speak to them this word: 'This is the nation that did not obey the voice of the Lord and did not accept discipline. Faithfulness has perished from their mouth.[29] *7:29 Shave the consecrated long hair of your Nazirite vow [see Symm.;*

---

29. MT 7:27–28: "And you will speak to them all these words, and they will not listen to you; and you will call to them, and they will not answer you. And you will say to them, 'This is the nation that did not obey the voice of the Lord its God and did not accept discipline [7:28a > Syr.]. Faithfulness has perished and has been cut off from their mouth.'"

LXX: your head; Syr.: your hair; Tg. Jon.: Tear away concerning your leaders who have gone into exile] and throw it away, and lift up upon lips [MT: bare places] a lament. For the LORD *has rejected and forsaken a generation doing this [LXX: the generation that did these things; MT: the generation of his fury; Syr.: the transitory generation; Tg. Jon.: the people of the generation who have transgressed his word].'"*

The temple gate speech in Jeremiah 7:1–15 concluded with the comparison to Shiloh (Jer. 7:12–15; 26:6), but chapter 7 will continue to develop the themes of the speech. A shift in address occurs at the beginning of verse 16a: ואתה ("And as for you"). Here the LORD prohibits Jeremiah from praying on behalf of the people (cf. Jer. 11:14; 14:11; see also Jer. 37:3; 42:2, 20; Lam. 3:8; 2 Macc. 15:14).[30] This is a striking prohibition for a prophet, given that a prophet was one whose role was in part to function as an intercessor (e.g., Gen. 20:7). It is even more striking when the reader remembers that Jeremiah has already been presented as a prophet like Moses (Jer. 1:4–10) whose success as an intercessor is well documented (Exod. 32:11–14; Deut. 9:25–29; Jer. 15:1). The rhetorical effect of this suggests that the judgment announced in Jeremiah 7:13–15 is inevitable despite the efforts of the prophet (cf. Ezek. 14:12–23). Jeremiah is not to lift up a cry or a prayer on the people's behalf (but see Jer. 14:7–9, 19–22). He is not to meet with the LORD for them (cf. Jer. 15:11). According to Jeremiah 14:11, Jeremiah is not to pray on behalf of the people for good. In the Hebrew source behind Greek Jeremiah, the reason for the prohibition is simply that the LORD is not listening (Jer. 7:16b). The MT, however, says that LORD is not listening to Jeremiah in particular. This clause is different in the parallel text of Jeremiah 11:14, which says that the LORD will not hear when the people call (see Jer. 7:27; 11:11; cf. Isa. 1:15; Amos 5:23; see also Jer. 29:12; 33:3).[31]

The rhetorical question in 7:17 ("Do you not see what they are doing in the cities of Judah and in the streets of Jerusalem?") suggests that the reason for the LORD's refusal to listen to Jeremiah's prayer on behalf of the people should be self-evident (see Jer. 7:34; 11:6; 33:10; 44:6, 17, 21). On the surface this sounds like the behavior of the people

---

30. Robert R. Wilson sees a parallel with Ezekiel who is largely limited to words of judgment from the time of his call (Ezek. 3:22–27) until the fall of Jerusalem (Ezek. 24:25–27; 33:21–22). His dumbness prevents him from interceding for the people ("An Interpretation of Ezekiel's Dumbness," *VT* 22 [1972]: 91–104).

31. See Parke-Taylor, *Formation of the Book of Jeremiah*, 190–92.

is out in the open for all to see (cf. Jer. 2:28 [LXX]; 11:13), but 7:18 describes the activity as occurring in the home (cf. Deut. 6:4–9). Everyone in the family is involved (cf. Exod. 32:2). The sons gather wood; the fathers kindle the fire; and the women or wives knead dough (Jer. 7:18a). According to the MT accentuation, which has the *athnach* under בצק ("dough"), all these actions (and not just the kneading of dough) are for the purpose of making "sacrificial cakes" (כונים) (Jer. 7:18b). This term is perhaps related to כיון in Amos 5:26: "And you will lift up the tent of your king and the pedestal/shrine [כיון] of your images, the star of your god(s) that you made for yourselves."[32] Rashi suggests that the cakes in Jeremiah 7:18 are in the shape of a star (cf. MT Jer. 44:19, which says that the cakes are made in the image of the one for whom they are made; see also Exod. 20:4; Deut. 5:8).[33] According to the Hebrew source behind Greek Jeremiah, these cakes are "for the host of the sky" (לצבא השמים), which refers to the forbidden worship of the sun, moon, and stars (Deut. 4:19; 2 Kgs. 21:5; Jer. 8:2; 19:13; Acts 7:42; see also Jer. 10:11–12). According to the MT, they are "for the work of the sky" (לִמְלֶכֶת [לִמְלֶאכֶת] השמים), which is presumably a reference to the same luminaries (cf. *Tg. Jon.*: "the star[s] of the sky" [= Venus]), but the same consonantal text can be revocalized to mean "for the queen of the sky" (לִמַלְכַּת השמים) (see Vulg.), which would likely be a reference to the goddess Ishtar ("star") (cf. Jer. 44:17, 19; see Judg. 2:13).[34] The second half of 7:18b adds that the family also pours out drink offerings to other gods in order to provoke the LORD (cf. Deut. 4:25; 31:29; 32:16; Jer. 8:19; 11:17; 25:7b [MT]). Such religious practice explains the unacceptable nature of the people's temple worship (Jer. 7:8–11). The people worship the host of the sky at home and then come to the temple to perform its rituals. It is difficult to think of the people consciously doing this "in order to" (למען) provoke the LORD. Thus, it is tempting to understand this to indicate result ("so that") rather than purpose ("in order that"), but BDB (775) interprets this word in a manner that is consistent with its meaning elsewhere: "in rhetorical passages, the issue of a line of action, though really undesigned, is represented by it ironically as if it were designed."

---

32. BDB (475) says that the term in Amos 5:26 is equivalent to the Assyrian name of the planet Saturn. The Masoretes have vocalized it according to the pattern of שקוץ ("detested thing").

33. Rosenberg, trans., *Mikraoth Gedoloth: Jeremiah Volume One*, 68.

34. See also James B. Pritchard, ed., *Ancient Near Eastern Texts Relating to the Old Testament*, 3rd ed. (Princeton, NJ: Princeton University Press, 1969), 95, 250, 578.

The first question in 7:19a—"Is it I whom they are provoking?" (note the fronting of the pronoun "I")—expects a negative answer. Of course, the announcement of judgment in 7:20 shows that the people's actions have indeed provoked the LORD to anger, but the real harm will come to the people themselves for what they have done (see Jer. 2:5, 17, 19; cf. Jer. 44:7–8). Thus, the second question in 7:19b—"(Are they) not (provoking) themselves for the sake of the shame of their faces?" (again, note the fronting of the pronoun "themselves" in contrast to the pronoun "I" in 7:19a)—expects a positive answer. The people certainly do not intend to provoke themselves "for the sake of the shame of their faces" (see Ps. 44:16 [Eng., 44:15]; Dan. 9:7–8; Ezra 9:7; 2 Chr. 32:21; see also Jer. 3:24; 11:13), but the question is given ironically as if the people were bringing about their own demise by design. The wording of 7:19 is not unlike that of Deuteronomy 32:21: "As for them, they have made me jealous with a non-god, they have provoked me with their empty idols. As for me, I will cause them to be jealous with a non-people, with a senseless nation I will provoke them." Therefore, the LORD announces in 7:20a that his anger and wrath are being poured out on "this place" (i.e., both the land of the covenant [Jer. 7:8, 14] and the temple [Jer. 7:3, 4, 12]), on the humans and animals, and on all the trees of the field and the fruit of the ground (cf. Jer. 4:23–28; 9:9 [Eng., 9:10]; 12:4; 15:3; Ezek. 38:20; Joel 1:12; Nah. 1:6; Zeph. 1:3). The completeness of the destruction is reminiscent of the plagues in Egypt (Exod. 8:13, 14 [Eng., 8:17, 18]; 9:9, 25, 33; 10:12, 15; 12:12; cf. Rev. 6; 8–9; 16). The fire of judgment will burn and not be extinguished (Jer. 7:20b; cf. Gen. 19:24; 2 Kgs. 22:17 [= 2 Chr. 34:25]; Isa. 1:31; 66:15, 24; Jer. 4:4b; 17:27; 21:12b; 39:8; 52:13; Dan. 7:9–10).

Jeremiah 7:21a begins a new subunit with the formula, "Thus says the LORD." In light of the abuses outlined in 7:8–11, 18, the LORD essentially commands the people here to disobey the sacrificial laws of Leviticus 1–7.[35] They are offering their sacrifices in vain (see Jer. 6:20; 14:12; cf. Jer. 44:25b).[36] Because the people have violated the Decalogue, it matters very little that they adhere to the cultic laws (cf. 1 Sam. 15:22; Isa. 1:10–17; Hos. 6:6; Amos 5:21–24; Mic. 6:6–8; Ps. 40:7–9 [Eng., 40:6–8]; Prov. 21:3; Mark 12:33).[37] Their behavior has

---

35. "The imperative is used in the sense of an ironical challenge" (GKC §110a). See also Ezekiel 9:7; 20:39.
36. Redak: "Do whatever you wish; it will be of no use" (Rosenberg, trans., *Mikraoth Gedoloth: Jeremiah Volume One*, 70).
37. Of course, when the heart is right, such sacrifices are an acceptable form of worship (Ps. 51:18–21 [Eng., 51:16–19]).

negated the substance of their sacrifices. "As for your burnt offerings, add them to your sacrifices and eat meat" (Jer. 7:21b). The fronting of "burnt offerings" in the Hebrew syntax indicates the topic or focus. The imperative ספו comes from the root יסף ("add") rather than the root ספה ("sweep away"). The adding of burnt offerings to other sacrifices could refer to the mingling of offerings and sacrifices that were to be kept separate. It could also refer to the empty multiplication of offerings and sacrifices to no avail (cf. Isa. 29:1; Hos. 8:13; Amos 4:4–5). The command to eat meat is in clear violation of the instruction for burnt offerings (Lev. 1), which were to be consumed by fire completely.[38]

The reason for the commands in 7:21 is stated in 7:22–23: "For I did not speak with your forefathers and I did not command them when I brought [MT *kethiv*: when bringing] them out of the land of Egypt concerning matters of burnt offering and sacrifice. But this word is what I commanded them, saying, 'Obey my voice, and I will become your God; and as for you, you will become my people, and you will walk in all my ways [MT: the way] that I command you in order that it may go well for you'" (see BDB, 405).[39] When the LORD brought Israel out of Egypt, he said, "And now, if you will indeed obey my voice and keep my covenant, you will be my special possession apart from all the peoples, for all the inhabited land is mine" (Exod. 19:5; cf. Jer. 11:4).[40] Israel had received the instruction for the Passover (Exod. 12), the Sabbath (Exod. 16), and the unidentified "statute and judgment" in Exodus 15:25, but the law of the old covenant (including the instructions for burnt offerings and sacrifices) had not been given. The people already had a covenant relationship with the LORD—the covenant with the patriarchs Abraham, Isaac, and Jacob (Gen. 15:18; Exod. 2:24), which was based on simple faith and obedience (Gen. 15:6; 26:5).[41] They were to be a "kingdom of priests" in the context of that covenant (Exod. 19:6), but when the

---

38. Worshipers were allowed to partake of peace/fellowship offerings (Lev. 3), and this is apparently what the instruction to eat meat in Deuteronomy 12:15 is referencing in the context of bringing burnt offerings and sacrifices to the central place of worship (Deut. 12:11, 14). Holladay, citing Calvin, suggests in his commentary on Jeremiah 7:21 that sacrificial observance had become a pretext for eating meat (*Jeremiah 1*, 261; cf. Hos. 9:4; 1 Cor. 11:20–22).

39. See Exodus 6:7; Leviticus 26:12; Deuteronomy 5:33; 29:12 (Eng., 29:13); Jeremiah 11:4; 24:7; 30:22; 31:1, 33; 32:38.

40. See Rashi in Rosenberg, trans., *Mikraoth Gedoloth: Jeremiah Volume One*, 70.

41. Circumcision was the sign of the covenant (Gen. 17; see 1 Cor. 7:19; Gal. 5:6; 6:15).

Lord gave the instruction to the people to meet with him on Mount Sinai (Exod. 19:10–13), the people transgressed (Exod. 19:16b), and their relationship with the Lord fundamentally changed.[42] No longer were they allowed to meet with the Lord on the mountain (Exod. 19:17, 23), and they were now a "kingdom with priests" (Exod. 19:22) rather than a "kingdom of priests." Furthermore, the law was added secondarily in Exodus 20–Leviticus 27 (also Deut. 12–26) because of transgression (Gal. 3:19). The making of the Sinai covenant in Exodus 24 was based on the Decalogue and Covenant Code in Exodus 20–23 (cf. Deut. 4:13), not on the sacrificial laws in Leviticus 1–7.[43] Thus, the burnt offerings and sacrifices were not an original or essential part of the covenant relationship, yet they were the only part of the law that the people in Jeremiah's day practiced, precisely because they thought that they could go through the motions of the rituals without a right heart for the Lord and still maintain their lifestyle of idolatry and immoral behavior.

The forefathers, much like the present generation (cf. Jer. 2:1–13), did not listen to the Lord or incline their ear (Jer. 7:24a; cf. Jer. 6:10, 17; 11:8). They walked or went in "the stubbornness of their evil heart/ mind" (see Jer. 3:17; 5:23; 9:13 [Eng., 9:14]; 11:8; 13:10; 16:12; 18:12; 23:17; see also Jer. 2:20; 5:5). The MT says that they went "in counsels, in the stubbornness of their evil heart/mind." Rudolph suggests in the *BHS* apparatus that "in counsels" (במעצות) has been added from Psalm 81:13 (Eng., 81:12).[44] The text of Jeremiah 7:24b ("and they were

---

42. See the discussion in Sailhamer, *Pentateuch as Narrative*, 51–57. According to Exodus 19:12, the people were to watch themselves "going up in/on the mountain" (עלות בהר) on a designated path. The text does not say that they were to keep themselves "from going up in/on the mountain" (מעלות בהר; *Tg. Onk.*; *Tg. Ps.-J.*). At the blast of the horn (Exod. 19:13), they were to go up "in/on the mountain" (בהר), not merely "to the mountain." Working out the logistical problem of having such a large group (Exod. 12:37) on the mountain is beside the point. The meaning of the phrase בהר is well established in Hebrew usage. But when the horn blasted in Exodus 19:16a, the people did not go up in/on the mountain as instructed. Rather, they trembled in the camp (Exod. 19:16b). Subsequently, they were only able to stand "at the foot of the mountain" (בתחתית ההר; Exod. 19:17). No longer would they be able to go up in/on the mountain (Exod. 19:23).

43. See Redak in Rosenberg, trans., *Mikraoth Gedoloth: Jeremiah Volume One*, 70 (but see also Exod. 20:24).

44. The context of the psalm is similar to that of the Jeremiah passage: "'I am the Lord your God who brought you up out of the land of Egypt. Open

backward and not forward") could be read with what precedes as an explanation of what it meant to go in the stubbornness of an evil heart/mind. It could also be read with the following text of 7:25a, which would indicate that the people have gone backward and not forward from the time of the exodus to the present day (cf. Deut. 9:24; Jer. 3:25; 32:30), but 7:25a is normally read as the subordinate temporal clause to the main clause in 7:25b. According to *Targum Jonathan*, the expression "backward and not forward" means that they turned a stubborn, resistant neck or back against the worship of the LORD and did not put the fear of the LORD in front of them (see Jer. 2:27; 7:26; 15:6; 32:33; Neh. 9:16–17).

From the time that the forefathers came out of the land of Egypt to the present period (cf. Jer. 11:7; 32:20), the LORD has sent his servants the prophets "daily" (יום ["day"] = יומם ["daily"] or יום יום ["each day"]; see Syr.), urgently sending them (Jer. 7:25; cf. 2 Kgs. 17:13; Jer. 7:13 [MT]; 11:7 [MT] 25:4, 5; 26:5; 29:19 [MT]; 32:33; 35:14–15; 44:4; Dan. 9:10; Ezra 9:10–11), but the people have not listened or inclined their ear (Jer. 7:26a; cf. Jer. 7:24a). The present generation has even hardened or stiffened its neck like a stubborn animal more than their forefathers did (Jer. 7:26b; cf. Judg. 2:19; Jer. 11:10; 16:12; 17:23; 19:15; see also Jer. 2:20, 27; 5:5). This language of the stiff neck likely comes from the description of the people involved in the golden calf incident at Sinai (Exod. 32:9; 33:3, 5; 34:9; Deut. 9:6, 13). The people in Jeremiah's day have surpassed such an iconic moment in their history with their rampant idolatry (Jer. 2:28b). The MT adds an extra verb ("they acted evilly" [הרעו]) to 7:26b: "and they hardened/stiffened their neck, they acted evilly more than their forefathers."

The LORD's message to the people, which began in 7:21, concludes at the end of 7:26. He now addresses the prophet in 7:27–28. There are, however, three different versions of these two verses. The Hebrew source behind Greek Jeremiah only has the first clause of 7:27 ("And you will speak to them this word [MT: all these words]") and the reported discourse of 7:28 ('This is the nation that did not obey the voice of the LORD [MT adds: its God] and did not accept discipline. Faithfulness has perished [MT adds: and has been cut off] from their mouth'). The Syriac has all of 7:27 ("And you will speak to them all these words, and they will not listen to you; and you will call to them, and they will

---

wide your mouth that I may fill it.' But my people did not obey my voice, and Israel did not yield to me [cf. Ps. 81:9–10 (Eng., 81:8–9)]. And I sent them away in the stubbornness of their heart. They went in their counsels (במועצותיהם)" (Ps. 81:11–13 [Eng., 81:10–12]).

not answer you"), but it lacks 7:28a (MT: "And you will say to them, 'This is the nation that did not obey the voice of the LORD its God and did not accept discipline'") and only has 7:28b ("Faithfulness has perished and has been cut off from their mouth"). The MT has the longer text, including what is missing from the Greek in 7:27 and what is missing from the Syriac in 7:28a: "And you will speak to them all these words, and they will not listen to you; and you will call to them, and they will not answer you. And you will say to them, 'This is the nation that did not obey the voice of the LORD its God and did not accept discipline. Faithfulness has perished and has been cut off from their mouth.'" Gerald Janzen has proposed that the text of 7:27, which is preserved in the Syriac ("and they will not listen to you; and you will call to them, and they will not answer you"), and the text of 7:28a, which is preserved in the Greek ("This is the nation that did not obey the voice of the LORD [MT adds: its God] and did not accept discipline"), are variant readings that now appear together in the conflate text of the MT.[45] As anticipated in Jeremiah 1:16–19, the people will not listen to the prophet when he calls to them (Jer. 7:27; cf. Isa. 6:9–10; Jer. 7:13; Ezek. 3:7–11). Rather, they will actively oppose him. Therefore, the LORD will not answer when the people call (Jer. 11:11; cf. Jer. 29:12; 33:3). Jeremiah's function will be to point out the failure of the people to obey the LORD's voice and receive his discipline (Jer. 7:28a; cf. Jer. 2:30; 4Q439, 469; see also Jer. 31:18). "Faithfulness" has perished (and, according to the MT, has been "cut off") from their mouth (Jer. 7:28b; cf. Isa. 57:1; see also Deut. 32:20; Ps. 78:8). This refers to the manner in which the people speak their oaths (Jer. 5:1–3) and to the way in which they speak to one another (Jer. 9:2, 4 [Eng., 9:3, 5]).[46] They do so in "deception" (שֶׁקֶר) rather than faithfulness.

There is a difference of opinion about whether Jeremiah 7:29 belongs with what precedes or with what follows. On the one hand, the text appears to be a continuation from 7:28 of the words Jeremiah is to speak to the people. On the other hand, some understand the conjunction כִּי at the beginning of 7:30 to introduce an explanation of 7:29, but the conjunction כִּי at the beginning of 7:30 likely introduces the

---

45. Gerald H. Janzen, *Studies in the Text of Jeremiah*, Harvard Semitic Monographs 6 (Cambridge, MA: Harvard University Press, 1973), 204n8.

46. It is also possible that this refers to the departure of "murmuring in" the Torah (private reading; Josh. 1:8; Isa. 59:21; Ps. 1:2) and "calling in" the Torah (public reading; Deut. 31:12; 2 Kgs. 23:2b; Neh. 8:3, 8) from the mouths of the people. Note the relationship between Jeremiah 17:5–8 and Psalm 1.

reason given in 7:30–31 for the announcement of judgment that begins in 7:32.[47] Therefore, the present commentary reads 7:29 as a continuation of 7:28. The commands, "Shave the consecrated long hair of your Nazirite vow and throw it away, and lift up upon lips [MT: bare places] a lament," are all feminine singular, referring to Judah as a woman (Jer. 7:29a; cf. Jer. 2:2; 3:1; etc.). A man or a woman could take a Nazirite vow (Num. 6:2). Cutting the long hair of the vow (Num. 6:5) indicated either defilement (Num. 6:9) or completion (Num. 6:13, 18). Keil comments, "The Nazarite, defiled by the sudden occurrence of death near to his person, was bound to cut off his long hair, because by this defilement his consecrated hair had been defiled; and just so must the daughter of Zion cut off her hair and cast it from her, because by her sins she had defiled herself, and must be held as unconsecrated."[48] This is also considered an act of mourning (cf. Mic. 1:16; Job 1:20), lifting up upon "lips" (שפתים), according to Greek Jeremiah, or upon "bare places" (שפים), according to the MT, a lament (cf. Jer. 3:21; 9:9 [Eng., 9:10]). The reason for the commands in 7:29a is given in 7:29b. The Lord has rejected (cf. Jer. 6:30) and forsaken (cf. Jer. 12:7; 23:33, 39) "a generation doing this" (דור עבד דנה; see *BHS* apparatus; LXX: the generation that did these things), which is apparently a reference back to the behavior described in the present chapter. The MT, however, has "the generation of his fury" (דור עברתו; cf. Isa. 10:6). The Syriac interprets the same text as "the transitory generation" (see BDB, 716–720). *Targum Jonathan* has "the people of the generation who have transgressed (עבר) his word."

7:30 "Because the sons of Judah did what was evil in my eyes," the prophetic utterance of the Lord, "they set up their detested idols in the house upon which my name is called to defile it [or, to make it ceremonially unclean], 7:31 and they built the high place [MT: high places] of Topheth, which is in the valley of Ben Hinnom, to burn their sons and their daughters in the fire, which I did not command them [them > Codex L; Tg. Jon. adds: in my Torah], and it did not enter my mind, 7:32 therefore, look, days are coming," the prophetic utterance of the Lord, "and they will never say again [MT: and it will never be said again] 'the high place of Topheth' [MT: 'Topheth'] or 'the valley of Ben Hinnom,' but 'the valley of the slain' [MT: 'the valley of slaughter'], and

---

47. The text of Jeremiah 7:30–8:3 as a unit has been added by a second hand in 4QJer[a].
48. Keil, *Jeremiah*, 105. See also 1 Samuel 1:11; Judges 13:5; 16:17; Jeremiah 35:5–6; Acts 21:23–24.

*they will bury in Topheth without place [LXX: because there is no place],
7:33 and the corpse [LXX: the dead; Syr.: corpses] of this people will
become food for the flying creatures of the sky and for the large land
animals, and there will be no one to scare them off [Syr.: no one to de-
liver], 7:34 and I will cause to cease from the cities of Judah and from
the streets of Jerusalem sound of rejoicing and sound of joy, sound of
bridegroom and sound of bride, for a waste place will all [all > Codex L]
the land become. 8:1 At that time," the prophetic utterance of the* LORD,
*"they will bring out [kethiv: and they will bring out] the bones of the
kings of Judah and the bones of its leaders and the bones of the priests
and the bones of the prophets [Tg. Jon.: false prophets] and the bones of
the inhabitants of Jerusalem from their graves, 8:2 and they will spread
them to the sun and to the moon and to all the stars [and to all the stars
> MT] and to all the host of the sky, which they prefer and which they
serve/worship and after which they go and which they seek [LXX: cling
to] and to which they prostrate themselves. They [4QJer^c: And they] will
not be mourned [MT: collected; cf. Jer. 16:4], and they will not be buried;
and they will be as a likeness [LXX: pattern, example] on the surface of
the ground [MT: as dung on the surface of the ground will they be], 8:3
for they have chosen death rather than life [cf. Syr., Tg. Jon., Vulg.; MT:
and death is chosen rather than life], and [they have done so] for all
the remnant [MT: by all the remnant], those who are left from [4QJer^c:
למן] this family [LXX: that generation; MT: this evil family] in all the
places [or, in every place; MT: in all the remaining places^49] where I have
driven [4QJer^c: scattered; cf. Jer. 23:1; Tg. Jon. exiled] them," [MT adds:
the prophetic utterance of the* LORD *of hosts].*

This unit has been added by a second hand in 4QJer^a, but its presence in all other textual witnesses strongly suggests that its omission

---

49. 4QJer^c has הנשארות instead of the MT's הנשארים written above the line
between המקמות and אשר. This supralinear insertion and the absence of
either reading in the Hebrew source behind Greek Jeremiah suggest that
the original text had no modifier here. The noun מקום is a masculine noun
that forms its plural with a feminine ending. The MT's masculine modifier agrees with the actual grammatical gender of the noun. The reading
in 4QJer^c agrees morphologically with the feminine ending. Redak notes
the strangeness of the MT wording (Rosenberg, trans., *Mikraoth Gedoloth:
Jeremiah Volume One*, 75. Keil (*Jeremiah*, 107), despite the presence of the
article on המקמות ("the places"), suggests that it is in the construct state:
"in all the places of those who remain whither I have driven them." This is
in violation of Hebrew grammar and syntax.

by the first hand is due to scribal oversight.[50] Therefore, 4QJer[a] likely does not bear witness to a shorter, more original text. As suggested in the commentary on 7:29, verses 30 and 31 of chapter 7 should be read as the reason for the judgment announced in 7:32–34 rather than as an explanation for the rejection in 7:29. The use of נאם יהוה ("the prophetic utterance of the LORD") helps to delineate the subunits in this section (Jer. 7:30, 32; 8:1).[51] Verse 30 begins, "Because the sons of Judah [see Jer. 32:30–32; 50:4, 33; Hos. 2:2 [Eng., 1:11]; Obad. 12) did what was evil in my eyes [cf. Deut. 17:2; Judg. 2:11; 1 Kgs. 11:6; et al.]." This is explained to mean that "they set up their detested idols [see Deut. 29:16 [Eng., 29:17]; 1 Kgs. 11:5, 7; 2 Kgs. 23:24; Jer. 4:1; 13:27; 16:18; 32:34; Ezek. 5:11; et al.; cf. Dan. 9:27; 11:31; 12:11] in the house upon which my name is called [cf. Jer. 7:10–11; 32:34] to defile it [or, to make it ceremonially unclean (i.e., common/unholy and unfit for worship)]," as if by design (cf. Jer. 2:7b; 7:10, 18). This is precisely the problem addressed in Jeremiah's temple speech (e.g., Jer. 7:9).

7:31a adds that "they built[52] the high place [MT: high places] of Topheth, which is in the valley of Ben Hinnom, to burn their sons and their daughters in the fire." High places were alternative places of worship to the central location in the Jerusalem temple (e.g., 1 Kgs. 14:23; 2 Kgs. 17:9–10; 21:3; see BDB, 119). The place name "Topheth" has been variously explained (see 2 Kgs. 23:10; Isa. 30:33; Jer. 19:6–14). Rashi comments, "That is Molech, which was of copper, and they would heat it up from underneath it with its hands spread out and heated. And they would place the child on his hands, and he would be burnt and moan, and the priests would beat drums so that the father should not hear his son's voice and take pity. It is called Topheth because of the drum (תוֹף), Hinnom because of the child's moaning (נָהֲמַת)."[53] On the other hand, Keil suggests, "It is formed from תּוּף, to spit out, like נֹפֶת from נוּף; and means properly a spitting out, then that before or on which one spits (as in Job 17:6), object of deepest abhorrence. It is transferred

---

50. See Janzen, *Studies in the Text of Jeremiah*, 174.

51. The occurrence in MT 8:3 is absent from the Hebrew source behind Greek Jeremiah.

52. This is a *qatal* (not *weqatal*) verb coordinated with the *qatal* verbs in 7:30 and under the governance of the causal conjunction. It should not be emended to *wayyiqtol* as if this were giving a narrative account. These are simply back references to actions that warrant the judgment announced in 7:32–34. Cf. Jeremiah 19:5.

53. Rosenberg, trans., *Mikraoth Gedoloth: Jeremiah Volume One*, 72.

to the worship of Moloch here and 19:6, 13ff., and in 2 Kings 23:10."[54] According to Thompson, however, "The name Topheth may derive from an Aramaic word *tēpaṯ*, 'fireplace,' while the name Ben-hinnom may derive from the former owner of the valley. The Hebrew vocalization of *Tēpaṯ* into *Tōpeṯ* was probably a deliberate change in which the vowels of the word *bōšeṯ*, 'shame,' were transferred to other consonants in order to emphasize the shameful character of the altar in question."[55] This last suggestion, that the Masoretic vocalization of תפת ("Topheth") is patterned after בשת ("shame"), finds warrant from the parallel text in Jeremiah 19:5 (see also Jer. 32:35): "and they built the high places of Baal to burn their children in the fire [MT adds: burnt offerings to Baal]." The name "Baal," for which בשת ("shame") appears in 3:24 and MT 11:13 (cf. Ishbaal/Ishbosheth [MT and LXX[Ms] 2 Sam. 2:8]), is in place of the name "Topheth." The vowels of the name "Molech" (מֹלֶךְ), whose consonants can also be read as "king" (מֶלֶךְ), are also patterned after בֹּשֶׁת ("shame"). Molech, also known as Milcom (1 Kgs. 11:5; Jer. 49:1, 3 [LXX 30:1, 3]), was the detested idol of the Ammonites (1 Kgs. 11:7) to whom the people sacrificed their children by fire (2 Kgs. 23:10; Jer. 32:25) contrary to the Torah (Lev. 18:21; 20:2–4; Deut. 12:31; 18:10). This practice was particularly prominent during the time of Manasseh (2 Kgs. 21:6; cf. 2 Kgs. 16:3; 17:17; Ezek. 16:20–21; 20:26, 31; 23:37, 39; Ps. 106:38; 2 Chr. 28:3) and was then forbidden during the time of Josiah (2 Kgs. 23:10), but it persisted among the people (see Isa. 57:5). Thus, "the valley of Ben Hinnom" (גיא בן הנם) (see Josh. 15:8; see also Jer. 2:23), from which comes the name "Gehenna," became associated with a hellish place of torment and the eternal destination of the wicked (e.g., Matt. 5:22, 29, 30). In Jeremiah 7:31b, the LORD stresses that he did not command the people to perform child sacrifice (cf. Jer. 19:5; 32:35). He says that this never entered his mind. The manner in which this is stated suggests that the people may have thought that they were in fact offering their children in obedience to the LORD's instruction (see Gen. 22:2).[56] The question is asked in Micah 6:7b, "Should I give my firstborn for my transgression, the fruit of my womb for the sin of my soul?" It appears that the instruction in Exodus 13:2 (cf. Exod. 22:28 [Eng., 22:29]; Neh. 10:37) to set apart the firstborn

---

54. Keil, *Jeremiah*, 106.

55. Thompson, *Book of Jeremiah*, 294.

56. Rashi: "and when I did speak to Abraham to slaughter his son, it did not enter My mind that he slaughter, but only to make his righteousness known" (Rosenberg, trans., *Mikraoth Gedoloth: Jeremiah Volume One*, 73). Cf. James 2:21–24.

of humans and animals to the LORD was read in isolation from the later instruction about the redemption of the firstborn (Exod. 13:13; Num. 18:15–16) and the replacement of the firstborn by the tribe of Levi (Num. 3:12–13, 41; 8:16–17).

לכן ("therefore") at the beginning of 7:32 introduces the announcement of judgment for the accusations made in 7:30–31 (cf. Jer. 7:20). The LORD points out ("look") that "days are coming" (cf. Jer. 9:24 [Eng., 9:25]; 16:14; 19:6; 23:5, 7; 30:3; 31:27, 31; MT 33:14; 48:12; 49:2; 51:47, 52) when "they will never say again [MT: and it will never be said again] 'the high place of Topheth' [MT: 'Topheth'] or 'the valley of Ben Hinnom,' but 'the valley of the slain [הַהֲרֵגָה]' [MT: 'the valley of slaughter (הַהֲרֵגָה)']" (Jer. 7:32a; cf. Jer. 3:16; 16:14; 19:6; 23:7; 31:29). These will no longer be simple place names known for shameful and detestable acts of idolatry and child sacrifice. They will be known as places of judgment (capital punishment [cf. Exod. 32:27]) for crimes committed against the LORD. The punishment will fit the crime (Exod. 21:23–25; Lev. 24:20). They will bury people in Topheth "without place" (cf. MT Jer. 19:11b). According to the LXX, this means they will bury people there because there is no other place, presumably because of the "vast numbers of the slain" elsewhere.[57] Bright, however, says that the place is "so full that many bodies cannot be buried at all" (cf. the expressions in Josh. 17:16a; Isa. 5:8b; Zech. 10:10b).[58] Holladay has yet another suggestion: "I suspect that the clue lies in the meaning of מָקוֹם as 'special place, cultic place.' This is the meaning in 7:3, 7, and 12, and in 7:20. Jrm has in mind the principle of 'let the punishment fit the crime.' If Yahweh has withdrawn his support from the people, then he will reverse Deut 12:5—there will be no more 'place' that Yahweh has chosen."[59]

The corpse(s) of the people will become food for the flying creatures of the sky and for the large land animals (Jer. 7:33a; cf. Deut. 28:26; 1 Sam. 17:44, 46; 1 Kgs. 14:11; 16:4; 21:24; Jer. 15:3; 16:4; 19:7; 34:20; Ezek. 29:5; Ps. 79:2). This is also an eschatological image in Ezekiel 39:4, 17–20 and Revelation 19:17–18. There will be no one to scare off such scavengers (Jer. 7:33b; cf. Gen. 15:11; 2 Sam. 21:10). The fate of the people here is the covenant curse for disobedience articulated in Deuteronomy 28:26. The LORD will cause the joyous sounds of wedding festivities to stop from the cities of Judah and the streets of Jerusalem (Jer. 7:34a; cf. Jer. 16:9; 25:10; 33:11; Hos. 2:13 [Eng., 2:11]; Bar. 2:23; Rev. 18:23; see also Jer. 7:17). McKane comments, "Weddings are not

---

57. See Keil, *Jeremiah*, 106.
58. Bright, *Jeremiah*, 57.
59. Holladay, *Jeremiah 1*, 269.

only occasions of joy, but are signs that the life of the community is always being renewed. They are acts of faith in its future and a promise that there will be new families and new generations to carry on its life."[60] All this will be lost, for the whole land will become a "waste place" (Jer. 7:34b; cf. Lev. 26:31, 33; Jer. 4:23–31; 22:5; MT 25:11, 18; 27:17; 44:2, 6, 22; Ezek. 5:14; 35:4).

"At that time" (Jer. 8:1; cf. Jer. 3:17; 4:11; 31:1; MT 33:15; 50:4, 20; see also "in those days" [Jer. 7:32]) the bones of the kings of Judah, its leaders, the priests, the false prophets, and the inhabitants of Jerusalem will be brought out of their graves (see Lev. 26:30; 2 Kgs. 23:16; Jer. 1:18; 2:8; 4:9; 5:31; 6:13; 8:10; 36:30; Ezek. 6:5; 43:7; Bar. 2:24; *b. Sanh.* 96b). These bones will be spread to the sun, moon, and stars (> MT)—all the host of the sky, which those listed in 8:1 prefer to the Lord (Jer. 8:2a). They serve or worship them (see Deut. 4:19; 2 Kgs. 21:3, 5; 23:4; Jer. 7:18; 19:13; 44:17, 19; Ezek. 8:16; Amos 5:26; Zeph. 1:5), follow after them (cf. Jer. 2:5b, 8b), seek them (Deut. 12:30; 2 Chr. 17:3; 25:15, 20), and prostrate themselves to them (Exod. 20:5; Deut. 5:9). Thus, it is only fitting that the objects of their worship will become the means of their judgment. Not only will the graves and remains of the dead be desecrated, but also the bones of the luminary worshipers will be exposed to the elements and will lie there unaided before the so-called gods and goddesses of the sky. According to the Hebrew source behind Greek Jeremiah, these people will not be "mourned" (יסּפדו) or buried (Jer. 8:2b; cf. Jer. 14:16; 22:10; *Jub.* 23:23). They will be as a "likeness" (דמין; LXX: "pattern, example") on the surface of the ground. The MT says that they will not be "collected" (יאספו) or buried. They will be as "dung" (דמן) on the surface of the ground (cf. 2 Kgs. 9:37; Ps. 83:11 [Eng., 83:10]; see also Isa. 5:25). The parallel text in MT Jeremiah 16:4a says that they will not "be mourned" (יסּפדו) or buried. They will be as "dung" (דמן; LXX: "pattern, example" = דמין ["likeness"]) on the surface of the ground. MT Jeremiah 25:33b conflates MT 8:2b and 16:4a: they will not "mourned" (יסּפדו) or "collected" (יאספו; > LXX) or buried. Both the MT and Greek Jeremiah agree in 25:33b that they will be as "dung" (דמן) on the surface of the ground (see also Jer. 9:21 [Eng., 9:22]: MT דמן ["dung"]; LXX "pattern, example" = דמין ["likeness"]).

The MT of Jeremiah 8:3 speaks of a remnant distinct from those who will suffer the fate of 8:1–2. They are those who are left from "this evil family" in all the places where the Lord has driven them (cf. Jer. 16:15; 23:3, 8; 24:9; 29:14, 18; 30:11; 32:37; 40:12; 43:5; 46:28). Death will be chosen by them rather than life (cf. Gen. 27:46; 30:1; Num.

---

60. McKane, *Jeremiah I–XXV*, 180.

11:15; 1 Kgs. 18:4; Jer. 20:14–18; Jon. 4:3, 8; Job 3; Lam. 4:9). It is thought that this refers to the horrors of exile that will drive the people to despair (Lev. 26:36–39; Deut. 28:65–67; see also the response to the horrors of the tribulation [Hos. 10:8; Luke 23:30; Rev. 6:16; 9:6]). Rashi comments, "Although they see the dead being subjected to disgrace, the distress of the living is worse than that, and they will choose death."[61] On the other hand, the Hebrew text behind Greek Jeremiah begins 8:3 with the causal conjunction "for" (כִּי) as if the verse were providing an explanation for the fate of those in 8:1–2. They have chosen death rather than life and have done so for all who remain in the sense that those who are left will follow in their footsteps (see Exod. 20:5; Deut. 5:9). The choice of death rather than life here is not a preference for one over the other out of despair. It is a failure to heed the instruction to choose life (the LORD and his blessing) rather than death (other gods and the curse), instruction found in the text of Deuteronomy 30:15–20. The words of Deuteronomy 30:15 are repeated in Jeremiah 21:8.

---

61. Rosenberg, trans., *Mikraoth Gedoloth: Jeremiah Volume One*, 75.

JEREMIAH 8:4–9:26 (MT 9:25)

8:4 For thus says the Lord *[MT: "And you will say to them, 'Thus says the* Lord*'], "Does one fall and not rise up [MT: Do people fall and not rise up]? Does one turn back and not return [Syr.: Do people turn back and not return; Tg. Jon.: If to return, it is revealed before me that they will not return; see GKC §150h, m]?*[1] *8:5 Why does my people [MT: this people, Jerusalem] apostatize in enduring [LXX: shameless] apostasy and [and > MT] hold on to their [their > MT] deceitfulness [LXX: are held by their inclination] and [and > MT] refuse to return? 8:6 Pay attention and listen [MT: I paid attention and listened]. Not rightly [or, What is not right; LXX: οὐχ οὕτως] do they speak. There is no person repenting concerning [LXX: from] his evil saying, 'What have I done?' A returner [LXX: runner] stops from his course like a horse sweating [LXX] in its neighing [cf. 8:16a; MT qere: Each one returns in their course (kethiv: courses; 4QJer*: במרצתם) like a horse rushing into battle]. 8:7 Even a stork in the sky, it knows its appointed time [Codex L: times]. Turtledove and swallow/swift [MT kethiv: horse], crane/sparrow [Rahlfs: field sparrows; MT: and crane/sparrow], they keep [4QJer*: ישמרו] the time of their coming [LXX: the times of their comings]; but my people, they do not know [or, acknowledge] the ordinances [MT: ordinance] of the* Lord.

8:8 How can you say, 'We are wise, and the Torah of the Lord *is with us'? Deception is what a pen of scribal deception has become [NETS: A false pen has become of no use to scribes; MT: But look, deceptively/falsely has a pen of scribal deception performed; ESV: But behold, the lying pen of the scribes has made it into a lie].*[2] *8:9 Wise men were ashamed [or, were put to shame] and [and > MT] dismayed, and they were caught [or, were captured]. For [MT: Look] it was the word of the* Lord *that they rejected, and wisdom of what do they have [or, Because it was the word of the* Lord *that they rejected, wisdom of what kind do they have]? 8:10 Therefore, I will give their wives to others and [and > MT] their fields to dispossessors.*[3]

---

1. 4QJer* appears to have had a shorter text here, perhaps lacking ולא ישוב.
2. See *BHS* apparatus.
3. MT adds: "'For from small to great [cf. 6:13: from their least to their greatest], each one makes unjust gain. From prophet [Syr.: false prophet; *Tg. Jon.*: scribe; cf. 6:13: And from prophet] to priest [cf. LXX 6:13], each one practices deception. And they healed [cf. 6:14; see GKC §23f, 75qq] the breaking/fracture of the daughter of my people [cf. 6:14] lightly [or, superficially; Syr.: with mocking; *Tg. Jon.*: with their false words], saying, "Peace, peace," and there is no peace [or, "Well-being, well-being," and there is

8:13 And [> MT] gathering and taking away, I will make an end of them [NETS: And they will gather their produce; Syr., Tg. Jon.: Destroying, I will destroy them; Vulg.: congregans congregabo]," the prophetic utterance of the Lord.[4] *There are no grapes on the grapevine, and there are no figs on the fig tree; and as for the leaf, it has fallen [MT: withered; MT also adds: and I gave to them, they pass over them (mlt Mss: they serve them; Ms: and they serve them)]." 8:14 [Syr. adds: And they will say,] "Why are we sitting? Gather together that we may enter the fortified cities and be cast [MT: and perish (or, be still / silent; cf. Syr., Vulg.) there], for it is God [MT: the* Lord *our God] who cast us [MT: caused us to perish (or, silenced us; cf. Syr., Vulg.) and made us drink bitter water [Tg. Jon.: a cup of curse, as bad as snake venom (cf. 8:17)], for we have sinned against him [MT: against the* Lord*]. 8:15 We waited [LXX: gathered] for peace, but there was no good; for a time of healing [Tg. Jon.: forgiveness of sins], and look, terror [LXX: haste; Tg. Jon.: repayment of sins]. 8:16 From Dan was heard [LXX: we will hear][5] the snorting [LXX: sharpness / swiftness (= חֲדַת?)] of his horses [Tg. Jon.: Because they worshiped the calves that were at Dan, a king with his army will go up against them and take them into exile]. From the sound of the neighing of his mighty ones [i.e., his horses] all the land [Tg. Jon.: all the inhabitants of the land] quaked [or, shook]. And he will come and devour [MT: And they came and devoured] land and its fullness, city and inhabitants*

---

no well-being]. They are put to shame, for an abomination is what they committed [or, Are they ashamed that an abomination is what they committed?]. Indeed, they are certainly not ashamed, and they do not know to be ashamed [MT 6:15: to exhibit shame; Syr.: to hinder themselves]. Therefore, they will fall among the fallen. At the time of their visitation [MT 6:15: At the time that I visit them] they will stumble,' says the Lord."

4. The LXX translator apparently had the same consonantal text as the MT (with the exception of the initial *waw* conjunction), but he interpreted it differently. The infinitive absolute is understood to play the role of a finite verb rather than an adverb (see GKC §113y). The form אֹסִיפֵם is understood to be the noun אָסִיף ("gathering") plus a third masculine plural pronominal suffix ("their") rather than a *hiphil* verb from סוף. The citation of this text in Zephaniah 1:2 favors the MT vocalization. Jason DeRouchie, discussing the oft-noted problem of the combination of the infinitive absolute of אָסֹף with a finite verb form of סוּף (see GKC §113w³), suggests that the finite verb should be reanalyzed as *hiphil* of אָסֹף ("YHWH's Future Ingathering in Zephaniah 1:2," *HS* 59 [2018]: 173–91). Since the root אָסֹף never occurs in the *hiphil* stem elsewhere, this proposal essentially trades one unresolved problem for another.

5. The verb נשׁמע can be parsed either as a *niphal qatal* 3ms or as a *qal yiqtol* 1cp.

therein." 8:17 "For [or, Indeed] look, I am about to send among/against you poisonous [LXX: deadly] serpents/snakes [Tg. Jon.: peoples, killers like poisonous snakes] for which there is no charm, and they will bite [Tg. Jon.: kill] you," [MT adds: the prophetic utterance of the Lord*].*

The subunits in Jeremiah 8:4–9:25 (Eng., 9:26) are notoriously difficult to divide, and it is almost a lost cause to find two commentators who agree on what they should be. The Hebrew source behind Greek Jeremiah introduces the Lord's discourse in 8:4 as an explanation of what precedes it: "For thus says the Lord." The MT, however, simply continues what precedes it: "And you will say to them, 'Thus says the Lord.'" The consistent use of singular verbs in the following questions found in the Hebrew source behind Greek Jeremiah encourages the reader to understand them in a general, proverbial manner (cf. Amos 3:3–6; Eccl. 4:10): "Does one fall and not rise up? Does one turn back and not return?"[6] The expected answer to both questions is normally yes, which makes the description of the people's failure to return to the Lord in 8:5–7 appear so out of sorts (cf. Jer. 3:7). On the other hand, the change from plural ("Do people fall and not rise up?") to singular verbs in the MT of 8:4 has suggested to some interpreters that the application is already being made to the people's relationship to the Lord (cf. Jer. 4:1). For example, *Targum Jonathan* renders the second question as an if-then statement: "If to return, it is revealed before me that they will not return" (cf. Rashi, Redak). Bullinger follows the eastern *qere*, which has a plural verb for the first half of the second question: "Shall they return [*to the Lord*] and He not return [*to them*]?"[7] Holladay believes that the plural verbs in the MT have Israel as their subject, and the singular verbs have the Lord as their subject.[8] He points to the pairing of the verbs "fall" and "rise" elsewhere in the prophetic literature (Isa. 24:20; 26:18–19; Jer. 25:27; Amos 5:2; 8:14; Mic. 7:8) and suggests that the questions in 8:4 are the Lord's quotation of the optimistic prophets: "If Israel falls, she will rise again, will she not? And if Yahweh turns away from us, he will turn back to us, will he not?" But the question in 8:5 only makes sense if the questions in 8:4 assume a general principle, which suggests that the Hebrew source behind Greek Jeremiah represents the original text in 8:4. In other words, if one normally rises up after falling and returns after turning back (8:4), then why does the Lord's people (which the MT identifies as the people of Jerusalem) endure in apostasy

---

6. See Calvin, *Jeremiah*, 1:424.
7. Bullinger, *Figures of Speech*, 11–12, 268.
8. Holladay, *Jeremiah 1*, 278.

(cf. Jer. 3:6) and hold on to deceitfulness and refuse to return (8:5)?[9] The term for "deceitfulness" (תרמית) in 8:5 appears elsewhere in the book in descriptions of the false prophets (Jer. 14:14; 23:26). A related noun (מרמה) occurs in Jeremiah 9:5 (Eng., 9:6), which says that the people refuse to acknowledge the LORD in their deceit.

The Hebrew source behind Greek Jeremiah begins 8:6 with two plural imperatives: "Pay attention and listen." It is not clear to whom these are directed. The MT has first person verbs: "I paid attention and listened" (cf. Num. 11:1). There is no definitive reason to think that there has been a change of speaker here from the LORD to someone else such as Jeremiah. The LORD says that the people speak what is "not right" (לוא כן) (cf. Jer. 23:10b), although it is possible that this expression means "not so" (see LXX), either in the sense that they do not speak with words of repentance, or in the form of a question ("They do not speak so, do they?").[10] "There is no person repenting concerning his evil saying, 'What have I done?'"[11] The LXX translator expected the idiom, "There is no person repenting from his evil,"[12] but Holladay has shown that the Hebrew phrase "relenting concerning evil" comes from descriptions of the LORD (Joel 2:13; Jon. 4:2).[13] The LORD has shown a willingness to relent concerning the evil or calamity of judgment, but the people have not responded with a willingness to repent concerning their moral evil (but see Jer. 31:19). There is no one doing justice, seeking faithfulness, or willing to return (see Jer. 5:1–3). According to the Hebrew source behind Greek Jeremiah 8:6b, "A returner stops (כְּלֹה) from his course (ממרצתו) like a horse sweating (שוטף) in its neighing (במצהלותיו)" (cf. Jer. 5:8; 8:16a). This conjures up an image of one who refuses to return due to preoccupation with other activity, but according to the MT *qere*, "Each one (כֻּלֹּה) returns in their course (במרוצתם) like a horse rushing (שוטף) into battle (במלחמה)" (cf. Jer. 22:17; 23:10). This is an image of one recklessly going down the path of destruction, unwilling to turn back.

In Jeremiah 5:21–25, the LORD contrasted the people with the ocean. The ocean obeys the LORD. The people do not. Now in 8:7 he

---

9. The answer, of course, is that they do not yet have the heart/mind to acknowledge the LORD (Deut. 29:3 [Eng., 29:4]; 30:6; Jer. 4:4; 31:31–34; Ezek. 11:19–20).

10. See Bright, *Jeremiah*, 63.

11. Bullinger suggests that the universal negative here does not deny particular examples of repentance (*Figures of Speech*, 618).

12. See Walser, *Jeremiah*, 250.

13. Holladay, *Jeremiah 1*, 279.

contrasts the people with various kinds of birds whose precise identification is hardly necessary to make the point: "Even a stork in the sky, it knows its appointed time [Codex L: times]. Turtledove and swallow/swift [MT *kethiv*: horse], crane/sparrow [Rahlfs: field sparrows; MT: and crane/sparrow],[14] they keep [4QJerᵃ: ישמרו] the time of their coming [LXX: the times of their comings]; but my people, they do not know [or, acknowledge] the ordinances [MT: ordinance] of the LORD" (cf. Isa. 1:3; Jer. 2:32; 5:4–5). It is possible that this alludes to the "appointed times" of Leviticus 23, which the people did not keep (see, e.g., Jer. 17:19–27).

In light of Jeremiah 8:6–7, the LORD asks in 8:8a (cf. Isa. 19:11; Jer. 2:23), "How can you say, 'We are wise, and the Torah of the LORD is with us'?" This appears to be a thought rooted in Deuteronomy 4:6, which says that the Torah is the people's wisdom. Yet the mere presence or possession of the text of the Torah has not made the people wise (see Jer. 2:8; 4:22; 6:19; 9:12, 22–23 [Eng., 9:13, 23–24]).[15] The Torah is not written on their hearts (Jer. 31:33; cf. Exod. 31:18). Rather, their sin is engraved with an iron stylus on their hard hearts (MT Jer. 17:1). It is possible that 8:8b ("Deception is what a pen of scribal deception has become [היה]")[16] is a continuation of what the people say (see Kara), in which case it would be an accusation of falsehood against scribes like Baruch and the true prophets of judgment whom they represent (cf. Jer. 43:2–3), but most understand 8:8b to be a comment from the LORD. Rashi and Redak differ on what this comment is.[17] According to Rashi, the wisdom of the Torah that the people possess is of no use because it is forged by their own false prophet of peace. According to Redak, the scribes who produced the Torah did so in vain because the people do not keep the Torah (cf. NJPS). Keil suggests that the text speaks not only of authors and composers but also of those who made the Torah the object of their study: "But inasmuch as such persons, by false interpretation and application, perverted the truth of the law into a lie, he calls their work the work of the lying style (pen)."[18] The scribes in 8:8b

---

14. Cf. Isaiah 38:14. McKane suggests that στρουθία in the LXX is "an insertion consequent on the corruption of αγουρ to ἀγροῦ" (*Jeremiah I–XXV*, 184).

15. "Indeed, the delusion, or falsehood, which the scribes have created seems to be not so much the law itself, as the resultant conceit that possession of the law gives all necessary wisdom" (Bright, *Jeremiah*, 64).

16. NET: "A false pen has become of no use to scribes"; MT: "But look, deceptively/falsely has a pen of scribal deception performed (עשה)"; ESV: "But behold, the lying pen of the scribes has made it into a lie."

17. Rosenberg, trans., *Mikraoth Gedoloth: Jeremiah Volume One*, 77.

18. Keil, *Jeremiah*, 110.

are presumably priestly scribes (e.g., Ezra 7:6, 10; Neh. 8–9) who have the privilege and duty of handling, copying, and teaching the Torah but do not know or acknowledge the LORD (Jer. 2:8; see Deut. 31:9; 33:10; but 2 Kgs. 17:13; 22:8; Dan. 9:10; Ezra 9:10–11; see also BDB, 708). Holladay suggests that these have come under the influence of the false prophets of peace (see Jer. 5:31; 6:13–14; 23:25–32).[19] Their עט שקר ("pen of deception" or "false pen") is a עד שקר ("false witness") (Exod. 20:16). On the other hand, William Schniedewind argues that 8:8b "is a protest against the authority of the written texts that were understood as subverting oral tradition and the authority of the prophets."[20] This hardly seems correct, however, given Jeremiah's own devotion to the text of the Torah and the book's emphasis on the writing of Jeremiah's words (Jer. 36). It appears more likely that the text speaks of scribal tampering in the transmission of the text of the Torah,[21] which is known from the available witnesses to have occurred in the transmission of all biblical books, including the book of Jeremiah.[22]

The verbs in Jeremiah 8:9a show the pattern of the beginning of a typical Hebrew narrative: *qatal* verb(s) establishing the background followed by *wayyiqtol* verb(s) for narrative sequence (cf. Gen. 1:1–3; 3:1; 4:1; etc.). The term "wise men" (חכמים) is presumably another way to describe the elite class known as the "scribes" in 8:8b. They are the

---

19. Holladay, *Jeremiah 1*, 282–83.

20. William M. Schniedewind, *How the Bible Became a Book: The Textualization of Ancient Israel* (Cambridge: Cambridge University Press, 2004), 117.

21. See Chad L. Eggleston, *See and Read All These Words: The Concept of the Written in the Book of Jeremiah*, Siphrut: Literature and Theology of the Hebrew Scriptures 18 (Winona Lake, IN: Eisenbrauns, 2016), 63–65. An example of such tampering would be the transformation of eschatological prophecies (e.g., LXX, SP Num. 24:7 ["Gog"]; see Ezek. 38–39) into historical prophecies (MT Num. 24:7 ["Agag"]; see 1 Sam. 15), putting messages of a final reckoning at arm's length (see the nearby reference to Num. 21:6–9 in Jer. 8:17 and the references to Num. 21:28–29 and Num. 24:17 in Jer. 48:45). The book of Jeremiah has undergone a similar change from its eschatological first edition represented by the LXX to its historicized second edition represented by the MT (see Introduction). Once the text is rendered a mere documentary of past events, it fails to speak with genuine force to the present generation.

22. See, e.g., the addition of Jeremiah 33:14–26, which is not in the Hebrew source behind Greek Jeremiah, in the MT. This addition apparently comes from priestly scribes who attempted to leverage the text of Jeremiah 23:5–6, which is based on the covenant with David, in order to introduce the idea of a covenant with the Levites alongside the biblical covenant with the priesthood of Aaron.

sages and scholars, yet they have been shamed and dismayed, ensnared by their own actions (see Jer. 5:26; 6:11). This is because they have rejected the prophetic word of the LORD that has come to them through true prophets like Jeremiah (Jer. 8:9b; cf. Jer. 6:19). The prophetic word of the LORD goes hand in hand with the Torah that they claim is with them (Isa. 1:10; 2:3; 8:16; Zech. 7:12; cf. John 5:39–40, 46–47). In fact, the true prophet is essentially a faithful exegete of the Torah (see LXX Prov. 29:18). Thus, if the so-called wise men or scribes implicitly reject the Torah, their source of wisdom, by their deceptive alteration of it (Jer. 8:8b), and they outwardly reject the prophetic word of the LORD through which exegesis of the Torah comes to them, what kind of wisdom do they really have (for the construction חכמת מה, cf. מה דבר in Num. 23:3)?

The announcement of judgment in Jeremiah 8:10a1 ("Therefore, I will give their wives to others and [and > MT] their fields to dispossessors") has an earlier parallel in 6:12a. The text of MT 8:10a2–12, which does not appear in the Hebrew source behind Greek Jeremiah, is a doublet of 6:13–15 (see the commentary on Jer. 6:12–15). It has been inserted secondarily here because of connections perceived in the surrounding context. Thus, the reference to those "from the least to the greatest" and "from the prophet to the priest" (and their practice of "deception") in 8:10 not only recalls the list in 8:1 but also the priestly scribes/wise men in 8:8–9 who handle the Torah with "deception" under the influence of the false prophets (see Syr.). *Targum Jonathan* even translates the word "prophet" here and in 6:13 as "scribe." Verse 11 says, "And they healed [וירפו; cf. pc Mss, 6:14: וירפאו] the breaking/fracture of the daughter of my people lightly saying, 'Peace, peace,' and there is no peace." This anticipates 8:15 (and 8:21–22; see also 14:17): "We waited for peace, but there was no good; for a time of healing [מרפה; cf. mlt Mss: מרפא], and look, terror." The spelling of ירפו and מרפה on the analogy of the root רפה (rather than רפא) makes the connection even more conspicuous. The announcement of judgment in 8:12b (introduced by לכן) forms a nice segue into 8:13–17 much the same way that the announcement of judgment (introduced by לכן) in 8:10a1 makes the transition into 8:13–17 in the Hebrew source behind Greek Jeremiah.

Despite the many efforts to reanalyze, revocalize, or emend אסף אסיפם ("gathering and taking away, I will make an end of them") at the beginning of 8:13, McKane concludes, "There is good reason for retaining MT," and he translates, "I will gather them for final destruction."[23] The reference to the lack of grapes on the grapevine, the lack of figs on the fig tree, and "fallen" (נפל; MT: "withered" [נבל]) leaves is not a metaphor

---

23. McKane, *Jeremiah I–XXV*, 188–89.

for the people (as in Jer. 2:21; 6:9) but a picture of the devastated land (cf. Jer. 4:23–31).[24] It is the opposite of the golden age of Solomon (see 1 Kgs. 5:5 [Eng., 4:25]) and what the prophets envision for the messianic kingdom (Mic. 4:4; Zech. 3:10). It is often assumed that 8:13 is a citation of Zephaniah 1:2–3, but a good case has been made that the prophetic author/composer of the Twelve (Hos.–Mal.) is citing from Jeremiah 7:20; 8:13; 15:3 in Zephaniah 1:2–3.[25] The seam work that this composer employs to combine the books of the Twelve features material distinct from its surroundings, development of the program set forth in Hosea 3:4–5, and citation from the book of Jeremiah. In the case of the Habakkuk-Zephaniah sequence, Zephaniah 1:7 picks up the language of Habakkuk 2:20b and reintroduces the Day of the LORD theme from Joel-Amos-Obadiah. Zephaniah 1:15 uses the phrase "day of distress" from Habakkuk 3:16b (cf. Nah. 1:7) to describe the Day of the LORD.[26] Habakkuk 3:17 mentions the failure of fig trees and grapevines anticipated in Jeremiah 8:13, and Zephaniah 1:2 is the only text other than Jeremiah 8:13 that combines the *qal* infinitive absolute of אסף with a *hiphil* first person singular prefixed verb of סוף.

The MT adds text to the end of Jeremiah 8:13, which is not in the Hebrew source behind Greek Jeremiah: "and I gave to them, they pass over them (יעברום) [mlt Mss: they serve them (יעבדום); Ms: and they serve them (ועבדום)]." Holladay mentions four ways in which this text has been understood: (1) *Targum Jonathan* and Rashi: "And I have given to them that which they [Israel] have been transgressing (= the commandments)" (see Ps. 148:6; cf. Jer. 5:22); (2) Redak: "And I have given to them that [the land, the gifts] which shall pass in ownership to them [the enemy]" (cf. Num. 27:7, 8); (3) "And I have given to them those (= the enemy) who shall overrun, violate them (= Israel)" (cf. Isa. 51:23); and (4) Vulgate: "And I have given to them that [the land, the gifts] which shall pass away, disappear in their [Israel's] regard" (cf. Jer. 5:22; 13:24).[27]

The text of Jeremiah 8:14–16 features the voice of the people (see Syr.: "And they will say"): "Why are we sitting? Gather together that we may enter the fortified cities and be cast [MT: and perish (or, be still/silent; cf. Syr., Vulg.) there]" (Jer. 8:14a). This is very close to the language of Jeremiah 4:5b (see also Lev. 26:25; Jer. 35:11). The thought of going

---

24. Contra Keil, *Jeremiah*, 111.

25. See Shepherd, *Commentary on the Book of the Twelve*, 22–36, 354.

26. Note also how Habakkuk 3:16–19 (cf. Hab. 3:1–2) stands apart from Habakkuk 3:3–15 and how the universal judgment in Zephaniah 1:2–3 stands apart from the particular application to Judah in Zephaniah 1:4–6.

27. Holladay, *Jeremiah 1*, 285–86.

to the city to meet fate one way or another rather than facing certain doom outside is not unlike the sentiment of the four skin-diseased men in 2 Kings 7:3–4. The Hebrew source behind Greek Jeremiah has the verb נרמה ("be cast"). The MT has נדמה ("perish" or "be still/silent") (cf. MT 1 Sam. 2:9a). The letters ר and ד are commonly confused in textual transmission. The rationale for 8:14a is given in 8:14b: "for it is God [MT: the LORD our God] who cast us [הרמנו; MT: caused us to perish (or, silenced us [הדמנו]; cf. Syr., Vulg.) and made us drink bitter water [*Tg. Jon.*: a cup of curse, as bad as snake venom (cf. 8:17)], for we have sinned against him [MT: against the LORD]" (cf. Jer. 3:25; 14:7, 20). McKane suggests a connection to Numbers 5 on the basis of *Targum Jonathan's* rendering: "Targ.'s paraphrase of מי ראש at 8.14 ('A cup of curse as toxic as a snake's venom') indicates that a connection is being established between מי ראש and המים המאררים in Num 5.18, 19, 22, 24, 27 (Targ. מיא מלטטא). According to Targ. (Jer. 8:14) the reason why the cup contains a poison is because it incorporates a curse, and it incorporates a curse (cf. Num chapter 5) because those who drink it are guilty. If they were innocent, their innocence would be established by the circumstance that the cup did them no harm (like the woman suspected of adultery in Num chapter 5)."[28]

By the people's own admission in 8:15, they "waited"[29] (cf. Isa. 25:9; Jer. 13:16) for the "peace" (שלום) promised by the false prophets (Jer. 6:14; MT 8:11), but nothing "good" (טוב) came (see שלום in MT Isa. 45:7 for which 1QIsa[a] has טוב). They waited for a time of "healing" (מרפא),[30] which *Targum Jonathan* interprets to be "forgiveness of sins," but there was only "terror" (בעתה), which *Targum Jonathan* interprets to be "repayment of sins" (LXX: "haste" [= בהלה? cf. MT/LXX Jer. 15:8b: בהלות/σπουδή; see also MT/LXX Jer. 14:9b: בעתה/ταραχή]). This verse has a very close parallel in Jeremiah 14:19 (see also Isa. 59:9, 11). The text of Jeremiah 8:21–22 asks why there has been no balm or "healer" (רפא) as expected from Gilead for the "breaking" or "fracture" (שבר) of the people (cf. Jer. 19:11). The false prophets have "healed" this "fracture" of the people only superficially with their message of "peace" (Jer. 6:14; 8:11 [MT]).

---

28. McKane, *Jeremiah I–XXV*, 191. See also Exodus 32:20; Deuteronomy 29:17 (Eng., 29:18); 32:32; Jeremiah 9:14 (Eng., 9:15); 23:15; 25:15; Habakkuk 2:15–16; Lamentations 3:19; Mark 16:18.

29. The LXX translator misread קוה ("wait") as the homonym קוה ("collect") (see Jer. 3:17). The infinitive absolute can stand in the place of a finite verb (GKC §113y).

30. For רפא in the Prophets, see Isaiah 6:10; 19:22; 57:19; Jeremiah 3:22; 6:14; MT 8:11; 8:22; 15:18; 17:14; 19:11; 30:17; 33:6; 51:9; Ezekiel 47:8, 9; Hosea 6:1; 14:5 (Eng., 14:4); Zechariah 11:16.

Already in Jeremiah 4:15 it was anticipated that a report would come from Dan in the north about the advancement of the enemy (Jer. 4:6; 5:15; 6:1, 22). Now in 8:16 it is said that the "snorting" (נחרת; LXX: "sharpness/swiftness" [= חַדַּת?]) of the enemy's horses was heard or would be heard from Dan (cf. Jer. 4:13; 6:23). As in 4:15, *Targum Jonathan* suggests that "because they worshiped the calves that were at Dan [1 Kgs. 12:28–29; 2 Kgs. 10:29; Amos 8:14], a king with his army will go up against them and take them into exile." That is, just as Israel's idolatry led to Assyrian exile, so Judah's idolatry will lead to Babylonian exile (2 Kgs. 17:13–23). "From [or, because of] the sound of the neighing of his mighty ones [i.e., his horses] all the land [*Tg. Jon.*: all the inhabitants of the land] quaked [or, shook]" (cf. LXX Jer. 8:6). The enemy "will come and devour" (MT: "came and devoured") the "land and its fullness, city and inhabitants therein" (cf. Hab. 2:8, 17). The text of 8:16 and its surrounding context bear an interesting relationship to Jacob's blessing of Dan in Genesis 49:16–18. Jacob desires Dan to be a "serpent" or "snake" (נחש) along a path that "bites" (נשך) a horse's heels (Gen. 49:17; cf. "Dan" and "horses" in Jer. 8:16 and "serpents/snakes" [נחשים] that "bite" [ונשכו] in Jer. 8:17). Then Jacob prays, "For your salvation I wait (קויתי), O LORD" (Gen. 49:18; see Gen. 3:15; cf. "We waited [קוה] for peace" [Jer. 8:15]). Thus, the LORD says in Jeremiah 8:17, "For/ Indeed look, I am about to send among/against you poisonous serpents/ snakes [*Tg. Jon.*: peoples, killers like poisonous snakes] for which there is no charm, and they will bite [*Tg. Jon.*: kill] you" (cf. *Tg. Jon.* Jer. 8:14). This alludes to the story of the biting serpents in Numbers 21:6–9 but without any means of deliverance corresponding to the bronze serpent (see also Deut. 32:24; Mark 16:18; Luke 10:19; John 3:14; Acts 28:3–6).[31]

8:18 Without healing [LXX: Incurable; Theod. = מבלי גאות: Without pride; MT: My source of brightening? Syr.: I grow old] with the grief of your heart, which is faint [MT: upon grief, upon me my heart is faint].[32] 8:19 Look, the voice [MT adds: of the cry] of the daughter of my people [or, of

---

31. Thompson, *Jeremiah*, 303.
32. *Tg. Jon.*: "Because they were mocking before the prophets who prophesied to them, sorrow and sighing I will bring to them because of their sins. The prophet says, 'My heart is faint.'" *Lamentations Rabbah* says that the grief in this verse is the LORD's grief because there is no one to study the Torah, keep the commandments, and perform good deeds (see Neusner, *Jeremiah in Talmud and Midrash*, 241). Holladay reconstructs this verse to say that Jeremiah's "joys have gone up and away, while grief has come down on him" (*Jeremiah 1*, 292).

my daughter-my people; NET: of my dear people] from a land of distances [or, wide extent; LXX: far away; Tg. Jon. adds: the prophet has rebuked them]: "Is the LORD not in Zion? Is there no king there [MT: Is her king not in it]?" "Why do they provoke me with their idols [or, carved / sculpted images] and with foreign idols [or, empty things]?" 8:20 [Tg. Jon. adds: The congregation of Israel said,] "Harvest has passed, summer [Syr.: ingathering] has ended; and as for us, we are not delivered."[33] 8:21 [Tg. Jon. adds: Jerusalem said,] Concerning [or, Because of] the breaking / fracture of the daughter of my people [MT adds: I am broken] I mourn [i.e., I am in dark clothing; Tg. Jon.: my face was covered with a black coating like a pot]. Horror, it has gripped me, writhing [or, anguish] like a woman in labor [writhing like a woman in labor > MT]. 8:22 Is there no balm in Gilead? Is there no healer / physician there? Why [Codex L, 4QJer^c: For why] has the healing / restoration of the daughter of my people [or, of my daughter—my people] not come up?[34]

9:1 (MT 8:23) I wish that my head were water [see GKC §151b], and my eyes [Codex L: my eye] a fountain of tears so that I could weep for my people [my people > MT] day and night, the slain [pc Mss: concerning the slain] of the daughter of my people [or, of my daughter-my people]. 9:2 (MT 9:1) I wish that I were in the wilderness a distant lodge [MT: a travelers' lodge] so that I could leave / forsake my people and go away from them, for all of them are adulterers, an assembly of treacherous / unfaithful people. 9:3 (MT 9:2) "And they bent their tongue like a bow [MT: their bow] in deception, and not in faithfulness / reliability was it mighty [MT: were they mighty] in the land.[35] For from evil to evil they went forth, and me they did not acknowledge," [MT adds: the prophetic utterance of the LORD (4QJer^c adds: of hosts)]. 9:4 (MT 9:3) "Each [MT: And each] from his friend / neighbor keep yourselves, and in any brother / relative do not trust. For every brother / relative surely follows at the heel [or, acts like Jacob (i.e., deceptively)], and every friend / neighbor as a slanderer goes. 9:5 (MT 9:4) Each with his friend / neighbor mocks /

---

33. It is possible that קָצִיר ("harvest") and קַיִץ ("summer") should be transposed in the Hebrew source behind Greek Jeremiah.

34. *Tg. Jon.*: "Jeremiah the prophet said, 'If I did not have good works to intercede for the house of Israel, would I not have desired the teaching of Elijah the prophet from Gilead whose words were healing? Because they have not returned, healing has not come up for the wound of the congregation of my people.'"

35. Cf. *Tg. Jon.*, Vulg., ASV. The ESV ("falsehood and not truth has grown strong in the land") has a problem with subject-verb agreement in the Hebrew text (see also NET).

deceives / trifles. Truth / Faithfulness [MT: And truth / faithfulness] they do not speak. Their tongue has learned to speak deception [MT: They have taught their tongue to speak deception]. They have committed iniquity and are weary of returning [MT: They have wearied themselves committing iniquity].[36] *9:6 (MT 9:5) Injury upon injury, deceit upon deceit, they have refused to acknowledge me [MT: Your dwelling is in the midst of deceit. In deceit they have refused to acknowledge me]," [MT adds: the prophetic utterance of the Lord]. 9:7 (MT 9:6) Therefore, thus says the Lord [MT adds: of hosts], "Look, I am about to refine them and test them, for I will act [MT: for how else can I act? (or, for how I will act!)] from before [or, because of] the evil [the evil > MT] of the daughter of my people [or, of my daughter—my people]. 9:8 (MT 9:7) A slaughtering [MT qere, Syr.: hammered / sharpened] arrow is their tongue, deceit is what the words of their mouth are [MT: deceit he speaks with his mouth].*[37] *Peace with his friend / neighbor is what he speaks, but in his inward part he puts enmity [MT: his ambush]. 9:9 (MT 9:8) Concerning these things will I not visit / punish [or, Upon these will I not visit (i.e., Will I not punish these); MT adds: them]?" the prophetic utterance of the Lord. "On a nation such as this will I not avenge myself?"*

The MT has added נאם יהוה ("the prophetic utterance of the Lord") at the end of 8:17 to indicate the close of the Lord's discourse. Verse 18 is the lament of the prophet Jeremiah. According to the Hebrew source behind Greek Jeremiah, he says, "Without healing (מבלי גהה) with the grief of your heart, which is faint (עם יגון לבכם דוי)."[38] This comes across more as

---

36. The Hebrew source behind Greek Jeremiah and the MT differ in their arrangement of the text at the end of 9:5 (MT 9:4) and the beginning of 9:6 (MT 9:5). The Hebrew source behind Greek Jeremiah has העוו ונלאו שב תך בתוך מרמה במרמה ("They have committed iniquity and are weary of returning. Injury upon injury, deceit upon deceit . . ."). The MT has העוה נלאו שבתך בתוך מרמה במרמה ("They have wearied themselves committing iniquity. Your dwelling is in the midst of deceit. In deceit . . ."). The LXX has τόκος for תך/תוך. This word means "interest/usury" in Greek, but it is likely a transliteration for the Hebrew original. McKane suggests that it is a word play that explains the injury or wrong as "money-lending on harsh terms" (*Jeremiah I–XXV*, 201).

37. Contrary to the arrangement of the text in *BHS*, the MT accentuation puts the phrase "with his mouth" with what follows: "With his mouth, peace with his friend/neighbor is what he speaks."

38. See the use of the root גהה (BDB, 155) in the Hebrew source behind Greek Jeremiah 14:19.

an interjection than as a complete thought (cf. Isa. 1:5; Hos. 5:13; Prov. 17:22; Lam. 1:22). Bright, following Rudolph, suggests putting מבלי גהת ("without healing") at the end of the Lord's discourse in 8:17: "And they will bite you—fatally!—Yahweh's word."[39] The MT of 8:18 is difficult: "My source of brightening (מבליגיתי) upon grief (עלי יגון), upon me my heart is faint (עלי לבי דוי)." This translation is based on the meaning of the root בלג ("gleam, smile") and the division of the verse by the Masoretic accent *athnach* (but see *BHS*). Rashi understands מבליגיתי to mean "my suppression": "That is to say, if I said, 'I will suppress and keep in my grief.'"[40]

In 8:19, the prophet points to the voice of the people. The phrase בת עמי ("the daughter of my people"; NET: "my dear people") occurs several times in this section (Jer. 8:19, 21, 22, 23 [Eng., LXX, 9:1]; see also Jer. 4:11; 6:26; 8:11 [MT]; 9:6 [Eng., LXX, 9:7]; 14:17). This sound of the people's cry (see MT) comes "from a land of distances" (מארץ מרחקים). The LXX interprets this phrase to mean "far away," which either anticipates or presupposes exile.[41] Bright, however, is likely correct to render "far and wide through the land" (cf. Isa. 33:17).[42] The pattern of the following questions (ה . . . אם . . . מדוע . . .) is identical to Jeremiah 2:14 and 8:22 with the exception that the third question comes from a different speaker (i.e., the Lord). The people ask, "Is the Lord not in Zion? Is there no king there [MT: Is her king not in it]?" Are these two separate questions about the presence of the Lord and the presence of the Davidic king in Zion (cf. Hos. 10:3), or is the second question a reiteration of the first, asking whether the Lord is present as king in Zion?[43] Furthermore, do these questions expect a positive answer or a negative answer? Contextually, it seems best to understand these questions to be about the presence of the Lord as king in Zion (cf. Zeph. 3:14–15; Zech. 2:14 [Eng., 2:10]; 9:9–10), expecting a positive answer. That is, the people have put their confidence in the kingship of the Lord just as they have put their confidence in the temple (Jer. 7:4). The problem is that they are in active rebellion against the Lord in whom they claim to put their trust. This is why the Lord then asks, "Why do they provoke me with their idols [or, carved/sculpted images]

---

39. Bright, *Jeremiah*, 62.
40. Rosenberg, trans., *Mikraoth Gedoloth: Jeremiah Volume One*, 80. The Syriac interprets this same word to be from the root בלה ("become old and worn out").
41. See Rosenberg, trans., *Mikraoth Gedoloth: Jeremiah Volume One*, 80; Calvin, *Jeremiah*, 1:448–49.
42. Bright, *Jeremiah*, 62, 64.
43. See Keil, *Jeremiah*, 113.

and with foreign idols [or, empty things]" (cf. Deut. 32:21; 2 Kgs. 22:17; Jer. 2:5; 5:19; 7:19; 14:22)? If their confidence is in the LORD, why do they worship other gods (see also Deut. 32:38; Judg. 10:14; Isa. 57:13; Jer. 2:28; 11:12)?

Jeremiah's report of the people's discourse resumes in 8:20: "Harvest has passed, summer has ended; and as for us, we are not delivered" (cf. Matt. 24:32; Mark 13:28; Luke 21:30). Rashi understands this to be a metaphor for the expectation of aid from Egypt, which has not come.[44] Keil, however, takes it to be a proverb: "As a country-man, hoping for a good harvest, falls into despair as to his chances, so the people have been in vain looking for its rescue and deliverance."[45] Holladay interprets the text more literally, suggesting that there is a reference to a real drought under way.[46] The people's false sense of security in the temple (Jer. 7:4) and in the presence of the LORD's kingship in Zion (Jer. 8:19) has left them befuddled now that their expectation of deliverance has not come to fruition. Thus, the prophet laments, "Concerning [or, Because of] the breaking/fracture of the daughter of my people [MT adds: I am broken] I mourn [i.e., I am in dark clothing]. Horror, it has gripped me, writhing [or, anguish] like a woman in labor [writhing like a woman in labor > MT]" (Jer. 8:21; cf. Jer. 14:17; Lam. 2:11). The MT adds הִשְׁבַּרְתִּי ("I am broken") to play on שׁבר ("breaking/fracture") (see Jer. 6:14; MT 8:11). The root קדר means "be dark" and likely refers to the dark clothing of a mourner (cf. Jer. 14:2). The "horror" of the people's fate has gripped Jeremiah (see Jer. 2:15; 4:7; 5:30; 18:16; 19:8; 25:9, 11, 18, 38; 29:18; 42:18; 44:12, 22; cf. Deut. 28:37). The phrase חִיל כַּיּוֹלֵדָה ("writhing/anguish like a woman in labor"), which is in the Hebrew source behind Greek Jeremiah but not in the MT, is identical to the end of Jeremiah 6:24.

In 8:22a, Jeremiah asks, "Is there no balm in Gilead? Is there no healer/physician there?" Gilead was apparently well known for its medicinal balm (see Gen. 37:25; Jer. 46:11; see also Gen. 43:11; Jer. 51:8; Ezek. 27:17; but cf. Hos. 6:8; 12:12 [Eng., 12:11]), but in this context the need is for spiritual healing and restoration (Jer. 8:15; 30:12–17; cf. Isa. 1:5–6; Lam. 2:13). Given the similarity to the pattern of questions

---

44. Rosenberg, trans., *Mikraoth Gedoloth: Jeremiah Volume One*, 81.

45. Keil, *Jeremiah*, 113. "*Redak* explains that the harvest season is a joyous time when people expect to be saved from hunger, as is the summer season, when people rejoice with the summer fruits. The people say: These joyous times have passed, when we expected to be saved, but we were not saved" (Rosenberg, trans., *Mikraoth Gedoloth: Jeremiah Volume One*, 81).

46. Holladay, *Jeremiah 1*, 293. See Jeremiah 8:23 (Eng., LXX, 9:1); 14:1, 17. See also Jeremiah 9:18, 21 (Eng., LXX, 9:19, 22).

in Jeremiah 2:14 and 8:19, the expected answer to the inquiries in 8:22a appears to be yes.[47] The remedy for which the balm in Gilead serves as a metaphor is available. This raises the follow-up question in 8:22b, "Why has the healing/restoration of the daughter of my people not come up?" If healing is available, why are the people not healed? The presupposed answer seems to be that the people have refused to take advantage of what has been available to them, but what exactly is the balm in Gilead (i.e., the spiritual remedy)? According to *Targum Jonathan*, in the absence of good works to intercede for Israel, the balm would be the teaching of Elijah the prophet from Gilead whose words were healing (1 Kgs. 17), but then it goes on to say that healing has not come because the people have not returned or repented. Thus, the balm is the prophetic call to return from idolatry (1 Kgs. 18).[48] The Talmud suggests that the balm is a sage or wise man, referring to the story of Jephthah the son of Gilead who made a foolish vow and had no wise man to remit it (Judg. 11:29–40).[49] There may be, however, an intentional correspondence between the questions in 8:19 and those in 8:22 that provides a clue to what the balm is: (1) "Is the LORD not in Zion?" (2) "Is there no king there?" (3) "Why do they provoke me with their idols and with foreign idols?" (1a) "Is there no balm in Gilead?" (2a) "Is there no healer/physician there?" (3a) "Why has the healing/ restoration of the daughter of my people not come up?" These parallels suggest that the divine kingship is the balm (Exod. 15:18; Zeph. 3:14–15; Zech. 2:14 [Eng., 2:10]; 9:9–10; Matt. 21:5; John 12:15), but the people have rejected their true king in favor of idols.[50]

---

47. Contra Calvin, *Jeremiah*, 1:455–56. Edgar Allen Poe's "The Raven," which cites Jeremiah in a very different context, also (like Calvin) expects a negative answer: "Is there—*is* there balm in Gilead?—tell me—tell me, I implore!" Quoth the Raven, "Nevermore."

48. This is also the view of Kara: "Since God is found among them, who is analogous to the physician, and the prophets admonish them daily to repent—repentance is analogous to balm—why, then, has the spiritual health of my people not been restored" (Rosenberg, trans., *Mikraoth Gedoloth: Jeremiah Volume One*, 81)?

49. See Neusner, *Jeremiah in Talmud and Midrash*, 294. *Targum Jonathan's* rendering of Judges 11:39 suggests that Jephthah could have inquired of Phineas the priest and redeemed his daughter.

50. See Jeremiah 22:6, where the king's palace is compared to Gilead. The traditional spiritual "There Is a Balm in Gilead" interprets the balm to be the substitutionary death of Jesus and the gift of the Holy Spirit. According to this reading, Jesus, the Davidic Messiah, is the divine king in the flesh (see Jer. 23:5–6; 30:9).

Both 9:1 (MT 8:23) and 9:2 (MT 9:1) express the desire or longing of the prophet.[51] First, Jeremiah wishes that his head were water and his eyes a fountain of tears so that he could weep for his people (specifically the slain) day and night (Jer. 9:1 [MT 8:23]; cf. Isa. 22:4; Jer. 9:10, 17–19 [MT 9:9, 16–18]; 13:17; Lam. 2:11; 4Q439; *1 En.* 95:1; *2 Bar.* 35:2; *4 Bar.* 2:5). This text is particularly close to Jeremiah 14:17–18. It is not clear if it is in response to a slaying of the people or in anticipation of it. Second, Jeremiah wishes that he were a "distant lodge" (מלון אחרון; MT: "travelers' lodge" [מלון ארחים]) in the wilderness so that he could leave or forsake his people and go away from them (Jer. 9:2 [MT 9:1]; cf. Jer. 14:8; Ps. 55:8 [Eng., 55:7]). He explains that this is because they are all adulterers (cf. Hos. 7:4; Jer. 23:10), literally (Jer. 5:8) and spiritually (Jer. 3:9b; 5:7). They are "an assembly of treacherous/unfaithful people" (see Jer. 3:7b, 8b, 10, 11; cf. Hab. 1:5). The use of the term עצרת ("assembly") suggests a sacred assembly of idolaters rejected by the LORD (2 Kgs. 10:20; Isa. 1:13; Amos 5:21; see BDB, 783).

The LORD speaks in 9:3a (MT 9:2a): "And they bent their tongue like a bow [MT: their bow] in deception, and not in faithfulness/reliability was it mighty [MT: were they mighty] in the land" (cf. Ps. 64:4 [Eng., 64:3]). This translation follows the guidance of the Masoretic accentuation. The tongue of the people is likened to a deceptive (i.e., malfunctioning) bow that fails the archer (cf. Jer. 9:5, 8 [MT 9:4, 7]).[52] This bow (i.e., their tongue) was mighty in the land but not in faithfulness/reliability. It was mighty in deception (i.e., failure). This comparison is similar to what is said about the sons of Ephraim in Psalm 78:8–9. They were unfaithful/unreliable archers who turned back in the day of battle. According to Psalm 78:57, they acted treacherously/unfaithfully (cf. Jer. 9:2b [MT 9:1b]) like their forefathers and were like a deceptive/unreliable (i.e., malfunctioning) bow (cf. Hos. 7:16). The term שקר ("deception") has been used in a variety of contexts thus far in Jeremiah (Jer. 3:10, 23; 5:2, 31; 6:13; 7:4, 8, 9; 8:8, 10), but it is in 5:2 that it describes the speech of the people in contrast to אמונה ("faithfulness") (Jer. 5:1, 3; cf. Jer. 4:2). The people swear disingenuously in the name of the LORD and swear by the non-god Baal (Jer. 5:7; 7:9; 12:16; Amos 8:14; Zeph. 1:5) and thus follow the false prophets of Baal (Jer.

---

51. *Lamentations Rabbah* suggests that the speaker in 9:1 (MT 8:23) must be God because only he can stay awake to weep day and night (Ps. 121:4) (see Neusner, *Jeremiah in Talmud and Midrash*, 256), but see 4Q483.

52. Holladay insists that 9:8 (MT 9:7) requires the tongue to be compared to an arrow in 9:3 (MT 9:2) (*Jeremiah 1*, 300), but there is no reason why it cannot be compared to a bow in one verse and an arrow in another.

2:8b; 5:31; 6:13; 8:10; 13:25; 23:14). The Lord explains, "For from evil to evil they went forth, and me they did not acknowledge" (Jer. 9:3b [MT 9:2b]). The expression "from evil to evil" appears to indicate ever-increasing idolatrous activity (see Judg. 2:11; 3:6, 12; 4:1; 6:1; 10:6; 13:1; cf. Ps. 84:8 [Eng., 84:7]). As for the Lord, the people have not acknowledged him as their God (cf. Isa. 5:13; Jer. 2:8; 4:22; 9:6, 24 [MT 9:5, 23]; Hos. 2:10 [Eng., 2:8]; 4:1, 6).[53]

The situation described in Jeremiah 9:4 (MT 9:3) shows the extent of the people's deception. No one can be trusted, not even friends and family (see Jer. 12:6; cf. Mic. 7:5–7). The structure of the verse is chiastic: (A) friend/neighbor, (B) brother/relative, (B1) brother/relative, and (A1) friend/neighbor. No one can be trusted because every brother or relative "surely follows at the heel" (עקוב יעקב), and every friend or neighbor goes about as a slanderer (see Lev. 19:16–18; Jer. 6:28). This language draws a comparison between the people of Judah and their patriarch "Jacob" (יעקב) who grabbed the "heel" (עקב) of his brother Esau at birth (Gen. 25:26) and later acted in "deceit" (מרמה) against him to obtain his father's blessing (Gen. 27:35; see Jer. 9:6, 8 [MT 9:5, 7]) and thus "followed at the heel" (עקב) of his brother twice in order to obtain both the birthright and the blessing (Gen. 27:36).[54] Such a comparison has a precedent in Hosea 12 where the "deceit" (מרמה) of the northern kingdom of Israel (Hos. 12:8 [Eng., 12:7]) is analogous to the "deceit" (מרמה) of Jacob/Israel (Gen. 27:35) who "followed at the heel" (עקב) of his brother (Hos. 12:4 [Eng., 12:3]).[55]

Jeremiah 9:5 (MT 9:4) continues the thought of 9:4 (MT 9:3): "Each with his friend/neighbor mocks/deceives/trifles [cf. Gen. 31:7]. Truth/Faithfulness (אמת) they do not speak [see Zech. 7:8–10; 8:16–17]. Their tongue has learned to speak deception (שקר) [MT: They have taught their tongue to speak deception; cf. Jer. 9:3, 8 (MT 9:2, 7)]. They have committed iniquity and are weary of returning [cf. Exod. 7:18b; Jer. 3:7, 19; 8:5; MT: They have wearied themselves committing iniquity]." The last two consonants in the Hebrew source behind Greek Jeremiah (שב), which form the infinitive in the expression "and are weary of returning (שב)," are the first two consonants of the word at the beginning of MT 9:5 (LXX 9:6): שבתך ("Your dwelling"). The beginning of LXX 9:6 (MT 9:5) reflects תך ("injury, wrong"), which is rendered into Greek as

---

53. It is not a question of whether they have known him but whether they have recognized and acknowledged him as the one true God.

54. See Keil, *Jeremiah*, 115; Bright, *Jeremiah*, 67, 71–72; Holladay, *Jeremiah 1*, 300. See also MT Jeremiah 17:9 and LXX Malachi 3:8.

55. See Shepherd, *Commentary on the Book of the Twelve*, 98–103.

τόκος ("interest, usury"). This results in two very different translations for 9:5–6 (MT 9:4–5) (see note to translation above). According to the Hebrew source behind Greek Jeremiah 9:6 (MT 9:5), the LORD says, "Injury upon injury, deceit upon deceit [cf. Hos. 4:2b; Pss. 10:7; 55:12 (Eng., 55:1)], they have refused to acknowledge me [cf. Jer. 4:22; 8:5; 9:3, 24 (MT 9:2, 23); Isa. 5:13; Hos. 4:1, 6; 6:6]." According to MT 9:5 (LXX 9:6), he says, "Your dwelling is in the midst of deceit. In deceit they have refused to acknowledge me," the prophetic utterance of the LORD.[56] The use of the term מרמה ("deceit") provides another allusion to the Jacob story (Gen. 27:35; cf. Hos. 12:8 [Eng., 12:7]; see also Jer. 8:5; 9:8 [MT 9:7]).

Jeremiah 9:7 (MT 9:6) introduces the announcement of judgment: Therefore [לכן], thus says the LORD [MT adds: of hosts], "Look, I am about to refine them and test them, for I will act [MT: for how else can I act? (or, for how I will act!)] from before [or, because of] the evil [the evil > MT] of the daughter of my people." For the image of refining and testing, see the commentary on Jeremiah 6:27–30 (see also Jer. 11:20; 12:3; 17:10; 20:12; cf. Isa. 1:25; 48:9–11; Zech. 13:9; Prov. 17:3). According to the Hebrew source behind Greek Jeremiah 9:8 (and MT *kethiv* 9:7), the tongue of the people is a "slaughtering" (שוחט) arrow (cf. Jer. 9:3 [MT 9:2]), but according to the MT *qere* 9:7, it is a "hammered/sharpened" (שחוט) arrow (cf. Syr.). The comparison of the tongue to the arrow symbolizes the deceit of the deadly words of their mouth (cf. Jer. 9:3–6 [MT 9:2–5]; Ps. 5:10 [Eng., 5:9]; Jas. 3). Following the model of the false prophets of peace (Jer. 6:14; 8:11 [MT]), each person speaks peace or well-being with his friend or neighbor, but inside he has "enmity" (איבה; MT: "his ambush" [ארבו]; cf. Mic. 7:2). Other texts express this idea equally well: "Near are you in their mouth but far from their kidneys/inner parts" (Jer. 12:2b; cf. Isa. 29:13); "speakers of peace with their friends/neighbors, but evil is in their heart" (Ps. 28:3; cf. Pss. 55:22 [Eng., 55:21]; 62:5 [Eng., 62:4]); "with his lip(s) a hater disguises himself, but in his inward part he puts deceit; when he makes his voice gracious, do not believe in him, for seven abominations are in his heart" (Prov. 26:24–25; cf. Prov. 10:6, 11, 18). For Jeremiah 9:9 (MT 9:8)—"Concerning these things will I not visit/punish [or, Upon these will I not visit (i.e., Will I not punish these); MT adds: them]?" the prophetic utterance of the LORD. "On a nation such as this will I

---

56. There may be a connection here to Deuteronomy 6:7: "and you will speak of them when you sit/dwell (בשבתך) in your house." The people were to speak the words of the Torah in their homes, but the false pen of the scribes has corrupted the transmission of the text of the Torah (Jer. 8:8).

not avenge myself?"—see the commentary on the use of the refrain in Jeremiah 5:9, 29.[57]

9:10 (MT 9:9) "Concerning the mountains [4QJer[a]*: הרים] lift up [m. pl.; cf. Syr.; MT: I will lift up] weeping [MT adds: and wailing], and concerning wilderness pastures [LXX: paths] a lament. For they are burned [LXX: they failed] so that there is no person [MT adds: passing through]. They [MT: And they] do not hear a sound of livestock. From the flying creatures of the sky to the large land animals, they flee, they go. 9:11 (MT 9:10) And I will make Jerusalem into exile(s) [MT: heaps] and a habitation for jackals [LXX: dragons]. And the cities of Judah I will make a desolation so that there is no inhabitant." 9:12 (MT 9:11) Who is the wise man that he may understand/explain this [or, Whoever is wise, let him understand/explain this]? And to whom has the word of the mouth of the LORD come [MT: And to whom has the mouth of the LORD spoken] that he may declare it [LXX adds: to you; or, And to whomever the word of the mouth of the LORD has come, let him declare it]? Why does the land perish? (Why) is it burned like the wilderness so that no one passes through?*

9:13 (MT 9:12) And the LORD said to me [to me > MT], "Because they forsook my Torah [or, instruction], which I set before them [Syr.: which I gave to them and to their forefathers], and did not obey my voice [MT adds: and did not walk in it], 9:14 (MT 9:13) and they walked/went after the stubbornness [LXX: pleasing things; cf. Syr.] of their evil [evil > Codex L] heart and after the Baals [LXX: idols; cf. Syr.] that their forefathers taught them." 9:15 (MT 9:14) Therefore, thus says the LORD [MT adds: of hosts], the God of Israel, "Look, I am about to make them [MT adds: this people] eat wormwood [LXX: distress] and make them drink bitter water [Tg. Jon.: a cup of curse, as bad as snake venom], 9:16 (MT 9:15) and I will scatter them among the nations whom they and their forefathers have not known, and I will send after them the sword until I finish them with it [with it > MT],"

---

57. "The refrain is used structurally after passages in which Yahweh's people are indicted for their transgressions (5:7–8; 5:20–28; 9:1–8). Pohlmann suggests the possibility that Jeremiah 7–8 have been inserted supplementarily, disturbing the close relationship between the passages which end with the refrain. In any case, the threefold use of the refrain indicates the care with which the material in these early chapters has been brought together in a unified way" (Parke-Taylor, *Formation of the Book of Jeremiah*, 188).

9:17 (MT 9:16) says the Lord *[MT: Thus says the* Lord *of hosts]. Summon [MT: Consider carefully and summon] the lamenting women that they may come [lit., and let them come], and to the wise/skilled women send that they may speak [lit., and let them speak; MT: that they may come], 9:18 (MT 9:17) that they may lift up over/for us wailing [lit., and let them lift up over us wailing; MT: and make haste, that they may lift up over/for us wailing], that our eyes may go down with tears [lit., and let our eyes go down with tears], and our eyelids, that they may flow with water [lit., and our eyelids, let them flow with water]. 9:19 (MT 9:18) For a sound of wailing is heard in Zion [Codex L: from Zion], "How we are ruined! We are very ashamed, for we have left the land and [Codex L: for; mlt Mss: and for] cast down [MT: they have cast down] our dwelling places [Syr.: and our dwelling places have fallen]." 9:20 (MT 9:19) [MT adds* כי*] Hear,*[58] *O women, the word of God [MT: the word of the* Lord*], and let your ear receive the words [MT: word] of his mouth [Tg. Jon.: the words of his prophets], and teach [or, in order that you may teach] your daughters wailing, and each her companion [i.e., female friend or neighbor] lament. 9:21 (MT 9:20) For death has gone up through our windows, it has entered our land [MT: our prominent buildings] to cut off infant from outside [or, street] and [and > MT] choice, young men from squares. 9:22 (MT 9:21) [MT adds: Speak (*דַּבֵּר*;* LXX[OL]*, Theod. =* דֶּבֶר*), Thus the prophetic utterance of the* Lord*] And the human corpses will be [MT: And the human corpse will fall] as a likeness [*דמין*;* LXX: *pattern, example; MT: dung (*דמן*)] on the surface of the ground [Codex L: field] and [and > Ms, LXX[B]] as a swath/row of fallen grain from after the harvester, and there is no one gathering.*

9:23 (MT 9:22) Thus says the Lord*, "Let not a wise man boast in his wisdom, and let not the mighty man boast in his might, and [and > Codex L] let not a rich man boast in his riches. 9:24 (MT 9:23) But in this let the one who boasts boast: having insight and knowing/acknowledging [MT adds: me] that I am the* Lord *[or, that I, the* Lord*, am] doing covenant loyalty and [and > MT] justice and righteousness in the land [LXX 1 Sam 2:10: having insight and knowing the Lord and doing justice and righteousness in the land], for in these things is my delight [MT: I delight]," the prophetic utterance of the* Lord*. 9:25 (MT 9:24) "Look, days are coming," the prophetic utterance of the* Lord*, "and I will visit upon [i.e., punish] every person circumcised in foreskin [Tg. Jon.: all the uncircumcised peoples and the house of Israel whose deeds resemble those of*

---

58. The Greek text ἀκούσατε δή may reflect Hebrew שמענה נא.

the uncircumcised; Luther: the circumcised with the uncircumcised], 9:26 (MT 9:25) upon Egypt and upon Judah and upon Edom and upon the sons of Ammon and upon the sons of [the sons of > MT] Moab and upon all people who are cut off of side / corner [i.e., those with hair clipped on the temples] who live in the wilderness [i.e., Arabian tribes], for all the nations are uncircumcised in flesh [in flesh > MT; Syr., Tg. Jon.: in their flesh], and all the members of the house of Israel are uncircumcised in their heart [cf. Syr., Tg. Jon.; MT: uncircumcised of heart]."

A decision about the identity of the speaker in 9:10 (MT 9:9) hinges in part on the textual variation in 9:10a (MT 9:9a). According to the Hebrew source behind Greek Jeremiah, the use of a masculine plural imperative suggests that the LORD is the speaker making a general address (but see Jer. 7:29): "Concerning the mountains lift up (שאו) weeping, and concerning wilderness pastures a lament" (cf. Jer. 9:18 [MT 9:17]; 23:10; Amos 5:1). This is followed by the Syriac. But the first-person singular verb of the MT might suggest that Jeremiah is the speaker: "Concerning the mountains I will lift up (אשא) weeping and wailing, and concerning wilderness pastures a lament" (cf. Jer. 9:1, 19, 20 [MT 8:23; 9:18, 19]; Ezek. 2:10; 2 Chr. 35:25). Since the LORD is the speaker in 9:11 (MT 9:10), it may be that the Hebrew source behind Greek Jeremiah has adjusted 9:10 (MT 9:9) so that the LORD is the speaker in both verses,[59] but Holladay accepts the reading of the MT and argues that the LORD is still the speaker.[60] The present commentary accepts the reading of the Hebrew source behind Greek Jeremiah and assumes the LORD to be the speaker in 9:10–11 (MT 9:9–10). The MT is likely an adjustment based on the first-person voice in 9:1 (MT 8:23). Weeping, wailing, and lamenting are important features of the immediate context (Jer. 7:29; 9:1, 17–22 [MT 8:23; 9:16–21]). The reason for such behavior here is that the fertile mountains and wild pastures are "burned" (נצתו) so that there are no people there (MT adds עבר ["passing through"]; cf. Jer. 9:12b [MT 9:11b]). A comparison with the language of witnesses to Jeremiah 2:15; 4:7, 26; 9:12 (MT 9:11) suggests that the verb נצתו ("burned") could be either נתצו ("torn down") or a form of נצה ("fall in ruins"). The remainder of Jeremiah 9:10 (MT 9:9) envisions a land not only void of humans but also missing the sound of livestock. Animal life in general is absent: "From the flying creatures of the sky to the large land animals, they flee, they go." This picture of desolation is reminiscent of Jeremiah 4:23–29 (cf. Jer. 7:20; Zeph. 1:3). According to MT 9:10a (LXX, Eng., 9:11a), the LORD will

---

59. McKane, *Jeremiah I–XXV*, 203–4.
60. Holladay, *Jeremiah 1*, 303–4.

make Jerusalem into "heaps" (גלים) and a habitation for jackals (cf. Isa. 13:22; 34:13; Jer. 10:22; 49:33; 51:37). According to the Hebrew source behind Greek Jeremiah, the LORD will make Jerusalem into "exile(s)" (גלות) (see Jer. 24:5; 28:4; 29:22; 40:1; 52:31). The cities of Judah will be made into a desolation without inhabitants (Jer. 9:11b [MT 9:10b]; cf. Isa. 6:11; Jer. 2:15; 4:7, 29; 9:12 [Eng., 9:11]). In other words, not only will the mountains and pastures of the wilderness be destroyed (Jer. 9:10 [MT 9:9]) but also the densely populated cities (Jer. 9:11 [MT 9:10]).

There is more than one legitimate way to render the text of Jeremiah 9:12a (MT 9:11a): (1) "Who is the wise man that he may understand/explain this? And to whom has the word of the mouth of the LORD come[61] that he may declare it?" (2) "Whoever is wise, let him understand/explain this. And to whomever the word of the mouth of the LORD has come, let him declare it." (3) "Who is the wise man? Let him understand/explain this, and let him to whom the word of the mouth of the LORD has come declare it."[62] The demonstrative "this" and the pronoun "it" refer back to the judgment described in 9:10–11 (MT 9:9–10). This is indicated by 9:12b (MT 9:11b): "Why does the land perish? (Why) is it burned like the wilderness so that no one passes through?" Who can comprehend or explain this situation and declare it to others (cf. Jer. 5:19; 13:22)? Both Rashi and Redak suggest that the wise man is distinct from the one to whom the word of the LORD comes, namely, a prophet (cf. Jer. 1:1–4, 11, 13).[63] Given the lack of true wise men (Jer. 4:22; 8:8–9) and the presence of false prophets (Jer. 2:8b; 5:31; 6:13–15), those who could understand/explain and declare what is happening would seem to be in short supply. As Calvin suggests, this is all the more reason for the faithful few to step up and respond to the call.[64] Only those who have the fear of the LORD are wise enough to comprehend and explain the judgment (see Deut. 31:13; Jer. 9:23–24 [MT 9:22–23]; Prov. 1:7; 9:10; Job 28:28). Only those to whom the revelatory word of the LORD has come can declare it. The language of Jeremiah 9:12a (MT 9:11a) is very close to that of Hosea 14:10 (Eng., 14:9) and Psalm 107:43 (see also Jas 3:13), but Jeremiah is not

---

61. Greek Jeremiah reflects דְּבַר פִּי יהוה ("the word of the mouth of the LORD") rather than MT דִּבֶּר פִּי יהוה ("has the mouth of the LORD spoken").

62. See Holladay, *Jeremiah 1*, 306–7. It is also possible to disregard the *athnach* of the MT and interpret the pronoun "it" proleptically: "that he may declare [or, let him declare] why the land perishes."

63. Rosenberg, trans., *Mikraoth Gedoloth: Jeremiah Volume One*, 85; see also McKane, *Jeremiah I–XXV*, 206.

64. Calvin, *Jeremiah*, 1:478.

dependent upon Hosea or the Psalter here. The Hosea text is part of a compositional seam that connects the end of Hosea to the beginning of Joel (Joel 1:2–3) by employing the language of the wisdom literature (cf. Ps. 78:1–8; Prov. 1–9; 10:1–22:16). The composer of the Twelve typically uses such distinct material along with citation from the book of Jeremiah in order to develop the program set forth in Hosea 3:4–5.[65] The citation from Jeremiah 9:12 (MT 9:11) in Hosea 14:10 (Eng., 14:9) helps to establish a wisdom reading strategy for the Twelve.[66]

The Lord answers the question posed in 9:12b (MT 9:11b): "Because they forsook my Torah, which I set before them, and did not obey my voice [MT adds: and did not walk in it], and they walked/went after the stubbornness of their evil heart and after the Baals that their forefathers taught them" (Jer. 9:13–14 [MT 9:12–13]; cf. Jer. 5:19; 16:10–13). The people face the judgment of 9:10–11 (MT 9:9–10) because they have abandoned the Lord's instruction in the written text of the Torah (see Jer. 2:8; 6:19; 8:8–9), the very Torah that has been set before them (cf. Deut. 4:8; 30:1; Jer. 26:4; 44:10).[67] To forsake the Torah is to forsake the Lord himself (cf. Jer. 1:16) and disobey his voice (cf. Jer. 3:13; 7:28; 22:21). The MT adds "and did not walk in it" (ולא הלכו בה) to the end of 9:13 (MT 9:12), which Janzen suggests is a gloss for על עזבם את תורתי ("because they forsook my Torah") on the basis of Jeremiah 26:4 and 44:10.[68] This addition anticipates the language of 9:14 (MT 9:13), which says that the people "walked" after the stubbornness of their evil heart (cf. Jer. 3:17; 7:24; 13:10; 23:17) and after the Baals that their fathers taught them (see Jer. 2:23; 12:16; cf. Jer. 2:5b, 8b).

Having answered the question from 9:12b (MT 9:11b) in 9:13–14 (MT 9:12–13), the Lord again announces judgment in 9:15–16 (MT 9:14–15; cf. Jer. 9:7–11 [MT 9:6–10]): "Look, I am about to make them [MT adds: this people] eat wormwood and make them drink bitter water, and I will scatter them among the nations whom they and their forefathers have not known, and I will send after them the sword until I finish them with it [with it > MT]." The language of 9:15 (MT 9:14) is very close to that of the people's words in 8:14 and to that of the announcement

---

65. See Shepherd, *Commentary on the Book of the Twelve*, 23–36.
66. Shepherd, *Commentary on the Book of the Twelve*, 112–13.
67. "The Talmud, therefore, deduces that they indeed studied the Torah, but they did not study it for its own sake but for their own interests. . . . Had they learned the Torah for its own sake, they would never have come to that state" (Rosenberg, trans., *Mikraoth Gedoloth: Jeremiah Volume One*, 86). See also Jeremiah 22:9; Psalm 89:31 (Eng., 89:30); Proverbs 4:2; 2 Chronicles 12:1.
68. Janzen, *Studies in the Text of Jeremiah*, 38.

of judgment against the false prophets in 23:15 (cf. Deut. 29:17 [Eng., 29:18]; Lam. 3:19; Rev. 8:11). In all three places, *Targum Jonathan* interprets the bitter water to be "a cup of curse, as bad as snake venom" (see Deut. 32:32–33; cf. Jer. 25:15; see also *Tg. Jon.* Jer. 11:19). The Lord will "scatter them among the nations" (Jer. 9:16a [MT 9:15a]; cf. Deut. 4:27; 28:64; 30:3; Jer. 13:24; 18:17; 30:11 [MT]) "whom they and their forefathers have not known" (cf. Deut. 28:36, 64; Jer. 5:15; 16:13; 17:4 [MT]; 22:28; Ezek. 32:9). The Lord will send the sword after them until he finishes them off (see Lev. 26:33; Jer. 14:12; 49:37), but not without a remnant (see Jer. 4:27; 5:10, 18; 30:11 [MT]; 46:28).

The Hebrew source behind Greek Jeremiah concludes the Lord's discourse from 9:15–16 (MT 9:14–15) at the beginning of 9:17 (MT 9:16): "says the Lord." The MT, on the other hand, introduces new discourse from the Lord here: "Thus says the Lord of hosts." But the use of the pronouns "us" and "our" in 9:18, 21 (MT 9:17, 20) suggests that Jeremiah is the speaker in 9:17–22 (MT 9:16–21).[69] These verses pick up the theme of lament from Jeremiah 9:1, 10 (MT 8:23; 9:9). McKane is likely correct that the call for lament here is not in response to events that have already occurred but in anticipation of things to come (cf. Amos 5:1).[70] The prophet gives the general call to summon the professional lamenting women (Jer. 9:17 [MT 9:16]; cf. Amos 5:16b; Matt. 9:23; Mark 5:38), those skilled in the practice, so that they might come, speak, and lift up wailing for everyone (Jer. 9:18 [MT 9:17]; cf. Jer. 9:10 [9:9]) in order that the eyes of the people may run with tears and that their eyelids may run with water (cf. Jer. 9:1 [MT 8:23]; 13:17; 14:17; Ps. 119:136; Lam. 1:16; 2:18; 3:48).[71] This is because a sound of wailing is heard in Zion (Codex L: "from Zion"), which Jeremiah quotes: "How we are ruined! We are very ashamed, for we have left the land and

---

69. These pronouns are in the MT and in Ziegler's Greek text (Göttingen Septuagint). Rahlfs' Greek text has "you" and "your." Note also that דבר כה נאם יהוה does not appear at the beginning of 9:22 (MT 9:21) in the Hebrew source behind the Old Greek.

70. "On the whole, it seems better to assume that they are a prophetic projection and so an expression of Jeremiah's absolute conviction that nothing can now save Jerusalem and Judah. Hence, even before the blow has fallen, there is nothing left for the prophet but to call for a public act of lamentation" (McKane, *Jeremiah I–XXV*, 209). See also Keil, *Jeremiah*, 118.

71. "There is another possibility, and that is that Jeremiah is here mocking the women who lament the dead Baal. There is precedent in Elijah's mocking of the prophets of Baal: Elijah characterized the god as sleeping or otherwise unavailable (1 Kgs 18:27)" (Holladay, *Jeremiah 1*, 312–13). Cf. Ezekiel 8:14.

cast down [MT: they have cast down] our dwelling places [Syr.: and our dwelling places have fallen]" (Jer. 9:19 [MT: 9:18]; cf. Jer. 2:26; 4:13; 8:9; 31:15).[72] The people who have not known to be ashamed (Jer. 6:15; 8:12 [MT]) are now ashamed.

In 9:20 (MT 9:19), Jeremiah calls on the professional mourning women to hear the word of God (MT: "the word of the LORD") and to receive the words (MT: "word") of his mouth and teach their daughters wailing and their female friends lament (cf. Ezek. 32:16). According to *Targum Jonathan*, these women are to receive the words of the LORD's prophets (as in Jer. 9:10, 17–18 [MT 9:9, 16–17]) and teach wailing and lament accordingly. Mishnah tractate *Mo'ed Qatan* 3:9 cites Jeremiah 9:20 (MT 9:19) and anticipates a time when there will be no more death or tears according to Isaiah 25:8, but for the present context the reason for the teaching of wailing and lament is that death has gone up through the windows and has entered the land (באדמתנו; MT: "prominent buildings" [בארמנותינו])[73] to cut off infants from the streets and young men from the squares (Jer. 9:21 [MT 9:20]). Some commentators have suggested that this has a parallel in a story from Canaanite mythology in which Baal is hesitant to put a window in his palace because he wants to keep Mot (the god of death) from kidnapping his daughters.[74] More recent commentators, however, have rejected this parallel.[75] The imagery in 9:21 (MT 9:20) has a better parallel in the prophetic literature of the Bible: "Against the city they rush, upon the city wall they run; on the houses they go up, through the windows they enter like the thief" (Joel 2:9). The enemy who brings death swarms upon the city like locusts and enters the very windows of the houses. Death has gone up through the windows (having entered the land) to kill the infants inside and those in the prime of life, making them absent from the streets and squares where they would normally be found (cf. Exod. 12:12, 23, 29). "And the human corpses will be [MT: And the human corpse will fall] as

---

72. The Hebrew source behind Greek Jeremiah says that the people have cast down and thus forsaken their dwelling places (i.e., gone into exile). The MT can be read in two different ways. One is to say that the enemies have cast down the people's dwelling places. The other is to say that the dwelling places have cast out the people (cf. Lev. 18:25). The Syriac is ambiguous about who casts down the dwelling places (cf. the suggested revocalization to *hophal* in the *BHS* apparatus).

73. It has been suggested that MT בארמנותינו is a corruption of בארבותינו ("through our lattices"). See McKane, *Jeremiah I–XXV*, 211.

74. E.g., Thompson, *Book of Jeremiah*, 317.

75. See Holladay, *Jeremiah 1*, 314; McKane, *Jeremiah I–XXV*, 211.

a likeness [דמין; LXX: pattern, example; MT: dung (דמן)] on the surface of the ground [Codex L: field] and [and > Ms, LXX[B]] as a swath/row of fallen grain from after the harvester, and there is no one gathering" (Jer. 9:22 [MT 9:21]).[76] The image of corpses in this latter verse has already been anticipated in Jeremiah 7:33 and 8:2 (see also Jer. 16:4; 25:33). Whereas the MT compares the corpses to "dung" (דמן) (cf. Isa. 5:25),[77] the Greek text indicates that an "example" (דמין) has been made of these people. Just as the people have witnessed the passing of the harvest without salvation (Jer. 8:20), so are they like a swath or row of fallen grain left behind the harvester without anyone to gather them.

It is often thought that 9:23–24 (MT 9:22–23) bears no relationship to the preceding material,[78] but the connection lies in the question posed in 9:12 (MT 9:11): "Who is the wise man?"[79] A wise person should not boast in his/her wisdom nor a mighty man in his might nor a rich man in his riches (Jer. 9:23 [MT 9:22]; see Isa. 5:21; 29:14; Pss. 52:3, 9 [Eng., 52:2, 8]; 75:5–6, 11 [Eng., 75:4–5, 10]; *Ahiqar* 207; 4Q460 8:2; Jas. 1:9–10).[80] Rather, the wise person is one who boasts in knowing or acknowledging the LORD (Jer. 9:24 [MT 9:23]; cf. Job 28:28;

------

76. The MT adds at the beginning of this verse: "Speak (דַּבֵּר; LXX[OL], Theod. = דְּבָר), 'Thus the prophetic utterance of the LORD.'" This is not in the Hebrew text behind the Old Greek and should be rejected as a secondary, editorial addition. Jeremiah is still the speaker in this verse.

77. Holladay sees an interesting parallel here with the story of Jezebel since the only earlier use of this term is in 2 Kings 9:37 where Elijah says that the corpse of Jezebel will be like dung on the open field: "Jeremiah is suggesting that the people are all comparable to Jezebel. Indeed is the parallel with Jezebel not reinforced by the reference to 'windows' in v 20?—Jezebel looked out her window before she was assassinated, and was doubtless thrown to her death through her window (2 Kgs 9:30, 32): compare the theme of the harlot peering through the window, already referred to (4:30)" (Holladay, *Jeremiah 1*, 315).

78. See, e.g., McKane, *Jeremiah I–XXV*, 213.

79. Note also the summoning of "the wise women" in Jeremiah 9:17 (MT 9:16).

80. "There is a sharp contrast between the antithesis of חכמה and גבורה in some wisdom sentences, or the representation in others that חכמה and עשר are complementary, and the condemnatory lumping together of wisdom, power and wealth in vv. 22–23 (cf. Prov 16.32; 21.22; Eccles 9.16ff.). A pejorative attitude to wealth is not normal in the book of Proverbs, although it is attested in 11.28 and 28.11. In 28.11 we have a correlation of impiety and wealth, and of piety and poverty which is more characteristic of certain Psalms than of the book of Proverbs. The impression which is to be had elsewhere in Proverbs is a different one. Wisdom has length of days in her right hand,

Prov. 1:7; 9:10)—something the people of Judah and Jerusalem have not done (Jer. 9:13–14 [MT 9:12–13]; see also Jer. 5:1). To their shame they have boasted in their own wisdom (Jer. 8:8–9), which is really a lack of wisdom (Jer. 4:22). They have not known or acknowledged the LORD (Jer. 9:3, 6 [MT 9:2, 5]).

According to 9:24 (MT 9:23), the one who boasts must be one "having insight" (השכל). This infinitive absolute is coordinated with the following ידע ("knowing/acknowledging"), but it does not share the same object. השכל is intransitive and thus has no object (and therefore should not be translated as "understanding" with a following object). Such insight comes from the reading of the Torah (Josh. 1:8 [ואז תשכיל]). What or whom the one who boasts must acknowledge can be rendered in more than one way. In the Hebrew source behind Greek Jeremiah, which does not have the object "me" (אותי), כי אני יהוה can be translated like the recognition formula in Ezekiel: "that I am the LORD" (cf. Ezek. 6:7b et al.).[81] This would require the following participle (עֹשֶׂה ["doing"]) to be attributive. The same construction could be rendered so that the participle is a predicate: "that I, the LORD, am doing." In the MT, which does have the object "me" (אותי),[82] the כי could also be a causal conjunction: "for I am the LORD doing"; "for I, the LORD, am doing." Both the Hebrew source behind Greek Jeremiah and the MT describe the LORD as the one "doing covenant loyalty and [and > MT] justice and righteousness in the land" (עשה חסד ומשפט וצדקה בארץ), but elsewhere in the book of Jeremiah "justice and righteousness" (משפט וצדקה) are expressions of knowing or acknowledging the LORD (see also Isa. 64:4; Ps. 106:3; Prov. 21:3). In MT Jeremiah 22:15b (cf. Jer. 22:3; see also Jer. 4:2), the LORD points out that Josiah, in contrast to his sons, "did justice and righteousness" (עשה משפט וצדקה). He then asks in Jeremiah 22:16b, "Is not that what it is to know me (הלוא היא הדעת אתי)?" Also, the Davidic Messiah in Jeremiah 23:5b "will have insight and do justice and righteousness in the land" (והשכיל ועשה משפט וצדקה בארץ).[83] Thus, it has been

---

wealth and honour (עשר וכבוד) in her left hand (3.16; cf. 8.18). Wealth is the crown of wise men (14.24)" (McKane, *Jeremiah I–XXV*, 212).

81. This would be an acknowledgment that he is Yahweh, the God who is present with his people (Exod. 3:12, 14). See Rolf Rendtorff, *The Canonical Hebrew Bible: A Theology of the Old Testament*, trans. David E. Orton (Leiden: Deo, 2005), 40.

82. Cf. Jeremiah 31:34.

83. Cf. Isaiah 9:5–6 (Eng., 9:6–7); 11:3–5; Psalm 72:1–4. This connection has likely prompted Paul's references to Jeremiah in 1 Corinthians 1:31 and

suggested that the Greek text of 1 Samuel 2:10 (cf. 4QSam[a]), which is substantially longer than the MT and features a version of the same text as Jeremiah 9:24 (MT 9:23), preserves a witness to a more original Hebrew text for Jeremiah (see also Ode 3:10): "having insight and knowing the Lord (= את יהוה) and doing (= וְעָשֹׂה or וַעֲשֹׂה) justice and righteousness in the land" (συνίειν καὶ γινώσκειν τὸν κύριον καὶ ποιεῖν κρίμα καὶ δικαιοσύνην ἐν μέσῳ τῆς γῆς).[84] The one who knows the Lord is the one who does justice and righteousness in the land. The Lord delights in these things and is pleased with the one who does them.

---

2 Corinthians 10:17 ("Let the one boasts boast in the Lord"). For Paul, Christ (the Lord in the flesh as the Davidic Messiah) is wisdom from God (1 Cor. 1:24, 30; cf. Matt. 11:19; see also Prov. 8:22–31; Col. 1:15–20). See Shepherd, *Text in the Middle*, 9–11.

84. See Isac Leo Seeligmann, *Gesammelte Studien zur Hebräischen Bibel*, FAT 41 (Tübingen: Mohr Siebeck, 2004), 454–55; Emanuel Tov, *The Greek and Hebrew Bible: Collected Essays on the Septuagint* (Atlanta: SBL, 2006), 448–52. S. R. Driver considers the longer text of LXX 1 Samuel 2:10 to be the result of an insertion from Jeremiah (*Notes on the Hebrew Text and the Topography of the Books of Samuel*, 2nd ed. [Oxford: Oxford University Press, 1912; repr., Eugene, OR: Wipf & Stock, 2004], 27). This insertion, which also includes the exhortation not to boast in wisdom, might, or riches, was likely prompted by the content of Hannah's prayer (1 Sam. 2:1–10), which encourages boasting in the Lord (1 Sam. 2:1–3) and discourages boasting in might (1 Sam. 2:4, 9b) and riches (1 Sam. 2:7). The source for the translated insertion was a superior Hebrew text of Jeremiah. The development from the form of the text in this source to the forms represented by LXX and MT Jeremiah probably began with the abbreviation of את יהוה to אתי (cf. Jer. 6:11 MT: חמת יהוה; LXX = חמתי), which was misinterpreted in the MT as the pronominal object "me" (אותי) and dropped altogether in the Hebrew source behind Greek Jeremiah. This led to the expansion כי אני יהוה, which separated וְעָשֹׂה or וַעֲשֹׂה from the other two infinitives and resulted in the change to the participle עֹשֶׂה to describe the Lord's action. The final step was the addition of חסד to the list of things done. On the other hand, P. Kyle McCarter Jr. argues that both the LXX *Vorlage* and the MT of 1 Samuel 2:10 suffered haplography and partial restoration (*1 Samuel: A New Translation with Introduction and Commentary*, Anchor Yale Bible 8 [New Haven, CT: Yale University Press, 1980], 70). This raises this question of whether a longer Hebrew version of 1 Samuel 2:10 was a source for Jeremiah. It is worth noting that the hope of an anointed king expressed in 1 Samuel 2:10 sets the trajectory for the book as a whole, which includes the covenant with David (2 Sam. 7). This same hope finds expression in the text of Jeremiah 23:5 cited above.

The following unit in Jeremiah 9:25–26 (MT 9:24–25) is also thought to be unrelated to the preceding context, but the connection goes back to Jeremiah 4:1–4 and runs through 9:23–24 (MT 9:22–23). According to 4:1–4, those who have circumcised hearts (Jer. 4:4) will swear by the LORD in "justice and righteousness" and be blessed (Jer. 4:2). According to 9:24 (MT 9:23), those who do "justice and righteousness" are pleasing to the LORD. The issue at hand in 9:25–26 (MT 9:24–25) is the difference between mere physical circumcision of the foreskin and spiritual circumcision of the heart. The unit begins with a future reference: "Look, days are coming" (Jer. 9:25 [MT 9:24]; cf. Jer. 7:32; 16:14; 19:6; 23:5, 7; 30:3; 31:27, 31; 33:14 [MT]; 48:12; 49:2; 51:47, 52). The LORD will visit upon or punish every person "circumcised in foreskin" (מול בערלה). *Targum Jonathan* interprets this to mean "all the uncircumcised peoples and the house of Israel whose deeds resemble those of the uncircumcised."[85] In other words, every unrighteous person "circumcised" (מול) along with every "foreskin" (ערלה; i.e., "uncircumcised person"). Luther and Calvin likewise render it "the circumcised with the uncircumcised."[86] Keil prefers to translate it as an oxymoron: "circumcised and yet possessed of the foreskin" or "uncircumcised-circumcised."[87] On the other hand, Bright simply renders the phrase "circumcised physically" (lit., "circumcised as to the foreskin").[88] This latter understanding is more in accordance with usage of the terminology elsewhere (see Gen. 17:14, 23, 24, 25; Lev. 12:3).

Verse 26 (MT v. 25) then lists those "circumcised in foreskin" who will be judged: Egypt, Judah, Ammon, Moab, and those with hair clipped on the temples who live in the wilderness. According to Josephus (*Ant.* 8:262), the Egyptians did indeed practice physical circumcision, and others learned it from them.[89] Rashi understands the phrase קצוצי פאה (lit., "cut off of side/corner") to mean "those cast off to the corner

---

85. "With the exegesis of Targ. and Kimchi vv. 24–25 can be explained as a consistent unit. Yahweh threatens circumcised and uncircumcised alike with a punitive judgement; the nations mentioned in v. 25 other than Judah are the 'uncircumcised' and Judah alone is 'circumcised.' There follows the statement that all the nations are uncircumcised and that the house of Israel, despite its having the physical mark of circumcision, is uncircumcised in heart" (McKane, *Jeremiah I–XXV*, 214).
86. Calvin, *Jeremiah*, 1:504.
87. Keil, *Jeremiah*, 120.
88. Bright, *Jeremiah*, 78.
89. Thus, it was a disgrace for Egyptians to die the death of the uncircumcised (see Ezek. 28:10; 32:19, 21, 24–30, 32).

of the desert,"[90] but most modern interpreters take it to mean "those with hair clipped on the temples" who live in the wilderness—that is, Arabian tribes (Jer. 25:23; 49:32; see BDB, 802; cf. Lev. 13:41; 19:27). This list of peoples is followed by an explanation for the judgment: "for all the nations are uncircumcised in flesh [in flesh > MT; Syr., *Tg. Jon.*: in their flesh], and all the members of the house of Israel are uncircumcised in their heart [cf. Syr., *Tg. Jon.*; MT: uncircumcised of heart]." The phrase "all the nations" does not refer back to the preceding list (as in "all these nations").[91] Judah is part of the preceding list of peoples, but here "all the nations" is set over against "all the members of the house of Israel," which in this context refers to Judah (see Jer. 10:1). "All the nations" refers to all nations other than Judah/Israel who do not practice physical circumcision specifically as a sign of the covenant with Abraham (Gen. 17) or as part of the Sinai law (Lev. 12). Thus, regardless of the practice of circumcision by nations like Egypt, they are all uncircumcised in the flesh. This is only implied in the MT ("uncircumcised") but made explicit in the Hebrew source behind Greek Jeremiah ("uncircumcised in flesh") and in the Syriac and *Targum Jonathan* ("uncircumcised in their flesh"). As Bright puts it, they are not members of the covenant people.[92] On the other hand, all the members of the house of Israel are "uncircumcised in their heart." That is, they are in need of the new covenant transformation of the heart (Lev. 26:41; Deut. 29:3 [Eng., 29:4]; 30:6; Jer. 4:4; 6:10; 31:31–34; Ezek. 11:19–20; 36:26; Acts 7:51; Rom. 2:25, 28–29; 1 Cor. 7:19; Gal. 5:6; 6:15; Col. 2:11). This is not to say that all the nations are circumcised in their heart. Their lack of spiritual circumcision is taken for granted. The point is that the physical circumcision of the Abrahamic or Mosaic covenant will ultimately be of no use to those whose hearts are not circumcised.[93]

---

90. Rosenberg, trans., *Mikraoth Gedoloth: Jeremiah Volume One*, 90.

91. See Keil, *Jeremiah*, 120.

92. Bright, *Jeremiah*, 78. See Neusner, *Jeremiah in Talmud and Midrash*, 1. See also Ezekiel 32:19–32; 44:7, 9. Calvin, on the other hand, thinks that Judah has become one of the nations (*Jeremiah*, 1:507).

93. Despite the lack of historical evidence, recent commentators have been inclined to follow Rudolph's suggestion of a coalition of circumcised peoples led by Egypt against the uncircumcised Babylonians (e.g., Holladay, *Jeremiah 1*, 319; see also Isa. 52:1). The point would then be that it is not enough merely to be on the side of the physically circumcised.

JEREMIAH 10

10:1 Hear the word of the LORD that he speaks to you [MT: Hear the word that the LORD speaks to you], O house of Israel. 10:2 Thus says the LORD, "According to the ways [MT: way] of the nations do not learn [LXX[A]: go], and by reason of the signs of the sky do not be dismayed. For they are dismayed before them [MT: For the nations are dismayed by reason of them]. 10:3 For the statutes/customs of the peoples [Syr.: the fear of the peoples] are vanity. There is a tree from a forest cut [MT: For a tree from a forest, he cuts it], a craftsman's work and a molten image [MT: a work of a craftsman's hands with an axe]. 10:4 With silver and gold he makes it beautiful [LXX: they are adorned; Syr.: they are overlaid; Tg. Jon.: he overlays it]. With hammers and nails [MT: With nails and hammers] he makes them firm, and they do not totter [or, so that they do not totter; LXX: and they will not be moved; MT: and it does not totter]. 10:5a Gold of hammered work [LXX: Wrought silver; MT: Like a post (or, scarecrow) in a cucumber field] is it [MT: are they], they do not walk [MT: and they do not speak]. 10:9 Beaten silver [Syr.: Good silver; Tg. Jon.: Overlaid silver], from Tarshish it comes [MT: it is brought], gold from Uphaz [LXX: gold of Mophas; Syr., Tg. Jon.: gold from Ophir], [MT adds: a craftsman's work] and a refiner's handiwork, works of wise/skilled men all of them, with violet/blue and purple they clothe them [MT: violet/blue and purple is their clothing, a work of wise/skilled men all of them]. 10:5b They must surely be carried, for they cannot march [Tg. Jon.: for there is no spirit/breath in them to walk]. Do not be afraid of them, for they cannot cause harm, and also causing good is not with them [LXX: and there is no good in them; Tg. Jon.: and also to do good they do not know]."[1]

10:11 Thus will you say to them, "The gods that did not make the sky and the land, may they perish [cf. LXX; or, they will perish] from the

---

1. Verses 6–8 and 10 of Jeremiah chapter 10 are not in the Hebrew source behind Greek Jeremiah. A translation of the MT of these verses is provided here: "There is no one like you, O LORD. You are great, and great is your name in might. Who will not fear you, O king of the nations? For for you it is befitting [Syr.: the kingdom is befitting (cf. *Tg. Jon.*)]. For among all the wise of the nations and in all their kingdom [Theod.: among all their kings] there is no one like you. And at once [Syr., *Tg. Jon.*: as one] they are brutish and foolish. Instruction from empty idols is wood. But the LORD God is truth [see GKC §141c; Syr.: But the Lord is the God of truth]. He is a living God and an everlasting king [cf. Theod.; Rev. 15:3]. Because of his anger the land quakes, and nations cannot endure his indignation."

land and from beneath this sky."[2] *10:12 The* LORD *[The* LORD *> MT] is the one who [Tg. Jon.: Thus will you say to them, We worship the one who] made land by his strength, established a world by his wisdom, and by his understanding stretched out sky. 10:13 [MT adds: At the sound of his giving] And [> MT] a roar of water was in the sky, and he brought up clouds from the end of the land [MT kethiv: from land's end]. Lightning for the rain he made, and he brought forth light [MT: wind] from his storehouses. 10:14 Every man [or, All mankind; Tg. Jon.: All the peoples] is brutish without knowledge. Every refiner is put to shame by/because of [or, is ashamed of] his carved/sculpted images [MT: a carved/sculpted image]. For deception is what they pour out, no breath is in them [MT: For deception is his molten image, and no breath is in them]. 10:15 Vanity are they, works [MT: work] of mockery. At the time of their visitation they will perish. 10:16 Not like these is the portion of Jacob; for the fashioner of all, he is his inheritance [MT: for the fashioner of all is he, and Israel is the tribe of his inheritance], the* LORD *[MT adds: of hosts] is his name.*

The heading in Jeremiah 10:1 begins a new section: "Hear the word of the LORD that he speaks to you [MT: Hear the word that the LORD speaks to you], O house of Israel." This address is to "the house of Israel," which in the present context refers to Judah just as it did in Jeremiah 9:26 (MT 9:25). The chapter condemns idolatry (Jer. 1:16) and commends worship of the one true God in the manner of Isaiah 40:12–16 and 44:9–20. It continues the line of thought from Jeremiah 9:12 ("Who is the wise man?") and 9:23 ("Let not a wise man boast in his wisdom") in its contrast of "the works of the wise/skilled" (Jer. 10:9; see also MT 10:7b ["the wise of the nations"]) with the creative work of the LORD done "by his wisdom" (Jer. 10:12).

Noam Mizrahi has recently argued that MT Jeremiah 10:1–16 consists of "satirical" and "hymnic" strands: superscription (Jer. 10:1),

---

2. *Tg. Jon.*: "This is a copy of the letter which Jeremiah the prophet sent to the remnant of the elders of the Exile who were in Babylon. 'If the nations among whom you are should say to you, "Worship the idols, O house of Israel: thus you shall answer them and thus you shall say to them: 'The idols which you worship are idols in which there is no profit. They cannot bring down rain from heaven, and they cannot make fruits sprout forth from the earth. They and those who worship them shall perish from the earth, and shall be destroyed from under these heavens'"'" (Robert Hayward, *The Targum of Jeremiah: Translation, with a Critical Introduction, Apparatus and Notes*, The Aramaic Bible 12 [Collegeville, MN: Liturgical, 1990], 79).

first satirical (Jer. 10:2–5), first hymnic (Jer. 10:6–7), second satirical (Jer. 10:8–9), second hymnic (Jer. 10:10), Aramaic (Jer. 10:11), third hymnic (Jer. 10:12–13), and third satirical (Jer. 10:14–16).[3] According to Mizrahi, the main strand is the satirical material (Jer. 10:2–5, 8–9, 14–16), which has been developed to move from critique of the idols to that of their makers. The present form of the text in the MT is now something of a "monotheistic creed."[4] For the purposes of the present commentary, the task is to explain the final form of the text rather to offer hypotheses about the way in which the text originated and developed. The problem is that there are two forms of the text. Both 4QJer[b] and the LXX bear witness to a shorter, differently arranged text than that found in the MT. The chapter begins with the sequence 10:1–4, 5a, 9, 5b and does not have 10:6–8, 10. According to McKane, 4QJer[b] and the LXX are witnesses to an earlier stage of a "rolling corpus" that reaches its final form in the MT,[5] but the present commentary works under the assumption that there are two final forms of the book of Jeremiah (see Introduction): the shorter, earlier (and eschatological) text of the Hebrew source behind Greek Jeremiah and the longer, later (and historicized) text of the MT. The MT was not a natural development of the Hebrew source behind Greek Jeremiah but a systematic revision. The two texts had their own separate processes of transmission. The shortness and different arrangement of Jeremiah 10:1–16 in the Hebrew source behind Greek Jeremiah are consistent with the character of this source for the book as a whole. The present commentary follows the earlier, more original form of the text in the Hebrew source behind Greek Jeremiah but also comments on the MT.

After the introductory formula ("Thus says the LORD"), the LORD exhorts the people not to learn [LXX[A]: "go"] the ways of the nations nor to be dismayed because of the "signs" (אתות) of the sky (Jer. 10:2a). According to Jeremiah 12:16, the people had learned from the nations to swear by Baal, the storm/fertility god whose work was supposedly manifested in the lightning and rain of the sky (see 1 Kgs. 18). The Torah, however, taught that the luminaries (sun, moon, and stars) in the sky were for "signs and appointed times and days and years" (Gen. 1:14). These "appointed times" (מועדים) are listed in Leviticus 23: the Sabbath, Passover, Pentecost, Rosh Hashanah, Yom Kippur, and the Feast of Tabernacles.

---

3. Noam Mizrahi, *Witnessing a Prophetic Text in the Making: The Literary, Textual, and Linguistic Development of Jeremiah 10:1–16*, BZAW 502 (Berlin: de Gruyter, 2017).
4. Mizrahi, *Witnessing a Prophetic Text in the Making*, 203.
5. McKane, *Jeremiah I–XXV*, 1–lxxxiii.

The luminaries were not to be feared as bad omens or used for astrology or worshiped as gods (Deut. 4:19),[6] but the people had fallen prey to the making of star images for "the queen of heaven" (Ishtar) and worshiped the sun, moon, and stars (see commentary on Jer. 7:18; 8:2). Nevertheless, just as the LORD told Jeremiah not to be "dismayed" at the opposition he would face (Jer. 1:17), so he now tells the people not to be "dismayed" at the signs of the sky, because such dismay is for unbelieving Gentiles (Jer. 10:2b; cf. Jer. 10:5b; Matt. 6:32).

The follow-up rationale for the exhortation in 10:2a is that the "statutes" or "customs" (חקות) of the peoples are "vanity" (הבל) (Jer. 10:3a; see GKC §145u[3]). This is a reference to the religious practices of the nations (cf. Lev. 18:3; 20:23; 2 Kgs. 17:8; Mic. 6:16).[7] Such practices are empty (see Deut. 32:21; Jer. 8:19). According to Jeremiah 2:5, the forefathers went after "what was empty" (ההבל) "and became empty" (ויהבלו). They became like the empty idols that they fashioned in their own image and worshiped—dumb, unresponsive, and destined for destruction (see Jer. 10:5, 11, 14, 15; see also MT 10:8; cf. Jer. 5:21). *BHS* arranges the clauses in 10:3–4 so that 10:3b1 is parallel to 10:3a and so that 10:3b2 (which is not a clause) and 10:4a are parallel. It is advisable, however, to respect the MT accentuation and keep the material prior to the *athnach* and *silluq* in both verses separate from the material that follows them. The Hebrew source behind Greek Jeremiah 10:3b begins, "There is a tree from a forest cut" (עץ מיער כרות; cf. MT: "For a tree from a forest, he cuts it" [כי עץ מיער כרתו]) (cf. Isa. 40:20a; 44:14; Jer. 2:27). Placed in apposition to this is a description: "a craftsman's work and a molten image" (מעשה חרש ומסכה; cf. MT: "a work of a craftsman's hands with an axe" [מעשה ידי חרש במעצד]) (cf. Isa. 40:20b; 44:12–13).[8] The craftsman then "makes it beautiful" (ייפהו) with silver and gold (Jer. 10:4a; cf. Isa. 2:20; 40:19; Jer. 10:9).[9] According to *Targum Jonathan* (cf. Syr.), he "overlays it" (= יצפהו) with silver and gold (cf.

---

6. According to Tosefta-Tractate Sukkah 2:6, "When Israel is occupied with Torah, they do not have to worry about all these omens" (Neusner, *Jeremiah in Talmud and Midrash*, 10).

7. The Syriac has "the fear of the peoples" in place of "the statutes/customs of the peoples," but this probably does not follow a different Hebrew text (as proposed in *BHS*: prp חַתַּת cf Gn 35,5). It is an interpretation of the same Hebrew text.

8. According to the Hebrew source behind Greek Jeremiah, the wood is carved and then cast in precious metal (see Jer. 10:4a) and sculpted.

9. The LXX translator interprets this verb as if it were a passive third plural: "they are adorned" (cf. Syr.).

Hab. 2:19b).[10] "With hammers and nails [MT: With nails and hammers] he makes them firm,[11] and they do not totter [or, so that they do not totter; LXX: and they will not be moved; MT: and it does not totter]" (Jer. 10:4b; Isa. 40:20b; 41:7; 44:12). This essentially makes a mockery of the idol, not only because it is a human creation but also because it cannot even hold itself up (cf. 1 Sam. 5:3).

According to the Hebrew source behind Greek Jeremiah 10:5a, the idol is "gold of hammered work" (כתם מקשה; LXX: "wrought silver" [cf. Jer. 10:9]). The MT, on the other hand, says that the silver and gold of the idol are "like a post/scarecrow in a cucumber field" (כתמר מקשה) (cf. Ep. Jer. 69). The LXX then renders ידברו according to its Syriac meaning ("they do not walk"), while the MT vocalizes it as "they do not speak." Either way the point is that these are lifeless objects (see Pss. 115:4–7; 135:15–17). Verse 9 continues the description of the material out of which the idol is made: "Beaten silver [Syr.: Good silver; *Tg. Jon.*: Overlaid silver], from Tarshish it comes [יבוא; MT: it is brought (יבא)], gold from Uphaz [אופז; LXX: gold of Mophas; Syr., *Tg. Jon.*: gold from Ophir (אופיר)], [MT adds: a craftsman's work] and a refiner's handiwork, works of wise/skilled men all of them, with violet/blue and purple they clothe them [MT: violet/blue and purple is their clothing, a work of wise/skilled men all of them]." It is evident from this translation that the text of this verse has undergone some addition and re-arrangement in the MT. The beaten silver comes from Tarshish, not necessarily in the sense that a place named Tarshish is its place of origin (but see Ezek. 27:12), but in the sense that the silver is delivered by sea (see the expression "ships of Tarshish" [= "sea-going ships"]; BDB, 1077). The gold is from Uphaz, an unknown location only mentioned elsewhere in Daniel 10:5 (but see 1 Kgs. 10:18; 2 Chr. 9:17). The Syriac and *Targum Jonathan* have "Ophir," which is well known for its gold (see 1 Kgs. 9:27–28; Isa. 13:12; Ps. 45:10 [Eng., 45:9]; Job 28:16; 1 Chr. 29:4). The point of saying such things about the silver and gold seems to be that they have been acquired with great effort and expense yet without any benefit (see Isa. 55:1–2; Jer. 2:8b, 11b, 13b). The MT

---

10. The letters י and צ were easily confused in Old Hebrew script (see Shemaryahu Talmon, *Text and Canon of the Hebrew Bible: Collected Studies* [Winona Lake, IN: Eisenbrauns, 2010], 163).

11. The plural pronoun "them" refers back to the silver and gold. In the following plural verb ("they do not totter") of the Hebrew source behind Greek Jeremiah, the antecedent of "they" is also the silver and gold. The MT, however, has a singular verb ("it does not totter"), in which case the antecedent of "it" is the wooden idol.

adds that they are a mere "craftsman's work" (cf. Isa. 44:12–13; Jer. 10:3). They are "a refiner's handiwork" (cf. Isa. 40:19; 46:6), "works of wise/skilled men all of them" (cf. Isa. 40:20). They clothe them with "violet/blue and purple," material mostly reserved elsewhere for the tabernacle and the temple (BDB, 71, 1067). Jeremiah 10:5b continues the mockery of the idols. The idols have to be carried (cf. Isa. 46:3, 7). They are unable to move themselves (cf. Jer. 10:5a). *Targum Jonathan* explains that this is because there is no spirit/breath in them to walk. There is thus no need to be afraid of them (cf. Jer. 10:2). Such idols are unable to cause any harm, nor is it in them to cause good (cf. Isa. 41:23; Zeph. 1:12).

The text of Jeremiah 10:6–8, 10 in the MT is a secondary addition not only because it creates a substantially longer text than that found in 4QJer[b] and the LXX but also because it is intrusive. It is true that it makes for a passage that alternates between mockery of idols and hymnic descriptions of the LORD, but this is at the cost of interrupting and rearranging texts that belong together. If it is argued that for this reason this longer text was original and then deliberately omitted, it must be said that such a concern for an ancient scribe or translator would not have sufficed to excise hymnic material that exalted the LORD as the one true God. The hymnic material in 10:6–7 begins with an affirmation: "There is no one (מֵאַיִן) like you, O LORD" (Jer. 10:6a; cf. Exod. 15:11; 1 Sam. 2:2; 2 Sam. 7:22; 22:32; 1 Kgs. 8:23; Isa. 46:5; Jer. 10:7b; Ps. 86:8; Bar. 3:36). It is possible, however, that this should be revocalized as follows: "From where (מֵאַיִן) is any like you, O LORD" (see BDB, 35)? This is followed by an affirmation of the LORD's greatness and the great reputation of his might: "You are great, and great is your name in might" (Jer. 10:6b; cf. Jer. 16:21). Idols cannot compare to such greatness. Whereas the idols are not to be feared (Jer. 10:5b), verse 7a asks, "Who will not fear you, O king of the nations" (cf. Ps. 96:10; Rev. 15:3–4)?[12] For such fear, while inappropriate for idols, is fitting for the LORD (see NET). The Syriac, on the other hand, understands the text to mean that the kingdom is fitting for the LORD, since he is the king of the nations (cf. *Tg. Jon.*). It is fitting because there is no one like the LORD "among all the wise of the nations and in all their kingdom [Theod.: among all their kings]" (Jer. 10:7b; cf. 1 Kgs. 5:10 [Eng., 4:30]; Isa. 19:12; Jer. 9:12, 23–24 [MT 9:11, 22–23]).[13] (Note how מאין כמוך at the end of 10:7b forms an inclusio with מאין כמוך at the beginning of 10:6a.)

---

12. Of course, there are those who do not fear the LORD (Jer. 5:24), but the gist of this question is, "Who in their right mind would not fear you?"

13. See also Jeremiah 1:5, 10; 3:17; 4:2; 12:14–17; 16:19; 25:15–26; 46–51.

The hymnic material in 10:6–7 is followed by mockery of the idols and their makers: "And at once [באחת (cf. Prov. 28:18); Syr., *Tg. Jon.*: as one (= כאחת?)] they are brutish and foolish. Instruction from empty idols is wood." Idol makers and worshipers are brutish and foolish (cf. Jer. 10:14) because the instruction that they receive comes from dumb idols (see Isa. 44:19; Jer. 10:3). According to Habakkuk 2:18–19, an idol is a teacher of deception, perpetuating the lie that it represents (cf. Isa. 9:14 [Eng., 9:15]). Finally, Jeremiah 10:10 adds another piece of hymnic material: "But the Lord God is truth. He is a living God and an everlasting king. Because of his anger the land quakes, and nations cannot endure his indignation." The first clause (ויהוה אלהים אמת) is a straightforward subject-predicate nominal clause ("But the Lord God is truth" [cf. John 14:6]), but not all versions see it this way. The Syriac reads אלהים אמת as if it were אלהי האמת ("But the Lord is the God of truth"). Others read אמת as if it were an adjective (e.g., ESV: "But the Lord is the true God"). The Lord is also "a living God" (Deut. 5:26; 1 Sam. 17:26, 36; Jer. 23:36), not a dumb idol, and he is "an everlasting king" (cf. Jer. 10:7a; Bar. 4:10), not a finite object. Unlike the idols, which are not able to cause bad or good (Jer. 10:5b), the Lord makes the land quake with his anger, and the very nations who worship idols are unable to endure his indignation (see Nah. 1:5–6; Mal. 3:2).

The text of Jeremiah 10:11 is in Aramaic, featuring both an earlier (ארקא) and a later (ארעא) form of "the land."[14] *Targum Jonathan* suggests that it is a letter from Jeremiah to the remnant in Babylon (cf. Jer. 24:5–7; 29:1–23; Ep. Jer.). This is plausible given the fact that Aramaic was becoming the official language of international correspondence (see 2 Kgs. 18:26; Ezra 4:8–6:18; 7:12–26). According to *Targum Jonathan's* expanded version of the letter, the text of 10:11 is what those in exile are to say to their captors who encourage them to worship idols. Such idols are of no benefit. They cannot bring down rain from the sky nor bring forth fruit from the ground. Redak suggests that the reply actually continues through Jeremiah 10:16, even though 10:12–16 is in Hebrew.[15] It is worth noting that the use of

---

14. "R. Samuel bar Nahman in the name of R. Yohanan: 'It is so that the Sursi language [Aramaic] should not be cheap in your eyes. For in the Torah, Prophets, and Writings, that language is to be found. In the Torah: it is written, "And Laban called it, Yagar Sahaduta" (Gen. 31:47). In the Prophets it is written, "Thus will you say to them" [in Aramaic] (Jer. 10:11). And in the Writings, it is written, "And the Chaldeans spoke to the king [in Aramaic]"' (Dan. 2:4)" (*y. Sot.* 7:2; Neusner, *Jeremiah in Talmud and Midrash*, 88).

15. Rosenberg, trans., *Mikraoth Gedoloth: Jeremiah Volume One*, 94.

יאבדו in 10:11b ("may they perish") and 10:15b ("they will perish") arguably forms a kind of inclusio. There is another way, however, to explain the relationship of Aramaic 10:11 to Hebrew 10:12–16. It is quite possible and likely that the Hebrew unit is intended to provide commentary on the Aramaic, explaining why it is that the creator God is superior to the so-called gods who did not create the world (cf. Isa. 40:21–26; Jer. 14:22; Ps. 96:5).[16] This arrangement of the text would then be analogous to the relationship between Hebrew and Aramaic in the book of Daniel where the Hebrew framework (Dan. 1:1–2:4a; 8–12) introduces, explains, and fills in the gaps of the Aramaic section (Dan. 2:4b–7:28).[17]

Holladay has noted well several features of the Aramaic syntax in 10:11.[18] First, the subject-verb word order and the fronting of אלהיא די שמיא וארקא ("The God/the gods who the sky and the land") creates the expectation that the verse will be about the creator God before the negation of the verb in the relative clause ("did not make"). Second, לא עבדו ("did not make") then forms a wordplay with the main verb יאבדו ("may they perish" or "they will perish").[19] The LXX renders this main verb with a third-person imperative, expressing a wish or desire ("may they perish"),[20] but a comparison with the use of this verb in the Hebrew text of 10:15b suggests that it may be indicative ("they will perish"). Third, אלה ("these"), once thought to be Hebrew but now considered "good Aramaic for the period," occurs at the end of the verse and has been understood in at least three different ways: (1) a modifier of "heavens" or "sky" ("these heavens" or "this sky"); (2) a reference back to "gods" ("these will perish"); or (3) according to the Latin Vulgate, "from these that are under the heavens." The third option is the least likely. Option two is possible but not very likely given the separation between the main verb and the demonstrative אלה. The first option is

---

16. See Michael B. Shepherd, *The Verbal System of Biblical Aramaic: A Distributional Approach*, StBibLit 116 (New York: Lang, 2008), 10–18.

17. See Michael B. Shepherd, *Daniel in the Context of the Hebrew Bible*, StBibLit 123 (New York: Lang, 2009), 66–67.

18. Holladay, *Jeremiah 1*, 334–35.

19. See also Bullinger, *Figures of Speech*, 316. This wordplay would not have been possible with Hebrew עשה ("make").

20. Normally a short *yiqtul* form in biblical Aramaic is a volitional form (Hans Bauer and Pontus Leander, *Grammatik des Biblisch-Aramäischen* [Halle: Niemeyer, 1927; repr., Hildesheim: Georg Olms, 1995], 283–84). See Daniel 2:24; 4:16; 5:10.

to be favored due to the placement of the demonstrative directly after the noun שְׁמַיָּא ("heavens" or "sky").

The MT of Jeremiah 10:12–16 finds a close parallel in MT 51:15–19 (= LXX 28:15–19). Parke-Taylor suggests that 10:12–16 is quoted in 51:15–19 in order to declare the incomparability and almighty power of the LORD as the creator, "denouncing idolatry and asserting that Israel has a secure future."[21] Walser, who places the Greek texts of these passages side by side, observes that most of the differences between the two passages in Greek are due to the process of translation and are on the level of vocabulary, while a few could be attributed to different sources.[22] He concludes, "Anyhow, it is hard to see that the translator had one of the translated texts in front of him while translating the other." Jeremiah 10:12, with its use of participles to describe the LORD's activity (cf. Pss. 146:6–9; 147:2–4, 6, 8–9, 11, 14–17, 19), takes the form of a little hymn, which sometimes occurs in prophetic literature (e.g., Amos 4:13; 5:8; 9:5–6): "The LORD [The LORD > MT] is the one who made land by his strength, established a world by his wisdom, and by his understanding stretched out sky" (cf. Isa. 40:22; 42:5; 44:24; 45:18; 51:13; Jer. 27:5; 32:17; Zech. 12:1; Pss. 24:2; 65:7 [Eng., 65:6]; 89:12 [Eng., 89:11]; 104:2, 24; 136:5; Prov. 3:19–20; 11QPsª 26:13–15; 1QHª 9:13–14).[23] This is in contrast to the "gods," idols made by human hands, who did not make the sky or the land (Jer. 10:11). The wisdom by which the LORD created the world is greater than that of those who make and worship idols (Jer. 10:7, 9; see again Jer. 9:12, 23–24 [MT 9:11, 22–23]; see also Rom. 1:18–32). According to Proverbs 8:22, the LORD "fathered" (קָנָה; see Gen. 4:1; Deut. 32:6; Prov. 8:24, 25; 30:4) wisdom, the "beginning" (רֵאשִׁית; see Gen. 1:1) of his way (cf. *Tg. Neof.* Gen. 1:1: "In the beginning, with wisdom, the Son of the Lord completed the sky and the land"). Wisdom was thus already present in the beginning as the firstborn of creation and the agent of creation (Prov. 8:30).[24]

---

21. Parke-Taylor, *Formation of the Book of Jeremiah*, 180.

22. Walser, *Jeremiah*, 260–61.

23. For the construction of a definite head followed by an indefinite participle, as in the Hebrew source behind Greek Jeremiah, see Cynthia L. Miller-Naudé, "Mismatches of Definiteness within Appositional Expressions Used as Vocatives in Biblical Hebrew," *JNSL* 40, no. 2 (2014): 103–5. This article deals primarily with vocatives, but some of the discussion is applicable to the pattern at hand in Jeremiah 10:12.

24. See Shepherd, *Text in the Middle*, 9–11. According to Sirach 24, the word of the Torah is the wisdom by which the LORD created the world (cf. Deut.

Calvin expresses the commonly held view that 10:12 refers to "the fixed and regular government of the world" established at creation, while 10:13 describes things that God continues to do,[25] but the pattern of 10:13—nominal clause, *wayyiqtol*, "x + *qatal*," *wayyiqtol*—suggests a double occurrence of a background-narrative sequence,[26] perhaps referring to the account in Genesis 7:11–12 (for mixture of imagery from the creation and flood accounts in Genesis, see Ps. 104): "[MT adds: At the sound of his giving] And [> MT] a roar of water was in the sky, and he brought up clouds from the end of the land [MT *kethiv*: from land's end]. Lightning for the rain he made, and he brought forth light [MT: wind] from his storehouses" (cf. Deut. 28:12; Jer. 5:24; Hab. 3:11; Pss. 33:7; 135:7; Job 38:22).[27] The Hebrew source behind Greek Jeremiah does not have the difficult לקול תתו ("At the sound of his giving") of the MT. These two Hebrew texts also differ in what the Lord brought forth from his storehouses.[28] The Hebrew source behind Greek Jeremiah has אור ("light"), which is parallel to "lightning," while the MT has רוח ("wind").

כל אדם (Jer. 10:14a) can be translated "every man" or "all mankind" (= all the nations or Gentiles; cf. *Tg. Jon.*: "all the peoples"). In context, it is not that every single human being is brutish without knowledge but that all those who make and/or worship idols in the manner of the nations are brutish (cf. Jer. 10:8, 21; Rom. 1:22). "Every refiner is put to shame by/because of [or, is ashamed of] his carved/sculpted images [MT: a carved/sculpted image]" (cf. Jer. 2:26–27; 10:9). The molten images that these refiners pour out are a lie (cf. Hab. 2:18). There is no breath of life in them (Jer. 10:14b; cf. Hab. 2:19; Ep. Jer. 24). Such idols are "vanity" (הבל), "work(s) of mockery" (Jer. 10:15a; cf. Jer. 10:3, 8). "At the time of their visitation they will perish" (Jer. 10:15b). This reiterates the thought of 10:11 that the gods/idols will perish, but the "time of visitation" in Jeremiah is normally for people (see Jer. 6:15; 8:12; 11:23; 23:12; 46:21; 48:44; 50:27), which suggests that the implication of 10:14–15 is that idol worshipers will not only become dumb

---

4:6; Ps. 33:6). According to Colossians 1:15–20, Christ is the firstborn of creation, the agent of creation, and the beginning (cf. Matt. 11:19; 1 Cor. 1:24, 30). These are not mutually exclusive ideas (see John 1:1–3).

25. Calvin, *Jeremiah*, 2:36.

26. See Niccacci, *Syntax of the Verb*, 47–62.

27. See the contrast between Baal and the Lord in their abilities to send forth fire from the sky (1 Kgs. 18:20–40).

28. The poetic image of the Lord with storehouses is not a primitive view of the deity. It is an anthropomorphism.

like the idols (see Isa. 6:9–10; Jer. 5:21; Pss. 115:5–8; 135:15–18) but also perish like them (see Lev. 26:30; Deut. 7:26; Isa. 1:31).

The text of Jeremiah 10:16 differs considerably between the Hebrew source behind Greek Jeremiah and the MT. According to the former, the focus is entirely on the LORD as the portion and inheritance of Jacob: "Not like these is the portion of Jacob; for the fashioner of all, he is his inheritance, the LORD of hosts is his name."[29] This language derives originally from the covenant with the high priesthood of Aaron, which, as part of the tribe of Levi, did not have a land portion allotted like the other tribes (Num. 18:19–20; Josh. 13:14, 33). The sons of Aaron and the priestly tribe of Levi would have the LORD himself as their portion and inheritance (i.e., in their service to the sanctuary): "And the LORD said to Aaron, 'In their land you will not inherit, and a portion you will not have in their midst. I am your portion and inheritance in the midst of the sons of Israel'" (Num. 18:20; cf. Josh. 13:14, 33; Ezek. 44:28). This was subsequently spiritualized and reapplied to all who trust in the LORD (see Pss. 16:5; 73:26; 119:57; 142:6 [Eng., 142:5]; Luke 10:42; John 13:8), which would be especially appropriate with the loss of everyone's land portion in the Babylonian exile: "The LORD is my portion, says my soul. Therefore, I will wait for him" (Lam. 3:24). According to the Hebrew source behind Greek Jeremiah 10:16, the "fashioner" of all is the inheritance of the people of God (see Gen. 2:7, 8, 19; Isa. 45:18; cf. Jer. 1:5; 18:2–6). The LORD (Yahweh) is his name (cf. Jer. 16:21b; Amos 4:13; 9:6; see also Exod. 3:12, 14, 15).[30] He is not like the dumb idols who did not make the world and whose makers and worshipers will perish with them. He is the creator of all. The MT, on the other hand, adds ‏וישראל שבט‎ to this text: "for the fashioner of all is he, and Israel is the tribe of his inheritance" (cf. Deut. 32:9; Isa. 19:25; 63:17; Jer. 12:7; Zech. 2:16 [Eng., 2:12]; Pss. 74:2; 78:71; *Pss. Sol.* 14:5). According to Deuteronomy 32:9, the people of Israel are the LORD's portion; Jacob is the territory of his inheritance apart from all the nations (see Gen. 12:1–3; Exod. 19:5). Thus, the addition in the MT of Jeremiah 10:16

---

29. According to Deuteronomy 4:19, the LORD apportioned the luminaries in the sky (see Jer. 10:2) to all the peoples. According to 4QDeutʲ 32:8, he gave the nations their inheritance according to the number of "the sons of God," which the MT interprets to be the seventy sons of Israel (see Gen. 46:27; Exod. 1:5; see the seventy nations in Gen. 10; see also Hos. 2:1 [Eng., 2:10]) and the LXX interprets to be the angels (see Job 1:6; nations have angels assigned to them in Dan. 10:13, 20, 21; 12:1).

30. See Isaiah 47:4; 48:2; 51:15; 54:5; Jeremiah 31:35; 32:18; 46:18; 48:15; 50:34; 51:19, 57.

shifts the text of the Hebrew source behind Greek Jeremiah from a singular focus on the LORD as Israel's portion and inheritance to a two-fold affirmation: the LORD is the people's portion, and the people are the LORD's inheritance.

10:17 He gathered from outside [MT: Gather from land/ground] your bundle/pack [LXX: substance/possession; Syr.: shame; Tg. Jon.: merchandise; Vulg.: confusion] dwelling [see GKC §90n; Vulg.: quae habitas] in a choice place [or, O one dwelling in a choice place (LXX: choice places; MT: the siege)]. 10:18 For thus says the LORD, "Look, I am about to sling [Tg. Jon.: as those who throw the stone with the sling so I will scatter] the inhabitants of this land [MT: the inhabitants of the land at this time] in distress in order that your wound may be found [MT: and I will cause distress for them in order that they may find (Vulg.: be found; Luther: feel it); Syr.: and they will seek me and find me; Tg. Jon.: and I will cause distress for them in order that they may receive repayment for their sins/debts]. 10:19 Woe because of your breaking/fracture, your wound is severe" [MT: Woe to me because of my breaking/fracture, my wound is severe]. And as for me, I said, "Surely this is my sickness, and it took me [MT: Surely this is a sickness, and I must bear it]." 10:20 My tent [Tg. Jon.: My land], it is destroyed [LXX: it suffers distress]; and all my tent cords [LXX: skins; Syr.: its tent cords; Tg. Jon.: my cities], they are torn apart. My children and my flock are no more [MT: My children (Tg. Jon.: My people), they have gone from me (Tg. Jon.: have gone into exile) and are no more]. There is no longer a place for my tent, a place for my tent curtains [MT: There is no longer anyone stretching out my tent or raising my tent curtains]. 10:21 For the shepherds [Tg. Jon.: the kings] have been brutish, and the LORD [Tg. Jon.: instruction from before the LORD] they have not sought. Therefore, all pasturing/shepherding [i.e., flock; LXX: the whole pasture] has not had insight, and they are scattered [MT: Therefore, they have not had insight (Tg. Jon.: have not prospered), and all their pasturing/shepherding is scattered]. 10:22 A sound of a report [see GKC §146b]! Look, it is coming, and great quaking/shaking from (the) land of north, to make the cities of Judah a desolation and [and > MT] a habitation for jackals [LXX: sparrows]. 10:23 I know, O LORD, that mankind's way does not belong to him [Syr.: I know that the way of the Lord is not like that of man], and [and > Codex L] man does not go and establish his step [MT: going and establishing his step does not belong to man; Tg. Jon.: not to man who goes and establishes his step]. 10:24 Discipline us [MT: me], O LORD, but in justice and [and > MT] not in anger lest you make us [MT: me] small. 10:25 Pour out your wrath upon nations [MT: the nations] who do not know/acknowledge you and upon families [nonn Mss, Tg. Jon., Ps. 79:6: kingdoms] who on your name do not call. For they devoured Jacob [Codex L adds: and devoured him] and destroyed him, and his pasture they have made desolate.

The unit in Jeremiah 10:17–25 revisits the theme of the enemy from the north (Jer. 10:22), which was last mentioned in 6:22, and ties it to the divine judgment of the "brutish" idol worship outlined in 10:1–16 (see Jer. 10:8, 14, 21). The shifts in speaker are somewhat difficult to follow in this section. Holladay identifies the speakers as follows: Jeremiah (Jer. 10:17), Yahweh (Jer. 10:18), the people (Jer. 10:19–20), Jeremiah (Jer. 10:21), Yahweh (Jer. 10:22), and the people (Jer. 10:23–25).[31] It is perhaps preferable, however, to simplify this and see two speakers in the passage: Jeremiah (Jer. 10:17, 19b–25 [MT 10:17, 19–25]) and the Lord (Jer. 10:18–19a [MT Jer. 10:18]). Jeremiah speaks on behalf of the people in 10:20–25 (cf. Jer. 3:22b–25; Lam. 1:11–22; 2:11; 3; 5).[32]

The Hebrew source behind Greek Jeremiah 10:17 and MT 10:17 are considerably different. According to the former, the text says, "He gathered (אסף) from outside (מחוץ) your bundle/pack dwelling [or, O one dwelling] in a choice place (במבחר)." According to the latter, it says, "Gather (אספי) from land/ground (מארץ) your bundle/pack dwelling [or, O one dwelling] in the siege (במצור)." It is not clear who the subject of the verb אסף ("He gathered") is in the Hebrew source behind Greek Jeremiah, whether the Lord or the enemy. It is possible that the image is that of gathering from outside to a place of safety inside (cf. Jer. 4:5; but see Jer. 5:17b), but it is more likely that it is one of an outsider who comes inside to remove the "bundle/pack" of the people of the land/city. The feminine participle ישבת ("dwelling") could modify the feminine noun כנעה ("bundle/pack"), but it could also function as a vocative describing the inhabitant(s) of Judah and/or Jerusalem ("O one dwelling"). The "choice place" (מבחר) would then be either the land of Judah (cf. Ps. 78:68) or the city of Jerusalem (cf. Deut. 12:5) or both. In the MT, however, the imperative אספי ("Gather") is directed to the

---

31. Holladay, *Jeremiah 1*, 338.
32. See McKane, *Jeremiah I–XXV*, 233–35. According to Calvin, 10:19 is also included in this: "We must then bear in mind that the Prophet speaks not here according to the feeling which the people had, for they were so stupefied that they felt nothing; but that he speaks of what they ought to have felt" (Calvin, *Jeremiah*, 2:47).

people of the land/city (f.). They are to take from the land/ground their bundle/pack dwelling in the "siege" (מבצר) or as those dwelling in the siege. Despite the various efforts of the early versions (Syr.: "shame" [from כנע "be humble"]; *Tg. Jon.*: "merchandise" [cf. כנען "merchant(s)"]; Vulg.: confusion), the sense of כנעה is likely that of a "bundle" or "pack" of possessions taken into exile (LXX: "substance/possession"; cf. Ezek. 12:3; see also Jer. 46:19). The image of 10:17 thus anticipates exile from the land/city.

Jeremiah 10:18 introduces the Lord's discourse ("For thus says the Lord") as an explanation of 10:17: "Look, I am about to sling [*Tg. Jon.*: as those who throw the stone with the sling so I will scatter] the inhabitants of this land [MT: the inhabitants of the land at this time] in distress in order that your wound may be found [MT: and I will cause distress for them in order that they may find]." According to Leviticus 18:24–30, the land would vomit out the people if they acted according to the abominations of the former inhabitants. Now the Lord employs a different metaphor—that of a slingshot. In the Hebrew source behind Greek Jeremiah, the purpose given for this is "in order that your wound may be found" (למען תמצא מכתך), which anticipates the reference to the severe wound in 10:19. The exile will expose the people's wound in a manner not previously discovered. The MT ("in order that they may find [ימצאו]") has no object for the *qal* verb. Thus, the Vulgate renders it as a *niphal* (יִמָּצְאוּ): "in order that they may be found" (presumably by the enemy). The Syriac paraphrases, "and they will seek me and find me," assuming that the punishment/discipline will be corrective (see MT Jer. 29:13). *Targum Jonathan* renders, "and I will cause distress for them in order that they may receive repayment for their sins/debts." McKane, on the other hand, follows the proposal of G. R. Driver that ימצאו equals ימצו (from מצה "drain") and should be vocalized as a *niphal*: "I will press them until they are squeezed dry."[33]

Jeremiah 10:19a is still part of the Lord's discourse in the Hebrew source behind Greek Jeremiah: "Woe because of your breaking/fracture, your wound is severe" (cf. Jer. 30:12). According to the MT, it is the speech of Jeremiah—"Woe to me because of my breaking/fracture, my wound is severe" (cf. Jer. 4:19; 14:17)—perhaps speaking on behalf of the people (cf. Jer. 4:13, 31; 6:14; 8:11). 10:19b then clearly introduces Jeremiah's speech with the fronted pronoun אני: And as for me, I said, "Surely this is my sickness, and it took me [MT: Surely this is

---

33. G. R. Driver, "Linguistic and Textual Problems: Jeremiah," *JQR* 28 (1938): 107; McKane, *Jeremiah I–XXV*, 228–30.

a sickness, and I must bear it]." The sense of the Hebrew source behind Greek Jeremiah seems to be that the prophet himself (or perhaps the prophet on behalf of the people) is taken by the "sickness" (חלי) of the "severe" or "incurable" (נחלה) wound of 10:19a. The prospect of the judgment announced in 10:18 is overwhelming. On the other hand, the sense of the MT is either resignation ("and I must bear it") or overconfidence ("and I will bear it").[34]

In Jeremiah 10:20a, the fronting of "My tent" and "all my tent cords" in their respective clauses is for topicalization.[35] *Targum Jonathan* interprets "My tent" to be "My land." According to this reading, the prophet Jeremiah speaks on behalf of the people about the land of Judah.[36] In Ezekiel 23:4, Jerusalem is known as "Oholibah" ("My tent is in her") because of the location of the sanctuary there. This tent is destroyed (cf. Jer. 4:20). *Targum Jonathan* interprets "all my tent cords" to be "all my cities." They are torn apart. The Hebrew source behind Greek Jeremiah 10:20b then begins, "My children and my flock are no more" (בני וצאני אינם) (cf. Jer. 16:2; 31:15). The MT has, "My children, they have gone from me and are no more" (בני יצאני ואינם). *Targum Jonathan* interprets this to mean that the people have gone into exile. The Hebrew source behind Greek Jeremiah then concludes, "There is no longer a place for my tent, a place for my tent curtains" (אין עוד מקום אהלי מקום יריעותי) (see Jer. 7:3b, 6a, 7a, 12a, 14a). The MT says, "There is no longer anyone stretching out my tent or raising my tent curtains" (אין נטה עוד אהלי ומקים יריעותי). McKane rightly observes that these words are proleptic and not indicative of a disaster that has already occurred.[37]

The explanation given for the disaster anticipated in 10:20 is that the shepherds are "brutish" and have not sought the LORD (Jer. 10:21a). This is not necessarily something that the people would say, although

---

34. See McKane, *Jeremiah I–XXV*, 230–31.
35. See Moshavi, *Word Order in the Biblical Hebrew Finite Clause*, 97–103.
36. Holladay, following Kumaki, says that "My tent" refers to the temple in Jerusalem wherein the tent of the tabernacle may have been erected in the Holy of Holies (*Jeremiah 1*, 342). Cf. Exodus 26; Jeremiah 4:20.
37. "The ruined tent and severed tent ropes are indicative of a disaster proleptically experienced, to which there will be no quick reaction, and no possibility of speedy reconstruction and rehabilitation will emerge. The prophet makes the community speak these words not because it is aware of such a hard destiny but because he knows and feels that this is the future which will eventuate. 'Sons' will go away—disappear into the oblivion of exile" (McKane, *Jeremiah I–XXV*, 231).

it is possible that they could reach a point where they would shift the blame to their leadership. Rather, this is the prophet giving utterance to what the people ought to admit. *Targum Jonathan* correctly identifies the shepherds here as the kings (see Jer. 2:8; 23:1–4; Ezek. 34). Just as every person who makes and/or worships an idol is "brutish" (Jer. 10:8, 14), so are the kings who rule over an idolatrous people. They have not sought prophetic instruction from the true God. This is well illustrated later in the book of Jeremiah when Zedekiah asks the prophet Jeremiah to "seek" the LORD on behalf of everyone (Jer. 21:2). The king's request is disingenuous in the sense that he is only interested in deliverance, not the LORD's will. This becomes apparent in Jeremiah 37:2 where the text clearly states that Zedekiah did not listen to "the words of the LORD that he spoke by Jeremiah the prophet" (see also 2 Chr. 36:12). For this reason, the whole flock (i.e., all the people) "has not had insight" (לא השכילה) (Jer. 10:21b; cf. Jer. 9:24 [MT 9:23]). Some versions take this to mean that the flock has not prospered (e.g., ESV), but the issue at hand is that the people are foolish and without insight because their leadership is brutish. Insight comes from study of the Torah (Deut. 17:18–20; Josh. 1:8), which has been rejected (Jer. 6:19b; 9:13 [MT 9:12]) and corrupted (Jer. 2:8; 8:8). The people are thus scattered like sheep without a shepherd (cf. 1 Kgs. 22:17; Zech. 13:7; Matt. 9:36; see also Num. 27:17; Zech. 10:2). They are in need of a Josiah-like king (2 Kgs. 22–23), a messianic ruler devoted to the true message of the Torah (John 5:46–47)—one who will reign "and have insight" (והשכיל) and perform justice and righteousness in the land (Jer. 3:15; 23:5b; cf. Isa. 52:13).

The exclamation ("A sound of a report!") at the beginning of 10:22 is parallel to the "great quaking/shaking" but not equivalent to it. Parallelism is not always synonymous or reiterative parallelism. The "report" (שמועה) here is a message about coming disaster (cf. Jer. 49:14; Obad. 1). The following, "Look, it is coming," is either a reference to the coming of the report itself by means of a messenger or a quote of the report about the impending desolation. The "great quaking/shaking" is made by the horses and chariots of the enemy army (cf. Jer. 6:23; 8:16; 47:3; Nah. 3:2). This enemy is the by now well-known eschatological enemy from the land of the north (see Jer. 1:14; 4:6, 13; 5:15; 6:1, 22).[38] The great quaking from the land of the north is coming "to make the

---

38. This verse "contains a reference to the enemy from the north, but this has mythological-liturgical character and is not a reference to a specific, historical threat" (McKane, *Jeremiah I–XXV*, 233).

cities of Judah a desolation" (cf. Jer. 4:7, 27; 6:8) and "a habitation for jackals" (cf. Jer. 9:11 [MT 9:10]; 49:33; 51:37).

Holladay argues that Jeremiah 10:23–25 is Jeremiah's quotation of the people citing Scripture (Prov. 16:9 and 20:24 then Pss. 6:2 and 38:2 [Eng., 6:1 and 38:1] then Ps. 79:6–7) and misappropriating it in a self-serving manner.[39] This may very well be right, but there is more than one way to explain these verses. Proverbs 16:9 and 20:24 are cited from the collection of Solomon's proverbs in Proverbs 10:1–22:16. Proverbs 16:9 says, "A man's mind is what plans his way, but the LORD is the one who establishes his step" (לב אדם יחשב דרכו ויהוה יכין צעדו). Proverbs 20:24 says, "From the LORD are a man's steps; and as for man, how can he understand his way" (מיהוה מצעדי גבר ואדם מה יבין דרכו)?[40] Thus, the Hebrew source behind Greek Jeremiah 10:23 says, "I know, O LORD, that mankind's way does not belong to him,[41] and man does not go and establish his step" (ידעתי יהוה כי לא לאדם דרכו ולא איש הלך והכין את צעדו).[42] This could be, as Holladay suggests, the voice of the people essentially saying that they cannot be held responsible for their actions since their way does not really belong to them (cf. Rom. 9:19). The LORD is the one who establishes their steps. But it could also be Jeremiah's acknowledgment of the providential will of God despite his concerns about the fate of the people. McKane comments, "Man may plan the course of his life, but he does not have the power to command circumstances to bend to his purpose" (cf. Jas. 4:13–17).[43]

---

39. Holladay, *Jeremiah 1*, 343–44.
40. See also Psalm 37:23: "By the LORD are a man's steps established, and in his way he delights" (מיהוה מצעדי גבר כוננו ודרכו יחפץ).
41. The Syriac interprets this to mean that the way of the Lord is not like that of man.
42. See 1QH[a] 7:24–25; 12:31–32; 1QS 11:10. The MT has a slightly different text for 10:23b: "going and establishing his step does not belong to man" (לא לאיש הלך והכין את צעדו). *Targum Jonathan* interprets this to mean that the way of mankind does not belong to man who goes and establishes his step.
43. McKane, *Jeremiah I–XXV*, 232. "Rabbi Joseph Kimchi interprets this verse as an allusion to Nebuchadnezzar, who had intended to march against Ammon. As Ezekiel states (21:26): 'For the king of Babylon stands at the parting of the way,' for his intention was to march on Ammon when he left his place, but when he came to the parting of the way, and there were two roads, one to Ammon and one to Jerusalem, God changed his mind and his divination so that he should march on Jerusalem in order to punish Zedekiah for transgressing his oath and profaning God's name. Concerning this, the prophet states: 'I know, O Lord, that *the* man's way is not his.'

Jeremiah 10:24 cites from the following Davidic lament/petition psalms: (1) "O LORD, do not in your anger rebuke me, and do not in your wrath discipline me" (יהוה אל באפך תוכיחני ואל בחמתך תיסרני) (Ps. 6:2 [Eng., 6:1]); and (2) "O LORD, do not in your divine anger rebuke me, nor in your wrath discipline me" (יהוה אל בקצפך תוכיחני ובחמתך תיסרני) (Ps. 38:2 [Eng., 38:1]). Thus, the text of Jeremiah 10:24 says, "Discipline us [MT: Discipline me (יסרני)], O LORD, but in justice and [and > MT] not in anger lest you make us small [MT: you make me small (יסרנו יהוה אך במשפט ואל באף פן תמעטנו) [(תמעטני)]" (cf. Jer. 15:15). The interchange between first common plural ("us") and first common singular ("me") in the Hebrew source behind Greek Jeremiah and the MT is illustrative of Jeremiah's representative role. Again, Holladay may be correct to say that this is the voice of the people implying that the LORD would be unjust to discipline them with such anger that they would become small again (cf. Gen. 18:25; Deut. 26:5; see also Jer. 29:6; 30:19; 44:28; Hos. 8:10), but the voice in the cited psalms is that of a member of the faithful remnant of the people of God genuinely seeking restoration after a failure for which he has received discipline (cf. Jer. 31:18). This cannot be said of the general populace in Jeremiah's day. Therefore, it appears likely that Jeremiah is praying on behalf of the remnant (despite Jer. 7:16; 11:14; 14:11; cf. Jer. 14:7–9, 19–22). He asks for the LORD to bring his judgment in just measure according to his word, but he also wants the LORD to preserve a remnant for himself according to his word (see Jer. 4:27; 5:10, 18; see also Jer. 30:11; 46:28).

According to Calvin, Psalm 79:6–7 is a citation from Jeremiah 10:25 or a psalm that Jeremiah wrote after he was taken to Egypt.[44] Holladay, on the other hand, believes Jeremiah 10:25 is a citation of Psalm 79:6–7 in which the people attempt to redirect divine judgment from themselves to the nations. Of course, as in the case of Jeremiah 10:23 and 10:24, this would be a misuse of the cited Scripture, but it is problematic that Jeremiah would cite from a psalm in this context that presupposes Jerusalem to be in ruins (Ps. 79:1; cf. Jer. 26:18; Mic. 3:12). Parke-Taylor suggests that the text of Psalm 79:6–7 now found in Jeremiah 10:25 was originally a later scribal comment in the margin of Jeremiah 10 that eventually found its way into the body

---

Since the *lammed* is vowelized with a *kamatz*, the definite article is meant. *The man* refers to Nebuchadnezzar" (Rosenberg, trans., *Mikraoth Gedoloth: Jeremiah Volume One*, 98).

44. Calvin, *Jeremiah*, 2:65. He also suggests that the psalm could have been written during the time of Antiochus Epiphanes.

of the text,[45] but perhaps it is better to go with the guidance of the texts themselves. The text of Jeremiah 10:25 comes under the general heading of the word of God that came to Jeremiah (Jer. 1:1–3). Psalm 79 is a psalm of Asaph, which, however it is related to the historical Asaph, comes from the perspective of someone living in the wake of the Babylonian invasion of Jerusalem. This may very well be Jeremiah (see Jer. 39–44), but since Jeremiah 10:25 does not presuppose the invasion, it has to be considered the primary version of the text. Thus, Jeremiah 10:25 is not a citation of Psalm 79:6–7. It is a text cited and interpreted in Psalm 79:6–7.

The prayer for the Lord to pour out his wrath on the nations who do not know or acknowledge him and on the families or kingdoms who do not call on his name is an imprecatory prayer (Jer. 10:25a; Ps. 79:6; cf. 1 Thess. 4:5; 2 Thess. 1:8; Rev. 16:1). In Jeremiah 10:25, it anticipates that the Lord will carry out his judgment on his people (Jer. 6:11; 25:1–11) who have sworn falsely in his name and have failed to acknowledge him (see Jer. 2:8; 4:22; 5:2; 9:3, 6, 24 [MT 9:2, 5, 23]). He will then turn around to judge his instrument of judgment—the wicked nations (see Jer. 25:12–13, 15–26). Psalm 79:6–7 simply presupposes that the judgment of Judah has already occurred and that the judgment of the nations is yet to come. This is analogous to the fourth beast and the little horn who bring tribulation and then face judgment (Dan. 7:8–12, 25–26; 9:24–27; cf. Ezek. 38–39; Rev. 20:7–10; see also Isa. 10:12). According to Jeremiah 10:25b (Ps. 79:7), it is a just judgment because "they devoured Jacob and destroyed him, and his pasture they have made desolate" (cf. Jer. 10:22b). In the beginning, anyone who tried to devour Israel was considered guilty, and calamity came upon them (Jer. 2:3b), but because of the broken covenant relationship, the Lord will give the people over to be devoured (Jer. 5:17). In the end, however, he will vindicate the faithful remnant of Israel and all those joined to her by faith (Jer. 3:17–18; 30:16).

---

45. Parke-Taylor, *Formation of the Book of Jeremiah*, 218.

JEREMIAH 11:1–17

11:1 The word that came from the LORD *to Jeremiah [MT: to Jeremiah from the* LORD*], saying, 11:2 "Hear [m. pl.] the words of this covenant and speak [GKC §112r; cf. Syr.: impv.; Tg. Jon., Vulg.: pl.; MT adds: them] to the people of Judah and to the inhabitants of Jerusalem. 11:3 And you will say to them, 'Thus says the* LORD*, the God of Israel, "Cursed is the person who does not hear/heed [Tg. Jon.: receive/accept] the words of this covenant, 11:4 which I commanded your forefathers [or, ancestors] when I brought them out of the land of Egypt from the iron furnace saying, 'Obey my voice and do [MT adds: them according to] all that I command you. And you will become my people; and I, I will become your God 11:5 in order to establish/confirm my oath [MT: the oath] that I swore to your forefathers [or, ancestors] to give to them a land flowing with milk and honey as this day.'"'" And I answered and said, "Amen [LXX: May it be],* LORD*." 11:6 And the* LORD *said to me, "Proclaim [LXX: Read] these words [MT: all these words] in the cities of Judah and in the streets of Jerusalem saying, 'Hear the words of this covenant and do them.'" 11:8 And they did not do.*[1] *11:9 And the* LORD *said to me, "Conspiracy [Syr.: Rebellion; cf. Tg. Jon.] has been found among the people of Judah and the inhabitants of Jerusalem. 11:10 They have turned back to the iniquities of their forefathers [or, ancestors] who refused to hear/heed my words. And look [look > MT], they, they have gone after other gods to serve/worship them, and [and > MT] the house of Israel and the house of Judah have broken my covenant that I made with their forefathers [or, ancestors]. 11:11 Therefore, thus says the* LORD*, 'Look, I am about to bring upon/against this people [Codex L: to them; nonn Mss: upon/against them] calamity from which they will not be able to depart. And they will cry out to me, but I will not listen to them. 11:12 And the cities of Judah and the inhabitants of Jerusalem will go and cry out to the gods to whom they have been sending sacrifices up in smoke. They will not deliver them [MT: And they will surely*

---

1. MT 11:6–8: "And the LORD said to me, 'Proclaim all these words in the cities of Judah and in the streets of Jerusalem saying, "Hear the words of this covenant and do them. For I solemnly warned your forefathers [or, ancestors] when I brought them out of the land of Egypt and [and > mlt Mss] until this day rising early and warning [i.e., urgently warning], saying, 'Obey my voice.' But they did not listen and they did not incline their ear and they went/walked in the stubbornness of their evil heart/mind. And I brought upon them all the words of this covenant that I commanded to do, and they did not do."'"

not deliver them] in the time of their calamity [LXX: They will not deliver them in the time of their calamity, will they?]. 11:13 For according to the number of your cities are your gods, O Judah, and according to the number of the streets [LXX: exits] of Jerusalem have you set up [MT adds: altars to shame] altars to send sacrifices up in smoke to Baal.' 11:14 And as for you, do not pray on behalf of this people, and do not lift up on their behalf a cry or a prayer, for I am not listening in the time of their calling to me in the time of [Codex L: on behalf of] their calamity."

11:15 "Why has the beloved in my house done [Syr.: 2fs] the wickedness [LXX: abomination; see GKC §90g; MT: What to my beloved in my house in her doing the wickedness]? Will vows and holy meat remove [see GKC §53n] from upon you [MT: the many and holy meat, they pass over from you] your evil / calamity [see GKC §91e]? Or in this will you be clear / justified [or, clean / pure; LXX: escape; MT: When your evil, then you exult; cf. Syr., Tg. Jon.]? 11:16 A flourishing olive tree, beautiful in form [MT: beautiful of fruit of form; Syr.: beautiful of fruit and beautiful in appearance], is what the LORD called your name. At the sound of its circumcision [NETS: its pruning] great was the distress upon you [MT: At (the) sound of a great roar / storm he kindled a fire upon her; Tg. Jon.: But now that you have transgressed the Torah, armies of peoples who are as strong as fire will come against you], and they broke its branches [or, and its branches were evil / worthless (Vulg.: were burned)]. 11:17 And the LORD [MT adds: of hosts] who planted you, he has spoken evil / calamity against you because of the evil of the house of Israel and the house of Judah, which [LXX: because] they made for themselves to provoke me by sending sacrifices up in smoke to Baal."

Jeremiah 11:2–5 is designated, "The word that came from the LORD to Jeremiah [MT: to Jeremiah from the LORD]" (Jer. 11:1; cf. Jer. 7:1). Given that this is an address from the LORD to the prophet Jeremiah, the plural imperative שמעו ("Hear") at the beginning of 11:2 is unexpected. Calvin suggests that colleagues such as Baruch are included in the address.[2] Keil proposes that the prophets are addressed in general and then Jeremiah in particular.[3] The following ודברת ("and speak") in the Hebrew source behind Greek Jeremiah is a second masculine singular *weqatal* form (the Syriac has a singular imperative). The Masoretic consonantal text has ודברתם, which can be vocalized according to the MT as וְדִבַּרְתָּם ("and speak them") or according to *Targum Jonathan*

---

2. Calvin, *Jeremiah*, 2:70.
3. Keil, *Jeremiah*, 132.

and the Latin Vulgate as וְדִבַּרְתֶּם ("and speak [m. pl.]"). It is not immediately obvious what covenant is referenced in the phrase "the words of this covenant" (cf. 1QS 2:12–13). There is some support for the thought that it may be the covenant that Josiah made (2 Kgs. 23:3), but most commentators understand it to be the Sinai covenant.[4] There is very little material difference between these two views since Josiah's covenant was made on the basis of the "words" found in the book of the Torah (Exod. 24:7–8). The following context, however, suggests that "this covenant" is used in two different ways in this chapter. In 11:3b, it refers to the covenant with the patriarchs that was assumed when the people came out of Egypt and arrived at Sinai (Exod. 19:4–6; Jer. 7:22–26; 11:4–5). In 11:6b, 8b, it refers to the Sinai covenant that was added secondarily because of transgression (Exod. 19:12, 13, 16; Jer. 7:22; Gal. 3:19). Jeremiah is to speak about these matters "to the people of Judah and the inhabitants of Jerusalem" (cf. Jer. 11:9).

The pattern of 11:3b ("Cursed [אָרוּר] is the person who does not hear/heed the words of this covenant") and 11:5b (And I answered and said, "Amen [אָמֵן], LORD") strongly suggests an allusion to the pattern of the Dodecalogue (Deut. 27:15–26): e.g., "'Cursed (אָרוּר) is the one who does not confirm the words of this Torah by doing them.' And all the people will say, 'Amen (אָמֵן)'" (Deut. 27:26; see also 1 Kgs. 1:36). Thus, the majority of interpreters understand "this covenant" in 11:3b to be the Sinai covenant, but there is more to it than this. Similar language is also a feature of the covenant relationship with the patriarchs: "every person who curses you is cursed (אָרוּר אֹרְרֶיךָ)" (Gen. 27:29b; cf. Gen. 12:3a; Num. 24:9b). Furthermore, 11:4 describes "this covenant" as the one commanded to the exodus generation when the people were brought out of the iron furnace of Egypt (cf. Deut. 4:20; 1 Kgs. 8:51).[5] At that time, the LORD simply said, "Obey my voice and

---

4. See Holladay, *Jeremiah 1*, 349. Abarbanel explains, "They would think that he meant a new covenant and would come to listen attentively. Then he would tell them that he meant the covenant of the Torah" (Rosenberg, trans., *Mikraoth Gedoloth: Jeremiah Volume One*, 99).

5. Contrast this with Jeremiah 31:32, which speaks of a covenant that was actually made when the people were brought out of Egypt (cf. 1 Kgs. 8:21). This cannot be the covenant with the patriarchs, which already existed. Furthermore, the covenant referenced in Jeremiah 31:32 was broken, which could only be said of the Sinai covenant. The reference to breaking the Abrahamic covenant in Genesis 17:14 is a reference to failure to keep the sign of the covenant, circumcision (Gen. 17:10–11). This would result in the cutting off of the individual but not the loss of the covenant relationship between God and his people in general.

do all that I command you. And you will become my people; and I, I will become your God" (cf. Jer. 7:22–23; 24:7; 31:33). These were the words that the LORD spoke to the people through Moses when they came to Mount Sinai prior to the giving of the law and the making of the Sinai covenant (Exod. 24:8): "And now, if you will indeed obey my voice and keep my covenant, you will be my treasured possession apart from all the peoples, for all the earth is mine" (Exod. 19:5). While many interpreters take these words to be proleptic (i.e., in anticipation of the Sinai covenant), the fact is that the people already had a covenant relationship with the LORD that had been the basis for the exodus—the covenant with the patriarchs (Exod. 2:23–25; cf. Lev. 26:42–45; see also Deut. 5:3). This is why 11:5a says that the purpose for commanding the words of this covenant to the exodus generation was to confirm the oath sworn to the patriarchs "to give them a land flowing with milk and honey as this day" (see Gen. 15:18; 26:3; Exod. 3:8, 17).[6] The law was then added secondarily because of transgression (Exod. 19:16b; Gal. 3:19; see commentary on Jer. 7:21–28), exacerbating and exposing the sin problem in order to point to the need for a new covenant relationship (Deut. 28:69 [Eng., 29:1]; 30:6; Jer. 4:4; 31:31–34). Thus, Jeremiah, even when referring to the covenant with the patriarchs, must address his own generation as those who are under the terms of the conditional, temporal covenant made at Sinai. They are like those who rejected the simple covenant of faith and obedience. They thus fall under the curses for disobedience in a broken covenant relationship (Lev. 26:14–41; Deut. 28:15–68; Jer. 11:10).

The short text found in the Hebrew source behind Greek Jeremiah 11:6–8 lacks 11:7 and all but the very end of 11:8: "And the LORD said to me, 'Proclaim[7] these words in the cities of Judah and in the streets of Jerusalem saying, "Hear the words of this covenant and do them."' And they did not do." According to this text, Jeremiah is instructed to make a simple call to the people of Judah and Jerusalem to hear the words of the covenant (presumably the Sinai covenant; see Exod. 24:8; Deut. 4:13) and do them. It is then stated plainly that the people did not do the words of the covenant (cf. Jer. 34:14). The LORD goes on to say that the present generation has returned to the iniquity of the forefathers who broke the covenant (Jer. 11:9–10; cf. Jer. 31:32; Zech. 7:11–14). The longer text of the MT, however, explains how the LORD commanded the exodus generation "and until this day" to obey

---

6. See McKane, *Jeremiah I–XXV*, 238.
7. The LXX translates this imperative as "Read," as if Jeremiah were to read the words aloud publicly from a written text (cf. Jer. 36:6; 51:61).

his voice (Jer. 11:7; cf. Exod. 19:5; Jer. 7:23; 11:4); they did not obey but went in the stubbornness of their evil heart (cf. Jer. 3:13b, 17b, 25b; 7:24a; 16:12b; 18:12b), and the LORD brought upon them the "words" of the Sinai covenant that he commanded them to do (Jer. 11:8): "And the LORD said to me, 'Proclaim all these words in the cities of Judah and in the streets of Jerusalem saying, "Hear the words of this covenant and do them. For I solemnly warned your forefathers [or, ancestors] when I brought them out of the land of Egypt and [and > mlt Mss] until this day[8] rising early and warning [i.e., urgently warning], saying, 'Obey my voice.'[9] But they did not listen, and they did not incline their ear and they went/walked in the stubbornness of their evil heart/mind. And I brought upon them all the words of this covenant that I commanded to do, and they did not do."'" It is usually assumed that the "words" brought upon the people were the curses of the Sinai covenant (Deut. 30:1), but this is problematic for at least two reasons. First, these were the words that the LORD commanded them to do (i.e., instructions), not the consequences of disobedience to laws already given (i.e., curses).[10] Second, neither for the exodus generation nor for Jeremiah's generation at the time of this message had the curses of Deuteronomy 27 and 28 (including exile) been brought upon the people.[11] Indeed, Jeremiah 11:11 makes it very clear that such curses are yet to come (cf. Jer. 39:16). Attempts to resolve this difficulty either by explaining the *wayyiqtol* וָאָבִיא ("and I brought") as a prophetic tense[12] or by revocalizing it as *waw* + *yiqtol* וְאָבִיא ("and I

---

8. "The conjunction *waw* in וְעַד (*wĕʿad*, 'even to') divides God's actions between his bringing the 'words of the covenant' against the people at Sinai 'and even to' the prophet Jeremiah's own day. In the parallel text, Jeremiah 7:25, the use of the preposition מִן (*min*, 'from') and the lack of a similar *waw* with עַד (*ʿad*, 'until') shows that Jeremiah 7:25 looks primarily to the giving of the law by the prophets throughout Israel's history and not principally at Sinai. Thus, 'From *[min]* the day your fathers came out of the land of Egypt until *[ʿad]* this day' shows that the verse looks to the giving of the law by the prophets (Jer 7:25) throughout Israel's history and not specifically at Sinai" (Sailhamer, *Meaning of the Pentateuch*, 410). Cf. Jeremiah 32:20, 31.

9. Cf. Jeremiah 7:13 [MT], 25; 25:3, 4; 26:5; 29:19 [MT]; 32:33; 35:14–15; 44:4.

10. Calvin senses this problem but does not satisfactorily resolve it (*Jeremiah*, 2:84).

11. See McKane, *Jeremiah I–XXV*, 238.

12. See Rosenberg, trans., *Mikraoth Gedoloth: Jeremiah Volume One*, 101.

will bring") are ultimately unsuccessful. A *weqatal* form וְהֵבֵאתִי ("and I will bring") would be expected for this meaning (cf. Jer. 25:13). Thus, the best explanation is that offered by Sailhamer: "Jeremiah 11:8 thus further clarifies the sense of Jeremiah 7:21–28. God entered a covenant with his people at Sinai. As suggested already in Exodus 19:1–9, originally there were no stipulations or collections of laws associated with that covenant. It was cast as a continuation of the Abrahamic covenant, which also had no laws, but rather was based on the call to faith, as Exodus 19:9 *(yăʾămînû)* clearly states. Then the people disobeyed God, and God brought stipulations/laws upon them to govern their relationship within the covenant."[13] The people disobeyed God's voice at Sinai (Exod. 19:5, 12, 13, 16), and the words of Exodus 20 and following were added because of their transgression (Jer. 7:21–23; Gal. 3:19; see again the commentary on Jer. 7:21–28), but neither they nor any generation down to the time of Jeremiah has done the words that the LORD commanded them, and so the prospect of judgment is imminent (Jer. 11:11).

The LORD says to Jeremiah in 11:9 that "conspiracy" (קֶשֶׁר) has been found among the people of Judah and the inhabitants of Jerusalem. This seems like a strange choice of terms given its usage in political contexts (2 Sam. 15:12; 1 Kgs. 16:20; 2 Kgs. 11:14; 12:21; 14:19; 15:15, 30) where "it is associated with the overthrow of government" (see also Isa. 8:12; Ezek. 22:25).[14] The Syriac and *Targum Jonathan* render it as if it were a more general word for rebellion. The following context of 11:10 explains that the "conspiracy" is the people's turning to the iniquities of the forefathers (cf. Ps. 79:8) and their following after other gods. While it is possible that the choice of the term "conspiracy" is intended to depict the breaking of the covenant as an overthrow of the LORD's government of the people in some sense, it appears more likely that קֶשֶׁר ("conspiracy") is a play on Jeremiah's frequently used term שֶׁקֶר ("deception").[15] The people have been disingenuous (Jer. 3:10). They have sworn falsely (Jer. 5:2; 7:9). They have trusted in false prophets (Jer. 5:31; 6:13; 8:10). They have worshiped false gods (Jer. 10:14). All this has amounted to a return to the iniquities of their forefathers who refused to hear/heed the LORD's words (Jer. 11:10; cf. Isa. 65:12; 66:4b; Jer. 7:26; 13:10). They have gone after other gods to

---

13. Sailhamer, *Meaning of the Pentateuch*, 409–10.

14. McKane, *Jeremiah I–XXV*, 239.

15. For this exegetical technique, see Wilhelm Bacher, *Die exegetische Terminologie der jüdischen Traditionsliteratur* (Hildesheim: Georg Olms, 1965), 44.

worship them (cf. Jer. 2:5) and have broken the Sinai covenant made with their ancestors (see Exod. 20:2–6; Lev. 26:15; Deut. 31:16; cf. Jer. 22:9).[16] It is important to acknowledge the force of this statement. The old covenant made at Sinai with its terms and conditions and inherent temporality is done. It was an "indefinite covenant" (ברית עולם) only in the sense that the time of its breaking could not be predicted (Exod. 31:16). All that is left is the consequence of the people's failure. Any hope for a future covenant relationship with the LORD does not lie in a renewal of the Sinai covenant, which is now broken (Jer. 31:32), but in a new covenant relationship that depends upon divine faithfulness and transformation of the human heart (Jer. 31:31, 33–34).

An announcement of judgment begins in 11:11: "Therefore, thus says the LORD, 'Look, I am about to bring upon/against this people [Codex L: to them; nonn Mss: upon/against them] calamity from which they will not be able to depart. And they will cry out to me, but I will not listen to them'" (cf. Jer. 19:3, 15; 35:17; 39:16; 45:5). Unlike the time of the exodus (Exod. 3:7–10) or the period of the Judges (Judg. 2:18; 3:9), the LORD will not listen to the people when they cry out to him (cf. 1 Sam. 8:18; Isa. 1:15; Ezek. 8:18; Mic. 3:4; Job 35:12–13).[17] Just as the people have refused to hear/heed the LORD's voice (Jer. 11:10; cf. Jer. 7:13, 27), so he will refuse to hear/heed the people's voice (see Zech. 7:13).[18] Since the people have disobeyed and broken the covenant, the LORD is under no obligation to bless them. He is only under obligation to curse them for disobedience (Lev. 26; Deut. 28). The people will then go and cry out to the gods to whom they have been sending sacrifices up in smoke, but those non-gods will not be able to deliver them in the time of their calamity (Jer. 11:12; cf. Deut. 32:37–38; Isa. 57:13). The people have historically only cried out to the LORD when they felt that they really needed him (e.g., Judg. 10:11–12), but when they have found their distress alleviated, they have quickly turned to the worship of other gods (e.g., Judg. 11:13). Thus, the LORD leaves the people in their time of trouble to the useless gods that they seem to prefer (e.g., Judg. 11:14). The causal conjunction כי at the beginning of 11:13 introduces what is

---

16. "With the extant form of MT there appears a more general reference to a history of apostasy involving both Northern and Southern Kingdoms, and את בריתי אשר כרתי את אבותם would then refer more naturally to the Sinai covenant" (McKane, *Jeremiah I–XXV*, 239).

17. Cf. Jeremiah 7:16; 11:14; 14:11. For the reversal of this in the new covenant, see Jeremiah 33:3.

18. "He who turns his ear away from Torah, even his prayer is an abomination" (Prov. 28:9).

likely a sarcastic rationale, as if to say, "Surely the people should cry out to the gods that they worship for help, because there are so many of them!" But idolatry is now a luxury that the people will no longer be able to afford in their time of distress. Their idols will prove to be of no benefit to them no matter what their number. The text of Jeremiah 11:12–13 is very close to that of Jeremiah 2:28 (see LXX and MT) in its suggestion that the people should try appealing to their so-called gods whose number is according to that of Judah's cities. The altars that the people have set up to Baal are according to the number of the streets of Jerusalem (cf. Hos. 10:1). The MT adds מזבחות לבשת ("altars to shame") prior to מזבחות לקטר לבעל ("altars to make sacrifices smoke [or, burn incense] to Baal"). These are more or less interchangeable variants now conflated in the MT. The term בשת *bōsheth* ("shame") became a substitute for בעל *baal* ("Baal") as evidenced in names like איש בשת ("Ishbosheth"), which appears in LXX[Ms] and in Aquila, Symmachus, and Theodotion as Εισβααλ ("Ishbaal") (see also Jer. 3:24). This change occurred because the meaning "lord" for *baal* gave way to a more negative connotation via its association with the Canaanite storm/fertility god "Baal," whose worship became a cause for great "shame" (*bōsheth*). This also explains the use of the feminine article with the male deity "Baal" in the Old Greek. The feminine article reminds the reader of ἡ αἰσχύνη ("shame"). Finally, because the Lord will not listen in the time that the people call to him, Jeremiah himself is instructed not to pray on behalf of the people (Jer. 11:14; see Lam. 3:28). This instruction echoes the language of Jeremiah 7:16 and anticipates that of Jeremiah 14:11. Despite the fact that Jeremiah is a prophet like Moses (Jer. 1:4–10; see also 2 Macc. 15:14), the time for intercession for the people's good has passed (cf. Jer. 6:8). Their fate has been sealed by their breaking of the covenant. The Lord is no longer willing to hear an intercessory prayer as in the time of Moses (Exod. 32:11–14) or Samuel (1 Sam. 12:23; Jer. 15:1). Of course, this does not necessarily prevent Jeremiah from praying (Jer. 14:7–9, 19–22; 37:3; 42:2), but it does mean that such prayer will not alter the Lord's course of action.

There is a difference of opinion about who might be the speaker in Jeremiah 11:15. Rashi considers God to be the speaker: "What has My people, who were beloved to Me, to do in My house, seeing that many of them perform evil design and sin intentionally?"[19] Redak, on the other hand, says that Jeremiah addresses God: "What has my Beloved to do in my house? What does God have to do any longer in the Temple, to

---

19. Rosenberg, trans., *Mikraoth Gedoloth: Jeremiah Volume One*, 103.

cause His presence to rest there?"[20] It is decidedly less difficult to hear "my house" with reference to the temple coming from God than it is to hear it from Jeremiah. The opening question according to the Hebrew source behind Greek Jeremiah is as follows: "Why has the beloved in my house done the wickedness (מה הידידה בביתי עשתה המזמתה)?"[21] The MT has, "What to my beloved in my house in her doing the wickedness (מה לידידי בביתי עשותה המזמתה)?"[22] This language is reminiscent of Isaiah 5:1a: "I will sing to my beloved (לידידי) the song of my beloved (דודי) to his vineyard." But there the LORD is clearly the beloved (cf. Isa. 5:7). The present text has more in common with Jeremiah 12:7: "I have left my house (ביתי); I have forsaken my inheritance; I have given the beloved (ידדות) of my soul into the palm of her enemies." According to the MT accentuation of Jeremiah 11:15a (*zaqeph*), הרבים ("the many") should be read with what precedes it, but the precise syntactical relationship of this word to the preceding text is unclear.[23] The LXX reflects Hebrew הנדרים ("vows"): "Will vows and holy meat remove (יַעֲבְרוּ) from upon you your evil/calamity (רעתכי)?"[24] In other words, empty religious ritual will not avert the coming disaster (cf. Isa. 1:10–17; Jer. 7:1–15). The Hebrew source behind Greek Jeremiah continues, "Or in this will you be clear/justified (או זאת התזכי)?" On the other hand, the elliptical MT 11:15b has, "When your evil, then you exult (כי רעתכי אז תעלזי)."

The Hebrew Bible on several occasions compares the people of God to a vineyard (Isa. 5:1–7; 27:2–6; Jer. 12:10; see also Matt. 21:33–46) or vine (Jer. 2:21; 5:10; 6:9; Ezek. 15; 17; 19:10–14; Hos. 10:1; 14:8 [Eng., 14:7]; Ps. 80:9–14 [Eng., 80:8–13]; see also John 15:1–17; Rom. 11:17–24). In Jeremiah 11:16, the comparison is to "a flourishing olive tree, beautiful in form (זית רענן יפה תאר)" (cf. Hos. 14:7 [Eng., 14:6]; see also Pss. 52:10 [Eng., 52:8]; 128:3). For the second phrase, the MT has יפה פרי תאר ("beautiful of fruit of form"; cf. Syr.: "beautiful of fruit and beautiful in appearance"). This is the name/reputation that the LORD gave the people. It speaks to the good preparation and potential that the people once had (cf. Isa. 5:1–2; Jer. 2:2–3). The Hebrew

---

20. Rosenberg, trans., *Mikraoth Gedoloth: Jeremiah Volume One*, 103.

21. Syriac: "Why, O beloved of my house, have you done (= עשית) the uncleanness?"

22. Or, "What right does my beloved have in my house . . . ?"

23. "הָרַבִּים makes no sense. It belongs manifestly to the words which follow" (Keil, *Jeremiah*, 134–35). *BHS* thus disregards the accentuation. It also disregards the placement of the *athnach*.

24. Cf. MT: "the many and holy meat, they pass over (יַעֲבְרוּ) from you" (but see GKC §53n).

source behind Greek Jeremiah then says, "At the sound of its circumcision [NETS: its pruning] great was the distress upon you (לקול מולתו נדלה הצרה עליך)." According to the MT, the text says, "At (the) sound of a great roar/storm he kindled a fire upon her (לקול המולה גדלה הצית אש עליה)" (see Jer. 4:4).[25] *Targum Jonathan* interprets this to mean: "But now that you have transgressed the Torah, armies of peoples who are as strong as fire will come against you." Interpretation of the final clause of 11:16 varies depending on whether the verb comes from רעע ("to be evil") or the homonym רעע ("to break"). Thus, the text either describes the reason for judgment ("and its branches were evil/worthless") or the judgment itself ("and they broke its branches").

The same God who planted the people (Isa. 5:1–2; Jer. 2:21; see also Jer. 1:10; 24:6; 31:28; 32:41; Amos 9:15) has now spoken "evil/calamity" (רעה) against them because of their "evil" (רעה) (Jer. 11:17; cf. Jer. 1:14, 16). This includes both the house of Israel and the house of Judah (see Jer. 3:6–13; 11:10; Bar. 2:26). The relative clause describes this "evil" as that "which they made for themselves." This is not to be rendered as "because they made for themselves [*BHS* proposes the addition of 'gods']" or as "which they did to themselves." Rather, the gods/idols are the "evil" that the people made for themselves with their own hands (see Jer. 1:16; 11:10), thus provoking (ironically, as if by design) the LORD by sending sacrifices up in smoke to Baal (see Jer. 7:18–19; 8:19b; 11:13).

APPLICATION OF JEREMIAH 7:1–11:17

This section of text (Jer. 7:1–11:17), though varied in its presentation, is clearly set apart from the preceding section on the enemy

---

25. "ἀνήφθη πῦρ ἐπ' αὐτήν is deleted in Gött. as doublet of μεγάλη θλεῖψις ἐπὶ σέ, though the words are only missing in the text of Origen. According to Ziegler, both ἀνήφθη πῦρ ἐπ' αὐτήν and μεγάλη θλεῖψις ἐπὶ σέ are renderings of גדלה הצית אש עליה. Further, according to Ziegler, it is strange that the words which correspond to MT are missing in the text of Origen, who usually corrects according to MT, and thus could not have deleted them. Hence Ziegler supposes that the words were missing in the *Vorlage* of Origen. Moreover, Ziegler notes that it is strange that in the second rendering אש is not translated, and he supposes that the translator of Jeremiah had another *Vorlage* than MT. See Ziegler 1958, 100. McKane 1986, 250, on the other hand, calls Ziegler's conclusion into doubt and suggests that μεγάλη θλεῖψις ἐπὶ σέ 'is a free expansion of MT גדלה.' However, such expansions seem to be at least very rare in the quite literal translation of Jeremiah" (Walser, *Jeremiah*, 268).

from the north (Jer. 4:5–6:30) and from the following section featuring Jeremiah's confessions (Jer. 11:18–20:18). It is framed by the rebuke of trust in empty temple ritual in Jeremiah 7:1–15 and 11:15 and by the exegesis of Exodus 19:5 in Jeremiah 7:21–28 and 11:1–8, showing that the law was added secondarily because of transgression (see also the shared language in Jer. 7:18–19 and 11:17). With regard to the program set forth in Jeremiah 1, the text of Jeremiah 7:1–11:17 is largely devoted to the development of the theme introduced in Jeremiah 1:16—the people's abandonment of the LORD and his covenant in their worship of other gods. Of course, this theme was also developed in Jeremiah 2:14–4:4 but in a different way. There the development was largely driven by exegesis of the divorce law in Deuteronomy 24:1–4 (Jer. 3:1–5). Interestingly, both Jeremiah 2:14–4:4 and 7:1–11:17 have shown an interest in the relationship between the house of Israel and the house of Judah (Jer. 3:6–18; 11:10, 17).

The exegesis of Exodus 19:5 in Jeremiah 7:21–28 and 11:1–8 remains profoundly relevant for new covenant readers of the book of Jeremiah. Christian theologians have long struggled to articulate what role the Mosaic law continues to have in the lives of believers, but this is in large part due to the fact that theologians have not always asked the same question that the Pentateuch is answering. The Pentateuch does not answer the question, "Do I still have to keep the laws?" The Pentateuch answers the question, "What role does the law play in the composition of the Pentateuch?"[26] The text of Jeremiah 7:21–28 and 11:1–8 expounds the answer to this question and shows that the law was added because of transgression not to solve the people's sin problem but to expose and exacerbate it in order to point to the need for a new covenant relationship. The old covenant is broken. Thus, new covenant believers are not under law but under grace (Rom. 6:14) in the sense that their blessing is not found in their own work of keeping the law but in the person and work of Christ (Jer. 4:2b). New covenant believers are enabled by the Spirit of God to do the will of God (Jer. 31:31–34; 32:39; Ezek. 11:19–20; 36:26–27; Rom. 8:4).

Does this mean that the character and will of God revealed in the laws of the Pentateuch are now irrelevant? By no means! In fact, the material accompanying Jeremiah 7:21–28 and 11:1–8 in this section addresses this very issue. It discusses the שֶׁקֶר ("deception") of the people: false trust in the temple (Jer. 7:4, 8), swearing falsely in violation of the Decalogue revealed in the Pentateuch (Jer. 7:9), the false

---

26. See Sailhamer, *Pentateuch as Narrative*, 47–59; *Introduction to Old Testament Theology*, 253–71; *Meaning of the Pentateuch*, 537–62.

pen of the scribes who claim to have wisdom and Torah (Jer. 8:8–9), prophets and priests acting deceptively (Jer. 8:10), people lying to one another (Jer. 9:2, 4 [MT 9:3, 5]), and worship of false gods/idols (Jer. 10:14). The alternative to such behavior is the wisdom of God (Jer. 9:12, 23–24 [MT 9:11, 22–23]; 10:7, 12). Such "wisdom" (חכמה) is found in the Torah itself (Deut. 4:6). Much like the wisdom literature (e.g., Job 28:28; Prov. 1:7; 9:10), the Torah instructs its readers in the fear of the LORD (Deut. 31:13; Ps. 19:10 [Eng., 19:9]).

JEREMIAH 11:18–12:6

*11:18 "O L*ORD*, cause me to know, and I will know [or, that I may know]" [MT: And the L*ORD*, he caused me to know, and I knew]. At that time I saw their deeds [MT: "At that time you showed me their deeds"]. 11:19 And I like a docile lamb that is led to slaughter [see Syr.; LXX: to be slaughtered], I did not know [MT: And I was like a docile lamb that is led to slaughter, and I did not know that against me they made plans]. Against me they made plans [LXX: they made an evil plan, saying], "Let us cast [LXX: Come and let us cast; cf. Tg. Jon.] wood [Tg. Jon.: deadly poison] into his food [MT: Let us destroy (the) tree with its food (BHS apparatus: in its freshness)], and cut him off [or, that we may cut him off] from the land of the living; and as for his name, it will never again be remembered." 11:20 "O L*ORD *[MT: And O L*ORD *of hosts], righteous judge, tester of kidneys and heart, let me see your vengeance from them [or, let me see you exact vengeance from them], for it is to you that I have revealed [BHS apparatus: rolled] my contention." 11:21 Therefore, thus says the L*ORD *concerning the men of Anathoth who seek my life [MT: your life] saying, "Do not prophesy in the name of the L*ORD*. And if not, you will die by our hand [MT: and you will not die by our hand (or, lest you die by our hand)]": 11:22 [MT adds: Therefore, thus says the L*ORD *of hosts] "Look, I am about to visit upon them [i.e., punish them]. Their choice, young men, they will die by the sword; and as for their sons and their daughters, they will die by famine. 11:23 And a remnant they will not have, for I will bring evil / calamity to / upon the men of Anathoth in the year of their visitation."*

*12:1 "You are righteous, O L*ORD*, when I complain [LXX: defend myself] to you. But matters of justice must I speak with you. Why is it the way of the wicked that prospers? Why are all those who commit treachery at ease? 12:2 You plant them; yea, they take root. They give birth [MT: go / grow; Tg. Jon.: become rich]; yea, they produce fruit [Tg. Jon.: acquire property]. You are near in their mouth but far from their kidneys [Tg. Jon.: The words of your Torah are near in their mouth, but the fear of you is far from their kidneys]. 12:3 And you, O L*ORD*, you know me [MT adds: you see me (Syr.: and you see me); Tg. Jon.: all is known and revealed before you], you test [MT: and you test] my heart with you [LXX: before you; Tg. Jon.: you test the hearts of those who desire the fear of you]. [MT adds: Drag them away like sheep to slaughter] Set them apart [LXX: Purify them; MT: and set them apart] for the day of their [their > MT] slaughter. 12:4 How long must the land languish [LXX: mourn] and the herbage of every field [LXX: all the grass of the field] be* *dry because of the evil of those who live in it. Large land animal [Codex L: animals (see GKC §145k)] is swept away [Syr.: perishes], and flying creature, for they say, 'God[1] does not see our ways [MT: He does not see our end].'"[2] 12:5 "[MT adds: כי][3] With your feet [MT: footmen] you ran, and they wearied you. How will you contend with [LXX: prepare for] the horses? And in a land of peace / well-being you are trusting, [MT adds: and] how will you do in the pride / majesty of the Jordan?[4] 12:6 For / Indeed even your brothers and the house of your father, they too have acted treacherously against you. They too have called, after you they have filled in [i.e., followed / pursued; LXX: were gathered; MT: They too have called after you fully]. Do not believe in them when they speak to you good things."*

These two units (Jer. 11:18–23 and 12:1–6) begin a new section (Jer. 11:18–20:18) that features the "confessions" of Jeremiah (Jer. 11:18–23; 12:1–6; 15:10–14, 15–21; 17:14–18; 18:18–23; 20:7–12, 14–18).[5] Several monographs have been devoted to the study of these confessions.[6] The results of these studies vary in detail, but there is a

---

1. 4QJer[a]: יה]וה
2. The placement of the *athnach* in the MT suggests a different arrangement of the syntax for 12:4b: "Because of the evil of those who live in it, large land animal(s) is/are swept away, and flying creature. For they say, 'He does not see our end.'"
3. *Targum Jonathan* prefaces this verse with the following: "This is the reply to Jeremiah the prophet concerning his request."
4. *Tg. Jon.* adds: "And if you see and are amazed at the good things that I do for Nebuchadnezzar the king of Babylon, the foot soldier, O prophet, then what if I were to show you what I will do to your righteous fathers who were from of old, who ran like the horses, doing good deeds before me? And I even said to them that I will bring blessings and consolations upon your children, look, like water flowing down flooding into the Jordan."
5. Very few see a connection between Jeremiah 11:18 and the immediately preceding material. Calvin is an exception (*Jeremiah*, 2:108–9).
6. See, e.g., Walter Baumgartner, *Die Klagegedichte des Jeremia*, BZAW 32 (Giessen: Töppelmann, 1917); A. R. Diamond, *The Confessions of Jeremiah in Context: Scenes of Prophetic Drama*, JSOTSup 45 (Sheffield: Sheffield Academic, 1987); Kathleen M. O'Connor, *The Confessions of Jeremiah: Their Interpretation and Role in Chapters 1–25*, SBLDS 94 (Atlanta: Scholars, 1988); Mark S. Smith, *The Laments of Jeremiah and Their Contexts*, SBLMS (Atlanta; Scholars, 1990). For a helpful summary of research, see Catherine Sze Wing So, "Structure in the Confessions of Jeremiah," in *The Book of Jeremiah: Composition, Reception, and Interpretation*, eds.

general consensus that the confessions do not stand in isolation from one another nor are they randomly scattered across the landscape of the book. They are integrally related to one another and are in dialogue with the intervening material. Some even see a kind of linear development from the beginning of this section to its end. The following commentary will work under the assumption that these confessions are a development of the theme of opposition and persecution set forth in Jeremiah 1:17–19, but these passages are not merely about the personal struggles of the prophet. Rather, Jeremiah is an example or paradigm of the suffering righteous—a representative of the faithful remnant and a model for the ideal readership of the book.[7] The following exposition will also keep a close eye on the relationship between the confessions and other laments in biblical literature such as those found in the Psalter and the book of Job.

Attempts to rearrange the text of Jeremiah 11:18–23 and 12:1–6 are not based on extant manuscript evidence and should be rejected as subjective and unfounded.[8] (The task is to explain the text or texts that we have, not the one[s] that we do not have.) As it stands, the repetition of 11:20 from the first confession (11:18–23) in 20:12 at the end of the next to last confession (20:7–12) forms an inclusio for the collection as a whole, thus showing signs of intentional design.[9] The text of 11:18a is vocalized differently in the LXX and the MT. LXX: "O Lord, cause me to know, and I will know [or, that I may know]" (= יְהוָה הוֹדִיעֵנִי וְאֵדָעָה); MT: And the Lord, he caused me to know, and I knew (וַיהוָה הוֹדִיעַנִי וָאֵדָעָה). The first features direct discourse from the prophet to the Lord. The second is the prophet's account of what the Lord did. At this point it is not clear what Jeremiah did not know or what he was made to know. The reader is initially kept in the dark just as the prophet once was. The Hebrew source behind Greek Jeremiah then switches from direct discourse in 11:18a to the prophet's personal account of what happened in 11:18b: At that time I saw (רָאִיתִי) their deeds. The MT, on the other hand, switches from an account of what the Lord did in 11:18a to direct discourse in 11:18b: "At that time you showed me (הִרְאִיתַנִי) their deeds." Again, the reader does

---

Jack R. Lundbom, Craig A. Evans, and Bradford A. Anderson (Leiden: Brill, 2018), 126–48.

7. See Hannes Bezzel, "The Suffering of the Elect. Variations on a Theological Problem in Jer 15, 10–21," in *Prophecy in the Book of Jeremiah*, eds. Hans M. Barstad and Reinhard G. Kratz, BZAW 288 (Berlin: de Gruyter, 2009), 48–73.

8. See the discussion in McKane, *Jeremiah I–XXV*, 253–55.

9. See Parke-Taylor, *Formation of the Book of Jeremiah*, 16–17.

not know at this juncture who the referent of the pronoun "their" might be, nor does he/she know about the deeds mentioned. This is an effective way to start the confession, enabling the reader to experience the prophet's lack of knowledge. The reader only gains knowledge of what the LORD revealed to Jeremiah by continuing to read the confession.

The syntactical arrangement of the Hebrew source behind Greek Jeremiah for the first part of 11:19 translates as follows: "And I like a docile lamb that is led to slaughter, I did not know (לא ידעתי). Against me they made plans." The MT, however, has a different arrangement (see the placement of the *athnach*): "And I was like a docile lamb that is led to slaughter, and I did not know (ולא ידעתי) that (כי) against me they made plans." Jeremiah compares himself to an unsuspecting lamb being led to slaughter (cf. Isa. 53:7; Jer. 12:3; Ps. 44:12, 23 [Eng., 44:11, 22]; Acts 8:32–33; Rom. 8:36).[10] He says that he was completely unaware of the plans made against him (cf. Jer. 18:18; see also Lam. 3:60–61). The MT has no formal introduction to the following quote of those who plotted against him. The LXX adds the introductory "saying" (= לאמר?). The Hebrew source behind Greek Jeremiah and the MT differ in the content of the quote. The Hebrew source behind Greek Jeremiah says, "Let us cast [נשליכה; LXX: Come and let us cast (= לכו ונשליכה?)] wood [עץ] into his food [בלחמו], and cut him off [or, that we may cut him off] from the land of the living; and as for his name, it will never again be remembered." *Targum Jonathan*, which normally agrees with the MT, appears to follow the Hebrew source behind Greek Jeremiah in this instance. It interprets the "wood" to be cast into Jeremiah's food as "deadly poison" (cf. Deut. 29:17b [Eng., 29:18b]; Jer. 9:14 [Eng., 9:15]; 23:15; Ps. 69:22 [Eng., 69:21]). The intended result is the cutting off of Jeremiah from "the land of the living" (cf. Isa. 53:8; Ps. 52:7 [Eng., 52:5]). His name will never again be remembered (cf. Ps. 83:5 [Eng., 83:4]). On the other hand, the MT says, "Let us destroy [נשחיתה] (the) tree [עץ] with its food [בלחמו; *BHS* apparatus: in its freshness (בלחו)], and cut him off [or, that we may cut him off] from the land of the living; and as for his name, it will never again be remembered." This text

---

10. Jerome: "It is the consensus of all the church that these words are spoken by Christ through the person of Jeremiah" (Wenthe, ed., *Jeremiah, Lamentations*, 98). The language of a lamb led to slaughter describes the suffering servant of the LORD in Isaiah 53:7–8 and is identified with Christ in Acts 8:32–33. This kind of association may have prompted the disciples' answer to Jesus' question about who the people say the Son of Man is: "Some John the Baptist, others Elijah, others Jeremiah or one of the prophets" (Matt. 16:14).

speaks of killing Jeremiah in the prime of life like the destruction of a healthy, fruit-bearing tree (cf. Deut. 20:19).

The prophet then addresses the Lord in 11:20 (cf. Jer. 20:12). He describes the Lord as a "righteous judge" (שפט צדק [see GKC §128p; cf. Ps. 7:12; 9:5 (Eng., 9:4)]) and "tester of kidneys and heart" (בחן כליות ולב). The parallel text in 20:12 has "righteous tester" (בחן צדיק) and "seer of kidneys and heart" (ראה כליות ולב). The Lord has already been introduced as one who tests the people (Jer. 6:27; cf. Isa. 48:9–11; Jer. 9:6 [Eng., 9:7]; 12:2–3; 17:10; Zech. 13:9; Pss. 7:10; 26:2; Prov. 17:3; 1 Thess. 2:4; Rev. 2:23). He is able to judge the people righteously (cf. Jer. 12:1) precisely because he is able to see into their mind, represented here by their kidneys and heart (see BDB, 480, 524–525; see also 1 Sam. 16:7; Isa. 11:4; Jer. 23:5; Prov. 20:27). Jeremiah prays an imprecatory prayer: "let me see your vengeance from them [or, let me see you exact vengeance from them]" (cf. Jer. 12:3; 17:18; 18:21–23; see also Jer. 20:10b). Such prayers (e.g., Ps. 10) are often considered the antithesis of love for enemies (Matt. 5:44), but they are in fact efforts not to take matters into one's own hands. They are expressions of trust that the Lord will bring about true justice in his own righteous way. The prophet explains: "for it is to you that I have revealed [גִּלִּיתִי; *BHS* apparatus: גַּלּוֹתִי (I have rolled)] my contention [רִיבִי]" (see Jer. 12:1; see also Lam. 3:58). The suggestion that the *piel* of גלה (גִּלִּיתִי ["I have revealed"]) should be read as a *qal* from גלל (גַּלּוֹתִי ["I have rolled"]) is based in part on confusion between the two in witnesses to Psalms 22:9 [Eng., 22:8]; 37:5; Proverbs 16:3. It is also considered problematic that Jeremiah would have to reveal something to the Lord who already knows the hearts of men, but the point is probably not that Jeremiah has made something known to the Lord that was previously unknown to him. Rather, it is that Jeremiah has confessed something previously unconfessed, namely, a particular point of contention (see Jer. 15:10).

Jeremiah 11:21 introduces the announcement of judgment: "Therefore, thus says the Lord concerning the men of Anathoth who seek my life [MT: your life] saying, 'Do not prophesy in the name of the Lord. And if not, you will die by our hand [MT: and you will not die by our hand (or, lest you die by our hand)].'" This introduction identifies the men of Jeremiah's own hometown, Anathoth, as those who seek the prophet's life (see Jer. 1:1; cf. 1 Kgs. 2:26; Jer. 20:10; Luke 4:24). It does not necessarily mean that all the men of Anathoth or even all the priests at Anathoth plotted against Jeremiah. The conspirators are quoted as threatening to kill Jeremiah if he does not cease to prophesy in the Lord's name (cf. Isa. 30:10; Amos 2:12; 7:13,

16; Mic. 2:6).[11] They no longer want to hear Jeremiah's words of rebuke or his warnings of judgment. They would rather hear messages of peace (Jer. 6:14; 8:11 [MT]). The announcement of judgment itself begins in Jeremiah 11:22: [MT adds: Therefore, thus says the LORD of hosts] "Look, I am about to visit upon them [i.e., punish them]. Their choice, young men, they will die by the sword; and as for their sons and their daughters, they will die by famine." The addition in the MT is an unnecessary repetition of the beginning of 11:21. The LORD is about to punish the conspirators from Anathoth. Their choice, young men will die by the sword, and their sons and daughters will die by famine (cf. Jer. 18:21; see also Jer. 5:12; 14:12, 16). If the strong and healthy will perish, surely those who are weak and sick will not survive (see Jer. 6:11). Even though they do not successfully carry out their plot, they will be judged for the plot itself (cf. Matt. 5:21–22). The text of 11:23 adds that the conspirators will not have a remnant (cf. Jer. 15:9; 50:26), for the LORD will bring evil/calamity upon them in the year of their "visitation" (cf. Jer. 6:15; 8:12; 23:12; 46:21; 48:44; 50:27). Again, this does not mean that no people at all from Anathoth will survive. Ezra 2:23 and Nehemiah 7:27 list "the men of Anathoth" (128) among those who eventually returned from Babylonian exile under the leadership of Zerubbabel and Joshua.[12]

The second confession (Jer. 12:1–6) begins with a declaration in 12:1a: "You are righteous, O LORD, when I complain [LXX: defend myself] to you" (cf. Ps. 119:137; see also Jer. 2:29; 11:20b; 18:19; 20:12b; BDB, 937). This is offset by the following clause introduced by אַךְ: "But matters of justice must I speak with you" (Jer. 12:1b; cf. Job 9:2–3, 14–20, 32–33).[13] According to Bright, "Jeremiah will not in principle question

---

11. Redak: "Now, how did Jeremiah state that God informed him of the plot if the people of Anathoth openly threatened him with death if he continued to prophesy in the name of God? The answer is that he considered it a mere threat that they would kill him in public, and he had no fear of that. That they should poison him was still possible, but he was completely unaware of such a plot" (Rosenberg, trans., *Mikraoth Gedoloth: Jeremiah Volume One*, 106).

12. Midrash explains that this is because the men of Anathoth repented (Neusner, *Jeremiah in Talmud and Midrash*, 139, 188), but such an explanation is unnecessary. Only the conspirators were judged, and for them there was no remnant, but those who did not plot against Jeremiah's life survived.

13. Rashi: "When I debate with You, I know that you will be right in Your words, but I wish to argue with You so that You will let me know Your way" (Rosenberg, trans., *Mikraoth Gedoloth: Jeremiah Volume One*, 107).

the justice of God, who is ever 'in the right, just' (*ṣaddīq*); no legal complaint (*rīb*) can be brought against him. Yet (next colon) there are specific cases of right (*mišpāṭīm*) that Jeremiah wishes to discuss."[14] McKane presses this even further: "Over against the unthinkable thought that Yahweh's righteousness can be impugned, there is dissatisfaction with a faith which seems to be merely obscurantist, and there is an unwillingness to make lack of comprehension into a theological virtue: 'If we are to use this language, why can we not press its implications and have a debate about its validity?'"[15] This is consistent with the nature of lament/petition psalms (e.g., Ps. 13), which tend to express the psalmist's experience in brutally honest terms while still affirming the trustworthiness of what God has revealed about himself. Thus, Jeremiah asks, "Why is it the way of the wicked that prospers? Why are all those who commit treachery at ease?" In other words, if God is righteous, why are the wicked and not the righteous allowed to prosper (cf. Jer 15:18 [LXX]; Hab. 1:13; Job 21:7–16)? Why do the righteous suffer? The wicked in this context are not the Babylonians (contra Rashi) but the men of Anathoth (Jer. 11:21). Jeremiah is trying to reconcile the fact that God has announced judgment in response to his complaint (Jer. 11:20–23) with the fact that he must currently endure the prosperity of his enemies and the persecution that comes from them.[16]

Jeremiah appears to accuse God at the outset of 12:2, as if God were to be held responsible for injustice: "You plant them; yea, they take root" (cf. Jer. 11:17).[17] Calvin, however, takes this as an affirmation of

---

Keil understands אַךְ to introduce a limitation: "only he will speak pleas of right" (Keil, *Jeremiah*, 137).

14. Bright, *Jeremiah*, 86–87.

15. McKane, *Jeremiah I–XXV*, 261.

16. Holladay suggests that Jeremiah 12:1b is a variation on Psalm 1, which affirms that the way of the righteous prospers while the way of wicked perishes, as if Jeremiah were asking why the affirmation of the psalm is no longer valid (*Jeremiah 1*, 376), but the basis for Jeremiah's question is not the promise of prosperity for the righteous. Rather, it is the fact that God himself is righteous, which is not an explicit declaration of Psalm 1. It appears unlikely that there is textual dependence between Jeremiah 12:1b and Psalm 1, especially given the fact that the two are saying very different things. It is more likely that the two simply share language that commonly surfaces in biblical discussions about the fate of the righteous and the wicked.

17. Holladay also sees this verse as a variation on Psalm 1 (Holladay, *Jeremiah 1*, 376–77), but this time not only are the thoughts different but also the Hebrew words are not the same. Furthermore, certain key words

divine providence: "But the Prophet here takes it as granted, that the world is governed by God's providence; he therefore does not touch the false notion, which yet harasses pious minds, that fortune governs the world" (cf. Isa. 40:24).[18] The Hebrew source behind Greek Jeremiah then says, "They give birth (ילדו); yea, they produce fruit," while the MT has, "They go/grow (ילכו); yea, they produce fruit" (cf. Hos. 14:7 [Eng., 14:6]). *Targum Jonathan* interprets this to mean that they become rich and acquire property. Jeremiah, however, sees through their false piety: "You are near in their mouth but far from their kidneys [*Tg. Jon.*: The words of your Torah are near in their mouth, but the fear of you is far from their kidneys]" (cf. Isa. 29:13; Jer. 11:20a; see also Ps. 119:151).

The text of 12:3a—"And you, O LORD, you know me (ידעתני) [MT adds: you see me (תראני)], you test (בחנת) my heart (לבי) with you" (cf. Jer. 11:20; 17:10)—is similar to that of Psalm 139:23–24a: "Search me, O God, and know my heart (ודע לבי); test me and know (בחנני ודע) my thoughts. And see (וראה) if there is a hurtful [or, idolatrous] way in me." Much like Jeremiah (see Jer. 11:20), the psalmist has just prayed an imprecatory prayer (Ps. 139:19–22), and now he lays himself bare and invites the LORD to test his heart to see if there is any wrong motive in his request for justice. Both the psalmist and Jeremiah are confident that they are in the right. Jeremiah then reiterates his imprecation from 11:20b in 12:3b. The MT begins 12:3b with an added clause not found in the Hebrew source behind Greek Jeremiah: "Drag them away like sheep to slaughter (לטבחה)." This addition makes explicit the connection to 11:19 where Jeremiah described himself as "a docile lamb led to slaughter (לטבוח)." Jeremiah is essentially praying that what his enemies planned for him would be done to them. The final clause of 12:3b then says, "Set them apart for the day of their slaughter (הרגם; MT: הרגה)" (cf. Jas. 5:5).

The phrase עד מתי ("How long?") at the beginning of 12:4 is common to biblical laments (e.g., Num. 14:27; Isa. 6:11; Jer. 4:14, 21; 23:26; 31:22; 47:5; Hos. 8:5; Hab. 2:6; Zech. 1:12; Pss. 6:4 [Eng., 6:3]; 74:10; 80:5 [Eng., 80:4]; 82:2; 90:13; 94:3). Here Jeremiah wonders how long the land must languish or mourn (cf. 1 Sam. 16:1; Isa. 24:4; 33:9; Jer. 23:10) and how long the wild herbage must be dry due to the evil of those who live in it (cf. Deut. 28:23–24; Jer. 4:23, 28; 14:1–9; Amos

---

and meanings necessary for the connection are absent. It is too much of a stretch to say that there is textual dependence here.

18. Calvin, *Jeremiah*, 2:122.

4:7–8; Ps. 107:34).[19] In the immediate context, this refers to the evil plot against Jeremiah's life by the conspirators from Anathoth. Their action has brought the covenant curse of drought to the land. Large land animals and flying creatures are swept away (cf. Jer. 4:25; 7:20; Zeph. 1:3) because the men of Anathoth say, "God does not see our ways (ארחותינו) [MT: He does not see our end (אחריתנו)]."[20] In other words, the men of Anathoth continue in their self-destructive evil because they think that their ways are hidden from God and his judgment (cf. Isa. 29:15; Jer. 16:17; 23:24; Ezek. 8:12; Pss. 10:11; 73:11; 94:7). According to the MT, they think that God does not see their "end" or destiny, but the reality is that they themselves are blind to this (see Deut. 32:20, 29; Jer. 5:31), for judgment will be their end (Jer. 11:21–23).

When the LORD speaks in 12:5, he essentially asks the same question twice, using two different metaphors. If Jeremiah is worn out from running on foot (MT: "with footmen" = "with foot-soldiers"; see BDB, 920), how can he expect to contend with horses (i.e., army horses; see Jer. 4:13; 6:23; 8:16; see also Jer. 22:15)?[21] If Jeremiah is trusting in "a land of peace/well-being," how will he manage in "the pride/majesty of the Jordan"? The pride/majesty of the Jordan refers to the thick overgrowth along the banks of the Jordan River where lions hid (see Jer. 49:19; 50:44; Zech. 11:3). It is thus symbolic of a dangerous place. On the one hand, what do running on foot or with footmen and trusting in a land of peace/well-being represent? On the other hand, what do horses and the pride/majesty of the Jordan represent? *Targum Jonathan* says that Nebuchadnezzar is the foot soldier; the righteous fathers are like the horses; and the coming blessings are like water flooding into the Jordan: "And if you see and are amazed at the good things that I do for Nebuchadnezzar the king of Babylon, the foot soldier, O prophet, then what if I were to show you what I will do to your righteous fathers who were from of old, who ran like the horses, doing good deeds before me? And I even said to them that I will bring blessings and consolations upon your children, look, like water flowing down flooding into the Jordan."[22] While it is possible to see the exegetical rationale behind this rendering,

---

19. As noted in the translation above, the MT accentuation (see the *athnach*) arranges the syntax differently for 12:4b: "Because of the evil of those who live in it, large land animal(s) is/are swept away, and flying creature. For they say, 'He does not see our end.'"

20. Cf. Job 8:13a: "Thus are the ways (ארחות) [LXX: τὰ ἔσχατα = אחרית] of all those who forget God."

21. See Holladay, *Jeremiah 1*, 379.

22. See also Neusner, *Jeremiah in Talmud and Midrash*, 357.

it ultimately does not do justice to the immediate context. Calvin takes the first question literally and comments that the oppression to which the city had thus far been subjected would be nothing compared to the attack of the horsemen in the Babylonian army, but this interpretation misses the metaphorical nature of the questions. Thompson suggests that Jeremiah's running refers to his encounters with false prophets (see Jer. 23:21; see also Ps. 147:15); the horses ("the military might of Babylon") were yet to come.[23] Again, it seems like a violation of the immediate context suddenly to introduce false prophets. McKane refers to an approach that says "the vindictiveness and hostility offered to Jeremiah in Anathoth (the safe country) will be nothing compared to the powerful opposition which he will awaken in the circles of the great in Jerusalem ('the swelling of the Jordan')."[24] Keil is closest to the mark when he suggests that the footmen are the conspirators of Anathoth; the land of peace or well-being is Jeremiah's hometown; and according to 12:6, the horses and the pride or majesty of the Jordan represent the members of Jeremiah's own family.[25] Thus, when Jeremiah complains about the men of Anathoth (Jer. 11:20; 12:1–4), the LORD not only offers an announcement of judgment for those men (Jer. 11:21–23) but also issues a warning to prepare Jeremiah for what is to come (Jer. 12:5–6). If Jeremiah thinks it is difficult to have people from his own hometown plot against his life, how much worse will it be to have his relatives against him? This is no time to grow weary. It is a time to remember the message of Jeremiah 1:10 and the promise of Jeremiah 1:17–19.[26] For even Jeremiah's brothers and the house of his father have acted treacherously against him (Jer. 12:6; cf. Jer. 9:4–5, 8 [MT 9:3–4, 7]; Mic. 7:5–7). According to the Hebrew source behind Greek Jeremiah, the text then says, "They too have called, after you they have filled in (אחריך מִלְאוּ) [i.e., followed/pursued; LXX: were gathered]." (For the sense of this Hebrew text, see Num. 14:24.) The MT has, "They too have called after you fully (אחריך מָלֵא)," which apparently means that they have raised their voices in pursuit of Jeremiah. Jeremiah is not to trust them even when they speak good things to him (cf. Pss. 28:3; 55:22 [Eng., 55:21]; 62:5 [Eng., 62:4]; Prov. 10:6, 11, 18; 26:24–26). The LORD may be near to their mouth, but he is far from what they are thinking (Jer. 12:2b). Their good words are disingenuous, putting Jeremiah at ease in order to carry out the evil plans of their hearts.

---

23. Thompson, *Book of Jeremiah*, 355.
24. McKane, *Jeremiah I–XXV*, 265.
25. Keil, *Jeremiah*, 139.
26. See the LORD's words to Baruch in Jeremiah 45.

JEREMIAH 12:7–17

*12:7 "I have abandoned my house; I have forsaken my inheritance; I have given my beloved [lit., the beloved of my soul (see BDB, 660); LXX: my beloved soul] into the palm of her enemies. 12:8 My inheritance has become to me like a lion in the forest. She has roared against me with her voice [see GKC §119q]. Therefore, I have rejected her. 12:9 Is a colored bird of prey [LXX: a hyena's cave/den] my inheritance to me? Are birds of prey around about her [LXX: or a cave/den around her]? Go, gather all the wild animals [lit., all the creatures of the field] and bring (them) to devour her [LXX: and let them come to devour her; Codex L: bring to eat/devour (or, to/for food); pc Mss, Vulg.: come to eat/devour]. 12:10 Many shepherds, they have destroyed my vineyard; they have trampled [LXX: defiled] my portion [nonn Mss: my inheritance]; they have made the portion of my desire into a desolate wilderness. 12:11 He has made it [LXX: It was made; Tg. Jon., Vulg.: They have made it (cf. Syr.)] into a desolation of destruction. Because of me, all the land is desolated with desolation, for there is no person setting to heart/mind [i.e., considering].¹ 12:12 Upon all bare places [LXX: every passage; cf. Tg. Jon., Syr., Vulg: all paths] in the wilderness have destroyers [NETS: spoilers] come, for a sword of the L*ORD* *is devouring from one end of the land to the other. There is no peace for all flesh. 12:13 Sow wheat, but thorns reap [cf. Syr.; MT: They have sown wheat, but thorns have they reaped]. As for their inheritances [LXX: lots/portions; MT: They make themselves sick; Syr.: And toil], they will not benefit them [Codex L: they will not benefit; pc Mss: but they will not benefit].² Be ashamed of your boasting [MT: And be ashamed of your produce/harvests], of reproach before the L*ORD* *[MT: because of the burning of the L*ORD*'s anger].*

*12:14 For [> MT] thus says the L*ORD* *concerning all the evil neighbors [MT: all my evil neighbors; Syr.: all my neighbors, the shepherds] who touch/harm [Syr.: are near] my inheritance [MT: the inheritance] that I caused my people Israel to inherit. Look, I am about to pluck them from upon their land, and Judah [MT: the house of Judah] will I pluck from their midst. 12:15 And then, after I pluck them, I will return and have compassion on them [or, I will have compassion on them again (see BDB,*

---

1. MT: "He has made it into a desolation. It mourns/languishes to me desolate. All the land is desolated, for there is no person setting to heart/mind."
2. "Do not be like those who sow wheat in untilled ground, and find nothing to gather except thorns, and from whose harvest there is no profit for them" (Hayward, *Targum of Jeremiah*, 86).

*998)] and settle them [MT: and restore them] each to his inheritance and
each to his land. 12:16 And so, if they will indeed learn the way [MT:
ways] of my people to swear by my name, 'As the* Lord *lives [or, By the life
of the* Lord*],' just as they taught my people to swear by Baal, they will be
built [Syr.: they will dwell] in the midst of my people. 12:17 And if they
do not turn [MT: listen], I will pluck up that nation, plucking up and
destroying," [MT adds: the prophetic utterance of the* Lord*].*

The remainder of chapter 12 consists of two units: 12:7–13 and
12:14–17. The Lord is the main speaker in both. These units are not
unrelated to Jeremiah's confessions in 11:18–23 and 12:1–6. Thus, just
as the "house" of Jeremiah's father has acted treacherously against
him (Jer. 12:6a), so the Lord says, "I have abandoned my house; I have
forsaken my inheritance; I have given my beloved into the palm of her
enemies" (Jer. 12:7; cf. Jer. 15:6; Matt. 23:38). The Lord's "house" here
is not the temple but his "inheritance" (cf. MT Jer. 10:16), his "beloved"
(cf. Jer. 11:15)—namely, the people. He has given them into their enemies' hands. This is not a description of something that has already
transpired but a decision that has already been made about the people's future.

Just as Jeremiah's own house has become like a dangerous place
where lions hide (Jer. 12:5b), so the Lord's house/inheritance has become to him like "a lion in the forest" (Jer. 12:8a). Because she has
roared against him (cf. Jer. 12:6a), he has rejected her (Jer. 12:8b; cf.
Hos. 9:15). When the Lord brought Israel out of Egypt, she was like
a lion (Num. 23:22–24), but now she has turned against him. Verse 9
then compares the Lord's inheritance to "a colored bird of prey" (עיט):
"Is a colored bird of prey [LXX: a hyena's cave/den] my inheritance to
me? Are birds of prey around about her [LXX: or a cave/den around
her]" (Jer. 12:9a)?[3] In a form of poetic justice, that which the Lord's
inheritance has become to him will be her judgment.[4] This is the
most straightforward explanation of the text without appeal to textual emendation or comparative philology. It has been suggested on
the basis of an Arabic cognate that the first occurrence of עיט is not "a
colored bird of prey" but a homonym meaning "lair/den."[5] צבוע is then
interpreted to be not "colored" but "hyena" (see Sir. 13:18): "Is my

---

3. In the account of the covenant with Abram, Abram drives away the birds
    of prey (Gen. 15:11; but see the LXX).

4. The point of the imagery is not that such a scenario would have to be de-
    monstrable in nature.

5. See Barr, *Comparative Philology*, 128–29.

inheritance a hyena's den to me" (cf. LXX; see also Jer. 7:11)?[6] The plural imperatives in 12:9b are not directed to any group in particular. They constitute a general summons: "Go, gather all the wild animals and bring [them] to devour her" (cf. Isa. 56:9). This anticipates the coming of the "destroyers" mentioned in 12:12.

Jeremiah 12:10 envisions many "shepherds" who have destroyed the Lord's "vineyard" (cf. Isa. 5:1–7; see also Jer. 2:21; 5:10; 6:9). They have trampled the Lord's desired "portion" (cf. Deut. 32:9) and made it into a "desolate wilderness" (cf. Jer. 9:10 [Eng., 9:11]). Most interpreters understand the "shepherds" here to be foreign rulers (as in Jer. 6:3; see also Syr. Jer. 12:14) rather than unrighteous Judean kings (as in Jer. 2:8; 10:21). The "vineyard" and the desirable or chosen land "portion" represent the people of the land of the covenant. The singular verb שָׂמָהּ ("He has made it") at the beginning of 12:11 suggests that God is the subject (the Lord refers to himself in the third person as in 12:12–14). He is ultimately responsible for the desolation (see Jer. 12:12). The LXX, however, renders it as a passive verb ("It was made"). *Targum Jonathan* and the Latin Vulgate translate the verb as if it were the plural שָׂמֻהָ ("They have made it"), continuing the subject from 12:10. The Hebrew source behind Greek Jeremiah 12:11 and the MT differ slightly in the wording and syntax. The former has, "He has made it into a desolation of destruction (לשממת אבדה). Because of me (עלי), all the land is desolated with desolation (שממה נשמה), for there is no person setting to heart/mind." The latter has, "He has made it into a desolation (לשממה). It mourns/languishes (אבלה) to me (עלי) desolate (שממה). All the land is desolated (נשמה), for there is no person setting to heart/mind" (cf. Jer. 4:27–28; 12:4). It is not entirely clear whether this is about the destruction of the land itself or the destruction of the people for whom the land is a metaphor (or some combination of the two). It is also not clear whether the final explanatory clause ("for there is no person setting to heart/mind") refers to lack of consideration on the part of the destroyers or to Judah's failure to pay attention to the Lord's instruction. Upon all "bare places" (cf. Jer. 3:2, 21) in the wilderness destroyers have come, for "a sword of the Lord" (cf. Deut. 32:41–42; Judg. 7:20; Isa. 34:6; 66:16; Jer. 46:10; 47:6) is devouring "from one end of the land to the other" (Jer. 12:12a; cf. Jer. 25:29, 33). "There is no peace for all flesh" (Jer. 12:12b; cf. Isa. 48:22; 57:21; Jer. 6:14; 8:11 [MT]).

The LXX and Syriac translate the first two verbs of 12:13 as imperatives: "Sow wheat, but thorns reap." The MT vocalizes the same

---

6. Barr, *Comparative Philology*, 235.

consonantal text as two *qatal* verbs: "They have sown wheat, but thorns have they reaped" (cf. Gen. 3:18; Hos. 8:7).[7] *Targum Jonathan* renders the text with prohibitions: "Do not be like those who sow wheat in uncultivated land and do not find anything to gather except thorns" (cf. Jer. 4:3; Hos. 10:8, 12–13). Imperatives here would communicate a directive to the people to face their judgment. The land will not produce for them because of the devastation brought to it. On the other hand, *qatal* verbs simply envision the consequences of the people's actions.[8] Commentators are divided on whether the sowing and reaping are literal or figurative (cf. Prov. 22:8; Gal. 6:8). Calvin, for example, thinks the expression is metaphorical, but he does not take it to mean according to the common view of his day that the prophets had sown good seed among the people only to see thorns grow. Rather, "the Jews are said to sow in seeking aids here and there, in strengthening themselves by confederacies, and in devising means to repel dangers."[9] Likewise, Keil insists that to reap thorns is not "to have a bad harvest by reason of drought, blight, or the ravaging of enemies" but proverbially to "reap the contrary of what they have sowed" in the sense that "the people's sinful ongoings will bring them sore suffering."[10] This interpretation has in its favor the fact that "vineyard" and land "portion" have already been used in the immediate context as figures for the people (Jer. 12:10). They are the ones who, contrary to expectation, have failed to produce acceptable fruit metaphorically speaking (cf. Isa. 5:1–7). Other commentators differ. According to Thompson, "This verse is best understood as a simple statement that as the result of the invasion of Judah by the Chaldeans, the people would be prevented from caring for their crops so that the weeds choked out the grain. Foreign armies often destroyed crops as well" (see Isa. 1:8).[11] This has in its favor passages that describe the literal devastation of the land itself (e.g., Jer.

---

7. Rashi argues that the imperative "sow" is inappropriate here. He interprets the verse as follows: "They prayed, but their prayer was not accepted. Why? Because they did not plow for themselves a furrow of repentance and good deeds. Therefore, they sowed seeds resulting in thorns" (Rosenberg, trans., *Mikraoth Gedoloth: Jeremiah Volume One*, 112).

8. "The passage is probably a premonition rather than a description of what has taken place and it will defeat attempts to locate it in a particular set of historical events" (McKane, *Jeremiah I–XXV*, 278).

9. Calvin, *Jeremiah*, 2:146. See Jeremiah 2:36.

10. Keil, *Jeremiah*, 142.

11. Thompson, *Book of Jeremiah*, 359; see also McKane, *Jeremiah I–XXV*, 277.

4:23–29; 12:4). It is perhaps best not to create a false dichotomy here. The two views are not mutually exclusive, and it is possible for the two to coexist in the same passage (see, e.g., the [intentional?] ambiguity of Jer. 12:11). In any case, the failure of the people to produce spiritual fruit and the failure of the land due to its devastation are both realities in the book of Jeremiah. The remainder of 12:13 in the Hebrew source behind Greek Jeremiah says, "As for their inheritances (נחלתיהם), they will not benefit them (לא יועלום). Be ashamed of your boasting (בשו מתפארתכם), of reproach before the LORD (מחרפה לאפי יהוה)" (cf. Jer. 2:8b, 11b). This seems to mean that the people will not benefit from the land portions inherited by them from their forefathers.[12] The unfruitful land will not be cause for boasting but cause for reproach. The MT, however, says, "They make themselves sick (נחלו), they will not benefit (לא יועלו) [pc Mss: but they will not benefit (ולא יועלו)]. And be ashamed of your produce/harvests (ובשו מתבואתיכם), because of the burning of the LORD's anger (מחרון אף יהוה)" (cf. Jer. 4:26b). This indicates that the people toil in vain either to produce a literal harvest or a metaphorical one. They are thus directed to be ashamed because of divine judgment.

Jeremiah 12:14a begins a new subunit: "For [> MT] thus says the LORD concerning all the evil neighbors (כָּל־הַשְּׁכֵנִים הָרָעִים) [MT: all my evil neighbors (כָּל־שְׁכֵנַי הָרָעִים); Syr.: all my neighbors, the shepherds (= כָּל־שְׁכֵנַי הָרֹעִים)] who touch/harm [Syr.: are near] my inheritance [MT: the inheritance] that I caused my people Israel to inherit."[13] The evil neighbors are generally understood to be the nations along the borders of Israel such as Egypt, Philistia, Edom, Ammon, Moab, Phoenicia (Tyre and Sidon), and Syria (see 2 Kgs. 24:2; Isa. 14:28–23:18; Jer. 46–49; Ezek. 25–32; Amos 1–2; Zeph. 2). The Syriac understands הרעים to be "the shepherds" or the kings of these neighboring nations (cf. Jer. 12:10). The sense of הנגעים ("who touch") is either "who harm" (cf. Zech. 2:12b [Eng., 2:8b]; 4Q372 3:10–11; see also Jer. 2:3) or "who border" (Syr.: "who are near"). It is not immediately clear then whether this text speaks of invasion of the land of Israel by these nations or negative influence on Israel from these nations (but see Jer. 12:16). The LORD draws attention to the fact that he is about "to pluck them from upon their land" (Jer. 12:14b). This is the language of judgment (both historical and eschatological) for "the nations" in the programmatic text of Jeremiah 1:10. It presumably envisions exile for such enemies, but

---

12. Note also that the people are called the LORD's inheritance in the immediate context (Jer. 12:7–8). See, however, Jeremiah 12:14.

13. In contrast to Jeremiah 12:7–8, "inheritance" here is not the people but the land given to the people.

then in a surprising turn of phrase the text adds: "and Judah [MT: the house of Judah] will I pluck from their midst." Here the same term "pluck" or "uproot" (נתש), which normally has a negative connotation, apparently speaks of deliverance from the evil neighbors.[14] McKane suggests that this does not refer to Judeans exiled in neighboring lands who will be repatriated to Judah but to those intermingled with their evil neighbors in Babylonian exile who will be separated from them in the return from Babylon.[15]

There is some ambiguity about the antecedent of the pronoun "them" (3x) in 12:15. Is it Judah or the neighboring nations? If it is Judah, as Thompson suggests,[16] then it would be appropriate to render, "And then, after I pluck them, I will have compassion on them again [see BDB, 998] and settle them (וְהֲשִׁבֹתִים) [MT: and restore them (וַהֲשִׁבֹתִים)] each to his inheritance and each to his land" (cf. Zech. 10:6, 10). According to this understanding, the Lᴏʀᴅ will have compassion on Judah again as he once did. The expression "each to his inheritance and each to his land" would mean that the people of Judah will return to their allotted portions in the land of the covenant. Rashi and Redak, however, interpret 12:15 as if the neighboring nations were the antecedent of "them."[17] If this is correct, then אשוב ורחמתים cannot mean "I will have compassion on them again" but "I will return and have compassion on them." The neighboring nations will be resettled in or restored to their respective countries. Such an interpretation of 12:15 would work well with 12:16, which assumes the nations to be the main subject. It is important to keep in mind that Jeremiah is a prophet to the nations (Jer. 1:5b), not only with words of judgment (Jer. 1:10; 46–51) but also with words of restoration (Jer. 1:10; 3:14–18; 16:19; 46:26 [MT]; 48:47; 49:6 [MT]). Restoration, however, whether for Judah/Israel or for the nations, has a prerequisite: to learn "the way" of the true people of God. If the nations will learn to swear by the Lᴏʀᴅ's name just as they taught his people to swear by Baal (see Jer. 5:2, 7; 10:2; 16:19), then they will be "built" in the midst of his people (Jer. 12:16; cf. Zech. 10:9). This is the same requirement placed on Israel in Jeremiah 4:1–2 in order for the nations to be blessed in Christ (see commentary on Jer. 4:1–2). The verb ונבנו ("they will be built") is often understood to mean that they will have progeny (cf. Gen. 16:2; 30:3), but given the connection already established with

---

14. See Calvin, *Jeremiah*, 2:153.
15. McKane, *Jeremiah I–XXV*, 280.
16. Thompson, *Book of Jeremiah*, 361. See Jeremiah 16:15; 23:3; 24:6; 27:22; 29:10, 14; 30:3; 32:37; 33:10–11, 26. See also Amos 9:14–15.
17. See Rosenberg, trans., *Mikraoth Gedoloth: Jeremiah Volume One*, 113.

Jeremiah 1:10 in this passage, it seems more likely that this refers to the "building" and "planting" (i.e., restoration) mentioned there (see also Jer. 31:4). Thus, the LORD will "pluck up" or judge the evil nations, but he will "build" or restore those who swear by his name. The book of Jeremiah ultimately looks beyond the historical return from Babylonian exile (Jer. 29:10–14) to a messianic and eschatological future in which full restoration of the lost blessing of life and dominion to all the nations will occur (Jer. 23:5–8; 25:11–13 [LXX]; 30–33; see Dan. 9:1–2, 24–27). Only with the spiritual circumcision of the new covenant will Judah/Israel and the nations have hearts/minds to swear by the LORD's name (Deut. 28:69 [Eng., 29:1]; 30:6; Jer. 4:4; 9:24–25 [Eng., 9:25–26]; 31:31–34; Ezek. 11:19–20; 36:26–27; Rom. 2:28–29; Col. 2:11). If any nation (including Judah/Israel) does not "turn" (MT: "listen"), the LORD will "pluck up" that nation (Jer. 12:17), but not in the positive sense in which he will "pluck up" Judah according to Jeremiah 12:14b. Rather, the LORD is "plucking up and destroying" any who do not genuinely swear by his name.

JEREMIAH 13

13:1 Thus the Lord *said [MT, 4QJer*ᵃ *add: to me], "Go and purchase for yourself a linen waistcloth and put it on your loins, but in the water do not bring it [LXX: and through water it will not pass]." 13:2 And I purchased the waistcloth according to the word of the* Lord *and put [it] on my loins. 13:3 And the word of the* Lord *came to me [MT, 4QJer*ᵃ *add: a second time], saying, 13:4 "Take the waistcloth [MT, 4QJer*ᵃ *add: that you purchased] that is on your loins and rise up, go [LXX: and go] to the Euphrates [or, Parah; Aq.: Paran] and hide it there in the cleft [LXX: hole] of the rock [or, a cleft of the rock (see GKC §127e)]." 13:5 And I hid it [MT, 4QJer*ᵃ*: And I went and I hid it] by the Euphrates [4QJer*ᵃ*:* בפרתה] *just as the* Lord *commanded me. 13:6 And then, after many days, the* Lord *said to me, "Rise up, go to the Euphrates and take from there the waistcloth that I commanded you to hide there." 13:7 And I went to the Euphrates [LXX adds: river] and dug, and I took the waistcloth from the place where I hid it. And look, it was ruined [MT: the waistcloth was ruined], something that would not be good for anything [Codex L: so that it would not be good for anything (GKC §152b); mlt Mss, LXX*⁵³⁴*, Syr.: and it would not be good for anything].*

13:8 And the word of the Lord *came to me saying, "Thus says the* Lord,[1] *13:9 'Thus will I ruin the pride/majesty [Tg. Jon.: strength] of Judah and the pride/majesty of Jerusalem [MT: the great pride/majesty of Jerusalem], 13:10 this great thing [LXX: this great pride; MT: this evil people], those who refused to hear my words [MT adds: who went in the stubbornness of their heart/mind] and went after other gods to serve/ worship them and to bow down to them, and they will be like this waistcloth [MT: so that it (the people) might become like this waistcloth], which will not be good for anything, 13:11 for just as the waistcloth clings to a person's loins, so did I cause [MT adds: all] the house of Israel and all the house of Judah to cling to me [MT adds: the prophetic utterance of the* Lord*] to become for me a people of name both for praise and for glory [or, to become my people of name and my praise and glory; MT: to be to me for a people and for a name and for praise and for glory], but they did not listen to me [to me > MT]. 13:12 And you will say to this people [MT: to them this word: "Thus says the* Lord *the God of Israel"], "Every skin-bottle [or, earthen jar/pitcher], it is filled with wine." And then, if they say to you, "Do we not indeed know that every*

---

1. Editions of the MT and English translations (except NETS) have "Thus says the Lord" at the beginning of 13:9.

skin-bottle [or, earthen jar/pitcher], it is filled with wine?" 13:13 then you will say to them, "Thus says the LORD, *'Look, I am about to fill [MT adds: all] the inhabitants of this land and their kings who sit as sons of David [MT: who sit for David; Syr.: who sit] on their throne [MT: on his throne; Syr.: on the throne of David] and the priests and the prophets and Judah [and Judah > MT] and all the inhabitants of Jerusalem with drunkenness. 13:14 And I will scatter [see LXX, Syr.; or, shatter] them, each man and his brother [MT: each man to/against his brother], and their fathers and their sons together [LXX: in the same way]. I will not spare,' the prophetic utterance of the* LORD *[MT: and their fathers and their sons together,' the prophetic utterance of the* LORD. *'I will not spare], 'and I will not pity and I will not have compassion from ruining them [LXX: from their ruin].'"''*

These two units—Jeremiah 13:1–11 and 13:12–14—feature two different metaphors, the ruined waistcloth (Jer. 13:1–11) and the skin or jar filled with wine (Jer. 13:12–14), but they are now joined by the key words "ruined," "ruin," and "ruining" from the root שחת (Jer. 13:7b, 9b, 14b). The segments of society mentioned in 13:13 are those who form the opposition to Jeremiah throughout the book in general (Jer. 1:17–19) and in the surrounding confessions of Jeremiah in particular (Jer. 11:18–20:18). The history of interpretation has wrestled with the question of whether 13:1–11 might be a prophetic vision rather than a historical account of something that Jeremiah actually did in response to divine instruction. Maimonides and Calvin among others have held this view, largely motivated by the thought that two round trips to the Euphrates River and back would be too much to ask of the prophet. The most glaring problem with this interpretation is the lack of any formal marker of the vision genre such as use of the root ראה (cf. Jer. 1:11–14; Ezek. 1:4; 8:2; 37:8; 40:2; Amos 7:1, 4, 7; 8:1; 9:1; Zech. 2:1, 3, 5 [Eng., 1:18, 20; 2:1]; 3:1; 4:2; 5:1, 2, 5; 6:1). It is more likely that the present passage is an example of a symbolic sign act (cf. Isa. 20; Jer. 16:1–9; 18:1–12; 19:1–13; 27–28; 32; 43:8–13; 51:59–64; Ezek. 4; 5; 12; 21; 24; Zech. 6:9–15). If this is rejected on the grounds that the text gives no explicit indication that the act was publicly performed and explained, then it should be noted that the text gives no explicit indication that the act was not publicly performed. Furthermore, the text of 13:1–11 is now linked to that of 13:12–14 where a message is given for the people. What matters is that the sign act and its meaning are now publicly accessible in textual form to readers of the book of Jeremiah. Prophetic sign acts typically come with their own built-in interpretation. Thus, the hermeneutical task is not to assign a symbolic meaning to every part of the act.[2] Rather, it is simply to identify the interpretation already provided.[3] Details left uninterpreted by the text should be left uninterpreted by the reader. To fill in such gaps is to obscure the focus of the text. Commentators, however, have rarely resisted the temptation to go beyond what the text says. Therefore, much of the following exposition will give attention to deciphering what has or has not distracted from the text in the history of interpretation.

The LORD instructs Jeremiah to go and purchase for himself a linen "waistcloth" (אזור) to be put on his loins (Jer. 13:1a; cf. Isa. 11:5; Jer. 19:1). This term is distinct from "belt, girdle" (חגור). Some commentators have suggested that this simple garment is symbolic of Israel's priesthood (Exod. 19:6) because linen was the material of the priests' clothing (Exod. 28:39),[4] but no such association is made within the text itself. The interpretation provided in 13:11 is simply that the waistcloth symbolizes Israel/Judah clinging to the LORD (who is represented here by the prophet). Jeremiah, however, is not to bring the waistcloth in the water (Jer. 13:1b). Various suggestions have been made for the explanation of this instruction. Rashi comments that Jeremiah is not "to wash it when it will be soaked with sweat, in order that it hasten to decay"; but Abarbanel says that wetting the garment in any way is

---

2. "As in the case of all parables it is wrong in principle to search for a meaning in every detail. Such a procedure only leads to allegorism, which is fraught with danger and is a hindrance to sound exegesis and proper interpretation" (Thompson, *Book of Jeremiah*, 363). Thompson unfortunately does not follow his own advice.

3. McKane is not content with this approach. He asserts that verses 9–11 of chapter 13 represent "secondary and misguided efforts to explain the imagery of vv. 1–7" (*Jeremiah I–XXV*, 288–89). Of course, McKane has no extant text-critical evidence for the secondary status of 13:9–11. His dismissal of the text's own interpretation of itself is contrary to the whole enterprise of discerning authorial intent through the verbal meaning (see E. D. Hirsch Jr., *Validity in Interpretation* [New Haven, CT: Yale University Press, 1967], 18). The entire operation breaks down if the interpreter is allowed to substitute his or her own interpretation for the text's given meaning. McKane's position is that he has respected the meaning of 13:1–7, which is why he thinks he must reject 13:9–11, but such a fracturing of the text must be demonstrated on the basis of textual evidence; it cannot merely be posited on the basis of personal opinion. The task is not to interpret the text we imagine but to interpret the text that we actually have, which requires us to live with the coexistence of 13:1–7 and 13:9–11.

4. See Keil, *Jeremiah*, 145; Holladay, *Jeremiah 1*, 397.

forbidden, "since this would strengthen the fibers."[5] Keil suggests that the waistcloth is to remain dirty in order to symbolize the moral decay of the people prior to exile.[6] The subsequent decay in 13:7b is physical, but according to Thompson, the garment is to come straight from the merchant without touching water, thus ensuring that it will be clean, dry, and undamaged.[7] These explanations seem to depend more on the commentators' ingenuity than on anything demonstrable from the text. In the end, McKane's exposition is the most straightforward. Given the fact that the waistcloth represents Israel/Judah clinging to the LORD (Jer. 13:11), the instruction not to bring it in the water is a way to say, "On no account and in no circumstances are you to take off this loin-cloth, not even for what might seem the most elementary and necessary reason—to wash it."[8]

Jeremiah follows the instruction "according to the word of the LORD" (Jer. 13:2). Then the word of the LORD comes to him "a second time" (Jer. 13:3; see MT, 4QJer[a]; cf. Jer. 1:13). The LORD instructs Jeremiah to take the waistcloth and go פרתה and hide it there in the cleft of the rock (Jer. 13:4; cf. Jer. 43:9). Jeremiah then dutifully follows his orders (Jer. 13:5). All ancient versions with the exception of Aquila ("to Paran") interpret פרתה to be פרת ("Euphrates") plus a directional ה. The more recent history of interpretation has favored the understanding that פרתה is פרה ("Parah") plus a directional ה (see Josh. 18:23).[9] According to this interpretation, Parah would make for a more reasonable journey for Jeremiah, being just a few miles north of his hometown Anathoth. Furthermore, the fact that פרתה ("to Parah") and פרתה ("to the Euphrates") are identical in orthography and vocalization would make for an easy wordplay that would presumably signal to readers that "Parah" symbolizes the Euphrates River in the land of Babylon from which the corrupting influence of idolatry has come and where Judah will be ruined in exile. There are, however, several problems with this view. The reading בפרת in the MT of 13:5 can only be translated "by the Euphrates," not "in Parah." This difficulty is thought to be alleviated by the reading found in 4QJer[a]: בפרתה. It is

---

5.   Rosenberg, trans., *Mikraoth Gedoloth: Jeremiah Volume One*, 114.

6.   Keil, *Jeremiah*, 145.

7.   Thompson, *Book of Jeremiah*, 364.

8.   McKane, *Jeremiah I–XXV*, 290.

9.   See Rosenberg, trans., *Mikraoth Gedoloth: Jeremiah Volume One*, 114; Thompson, *Book of Jeremiah*, 364–65; Holladay, *Jeremiah 1*, 396. The other alternative, that פרת is אפרת (Gen. 48:7), has never gained much traction.

also problematic that פרת in the Hebrew Bible is always "Euphrates" (BDB, 832). The place name "Parah" only occurs once in Joshua 18:23 where it appears with the definite article. The main reason commentators prefer "Parah" to "Euphrates" in Jeremiah 13 is that they consider the Euphrates to be too great of a distance for Jeremiah to travel (see Ezra 7:9), but this is not an argument based on word usage. It is not the task of the interpreter to imagine the convenience of the situation and only then to determine word meanings accordingly.[10] Linguistic usage in texts determines word meanings. Thus, regardless of the consequences, the most plausible translation of פרתה in Jeremiah 13:4 is "to the Euphrates."

Jeremiah then recounts that the Lord directed him "after many days" to go back to the Euphrates and to take from there the waistcloth that he commanded him to hide there (Jer. 13:6). There is no indication from the interpretation in 13:9–11 that this is supposed to signify return from exile. Jeremiah adds that he went to the Euphrates and dug up the waistcloth from the place where he hid it (Jer. 13:7a), which implies either that he had buried the object or that it had somehow been covered with the passage of time. He then draws the reader's attention to see what he saw with his own eyes: "And look (והנה), it was ruined (נשחת) [MT: the waistcloth (האזור) was ruined], something that (אשר) would not be good for anything [Codex L: so that it would not be good for anything (GKC §152b); mlt Mss, LXX[534], Syr.: and it would not be good for anything]" (Jer. 13:7b; cf. Jer. 18:3). Attempts to interpret this either as the decay of the people in Babylonian exile (Lev. 26:36, 39) or as the corrupting influence of Babylonian religion fall flat when the reader arrives at the interpretation in 13:9–11. These verses make no reference to the exile,[11] nor do they attribute the worship of other gods to the corruption of Judah in Babylon, which is what the waistcloth (Judah) by the Euphrates (Babylon) would have to represent.[12] Rather, the worship of

---

10. See Keil, *Jeremiah*, 144. This also applies to the argument that the banks of the Euphrates would not provide a "cleft in the rock" for Jeremiah, whereas Parah would have this. Whatever the case may have been (e.g., rocky soil from which Jeremiah would have to dig [Jer. 13:7]), the words mean what they mean quite apart from what the interpreter envisions the referent to be. The hermeneutical task is not to work out the logistics of the situation but to determine word meanings according to usage.

11. It is worth noting here that those who go into exile in 597 with Jehoiachin are considered "good figs" (Jer. 24).

12. Holladay has suggested that Jeremiah 13:1–7 is based on exegesis of Isaiah 7:18–19 and 8:7–8: "The act symbolizes the threat of the Euphrates to

other gods is given as the reason for their ruin, not the ruin itself. What then does the Euphrates represent in Jeremiah's symbolic act? Why is it such a seemingly significant part of the picture? These are fair questions, but the answer according to 13:9–11 is that the Euphrates symbolizes nothing. The interpretation provided in 13:9–11 focuses solely on what the ruined waistcloth signifies and gives no attention to the symbolic significance of the Euphrates.[13] Since the text assigns no symbolic value to the Euphrates, the reader should be content to leave the matter alone, being careful not to force the text to go beyond its intended design. It is not the reader's job to raise and answer questions that the text neither raises nor answers. Rather, it is the reader's job to discover what questions the text is raising and answering.

Jeremiah introduces the interpretation of the symbolic sign act in 13:9–11 as "the word of the LORD" that came to him (Jer. 13:8; cf. Jer. 13:2, 3). The "ruined" (נשחת) waistcloth from 13:7b is interpreted as follows: "Thus will I ruin (אשחית) the pride/majesty [*Tg. Jon.*: strength] of Judah and the pride/majesty of Jerusalem [MT: the great pride/majesty of Jerusalem]" (Jer. 13:9; cf. Lev. 26:19). The term גאון can be "pride" (e.g., Isa. 16:6; Jer. 48:29; see also Jer. 13:17), in which case the ruin of Judah and Jerusalem would mean primarily humiliation. This word can also be "majesty": "of nations, their wealth, power, magnificence of buildings" (BDB, 144). With this latter meaning, the ruin of Judah and Jerusalem would be the destruction of the land. Of course, these are closely related ideas, and both would be true. The destruction of the majesty of the land of Judah and Jerusalem would result in the humiliation of the pride of Judah and Jerusalem. It is simply a question of which sense of the term is mainly in view.

The last phrase of 13:9 in the MT ("and the great pride/majesty of Jerusalem") features the arthrous adjective הרב ("the great"). The

---

inundate Judah even though Judah might want to wish to hide. . . . Parah represents the Euphrates on Judah's soil, the symbolic fulfillment of Isaiah's words in Isa 8:7–8" (*Jeremiah 1*, 398). The connection to the Isaiah texts, which speak of an earlier time and the threat of the Assyrians, is very strained. Furthermore, it is difficult to see how taking the waistcloth (Judah) to the Euphrates (Babylon) represents Babylon (the Euphrates) coming to Judah (the waistcloth). Even if it is conceded that Parah, which is near Anathoth, represents the Euphrates, the direction of the movement in Jeremiah's symbolic act is wrong for this view of Holladay.

13. Abarbanel: "Although all the details were symbolic, God explained only two of them, the meaning of the girdle and the meaning of its decay" (Rosenberg, trans., *Mikraoth Gedoloth: Jeremiah Volume One*, 115). See Deuteronomy 29:28 (Eng., 29:29).

Hebrew source behind Greek Jeremiah has this at the beginning of 13:10 as a substantive with a following demonstrative, "this great thing" (הרב הזה), which the LXX translates as a reference back to 13:9: "this great pride." The remainder of 13:10 then describes "this great thing" in terms of the people who expressed their pride in their rebellion against God. On the other hand, the MT has "this evil people" (העם הזה הרע) in place of "this great thing." The people are described as those who refused to hear God's words (cf. Jer. 11:10). The MT adds: "who went in the stubbornness of their heart/mind" (cf. Jer. 5:23; 7:24; 9:13 [Eng., 9:14]; 11:8; 16:12; 23:17). The people also "went after other gods to serve/worship them and to bow down to them" (cf. Jer. 1:16; 2:5; 7:9; 16:11). The result is that they will be like the ruined waistcloth—their great pride humiliated and/or their land destroyed, no good for anything.

13:11 explains the demise of Israel and Judah (cf. Jer. 3). Just as a waistcloth "clings" (דבק) to a person's loins, so did the Lord make Israel and Judah cling to him. This terminology comes from Deuteronomy (Deut. 4:4; 10:20; 11:22; 13:5; 30:20). They were to become for the Lord "a people of name both for praise and for glory" (לעם לשם ולתהלה ולתפארת) (cf. Jer. 33:9; Zeph. 3:19–20). The MT has "for a people and for a name and for praise and for glory" (לעם ולשם ולתהלה ולתפארת). In other words, the people were set apart to bring renown and praise and glory to the Lord (see Isa. 43:21). This language comes from Deuteronomy 26:19. It is not merely that the people were to receive positive attention from the nations (cf. Isa. 62:7) but that the nations would be pointed to the name of the Lord that the people bore (Deut. 4:6–8; 10:21; Jer. 17:14). The people did not listen to the Lord and thus did not bring honor to him. Therefore, they must face the ruin illustrated by Jeremiah. This has already happened for the northern kingdom of Israel, but it still lies in the future for Judah and Jerusalem from Jeremiah's perspective. Furthermore, the lack of any explicit historical reference to Babylonian exile in this passage lends itself well to prefiguration, especially given the foregrounding of eschatological judgment in the early chapters of Jeremiah (e.g., Jer. 4:5–6:30).

The Hebrew source behind Greek Jeremiah and the MT differ in the introductory words of 13:12. The former says, "And you will say to this people." The latter says, "And you will say to them this word: 'Thus says the Lord the God of Israel.'" The phrase "to them" (אליהם) in the MT creates a link to the foregoing 13:1–11 where an antecedent for the pronoun "them" may be found (i.e., the people of Judah and Jerusalem),[14] but a link between 13:1–11 and 13:12–14 is

---

14. See McKane, *Jeremiah I–XXV*, 292.

already present in the use of the root שׁחת (Jer. 13:14b; cf. Jer. 13:7b, 9a). Jeremiah is to say to the people that every נבל is filled with wine (Jer. 13:12a). The LXX translates נבל with ἀσκός ("skin") (cf. 1 Sam. 1:24; 10:3; 25:18; 2 Sam. 16:1). The other versions understand it to be an earthen or clay jar/pitcher of some sort (cf. Isa. 22:24; 30:14; Jer. 48:12; Lam. 4:2).[15] A decision here will affect translation of the verb from נפץ in 13:14 as either "scatter" (i.e., pour out the contents of the skin-bottle) or "shatter" (i.e., break the clay jar/pitcher). It is anticipated in 13:12b that the people will respond, "Do we not indeed know that every skin-bottle [or, earthen jar/pitcher], it is filled with wine?" There is no indication (or evidence from elsewhere) that this is a popular proverb ("Everything has its purpose") or a drinker's saying, as some have suggested.[16] Rather, Jeremiah's assignment is to point out something painfully obvious, which the people will take as an insult to their intelligence. They do not yet know the symbolic significance of the prophet's seemingly banal comment.

At this point in the conversation Jeremiah is to inform the people that they are the skin-bottle or earthen jar/pitcher (cf. 2 Sam. 12:7a): "Thus says the LORD, 'Look, I am about to fill [MT adds: all] the inhabitants of this land and their kings who sit as sons of David [MT: who sit for David; Syr.: who sit] on their throne [MT: on his throne; Syr.: on the throne of David; cf. Jer. 17:25] and the priests and the prophets and Judah [and Judah > MT] and all the inhabitants of Jerusalem with drunkenness'" (Jer. 13:13). These are the groups identified thus far in the book who have opposed Jeremiah and rebelled against God: the general populace of Judah and Jerusalem, the Davidic kings, the priests, and the false prophets (Jer. 1:17–19; 2:8; 5:31; 6:13; 8:10; 10:16; 14:18; et al.). They will all drink the cup of the LORD's judgment (see Isa. 51:17; Jer. 25:15; 48:26; 49:12; 51:57; Hab. 2:16; Ps. 60:5 [Eng., 60:4]; Rev. 14:10; 16:19).

The LORD will then either "scatter" (II. נפץ) the people as in the bursting of a skin-bottle and the spilling of its contents (see LXX, Syr.; Jer. 13:24) or "shatter" (I. נפץ) them as in the breaking of a clay jar or pitcher (see Judg. 7:19; Jer. 19:10–11; 48:12; see also BDB, 658–59) (Jer. 13:14). II. נפץ ("disperse, be scattered") does not occur in the *piel* stem anywhere else in the Hebrew Bible, but this apparently did not deter the translators of the LXX and the Syriac. According to the Hebrew source behind Greek Jeremiah, this will be done to "each man and his brother (אישׁ ואחיו), and their fathers and their sons together."

---

15. See McKane, *Jeremiah I–XXV*, 293–94.
16. See the discussion McKane, *Jeremiah I–XXV*, 295–96.

The MT, however, has "each man to/against his brother (איש אל אחיו), and their fathers and their sons together." This latter reading has suggested internal strife (see Jer. 9:3–4 [Eng., 9:4–5]; 12:6; Mic. 7:5–7). The LORD will not spare, nor will he pity or have compassion (cf. Jer. 21:7) "from ruining them" (מהשחיתם). This last phrase links the metaphor of the ruined waistcloth (Jer. 13:7b, 9a) with that of the ruined skin-bottle or earthen jar/pitcher.

13:15 Hear and give ear and [and > MT] do not be haughty, for it is the LORD who has spoken. 13:16 Give to the LORD your God glory before he causes darkness and before your feet stumble [see GKC §145p] on mountains of twilight [i.e., dimly lit mountains], and you wait for light [m.], and there deep darkness [LXX: and there shadow of death; MT: and he makes it (f.) into deep darkness], and it is made into deep darkness [see MT qere; MT kethiv: he makes into deep darkness; LXX: and they are put into darkness]. 13:17 If you do not listen [MT: And if you do not listen to it], in secret places you [lit., your soul / self / being; MT: my soul / self / being] will weep because of pride [Syr.: because of sorrow / distress; MT adds: and weeping it will weep], and your eyes will go down with tears [MT: and my eye will go down with tears], for the flock of the LORD has been broken [MT: taken captive]. 13:18 Say [pl.; MT: sg.] to the king and to the mighty men [MT: the queen(-mother)], "Make low and sit [MT: Make low, sit; BDB, 1050: take a low seat (see GKC §120g); Syr.: Humble yourselves and return], for from your head [MT: your head places] your beautiful crown has come down [Tg. Jon.: for your glory has gone into exile from you, the crown of your praise has fallen]." 13:19 As for the cities of the Negev [Syr., Tg. Jon.: the cities of the south], they are shut up, and there is no one opening. Judah is taken into exile, he has completed a complete exile [MT: Judah is taken into exile, all of it, she is taken into exile completely; Tg. Jon. adds: they have received the payment for their deeds].

13:20 Lift up [MT kethiv: f. sg.; MT qere: m. pl.] your [LXX: sg.; MT: m. pl.] eyes, O Jerusalem [> MT], and see [MT kethiv: f. sg.; MT qere: m. pl.] those coming from the north. Where is the flock [Tg. Jon.: the people] that was given to you, your beautiful sheep [Tg. Jon.: people]? 13:21 What will you say when they appoint over you [or, when they visit upon you; MT: when he appoints over you (or, when he visits upon you)]—and you, you taught them over you as friends / allies [LXX: lessons]—as head [Tg. Jon.: and you, you taught them to do harm to you; they have been leaders as from the beginning]? Will not pains grip you like a woman in childbirth?[17] *13:22 And when [LXX: if] you say in your heart/mind, "Why have these things happened to me?" Because of the abundance of your iniquity your skirts [LXX: hind parts] are uncovered, your heels are violated [LXX: publicly displayed]. 13:23 Can a Cushite [LXX: Ethiopian] change his skin, or a leopard its spots? Also you, are you able to do good, being taught/accustomed to do evil? 13:24 "And I scattered [MT: And I will scatter] them like chaff passing away [LXX: carried] to/by [Syr., Tg. Jon.: before; Vulg.: in] desert wind. 13:25 This is your lot and the portion of your rebellion [MT: the portion of your measure (or, your measured apportionment); Syr., Tg. Jon.: the portion of your inheritance] from me," the prophetic utterance of the* Lord, *"because you forgot me and trusted in deception [or, whom you forgot and trusted in deception].*[18] *13:26 And also I, I have stripped off your skirts [LXX: hind parts] over your face, and your disgrace will be seen. 13:27 And [And > MT] as for your adulteries and your neighings and the wickedness [LXX: estrangement] of your fornication on hills and [and > MT] in the field/country, I have seen your detested acts. Woe to you, Jerusalem, for you will not be clean after me. How long still [Syr.: How long? Return! MT: Woe to you, Jerusalem, you will not be clean after when still]?"*[19]

Modern commentators typically group the remaining verses of chapter 13 in the following way: 15–17, 18–19, and 20–27. Jeremiah's general summons in 13:15a ("Hear and give ear and do not be haughty") assumes a contrast between paying attention and pride. This builds on the interpretation of the prophet's sign act in 13:9–11 where the Lord says that he will ruin the pride of the people of Judah and Jerusalem who have refused to listen to him (see also Jer. 13:17). Thus, Jeremiah grounds his call to hear in the fact that "it is the Lord who has spoken" (Jer. 13:15b; cf. Isa. 1:2a, 19–20; 40:5; 58:14; Mic. 4:4).

The expression, "Give to the Lord your God glory," at the beginning of 13:16 is likely the idiom for, "Confess your sins" (cf. Josh. 7:19; 1 Sam. 6:5; Ezra 10:11; John 9:24).[20] The people are to do this before the Lord causes the darkness of judgment (cf. Joel 2:2; Amos 5:18–20; 8:9;

---

17. TEV: "What will you say when people you thought were your friends conquer you and rule over you? You will be in pain like a woman giving birth."

18. See Robert D. Holmstedt, *The Relative Clause in Biblical Hebrew*, LSAWS 10 (Winona Lake, IN: Eisenbrauns, 2016), 180.

19. *Tg. Jon.*: "Woe to you, Jerusalem, you will not be clean. Up to now you have a respite, many days."

20. See Kara: "Give Him honor by repenting of your sins" (Rosenberg, trans., *Mikraoth Gedoloth: Jeremiah Volume One*, 117); Keil, *Jeremiah*, 147. For

Zeph. 1:15),[21] which will make their feet stumble on dimly lit mountains (cf. Isa. 59:10; Ps. 91:12). At that time, the people will "wait" (קוה) in vain for light, only to find that there is "deep darkness" (צלמות).[22] It is not clear if "light" and "darkness" represent anything more than "salvation" and "judgment." The expected light could be help from foreign allies (Jer. 2:18, 36; 13:21; Redak), help from other gods (Jer. 2:28; 5:31; 10:14; 13:25; 23:14), a false sense of security in cherished institutions (Jer. 7:4), or the message of the false prophets (Jer. 6:14; 8:11). *Lamentations Rabbah* suggests that the darkness represents lack of teaching from the Torah and lack of prophecy (see Jer. 6:19; 8:8–9; Lam. 2:9),[23] in which case the light would represent the presence of both (see Isa. 2:3, 5; Ps. 119:105). According to Isaiah 8:16–18, only those who bind "Testimony" (i.e., the prophetic witness) and seal "Torah" and "wait" (קוה) for the LORD will see the light at the end of the tunnel (Isa. 9:1, 5–6; 42:6; 49:6; 60:1–3, 19–20). Those who turn to alternative revelation will find themselves in darkness (Isa. 8:19–22).

The fundamental difference between the Hebrew source behind Greek Jeremiah 13:17 and the MT is the subject of the weeping. According to the former, if the people do not heed the words of

---

a different view, see Malachi 2:2 (cf. Mal. 1:6); Calvin, *Jeremiah*, 2:177; Holladay, *Jeremiah 1*, 406–7.

21. This suggests that there is still opportunity for repentance, but the following context indicates that the people's fate is sealed and their judgment inevitable (e.g., Jer. 13:23–25).

22. The MT vocalizes צלמות as צַלְמָוֶת, and the LXX translates it as "shadow of death," as if it were a combination of צל ("shadow") and מות ("death"). The word has more recently been analyzed as a combination of the root צלם ("darkness") and the abstract noun ending: צַלְמוּת, ות. Either way, the sense of the term is "deep darkness." See Barr, *Comparative Philology*, 375–80. See also D. Winton Thomas, "Ṣalmāwet in the OT," *JSS* 7 (1962): 191–200. The Hebrew source behind Greek Jeremiah has וְשָׁם צַלְמָוֶת וְשִׁית לַעֲרָפֶּל ("and there deep darkness, and it is made into deep darkness"), featuring two different words for "deep darkness." שִׁית should be analyzed as a passive participle (BDB, 1011). The MT *qere* has וְשָׂמָה לְצַלְמָוֶת וְשִׁית לַעֲרָפֶּל ("and he makes it into deep darkness, and it is made into deep darkness"). "Driver's explanation of ושׂמה (*JQR* 28, p. 112) that ה here and elsewhere represents the masculine suffix (וְשָׂמֹה) is the correct one (ה is an earlier orthography than ו. . . . Driver's other proposal is linked to an appeal to Sept. (καὶ τεθήσονται εἰς σκότος) which he explains as a misreading of וְשָׁתוֹ (taken as וְשָׁתוּ)" (McKane, *Jeremiah I–XXV*, 298).

23. See Neusner, *Jeremiah in Talmud and Midrash*, 238.

13:15–16, then they will be the ones to weep in secret places (i.e., in shame) because of their pride (i.e., the consequences of their pride), and their eyes will run with tears (cf. Jer. 9:17 [Eng., 9:18]; Lam. 2:18).[24] According to the latter, if the people do not listen, then the prophet Jeremiah will weep in secret places (i.e., alone, although the knowledge of such is public) because of the people's pride (i.e., their refusal to listen [cf. Jer. 13:15]),[25] and his eyes will run with tears (cf. Jer. 8:23 [Eng., 9:1]; 14:17; Ps. 119:136; Lam. 1:16; 3:48; Luke 19:41).[26] The LORD will ruin the pride of the people (Jer. 13:9).[27] Therefore, either the people or Jeremiah (or both) will weep because "the flock of the LORD" (cf. Jer. 13:20b; Pss. 80:2 [Eng., 80:1]; 95:7; 100:3) has been "broken" (נשבר) (cf. Jer. 4:6; 6:14; 8:11, 21; 10:19; 14:17; 30:12).[28] The people of God are "scattered" (see Jer. 13:14, 24) like sheep without a shepherd/king (cf. Num. 27:17; 1 Kgs. 22:17; Ezek. 34:5; Zech. 10:2; Matt. 9:36), wandering in the darkness and stumbling on the mountains (Jer. 13:16) without anyone to lead them on the right path (see Ps. 23:1–4).[29]

The Hebrew source behind Greek Jeremiah 13:18 begins with the plural imperative אמרו ("Say"), while the MT has the singular אמר. This instruction does not appear to be for any group or person in particular, although it has been suggested that the singular imperative of the MT is the LORD's word to Jeremiah, which would require an unmarked shift of speaker from Jeremiah in 13:15–17 to the LORD in 13:18.[30] According to the Hebrew source behind Greek Jeremiah (cf. Syr.), the words to be said are to be addressed "to the king and to the mighty men (למלך ולגבורים)." According to the MT, they are to be addressed "to the king and to the queen-mother (למלך ולגבירה)." This latter reading is usually thought to refer to Jehoiachin and his

---

24. For the reversal of this image, see Isaiah 25:8; 30:19. Rudolph (*BHS*), contrary to the MT accentuation, reads במסתרים ("in secret places") with what precedes and proposes changing it to either במסררים or במסרבים ("in rebelliousness").

25. The MT adds ודמע תדמע ("and weeping it will weep") (> LXX).

26. See *b. Hagigah* 5b.

27. גאון "pride" (Jer. 13:9) and גוה "pride" (Jer. 13:17) are from the same root גאה.

28. The MT says the flock of the LORD has been "taken captive" (נשבה).

29. "It is impossible to decide with any assurance whether the passage is wholly proleptic or whether it is partly retrospective and partly proleptic" (McKane, *Jeremiah I–XXV*, 300–301).

30. See McKane, *Jeremiah I–XXV*, 302.

mother Nehushta (see 2 Kgs. 24:8, 14–16; Jer. 22:26; cf. 1 Kgs. 2:19; 15:13), although the text of 2 Kings 24:14–16, which describes the exile of the king and his mother, does not refer to Nehushta as גבירה ("queen-mother"). It does, however, mention "mighty men" (גבורים) twice (2 Kgs. 24:14, 16). On the other hand, Jeremiah 29:2, which refers to the exile of Jehoiachin and his mother, does use the term גבירה. McKane suggests the possibility of inner-Greek corruption of Jeremiah 13:18.[31] What was originally τῇ δυναστευούσῃ ("to the queen-mother"), now preserved in Aquila, has become τοῖς δυναστεύουσι(ν) ("to the mighty men"). But since LXX Jeremiah 36:2 (MT 29:2) uses βασίλισσα for גבירה, it appears that Aquila's rendering of 13:18 is an adjustment of an earlier Greek text in order to make it fit with a proto-MT reading. The similarity of גבורים and גבירה points to inner-Hebrew variation. Either the MT is original, and the Hebrew source behind Greek Jeremiah is an adjustment to 2 Kings 24:14, 16, or the Hebrew source behind Greek Jeremiah is original, and the MT is an adjustment to Jeremiah 29:2.

The king and his mighty men (or the queen-mother) are to be instructed, "Make low and sit" (הַשְׁפִּילוּ וְשֵׁבוּ) [MT: Make low, sit (הַשְׁפִּילוּ שֵׁבוּ); Syr.: Humble yourselves and return (= הַשְׁפִּילוּ וְשֵׁבוּ)]. That is, they are to take the low place because of the loss of their position of power (cf. Isa. 47:1). For from their head their "beautiful crown" has come down (cf. Isa. 28:1–4; Ps. 89:40 [Eng., 89:39]; Lam. 5:16; see also Jer. 13:20b). *Targum Jonathan* interprets this to mean that their glory has gone into exile. This does not necessarily mean that the event itself has already occurred, only that the certainty of it is affirmed. In like manner, Jeremiah 13:19 adds that "the cities of the Negev" (Syr., *Tg. Jon.*: "the cities of the south") are shut up without anyone opening them (cf. Isa. 24:10). Judah is taken into exile. There is a debate about whether ערי הנגב refers to cities in the southern region of Judah (i.e., the Negev) or to cities in the land of Egypt. According to Calvin, the text refers to the cities of Egypt where the people of Judah looked for refuge.[32] Keil, however, is likely correct when he comments, "The cities of the south are mentioned, not because the enemy, avoiding the capital, had first brought the southern part of the land under his power, as Sennacherib had once advanced against Jerusalem from the south, 2 Kings 18:13f., 19:8 (Graf, Näg., etc.), but because they were the part of the kingdom most remote for an enemy approaching from the north; so that when they were taken,

---

31. McKane, *Jeremiah I–XXV*, 303.
32. Calvin, *Jeremiah*, 2:185.

the land was reduced and the captivity of all Judah accomplished" (see Jer. 13:20).[33] Jeremiah 13:19b in the Hebrew source behind Greek Jeremiah says, "Judah is taken into exile, he has completed a complete exile (כָּלָה גָּלוּת שְׁלֵמָה)" (cf. Amos 1:6b, 9b). The MT has, "Judah is taken into exile, all of it (כֻּלָּה), she is taken into exile completely (הָגְלָת שְׁלוֹמִים)."

The imperatives in 13:20a are feminine singular in the Hebrew source behind Greek Jeremiah, which also supplies the addressee (Jerusalem), and in the MT *kethiv*: "Lift up your eyes, O Jerusalem, and see those coming from the north." The Hebrew source behind Greek Jeremiah also has the feminine singular pronominal suffix on עֵינַיִךְ ("your eyes").[34] The MT *qere*, however, has masculine plural imperatives to match the masculine plural pronominal suffix on the MT's עֵינֵיכֶם ("your eyes").[35] The reference to those coming from the north picks up the theme of the enemy from the north (Jer. 1:14; 4:6, 13; 5:15; 6:1, 22; 10:22). As noted previously, it is customary to identify this enemy as Babylon, but no such historical identification has as yet been made in the text of Jeremiah. The question in 13:20b—"Where is the flock [*Tg. Jon.*: the people] that was given to you, your beautiful sheep [*Tg. Jon.*: people]?"—revisits the language of 13:17b, 18b. The flock is scattered. The sheep (i.e., the people) given to Jerusalem under the leadership of the Davidic shepherds/kings (see Jer. 2:8; 10:21) are gone.

Despite the difficulties of the Hebrew text of Jeremiah 13:21, the general sense of the verse is fairly clear (see the TEV cited with the translation above).[36] Those foreigners courted as allies by Jerusalem will be the very ones to subject Jerusalem to their will (see Jer. 2:18,

---

33. Keil, *Jeremiah*, 148–49. See also McKane, *Jeremiah I–XXV*, 304.

34. Note also the second feminine singular pronominal suffix in 13:20b.

35. Redak: "The 'kethib' is in the feminine singular, referring to the nation; the 'keri' is in the masculine plural, referring to the individuals. I feel that the plural form is addressed to the king and the queen-mother, mentioned above, for the flock was given to them, they being the shepherds. The 'kethib' is addressed to the gathering of the great princes who were exiled with Jeconiah and the craftsmen and the sentries of the gate, for the 'flock was given to them,' and they were included among the shepherds" (Rosenberg, trans., *Mikraoth Gedoloth: Jeremiah Volume One*, 119).

36. Holladay, however, has given up all hope of making any sense of the MT or the LXX. His emendation renders the verse virtually unrecognizable: "What will you say when your lambs are missing?—and it was you who trained them!—your sucklings, as if trained by the poor man" (Holladay, *Jeremiah 1*, 411, 413–14).

36), and this will be a difficult pill for Jerusalem to swallow.[37] The leadership and the people will have nothing to say at that point. They will be like a woman in childbirth gripped by her pains (cf. Jer. 4:31; 6:24; 22:23; 30:6; 1QHᵃ 11:7). The expression לראש . . . כי יפקדו עליך can be rendered as "when they appoint over you . . . as head" (i.e., when the foreigners designate a leader or leaders over them) or as "when they visit upon you . . . as head" (i.e., when the foreigners inflict punishment on them as their ruler). The MT has the singular כי יפקד עליך ("when he appoints over [or visits upon] you"), in which case either the LORD or a foreign leader is anticipated to designate a leader or leaders over them or to inflict punishment on them as their ruler. The parenthetical comment—"and you, you taught them over you as friends/ allies [LXX: lessons]"—is interpreted by *Targum Jonathan* to mean, "and you, you taught them to do harm to you." This perhaps takes its cue from Jeremiah 13:23b, which describes the people as those "taught/ accustomed to do evil" (see also Jer. 2:33).

If Jerusalem should play the fool and think, "Why have these things happened to me?" (Jer. 13:22a; cf. Jer. 2:23, 35) then the answer is simple. It is because of the abundance of Jerusalem's iniquity (Jer. 13:22b; cf. Jer. 5:6, 19; 9:11–12 [Eng., 9:12–13]; 14:7; 16:10–13; 22:8–9; 30:14–15). For this reason Jerusalem's "skirts [LXX: hind parts] are uncovered" and her "heels are violated [LXX: publicly displayed]" (cf. Jer. 13:26; Ezek. 23:29). Bright interprets these to be euphemistic expressions and translates, "That your limbs are exposed, Your body ravished."[38] According to Thompson, the imagery may allude to "the practice of stripping an adulterous woman of her garments" (Isa. 47:2–3; Ezek. 16:37, 39; 23:26, 29; Hos. 2:5 [Eng., 2:3]; Nah. 3:5; see also Jer. 13:26–27).[39] McKane contends

---

37. Rashi references Ezekiel 23:16 ("And she lusted for them to the sight of her eyes, and she sent emissaries to them, to the Chaldees") and Isaiah 39:2 (// 2 Kgs. 20:13)—the story of Hezekiah showing the emissaries of Merodach-baladan his treasures. Redak refers to the story of 2 Kings 16:7 where Ahaz appeals to the king of Assyria for help against the kings of Aram and Israel (Rosenberg, trans., *Mikraoth Gedoloth: Jeremiah Volume One*, 119). According to Keil, "The prophet means the heathen kings, for whose favour Judah had hitherto been intriguing, the Babylonians and Egyptians" (*Jeremiah*, 150).

38. Bright, *Jeremiah*, 93, 95. Likewise, Holladay believes sexual violence is in view here (*Jeremiah 1*, 414). עקביך ("your heels") may be like רגלים ("heels"), a euphemism for genitals (BDB, 920).

39. "Judah is a prostitute because of her idolatrous practices and as such will be exposed nude" (Thompson, *Book of Jeremiah*, 374).

285

that the entirety of 13:22b is like 13:26, arguing that it only speaks of "judicial punishment" and does not refer to rape,[40] but this does not seem to do justice to the verb נחמסו ("violated"), which is unique to 13:22b.

The above translation of Jeremiah 13:23 assumes that both halves of the verse are rhetorical questions expecting the obvious answer of no (cf. Amos 3:3–6): "Can a Cushite [LXX: Ethiopian] change his skin, or a leopard its spots? Also you, are you able to do good, being taught/accustomed to do evil" (see Amos 9:7; see also Gen. 6:5)?[41] Other translations assume that the first half of the verse expects a positive answer for the sake of argument (e.g., ESV: "Can the Ethiopian change his skin or the leopard his spots? Then also you can do good who are accustomed to do evil"). This latter option is essentially equivalent to an if-then statement: "If the Cushite/Ethiopian could change his skin or a leopard its spots, then you too could do good, even though you are trained to do evil." A Cushite cannot change his dark complexion nor a leopard its spots. Likewise, the people are unable to cease to do evil and learn to do good (see Isa. 1:16b–17a). They are taught or accustomed to evil rather than taught of God (see Isa. 54:13; 1 Thess. 4:9). Calvin comments, "Learned men in our age do not wisely refer to this passage, when they seek to prove that there is no free-will in man; for it is not simply the nature of man that is spoken of here, but the habit that is contracted by long practice."[42] Because such self-transformation is hopeless, the LORD, who begins to speak in Jeremiah 13:24, says that he will scatter the people like chaff in the desert wind (cf. Jer. 9:15

---

40. McKane, *Jeremiah I–XXV*, 311. According to BDB (784), the expression נחמסו עקביך ("[your heels] are treated violently, i.e., are rudely exposed") refers to "an attack from behind."

41. Francis Andersen calls this type of construction "double coordination": "When an inclusive phrase (gam-)X . . . gam-Y is distributed between two clauses, and gam-Y is clause-initial, and the second clause is coordinated, the second clause begins *wĕgam*-Y. Here *wĕgam* is not a compound conjunction. Each conjunction operates independently on a different level of the grammatical hierarchy. *wĕ*- is a sentence-level conjunction joining two clauses; gam is a phrase-level conjunction joining Y to X in a phrase that cuts across a sentence" (Francis I. Andersen, *The Sentence in Biblical Hebrew* [The Hague: Mouton, 1974], 157).

42. "Aristotle, a strong advocate of free will, confesses that it is not in man's power to do right, when he is so immersed in his own vices as to have lost a free choice (7. *Lib. Ethicōn*), and this also is what experience proves. We hence see that this passage is improperly adduced to prove a sentiment which is yet true, and fully confirmed by many passages of Scripture" (Calvin, *Jeremiah*, 2:191).

[Eng., 9:16]; 13:14, 17b, 20b; 18:17; see also Isa. 29:5; 40:24; MT Jer. 4:11–12; Pss. 1:4; 83:14 [Eng., 83:13]; Dan. 2:35).

According to the LORD's words in the Hebrew source behind Greek Jeremiah 13:25, the judgment anticipated in 13:24 is Jerusalem's "lot" (cf. Isa. 17:14; 57:6): "This is your lot and the portion of your rebellion (וּמְנָת מִרְיֵךְ) from me." That is, what the LORD has allotted Jerusalem in judgment is commensurate with the people's rebellion. The MT has, "This is your lot and the portion of your measure (וּמְנָת מִדַּיִךְ) from me" (cf. Isa. 65:7).[43] With only a slight change in the consonantal text, this shifts the focus from what is due Jerusalem for its rebellion to the just nature of what is measured and dealt to the people. The Syriac and *Targum Jonathan* have the phrase in question as "the portion of your inheritance," which would seem to turn LXX Jeremiah 10:16 on its head. The LORD himself is supposed to be the people's inheritance, but instead they receive judgment. This is because they forgot the LORD (cf. Jer. 2:32; 3:21; 18:15; 23:27) and trusted in "deception" (שׁקר). The term שׁקר has been used in various ways thus far in the book of Jeremiah, but the immediate context of 13:25, which speaks of the people's "adultery" (i.e., idolatry; Jer. 13:27), and the reference to forgetting the LORD strongly suggest that false worship of Baal is in view (see Jer. 5:31; 10:14; 23:14; cf. Rom. 1:25).[44] Therefore, the LORD, in addition to what is said in 13:22b, says that he has stripped off Jerusalem's "skirts" (LXX: "hind parts") in order to expose the disgrace of Jerusalem's adultery/idolatry (Jer. 13:26; cf. Isa. 47:2–3; Ezek. 16:37, 39; 23:26, 29; Hos. 2:5 [Eng., 2:3]; Nah. 3:5).

As for Jerusalem's acts of adultery/idolatry (cf. Jer. 3:9) and her neighings (cf. Jer. 5:7–8) and the wickedness (LXX: estrangement)[45] of her fornication on hills and in the field/country (cf. Deut. 12:2; Isa. 65:7; Jer. 2:20; 3:2, 23), such "detested acts" (see Jer. 4:1; 7:30; 16:18; 32:34) have not gone unnoticed by the LORD (Jer. 13:27a; cf. Jer. 13:26b). Woe to Jerusalem (cf. Jer. 48:46), "for you will not be clean after me (אַחֲרֵי)," says the LORD (Jer. 13:27b). That is, Jerusalem is doomed because the people refuse to be cleansed of their spiritual adultery in order to follow

---

43. "Hitz. renders מְנָת מִדַּיִךְ: portion of thy garment, that is allotted for the swelling folds of thy garment (cf. Ruth 3:15, 2 Kings 4:39), on the ground that מַד never means *mensura*, but garment only" (Keil, *Jeremiah*, 150).

44. See Bright, *Jeremiah*, 95. Kara interprets the "deception" to be "the false help of the nations" (Rosenberg, trans., *Mikraoth Gedoloth: Jeremiah Volume One*, 121; see Jer. 13:21). See Judges 20:6.

45. "Hence Sept. ἀπαλλοτρίωσις at Jer 13.27 probably indicates an addiction to foreign gods (apostasy) and so is an exegesis of זמה" (McKane, *Jeremiah I–XXV*, 312–13).

after the LORD (see BDB, 372; cf. Jer. 33:8). The final, "How long still (עַד מָתַי עֹד)?" is not a genuine expectation that things might eventually change (see Jer. 13:23) but a lament over the sealed fate of the city (cf. Isa. 6:11; Jer. 12:4; Hab. 2:6b). MT 13:27b has a slightly different text and vocalization: "Woe to you, Jerusalem, you will not be clean after when still (אַחֲרֵי מָתַי עֹד)?"[46]

---

46. Holladay's emendation of this text results in the following translation: "Woe to you, Jerusalem, (that) you are not clean!—other (partners) you designate (אֲחֵרִים תִּיעָדִי)" (*Jeremiah 1*, 412, 417).

JEREMIAH 14:1–15:9

14:1 And the word of the LORD *came to Jeremiah concerning the drought [MT: That which was the word of the* LORD *to Jeremiah because of the drought]. 14:2 "Judah mourns; and her gates, they languish. And [> MT] they are dark on the ground [Tg. Jon.: their faces are covered with a black coating like a pot; they are left alone on the ground]; and the outcry of Jerusalem, it goes up. 14:3 And her [MT: their] nobles [lit., majestic ones], they send their servants [lit., insignificant ones] for water. They come to cisterns, but [> Codex L] they do not find water; and their vessels return empty. [MT adds: They are ashamed and humiliated (NET: Disappointed and dismayed), and they cover their head.] 14:4 And the produce of the ground, it is dismayed [LXX: it fails; MT: Because of the ground that is dismayed (NET: cracked)], for there is no rain [MT adds: in the land], farmers are ashamed/disappointed, [mlt Mss, Syr. add: and] they cover their head. 14:5 [MT adds: כִּי] Even a doe in the field, it gives birth and forsakes, for there is no grass. 14:6 And wild donkeys, they stand on bare places. They pant for air [4QJerᵃ, MT add: like jackals]. Their eyes fail, for there is no herbage."*

14:7 If [or, Though] our iniquities testify against us [LXX: oppose us], O LORD*, act for the sake of your name [LXX: do to us for your sake]. For [or, Indeed] our apostasies are many [LXX adds: before you; Syr.: great is your goodness], [LXX adds: for] it is against you that we have sinned. 14:8 O hope of Israel, O* LORD *[> Codex L], and savior [LXX: and you save; MT: his savior] in time of distress, why should you be like a resident foreigner in the land and like a native [MT: traveler] turning aside [or, pitching a tent] to lodge for the night [MT: who turns aside (or, pitches a tent) to lodge for the night; Tg. Jon.: why should your anger rest on us, and we are like resident foreigners in the land and like a traveler who turns aside to lodge for the night]? 14:9 You will not be like a man sleeping, like a man who is unable to save, will you [MT: Why should you be like a man astonished (or, surprised, confused; Holladay: helpless), like a mighty man who is unable to save]? And you are in our midst, O* LORD*, and your name upon us is called. Do not abandon [LXX: forget] us.*[1]

---

1. "Why *does your anger hover over us when we are taken into exile and forsaken? You,* O mighty One, *are* able to redeem, and as for you, *your Shekhina is among us*, O Lord, and your Name has been called over us: you will not forsake us" (Hayward, *Targum of Jeremiah*, 90).

14:10 Thus says the Lord *to this people, "[MT adds: Thus] They love to wander with their feet [LXX: to move their feet], and they do not restrain [LXX: spare; MT: they love to wander; their feet they do not restrain]. And the* Lord, *he does not accept them. Now he will remember their iniquity [MT adds: and he will visit their sins]."*[2]

14:11 And the Lord *said to me, "Do not pray on behalf of this people for good. 14:12 If they fast, I am not listening to their cry; and if they offer burnt offering and grain offering [LXX: sacrifices], I am not accepting them. For by sword and by famine and by plague [LXX: death] am I making an end of them." 14:13 And I said, "Ah [LXX: The one who is],*[3] Lord *[MT: Lord* God*]! Look, their prophets are prophesying and saying [MT: the prophets (Tg. Jon.: the false prophets) are saying to them], 'You will not see a sword; and as for famine, it will not come to you. For stability and peace / well-being [Codex L: lasting peace / well-being; pc Mss: peace / well-being and stability] are what I will give on the land and in this place [MT: I will give to you in this place].'" 14:14 And the* Lord *said to me, "Deception is what the prophets [Tg. Jon.: false prophets] are prophesying in my name. I did not send them, and I did not command them, and I did not speak to them. For [> MT] false vision and divination and worthlessness [LXX: omens; NET: worthless predictions] and the deceit of their heart / mind are what they are prophesying to you [mlt Mss: to them]. 14:15 Therefore, thus says the* Lord *concerning the prophets [Tg. Jon.: false prophets] who prophesy in my name deception [deception > MT], and I did not send them, who say [MT: and they say], 'Neither sword nor famine will come in this land': Deaths by diseases will they die [> MT], and by famine will the prophets be finished [MT: By sword and by famine will those prophets (Tg. Jon.: those false prophets) be finished]. 14:16 And as for the people to whom they prophesy, they will be [*והיו*; MT: *יהיו*] cast in the streets of Jerusalem from before the sword and the famine [Syr. adds: and the plague], and there will be no one burying them [cf. Syr.; or, for them]—[MT adds: them] and [> MT] their wives and their sons and their daughters. And I will pour out on them the punishment for their evil."*

---

2. "Thus says the Lord to this people: 'As they have loved, *so I will require of them that they should* go into exile *from the land of the house of my Shekhina; and just as they were partaking of the worship of idols* and have not withheld their feet *from the house of my sanctuary, so that there is no* pleasure *in them before* the Lord, so he will *visit* their *sins* and *punish* their iniquities'" (Hayward, *Targum of Jeremiah*, 90–91).

3. See commentary on Jeremiah 1:6.

BHS (Rudolph) arranges Jeremiah 14:1–15:9 in alternating sections of poetry and prose: superscription (Jer. 14:1), poetry (Jer. 14:2–9), prose (Jer. 14:10–16), poetry (Jer. 14:17–22), prose (Jer. 15:1–4), and poetry (Jer. 15:5–9). The following structure emerges from the content: (1a) the word of the LORD concerning the drought (Jer. 14:1–6); (1b) Jeremiah's prayer (Jer. 14:7–9); (1c) the LORD's judgment of the people and the false prophets by sword, famine, and plague and his rejection of Jeremiah's intercession (Jer. 14:10–16); (2a) the word of the LORD through Jeremiah to the people concerning sword and famine (Jer. 14:17–18); (2b) Jeremiah's prayer (Jer. 14:19–22); the LORD's rejection of Jeremiah's intercession and his judgment of the people by death, sword, famine, and captivity (Jer. 15:1–4); and divine judgment (Jer. 15:5–9).[4]

The superscription in 14:1 marks off a new section from what precedes it. Codex Sinaiticus indents this verse on the left and the right. The form of the superscription differs between the Hebrew source behind Greek Jeremiah and the MT. The Hebrew source behind Greek Jeremiah says, "And the word of the LORD came to Jeremiah concerning the drought" (ויהי דבר יהוה אל ירמיהו על הבצרה) (cf. Jer. 29:30; 32:26 [MT]; 33:1; 33:19, 23 [MT]; 34:12; 35:12 [MT]; 36:27; 37:6; 42:7; 43:8). The MT has, "That which was the word of the LORD to Jeremiah because of the drought" (אשר היה דבר יהוה אל ירמיהו על דברי הבצרות) (cf. MT Jer. 46:1; 47:1; 49:34). The singular forms בצרה and בצרת (see Jer. 17:8) and the plural form בצרות apparently all mean "dearth, destitution, diminution, cutting off" (see *HALOT* 1:149). Drought is one of the covenant curses according to Leviticus 26:18–20 and Deuteronomy 28:22–24 (see Jer. 3:3a [MT]; Amos 4:6–11). No date or historical reference is given for this particular drought.

Jeremiah 14:2 begins the description of the drought: "Judah mourns; and her gates, they languish. And [> MT] they are dark on the ground; and the outcry of Jerusalem, it goes up" (cf. Isa. 3:26). As McKane notes, "There are passages relating to vegetation and crops, where 'wither' and 'wilt' would seem to be appropriate renderings for אבל and אמלל (Isa 24.4, 7; 33:9; Joel 1.10), and there are others where these verbs are used of human feelings (Isa 19.8; Jer 14.2; Lam 2.8)."[5] "Judah" here stands

---

4. Cf. Holladay, *Jeremiah 1*, 423.

5. "In Hos 4.3 אבל is used of הארץ and אמלל of כל יושב בה, so that 'wither' is appropriate for the first and 'mourn' for the second (although 'mourn' is also a possibility for the first). KB³ postulates two roots: Jer 14.2 is assigned to I אבל 'mourn,' and Jer 12.4 and 23.10, where אבל is associated with הארץ, is assigned to II אבל 'wither'" (McKane, *Jeremiah I–XXV*, 316). See also Jeremiah 4:28.

for the people of the land who mourn, although the mourning is in fact due to the withering of the land itself. The "gates" represent the cities of Judah and the people therein (see Deut. 12:12, 15, 17, 18; 14:21; 15:7; Jer. 15:7; Lam. 1:4), although it is possible that "gates" more precisely refers to the leading elders who meet in the gates of the cities to make decisions (see Ruth 4:1–2; Lam. 2:10; 5:14). The gates are "dark on the ground" in the sense that the people and/or leadership are clothed in black and bowed low to the ground to express their mourning (see BDB 871; see also Jer. 8:21; Pss. 35:14; 38:7 [Eng., 38:6]; Lam. 2:9). *Targum Jonathan* says: "their faces are covered with a black coating like a pot; they are left alone on the ground." McKane is likely correct to say that the outcry of Jerusalem that goes up in this context is not a cry for deliverance but a cry of distress (see Isa. 24:11; Jer. 46:12; Ps. 144:14).[6] According to Jeremiah 14:3, the nobles send their servants for water, but when these servants come to the cisterns designed to catch rainwater (cf. Jer. 2:13), there is no water to be found (cf. Exod. 16:22). Thus, the vessels for water return empty. The MT adds, "They are ashamed and humiliated [NET: disappointed and dismayed], and they cover their head" (cf. Isa. 54:4; Jer. 14:4b; 22:22b; 31:19).

There are several different options for the beginning of Jeremiah 14:4. It is usually thought that the LXX καὶ τὰ ἔργα τῆς γῆς ἐξέλιπεν ("And the works of the ground, it fails") reflects וַעֲבוֹדַת הָאֲדָמָה חָדְלָה,[7] but τὰ ἔργα in this context probably means "produce" and thus reflects עבור in the phrase וַעֲבוּר הָאֲדָמָה ("And the produce of the ground"; cf. Josh. 5:11, 12).[8] ἐξέλιπεν is not necessarily a reflection of חָדְלָה. It could be a translation of חַתָּה. The verb חַתָּה is either a personification of the ground's produce ("it is dismayed"; cf. Jon. 1:4b) or (in the MT) an indication that the ground itself is broken or "cracked" (NET). The MT בַּעֲבוּר הָאֲדָמָה ("because of the ground") can be read with what precedes it ("and they cover their head because of the ground") or with what follows it ("Because of the ground that is dismayed/cracked"). A third option is to read בַּעֲבוּרָהּ הָאֲדָמָה חַתָּה ("Because of it [i.e., the drought] the ground is dismayed/cracked"), assuming that the ה suffix on בעבורה has been lost due to haplography (see the ה prefix on the beginning of the following word האדמה). The produce of the ground fails because there is no rain (MT adds: "in the land"; cf. 1 Kgs. 17:7), which is due to divine

---

6. McKane, *Jeremiah I–XXV*, 317.

7. It is a common idiom in Greek for a neuter plural subject to take a singular verb.

8. See Takamitsu Muraoka, *A Greek-English Lexicon of the Septuagint* (Leuven: Peeters, 2009), 290.

judgment (see Jer. 5:24; 14:22). Therefore, farmers are "ashamed" or disappointed. They cover their head in shame (cf. 2 Sam. 15:30; Jer. 2:36–37; 12:13 [MT]; Est. 6:12).

Not only does the drought (Jer. 14:1) affect the people (Jer. 14:2–3) and the produce (Jer. 14:4) of the land, but also, according to Jeremiah 14:5–6, it affects the animal life. Even a doe in the field, which would normally care for its young, abandons its offspring after giving birth simply because there is no grass on which to feed and sustain life (Jer. 14:5). Wild donkeys stand on bare places panting for air (4QJer[a], MT add: "like jackals") (Jer. 14:6a; cf. Jer. 2:24). "Their eyes fail, for there is no herbage" (Jer. 14:6b; cf. Lam. 2:11; 4:17). The land is bare, and the wildlife is out of breath either due to exhaustion in search of food or due to hunger and failing health. Likewise, the animals' eyes fail either because they are strained looking for herbage or because they lack the proper nutrition.

The juxtaposition of Jeremiah's prayer (Jer. 14:7–9) next to the description of the drought (Jer. 14:2–6) suggests that it is a prayer for mercy in the context of the drought, even though the prayer itself makes no direct reference to the drought. The prayer has several features in common with other biblical prayers. First, although Jeremiah is presumably to be counted among the righteous remnant, he nevertheless sees himself in solidarity with the people in general and includes himself in the confession of sin: "If/Though our iniquities testify against us" (Jer. 14:7a; cf. Exod. 34:9; Dan. 9:5; Ezra 9:6; Neh. 1:6; see also Jer. 3:22b–25; 14:10; Ps. 44). The language of iniquities/transgressions/sins or pride testifying against the people also occurs in Isaiah 3:9; 59:12; Hosea 5:5; 7:10. Second, Jeremiah appeals to God's primary motive for action, namely, his reputation and glory: "O Lord, act for the sake of your name" (Jer. 14:7a; cf. Isa. 48:9–11; Jer. 3:21; 14:21; Ezek. 20:9; 36:20–23; Pss. 25:11; 79:9; 109:21; 143:11). Of course, it would not be contrary to God's character to judge the people for breaking the covenant, but the concern here may be the potential misunderstanding of God's judgment by the watching nations (see, e.g., Exod. 32:12; Deut. 9:28; 32:27; *4 Bar.* 1:6; but see also Ezek. 39:23). Third, Jeremiah recognizes that an appeal to God's pursuit of his own glory is the only card that he has to play. The "apostasies" of the people are many (see Jer. 2:19; 5:6; 8:5; 13:22; 30:14), and it is against the Lord that they have sinned (Jer. 14:7b, 20; cf. Jer. 3:25; 8:14).[9] Thus, no appeal for grace or mercy can be made on the basis of the people's own merit.

---

9. The Syriac has "great is your goodness (ܒܣܝܡܘܬܟ)" instead of "our apostasies are many." This may be an inner-Syriac variant given the similarity

The Lord is the "hope of Israel" (cf. Jer. 17:13; 50:7; Ps. 71:5) and his "savior" (cf. 2 Sam. 22:3; Isa. 43:3, 11; 45:15; 49:26; 60:16; 63:8; Hos. 13:4; Ps. 106:21) "in time of distress" (Jer. 14:8a; cf. Isa. 33:2; 63:9; Jer. 15:11; 30:7; Nah. 1:7; Ps. 37:39; Neh. 9:27).[10] Why should he be "like a resident foreigner in the land and like a native [MT: traveler] turning aside [or, pitching a tent] to lodge for the night" (Jer. 14:8b; cf. Jer. 9:1 [Eng., 9:2])?[11] The Hebrew source behind Greek Jeremiah has אזרח ("native") where the MT has ארח ("traveler"). At first glance, the MT's reading would seem to be the more natural fit for the context, but this is also why it is probably secondary. It is more likely that a scribe would have changed "native" to "traveler" than it is for one to have changed "traveler" to "native." God is like a "native" spending the night either in the sense that he is like a native of another land or, more strikingly, in the sense that he is like a native of the land of Israel who chooses not to stay more than a night. *Targum Jonathan's* rendering gives 14:8b a different sense based on Leviticus 25:23: "why should your anger rest on us, and we are like resident foreigners in the land and like a traveler who turns aside to lodge for the night?" This seems to acknowledge that the people do not really possess the land. They are more like tenants. The Lord is the one who owns the land. Thus, the Targum suggests, the Lord's anger should not rest on the people as if they were the owners. Jeremiah 14:9a adds to this line of questioning: "You will not be like a man sleeping (נרדם), like a man (גבר) who is unable to save, will you [MT: Why should you be like a man astonished (נדהם; or, surprised, confused; Holladay: helpless), like a mighty man (גבור) who is unable to save]" (cf. Pss. 44:24 [Eng., 44:23]; 78:65; see also Zeph. 3:17)? This likely anticipates the kind of question that the

---

between *tybwtk* ("your goodness") and *tybwtn* ("our apostasies"), but see 1QM(33) 18:8.

10. The term מקוה ("hope") has a homonym that means "collection (of water)" or "pool." "It is appropriate to address Yahweh as the source of hope for Israel, but it is particularly appropriate in the context of a drought to address Yahweh as the true pool of water for Israel. There is of course no way to render the double meaning into English" (Holladay, *Jeremiah 1*, 433). See Jeremiah 2:13; 17:13.

11. Redak: "The wayfarer is even less concerned than the stranger, since he is here today and not tomorrow. You are like them in this respect when You hide Your face from the land and do not concern Yourself with the misfortunes befalling it. Yet, in reality, the land is Yours, and we are the strangers who have become inhabitants with You" (Rosenberg, trans., *Mikraoth Gedoloth: Jeremiah Volume One*, 124).

nations might ask (see Deut. 9:28; cf. 1 Kgs. 18:27), but the Lord is in the midst of the people (cf. Mic. 3:11b), and his name is called upon them (Jer. 14:9b; cf. Deut. 28:10; Dan. 9:19; 2 Chr. 7:14). This probably refers to the fact that the temple, which also has the name of the Lord on it (see Jer. 7:10, 11, 14, 30), marks the special presence of the Lord with his people. Therefore, since the temple (and thus the city of Jerusalem [Deut. 12:5]) and the people of the land of Judah bear the Lord's name, whatever happens to them also reflects upon the Lord's reputation. A prayer for the Lord to act for the sake of his name is also a prayer for him to act on behalf of those who bear his name (see Dan. 9:15–19). Thus, the final request is, "Do not abandon [LXX: forget] us" (cf. Lam. 5:20), which *Targum Jonathan* renders more confidently: "you will not forsake us."[12]

The Lord's response to Jeremiah's prayer is not positive, despite the strength of the prophet's appeal. In the Hebrew source behind Greek Jeremiah 14:10a, the Lord says, "They love to wander with their feet, and they do not restrain" (cf. Prov. 7:11). In the MT he says, "Thus they love to wander; their feet they do not restrain" (cf. Jer. 5:31; Amos 4:5). *Targum Jonathan* renders, "As they have loved, *so I will require of them that they should* go into exile *from the land of the house of my Shekhina; and just as they were partaking of the worship of idols* and have not withheld their feet *from the house of my sanctuary*" (cf. Jer. 7:9–11).[13] "The intention is that God will exile them just as they loved to wander, according to *Rashi*, to worship foreign deities, and, according to *Redak*, to enlist aid from Egypt or Assyria."[14] Keil, citing Graf, argues that the adverb כֵן ("Thus") in the MT must refer back to the content of Jeremiah's prayer in 14:7–9: "*Thus*, in the same degree as Jahveh has estranged Himself from His people (cf. vv. 8 and 9), have they estranged themselves from their God" (see Jer. 2:23, 25, 31).[15] The Lord does not accept them (Jer. 14:10b). Their iniquities do testify against them (Jer. 14:7), so now he will remember their iniquity (MT adds: "and he will visit their sins"). He will act for the sake of his name but not solely to defend his actions against being misconstrued. Rather, he will act in the interest of vindicating his holy character (Exod. 34:6–7), maintaining his fidelity to the terms of the covenant (Lev. 26; Deut. 28). His refusal to heed Jeremiah's

---

12. According to Rashi, תַּנִּחֵנוּ is equivalent to תַּעַזְבֵנוּ (Rosenberg, trans., *Mikraoth Gedoloth: Jeremiah Volume One*, 124).
13. Hayward, *Targum of Jeremiah*, 90–91.
14. Rosenberg, trans., *Mikraoth Gedoloth: Jeremiah Volume One*, 125. See also Calvin, *Jeremiah*, 2:216.
15. Keil, *Jeremiah*, 155.

plea is not an indication that he is somehow absent or incapacitated (Jer. 14:8–9). Jeremiah 14:10b is a citation of Hosea 8:13; 9:9. The addition in the MT ("and he will visit their sins") makes the citation even more explicit. In the Hosea context, Israel is accused of being like Gibeah of Benjamin in the story of Judges 19 where the people sink to the level of Sodom and Gomorrah (Hos. 9:9; see Gen. 19). Their judgment will be a recapitulation of their history, a metaphorical "return to Egypt" (Hos. 8:13; 9:3; 11:5; cf. Deut. 28:68).

The LORD's discourse is reintroduced in 14:11a. His prohibition in 14:11b ("Do not pray on behalf of this people for good") is a reprisal of Jeremiah 7:16 and 11:14 (see also Jer. 15:1–4; 2 Macc. 15:14). What makes 14:11b especially poignant is the fact that it comes on the heels of a prayer from Jeremiah on behalf of the people (Jer. 14:7–9; see also Jer. 14:19–22; 37:3; 42:2). It is clear from 14:10 that such prayer will be met with rejection. Jeremiah, a prophet like Moses (Jer. 1:4–9), is unable to intercede successfully for his people in the manner of Moses (Exod. 32:11–14; Deut. 9:25–29)—a point made explicit in Jeremiah 15:1–4. That Jeremiah has continued to pray for the people in the book despite 7:16 and 11:14 suggests that such prohibitions are not to be understood as strict warnings to be heeded. Jeremiah's prayer in 14:7–9 is not an act of disobedience. Rather, the understanding is that Jeremiah's intercessions will face negative replies. The text of 14:11b does add one new element. Jeremiah is not to pray on behalf of the people "for good" (cf. Jer. 18:20; 24:5–6; 44:27; see also LXX 15:11). This suggests that imprecatory prayers (e.g., Jer. 11:20) may very well be answered as requested (e.g., Jer. 11:21–23).[16]

If the people fast, the LORD is not listening to their cry (Jer. 14:12a).[17] This is because they do not fast in right relationship to him (cf. Isa. 58; Zech. 7). If they offer burnt offerings and grain offerings, the LORD is not accepting them (cf. Jer. 7:21–23; 17:24–27; see also Amos 5:21–24). That is, such offerings by themselves do not make the people acceptable to the LORD (see Jer. 6:20; 14:10b). He cannot accept them. This is because he has determined to make an end of them "by sword and by famine and by plague [LXX: death]" (Jer. 14:12b; cf. Lev. 26:25–26; Jer. 9:15 [Eng., 9:16]; 11:22; 18:21; Ezek. 5:12, 17; 6:11–12; 7:15; 12:16; 14:13, 17, 19, 21;

---

16. See Redak in Rosenberg, trans., *Mikraoth Gedoloth: Jeremiah Volume One*, 125. See also Thompson, *Book of Jeremiah*, 382.

17. "*Redak* notes that there is no fast without prayer. Therefore, He mentions their prayer without previously mentioning that they will pray" (Rosenberg, trans., *Mikraoth Gedoloth: Jeremiah Volume One*, 125).

Bar. 2:25; Rev. 6:8).[18] Parke-Taylor provides some helpful data on the use of this triad:[19] "the triad חרב, רעב and דֶּבֶר (*sic*) . . . occurs very frequently and mostly in prose passages, e.g., 14:12; 21:9 = 38:2; 24:10; 27:8, 13; 32:24, 36; 42:17, 22; 44:13. Sometimes the nouns occur in a different order: 21:7 ('pestilence, sword, famine'); 15:2, which adds שְׁבִי ('captivity') as a fourth term; 34:17 ('sword, pestilence, famine'). Jeremiah 28:8 has the sequence 'war, famine and pestilence.'"[20] McKane suggests that the term "famine" (רעב) in this triad is not to be confused with the "drought" (בצרה) mentioned in Jeremiah 14:1 (see Jer. 52:6).[21]

Jeremiah responds with an expression of grief: "Ah, LORD" (Jer. 14:13; cf. Jer. 1:6; 4:10; 32:17). He points out that people's prophets (*Tg. Jon.*: "the false prophets") are misleading the people by saying, "You will not see a sword; and as for famine, it will not come to you. For stability and peace/well-being [Codex L: lasting peace/well-being; pc Mss: peace/well-being and stability] are what I will give on the land and in this place [MT: I will give to you in this place]" (cf. Jer. 5:12).[22] Jeremiah 14:13 is usually understood to be the prophet's "plea of extenuation" after the failure of his prayer in 14:7–9.[23] He implicitly claims that the people cannot be faulted for what the false prophets have led them to do. The LORD will indeed address the problem of the false prophets (Jer. 14:14–15), but he will also hold the people responsible for their actions (Jer. 14:16). The quote of the false prophets in 14:13 depicts them speaking on behalf of the LORD, using the first-person

---

18. "Sept., Pesh. and Targ. understand דבר as 'deadly pestilence,' and this should be noted in connection with Weippert's contention (p. 165n256) that מות is a variant of דבר in 15.2, 18.21 and 43.11" (McKane, *Jeremiah I–XXV*, 324).

19. Parke-Taylor, *Formation of the Book of Jeremiah*, 21–23, 201–2.

20. Parke-Taylor, *Formation of the Book of Jeremiah*, 22. Parke-Taylor considers חרב and רעב to be the primary terms. The addition of דבר to make the triad is an expansion of an original dyad (Parke-Taylor, *Formation of the Book of Jeremiah*, 202).

21. The kind of famine mentioned in association with the sword "results rather from a 'scorched earth' policy by an invader, or from destruction and expropriation of crops, coupled with siege conditions" (McKane, *Jeremiah I–XXV*, 316).

22. "The derivation of הראו (v. 13) from ראה is confirmed by 5.12) נראה) and this is how 14.13 was understood by the versions, but 42.16 (החרב אשר אתם יראים) gives a different indication and 'see' and 'fear' may be variants in this type of expression" (McKane, *Jeremiah I–XXV*, 325).

23. Holladay, *Jeremiah 1*, 435.

pronoun "I" (i.e., they claim to speak in the Lord's name [Jer. 14:14–15]). According to the Hebrew source behind Greek Jeremiah, they represent the Lord as saying that there will be "stability and peace/well-being" (אֱמֶת וְשָׁלוֹם) (cf. Jer. 6:14; 8:11; 28). The Leningrad Codex has "lasting peace/well-being" (שָׁלוֹם אֱמֶת) (see Redak). A few Masoretic manuscripts have "peace/well-being and stability" (שָׁלוֹם וֶאֱמֶת) (cf. Isa. 39:8; Jer. 33:6).[24] This stability and well-being are said to be what the Lord will give "on the land and in this place" according to the Hebrew source behind Greek Jeremiah, which suggests "place" (מקום) refers to the temple (cf. Jer. 7:3, 12, 14) insofar as it is coordinated with "the land" of Israel. On the other hand, the MT simply says that the Lord will give well-being "in this place," in which case "place" could refer either to the temple or to the land (cf. Jer. 7:7; 14:15).

The Lord says to Jeremiah that "deception" (שקר) is what the false prophets are prophesying in his name (Jer. 14:14a; cf. Jer. 23:25; Matt. 7:22).[25] Not only do they speak false words of hope (Jer. 6:14–14; 8:10–11; 14:13), but also they prophesy by a false god (Jer. 2:8b; 5:31; 23:13–14). These so-called prophets are not like Jeremiah (Jer. 1:7). The Lord did not send them or command them or speak to them (cf. Jer. 23:32; 27:15; 28:15; 29:9, 31; see also Deut. 18:20). They "prophesy" to the people "false vision" (חזון שקר), "divination" (קסם), "worthlessness" (אליל), and "the deceit of their heart/mind" (תרמית לבם) (Jer. 14:14b; cf. Ezek. 13:2, 6–9).[26] Their "false vision" (חזון שקר) is "the vision of their heart/mind" (חזון לבם) (see Jer. 23:16b). That is, it originates with them. It does not come from the mouth of the Lord. The NET translates קסם ואליל ("divination and

---

24. Perhaps the original reading was אֱמֶת וְשָׁלוֹם, which was changed to שָׁלוֹם וֶאֱמֶת on the basis of Jeremiah 33:6. The *waw* conjunction then dropped by accident, which required the first word to be in the construct state: שָׁלוֹם אֱמֶת.

25. Holladay notes the two different stems used for "prophesying," the *niphal* (Jer. 14:14a) and the *hithpael* (Jer. 14:14b) (Holladay, *Jeremiah 1*, 435). The first is the usual stem for "prophesying." The second sometimes refers to ecstatic behavior (e.g., 1 Sam. 19:24). The two can be used interchangeably or synonymously, but Holladay suggests that the shift to *hithpael* here may indicate "aberrant behavior."

26. "*Malbim* classifies these false prophets into four categories. One group prophesied by 'the false vision,' the product of their imagination. The second group by 'divination' through star-gazing or lots. The third group by 'the thing of nought,' the reply of the teraphim, or oracles, which are of no value. Others misled the people by 'the deceit of their heart' (i.e., by intentional lies, prophecies fabricated by the prophet" (Rosenberg, trans., *Mikraoth Gedoloth: Jeremiah Volume One*, 126).

worthlessness") as an example of hendiadys: "worthless predictions."[27] Divination is a forbidden practice according to Deuteronomy 18:10. The deceit of these false prophets comes from their own mind and not from the mind of God (see Jer. 23:26), yet they deliver their deceit in the name of the LORD. "Therefore," the LORD announces judgment for the prophets who prophesy falsely in his name that neither sword nor famine will come to the land (Jer. 14:15a; cf. Jer. 14:13; see also Mic. 3:5–8). The Hebrew source behind Greek Jeremiah says, "Deaths by diseases will they die" (ממותי תחלאים ימתו) (cf. Jer. 16:4a). The MT does not have this text. The Hebrew source behind Greek Jeremiah then continues: "and by famine will the prophets be finished." The MT has, "By sword and by famine will those prophets be finished" (Jer. 14:15b). In other words, the very judgment that the false prophets predict the people will avoid (i.e., sword and famine) is the one that will come upon them.

As for the people to whom the false prophets prophesy, they too are culpable (Jer. 14:16).[28] They too have said that they will see no harm such as sword or famine (Jer. 5:12; cf. Jer. 14:13). They have willingly embraced the message of the false prophets (Jer. 5:31; Mic. 2:11). Thus, "they will be cast in the streets of Jerusalem from before the sword and the famine [Syr. adds: and the plague (cf. Jer. 14:12)]" (cf. Bar. 2:25; see also Isa. 5:25; Jer. 15:2). There will be no one to bury them (cf. Jer. 7:33; 8:1–3; see also 2 Kgs. 9:10; Ps. 79:3), including their wives and their sons and their daughters (cf. Jer. 11:22; 18:21), because all have been involved in the lie (Jer. 7:18). The LORD will "pour out" on them the punishment for their evil (cf. Jer. 6:11).

14:17 "And you will say to them this word: 'Let your eyes go down with tears [MT: Let my eyes go down with tears] day and night [MT: night and day], and let them not cease [Syr., Tg. Jon., Vulg.: and let them not be silent; NET: My eyes overflow with tears day and night without ceasing (see GKC §109e)]. For with breaking/fracture the daughter of my people [or, my daughter—my people] is broken/fractured [MT: For with great breaking the virgin daughter of my people is broken; see GKC §117q] and [> MT] with a very severe wound. 14:18 If I go out to the

---

27. It is also possible that this should be rendered "idolatrous predictions" (see BDB, 47).
28. Redak: "Although they were misled by the false prophets, they should have been able to distinguish between true prophets and false ones since the true prophet bases his words on Mosaic Law, whereas the false prophets praise idol worship, which is a direct negation of Mosaic Law" (Rosenberg, trans., *Mikraoth Gedoloth: Jeremiah Volume One*, 126).

*field / country, look, those slain by a sword. And if I enter the city, look, diseases of famine. For priest and prophet [MT: both prophet (Tg. Jon.: scribe) and priest], they go to a land that they do not know [Codex L: they go about their business in a land and they do not know].'" 14:19 Have you completely rejected Judah? And from Zion have you departed [MT: Do you loathe Zion]? Why do you strike us, and we have no healing? We wait for peace / well-being, but there is no good; for a time of healing [Codex L: and for a time of healing], but look, terror. 14:20 We know, O L*ORD*, our wickedness, the iniquity of our fathers [i.e., forefathers, ancestors], for / indeed [or, that] we have sinned against you. 14:21 Stop for the sake of your name [MT: Do not spurn for the sake of your name]. Do not destroy [MT: Do not treat with contempt] the throne of your glory [or, your glorious throne]. Remember [Tg. Jon.: Let the memory of the covenant of our fathers come before you], do not break your covenant with us. 14:22 Are there among the empty idols of the nations those who cause rain? And is it the sky that gives copious showers? Is it not you [MT adds: the L*ORD* our God]? And [> LXX[51], Bo] we wait for you, for you are the one who made all these.*

*15:1 And the L*ORD* said to me, "If Moses were to stand, or Samuel [LXX[A]: or Aaron], before me [Tg. Jon.: to seek from before me], I would not be toward them [MT: this people; Tg. Jon.: there would be no pleasure before me in this people]. Send this people away that they may go out [MT: Send away from before me that they may go out; Tg. Jon.: Send away from the house of my dwelling presence that they may go into exile]. 15:2 And so, when / if they say to you, 'Where will we go out?' you will say to them, 'Thus says the L*ORD*, "Whoever to death, to death; and whoever to the sword, to the sword; and whoever to famine, to famine; and whoever to captivity, to captivity."' 15:3 And I will visit upon them four families [LXX: kinds]," the prophetic utterance of the L*ORD*: "the sword to slaughter and the dogs to drag [LXX: for tearing apart] and the animals of the land and the flying creatures of the sky [MT: and the flying creatures of the sky and the animals of the land] to devour and to destroy. 15:4 And I will give them as an object of terror to all the kingdoms of the inhabited earth on account of Manasseh [Tg. Jon.: because they did not repent like Manasseh] the son of Hezekiah the king of Judah for all [all > Codex L] that he did in Jerusalem.*

*15:5 [MT adds: כִּי] Who will have pity on you, Jerusalem? And who will mourn for you [NETS: and who will be in dread over you]? And who will turn aside [MT adds: to ask] for your well-being? 15:6 You are the one who has forsaken me," the prophetic utterance of the L*ORD*, "backward you go.*

And I will stretch out my hand and destroy you [MT: And I stretched out my hand against you and destroyed you (GKC §111w¹)], and I will not let them remain [MT: I am weary of relenting; Tg. Jon.: because you could have turned but you did not turn]. 15:7 And I will scatter them [MT: And I scattered them] with a winnowing fork [LXX: in dispersion] in the gates of my people [MT: in the gates of the land]. I am bereaved [MT: I bereave(d)]. I have destroyed my people because of their evil [MT: I have destroyed my people. From their ways they have not turned]. 15:8 Their widows are more numerous than the sand of the sea [MT: His widows are more numerous to me than the sand of the sea]. I have brought upon a young man's mother destruction at noon [MT: I have brought to / against them, against a young man's mother (Syr.: against mother and against young man; Tg. Jon.: against the troop of their young men), a destroyer at noon]. I have caused to fall upon her [Ms, Syr., Tg. Jon.: upon them] suddenly agitation and terror [LXX: trembling and haste; Tg. Jon.: armies, and they will destroy their cities]. 15:9 The woman who gives birth to seven languishes [Tg. Jon.: Their land is desolate without her people]; her life breathes out [or, she breathes out her life; ESV: she has fainted away; Tg. Jon.: they have become anguish of life]. Her sun sets [MT qere: m. sg.; MT kethiv: f. sg.] while it is still day [Tg. Jon.: Their glory has gone into exile during their lifetime]. She is ashamed and humiliated. And the rest of them to the sword will I give before their enemies," [MT adds: the prophetic utterance of the Lord].

The first clause of 14:17 ("And you will say to them this word") is often taken by modern interpreters as a conclusion to the preceding material on the grounds that what follows does not qualify as a divine oracle.[29] There are at least two problems with this understanding. First, it only applies to the text of the MT in which Jeremiah expresses his desire to weep ("Let my eyes go down with tears night and day") (cf. Jer. 8:23 [Eng., 9:1]; 13:17 [MT]; Ps. 119:136; Lam. 1:16; 3:48). This sounds more like a personal lament than a divine oracle to the people. It does not apply, however, to the Hebrew source behind Greek Jeremiah, which calls on the people to weep ("Let your eyes go down with tears day and night") (cf. Jer. 9:17 [Eng., 9:18]; 13:17 [LXX]; Lam. 2:18). Second, even if the interpreter were to accept the text of the MT, it is not the job of the interpreter to decide in advance what qualifies as a divine oracle and then to rearrange the text accordingly. It is the

---

29. See, e.g., Holladay, *Jeremiah 1*, 436. Holladay considers this to be analogous to 13:12, but the clause at the beginning of 13:12 does not settle the matter. It too can be read with what precedes or with what follows.

job of the interpreter to accept the introduction of 14:17–18 as a divine oracle and then to do the work of sorting out the implications of such an introduction.[30] The last clause of 14:17a adds: "and let them [i.e., your/my eyes] not cease" (וְאַל־תִּדְמֶינָה) (cf. MT Lam. 3:49). The Syriac, *Targum Jonathan*, and Latin Vulgate read: "and let them not be silent" (וְאַל־תִּדְמֶינָה) (cf. Lam. 2:18; 3:49 [LXX]). The negation אל strongly suggests the presence of jussive forms in 14:17a, but the NET translates as follows on the basis of GKC §109e: "My eyes overflow with tears day and night without ceasing." Jeremiah 14:17b revisits language from earlier in the book: "For with breaking/fracture the daughter of my people [cf. Jer. 6:14; 8:11, 21] is broken/fractured [MT: For with great breaking (cf. Jer. 4:6; 6:1) the virgin daughter of my people is broken] and [> MT] with a very severe wound [cf. Jer. 10:19; 30:12]" (see also Jer. 17:18). The construct phrase "the daughter of my people" (MT: "the virgin daughter of my people") is a term of affection in which the final noun in the absolute state is appositional or epexegetical: "daughter, my people" (MT: "virgin daughter, my people") (see Jer. 4:11; 6:26; 8:11 [MT], 19, 21, 22; 9:1 [MT 8:23], 6 [MT 9:7]).

In 14:18a, Jeremiah reports that if he goes out to the field or country, he sees those slain by a sword; if he enters a city, he sees diseases of famine (see Deut. 28:16; 1 Kgs. 14:11; 16:4; 21:24; Jer. 14:15–16). It is not clear whether he actually witnesses these things. It is possible that he envisions them. 14:18b is offered as an explanation of this situation: "For priest and prophet [MT: both prophet (*Tg. Jon.*: scribe) and priest], they go to a land that they do not know [Codex L: they go about their business in a land and they do not know]" (see Jer. 2:8; 5:31; 13:13; 23:11). According to the Hebrew source behind Greek Jeremiah, these leaders who have led the people astray "go to a land that they do not know" (סחרו אל ארץ לא ידעו) (cf. Jer. 15:14; 16:13; 22:28b). The LXX translator understands the verb סחרו simply to mean "they go." That is, they go into exile, leaving the land and the people they have deceived to be devastated.[31] Codex L, however, says: "they go about their business in a land and they do not know" (סחרו אל ארץ ולא ידעו). The only difference in this text is the presence of the conjunction *waw* prior to the last clause, but it requires the verb סחרו to have the sense "they go about their business" (see BDB, 695). According to Calvin, this means "that the priests and prophets would go round to seek subterfuges, as they would be destitute

---

30. Calvin suggests that the prophet's weeping was to be a kind of "word" or message to the people that could turn them to repentance (*Jeremiah*, 2:230–31).

31. Holladay argues that they go to Sheol (*Jeremiah 1*, 437–38).

of all means of escape, not knowing what to do; and *they shall not know*, that is, they shall find that a sound mind is by God taken from them, because they had demented others."[32] It is more straightforward to say that Jeremiah finds the country slain by the sword and the city diseased by famine because the prophets and priests do not pay attention to the warning signs. They simply go about their usual business of false religion, delivering messages of false security. They act in ignorance of what befalls them (cf. Lam. 4:13–15).

Jeremiah's prayer in 14:19–22 covers much of the same ground as the one in 14:7–9, even though his previous request was not granted (Jer. 14:10) and despite the fact that he has been told not to pray for the good of the people (Jer. 14:11). The first two questions in 14:19 expect negative answers (see the use of μή in the LXX). The first of these two ("Have you completely rejected Judah?") is not ignorant of the statements made in Jeremiah 6:30 and 7:29b about the fact that the Lord has rejected the people. Rather, the use of the infinitive absolute nuances the question so that it asks whether Judah is "completely" rejected. According to texts like 4:27; 5:10, 18, there seems to be hope for a faithful remnant (see also Lev. 26:44; Lam. 5:22). The second question differs between the Hebrew source behind Greek Jeremiah and the MT. The former has, "And from Zion have you departed" (ומציון גהתה נפשך) (see גהה in BDB, 155; see also Ezek. 11:23)? The latter has, "Do you loathe Zion" (אם בציון געלה נפשך) (cf. Lev. 26:30; LXX Jer. 31:32b)? The following "why" question ("Why do you strike us, and we have no healing?") is not the same as those found in 5:19; 13:22; 16:10. It concedes that the strike is just but wonders why no healing follows (cf. Jer. 8:22; see also Isa. 1:5–6). Jeremiah 14:19b repeats 8:15: "We wait for peace/well-being, but there is no good; for a time of healing [Codex L: and for a time of healing], but look, terror" (see also Jer. 14:22b).

The confession in 14:20—"We know, O Lord, our wickedness, the iniquity of our fathers, for/indeed [or, that] we have sinned against you"— is a model for all the people to follow (cf. Jer. 3:25; 14:7; Bar. 3:7; see also Jer. 8:14b). According to the Hebrew source behind Greek Jeremiah 14:21a, the specific request of this prayer is: "Stop (חדל נא) for the sake of your name" (cf. Amos 7:5; see LXX^S Jer. 14:21 and LXX Amos 7:5).[33] The parallel is: "Do not destroy (אל תחבל) your glorious throne." On the other hand, the MT has: "Do not spurn (אל תנאץ) for the sake of your name. Do not treat with contempt (אל תנבל)[34] your glorious throne" (cf.

---

32. Calvin, *Jeremiah*, 2:234.
33. See also Ezekiel's concern in Ezekiel 9:8; 11:13.
34. Mlt Mss: ואל תנבל

Deut. 32:15, 19). The prayer for the LORD to act for the sake of his name has been discussed in the commentary on 14:7. The "glorious throne" (cf. Jer. 17:12; Ps. 47:9 [Eng., 47:8]; Lam. 5:19) here is not the same as the throne anticipated in 3:17, which presupposes the absence of the ark of the covenant (Jer. 3:16) and envisions a new Jerusalem in a new creation (Isa. 65:17–25) without the temporary structure of the temple (Isa. 66:1a); nor is it the throne of the Davidic king (Jer. 13:13; 17:25). The glorious throne in 14:21 is the ark of the covenant (see references in the commentary on 3:17). The prayer is that the ark of the covenant and the temple that houses it would not be lost, not because these things should be trusted in the manner of Jeremiah 7:4, but because they are symbols of God's special presence with his people (Exod. 25:22; 1 Kgs. 8:27–30). Thus, Jeremiah prays, "Remember, do not break your covenant with us" (cf. Add. Dan. 3:34).[35] The irony is that the people are the ones who have broken the covenant (Jer. 11:10; 15:6). The LORD has remained faithful (see Lev. 26:44). This includes faithfulness to judge the people according to the terms of the old covenant (Lev. 26; Deut. 28). It also includes faithfulness to restore the people according to his word concerning a new covenant relationship (Jer. 31:31–34).[36]

The questions in Jeremiah 14:22a also expect negative answers (cf. Jer. 14:19a). "Are there among the empty idols of the nations those who cause rain" (cf. Jer. 2:5b; 8:19b; 16:19b; Ep. Jer. 52)? The answer is no. Only the one true God does this (see Jer. 5:24). "And is it the sky that gives copious showers?" The forces of nature do not act by themselves (Jer. 8:2; 10:2). They depend upon the providence

---

35. McKane asks whether this covenant is the covenant with David (see Pss. 89:4, 29, 34 [Eng., 89:3, 28, 33]; 132:12; Jer. 33:21) or Josiah's covenant (2 Kgs. 23:3) (*Jeremiah I–XXV*, 334), but *Targum Jonathan* is undoubtedly correct to assume a reference to the Sinai covenant ("Let the memory of the covenant of our fathers come before you"). The Sinai covenant is the only major divine-human covenant in the Bible that is conditional and thus breakable. The covenant with David (2 Sam. 7:12–16), which is about one particular son of David who will build the temple and reign over an everlasting kingdom, is unconditional (see Ps. 89:34 [Eng., 89:33]). It is only conditional when reapplied to the plurality of sons of David who reign on the throne in the meantime (see Ps. 89:31–33 [Eng., 89:30–32]). See Shepherd, *Text in the Middle*, 122–29.

36. "But God had hidden means of accomplishing his purpose; for he did, according to the common apprehension of men, abolish the covenant by which the Jews thought him to be bound to them; and yet he remained true; for his truth shone forth at length from darkness, after the time of exile was completed" (Calvin, *Jeremiah*, 2:243).

of God.[37] Thus, Jeremiah prays, "Is it not you [MT adds: the LORD our God]? And [> LXX[51], Bo] we wait for you, for you are the one who made all these" (cf. Isa. 25:9; 26:8; Jer. 14:19b). The LORD, not the idols, is the one who made "all these" (i.e., the rain, the sky, and the copious showers; cf. Zech. 8:12; see also Isa. 37:16; Jer. 10:11–13; 32:17).[38]

When the LORD begins to speak in 15:1, the syntax of the protasis in the Hebrew text indicates that it should not be translated as if there were a compound subject with a plural verb ("If Moses and Samuel were to stand before me"). Rather, the verb is singular; Moses is the main subject; and Samuel is given as an alternative ("If Moses were to stand, or Samuel, before me").[39] Codex Alexandrinus has "Aaron" in place of "Samuel" (cf. Exod. 4:29; 7:6, 10; 8:8 [Eng., 8:12]; 10:3, 8; 16:6; 19:24; Lev. 9:23; Num. 1:17, 44; 3:39; 4:34, 37, 45, 46; 8:20; 14:5; 17:8; 20:6, 8). Psalm 99:6 names Moses, Aaron, and Samuel together. To "stand before" (i.e., serve) the LORD here is to intercede in the role of a prophet on behalf of the people before the LORD (*Tg. Jon.*: "to seek from before me"; cf. 1 Kgs. 17:1; 18:15; 2 Kgs. 3:14; 5:16; Jer. 15:19; 18:20; see also Jer. 35:19). Moses (Exod. 17:11; 32:11–14; Num. 14:13–20; Deut. 9:25–29) and Samuel (1 Sam. 7:5, 9; 12:19, 23) are well known for such intercession,[40] but not even they could successfully intercede on behalf of the people in the present situation.[41] Thus, it will be no different for Jeremiah, a prophet like Moses (Jer. 1:4–9;

---

37. McKane appears to be unsettled as to whether this verse alludes to the drought referenced in 14:1–6 (*Jeremiah I–XXV*, 316, 332–33). It is true that the text is more of a general statement that the LORD who alone has control over nature is the one for whom the people should wait (cf. 1 Kgs. 18), but the specific focus on rain and the parallel structuring of 14:1–16 and 14:17–15:4 make it very difficult to expect careful readers not to make the connection.

38. See Keil, *Jeremiah*, 159. Calvin thinks that "all these" refers to God's punishments (*Jeremiah*, 2:246). Holladay thinks אֵלֶּה ("these") should be revocalized as אָלָה ("curse") (*Jeremiah 1*, 439).

39. See Michael B. Shepherd, "The Compound Subject in Biblical Hebrew," *HS* 52 (2011): 107–20.

40. Rashi: "Both were needed to beg mercy for Israel, but first they induced them to repent, and afterwards they prayed on their behalf, but they had no idea of turning away My wrath until they had induced them to repent" (Rosenberg, trans., *Mikraoth Gedoloth: Jeremiah Volume One*, 129).

41. The sentiment is very similar to that of Ezekiel 14:14: "And even if these three men were in its midst—Noah, Daniel, and Job—they by their own righteousness would only deliver themselves" (cf. Ezek. 18). See Jeremiah 5:1.

see Jer. 7:16; 11:14; 14:11). Despite his efforts in prayer (Jer. 14:7–9, 19–22), the LORD will judge the people. Nevertheless, Jeremiah will continue to pray for them (see, e.g., Jer. 42:4). According to the Hebrew source behind Greek Jeremiah, the LORD says that he would not be toward "them," which presumably refers back to Moses and Samuel. That is, he would not heed their prayer. The MT, however, says that he would not be toward "this people" (*Tg. Jon.*: "there would be no pleasure before me in this people"). He would turn his back on the people despite the intercession of Moses or Samuel. The Hebrew source behind Greek Jeremiah puts the phrase "this people" as the object of the following imperative: "Send this people away that they may go out [MT: Send away from before me that they may go out; *Tg. Jon.*: Send away from the house of my dwelling presence that they may go into exile]." This is an ironic twist of the LORD's words through Moses in Exodus 5:1; 7:16, 26; 8:16 (Eng., 8:20); 9:1, 13; 10:3: "Send my people away."[42] The expected response from the people is, "Where will we go out" (Jer. 15:2a)? Jeremiah is then to say to them, "Thus says the LORD, 'Whoever to death, to death; and whoever to the sword, to the sword; and whoever to famine, to famine; and whoever to captivity, to captivity'" (Jer. 15:2b; cf. Jer. 14:12, 16; 18:21; 43:11; Ezek. 14:21; Ezra 7:26; Rev. 13:10). "Death" here stands for the "plague" (cf. Jer. 14:12). This is not a series of graded judgments but a collection of varied yet equally deadly judgments. Critical scholars usually assume that the fourth item ("captivity") is an addition to the usual triad,[43] but there is no textual evidence for this secondary classification.

Jeremiah 15:3 adds four more kinds of judgment to the list: "the sword to slaughter and the dogs to drag [LXX: for tearing apart] and the animals of the land and the flying creatures of the sky [MT: and the flying creatures of the sky and the animals of the land] to devour and to destroy" (cf. 2 Kgs. 9:36; Jer. 7:33; 19:7; 22:19; Ezek. 14:21; Rev. 6:8; *T. Jud.* 23:3). The sword is a repeat from 15:2. Jeremiah 15:4 then concludes, "And I will give them as an object of terror[44] to all the kingdoms of the inhabited earth on account of Manasseh [*Tg. Jon.*:

---

42. "Moses' task was to get the people out of Egypt; Jrm's task is to get the people of out Yahweh's presence" (Holladay, *Jeremiah 1*, 440).

43. E.g., McKane, *Jeremiah I–XXV*, 335.

44. The *kethiv* (זועה) and *qere* (זעוה) are interchangeable (BDB, 266). See Deuteronomy 28:25; Isaiah 28:19; Jeremiah 24:9; 29:18; 34:17; Ezekiel 23:46; 2 Chronicles 29:8. This is a case of metathesis or transposition (cf. כבש and כשב). See also Barr, *Comparative Philology*, 96–101.

because they did not repent like Manasseh][45] the son of Hezekiah the king of Judah for all [all > Codex L] that he did in Jerusalem." *Targum Jonathan* interprets the text to mean that the people will face judgment because they have not repented like Manasseh (see 2 Chr. 33:12–13; *Pr. Man.*; 4Q381; *m. Sanh.* 10:2), but the book of Kings repeatedly identifies Manasseh and the influence of his religious aberrations as the cause of the exile (2 Kgs. 21:10–16; 23:26–27; 24:3–4). Manasseh did not follow in the footsteps of his father Hezekiah (2 Kgs. 21:2). The reforms of his grandson Josiah (2 Kgs. 23), which were designed to eradicate the practices established by Manasseh (2 Kgs. 21), were unable to overcome completely the persistence of what had become so deeply ingrained among the people (see, e.g., Jer. 7:30–8:3).

The final poem in 15:5–9 opens with a series of questions from the LORD for Jerusalem: "Who will have pity on you, Jerusalem? And who will mourn for you?[46] And who will turn aside [MT adds: to ask] for your well-being" (Jer. 15:5; cf. Isa. 51:19; Nah. 3:7; see also Jer. 16:5; Ps. 69:21 [Eng., 69:20])? According to McKane, the added כִּי at the beginning of 15:5 in the MT is a redactional link.[47] Of course, the implied answer to these questions is that no one will do these things (see Lam. 1:2, 16, 17, 21). The sense of the third question is usually taken to be, "Who will turn aside to ask how you are doing" (e.g., NET, ESV)?[48] This may very well be correct, but a comparison with Jeremiah 29:7 and Psalm 122:6–7 suggests another possibility: "Who will turn aside to pray for your well-being?"

The fronting of the pronoun אַתְּ ("You") at the beginning of 15:6a suggests a contrast, as if to say, "It is not I who have forsaken you. You are the one who has forsaken me" (see Deut. 32:15). This is in response to the prayer that the LORD not break his covenant with the people (Jer. 14:21b). It is not the LORD who has broken the covenant (Lev. 26:44). The people are the ones who have broken the covenant (Jer. 11:10). It is only because the people have forsaken the LORD that he has forsaken them (Jer. 7:29; 12:7; 23:33, 39). It is Jerusalem that goes "backward" and not forward, refusing to heed the LORD's voice and persisting in stubbornness (see Jer. 7:24). Therefore, the LORD is not

---

45. See Neusner, *Jeremiah in Talmud and Midrash*, 363.

46. The LXX translation—"and who will be in dread over you?" (NETS)—is perhaps based on reading נוד as "flee" (cf. Jer. 49:30) rather than "mourn."

47. McKane, *Jeremiah I–XXV*, 337.

48. Rudolph (*BHS* apparatus) suggests that לִשְׁאֹל ("to ask") has fallen out of the Hebrew source behind Greek Jeremiah due to homoioarchton (see לִשְׁלֹם).

"toward" this people nor those who intercede for them (Jer. 15:1). He will stretch out his hand and destroy them (Jer. 15:6b; cf. Jer. 6:12b). The LXX translates the first two verbs of 15:6b and the first verb of 15:7a as if they were *waw + yiqtol* forms ("And I will stretch out my hand and destroy you . . . And I will scatter them . . ."). The MT, however, has *wayyiqtol* forms ("And I stretched out my hand against you and destroyed you . . . And I scattered them . . .").[49] According to the Hebrew source behind Greek Jeremiah, the last clause of 15:6b says: "and I will not let them remain" (וְלֹא אֲנַחֵם [Rudolph: (נִלְאֵיתִי הַנָּחֵם]). The MT says: "I am weary of relenting" (נִלְאֵיתִי הִנָּחֵם) (cf. Jer. 6:11a).

The LORD will "scatter" the people with a winnowing fork (Jer. 15:7a; cf. Jer. 4:11–12; 13:14, 24; 31:10). According to the Hebrew source behind Greek Jeremiah, he says that he will do this "in the gates of my people"; that is, in the cities of the land of Judah (cf. Jer. 14:2). On the other hand, the MT has the phrase "in the gates of the land." It is not clear whether this refers to the cities of the land of Judah or to the cities of the inhabited earth (i.e., exile).[50] LXX Jeremiah 15:7b reflects שָׁכַלְתִּי (*qal* stem): "I am bereaved." The MT has שִׁכַּלְתִּי (*piel* stem): "I bereave(d)" (cf. Deut. 32:25). This language anticipates the image of mothers losing their sons in 15:8–9 (cf. 1 Sam. 15:33). The last clause of the Hebrew source behind Greek Jeremiah 15:7b says, "I have destroyed my people because of their evil (מרעתם)." The MT says, "I have destroyed my people. From their ways they have not turned (מדרכיהם לוא שבו)" (cf. Jer. 7:5–6; Amos 4:6–11).

---

49. "The perplexities which are encountered, both historical and translational, with Hebrew verbs in a passage like this have a more general application. Even if the correct translational procedure is to render verbs in the past tense, it does not follow that the events which a prophet describes as past actually lie in the past. The question arises whether when a judgement is made that verbs are 'prophetic perfects,' it is right to render them as future tenses or as past tenses, and there are clearly disadvantages in both procedures. If they are translated as past tenses, there is no overt indication that they refer to events which still lie in the future. If they are translated as future tenses, the exceptional nature of the prophetic utterance and perhaps of the interior state of the prophet are lost. The oddness which should be preserved is precisely that he speaks of future events as if they were past events. Thus we may be misrepresenting his intention, if we suppose that he is 'predicting' future events. We should consider whether he speaks of future events as if they were past because their unfolding is so inevitable for him" (McKane, *Jeremiah I–XXV*, 342–43).
50. Holladay argues that it refers to the gates of Sheol (*Jeremiah 1*, 442).

The Lord says in 15:8a that the widows of the people are more numerous than the sand of the sea.[51] The descendants of Abraham and Jacob were to be as numerous as the sand on the seashore (Gen. 22:17; 32:13), but now their widows will surpass that number (cf. Isa. 10:22; see also Jer. 10:24). The ravaging judgments of 15:2–3 have so decimated the male population that wives are without husbands and young maidens are presumably without young men to marry. This recalls the image of Isaiah 4:1 in which seven women grab one man and say that they will provide their own food and clothing if only his name would be called upon them (i.e., if only he would be their husband) so that their reproach might be removed. The Hebrew source behind Greek Jeremiah 15:8a then adds, "I have brought upon a young man's mother destruction at noon" (הבאתי על אם בחור שוד בצהרים) (cf. Jer. 6:26). The MT says, "I have brought to/against them, against a young man's mother, a destroyer at noon" (הבאתי להם על אם בחור שדד בצהרים). Rashi suggests that the mother here is Jerusalem,[52] but it is more likely that this is a continuation of the first clause of 15:8a. Not only have wives lost their husbands, but also mothers have lost their young sons in battle "at noon" (see commentary on Jer. 6:4; cf. Zeph. 2:4; see also Jer. 18:21). According to the Hebrew source behind Greek Jeremiah 15:8b and most Masoretic manuscripts, the Lord has caused to fall upon "her" (i.e., the mother) suddenly "agitation and terror" (LXX: "trembling and haste"; *Tg. Jon.*: "armies, and they will destroy their cities").[53] One Masoretic manuscript, the Syriac, and *Targum Jonathan* say that he has caused these things to fall upon "them" (i.e., either the young men or both the young men and the husbands).

"The woman who gives birth to seven languishes" (Jer. 15:9a; *Tg. Jon.*: "Their land is desolate without her people"; cf. 1 Sam. 2:5; Ruth 4:15; 2 Macc. 7; see also Jer. 14:2). The mother who is blessed and fruitful becomes cursed and bereaved. Translation of the next clause (נפחה נפשה) depends upon whether נפשה is the subject ("her life breathes out") or the object ("she breathes out her life"). Since the remainder of 15:9a speaks of her shame and humiliation, it is generally considered desirable not to understand נפחה נפשה to mean that she dies but that she swoons (e.g., ESV: "she has fainted away"). "Her sun sets while it is still day.[54] She is ashamed and humiliated" (cf. Jer. 14:3–4). This

---

51. This is hyperbole according to Bullinger, *Figures of Speech*, 427, 758.
52. See Rosenberg, trans., *Mikraoth Gedoloth: Jeremiah Volume One*, 132.
53. Note how the Targum has found a way to incorporate עיר ("city"), the more frequently occurring homonym of עיר ("agitation").
54. *Tg. Jon.*: "Their glory has gone into exile during their lifetime."

language is very close to that of Micah 3:6–7 (see also Amos 8:9–10), which announces judgment on the false prophets: "Therefore, it will be night for you without a prophetic vision, and it will grow dark for you without divination by casting lots. And the sun will set on the prophets, and the day will be dark on them. And those who see prophetic visions will be ashamed, and those who divine by casting lots will feel humiliation. And they will cover over moustache, all of them, for there will be no answer from God."[55] As for the rest of the people, the LORD will give them to the sword before their enemies (Jer. 15:9b; cf. Jer. 6:9). A comparison with Jeremiah 11:23 suggests that this is the remnant of the wicked, not the righteous remnant.

---

55. See Shepherd, *Commentary on the Book of the Twelve*, 249–51.

JEREMIAH 15:10–21

15:10 Woe to me, O my mother! As whom did you bear me? A man of contention and strife to all the land [MT: Woe to me, O my mother, that/ because you bore me, a man of contention and strife to all the land]. I have not lent, and they have not lent to me [LXX: I neither owed nor did anyone owe me]. As for my strength, it has failed among those who curse/despise me [MT qere: Each one of them curses/despises me]. 15:11 Amen, O LORD, when they advance, if I have not entreated you in the time of their calamity and in the time of their distress for good against the enemy [MT: The LORD said, "Have I not let you loose for good? Have I not caused the enemy (Syr. adds: from the north) to entreat you in time of calamity and in time of distress?"].[1] 15:12 "Will iron be known? And a bronze covering is your strength [MT: Will one break (pc Mss: know; Symm.: harm; Aq., Vulg.: join) iron, iron from the north, and bronze (or, Will iron break [pc Mss: know; Symm.: harm; Aq., Vulg.: join] iron from the north, and bronze)?].[2] 15:13 And your treasures will I give as plunder in exchange for all your sins and in all your borders [MT: Your wealth and your treasures as plunder will I give not for a price but (but > 2 Mss) for all your sins and in all your borders (mlt Mss: border)]. 15:14 And I will cause you to serve [cf. pc Mss, Syr.] all around your enemies in a land that you do not know [Codex L: And I will cause your enemies to pass through (mlt Mss: to serve in) a land (mlt Mss add: that) you do not know]. For a fire is kindled in my anger; against you [pc Mss: forever] will it burn."

15:15 [MT adds: As for you, you know] O LORD, remember me and visit me and avenge yourself for me [NETS: hold me guiltless] against those who pursue/persecute me. Not to forbearance [MT: Do not as one who is patient take me]. Know [or, Acknowledge] my bearing for you reproach 15:16 from those who spurn your words [MT: Your words were found; Syr.: And I kept your commands; Tg. Jon.: I received your word(s)]. Make an end of them [MT: and I ate them; Syr.: and I did them; Tg. Jon.: and I confirmed them] that your word may become to me a reason for rejoicing [MT: and your word (kethiv: words) became to me a reason for rejoicing] and a cause for the joy of my heart. For your name is

---

1. *Tg. Jon.:* "The Lord said, 'Will it not end well for you if they come and seek you when I bring the enemy against them and he oppresses them?'"
2. *Tg. Jon.:* "A king who is strong like iron will come up to help a king who is strong like iron and bronze. He will come from the north against him to break him."

called upon me, O LORD *[MT adds: the God of] hosts. 15:17 I did not sit in the council of merrymakers, but I exulted [LXX: acted reverently] before [or, because of] your hand [Syr.: and I did not fear before / because of your hand; Tg. Jon.: and I did not rejoice before / because of your word]. Alone I sat, for it was with indignation [LXX: bitterness; Tg. Jon.: prophecies of curse] that I was filled [MT: I did not sit in the council of merrymakers and exult. Before (or, Because of) your hand I sat alone, for it was with indignation that you filled me.] 15:18 Why do those who cause me pain have victory over me [MT: Why has my pain been perpetual]? My wound [MT: And my wound] is incurable. Whence will I be healed [MT: It refuses to be healed.]? Will you indeed be to me like a deceptive water source, that is, unreliable water? 15:19 Therefore, thus says the* LORD, *"If you will return, I will restore you, and [and > MT] before me you will stand. And if you bring forth what is precious from what is worthless [Tg. Jon.: if you cause the wicked to return to be righteous], like my mouth [or, according to my command] will you be. And [And > MT] they will turn to you; but you, you will not turn to them. 15:20 And I will make [or, appoint; lit., give] you to this people as a fortified bronze wall; and they will fight against you, but they will not prevail against you, for with you am I to deliver you 15:21[3] and to rescue you from the hand of evil men and from the palm of terror-striking men."*

This section features the third (Jer. 15:10–14) and fourth (Jer. 15:15–21) of Jeremiah's confessions (cf. Jer. 11:18–23 and 12:1–6). The word אֵם ("mother") in 15:10 establishes a catchword link to the previous section (Jer. 15:8). Just as the LORD bereaves mothers of their young sons in battle (Jer. 15:7b–9), so Jeremiah says, "Woe to me, O my mother!" The MT follows this with כִּי יְלִדְתִּנִי ("that/because you bore me"), as if the prophet were cursing the day of his birth (cf. Isa. 45:10; Jer. 20:14–18; Job 3; see also Jer. 16:1–4). That is, Jeremiah wishes his mother had been bereaved from the beginning. The Hebrew source behind Greek Jeremiah, however, poses a question: מִי יְלִדְתָּנִי ("As whom did you bear me?"). The answer is, "A man of contention and strife to all the land" (see Jer. 11:20b; 12:1a; 20:12b; cf. Hab. 1:3).[4] Jeremiah then

---

3. MT 15:20b–21: "for with you am I to deliver you and to rescue you," the prophetic utterance of the LORD, "and I will rescue you from the hand of evil men and purchase/redeem you from the palm of terror-striking men."

4. According to Holladay, Jeremiah is "both the victim of the people's quarrels and the mediator of Yahweh's quarrel with the people" (*Jeremiah 1*, 452). See Jeremiah 2:9.

adds, "I have not lent, and they have not lent to me" (see Exod. 22:24).[5] In other words, he asserts that he has acted above reproach in his role as prophet among the people (cf. 1 Sam. 12:1–5; see also Neh. 5), but his strength has failed among those who curse/despise him (כחי כָּלָה [מקללני]) (MT *qere*: "Each one of them curses/despises me" [כֻּלֹּה מְקַלְלַנִי]). The MT *kethiv* כלה מקללוני is usually emended to כֻּלְּהֶם קִלְלוּנִי ("All of them curse/despise me"). The choice of the *piel* of קלל ("despise, treat lightly or with contempt") here rather than ארר ("curse") may allude to Genesis 12:3a: "I will bless those who bless you, and each one who despises you (וּמְקַלֶּלְךָ) will I curse."

The MT presents Jeremiah 15:11 as the Lord's discourse: "The Lord said (אמר יהוה), 'Have I not let you loose (*kethiv*: שֵׁרוֹתִךָ; *qere*: שֵׁרִיתִיךָ)[6] for good (לטובה)? Have I not caused the enemy (אֵת הָאֹיֵב) [Syr. adds: from the north (cf. MT 15:12)] to entreat you in time of calamity and in time of distress?'"[7] If the people of Judah are the enemy, then this means that despite their persecution of Jeremiah they will eventually turn to him for guidance, thus setting him free (e.g., Jer. 37:3; 42:2).[8] If the enemy is Babylon, then perhaps this is in anticipation of the setting free of Jeremiah (Jer. 39:11–14) and the option given to him to stay in the land or not (Jer. 40:1–6).[9] On the other hand, the Hebrew source behind Greek Jeremiah presents 15:11 as Jeremiah's discourse: "Amen, O Lord (אמן יהוה), when they advance (בְּאַשְׁרָם), if I have not entreated you in the time of their calamity and in the time of their distress for good (לטובה) against the enemy (אֶל הָאֹיֵב)" (cf. 28:6; see also LXX Jer. 3:19). In other words, may his persecutors' words of contempt (Jer. 15:10) come upon him if he has not been faithful to perform his role as prophetic intercessor for their good in their time of need against the enemy (see Jer. 14:7–9, 11, 19–22; 17:16; 18:20).[10]

---

5. Bullinger says this is synecdoche "for all kinds of business transactions and contracts which are liable to gender strife" (*Figures of Speech*, 634).

6. For proposals for this verb, see Rudolph's *BHS* apparatus. See also Holladay, *Jeremiah 1*, 446, 453 ("I have armored you").

7. Following Isaiah 53:6, Holladay proposes Jeremiah 15:11b to mean: "I have imposed on you in a time of disaster and a time of distress the enemy" (Holladay, *Jeremiah 1*, 453). For the phrases "time of calamity" and "time of distress," see Jeremiah 14:8; 17:17; 30:7.

8. See Rashi (Rosenberg, trans., *Mikraoth Gedoloth: Jeremiah Volume One*, 134).

9. See Calvin, *Jeremiah*, 2:272.

10. Bright takes a somewhat similar view, but his translation is a combination of Greek Jeremiah and an emended MT: "But I swear, O Yahweh, for their good I have served [שֵׁרַתִּיךָ] thee, and with thee for the foe interceded in

Jeremiah 15:12 is a notoriously difficult verse, and a commentator can only hope to lay out the different options for interpretation well. Part of the difficulty is the textual variation in witnesses to the main verb, which involves confusion of ד and ר: "Will iron be known (הֲיִוָּדַע)? And a bronze covering is your strength [MT: Will one break (הֲיָרֹעַ); pc Mss: know [הֲיֵדַע]; Symm.: harm [= הֲיֵרַע]; Aq., Vulg.: join [from רעה]) iron, iron from the north, and bronze (or, Will iron break [pc Mss: know; Symm.: harm; Aq., Vulg.: join] iron from the north, and bronze)?]." The LORD is apparently the speaker here in both the MT (see MT 15:11) and the LXX (see "your strength," addressed to Jeremiah at the end of 15:12). If the MT of 15:12 represented by Codex L is accepted, there are essentially two options for translation: (1) "Will one break iron, iron from the north, and bronze?" or (2) "Will iron break iron from the north, and bronze?" Rashi adopts the second option and interprets the first "iron" to be the people and the second "iron" to be Jeremiah: "I say that iron that comes from the north is harder than other iron, and this is its interpretation: They were compared to iron, '(above 6:28) Going tale bearing like copper and iron.' And concerning Jeremiah it is stated: '(above 1:18) I have made you . . . into an iron pillar and into copper walls,' and his is stronger than theirs, for Nebuchadnezzar will come upon them according to his words."[11] Keil, however, suggests the following sense: "As little as a man can break iron, will the Jewish people be able to break the hostile power of the north."[12] Holladay proposes a variation on option one in which the indefinite subject "one" becomes "he" (Hananiah from Jer. 28, specifically 28:13–14): "Can he break iron [that is, the theoretical iron pegs], iron from the north [that is, the yoke of Nebuchadrezzar], and bronze [that is, the fortified wall of bronze into which Yahweh had made Jrm,

---

the time of his trouble and woe" (*Jeremiah*, 106, 109). This translation also assumes that "the foe" is the same as those who curse/despise Jeremiah. Greek Jeremiah and the Syriac require the enemy to be a foreign nation.

11. Rosenberg, trans., *Mikraoth Gedoloth: Jeremiah Volume One*, 134. Rashi also mentions the interpretation of *Targum Jonathan*, according to which the first "iron" is Pharaoh and the second "iron" is Nebuchadnezzar: "A king who is strong like iron will come up to help a king who is strong like iron and bronze. He will come from the north against him to break him." McKane wonders if readers of the phrase "iron from the north" in the MT can realistically be expected to think of iron that is known to be "harder" rather than the enemy from the north so well-established thus far in the book (*Jeremiah I–XXV*, 349). Rashi has cleverly incorporated an understanding of both into his commentary.

12. Keil, *Jeremiah*, 163.

15:20]?"[13] But the Hebrew source behind Greek Jeremiah 15:12 makes no reference to iron from the north or the enemy from the north: "Will iron be known? And a bronze covering is your strength." This text includes חילך ("your strength") from the beginning of MT 15:13. The answer to the question, "Will iron be known?" is found in Jeremiah 6:27–30. The people are stubborn like "bronze and iron" (Jer. 6:28), but they are also like "rejected silver" (Jer. 6:30). Their impurities are known (Jer. 6:29). On the other hand, Jeremiah is strong like a bronze wall (Jer. 1:18; 15:20). Thus, 15:12 is the LORD's encouragement to the prophet in light of his concerns expressed in 15:10–11.

The text of 15:13–14 bears a striking resemblance to that of MT 17:3–4.[14] According to Parke-Taylor, "there is a consensus among exegetes that 17:3–4 is the primary passage, secondarily inserted after 15:12."[15] In these verses (15:13–14), the LORD either addresses Judah (as in 17:3–4) or Jeremiah as representative of the people.[16] He says that he will give Judah's treasures (cf. Isa. 39:2, 6; Jer. 20:5) as plunder in exchange for its sins, and this will take place in all its borders. According to the MT, this will be done "not for a price" that the LORD owes but for all Judah's sins (cf. Isa. 50:1; 55:1). The Hebrew source behind Greek Jeremiah 15:14a says, "And I will cause you to serve (והעבדתיך) all around your enemies in a land that you do not know" (cf. Jer. 16:13; 22:28; see also LXX 14:18b). This anticipates exile. Codex L, however, says, "And I will cause your enemies to pass (והעברתי) through a land you do not know." It is not clear what this means, and the reading appears to be in part the result of scribal confusion of ד and ר. The reason for the judgment announced in 15:13–14a is given in 15:14b: "For a fire is kindled in my anger; against you [pc Mss: forever] will it burn" (cf. Deut. 32:22).

---

13. Holladay, *Jeremiah 1*, 455.

14. For an analysis of the textual variation between the two, see Parke-Taylor, *Formation of the Book of Jeremiah*, 23–31. MT 17:1–4 does not appear in the LXX. It is possible that a Hebrew scribe or the Greek translator accidentally skipped from יהוה in 16:21b to יהוה in 17:5a (see Janzen, *Studies in the Text of Jeremiah*, 117), but see commentary on these verses.

15. Parke-Taylor, *Formation of the Book of Jeremiah*, 28. But see again the commentary on Jeremiah 17:1–4.

16. Holladay argues that Jeremiah is addressed exclusively: "Your strength and your treasures I will give away, with no recompense: but at least this loot will not be recompense for your sins, as is the case with the people, nor to buy territorial integrity, as is the case with the monarchy" (*Jeremiah 1*, 456). Cf. Jeremiah 45:5.

When the next confession begins in 15:15, it is clear that Jeremiah is the speaker again. The beginning of this verse in the MT (אתה ידעת ["As for you, you know"]) is not present in the Hebrew source behind Greek Jeremiah. Jeremiah prays that the Lord would "remember" him (i.e., with kindness) and "visit" him (i.e., care for him) and "avenge" himself for him against those who pursue/persecute him (cf. Ps. 106:4). This is not unlike Jeremiah's prayers for vengeance in 11:20 and 12:3 (see also Jer. 17:18), except here he suggests that the Lord would be avenging himself on his behalf. This is because Jeremiah bears the Lord's name (Jer. 15:16). Any reproach on Jeremiah is a reproach on the Lord's name. Therefore, to avenge Jeremiah is to avenge the name of the Lord (cf. Jer. 14:7, 21). The elliptical text of the Hebrew source behind Greek Jeremiah (אל לארך אפים ["Not to forbearance"]) finds its interpretation in the MT: אל לארך אפך תקחני ("Do not as one who is patient take me").[17] The negation אל does not negate the verb but the immediately following phrase (see GKC §152h; cf. Jer. 10:24b; Pss. 6:2; 38:2 [Eng., 6:1; 38:1]). Thus, the MT is not, "Do not take me as one who is patient," but, "Do not as one who is patient take me." That is, Jeremiah prays not that he would avoid death altogether but that he would not as a result of divine forbearance toward his persecutors be "taken" (cf. Gen. 5:24; 2 Kgs. 2:10; Isa. 53:8; Ps. 49:16 [Eng., 49:15]; Job 1:21). He asks that the Lord "know" or acknowledge how he has born reproach for him (Jer. 15:15b; cf. Ps. 69:8 [Eng., 69:7]; see also Jer. 31:19; Zeph. 3:18).

The text of the Hebrew source behind Greek Jeremiah 15:15b continues into 15:16a: "Know [or, Acknowledge] my bearing for you reproach from those who spurn your words (מנאצי דבריך)" (cf. Isa. 5:24; Jer. 23:17). The MT, however, begins a new clause in 15:16a: "Your words were found" (נמצאו דבריך). This latter reading appears to be a reference to the discovery of the book of the Torah during the reign of Josiah in 622 BC (see 2 Kgs. 22:13; 23:2).[18] The Hebrew source behind

---

17. "I.e., through being so lenient with my persecutors that they have time to destroy me" (Bright, *Jeremiah*, 110). See Exodus 34:6.

18. See Thompson, *Book of Jeremiah*, 396; Holladay, *Jeremiah 1*, 458. This does not require that the events of 622 predate or occur simultaneously with the call of Jeremiah (627 BC). The placement of words in Jeremiah's mouth (Jer. 1:9) and Jeremiah's eating of the words of the Torah (MT Jer. 15:16) are complementary but not identical. The former is primarily to identify Jeremiah as a prophet like Moses (Deut. 18:18). The latter describes Jeremiah's acceptance of the Torah and thus his agreement with the reforms of Josiah. His previous call as a prophet is precisely what makes him so receptive to the words of the Torah.

Greek Jeremiah then says, "Make an end of them (כַּלֵּם) that your word may become (וִיהִי דְבָרְךָ) to me a reason for rejoicing and a cause for the joy of my heart." This suggests that Jeremiah's ability to rejoice in the LORD's word is contingent upon the demise of his persecutors. The MT says: "and I ate them (וָאֹכְלֵם), and your word became (וַיְהִי דְבָרְךָ)[19] to me a reason for rejoicing and a cause for the joy of my heart." Jeremiah says that he "ate" (i.e., received, accepted) the recently discovered words of the Torah, and this word of the LORD became to him a reason to rejoice (cf. Deut. 8:3; 28:47; Pss. 19:11 [Eng., 19:10]; 119:103; Ezek. 2:8–3:3; Neh. 8:12; Rev. 10; see also Deut. 30:14; Josh. 1:8; Isa. 59:21; Ps. 1:2).[20] This is because the LORD's name is called upon him, and he belongs to the LORD as his true prophet (Jer. 15:16b). This language is ordinarily reserved in the book of Jeremiah for the temple (e.g., Jer. 7:10, 14) and the people (e.g., Jer. 14:9; see also the city in Jer. 25:29),[21] but Jeremiah stands here as a representative of the people of God, especially the faithful remnant of this people.

In Jeremiah 15:17, the prophet recounts his former conduct, which becomes the basis for his question in 15:18. The syntax of 15:17 differs between the MT (see the placement of the *athnach*) and the early versions (LXX, Syr., *Tg. Jon.*), primarily in the location of the phrase "before [or, because of] your hand." The MT places this phrase with what follows it: "I did not sit in the council of merrymakers and exult. Before [or, Because of] your hand I sat alone, for it was with indignation that you filled me." The above translation of the Hebrew source

---

19. The *kethiv* of Codex L (ויהי דבריך) lacks subject-verb agreement.

20. This word, however, has also become a reproach to Jeremiah (Jer. 15:15b; 20:8–9). Ezekiel also "eats" a scroll, which becomes sweet like honey in his mouth. "Like Jeremiah, Ezekiel's own reception of the scroll is positive (Jer 15:16; Ezek 3:3), but the message of the scroll is hard for the people and leads to their rejection of the prophet (Jer 20:8–9; Ezek 2:5, 8–10). This text serves as a bridge between the Jeremiah text and Revelation 10. In the Revelation passage, John says that he saw an angel with a little scroll opened in his hand (Rev 10:2; cf. Jer 32:11, 14). The voice from heaven instructed him to take the scroll and eat it (Rev 10:8–9). It was sweet like honey in his mouth, but it made his stomach bitter (Rev 10:10). The word 'bitter' is likely a play on the Hebrew words מַר ('bitter') and מְרִי ('rebellion') (Ezek 2:8; cf. Exod 15:23). Much like the prophets before him, John found that he was able to accept the scroll, but he would later find that it was hard to handle (Rev 1:9). The Revelation 10 passage is largely based on the Ezekiel text, but that text is itself a reading of another prophet" (Shepherd, *Text in the Middle*, 146).

21. See Deuteronomy 28:10; Isaiah 63:19; Daniel 9:19; 2 Chronicles 7:14.

behind Greek Jeremiah places it with what precedes it: "I did not sit in the council of merrymakers, but I exulted [LXX: acted reverently] before [or, because of] your hand [cf. Jer. 15:16]. Alone I sat, for it was with indignation that I was filled."[22] Thus, Jeremiah either sat alone or exulted because of divine compulsion (see 1 Kgs. 18:46; 2 Kgs. 3:15; Isa. 8:11; Ezek. 1:3; 3:14, 22; 8:1; 33:22; 37:1; 40:1; Pss. 32:4; 38:3–4 [Eng., 38:2–3]). Either way, Jeremiah's activity was set apart from that of the "merrymakers" (מְשַׂחֲקִים). According to McKane, this term does not necessarily indicate impiety: "The sense of the verse is rather that the prophetic vocation requires of Jeremiah an unnatural way of life and that he is set apart in loneliness from normal social pleasantries" (see Jer. 16:8; Eccl. 3:4; 7:3–4; see also Jer. 30:19; 31:4).[23] Holladay, however, has noted the connection with the term "laughingstock" (שְׂחוֹק) in 20:7: "One senses then that the merrymakers were not making merry in general but were making merry at Jrm's expense, or at the expense of his message."[24] Thus, the "council of merrymakers" here is more like the "assembly of scoffers" in which the blessed person does not sit (Ps. 1:1b; see also Ps. 26:4–5). Such a person prefers to "murmur" (i.e., read aloud quietly to himself) in the text of the Torah day and night (Ps. 1:2; cf. Josh. 1:8). This is the kind of activity that gave Jeremiah's heart joy (Jer. 15:16). Thus, he sat alone (cf. Lev. 13:46; Lam. 1:1; 3:28) because, as he says, "it was with indignation [LXX: bitterness; *Tg. Jon.*: prophecies of curse] that I was filled (מָלֵאתִי)" (cf. Jer. 6:11). The MT makes it explicit that it was the LORD who filled Jeremiah with this indignation: "for it was with indignation that you filled me (מִלֵּאתָנִי)" (cf. Jer. 10:10b). Jeremiah's acceptance of the words of the Torah has given him great joy (as opposed to the mockery from those who persecute him), but its message has filled him with indignation at the infidelity of the people (cf. 2 Kgs. 22:11–13). This situation has put him at odds with virtually everyone around him and made him incompatible with society in general (see Ps. 119:22–24; see also Num. 23:9; Deut. 33:28).

---

22. The Syriac ("and I did not fear before/because of your hand") and *Targum Jonathan* ("and I did not rejoice before/because of your word") also place this phrase with what precedes it, but they carry over the negation from the first clause to the second clause. The Syriac translates the verb "exult" as "fear," giving the sense that Jeremiah did not shrink back from divine compulsion. *Targum Jonathan* renders the word "hand" as "word," giving the sense that Jeremiah did not celebrate in the downfall of others (see Prov. 24:17–18).

23. McKane, *Jeremiah I–XXV*, 354.

24. Holladay, *Jeremiah 1*, 459.

Given Jeremiah's record of fidelity to his calling despite the cost, he wonders why he must endure so much trouble. His question in 15:18a ("Why do those who cause me pain have victory over me [לָמָּה הַמַּכְאִבַי יְנַצְּחוּנִי]?" MT: "Why has my pain been perpetual [לָמָּה הָיָה כְאֵבִי נֶצַח]?") is reminiscent of Moses' complaint: "Why have you treated your servant badly, and why have I not found favor in your eyes, putting the burden of all this people on me" (Num. 11:11; cf. Exod. 5:22–23; see also Jer. 12:1; 45:3)? Jeremiah says that his wound, like that of the people, is "incurable" (cf. Jer. 30:12). According to the Hebrew source behind Greek Jeremiah 15:18b, he asks, "Whence will I be healed (מֵאַיִן אֶרָפֵא)?" The MT, however, has a statement: "It [i.e., his wound] refuses to be healed (מֵאֲנָה הֵרָפֵא)." The incurable wound here is likely not a physical affliction but a metaphor for the persecution that Jeremiah continually faces. The verse concludes with a bold question, calling into doubt the LORD's transparency in his dealings with Jeremiah: "Will you indeed be to me like a deceptive water source, that is, unreliable water" (cf. Jer. 20:7)? This refers to a promising source from which people expect water, only to find that the source is dry and thus "deceptive" and "unreliable" (see Job 6:15–21). It suggests that the LORD has somehow not been forthright or honest, misleading Jeremiah into thinking that his relationship to the people on behalf of the LORD would not be so difficult. But this is not the case. The LORD informed Jeremiah of this when he called him to be his prophet (Jer. 1:17–19). The LORD is a reliable water source (Isa. 58:11; Jer. 14:22). He is indeed a fountain of living water (Jer. 2:13; 17:13) in contrast to the broken cisterns (i.e., other "gods"). Thus, Jeremiah's question in 15:18b will prompt the LORD to rebuke him in 15:19 and to call on him to repent.

"If you will return" (Jer. 15:19a) is an implied rebuke of Jeremiah's insinuation in 15:18b. It assumes that Jeremiah has turned away in some manner and must now come back.[25] The language of the protasis-apodosis construction in 15:19a is reminiscent of what was addressed to the people in 4:1–2 (see also Jer. 18:11b; 25:5; 31:18b). If Jeremiah repents of his words in 15:18b, then the LORD will restore him to stand before him, that is, to serve the LORD as his prophet (cf. Jer. 15:1; 18:20).

---

25. "*Redak* explains that God takes the prophet to task for his complaint. You said false words to me when you said that I was like a failing spring. You sinned against Me. Now if you completely repent before Me and regret what you said to Me, I will return you in repentance and I will forgive you, and you shall stand before Me as before. Standing before God includes prayer and thanksgiving before Him, as well as the reception of prophecy" (Rosenberg, trans., *Mikraoth Gedoloth: Jeremiah Volume One*, 137).

If Jeremiah "brings forth" (תוֹצִיא) what is "precious" from what is "worthless" (cf. Lam. 1:11b), then he will be like the LORD's "mouth" (or, according to his command). *Targum Jonathan* interprets this to mean: "if you cause the wicked to return to be righteous." It is more likely, however, that what is "worthless" here is the content of Jeremiah's words in 15:18b. That which is "precious" is the message that he must put in place of those words. According to Tosefta-tractate Horayot 2:7, this message is that of the Torah, whose wisdom is more "precious" than jewels (Prov. 3:15).[26] Man must live not on bread alone but on all "that goes forth" (מוֹצָא) from the LORD's "mouth" (Deut. 8:3b; cf. Jer. 17:16b). The LORD has put his words in Jeremiah's mouth (Jer. 1:9b), and Jeremiah has "eaten" the words of the Torah (MT Jer. 15:16a). If Jeremiah will only speak these words, his mouth will be like the LORD's mouth and in accordance with his will (see Pss. 1:2; 19:15 [Eng., 19:14]). The people will turn to Jeremiah, but Jeremiah must not turn to them (Jer. 15:19b; cf. 1 Sam. 12:23). In other words, if Jeremiah speaks the words of the Torah as a faithful prophet, and if any of the people actually repent, they will turn to him, but Jeremiah must be careful not to capitulate to the ways of the people and thus become like them.

The last two verses of chapter 15 revisit the language of Jeremiah 1:8, 17–19 (see commentary there; see also Jer. 20:11): "And I will make [or, appoint; lit., give] you to this people as a fortified bronze wall; and they will fight against you, but they will not prevail against you, for with you am I to deliver you and to rescue you from the hand of evil men and from the palm of terror-striking men" (Jer. 15:20–21; cf. Jer. 20:13). The MT has a longer text for 15:20b–21: "for with you am I to deliver you and to rescue you," the prophetic utterance of the LORD, "and I will rescue you from the hand of evil men and purchase/redeem [or, "ransom" (see BDB, 804)] you from the palm of terror-striking men." Janzen explains the shorter text of the Hebrew source behind Greek Jeremiah as a case of haplography (see וּלְהַצִּילְךָ [15:20b] and וְהִצַּלְתִּיךָ [15:21a] in the MT),[27] but this does not explain the absence of the verb וּפְדִתִיךָ ("and purchase/redeem you"). Furthermore, the parallel texts in 1:8b and 1:19b (see also LXX 1:17b) only use the infinitive forms לְהַצִּלֶךָ and לְהַצִּילְךָ ("to rescue you"), not the finite verb וְהִצַּלְתִּיךָ ("and I will rescue you"). It is more likely that MT 15:20b–21 is an expansion of the shorter Hebrew text behind Greek Jeremiah, complete with the addition of נְאֻם יְהוָה ("the prophetic utterance of the LORD"), which is a known expansion elsewhere in MT Jeremiah.[28]

---

26. See Neusner, *Jeremiah in Talmud and Midrash*, 5.
27. Janzen, *Studies in the Text of Jeremiah*, 117.
28. Janzen, *Studies in the Text of Jeremiah*, 78–79.

JEREMIAH 16

16:1 "And as for you, you will not take for yourself a wife [LXX: do not take a wife]," says the LORD *the God of hosts, 16:2 "and you will not have a son or a daughter in this place."[1] 16:3 For thus says the* LORD *concerning the sons and concerning the daughters who are born in this place and concerning their mothers who give birth to them and concerning their fathers who father them in this land, 16:4 "Deaths by diseases will they die. They will not be mourned, and they will not be buried. As a likeness [LXX: pattern, example; MT: dung] on the surface of the ground will they be, both for the animals of the land and for the flying creatures of the sky. By the sword will they fall, and by famine will they come to an end [MT: And by sword and by famine will they come to an end, and their corpse will become food for the flying creatures of the sky and for the animals of the land]." 16:5 [MT adds: כִּי] Thus says the* LORD*, "Do not enter a feast house [LXX: their group / banquet / revel; NET: a house where they are having a funeral meal; Syr.: a house of mourning], and do not go to mourn, and do not mourn for them. For I have gathered my peace from this people [MT adds: the prophetic utterance of the* LORD*, the covenant loyalty and the compassion]. 16:6 [MT adds: And great and small will die in this land. They will not be buried,] They will not mourn for them [MT: and they will not mourn for them], and they will not cut themselves [Syr.: wail], and they will not make themselves bald [MT: and he will not cut himself, and he will not make himself bald for them]. 16:7 And bread will not be divided / broken for / in their mourning to give comfort concerning the dead [Codex L: And they will not divide / break for them (pc Mss: divide / break bread) for / in mourning (Vulg.: for a mourner) to comfort him (Syr.: that they may comfort them; Tg. Jon.: to comfort them) concerning the dead]. And they will not give him [MT: them] a cup of comfort to drink concerning his [Syr.: their] father or his [Syr.: their] mother [Tg. Jon.: each concerning his father or his mother]. 16:8 And a feast house you will not enter to sit with them to eat and to drink." 16:9 For thus says the* LORD *[MT adds: of hosts] the God of Israel, "Look, I am about to cause to cease from this place before your eyes and in your days sound of rejoicing and sound of joy, sound of bridegroom and sound of bride."*

The MT begins chapter 16 with a standard introductory formula: "And the word of the LORD came to me, saying" (MT Jer. 16:1; cf. MT Jer.

---

1. MT: "And the word of the LORD came to me, saying, 'You will not take for yourself a wife, and you will not have sons or daughters in this place.'"

1:4, 11, 13; 2:1; etc.). The Hebrew source behind Greek Jeremiah, however, starts directly into the LORD's address to Jeremiah: "And as for you [> MT], you will not take for yourself a wife [LXX: do not take a wife]," says the LORD the God of hosts [> MT], "and you will not have a son [MT: sons] or a daughter [MT: daughters] in this place." This opening prohibition forms an inclusio with the final verse of the unit in which the LORD says that he will cause the sounds of wedding festivities to cease from this place (Jer. 16:9). According to Jeremiah 16:10, the prophet is to declare the words of this unit (Jer. 16:1–9) to the people and anticipate their response. Thus, the repeated use of כה אמר יהוה ("Thus says the LORD") in these verses (Jer. 16:3, 5, 9) is not for the LORD's introduction of his own discourse (as in most English translations) but for Jeremiah's introduction of the LORD's discourse (as is commonly the case throughout the book).

The instruction not to marry and not to have children is another example of a symbolic prophetic sign act (see commentary on Jer. 13:1–14).[2] Just as Hosea's sequestering of his wife was symbolic of the LORD's judgment of Israel (Hos. 3:3–4), so Jeremiah's lack of a wife will be symbolic of the LORD's judgment of Judah. Just as the names of the children of Hosea (Hos. 1) and Isaiah (Isa. 8:18) were signs of things to come, so Jeremiah's lack of children anticipates terrible loss on the horizon. The prophet Ezekiel will lose the desire of his eyes (i.e., his wife) and have no chance to mourn her death (Ezek. 24:16). This will be symbolic of how Judah will lose the desire of its eyes (i.e., the temple) and its children and have no opportunity to mourn (Ezek. 24:21–25). The fact that Jeremiah is told not to take a wife or have children "in this place" (i.e., in the land of Judah [cf. Jer. 7:7]) is not an invitation to speculate about the possibility of Jeremiah having a family somewhere else. It is simply a way to stress that what Jeremiah experiences in the land is symbolic of what the people will experience in the land.

As for the children born in the land, along with their mothers and fathers (Jer. 16:3; see Jer. 11:22b; 14:16; 15:7b–9, 10a), they will die "deaths by diseases" (Jer. 16:4a; cf. LXX Jer. 14:15, 18). They will neither be mourned nor buried (cf. Jer. 8:1–3; 14:16; 25:33). Mass destruction and exile will leave no motivation or time for such ceremony,

---

2.　"That he abstained from marriage and children was a powerful sign that the end of Judah was at hand. People would die in the land before many days were past. Jeremiah, who never had a wife or children, was as those would be who had married and had produced children but would lose them all in the calamity that would befall Judah" (Thompson, *Book of Jeremiah*, 404). See Jeremiah 10:20; 15:8–9.

despite the honor and respect attached to it. Disgrace brought by the absence of proper grief and the lack of decent burial is part of the judgment. According to the Hebrew source behind Greek Jeremiah, the people will lie on the ground as an "example" (דמין) for all to see. On the other hand, the MT says that they will be like "dung" (דמן) on the ground's surface (cf. Jer. 8:2; 9:21 [Eng., 9:22]; 25:33; see also Isa. 5:25). Their bodies will be there for the animals and birds to consume (Jer. 16:4b; cf. Deut. 28:26; 1 Sam. 17:44, 46; 1 Kgs. 14:11; 16:4; 21:24; Jer. 7:33; 15:3; 19:7; 34:20; Ezek. 29:5; 39:4, 17–20; Ps. 79:2; Rev. 19:17–18). They will fall by the sword and come to an end by famine (cf. Deut. 28:21–25; Jer. 14:12, 15, 16; 15:2; et al.). The rearrangement of the clauses in MT 16:4b seems to be driven by the desire to see a logical sequence from death by sword and famine to corpses made into animal food. This would parallel the sequence of 16:4a from death by disease to bodies lying on the ground. Such a rationale for order suggests that the arrangement of the Hebrew source behind Greek Jeremiah reflected in the translation above is more original and has subsequently been altered into what now appears in the MT.

In Jeremiah 16:5a, the Lord forbids Jeremiah to enter a "feast house" (בית מרזח). This term is apparently interchangeable with "feast house" (בית משתה) in 16:8, a place to eat and drink (see Vulg., Rashi; see also Jer. 16:7).[3] Both terms can be used in more than one kind of context. Thus, in Amos 6:7 מרזח refers to revelry and drinking without restraint, but in the present context a בית מרזח is "a house of mourning" (Syr.) or "a house where they are having a funeral meal" (NET; see Ep. Jer. 31).[4] Likewise, a משתה can be the kind of feast or banquet described in Esther 1, in which case a בית משתה would be the very opposite of a בית אבל, "house of mourning" (Eccl. 7:2), but again the present context suggests that it is broad enough in its usage to refer to a place to have a funeral meal.[5] Jeremiah is further instructed: "and do not go to mourn

---

3. According to Bordreuil and Pardee, a *mrzḥ* in Ugaritic is a "societal group devoted to the drinking of wine" (Pierre Bordreuil and Dennis Pardee, *A Manual of Ugaritic*, LSAWS 3 [Winona Lake, IN: Eisenbrauns, 2009], 348). There is perhaps also a religious association (195, 261).

4. This dual usage continues in post-biblical Hebrew and Aramaic. See Marcus Jastrow, *A Dictionary of the Targumim, the Talmud Babli and Yerushalmi, and the Midrashic Literature*, 2nd ed. (New York: Judaica, 1903), 840. See also Wisdom of Solomon 12:5 for the Greek term that the LXX uses for this word in Jeremiah 16:5.

5. Holladay suggests the possibility that "feast house" in 16:8 refers to a place to have a wedding feast (*Jeremiah 1*, 470; see Jer. 16:9), but 16:9

(לספוד), and do not mourn (תנד) for them" (cf. Jer. 16:4a; Ezek. 24:16). This is because the LORD has gathered his "peace" or "well-being" (שלום) from the people (Jer. 16:5b; cf. Jer. 6:14; 14:13; see also Jer. 16:9). The addition in the MT (the prophetic utterance of the LORD, "the covenant loyalty [החסד] and the compassion [הרחמים]") is apparently intended to explain what is meant here by the removal of שלום. The covenant relationship is broken (Jer. 11:10), and the LORD will no longer have compassion on his people (cf. Hos. 1:6). There will be no mourning over the deaths of those in 16:3–4 as if they were people in right standing with the LORD. Their deaths are a divine judgment brought about by their refusal to heed the LORD's voice.

The MT adds at the beginning of 16:6 that both great and small will die in the land and remain unburied (cf. Jer. 6:13; 16:4). This addition, which does not appear in the Hebrew source behind Greek Jeremiah, indicates that the coming judgment will be an indiscriminate one. All are guilty, and none will be spared, regardless of position or status. The shorter text of the Hebrew source behind Greek Jeremiah simply resumes the thought of 16:4a ("They will not mourn for them") and adds that the people will also not mingle pagan religious practices ("and they will not cut themselves, and they will not make themselves bald")[6] with their mourning (see Lev. 19:27–28; 21:5; Deut. 14:1; 1 Kgs. 18:28; Isa. 15:2; Jer. 5:7 [MT]; 41:5; 47:5; 48:37). The presence of such behavior in rituals mourning the dead is likely part of the reason why they are not allowed and why Jeremiah is forbidden to participate or to associate with those who do participate. Jeremiah 16:7a adds that "bread" (לחם) will not "be broken" (יפרס) in "their mourning" (אבלם) "to give comfort" (לנחם) concerning the dead (cf. Isa. 58:7; Lam. 4:4). The Leningrad Codex says that they will not "break" (יפרסו) "for them" (להם) in "mourning" (אֵבֶל) "to comfort him" (לנחמו) concerning the dead. The Latin Vulgate has "for a mourner" (= עַל אָבֵל) instead of "in mourning" (עַל אֵבֶל). This provides an antecedent for the third masculine singular pronominal suffix on the infinitive לנחמו ("to comfort him"). The Syriac ("that they may comfort them") and *Targum Jonathan* ("to comfort them") have plural pronouns. There is no pronominal suffix on the

---

is not designed to define the meaning of "feast house." Rather, the cessation of wedding festivities in 16:9 is parallel to the removal of "peace" or "well-being" in 16:5b. Thus, the prohibitions in 16:6a and 16:8 are not two separate instructions but the same instruction given in different terms.

6. The MT uses singular verbs ("and he will not cut himself, and he will not make himself bald for them"), perhaps in a distributive sense: "and each will not cut himself, and each will not make himself bald for them."

infinitive in the Hebrew source behind Greek Jeremiah, but it does have a third masculine singular object suffix in 16:7b, which seems to presuppose that "mourner" is the antecedent: "And they will not give him [MT: them] a cup of comfort to drink concerning his [Syr.: their] father or his [Syr.: their] mother [*Tg. Jon.*: each concerning his father or his mother]." The use of the plural pronoun "them" in the MT has prompted the Syriac to use plural pronouns in the remainder of the verse ("their father or their mother"). *Targum Jonathan* resolves the matter with the distributive "each concerning his father or his mother." This text speaks of the eating and drinking that would occur in a "feast house" (Jer. 16:5a, 8) or in a place to have a funeral meal. The custom of encouraging those in mourning to take food is referenced in several places (2 Sam. 3:35; 12:16–23; Ezek. 24:17, 22).

In Jeremiah 16:8 ("And a feast house you will not enter" [ובית משתה לא תבוא]) reiterates the prohibition of 16:5a ("Do not enter a feast house" [אל תבוא בית מרזח]), albeit in different terms.[7] Jeremiah 16:9 (cessation of wedding festivities) then reiterates the reason for the prohibition from 16:5b (removal of "peace" or "well-being"), again in different terms, but this is not merely gratuitous repetition. The specific wording of 16:8 is that Jeremiah will not enter a feast house "to sit (לשבת) with them to eat and to drink." This creates a link with the preceding confession of Jeremiah in 15:15–21: "I did not sit (ישבתי) in the council of merrymakers" (Jer. 15:17). Jeremiah did not sit with those who made merry at his expense (cf. Jer. 20:7b). Rather, he says, "Alone I sat (ישבתי)." As noted in the commentary on that text, Jeremiah prefers to be alone with the text of the Torah (Jer. 15:16–17; cf. Ps. 1:1–2).[8] Now he is to separate himself from those who mourn in the manner described in 16:6–7. The LORD explains, "Look, I am about to cause to cease from this place before your eyes and in your days sound of rejoicing and sound of joy, sound of bridegroom and sound of bride" (Jer. 16:9; cf. Jer. 7:34; 25:10; 33:11; Rev. 18:23). As noted in the commentary on Jeremiah 7:34, these sounds are representative of the life of the community. Their cessation is a picture of what it means for the

---

7. Note the chiastic structuring of these clauses. "In a chiastic sentence, a chiastic clause combines with the lead clause to give a single picture of two simultaneously occurring aspects of the same situation or event." (Andersen, *Sentence in Biblical Hebrew*, 121). Cf. the parallel prohibitions in Genesis 37:22 arranged in a chiastic structure.

8. Rembrandt's "Jeremiah Lamenting the Destruction of Jerusalem" captures this beautifully, depicting Jeremiah alone with his Bible.

LORD to gather his שלום ("peace" or "well-being") from the people (Jer. 16:5b).[9]

16:10 "And then, when you declare to this people all these words/ things, and they say to you, 'Why has the LORD spoken against us all this calamity [MT: all this great calamity]? What [MT: And what] is our iniquity? And what is our sin that we have committed against the LORD our God?' 16:11 you will say to them, 'Because your forefathers forsook me [Tg. Jon.: the worship of me],' the prophetic utterance of the LORD, 'and went after other gods [Tg. Jon.: the idols of the peoples] and served/worshiped them and prostrated themselves to them [or, worshiped them]; but me they forsook, and my instruction [or, my Torah; LXX: my law] they did not keep. 16:12 And as for you, you have acted more evilly [MT adds: to do] than your forefathers. And look, you are going each after the stubbornness of his evil heart [NETS: after the things that please your evil heart; cf. Syr., Tg. Jon.], not listening to me. 16:13 And I will hurl you from upon this land to the land that you have not known/experienced, neither you nor your forefathers, and you will serve/worship there other gods [Tg. Jon.: and you will serve there the peoples, the worshipers of idols; MT adds: day and night] that will not give [MT: where/when I will not give] to you grace/favor.'"

16:14 "Therefore, look, days are coming," the prophetic utterance of the LORD, "and they will never say again [MT: and it will never be said again], 'As the LORD lives [or, By the life of the LORD; Tg. Jon.: and they will never talk again about the might of the Lord] who brought up the sons of Israel [Syr.: the house of Israel] from the land of Egypt . . . ,' 16:15 but, 'As the LORD lives [or, By the life of the LORD; Tg. Jon.: but they will talk about the might of the Lord] who brought up the house of Israel [MT: the sons of Israel] from the land of the north and from all the lands where he [pc Mss: I] banished them . . . .' And I will restore them to their land that I gave to their forefathers."

16:16 "Look, I am about to send for many fishermen [Tg. Jon.: for peoples, killers (or, to people's killers)]," the prophetic utterance of the LORD, "and they will fish for [Tg. Jon.: kill] them. And afterward I will send for many hunters, and they will hunt them from upon every mountain

---

9. The sounds of "rejoicing" (ששון) and "joy" (שמחה) will cease, but Jeremiah's cause for "rejoicing" (ששון) and "joy" (שמחה)—namely, the words of the Torah (Jer. 15:16)—will remain.

and from upon every hill and from the clefts of the rocks. 16:17 For my eyes are on all their ways [MT adds: they are not hidden from before me], and their iniquity is not hidden from before my eyes. 16:18 And I will pay back [MT adds: first] double [NET: in full] for their iniquity and their sin [Tg. Jon.: And I will pay back to the second like the first their debts and their sins] because they profaned/polluted my land [Tg. Jon.: the land of the house of my dwelling presence] with the corpse of their detested idols [Syr.: with the sacrifices of their idols]; and as for their abominations, they filled my inheritance [ESV: and have filled my inheritance with their abominations]."[10]

16:19 O L*ORD, my strength and my stronghold [LXX: my help] and my refuge in a day of distress. [Tg. Jon. adds: At the report of your might] To you nations will come from the ends of the inhabited earth and say, "How [MT: Surely/Only] deception our forefathers inherited, that which was empty, and there was not among them one benefiting (them)!*[11] *16:20 Will mankind make for himself gods, and they are non-gods [Tg. Jon.: Is it possible that mankind should make for himself objects of worship, and they are idols for which there is no need]?" 16:21 "Therefore, look, I am about to make known to them at this time my hand/power, and I will make known to them my might [MT: Therefore, look, I am about to make known to them. At this time I will make known to them my hand/power and my might], and they will know/acknowledge that my name is the* LORD *[Yahweh]."*

It is expected at the outset of 16:10 that Jeremiah will declare to the people all the "words/things" (דברים) of 16:1–9 (Jer. 16:10a). Perhaps it is anticipated that the people will require an explanation for Jeremiah's symbolic action of not having a family (cf. Ezek. 12:9–10; 24:19; 37:18). It is also expected that the people will ask in response to Jeremiah's declaration of the words, "Why has the LORD

---

10. The MT accentuation seems to favor the following translation: "And I will pay back first double for their iniquity and their sin because they profaned my land. With the corpse of their detested idols and their abominations they filled my inheritance." The NETS provides another option: "And I will doubly repay their injustices and their sins with which they have polluted my land with the carcasses of their abominations and with their lawless acts, by which they erred [ἐπλημμέλησαν] against my inheritance." ἐπλημμέλησαν ("erred") is likely an inner-Greek variant for επλησαν ("filled").

11. NETS: "How have our fathers acquired false idols, and there is no profit in them!"

spoken against us all this calamity [MT: all this great calamity]? What [MT: And what] is our iniquity? And what is our sin that we have committed against the LORD our God" (Jer. 16:10b)? The question-and-answer pattern of 16:10–11 has already occurred twice in the book of Jeremiah (Jer. 5:19; 9:11–13 [Eng., 9:12–14]; cf. Deut. 29:23–27 [Eng., 29:24–28]; 1 Kgs. 9:8–9; Jer. 22:8–9; 2 Chr. 7:21–22).[12] It may seem beyond remarkable at this juncture that the people could plead such ignorance, but it is their nature to do so (see Jer. 2:23, 35; 13:22–23). When the people ask Jeremiah these questions, he is to respond first of all with a reference to their forefathers: "'Because your forefathers forsook me [*Tg. Jon.*: the worship of me],' the prophetic utterance of the LORD, 'and went after other gods [*Tg. Jon.*: the idols of the peoples] and served/worshiped them and prostrated themselves to them [or, worshiped them]; but me they forsook, and my instruction [or, my Torah; LXX: my law] they did not keep'" (Jer. 16:11; cf. Jer. 1:16; 2:5, 8, 11, 13; 6:19; 11:10). This is not because the present generation must pay for the sins of its forefathers (see Deut. 24:16) but because the current generation has learned the ways of its forefathers and continued in them (Jer. 9:12–13 [Eng., 9:13–14]; see Exod. 20:5; see also the commentary on Jer. 31:29–30).

When Jeremiah turns to the present generation in 16:12 ("And as for you"), he is to say that the people have behaved even worse than their forefathers (cf. Jer. 7:26; see also 1 Kgs. 14:9), pointing out that they are going after the stubbornness of their evil hearts (i.e., after "other gods" or idols; cf. Jer. 3:17; 7:24; 9:13 [Eng., 9:14]; 13:10; 18:12; 23:17) and not listening to the LORD (thus breaking the covenant in the manner of their forefathers). What is it that makes the sin of the current generation worse than that of the forefathers? Malbim suggests that the forefathers forgot the Torah and thus acted in ignorance (see, e.g., Deut. 8:14; 1 Sam 12:9; Pss. 78:11, 42; 106:7, 21; Neh. 9:17), while the present generation has deliberately and wittingly gone after their own hearts (but see Jer. 7:24).[13] According to Calvin, the present generation has rejected not only the Torah (like the forefathers) but also the Prophets (see Jer. 7:25–26).[14] Perhaps the true explanation of this lies not so much in downplaying the sin of the forefathers or in differentiating the sin of the present generation but in observing that the present generation has maintained the trajectory of the sin of the forefathers in an ever-increasing fashion.

---

12. See also Malachi 1:6–7; 2:17; 3:7–8, 13–14.
13. Rosenberg, trans., *Mikraoth Gedoloth: Jeremiah Volume One*, 141.
14. Calvin, *Jeremiah*, 2:318–19.

The conclusion to the Lord's response to the people through Jeremiah is that he will "hurl" them from the land of the covenant to "the land" (i.e., Babylon) that neither they nor their forefathers have known by experience (Jer. 16:13a; cf. Jer. 7:15; 9:15 [Eng., 9:16]; 14:18b; 15:14; 17:4; 22:26, 28). It is there that they will serve/worship "other gods" (Jer. 16:13b; cf. Deut. 4:28; 28:36, 64). It is possible that this means the Lord will give the people what they want as a form of judgment (cf. 1 Sam. 8:7–9; Rom. 1:18–32). What they have so casually worshiped in their own land they will now be forced to worship in a foreign land. Another possibility is the rendering of 16:13b in *Targum Jonathan*: "and you will serve there the peoples, the worshipers of idols" (cf. Jer. 15:14; 17:4). The parallel text in Jeremiah 5:19 says that they will serve זרים, which can be either "strange gods" (Deut. 32:12, 16; Jer. 2:25) or simply "strangers, foreigners" (Jer. 30:8). In the Hebrew source behind Greek Jeremiah, the relative clause at the end of 16:13b modifies "other gods": "and you will serve/worship there other gods that (אשר) will not give (לא יתנו) to you grace/favor." English translations usually render the relative in the longer text of the MT as if it were a causal conjunction: "and you will serve/worship there other gods day and night because (אשר) I will not give (לא אתן) to you grace/favor."[15] Holmstedt, however, has made a good case that the relative in the MT modifies either שם "there" ("and you will serve/worship there other gods day and night where [אשר] I will not give to you grace/favor") or the phrase "day and night," which is not in the LXX ("and you will serve/worship there other gods day and night when [אשר] I will not give to you grace/favor").[16]

The text of 16:14–15 recurs with some variation in MT 23:7–8. The Hebrew source behind Greek Jeremiah 23 places verses 7–8 at the end of the chapter after verse 40. The primary difference between 16:14–15 and MT 23:7–8 is that the former occurs in the context of judgment (Jer. 16:10–13, 16–18) while the latter appears in a context of deliverance (Jer. 23:5–6). The placement of verses 7–8 of chapter 23 at the end of the chapter in the Hebrew source behind Greek Jeremiah also puts them in a judgment context (Jer. 23:33–40). Thus, for 16:14–15 and the Hebrew source behind Greek Jeremiah 23, the focus of these verses is not so much the new exodus as it is the new captivity.[17] The future

---

15. According to *Pesiqta de Rab Kahana*, this is part of a conglomeration of texts in the book of Jeremiah that contradicts the priestly blessing in Numbers 6:24–26 (see Neusner, *Jeremiah in Talmud and Midrash*, 167). Cf. Malachi 1:6–2:9 (see Shepherd, *Commentary on the Book of the Twelve*, 485–86).
16. Holmstedt, *Relative Clause*, 233, 376.
17. See Keil, *Jeremiah*, 168–69.

place of judgment (i.e., the land of the north) will be harsher than the past (i.e., Egypt). Of course, this also means that the future deliverance will be far greater than the former one. Enslavement in Egypt was the darkest period in the life of ancient Israel, and the departure from that place of bondage became the paradigm for all subsequent deliverance.[18] Thus, to say that there would be an even darker time from which there would be an even greater deliverance was to speak in almost hyperbolic terms.

On several occasions in the book of Jeremiah the reader finds that "days are coming" (cf. Jer. 9:24 [Eng., 9:25]; 30:3; 31:27, 31; 33:14 [MT]; 48:12; 49:2; 51:47, 52) when certain things will no longer be said (Jer. 3:16; 7:32; 16:14–15; 19:6; 23:7–8; 31:29; see also Jer. 31:23). A time is coming when people will no longer reference the exodus from Egypt to describe the LORD when formulating an oath (Jer. 16:14; cf. Jer. 4:2; 5:2; 38:16; see also Isa. 43:16–18). Indeed, the coming judgment will be so devastating that Egypt will no longer be remembered (cf. Ezek. 23:27). Rather, people will reference the new exodus from the land of the north in their oath formulas (Jer. 16:15a; cf. Isa. 43:19–20).[19] This new exodus will result in full restoration to the land of the covenant (Jer. 16:15b). Whatever decision the interpreter has made about the enemy from the north thus far in the book of Jeremiah (Jer. 1:13–15 et al.) will affect the manner in which this reference is received. If the enemy from the north is Babylon, then it is a reference to the Babylonian captivity and the subsequent return to the land in the latter part of the sixth century BC. The problem with this is that there was no such restoration in any full sense, only subjection to Persian rule, Greek rule, and Roman rule. Even the modern political state of Israel is not a full restoration of the land of the covenant (see the boundaries in Gen. 15:18). On the other hand, if the enemy from the north is an eschatological enemy (Ezek. 38:14–17; Dan. 9:24–27), then the greatest tribulation (and thus the greatest salvation) for which the Babylonian captivity is only a prefiguration is yet to come. This is the sense in which Redak understands the text.[20] Jeremiah 16:15 speaks of what will happen "at the end of days"

---

18. See Shepherd, *Textual World of the Bible*, 5, 9–10; "The New Exodus in the Composition of the Twelve," in *Text and Canon: Essays in Honor of John H. Sailhamer*, eds. Robert L. Cole and Paul J. Kissling (Eugene, OR: Pickwick, 2017), 120–36. See also Isaiah 43:16–21; 48:20–21; 51:9–11.

19. In Isaiah 43:18, the LORD urges the people not to remember the former things such as the original exodus (Isa. 43:16–17; but see Isa. 46:9). This is because he is about to do a new thing—a new exodus (Isa. 43:19–20).

20. Rosenberg, trans., *Mikraoth Gedoloth: Jeremiah Volume One*, 142.

(בְּאַחֲרִית הַיָּמִים) during the messianic era when the final redemption occurs (see Gen. 49:1, 8–12; Num. 24:7–9, 14, 17–24; Deut. 4:30; 31:29; 33:5, 7; Isa. 2:1–5; Jer. 23:5–6, 19–20; 30:23–24; 48:47; 49:39; Ezek. 38:14–17; Hos. 3:4–5; Mic. 4:1–5; Dan. 2:28; 10:14). According to McKane, the addition of "and from all the lands where he [pc Mss: I] drove them" in Jeremiah 16:15a (cf. Dan. 9:7) is an "umbrella device which indicates that the oath can be used comprehensively."[21] Thus, even for those who understand the enemy from the north to be Babylon, the text has application beyond the Babylonian captivity.

In Jeremiah 16:16, the LORD says that he is about to send for many fishermen who will fish for the people; and afterward he will send for many hunters who "will hunt them from upon every mountain and from upon every hill and from the clefts of the rocks."[22] Fishing and hunting are metaphors elsewhere for enemy invasion (see Ezek. 12:13; 17:20; 29:4–5; 32:3; Amos 4:2; Hab. 1:15–17; see also 1QH[a] 13:10).[23] Rashi and Redak suggest that the fishermen are the killers of the people (cf. *Tg. Jon.*) and that the hunters are the captors of the survivors.[24] According to Joseph Kara, the fishers represent Nebuchadnezzar, while the hunters represent neighboring peoples who would pursue fleeing Judeans and deliver them to the enemy.[25] Others (e.g., Duhm) see in the figures of fishing and hunting (and in the word "double" [מִשְׁנֶה] in 16:18) an allusion to the events of 597 and 587. Holladay argues that the fishermen represent the Egyptians (Isa. 19:8) and that the hunters represent the Babylonians (Lam. 4:18–19),[26] a suggestion that makes for an interesting connection with Jeremiah 16:14–15. The text itself, however, is not so specific. The most that can be said is that there is a distinction between the fishermen and the hunters. Only "afterward" will the hunters come. The mountains, hills, and clefts are certainly places to which people would flee (e.g., 1 Sam. 13:6; Isa. 7:19), but they

---

21. McKane, *Jeremiah I–XXV*, 375–76. The third person ("where he drove them") keeps this addition as part of the oath formula. The first person ("where I drove them") does not.
22. For evidence of a shorter Hebrew text here, see McKane, *Jeremiah I–XXV*, 379.
23. Contrary to Augustine, fishing for people in this context is not the same as that found in Matthew 4:19 (Wenthe, ed., *Jeremiah, Lamentations*, 125).
24. Rosenberg, trans., *Mikraoth Gedoloth: Jeremiah Volume One*, 143. Malbim says the fishermen capture the bulk of the people; the hunters pursue the remaining people.
25. Rosenberg, trans., *Mikraoth Gedoloth: Jeremiah Volume One*, 143.
26. Holladay, *Jeremiah 1*, 478–79.

are also the places where they would practice their false religion (e.g., Jer. 2:20; Ezek. 6:13). Thus, in the places where they have brought judgment upon themselves, they will be judged.

The LORD explains the judgment announced in 16:16 first of all by saying in 16:17 that his eyes are on all their ways, and their iniquity is not hidden from him (cf. Isa. 29:15; Jer. 3:13; 12:4; 17:10; 23:24; 32:19; Ezek. 8:12; Prov. 5:21). He then adds in 16:18 that he will pay back "double" (משנה) for their iniquity and sin. The MT says that he will do this "first" (ראשונה), as if to say that judgment is necessary before restoration is possible, but the Hebrew source behind Greek Jeremiah does not have this word. *Targum Jonathan* (and likewise Rashi) interprets "double" as a reference to the iniquity of the forefathers and the repetition of this iniquity by the present generation. Others see in it a reference to the fishing and hunting of 16:16 (see above).[27] But the term משנה ("double") here likely has the sense "in full" (see Deut. 15:18; Jer. 17:18b; cf. Isa. 40:2; see also Exod. 22:3, 6, 8 [Eng., 22:4, 7, 9]).[28] The LORD will pay back the people in full for their iniquity and sin because they have "profaned/polluted" the land of the covenant (cf. Lev. 18:24–30; Num. 35:33–34; Isa. 47:6; Jer. 2:7; Ps. 106:38). English translations typically ignore the Masoretic accentuation (see note to translation above) and render the phrase "with the corpse of their detested idols" with what precedes it: "because they profaned/polluted my land with the corpse of their detested idols." The closest parallel to נבלת שקוציהם ("the corpse of their detested idols") is פגרי גלוליכם ("the corpses of your dung idols") in Leviticus 26:30 (see also Jer. 4:1; 7:30). This refers to the fact that the idols that the people have worshiped are nothing more than lifeless objects (cf. Num. 25:2; Ps. 106:28). English translations usually render the last clause of 16:18 as if the preposition ב ("with") were prefixed to תועבותיהם ("their abominations"): "and have filled my inheritance with their abominations" (ESV). The above translation renders תועבותיהם as the fronted subject of the verb: "and as for their abominations, they filled my inheritance" (see Jer. 2:7; 7:10; Ezek. 11:21; see also Exod. 15:17; Ps. 79:1).

The abrupt insertion of Jeremiah's words in 16:19–20 has led some to conclude that 16:21 is properly the end of the words of judgment in 16:16–18.[29] It is possible, however, to read 16:19–21 as a coherent unit. Jeremiah's opening address in 16:19a ("O LORD, my strength and my

---

27. Holladay, *Jeremiah 1*, 479.
28. See NET; Bullinger, *Figures of Speech*, 586; McKane, *Jeremiah I–XXV*, 378.
29. McKane, *Jeremiah I–XXV*, 383.

stronghold and my refuge in a day of distress") has several parallels elsewhere (2 Sam. 22:3; Isa. 59:17; Jer. 17:17; Nah. 1:7; Pss. 18:3 [Eng., 18:2]; 28:8; 37:39; 46:2 [Eng., 46:1]). This is the representative voice of the righteous remnant in the midst of tribulation. Jeremiah then adds in 16:19b, "To you nations will come from the ends of the inhabited earth and say, 'How [MT: Surely/Only] deception our forefathers inherited, that which was empty, and there was not among them one benefiting (them)!'"[30] According to Redak, this will take place in the messianic era (cf. Isa. 2:1–5; 66:18–24; Mic. 4:1–5; Zech. 8:20–23).[31] As noted earlier in this commentary, such a concern for the nations is not an isolated one in the book of Jeremiah (see Jer. 1:5, 10; 3:14–18; 4:2; 12:14–17; 25:15–26; 46–51). Calvin proposes that the logic of this concern at the present juncture is comparable to the apostle Paul's thinking in Romans 11.[32] The setting aside of Israel results in the conversion of the nations. Meanwhile, God preserves a faithful remnant of Israel. The conversion of the nations provokes Israel to jealousy, and eventually in this manner all true or believing Israel will be saved. If God turns the nations to himself, surely he will turn to himself his chosen instrument to reach the nations.

The reported discourse of the converted nations continues in 16:20: "Will mankind make for himself gods, and they are non-gods [*Tg. Jon.*: Is it possible that mankind should make for himself objects of worship, and they are idols for which there is no need]?"[33] The language of this verse if very close to that of Jeremiah 2:11 (see also Deut. 32:17, 21; 2 Kgs. 19:18; Hos. 8:6; Jer. 5:7; Ps. 96:5; GKC §152a¹), but McKane has noted a key difference between these two verses: "In 2.11 it is the abysmal lack of a sense of values among Yahweh's own people who barter the true God for worthless idols. In 16.20 it is the stupidity of the Gentiles who suppose that men can construct a God and are not aware of the vacuity of idols."[34] It is God who makes mankind (Gen. 1:26). Mankind does not make God (see again Jer. 10:1–16).

When the Lord speaks again in Jeremiah 16:21, there is a difference of opinion about what the antecedent of the pronoun "them"

---

30. Cf. Jeremiah 2:5, 8; 10:3, 14, 15; 12:16; 13:25; 14:22; Romans 1:25; 1 Thessalonians 1:9. Interestingly, Rashi appears to follow a Hebrew text similar to that of the source behind Greek Jeremiah, which has אֵיךְ ("How"), as in a lament, rather than the MT's אַךְ ("Surely/Only").
31. Rosenberg, trans., *Mikraoth Gedoloth: Jeremiah Volume One*, 144.
32. Calvin, *Jeremiah*, 2:330.
33. On the other hand, it is possible that this is Jeremiah's comment.
34. McKane, *Jeremiah I–XXV*, 382.

might be: "Therefore, look, I am about to make known to them at this time my hand/power, and I will make known to them my might [MT: Therefore, look, I am about to make known to them. At this time I will make known to them my hand/power and my might], and they will know/acknowledge that my name is the LORD [Yahweh]." If this verse is a continuation of the words of judgment in 16:16–18, then the referent would be the people of Judah.[35] According to this reading, the LORD is about to make known to the people of Judah his power in judgment, and they will acknowledge his name. On the other hand, if this verse is a continuation of 16:19–20, then the nations would be the most likely antecedent.[36] The LORD is about to make known to the nations his power in such a way that they will acknowledge him and confess the folly of their idol worship (cf. Ezek. 39:21). A third option is to say that the LORD is about to make known to the people of Judah his power in converting the nations in such a way that Judah will have to acknowledge the LORD's name. The one true God will be acknowledged as Yahweh, the God who is present with his people (Exod. 3:12, 14) whether in judgment or in restoration.[37]

---

35. See Calvin, *Jeremiah*, 2:334.

36. See Thompson, *Book of Jeremiah*, 415.

37. See Rendtorff, *Canonical Hebrew Bible*, 40. See also Exodus 6:2, 6–8, 29; 7:5, 17; 8:18 (Eng., 8:22); 10:2; 12:12; 14:4, 18; 16:12; Leviticus 18:2, 4–6, 21, 30; 19:2–4, 10, 12, 14, 16, 18, 25, 28, 30–32, 34, 36–37; 20:7–8, 24, 26; 21:8, 12, 15, 23; 22:2–3, 8–9, 16, 30–33; 23:22; 24:22; 25:17, 55; 26:1–2, 44–45; Ezekiel 5:13, 15, 17; 6:7, 10, 13, 14; 7:4, 9, 27; 11:10, 12; 12:15, 16, 20; 13:9, 14, 21, 23; 14:8–9; 15:7; 16:62; 17:21, 24; 20:5, 7, 12, 19, 20, 26, 38, 42, 44; 21:4, 10, 37 (Eng., 20:48; 21:5, 32); 22:16, 22; 23:49; 24:14, 24, 27; 25:5, 7, 11, 17; 26:6, 14; 28:22–24, 26; 29:6, 9, 16, 21; 30:8, 12, 19, 25, 26; 32:15; 33:29; 34:27, 30; 35:4, 9, 12, 15; 36:11, 23, 36, 38; 37:6, 13, 28; 38:23; 39:6–7, 22, 28.

JEREMIAH 17

[MT 17:1–4 > LXX][1]

17:5 [MT adds: Thus says the LORD] Cursed is the man who trusts in mankind and puts the flesh of his arm on him [MT: and makes flesh his arm / strength] and whose heart turns aside from the LORD. 17:6 And he will be like a shrub in the desert plain, [MT adds: and] he will not see when good comes; and he will inhabit parched places in the wilderness, a salty / barren and uninhabited land. 17:7 But [> MT] blessed is the man who trusts in the LORD and whose object of trust is the LORD. 17:8 And he will be like a tree planted [LXX: thriving] by water, which by a stream [LXX: to moisture] sends its roots, and does not fear [MT qere: see] when heat comes, and whose leaf is flourishing; [MT adds: and] in a year of drought it is not anxious and does not move [LXX: cease] from producing fruit.

17:9 The heart is deeper [MT: more deceptive; Syr.: stronger] than all, and (hu)man is he / it [MT: and incurable (Tg. Jon.: strong) is it], and who can know him / it [MT: it]? 17:10 "I the LORD search heart(s) and [and > Codex L] test kidneys [Codex L adds: and] to give to each according to his ways [MT kethiv: his way] and [and > Codex L] according to the fruit of his deeds."

---

1. MT 17:1–4: (17:1): "The sin of Judah is written with an iron stylus, with a hard point [Rudolph (*BHS*) joins this phrase with the following clause], engraved on the tablet [Theod., LXX^{OL}: chest] of their heart and on the horns of your [mlt Mss: their] altars, (17:2) as their sons/children [Syr.: in their heart] remember their altars and their Asherah poles beside flourishing trees [nonn Mss: beside every flourishing tree; Syr., *Tg. Jon.*: under every flourishing tree] on [mlt Mss: and on] the high hills [see GKC §126x]. (17:3) My mountain in the field [Rudolph (*BHS*) joins this with the end of 17:2 and reads: mountains in the field/country (cf. Syr.)], your wealth, all your treasures [mlt Mss: and all your treasures] as plunder will I give, your high places, for sin in all [mlt Mss: for the sin of all] your borders [mlt Mss: your border]. (17:4) And you will release your hand [יָדְךָ (cf. Deut. 15:3); MT: וּבְךָ (?); LXX^L, Vulg. = לְבַדְּךָ (alone)] from your inheritance that I gave to you [*Tg. Jon.*: And I will bring the enemy against your land, and it will be desolate like the (year of) release/remission; and then I will make repayment of judgments until I exile you from your inheritance that I gave to you]. And I will cause you to serve [pc Mss: to pass through] your enemies in the land that you do not know. For a fire have you kindled [pc Mss: is kindled] in my anger; forever will it burn."

17:11 A partridge[2] [Syr.: Like a partridge (cf. Tg. Jon.)] that gathers [i.e., gathers eggs; or, broods] and does not give birth [i.e., hatch/lay them][3] is one who makes riches without justice [MT: and not with justice]. In the middle of his days [MT kethiv: his day] they will leave him [MT: it will leave him (or, he will leave it); Tg. Jon., Vulg.: he leaves them], and at his end he will be a fool [Tg. Jon.: wicked].

17:12 [Tg. Jon. adds: Vengeance will be made from him before the one whose dwelling presence is on] An exalted throne of glory (is) our sanctuary [NETS: O exalted throne of glory, our sanctity (or, holy precinct)! MT: A throne of glory on high from (the) beginning (is) the place of our sanctuary]. 17:13 O hope of Israel! O Lord! All those who forsake you, they will be ashamed. Those who turn aside [Codex L kethiv: My reprovers/faultfinders; Codex L qere (mlt Mss): And my turned aside ones (or, And those who turn aside from me); Syr.: And the rebellious; Tg. Jon.: And the wicked who have transgressed your word],[4] in the land[5] they will be written/recorded [or, in the land let them be written/recorded; Tg. Jon.: into Gehenna they are about to fall], for they have forsaken the fountain of living water, the Lord.

17:14 Heal me, O Lord, and I will be healed [or, so that I will be healed]. Deliver me, and I will be delivered [or, so that I will be delivered], for the object of my praise is what you are. 17:15 Look, they are saying to me, "Where is the word of the Lord? Let it come." 17:16 And as for me, I have not hastened [LXX: grown tired] from grazing [or, from shepherding; LXX: following; Aq., Symm.: from evil (cf. Syr.: in evil I have not remained)] after you [Tg. Jon.: I have not held back concerning your word from prophesying to them to turn them back to the worship of you], and man's day [MT: an incurable day] I have not desired. You, you know. What has gone forth from my lips has been before your face [BHS: You, you know what has gone forth from my lips; it has been before your

---

2. Greek witnesses have a double reading for קֹרֵא: ἐφώνησε (= קָרָא) and πέρδιξ (= קֹרֵא).

3. *Tg. Jon.:* "Look, like a partridge that gathers eggs that do not belong to it and warms chicks that after it will not go."

4. *BHS* prp: "And your turned aside ones [or, And those who turn aside from you]."

5. It is possible that the phrase "in the land" modifies what precedes it ("Those who turn aside in the land") rather than what follows it ("in the land they will be written/recorded"), although this would be contrary to the Masoretic accentuation.

face]. 17:17 Do not become to me a terror [LXX: alienation]. My refuge [MT adds: are you] in a day of evil/calamity [NETS: when you spare me in an evil day]. 17:18 Let those who persecute me be ashamed, but do not let me be ashamed. Let them be dismayed, but do not let me be dismayed. Bring upon them a day of evil/calamity, and with a double breaking [or, full breaking] break them.

The text of MT Jeremiah 17:1–4 and the introductory formula ("Thus says the Lord") at the beginning of MT 17:5 do not appear in Greek Jeremiah. It is usually assumed that this is the result of oversight (homoioteleuton) on the part of the Hebrew scribe who produced the source text of Greek Jeremiah or on the part of the Greek translator himself. According to this theory, either the scribe or the translator accidentally skipped from יהוה at the end of 16:21 to יהוה in כה אמר יהוה ("Thus says the Lord") at the beginning of 17:5 and inadvertently omitted the intervening text.[6] Upon further examination, however, this does not appear to be the most plausible explanation of the textual evidence. Apart from the fact that this is a substantial piece of text to overlook (and not just a verse or two), it is important to note that both the MT and 4QJer[a] have a section break after 17:4. This suggests that the break is ancient and not a later scribal innovation, which means that a scribe or a translator would have had to overlook the break in order to skip from 16:21 to 17:5. Furthermore, the introductory formula at the beginning of 17:5 is clearly a secondary editorial insertion. The Lord is not the speaker in 17:5–8. Thus, it seems likely that 17:1–4 and the introductory formula in 17:5 have been added as part of the second edition of the book represented by the MT and were never a part of the first edition of the book represented by Greek Jeremiah. The text of 17:1–2 expands upon the reference to the people's sin in 16:18 and anticipates the heart theme in 17:5, 9, 10, while 17:3–4 reuses material from 15:13–14. As for the introductory formula in 17:5, it prematurely anticipates the Lord's speech in 17:10.

According to the Masoretic accentuation of 17:1 (see the *athnach*), the phrase "with a hard point" is in apposition to the phrase "with an iron stylus": "The sin of Judah is written with an iron stylus, with a hard point." *BHS*, however, arranges the text so that the phrase "with a hard point" is read with what follows it: "With a hard point it is engraved on the tablet of their heart," thus creating two parallel clauses in chiastic structure. The term שמיר is variously rendered "flint," "diamond," or "adamant," but it is likely just a way to describe the hardness

---

6. See, e.g., Janzen, *Studies in the Text of Jeremiah*, 117.

or perhaps sharpness of the engraving instrument (cf. Ezek. 3:9; Zech. 7:12).[7] The sin of Judah (i.e., idolatry; see Jer. 16:18) is written with an iron stylus (i.e., a hard point; see Job 19:24), engraved on the tablet of their heart (see Prov. 3:3; 7:3), and thus not easily altered or removed (see Jer. 13:23). Their heart has turned aside from the LORD and failed to trust in him (Jer. 17:5, 9, 10). Only the transformative power of the new covenant relationship can change this situation so that it is the Torah that is written on the hearts and minds of the people (see Jer. 4:4; 31:31–34; Ezek. 11:19–20; see also Deut. 6:5; 29:3 [Eng., 29:4; cf. Jer. 6:19; 8:8; 16:11–12]; 30:6).

The last phrase of 17:1 ("and on the horns of your [mlt Mss: their] altars") adds that the sin of Judah is also written or engraved on the horns of the people's altars.[8] These are not the LORD's altars in the temple but "your altars" (mlt Mss: "their altars"), that is, the altars of idolatry that the people have multiplied for themselves (see Jer. 2:28; 11:13; Hos. 8:11; 10:1).[9] Josiah attempted to remove these altars with his religious reforms (2 Kgs. 23:12, 15), but they persisted in the land after his reign. Jeremiah 17:2 explains what is meant by this reference to the horns of the altars: "as their sons/children [Syr.: in their heart] remember their altars and their Asherah poles beside flourishing trees [nonn Mss: beside every flourishing tree; Syr., *Tg. Jon.*: under every flourishing tree] on [mlt Mss: and on] the high hills [see GKC §126x]."[10] The evidence of Judah's sin is manifest in the false worship practices of each subsequent generation at alternative worship sites (i.e., forbidden alternatives to the temple [see Deut. 12:2, 5]). The phrases "beside flourishing trees, on the high hills" do not modify "remember" but "their altars and their Asherah poles" (see commentary on Jer. 2:20 and references there).[11] These were altars to local manifestations of Baal (the Canaanite storm/fertility god) and poles to symbolize the

---

7. Rashi quotes from an obscure Midrash: "with a pen of iron, with a diamond point, preserved by Jeremiah, called 'an iron wall,' and by Ezekiel, to whom it was said: '(3:9) As a diamond, harder than flint have I made your forehead'" (Rosenberg, trans., *Mikraoth Gedoloth: Jeremiah Volume One*, 145).

8. "He had spoken of the heart, he now proceeds farther—that there appeared openly an evidence of hidden iniquity" (Calvin, *Jeremiah*, 2:338).

9. Contra Keil, *Jeremiah*, 172.

10. It is not really possible grammatically or syntactically to render as Rashi does, "Like the remembrance of their children, so was the remembrance of their altars to them" (Rosenberg, trans., *Mikraoth Gedoloth: Jeremiah Volume One*, 145).

11. Contra Keil, *Jeremiah*, 173.

Canaanite goddess of fortune (see BDB, 81). It is thus not necessary to find in the reference to the horns of these altars practices associated with the altars in the temple such as the priestly act of putting the blood of a sin offering on the horns (Exod. 29:12; Lev. 4:7, 30, 34; 8:15; 16:18).[12] Even less plausible is a connection with the stories of Adonijah and Joab who fled to the altar in the temple to take hold of its horns (1 Kgs. 1:50; 2:28).[13]

The text of Jeremiah 17:3–4 is very close to that of 15:13–14 in many ways, but there is no reason to assume that they should be identical in every detail. Each passage has its own textual history in the transmission of the book. Rudolph takes הֲרָרִי בַּשָּׂדֶה ("My mountain in the field") from the beginning of 17:3 and alters it to הָרֲרֵי בַּשָּׂדֶה ("mountains in the field/country") in order to join it to the end of 17:2 with the description of the alternative places of worship. As it stands, the MT ("My mountain in the field") is a reference to Mount Zion (Jerusalem; cf. Jer. 21:13), the chosen site of the temple to be exalted above all others (Isa. 2:2; Mic. 4:1; Zech. 14:10); but because of the sin of Judah throughout the land ("in all your borders"), the wealth and treasures of the temple will be given as plunder to the enemy (see 2 Kgs. 24:13; Isa. 39:6; Jer. 15:13; 20:5), and Jerusalem will be reduced to a field (Jer. 26:18; Mic. 3:12). This includes the people's alternative worship sites ("your high places") mentioned in 17:2.

The opening line of Jeremiah 17:4a appears to allude to the instruction for the year of remission: "And you will release your hand [יָדְךָ (cf. Deut. 15:3); MT: וּבָךְ (?); LXX[L], Vulg. = לבדך (alone)] from your inheritance that I gave to you [*Tg. Jon.*: And I will bring the enemy against your land, and it will be desolate like the (year of) release/remission; and then I will make repayment of judgments until I exile you from your inheritance that I gave to you]" (see Exod. 23:10–11; Lev. 25:3–4; Deut. 15:1).[14] Rashi paraphrases, "Perforce you will release your land for the time that it did not rest on your Sabbaths, which I said to you, '(Lev. 25:2) And the land shall rest a Sabbath for the Lord'" (see 2 Chr. 36:21).[15] The LORD will make the people serve their enemies in the land that they have not experienced (cf. Jer. 9:15 [Eng., 9:16]; 16:13; 22:28;

---

12. "The scene seems to be an occasion of atonement when the blood of the sin offering (see the regulations in Lev iv–v) was smeared on the 'horns' of the altar (protuberances at its four corners); but the sin is as it were engraved there, and will not come off" (Bright, *Jeremiah*, 117).

13. Contra Holladay, *Jeremiah 1*, 484.

14. For "your inheritance," see "my inheritance" in Jeremiah 16:18b.

15. Rosenberg, trans., *Mikraoth Gedoloth: Jeremiah Volume One*, 146.

Ezek. 32:9). For they have kindled a fire in his anger that will burn indefinitely (Jer. 17:4b; cf. Isa. 66:24).

The text of Jeremiah 17:5–8 appears to be the basis for Psalm 1. Jeremiah contrasts the cursed man who trusts in mankind and ends up like a shrub in the desert (Jer. 17:5–6) with the blessed man who trusts in the LORD and so is like a fruitful tree planted by water (Jer. 17:7–8). Psalm 1 contrasts the blessed person who "murmurs" (i.e., reads aloud quietly to himself) in the text of the Torah day and night and thus is like a fruitful tree planted by water (Ps. 1:1–3) with the wicked who are like the chaff that the wind drives away and who will not stand in the final judgment (Ps. 1:4–6). Holladay argues that Jeremiah 12:1–2 and 17:5–8 are both variations on the theme of Psalm 1,[16] but there is no demonstrable literary dependence between Jeremiah 12:1–2 and Psalm 1. Furthermore, it is highly unlikely that a passage like Jeremiah 17:5–8 would be dependent upon Psalm 1 and make no reference to the Torah. Rather, what seems to be the case is that Psalm 1 has taken the abstract from the Jeremiah text (trust in the LORD) and given it concrete expression (Torah study).[17]

Rashi attempts to connect Jeremiah 17:5–8 with 17:1–4 by identifying the man who fails to trust in the LORD with one who sows the land during the seventh year and does not allow it to rest (see comments on 17:4).[18] Calvin proposes that 17:5 refers to trust in Assyria and Egypt (see Isa. 31:3; Jer. 2:18, 37), and this reference may very well have been prompted by the threat of exile in 17:4, but Calvin quickly adds that 17:5 expresses a general truth that may be applied to individual cases.[19] Perhaps a Judean king like Zedekiah is such a case (cf. Ezek. 17:5–10). Another possibility is that 17:5–8 describes Jeremiah's journey from despair over what he suffered at the hands of men to deep-seated trust in the LORD (see Jer. 15:15–21). On the other hand, McKane suggests that 17:5–8 is an isolated unit.[20] It focuses on the individual rather than the corporate life of Judah and has potential for universal application (cf. Ps. 1).[21] Another way to say this is that text is ultimately for the reader of the book of Jeremiah, but 17:5–8 does not stand in isolation from its surroundings. The passage must be related to the text that originally preceded it, namely, Jeremiah 16:19–21 (17:1–4 >

---

16. Holladay, *Jeremiah 1*, 489–90.

17. See Seeligmann, *Gesammelte Studien*, 17–18.

18. Rosenberg, trans., *Mikraoth Gedoloth: Jeremiah Volume One*, 146–47.

19. Calvin, *Jeremiah*, 2:344–45.

20. McKane, *Jeremiah I–XXV*, 389.

21. McKane, *Jeremiah I–XXV*, 392–93.

LXX). According to that passage, the nations will turn from idols made by "mankind" (אדם) and come to the LORD. And so, the implied instruction in 17:5–8 is to forsake trust in "mankind" (אדם) and to make the LORD the object of trust.

Jeremiah 17:5 and 17:7 are not wishes that certain types of people would be either cursed or blessed. Rather, they are statements of fact.[22] "Cursed is the man who trusts in mankind and puts the flesh of his arm on him [MT: and makes flesh his arm/strength] and whose heart turns aside from the LORD" (Jer. 17:5; cf. Pss. 56:5 [Eng., 56:4]; 118:8; see also Jer. 17:1, 9, 10, 13). Such a person will be like a shrub in the desert plain (Jer. 17:6; cf. Jer. 48:6; see also *m. Avot* 3:17). He will not see when "good" (טוב) comes (cf. Jer. 29:32), perhaps a reference to rain (see Deut. 28:12). He will inhabit parched places in the wilderness, a salty/barren and uninhabited land (cf. Deut. 29:22 [Eng., 29:23]; Judg. 9:45; Job 39:6). It is possible that these are descriptions of the shrub to which the cursed man is compared (see Redak); that is, the shrub is the grammatical subject of the verbs "see" and "inhabit." This would make for nice symmetry with 17:8 where the blessed man is compared to a tree, which is then described in terms opposite to those in 17:6. Modern commentators, however, have favored the cursed man as the grammatical subject of the verbs. McKane argues that ערער does not even mean "shrub" but "one living destitute" (cf. Gen. 15:2): "The right conclusion is rather that there is no tree imagery in v. 6 and that its simile has a different character from that of v. 8: the man who trusts in human power is likened to a destitute person who knows nothing of the good life and suffers a solitary existence in a wasteland."[23] Nevertheless, the early versions and modern lexicons all take ערער to be a type of plant or shrub. It is worth noting that the wicked in Psalm 1:4 are compared to chaff.

The man who trusts in the LORD and makes the LORD the object of his trust is blessed (Jer. 17:7; cf. Pss. 34:9; 40:5; 52:10; 84:13 [Eng., 34:8; 40:4; 52:8; 84:12]; Prov. 16:20; *m. Pe'ah* 8:9).[24] "And he will be

---

22. Although the wicked appear to prosper as blessed people for a time (Jer. 12:1–2; cf. Jer. 17:7–8), their ultimate fate is that of the cursed (see Jer. 11:22–23). Likewise, the righteous like Jeremiah or Job may suffer for a season, but in the end their confidence in the LORD will not be in vain (e.g., Jer. 15:19–21).

23. McKane, *Jeremiah I–XXV*, 390.

24. "What then seems to us so easy, we find in reality to be very difficult: and hence the Prophet, after having said, that they are blessed who trust in God, has mentioned this in the second place, *And whose hope is God*; as though he had said, 'The world knows not what it is to trust in God: though

like a tree planted [LXX: thriving] by water, which by a stream [LXX: to moisture] sends its roots, and does not fear [MT *qere*: see] when heat comes, and whose leaf is flourishing; [MT adds: and] in a year of drought it is not anxious and does not move [LXX: cease] from producing fruit" (Jer. 17:8; cf. Num. 24:6; Jer. 31:12; *Tg. Neof.* Gen. 49:22).[25] This person is not like a shrub with shallow roots in a desert plain but like a tree that sends down its roots deep next to a reliable water source. The cursed man (or shrub) "does not see when good comes" (לֹא יִרְאֶה כִּי יָבוֹא טוֹב). The tree, on the other hand, "does not fear when heat comes" (לֹא יִרָא כִּי יָבֹא חֹם). The MT *qere* (יִרְאֶ) vocalizes the text of 17:8 so that יִרְאֶה ("see") is read instead of יִרָא ("fear"): "does not see when heat comes." This suggests that the tree is so well nourished that it does not even notice the heat, but the original text features a wordplay between יִרְאֶה ("see") in 17:6 and יִרָא ("fear") in 17:8 (see also Job 5:21b).[26] When heat comes, there is no reason for the consistently watered tree to fear. Its leaves flourish. In a year of drought such as the one mentioned in Jeremiah 14:1, the tree is not anxious, nor does it fail to produce fruit. This personification of the tree lends itself well to the comparison with the blessed person.

There is no better commentary on the imagery of Jeremiah 17:7–8 than the one found in Psalm 1:1–3. The Jeremiah text naturally raises the question, "How does someone trust in the LORD?" What does it look like to be as a tree planted by water? Psalm 1 gives this trust concrete expression: Torah study.[27] To live the ideal life of a scribe (e.g., Ezra

---

every one boldly testifies this, and even boastingly declares that he trusts in God, yet not one in a thousand finds that he understands this, or has ever known that it is from the heart to hope in God.' We now see that this repetition is not superfluous or unmeaning" (Calvin, *Jeremiah*, 2:351).

25. Contrary to what Jeremiah felt in 15:18, the LORD is not like an unreliable water source (see Jer. 2:13; 17:13).

26. For the combination of these two verbs elsewhere, see Isaiah 41:5; Psalms 40:4; 52:8 (Eng., 40:3; 52:6).

27. Translations of "Torah" in Psalm 1:2 as "law" give the impression that the blessed person only delights in the collections of law found in Exodus 20–Leviticus 27. But the giving of the law at Sinai was cause for fear rather than delight (Exod. 20:18–21; Deut. 5:23–30). It is the message of the Pentateuch (Gen.–Deut.) that gives reason for delight—a message of faith (e.g., Gen. 15:6), eschatological and messianic salvation (e.g., Gen. 49:1, 8–12; Num. 24:7–9, 14, 17), and hope in a new covenant relationship (Deut. 28:69; 29:3 [Eng., 29:1, 4]; 30:6). Thus, Ezra the scribe makes the entire Pentateuch the object of his study (Neh. 8–9). Psalms 1 and 2 form an introduction to the Psalter in which Psalm 1 identifies the Torah as

7:6, 10) and sit in front of the written text of the Torah throughout the day is to trust in the LORD. It is the very act of faith, obedience, and worship.[28] The believer is the tree, and the Torah is the water—a constant source of nourishment for spiritual growth. The LORD, contrary to Jeremiah's thought in 15:18, is a fountain of living water (Jer. 2:13; 17:13) through his revealed word. Jeremiah himself has learned in the midst of his struggles to delight in the words of the Torah (Jer. 15:16).

The text of Jeremiah 17:9–10 is not unrelated to that of 17:5–8. It speaks to the issue of the human "heart/mind" (לב) that turns aside from the LORD (Jer. 17:5b; see also Jer. 17:1, 13b). The Hebrew source behind Greek Jeremiah 17:9 says, "The heart is deeper (עמק) than all, and (hu)man (אָנֹשׁ) is he/it, and who can know him/it" (cf. Ps. 64:7 [Eng., 64:6]; Prov. 18:4; 20:5)?[29] According to this, the human heart is too deep to be known (see Jud. 8:14). Human sin is concealed, engraved on the tablet of the heart (Jer. 17:1), so that it is not known whether the object of a person's trust is mankind (Jer. 17:5) or the LORD (Jer. 17:7). On the other hand, MT 17:19 says, "The heart is more deceptive (עקב) than all, and incurable (אָנֻשׁ) is it, and who can know it?"[30] This change is likely based on the language of Jeremiah 9:3b (Eng., 9:4b): "For every brother/relative surely follows at the heel (עקוב יעקב) [or, acts like

---

the Psalter's object of study (e.g., Pss. 19; 78; 105; 106; 119; 135; 136), and Psalm 2 identifies the Messiah as the principal subject of the Torah (see, e.g., Pss. 40–41; 72; 89; 110; 118). Just as the Pentateuch concludes with the expectation of a messianic prophet like Moses (Deut. 18:15, 18; 34:10) followed by instruction to "murmur" in the book of the Torah day and night at the beginning of the Prophets (Josh. 1:8), so the Prophets conclude with the expectation of a forerunner prophet like Elijah (Mal. 3:1, 23 [Eng., 3:1; 4:5]) followed by instruction to "murmur" in the Torah day and night at the beginning of the Writings (Ps. 1:2).

28. "Once Rabbi Tarfon and the elders were reclining at a banquet in the upper room of the house of Nitezeh in Lud. This question was raised for them: 'Is study greater, or is action greater?' Rabbi Tarfon answered, 'Action is greater.' Rabbi Aqiba answered, 'Study is greater.' All answered, saying, 'Study is greater, because study brings about action'" (*b. Qidd.* 40b). See also Shepherd, *Textual World of the Bible*, 97–107; *Textuality and the Bible*, 38–39.

29. Early church fathers mistakenly thought the "man" in Greek Jeremiah 17:19 was Christ (see Wenthe, ed., *Jeremiah, Lamentations*, 136–38). Cf. LXX Numbers 24:7, 17.

30. There is also variation between אָנֹשׁ "man" (see LXX) and אָנוּשׁ "incurable" (MT) in Jeremiah 17:16.

Jacob (i.e., deceptively)]."[31] The term "incurable" comes from Jeremiah 15:18 (אנושה) and 30:12 (אנוש). The answer to the question, "Who can know it?" comes directly from the Lord himself in 17:10: "I the Lord search heart(s) and [and > Codex L] test kidneys [Codex L adds: and] to give to each according to his ways [MT *kethiv*: his way] and [and > Codex L] according to the fruit of his deeds."[32] The human heart may be hidden from others who only see what is on the outside, but the Lord is able to see what is inside (see 1 Sam. 16:7; Prov. 20:27). Both the heart and the kidneys represent the control center of the human. Only those who trust in the Lord will have hearts that bear the kind of "fruit" (פרי) that will pass the test (Jer. 17:7–8; see also Gal. 5:22–23).

Jeremiah 17:11 appears to be a kind of proverbial saying (cf. Prov. 23:4–5) that illustrates the fate of those who trust in humanity rather than the Lord—those to whom the Lord will give according to their evil deeds. The key word "leave/forsake" (עזב) links the verse with the following context (Jer. 17:13). The metaphor of the partridge has been variously understood throughout the history of interpretation. It is not an invitation to study the behavior of partridges, as if readers were expected to have scientific knowledge of these creatures. Rather, the proverb appeals to common knowledge, and the hermeneutical task is to understand the words rather than the referent.[33] According to *Targum Jonathan*, the image is that of a partridge that gathers eggs that do not belong it and warms chicks that will eventually not follow after it once they realize that they do not belong to it (cf. Rashi).[34] So it is with one who makes riches unjustly (see Jer. 5:27;

---

31. It is less plausible that MT 17:9, which has language native to the book of Jeremiah elsewhere, was the original text and then was altered deliberately to the text that lies behind Greek Jeremiah, whose language does not appear elsewhere in the book.

32. "The connections of the vocabulary of vv. 9f. may be investigated in the following ways: (a) with reference to חקר (b) with reference to חקר and בחן (c) with reference to בחן (d) with reference to כפרי מעלליו. (a) Ps 139.1; (b) Jer 17.10; Ps 139.23; (c) Jer 11.20 (20.12); 12.3; Ps 7.10; 17.3; 26.2; 66.10; Prov 17.3; 1 Chr 29.17; (d) Isa 3.10; Mic 7.13; Jer 6.19; 17.10 (32.19); 21.14" (McKane, *Jeremiah I–XXV*, 395–96). See also Jeremiah 6:27; Revelation 2:23. McKane also lists passages from Jeremiah with the coupling of "ways" and "deeds" (Jer. 4:18; 7:3, 5; 18:11; 23:22; 25:5; 26:13; 35:15). See also Jeremiah 16:17; Hosea 12:3 (Eng., 12:2); 1 Peter 1:17; Revelation 22:12.

33. "Words" (*verba*) explain "things" (*res*). "Things" (*res*) do not explain "words" (*verba*).

34. "We reach the conclusion that the figure is that of a partridge (?) sitting on or hatching eggs which it has not itself laid, since this enables the simile

1 En. 97:8–10). In the middle of his days, they will "leave" (עזב) him (cf. Ps. 49:18 [Eng., 49:17]). According to Calvin, "While partridges so burn with love to their brood, they are at the same time led away by their own lust, and that while they conceal their eggs, the male cunningly steals them, so that their labor proves useless."[35] Both of these explanations assume that the point of the analogy is to highlight the act of doing something unjustly. Therefore, they look for something "unjust" in the description of the partridge.

What if the point of the analogy is not lack of justice but loss of gain?[36] Of course, it is the one who makes riches without justice who loses his gain, but perhaps the lack of justice is not a feature of the partridge metaphor. All analogies break down at some point. They typically do not correspond in every detail. The verb דגר can mean "gather" (as in Aramaic) or "brood" (cf. Isa. 34:15): "A partridge that gathers [i.e., gathers eggs; or, broods]." But the following ולא ילד cannot be rendered as a relative clause as if אשר were in the place of ו (contra LXX). Thus, it is not possible to say: "A partridge that gathers eggs that it did not lay." The verb ילד ("give birth") in this context presumably refers either to the laying of eggs or the hatching of them, although the hatching of eggs is more analogous to the kind of giving birth to which ילד normally refers. There is no indication of whether the eggs belong to the partridge or not. Thus, the metaphor speaks of a partridge that gathers eggs or broods but does not hatch them for whatever reason. Likewise, an unjust person gathers and/or protects his riches but loses them prematurely. In the demise of such a person, he/she will be considered a "fool" (נבל) like "Nabal" (נבל), a wealthy man (1 Sam. 25:2–3) who died and lost everything prematurely (1 Sam. 25:37–38) because he mistreated people in his protection of his wealth (1 Sam. 25:4–12) and thus lived up to his name (1 Sam. 25:25). Ironically, Nabal's wise wife Abigail (1 Sam. 25:3) became the wife of king David whom Nabal disrespected (1 Sam. 25:42)—a fitting picture of the way in which

---

to function in the way that is desiderated: the partridge acquires chicks by the misappropriation of eggs and the unjust man acquires ill-gotten wealth" (McKane, *Jeremiah I–XXV*, 401).

35. Calvin, *Jeremiah*, 2:358.
36. "But if the first colon is to be translated 'The partridge broods but does not hatch,' then the point of the passage is not so much that the rich man has gathered his riches unjustly, but rather that, having gathered his riches unjustly, the punishment will fit the crime, and he will lose what he has amassed, so that he should not count on holding on to what he has gained" (Holladay, *Jeremiah 1*, 498).

divine justice rewards the wise who trust in the LORD and judges the foolish who do not (see 1 Sam. 25:30–34, 39).

Targum Jonathan attempts to connect 17:12 with 17:11 by adding at the beginning of the verse: "Vengeance will be made from him [i.e., the fool from 17:11] before the one whose dwelling presence is on the throne of glory." But 17:12–13 is a unit, and the connection to the preceding material will come primarily in verse 13. The syntax of the Hebrew source behind Greek Jeremiah 17:12 can be read in at least two different ways: (1) "An exalted (מוּרָם) throne of glory (is) our sanctuary"; or (2) "O exalted (מוּרָם) throne of glory, our sanctuary."[37] According to the first option, the verse is a statement about the temple being an exalted throne of glory (cf. Jer. 3:17; 14:21). According to the second, the LORD is addressed as an exalted throne of glory, the people's sanctuary (cf. Isa. 6:1; 8:14; Jer. 2:11b). This second option works well with the address to the LORD at the beginning of 17:13: "O hope of Israel! O LORD!" The MT has an expanded text for 17:12:[38] (1) "A throne of glory on high (מָרוֹם) from (the) beginning (מֵרִאשׁוֹן) (is) the place (מְקוֹם) of our sanctuary"; or (2) "O throne of glory on high (מָרוֹם) from (the) beginning (מֵרִאשׁוֹן), the place (מְקוֹם) of our sanctuary" (cf. Jer. 7:3–4; Ezek. 43:7).[39]

Jeremiah 17:13a is clearly addressed to the LORD: "O hope of Israel! O LORD! All those who forsake you (עֹזְבֶיךָ), they will be ashamed (יֵבֹשׁוּ)" (cf. Jer. 14:8; 50:7).[40] Just as the riches of the unjust man "leave" (עזב) him to the shame of his folly (Jer. 17:11), so those

---

37. The phrase "throne of glory" can also be rendered "glorious throne."

38. The suggestion that the Greek translator or the scribe who produced his Hebrew source accidentally skipped from מרום to מקום and thus omitted מראשׁון מקום is not plausible for two reasons. First, the Hebrew source behind Greek Jeremiah had מורם, not מרום. Second, the letters ר and ק are not commonly confused in transmission or translation of biblical Hebrew texts.

39. The rabbinic literature interprets the phrase מראשׁון ("from the beginning") as a reference to Genesis 1:1 (Neusner, *Jeremiah in Talmud and Midrash*, 101, 186, 286, 318), but the word in Genesis 1:1 is ראשׁית, not ראשׁון. "Zion is called loftiness from the beginning, i.e., from immemorial time, as having been from eternity chosen to be the abode of God's glory upon earth; cf. Ex. 15:17, where in the song of Moses by the Red Sea, Mount Zion is pointed out prophetically as the place of the abode of Jahveh, inasmuch as it had been set apart thereto by the sacrifice of Isaac" (Keil, *Jeremiah*, 177).

40. The word מִקְוֵה ("hope") has a homonym that means "collection (of water)." This is worth noting in light of the designation of the LORD at the end of the verse as a fountain of living water.

who "leave" or "forsake" (עזב) the L ord will be ashamed. Likewise, Jeremiah's persecutors "will be ashamed" (יבשׁו), but Jeremiah's trust in the L ord will keep him from such shame (Jer. 17:18). According to the Hebrew source behind Greek Jeremiah 17:13b, "Those who turn aside (סָרִים),[41] in the land they will be written/recorded [or, in the land let them be written/recorded]."[42] These are the ones who trust in mankind and whose hearts "turn aside" (סור) from the L ord (Jer. 17:5). It is possible that the phrase "in the land" should be read with what precedes it ("Those who turn aside in the land"), although most follow the MT accentuation, which puts it with what follows: "in the land they will be written/recorded." It is not immediately clear, however, what this means. According to *Targum Jonathan*, it means that they are about to fall into Gehenna. The idea that they will be registered in the land of the dead has been taken up by modern interpreters on the basis of Ugaritic evidence.[43] On the other hand, McKane thinks it odd that a penal significance would be attached to Sheol, since all people must die at some point.[44] He cites Rudolph's position that there is a contrast here between ineffaceable and effaceable writing (cf. Jer. 18:23): "The sins of Israelites are incised on their hearts with a diamond point (v. 1), but the record which might preserve a memorial of them and save them from oblivion is written with a finger on rootless dust."[45] The judgment that they will receive is due to the fact that they have "forsaken" (עזב) the fountain of living water, the L ord (see commentary on Jer. 2:13). Again, contrary to the thought that the L ord is an unreliable water source (Jer. 15:18), he is indeed a fountain of living water.

---

41. It is possible that this source had סָרֵי, which would connect with the following phrase בארץ ("in the land"): "Those who turn aside in the land."
42. Neither the *kethiv* יְסוֹרַי ("My reprovers/faultfinders") or the *qere* וְסוּרֵי ("And my turned aside ones" or "And those who turn aside from me") of the Leningrad Codex are satisfactory (see Jer. 2:21; 6:28; GKC §50f), prompting the proposal in the *BHS* apparatus: וְסוּרֶיךָ ("And your turned aside ones" or "And those who turn aside from you"). The Syriac interprets this word as if it were from the root סרר ("And the rebellious") (see Jer. 6:28).
43. See Thompson, *Book of Jeremiah*, 423. See also Keil (*Jeremiah*, 177), who suggests that "land" here is synonymous with "dust" (cf. Job 14:8) and thus refers to death. According to Keil, to be written in the land is the opposite of being written in the book of life (Dan. 12:1; see also Exod. 32:32; Isa. 4:3).
44. McKane, *Jeremiah I–XXV*, 407. Of course, the Targum is not saying that the people will simply die but that they will go to a place of punishment.
45. McKane, *Jeremiah I–XXV*, 408.

Jeremiah 17:14–18 constitutes the fifth confession of Jeremiah. It hearkens back to the fourth confession in 15:15–21. Thus, in 17:14 Jeremiah prays, "Heal me, O LORD, and I will be healed [or, so that I will be healed]. Deliver me, and I will be delivered [or, so that I will be delivered], for the object of my praise is what you are" (cf. Jer. 8:20, 22; 14:19; Ps. 6:3 [Eng., 6:2]; see also Deut. 10:21; Jer. 14:8; Ps. 71:6). This is a follow-up prayer to what Jeremiah said in 15:18: "Why do those who cause me pain have victory over me [MT: Why has my pain been perpetual]? [MT adds: And] My wound is incurable. Whence will I be healed [MT: It refuses to be healed.]? Will you indeed be to me like a deceptive water source, that is, unreliable water?"[46] Jeremiah's prayer for healing in 17:14 is a prayer for deliverance from his enemies—those who persecute him in the land of Judah for his faithfulness to his prophetic calling.[47] What he has to say to them is too difficult for them to hear. They are saying to him, "Where is the word of the LORD? Let it come" (Jer. 17:15; cf. Isa. 5:19; 66:5; Ezek. 12:22), taunting and challenging him, accusing him of being a false prophet (see Deut. 18:22).[48]

Jeremiah says that he has not hastened "from grazing" (מֵרֹעֶה) after the LORD (Jer. 17:16). Like a sheep that follows its shepherd (Ps. 23), Jeremiah has faithfully followed the LORD (cf. LXX Jer. 17:16) despite the difficulties of his calling.[49] The paraphrase of *Targum Jonathan* says, "I have not held back concerning your word from prophesying to them to turn them back to the worship of you" (cf. Jer. 15:11). It is not likely that Jeremiah is saying that he has not hastened "from shepherding" after the LORD. The figure of a shepherd is normally used for kings (e.g., Jer. 2:8; 3:15; 6:3; 10:21; 23:1–4), not prophets. Even less likely is any rendering that suggests Jeremiah is claiming not to have pressed himself into the position of prophet in order to speak out against the people, however well this may fit with what

---

46. See Holladay, *Jeremiah 1*, 505.

47. "The experience Jeremiah had had in his calling seemed to contradict the truth, that trust in the Lord brings blessing (v. 7ff.); for his preaching of God's word had brought him nothing but persecution and suffering. Therefore he prays the Lord to remove this contradiction and to verify that truth in his case also" (Keil, *Jeremiah*, 178).

48. "So long as his announcements were not fulfilled, the unbelieving were free to persecute him as a false prophet (cf. Deut. 18:22), and to give out that his prophecies were inspired by his own spite against the people" (Keil, *Jeremiah*, 178).

49. See McKane, *Jeremiah I–XXV*, 410. See also Jeremiah 11:19.

follows.[50] The Greek renderings of Aquila and Symmachus appear to reflect מֵרָעָה ("from evil") rather than מֵרֹעֶה ("from grazing"), as if to say that Jeremiah has not quickly turned aside from the trouble of his prophetic office. The Syriac seems to read ברעה ("in evil"), in which case Jeremiah is making the case that he is not guilty of any wrongdoing in his prophetic ministry. Jeremiah then adds: "and man's day [MT: an incurable day] I have not desired." The variation between "man's day" (יוֹם אֱנוֹשׁ) and "an incurable day" (יוֹם אָנוּשׁ) is similar to the textual problem in 17:9 (see commentary above). Jeremiah is saying that he has not desired the day of judgment for his enemies (cf. Ezek. 18:23, 32; 33:11; see Jer. 17:18b). He has sought the LORD's justice for his persecutors (see Jer. 11:20; 12:3; cf. Deut. 28:63), but he has not in a bloodthirsty manner longed to see their destruction for its own sake (cf. Ps. 139:19–24). According to the Masoretic accentuation (*athnach*), Jeremiah states that the LORD knows this: "You, you know. What has gone forth from my lips has been before your face." According to the arrangement of the text in *BHS*, the object of the verb "know" is what follows: "You, you know what has gone forth from my lips; it has been before your face." The LORD knows that Jeremiah has prayed on behalf of the people (Jer. 14:7–9, 19–22; 18:20b) despite indications that such prayer would be in vain (Jer. 7:16; 11:14; 14:11).

Jeremiah prays that the LORD would not be a "terror" to him (Jer. 17:17a; cf. Jer. 15:18b). He declares that the LORD is his "refuge in a day of evil/calamity" (Jer. 17:17b; cf. Jer. 15:11; 16:19; 18:23b). This could be a reference either to the present day of trouble or to the final time of judgment. Jeremiah expects to be vindicated: "Let those who persecute me be ashamed, but do not let me be ashamed. Let them be dismayed, but do not let me be dismayed. Bring upon them a day of evil/calamity, and with a double breaking [or, full breaking] break them" (Jer. 17:18; see Jer. 15:15; 17:13; see also Jer. 11:20; 12:3; 18:23). This language comes straight out of the programmatic text of the book (see Jer. 1:17b). The day of evil/calamity will come upon his enemies, but he will take refuge in the LORD. In asking for a "full breaking,"[51] Jeremiah is only requesting what the LORD himself has said he will do (see Jer. 14:17; 16:18). The LORD has instructed Jeremiah not to pray on behalf of the people "for good" (Jer. 14:11), but a prayer for righteous judgment will be answered.[52]

---

50. See Keil, *Jeremiah*, 178.

51. See Bullinger, *Figures of Speech*, 586.

52. Ibn Nachmiash comments, "Although it was previously stated that Jeremiah prayed for their good, it is possible that he prayed for the people in

17:19 Thus said the LORD [MT adds: to me], "Go and stand in the gates [MT: gate] of the sons of your people [4QJer^a, MT kethiv: of sons of people; MT qere: of the sons of the people] through which the kings of Judah enter and through which they exit, and in all the gates of Jerusalem, 17:20 and say to them, 'Hear the word of the LORD, O kings of Judah and all Judah and all [4QJer^a, MT add: inhabitants of] Jerusalem who enter through these gates. 17:21 Thus says the LORD, "Watch yourselves for your lives, and do not lift up a burden on the Sabbath day and bring in [LXX: enter; see 17:24, 27] through the gates of Jerusalem. 17:22 And do not bring out a burden from your houses on the Sabbath day; and as for any work, do not do it. And set apart the Sabbath day just as I commanded your forefathers. (17:23) But they did not listen, and they did not incline their ear, 17:23 and they hardened / stiffened their neck more than their forefathers [more than their forefathers > 4QJer^a, MT] so as not to listen to me and so as not to receive discipline / instruction. 17:24 And so, if you will indeed listen to me," the prophetic utterance of the LORD, "not to bring in a burden through the gates of this city on the Sabbath day and to set apart the Sabbath not to do [MT kethiv adds: בָּה (in it) or בֹּה (on it); MT qere adds: בֹּו (on it)] any work, 17:25 then kings and princes sitting on the throne of David and [and > 4QJer^a, MT] riding on chariots and on horses will enter through the gates of this city, they and their officials, the men of Judah and the inhabitants of Jerusalem, and this city will be inhabited forever. 17:26 And they will come from the cities of Judah and from the places surrounding Jerusalem and from the land of Benjamin and from the lowland and from the hill country and from the south bringing burnt offerings and sacrifices and grain offerings and frankincense, [MT adds: and] bringing thanksgiving offerings to the house of the LORD. 17:27 But if you do not listen to me, to keep the Sabbath day, [MT adds: and] not to lift up a burden and enter through the gates of Jerusalem on the Sabbath day, I will kindle a fire in its gates, and it will consume the prominent buildings of Jerusalem, and it will not be extinguished."'"

It may seem strange at first to find at this juncture of the book of Jeremiah a passage about the Sabbath day, but it is important to remember that the Sabbath is the "sign" (אות) of the covenant that was made at Sinai (Exod. 31:12–17), just as the rainbow is the sign of the

---

general, but not for his pursuers. It is also possible that, at first, he prayed for their good, but after they humiliated him and abused him considerably, he changed his tactics and prayed for their retribution" (Rosenberg, trans., *Mikraoth Gedoloth: Jeremiah Volume One*, 151).

Noahic covenant (Gen. 9:12–13), and just as circumcision is the sign of the covenant with Abraham (Gen. 17:11). Thus, the Sabbath can stand for the whole of the Mosaic covenant and represent covenant fidelity in general (see, e.g., Isa. 56:2, 4, 6). Just as the Sabbath day is to be set apart, so the people of God are to be set apart (Exod. 31:13–14). Even for new covenant believers who are no longer under the law (Rom. 6:14), the reading of the Sabbath instruction in the larger context of the Pentateuch serves as a reminder of the original rest granted in the garden of Eden (Gen. 2:2–3; Exod. 20:8–11), the rest that came as a result of the exodus from Egypt (Deut. 5:12–15), and the future rest that remains for the people of God (Heb. 4:1–11). Therefore, in a book like Jeremiah, which is concerned with the breaking of the covenant (Jer. 11:10), the failure to keep the Torah (Jer. 16:11), and the forsaking of the LORD (Jer. 16:11; 17:13), it is only fitting that the Sabbath would be brought into the mix.

According to the MT *qere* of Jeremiah 17:19, the prophet recounts how the LORD instructed him to go and stand "in the gate of the sons of the people" (בשער בני העם) (cf. Jer. 7:2; 19:2; 22:1–2). Since no such gate is known, it has been suggested that בני העם ("the sons of the people") should be emended to בנימין ("Benjamin"; see Jer. 37:13; 38:7). This reading is adopted in the RSV, but it lacks extant textual support. 4QJer[a] and MT *kethiv* have the indefinite phrase "in gate of sons of people" (בשער בני עם). Such variation in MT tradition suggests the possibility that both readings may be corruptions of an earlier, more original reading. The Hebrew source behind Greek Jeremiah has the phrase "in the gates of the sons of your people" (בשערי בני עמך), which does not make reference to one specific gate by an unknown name. These are the gates through which the general populace and the royalty (i.e., the laity as opposed to the priests) enter and exit (cf. 2 Chr. 35:5, 12, 13; see also 2 Kgs. 23:6; Jer. 26:23). It is not clear whether these are city gates or temple gates. Lest the reader think that this makes 17:19b ("and in all the gates of Jerusalem") redundant, there are several possibilities for this latter phrase: (1) gates through which only the general populace passes; (2) gates through which only the royalty passes; (3) gates through which only the priests pass or gates through which only the priests and another group or other groups pass; (4) gates for foreigners or gates through which all may pass indiscriminately; and/or (5) city gates as opposed to temple gates or vice versa. In accordance with the LORD's instruction, Jeremiah is to address the kings of Judah, all Judah, and all Jerusalem who enter through these gates (Jer. 17:20). Since only one king can rule on the throne at a time, the intention must be to deliver a message that would be relevant to each king who reigns in succession.

The message begins with a warning: "Watch yourselves for your lives" (השמרו בנפשותיכם) (Jer. 17:21a).[53] This is because violation of the Sabbath law results in capital punishment (see Exod. 31:14–15; 35:2; Num. 15:32–36). According to MT 17:21b, the prohibition is not to lift up a "burden" (משא) on the Sabbath day and bring it in through the gates of Jerusalem (cf. Jer. 17:24). The LXX translates that the people are not to lift up a burden on the Sabbath and "enter" through the gates of Jerusalem (cf. Jer. 17:27). The terminology of lifting up a burden is not a feature of the Sabbath law in Exodus 20:8–11 or Deuteronomy 5:12–15 (cf. Exod. 23:12; 31:12–17; 34:21; 35:2; Lev. 23:3). In fact, the instruction in the Pentateuch is so ambiguous (speaking only of rest from work) that special consultation of the LORD has to be made in the case of the man caught gathering wood on the Sabbath (Num. 15:32–36; cf. Lev. 24:10–23; Num. 9:6–14; 27:1–11). A specific prohibition such as the one against kindling a fire in a dwelling place on the Sabbath is very rare (Exod. 35:3). Later Judaism would understand the lifting of a burden on the Sabbath to include the mere transportation of any object (see Jub. 2:29–30; John 5:10),[54] but this is not the inner-biblical understanding of these terms. Nehemiah 13:15–22 uses the term "burden" (משא) for items brought into the city of Jerusalem on the Sabbath day for commerce: grain, wine, grapes, figs, fish, and all kinds of merchandise (see also Neh. 10:32 [Eng., 10:31]). Thus, whereas those referenced in Amos 8:5 impatiently waited out the Sabbath in order to resume their dishonest trade, the problem that both Jeremiah and Nehemiah seek to address is the brazen disregard for the Sabbath day by those who would rather buy and sell than rest in accordance with God's revealed will.[55]

Jeremiah 17:22 adds that the people are not to bring out a burden from their houses on the Sabbath day. Again, this would be any load carried out for the purpose of commerce. And as for any other kind of work, it is not to be done on the Sabbath day (וכל מלאכה לא תעשו). This latter clause contains the language of the Sabbath law from the Pentateuch (see Exod. 20:10; 31:14–15; 35:2; Lev. 23:3; Deut. 5:14). The general rule still applies, but the special concern of this passage is to deal with a particular kind of work that has been done on the Sabbath. The people are to "set apart" the Sabbath day just as the LORD commanded their forefathers (see Gen. 2:3; Exod. 20:8, 11b; 31:13–15; Lev.

---

53. Cf. "And you must watch yourselves very carefully" (ונשמרתם מאד לנפשתיכם) (Deut. 4:15a).

54. See also Neusner, *Jeremiah in Talmud and Midrash*, 69, 97.

55. See Calvin, *Jeremiah*, 2:377, 379. See also Zechariah 14:21b.

23:3; Deut. 5:12); but their forefathers did not listen, nor did they incline their ear (cf. Neh. 13:18). They hardened/stiffened their neck like a stubborn animal so as not to listen or receive discipline/instruction (Jer. 17:23; cf. Jer. 19:15; 32:33; see Exod. 32:9; see also Prov. 1:3). The Hebrew source behind Greek Jeremiah adds that the forefathers did this "more than their forefathers" (cf. Jer. 7:26; 16:12).

The if-then constructions of 17:24–26 and 17:27 follow the pattern of Leviticus 26 and Deuteronomy 28: blessing for obedience and curse for disobedience (cf. Jer. 22:4–5; see also commentary on Jer. 6:8). This is one of the hallmarks of the conditional covenant made at Sinai as opposed to the unconditional new covenant, which depends upon divine faithfulness rather than unreliable human fidelity. If the people listen to the LORD so as not to bring in a burden through the gates of the city of Jerusalem on the Sabbath day and so as to set apart this day by not doing any work (Jer. 17:24),[56] then "kings and princes sitting on the throne of David and [and > 4QJer[a], MT] riding on chariots and on horses will enter through the gates of this city, they and their officials, the men of Judah and the inhabitants of Jerusalem, and this city will be inhabited forever" (Jer. 17:25). The combination of kings and "princes" (שרים) refers to successive kings on the throne and their sons who succeed them. The descriptions of the kings and princes as those "sitting on the throne of David" (cf. Jer. 13:13; 22:2) and "riding on chariots and on horses" are coordinated by the conjunction *waw* ("and") in the Hebrew source behind Greek Jeremiah (cf. LXX Jer. 22:4). On the other hand, the MT lacks this conjunction, perhaps indicating that "riding on chariots and on horses" does not describe the kings and princes but the manner in which they enter through the gates of the city (cf. MT Jer. 22:4). שריהם ("their officials") does not refer to princes but to the officials of the royalty. Finally, there is a general reference to the men of Judah and the inhabitants of Jerusalem. The last thought in 17:25b is that the city of Jerusalem will be inhabited forever. McKane comments, "More allowance should be made for the splendour of an eschatological consummation (a Messianic Age) in v. 25, even if it is the protocol of the pre-exilic Judaean court, and the way in which royal processions were organized in that context, which dominates the description."[57] Verse 26 adds, "And they will come from the

---

56. The MT *kethiv* adds בה after לבלתי עשות ("not to do"), which can be read as בָּה ("in it"; i.e., not to do in the city [f.] any work) or as בֹּה ("on it"; cf. *qere*: בֹו; i.e., not to do on the Sabbath day [m.] any work).

57. McKane, *Jeremiah I–XXV*, 419. See Jeremiah 3:15; 23:4, 5–6. For images of the entry of the ideal king, see Psalms 24:7–10; 118:19–26; Zechariah 9:9–10.

cities of Judah and from the places surrounding Jerusalem and from the land of Benjamin and from the lowland and from the hill country and from the south bringing burnt offerings and sacrifices and grain offerings and frankincense, [MT adds: and] bringing thanksgiving offerings to the house of the LORD" (cf. Jer. 32:44; 33:11, 13; see also Deut. 12:5; Jer. 14:12).[58]

On the other hand, if the people do not listen to the LORD, "to keep the Sabbath day, [MT adds: and] not to lift up a burden and enter through the gates of Jerusalem on the Sabbath day" (cf. LXX Jer. 17:21), the LORD will kindle a fire in the city's gates that will consume the "prominent buildings" (BDB, 74) of Jerusalem (see also Jer. 9:20 [Eng., 9:21]), a fire that will not be extinguished (Jer. 17:27; cf. Jer. 7:20; 21:12, 14; 22:5; 49:27; 50:32; Amos 2:5).[59] The accounts of the burning of Jerusalem in Jeremiah 39:8 (MT) and 52:13 confirm that the people did not heed this warning. This consequence may be an ironic twist of fate based on the prohibition in Exodus 35:3: "Do not kindle a fire in any of your dwellings on the Sabbath day."

---

58. "In v. 26 the main codices of Sept. read καὶ θυσίαν καὶ θυμιάματα, apparently a double rendering of וזבח. The reading in Sept.[OL] (see Ziegler) is καὶ θυμιάματα, and Ziegler supposes that the original text was καὶ θύματα of which καὶ θυμιάματα ('and incense') is a corruption and καὶ θυσίαν a doublet. Ziegler (*Beiträge*, pp. 103f.) has turned the argument on its head: if the Greek translator of the book of Jeremiah elsewhere uses θυσία to render זבח, there is reason for urging the originality of καὶ θυσίαν, and Janzen's view (pp. 202f.) that καὶ θυμιάματα is a doublet deriving from a rendering of וזבח as καὶ θύματα is probably correct. Since θυμίαμα/θυμιάματα does not appear in Sept. as a rendering of מנחה, the possibility that καὶ θυμιάματα is an alternative to the transcription καὶ μαναα (so Ziegler) can be dismissed" (McKane, *Jeremiah I–XXV*, 415).

59. On the basis of this verse the Talmud teaches that a fire occurs only in a place where there is desecration of the Sabbath (*b. Shabb.* 119b).

JEREMIAH 18

18:1 The word that came from the LORD *to Jeremiah [MT: to Jeremiah from the* LORD*], saying, 18:2 "Arise and go down to the potter's house, and thither [or, there] you will hear my words [MT: I will cause you to hear my words]." 18:3 And I went down to the potter's house, and look, he was making a work on the two stones [LXX: the stones; Syr., Tg. Jon.: the block; Vulg.: wheel]. 18:4 And the vessel that he was making [Codex L, mlt Mss add: with clay; nonn Mss add: as clay] in his hands [MT: in the potter's hand] would be ruined [or, was ruined], and he would make [or, he made] it again into another vessel just as it was right in his eyes to do. 18:5 And the word of the* LORD *came to me, saying, 18:6 "Like this potter am I not able to do to you, O house of Israel? [MT adds: the prophetic utterance of the* LORD*] Look, like the potter's clay [MT: like the clay in the potter's hand] are you in my hand [MT: so are you in my hand, O house of Israel]. 18:7 At one moment [NETS: At last; Syr.: If from the calm; Vulg., Luther: Suddenly] I speak concerning a nation or concerning a kingdom to pluck them up and to destroy [MT: to pluck up and to tear down and to destroy], 18:8 and if that nation turns from their [MT: its] evil [MT adds: about which I have spoken], I will relent concerning the evil/calamity that I planned to do to them [MT: it]. 18:9 And at another moment [see 18:7] I speak concerning a nation or a kingdom to build and to plant, 18:10 and if they do [MT: and if it does] what is evil in my eyes not to obey my voice, I will relent concerning the good that I said to do them [MT: it]. 18:11 And now, say to the men of Judah and to the inhabitants of Jerusalem [MT adds: saying, 'Thus says the* LORD*'], 'Look, I am about to fashion against you evil/calamity and make against you a plan. Return, each from his evil way, and improve your deeds [MT: your ways and your deeds].'" 18:12 And they said [MT: And they will say], "It is hopeless [LXX: We will act like a man;[1] Tg. Jon.: We have turned from the worship of you]! For after our plans [LXX: turnings away] we will go, and each the stubbornness [LXX: pleasing things] of his evil heart/mind we will do."*

The most obvious connection between Jeremiah 17:19–27 and 18:1–12 is the "if-then" pattern of 17:24–27 and 18:7–10.[2] Apart from that, the term "work" (מלאכה) in 17:22, 24 and 18:3 provides another

---

1. The translator mistakenly thought נואש to be from the root איש or אנש. Cf. Syriac. See also Jeremiah 2:25.

2. See Thompson, *Book of Jeremiah*, 432.

link. If the people refrain from "work" on the Sabbath day, they will experience blessing; if not, they will experience a curse. If the potter (the LORD) makes a "work" (a nation or kingdom such as Judah) for one purpose and finds that it is suited for another, he will remake it accordingly. These two are linked insofar as the success of the "work" (the kingdom of Judah) depends upon whether it keeps itself from "work" on the Sabbath (i.e., is faithful to the terms of the covenant).[3] The connection to the following chapter then comes in the reference to the earthenware flask fashioned by a potter (Jer. 19:1, 11).

The syntactical variation between the Hebrew source behind Greek Jeremiah 18:1 ("The word that came from the LORD to Jeremiah, saying") and MT 18:1 ("The word that came to Jeremiah from the LORD, saying") is also a feature of Jeremiah 11:1; 32:1; 40:1 (LXX 11:1; 39:1; 47:1) (but not Jer. 30:1; 34:1, 8; 35:1 [LXX 37:1; 41:1, 8; 42:1]; see also MT 7:1). Since the third-person reference to Jeremiah appears to be at odds with 18:5 ("And the word of the LORD came to me, saying"), it is possible that אל ירמיהו ("to Jeremiah") is the result of reading אלי ("to me") as an abbreviation (אל י) for אל ירמיהו (cf. Jer. 32:6, 26 [LXX 39:6, 26]; see also MT and LXX Jer. 1:4).

The LORD instructs Jeremiah to go to the local potter's house where he will hear the LORD's words in the form of an object lesson (Jer. 18:2; cf. Zech. 11:13). Jeremiah then narrates that he went down to the potter's house in accordance with the LORD's instruction (Jer. 18:3a). Using the word הנה ("look"), he vividly depicts what he saw there and brings the reader into his viewpoint: "and look, he was making a work on the two stones." The term translated here as "the two stones" (הָאָבְנָיִם) is variously rendered by the early versions: LXX "the stones" (= הָאֲבָנִים); Syr., *Tg. Jon.* "the block"; Vulg. "wheel." Bright comments, "The apparatus consisted of two stone wheels on a vertical axle, the lower of which was spun by the feet, while the upper carried the clay which the potter shaped as the wheel revolved."[4]

---

3. Malbim: "Since after all the evil decrees, God revealed to the prophet that if they observe the Sabbath, He would repeal the decree, He calls him to the house of the potter to illustrate His words graphically" (Rosenberg, trans., *Mikraoth Gedoloth: Jeremiah Volume One*, 154).

4. Bright, *Jeremiah*, 124. See also *DCH* 1:114. "So a potter sitting at his work and turning a wheel with his feet, who always lies down in anxiety about his work, and every work of his is taken into account. With his arm he will mold clay and in front of his feet he will bend its strength; he will give over his heart to completing the glazing, and his sleeplessness is about cleaning the kiln" (Sir. 38:29–30 NETS). Keil wonders whether the derivation is

The first two verbs in Jeremiah 18:4 are either *weqatal* forms or simple "*waw* + *qatal*" forms. If they are *weqatal* verbs, then Jeremiah is describing what the potter would customarily do: "And the vessel that he was making in his hands would be ruined (ונשחת), and he would make it again (ושב)[5] into another vessel just as it was right in his eyes to do" (cf. NET).[6] This perhaps indicates that Jeremiah himself witnessed the potter doing this repeatedly. The difficulty with this view is that the following verbal form is a *wayyiqtol* (ויעשהו), suggesting a narrative account of a single event. If the first two verbs are simple "*waw* + *qatal*" forms, then they provide background information for narration that continues with the *wayyiqtol*: "And the vessel that he was making in his hands was ruined, and he made it again into another vessel just as it was right in his eyes to do" (cf. ESV). The difficulty with this view is that the reader would expect to find one "*waw* + *qatal*" form (ונשחת) and two *wayyiqtol* forms (וישב ויעשהו) (cf. Gen. 26:18).

Many Masoretic manuscripts, including the Leningrad Codex, add the phrase בחמר ("with clay"; see BDB, 90) to 18:4a: "And the vessel that he was making with clay." This seems like an unnecessary addition since it can be assumed that a potter would be working with clay, but it does provide another possible antecedent (in addition to "the vessel") for the pronoun "it" when 18:4b later says: "and he would make it again" (or, "and he made it again"). Does the potter remake the vessel or the clay (see Jer. 19:11)? Some Masoretic witnesses have the phrase כחמר ("as clay"), which Bright renders, "as clay sometimes will in the potter's hands,"[7] which suggests a problem with the clay itself. This kind of textual variation may simply be due to accidental confusion of the similar letters ב and כ, but it is possible that בחמר was deliberately altered to כחמר because of the occurrence of כחמר in 18:6b.[8]

When Jeremiah says 18:4a that the vessel that the potter was making "would be ruined" or "was ruined" (ונשחת), the verb ונשחת does not automatically have a negative connotation as נשחת does in Jeremiah

---

from אֶבֶן ("stone") or אוֹפָן ("wheel") (*Jeremiah*, 183). See also Wisdom of Solomon 15:7–8.

5. Lit., "and he would return (ושב) and make it (ויעשהו)."

6. The phrase בידיו (MT: ביד היוצר) should be rendered "in his hands" (MT: "in the potter's hand") rather than "with his hands" (MT: "with the potter's hand") in order to correspond with the analogy in 18:6b: "Look, like the potter's clay [MT: like the clay in the potter's hand] are you in my hand [MT: so are you in my hand, O house of Israel]."

7. Bright, *Jeremiah*, 121.

8. See McKane, *Jeremiah I–XXV*, 421.

13:7. According to the exposition of this object lesson in 18:7–10, the "ruining" of the vessel simply represents a deviation from the original design. A vessel intended for "evil/calamity" may be "ruined" in the sense that its course is altered so that it is intended for "good" (Jer. 18:7–8). A vessel intended for "good" may be "ruined" in the sense that its course is altered so that it is intended for "evil/calamity" (Jer. 18:9–10; cf. Jer. 19:11). Thus, when Jeremiah says that the potter "would make" or "made" it (i.e., the vessel) again into another vessel just as it was "right" (ישר) in his eyes to do, it does not mean that the remade vessel was "pleasing" or "chosen" but that it was "fitting" or "appropriate" for its new design.

When the word of the LORD comes to Jeremiah again (Jer. 18:5; cf. Jer. 1:4, 11; 2:1; 13:8; 16:1), the LORD explains the meaning of the object lesson in the form of an address to Israel (i.e., Judah): "Like this potter am I not able to do to you, O house of Israel? [MT adds: the prophetic utterance of the LORD] Look, like the potter's clay [MT: like the clay in the potter's hand] are you in my hand [MT: so are you in my hand, O house of Israel]" (Jer. 18:6). The LORD is like the "potter" (יוצר), and the people are like the clay vessel in his hand (cf. Isa. 27:11; 43:1, 21; 44:2, 21, 24; 64:7; Lam. 4:2; see also 2 Cor. 4:7). The LORD is the original "potter" who "fashioned" (יצר) mankind out of the dust of the ground (Gen. 2:7; Sir. 33[36]:13). He "formed" (יצר) Jeremiah in the belly of his mother (Jer. 1:5; cf. Isa. 43:7; 49:5; Zech. 12:1; Ps. 33:15). The potter should not be regarded as the clay, nor should the vessel made out of clay deny that the potter made it or claim that the potter lacks understanding (Isa. 29:16). The clay vessel is in no position to question the potter (Isa. 45:9, 11; Rom. 9:20–21). The potter is the creator, and the vessel is the creation (Isa. 45:7, 18; Jer. 10:16; 51:19; Amos 4:13; Pss. 74:17; 94:9; 95:5).[9]

"At one moment" (רגע) the LORD may speak concerning a nation or concerning a kingdom "to pluck them up and to destroy" (לנתוש אתם ולהאביד; MT: "to pluck up and to tear down and to destroy" [לנתוש ולנתוץ ולהאביד]) (Jer. 18:7). This is the language of the programmatic text in Jeremiah 1:10 (see commentary there). The first thing to be observed about this is that it applies not only to Judah but also to any nation or kingdom. If a nation turns from its "evil" (רעה), the LORD will "relent" (נחם) concerning the "evil/calamity" (רעה) that he planned to do to it (Jer. 18:8; cf. Jer.

---

9. John Chrysostom: "For the distance between God and man is as great as the distance between the potter and the clay. Rather the distance is not merely as great but much greater. The potter and the clay are of one and the same substance" (Wenthe, ed., *Jeremiah, Lamentations*, 147). See also Calvin, *Jeremiah*, 2:395.

31:28; Joel 2:14; Jon. 3:9–10; 4:2). The Lord does not change his mind in a fickle manner like humans (see Num. 23:19 and comments on Jer. 4:28), but he does relent in accordance with opportunities for repentance established in advance.[10] The teaching about personal responsibility in Ezekiel 18 shares this sentiment. If the wicked person turns from his sin and keeps the Lord's statutes and does justice and righteousness, that person will live and not die, for the Lord does not delight in the death of the wicked but in his/her repentance (Ezek. 18:21–23, 27–29, 32).

"And at another moment" (ורגע) the Lord may speak concerning a nation or a kingdom "to build and to plant" (לבנת ולנטע) (Jer. 18:9). Again, this is the language of the programmatic text in Jeremiah 1:10. If such a nation does what is evil in the Lord's eyes, he will relent concerning the good that he said he would do (Jer. 18:10). Likewise, the teaching in Ezekiel 18 says that if a righteous person turns from his/her righteousness and behaves like the wicked, that person's former righteousness will be forgotten, and he/she will die (Ezek. 18:24). If it is objected that this is somehow "unfair" (Ezek. 18:25a), the response is that it is not the way of the Lord that is unfair but the way of the people (Ezek. 18:25b). This is because the people expect their past to determine their future regardless of what happens in the present (Jer. 31:29; Ezek. 18:2).

ועתה ("And now") marks the logical conclusion to the discourse thus far (Jer. 18:11). Jeremiah is to say to the men of Judah and the

---

10. Jerome: "Our point here is not that God was ignorant of what the nations and kings would do, but rather that he had endowed the human person with his own will, so that he would receive either a reward or a punishment on the basis of his own merit" (Wenthe, ed., *Jeremiah, Lamentations*, 146). Origen: "To repent seems to be culpable and unworthy not only of God but also of the wise person. For I cannot conceive of a wise person repenting. Rather, when a person repents, supposing the customary use of the word, he repents for not having decided to be good. But God, who knows in advance what happens in the future, is unable not to have decided to be good and to repent for this. How, then, has the Scripture brought forth this phrase that says, 'I will repent'? . . . Whenever the Scriptures speak theologically about God in relation to himself and do not involve his plan for human matters, they say that he is 'not as a human.' . . . But whenever the divine plan involves human matters, it carries the human intellect and manners and way of speaking. If we are talking with a two-year-old child, we speak inarticulately because of the child. . . . Something of this sort also seems to me the case with God, whenever he manages the race of humankind and especially those still infants" (Wenthe, ed., *Jeremiah, Lamentations*, 148).

inhabitants of Jerusalem (cf. Jer. 4:3; 11:2; see also Jer. 13:18), "Look, I am about to fashion against you evil/calamity and make against you a plan. Return, each from his evil way, and improve your deeds [MT: your ways and your deeds]." The Hebrew word translated "fashion" (יוצר) here is the same word translated "potter" (יוצר) in 18:3, 6 (and MT 18:4). The translation "fashion," "form," or "shape" helps the English reader make the connection, but the precise semantic nuance in this context is "frame," "pre-ordain," or "plan" (see BDB, 427; cf. 2 Kgs. 19:25; Isa. 22:11; 37:26; 46:11; Jer. 33:2). That is, just as a potter shapes clay, so the LORD "shapes" situations. In this case, he is planning "disaster" (רעה) for the "evil" (רעה) of the people of Judah (see Jer. 1:14, 16; 18:7; 21:10; 36:3; 44:27; cf. Jer. 29:11; see also Jer. 18:18). Thus, the people are urged to return from their evil ways and to improve their deeds (cf. Jer. 7:5–7; 18:8; 25:5; see also Jer. 4:1; 15:19). It is natural to think that this comes from a time early in Jeremiah's ministry when Judah's fate was not sealed and when there was still opportunity for repentance (see commentary on Jer. 6:8),[11] but it may simply be a way to elicit a response (i.e., refusal to repent) such as the one in 18:12, which shows the coming judgment to be a just one. Repentance and obedience will not happen under the old covenant because they depend upon human initiative and faithfulness. True change will only occur in the new covenant when the LORD restores the people and gives them hearts and minds to believe and obey (Jer. 4:1–4; 29:14; 30:3, 18; 31:18, 23, 31–34; 32:44; 33:7, 11).

The Hebrew source behind Greek Jeremiah 18:12 introduces the reply of the people with the narrative form ויאמרו ("And they said") (cf. Jer. 18:18). According to this reading, the text of this verse is a report from the prophet to the LORD after his delivery of the message to the people. The MT, however, has the discourse form ואמרו ("And they will say"), which is either a continuation of the LORD's discourse that indicates what he anticipates the people's response to be, or it is Jeremiah's introduction to what he anticipates the people will say.[12] The expression, "It is hopeless" (נואש), also occurs in MT 2:25 (cf. Isa. 57:10). The people are too committed to following after their own "plans, thoughts" to pay attention to those of the LORD and repent (see Isa. 55:7–9). This refers to the way in which they follow after idols or strange gods (Jer. 2:5b, 8b, 25b; see also the "plan" being made against Jeremiah in Jer. 18:18). They each do "the stubbornness of his evil heart/mind" (cf. Deut. 29:18; Jer. 3:17; 7:24; 9:13 [Eng., 9:14]; 11:8; 13:10; 16:12; 23:17).

---

11. See Keil, *Jeremiah*, 182; Thompson, *Book of Jeremiah*, 432.
12. Holladay, *Jeremiah 1*, 517.

18:13 Therefore, thus says the LORD, "Ask among the nations, 'Who has heard [Syr.: done] such things?' It is a horrible thing that virgin Israel has done greatly. 18:14 Do breast-shaped crags depart from a rock? Does the snow of Lebanon leave [MT: Does the snow of Lebanon depart from a rock of a field]? Will presumptuous waters brought by an east wind be plucked up [MT: Will strange, cold flowing waters be plucked up]? 18:15 For my people have forgotten me. In vain [or, To that which is nothing] do they send sacrifices up in smoke. And they will stumble [LXX: be weak; Codex L: And they caused them to stumble] in their ways, ancient paths, to walk paths, a way not built up [LXX: not having a way for travel], 18:16 to make their land into an object of horror and [and > MT] everlasting hissing. All those who pass by it will be appalled and shake their head [MT: Every person who passes by it will be appalled and shake his head]. 18:17 Like [mlt Mss: With] an east wind [LXX, Syr., Vulg.: scorching wind] I will scatter them before their enemies [MT: before enemies]. I will show them the day of their distress/ calamity [MT: Back of neck and not face I will see (Or: show) them in the day of their distress/calamity]."

18:18 And they said, "Come, and let us make against Jeremiah a plan [MT: plans], for Torah [or, instruction] will not perish from priest nor counsel from wise man nor word from prophet. Come, and let us strike him with the tongue [Syr.: his tongue; Tg. Jon.: and let us bear false testimony against him], and let us [MT adds: not] pay attention to all his words." 18:19 Pay attention to me, O LORD [MT: Pay attention, O LORD, to me], and listen to the voice of my contention [MT: those who contend with me]. 18:20 Should a man be repaid [Syr.: Should I be repaid; Tg. Jon.: Is it possible to repay] evil for good? For they have spoken word(s) [שִׂיחָה] against my life, and their stumbling block have they hidden for me [MT: For they have dug a pit for my life]. Remember my standing before you to speak for them good to turn back your wrath from them. 18:21 Therefore, give their sons [or, children] to famine and pour them out [LXX: gather them (from אגר?); Syr.: deliver them] to a sword's hands [i.e., a sword's power]. Let [MT: And let] their women be bereaved and widows; and as for their men, let them be slaughtered by death [i.e., plague], and let their choice, young men be stricken by sword in battle. 18:22 Let a cry of distress be heard [LXX: Let there be a cry of distress] in their houses [MT: from their houses]. You will bring [MT: when you bring] against them a band/troop suddenly. For they dug a pit [LXX: undertook a word/plan (= שִׂיחָה)] to capture me, and snares they hid for me [MT: for my feet]. 18:23 And you, O LORD, you know all their counsel against me for death. Do not cover their iniquity [cf. Neh.

3:37 (Eng., 4:5)], and their sin from before you do not blot out. Let their stumbling block [LXX: weakness] be before you [MT: And let them be (qere: that they may be) caused to stumble (Ms, Syr.: cast out) before you]. In the time of your anger deal with them.

The conjunction לכן ("Therefore") at the beginning of 18:13 introduces not an announcement of judgment (as in Jer. 5:14) but an invitation to consider the manner in which the people have responded to the LORD according to 18:11–12 (cf. Jer. 2:9): "Ask among the nations, 'Who has heard [Syr.: done] such things?' It is a horrible thing that virgin Israel has done greatly." This implies that Israel (i.e., Judah) has done something so terrible that it is unprecedented even among the nations. Behavior that might have been expected elsewhere has occurred in the least expected place—among God's chosen, privileged people. The juxtaposition of "horrible thing" (שערת) and "virgin Israel" makes for a particularly striking contrast (see Jer. 5:30; 14:17; 23:14). She who had such great potential to be the pure bride (Jer. 2:2–3) has become the worst kind of whore (Jer. 3:1–11). She has gone after her own "plans, thoughts" (i.e., idols, strange gods) and forsaken her faithful husband, the LORD (Jer. 18:12). Even the nations, who worship non-gods, do not abandon their idols: "For cross over to the isles of Kittim and see, and to Kedar send and consider carefully; and see if it has happened like this. Do nations exchange their gods [MT: Does a nation exchange gods], and they are non-gods [or, even though they are non-gods]? And my people, it exchanges its glory for those that do not benefit [MT: for that which does not benefit]" (Jer. 2:10–11). How unthinkable it is that Israel would leave the one true God!

The number of interpretations and emendations of Jeremiah 18:14 may give the impression that what is done with the text is something of a free for all, but the reality is that there is general agreement on the point of the analogies.[13] The somewhat subtle differences between the two Hebrew editions of the book make for substantial differences in translation. The Hebrew source behind Greek Jeremiah 18:14a says, "Do breast-shaped crags depart from a rock? Does the snow of Lebanon leave (הֲיַעַזְבוּ מִצּוּר שָׁדַיִם שֶׁלֶג לבנון)?" MT 18:14a says, "Does the snow of Lebanon depart from a rock of a field (הֲיַעֲזֹב מִצּוּר שָׂדַי שֶׁלֶג לבנון)?"[14] Some

---

13. See McKane, *Jeremiah I–XXV*, 428–32.

14. The combination of the root עזב ("leave") and the preposition מן ("from") is unusual. Bullinger (*Figures of Speech*, 29) suggests an ellipsis: "Will *a man* leave the snow of Lebanon for the rock of the field?" Cf. Rashi (Rosenberg, trans., *Mikraoth Gedoloth: Jeremiah Volume One*, 157): "Shall a man

prefer to adjust שָׂדַי ("field") to שִׂרְיוֹן ("Sirion" = "Hermon"). According to Keil, the rock of the field is not Zion (Jer. 17:3; 21:13; Ps. 133:3); rather, the field is "the land of Israel, whence seen, the summit of Lebanon, and especially the peak of Hermon covered with eternal snow might very well be called the rock of the field."[15] The Hebrew source behind Greek Jeremiah 18:14b says, "Will presumptuous waters brought by an east wind be plucked up (אם ינתשו מים זדים קדים נוזלים)?"[16] The "presumptuous waters" (מים זדים) are "boiling" or "turbulent" waters. To ask if they will be "plucked up" (ינתשו) is odd, but not unintelligible. Many prefer emendation to ינשתו ("dried up") (see Rudolph, *BHS* apparatus).[17] MT 18:14b says, "Will strange, cold flowing waters be plucked up (אם ינתשו מים זרים קרים נוזלים)?"[18] The "strange waters" (מים זרים) are waters that come from a distant place (cf. 2 Kgs. 19:24) and thus seem perennial. Just as these constant features of nature do not fail, so the Lord, the fountain of living water (Jer. 2:13; 17:13), does not fail (see Isa. 49:15; Jer. 31:35–37).[19] Therefore, it is inexplicable that Israel would prefer idols, which are broken cisterns (Jer. 2:13; see also Isa. 1:3; Jer. 2:32; 8:7; 13:23; Amos 6:12).

The conjunction כי ("For") at the beginning of 18:15a introduces an explanation for the call to ask among the nations in 18:13 and the subsequent illustration in 18:14. It answers the question, "Why are these things being said?" It is because the people have forgotten the Lord (cf.

---

who needs to drink abandon water that flows from the rock in the fields that comes from the snow of the Lebanon, which is clean?"

15. Keil, *Jeremiah*, 185. Bright (*Jeremiah*, 122) reads צוֹר ("flint") instead of צוּר ("rock"): "Do flints depart from the fields, Or the snow from Lebanon? Do flowing streams run dry, Or bubbling springs?"

16. The LXX translator rendered נוזלים ("flowing") as a passive participle ("brought"), perhaps because he read this word as a *niphal* participle from the root אזל ("go") rather than a *qal* participle from the root נזל.

17. The verb ינטשו ("abandoned" or "spread abroad") has also been suggested (see Redak).

18. Holladay (*Jeremiah 1*, 519): "Or are cities [ערים] uprooted by the waters, the capital [קריה] by floods?"

19. See Calvin, *Jeremiah*, 2:407; Keil, *Jeremiah*, 186. It is possible, though less likely, that the analogies are intended to say that Israel should be like the snow that never leaves Lebanon or like the waters that never dry up. This might work well with 18:15, which would then be the contrast to what should have been expected, but it does not work so well with 18:13 (cf. Jer. 2:9–13) where it is the faithfulness of the Lord (illustrated by 18:14) that makes Israel's apostasy so horrible (see Jer. 2:5; Mic. 6:3).

Jer. 2:32; 3:21; 13:25). "In vain [or, To that which is nothing] do they send sacrifices up in smoke" (cf. Jer. 2:30; 4:30; 6:29; see also Jer. 1:16; 7:9; 11:13, 17; Ps. 31:7 [Eng., 31:6]). According to the Hebrew source behind Greek Jeremiah 18:15b and one Masoretic manuscript, the text says, "And they will stumble (וְיִכָּשְׁלוּ) in their ways, ancient paths, to walk paths, a way not built up" (cf. Jer. 6:15, 21; LXX Jer. 18:20, 23). The Leningrad Codex says, "And they caused them to stumble (וַיַּכְשִׁלוּם) in their ways, ancient paths, to walk paths, a way not built up." The non-gods are presumably the subject of the main verb in this latter reading (cf. 2 Chr. 28:23), with the people of Judah as the object.[20] The "ancient paths" (שבילי עולם; mlt Mss: שבולי עולם) are generally thought to be the same as those in Jeremiah 6:16—the teachings of the Torah (see also Ps. 139:24).[21] In the present context, however, the phrase "ancient paths" is in apposition to "their ways" (cf. Jer. 2:23, 33; 3:13, 21; 15:7; 16:17; 18:11). Thus, the "ancient paths" here are the paths of the wicked followed since long ago (cf. Job 22:15; see Jer. 3:25; 32:30).[22] The end result of walking such paths is that they make their land into "an object of horror and everlasting hissing" (Jer. 18:16a; cf. 1 Kgs. 9:8; Jer. 5:30; 19:8; 25:9, 18; 29:18; 49:17; 50:13; 51:37; Lam. 2:15–16). "All those who pass by it will be appalled and shake their head [MT: Every person who passes by it will be appalled and shake his head]" (Jer. 18:16b; cf. 1 Kgs. 9:8; Jer. 19:8; 49:17; 50:13; Pss. 22:8; 44:15 [Eng., 22:7; 44:14]; 109:25; Lam. 2:15–16).

The Lord says in 18:17a that he will scatter the people before their enemies "like an east wind" (כרוח קדים; mlt Mss: "with an east wind" [ברוח קדים]) (cf. Jer. 9:15 [Eng., 9:16]; 13:24). According to the Hebrew source behind Greek Jeremiah 18:17b, he says, "I will show them (אַרְאֵם) the day of their distress/calamity" (cf. Jer. 2:28; 11:12, 14; 14:8; 15:11; 16:19; 17:17; Ezek. 35:5; Obad. 13), but in the expanded text of the MT he says, "Back of neck and not face I will see them (אֶרְאֵם) in the day of their distress/calamity" (Exod. 23:27; 2 Sam. 22:41; Ps. 18:41 [Eng., 18:40]). Rashi interprets this to mean: "when they flee from before the enemy, I will look upon them and I will not save them."[23] The "Eastern Masoretes" (Orientales) vocalize the text so that it says,

---

20. See McKane, *Jeremiah I–XXV*, 432. Keil (*Jeremiah*, 186) prefers the false prophets as the subject (cf. Jer. 23:27). The priests may also be considered a possibility (Mal. 2:8).
21. An ellipsis is required for this: "[*so that they forsake*] the ancient paths" (Bullinger, *Figures of Speech*, 60).
22. See Holladay, *Jeremiah 1*, 525.
23. Rosenberg, trans., *Mikraoth Gedoloth: Jeremiah Volume One*, 158.

"Back of neck and not face I will show them (אֶרְאֵם) in the day of their distress/calamity." According to this, just as the people have turned to the LORD the back of their neck and not their face (Jer. 2:27; 7:24; 32:33), so he will turn his back on them and not shine his face on them (Num. 6:24–26; Jer. 21:10).[24]

Jeremiah 18:18–23 is the sixth confession of Jeremiah. It initially comes across as a continuation of the preceding material ("And they said, 'Come, and let us make against Jeremiah a plan [MT: plans]'"), as if the plotting against Jeremiah were prompted specifically by the prophet's report of the LORD's words in 18:13–17, but the reality is that 18:13–17 is but a sample of the larger prophetic ministry of Jeremiah to which the people are reacting. The key word that connects 18:18–23 to the first half of the chapter is מחשבה ("plan, thought"). In 18:11, the LORD says that he is about to make against the people a "plan." The people respond in 18:12 that they will go after their own "plans." Now in 18:18 the people intend to make a "plan" against Jeremiah (cf. Ps. 56:6 [Eng., 56:5]; Lam. 3:60–61). It is not clear who is involved in the making of this plan, although the impression is that the opposition comes from the people in general or from several segments of society (as in Jer. 1:18b) rather than from a specific group such as the people of Jeremiah's hometown or his family (as in Jer. 11:18–23; 12:1–6). It is also not clear what the nature of the plot against Jeremiah will be. The latter part of 18:18 seems to presuppose an attempt to remove Jeremiah in some way, although it is not initially evident if this is the same as the "plan" to take the prophet's very life in Jeremiah 11:19 (but see Jer. 18:23).

The rationale for the plot against Jeremiah is that "Torah [or, instruction] will not perish from priest nor counsel from wise man nor word from prophet" (cf. Ezek. 7:26; 4Q177 4:6).[25] It is possible that this refers to an unfulfilled prediction from Jeremiah that such things would perish, in which case Jeremiah's opponents are laying the charge of false prophecy against him in order to subject him to the death penalty (Deut. 18:20–22);[26] but in the absence of a clear example of such a prediction (e.g., Ezek. 7:26; Amos 8:11; see also Lam. 2:9), it is preferable to see

---

24. This differs from the context of Exodus 33:23, where the LORD tells Moses that he will see his back but not his face. In Jeremiah 18:17b, turning the back to someone is rejection of that person. In Exodus 33:23, God prevents Moses from seeing his face in order to protect his life (Exod. 33:20).

25. The Ezekiel 7:26 text uses "elders" in place of "wise man" and "prophetic vision" in place of "word."

26. See Bright, *Jeremiah*, 124.

in these words a kind of reasoning that suggests that the removal of Jeremiah would ultimately not be any real loss. If Jeremiah were gone, they surmise, the teaching of the Torah would still be available from the priests; there would still be advice from wise men and messages from prophets.[27] The problem that they do not recognize is that the priests and those responsible for handling the Torah do not acknowledge the LORD (Jer. 2:8); the so-called wise men are not wise at all, because they have rejected the word of the LORD (Jer. 8:8–9); and the prophets prophesy by Baal (Jer. 2:8). All three groups—priests, wise men, and prophets—are caught up in the same deception (Jer. 5:31; 6:13–15). They tell the people what they want to hear but not what they need to hear. Jeremiah's presence is much more of a necessity than his opponents realize.

When those making plans against Jeremiah say, "Come, and let us strike him with the tongue" (Jer. 18:18b; see Jer. 9:2, 4, 7 [Eng., 9:3, 5, 8]), *Targum Jonathan* interprets their words to mean that they will bear false testimony against him.[28] In other words, the plan is not to make a legitimate accusation of false prophecy against him but to concoct a false accusation of some sort (cf. 1 Kgs. 20:9–10; see also Exod. 20:16; Deut. 5:20; Jer. 7:9). On the other hand, the Syriac says, "Come, and let us strike him with his tongue," in which case Jeremiah's opponents plan to use his own words against him in some way. The last clause of 18:18b in the Hebrew source behind Greek Jeremiah does not have a negation: "and let us pay attention to all his words." According to this reading, Jeremiah's enemies plan to pay careful attention to his words in order to find a way to trap him in what he says (cf. Matt. 22:15). The MT, however, does include a negation: "and let us not pay attention to all his words." According to this reading, those who are against Jeremiah look forward to ridding themselves of him so that they no longer have to give any attention to what he says.

The end of 18:18b ("and let us [MT adds: not] pay attention [ונקשיבה] to all his words") connects to the beginning of 18:19a: "Pay attention

---

27. The irony of this thought is that the Torah was lost by the priests in the period leading up to its discovery in the time of Josiah (2 Kgs. 22–23). The responsibility of transmitting and teaching the Torah fell to true prophets like Jeremiah (2 Kgs. 17:13; Dan. 9:10; Ezra 9:10–11).

28. It is perhaps possible that the text should be translated, "Come, and let us strike him in the tongue," in which case the idea would be to assault Jeremiah physically in such a way that he would be unable to speak (cf. Jer. 11:19; 20:2; 37:15). The text is normally not understood in this manner since the preposition ב after the *hiphil* of the verbal root נכה typically means "with" rather than "in" (see 2 Sam. 2:23).

(הַקְשִׁיבָה) to me, O LORD [MT: Pay attention, O LORD, to me]" (cf. Pss. 5:3 [Eng., 5:2]; 17:1; 55:3; 61:2 [Eng., 55:2; 61:1]; 86:6; 142:7 [Eng., 142:6]; Dan. 9:19). The prophet then adds the parallel clause in 18:19b: "and listen to the voice of my contention [MT: those who contend with me]" (see Jer. 12:1). The difference between "my contention" (רִיבִי) and "those who contend with me" (יְרִיבָי) can also be seen in witnesses to Psalm 35:1 where the Leningrad Codex has "those who contend with me" (יְרִיבָי) and a few Masoretic manuscripts have "my contention" (רִיבִי; cf. Syr.; see also Pss. 35:23; 43:1; Lam. 3:58).

Jeremiah then asks, "Should a man be repaid [Syr.: Should I be repaid; *Tg. Jon.*: Is it possible to repay] evil for good" (Jer. 18:20a; cf. Gen. 44:4; 1 Sam. 25:21; Pss. 35:12; 38:21 [Eng., 38:20]; 109:5; Prov. 17:13; see also Prov. 20:22; 24:29; Rom. 12:21)? Holladay suggests that this is a quote from Jeremiah's opponents in which they ask whether disaster should be repaid for the good they have done (according to the false prophets of peace),[29] but in the absence of any explicit indication of this, it is perhaps best to take these words as Jeremiah's rhetorical question (expecting a negative answer) about whether he deserves the kind of opposition expressed in 18:18 for the good that he has done on behalf of the people. According to the Hebrew source behind Greek Jeremiah, the prophet explains, "For they have spoken words (דִּבְּרוּ שִׂיחָה) against my life, and their stumbling block have they hidden for me."[30] The shorter text of the MT simply says, "For they have dug a pit (כָּרוּ שׁוּחָה) for my life" (cf. Jer. 18:22b; Pss. 7:16; 57:7 [Eng., 7:15; 57:6]; 119:85). The former reading works well as a reference to the words of 18:18. The latter reading is better suited to the immediate context of 18:22b. Jeremiah prays that the LORD would remember how he has stood in his service as his prophet like Moses (cf. Exod. 32:11–14; Deut. 9:25–29) to speak good on behalf of the people in order to turn back divine wrath from them despite every indication that such intercession would go unheeded (see Jer. 14:7–9, 11, 19–22; 15:1, 11, 19; 17:16; cf. 2 Kgs. 20:3; Neh. 5:19; 6:14; 13:14, 22b, 31b).

Because of the wrong done to him ("Therefore"), Jeremiah requests that the children of his enemies be given to famine and delivered to the power of the sword (Jer. 18:21; cf. Ezek. 35:5; Pss. 63:11 [Eng., 63:10]; 109:9–10). He asks that their women be bereaved and widowed. He prays for their men to be slaughtered by "death" (דבר = מות ["plague"]; see Jer. 14:12; 15:2; 43:11) and for their young men to be stricken by

---

29. Holladay, *Jeremiah 1*, 531.
30. The LXX uses κόλασις ("punishment") for מַכְשׁוֹל ("stumbling block") in Ezekiel 14:3, 4, 7; 18:30; 44:12. See also the root כשל in Jeremiah 18:15b, 23b.

the sword in battle. This is not the first of Jeremiah's imprecatory prayers (see Jer. 11:20; 12:3; 17:18). Lest the reader think that such prayers are motivated by personal vengeance, it is important to keep in mind that through prayer Jeremiah is entrusting his vindication to the LORD rather than taking matters into his own hands. Furthermore, Jeremiah only requests what the LORD himself has said that he will do (see Jer. 6:11–12; 11:22; 14:12, 16; 15:7–9). The LORD has made it very clear that Jeremiah's prayers for the people's good will not be met with a positive answer (Jer. 14:11).

Jeremiah continues, "Let a cry of distress be heard [LXX: Let there be a cry of distress] in their houses (בבתיהם) [MT: from their houses (מבתיהם)]. You will bring [MT: when you bring] against them a band/troop suddenly" (Jer. 18:22a; cf. Jer. 4:20; 6:26; 15:8; 20:10 [LXX]). "For," he explains, "they dug a pit (כָרוּ שִׁיחָה) to capture me, and snares they hid for me [MT: for my feet]" (Jer. 18:22b; cf. MT Jer. 18:20; Pss. 57:7 [Eng., 57:6]; 119:85, 110; 140:6; 142:4 [Eng., 140:5; 142:3]; 1QH[a] 10:29).[31] The word for "pit" (*kethiv*: שיחה; *qere*: שוחה) here is different from the one in 38:6 (בור), but in both cases Jeremiah's life is at stake (see Jer. 38:9). The LXX translator read כרו שיחה as if it were כָרוּ שִׂיחָה ("they undertook a word/plan") rather than כָרוּ שִׁיחָה ("they dug a pit") (cf. Jer. 18:20).

According to Jeremiah, the LORD is fully aware of the counsel of his enemies against him for death (Jer. 18:23a; cf. Jer. 11:18–19; 12:3; 15:15 [MT]). Jeremiah thus prays, "Do not cover (תכפר) their iniquity, and their sin from before you do not blot out (תֶּמַח)."[32] This prayer is cited by Nehemiah who makes it into his own imprecation against his enemies: "Do not cover (תכס) their iniquity, and their sin from before you let it not be blotted out (תִּמָּחֶה)" (Neh. 3:37 [Eng., 4:5]).[33] Nehemiah's citation of Jeremiah is instructive in several ways. First, it shows that from a very early time in the inner-biblical reception history of the book of Jeremiah the confessions were not read merely as a record of the prophet's personal situation. Rather, it was understood that, much like the prayers in the Psalter, Jeremiah's words were being presented

---

31. On the basis of Proverbs 23:27a ("For a fornicating woman [LXX: stranger] is a deep pit"), the Talmud suggests that Jeremiah's opponents suspected him of sexual immorality (*b. B. Qam.* 16b). Since sex with a prostitute was not punishable by death, the thought is that they accused him of sex with a married woman, which does warrant the death penalty (see Jer. 18:23).

32. For the MT's תֶּמְחִי see GKC §75ii (cf. Jer. 3:6; Neh. 13:14). For the image of blotting out, see Exodus 32:32–33. See also Jeremiah 17:13.

33. Nehemiah 3:37a2–38 is not present in the LXX.

as exemplary models for the faithful readership of the book to follow. This understanding was due to the prophet's role in the book as a representative of the people of God. Second, the use of the verb תכס (from כסה) in the Nehemiah citation for the verb תכפר (from כפר) in Jeremiah 18:23a demonstrates an early inner-biblical understanding of the *piel* of כפר as "cover" rather than "forgive" or "atone."[34] Third, as Rashi notes, the Nehemiah text interprets the strange תמחי of the MT not as an unusual *qal* or *hiphil* second masculine singular but as a *niphal* third feminine singular (תִּמָּחֶה).[35] Jeremiah then concludes, "Let their stumbling block [LXX: weakness] be before you [MT: And let them be (*qere*: that they may be) caused to stumble (Ms, Syr.: cast out) before you]. In the time of your anger deal with them" (Jer. 18:23b; cf. Jer. 17:17–18; 18:17; see also Jer. 10:24; Ps. 6:2 [Eng., 6:1]). According to the Hebrew source behind Greek Jeremiah, he prays that "their stumbling block" (מכשולם), which they hid for Jeremiah according to LXX 18:20, would not escape the LORD's notice, so that in the time of his anger he might deal with them accordingly. According to the Leningrad Codex, he prays that his enemies might be "caused to stumble" (מְכְשָׁלִים) before the LORD (cf. Jer. 18:15b). According to one Masoretic manuscript and the Syriac, he prays that they might be "cast out" (מֻשְׁלָכִים) before the LORD (cf. Jer. 14:16). Thompson notes that there is no response to Jeremiah from the LORD here as in 11:21–23; 12:5–6; 15:19.[36]

---

34. See Holladay, *Jeremiah 1*, 533. But see also Psalm 32:1.
35. Rosenberg, trans., *Mikraoth Gedoloth: Jeremiah Volume One*, 161.
36. Thompson, *Book of Jeremiah*, 444.

JEREMIAH 19

19:1 Then [MT: Thus] the LORD said to me [to me > Codex L], "Go and purchase a flask fashioned of earthenware [MT: a potter's earthenware flask (earthenware > Syr.)], and [> pc Mss] take [take > MT; Syr., Tg. Jon. add: with you] some of the elders of the people and some of the [MT adds: elders of the] priests, 19:2 and go out to the valley [LXX: common burial place] of the sons of their children [MT: Ben Hinnom], which is outside the entrance of the Potsherd Gate [Tg. Jon.: in front of the Dung Gate], and proclaim [LXX: read] there all the words [pc Mss: all these words] that I will speak to you, 19:3 and say, 'Hear the word of the LORD, O kings of Judah and men of Judah [and men of Judah > MT] and inhabitants of Jerusalem and those who enter through these gates [and those who enter through these gates > MT]. Thus says the LORD [MT adds: of hosts] the God of Israel, "Look, I am about to bring upon this place calamity [MT: I am about to bring calamity upon this place], which, every person who hears it, his ears will tingle / ring, 19:4 because they forsook me and treated this place as foreign [Syr., Tg. Jon.: defiled this place] and sent sacrifices up in smoke in it to other gods, which they did not know, they and their forefathers; and as for the kings of Judah, they have filled this place with blood of innocent ones [MT: which they did not know, they and their forefathers and the kings of Judah, and they have filled this place with blood of innocent ones] 19:5 and have built the high places of Baal to burn their children in the fire [MT adds: as burnt offerings to Baal], which I did not command [MT adds: and I did not speak; Tg. Jon.: which I did not command in my Torah or send by the hand of my servants the prophets], and it did not enter my mind [see GKC §144b; Tg. Jon.: and not pleasure before me].

19:6 Therefore, look, days are coming," the prophetic utterance of the LORD, "and this place will never again be called Topheth [LXX: fall] or the valley [LXX: common burial place] of Ben Hinnom but the valley [LXX: common burial place] of slaughter [Syr., Tg. Jon.: slain], 19:7 and I will make void [LXX: slaughter] the counsel of Judah and the counsel of [the counsel of > MT] Jerusalem in this place, and I will cause them to fall by the sword before their enemies and by the hand of those who seek their life, and I will give their corpse as food to the flying creatures of the sky and to the large land animals, 19:8 and I will make this city into an object of horror and into an object of hissing; every person who passes by it will be appalled and hiss because of all its wound [Codex L: wounds]; 19:9 and they will eat [cf. 4QJer^c; MT: and I will cause them to eat] the flesh of their sons and the flesh of their daughters, and each

the flesh of his neighbor they will eat [Tg. Jon.: and each the possessions of his neighbor they will plunder], in siege and in distress with which their enemies [MT adds: and those who seek their life] oppress them."'
19:10 And you will break the flask before the eyes of the men who are going with you [אִתָּךְ; MT: who are going you (אוֹתָךְ)],[1] 19:11 and you will say, 'Thus says the Lord [MT adds: of hosts], "Thus I will break this people and this city. Just as is broken an earthenware vessel [MT: Just as he breaks the potter's vessel], which can never be repaired again [MT adds: and in Topheth they will bury without place to bury], 19:12 so I will do," the prophetic utterance of the Lord, "to this place and to its inhabitants to make [LXX: to be made; MT: and to make; Syr.: and I will make; Vulg.: so that I can make] this city like Topheth [LXX: like one falling], 19:13 and the houses of Jerusalem and the houses of the kings of Judah will be like the place of Topheth of unclean things [LXX: like the falling place of unclean things; MT: like the place of Topheth, the unclean (pl.)], all the houses [see DCH 4:483] on whose roofs they have sent sacrifices up in smoke to all the host of the sky and poured out drink offerings to other gods."'"

19:14 And Jeremiah came from Topheth [LXX: the fall] where the Lord sent him to prophesy, and he stood in the court of the house of the Lord and said to all the people, 19:15 "Thus says the Lord [MT adds: of hosts the God of Israel], 'Look, I am about to bring upon this city and upon its cities [LXX: its villages; MT: all its cities] all the calamity that I spoke against it, for they have hardened/stiffened their neck not to hear/heed my words.'"

Chapter 19 features yet another symbolic sign act (cf. Jer. 13:1–14; 16:1–9; 18:1–12), which fits nicely within the sequence of Jeremiah 18–20. After the visit to the potter's house in 18:1–12, Jeremiah receives instruction to purchase "a flask fashioned of earthenware [MT: a potter's earthenware flask]" (Jer. 19:1). The brief narrative in 19:14–15 then serves to connect 19:1–13 to the following chapter 20 where the story continues in 20:1–6 with Pashhur's response to Jeremiah's words. According to Rudolph (see *BHS* apparatus), the core material in 19:1–2a (minus the reference to the valley of Ben Hinnom) continues in 19:10–11a, 14–15 where Jeremiah is instructed to break the flask. The material in 19:2b–9, 11b–13 largely consists of text interpolated from Deuteronomic or Deuteronomistic prose (e.g., Deut. 28:26, 53, 55, 57; Jer. 19:7b, 9) and from elsewhere in the book of Jeremiah (e.g.,

---

1. See Shepherd, *Textuality and the Bible*, 78–93.

Jer. 7:31–33; 19:5–7, 11b, 13; 32:29, 35).[2] Holladay, however, suggests that 19:2b–9 also includes unique material such as 19:3b, which is distinct from Deuteronomistic diction, even though it appears in the Deuteronomistic History (see 1 Sam. 3:11; 2 Kgs. 21:12).[3] There is also the unusual use of בקק ("make void") in 19:7 that appears to be a play on the word בקבק ("flask") in 19:1, 10, not unlike the use of חרסית ("pot-sherd") in 19:2a to play on the word חרש ("earthenware") in 19:1. This suggests more than a supplementary relationship between the parts of the chapter now separated by critical scholarship. Furthermore, there is no extant textual evidence that suggests 19:1–2a, 10–11a, 14–15 ever existed apart from 19:2b–9, 11b–13. The use of Deuteronomic or Deuteronomistic language and the repetition of material within the book of Jeremiah has already been well established as standard practice in the compositional process. Whatever text and commentary relationship that exists between 19:1–2a, 10–11a, 14–15 and 19:2b–9, 11b–13 is one that occurs within an integrated whole. The fact that Jeremiah is instructed to take some of the elders and priests to witness the sign act in 19:1 and then told to speak to the kings of Judah (the multiple kings during Jeremiah's tenure) and the inhabitants of Jerusalem in 19:3a is not an example of incongruence. The message that Jeremiah initially delivered to a small audience was ultimately intended to find its way to the masses.[4]

The Hebrew source behind Greek Jeremiah 19:1a begins with אז (τότε, "Then") rather than the MT's כה (τάδε, "Thus").[5] Some Masoretic manuscripts, the LXX, and the Syriac introduce the discourse as what the LORD said "to me" (i.e., Jeremiah). The Leningrad Codex does not

---

2. According to McKane (see *Jeremiah I–XXV*, 451–59), the nucleus of the chapter is 19:1, 2a (minus the reference to the valley of Ben Hinnom), 10, 11a. Next, he believes, a "sermon" was added in 19:2b, 3–4, 7–9 to explicate the symbolic action. Then came the addition of 19:12 (where he says "Topheth" made its first entrance into the passage only as a place with which Jerusalem was compared) followed by the insertion of 19:5–6, which he considers to be erroneous exegesis of 19:4 (on the basis of his own erroneous assumption that the references to idolatry in v. 4 "were understood as allusions to the sacrifice of children in the valley of Ben Hinnom"). The reference to the valley of Ben Hinnom in 19:2a was then added along with 19:14–15 (which connected the passage to 20:1–6). McKane does not see a place for 19:11b, which is absent from the LXX.

3. Holladay, *Jeremiah 1*, 537.

4. See Thompson, *Book of Jeremiah*, 446, 448–49. Contra Bright, *Jeremiah*, 131.

5. See Walser, *Jeremiah*, 310.

have "to me" (note that the narration in 19:14 refers to Jeremiah in the third person). The instruction to go and purchase "a flask fashioned (יָצוּר) of earthenware [MT: a potter's (יוֹצֵר) earthenware flask]" is reminiscent of the one in 13:1 to go and purchase "a linen waistcloth."[6] The omission of "earthenware" (חרש) in the Syriac version may be due to a perception of redundancy. It was possible for a flask to be made out of material other than clay, but it is safe to assume that one produced by a potter would have been made of clay. The word חרסית ("potsherd") in 19:2 seems to presuppose the presence of חרש ("earthenware") in 19:1, but the Syriac renders חרסית as if it were חדסית ("Hadsith").

The MT of 19:1b lacks a main verb: "and [> pc Mss] some of the elders of the people and some of the elders of the priests." All other witnesses agree with the inclusion of ולקחת ("and take") in the Hebrew source behind Greek Jeremiah: "and take some of the elders of the people and some of the priests." The Syriac and *Targum Jonathan* add the phrase "with you" after this verb: "and take with you some of the elders of the people and some of the elders of the priests." It is not evident whether the verb "take" has been added to supply what seems to be lacking in the MT. It is possible that the verb has been accidentally omitted in the MT. Jeremiah is to take some of the elders of the people and some of the priests to witness the sign act that he is about to perform. They will be able to bear testimony to the kings and the inhabitants of Jerusalem concerning the message that the act symbolizes (see Jer. 19:3). The Hebrew source behind Greek Jeremiah has "some of the priests" where the MT has "some of the elders of the priests." The phrasing of the MT seems to be on the analogy of the preceding "some of the elders of the people." Thompson raises a valid question about how someone as unpopular as Jeremiah could summon such an audience.[7] He suggests that the elders and the priests came looking for "incriminatory utterances" against Jeremiah (see Jer. 18:18).

According to the Hebrew source behind Greek Jeremiah 19:2a, Jeremiah is to go out to "the valley [LXX: common burial place (see MT Jer. 19:11b)] of the sons of their children (בני בניהם), which is outside the entrance of the Potsherd Gate" (cf. Jer. 7:2; 17:19; 22:1–2). The MT has "Ben Hinnom" (בן הנם) instead of "the sons of their children" (see Jer. 19:6; see also commentary on Jer. 7:31). The phrase "their children" (בניהם) also occurs in 19:5, 9. The שער החרסית ("Potsherd Gate"), which plays on the term חרש ("earthenware") from 19:1, was apparently a place where broken pottery was deposited (see Jer. 19:10).

---

6. A בקבק ("flask/jar/jug/bottle") is used for honey in 1 Kings 14:3.

7. Thompson, *Book of Jeremiah*, 448.

Targum Jonathan identifies it as the "Dung Gate" (see Neh. 2:13; 3:13–14; 12:31) on the southwest side of Jerusalem leading into the valley of Ben Hinnom.[8] Jeremiah is to proclaim (LXX: "read") there all the words (pc Mss: "all these words") that the LORD speaks to him (Jer. 19:2b). The LXX ("read") presupposes the presence of a written text (cf. Jer. 3:12; 11:6; 29:29; 32:11, 14; 36:6, 8, 10, 13–15, 21, 23; 51:61, 63).

Jeremiah will say via the witness of the elders and priests, "Hear the word of the LORD," to the kings of Judah who reign during the time of his prophetic ministry and to the inhabitants of Jerusalem (Jer. 19:3a). The Hebrew source behind Greek Jeremiah adds "and men of Judah" after "kings of Judah." It also adds "and those who enter through these gates" after "inhabitants of Jerusalem" (see Jer. 7:2; 17:20; 22:2). The word of the LORD says, "Look, I am about to bring upon this place calamity [MT: I am about to bring calamity upon this place], which, every person who hears it, his ears will tingle/ring" (Jer. 19:3b). This latter expression occurs only two other times in the Hebrew Bible. Once in 1 Samuel 3:11 where the LORD tells the boy Samuel that he is about to do something, "which, every person who hears it, his two ears will tingle/ring" (see the reference to Samuel in Jer. 15:1). At that time, the LORD would establish against Eli all that he had spoken against his house. The second occurrence is in 2 Kings 21:12 where the LORD announces judgment for what Manasseh has done (see the reference to Manasseh in Jer. 15:4): "Look, I am about to bring calamity upon Jerusalem and Judah, which, every person who hears it, his two ears will tingle/ring." The phrase "this place" (המקום הזה) in Jeremiah 19:3b is not a reference to the land of the covenant (as in Jer. 7:7) or to the place of the sanctuary (cf. Jer. 7:12) but a reference to Jerusalem (see Jer. 19:4, 12–13).

The phrase יען אשר at the beginning of 19:4 functions as a causal conjunction ("because"). The question is whether it introduces the cause for what is said in 19:3b (cf. Jer. 29:23) or the cause for the announcement of judgment introduced in 19:6 (cf. Jer. 25:8–9; 29:25, 31–32; 35:18–19). The Masoretes make an open paragraph division (פתוחא) after 19:5, starting 19:6 flush right. This suggests 19:4–5 should be read together as the cause for what is said is 19:3b. The LORD is about to bring calamity upon Jerusalem, he says, "because they forsook me and treated this place as foreign (וינכרו) and sent sacrifices up in smoke in it to other gods" (Jer. 19:4a; cf. Jer. 1:16). The people treated Jerusalem ("this place") as foreign in the sense that they worshiped

---

8. Calvin's identification of this gate as the "solar" or "east" gate (from חרס, "sun") cannot be correct (*Jeremiah*, 2:432). It would be facing the wrong direction.

foreign gods there (see Jer. 5:19; 8:19). The syntax of the remainder of 19:4 differs between the Hebrew source behind Greek Jeremiah and the MT. According to the former, the text is to be translated as follows: "which they did not know, they and their forefathers; and as for the kings of Judah, they have filled this place with blood of innocent ones." Here "the kings of Judah" are separated from "they and their forefathers" and become the subject of the following verbs in 19:4b, 5a. According to the MT (see the placement of the *athnach* accent), the text is to be translated: "which they did not know, they and their forefathers and the kings of Judah, and they have filled this place with blood of innocent ones."[9] Here "the kings of Judah" are included in the same list as "they and their forefathers." Jerusalem ("this place") has been filled with blood of "innocent ones." While the wording of Psalm 106:37–38 might seem to lend support to the idea that this already speaks of the kind of child sacrifice referenced in Jeremiah 19:5, it is to be noted that shedding of innocent blood in the book of Jeremiah normally refers to "judicial murder" (see Jer. 2:34; 7:6; 22:3, 17; 26:15; see also 2 Kgs. 21:16; 24:4; Sir. 34:21–22).[10]

The text of 19:5 is very close to that of 7:31 (see commentary there). The main difference between the two is that 19:5 has "the high places of Baal" where 7:31 has "the high place [MT: high places] of Topheth, which is in the valley of Ben Hinnom." Jeremiah 19:5 is not specifically or explicitly about Topheth, nor is it an explication of 19:4 (contra McKane). It simply adds that the members of the guilty party or parties of 19:4 built the high places of Baal for child sacrifice that the LORD did not command.[11] According to Jeremiah 32:35, the people built the high places of Baal in the valley of Ben Hinnom to practice child sacrifice to Molech. It is this connection that allows for the comparison of Jerusalem to Topheth (which is in the vicinity of Jerusalem) in 19:6, 12, 13.

Therefore, the LORD says that days are coming when "this place" will never again be called "Topheth" or "the valley of Ben Hinnom" but "the valley of slaughter [Syr., *Tg. Jon.*: slain]" (Jer. 19:6; cf. Jer. 7:32;

---

9. According to Keil (*Jeremiah*, 191), "The words: they and their forefathers, and the kings of Judah, are not the subject to 'knew not,' as is 'they and their,' etc., in 9:15; 16:13, but to the preceding verb of the principal clause."
10. See Keil, *Jeremiah*, 191; McKane, *Jeremiah I–XXV*, 452. See also Deuteronomy 19:10; 1 Samuel 19:5; Isaiah 59:7; Joel 4:19 (Eng., 3:19); Proverbs 6:17.
11. See Neusner, *Jeremiah in Talmud in Midrash*, 25, 294.

20:3).[12] The phrase "this place" cannot refer to Topheth or the valley of Ben Hinnom in the Hebrew source behind Greek Jeremiah since neither location has been mentioned thus far in the text of chapter 19. Rather, "this place" must be Jerusalem, as in 19:3, 4, 7, 12. In other words, Jerusalem has become so associated with the idolatrous practices of nearby Topheth in the valley of Ben Hinnom that it has been called "Topheth," but days are coming when it will cease to be called "Topheth" and commence being called "the valley of slaughter" because of the great loss of life that will come with divine judgment. Thus, 19:5–6 takes the text of 7:31–32 in a slightly different direction.

According to the LXX, the LORD says in 19:7a that he will "slaughter" the counsel of Judah and the counsel of Jerusalem "in this place." This makes for a nice link to "the valley of slaughter" at the end of 19:6, but it is a poor rendering of וּבַקֹּתִי ("and I will make void") from the root בקק. Such an uncommon use of this verb (cf. Isa. 19:3), which normally means to "empty" or "lay waste" land (see Isa. 24:1, 3; Jer. 51:2; Nah. 2:3 [Eng., 2:2]), draws attention to itself and appears to be a deliberate play on the word בקבק ("flask") found in 19:1, 10.[13] The reference to the "counsel" (עצה) of Judah and Jerusalem recalls the "counsel" of the so-called wise men in 18:18 and the "counsel" of Jeremiah's enemies against him in 18:23.[14] The phrase "in this place" in 19:7a is not a redundancy or a reference to a place other than Jerusalem but a way to say: "I will make null and void the policies which the statesmen formulate here in Jerusalem for the state of Judah."[15] The LORD will cause the people to "fall by the sword before their enemies and by the hand of those seek their life" (see Jer. 14:12, 16; 15:3; 19:9; 21:7; 34:20; 38:16; 44:30). He will give "their corpse as food to the flying creatures of the sky and to the large land animals" (Jer. 19:7b; cf. Deut. 28:26; Jer. 7:33; 16:4; 34:20; Ps. 79:2). As McKane observes, this "is not introduced here in the context of unburied corpses in the valley of Ben Hinnom, but in the context of carnage on a battlefield."[16]

The LORD will make the city of Jerusalem into "an object of horror and into an object of hissing" (Jer. 19:8a; cf. Jer. 18:16a; 49:17a; 50:13a);

---

12. Outside of Jeremiah 19 the LXX transliterates the place name "Topheth," but within chapter 19 Topheth is variously rendered as "fall" (Jer. 19:6), "one falling" (Jer. 19:12), "the falling" (Jer. 19:13), and "the fall" (Jer. 19:14).

13. See Rashi and Kara in Rosenberg, trans., *Mikraoth Gedoloth: Jeremiah Volume One*, 162.

14. Rosenberg, trans., *Mikraoth Gedoloth: Jeremiah Volume One*, 162.

15. McKane, *Jeremiah I–XXV*, 453.

16. McKane, *Jeremiah I–XXV*, 453.

"every person who passes by it will be appalled and hiss because of all its wound [Codex L: wounds]" (Jer. 19:8b; cf. 1 Kgs. 9:8; Jer. 18:16b; 49:17b; 50:13b; Zeph. 2:15; Lam. 2:15–16). Due to the extreme conditions, the people of the city will resort to cannibalism (one of the covenant curses according to Lev. 26:29; Deut. 28:53, 55, 57): "and they will eat [MT: and I will cause them to eat] the flesh of their sons and the flesh of their daughters, and each the flesh of his neighbor they will eat [*Tg. Jon.*: and each the possessions of his neighbor they will plunder], in siege and in distress with which their enemies [MT adds: and those who seek their life (cf. 19:7a)] oppress them" (Jer. 19:9; cf. Isa. 9:19 [Eng., 9:20]; 49:26; Ezek. 5:10; Zech. 11:9; 4Q248; see in particular 2 Kgs. 6:28–29; Jer. 30:16 [LXX 37:16]; Lam. 2:20; 4:10; Bar. 2:3).[17] They will be forced to eat the very children that they once sought to sacrifice.[18]

After instructing Jeremiah to purchase a flask and take witnesses (i.e., the elders and the priests) to the valley outside the Potsherd Gate (Jer. 19:1–2a) and to proclaim words that will ultimately reach the kings of Judah and the inhabitants of Jerusalem (Jer. 19:2b–9), the LORD adds in 19:10–11a that Jeremiah is to break the flask before the eyes of those going with him (i.e., the elders and the priests) and say on behalf of the LORD, "Thus I will break this people and this city" (cf. Jer. 13:14).[19] The remainder of 19:11a and 19:12 form a comparative construction ("Just as [כאשר] . . . so [כן]"), which is interrupted by the MT's addition of 19:11b ("and in Topheth they will bury without place to bury") from 7:32b:[20] "Just as is broken an earthenware vessel [MT: Just as he breaks the potter's vessel], which can never be repaired

---

17. *Targum Jonathan* softens the force of this considerably, rendering the text so that it speaks of the plundering of possessions rather than cannibalism.
18. Abarbanel: "As payment in kind for sacrificing their children to Baal, they will be forced to eat them because of their intense hunger" (Rosenberg, trans., *Mikraoth Gedoloth: Jeremiah Volume One*, 163). Where the Hebrew source behind Greek Jeremiah has ואכלו ("and they will eat"), the MT has והאכלתים ("and I will cause them to eat"), which may be an ironic allusion to Deuteronomy 8:3: "and he caused you to eat the manna."
19. There may be an allusion here to the instruction in Leviticus 15:12 to break an earthenware vessel made unclean.
20. The addition in MT 19:11b, which does not appear in the Hebrew source behind Greek Jeremiah, has long been considered an interpolation from 7:32b that began either as a marginal correction to the end of 19:6 or as a marginal comment on 19:12 (see McKane, *Jeremiah I–XXV*, 446). Lucian's recension of the LXX inserts this addition at 19:13. The meaning of this addition is either that so many bodies will be buried in Topheth that there will be no more room or that bodies will be buried in Topheth because

again [MT adds: and in Topheth they will bury without place to bury], so I will do," the prophetic utterance of the LORD, "to this place and to its inhabitants to make [LXX: to be made; MT: and to make; Syr.: and I will make; Vulg.: so that I can make] this city like Topheth [LXX: like one falling]" (cf. Jer. 8:15; 22:28; Ps. 31:13 [Eng., 31:12]). Malbim comments, "Unlike the clay in the potter's hand, which can be formed into a different shape, the finished jar cannot be repaired" (see Jer. 18:4–8).[21]

In what way will the city of Jerusalem be like Topheth? On the one hand, Jerusalem will become known as the valley of slaughter or the valley of the slain like Topheth (Jer. 7:32; 19:6),[22] which will make the city ceremonially "unclean" (Lev. 21:1; Num 5:2–3). On the other hand, just as Josiah rendered Topheth "unclean" (2 Kgs. 23:10), so the city of Jerusalem (the site of the temple) will be religiously unclean and unfit as a place of worship (cf. Jer. 2:7). According to Jeremiah 19:13a, the houses of Jerusalem and those of the kings of Judah will be "like the place of Topheth of unclean things" (כמקום תפת הטמאים). The MT says that they will be "like the place of Topheth, the unclean" (כמקום התפת הטמאים). McKane suggests that the unusual syntax of the MT may be designed to indicate that not all the houses of the city will be like Topheth, only the unclean ones.[23] The text of 19:13b further clarifies that the houses that will be like Topheth will be the ones "on whose roofs they have sent sacrifices up in smoke to all the host of the sky and poured out drink offerings to other gods" (see Deut. 4:19; 2 Kgs. 21:3; 23:12; Jer. 7:18; 8:2; 10:2; 32:29; Zeph. 1:5; Acts 7:42). The ל preposition in the phrase לכל הבתים ("all the houses") at the beginning of 19:13b has a specifying function: "namely" or "that is to say" (see *DCH* 4:483).

The brief narrative in 19:14–15 provides an account of Jeremiah's return from Topheth and serves to connect 19:1–13 to 20:1–6. Much the same way that Jeremiah's temple gate speech in 7:1–15 provokes a negative response from the people (Jer. 26), so his words spoken in the court of the temple (Jer. 19:14–15) set up a confrontation with Pashhur (Jer. 20:1–6),[24] yet Jeremiah's words in 19:15 are characteristic of his prophetic ministry in general (see Jer. 11:11; 19:3; 35:17; 39:16; 45:5;

---

there will be no more room elsewhere (see Rosenberg, trans., *Mikraoth Gedoloth: Jeremiah Volume One*, 164).

21. Rosenberg, trans., *Mikraoth Gedoloth: Jeremiah Volume One*, 164.
22. See Rashi (Rosenberg, trans., *Mikraoth Gedoloth: Jeremiah Volume One*, 164).
23. McKane, *Jeremiah I–XXV*, 447.
24. See McKane, *Jeremiah I–XXV*, 449.

see also Jer. 7:26; 17:23).[25] Thus, it is likely that Pashhur responds not merely to the words spoken in the temple court but to the larger message that they represent. What Jeremiah says in the temple court simply provides the occasion or the opportunity for Pashhur to rein in the prophet: "Thus says the LORD [MT adds: of hosts the God of Israel], 'Look, I am about to bring upon this city and upon its cities [LXX: its villages; MT: all its cities] all the calamity that I spoke against it, for they have hardened/stiffened their neck not to hear/heed my words'" (Jer. 19:15). Redak explains the MT's "all its cities" to refer to "all the cities of Judah, which depended upon Jerusalem, the mother city."[26] McKane, however, argues that "v. 15 refers to the capital city Jerusalem and its dependent villages, not to the capital city and all the towns of Judah."[27] Following Ziegler, he notes that the LXX doublet "and upon all its cities and upon its villages" includes the original rendering ("and upon its villages"), which captures the sense of the Hebrew text, and a secondary insertion ("and upon all its cities") that provides a more formally equivalent yet misleading rendering of the Hebrew text found in the MT.

---

25. "All the evil that I have pronounced against it, not merely in the valley of Benhinnom (vv. 3–13), but generally up till this time, by the mouth of Jeremiah. If we limit this reference of this view to the prophecy in Topheth, we must assume, with Näg., that Jeremiah repeated the substance of it here; and besides, that prophecy is not in keeping with 'all its cities,' inasmuch as it (vv. 3–13) deals with Jerusalem alone" (Keil, *Jeremiah*, 193).
26. Rosenberg, trans., *Mikraoth Gedoloth: Jeremiah Volume One*, 165.
27. McKane, *Jeremiah I–XXV*, 447.

JEREMIAH 20

20:1 And Pashhur, the son of Immer [Syr.: Amariah], the priest [LXX^{min}: the false prophet]—and he was overseer, ruler [Tg. Jon.: the ruler of the priests] in the house of the LORD—heard Jeremiah [Syr. adds: the prophet] prophesying these words. 20:2 And he struck him [MT: And Pashhur struck Jeremiah the prophet] and put him in the stocks [Syr.: enclosure] that were in a gate of a house designated "the upper" [MT: in the upper Benjamin Gate], which was in the house of the LORD. 20:3 And Pashhur brought Jeremiah out of the stocks [MT: And then, on the next day, Pashhur brought Jeremiah out of the stocks], and Jeremiah said to him, "Not 'Pashhur' does the LORD call your name but 'Sojourner' [MT: Terror on Every Side; Tg. Jon.: Those who kill will be gathered against you all around]. 20:4 For thus says the LORD, 'Look, I am giving you to a sojourning-place in addition to all your friends [MT: I am about to make you into an object of terror to you and to all your friends], and they will fall by the sword of their enemies while you watch [lit., and your eyes seeing; LXX: and your eyes will see]. And you [> MT] and all Judah I will give into the hand of the king of Babylon, and he will exile them [MT adds: to Babylon] and strike them with the sword. 20:5 And I will give all the wealth of this city and all the product of its toil [MT adds: and all its preciousness] and all the treasures of the king [MT: kings] of Judah [MT adds: I will give] into the hand of his enemies [MT: their enemies], [MT adds: and they will plunder them and take them] and they will bring them to Babylon. 20:6 And as for you [MT adds: Pashhur] and all those who live in your house, you will go into captivity, and in Babylon you will die [MT: and to Babylon you will go, and there you will die], and there you will be buried, you and all your friends to whom you have prophesied in / with / by deception.'"

20:7 You deceived me, O LORD, and I was deceived. You were too strong for me,[1] *and you prevailed. I became a laughingstock all the day. Everyone mocks me [LXX: I continued to be mocked].*[2] *20:8 For in the bitterness of*

---

1.   Ziegler and Rahlfs do not include the pronoun "me" in their editions of LXX Jeremiah, but it is present in Codex Sinaiticus.

2.   It is possible that the LXX translator read the consonantal text that appears in the MT as כֻּלֹּה ("Everyone") as a verbal form (perhaps an infinitive) from the root כלה ("to be complete"), which he translated as "I continued" (see Jer. 20:18b, where the translator uses the same verb [διατελέω] to translate a *qal wayyiqtol* from the root כלה). This led to the passive rendering of the participle "mocking" as "mocked."

my word I laugh [MT: For as often as I speak I cry out]. "Violence and destruction," I call. For the word of the LORD has become a reproach for me [MT: for me a reproach] and derision all my day [MT: all the day]. 20:9 And if I say, "I will not mention the name of the LORD [MT: I will not mention him/it], and I will never again speak in his name," then it becomes [MT adds: in my heart] like a burning fire flaming [MT: shut up] in my bones, and I am weary of all of it [MT: weary of holding (it) in], and I am not able [LXX adds: to bear]. 20:10 For I hear the whispering [LXX: blame] of many gathered on every side [MT: For I hear the whispering of many. Terror is on every side]. "Band together, and let us band together against him, every man of his friends. Watch his intent so that we can prevail over him and take our revenge on him" [MT: "Denounce, and let us denounce him," every man of my friendship, those watching for my stumbling, "Perhaps he will be deceived so that we can prevail over him and take our revenge on him"]. 20:11 But the LORD is with me like a terror-striking mighty man. Therefore, they pursue but are not able to succeed [MT: Therefore, my pursuers are the ones who will stumble and not prevail]. They are very ashamed, for they have not succeeded. Their humiliation will never be forgotten [MT: Eternal humiliation will not be forgotten].[3] *20:12 O LORD [MT adds: of hosts], who tests the righteous [pc Mss: righteous tester (lit., tester of righteousness)], who sees kidneys and heart, let me see your vengeance against them [MT: let me see you exact vengeance from them], for it is to you that I have revealed [BHS apparatus: rolled] my contention.*

20:13 Sing to the LORD, praise him [MT: praise the LORD]. For he rescues the life of the needy from the hand of evildoers.

20:14 Cursed be the day in which I was born. The day that my mother bore me, let it not be blessed. 20:15 Cursed be the man who told my father the news, saying, "A male [MT: male child] has been born to you," making glad [LXX: being glad; MT: making glad he made him glad]. 20:16 Let that man be [MT: And that man will be] like the cities that the LORD overthrew, and he did not relent [or, without relenting]. Let him hear [MT: And he will hear] an outcry [NET: cry of distress] in the morning and a shout [NET: battle cry] at noontime, 20:17 who [LXX:

---

3. The LXX uses νοέω ("understand") to render both instances of *hiphil* שׂכל in this verse, which in this context has the sense "succeed." This creates a difference in the rendering of the syntax in 20:11b: "They were greatly ashamed, because they did not consider their dishonor, which will never be forgotten" (NETS).

*because he] did not put me to death in the womb [MT: from the womb]
so that my mother would become for me my grave [see GKC §111l] and
her womb [LXX: the womb] eternally pregnant. 20:18 Why[4] did I come
forth from the womb [MT: Why from the womb did I come forth] to see
toil and grief and that my days be finished in shame [LXX: and my days
continued in shame]?*

The narrative in 20:1–6 is a continuation of 19:14–15. When 20:1
says that Pashhur heard Jeremiah prophesying "these words," it is a
reference back to the prophecy of judgment upon the city of Jerusalem
in 19:15. This prophecy was spoken in the court of the temple in
Jerusalem according to 19:14 (cf. Jer. 26:7).[5] Pashhur the son of Immer
(Jer. 20:1, 2, 3, 6) is distinct from Pashhur the son of Malchiah (Jer.
21:1; 38:1b; Neh. 11:12; see also 1 Chr. 9:12a).[6] He may be the same
Pashhur who is the father of Gedaliah in Jeremiah 38:1a. Immer is
the name of a priest or priestly house from the time of David (1 Chr.
24:14; see also 1 Chr. 9:12b). The names Pashhur and Immer also appear together in postexilic lists of priests (Ezra 2:37–38; 10:20, 22; Neh.
7:40–41; see also Neh. 10:4). Pashhur the son of Immer is not "the
high priest" (הכהן הגדול) but "overseer, ruler" (פקיד נגיד) in the temple,
which, according to *Targum Jonathan*, makes him "the ruler of the
priests."[7] The person who held this position was directly under the authority of the high priest and had the responsibility to keep order in the
temple (see Jer. 29:26–27; 52:24 [= 2 Kgs. 25:18]; see also Deut. 17:12).

According to Jeremiah 20:2, Pashhur struck Jeremiah and put him
in "the stocks" (המהפכת). The *hiphil* of נכה ("to strike") does not mean
"to beat" or "to have someone beaten by someone else," as is frequently
suggested in the commentaries. Rather, this was a physical rebuke, a
one-time strike of the hand perhaps to the jaw or the mouth (cf. 1 Kgs.
22:24; John 18:22; Acts 23:2; see also Jer. 18:18; 37:15). The term מהפכת

---

4. See Michael B. Shepherd, "So-called Emphasis and the Lack Thereof in
   Biblical Hebrew," *Maarav* 19 (2012): 185–86.

5. It is also worth noting that Jeremiah had taken some of the priests with
   him to the valley to witness the sign act of the breaking of the flask (Jer.
   19:1–2). Jeremiah himself was of priestly stock (Jer. 1:1). See also MT Jeremiah 1:18b.

6. It has been suggested that "Pashhur" is an Egyptian name meaning "son
   of Horus" (Holladay, *Jeremiah 1*, 542).

7. "It will be remembered that at his call (i 10) Jeremiah had been made
   'overseer' over nations. Now, ironically, the ecclesiastical 'overseer' takes
   steps to silence God's 'overseer'" (Bright, *Jeremiah*, 132).

("stocks") apparently does not describe a place of confinement (such as the pit in Jer. 37:15–16; 38:6–13) but an instrument of confinement (not an instrument of torture; see Jer. 29:26 where this word is paired with צינק, another instrument of confinement). There is also such a thing as בית המהפכת ("the house of stocks") (see 2 Chr. 16:10). The particular instrument referenced in Jeremiah 20:2 was located according to the Hebrew source behind Greek Jeremiah "in a gate of a house designated 'the upper'" (בשער בית מני העליון), which was in the house of the LORD." According to the MT, it was located "in the upper Benjamin Gate (בשער בנימן העליון)." This gate in the house of the LORD (see Ezek. 8:3; 9:2) is to be distinguished from the city gate by the same name (Jer. 37:13; 38:7).

Jeremiah 20:3 narrates that when Pashhur brought Jeremiah out of the stocks (according to the MT, "on the next day"), Jeremiah said to him, "Not 'Pashhur' does the LORD call your name but 'Sojourner' [גר from the root גור ('sojourn')]." This is according to the Hebrew source behind Greek Jeremiah. It is comparable to the account of Amos' encounter with Amaziah the priest of Bethel (Amos 7:10–17) in which Amos prophesies that Amaziah will die in an unclean land (Amos 7:17). It is also appropriate in the present context because Jeremiah says in 20:6 that Pashhur will go into captivity and die in Babylon. According to the MT, however, Pashhur's name will be מגור מסביב ("Terror on Every Side") (see Jer. 6:25; 20:10; 46:5; 49:29; Ps. 31:14 [Eng., 31:13]; Lam. 2:22).[8] Here מגור is from the homonymic root גור ("dread"), but *Targum Jonathan* interprets the text as if this word were from the homonymic root גור ("gather together"): "Those who kill will be gathered against you all around."[9] Older interpreters generally assumed that the meaning (or at least the understood meaning) of the name "Pashhur" must somehow be the opposite of whatever מגור מסביב means. Thus, Rashi notes two interpretations of the name.[10] One says that פשחור, which is a combination of פש ("great") and חור ("nobility"), has become a combination of פשח ("cut off") and שחור ("black"), like a cut off tree. Another says that

---

8. The development of this expression in the present context may have started with dittography of non-final *mem*: אם מגור, אם מגר אם, אם גר. Once this took place, מסביב was added to make sense of the new formation.

9. Holladay argues that three different senses of מגור are explicated in 20:4–6: "Thus Jrm is saying, 'You will be a מָגוֹר = "terror" to all your friends; your friends will be an occasion of מָגוֹר = "attack" to you by falling by the sword of the enemy, and you and they will be an occasion of מָגוֹר = "sojourning" by exile in Babylon'" (*Jeremiah 1*, 544).

10. Rosenberg, trans., *Mikraoth Gedoloth: Jeremiah Volume One*, 166.

פַשְׁחוּר is פַשׁ סָחוּר ("Many will be around you to slay you"), in which case the name is synonymous with *Targum Jonathan's* interpretation of מָגוֹר מִסָּבִיב. On the other hand, modern interpreters tend to deny that there is any wordplay between פַשְׁחוּר and מָגוֹר מִסָּבִיב.[11] One exception to this trend is Holladay who suggests that Jeremiah's understanding of פַשְׁחוּר is not based on the actual derivation of the name but on a "deformation" of the name as the Aramaic פַּשׁ־סָחוֹר ("fruitful all around"), which is thought to be the opposite of מָגוֹר מִסָּבִיב.[12]

The text of 20:4–6 then offers explanation of the renaming of Pashhur. According to the Hebrew source behind Greek Jeremiah 20:4a, Jeremiah explains that the Lord says, "Look, I am giving you to a sojourning-place (מָגוּר) in addition to all your friends [see BDB, 511], and they will fall by the sword of their enemies while you watch" (cf. Deut. 28:32; 2 Kgs. 25:7; Jer. 52:10). This corresponds to the renaming of "Pashhur" as "Sojourner" (גֵּר) in the Hebrew source behind Greek Jeremiah 20:3 and to the description of Pashhur's fate in 20:6. In the MT, however, the Lord says, "Look, I am about to make you into an object of terror (מָגוֹר) to you and to all your friends," which is consistent with מָגוֹר מִסָּבִיב ("Terror on Every Side") in its version of 20:3. Pashhur's "friends" here are his allies against Jeremiah (cf. Jer. 20:6).[13] The text of 20:4b adds, "And you [> MT] and all Judah I will give into the hand of the king of Babylon, and he will exile them [MT adds: to Babylon] and strike them with the sword" (cf. Jer. 20:2). This is the first mention of Babylon in the book of Jeremiah.

It is added in 20:5 that the Lord will give "all the wealth of this city and all the product of its toil [MT adds: and all its preciousness] and all the treasures of the king [MT: kings] of Judah [MT adds: I will give] into the hand of his enemies [MT: their enemies], [MT adds: and they will plunder them and take them] and they will bring them to Babylon" (see 2 Kgs. 20:17; 25:13–17; Isa. 39:6; Jer. 3:24; 15:13; 17:3; 52:17–23; Dan. 1:2; 2 Chr. 36:6–7, 18). The MT has expanded the more original Hebrew source behind Greek Jeremiah. As for Pashhur ("you") and his family ("all those who live in your house"), they will go into captivity ("you [pl.] will go into captivity"), and in Babylon Pashhur will die ("you

---

11. See Keil, *Jeremiah*, 194; Bright, *Jeremiah*, 132; Thompson, *Book of Jeremiah*, 455; McKane, *Jeremiah I–XXV*, 464. See also Jeremiah 7:32; 19:6.
12. Holladay, *Jeremiah 1*, 543–44.
13. With regard to the apparent discrepancy between 20:4 and 20:6, "the meaning is simply that some will die in Judah and some will go into exile, while Pashhur himself and his family will suffer exile, and will die and be buried in a foreign land" (McKane, *Jeremiah I–XXV*, 465).

[sg.] will die") and be buried ("you [sg.] will be buried")—a priest in an unclean land (Jer. 20:6; cf. Amos 7:17). The latter part of 20:6 adds that this applies not only to Pashhur but also to all his friends to whom he has prophesied in/with/by deception (cf. Jer. 20:4).[14] This does not necessarily imply that Pashhur was both prophet and priest (cf. Jer. 1:1; Ezek. 1:3; Zech. 1:1). It only indicates that he perpetuated the message of the false prophets (see Jer. 6:13–15; 8:10–12), which included a false sense of security in the temple (Jer. 7:4, 8), prophecy by Baal (Jer. 2:8b; 5:31), and a general denial of true prophecy about coming judgment (Jer. 14:13–14; see also Jer. 29:9).

Jeremiah 20:7–12 is the seventh confession of the prophet Jeremiah. Its current placement in the book strongly suggests that it is to be read as a response to the persecution narrated in 20:1–6.[15] Indeed, the MT makes the connection between the two passages explicit with its repetition of מגור מסביב ("Terror [is] on every side") in 20:3 and 20:10. The text of 20:7–12 roughly takes the form of a lament psalm (cf. Ps. 13) in which there is movement from an accusatory outcry (Jer. 20:7) to an expression of trust (Jer. 20:11–12), which is then reiterated by the brief hymnic material that follows in 20:13. This form-critical observation helps to guard the reader against two extremes in interpretation. On the one hand, it is not necessary to soften Jeremiah's words in 20:7.[16] Lament psalms are well known for their brutal honesty, especially in their opening words. The speaker is not necessarily articulating what he believes to be true about God.[17] Rather, it is an expression of what is genuinely felt in the moment. In presenting lament psalms as model prayers to their readers,

---

14. "In verse 4, Jeremiah prophesies that Pashhur's friends will fall by the sword and here he says that they will be taken in captivity to Babylon and die and be buried there. *Redak* reconciles this difficulty by explaining that those who will escape the sword of the Babylonians will be taken captive to Babylon, where they will die and be buried" (Rosenberg, trans., *Mikraoth Gedoloth: Jeremiah Volume One*, 167). See also Jeremiah 15:2.

15. Redak: "Since Pashhur struck him and had him imprisoned, he cried out in complaint about the injustice done him" (Rosenberg, trans., *Mikraoth Gedoloth: Jeremiah Volume One*, 167).

16. Calvin argues that Jeremiah is being "ironical": "He assumes the character of his enemies, who boasted that he presumptuously prophesied of the calamity and ruin of the city, as no such thing would take place" (*Jeremiah*, 3:26).

17. Origen, however, believes that God really did deceive Jeremiah for his own good, knowing that he would not have accepted his call unless certain information were withheld from him (Wenthe, ed., *Jeremiah, Lamentations*, 153–55). He likens this to the way a parent often has to deal with a child.

the biblical authors encourage such honesty (rather than disingenuous lip service), which then progresses to affirmation of revealed theological truth. On the other hand, it is important not to charge Jeremiah with blasphemy. Again, his honesty about his feelings is not out of bounds as long as he does not merely stay in such a state of mind so that his emotion becomes what he actually believes about God.

The translation, "You deceived me, O LORD, and I was deceived" (Jer. 20:7a; cf. Jer. 4:10), is a rendering of the *piel* ("deceived") and *niphal* ("was deceived") stems of the same root פתה ("to be simple"). The *piel* of this root essentially means "to make someone naïve or easily misled." The *niphal*, like the *pual* (cf. Jer. 20:10b; Ezek. 14:9), is the passive of this meaning.[18] In some contexts, the sense of the *piel* is more accurately rendered as "entice" (e.g., Judg. 14:15; 16:5; Hos. 2:16 [Eng., 2:15]; see also the *niphal* in Job 31:9) or even "seduce" (e.g., Exod. 22:15 [Eng., 22:16]). Some commentators prefer this sense for Jeremiah 20:7 and see a correlation between it and the following verb חזקתני ("You were too strong for me"; cf. 2 Sam. 13:14: "And he [Amnon] was not willing to listen to her [Tamar], and he was stronger [ויחזק] than she, and he afflicted her and lay with her"),[19] although normally the *hiphil* of חזק rather than the *qal* appears for forced or coerced relationships in contexts of sexual seduction (see Deut. 22:25; 2 Sam. 13:11).[20] Jeremiah's particular accusation seems to be that God "deceived" him in such a way that he prevailed upon him to be his prophet (cf. 2 Sam. 3:25; 1 Kgs. 22:20–22; Ezek. 14:9; Ps. 78:36; Prov. 24:28; 2 Chr. 18:19–21; 2 Thess. 2:11; see also Jer. 20:9b).[21] Both Origen and Jerome suggest that Jeremiah thought the message of judgment was only for the nations (see Jer. 1:5; 25:15).[22] Thus, when he found out that it was also for Judah, he felt deceived. According to Redak, Jeremiah has in mind in 20:7 the manner in which God responded to his initial objection to his calling (Jer. 1:6–7).[23] Given the context of opposition in 20:1–2, 10, however, it is likely that Jeremiah says that he feels deceived in the sense that he did not really know what he would

---

18. See Bruce K. Waltke and M. O'Connor, *An Introduction to Biblical Hebrew Syntax* (Winona Lake, IN: Eisenbrauns, 1990), 393–94.

19. See Thompson, *Book of Jeremiah*, 459; McKane, *Jeremiah I–XXV*, 470; Holladay, *Jeremiah 1*, 552–53. Holladay also suggests a connection between the outcry in MT Jeremiah 20:8 and the unheard cry of the violated woman in Deuteronomy 22:27.

20. See McKane, *Jeremiah I–XXV*, 469.

21. See similar language in Jeremiah 4:10; 15:18b.

22. Wenthe, ed., *Jeremiah, Lamentations*, 155.

23. Rosenberg, trans., *Mikraoth Gedoloth: Jeremiah Volume One*, 167.

be up against when he accepted his call (cf. Exod. 5:22–23). The reality, however, is that God was very forthright about what was in store for him (see Jer. 1:17–19). Jeremiah adds in 20:7b, "I became a laughingstock all the day. Everyone mocks me" (cf. Jer. 15:17; Job 12:4; Lam. 3:14; see also Ezek. 23:32).[24] This gives the reader a sense of the humiliation and insult that came with Jeremiah's occupation and role in society.

Jeremiah 20:8 provides an explanation for the comments in 20:7. According to the Hebrew source behind Greek Jeremiah, the prophet says, "For in the bitterness of my word I laugh" (כי מר דברי אצחק). Laughter is an ambiguous reaction. Therefore, the MT has adjusted the text to make the meaning more explicit: "For as often as I speak I cry out" (כי מדי אדבר אזעק) (cf. Jer. 31:20). What does he say when he cries out? He calls, "Violence and destruction" (חמס ושד) (cf. Jer. 6:7; Ezek. 45:9; Amos 3:10; Hab. 1:3). According to Rashi, this means that every time Jeremiah prophesies he must proclaim judgment rather than good for the people (cf. *Tg. Jon.*),[25] but Redak says that it means Jeremiah must call out to complain about the words of violence spoken against him.[26] McKane explains the logic of this latter option: "In v. 8a the prophet describes himself as one who is under constant siege, a beleaguered soul, hard-pressed and continually crying out for help. In v. 8b he explains why he has been reduced to this condition: it is the consequence of his obedience to his prophetic vocation."[27] The ministry of the prophetic word of the LORD has become a "reproach" for Jeremiah and a cause for constant "derision" (Jer. 20:8b; cf. Jer. 6:10; Ps. 69:11 [Eng., 69:10]; Lam. 3:61; see also Num. 11:11–15).[28] Jerome comments that the delay in the fulfillment of Jeremiah's prophecy about Babylonian invasion has made him look like a false prophet (see Jer. 17:15) and thus brought a reproach upon him from the people.[29]

---

24. See the MT *qere* for Jeremiah 15:10b.
25. Rosenberg, trans., *Mikraoth Gedoloth: Jeremiah Volume One*, 168. This may include both the denunciation of the people's violence and destruction as well as their punishment by violence and destruction (see Holladay, *Jeremiah 1*, 554).
26. Rosenberg, trans., *Mikraoth Gedoloth: Jeremiah Volume One*, 168.
27. McKane, *Jeremiah I–XXV*, 472.
28. Note how this contrasts with Jeremiah's joyful reception of the words of the Torah in Jeremiah 15:16. Now it is in the "bitterness" (מר) of his message that he laughs (LXX Jer. 20:8a). This is comparable to Ezekiel's sweet reception of the scroll (Ezek. 3:1–3), which is made bitter by the people's "rebellion" (מרי) (Ezek. 2:8; cf. Rev. 10:8–10).
29. Wenthe, ed., *Jeremiah, Lamentations*, 156.

Jeremiah then describes on the basis of his personal experience what it is like to take matters into his own hands and attempt to abandon his prophetic ministry (Jer. 20:9). The Hebrew source behind Greek Jeremiah 20:9 and the MT differ in several details. According to the former, Jeremiah says, "And if I say [cf. Ps. 94:18], 'I will not mention [or, remember] the name of the LORD (שם יהוה), and I will never again speak in his name,' then it [i.e., the name of the LORD] becomes like a burning fire flaming (להטת) in my bones [cf. Ps. 104:4], and I am weary of all of it (כלה), and I am not able [LXX adds: to bear]." This reading makes "the name of the LORD" what burns inside of Jeremiah and must come out (see Exod. 5:23; Deut. 18:19). In the MT, however, the prophet says, "And if I say, 'I will not mention him/it, and I will never again speak in his name,' then he/it becomes in my heart (בלבי) like a burning fire shut up (עצר) in my bones, and I am weary of holding (him/it) in (כלכל) [cf. Jer. 6:11], and I am not able."[30] While it is possible that the LORD is the antecedent of the pronoun "him/it" ("I will not mention him/it"), it is more likely that "the word of the LORD" is the referent.[31] The word (m.) of the LORD becomes like a burning fire (f.) (cf. Jer. 5:14; 23:29; see also Luke 24:32). The word (m.) of the LORD, not the fire (f.), is "shut up" (m.) inside Jeremiah, but he cannot contain it any longer (cf. Jer. 23:9; Ps. 39:4 [Eng., 39:3]; Lam. 1:13; 1QH[a] 16:30).[32] This speaks volumes about the nature of the prophetic call. The office of prophet is not a job that someone can simply choose or not choose (unlike that of the professional prophet for hire [Amos 7:14–15; Mic. 2:11; 3:5, 11]). Jeremiah was already set apart as a prophet before his birth (Jer. 1:5). Thus, as Amos says, if the LORD speaks, the true prophet has no choice but to speak (Amos 3:8). Likewise, the apostle Paul speaks of an inner compulsion that drives him to proclaim his message (1 Cor. 9:16).[33]

---

30. See the connection between "and you prevailed" (ותוכל) in 20:7a and "and I am not able" (ולא אוכל) in 20:9b.

31. Ambrose suggests that the Spirit is the referent (Wenthe, ed., *Jeremiah, Lamentations*, 157).

32. Redak: "The word of the Lord was in my heart like a burning fire, that I strive with all my might to take it out" (Rosenberg, trans., *Mikraoth Gedoloth: Jeremiah Volume One*, 168). See also GKC §132d and McKane, *Jeremiah I–XXV*, 473.

33. "May the power of the Holy Spirit be so revived, that we may to the end pursue the course of our office and never stand still, but assail even the whole world, knowing that God commands us and requires from us what others disapprove and condemn" (Calvin, *Jeremiah*, 3:35). See also Acts 4:20.

In 20:10, Jeremiah explains again the reason for his despair (cf. Jer. 20:8): "For I hear the whispering [LXX: blame] of many gathered on every side (גורים מסביב)" (cf. Syr., *Tg. Jon.*). The MT says, "For I hear the whispering of many. Terror is on every side (מגור מסביב)." This text is a citation of Psalm 31:14a (Eng., 31:13a), a lament psalm. The expression מגור מסביב ("Terror [is] on every side") is a repetition of the renaming of Pashhur in MT Jeremiah 20:3b. What is true for Jeremiah now will be true for Pashhur later. Others interpret מגור מסביב to be the first part of Jeremiah's following quote of what his enemies say about him. Thus, Bright comments, "Apparently Jeremiah had used the expression so often that it was becoming a nickname."[34] McKane, however, argues that the expression is normally an exclamation or interjection: "That מגור מסביב in 20.10 has to be understood as an asyndetic parenthesis by means of which Jeremiah expresses his feelings is a correct conclusion, and if the expression is to be justified as original in the verse, the justification has to be achieved on this basis."[35]

The remainder of 20:10 differs considerably between the Hebrew source behind Greek Jeremiah and the MT. According to the former, Jeremiah reports his enemies as saying, "Band together, and let us band together against him (התגדדו ונתגדנו), every man of his friends (כל אנוש שלומיו). Watch his intent so that we can prevail over him and take our revenge on him (שמרו יצרו ונוכלה לו ונקחה נקמתנו ממנו)" (cf. Jer. 18:18). This indicates that those who are considered Jeremiah's "friends" are summoned against him to look for an opportunity to take their revenge on him (cf. Pss. 55:21; 56:7 [Eng., 55:20; 56:6]; 71:10). Not only does Jeremiah feel that the LORD has prevailed over him (Jer. 20:7a), but also his so-called friends plan to do so (but see Jer. 1:19; 15:20). The MT says, "'Denounce, and let us denounce him (הגידו ונגידנו),' every man of my friendship (כל אנוש שלומי), those watching for my stumbling (שמרי צלעי),[36] 'Perhaps he will be deceived so that we can prevail over him and take our revenge on him (אולי יפתה ונוכלה לו ונקמה נקמתנו ממנו).'" Here the phrases "every man of my friendship, those watching for my stumbling" (cf. Pss. 35:15; 38:17–18; 41:10 [Eng., 38:16–17; 41:9] are interjected by Jeremiah in the middle of the quote to identify those who are against him. The translation "denounce" is an interpretive rendering of the *hiphil* of

---

34. Bright, *Jeremiah*, 132.

35. McKane, *Jeremiah I–XXV*, 477.

36. This phrase can also be rendered "those who watch at my side" (cf. "every man of my friendship"). See also the rendering of the Syriac version and compare to Proverbs 26:24–25.

נגד ("tell, declare"). It is apparently a call to report to the authorities anything that might be perceived as wrongdoing on Jeremiah's part. Jeremiah feels deceived by the LORD (Jer. 20:7a), and his friends who are really enemies hope that he will be deceived in some way so that they might take advantage of it.[37] Redak paraphrases, "Perhaps he will be enticed to eat and drink with us, and we will take our revenge from him by giving him poison to drink" (cf. *Tg. Jon.* Jer. 11:20).[38] Kara, however, characterizes their words differently: "Perhaps we will entice him to say evil prophecies about this place, and, thereby, we will prevail against him and wreak vengeance upon him."[39]

Despite the depth and seriousness of Jeremiah's sentiments in 20:7–10, he nevertheless moves to an affirmation of his confidence in the LORD in 20:11–12. From the very beginning, the LORD has said that he will be with Jeremiah to rescue him so that his opponents do not prevail over him (Jer. 1:8, 17–19; 15:20–21). He will redeem his prophet from "terror-striking men" (עריצים) (Jer. 15:21b). Thus, Jeremiah now affirms his belief that the LORD is indeed with him "like a terror-striking mighty man" (כגבור עריץ) (Jer. 20:11a). The LORD is not like a mighty man unable to save (MT Jer. 14:9). "Therefore," Jeremiah says, "they pursue but are not able to succeed (רדפו והשכל לא יכלו) [MT: my pursuers are the ones who will stumble and not prevail (רדפי יכשלו ולא יכלו)]." They are greatly ashamed because of their lack of success (Jer. 20:11b; cf. Jer. 6:15; 8:12; 17:18; Ps. 129:2, 5). "Their humiliation will never be forgotten (כלמתם עולם לא תשכח) [MT: Eternal humiliation will not be forgotten (כלמת עולם לא תשכח)]" (cf. Jer. 23:40). The text of Jeremiah 20:12 is, with some variation, very close to that of 11:20 (see commentary there) where Jeremiah expressed his faith that the LORD would vindicate him from the men of Anathoth who sought his life. Jeremiah reiterates his belief that the LORD knows the inner man and thus discerns the difference between the righteous and the wicked. He entrusts the matter to the LORD's hands and prays that he might see the LORD's vengeance against those who seek to take their revenge on him (see Jer. 20:10b).[40]

---

37. "The material in vv 7–10 gives the impression that Jrm is in a hall of mirrors: that Yahweh is his enemy (v 7) and that his enemies pretend to be his friends (v 10); that his enemies hope to do what Yahweh has already done—deceive him and best him (vv 7, 10); that he feels trapped, without any possibility of escape (v 9)" (Holladay, *Jeremiah 1*, 557).
38. Rosenberg, trans., *Mikraoth Gedoloth: Jeremiah Volume One*, 169.
39. Rosenberg, trans., *Mikraoth Gedoloth: Jeremiah Volume One*, 169.
40. See Calvin, *Jeremiah*, 3:42.

Jeremiah 20:13 is separated from what precedes and follows it by two closed paragraph divisions in the MT. It is a piece of hymnic material with a call to praise (featuring two plural imperatives) followed by a cause or reason for praise introduced by the conjunction כִּי (cf. Ps. 117): "Sing to the Lord, praise him [MT: praise the Lord]. For he rescues the life of the needy from the hand of evildoers" (cf. Jer. 15:21; Ps. 35:10; 4Q434). According to McKane, this is "the response of a pious reader or commentator to Jeremiah's affirmation of confidence, and certainty of victory over his enemies."[41] But there is no reason why it could not be Jeremiah's (or Baruch's) appendix to the confession in 20:7–12. The hymn in 20:13 prompts the appropriate response from the readership to the confession. Jeremiah represents the "needy" (אֶבְיוֹן) in the hymn not in terms of his socioeconomic status but in terms of his need for God to deliver him from his enemies (see BDB, 2).

Jeremiah 20:14–18 is the eighth and final confession of Jeremiah. The sudden shift from words of confidence (Jer. 20:11–12) and praise (Jer. 20:13) to the curses of this confession may be compared to the apostle Paul's sudden change from confidence that nothing can separate the people of God from the love of God that is in Christ Jesus (Rom. 8:39) to an expression of great grief (Rom. 9:1–2) and desire to be cursed for the sake of his Jewish brethren (Rom. 9:3; cf. Exod. 32:32).[42] Of course, the difference is that Jeremiah's confession is a personal struggle against the temptation of despair in the face of severe persecution. Paul, on the other hand, is articulating a Christlike, self-sacrificial evangelistic spirit. Perhaps a better comparison is the prophet Elijah's sudden shift from vindication in his showdown with the prophets of Baal (1 Kgs. 18) to his depression-laden flight from Jezebel (1 Kgs. 19). The closest biblical parallel to Jeremiah 20:14–18 is Job 3 (see also *Pss. Sol.* 3:9), although the precise literary relationship between the two is not known.[43] Job's initially pious response to his suffering in Job 1:20–22; 2:9–10 is suddenly replaced by his wish for the day of his birth to perish (Job 3:3).

---

41. McKane, *Jeremiah I–XXV*, 481.

42. "Thus he recites, in the latter passage, what had before happened to him, as though he had said, 'When I now declare that I have been rescued by God from the hand of the wicked, I cannot sufficiently express the greatness of that favour, until I make it more clearly known to all the godly how great and how dreadful agonies I suffered, so that I cursed my birth-day, and abhorred everything that ought to have stimulated me to give praise to God'" (Calvin, *Jeremiah*, 3:44–45).

43. See Bright, *Jeremiah*, 134. McKane suggests that it is not a matter of literary dependence but shared literary convention (*Jeremiah I–XXV*, 482–83).

The clauses of 20:14 are arranged as a chiastic structure: "(A) Cursed be (B) the day in which I was born. (B¹) The day that my mother bore me, (A¹) let it not be blessed" (cf. MT Jer. 15:10; Job 3:3–10). Of course, there is nothing that can be done about the day of Jeremiah's birth, but he is expressing his grief by wishing that he had never been born (cf. Mark 14:21).[44] What Jeremiah must fight to reaffirm is the divine design for his life that was already in place prior to his birth (see Jer. 1:5). Jeremiah also curses the unidentified man who told his father the good news that a son (i.e., an heir) was born to him, congratulating him (Jer. 20:15; cf. Job 3:3b). At first glance, this seems to be a rather arbitrary curse on an innocent man, but Jeremiah has nothing personal against the man himself. He is cursing what the man represents. For Jeremiah, the announcement of his birth was not good news. His birth was not something for which congratulations should have been offered.

In 20:16a, Jeremiah expresses his desire that the man who congratulated his father be like the cities that the LORD "overthrew" (הָפַךְ) without relenting (cf. Jer. 4:28b). This alludes to the story of the overthrow of Sodom and Gomorrah—"And he overthrew (וַיַּהֲפֹךְ) those cities" (Gen. 19:25a). "Let him hear," Jeremiah says, "an outcry (זְעָקָה) in the morning and a shout (תְּרוּעָה) at noontime" (Jer. 20:16b). This refers to the cries of distress and battle cries typically associated with enemy invasion (see Jer. 4:19b; 6:4a; 15:8a; 18:22a; 49:2a). The relative אֲשֶׁר at the beginning of 20:17 is often rendered as a causal conjunction (see LXX: ὅτι), but it works quite well as a simple relative ("who") with "that man" from 20:16a as the antecedent:[45] "who did not put me to death in the womb [MT: from the womb] so that my mother would become for me my grave [see GKC §111l] and her womb [LXX: the womb] eternally pregnant" (cf. Job 3:11–12, 16).[46] The difference between "in

---

44. McKane refers to the interpretation of Lowth who suggests that Jeremiah is cursing the recurring anniversary of his birthday—"the antitype of a birthday greeting" (*Jeremiah I–XXV*, 483). The difficulty with this view is that there is a phrase in biblical Hebrew for "birthday" (יוֹם הֻלֶּדֶת), but it does not appear in Jeremiah 20:14–18 (see Gen. 40:20).

45. See Holmstedt, *The Relative Clause*, 235

46. "The difficulty arising from simply accepting the literal meaning is solved by the consideration, that the curse is not levelled against any one particular person. The man that was present at the birth, so as to be able to bring the father news of it, might have killed the child in the mother's womb. Jeremiah is as little thinking how this could happen as, in the next words, he is of the possibility of everlasting pregnancy. His words must be taken rhetorically, not physiologically" (Keil, *Jeremiah*, 199). The lack of

the womb" (ברחם) and "from the womb" (מרחם) may be negligible, but there is perhaps a distinction between causing a miscarriage "in the womb" and putting to death a healthy baby born "from the womb." McKane notes that the Job 3 passage develops the idea of the grave differently as "the symbol of rest and repose and of release from the tempest of life" (see Job 3:13–15, 17–19; cf. Eccl. 7:1b).[47]

Jeremiah concludes his final confession by questioning why he ever came forth from the womb if it was only to see toil and grief and finish his days in shame (Jer. 20:18; cf. Job 3:20–26; 10:18; Eccl. 4:3; see also Isa. 45:10), yet neither Jeremiah nor Job succumbs to the temptation to take his own life (see 1 Sam. 31:4–6; 2 Sam. 17:23; Matt. 27:5; Acts 1:18). Job relearns the fear of the LORD (Job 1:1; 28:28) in the midst of his suffering and repents for losing sight of what he knew to be true about God (see Job 38–42). The reader has already seen Jeremiah in the previous confession make this journey from despair (Jer. 20:7–10) to hope (Jer. 20:11–12), and it need not be repeated here that the story of Jeremiah's life does not end in regret.

APPLICATION OF JEREMIAH 11:18–20:18

The above commentary has demonstrated Jeremiah 11:18–20:18 to be a tightly woven section most notably characterized by the prophet's confessions. These confessions are not only closely related to one another (e.g., Jer. 11:20; 20:12) but also linked directly to the material in the intervening texts such as the various sign acts. They contribute to the overall program of the book by developing the theme of opposition to Jeremiah (e.g., Jer. 1:17–19; 15:20–21). The prophet Jeremiah functions as a representative of the suffering remnant of the people of God and provides an example for the readers of the book to follow. Much like the lament psalms of the Psalter, his confessions instruct the reader in how to navigate from despair due to persecution to hope in the revealed word of God. Just as God is with Jeremiah (Jer. 1:8, 17–19; 15:18–21) who bears the LORD's name (Jer. 15:16b), so is he with his faithful followers (Jer. 30:11 [MT]; 46:28) who bear his name (Jer. 14:9b).

The confessions are applicable not in the sense that the reader must engage in a kind of existential interpretation of Jeremiah's situation but in the sense that the composer of the book has already done the work of connecting the program of the book not only to Jeremiah

---

agreement between the masculine noun רחם ("womb") and the feminine adjective הרה ("pregnant") may be resolved by the recognition that רחם ("womb") is metonymy for the woman (see Judg. 5:30).

47. McKane, *Jeremiah I–XXV*, 484.

but also to the readers. In other words, the confessions have already been made applicable within the book itself. Two examples of this will suffice. First, Nehemiah's citation of Jeremiah 18:23 (Neh. 3:37 [Eng., 4:4]) shows an inner-biblical understanding of the applicability of the prophet's confession. Nehemiah, a faithful member of the remnant of the people of God and a reader of the book of Jeremiah, finds himself in the midst of persecution and follows the clues of the book in order to adopt the prophet's words as his own. Second, the praise hymn in Jeremiah 20:13 is a direct invitation from the book to the reader to respond in like manner to Jeremiah's progression from lament to confidence in the LORD (Jer. 20:7–12). In fact, this self-applying text could not be a more fitting way to conclude the collection of Jeremiah's confessions as a whole.

JEREMIAH 21

21:1 The word that came from the LORD *to Jeremiah [MT: to Jeremiah from the* LORD*] when King Zedekiah sent to him Pashhur the son of Malkijah and Zephaniah the son of Maaseiah, the priest, saying, 21:2 "Seek on our behalf the* LORD*, for [MT adds: Nebuchadrezzar] the king of Babylon is fighting against us. Perhaps the* LORD *will do [MT adds: with us] according to all his wonderful acts, and he will withdraw from us." 21:3 And to them Jeremiah said [MT: And Jeremiah said to them], "Thus you will say to Zedekiah, the king of Judah [the king of Judah > MT; Syr.: Zedekiah, the king], 21:4 'Thus says the* LORD *[MT adds: the God of Israel], "Look, I am about to turn back the weapons of war [MT adds: that are in your (pl.) hand] with which you [pl.] are fighting [MT adds: the king of Babylon and] the Chaldeans who are besieging you [pl.] from outside the city wall [MT adds: and I will gather them] into the midst of this city. 21:5 And I will fight you [MT: with you] with an outstretched hand and with a strong arm [MT adds: and in anger and] in fury and in great wrath. 21:6 And I will strike all the inhabitants in this city [MT: of this city], man and animal [MT: both man and animal], with a great plague [LXX: death], and they will die [MT: by a great plague they will die]. 21:7 And afterwards," the prophetic utterance of the* LORD*, "I will give Zedekiah, the king of Judah, and his servants and the people who are left in this city [Codex L: and the people and those who are left in this city] from the plague [LXX: death] and from the famine and from the sword [Codex L: from the plague, from the sword, and from the famine] [MT adds: into the hand of Nebuchadrezzar, the king of Babylon, and] into the hand of their enemies, [MT adds: and into the hand of] those who seek their life, and they [MT: he] will strike them with the edge of the sword. I [MT: He] will not have pity on them, [MT adds: and he will not spare] and I [MT: he] will not have compassion on them [on them > MT]."'"*

21:8 "And to this people you will say, 'Thus says the LORD*, "Look, I am setting before you the way of life and the way of death. 21:9 The one who stays in this city, he will die by the sword or [or > mlt Mss] by famine [MT adds: or by plague]; but the one who goes out and falls [or, deserts / defects / surrenders; > Syr.] to the Chaldeans who are besieging you, he will live, and he will have his life as plunder [LXX: windfall], and he will live [and he will live > Codex L]. 21:10 For I have set my face against this city for evil / harm and not for good [MT adds: the prophetic utterance of the* LORD*]. Into the hand of the king of Babylon it will be given, and he will burn it with fire."'"*

21:11 O house of the king of Judah [MT: And to the house of the king of Judah], "Hear the word of the LORD. 21:12 O house of David, thus says the LORD, 'Judge in the morning [or, each morning] with justice and rescue [LXX: guide[1]] a robbed person from the hand of his oppressor [MT: from an oppressor's hand], lest my fury go forth like fire and burn without anyone to extinguish it [MT adds: because of the evil of their (mlt Mss: your) deeds]. 21:13 Look, I am against you, O inhabitant of the valley of Tyre, the plain [MT: O inhabitant of the valley, O rock of the plain,' the prophetic utterance of the LORD],[2] those who say, "Who will terrify us [MT: Who will come down against us], and who will enter our dwelling places [LXX: our dwelling place[3]]?" 21:14 [MT adds: And I will visit upon you (i.e., punish you) according to the fruit of your deeds,' the prophetic utterance of the LORD] And I will kindle a fire in its forest, and it will consume all its surroundings.'"

Jeremiah 21 begins a new literary complex that extends through chapter 24.[4] The word of the LORD to Zedekiah, the last king of Judah, in 21:1–7 is followed by two subunits addressed to the people (Jer. 21:8–10) and to the house of the king of Judah (Jer. 21:11–14) respectively. This leads into the material against the sons of Josiah in chapter 22, specifically Shallum or Jehoahaz (Jer. 22:11), Jehoiakim (Jer. 22:18), and Jehoiachin the grandson of Josiah (Jer. 22:24). Chapter 22 is capped by the judgment pronounced on these "shepherds" (i.e., kings) in Jeremiah 23:1–4, which is followed by the hope of an ideal, messianic king in 23:5–6.[5] The section against the false prophets then occurs in 23:9–40. Chapter 24 concludes with the vision of the two baskets of figs. The good figs represent those in Babylonian exile with Jehoiachin; and the bad figs represent those still in the land with Zedekiah. These chapters thus begin and end with Zedekiah and address the problems associated with the kings of Judah and the false prophets introduced in Jeremiah 1:18 and 2:8.

The word that came from the LORD to Jeremiah (Jer. 21:1a; cf. Jer. 7:1; 11:1; 18:1; 21:1; 25:1; 30:1; 32:1; 34:1, 8; 35:1; 40:1) does not

---

1. Walser suggests that the Greek translator may have had a form of צלח in his *Vorlage* (*Jeremiah*, 320).
2. *Tg. Jon.*: Look, I am about to send my rage against you who sits in the strong places, in fortified cities, says the Lord.
3. LXX Nahum 2:13b [Eng., 2:12b] also uses this singular noun for the same plural noun in the MT.
4. See Keil, *Jeremiah*, 202; McKane, *Jeremiah I–XXV*, 495.
5. Jeremiah 23:7–8 (cf. Jer. 16:14–15) appears directly after 23:6 in the MT, but these two verses occur at the end of the chapter in LXX Jeremiah.

formally begin until 21:4. The intervening material in 21:1b–3 is some-what parenthetical. This word came when King Zedekiah sent to him Pashhur the son of Malkijah and Zephaniah the son of Maaseiah, the priest (Jer. 21:1b; cf. Jer. 37:3a; 38:14). Pashhur the son of Malkijah (see MT Jer. 38:1; cf. Neh. 11:12) is not to be confused with Pashhur the son of Immer (Jer. 20:1–6). Zephaniah the son of Maaseiah is also mentioned in Jeremiah 29:25, 29; 37:3; 52:24 (= 2 Kgs. 25:18).

Zedekiah sent Pashhur and Zephaniah to Jeremiah to request that he "seek" (דרש) the LORD on their behalf because the king of Babylon, whom the MT identifies as "Nebuchadrezzar,"[6] was fighting against them (Jer. 21:2a). This refers to the siege of the city of Jerusalem nar-rated in 2 Kings 25:1–3 (see also Jer. 34:1; 39:1; 52:4–6). To "seek" (דרש) the LORD in this context is to inquire about a course of action specifically through a prophet (see 1 Sam. 9:9; 1 Kgs. 22:5–8; 2 Kgs. 3:11; 8:8; 22:13; cf. Jer. 37:3b; 42:2–3). It is apparent, however, from texts like Jeremiah 10:21 and 37:2 that Zedekiah, despite his con-sultation of Jeremiah, was not genuinely interested in the will of the LORD. Thus, he added, "Perhaps the LORD will do [MT adds: with us] ac-cording to all his wonderful acts, and he [i.e., the king of Babylon][7] will withdraw from us" (Jer. 21:2b; see Jer. 34:21 [MT]; 37:5, 11). Zedekiah only wanted a miraculous deliverance, nothing more and nothing less. The reference to "his wonderful acts" (נפלאתיו) is a reference to the great acts of God narrated in the Torah (Gen.–Deut.) and the Former Prophets (Josh.–Kgs.) (see Ps. 78:4, 11). Thompson and McKane sug-gest that Zedekiah was thinking of the deliverance from Sennacherib in the days of Hezekiah (2 Kgs. 19:32–37; Isa. 37:33–38),[8] but there is no explicit reference to this, and it is probably too specific for such a general phrase as "according to all his wonderful acts."

In Jeremiah 21:3, the prophet responds to Pashhur and Zephaniah with instruction to relay the word of the LORD to Zedekiah. The LORD says, "Look, I am about to turn back the weapons of war [MT adds: that are in your (pl.) hand] with which you [pl.] are fighting [MT adds: the king of Babylon and] the Chaldeans who are besieging you [pl.]

---

6. The spelling "Nebuchadrezzar" is normal in Jeremiah and Ezekiel with the exception of Jeremiah 27–29 (but not Jer. 29:21) and some editions of Jeremiah 34:1 and 39:5 where the spelling "Nebuchadnezzar" appears. "Nebuchadnezzar" is the usual spelling elsewhere in the Hebrew Bible. See Janzen, *Studies in the Text of Jeremiah*, 139–41.

7. It is possible that "he" is the LORD who is fighting against Jerusalem through the king of Babylon (see Jer. 21:4–7).

8. Thompson, *The Book of Jeremiah*, 467; McKane, *Jeremiah I–XXV*, 496.

from outside the city wall [MT adds: and I will gather them] into the midst of this city" (Jer. 21:4). The MT has expanded the shorter, more original text of the Hebrew source behind Greek Jeremiah (cf. Lev. 26:25). The use of second person plural pronouns in this verse indicates that the message is not only for Zedekiah but also for the people he represents. Turning back the weapons of war is usually understood to mean that the soldiers of Zedekiah's army will retreat from fighting the Chaldeans and come inside the city's defenses (see, e.g., NET; cf. Jer. 4:5; 8:14). McKane, however, takes the meaning of the text in a different direction: "Yahweh will fight against the defenders of Jerusalem, and the weapons which ought to be pointed against the besieging Babylonians will be directed by Yahweh against the city and its inhabitants."[9] Based on the usage of מחוץ elsewhere (see BDB, 299–300), the phrase מחוץ לחומה ("from outside the city wall") likely modifies "the Chaldeans who are besieging you" (i.e., they are besieging on the outside of the city wall, and the city wall has not yet been breached),[10] although it has been suggested that it could modify "I am about to turn back the weapons of war" (i.e., the weapons of war will be brought from outside the city wall into the city).[11]

The LORD adds, "And I will fight you [MT: with you] with an outstretched hand and with a strong arm [MT adds: and in anger and] in fury and in great wrath" (Jer. 21:5; cf. Deut. 29:27; Isa. 63:10; Jer. 32:37; 42:18; Lam. 2:4–5). Thus, the king of Babylon and the Chaldeans are merely instruments in the hand of the LORD to do his bidding. The language "with an outstretched hand and with a strong arm" (ביד נטויה ובזרוע חזקה) is normally reserved for descriptions of divine power against the mighty Egyptians in the deliverance of the people from Egyptian bondage (see, e.g., Exod. 6:6; Deut. 4:34; 5:15; 7:19; 26:8; Jer. 32:21; Ps. 136:12; see also Jer. 27:5) or for descriptions of the new exodus (Ezek. 20:33). Here there is an ironic reversal of usage in which the LORD fights not against the enemy but against his people "with an outstretched hand and with a strong arm"—a deconstructed exodus, as it were (see also Isa. 5:25b; 9:11b, 16b, 20b [Eng., 9:12b, 17b, 21b]; 10:4b). The LORD will strike all the inhabitants in the city of Jerusalem, "man and animal," with a great plague, and they will die (Jer. 21:6). This also alludes to the story of the exodus from Egypt (see Exod. 9:3, 15; 12:29; Ps. 135:8); but in place of sending the plague against the Egyptians and striking the firstborn of both man and beast in Egypt,

---

9. McKane, *Jeremiah I–XXV*, 498.
10. See Keil, *Jeremiah*, 203.
11. See Bright, *Jeremiah*, 215; Holladay, *Jeremiah 1*, 567, 571.

the Lord is now striking the people and animals of Jerusalem with a deadly plague (see Exod. 15:26).[12]

After the initial siege of the city (2 Kgs. 25:1–3; Jer. 21:4–6; 34:1; 39:1; 52:4–6), the Lord will give Zedekiah, his servants, and the people left in Jerusalem from the plague, famine, and sword into the hand of their enemies who seek their life (Jer. 21:7a; cf. Jer. 14:12b; 19:7, 9; 24:8–10; 27:8; 34:20–21; 38:16; 44:30). The MT's addition of "into the hand of Nebuchadrezzar, the king of Babylon" provides the subject for its following singular verb: "and he will strike them (וְהִכָּם) with the edge of the sword" (Jer. 21:7b; cf. Luke 21:24). The LXX, however, does not have this addition and thus assumes "their enemies" to be the subject: "and they will strike them (= וְהִכֻּם) with the edge of the sword." The MT and the Hebrew source behind Greek Jeremiah also differ in the remainder of 21:7b, primarily due to the previous addition of Nebuchadrezzar's name in the MT. In the MT, the verbs are third masculine singular (assuming Nebuchadrezzar to be the subject); but in the Hebrew source behind Greek Jeremiah, the verbs are first common singular (assuming the Lord to be the subject): "I [MT: He] will not have pity on them, [MT adds: and he will not spare] and I [MT: he] will not have compassion on them [on them > MT]" (cf. Jer. 13:14). The theological perspective of the Hebrew source behind Greek Jeremiah is consistent with the message of Jeremiah 21:4–6, which reveals the Lord to be the one fighting against Jerusalem by means of the Babylonians. Jeremiah 21:7 speaks generally of the fate of the people of Jerusalem. The specific details of Zedekiah's fate are recounted in multiple passages (see 2 Kgs. 25:4–7; Jer. 39:4–7; 52:7–11; see also Jer. 34:3–5; Ezek. 12:10–16). According to these accounts, Zedekiah is captured by the Babylonians in his attempt to flee, and his sons are executed before his eyes. He is then blinded and hauled off to Babylon. The details of Zedekiah's ultimate fate in Babylon are not provided, except for the manner in which he will be mourned (see Jer. 34:5). At first glance, the word of the Lord to Zedekiah in MT Jeremiah 34:4b ("You will not die by the sword") appears to be a contradiction of 21:7b ("and they [MT: he] will strike them with the edge of the sword"), but

---

12. McKane, following Weiser, suggests that the plague here is an allusion to the one that decimated Sennacherib's army (2 Kgs. 19:35; Isa. 37:36), even though the word "plague" does not appear in the accounts of that event (*Jeremiah I–XXV*, 500). McKane also suggests that the reference to the plague in Jeremiah 21:6 is intended to establish a correspondence between Jeremiah 21:4–6 and 2 Kings 25:1–3 (= Jer. 52:4–6), even though the latter passage speaks of a famine rather than a plague (ibid.).

this text from 34:4b is absent from the Hebrew source behind Greek Jeremiah. Furthermore, when Jeremiah 34:5a says that Zedekiah will die in peace, it does not mean anything more than that he will not die in the Babylonian invasion of Jerusalem. Zedekiah will not die in war but in Babylonian exile. The specific manner in which he will die (e.g., execution) is not stated.

Following the address to Zedekiah (Jer. 21:3–7) is an address to the people (Jer. 21:8–10): "And to this people you will say, 'Thus says the LORD, "Look, I am setting before you the way of life and the way of death"'" (Jer. 21:8; cf. Jer. 8:3; see also Prov. 9). This is a citation of Deuteronomy 30:15 (cf. Deut. 11:26; 30:1, 19): "See, I have set before you today life and well-being, and death and disaster." If the people choose the LORD, then they will be blessed (Deut. 30:16). If not, they will be cursed (Deut. 30:17). Thus, the options given to the people in Jeremiah 21:9 are offered in terms of reception or rejection of the will of the LORD.[13] The first option, which is the way of death, is to stay in the city and die "by the sword or [or > mlt Mss] by famine [MT adds: or by plague]" (Jer. 21:9a; cf. Jer. 27:13; 38:2a, 18).[14] The second option, which is the preferred option, the way of life, is to go out and fall (or, desert/defect/surrender) to the besieging Chaldeans (Jer. 21:9b; cf. Jer. 27:11–12; 37:13–14; 38:2b, 17, 19; 39:9; 52:15 [= 2 Kgs. 25:11). The person who does this will live, "and his life will be his as plunder" (Jer. 21:9b; cf. Jer. 38:2b; 39:18; 45:5). "For," the LORD explains, "I have set my face against this city for evil/harm [i.e., disaster] and not for good [i.e., well-being]. Into the hand of the king of Babylon it will be given, and he will burn it with fire" (Jer. 21:10; cf. Jer. 44:11, 27; Amos 9:4 [cf. Jer. 24:6; 39:12; 40:4]; see also Jer. 29:11; for burning with fire, see Jer. 21:12, 14; 32:29; 34:2, 22; 37:8; 38:18, 23; 52:13 [= 2 Kgs. 25:9]; 2 Chr. 36:19). Jeremiah 21:9 is a general description of the anticipated fate of the people. The specific details found in 2 Kings 25, Jeremiah 39, and Jeremiah 52 indicate that some of the people who remain in the city go into exile along with those who surrender (see 2 Kgs. 25:11; Jer. 39:9 [MT]; 52:15). Furthermore, some of the poor are left in the land of Judah to work vineyards and fields (2 Kgs. 25:12; Jer. 39:10 [MT]; 52:16). Jeremiah 40–44 provides an account of those who remain in the land (including Jeremiah) after Babylonian invasion and captivity.

After the address to Zedekiah (Jer. 21:3–7) and the address to the people (Jer. 21:8–10) comes an address to the house or dynasty of the

---

13. See Wenthe, ed., *Jeremiah, Lamentations*, 160–62; Calvin, *Jeremiah*, 3:62.
14. See McKane (*Jeremiah I–XXV*, 505) for statistics on the triad of sword, famine, and plague.

king of Judah—that is, the royal house of the Davidic monarchy: "O house of the king of Judah [MT: And to the house of the king of Judah], 'Hear the word of the LORD'" (Jer. 21:11). McKane follows Rudolph's view that the MT's לבית מלך יהודה ("to the house of the king of Judah") "refers to the collection of sayings which follow in 21.12–23.8, and that the attachment of ו is a secondary, editorial attempt to connect it also with what precedes by creating the impression that ולבית מלך יהודה follows on from ואל העם הזה תאמר" (see Jer. 22:1; cf. MT Jer. 23:9).[15] The Hebrew source behind Greek Jeremiah lacks the *waw* conjunction and the *lamedh* preposition: בית מלך יהודה ("O house of the king of Judah"). The use of the nominative case in the Greek translation may be understood as a nominative of address (e.g., Brenton: "O house of the king of Juda"; cf. Jer. 21:12: "O house of David"). The NETS renders the Greek text as an example of left-dislocation or fronting: "As for the house of the king of Iouda" (but see NETS Jer. 21:12: "O house of David!").

The LORD calls on the house of David to judge "in the morning" or "each morning" (לבקר; cf. Isa. 33:2b; Amos 4:4b) with "justice" (משפט) and rescue a robbed person from the hand of his oppressor (Jer. 21:12a; cf. Jer. 22:3, 15–16; Sir. 4:9).[16] It is the daily responsibility of the Davidic king to bring justice and righteousness to the people and to vindicate those who are wronged (see 2 Sam. 8:15; 1 Kgs. 3:16–28; cf. Exod. 18:13). Of course, this is precisely what the sons of Josiah have not done (see Jer. 5:28; 22:1–23:4). Only in the kingdom of the ideal, messianic son of David will there be perfect justice (see Jer. 23:5–6; cf. Isa. 9:5–6 [Eng., 9:6–7]; 11:3–5; Ps. 72:4). The consequence of current kings failing in this civic duty is that the LORD's fury will "go forth like fire and burn without anyone to extinguish it" (Jer. 21:12b; cf. Jer. 4:4b; 7:20; 17:27b; 21:10b, 14b). The MT adds at the end of 21:12b: "because of the evil of their deeds." This text does not appear in the Hebrew source behind Greek Jeremiah. The *qere* in the Leningrad Codex and the *kethiv* in a multitude of Masoretic manuscripts read: "because of the evil of your deeds" (cf. Jer. 4:4b). Redak comments on the divergent Masoretic readings: "Although the 'kethib' is מַעֲלָלֵיהֶם, *their deeds,*

---

15. McKane, *Jeremiah I–XXV*, 506. Redak comments on this text, "The words, 'you shall say,' are missing. This is true in many cases, where Scripture relies on the reader's understanding to insert the missing words" (Rosenberg, trans., *Mikraoth Gedoloth: Jeremiah Volume One*, 174).
16. According to McKane, the "oppressor" in this context is not simply someone who robs or steals in transgression of the law but someone involved in "judicial malpractice" (*Jeremiah I–XXV*, 509–510; cf. Isa. 10:2; 61:8; Eccl. 5:7; see also BDB, 798).

referring to the people, the 'keri' is מַעַלְלֵיכֶם, *your deeds*, referring to the royal family, who were negligent in their execution of justice."[17]

The MT of Jeremiah 21:13 appears to be an address to Mount Zion or Jerusalem, the city of David: "Look, I am against you, O inhabitant of the valley, O rock (צוּר) of the plain" (Jer. 21:13a; cf. Isa. 22:1; Jer. 17:3; Ps. 125:2). The Hebrew source behind Greek Jeremiah seems at first glance to be an address to Tyre: "Look, I am against you, O inhabitant of the valley of Tyre (צוֹר), the plain." But Tyre was the place from which the cedars of Lebanon were acquired for the building of Solomon's temple and the royal palace (see 1 Kgs. 5:15, 20, 23 [Eng., 5:1, 6, 9]). In fact, so many cedars went into the making of the king's house that it became known as "The House of the Forest of Lebanon" (see 1 Kgs. 7:2; 10:17; see also Isa. 22:8; Jer. 21:14; 22:6–7, 23). Thus, the Hebrew source behind Greek Jeremiah is also an address to the city of David. In particular, it is an address to "those who say, 'Who will terrify us (יְחַת) [MT: Who will come down (יֵחַת) against us], and who will enter our dwelling places?'" (Jer. 21:13b; cf. Jer. 37:9). Just as there is a false sense of security in the temple (Jer. 7:4), so there is a misguided confidence in the institution of the Davidic monarchy and in the fortifications of the city of David.[18] The MT adds a portion of text at the beginning of 21:14 that does not appear in the Hebrew source behind Greek Jeremiah: "And I will visit upon you (i.e., punish you) according to the fruit of your deeds," the prophetic utterance of the LORD (cf. Jer. 17:10; 23:2; 32:19; see also Zeph. 1:8). The LORD will kindle a fire in the "forest" (i.e., royal palace) of the city of David (see again 1 Kgs. 7:2; 10:17; Isa. 22:8; Jer. 21:13; 22:6–7, 23), and it will consume everything around it (see Jer. 11:16; Jer. 21:10, 12b; 39:8; 43:12; 49:27; 50:32; 52:13 [= 2 Kgs. 25:9]).

---

17. Rosenberg, trans., *Mikraoth Gedoloth: Jeremiah Volume One*, 174.

18. Psalm 89 is a good example of how the covenant with David could be misunderstood. The unconditional covenant is for the one messianic son of David who will build the temple and reign over an everlasting kingdom (2 Sam. 7:12–16; Ps. 89:34–38 [Eng., 89:33–37]; see also Zech. 6:12–13; Dan. 7:13–14). The terms of the covenant apply conditionally to the plurality of sons of David who reign on the throne in the meantime (Ps. 89:31–33 [Eng., 89:30–32]). The voice of the king (perhaps Zedekiah) in Psalm 89:39–52 (Eng., 89:38–51) reflects a failure to grasp this distinction. This king thinks that the covenant should apply unconditionally to him regardless of his behavior so that there are no negative consequences. See Shepherd, *Text in the Middle*, 122–29.

JEREMIAH 22

22:1 Thus said the Lord, *"Go and go down [MT: Go down] to the house of the king of Judah and speak there this word 22:2 and say, 'Hear the word of the* Lord, *O king of Judah who sits on the throne of David, you and your house [MT: your servants] and your people and [and > MT] those who enter through these gates. 22:3 Thus says the* Lord, *"Do justice and righteousness and rescue a robbed person from the hand of his oppressor [MT: from an oppressor's hand; cf. 4QJer*ᵃ*; Jer. 21:12a]; and as for a resident alien and [and > Codex L] an orphan [or, a fatherless child] and a widow, do not oppress (them) and [and > Codex L] do not treat (them) violently; and with regard to innocent blood, do not pour (it) out in this place. 22:4 For if you [pl.] will indeed do this word, kings sitting on the throne of David [MT: kings sitting for David on his throne] and riding on chariots and [and > 4QJer*ᵃ*] on horses will enter through the gates of this house, they and their servants and their people [MT: he and his servants (see 4QJer*ᶜ*) and his people]. 22:5 And if you [pl.] do not do [MT: hear/heed] these words, by myself I swear," the prophetic utterance of the* Lord, *"that a ruin will this house become [Tg. Jon.: to the sword will this house be]."*

22:6 For thus says the Lord *concerning/to/against the house of the king [of the king > Cairo Geniza] of Judah, "Gilead is what you are to me, the top of Lebanon [Tg. Jon.: If you were beloved before me like the house of the sanctuary, which is high on the tops of the mountains].*[1] *I swear that I will make you a wilderness [lit., If I do not make you a wilderness (see GKC §149b, c)], cities (that) are uninhabited [see GKC §44m]. 22:7 And I will set apart [LXX: bring] against you destroyers, each and his vessels [LXX: each and his axe; cf. Rahlfs: a destroying man and his axe], and they will cut down the choicest [cf. 4QJer*ᵃ*] of your cedars [Tg. Jon.: and they will kill the best of your warriors like those who cut the wood of the forest] and cause (them) to fall [or, cast (them)] into the fire.*

22:8 And nations [MT: many nations] will pass by this city and say to one another, 'Why did the Lord *do thus to this great city?' 22:9 And they will say, 'Because they forsook the covenant of the* Lord *their God and bowed down to other gods and served/worshiped them.'*

---

1. See Hayward, *Targum of Jeremiah*, 109, n. 2. See also Neusner, *Jeremiah in Talmud and Midrash*, 23, 38, 55.

22:10 Do not weep for the dead and do not mourn for him. Weep indeed [ESV: weep bitterly] for the one who goes [Tg. Jon.: for the one who goes into exile], for he will never return again and see the land of his kindred."

22:11 For thus says the LORD *concerning Shallum [LXX[L]: Jehoahaz] the son of Josiah [MT adds: the king of Judah] who reigned in place of Josiah his father, he who went out from this place, "He will never return there again, 22:12 but [Codex L: for] in the place where I [MT: they] exiled him, there he will die, and this land he will never see again."*

22:13 Woe [or Ah]! One who builds his house without righteousness [or, with unrighteousness] and his upper chambers without justice [or, with injustice], by his neighbor he serves for nothing [i.e., he makes his neighbor work for him for nothing],[2] and the pay for his work he does not give. 22:14 You built for yourself [MT: who says, "I will build for myself] a house of size [MT, 4QJer[a, c] add: and] (with) spacious upper chambers, cut with window(s) [cf. 4QJer[c]; MT: and cuts / widens for himself my windows] and paneled with cedar and painted [MT: paints] with vermilion.[3] 22:15 Will you be king because you are provoked by [or, strive to compete with] Ahaz your forefather [LXX[A]: Ahab; MT: because you strive to excel in cedar (see GKC §55h; BDB, 354); Tg. Jon.: Do you imagine to be like the former king]? Did they not eat and drink [LXX: They will not eat, and they will not drink]? It is good [LXX: better] for you to do justice and righteousness. [MT: Your father, did he not eat and drink and do justice and righteousness, then it was good for him?] 22:16 They did not know, they did not plead the cause of the afflicted and the needy [MT: He plead the cause of the afflicted and the needy, then it was good]. Is not that what it is to know [or, acknowledge] me [LXX: Is not this you not knowing me]?' the prophetic utterance of the LORD. *22:17 'Look [MT: For] your eyes and your heart / mind are not except upon your unjust gain and upon*

---

2. "It should be noticed that this is the first example of ἐργάζομαι in Jeremiah, and that it is a rendering of עבד. עבד is usually rendered by δουλεύω in the Septuagint, but from here on the translator of Jeremiah mostly renders עבד by ἐργάζομαι" (Walser, *Jeremiah*, 323).

3. The Hebrew words קרוע, ספון, and משוח are translated here as if they were all vocalized as masculine singular *qal* passive participles ("cut," "paneled," and "painted") modifying the masculine noun בית ("house"). The LXX translates these words as if they were all plural passive participles modifying "spacious upper chambers."

the blood of the innocent to pour out and upon oppression/extortion [LXX: unrighteousness] and upon the crushing/oppression [or, course; LXX: murder] to do. 22:18 Therefore, thus says the LORD *concerning Jehoiakim the son of Josiah, the king of Judah, "Woe to this man [> MT]! They will not mourn for him, 'Ah, brother [MT: Ah, my brother!' or 'Ah, sister]!' They will not mourn for him, 'Ah, lord/master [MT: Ah, lord/master!' or 'Ah, his royal splendor]!' 22:19 A donkey's burial will he be buried, dragged and cast [see GKC §113h] beyond the gate [MT: gates] of Jerusalem."*

22:20 Go up to Lebanon [4QJer^c: in Lebanon] and cry out, and in Bashan give your voice, and cry out on the other side of the sea [cf. Syr.; MT: from Abarim; Tg. Jon.: at the ford; Vulg.: to those passing by], for all your lovers/friends [or, allies] are broken [4QJer^c: poured out]. 22:21 I spoke to you [Tg. Jon.: I sent to you all my servants the prophets] in your neglect/error [LXX: transgression; MT: ease/prosperity] and [> MT] you said, "I will not listen." This has been your way since your youth, [MT adds: for] you have not obeyed my voice. 22:22 As for all your shepherds [Aq., Symm.: your friends], wind will shepherd (them). And as for your lovers/friends [or, allies], into captivity they will go. Indeed, at that time you will be ashamed and humiliated because of your friends [MT: your evil]. 22:23 O inhabitant [see GKC §90n] in Lebanon, nested among the cedars, [MT adds: how] you will groan [see GKC §23f^1] when pains come to you, writhing like a woman in labor.

22:24 "As I live," the prophetic utterance of the LORD *[Syr. adds: God], "Jeconiah [MT: Coniah; i.e., Jehoiachin] the son of Jehoiakim, the king of Judah, will certainly [> MT] not be a signet ring [or, seal] on my right hand. [MT adds: כִּי] From there I will tear you [Vulg.: him] off, 22:25 and I will give you into the hand of those who seek your life [MT adds: and into the hand of] before whom you are afraid, [MT adds: and into the hand of Nebuchadrezzar and] into the hand of the Chaldeans, 22:26 and I will hurl you and your mother who bore you to a land [MT: another land] where you [sg.; MT pl.] were not born, and there you [pl.] will die, 22:27 [MT, 4QJer^c add: and] to the land for which [MT: where] they long [lit., they lift up their soul/desire] [MT adds: to return], [MT adds: thither] they will not return."*

22:28 Jeconiah is despised like a vessel in which there is no delight [or, like an undesirable vessel; LXX: like a vessel for which there is no use; MT: Is this man, Coniah, a despised, shattered vessel/jar/pot? Is he a vessel in which there is no delight?]. Why[4] is he hurled and cast [MT: Why are they hurled, he and his seed/offspring, and cast] to a land [MT: the land] that he does not know [MT: that they do not know]? 22:29 O land, land [MT: O land, land, land], hear the word of the LORD [Tg. Jon.: From his land they have exiled him to another land. O land of Israel, receive the word of the Lord]! 22:30 [MT adds: Thus says the LORD] "Write [or, Record/Register] this man childless [LXX: banished] [MT adds: a man who will not prosper in his days], for a man sitting on the throne of David [MT adds: and] ruling again over Judah will not prosper from his seed/offspring."'

Chapter 22 follows the address to Zedekiah (Jer. 21:3–7) and the address to the house of the king of Judah (Jer. 21:11–14) with an address to the king of Judah (Jer. 22:1–5) and words concerning the house of the king of Judah (Jer. 22:6–7, 8–9, 10). The latter part of the chapter features messages specifically about three kings of Judah: Shallum/ Jehoahaz (Jer. 22:11–12), Jehoiakim (Jer. 22:13–19), and Jehoiachin (Jer. 22:24–27, 28–30). The small unit in 22:20–23 connects to the surrounding context through its reference to the royal palace as a house made of cedars from Lebanon (Jer. 22:23; cf. Jer. 22:6–7, 14).

In 22:1, the LORD instructs the prophet Jeremiah to "go down" to the house of the king of Judah, presumably from the temple (see Jer. 26:10; 36:12), and speak the message of the following verses. The word of the LORD is to be addressed to the king of Judah who sits on the throne of David and his "house" (MT: "servants") (Jer. 22:2; cf. Jer. 13:13; 17:25; 36:24). There is then a difference between the Hebrew source behind Greek Jeremiah and the MT as to whether one more group is included in the address or two: "and your people and [and > MT] those who enter through these gates." According to the MT, there is only one group—the king's people who enter through the gates; but the Hebrew source behind Greek Jeremiah indicates two groups—the king's people and those who enter the gates. It is not entirely clear who the king's people might be. "Your people" (i.e., the king's people) is more specific than "the people" (i.e., the general populace), but it is not as specific as a word like שָׂרֶיךָ ("your officials"). It is perhaps a reference to prominent supporters of the king from the general populace. The phrase "those who enter through these gates" appears to be a catch-all for any who come through the gates of the royal palace (cf. Jer. 7:2 [MT]; 17:19–20).

---

4. Rahlfs has ὅτι ("because"). The Göttingen Septuagint (Ziegler) has ὅ τι ("which"). See Walser, *Jeremiah*, 327.

The LORD says, "Do justice and righteousness and rescue a robbed person from the hand of his oppressor [MT: from an oppressor's hand]" (Jer. 22:3a). This text is very close to that of Jeremiah 21:12a (see commentary there), but it goes on to add: "and as for a resident alien and [and > Codex L] an orphan [or, a fatherless child] and a widow, do not oppress (them) and [and > Codex L] do not treat (them) violently; and with regard to innocent blood, do not pour (it) out in this place" (Jer. 22:3b; see Exod. 22:20; Lev. 19:13, 33; Jer. 7:6; 19:4; Sir. 4:9–10; Jas. 1:27). It is the responsibility of the king to bring justice and righteousness to the land and to defend those who cannot defend themselves (cf. Deut. 10:18–19), not to take advantage of them (Isa. 1:17, 23; Jer. 22:15–17). The reference to the pouring out of "innocent blood" (דם נקי) is likely not a reference to child sacrifice but a reference to judicial murder (see commentary on 19:4).

If those addressed in 22:2 will do what the LORD says in 22:3, then "kings sitting on the throne of David [MT: kings sitting for David on his throne] and riding on chariots and [and > 4QJerᵃ] on horses will enter through the gates of this house, they and their servants and their people [MT: he and his servants (see 4QJerᶜ) and his people]" (Jer. 22:4; cf. Jer. 17:24–26).[5] But if they do not do what the LORD requires, then the royal palace will become a "ruin" (Jer. 22:5; cf. Jer. 7:34; 17:27; 27:17; see also Isa. 45:23; Jer. 44:26; 49:13; 51:14 [MT]; Amos 6:8; Heb. 6:13).[6] This anticipates the prophecy of the destruction of the palace in 22:6–7. The similarities between Jeremiah 17:24–27 and 22:4–5 are striking, although the procession in 17:25 comes through the city gates rather than those of the royal palace. McKane notes well the key differences between the two passages: "the alternatives which are set out in 17.25–27 focus on Jerusalem and not the Davidic dynasty as in 22.4f. Moreover, the issue on which the destiny of Jerusalem hinges in chapter 17 is Sabbath observance and this is far removed from the matter of judicial impartiality and social justice on which 21.12 and 22.1–5 hang."[7]

Verses 6 and 7 essentially explain what is meant by the desolation of the royal palace in 22:5. The personified ("you") house of the king is compared to the densely wooded northern region of Gilead and to the top of the wooded mountain range of Lebanon on the northern border of

---

5. "The palace will be the hub of the kingdom and will be alive with the pomp and ceremony of a royal way of life for so long as the king is the defender of the just community demanded by Yahweh" (McKane, *Jeremiah I–XXV*, 517).

6. *Targum Jonathan* interprets חרבה ("ruin") as חרבא ("sword"): "to the sword will this house be."

7. McKane, *Jeremiah I–XXV*, 516.

the land of Israel, which was well known for its cedars (Jer. 22:6a). As noted in the commentary on Jeremiah 21:13–14, this is because of the large amount of cedars from Lebanon that went into the building of the royal palace (see 2 Sam. 7:2; 1 Kgs. 7:2; 10:17; Isa. 22:8; Jer. 22:23; 2 Chr. 9:16, 20). Assuming the failure of the kings of Judah and their associates, the LORD swears an oath that he will make this metaphorical forest into a wilderness (i.e., a desolate place), uninhabited cities (including Jerusalem and the surrounding daughter cities) (Jer. 22:6b; cf. Jer. 4:26, 29). He will "set apart" (cf. Jer. 6:4) against the king's house destroyers, "each and his vessels" (LXX: "each and his axe") (Jer. 22:7a). These destroyers will cut down the best of the cedars in the structure of the palace and cast them into the fire (Jer. 22:7b; cf. Jer. 21:14b; 39:8; 52:13; see also Jer. 6:6; 46:22–23). The LXX ("each and his axe") and *Targum Jonathan* ("and they will kill the best of your warriors like those who cut the wood of the forest") have both understood that the invasion of an enemy army and its destruction of the royal palace are given here under the figure of lumberjacks chopping down the trees of a forest (cf. Isa. 14:8; Ps. 74:5).

At that time, nations will pass by the uninhabited city of Jerusalem and its destroyed palace and say to one another, "Why did the LORD do thus to this great city" (Jer. 22:8; cf. Deut. 29:23; 1 Kgs. 9:8; see also Jer. 5:19a; 9:11b [Eng., 9:12b])? This presupposes an assumption on the part of the nations that the God of the Hebrews (Yahweh) is responsible for what happens to Jerusalem. The answer to this question is, "Because they forsook the covenant of the LORD their God and bowed down to other gods and served/worshiped them" (Jer. 22:9; cf. Deut. 29:24–27; 1 Kgs. 9:9; see also Jer. 1:16; 5:19b; 9:12–13 [Eng., 9:13–14]; 11:10; 16:11). Thus, there will be no need for the LORD to withhold his judgment in an effort to act for the sake of his name (Jer. 14:7, 21) and to protect his reputation from misrepresentation by the nations (see Exod. 32:12; Deut. 9:28; 32:27). The nations will understand exactly what has happened. The people of Judah and Jerusalem are accountable for their breaking of the covenant and their worship of other gods, and the righteous and holy God Yahweh will judge them accordingly.

The exhortation not to weep for the dead and not to mourn for him (Jer. 22:10a) refers to the premature death of the righteous king Josiah at the hands of Pharaoh Necho (see 2 Kgs. 23:29–30; 2 Chr. 35:20–24a) and the subsequent mourning over his loss (see 2 Chr. 35:24b; see also Zech. 12:11).[8] According to 2 Chronicles 35:25, Jeremiah himself la-

---

8. "But Josiah, on his chariot, did not turn away from him but went on to fight against him, and did not heed the words of the prophet Jeremiah from the mouth of the Lord" (1 Esd. 1:26).

mented the death of Josiah. Male and female singers continued to utter laments for Josiah to the point that such laments became customary and were recorded in a book of laments. But the instruction in Jeremiah 22:10b is to weep instead "for the one who goes" (להלך), since he will never return again to see the land of his kindred. The following context (Jer. 22:11–12) makes it clear that this refers to Shallum (i.e., Jehoahaz) (see also Jer. 22:27). *Targum Jonathan* interprets "for the one who goes" to mean "for the one who goes into exile." McKane, on the other hand, suggests that הלך in this context may mean "dying" rather than "going."[9] The intent of Jeremiah 22:10 is not to say that Josiah, like Jehoiakim (Jer. 22:18), is undeserving of mourning. Rather, it is to say that the fate of Shallum (Jehoahaz) is far worse than that of Josiah (cf. Luke 23:28). Josiah died prematurely, but he did not suffer and die in exile. He will see the land again in the resurrection (see Dan. 12:1–2, 13).

The text of Jeremiah 22:11–12 provides an explanation of what is said about the הלך ("one who goes") in 22:10b by putting a name with the description. It is what the LORD says about "Shallum" (LXX[L]: "Jehoahaz") who reigned in place of his father Josiah and who "went out" (יצא) from the royal palace, the city of Jerusalem, and the land of the covenant into exile (Jer. 22:11a). The LORD says, "He will never return there again, but [Codex L: for] in the place where I [MT: they] exiled him, there he will die, and this land he will never see again" (Jer. 22:11b–12). No explanation is given for the use of the name "Shallum" instead of "Jehoahaz" (see also 1 Chr. 3:15), but the phenomenon of multiple names for the same king may be compared to "Eliakim/Jehoiakim" (2 Kgs. 23:34a), "Coniah/Jeconiah/Jehoiachin" (Jer. 22:24; 24:1; 52:31), and "Mattaniah/Zedekiah" (2 Kgs. 24:17).[10] According to 2 Kings 23:30–34 (2 Chr. 36:1–4), the people of the land anointed Jehoahaz and made him king in place of his father Josiah. Jehoahaz reigned in Jerusalem for three months and did what was evil in the sight of the LORD. Pharaoh Necho imprisoned him in Riblah in the land of Hamath and made Eliakim king in his place and changed his name to Jehoiakim. Pharaoh Necho took Jehoahaz and brought him to Egypt where he died.

---

9. McKane, *Jeremiah I–XXV*, 523–24.
10. "According to Frc. Junius, Hitz., and Graf, Jeremiah compares Jehoahaz on account of his short reign with Shallum in Israel, who reigned but one month (2 Kings 15:13), and ironically calls him Shallum, as Jezebel called Jehu, *Zimri* murderer of his lord, 2 Kings 9:31" (Keil, *Jeremiah*, 208). Keil does not adopt this view, but it is as attractive as any other explanation that has been offered.

Jeremiah 22:13–19 takes the pattern of a "woe" oracle (הוֹי ["Woe!" or "Ah!"]; cf. Jer. 23:1–4): introduction (22:13), accusation (22:24–17), and announcement of judgment (22:18–19). It is not explicit that the accusation is against Jehoiakim until the announcement of judgment. Verse 13 describes Jehoiakim as one "who builds his house without righteousness and his upper chambers without justice" (cf. Hab. 2:12; Mic. 3:10; *1 En.* 94:7). He makes his neighbor (i.e., fellow Judean) work for him for nothing (see Lev. 19:13; 25:39, 46; Deut. 24:15; 1 Kgs. 5:27; 12:4; Jer. 30:8b; 34:9–10; Sir. 21:8; *1 En.* 99:13). He does not give the wages due for the work done. This speaks of the king's abuse of his position of power for his own personal gain. "If it is not the LORD who builds a house, then in vain do its builders work on it" (Ps. 127:1).

The Hebrew source behind Greek Jeremiah 22:14a begins the accusation as follows: "You built for yourself a house of size with spacious upper chambers."[11] The MT, however, gives this as a quote of Jehoiakim: "I will build for myself a house of size and spacious upper chambers." The Hebrew source behind Greek Jeremiah 22:14b goes on to describe this house as one "cut with window(s) and paneled with cedar and painted with vermilion" (cf. 1 Kgs. 6:9; 7:3, 7; Hag. 1:4). The MT, which appears to shift from description of Jehoiakim to description of the house and back, is difficult: "and cuts/widens for himself my windows and paneled with cedar and paints with vermilion." The NET suggests emendation of חַלּוֹנָי וְסָפוּן ("my windows and paneled") to חַלּוֹנָיו וְסָפֻן ("his windows and panels").

The Hebrew source behind Greek Jeremiah 22:15a says, "Will you be king because you are provoked by [or, strive to compete with] Ahaz (אחז) your forefather" (cf. Jer. 12:5)? Holladay favors this reading.[12] The MT says, "Will you be king because you strive to excel in cedar (ארז)?" *Targum Jonathan* interprets this to mean, "Do you imagine to be like the former king" (Solomon? Josiah?)? Thus, both the Hebrew source behind Greek Jeremiah and the MT question whether Jehoiakim's status as king depends upon his ability to compete with a previous king in his construction on the royal palace. The Hebrew source behind Greek Jeremiah 22:15b then appears to assume a plurality of previous kings: "Did they not eat and drink? It is good [LXX: better] for you to do justice and righteousness." The point of this reference to the eating and

---

11. "The Deuteronomic historian records that Jehoiakim had to exact silver and gold from the country gentry in the early years of his reign to pay tribute to Pharaoh (2 Kgs 23:35): his project for more luxurious palace quarters cannot have been popular" (Holladay, *Jeremiah 1*, 595).
12. Holladay, *Jeremiah 1*, 596.

drinking of Jehoiakim's forefathers is not immediately clear, although LXX 22:16 seems to indicate that they enjoyed the benefits of their position to the neglect of justice and righteousness. Thus, it would be better for Jehoiakim not to follow their example. MT 22:15b, however, refers specifically to Jehoiakim's father Josiah in a way that suggests more precisely the sense of the rhetorical question: "Your father, did he not eat and drink and do justice and righteousness, then it was good for him?" Josiah ate and drank (see Isa. 22:13; Eccl. 2:24; 3:13; 5:17 [Eng., 5:18]; 8:15), but he also did justice and righteousness (see Jer. 22:3; 23:5). Thus, things went well for him. Jehoiakim would do well to follow this model. Redak paraphrases, "I would not blame you for your pleasures if you performed justice and righteousness, for your father Josiah ate and drank in kingly manner and enjoyed his bounty, but since he performed justice and righteousness, it was well for him, and he enjoyed his bounty all his life."[13]

According to the Hebrew source behind Greek Jeremiah 22:16a, Jehoiakim's forefathers "did not know, they did not plead the cause of the afflicted" (cf. Jer. 5:28). On the other hand, the MT refers again to Josiah: "He pleaded the cause of the afflicted and the needy, then it was good" (cf. Prov. 31:9). Thus, the Hebrew source behind Greek Jeremiah 22:15–16 uses Jehoiakim's forefathers as negative examples, while the MT uses Josiah as a positive example. Doing justice and righteousness (i.e., pleading the cause of the afflicted) is what it is to know or acknowledge the LORD (Jer. 22:16b; see commentary on Jer. 9:23 [Eng., 9:24]). The LXX converts the final rhetorical question of the verse ("Is not that what it is to know [or, acknowledge] me?") to match more closely its source text in the first half of the verse: "Is not this you not knowing me?" This conversion probably does not reflect a different Hebrew text from the one found in the MT. It is the translator's decision. It is precisely what Jehoiakim's forefathers did not do that constitutes what it is to know or acknowledge the LORD. The translator considered it preferable to say that doing what the forefathers did would be not to know or acknowledge the LORD.

The Hebrew source behind Greek Jeremiah 22:17 begins with הנה ("Look"), pointing out something. The MT begins with כי ("For"), explaining something. Jehoiakim's eyes and heart/mind are only upon his "unjust gain" (cf. Jer. 6:13; 8:10), the pouring out of "innocent blood" (see 2 Kgs. 24:4; Jer. 22:3), "oppression/extortion" (see Jer. 6:6b; 21:12; 22:3), and "crushing/oppression" (LXX: "murder"; see Jer. 26:20–23; see also 1 Sam. 12:3). It is possible that מרוצה ("crushing/oppression") is

---

13. Rosenberg, trans., *Mikraoth Gedoloth: Jeremiah Volume One*, 180.

not from the root רצץ ("crush/oppress") but from the root רוץ ("run"), meaning "course," as in a bad course of action (see Jer. 8:6; 23:10).

The announcement of judgment in 22:18–19 explicitly names Jehoiakim as the king against whom the accusations have been brought in the previous verses. The first part of this announcement in the Hebrew source behind Greek Jeremiah does not appear in the MT: הוי על האיש הזה ("Woe to this man!") (Jer. 22:18a; cf. Jer. 22:13; 23:1). The text goes on to say that the people will not mourn for Jehoiakim as they did for his father Josiah (see Jer. 22:10; 2 Chr. 35:24b–25). According to the Hebrew source behind Greek Jeremiah, they will not mourn for him, saying, "Ah, brother!" (cf. 1 Kgs. 13:30). The MT says, "'Ah, my brother' or 'Ah, sister.'" There is some debate about whether the words "brother" and "sister" refer to those being mourned or to fellow mourners. It is also possible that this is simply a general representation of what would be heard at a funeral. If "brother" and "sister" specifically refer to those being mourned in the MT, then they perhaps refer to Jehoiakim and his mother respectively (cf. Jehoiachin and his mother in Jer. 22:26). Jeremiah 22:18b adds, "They will not mourn for him, 'Ah, lord/master [MT: Ah, lord/master!' or 'Ah, his royal splendor]'" (cf. Jer. 34:5)! The MT again expands upon the shorter text of the Hebrew source behind Greek Jeremiah. The terms "lord/master" and "his royal splendor" clearly refer to the king, Jehoiakim. The statement in 2 Kings 24:6a that Jehoiakim lay with his fathers does not indicate the manner of Jehoiakim's death or the nature of his burial. In fact, the TEV renders this idiom simply as, "Jehoiakim died." According to 2 Chronicles 36:6, Nebuchadnezzar bound him in bronze fetters to take him away to Babylon. Jeremiah 22:19a says that Jehoiakim will be given a donkey's burial, which is then explained to mean that he will be dragged and cast beyond the gate (MT: "gates") of Jerusalem (Jer. 22:19b). Jeremiah 36:30b says that his corpse will be cast out and exposed to the elements—heat by day and frost by night (cf. Jer. 8:1–2; 14:16; see Deut. 28:26; see also Isa. 14:19–20). This is perhaps poetic justice for the treatment of the prophet Uriah referenced in Jeremiah 26:23b.

In Jeremiah 22:1, the prophet received instruction from the Lord to "go down" to the house of the king of Judah, which was known as "The House of the Forest of Lebanon" (1 Kgs. 7:2; see Jer. 22:6–7, 23). Now in 22:20, Jeremiah issues feminine singular imperatives on behalf of the Lord to the city of Jerusalem to "go up" to Lebanon in the north and cry out. Additionally, the people of Jerusalem are to make their voice heard in Bashan to the northeast and cry out "on the other side of the sea" (מעבר ים). For this last phrase, the MT has "from Abarim"

(מעברים) to the southeast (cf. *Tg. Jon.*: "at the ford" [= מַעֲבָר]; Vulg.: "to those passing by" [= מֵעֹבְרִים]). The latter part of 22:20 explains that this will prove to be a vain appeal to Jerusalem's broken "allies" (cf. Hos. 8:9). According to the narrative in 2 Kings 24:7, Nebuchadnezzar prevented the king of Egypt (a potential ally) from going forth from his land when he took all the territory from the wadi of Egypt to the Euphrates, which formerly belonged to the king of Egypt.

The Lord says in 22:21a, "I spoke to you in your neglect/error (בְּשַׁלְוֹתֶךְ)" (see LXX: "in your transgression"; cf. Dan. 3:29; 6:5 [Eng., 6:4]; Ezra 4:22; 6:9). The MT has, "I spoke to you in your ease/prosperity (בְּשַׁלְוֹתַיִךְ or בְּשַׁלְוֹתֶךְ)." According to *Targum Jonathan*, this refers to the manner in which the Lord sent to the people all his servants the prophets, but the people refused to listen (cf. Jer. 7:25; 25:4; 26:5; 29:19). It has been the way of the people since their "youth" not to obey the voice of the Lord (Jer. 22:21b; see Jer. 2:2; 3:24–25; 32:30). Jeremiah 22:22a continues, "As for all your shepherds [Aq., Symm.: your friends (= רֵעַיִךְ)], wind will shepherd (them). And as for your lovers/friends [or, allies], into captivity they will go" (cf. Jer. 30:16). The first clause features a wordplay based on the root רעה ("to shepherd"): "As for all your shepherds (רעיך), wind will shepherd (תרעה) (them)." The shepherds are the kings (see, e.g., Jer. 2:8; 3:15; 10:21; 23:1)—Jehoahaz (2 Kgs. 23:34b; Jer. 22:11–12), Jehoiakim (2 Chr. 36:6), Jehoiachin (2 Kgs. 24:15; Jer. 22:26), and Zedekiah (2 Kgs. 25:7)—who will be driven as if by the wind into exile. The lovers/friends are allies like Egypt who will also go into captivity. According to the Hebrew source behind Greek Jeremiah 22:22b, the Lord says, "Indeed, at that time you will be ashamed and humiliated because of your friends (רֵעַיִךְ)" (cf. Jer. 2:36; Lam. 1:2; see also Jer. 14:3; 31:19). The MT has "your evil" (רָעָתֵךְ) instead of "your friends." The kings and allies in which the city of Jerusalem has put its trust will ultimately be of no help.

In Jeremiah 22:23a, the city of Jerusalem is addressed with feminine singular participles as "inhabitant in Lebanon, nested among the cedars" (cf. Jer. 21:13). This is because Jerusalem is the place of the royal palace, which is "the top of Lebanon" to the Lord due to the amount of cedars from Lebanon in its structure (Jer. 22:6–7, 14; see again 1 Kgs. 7:2; 10:17; Isa. 22:8). The irony of this form of address lies in its juxtaposition with 22:20–22. The city of Jerusalem is to go up to Lebanon to cry for help (Jer. 22:20a), but there will be no help from allies or from the kings in the royal palace (Jer. 22:20b, 22). Nevertheless, the people believe their nest is secure in a high place, unwilling to acknowledge that it will soon be brought down (cf. Jer. 49:16; Obad. 4). Jerusalem will groan when pains come to it, when writhing comes like that of a woman in labor (Jer. 22:23b; cf. Jer. 6:24; 13:21; 49:24; 50:43).

חי אני ("As I live") at the beginning of 22:24a introduces an oath. Thus, the following כי אם does not mean "though" (contra ESV et al.). Rather, it marks the start of the oath (see BDB, 474) and is normally untranslated unless the translator intends to bring out the elliptical nature of the oath (i.e., ". . . if Jeconiah the son of Jehoiakim, the king of Judah, will certainly be a signet ring on my right hand"; = "the Lord do so unto me, if Jeconiah . . . will certainly be a signet ring on my right hand"): "As I live," the prophetic utterance of the LORD [Syr. adds: God], "Jeconiah [MT: Coniah; i.e., Jehoiachin][14] the son of Jehoiakim, the king of Judah, will certainly [> MT] not be a signet ring [or, seal] on my right hand" (see GKC §149b).[15] The king is the signet ring or seal on the LORD's (anthropomorphic) dominant hand in the sense that he represents the LORD's authority on earth (see 1 Kgs. 21:8; Est. 8:8; see also Gen. 41:42; Est. 3:10; 8:2; Dan. 6:18 [Eng., 6:17]). Thus, the removal of Jehoiachin from his position as king also means his removal as the representative, authoritative signet ring or seal from the LORD's right hand: "From there I will tear you [Vulg.: him] off" (Jer. 22:24b). Haggai 2:23 cites this text in a remarkable fashion: "In that day," the prophetic utterance of the LORD of hosts, "I will take you, Zerubbabel the son of Shealtiel, my servant," the prophetic utterance of the LORD, "and I will make you like a signet ring [or, seal], for it is you whom I have chosen," the prophetic utterance of the LORD of hosts.[16] As for Jehoiachin, how-

---

14. For the different spellings of Jehoiachin's name, see Janzen, *Studies in the Text of Jeremiah*, 144.

15. See also Thompson, *Book of Jeremiah*, 483; McKane, *Jeremiah I–XXV*, 540–41; Holladay, *Jeremiah 1*, 604–5.

16. "The text of Haggai 2:23 is a citation and a reversal of Jeremiah 22:24. The LORD announced in Jeremiah 22:24 that he would tear Jehoiachin off his right hand as a seal/signet-ring. But now in Haggai 2:23 Zerubbabel, a descendant of the Davidic king Jehoiachin (1 Chr. 3:17–19), is the chosen seal/signet-ring. The messianic implications are hard to miss, especially when the LORD refers to Zerubbabel as 'my servant' (cf. Isa. 42:1–7; 49:1–9; 50:4–11; 52:13–53:12). It will be up to the following book of Zechariah to clarify that Zerubbabel is only a prefiguration of the real servant of the LORD. Zechariah uses the language of Haggai 2:23 in Zechariah 3:8; 6:12–13 to indicate that the servant is not a contemporary of Joshua. Rather, he is the messianic Branch from Jeremiah 23:5–6 who will build the temple in accordance with the Davidic covenant (2 Sam. 7:13) and occupy the offices of priest and king" (Shepherd, *Commentary on the Book of the Twelve*, 32–33, see also 389–90). Malbim: "for the King Messiah will

ever, the LORD will remove him from his own hand and give him into the hand of those who seek his life, those before whom he is afraid (Jer. 22:25a; cf. Jer. 19:7, 9; 21:7; 34:20–21; 39:17; 44:30; 46:26; 49:37)—that is, into the hand of the Chaldeans (Jer. 22:25b). The MT expands this text to include a reference to Nebuchadrezzar.

The LORD will "hurl" Jehoiachin and his mother (Nehushta) to a land where neither he nor his mother were born, and there they will die (Jer. 22:26; cf. Jer. 13:18–19; 16:13; 22:12; 24:1; 28:4; 29:2; see also Deut. 29:27; Isa. 22:17–18). They will not return to the land of the covenant for which they long (Jer. 22:27; cf. Jer. 22:10–11; 44:14). Indeed, this is where the reader finds Jehoiachin at the end of the book, in Babylonian exile (Jer. 52:31–34 [= 2 Kgs. 25:27–30]). According to the narrative in 2 Kings 24:8–17 (cf. 2 Chr. 36:9–10), Jehoiachin reigned only for three months and did what was evil in the sight of the LORD. He and his mother, along with his servants and officials, surrendered to Nebuchadnezzar. The king of Babylon then took a select group of people from Jerusalem into captivity.

The Hebrew source behind Greek Jeremiah 22:28a has a shorter text that makes a statement about Jehoiachin: "Jeconiah is despised like a vessel in which there is no delight" (נבזה יכניהו ככלי אין חפץ בו). Jehoiachin is like an undesirable vessel, or, as the LXX renders, "like a vessel which is without its use" (cf. Jer. 48:38; Hos. 8:8). The longer text of the MT asks two rhetorical questions: "Is this man, Coniah, a despised, shattered vessel/jar/pot? Is he a vessel in which there is no delight" (העצב נבזה נפוץ האיש הזה כניהו אם כלי אין חפץ בו) (cf. Jer. 13:14; 18:4; 19:10)?[17] The second half of 22:28 has singular verbs in the Hebrew source behind Greek Jeremiah (referring to Jehoiachin) and plural verbs in the MT (referring to Jehoiachin and his seed/offspring): "Why is he hurled and cast [MT: Why are they hurled, he and his seed/offspring, and cast] to a land [MT: the land] that he does not know [MT: that they do not know]" (cf. Jer. 14:18b; 15:14; 16:13; 17:4; 22:26)? Of course, the answer to this question is that Jehoiachin is a useless vessel to be thrown out.

---

be like a signet ring on God's right hand, so to speak. Just as the name of the owner of the ring is engraved on his signet ring, through which he makes himself known, so will God's name be known in the world through the King Messiah, through whom His miracles will be known" (Rosenberg, trans., *Mikraoth Gedoloth: Jeremiah Volume One*, 183).

17. McKane translates עצב as "idol" (*Jeremiah I–XXV*, 546). Holladay translates it as "puppet" (*Jeremiah 1*, 607, 610). The longer text of the MT has likely incorporated האיש הזה ("this man") from 22:30a.

It is not clear whether Jeremiah 22:29 refers to the preceding word of the LORD or to the following one. In favor of the former option is the threefold repetition of the word "land" in 22:26–28 (see also the closed paragraph division after 22:29 in the MT). In favor of the latter option is the MT's added introduction to 22:30 ("Thus says the LORD"). The Hebrew source behind Greek Jeremiah 22:29a says, "O land, land" (cf. 1QIsaᵃ 6:3; LXX Jer. 7:4; LXX Ezek. 21:32), while the MT says, "O land, land, land" (cf. MT Isa. 6:3; MT Jer. 7:4; MT Ezek. 21:32). *Targum Jonathan* interprets this repetition in light of the preceding context: "From his land they have exiled him to another land. O land of Israel, receive the word of the Lord." According to Redak, however, the repetition is for emphasis, and "land" is for the people of the land.[18] Thus, the feminine singular imperative שמעי ("hear") in 22:29b agrees with the feminine noun ארץ ("land"), but then the people are addressed more directly in 22:30 with the masculine plural imperative כתבו ("Write").

The instruction, "Write [or, Record/Register] this man [i.e., Jehoiachin] childless [ערירי (see Gen. 15:2); LXX: banished]," in 22:30a is initially explained by an addition in the MT: "a man who will not prosper in his days." It is clarified further by the following כי clause: "for a man sitting on the throne of David [MT adds: and] ruling again over Judah will not prosper from his seed/offspring" (Jer. 22:30b; cf. Jer. 29:32; see also Jer. 33:17–18 [MT]; 35:19; 36:30). Thus, Jehoiachin will not be literally childless (see 1 Chr. 3:17–24). Rather, it is that none of his sons will reign on the throne. The last king of Judah, Zedekiah, was Jehoiachin's uncle (2 Kgs. 24:17). Even Zerubbabel, a descendant of Jehoiachin and leader of the postexilic community of Judeans who returned from Babylonian exile (Ezra 2:2; 5:2), did not reign on the throne as king.

---

18. Rosenberg, trans., *Mikraoth Gedoloth: Jeremiah Volume One*, 184.

JEREMIAH 23

23:1 "Woe [or, Ah]! Shepherds [Tg. Jon.: Stewards] losing and scattering the sheep of their pasture [MT: the sheep of my pasture; Tg. Jon.: the people upon whom my name is called]," [MT adds: the prophetic utterance of the LORD]. 23:2 Therefore, thus says the LORD [MT adds: God of Israel] to / about / against those who shepherd [MT: the shepherds who shepherd] my people, "You are the ones who have scattered my sheep and banished them and not attended to them. Look, I am about to visit upon you the evil of your deeds [i.e., bring upon you the punishment for the evil of your deeds]," [MT adds: the prophetic utterance of the LORD]. 23:3 "But as for me, I will gather the remnant of my sheep from the whole of the land [MT: from all the lands] where I have banished them, and I will bring them [MT: f. pl.] back to their [MT: f. pl.] pasture, and they will be fruitful and multiply. 23:4 And I will establish over them shepherds, and they will shepherd them, and they will never be afraid again, and they will not be terrified [MT adds: and they will not be missing]," the prophetic utterance of the LORD.

23:5 "Look, days are coming," the prophetic utterance of the LORD, "and I will raise up for David a righteous Branch [LXX: a righteous sunrise / dawn; Syr.: the radiance of righteousness; Tg. Jon.: a Messiah of righteousness], and a king will reign [Syr.: and he will reign in the kingdom] and act wisely and do justice and righteousness [Syr.: judgment of righteousness] in the land. 23:6 In his days, Judah will be delivered; and Israel [LXX^S: and Jerusalem], he will dwell in security. And this is the name [MT: his name] that the LORD will call him [see GKC §74e; pc Mss: they will call; Syr., Tg. Jon., Vulg.: they will call him]: Iosedek [or, Jehozadak; MT: the LORD our righteousness; Symm.: O Lord, justify / vindicate us; Tg. Jon.: may merits be done for us from before the Lord in his days] among the prophets [MT has "to the prophets" and places the phrase at the beginning of 23:9]."[1]

This section concludes the material on the sons of Josiah in Jeremiah 21–22. It begins with an introductory הוֹי ("Woe!" or "Ah!"), as in 22:13 ("Woe [or Ah]! One who builds his house without righteousness"), and is addressed to "Shepherds losing and scattering the sheep of their pasture" (Jer. 23:1). The absence of the definite article on רעים ("Shepherds") does not make this a general address to shepherds. It

---

1. The MT has 23:7–8 here, but the Hebrew source behind Greek Jeremiah puts these two verses at the end of the chapter.

is clear from the context of Jeremiah 21–22 that the "shepherds" are the kings of Judah who have reigned on the throne since Josiah (see Jer. 2:8; 3:15; 10:21; 22:22; 25:34–38). Thus, the MT clarifies that "the sheep of their pasture" (צאן מרעיתם) are "the sheep of my pasture" (צאן מרעיתי). According to *Targum Jonathan*, the shepherds are "stewards," and the sheep of the pasture are "the people upon whom my name is called" (see Pss. 74:1; 79:13; 100:3). These shepherds (i.e., the kings) are "losing and scattering" the sheep (i.e., the people). The participle מאבדים is commonly translated as "destroying," but the context and the shepherd metaphor suggest that "losing" is more appropriate (see BDB, 2). When shepherds fail in their task, they do not directly destroy their flock. They lose their flock, which may or may not result in the destruction of the flock. The point of the metaphor here is not to say that the people are innocent. The book of Jeremiah has been clear thus far that the people are guilty too, but the focus of the present passage is on the failure of the kings in their responsibility. They have led the people astray, and such leadership has negative consequences not only for the people in general but also for the righteous remnant. Ezekiel 34 serves as a kind of extended commentary on Jeremiah 23:1–6. The address in Ezekiel 34 also begins with הוי: "Woe/Ah! Shepherds of Israel" (Ezek. 34:2b). It goes on to describe the shepherds as those who take advantage of the flock (Ezek. 34:3a; cf. John 10:8). They do not feed the flock, nor do they give attention to sheep that need special care (Ezek. 34:3b–4). The sheep are thus scattered without a true shepherd and left exposed to wild predators (Ezek. 34:5). They wander without anyone to seek them (Ezek. 34:6).

The conjunction לכן ("Therefore") at the beginning of 23:2 marks the announcement of judgment (cf. Ezek. 34:7, 9). The announcement is addressed "to" (אל = על) "those who shepherd [MT: the shepherds who shepherd] my people." Of course, it is also "about" or "against" them, but the use of second person pronouns in the announcement itself strongly suggests that it is specifically "to" them.[2] These shepherds (i.e., kings) are the ones (note the fronted pronoun אתם) who have scattered the LORD's sheep (i.e., the people) and driven them into exile (cf. Jer. 9:15 [Eng., 9:16]; 13:24; 18:17; 40:12; 43:5). They have not "attended to" (פקד) them. Thus, the LORD is about to "visit" (פקד) upon them the evil of their deeds (cf. Zeph. 1:8–9; Zech. 10:3). The MT of Jeremiah 21:12b, 14a also refers to the evil of the deeds for which the kings will face punishment. It is a reference to the lack of justice and righteousness that the LORD requires from them (see Jer. 21:12a, 22:3, 15).

---

2. See McKane, *Jeremiah I–XXV*, 553–54.

The fronted pronoun אני at the beginning of 23:3 sets the Lᴏʀᴅ in contrast to the shepherds (note again the fronted pronoun אתם in 23:2). The Lᴏʀᴅ will gather not all his sheep but the remnant of his sheep "from the whole of the land" (MT: "from all the lands") where he has banished them (cf. Jer. 29:14; 32:37; Mic. 2:12; Dan. 9:7).[3] He will restore them to their pasture (i.e., the land of the covenant) where they will be fruitful and multiply (cf. Gen. 1:26–28; Jer. 3:16). According to Redak, this speaks not merely of the return from Babylonian captivity but of the ultimate hope of the believing remnant in the messianic age.[4] There is likely very little difference between מכל הארץ ("from the whole of the land"), which is the Hebrew source behind Greek Jeremiah, and the MT's מכל הארצות ("from all the lands"), insofar as the former is not a reference to the whole land of Babylon but to the whole of the inhabited earth. As in Jeremiah 3:17–18, this includes not only the remnant of Israel and Judah but also a remnant of believers from all the nations. According to Ezekiel 34:11–16, the Lᴏʀᴅ will seek his sheep and rescue them from the places where they have been scattered (Ezek. 34:11–12). He will gather them and bring them to their land where they will enjoy good pasture (Ezek. 34:13–14). He will care for them in a way that the sons of Josiah have not (Ezek. 34:15–16; cf. Ps. 23), and the abusive shepherds will face judgment for their actions (Ezek. 34:17–22). The true people of God, however, will be fruitful and multiply (MT Ezek. 36:11). As noted in the commentary on Jeremiah 3:16, these are the original words of the blessing of life and dominion in the land from Genesis 1:28. The lost blessing will be restored through the messianic king who will bring justice and righteousness to the land (Jer. 4:2; 23:5–6).[5]

The Lᴏʀᴅ will establish over the remnant of his people shepherds who will tend them, and the remnant will never be afraid again or be terrified (Jer. 23:4; cf. Jer. 1:17b). The MT adds, "and they will not be

---

3. The shepherds (Jer. 23:2) and the Lᴏʀᴅ (Jer. 23:3) are said to have "banished" (*hiphil* of נדח) the people. The shepherds did this in the sense that they led the people astray. The Lᴏʀᴅ then drove the people out for their willing participation under such leadership, and the members of the righteous remnant were caught in the mix (e.g., Daniel and his friends).

4. Rosenberg, trans., *Mikraoth Gedoloth: Jeremiah Volume One*, 185–86. See also McKane, *Jeremiah I–XXV*, 558–59. The text of Jeremiah 23:3–4 is also part of the words of judgment for the failed shepherds to the extent that it highlights the fact that the kings are left in exile and replaced.

5. The deceased members of the remnant will participate in this in the resurrection (Dan. 12:2). See Walther Eichrodt, *Theology of the Old Testament*, trans. J. A. Baker (Philadelphia: Westminster, 1967), 2:514–15.

missing (*niphal* of פקד)," thus exploiting the semantic range of פקד in 23:2, 4: פקד, "attend to" (Jer. 23:2a); פקד, "visit," as in "visit upon" = "punish" (Jer. 23:2b); and *niphal* of פקד, "be missing" (Jer. 23:4b). The plurality of good shepherds mentioned here makes a nice contrast with the plurality of bad shepherds in 23:1–2 (cf. Isa. 32:1; Ezek. 45:8–12), but it raises a question about the relationship of this plurality to the "one shepherd" (רעה אחד) in MT Ezekiel 34:23 (LXX: "another shepherd" [= רעה אחר]) and the singular king in Jeremiah 23:5–6 (see also John 10:11, 14; Heb. 13:20; 1 Pet. 2:25; 5:4). Keil suggests that the good shepherds are "summed up in the person of the Messiah": "The relation of the good shepherds to the righteous branch is not so, that the latter is the most pre-eminent of the former, but that in that one branch of David the people should have given to them all the good shepherds needed for their deliverance" (cf. Mic. 5:1–5 [Eng., 5:2–6]).[6] As noted in the commentary on Jeremiah 3:15a ("And I will give to you shepherds according to my heart"), another possibility is that the restoration of the lost blessing of life and dominion in the land will occur when the Messiah reigns as the good shepherd and the saints or people of God reign with him as the good shepherds (see Isa. 32:1; Dan. 7:13–14, 27; Rev. 5:10; 20:6; 22:5).

The expression הנה ימים באים ("Look, days are coming") points forward to the future work of God (Jer. 23:5a; cf. Jer. 16:14; 23:7; 30:3; 31:27, 31; 33:14). In those days, the Lᴏʀᴅ will raise up the Messiah: "and I will raise up (והקמתי) for David a righteous Branch (צמח)" (cf. Ps. 132:17: "There I will cause to sprout [אצמיח] a horn for David").[7] This choice of verb (*hiphil* of קום) comes directly from the covenant with David: "When your days are fulfilled and you lie with your fathers, I will raise up (והקימתי) your seed after you who will go forth from you, and I will establish his kingdom" (2 Sam. 7:12; cf. 1 Chr. 17:11).[8] The title "Branch" (צמח) also appears in the phrase "the Branch of the Lᴏʀᴅ" in Isaiah 4:2, which *Targum Jonathan* translates as "the Messiah of the Lord." Isaiah 11:1 develops this to speak of a "branch/twig" (חטר) from

---

6. Keil, *Jeremiah*, 217.
7. Jeremiah 33:15a says, "I will cause to sprout for David a branch of righteousness" (אצמיח לדוד צמח צדקה). See also Ezekiel 29:21a1: "In that day, I will cause to sprout (אצמיח) a horn for the house of Israel [LXX: a horn will sprout (= תצמח) for all the house of Israel]" (cf. 2 Sam. 23:5). In the conclusion to Hannah's prayer, she expresses the desire that the Lᴏʀᴅ exalt the "horn" (i.e., strength) of his anointed king (1 Sam. 2:10).
8. See also Ezekiel 34:23a: "And I will raise up (והקמתי) over them one shepherd [LXX: another shepherd], and he will shepherd them, my servant David" (cf. 2 Sam. 23:1 [4QSamᵃ]; Jer. 30:9; Hos. 3:5).

the "stock/stem" (גזע) of Jesse, David's father, and a "sprout/shoot" (נצר) from his roots who will bring justice and righteousness to the people (Isa. 11:3–5; cf. Isa. 9:5–6 [Eng., 9:6–7]; see also "the root of Jesse" in Isa. 11:10; cf. Rev. 5:5; 22:16).[9] This has likely informed the use of the title "Branch" (צמח) in Jeremiah 23:5, which speaks of a newly formed "sprout" or "growth" from the family tree or lineage of David who will reign with justice and righteousness (cf. Ezek. 17:22–24).[10] Jeremiah 23:5 is then the basis for the use of this title in Zechariah. "Look, I am about to bring my servant Branch (צמח) [*Tg. Jon.*: my servant the Messiah]" (Zech. 3:8b).[11] "Look, a man whose name is Branch (צמח) [*Tg. Jon.*: the Messiah], and from his place he will sprout and build the temple of the LORD; and he is the one who will build the temple of the LORD [> LXX]; and he is the one who will bear royal splendor and sit and rule on his throne; and he will be a priest on his throne [LXX: and the priest will be at his right hand], and peaceful counsel will be between the two of them" (Zech. 6:12b–13). This latter text speaks of a man who will build the temple in fulfillment of the covenant with David (see 2 Sam. 7:13) and rule as king and priest (cf. Ps. 110:4; Heb. 7).[12]

Targum Jonathan translates "righteous Branch" (צמח צדיק) in Jeremiah 23:5a as "a Messiah of righteousness" (משיח דצדקא) or "righteous Messiah." The LXX translates this same phrase as "a righteous sunrise/dawn" (ἀνατολὴν δικαίαν) (cf. LXX Zech. 3:8; 6:12; see also Luke 1:78).[13] This rendering creates a link with the ancient Greek translation of the messianic prophecy in Numbers 24:17b: "A star [*Tg. Onk.*: king] will rise (ἀνατελεῖ) [MT: tread] from Jacob, and a man [MT: scepter; Syr.: head/leader; *Tg. Onk.*: the Messiah] will rise up from Israel" (cf. Mal. 3:20 [Eng., 4:2]; Matt. 2:2; 2 Pet. 1:19; Rev. 22:16). Thus, although the Greek noun ἀνατολή can be used for growth, it appears to be used in translation of Jeremiah 23:5a for a rising star as a messianic image.[14]

---

9. See Childs, *Isaiah*, 36.

10. 4Q252 calls the coming king from the tribe of Judah in Genesis 49:10 "the Messiah of righteousness, the Branch of David" (משיח הצדק צמח דויד). See also 4QFlor (4Q174).

11. See Shepherd, *Commentary on the Book of the Twelve*, 410–11.

12. Shepherd, *Commentary on the Book of the Twelve*, 426–29. This does not depend upon MT Jeremiah 33:14–26 (> LXX), which is saying something quite different about the priesthood (see commentary on Jer. 33:14–26).

13. The Syriac has "the radiance/sprout of righteousness" or "the righteousness radiance/sprout" (cf. Heb. 1:3).

14. See William Horbury, *Jewish Messianism and the Cult of Christ* (London: SCM, 1998), 94.

Recent commentators have opted on the basis of extra-biblical evidence to interpret צמח צדיק as "true/legitimate scion/descendant/heir,"[15] but the issue in the context of Jeremiah 21:1–23:6 is not legitimacy. Each of the sons of Josiah has a legitimate claim to the throne. The issue at hand is that the sons of Josiah have not done the justice and righteousness required of them (Jer. 21:12; 22:3, 15–16). The messianic king, on the other hand, will perform justice and righteousness (Jer. 23:5b), and for this reason it is appropriate to call him "a righteous Branch."

The messianic king will reign "and act wisely" (והשכיל) (Jer. 23:5b; cf. Isa. 52:13 [ישכיל]; Jer. 3:15b [והשכיל]). The Spirit of wisdom will rest upon him (Isa. 11:2; 42:1; Matt. 3:16; cf. Prov. 1:2–7). Such wisdom will come from reading the Torah in accordance with the instructions for the king in Deuteronomy 17:18–20 (see also Deut. 4:6). "And this book of the Torah should not move from your mouth, and you should murmur in it day and night in order to be careful to do according to all that is written in it, for then you will make your way prosperous and then you will act wisely (תשכיל)" (Josh. 1:8; cf. Ps. 1:2). In contrast to the sons of Josiah, who have not acted wisely (Jer. 10:21) or practiced justice and righteousness (Jer. 21:12; 22:3, 15–16), the messianic king will do justice and righteousness and act in right relationship to the LORD (Jer. 9:23 [Eng., 9:24]) and in right relationship to the people, bringing justice in defense of the defenseless (see Isa. 9:5–6 [Eng., 9:6–7]; 11:3–5; 42:1–4; Jer. 4:2; Ezek. 45:9; Ps. 72:1–4; cf. Gen. 18:19; 1 Sam. 18:15; 2 Sam. 8:15).

In the days of the Messiah, Judah will be delivered, and Israel[16] will live "in security" (לבטח) (Jer. 23:6a; cf. Jer. 32:37; see 4Q522 9 II 2–9). Ezekiel 34:25–28 explains that the LORD will make a covenant of peace and stop the wild animals from the land so that the people can live in the wilderness "in security" (לבטח; > LXX) and sleep in the forests (Ezek. 34:25; cf. Isa. 11:6–8; 65:25; Hos. 2:20 [Eng., 2:18]; see also Lev. 26:3–13). He will bless the land with rain so that the trees bear fruit and the land brings forth produce; and the people will live on the land "in security" (לבטח), acknowledging that the LORD has rescued them from those whom they served (Ezek. 34:26–27). They will never again be plunder for the nations or prey for the wild animals; they will

---

15. See Bright, *Jeremiah*, 144; Thompson, *Book of Jeremiah*, 489; McKane, *Jeremiah I–XXV*, 561.

16. Codex Sinaiticus has "Jerusalem" instead of "Israel." This comes from Jeremiah 33:16.

live "in security" (לבטח) (Ezek. 34:28; cf. Zech. 14:11).[17] Jeremiah 23:6a envisions a reunited kingdom of Judah and Israel under the rule of the Davidic Messiah (see also Zech. 8:13; 9:13; 10:6). This is the same kingdom envisioned by Jeremiah 3:17–18, which also includes the nations who are joined to the people of God (see also Isa. 2:1–5; 66:18–24; Jer. 1:10; 4:2; 12:14–17; 16:19; Amos 9:12; Mic. 4:1–5; Zech. 8:20–23).

Jeremiah 23:6b gives the "name" (שם) by which the Messiah will be called.[18] According to the Hebrew source behind Greek Jeremiah, the LORD will call his name "Iosedek" or "Jehozadak" (יהוצדק)[19] "among the prophets" (בנבאים). There are several indications that this text is secondary to the MT, which has "the LORD our righteousness" (יהוה צדקנו).[20] First, Ziegler's Greek text includes κύριος ("Lord") in brackets as the subject of the verb "will call."[21] This indicates a double reading of the divine name יהוה, once as a separate word and once as a theophoric element on the name יהוצדק. The original reading was יהוה צדקנו ("the LORD our righteousness"); but since this is not technically a "name," a Hebrew scribe altered the text to יהוה יהוצדק, making יהוה the subject of the verb "will call," and producing an actual name יהוצדק ("Jehozadak" ["the LORD is righteous"]), which is not unlike the name צדקיהו ("Zedekiah" ["the LORD is my righteousness"]). A further difficulty with the Hebrew source behind Greek Jeremiah is the alteration of the following heading לנבאים ("Concerning the prophets") for Jeremiah 23:9–40 (LXX has Jer. 23:7–8 at the end of the chapter)

---

17. The use of לבטח here differs from that of Ezekiel 38:11a, 14b where it has the sense "unsuspectingly" (cf. Judg. 18:7). "In Lev 26, it is clear that the covenant being described is contingent on human behavior (*'If* you walk in my statutes,' v. 3). In Ezek 34, however, the covenant blessings being described are both future and unconditional: they are unqualified guarantees of divine action" (Michael A. Lyons, *From Law to Prophecy: Ezekiel's Use of the Holiness Code*, LHBOTS 507 [London: T&T Clark, 2009], 124–25).

18. In MT Jeremiah 33:16 (> LXX), it is not the name of the Messiah but the name of the city of Jerusalem (cf. MT Ezek. 48:35).

19. See this name in Haggai 1:1b.

20. Since this text is not a feature native to the layer that makes the MT a revised edition of the book, it can inform restoration of the original text in this individual, isolated instance where the Hebrew source behind Greek Jeremiah has deviated from it.

21. The subject in the MT ("he will call him") is indefinite and is thus equal to witnesses that have third person plural verbs: "they will call" (pc Mss) or "they will call him" (Syr., *Tg. Jon.*, Vulg.).

to בנבאים ("among the prophets") (cf. Jer. 23:13), which is then included with the name Jehozadak: "Jehozadak among the prophets."

יהוה צדקנו ("the LORD our righteousness") is not a normal Hebrew name. Hebrew names with a theophoric element are typically descriptions of the LORD (e.g., "Zedekiah" ["the LORD is our righteousness"]) rather than descriptions of those bearing the names. יהוה צדקנו ("the LORD our righteousness") is comparable to עמנו אל ("God with us") (Isa. 7:14b), which is not a single name but two words separated by a space (but see 1QIsaᵃ). The text of Isaiah 7:14b says that עמנו אל ("God with us") is the "name" (שם) that the child is to be called, but its citation in Matthew 1:23 immediately follows the naming of the child as "Jesus" with the understanding that עמנו אל ("God with us") is not the child's name but a description of the child himself as one born of the Holy Spirit (Matt. 1:20; see the description of the child in Isa. 9:5 [Eng., 9:6] as "God Almighty" [cf. Isa. 10:21]). Thus, יהוה צדקנו ("the LORD our righteousness") is neither a name nor a description of the LORD but a description of the Messiah himself. The Messiah is "the LORD our righteousness" (cf. 1 Cor. 1:30), God in the flesh.[22] In what sense then is he "our righteousness"? Within the immediate context, he is the one who does "justice and righteousness" (Jer. 23:5b). More broadly, he will judge the wicked and vindicate the righteous (Isa. 11:3–5; see Symm. Jer. 23:6b: "O Lord, vindicate us [צִדְקֵנוּ]"). By faith in him and in his substitutionary death (Isa. 53:1, 4–6) the people of God will be declared righteous (Isa. 53:11; 60:21) and subsequently bear the fruit of righteousness (Isa. 61:3).[23] Thus, the apostle Paul can say, "He made him who knew no sin to be a sin offering for us in order that we might become the righteousness of God in him" (2 Cor. 5:21; see also 1 John 2:1–2, 29).

The text of MT Jeremiah 23:7–8 occurs with slight variation in wording in three different places among textual witnesses to the book of Jeremiah. The first is in MT and LXX Jeremiah 16:14–15. The second is in MT Jeremiah 23:7–8. The third is at the end of LXX Jeremiah

---

22. According to Jeremiah 3:17, the LORD will rule on his throne in Jerusalem as the messianic king (cf. Zeph. 3:14–15; Zech. 2:14 [Eng., 2:10]; 9:9–10).

23. For the verbal links between the descriptions of the Davidic Messiah in Isaiah 9:5–6 (Eng., 9:6–7); 11:1–10 and the descriptions of the servant of the LORD (Isa. 42:1–7; 49:1–9; 50:4–11; 52:13–53:12; 61:1–9), see Shepherd, *Text in the Middle*, 138. Just like the Davidic Messiah in Jeremiah 23:5, the servant of the LORD "will act wisely" (ישכיל) (Isa. 52:13a). Just as the Davidic Messiah is "the LORD our righteousness" in Jeremiah 23:6, the servant will be "high and lifted up" (Isa. 52:13b) like the LORD himself (Isa. 6:1; see John 12:41). See also Zechariah 12:10; John 19:37.

23. As noted in the commentary on 16:14–15 (see commentary there), the placement there and at the end of Jeremiah 23 is within the context of judgment, highlighting the new and harsher captivity (the land of the north versus Egypt). On the other hand, the placement in MT Jeremiah 23:7–8 depicts the messianic salvation of 23:5–6 as a new exodus, the new paradigm for deliverance among the people of God (cf. Num. 23:22; 24:8; Isa. 11:1–10, 16; 43:16–21; Hos. 11:1, 5, 11; Matt. 2:15).[24] Insofar as the enemy from the north is an eschatological enemy (and not merely Babylon), this salvation will take place in the last days, beginning with the defeat of the enemy and culminating with the restoration of the lost blessing of life and dominion in the land of the covenant and with the establishment of the messianic kingdom on earth (see Jer. 25:1–13; Ezek. 38–39; Joel 4 [Eng., 3]; Zech. 12–14; Dan. 9:1–2, 24–27; Rev. 17–22). (See the end of chapter 23 for further comment on these verses.)

23:9 [MT: Concerning the prophets:][25] My heart is broken within me; all my bones grow soft [HALOT 2:1220: tremble]. I am like a broken man [MT: drunken man] and like a man over whom wine has passed [or, overcome by wine] from before [or, because of] the LORD *and from before [or, because of] the splendor of his glory [MT: the words of his holiness (i.e., his holy words)]. 23:10 [MT adds: For the land is full of adulterers.] For from before [or, because of] these [MT: a curse] the land languishes, wilderness pastures are dry; and their course is evil, and their might is not right [LXX: not so]. 23:11 "For both priest and prophet [MT: both prophet (Tg. Jon.: scribe) and priest], they are polluted [Tg. Jon.: they have stolen their ways]. Even in my house have I found [LXX: seen][26] their evil," [MT adds: the prophetic utterance of the* LORD*]. 23:12 "Therefore, their path will be to them like slippery places in the darkness.[27] They [LXX: And they] will be thrust down, and they will fall in it [i.e., in the darkness]; for I will bring upon them calamity in the year of their visitation," [MT adds: the prophetic utterance of the* LORD*].*

---

24. See Shepherd, *Commentary on the Book of the Twelve*, 92–98.
25. *Targum Jonathan* renders, "From before [or, Because of] the false prophets." The Hebrew source behind Greek Jeremiah includes this phrase at the end of the 23:6 as "among the prophets" (בנבאים) (cf. Jer. 23:13).
26. The verb εἶδον ("I have seen") may be an inner-Greek variant for εὗρον ("I have found").
27. The Syriac reads the phrase "in the darkness" with what follows (cf. *BHS*): "And into the darkness they will be driven, and they will fall on them [i.e., the slippery places]."

23:13 *"And among the prophets of Samaria I saw unseemliness [LXX: lawlessness; Syr.: falsity; Tg. Jon.: wickedness; Vulg.: foolishness]. They prophesied by Baal and led my people Israel astray. 23:14 And among the prophets of Jerusalem I have seen something horrible. They commit adultery and live [lit., walk] in deception and strengthen the hands of evildoers [Syr.: the hands of their friends/lovers] so that each does not turn from his evil way [MT: so that they each do not turn from his evil]. All of them have become to me like Sodom, and its inhabitants like Gomorrah." 23:15 Therefore, thus says the Lord [MT adds: of hosts concerning the prophets (Tg. Jon.: false prophets)], "Look, I am about to make them eat wormwood [LXX: pain] and drink bitter water [Tg. Jon.: a cup of curse, as bad as snake venom], for from the prophets of Jerusalem pollution has gone forth to all the land."*

23:16 *Thus says the Lord of hosts, "Do not listen to the words of the prophets [Syr., Tg. Jon.: false prophets; MT adds: who are prophesying to you], for they make a prophetic vision empty [MT: they make you empty]. From their heart/mind they speak and not from the mouth of the Lord [MT: The prophetic vision of their heart/mind they speak, not from the mouth of the Lord]. 23:17 They say [MT adds: saying; Tg. Jon. adds: in their false prophecy] to those who spurn/reject the word of the Lord [MT: to those who spurn/reject me, 'The Lord has spoken'], 'Peace is what there will be for you.' And to all who go after their thoughts [> MT], to every person [MT: and every person] who goes in the stubbornness of his heart/mind, they say, 'Calamity will not come upon you.' 23:18 For who has stood in the counsel of the Lord and seen his word [MT: For who has stood in the counsel of the Lord to see and hear his word; Syr.: For who has stood in the counsel of the Lord and seen and heard his word]? Who has paid attention [Codex L kethiv adds: to my word; Codex L qere adds: to his word] and listened? 23:19 Look, the tempest [LXX: earthquake] of the Lord! And [> MT] fury, it goes forth, [MT adds: and] a whirling [MT Jer. 30:23:* מתגורר*] tempest [LXX: as an earthquake]. Upon the head of the wicked will it whirl [LXX: Being gathered, upon the ungodly it will come]. 23:20 And [> MT] the anger of the Lord [Jer. 30:24: the burning of the anger of the Lord] will not turn back until he accomplishes and until he makes happen the plan [LXX: undertaking; MT: plans] of his heart/mind. At the end of the days they [MT: you] will understand it [LXX: them (or, these things)] [MT adds: (with) understanding]. 23:21 I did not send the prophets [Tg. Jon.: false prophets]; but they, they ran. I did not speak to them; but they, they prophesied. 23:22 And if they had stood in my counsel and heard my words, my people they would have turned back from the evil of their* *deeds [MT: And if they had stood in my counsel, they would have caused my people to hear my words and turned them back from their evil way and from the evil of their deeds].*

23:23 A God[28] nearby am I," the prophetic utterance of the LORD, *"and not a God far off [Tg. Jon.: I, God, created the world from the beginning, says the Lord. I, God, am about to renew the world for the righteous]. 23:24 If a man hides in secret places, am I not the one who sees him [MT: Can a man hide in secret places and I not be the one who sees him]? [MT adds: the prophetic utterance of the* LORD.*] Are not the sky and the land [i.e., the whole world] what I fill?" the prophetic utterance of the* LORD.

23:25 "I have heard what the prophets who prophesy in my name deception have said, saying, 'I have had a dream [MT: I have dreamed, I have dreamed].' 23:26 How long will this be [MT: היש] in the heart/mind of the prophets who prophesy deception and when they prophesy the deceit of their heart/mind [MT: and the prophets of the deceit of their heart/mind], 23:27 those who plan to forget my name [Rahlfs: to forget my law; MT: to cause my people to forget my name; Syr.: to lead my people astray in my name] by their dreams that they recount to one another, just as their forefathers forgot my name by Baal [i.e., by the worship of Baal (cf. Syr., Tg. Jon.)]? 23:28 The prophet with whom is a dream, let him recount his dream; and the one with whom is my word, let him speak my word faithfully. What does straw have to do with grain? [Tg. Jon.: Look, just as someone makes a distinction between straw and grain, so he makes a distinction between the wicked and the righteous] [MT adds: the prophetic utterance of the LORD.*] 23:29 Are not my words like fire [MT: Is not thus my word like fire (Tg. Jon.: Are not all my words strong like fire)]," [MT adds: the prophetic utterance of the* LORD*], "and like a hammer that shatters rock [LXX: and like an ax that cuts rock]? 23:30 Therefore, look, I am against the prophets [Tg. Jon.: false prophets]," the prophetic utterance of the* LORD *God, "who steal my words from one another. 23:31 Look, I am against the prophets [Tg. Jon.: false prophets]," [MT adds: the prophetic utterance of the* LORD*], "who take [Rahlfs: cast out; Syr.: turn; Tg. Jon.: prophesy] their tongue [LXX: prophecies of tongue; Tg. Jon.: the will of their heart/mind] and slumber [MT: and utter prophecy; Syr.: and say,*

---

28. The MT has a prefixed interrogative ה at the beginning of this verse, which makes 23:23 the first member of a double question. אם introduces the second member in 23:24a (see BDB, 210; GKC §150g, h).

'The Lord said so' (cf. Tg. Jon.)]. 23:32 Look, I am against the prophets
who prophesy [Codex L: those who prophesy; mlt Mss: prophets of] false /
deceptive dreams," [MT adds: the prophetic utterance of the LORD], "and
recount them and lead my people astray with their deceptions and with
their wantonness. And as for me, I did not send them, and I did not command them, and they do not at all benefit this people," [MT adds: the
prophetic utterance of the LORD].

23:33 "And when this people or a priest or a prophet [MT: or the prophet
(Tg. Jon.: a scribe) or a priest] asks you [MT adds: saying], 'What is the
burden [NIV: oracle] of the LORD [Tg. Jon.: What is the prophecy in the
name of the Lord]?' you will say to them, 'You are the burden [MT: What
burden (NIV: oracle)?], and I will dash you to pieces [MT: and I will forsake you], the prophetic utterance of the LORD.' 23:34 And the prophet [Tg.
Jon.: scribe] and the priest and the people who say [MT: who says], 'The
burden [NIV: oracle] of the LORD [Tg. Jon.: The prophecy in the name of
the Lord],' I will visit upon [i.e., punish] that man and upon his house."
23:35 Thus you should say each to his neighbor and each to his brother,
"What has the LORD answered?" and "What has the LORD spoken?" 23:36
And as for "the burden [NIV: oracle] of the LORD [Tg. Jon.: the prophecy
in the name of the Lord]," do not ever mention [MT: remember] (it) again,
for the burden [NIV: oracle; Tg. Jon.: prophecy] is to the man [MT: a
man] the word [MT: his word], [MT adds: and you pervert the words of
the living God, the LORD of hosts, our God]. 23:37 And what has the LORD
our God spoken? [MT: Thus you should say to the prophet, "What has
the LORD answered you?" and "What has the LORD spoken?"] 23:38 [MT
adds: And if "the burden (NIV: oracle) of the LORD (Tg. Jon.: the prophecy
in the name of the Lord)" you say,] Therefore, thus says the LORD God
[God > MT], "Because you have said this word, 'The burden [NIV: oracle]
of the LORD [Tg. Jon.: The prophecy in the name of the Lord],' and I sent
to you, saying, 'Do not say, "The burden [NIV: oracle] of the LORD [Tg.
Jon.: The prophecy in the name of the Lord],"' 23:39 therefore, look, I am
about to take and dash to pieces [Codex L: therefore, look, I, and I will
forget (pc Mss: take) you completely and forsake] you and the city that
I gave to you and to your forefathers [MT adds: from before me]. 23:40
And I will put upon you everlasting reproach and everlasting humiliation, which will not be forgotten.

23:7 Therefore, look, days are coming," the prophetic utterance of the
LORD, "and they will never say again, 'As the LORD lives [or, By the life
of the LORD; Tg. Jon.: and they will never talk again about the might of
the Lord] who brought up the house [MT: sons] of Israel from the land

of Egypt . . . ,' 23:8 but, 'As the Lord *lives [or, By the life of the* Lord*; Tg. Jon.: but they will talk about the might of the Lord] who brought in [MT: who brought up and brought in] all [> MT] the seed[29] [> Syr.] of [MT adds: the house of] Israel from the land of the north and from all the lands where he [MT: I] banished them and restored them to their land . . .' [MT: drove them . . . .' And they will live on their land]."*

The phrase לנבאים at the beginning of MT Jeremiah 23:9 does not give the cause of the prophet's state of being ("Because of the prophets"). Rather, it provides a heading for the remainder of the chapter: "Concerning the prophets" (cf. Jer. 46:2; 48:1; 49:1, 7, 23, 28; see also Ezek. 13:2; Mic. 3:5). The cause for Jeremiah's troubled state is given in 23:9b. Jeremiah says that his heart is broken and that his bones "grow soft" or "tremble" (רחפו) (cf. Jer. 20:9; Ps. 22:15 [Eng., 22:14]). The prophet is not "heartbroken" (i.e., saddened). He is in a disturbed state of mind that affects him physically (cf. Jer. 4:19). He is "like a broken man" (כאיש שבור) (MT: "like a drunken man" [כאיש שכור]) and like a man overcome by wine. According to the Hebrew source behind Greek Jeremiah 23:9b, this is due to the Lord and "the splendor of his glory" (הדר כבודו). The MT, however, says that it is because of the Lord and "the words of his holiness" or "his holy words" (דברי קדשו). McKane suggests that these holy words are then found in 23:10–12,[30] but it is also possible that 23:10 is Jeremiah's initial explanation of what he means, which is followed by the Lord's words in 23:11–12.

The MT has an addition at the beginning of 23:10: "For the land is full of adulterers." This refers either to the spiritual adultery that has filled the land or to literal adultery, which is a symptom of spiritual adultery (see Jer. 5:7–8; 7:9; 23:14). The MT thus begins 23:10 with two כי clauses, which has resulted in attempts to explain one or both as something other than causal. The Hebrew source behind Greek Jeremiah, however, begins 23:10 with a single כי clause (which is the second clause in the MT) followed by its parallel clause: "For from before [or, because of] these [MT: a curse] the land languishes, wilderness pastures are dry." This picture of the land hearkens back to Jeremiah 12:4 (see also Jer. 4:28). The initial difficulty with this text is the lack of an antecedent for אלה, which the LXX translator has understood as אֵלֶּה ("these"). The prior clause in the MT ("For the land is full of adulterers") supplies "adulterers" as a possible antecedent, but this clause is not in the Hebrew source behind Greek Jeremiah. The MT vocalizes

---

29. See Isaiah 6:13; 53:10; 66:22.
30. McKane, *Jeremiah I–XXV*, 569.

אלה as אָלָה ("a curse"), which might seem to provide an easy solution to the problem: the land languishes because of a covenant curse (see Deut. 28:23–24). But a comparison with Jeremiah 4:26b suggests another option. There Jeremiah sees the land devastated "from before [or, because of] the LORD, and from before [or, because of] the burning of his anger they are desolated [they are desolated > MT]." The similarity between this text and that of 23:9b ("from before [or, because of] the LORD and from before [or, because of] the splendor of his glory [MT: the words of his holiness (i.e., his holy words)]") suggests that the antecedent of אלה as אֵלֶּה ("these") is "the LORD" and "the splendor of his glory" (MT: "his holy words"). It is because of these that the land languishes. Jeremiah 23:10b then concludes the verse: "and their course (מרוצתם) is evil, and their might is not right (כן) [LXX: not so (οὐχ οὕτως)]." Again, the use of the pronoun "their" would seem to require the MT's "adulterers" as an antecedent, which is not present in the Hebrew source behind Greek Jeremiah, but the shorter Hebrew text behind Greek Jeremiah either presupposes a reference to the people of the land and their "course" of action (see Jer. 8:6; see also Jer. 22:17) or uses the pronoun proleptically to refer to the false prophets and the course that they "run" (see רצו ["they ran"] in Jer. 23:21). The latter of these two options works well with the follow-up explanation found in the LORD's words of 23:11: "For both priest and prophet [MT: both prophet and priest], they are polluted. Even in my house have I found their evil" [MT adds: the prophetic utterance of the LORD]. This is not the first time that priests and prophets have been mentioned together (see Jer. 2:8; 5:31; 6:13; 8:10; 14:18). They are polluted in the sense that they have profaned the land with their spiritual adultery (i.e., worship of idols or other gods [see Jer. 3:1, 2, 9; 23:15]), even in the temple, the house of the LORD (see Jer. 7:9–11; 32:34; Ezek. 8:6).

"Therefore" (לכן), the LORD announces in 23:12a, the judgment will be that "their path will be to them like slippery places in the darkness" (יהיה דרכם להם כחלקלקות באפלה). They will be thrust down, and they will fall in the darkness. The language of this text appears to come from that of Psalm 35:6: "May their path be darkness and slippery places" (יהי דרכם חשך וחלקלקות). The LORD then explains in 23:12b: "for I will bring upon them calamity in the year of their visitation" (כי אביא עליהם רעה שנת פקדתם). This text is very close to Jeremiah 11:23b: "for I will bring calamity upon the men of Anathoth in the year of their visitation" (כי אביא רעה אל אנשי ענתות שנת פקדתם) (see also Jer. 6:15; 8:12; 46:21; 48:44; 50:27).

The following judgment oracle in 23:13–15 mentions the former prophets of Samaria (Jer. 23:13) and the current prophets of Jerusalem

(Jer. 23:14). The general assumption among commentators, with the exception of McKane,[31] has been that the design of this is to show how much more egregious the behavior of the prophets of Jerusalem has been in comparison to that of the prophets of Samaria. While such a comparison is not made explicit in the present passage, the assumption does have some warrant from the fact that Judah is said to have surpassed Israel in its apostasy (see Jer. 3:11; Ezek. 16:47; 23:11). The Lord saw among the prophets of Samaria "unseemliness" (תפלה) (Jer. 23:13a). This term may refer to unseemliness ascribed to God by the false prophets (see, e.g., תפלה in Job 1:22), or it may refer to the smearing of "whitewash" (תפל) with false visions (see Ezek. 22:28; Lam. 2:14). The explanation in 23:13b seems to have both senses in view: "They prophesied by Baal and led my people Israel astray" (see 1 Kgs. 16:32; 18:19). They prophesied by Baal rather than the Lord, thus ascribing unseemliness to the Lord by giving the impression that he had wronged them in some way (see Mic. 6:3), and they led the people astray with their false prophecies (see Jer. 3:6–8; 7:12–15). Of course, the false prophets of Jerusalem have done the same (see Jer. 2:5, 8; 23:27, 32; Mic. 3:5; see also Isa. 10:10–11; Mic. 1:5).

Among the prophets of Jerusalem the Lord has seen "something horrible" (שערורה) (Jer. 23:14a; cf. Jer. 5:30–31; 18:13). "They commit adultery (נאוף) and live [lit., walk] in deception (שקר)." The use of the infinitive absolute נאוף ("commit adultery") here and in Jeremiah 7:9, where it refers to the Decalogue (Exod. 20:14; Deut. 5:18), suggests that the reference here is to literal adultery (see Jer. 29:23), although this should be understood as a symptom of spiritual adultery (Jer. 5:7–8; 23:10 [MT]). Living or walking in שקר ("deception") may be equivalent to prophesying by בעל ("Baal") (see Jer. 2:5, 8; 5:31; 7:9; 13:25; 20:6), but in the present context it is preferable to understand this expression as a description of the generally deceptive nature of the life and message of the false prophets of Jerusalem (see Jer. 23:25; 27:15; 29:9, 21). These prophets also "strengthen the hands of evildoers so that each does not turn from his evil way" (cf. Ezek. 13:22), which is the opposite of what prophets are to do (see Jer. 23:22; 25:5; 26:3; 35:15). They have all become like Sodom to the Lord, and the inhabitants of Jerusalem whom they have deceived are like Gomorrah (Jer. 23:14b; cf. Deut. 32:32; Isa. 1:10). Holladay notes that this could mean that they are like Sodom and Gomorrah in that they are subject to destruction (see Jer. 20:16; cf. Gen. 19:25; Deut. 29:22 [Eng., 29:23]; see also 2 Pet. 2:6; Jude 7), but since the announcement of judgment does not come until 23:15,

---

31. McKane, *Jeremiah I–XXV*, 574.

he concludes that the comparison in 23:14b indicates that the prophets and inhabitants of Jerusalem are deserving of destruction.[32] Sodom and Gomorrah are well known for their sexual immorality (Gen. 19; cf. Judg. 19), but Ezekiel 16:49–50 further explains that the iniquity of Sodom consisted of failure to strengthen the hand of the afflicted and the needy (cf. Jer. 22:16); this failure was accompanied by the practice of תועבה ("abomination"), which can refer either to sexual immorality (e.g., Ezek. 22:11) or to idolatry (e.g., Ezek. 8:6).

"Therefore" (לכן), the LORD says, "Look, I am about to make them eat wormwood and drink bitter water" (Jer. 23:15a; cf. Jer. 8:14b, 9:14 [Eng., 9:15]; see also Deut. 29:17 [Eng., 29:18]; Lam. 3:19; Rev. 8:11). As in Jeremiah 8:14b and 9:14 [Eng., 9:15], *Targum Jonathan* interprets the bitter water to be "a cup of curse, as bad as snake venom" (see Deut. 32:32–33; Jer. 25:15). This is the judgment for the "pollution" (see Jer. 23:11) that has gone forth from the prophets to all the land (Jer. 23:15b). It will be bitter like the eating of wormwood and poisonous (or deadly) like the drinking of bitter/poisonous water.

The prohibition in 23:16a—"Do not listen to the words of the prophets"—employs a masculine plural verb but does not explicitly address any group in particular. The prophets to whom the people are not to listen are the ones not sent by the LORD (see Jer. 23:21, 32). According to the Hebrew source behind Greek Jeremiah, their words are not to be heeded because "they make a prophetic vision empty" (מהבלים המה חזון). In context, this apparently means that they make empty promises of peace or well-being (Jer. 23:17). The MT, however, says that it is because "they make you empty" (מהבלים המה אתכם). This is reminiscent of Jeremiah 2:5 (see also 2 Kgs. 17:15): "What injustice did your forefathers find in me that they became distant from me and went after what was empty (ההבל) and became empty (ויהבלו)?" As noted in the commentary on that text, it speaks of how the people went after "idols" (*Tg. Jon.*) or other gods and became like them (i.e., dumb, unresponsive, and subject to destruction). Within the same context, the prophets are said to have participated in this by prophesying by "Baal" (בעל) and going after things (i.e., idols, other gods) that do not benefit them (Jer. 2:8b). Thus, the MT of Jeremiah 23:16a may be designed to say that the false prophets make the people into empty idol worshipers. The Hebrew source behind Greek Jeremiah 23:16b then says, "From their heart/mind (מלבם) they speak and not from the mouth of the LORD" (Jer. 14:14b; 23:26; Ezek. 13:2). Since the MT does not put חזון ("prophetic vision") with the preceding text of 23:16a, it is included

---

32. Holladay, *Jeremiah 1*, 632.

with 23:16b in the construct state: "The prophetic vision of their heart/ mind (חזון לבם) they speak, not from the mouth of the LORD." The source of their message is their own mind, not the word of the LORD. The LORD has not put his words in their mouth (see Deut. 18:18; Jer. 1:9).

The Hebrew source behind Greek Jeremiah and the MT begin 23:17a quite differently from one another. According to the former, 23:17a begins, "They say to those who spurn the word of the LORD" (אמרים לִמְנַאֲצֵי דְּבַר יהוה) (cf. Isa. 5:24b; LXX Jer. 15:16). According to the latter, it begins, "They say saying to those who spurn me, 'The LORD has spoken'" (אמרים אמור לִמְנַאֲצַי דִּבֶּר יהוה). Thus, in the MT, the false prophets make a direct claim that the LORD has spoken what they are saying. The problem with the MT is that דִּבֶּר יהוה ("The LORD has spoken") is a very strange way to introduce the word of the LORD. Even false prophets know to say כה אמר יהוה ("Thus says the LORD") (see Jer. 28:2). The message of the false prophets for those who reject the true word of the LORD concerning judgment is a message of peace and well-being (שלום): "Peace is what there will be for you" (cf. Jer. 4:10; 6:14; 8:11 [MT]; see also Deut. 29:18 [Eng., 29:19]). The Hebrew source behind Greek Jeremiah 23:17b features a double version: (1) "And to all who go after their thoughts" (cf. Jer. 7:24; 18:12); and (2) "to every person who goes in the stubbornness of his heart/mind" (cf. Jer. 3:17; 7:24; 9:13 [Eng., 9:14]; 11:8; 13:10; 16:12; 18:12). The MT only has the second of these two and probably represents the more original text. The first of these two may be backtranslated either as ולכל הלכים אחרי מחשבותיהם (cf. Jer. 18:12) or as ולכל הלכים במעצותיהם (cf. Jer. 7:24). To those whose minds stubbornly resist the message of true prophets like Jeremiah, the false prophets not only promise peace but also say, "Calamity will not come upon you" (cf. Jer. 5:12–13; Mic. 3:11).

Calvin interprets the questions of 23:18 to be those of the false prophets directed toward the true prophets (cf. Job 15:8), which Jeremiah then turns against them in 23:22,[33] but most commentators have understood the speaker in 23:18 to be either the LORD or Jeremiah explaining why no one should listen to the false prophets. The wording of the questions in 23:18 varies in the early witnesses: "For who has stood in the counsel of the LORD and seen his word [MT: For who has stood in the counsel of the LORD to see and hear his word; Syr.: For who has stood in the counsel of the LORD and seen and heard his word]? Who has paid attention [Codex L *kethiv* adds: to my word; Codex L *qere* adds: to his word] and listened?" Since 23:22 presupposes that it is possible to stand in the counsel of the LORD, the questions in 23:18 are not

---

33. Calvin, *Jeremiah*, 3:170–72.

merely rhetorical (as in Rom. 11:34), as if to say that no one has stood in his counsel. Rather, the answer to the questions is that those who have called the people to repentance are the true prophets who have stood in the LORD's counsel and paid attention to his word. Those who simply promise peace have not stood in the LORD's counsel. The Hebrew word סוֹד can mean either "counsel" or "council" (BDB, 691). Thus, some commentators prefer to see a reference here to a divine assembly in which true prophets participate (see 1 Kgs. 22:19–22; Isa. 6:1–8; Ps. 89:6, 8 [Eng., 89:5, 7]; Job 1:6; 2:1; see also Ezek. 13:9),[34] but the usage in the present context corresponds more closely to that of Amos 3:7: "Certainly the LORD does not do a thing unless he reveals his counsel (סוֹד) to his servants the prophets" (cf. Ps. 25:14).

Verses 19 and 20 of chapter 23 form a doublet with verses 23 and 24 of chapter 30.[35] In the present context, these verses speak specifically of God's judgment of the false prophets. At the end of chapter 30, however, they speak more generally of God's judgment of the wicked in contrast to the restoration of his true people. The LORD's judgment is envisioned as a storm whirling on the head of the wicked (Jer. 23:19; cf. 2 Sam. 3:29; 22:8–16; Jer. 25:32; Nah. 1:2–8; Hab. 3:3–15; Ps. 18:8–16 [Eng., 18:7–15]; see also Obad. 15). The anger of the LORD will not turn back until he accomplishes his plans (Jer. 23:20a; cf. Isa. 5:25b; Jer. 4:8b; 1Q33 3:9). The Hebrew source behind Greek Jeremiah 23:20b says that "they" (i.e., the false prophets) will understand or comprehend this judgment "at the end of the days" (באחרית הימים). The MT says "you" (i.e., those told not to listen to the words of the false prophets in 23:16) will understand it (cf. Jer. 30:24b). Either way, comprehension of God's judgment of the wicked, specifically the false prophets, will not come presently. According to Redak, the phrase "at the end of the days" (באחרית הימים) denotes the messianic era (see Gen. 49:1, 8–12; Num. 24:7–9, 14, 17; Deut. 4:30; 31:29; 33:7; Isa. 2:2–5; Jer. 30:9, 21, 24; 48:47; 49:39; Ezek. 38:16; Hos. 3:5; Mic. 4:1–5; Dan. 2:28; 10:14): "Then you will understand this prophecy, for, until those days, you do not consider it since you do not witness the destruction of the wicked. The use of the second person rather than the third denotes the resurrection of the dead that will take place at that time. Therefore, he addresses his own generation, who will be present at the end of days."[36]

---

34. E.g., Bright, *Jeremiah*, 152; Holladay, *Jeremiah 1*, 635.

35. See Parke-Taylor, *Formation of the Book of Jeremiah*, 86–89.

36. Rosenberg, trans., *Mikraoth Gedoloth: Jeremiah Volume One*, 191. "'The end of the days' is not merely the completion of the period in which we now are (Hitz., Gr. Näg., etc.). but, as universally, the end of the times, i.e., the

Modern commentators who insist that this phrase does not have an eschatological sense in the present context must nevertheless concede that such comprehension of judgment did not come with Babylonian exile (see Jer. 29:21–23).[37] Only in the final judgment will there be a separation of the wheat from the chaff (Jer. 23:28b; Matt. 3:12; see also Ps. 1:6; Eccl. 12:14; Matt. 25:32; 2 Cor. 5:10; Rev. 20:11–15).[38]

Unlike true prophets like Moses (Exod. 3:10) and Jeremiah (Jer. 1:7), the false prophets were not "sent" (שלח) by the LORD (Jer. 23:21a; see also Jer. 14:15; 23:32). Nevertheless, they "ran" their course as if they were sent to deliver a message in the name of the LORD (see Jer. 23:10b; cf. Jer. 12:5; Ps. 147:15; 2 Thess. 3:1). The LORD did not speak to them, but they prophesied anyway (Jer. 23:21b). If those so-called "prophets" had stood in the LORD's counsel (see Jer. 23:18; Amos 3:7) and heard (וַיִּשְׁמְעוּ), they would have turned back (הֲשִׁבוּם) the people "from the evil of their deeds" (MT: "And if they had stood in my counsel, they would have caused my people to hear [וְיַשְׁמִעוּ] my words and turned them back [וִישִׁבוּם] from their evil way and from the evil of their deeds") (Jer. 23:22; cf. Jer. 23:14; Lam. 2:14). When the LORD threatens judgment, true prophets do not put the people at ease with messages of peace and well-being. Rather, they urge the people to repent (see Jer. 18:11; 25:5; 26:3; 28:8; 35:15; 36:3, 7).

The Hebrew source behind Greek Jeremiah 23:23 is a statement: "A God nearby am I," the prophetic utterance of the LORD, "and not a God far off." In the MT, however, this verse is a double question: "Am I a God nearby," the prophetic utterance of the LORD, "and not a God far off?" The Hebrew source behind Greek Jeremiah asserts that God is nearby (cf. Deut. 4:7; Acts 17:27; *Apocr. Ezek.* 5), while the rhetorical questions of the MT imply that God is far off (cf. 1 Kgs. 8:27; Isa. 66:1). Both versions relate directly to the questions in 23:24: "If a man hides in secret places, am I not the one who sees him [MT: Can a man hide in secret places and I not be the one who sees him]? [MT adds: the prophetic utterance of the LORD.] Are not the sky and the land [i.e., the whole world] what I fill?" the prophetic utterance of the LORD (cf. Isa. 6:3; 11:9; 29:15; Jer. 12:4b; Amos 9:2–3; Hab. 2:14; Ps. 113:5–6). According to the Hebrew source behind Greek Jeremiah 23:23–24, God

---

Messianic future, the last period of the world's history which opens at the close of the present aeon" (Keil, *Jeremiah*, 223).

37. E.g., Thompson, *Book of Jeremiah*, 498.

38. Despite the struggles of a true prophet like Jeremiah (see the confessions in Jer. 11–20), it is far better in the end to be accepted by the LORD and rejected by the people than vice versa.

is not far off and unaware of what the false prophets are doing. Rather, he is nearby and close enough even to see what happens in the secret places.[39] Indeed, there is no place in the world where he is absent (cf. Ps. 139:7–12). Redak suggests that the terms "nearby" and "far off" in the MT have a temporal sense (cf. Deut. 32:17): "Am I a recent God? Am I not a God from days of yore? Did people not know Me from the Creation of the world that I am an eternal God, not like the new gods who neither see nor hear, but I see people's deeds and hear their speech, and I hear the words of the prophets who prophesy falsely in My name."[40] On the other hand, both Rashi and Kara understand these terms in a spatial sense.[41] That is, God is not so close that he is like someone who suffers from myopia, seeing only those things nearby and directly in front of him. Rather, he is able to pan out, so to speak, and bring everything into view from a distance (cf. Ps. 139:2).[42]

The deception that the false prophets have prophesied in the LORD's name has not gone unheard or unnoticed (Jer. 23:25a; cf. Deut. 18:20; Jer. 14:14; 27:9–10; 29:8, 21; see also Exod. 20:7; Deut. 5:11; Jer. 7:9). These prophets claim to have received divine revelation through a dream (Jer. 23:25b; cf. Gen. 37:5; Dan. 2:3). True prophets sometimes do receive or interpret revelatory dreams (see Num. 12:6; Jer. 31:26; Joel 3:1 [Eng., 2:28]; Dan. 1:17; 5:12; 7:1; see also Gen. 28:12; 40:8; 41:12), so the issue here is not the legitimacy of the medium. It is a question of whether the dream is genuinely from the LORD or simply from the mind of the false prophets (see Deut. 13:2–6; Zech. 10:2; 13:2–6). Thus, the LORD laments, "How long (עד מתי) will this be in the heart/mind of the prophets who prophesy deception and when they prophesy the deceit of their heart/mind [MT: and the prophets of the deceit of their heart/mind]" (Jer. 23:26; cf. Isa. 6:11; Jer. 14:14b;

---

39. According to Deuteronomy 30:11–14, God's word is not "far off" but "nearby."

40. Rosenberg, trans., *Mikraoth Gedoloth: Jeremiah Volume One*, 192. See also Deuteronomy 32:17; Judges 5:8.

41. Rosenberg, trans., *Mikraoth Gedoloth: Jeremiah Volume One*, 191–92.

42. Cf. The Hymn to the Aton: "Thou has made the distant sky in order to rise therein, In order to see all that thou dost make" (Pritchard, *Ancient Near Eastern Texts*, 371). Holladay connects the language of 23:23–24 to 12:2b: "in 12:2b Jrm affirms that Yahweh is hidden from his opponents, while here Yahweh affirms that no one can be hidden from him. Both passages affirm the sovereignty of Yahweh over any complacent convictions of people, but here 'afar off' is used with the rather specialized nuance that Yahweh is aware of everything, no matter how remote or obscure" (Holladay, *Jeremiah 1*, 639).

23:16b)?[43] Jeremiah 23:27 describes the false prophets as "those who plan to forget my name [Rahlfs: to forget my law; MT: to cause my people to forget my name; Syr.: to lead my people astray in my name] by their dreams that they recount to one another, just as their forefathers forgot my name by Baal [i.e., by the worship of Baal (cf. Syr., *Tg. Jon.*)]," which is somewhat ironic given the fact that these prophets prophesy in the Lord's name (Jer. 23:25). Of course, the false prophets of Jerusalem in Jeremiah's day prophesied by Baal (Jer. 2:8) just as the previous generations and just as the false prophets of Samaria (Jer. 23:13), but the focus here seems to be the sharing of dreams that have messages of peace and well-being. Such dreams obscure the genuine word of the Lord (a message of judgment) and thus make the prophets' appeal to the Lord's name an empty one.

Modern commentators tend to understand Jeremiah 23:28a to mean that a prophet who has a dream is allowed to recount his dream as long as he does not claim that it is a word from the Lord, while one who has the word of the Lord must speak it faithfully.[44] The following proverb ("What does straw have to do with grain?")[45] in 23:28b is then interpreted to mean, "What does a dream have to do with my word?" The difficulty with this exegesis is that there is no clear separation in 23:28a between the recounting of a dream and the claim to prophesy in the Lord's name. In fact, 23:25 assumes that the two go hand in hand. Furthermore, 23:27 has already indicated that the mere recounting of dreams is the means by which the Lord's name is practically forgotten. Thus, it seems highly unlikely that 23:28a is granting permission to recount empty dreams of peace and well-being in the Lord's name as long as they are somehow not passed off as the word of the Lord. Since the issue in 23:25 is not the legitimacy of a dream as a medium but the question of whether it comes from the Lord, it is more likely the case that 23:28a encourages true prophets who receive genuinely prophetic dreams to recount those dreams.[46] True prophets to whom the word of the Lord genuinely comes have the responsibility to speak that word faithfully, even if it is an unpalatable message of judgment to which the people will react negatively (see Amos 3:8). This is in contrast to the false prophets who claim that the product of their own mind is a

---

43. The MT has an unusual construction in which עד מתי is followed by ה interrogative.
44. See, e.g., Bright, *Jeremiah*, 153; McKane, *Jeremiah I–XXV*, 590.
45. Bullinger, *Figures of Speech*, 763. Cf. 2 Samuel 16:10; Matthew 3:12.
46. See Redak in Rosenberg, trans., *Mikraoth Gedoloth: Jeremiah Volume One*, 193.

message from the LORD. Thus, the proverb in 23:28b means, "What do false dreams and messages have to do with genuinely prophetic dreams and the word of the LORD?"[47] Genuine words from the LORD are "like fire and like a hammer that shatters rock" (Jer. 23:29; see *b. Shabb.* 88b). This either describes the effect of the words on the true prophet's audience (i.e., fiery judgment and devastation [e.g., Jer. 5:14; 21:10]) or it describes their effect on the true prophet: the word of the LORD "becomes [MT adds: in my heart] like a burning fire flaming [MT: shut up] in my bones" (Jer. 20:9). For the false prophets, on the other hand, prophecy is a casual affair in which they tell the people what they want to hear. There is thus no real demand on the lives of the false prophets, nor is there any rebuke for the people (see again Jer. 23:22). The effect of false prophecy is negligible except for the fact that it gives the people a false sense of security and hides the truth from them (see again Jer. 23:27).

"Therefore" (לכן), the LORD announces three times, "Look, I am against the prophets" (Jer. 23:30a, 31a, 32a). Jeremiah 23:30b describes these prophets as those "who steal my words from one another" (cf. Jer. 2:26). According to Rashi, "They have spies who spy upon the true prophets, who listen to their expression with which they prophesy and say false prophecies with that same expression."[48] The example that Rashi uses is Hananiah's false prophecy, "I have broken the yoke of the king of Babylon" (Jer. 28:2b), which appears to be a reuse of Jeremiah's true prophecy, "Look, I am about to break the bow of Elam" (Jer. 49:35) (see *b. Sanh.* 89a). This view highlights the fact that the LORD's words are being stolen, but it does not account for the fact that the false prophets are stealing these words from one another, not from true prophets. Thus, Calvin comments, "I rather think that their secret arts are here pointed out, that they secretly and designedly conspired among themselves, and then that they spread abroad their own figments according to their usual manner."[49] Holladay, however, suggests that the false prophets were not deliberately deceiving the people but were claiming to speak the LORD's words when those were only the product of their own deceived minds: "Since it is not the true words of Yahweh, but only what they claim to be the true words of Yahweh, the expression 'my words' must be placed in quotation marks."[50]

---

47. Rashi (Rosenberg, trans., *Mikraoth Gedoloth: Jeremiah Volume One*, 193): "What has falsehood to do with truth?"
48. Rosenberg, trans., *Mikraoth Gedoloth: Jeremiah Volume One*, 194.
49. Calvin, *Jeremiah*, 3:201.
50. Holladay, *Jeremiah 1*, 645.

According to the Hebrew source behind Greek Jeremiah 23:31, the prophets opposed by the Lord are those "who take their tongue and slumber" (הלקחים לשונם וינומו נום).[51] This perhaps refers to the dreams that the false prophets claim to have in their sleep (Jer. 23:25). The MT, however, says that they are those "who take their tongue and utter prophecy" (הלקחים לשונם וינאמו נאם). These so-called prophets have not received the word of the Lord but the words of their own mouth ("their tongue") and the product of their own mind (Jer. 23:16, 26). The Lord is against the false prophets who recount deceptive dreams (cf. Jer. 23:27) and thus lead the people astray (cf. Jer. 23:13) with their deceptions and "wantonness" (Jer. 23:32a; cf. Zeph. 3:4; Jer. 23:14; *1 En.* 98:15). He did not send them or command them (cf. Jer. 14:14; 23:21; see also Deut. 18:20; Jer. 43:2; Ezek. 13:6–10; 22:28; Neh. 6:12), "and they do not at all benefit this people" (Jer. 23:32b; cf. Jer. 2:8b).

In Jeremiah 23:33a, the Lord gives a scenario in which the people or a priest or a prophet asks Jeremiah, "What is the burden (משא) of the Lord?" The Hebrew word משא, from the root נשא ("to lift up"), can be translated "burden" (i.e., that which is lifted up or burdensome [e.g., Jer. 17:21]) or "oracle" (i.e., a discourse that is taken up [e.g., Isa. 13:1]), depending on the context. Some English translations (e.g., NRSV) prefer to translate it as "burden" throughout the present passage (Jer. 23:33–40). Others (e.g., NIV) prefer to use "oracle" throughout the passage. Still others (e.g., TEV) see a play on the two uses of the term wherein it is to be translated "oracle" or "message" in 23:33a but "burden" in 23:33b–40. As McKane has noted, the difficulty with the latter two options is that they fail to account for the harshness of the response in 23:33b–34.[52] According to the Hebrew source behind Greek Jeremiah 23:33b, Jeremiah is to respond on the Lord's behalf, "You are the burden" (אתם המשא). This can hardly be translated, "You are the oracle." To call the people, priests, and prophets a burden simply because of a request for the oracle of the Lord seems unnecessarily aggressive, but if it is a response to a disingenuous request for something that is perceived to be burdensome from the Lord, such as a message of judgment, then it is a fitting reply. The word of the Lord is not the burden (see 1 John 5:3; see also Jer. 6:16; Matt. 11:28–30 [cf. Matt. 10:38; 23:4]); the people are the burden. According to the MT, however, Jeremiah is to respond, "What burden" (את מה משא)? Of course, this could be translated, "What oracle?" but the Hebrew text is

---

51. According to Tov (*Text-Critical Use*, 192), the Greek translator did etymo-
logical exegesis of וינאמו נאם, translating it as if it were וינומו נום.
52. McKane, *Jeremiah I–XXV*, 599.

strange (note the definite direct object marker prior to the question) and is probably the result of incorrect word division (see the Hebrew text behind Greek Jeremiah above). Furthermore, the reply, "You are the burden," fits better with the following clause: "and I will dash you to pieces (ורטשתי אתכם) [MT: and I will forsake you (ונטשתי אתכם)]" (see also Isa. 13:16; Jer. 23:39; Hos. 14:1 [Eng., 13:16]; Nah. 3:10).[53] It also works well with 23:24: "And the prophet and the priest and the people who say, 'The burden of the LORD,' I will visit upon that man and upon his house." Thus, the consequences are severe not only for the person who uses this phrase but also for his/her household.

Rather than asking, "What is the burden of the LORD?" (Jer. 23:33a) the people should be asking one another, "What has the LORD answered?" and "What has the LORD spoken?" (Jer. 23:35). Only in the MT of 23:37 is it suggested that these questions should be directed to the prophet. The fact that the people should be asking one another these questions suggests that a true prophet like Jeremiah has already delivered the LORD's message to the people. They need now only to inform and remind one another of what the LORD has answered and spoken. As for the phrase "the burden of the LORD," the LORD says, "Do not ever mention (תַזְכִּרוּ) [MT: remember (תִזְכְּרוּ)] (it) again" (Jer. 23:36a). The reason given for this prohibition is not entirely clear: "for the burden is to the man [MT: a man] the word [MT: his word]" (Jer. 23:36b).[54] Calvin comments, "By these words he shews that what is bitter in prophecies is as it were accidental; for God has nothing else in view in addressing men, but to call them to salvation."[55] Calvin's point seems to be that whatever is burdensome about the word of the LORD is due to the man, not to the word of the LORD itself. Holladay paraphrases, "You are to

---

53. In the Aramaic of *Targum Jonathan* Jeremiah 23:33b, the root רטש means "abandon" (see Jastrow, *Dictionary of the Targumim*, 1472). Perhaps an original Hebrew ורטשתי found in the source behind Greek Jeremiah has been interpreted in two ways. The LXX translator read it according to its normal Hebrew sense ("and I will dash to pieces"). The tradition behind the MT read it according to its Aramaic sense ("and I will abandon/forsake"), which resulted in the change to ונטשתי—Hebrew for "and I will forsake."

54. The MT can be translated in at least two other ways: (1) "for the burden/ oracle is to the man of his word"; and (2) "for his word will be the burden/ oracle to a man." According to the first, the word of the LORD only comes to the true prophet ("the man of his word") (see Rashi). According to the second, man's word is what has been passed off as the word of the LORD to each person (see Redak).

55. Calvin, *Jeremiah*, 3:211.

use the term 'burden of the Lord' no more—the term 'burden' is to be confined to human words, and to use the term to refer to divine words would be to insult the Lord."[56] Thus, the MT adds at the end of 23:36b: "and you pervert the words of the living God, the Lord of hosts, our God." The MT also has a longer text for 23:37: "Thus you should say to the prophet, 'What has the Lord answered you?' and 'What has the Lord spoken?'" This appears to be based on 23:35 with the exception that the questions are directed to the prophet rather than to one another (see Jer. 37:17). Also, the verb תאמר ("you should say") in 23:37 is singular, whereas 23:35 has the plural תאמרו ("you should say"). The Hebrew source behind Greek Jeremiah 23:37 simply asks, "And what has the Lord our God spoken?" That is, if the people are to ask one another what the Lord has answered and spoken in accordance with 23:35 and expect a response, then it is presupposed that there are those who have heard the Lord's word from a true prophet like Jeremiah and can give an adequate reply. Thus, the question in 23:37 prompts the audience to think about what that reply should be based on what has been revealed to them through genuine prophecy.

Because the people use the phrase "the burden of the Lord," even though the Lord has sent his prophet Jeremiah to tell them not to say it (Jer. 23:38), the Lord says: "therefore, look, I am about to take and dash to pieces (לכן הנני נֹשֶׁא ורטשתי) you and the city [i.e., Jerusalem] that I gave to you and to your forefathers" (Jer. 23:39; cf. Jer. 23:33). This features a play on the key word of the passage משא ("burden"). The Lord is about to "take" or "lift up" (נשא) the real "burden" (משא), namely, the people (Jer. 23:33), and dash them to pieces. The Leningrad Codex, however, says: "therefore, look, I, and I will forget you completely and forsake (לכן הנני וְנָשִׁיתִי אתכם נָשֹׁא ונטשתי) you and the city that I gave to you and to your forefathers from before me." A few Masoretic manuscripts have וְנָשִׂיתִי אתכם נָשֹׁא ("and I will take you completely") (נָשָׂאתִי = נָשִׂיתִי). The Lord will put upon the people "everlasting reproach and everlasting humiliation, which will not be forgotten" (Jer. 23:40; cf. Jer. 20:11b).

The final two verses of chapter 23 in the Hebrew source behind Greek Jeremiah appear as verses 7 and 8 of chapter 23 in the MT (see commentary after Jer. 23:6). These verses form a doublet with Jeremiah 16:14–15 (see commentary there). They anticipate a time when the greatest act of deliverance in Israel's history (the exodus from Egypt) will be superseded by an even greater act (an exodus from the land of the north), which will become the new way to describe the Lord in oaths taken in his name (cf. Isa. 43:16–21). As noted earlier in the

---

56. Holladay, *Jeremiah 1*, 652.

commentary on Jeremiah 16:14–15 and MT 23:7–8, there are two main issues involved in the interpretation of this doublet. The first is the identification of the enemy from the north. Those who follow the later edition of the book of Jeremiah represented by the MT will most likely identify this enemy as Babylon (Jer. 25:9). On the other hand, the earlier edition of the book represented by the Hebrew source behind Greek Jeremiah is open to the possibility that the enemy from the north is an eschatological one (see commentary on Jer. 1:13–15; 4:6; 5:15; 6:1, 22; 10:22; 13:20; 15:12; 25:9; 50:3; see also Jer. 31:8; Ezek. 38:14–17; 39:25–29). A decision on this identification will determine whether the new exodus envisioned here is a historical one or an eschatological one. The second issue is the placement of these verses. When they appear in a context of judgment, such as Jeremiah 16:14–15 or at the end of chapter 23, the focus is not so much on the greater act of deliverance as it is on the harsher place of judgment from which the people must be delivered. But when they appear in a context of deliverance, as in MT 23:7–8, they do in fact highlight a new and better exodus for the people of God.[57]

---

57. Ben Zoma considers the days that are coming in this context to be those of the messianic age (Neusner, *Jeremiah in Talmud and Midrash*, 3). See LXX Numbers 24:7–9, 14, 17 and Jeremiah 23:5–6.

JEREMIAH 24

24:1 The L*ORD* *showed me [MT adds: and look] two baskets of figs set before the temple of the* L*ORD* *after Nebuchadnezzar [MT: Nebuchadrezzar] the king of Babylon exiled Jeconiah [i.e., Jehoiachin] the son of Jehoiakim, the king of Judah, and the officials [MT adds: of Judah] and the craftsmen and the smiths [LXX: the prisoners] and the wealthy [and the wealthy > MT] from Jerusalem and brought them to Babylon. 24:2 The one basket [see GKC §134l] had very good figs like the first-ripe figs, and the other basket [see BDB, 25] had very bad figs, which could not be eaten because they were so bad. 24:3 And the* L*ORD* *said to me, "What do you see, Jeremiah?" And I said, "Figs. The good ones are very good, and the bad ones are very bad, which cannot be eaten because they are so bad."*

24:4 And the word of the L*ORD* *came to me, saying, 24:5 "Thus says the* L*ORD* *God of Israel, 'Like these good figs, so will I regard the exiles of Judah, whom I sent from this place to the land of the Chaldeans, for good. 24:6 And I will set my eyes [Codex L: my eye] on them for good, and I will restore them to this land, and I will build them and not tear down, and I will plant them and not pluck up. 24:7 And I will give to them a heart/mind to know me, that I am the* L*ORD*, *and they will become my people, and I, I will become their God, for they will return to me with all their heart/mind. 24:8 And like the bad figs, which cannot be eaten because they are so bad,' [MT adds: כִּי] thus says the* L*ORD*, *'so will I make Zedekiah the king of Judah and his officials and the rest of Jerusalem [Cairo Geniza: Judah], those who are left in this land and those living in Egypt. 24:9 And I will make them into an object of terror [LXX: a dispersion; MT adds: for evil] to all the kingdoms of the inhabited earth and [and > MT] an object of reproach and a proverb and an object of hatred/rejection [MT: an object of a sharp word] and an object of contempt [LXX: a curse; NET: an example to be used in curses] in all the places where I banish them. 24:10 And I will send among/against them the famine and the plague and the sword [Codex L: the sword, (mlt Mss add: and) the famine, and the plague] until they are finished from upon the land that I gave to them [MT adds: and to their forefathers].'"*

Chapter 24 is an account of a prophetic vision seen by Jeremiah (Jer. 24:1–3) and explained by the word of the L*ORD* (Jer. 24:4–10). The pattern of this account has points of contact with the visions in Jeremiah 1:11–14 but most closely follows the pattern in Amos 7:7–9 and 8:1–3 (see also Amos 7:1–6; Zech. 1–6). Jeremiah says that the

LORD "showed" (*hiphil* of ראה) him two baskets of figs set before the temple of the LORD (Jer. 24:1a; cf. Amos 7:1, 4, 7; 8:1). These baskets of figs were not actually in front of the temple in real time and space. Rather, the prophet saw them there in a vision. The two baskets of figs are in the foreground of the vision, while the temple is in the background. No significance is attached to the temple in the explanation of the vision (Jer. 24:4–10). Jeremiah received this vision after Nebuchadnezzar exiled "Jeconiah" (= Jehoiachin) in 597 BC along with his officials, the craftsmen, the smiths,[1] and the wealthy (> MT) from Jerusalem to Babylon (Jer. 24:1b; see 2 Kgs. 24:10–17; Jer. 13:18–19; 22:24–30; 27:20; 28:3–4; 29:1–2; Est. 2:6; 2 Chr. 36:9–10; Bar. 1:9).[2] Second Kings 24:14, 16 adds the military to this list. As in 605 BC (see Dan. 1), the Babylonians took the elite and the skilled from Judean society to assimilate them into Babylonian culture, and they left the poor behind to tend the land (see 2 Kgs. 24:14; cf. 2 Kgs. 25:11–12; see also Jer. 40; 52:15–16, 28–30).

One of the two baskets in the vision had very good figs comparable to "first-ripe figs" (Jer. 24:2a; cf. Isa. 28:4; Hos. 9:10). Keil comments that this has nothing to do with "first fruits," suggesting instead that the figs symbolize the people,[3] but the two are not mutually exclusive here. It is to be noted that Israel is called the "first fruits" of the LORD's produce in Jeremiah 2:3. The other basket had very bad figs, "which could not be eaten because they were so bad" (Jer. 24:2b). This recalls

---

1. The LXX translates מסגר ("smiths") as "prisoners," likely because of the homonym מסגר ("prison") (see *HALOT* 1:604), but such a rendering is out of sorts with the other members of the list. They are all "prisoners," so to speak, but the point of the list is to show that the various elite and skilled members of Judean society were taken, leaving only the poor and lowly behind. See also McKane, *Jeremiah I–XXV*, 608. Rashi refers to an explanation that says חרש ("craftsmen") and מסגר ("smiths") mean "silent" and "close" respectively and describe exiled Torah scholars: "That is to say, great sages in Torah, to the extent that when one of them would speak, everyone would remain silent. מַסְגֵּר means that when they would close the discussion, no one would reopen it" (Rosenberg, trans., *Mikraoth Gedoloth: Jeremiah Volume One*, 197).
2. "The King Jeconiah had been then carried away into exile, together with the chief men and artisans. The condition of the king and of the rest appeared indeed much worse than that of the people who remained in the country, for they still retained a hope that the royal dignity would again be restored" (Calvin, *Jeremiah*, 3:220). See Ezekiel 11:15.
3. Keil, *Jeremiah*, 227.

the song about the vineyard that produced bad or sour grapes (Isa. 5:1–7). The LORD then asks, "What do you see, Jeremiah?" to which the prophet responds, "Figs" (Jer. 24:3a; cf. Jer. 1:11, 13; Amos 7:8a; 8:2a; Zech. 4:2; 5:2). Jeremiah's description of the figs in 24:3b ("The good ones are very good, and the bad ones are very bad, which cannot be eaten because they are so bad") is almost identical to the one in 24:2 with the exception that he does not compare the good figs to first-ripe figs in 24:3b. Jeremiah is unable to interpret what he sees and thus relies upon the revelatory word of the LORD for an explanation (Jer. 24:4–10; cf. Jer. 1:12, 14; Amos 7:8b–9; 8:2b–3; Zech. 4:4–5, 10–13; 5:3–4).

When the word of the LORD comes (Jer. 24:4), he says, "Like these good figs, so will I regard the exiles of Judah, whom I sent from this place to the land of the Chaldeans, for good" (Jer. 25:5; see *4 Bar.* 5–6). Normally the phrase "for good" is read with the verb "regard" ("so will I regard . . . for good"), although Malbim reads it with the verb "sent" ("whom I sent . . . for good").[4] In what sense can Jehoiachin and those who went into exile with him be considered good figs? The words against Jehoiachin in Jeremiah 22:24–30 hardly give the impression that he is good. Furthermore, Jeremiah's earlier prophecies of judgment are directed against the various segments of society indiscriminately (Jer. 1:17–19). Calvin suggests that those in exile are not called good in themselves but "because God had chastened them more gently than he intended to chastise Zedekiah and the rest" (see Ezek. 11:16).[5] On the other hand, Bright comments that the officials who left with Jehoiachin were in fact the very best leaders who had on more than one occasion intervened on Jeremiah's behalf (see Jer. 26:17–24; 36:14–19, 25) and would be replaced by those hostile to the prophet and perhaps less competent than their predecessors (see Jer. 37–38; but note Jer. 38:8–13).[6] But the explanation of the good figs in 24:5 is not so much about the good quality of the exiles as it is about the good or beneficial purpose that the LORD has for them, which is expounded in 24:6–7. The LORD will regard them not "as good" but "for good" (cf. Jer. 29:11; see the contrast with Jer. 14:11; 21:10; 39:16; 44:11, 27, 29). He regards them for good in the sense that they are already on the other side of judgment awaiting future restoration (see Jer. 29:1–14).

---

4. See Rosenberg, trans., *Mikraoth Gedoloth: Jeremiah Volume One*, 198.
5. Calvin, *Jeremiah*, 3:222. See Jeremiah 52:31–34 (= 2 Kgs. 25:27–30) and contrast Jeremiah 39:4–7 and 52:7–11 (= 2 Kgs. 25:4–7). See also Jeremiah 29:4–7 and contrast Jeremiah 52:24–27 (= 2 Kgs. 25:18–21).
6. Bright, *Jeremiah*, 194.

The LORD will set his eyes (Codex L: "eye") on the exiles "for good" and restore them to the land of the covenant (Jer. 24:6a; cf. Jer. 21:10; 39:12; 40:4; Amos 9:4; see also Jer. 32:37). It is evident from the context of 24:6–7 that this does not merely anticipate the favor shown to Jehoiachin (2 Kgs. 25:27–30; Jer. 52:31–34) or the return to the land after Babylonian exile to rebuild the temple and the city of Jerusalem (Hag. 2:3; Ezra 1:1–4; 3:12; Neh. 4:4 [Eng., 4:10]). Rather, the good that the LORD plans to do for his people is also a spiritual and eschatological renewal that was never realized in the postexilic period (see Isa. 56–66; Zech. 1–6). He says, "I will build them and not tear down, and I will plant them and not pluck up" (Jer. 24:6b; cf. *Pss. Sol.* 14:4; 2 Cor. 13:10). This language comes directly from the programmatic text in Jeremiah 1:10 (see commentary there): "See, I have appointed you this day over the nations and over the kingdoms to pluck up and to tear down and to destroy [MT adds: and to throw down], and [and > MT] to build and to plant" (see also Jer. 12:14–17; 18:7–10; 31:27–28, 40; 42:10; 45:4). Thus, Jeremiah 24:6b looks beyond the judgment that has taken place to an irreversible restoration in the eschaton.

The LORD says that he will give the people a heart/mind to know him, that is, to acknowledge or recognize that he is Yahweh and not Baal (Jer. 24:7a; see Jer. 2:8b; 3:1–2; 4:22; cf. Isa. 5:13; Hos. 2:10, 18 [Eng., 2:8, 16]; 4:6; 6:3). According to Deuteronomy 29:3 (Eng., 29:4), the LORD had not yet given the people "a heart/mind to know" (לב לדעת) under the old covenant. They were in need of the circumcised heart/mind of the new covenant (Deut. 28:69 [Eng., 29:1]; 30:6; Jer. 4:4; 9:25 [Eng., 9:26]; 31:31, 33; 32:40; Ezek. 18:31; Rom. 2:28–29) in order to devote themselves wholly to the LORD. Only in this new covenant relationship will the people "know" the LORD (Jer. 31:31, 34; 1 John 2:27). Only in the new covenant will they do justice and righteousness, which is what it means to know him (see 1 Sam. 2:10 [LXX]; Jer. 9:23 [Eng., 9:24]; 22:15–16; Jas. 1:27). Only with a new heart/mind and the gift of the Spirit will they acknowledge that the one true God is Yahweh (see Jer. 32:39; Ezek. 11:19–20; 36:26–27; see also 2 Chr. 30:12), the one who is present with them (see Exod. 3:12, 14–15; 7:5; 9:16; Lev. 18:30b; et al.; see also the recognition formula in Ezek. 6–39 [e.g., Ezek. 6:7]). Only then will the Torah be on their hearts/minds to do the LORD's will (Jer. 31:33; 2 Cor. 3, 6; see also Ezek. 11:19–20; 36:26–27; Rom. 8:4). When the people have this new heart/mind, they will become the LORD's people, and he will become their God (Jer. 24:7a). This is known as the covenant formula (see Jer. 7:23; 11:4; 31:1; 30:22 [MT]; 31:33; 32:38; Ezek. 11:20; 36:28). According to Jeremiah 31:1, the new covenant relationship will be made "at that time," a reference back to the phrase "at the end of the days" in

30:24b.[7] The people will have this relationship because they will return to the LORD with all their heart/mind (Jer. 24:7b; cf. Deut. 6:5; 30:2, 10; 1 Kgs. 8:48; 2 Kgs. 23:25; Jer. 3:10; 29:13). As McKane comments, it "is not that Yahweh's work of rehabilitation is conditional on the wholehearted repentance of his people, but rather that this wholehearted repentance is part and parcel of his work of restoration."[8]

The LORD then says that he will make Zedekiah, his officials, and the rest of Jerusalem, "those who are left in this land and those living in Egypt," like the bad figs (Jer. 24:8). It is true that this was a very obstinate group (see Jer. 21; 27–28; 37–38; Ezek. 2:3–4; 3:7; 12:22; 14:3, 14; 15:2; 16:3; 17:5–10; 18:2; 19), but he does not say that those with Zedekiah are the bad figs, as if those with Jehoiachin were good and not bad, but that he will make Zedekiah and those with him like the bad figs. This includes those living in Egypt. According to Bright, this does not require a date after 587 BC when many Judeans settled in Egypt (see Jer. 43–44): "Undoubtedly Jews of the pro-Egyptian party, who had favored resistance to Babylon, had fled there when Jehoiakim became Nebuchadnezzar's vassal (ca. 603), or when Nebuchadnezzar invaded Judah in 598/7" (see also Jer. 37:7; Ezek. 17:7).[9]

Jeremiah 24:9–10 explains what it means for the LORD to "make" (נתן) Zedekiah and those with him like the bad figs. He will make them into "an object of terror" (זועה) to all the kingdoms of the inhabited earth (Jer. 24:9a; cf. Deut. 28:25; Isa. 28:19; Jer. 15:4; 29:18; 34:17; Ezek. 23:46; 2 Chr. 29:8). The MT adds that he will do this "for evil" (לרעה), which makes explicit the contrast with "for good" (לטובה) in 24:5–6 (see again Amos 9:4). The LORD will also make these people into an object of reproach, a proverb, an object of hatred/rejection, and an

---

7. The NT authors speak of the making of the new covenant in an "already, but not yet" form of eschatology (see Luke 22:16, 20; 1 Cor. 11:25–26).

8. McKane, *Jeremiah I–XXV*, 609. Cf. Deuteronomy 30:1–7. Most English translations divide Deuteronomy 30:1–7 between 30:1–2 (protasis) and 30:3–7 (apodosis) based on the shift from "you" (Deut. 30:1b–2) to "the LORD" (Deut. 30:3), but this makes the restoration of the people dependent on their ability to initiate their own return and does not improve upon the situation under the old covenant. "Therefore, it seems best to depend upon the shift in verbal forms from *yqtl* (protasis) to *wqtl* (apodosis). According to this view, once the covenant curses expected in Deuteronomy 28–29 come upon the people (Deut 30:1a), then everything in the chain of *wqtl* forms (Deut 30:1b–7) will happen. That is, repentance, restoration, and circumcision come as a package. There is no reference to temporal sequence, condition, or cause and effect" (Shepherd, *Text in the Middle*, 97).

9. Bright, *Jeremiah*, 193.

object of contempt in all the places where he banishes them (Jer. 24:9b; cf. Deut. 28:37; 1 Kgs. 9:7; 2 Chr. 7:20; see also Jer. 8:3; 16:15; 23:8).[10] They will be "a proverb" (משל) in the sense that their situation will be so notorious that they will become the subject of a popular saying, but not in a good way. According to the Hebrew source behind Greek Jeremiah, the people will be "an object of hatred/rejection" (שנאה). The MT has שנינה ("an object of a sharp word"). The last word in the list, קללה, is usually understood to mean "a curse," as in the LXX (cf. NET: "an example to be used in curses"), but given the meaning of קלל ("to be light"), it is possible and perhaps even more likely in this context that the sense of קללה is "an object of contempt" (cf. NEB: "a thing of ridicule").[11] Finally, the Lord says, "And I will send among/against them the famine and the plague and the sword [Codex L: the sword, (mlt Mss add: and) the famine, and the plague] until they are finished from upon the land that I gave to them [MT adds: and to their forefathers]" (Jer. 24:10; see Jer. 39; 52; see also Jer. 7:14; 12:14; 25:5). This is the same triad found elsewhere in the books of Jeremiah and Ezekiel (see, e.g., Jer. 14:12; 29:17 et al.; see commentary on Jer. 14:12).

---

10. See 2 Kings 22:19; Jeremiah 2:15; 4:17; 7:34; 19:8; 22:5; 26:6; 25:9, 11, 18; 29:18; 42:18; 44:6, 8, 12, 22; 43:13, 17; Micah 6:16; Psalms 44:15–15 (Eng., 44:13–14); 79:4; 2 Chronicles 29:8.
11. See also Holladay, *Jeremiah 1*, 660.

JEREMIAH 25:1–13

25:1 The word that came to Jeremiah concerning all the people of Judah in the fourth year of Jehoiakim the son of Josiah, the king of Judah [MT adds: that is, the first year of Nebuchadrezzar the king of Babylon], 25:2 which he [MT: Jeremiah the prophet] spoke to all the people of Judah and to [MT adds: all] the inhabitants of Jerusalem, saying, 25:3 "In [MT: From] the thirteenth year of Josiah the son of Amon [LXX: Amos], the king of Judah, and until this day, these twenty-three years [see DCH 3:88], [MT adds: the word of the LORD *came to me] I spoke [MT: and I spoke] to you rising early and speaking [i.e., urgently speaking] [MT adds: and you did not listen], 25:4 and I sent to you my servants the prophets [MT: and the* LORD *sent (or, used to send) to you all his servants the prophets] rising early and sending [i.e., urgently sending], (but you did not listen and you did not incline your ear [MT adds: to listen]), 25:5 saying, 'Turn, each from his evil way and from the evil of your deeds, so that [see GKC §110f] you may live upon the land that I gave [MT: that the* LORD *gave] to you and to your forefathers from everlasting to everlasting. 25:6 Do not go [MT: And do not go] after other gods to serve / worship them and to bow down [or, prostrate yourselves] to them, and do not provoke me with the works of your hands to cause you harm [MT: and I will not cause you harm].' 25:7 But you did not listen to me" [MT adds: the prophetic utterance of the* LORD, *"in order to provoke me with the works of your hands to your own harm"].*

25:8 Therefore, thus says the LORD *[MT adds: of hosts], "Because you have not believed in [MT: listened to] my words, 25:9 look, I am about to send and take a family from (the) north [MT: all families of north,"] [MT adds: the prophetic utterance of the* LORD, *"and to Nebuchadrezzar the king of Babylon, my servant] and bring them against this land and against its inhabitants and against all the nations [MT: these nations] around, and I will exterminate them and make them into an object of horror and hissing and lasting reproach [MT: lasting ruins], 25:10 and I will destroy from them sound of rejoicing and sound of joy, sound of bridegroom and sound of bride, scent of myrrh [MT: sound of millstones] and light of lamp [Tg. Jon.: sound of public assemblies that sing praises by lamp light], 25:11 and all the land will become a desolation [or, object of horror; MT: and all this land will become a ruin, a desolation (or, object of horror)], and they will serve among the nations for seventy years [MT: and these nations will serve the king of Babylon for seventy years], 25:12 and when seventy years are fulfilled [MT: and it will be as soon as seventy years are fulfilled], I will visit upon [i.e., punish] that nation and make them into a lasting desolation [MT: I will visit upon the king of Babylon and upon that nation," the prophetic utterance of the LORD, "their iniquity and upon the land of the Chaldeans, and I will make him into lasting desolations], 25:13 and I will bring upon that land all my words that I have spoken against it, everything written in this book."*[1]

According to the present commentary, this passage (Jer. 25:1–13) forms the conclusion to the scroll that Jeremiah dictated to Baruch (Jer. 36:1–4; 45:1).[2] Other scholars argue that it is an introduction either to the collection of oracles about the nations, which appears immediately after the present passage in the arrangement of the Hebrew source behind Greek Jeremiah,[3] or to the text of MT Jeremiah 25:15–26, which speaks of the cup of judgment that all the nations must drink. Still others contend that Jeremiah 25:1–13 began as a conclusion to the scroll but then shifted in its role to serve as an introduction to words of judgment against the nations.[4] Therefore, the following exposition will pay careful attention to details of the text that provide clues to the intended function of this passage.

Jeremiah 25:1–13 is "The word that came to Jeremiah concerning all the people of Judah in the fourth year of Jehoiakim the son of Josiah, the king of Judah" (Jer. 25:1). This was the year 605 BC. It was the same year in which Jeremiah dictated the scroll to Baruch (Jer.

---

1. In the MT, 25:13b2 is a relative clause that modifies "everything written in this book": "which Jeremiah prophesied against all the nations." In the Hebrew source behind Greek Jeremiah, this text is a heading to a following collection of oracles about the nations: "That which Jeremiah prophesied concerning the nations" (= LXX Jer. 29:14). MT Jeremiah 25:14 is an added verse not found in the Hebrew source behind Greek Jeremiah: "For they too, many nations and great kings, have served by them, and I will repay them according to their work and according to the work of their hands."

2. Cf. Holladay, *Jeremiah 1*, 661–69.

3. See Anneli Aejmelaeus, "Jeremiah at the Turning Point of History: The Function of Jer. XXV 1–14 in the Book of Jeremiah," *VT* 52 (2002): 459–82. Aejmelaeus makes the point in the conclusion of her article that the designation of Jeremiah as "a prophet to the nations" (Jer. 1:5) does not make sense "unless the oracles against the nations are part of the book." It is to be noted, however, that the book does have other things to say about the nations (e.g., Jer. 1:10; 3:17; 4:2; 12:14–17; 16:19). See also McKane, *Jeremiah I–XXV*, 633.

4. See, e.g., Bright, *Jeremiah*, 163.

36:1–4; 45:1).[5] This was also the year in which Nebuchadnezzar defeated Pharaoh Necho of Egypt at Carchemish (Jer. 46:2) and the year in which he besieged Jerusalem and took a group of elites to Babylon for assimilation, including Daniel and his three friends (2 Kgs. 24:1; Dan. 1:1–6).[6] Thus, the MT adds to the end of the verse: "that is, the first year of Nebuchadrezzar the king of Babylon" (see also Jer. 32:1; 52:12).[7] This is a fairly innocuous parenthetical comment marked by היא ("that is") (cf. Gen. 14:3b, 17b; 36:1; Josh. 18:13a; 1 Chr. 11:4a),[8] but it is consistent with other additions in MT Jeremiah 25:1–13 wherein Babylon (and King Nebuchadnezzar in particular) is explicitly identified as the enemy from the north (MT Jer. 25:9, 11, 12), whereas the Hebrew source behind Greek Jeremiah leaves this enemy unidentified.[9] The word or message that came to Jeremiah in the fourth year of Jehoiakim is further described in Jeremiah 25:2 as that "which he [MT: Jeremiah the prophet] spoke to all the people of Judah and to [MT adds: all] the inhabitants of Jerusalem."

Anneli Aejmelaeus has noted that Jeremiah 25:3–7 "contains no single phrase that does not occur elsewhere in the book," except for the dating in 25:3.[10] The main difference between the Hebrew source behind Greek Jeremiah and the MT in this passage is that the former presents these words as those of the LORD himself, which is consistent with 25:1–2, while the latter presents them as the discourse of the prophet Jeremiah. Beginning in the thirteenth year of Josiah (627 BC) and continuing to the present day (605 BC), twenty-three years (see Jer. 1:2–3; 36:2), the LORD spoke to the people urgently ("rising early

---

5. Note that 25:1–13 does not follow chapter 24 in chronological order (see Jer. 24:1; see also Jer. 26:1). Chronology is not always the determining factor in the ordering of the book's material. Sometimes the principle of arrangement is theological (see, e.g., Jer. 34–35).

6. Daniel 1:1 calls this the third year of Jehoiakim, presumably because it reckons the first full year of his reign to be his first year as king. If the year in which Jehoiakim took the throne is counted as the first year of his reign, then 605 BC is reckoned as his fourth year.

7. "Although Nebuchadnezzar's first official regnal year began in April 604 (at the New Year), he actually took the throne in September 605" (Bright, *Jeremiah*, 160).

8. Fishbane, *Biblical Interpretation*, 44–46.

9. "A comparison between the two text forms reveals that the 'enemy from the north' is still meant to be anonymous in Jeremiah's decisive address in the year 605 BC" (Aejmelaeus, "Jeremiah at the Turning Point of History," 464).

10. Aejmelaeus, "Jeremiah at the Turning Point of History," 468.

and speaking") (Jer. 25:3; cf. Jer. 7:13 [MT]; 11:7 [MT]; 32:33; 35:14). The MT's addition at the end of 25:3 ("and you did not listen") also appears in Jeremiah 7:13 and 35:14. During this time, the Lord sent not only Jeremiah the prophet but also a plurality of his servants the prophets (Jer. 25:4; e.g., Zeph. 1:1; cf. Jer. 7:25; 26:5; 29:19 [MT]; 35:15; 44:4; see also 2 Kgs. 17:13; 2 Chr. 36:15), but it is added parenthetically at the end of 25:4 that the people did not listen or incline their ear (cf. Jer. 7:24, 26; 11:8 [MT]; 17:23; 34:14; 35:15; 44:5; see also 2 Kgs. 17:14).

Jeremiah 25:5–6 then cites what the prophets would say when they were sent: "Turn, each from his evil way [cf. Jer. 18:11; 23:14, 22; 26:3; 35:15; 36:3, 7; see also Jon. 3:8b; Zech. 1:4; Acts 3:26] and from the evil of your deeds [cf. Jer. 4:4; 21:12; 23:22; 26:3; 44:22], so that you may live upon the land that I gave [MT: that the Lord gave] to you and to your forefathers [cf. Jer. 7:7; 24:10; 35:15] from everlasting to everlasting [cf. Jer. 7:7]. Do not go [MT: And do not go] after other gods to serve/worship them and to bow down [or, prostrate yourselves] to them [cf. Jer. 1:16; 7:6, 9; 11:10; 13:10; 16:11; 35:15; see also Exod. 20:2–6; Deut. 5:7–10], and do not provoke me with the works of your hands [cf. Jer. 32:30; 44:8][11] to cause you harm [MT: and I will not cause you harm] [cf. Jer. 7:6; see also Josh. 24:20]." Despite the best efforts of the prophets, the people did not listen to what the Lord had to say (Jer. 25:7; cf. Jer. 3:13; 7:13; 26:5; 34:17; 35:14, 15; 40:3; 42:21; 44:23; see also Bar. 1:21–22). The MT adds to the end of 25:7: "in order to provoke me with the works of your hands to your own harm" (see commentary on Jer. 7:18–19).

"Therefore" (לכן), the Lord announces in 25:8, "because you have not believed in my words" (יען אשר לא האמנתם בדברי) (cf. 2 Kgs. 17:13, 14b). The MT says, "Because you have not listened to my words" (יען אשר לא שמעתם את דברי) (cf. 2 Kgs. 17:13, 14a). Because of this, the Lord indicates in the Hebrew source behind Greek Jeremiah 25:9a that he is about "to send and take a family from (the) north and bring them against this land and against its inhabitants and against all the nations around." The MT makes several alterations and additions to this text: (1) "a family from (the) north" becomes "all families of north" (cf. MT Jer. 1:15); (2) addition of "the prophetic utterance of the Lord"; (3) awkward insertion of "and to Nebuchadrezzar the king of Babylon, my servant" (cf. MT Jer. 27:6; 43:10),[12] which does not fit into the Hebrew

---

11. The phrase "the works of your hands" can be used more broadly (see MT Jer. 25:14b), but in the immediate context of Jeremiah 25:6b it refers to manmade idols (i.e., "other gods").

12. The designation of Nebuchadnezzar as the Lord's "servant" (i.e., his instrument) never occurs in the Hebrew source behind Greek Jeremiah.

syntax and is thus foreign to the context; and (4) "the nations" becomes "these nations," presumably in anticipation of Jeremiah 25:15–26 and/or Jeremiah 46–51. English translations of the MT typically smooth over the difficulties in one way or another (e.g., ESV), but a translation that follows the rules of Hebrew grammar and syntax will make the problems evident: "look, I am about to send and take all families of north," the prophetic utterance of the LORD, "and to Nebuchadrezzar the king of Babylon, my servant, and bring them against this land and against its inhabitants and against all these nations around." This is a rather obvious and secondary attempt to make King Nebuchadnezzar and Babylon into the enemy from the north and thus does not represent the original Hebrew text. Such a historicization of the prophecy about this enemy has not happened up to this point in the book (see Jer. 1:13–15; 4:6, 13; 5:15; 6:1, 22; 10:22; 13:20; 15:12) and does not occur again after MT 25:9, 11, 12.[13] The MT even makes a distinction between "the kings of the north" and "the king of Sheshach" (= "the king of Babylon") in 25:26b (> LXX). Furthermore, the enemy from the north comes against Babylon in Jeremiah 50:3.[14] The more preferable text of the Hebrew source behind Greek Jeremiah leaves the enemy from the north unidentified and thus open to eschatological interpretation. It is the basis for Ezekiel's identification of Jeremiah's enemy from the north as "Gog" (Ezek. 38–39; see also LXX, SP Num. 24:7; Rev. 20:8),[15] an eschatological enemy who will come from the north with his horde of nations "at the end of the days" (Ezek. 38:15–16) in accordance with what the LORD spoke in former days through his prophets, namely, Jeremiah among the prophets (Ezek. 38:17; cf. Dan. 9:2).[16] This enemy will ultimately fall in defeat in the land of Israel (Ezek. 39:4; cf. Dan. 11:45).

---

13. Of course, Babylon was a historical enemy from the east that would attack Judah from the north (but see Gen. 14; see also Ezek. 21:23–25 [Eng., 23:18–20]), but this is beside the point. The issue is whether the intent of the book of Jeremiah is to identify Babylon as its enemy from the north.

14. This enemy is never explicitly identified as the Medes (Jer. 51:11, 28). That is, the Medes are mentioned, but they are never directly called the enemy from the north as Babylon is in MT 25:9 (see Jer. 50:9, 41; 51:48). The enemy from the north remains separate and unidentified.

15. For other depictions of a final battle with this enemy, see Joel 4 (Eng., 3); Zechariah 12; 14; Revelation 16; 19.

16. Ezekiel commentators have difficulty making the connection between Ezekiel 38:17 and the book of Jeremiah due to the fact that they assume MT Jeremiah, which does not present an eschatological enemy from the north but a historical one (Babylon). See, e.g., Daniel I. Block, *The Book of Ezekiel: Chapters 25–48*, NICOT (Grand Rapids: Eerdmans, 1997), 453–56.

The Lord will "exterminate" (חרם) the land, its inhabitants, and the surrounding nations by means of the enemy from the north (Jer. 25:9b). This is perhaps an allusion to the consequence for the worship of other gods in Deuteronomy 13:16 (see also Deut. 13:17 and Jer. 30:18). He will make them into "an object of horror and hissing and lasting reproach" (cf. Jer. 19:8; 25:18; 29:18; 42:18; 2 Chr. 29:8). The last term, "lasting reproach" (חרפת עולם), which is in the Hebrew source behind Greek Jeremiah, is replaced by "lasting ruins" (חרבות עולם) in the MT. The "reproach" (or the "ruins") is "lasting" rather than "everlasting" due to the time frame of "seventy years" indicated in Jeremiah 25:11. The Lord will destroy from these people the "sound of rejoicing and sound of joy, sound of bridegroom and sound of bride, scent of myrrh [MT: sound of millstones] and light of lamp" (Jer. 25:10; cf. Jer. 7:34; 16:9; 33:11; Bar. 2:23; Rev. 18:22–23). The sounds of vitality and well-being will no longer be present in the desolate land.[17] The Hebrew source behind Greek Jeremiah has "scent of myrrh" (ריח מור), whereas the MT has "sound of millstones" (קול רחים).[18] According to Redak, "they would grind spices for festive occasions and light many candles."[19]

The difference between the Hebrew source behind Greek Jeremiah 25:11–12 and the MT is once again a difference between a potentially eschatological prophecy and a historical one: "and all the land will become a desolation [MT: and all this land will become a ruin, a desolation], and they will serve among the nations for seventy years [MT: and these nations will serve the king of Babylon for seventy years]" (Jer. 25:11). The land of the covenant will become a desolation, and the people of the land will serve among the nations for "seventy years." This version of the prophecy is very nonspecific and leaves open the possibility that the seventy years may be symbolic of a complete, indefinite period of time (see Dan. 9:24–27). On the other hand, the MT specifically states that the nations (see Jer. 25:9) will serve the king of

---

They also consider Jeremiah and Ezekiel to be contemporaries, making it unlikely that the book of Ezekiel would refer to Jeremiah as one who prophesied in former days. There was overlap between the ministries of these two prophets, but Jeremiah's began in 627 BC, while Ezekiel's began in 593 BC (Ezek. 1:2). The prophecy of Jeremiah 25:1–13 came in 605 BC.

17. "The 'sound of millstones' and the 'light of the lamp' are doubtless intended to signify the beginning 'and the end of the day, and thus all activity between" (Holladay, *Jeremiah 1*, 668).

18. *Targum Jonathan* interprets MT's "sound of millstones and light of lamp" to mean "sound of public assemblies that sing praises by lamp light."

19. Rosenberg, trans., *Mikraoth Gedoloth: Jeremiah Volume One*, 204.

Babylon for seventy years. According to this version of the prophecy, the seventy years are more or less a literal period of time (i.e., a lifetime [see Ps. 90:10; see also Isa. 23:15, 17]) of servitude to the king of Babylon. This is the way the prophecy of seventy years appears in Jeremiah 29:10 in both the Hebrew source behind Greek Jeremiah and the MT. It is also the understanding of the seventy years in Zechariah 1:12 and 2 Chronicles 36:20–21 (see also Dan. 9:2; Ep. Jer. 2; *Sib. Or.* 3:280; *4 Bar.* 5–6).[20] Ezra 1:1 and 2 Chronicles 36:22 appear to identify the year of the decree of Cyrus (539 BC) as the *terminus ad quem* of Jeremiah's prophecy of seventy years (see also Isa. 44:28; 45:1). This would make the first year of Jehoiakim (609 BC) the *terminus a quo*. During this period (609–539 BC), Nebuchadnezzar initially invaded Jerusalem in 605 BC (2 Kgs. 24:1 Dan. 1:1) and subsequently took captives in the years 597 BC, 587 BC, and 582 BC (see MT Jer. 52:28–30). The book of Jeremiah concludes with Jehoiachin still in Babylonian exile in 561 BC (Jer. 52:31–34).

In Daniel 9:1–2, Daniel is reading the prophecy of seventy years in the book of Jeremiah among other prophetic books in the first year of Darius, a subordinate of Cyrus who was given reign over the Chaldean region of the new Medo-Persian empire (see Dan. 1:21; 6:1 [Eng., 5:31]; 7:29; 8:20; 10:1). Daniel considers this year of the decree of Cyrus (Ezra 1:1–4; 6:3–5; 2 Chr. 36:22–23) to be the *terminus ad quem* for Jeremiah's prophecy of seventy years and thus prays that the LORD would now restore the people in fulfillment of that prophecy (Dan. 9:3–19). Such an understanding of the prophecy presupposes that it speaks of a literal period of seventy years, as if Daniel were reading the version of the prophecy in Jeremiah 29:10 (or perhaps the MT version of Jer. 25:11); but when the angel Gabriel appears on the scene to help Daniel with the interpretation (Dan. 9:20–23), he pushes the prophecy into the future indefinitely and says that "seventy sevens" have been determined (Dan. 9:24).[21] Such an eschatological interpretation of

---

20. According to 2 Chronicles 36:21, the fulfilment of Jeremiah's prophecy of seventy years satisfied the land sabbath requirement that had been neglected (see Lev. 25:4; 26:33–35).

21. "Seventy sevens" is often translated "seventy weeks," but since the events of Daniel 9:24–27 did not transpire during the next 490 days, interpreters have opted to interpret "seventy weeks" to mean seventy weeks of years (i.e., 490 years). There are several problems with this interpretation. First, the Hebrew word translated "week" does not mean "week of years" in normal usage (but see *Jub.*; *DCH* 8:226–27). Second, the events of Daniel 9:24–27 did not transpire in the next 490 years beginning with the decree

Jeremiah's prophecy could only have its basis in the Hebrew source behind Greek Jeremiah 25:11. During this complete, indefinite period of "seventy sevens," the city of Jerusalem will be rebuilt in accordance with the decree of Cyrus (Dan. 9:25); the Messiah will be cut off (Dan. 9:26; cf. Isa. 50:4–11; 52:13–53:12; Zech. 12:10; Ps. 22); and the final enemy of the people of God will come to his end (Dan. 9:27; cf. Jer. 25:12–13; Ezek. 39). Thus, the *terminus ad quem* for the literal seventy years of servitude to Babylon becomes the *terminus a quo* for the symbolic seventy years. In the arrangement of the Hebrew Bible found in *Biblia Hebraica Stuttgartensia*, the last three books are Daniel, Ezra-Nehemiah, and Chronicles (see Matt. 23:35; *b. B. Bat.* 14b). The book of Ezra-Nehemiah gives the reader a picture of the postexilic community of Judeans who returned to the land of the covenant in response to the decree of Cyrus after the literal seventy years of servitude to Babylon, which is Daniel's expectation in Daniel 9:3–19. The book of Chronicles, however, provides a comprehensive account of biblical history from Adam in Genesis (1 Chr. 1:1) to the decree of Cyrus in Ezra 1:1–4 (2 Chr. 36:22–23).[22] Thus, the Hebrew Bible concludes with the very decree that begins the period of seventy sevens according to Daniel 9:1–2, 24–27. It is perhaps no accident then that 2 Chronicles

---

of Cyrus in 539 BC. Thus, interpreters have sought to find an appropriate end point from which to work backwards. Critical scholars see the fulfilment of the prophecy in the mid-second century BC during the time of Antiochus Epiphanes, requiring the period of seventy weeks of years to begin in the latter part of the seventh century BC. Conservative scholars see the fulfilment of sixty-nine weeks of years (483 years) in the first century AD, requiring the period to begin with the commissioning of Nehemiah (Neh. 2). This leaves one week of years for the eschaton. It is clear, however, that the decree to rebuild, the decree that begins the seventy sevens, is the decree of Cyrus (Dan. 9:1–2, 25; Ezra 1:1; 2 Chr. 36:22). It is thus preferable to interpret "seventy sevens" to represent a complete, indefinite period of time (cf. Gen. 4:24; Matt. 18:21) during which several delineated events will transpire prior to the establishment of Christ's kingdom on earth. This is in accordance with the characterization of prophecy in 1 Peter 1:10–12, which stresses that the prophets do not speak in terms of chronological timetables. See the discussion in Shepherd, *Daniel in the Context of the Hebrew Bible*, 95–99.

22. See Georg Steins, "Torah-Binding and Canon Closure: On the Origin and Canonical Function of the Book of Chronicles," in *The Shape of the Writings*, eds. Julius Steinberg and Timothy J. Stone, Siphrut: Literature and Theology of the Hebrew Scriptures 16 (Winona Lake, IN: Eisenbrauns, 2015), 237–80.

36:22–23 truncates the decree of Cyrus from Ezra 1:1–4 precisely at the point where an association might be made with the coming of the Messiah: "Whoever among you from all his people, may the LORD his God be with him so that he may go up [i.e., to build the temple]" (2 Chr. 36:23b; cf. "It is he who will build for me a temple" [1 Chr. 17:12a]; see also 2 Sam. 7:13; Zech. 6:12–13).[23]

When the seventy years are over, the LORD will punish the eschatological enemy nation from the north and make the people of that nation into a lasting desolation (Jer. 25:12; cf. Num. 24:7 [LXX]; Deut. 30:7; Ezek. 39; Dan. 9:27; 11:45; Rev. 18:6; 20:8–9). The MT historicizes this prophecy so that the punishment comes upon the king of Babylon and the land of the Chaldeans (cf. Jer. 50:15, 29). The LORD will bring upon "that land" all his words that he has spoken against it, "everything written in this book" (Jer. 25:13). According to the Hebrew source behind Greek Jeremiah, "that land" is the land of the eschatological enemy from the north. According to the MT, it is the land of Babylon. There is considerable debate then about what the referent of "this book" must be. Many commentators assume that a lack of words against a foreign enemy in Jeremiah 1:1–25:13 requires "this book" to include something that follows 25:13 in the present form of the book of Jeremiah—either the cup of judgment passage (Jer. 25:15–26), which includes judgment of the kings of the north (Jer. 25:26a) and, at least in MT 25:26b, judgment of Babylon, or the collection of oracles about the foreign nations in Jeremiah 46–51 (see Jer. 51:60–64), which appear in a different arrangement directly after 25:13 in the Hebrew source behind Greek Jeremiah, including the oracles against Babylon (Jer. 50–51) that serve to prefigure the downfall of the final enemy from the north (see, e.g., Jer. 50:15, 29; Rev. 18:6).[24] On the other hand, the phrasing of "everything written in this book" suggests that it is not proleptic; rather, it points to the preceding material as the content

---

23. See John H. Sailhamer, "Biblical Theology and the Composition of the Hebrew Bible," in *Biblical Theology: Retrospect and Prospect*, ed. Scott J. Hafemann (Downers Grove, IL: InterVarsity, 2002), 34–37.

24. In the arrangement of the oracles against the nations in the Hebrew source behind Greek Jeremiah, the first and last sections end with references to the last days (Jer. 49:39 [LXX 26:19] and 48:47 [the text of 48:45–47a, which would be the end of chapter 29 in the LXX, is missing in the LXX due to homoioteleuton; the following editorial note in MT 48:47b is also absent]). This creates an eschatological framework for these oracles so that the words of historical judgment (and restoration) may be read as illustrations of things to come.

of "this book" (cf. Deut. 28:58; 29:19, 26 [Eng., 29:20, 27]). Since the content of the scroll of Jeremiah thus far has primarily been about the judgment of Judah and Jerusalem (see Jer. 36), Holladay suggests that "that land" upon which the LORD will bring his words was originally "the land" (i.e., the land of Judah; cf. Rudolph in *BHS* apparatus: "this land").[25] Of course, the difficulty with this is that there is no evidence for such a reading among the extant textual witnesses. Furthermore, it is possible to make sense of 25:13 even if "that land" refers to the enemy (and even if "this book" refers to 1:1–25:13). While it is true that much of 1:1–25:13 anticipates the impending judgment of Judah and Jerusalem, it is also true that it anticipates the vindication of the true people of God (Jer. 1:10b; 3:14–17; 4:1–4; 23:5–8; 24:6–7) in such a manner that the tables will be turned on their enemies (see Jer. 12:14–17; 25:12). Just as their enemies have done to them, so will it be done to their enemies (see Jer. 50:15, 29; Rev. 18:6, 22–23; cf. Obad. 15). Thus, all the words against Judah and Jerusalem in 1:1–25:13 will become words against the enemy nation.

MT Jeremiah 25:13b2 is a relative clause that modifies "everything written in this book": "which Jeremiah prophesied against all the nations." But in the Hebrew source behind Greek Jeremiah, this text is a heading to a following collection of oracles about the nations: "That which Jeremiah prophesied concerning the nations" (= LXX Jer. 29:14). MT Jeremiah 25:14 is an added verse not found in the Hebrew source behind Greek Jeremiah: "For they too, many nations and great kings, have served by them, and I will repay them according to their work and according to the work of their hands." Many commentaries and translations assume the verb עבדו to be a so-called "prophetic perfect" ("will serve"). They also assume the pronoun "them" to refer to the Babylonians, in which case the Babylonians will be in servitude to many nations as repayment for what they have done (cf. Jer. 27:7). Another possibility is that the verb should be translated "have served" (background *qatal*). The first pronoun "them" refers to the people of Judah and Jerusalem. The second refers to the nations. According to this interpretation, the people of Judah and Jerusalem have been in servitude in various ways to many nations throughout their history, but the LORD will repay those nations according to what they have done (cf. Jer. 30:8). In the MT, this anticipates the cup of judgment for the nations in Jeremiah 25:15–26.

The original scroll of Jeremiah (Jer. 1:1–25:13), which was dictated to Baruch in 605 BC (Jer. 25:1; 36:1–4), likely concluded with the scribal

---

25. Holladay, *Jeremiah 1*, 669.

colophon featuring Baruch in Jeremiah 45, which is also dated to 605 BC (Jer. 45:1). As the book grew to include the oracles concerning the nations as well as the rest of the material that now constitutes the second half of the Hebrew source behind Greek Jeremiah (Jer. 36:32), this colophon always remained at the end until the addition of the appendix in Jeremiah 52. Of course, the MT has rearranged the oracles concerning the nations and moved them from after 25:13 to chapters 46–51 between the colophon (Jer. 45) and the appendix (Jer. 52).

APPLICATION OF JEREMIAH 21:1–25:13

This segment of the book of Jeremiah has featured the convergence of the messianic hope (Jer. 23:5–6) with the hope of redemption from the enemy from the north (Jer. 23:7–8; 24:6–7; 25:8–13). The righteous Davidic Messiah (Jer. 23:5–6) stands in stark contrast to the sons of Josiah who face judgment due to their lack of righteousness (Jer. 21:1–23:4; 24:8–10). As the prophet like Moses (Deut. 18:15, 18; 34:10; Luke 9:35; John 6:14; Acts 3:22; 7:37), this messianic figure also contrasts with the false prophets (Jer. 23:9–40). The enemy from the north (Jer. 1:13–15; 4:5–6:30) will come in the last days as God's instrument of judgment (Jer. 25:8–11; Ezek. 38:14–17), but this enemy will ultimately fall in defeat to the Messiah in a final battle (Jer. 25:12–13; see Gen. 49:11–12; Num. 24:7 [LXX]; Isa. 63:1–6; Ezek. 39; Joel 4 [Eng., 3]; Zech. 12; 14; Rev. 16:16; 19:11–21; 20:8–9). In this manner the two parts of the program of Jeremiah 1:10, judgment and restoration, will come to fruition (see Jer. 24:6). Thus, the book of Jeremiah is a messianic book not in the way that readers predetermine it should be, whether verse by verse or section by section, but in the textual portrait of the Messiah that emerges over the course of the book's composition as a whole in conversation with other books of the biblical canon. This does not consist of mere prediction but of revelatory imagery (1 Pet. 1:10–12); and much the same way that one part of a portrait does not give the whole picture, so one part of the text of Jeremiah does not give the whole image of the Messiah. It is the whole image of the Messiah to which the NT authors appeal for their explanation of the historical Jesus of Nazareth (e.g., Luke 24:25–27, 44).

The apostle Paul tells Timothy that from his youth he has known "the holy Scriptures, which are able to make you wise for salvation through faith in Christ Jesus" (2 Tim. 3:15). Since there were no NT documents in Timothy's youth, the "holy Scriptures" here are the Hebrew Scriptures, including the book of Jeremiah. All such Scripture is "God-breathed and beneficial for teaching, rebuking, correcting, and training in righteousness in order that the man of God may be complete, equipped for every good work" (2 Tim. 3:16–17; see also 2 Pet. 1:19–21). The biblical revelation of wisdom for salvation through faith in Christ Jesus is sufficient for the believer. Unfortunately, the temptation for many Bible teachers and preachers is to take the already applicable biblical text and add application to it, as if the task were to transform the Bible into one long set of instructions. Of course, the Bible contains legal and proverbial exhortation, propositional statements, and the like, but there is more to the Bible than that. There is narrative, poetry, and prophecy of a theological nature designed to be understood and believed for the renewing of the mind (Rom. 12:1–2) and for holy living (2 Pet. 3:11). The path from understanding and faith to the renewing of the mind and holiness cannot be short-circuited by added applications generated by teachers and preachers. Such applications are generally motivated by concerns stemming from tradition, contemporary Christian culture, or from the culture at large and are often the sort of generic application that could be made from any work of literature. The rule seems to be that any application is fair game as long as it does not go against any major systematic doctrine; but if the unique, special revelation of the Bible is desired, then the texts must be allowed to speak on their own terms and according to their own agenda.

THE NATIONS

part from overall length, the most substantial macrostructural difference between the Hebrew source behind Greek Jeremiah and MT Jeremiah is the arrangement and placement of the oracles concerning the nations. Both Isaiah (Isa. 13–23) and Ezekiel (Ezek. 25–32) have their collections of oracles about the nations earlier in their books rather than at the end. This is the way the oracles appear in the Hebrew source behind Greek Jeremiah. After the heading provided in Jeremiah 25:13b2 (= LXX 25:14), the oracles occur in the following order: Elam (Jer. 49:34–39), Egypt (Jer. 46:2–28), Babylon (Jer. 50–51), Philistia (Jer. 47), Edom (Jer. 49:7–22), Ammon (Jer. 49:1–6), Kedar (Jer. 49:28–33), Damascus (Jer. 49:23–27), and Moab (Jeremiah 48).[1] The first and last of these oracles conclude with the phrase "at the end of the days" (Jer. 49:39 and 48:47; cf. Jer. 23:20; 30:24),[2] thus providing an eschatological framework for the entire collection. This eschatological framework, which makes the historical messages into illustrations of things to come, has had a great influence on other biblical authors. In particular, the apostle John sees Babylon in Jeremiah 50–51 as a prefiguration of the final enemy (see Rev. 17–18).

---

1. Immediately following this collection is the passage about the cup of judgment for all the nations to drink (Jer. 25:15–38 [= LXX 32:1–24]).
2. Jeremiah 48:45–47 is lacking in the LXX, but this is likely due to scribal or translator oversight. The scribe or translator accidentally skipped from נאם יהוה at the end of 48:44b to נאם יהוה at the end of 48:47a, omitting the intervening text (homoioteleuton). נאם יהוה was subsequently dropped altogether from the end of 48:44b either from the source text or in translation. The note in 48:47b is an editorial addition in the MT.

The MT has rearranged these oracles, provided them with a new heading (MT Jer. 46:1 [> LXX]), and placed them at the end of the book (Jer. 46–51). This new arrangement appears to have its basis in the sequence of the nations to which the cup of judgment passes in MT Jeremiah 25:19–26: Egypt (Jer. 25:19; 46), Philistia (Jer. 25:20; 47), Edom/Moab/Ammon (Jer. 25:21; 48:1–49:22 [Moab/Ammon/Edom]), Elam (Jer. 25:25; 49:34–39), and Babylon (Jer. 25:26; 50–51).[3] The placement of this newly arranged collection after Jeremiah 42–44 is logical, although it does overlook the formal conclusion to the book in chapter 45, which is a short scribal colophon that now appears between 42–44 and 46–51 in the MT. Chapters 42–44 narrate the decision of the Judeans left in the land after the Babylonian invasion to flee to Egypt. The first oracle in the MT's collection is then about Egypt (Jer. 46:2). The last nation in the MT's collection, which receives two lengthy chapters, is Babylon (Jer. 50–51). Since the MT views Babylon as the enemy from the north (Jer. 25:9) whose invasion forms the culmination of the book's prophecy, it is only fitting that the MT would relocate chapters 50–51 to the climactic end of the book just prior to the appendix in chapter 52 (cf. 2 Kgs. 25), which gives a second account of the Babylonian invasion within the book (cf. MT Jer. 39). This historicization of the book's prophecy is one of the fundamental differences in message between MT Jeremiah and the Hebrew source behind Greek Jeremiah, which is eschatological in its orientation.

As noted in the commentary on Jeremiah 1:5, 10, Jeremiah is a prophet to the nations. His message for the nations is not solely one of judgment. It is also a message of restoration (Jer. 1:10b; 3:17; 4:2; 12:14–17; 16:19; 48:47; 49:39; see also MT 46:26b; 49:6). Thus, just as Jeremiah distinguishes between unbelievers to be judged and believers to be delivered among the people of Judah and Israel (Jer. 3:1–4:4), so he does with the nations.

---

3.   The only nations in Jeremiah 46–51 that do not appear in 25:19–26 are Damascus/Syria (Jer. 49:23–27) and Kedar (Jer. 49:28–33), although MT 25:23–24 mentions Dedan, Tema, and Arabia with which Kedar is associated in Isaiah 21:13–17. MT Jeremiah 25:19–26 also mentions Tyre, Sidon, and Media (Jer. 25:22, 25) who do not have oracles in Jeremiah 46–51.

ELAM

(Jer. 25:13b2; 49:34–39; 46:1 [= LXX 25:14–19; 26:1])

25:13b2 (25:14a)[1] That which Jeremiah prophesied concerning[2] the nations:

49:34 (25:14b) Concerning Elam:[3]

---

1. The Göttingen Septuagint and the NETS make the last verse of this unit the first verse of chapter 26 (= MT chapter 46), even though this verse clearly belongs with what precedes it rather than with what follows it. It is not equivalent to MT Jeremiah 46:1. Rahlfs more appropriately makes this verse the last verse of LXX chapter 25 (i.e., verse 20) and leaves LXX chapter 26 without a verse 1. The verse has no exact equivalent in the MT (but see MT 49:34). It is counted here as 46:1 only because of the arrangement in the Göttingen Septuagint and the NETS and because there is no way to indicate equivalent versification in the MT.
2. The preposition עַל is translated "concerning" here because the oracles are not simply "against" the nations (see Jer. 48:47; 49:6, 39) nor are they directly "to" the nations.
3. The NETS combines 25:13b2 (25:14a) and 49:34 (25:14b) in its translation: "What Ieremias prophesied against the nations of Ailam." The present translation is based on the understanding that there are two distinct headings here, one for the entire collection of oracles concerning the nations and one for the first oracle, which is about Elam (see William McKane, *A Critical and Exegetical Commentary on Jeremiah*, vol. 2, *Introduction and Commentary on Jeremiah XXVI–LII*, ICC [London: Bloomsbury T&T Clark, 1996], 1245). The MT has a much longer text for 49:34: "That which was the word of the LORD to Jeremiah the prophet concerning Elam in the beginning of the kingdom of Zedekiah the king of Judah, saying." A slightly different form of this text in MT 49:34 appears after 49:34–39 (25:14–19) in the Hebrew source behind Greek Jeremiah.

49:35 (25:15) Thus says the LORD *[MT adds: of hosts], "Break the bow of Elam [NETS: Let the bow of Ailam be crushed; MT: Look, I am about to break the bow (Tg. Jon.: strength) of Elam], the principal source of their might. 49:36 (25:16) And I will bring to Elam four winds [Tg. Jon.: four kingdoms] from the four ends of the sky, and I will scatter them to all these winds, and there will not be a nation [MT: the nation] where it will not come [nonn Mss: where they will not come], those banished from Elam [MT kethiv: those banished indefinitely]. 49:37 (25:17) And I will cause them [MT: Elam] to be dismayed [Syr., Tg. Jon.: And I will break Elam] before their enemies who seek their life [MT: before their enemies and before those who seek their life], and I will bring upon them calamity, the burning of my anger, [MT adds: the prophetic utterance of the* LORD*], and I will send after them my sword [MT: the sword] .until I finish them off. 49:38 (25:18) And I will set my throne in Elam and send away [MT: destroy][4] from there king and officials, [MT adds: the prophetic utterance of the* LORD*]. 49:39 (25:19) And then, at the end of the days, I will restore the fortunes [LXX: captivity] of Elam," the prophetic utterance of the* LORD*.*

46:1 (26:1) In the beginning of the kingdom of Zedekiah the king, this word came concerning Elam.

The Hebrew source behind Greek Jeremiah features a heading for the entire collection of oracles concerning the nations—"That which Jeremiah prophesied concerning the nations"[5] (Jer. 25:13b2 [LXX 25:14a]; cf. MT Jer. 14:1; 46:1; 47:1)—and a heading for the first section, which is about Elam: "Concerning Elam" (Jer. 49:34 [LXX 25:14b]). These oracles are not simply "against" the nations (see Jer. 48:47; 49:6, 39) nor are they "to" the nations. There is no indication that they were to be addressed and delivered to the nations in either oral or written form. Rather, they are designed to be read by readers of the book of Jeremiah. The text of MT Jeremiah 49:34 ("That which was the word of the LORD to Jeremiah the prophet concerning Elam in the beginning of the kingdom of Zedekiah the king of Judah, saying") is a reworked and relocated version of what appears at the end of 49:34–39 (LXX 25:14–19; see also MT 28:1) in the Hebrew source behind Greek Jeremiah: "In the beginning of the kingdom of Zedekiah the king, this word came

---

4.   Rudolph wonders whether καὶ ἐξαποστελῶ (= וֹשׁלחתי) is a corruption from καὶ ἐξαπολέσω (= והאבדתי) (see *BHS* apparatus).
5.   In the MT, this is a relative clause modifying "everything written in this book" (Jer. 25:13).

concerning Elam" (LXX 26:1). The MT's heading for the entire collection of oracles concerning the nations is in MT Jeremiah 46:1 (> LXX).

Elam appears elsewhere in the Bible as an early invader of Palestine (Gen. 14:1, 9), a place of dispersed Israelites (Isa. 11:11), a foe of Babylon (Isa. 21:2), and an ally of Assyria (Isa. 22:6) (BDB, 743; see also Gen. 10:22 [= 1 Chr. 1:17]; Jer. 25:25; Ezek. 32:24; Dan. 8:2). In response to the view of Heinrich Ewald that Elam had been an ally of the Babylonians in the deposition of Jehoiachin (see also *b. Sanh.* 89a), Keil comments, "The prophecy itself contains not the slightest indication of any hostility on the part of the Elamites towards Judah; nor is anything proved regarding this by the fact that the chastisement is not said to proceed from Nebuchadnezzar."[6]

In the Hebrew source behind Greek Jeremiah 49:35a (LXX 25:15a), the LORD gives a command (a masculine singular imperative): "Break (שְׁבֹר) the bow of Elam" (NETS: "Let the bow of Ailam be crushed"). The MT, however, has a participle: "Look, I am about to break (שֹׁבֵר) the bow of Elam."[7] The Elamites were apparently well known for their archery (see Isa. 22:6). Their "bow" here is synecdoche (part for the whole) for their military might (cf. Hos. 1:5). Thus, *Targum Jonathan* translates "bow" as "strength" (see also Rashi). By means of apposition, Jeremiah 49:35b (LXX 25:15b) calls the bow of Elam "the principal source (רֵאשִׁית) of their might" (Rashi: "the best of their might").

The LORD will bring to Elam "four winds from the four ends of the sky" and scatter them to all these winds (Jer. 49:36a [LXX 25:16a]; cf. Jer. 49:32 [LXX 30:27]; Ezek. 5:10; 12:14; 37:9; Zech. 2:10 [Eng., 2:6]; 6:5; Dan. 7:2; 8:8; Matt. 24:31; Rev. 7:1). *Targum Jonathan* interprets the four winds to be four kingdoms (see also Calvin), but it is possible that "far-flung dispersion" in every direction (north, south, east, and west) is all that is meant here.[8] "There will not be a nation [MT: the nation] where it will not come [nonn Mss: where they will not come], those banished from Elam [MT *kethiv*: those banished indefinitely]" (Jer. 49:36b [LXX 25:16b]). Calvin considers this language to be hyperbolic and comments that it likely refers to dispersion among

---

6. Keil, *Jeremiah*, 417.
7. According to the Talmud, the false prophet Hananiah constructed an argument *a fortiori* from these words (see Neusner, *Jeremiah in Talmud and Midrash*, 353). Since the LORD said that he would break the bow of Elam for helping the Babylonians, how much more would he break the bow of the Babylonians themselves (see Jer. 28:2)?
8. See McKane, *Jeremiah XXVI–LII*, 1246–47.

neighboring nations.[9] The language is perhaps hyperbolic, but it need not be limited to neighboring nations. The last phrase of 49:36b (LXX 25:16b), "those banished from Elam" (נדחי עילם), appears in the MT *kethiv* as "those banished indefinitely" (נדחי עולם).

At the beginning of 49:37a (LXX 25:17a), the LORD says, "And I will cause them [MT: Elam] to be dismayed" (cf. MT Jer. 1:17). The verb here is a *hiphil* of חתת ("to be shattered, dismayed, terrified"). The Syriac and *Targum Jonathan* both translate, "And I will break Elam." McKane argues that the verb should be translated "shatter" so that 49:37 (LXX 25:17) may be read as a continuation of 49:35 (LXX 25:15), which uses שבר ("break").[10] The LORD will either cause them to be dismayed or shatter them "before their enemies who seek their life" (לפני איביהם מבקשי נפשם) (cf. Jer. 22:25; 46:26 [MT]). The MT has "before their enemies and before those who seek their life" (לפני איביהם ולפני מבקשי נפשם). The LORD will bring upon them calamity, the burning of his anger (Jer. 49:37a [LXX 25:17a]) and send after them his sword to finish them off (Jer. 49:37b [LXX 25:17b]; cf. Jer. 9:15 [Eng., 9:16]).

The LORD will set his throne in Elam (Jer. 49:38a [LXX 25:18a]). That is, he will establish his authority in Elam (cf. Isa. 16:5; Jer. 1:15; 43:10; Dan. 7:9–10). Multiple passages in the rabbinic literature interpret this to be one of several biblical texts indicating that God went with his people everywhere they went into exile (1 Sam. 2:27; Isa. 43:14; 63:1),[11] but the present oracle does not speak of an exile of God's people (see, however, Isa. 11:11). According to the presumed Hebrew source behind Greek Jeremiah 49:38b (LXX 25:18b), the LORD will "send away" (*piel* of שלח) from Elam "king and officials." It is possible, however, that the Greek text here is misleading (see note to translation above). According to the MT, the LORD will "destroy" (*hiphil* of אבד) from there "king and officials."[12]

The oracle concerning Elam then takes an interesting turn: "And then, at the end of the days, I will restore the fortunes [LXX: captivity]

---

9. Calvin, *Jeremiah*, 5:116–17.

10. McKane, *Jeremiah XXVI–LII*, 1246–47.

11. Neusner, *Jeremiah in Talmud and Midrash*, 17, 22, 42, 74, 258.

12. Redak: "Our Rabbis explain the verse as an allusion to Vashti, Haman, and his sons, for the entire event was for the benefit of Israel in their exile. They identify the 'king' as Vashti and the 'princes' as Haman and his ten sons" (A. J. Rosenberg, trans., *Mikraoth Gedoloth: Jeremiah Volume Two* [Brooklyn: Judaica, 1989], 380). McKane also equates Elam with Persia (*Jeremiah XXVI–LII*, 1248).

of Elam" (Jer. 49:39 [LXX 25:19]; cf. Jer. 12:15; 46:26b; 48:47; 49:6; see also Ezek. 29:14). Ephrem the Syrian, appealing to Romans 15:4 ("Whatever was written of old was written for our instruction"), comments, "Thus, the Holy Spirit ordered Jeremiah and other prophets to record events of the captivity and of the return of magnificent and great nations in their own time, so that we would have a clear and vivid depiction of our slavery under the burden of Satan, as well as providing us with a picture of the divine household of our Lord who, through his death, bestowed on us life and redemption."[13] This shows a remarkable awareness of the influence of the phrase "at the end of the days" in the first (Jer. 49:39) and last (Jer. 48:47) of the oracles concerning the nations in the arrangement found within the Hebrew source behind Greek Jeremiah. The historical messages for the nations are now pictures of eschatological realities. Calvin sees the fulfilment of Jeremiah 49:39 (or at least its inauguration) in Luke's reference to the Elamites in his account of Pentecost (Acts 2:9).[14] Keil also understands Jeremiah 49:39 to be about the messianic future.[15] Indeed, he interprets the entire oracle concerning Elam to represent something much larger than the particular historical situation of the nation: "In this prophecy, Elam is not considered in its historical relation to the people of Israel, but as the representative of the heathen world lying beyond, which has not hitherto come into any relation towards the people of Israel, but which nevertheless, along with it, falls under the judgment coming on all nations, in order that, through the judgment, it may be led to the knowledge of the true God, and share in His salvation."[16]

The phrase "at the end of the days" (באחרית הימים) is the same one found with the major poems of the Pentateuch (Gen. 49:1; Num. 24:14; Deut. 31:29; see also Deut. 4:30), which interpret the blocks of narrative that precede them in an eschatological and messianic fashion.[17] It is the same phrase that appears in the programmatic passages (Isa. 2:2 [= Mic. 4:1]; Hos. 3:5) and restoration sections of the Prophets (Jer.

---

13. Wenthe, ed., *Jeremiah, Lamentations*, 258.
14. Calvin, *Jeremiah*, 5:119–20.
15. Keil, *Jeremiah*, 419. See also McKane, *Jeremiah XXVI–LII*, 1248.
16. Keil, *Jeremiah*, 420. Holladay likewise says that Elam symbolizes universality: "it is difficult to discern any motivation for this addition [i.e., Jer. 49:39] except an affirmation of ultimate universalism, an affirmation that must stem from a time well into the Persian period" (*Jeremiah 2: A Commentary on the Book of the Prophet Jeremiah Chapters 26–52*, Hermeneia [Minneapolis: Fortress, 1989], 389).
17. See Sailhamer, *Pentateuch as Narrative*, 35–37.

30:24 [= Jer. 23:20]; Ezek. 38:16).[18] It is also the same phrase that appears with the first and last visions of the book of Daniel (Dan. 2:28 [in Aramaic]; 10:14).[19] The expression "restore the fortunes" normally refers to restoration of the people of God (e.g., Deut. 30:3; Jer. 30:3). It is evident from the larger context of the book of Jeremiah that this includes believing Gentiles (Jer. 1:5, 10; 3:17; 4:2; 12:14–17; 16:19; 46:26 [MT]; 48:47; 49:6 [MT]). The LXX translates this same expression as "restore the captivity." A decision on this matter largely depends on two factors. First, there is the issue of the root for the noun שבות (*kethiv*: שבית). Does it come from שוב ("turn") and thus form a cognate object of the main verb, or does it come from שבה ("take captive")? The second factor is the context. There are some contexts where the translation of this expression as "restore the captivity" makes very little sense (e.g., Job 42:10). In the present context, there is no reference to the captivity of the general populace of Elam. There is only a reference to the scattering of the people (Jer. 49:36) and either the sending away or the destruction of their king and their officials (Jer. 49:38). Thus, it seems more appropriate to render the expression here as "restore the fortunes."[20]

As noted above, the concluding notice in the Hebrew source behind LXX 26:1 ("In the beginning of the kingdom of Zedekiah the king, this word came concerning Elam") has been reworked and relocated to 49:34 in the MT ("That which was the word of the LORD to Jeremiah the prophet concerning Elam in the beginning of the kingdom of Zedekiah the king of Judah, saying") (cf. Jer. 28:1).

---

18. See Shepherd, *Commentary on the Book of the Twelve*, 24–25, 53–54.
19. See Shepherd, *Daniel in the Context of the Hebrew Bible*, 72–75, 99–104.
20. See also McKane, *Jeremiah XXVI–LII*, 1247–48; *TLOT* 3:1314–15.

EGYPT

(Jer. 46:2–28 [= LXX 26:2–28])

[MT adds: 46:1 That which was the word of the Lord *to Jeremiah the prophet concerning (mlt Mss add: all) the nations:]*

46:2 (26:2) About Egypt:

Concerning the army of Pharaoh Necho [Syr., Tg. Jon.: the lame (= נָכֶה)][1] the king of Egypt, which was by the river Euphrates at Carchemish, which Nebuchadnezzar [MT: Nebuchadrezzar] the king of Babylon struck in the fourth year of Jehoiakim [MT adds: the son of Josiah] the king of Judah:

46:3 (26:3) [Syr. adds: Thus says the strong Lord, the God of Israel] "Arrange small shield and large shield [LXX: Take up weapons and shields] and draw near to the battle! 46:4 (26:4) Saddle the horses; mount [MT: and mount], O horsemen! And take your stations with your helmets [MT: with helmets]; throw [MT: polish] the spears, and [and > MT] put on the armor [LXX: your breastplates]! 46:5 (26:5) Why are they dismayed / terrified and turning back? [MT: Why do I see? They are dismayed / terrified (Syr., Tg. Jon.: broken), turning back.] Because their mighty men [MT: And their mighty men], they will be crushed. In flight [MT: And in flight] they have fled [or, A fleeing have they fled] and not returned, terror on every side [LXX: surrounded all around]," the prophetic utterance of the Lord. *46:6 (26:6) Let not the swift flee, and let*

---

1. The tradition behind the designation "Pharaoh the lame" in the Syriac and *Targum Jonathan* is explained in Rosenberg, trans., *Mikraoth Gedoloth: Jeremiah Volume Two*, 346 (see also Syr., *Tg. Jon.* Jer. 44:30).

not the mighty escape [or, The swift cannot flee, and the mighty cannot escape (see GKC §107p)]. Northward [Syr.: Among the mighty men] by the Euphrates [MT: by the river Euphrates] they have stumbled [LXX: they are weak], they have fallen [MT: and they have fallen].[2] *46:7 (26:7) Who is like the Nile [LXX: a river] that goes up [or, Who is this that goes up like the Nile; Tg. Jon.: Who is this who goes up with his armies like a cloud that goes up and covers the land],*[3] *and like the streams that toss about with water [MT: whose waters toss about]? 46:8 (26:8) The waters of Egypt are like the Nile [LXX: a river] that goes up [MT: Egypt (Syr.: The king of Egypt; Tg. Jon.: Pharaoh the king of Egypt) is like the Nile that goes up (or, Egypt like the Nile goes up)] [MT adds: and like the streams that toss about with water].*[4] *And he said, 'I will go up and [and > MT] cover land and [and > MT] destroy [MT adds: city and] inhabitants therein.'*[5] *46:9 (26:9) Mount on the horses [MT: Go up, O horses], [MT adds: and] go madly, O chariots [LXX: prepare the chariots]! Go forth, O mighty men [MT: And let the mighty men go forth], Cush and Put [LXX: of Ethiopians and Libyans], graspers of a small shield [LXX: armed with weapons], and Lydians, grasp, bend a bow [MT: graspers of benders of a bow]! 46:10 (26:10) And that day belongs to the LORD our God [MT: to the Lord GOD of hosts], a day of vengeance to take vengeance on his foes. And a sword of the LORD [of the LORD > MT] will devour and be sated and saturated from their blood, for a sacrifice of the LORD [MT: of the Lord GOD of hosts] will be from [MT: in] (the) land of the north by the river Euphrates. 46:11 (26:11) Go up to Gilead and take balm, O virgin daughter Egypt [LXX: Go up, O Gilead, and take balm to the virgin daughter of Egypt]! In vain have you increased [see GKC §44h; Syr.: have I increased] your [> MT] medicines. There is no healing [LXX: help] for you. 46:12 (26:12) Nations have heard your voice [MT: your disgrace], and the inhabited earth is full of your outcry [or, and*

---

2. "It is not clear to what τά refers. Brenton, who takes ἐπὶ βορρᾶν with the preceding, translates 'the *forces* at Euphrates,' thus adding 'forces.' If ἐπὶ βορρᾶν is taken with the following, τὰ παρὰ τὸν Εὐφράτην can be taken as a qualifier to ἐπὶ βορρᾶν. τά, then, refers to the place/places at Euphrates, hence it is rendered by 'by Euphrates' in the present translation" (Walser, *Jeremiah*, 342).

3. See Shepherd, "So-called Emphasis," 183–86.

4. Note how this addition in the MT matches the Hebrew source behind Greek Jeremiah 46:7b but not MT 46:7b.

5. The coordination of cohortative forms may express purpose: "I will go up in order to cover land and destroy inhabitants therein" (see GKC §108d). In the MT, the noncoordinated forms each express determination or resolve.

your outcry has filled the inhabited earth]. For one mighty man over another they stumble, together [Syr.: by the sword] they both fall."

MT Jeremiah 46:1, which does not appear in the Hebrew source behind Greek Jeremiah, is a newly added heading for the rearranged and relocated oracles concerning the nations in MT Jeremiah: "That which was the word of the LORD to Jeremiah the prophet concerning [mlt Mss add: all] the nations" (cf. Jer. 14:1; 47:1; 49:34). McKane considers it an elaboration of Jeremiah 25:13b2: "this should be taken as an indication that the place where the oracles against foreign nations are introduced in Sept. was once the place which they occupied in MT and that they were subsequently removed to their extant position at the end of the book of Jeremiah."[6]

The heading "About Egypt" (למצרים) at the beginning of 46:2 (LXX 26:2) is for the entire chapter (cf. Jer. 23:9; 48:1; 49:1, 7, 23, 28). The heading in the remainder of 46:2 ("Concerning the army of Pharaoh Necho") and the one in 46:13 are subheadings. Other prominent oracles about Egypt in the prophetic literature include Isaiah 19–20 and Ezekiel 29–32. The first subsection of the chapter in 46:2–12 (LXX 26:2–12) concerns Pharaoh Necho's army, which came to Carchemish by the river Euphrates and which Nebuchadnezzar struck in the fourth year of Jehoiakim (605 BC) (see also Jer. 25:1; 36:1; 45:1). In 609 BC, Pharaoh Necho went up to the Euphrates to aid the king of Assyria against the advancing Babylonian army (2 Kgs. 23:29a). According to 2 Chronicles 35:20a, he came specifically to Carchemish. When Josiah, whose great grandfather Hezekiah had been friendly with the Babylonians (2 Kgs. 20:12–13), came to confront Necho as he passed from Egypt through the land of Israel, Necho killed Josiah at Megiddo (2 Kgs. 23:29b; see 2 Chr. 35:23). According to the Chronicler, Josiah confronted Necho despite a proper warning from God that came through messengers sent by Necho to Josiah (2 Chr. 35:21–22). Josiah's son Jehoahaz/Shallum briefly reigned after his father's death but was subsequently removed by Necho and replaced by his brother Eliakim whom Necho renamed Jehoiakim (2 Kgs. 23:31–34; 2 Chr. 36:1–4). Jehoiakim was then required to pay Necho (2 Kgs. 23:35). Most commentators assume that Nebuchadnezzar's subsequent defeat of Necho in 605 BC was divine judgment for these actions (see, e.g., comments on Jer. 46:10), although the text of Jeremiah 46:2–12 does not make this explicit. In the larger context of the book of Jeremiah and in the subsequent history of relations between Egypt and Judah, Egypt proves to be an unreliable ally

---

6. McKane, *Jeremiah XXVI–LII*, 1109.

and refuge for Judah precisely because of its inability to withstand the Babylonians (see Jer. 37:5–8; 42:13–17; 43:8–13; 44:30).

Jeremiah 46:3–12 divides into two main parts: 46:3–6 and 46:7–12. In the first part, the soldiers of the Egyptian army are commanded to prepare for battle (Jer. 46:3–4) and then are depicted in flight from their enemies (Jer. 46:5–6). In the second, Egypt rises like the Nile to cover the land (Jer. 46:7–9) only to face defeat from which it cannot recover (Jer. 46:10–12). The whole of this first half of the chapter is neither a simple narrative of a past event nor a mere prediction of something yet to come. It is a poetic image of the LORD's day of vengeance against his enemies, including Egypt in particular (Jer. 46:10).

There is some question as to the identity of the speaker barking the imperatives in 46:3–4 (LXX 26:3–4). The Syriac begins 46:3 with an added introduction to the LORD as the speaker: "Thus says the strong Lord, the God of Israel." This addition agrees with נאם יהוה ("the prophetic utterance of the LORD") at the end of 46:5. If the LORD is the speaker here, then the commands form an ironic challenge to those who will eventually flee and fall in defeat (cf. Joel 4:9–15 [Eng., 3:9–15]).[7] Others suggest that the imperatives come from the Egyptian officers, in which case they are genuine orders to prepare for battle.[8] There is also a question about the group to whom the orders are given. Redak suggests that they could be addressed either to Nebuchadnezzar's army or to Pharaoh Necho's army,[9] but most commentators understand the soldiers in Necho's army to be the recipients. The commands to arrange small and large shields and draw near to the battle are essentially orders to arrange in battle array (Jer. 46:3 [LXX 26:3; cf. Jer. 50:14; see also 1 Kgs. 10:16–17). Holladay considers the orders to the horsemen to saddle their horses and mount them to be ironic (Jer. 46:4a [LXX 26:4a]).[10] The soldiers are commanded, "And take your stations with

---

7. This assumes that the commands are addressed to the Egyptian army. If they are addressed to the Babylonian army, then they are genuine orders for them to do the LORD's bidding against the Egyptians.

8. E.g., Bright, *Jeremiah*, 305.

9. Rosenberg, trans., *Mikraoth Gedoloth: Jeremiah Volume Two*, 346.

10. "The phraseology in Isa 31:1 suggests that the Egyptians boasted in their chariotry, but the skills and equipment necessary for cavalry evidently came from the steppes of Asia into Mesopotamia, and from there into Europe. These battle orders are thus ironic, reminding the hearer of this lack in the Egyptian forces (compare the mockery of the Assyrian commander to those in Jerusalem in regard to their depending on Egypt for chariots and horsemen, 2 Kgs 18:23–24)" (Holladay, *Jeremiah 2*, 319–20).

your helmets [MT: with helmets]" (cf. Jer. 46:14), and, according to the Hebrew source behind Greek Jeremiah, "throw (רמו) the spears, and [and > MT] put on the armor [LXX: your breastplates]" (Jer. 46:4 [LXX 26:4]; cf. 2 Chr. 26:14)! In place of "throw" (רמו), the MT has "polish" (מרקו). Rudolph refers to the proposal "draw out" (הרקו) based on Psalm 35:3 (see *BHS* apparatus). The armor that the soldiers are to wear is specifically scale-armor or a coat of mail.

As soon as the orders are given for the army to prepare for battle (Jer. 46:3–4), a question is asked about the army's flight: "Why are they dismayed/terrified and turning back" (Jer. 46:5 [LXX 26:5])? The MT inserts ראיתי after the initial interrogative: "Why do I see (ראיתי)? They are dismayed/terrified [Syr., *Tg. Jon.*: broken], turning back" (cf. Jer. 30:6b). McKane suggests that this secondary insertion is "connected with an intention to describe visionary experience" (cf. Jer. 4:23–26).[11] The Hebrew source behind Greek Jeremiah provides an answer to the question: "Because (כי) their mighty men, they will be crushed." The MT does not: "And their mighty men, they will be crushed." "In flight [MT: And in flight] they have fled [or, A fleeing have they fled] and not returned, terror on every side [LXX: surrounded all around]" (cf. Jer. 6:25b; 20:3b, 10; 49:29b; Ps. 31:14 [Eng., 31:13]; see also Jer. 46:15, 21 [LXX 26:15, 21]). What appear to be jussive forms in 46:6a ("Let not the swift flee, and let not the mighty escape") may "express the conviction that something cannot happen" (GKC §107p): "The swift cannot flee, and the mighty cannot escape" (cf. Amos 2:14–16). "Northward [Syr.: Among the mighty men] by the Euphrates [MT: by the river Euphrates] they have stumbled [LXX: they are weak], they have fallen [MT: and they have fallen]" (Jer. 46:6b [LXX 26:6b]; see Jer. 46:2, 12, 16 [LXX 26:2, 12, 16]).

The question-and-answer pattern of 46:7–8 (LXX 26:7–8) resets the imagery. No longer is the Egyptian army in flight (46:5–6). The army is confidently advancing along with its allies (or mercenaries; see Jer. 46:9, 21). As in 46:5, the question in 46:7 is somewhat rhetorical, although the expected answer is provided: "Who is like the Nile [LXX: a river] that goes up [or, Who is this that goes up like the Nile], and like the streams that toss about with water [MT: whose waters toss about]?" *Targum Jonathan* interprets this to be one "who goes up with his armies like a cloud that goes up and covers the land." The rising and turbulent waters of the Nile flood the land and sink again (see Amos 8:8; 9:5). Egypt's armies are like the Nile that "goes up" (Jer. 46:8a; cf. 2 Kgs. 23:29; 2 Chr. 35:20). The Hebrew source behind Greek Jeremiah

---

11. McKane, *Jeremiah XXVI–LII*, 1114.

46:8a (LXX 26:8a) does not have the expected parallel "and like the streams that toss about with water" (cf. Jer. 46:7), but it is added in the MT (see note to translation above).[12] This comparison to the Nile is not unlike the comparison of Assyria to flood waters in Isaiah 8:5–8. "I will go up," says Pharaoh, "and [and > MT] cover land and [and > MT] destroy [MT adds: city and] inhabitants therein" (Jer. 46:8b; see note to translation above).[13] This quote of Pharaoh Necho's intentions is reminiscent of the poetic characterization in Exodus 15:9 of the Pharaoh's thoughts when he considered pursuing the people of Israel who had departed from the land of Egypt: "Enemy said, 'I will pursue, I will overtake, I will divide plunder; I will have my fill of them, I will unsheathe my sword, my hand will dispossess them.'" Such thoughts ultimately came to nothing.

Despite the rather obvious differences between the Hebrew source behind Greek Jeremiah 46:9 (LXX 26:9) and the MT, there is a striking resemblance between the orders given here and those in 46:3–4. The Hebrew source behind Greek Jeremiah begins, "Mount on the horses" (עלו על הסוסים), whereas the MT has, "Go up, O horses" (עלו הסוסים). Just as Egypt "goes up" like the Nile, and just as Pharaoh Necho expresses his intention to "go up," so either the horsemen are ordered to "go up" on their horses, or the horses themselves are ordered to "go up." Then the chariots are commanded to go about madly (cf. Nah. 2:5 [Eng., 2:4]), and the warriors are ordered to go forth into battle: "Go forth (צאו), O mighty men [MT: And let the mighty men go forth (ויצאו)]." This includes not only the members of the Egyptian army but also their allies or foreign contingents (i.e., mercenaries [see Jer. 46:21]), Cush and Put, which the LXX identifies as the Ethiopians and Libyans (see Nah. 3:9; see also Gen. 10:6; Ezek. 30:5). These soldiers wield small shields (cf. Jer. 46:3). The text also mentions Lydians who are ordered to grasp and bend a bow. The MT describes them as "graspers of benders of a bow" (cf. Jer. 50:14, 29). These Lydians are likely not those of Asia Minor who are associated with Javan (Greece) in Isaiah 66:19, although the MT of that text does describe them as archers. Rather, they are the ones mentioned

---

12. "Parablepsis in the LXX-V is probably not the issue, as verses 7 and 8a are so tightly structured parallelistically that a scribe's inadvertent omission of one of the poetic members is surely unlikely. It may be that the MT shows a clarifying addition answering the rhetorical question posed in verse 7—an example of what Tov calls 'contextual exegesis'" (Sharp, "Take Another Scroll and Write," 492).
13. "Is there an ironic reminder here of the waters that 'covered' the Egyptian chariots at the exodus (Exod 14:28; 15:5, 10)" (Holladay, *Jeremiah 2*, 321)?

in Genesis 10:13. Bullinger considers the orders in 46:9 to be ironic, given the fate of the Egyptian army in 46:10.[14] McKane, however, is not so sure.[15] A decision on this matter largely depends on who the speaker is, the LORD or the Egyptian officers.

It is not immediately clear to what day the phrase "that day" (היום ההוא) refers at the beginning of 46:10 (LXX 26:10). The only specific time reference in the preceding context is in 46:2, namely, the fourth year of Jehoiakim (605 BC) in which Nebuchadnezzar struck Pharaoh Necho's army. Thus, many commentators understand the LORD's "day of vengeance" (יום נקמה) in 46:10 to be the day of judgment for Pharaoh Necho for what he did to Josiah in 609 BC (2 Kgs. 23:29). Yet the language of 46:10 and its usage elsewhere suggest a broader application (see also Jer. 46:21b; Ezek. 30:3–4). In particular, the connections to Isaiah 34:5–8 are very revealing. The Isaiah context sets forth the historical judgment of "Edom" (אדום) (Isa. 34:5–17) as a picture of the eschatological judgment of "all the nations," that is, all "mankind" (אדם) (Isa. 34:1–4). The day of Edom's judgment is called the LORD's "day of vengeance" (יום נקם) (Isa. 34:8), which elsewhere in Isaiah is a day of retribution when the LORD will pay back his enemies and redeem his people through the coming of the Messiah (Isa. 61:1–2 [cf. Luke 4:16–30; 21:22]; 63:1–6 [cf. Gen. 49:8–12; Rev. 14:14–20; 19:11–16]). This day in Jeremiah 46:10 is not specifically a day of judgment for Egypt but a day for the LORD to take vengeance on his foes generally, including Egypt but not limited to Egypt (cf. Nah. 1:2; see also Jer. 50:28). A "sword of the LORD" (חרב ליהוה) will "devour and be sated and saturated (ורותה) from their blood (מדמם)" (cf. Deut. 32:40–42; Jer. 12:12; 46:14; 47:6; see also Jer. 50:35–38). The phrase "sword of the LORD" (חרב ליהוה) does not appear in MT Jeremiah 46:10, but it does appear in Isaiah 34:6 where it says that the LORD's sword is "saturated" (רותה) and filled with blood (Isa 34:5–6). This will happen because a "sacrifice of the LORD" (זבח ליהוה)[16] will be "from the land of the north" (מארץ צפון) by the river Euphrates. The phrase

---

14. Bullinger, *Figures of Speech*, 810.

15. McKane, *Jeremiah XXVI–LII*, 1115.

16. The MT has "sacrifice of the Lord GOD of hosts" (זבח לאדני יהוה צבאות). Neither אדני ("Lord") nor צבאות ("hosts") is in the Hebrew source behind Greek Jeremiah. צבאות is commonly added in the MT. The vowels of אדני are normally given as the perpetual *qere* for יהוה, thus "LORD" for YHWH. But when אדני יהוה is written, the vowels of אלהים ("God") are given as the *qere* for the divine name, thus "GOD" for YHWH. The combination אדני יהוה goes back to a time prior to the written vocalization system of the MT when אדני was often written into the text in to indicate that it should be

"sacrifice of the LORD" (זבח ליהוה) also appears in Isaiah 34:6b where it refers to a great slaughter in the land of Edom (see Isa. 34:6b–7). MT Jeremiah 46:10 puts the sacrifice of the LORD "in (the) land of the north" (בארץ צפון) by the river Euphrates, which seems to connect this event with the fall of the Egyptian army to the Babylonians (see Jer. 46:2). The Hebrew source behind Greek Jeremiah, however, says that the sacrifice will be "from (the) land of the north" (מארץ צפון) by the river Euphrates. This suggests a reference to the coming of the eschatological enemy from the north and his ultimate demise (see commentary on Jer. 25:9, 12–13; see also Jer. 46:20–21). According to Ezekiel 39:17–20 (cf. Rev. 19:17–18), the great sacrifice will take place in the wake of the defeat of the final enemy Gog from the land of Magog in the last days (Ezek. 38:2, 16; 39:4; see also Num. 24:7 [LXX]; Rev. 20:8). According to Zephaniah 1:7, it will happen in the eschatological Day of the LORD (see also Zeph. 1:15; cf. Jer. 30:7; Nah. 1:7; Hab. 3:16). Such an eschatological reading of Jeremiah 46:10 (LXX 26:10) is encouraged not only by these connections with other prophetic texts but also by the framing of the oracles concerning the nations in the arrangement of the Hebrew source behind Greek Jeremiah where the first (Jer. 49:34–39) and last (Jer. 48) oracles both conclude with the phrase "at the end of the days" (Jer. 49:34 and Jer. 48:47). While it is true that these oracles contain historical words of judgment for the nations, their current presentation within the book of Jeremiah also commends them as depictions of things to come.

The command to virgin daughter Egypt to go up to Gilead and take balm is ironic (Jer. 46:11a [LXX 26:11a]; cf. Jer. 8:22; 51:8; see also Gen. 37:25).[17] This is because it is in vain that Egypt has increased its medicines (Jer. 46:11b [LXX 26:11b]). There is no healing (cf. Jer. 30:13). According to the Hebrew source behind Greek Jeremiah 46:12a (LXX 26:12a), the text says, "Nations have heard your voice (קולך), and the inhabited earth is full of your outcry." The MT says, "Nations have heard your disgrace (קלונך), and the inhabited earth is full of your outcry." Sharp suggests that the less common "your disgrace" has been changed to the more common "your voice" to make closer parallelism with "your outcry."[18] On the other hand, Bright notes the suggestion of

---

pronounced in place of the divine name YHWH (see throughout MT Ezekiel in comparison to LXX Ezekiel).

17. See again Bullinger, *Figures of Speech*, 810. Mezudath David says that Egypt is "yet unconquered by any other kingdom, like a virgin never possessed by a man" (Rosenberg, trans., *Mikraoth Gedoloth: Jeremiah Volume Two*, 348).

18. Sharp, "Take Another Scroll and Write," 493.

David Noel Freedman that "*qln* may here be an otherwise unattested elaboration of *qwl*, with the same meaning."[19] This great outcry that has reached the nations is due to the mighty warriors of Egypt stumbling over one another and falling "together" (יחדיו) (Jer. 46:12b [LXX 26:12b]; cf. Jer. 46:6, 16). The Syriac reflects a text that says they fall "by the sword" (בחרב) (cf. Lev. 26:37).

46:13 (26:13) That which the LORD *spoke by the hand of Jeremiah [MT: The word that the* LORD *spoke to Jeremiah the prophet] about the coming of [MT adds: Nebuchadrezzar] the king of Babylon to strike the land of Egypt:*

46:14 (26:14) "Declare [MT adds: in Egypt and proclaim] in Migdol and proclaim in Noph [LXX: Memphis; MT adds: and in Tahpanhes]. Say, 'Take your station and prepare [MT adds: yourself], for a sword has devoured your thicket [MT: around you].' 46:15 (26:15) Why has Apis your mighty one [LXX: your (choice) bull calf] fled [mlt Mss: Why is your mighty one (Codex L: mighty ones) prostrated / beaten down (or, swept away)]? He has not remained, for the LORD *is the one who has driven him out [LXX: paralyzed him]. 46:16 (26:16) And as for your multitude [Syr.: their multitude], it stumbled, also it fell; and to one another they would say [MT: He increased one stumbling. Also, each fell over his neighbor, and they said], 'Rise up[20] and let us return [or, Rise up that we may return] to our people, [MT adds: and] to the land of our kindred because of [lit., from before] a Greek sword [MT: a sword that oppresses; Tg. Jon.: the sword of the enemy, which is like wine that makes drunk].' 46:17 (26:17) Call the name of [MT: They called there] Pharaoh Necho [Necho > MT] the king of Egypt, 'Roar / Crash leaving / forsaking the appointed time [MT: Roar / Crash (who) let the appointed time pass by]."[21] 46:18 (26:18) As I live," the prophetic utterance of the* LORD *God [MT: the prophetic utterance of the king whose name is the* LORD *of hosts], "like Tabor among the mountains and like Carmel by the sea he will come [Syr.: Pharaoh will fall like the breaking of a mountain and like an orchard in the midst of the sea; see also Tg. Jon.]. 46:19 (26:19) Vessels*

---

19. "The spelling *ql* is attested in pre-Exilic Hebrew inscriptions and also in the Bible, while the ending in *n* is common; and cf. *qōlān* in late (and modern) Hebrew: 'one making a loud noise, a shouter, crier'" (Bright, *Jeremiah*, 302). See also McKane, *Jeremiah XXVI–LII*, 1120.
20. The MT has קוּמָה, but the Eastern *qere* is קוּמוּ.
21. Alternative translation of the MT: They proclaimed there, "Pharaoh the king of Egypt is a roar/crash (who) let the appointed time pass by."

of exile make for yourself, O inhabitant of daughter Egypt. For Noph [LXX: Memphis], a desolation will she become, and she will be burned [from יצת; or, and she will be ruined (from נצה); Ziegler: καὶ καυθήσεται (and she will be burned); Rahlfs: καὶ κληθήσεται οὐαί (and she will be called Woe)] without inhabitant in her. 46:20 (26:20) A beautiful heifer is Egypt. A nipper [Syr.: an army] from (the) north is entering her. 46:21 (26:21) Also/Even her hired ones [or, mercenaries; Tg. Jon.: leaders] in her midst are like stall calves [LXX: fattened calves]. For they too have turned and fled together. They have not remained. For the day of their distress/calamity is coming [or, has come] upon them, the time of their visitation. 46:22 (26:22) A sound [MT: Her sound; Syr.: The sound of the army; Tg. Jon.: The sound of the rattle of their weapons] like a serpent goes [LXX: as of a hissing serpent; Syr.: like a serpent that slithers; Vulg.: like bronze will sound], for in sand [MT: in strength (or, with an army)] they go, and with axes have they come [LXX: will they come] to her [mlt Mss: to you] like lumberjacks [lit., cutters of trees]. 46:23 (26:23) They have cut down [LXX: They will cut down; Syr.: Cut down; Tg. Jon.: Destroy] her forest [Tg. Jon.: her leaders]," the prophetic utterance of the Lord, *"for it cannot be searched, for they are more abundant than locusts [LXX: for it multiplies beyond locusts],[22] and they have no number. 46:24 (26:24) Daughter Egypt is put to shame, she is given into the hand of a people from the north." 46:25 (26:25) [MT: adds: The* Lord *of hosts, the God of Israel, said] "Look, I am about to visit upon Amon her son [MT: Amon of No/Thebes; Tg. Jon., Vulg.: the noisy crowd of Alexandria], [MT adds: and] upon Pharaoh [MT adds: and upon Egypt and upon her gods and upon her kings and upon Pharaoh] and upon those who trust in him. [MT adds 46:26: And I will give them (Syr. adds: into the hand of their enemies and) into the hand of those who seek their life and into the hand of Nebuchadrezzar the king of Babylon and into the hand of his servants, and afterwards she will dwell like days of old," the prophetic utterance of the* Lord.*] 46:27 (26:27) And as for you, do not fear, O my servant Jacob; and do not be dismayed/terrified [Syr., Tg. Jon.: and do not break], O Israel. For look, I am about to deliver you from far away, and your seed/offspring [Tg. Jon.: your sons] from the land of their captivity. And Jacob will return and be quiet and at ease [LXX: and sleep (from ישן?)], and there will be no one causing trembling [LXX: and there will be no one troubling him]. 46:28 (26:28) As for you, do not fear, O my servant Jacob," the prophetic utterance of the* Lord,

---

22. The singular verb in the LXX likely does not reflect a singular verb in its *Vorlage*. The *qal qatal* of רבב in the Hebrew Bible only occurs in 3fs and 3cp, not 3ms (see BDB, 912). See also Walser, *Jeremiah*, 347.

"for with you am I. For I will make a complete destruction among all the nations [LXX: among every nation] where I have banished you. But you I will not make a complete destruction, and I will discipline you justly [ESV: in just measure; Tg. Jon.: and I will bring against you sufferings to teach you but with judgment of restraint], and I will by no means leave you unpunished [Tg. Jon.: and I will not completely destroy you]."

Despite the similarities between 46:2–12 and 46:13–24, the subheadings in 46:2 and 46:13 refer to two different events. 46:2 refers to Nebuchadnezzar's strike of Pharaoh Necho's army by the river Euphrates at Carchemish in the fourth year of Jehoiakim (i.e., 605 BC). 46:13 does not provide a date but refers to the coming of the king of Babylon (MT: Nebuchadrezzar) to strike the land of Egypt (cf. Jer. 43:8–13). According to Rashi, this strike is to be associated with the word of the LORD that came to Ezekiel in the twenty-seventh year of Jehoiachin's exile (571 BC), which said that Egypt would be given to Nebuchadnezzar as a reward for his labor against Tyre (Ezek. 29:17–20).[23] This is only possible in MT Jeremiah, since the Hebrew source behind Greek Jeremiah refers to Pharaoh Necho (610–594 BC) in 46:17 (LXX 26:17; see also Syr.), unless the Babylonian strike against Egypt was not necessarily anticipated in the immediate future.[24] Likewise, if MT Jeremiah 46:17 is a play on the name of Pharaoh Hophra (589–574 BC) as some commentators suggest, then the conclusion would have to be that the threat of Babylonian invasion was issued in his time but did not come to fruition until afterwards (i.e., 568 BC) during the reign of Pharaoh Amasis (570–526 BC).[25] Thus, there are two somewhat unresolved issues involved in the interpretation of 46:13: (1) the date of the oracle, which is unknown, and (2) the date of the anticipated Babylonian strike of Egypt (568 BC?). "That which the LORD spoke by the hand of Jeremiah"[26] (Jer. 46:13a; cf. Jer. 50:1) has two main parts: 46:14–19 and 46:20–24. The prose material in MT 46:25–26 is substantially shorter in the Hebrew source behind Greek Jeremiah. The additional message for Israel in 46:27–28 has a parallel in MT 30:10–11 (but not in the Hebrew source behind Greek Jeremiah).[27]

---

23. Rosenberg, trans., *Mikraoth Gedoloth: Jeremiah Volume Two*, 349.
24. Thompson believes that Jeremiah composed the oracle of 46:14–24 at the end of 604 BC when Nebuchadnezzar was advancing toward Egypt (*Book of Jeremiah*, 691).
25. McKane, *Jeremiah XXVI–LII*, 1125, 1139.
26. MT: "The word that the LORD spoke to Jeremiah the prophet."
27. See Parke-Taylor, *Formation of the Book of Jeremiah*, 119–26. See also Paul R. Raabe, "What Is Israel's God Up to Among the Nations? Jeremiah

The plural imperatives in Jeremiah 46:14a (LXX 26:14a) are presumably addressed to the Egyptians in general or to the Egyptian officers in particular (cf. Jer. 46:3, 4, 9; see also Jer. 4:5): "Declare [MT adds: in Egypt and proclaim] in Migdol and proclaim in Noph [LXX: Memphis; MT adds: and in Tahpanhes]" (cf. Jer. 50:2). (For these place names, see Exod. 14:2; Jer. 2:16; 44:1; Ezek. 29:10; 30:6.) They are to say, "Take your station and prepare [MT adds: yourself], for a sword has devoured your thicket (סבכך) [MT: around you (סביביך)]" (cf. Jer. 21:14; 46:4; Ezek. 30:5–6). These imperatives are singular, perhaps directed to the soldiers in a distributive sense.[28] The image of a sword devouring Egypt's "thicket" according to the Hebrew source behind Greek Jeremiah is comparable to the image of lumberjacks cutting down Egypt's forest (Jer. 46:22–23; see also Jer. 22:7; Ps. 74:5). The thicket is the place from which the lion (Egypt) should be able to launch its attack (cf. Jer. 4:7), but the sword destroys its cover. Thus, Egypt's preparations for battle are in vain.[29]

According to the Hebrew source behind Greek Jeremiah 46:15a (LXX 26:15a), the Lord asks/taunts, "Why has Apis your mighty one [LXX: your (choice) bull calf][30] fled?" (מדוע נס חף אבירך) (cf. Jer. 46:5, 6, 21). McKane comments, "Apis is the bull of Memphis sacred to Ptah who was the chief deity of that city and was subsequently regarded as an incarnation of Osiris" (see Jer. 46:25; see also Exod. 9:3; 12:12; Num. 33:4).[31] On the other hand, the MT has, "Why is your mighty one [Codex L: your mighty ones (אביריך)][32] prostrated/beaten down [or, swept away] (מדוע נסחף אבירך)?" This so-called mighty one has not remained, "for the Lord is the one who has driven him out [LXX: paralyzed him]" (Jer. 46:15b [LXX 26:15b]).

The Hebrew source behind Greek Jeremiah 46:16 (LXX 26:16) begins, "And as for your multitude [Syr.: their multitude], it stumbled, also it fell; and to one another they would say" (והמונך כשל גם נפל ואיש אל רעהו יאמרו) (cf. Jer. 46:6, 12). The MT has, "He increased one stumbling. Also, each fell

---

46, 48, and 49," in *The Book of Jeremiah: Composition, Reception, and Interpretation*, eds. Jack R. Lundbom, Craig A. Evans, and Bradford A. Anderson (Leiden: Brill, 2018), 230–52.

28. See McKane, *Jeremiah XXVI–LII*, 1126.

29. See Calvin, *Jeremiah*, 4:587.

30. "ὁ ἐκλεκτός is either a doublet resting on a Hebrew variant of אבירך or an expansion—an epithet added to אבירך" (McKane, *Jeremiah XXVI–LII*, 1127).

31. McKane, *Jeremiah XXVI–LII*, 1128.

32. A "plural of majesty"?

over his neighbor, and they said" (הרבה כושל גם נפל איש אל רעהו ויאמרו).[33] This multitude of stumbling people said, "Rise up and let us return [or, Rise up that we may return] to our people, [MT adds: and] to the land of our kindred because of [lit., from before] a Greek (יוניה) sword [MT: a sword that oppresses (היונה); *Tg. Jon.*: the sword of the enemy, which is like wine (חמר = Heb. יין) that makes drunk]" (cf. Jer. 25:38b; 50:16b). Redak understands these people to be "those foreigners who came to Egypt to avoid the famine in their native land."[34] Calvin, on the other hand, suggests that they are mercenaries, soldiers hired from foreign lands, who abandoned their aid to the Egyptian army in the face of the threat of Babylonian invasion (see Jer. 46:9, 21).[35]

The Hebrew source behind Greek Jeremiah 46:17 (LXX 26:17) begins, "Call the name (קְרָאוּ שֵׁם) of Pharaoh Necho the king of Egypt." The MT has, "They called there (קָרְאוּ שָׁם) Pharaoh the king of Egypt." According to the former, the name of Pharaoh Necho is to be called "Roar/Crash leaving/forsaking (עָזְבִי) the appointed time."[36] According to the latter, an unidentified group in an unidentified place (the mercenaries in the land of their kindred?) called an unidentified Pharaoh "Roar/Crash (who) let the appointed time pass by (העביר)" (or, "They proclaimed there, 'Pharaoh the king of Egypt is a roar/crash (who) let the appointed time pass by'").[37] Some commentators consider the verb העביר in the MT to be a pun on the name of Pharaoh Hophra (cf. Jer. 20:3), which may allude to his failure to aid Judah against the Babylonians (see Jer. 37:5–10; 44:30).[38] Pharaoh is a loud boaster whose bark is worse than his bite (see Isa. 30:7). In what sense, though, has he missed the "appointed time"? Rashi explains, "For he had appointed a set time to go forth and wage war, and he did not go forth, and the day of the appointed time passed by."[39] Calvin, however,

---

33. Rudolph proposes emendation of הרבה ("He increased") to רהב הרב ("Rahab the great") (see *BHS* apparatus). See Isaiah 30:7; Psalm 87:4. Cf. Holladay, *Jeremiah 2,* 329.

34. Rosenberg, trans., *Mikraoth Gedoloth: Jeremiah Volume Two,* 350. See also Keil, *Jeremiah,* 374.

35. Calvin, *Jeremiah,* 4:589.

36. See the discussion of the Greek transliteration of עזבי in Sharp, "Take Another Scroll and Write," 495.

37. McKane: "'Boaster' a man who has let his chance slip" (*Jeremiah XXVI–LII,* 1124).

38. See, e.g., Thompson, *Book of Jeremiah,* 692; Holladay, *Jeremiah 2,* 304, 330. McKane disputes the pun (*Jeremiah XXVI–LII,* 1129).

39. Rosenberg, trans., *Mikraoth Gedoloth: Jeremiah Volume Two,* 350.

disagrees: "As, then, the destruction of Egypt had been predicted many years before, and as the Egyptians remained in safety after Judea was overthrown and laid waste, it is probable that they became more hardened, thinking that the time had elapsed."[40]

In 46:18 (LXX 26:18), the LORD God (MT: "the king whose name is the LORD of hosts")[41] swears that Nebuchadnezzar will come against Egypt as surely as Tabor is fixed among the mountains and as surely as Carmel is fixed by the sea.[42] Not everyone, however, has interpreted the comparisons to Tabor and Carmel in this manner. The Syriac version translates, "Pharaoh will fall like the breaking (ܐܛܘܪܐ) of a mountain and like an orchard (ܟܪܡܐ) in the midst of the sea." Thompson comments, "Both [Tabor and Carmel] seemed to Jeremiah to depict Nebuchadrezzar who towered over Egypt in his might like lofty mountains towering over a plain."[43] With the certainty of Babylonian invasion on the horizon, Egypt is instructed to make "vessels of exile" (Jer. 46:19a [LXX 26:19a]; cf. Jer. 10:17; Ezek. 12:3). For Memphis will become a desolation and will be "burned" (from יצת)[44] without any inhabitants left (Jer. 46:19b [LXX 26:19b]; see Jer. 43:12; Ezek. 30:13–19; 4Q386; cf. Jer. 2:15b; 4:7b; 9:9b, 11b [Eng., 9:10b, 12b]; see also Isa. 6:11b).

Jeremiah 46:20 (LXX 26:20) compares Egypt to a "beautiful heifer" (עגלה יפיפיה; cf. Jer. 46:15), but this beautiful heifer is susceptible to a "nipper" ("gadfly" or "horsefly"), which the Syriac interprets to be an army (i.e., the Babylonian army) entering Egypt from the north (cf. Jer. 46:10, 24). This metaphor is comparable to the LORD whistling for the fly from Egypt and the bee from Assyria in Isaiah 7:18. Egypt's hired ones (i.e., mercenaries) are also like "stall calves" (עגלי מרבק; LXX: "fattened calves") ready for slaughter (Jer. 46:21a [LXX 26:21a]).[45] "For they too have turned and fled together. They have not remained" (cf. Jer. 46:5, 6, 15; see also Jer. 47:3). This is because "the day of their distress/calamity" (cf. Deut. 32:35; Jer. 18:17b) is coming (or, has come), "the time of their visitation" (Jer. 46:21b [LXX 26:21b]; cf. Jer. 6:15b; 10:15b; 48:44b; 50:27). Such language reminds the reader of the way in which

---

40. Calvin, *Jeremiah*, 4:591.

41. Cf. MT Jeremiah 48:15b (> LXX) and 51:57b (LXX 28:57b).

42. See Rashi in Rosenberg, trans., *Mikraoth Gedoloth: Jeremiah Volume Two*, 351. See also *Targum Jonathan*; Calvin, *Jeremiah*, 4:593; McKane, *Jeremiah XXVI–LII*, 1130.

43. Thompson, *Book of Jeremiah*, 692.

44. Or "ruined" (from נצה); Ziegler: καὶ καυθήσεται ("and she will be burned"); Rahlfs: καὶ κληθήσεται οὐαί ("and she will be called Woe").

45. See McKane, *Jeremiah XXVI–LII*, 1132.

the historical invasion of Egypt by the Babylonians prefigures the eschatological judgment of the nations (see commentary on Jer. 46:10).

There are two comparisons made in 46:22 (LXX 26:22), one to a serpent and one to lumberjacks. It is clear that the second comparison to lumberjacks is intended to describe the invading Babylonian army. It is not clear, however, whether the first comparison to a serpent is designed to describe Egypt or the invading army. 46:22a says, "A sound [MT: Her sound] like a serpent goes" (cf. Gen. 3:14). The LXX interprets this to be a sound as of a "hissing" (= שרק?) serpent.[46] The Syriac translates, "The sound of the army is like a serpent that slithers." *Targum Jonathan* renders, "The sound of the rattle of their weapons is like serpents crawling." The Latin Vulgate says that its voice/sound like "bronze" (= נחשת) will sound. These early versions seem to suggest that the sound of the invading army is being compared to a sound that a serpent makes (or, in the case of the Latin Vulgate, the sound of a bronze gong), but the following clause in the Hebrew source behind Greek Jeremiah could be understood as a description of Egypt fleeing: "for in sand (חול) they go." The MT, however, appears to maintain a description of the Babylonian army: "for in strength (חיל) they go." Keil argues that the text pictures Egypt lying on the ground humbled (cf. Isa. 29:4), "making a sound like that of a serpent in a moss among fallen leaves, fleeing before the woodcutters."[47] It is somewhat forced, however, to see Egypt in the first half of the verse and Babylon in the second, requiring the Egyptians to be both the serpent and the trees. It is more natural to see the second half of the verse as a continuation of the first. The Babylonian army makes a threatening sound like a serpent, "and with axes have they come [LXX: will they come (= יבאו?)] to her [mlt Mss: to you] like lumberjacks [lit., cutters of trees]" (cf. Isa. 10:18–19, 33–34; Jer. 21:14; 22:6–7; Ps. 74:5; see also Deut. 20:19). This may be descriptive not only of cutting down people but also of structural damage. They have cut down (LXX: "They will cut down" [= יכרתו?]) her forest (*Tg. Jon.*: "her leaders"), because it cannot be "searched" (Jer. 46:23a [LXX 26:23a]).[48] In other words, given the size of Egypt, it is easier to demolish the whole than to locate specific targets within it, "for they are more abundant than locusts, and they have

---

46. Cf. LXX Deuteronomy 32:24b; Micah 7:17. See McKane, *Jeremiah XXVI–LII*, 1133.

47. Keil, *Jeremiah*, 376–77. "The snake hides in the forest, and since the woodcutters cannot search the forest to find it, they cut the forest down" (Thompson, *Book of Jeremiah*, 693).

48. The Syriac ("Cut down") and *Targum Jonathan* ("Destroy") both interpret כרתו as an imperative.

no number" (Jer. 46:23b [LXX 26:23b]). Daughter Egypt is thus "put to shame" (BDB, 102) and given into the hand of a people from the north (Jer. 46:24 [LXX 26:24]; cf. Jer. 46:20).

The Hebrew source behind Greek Jeremiah 46:25 (LXX 26:25) is substantially shorter than the MT. The MT has added an introduction to the verse: "The LORD of hosts, the God of Israel, said." It has also made an addition to the middle of the verse between the phrase "upon Pharaoh" and the phrase "and upon those who trust in him": "and upon Egypt and upon her gods and upon her kings and upon Pharaoh." The *BHS* apparatus suggests that the shorter text in the Greek version is due to homoioteleuton. That is, either the Hebrew scribe or the Greek translator accidentally skipped from the first instance of על פרעה ("upon Pharaoh") to the second and omitted the intervening text. This is unlikely for two reasons. First, the second occurrence of this phrase in the MT is redundant, suggesting that the plus in the MT has been added secondarily without due attention to what was already present in the context. Second, the added material seems to come from Exodus 12:12 and Numbers 33:4, which both indicate that the historical plagues in Egypt were judgments against the gods of Egypt. Thus, according to the MT, the impending judgment upon Egypt at the hands of the Babylonians is analogous to the historical judgment in the exodus story and is summative against all the people, gods, and kings of the land. The shorter text of 46:25 simply says, "Look, I am about to visit upon Amon her son (אמון בנה), upon Pharaoh and upon those who trust in him."[49] The MT has "Amon of No/Thebes" (אמון מנא) instead of "Amon her son" (see Ezek. 30:14; Nah. 3:8). Amon was the chief god or idol of Egypt (cf. Jer. 46:15). Both *Targum Jonathan* and the Latin Vulgate translate this same phrase as "the noisy crowd of Alexandria," as if reading המון ("noisy crowd" or "multitude") instead of אמון ("Amon").

MT Jeremiah 46:26 does not appear in the Hebrew source behind Greek Jeremiah at all, yet the language of the verse is consistent with what the reader finds elsewhere in the book. MT 46:26a says, "And I will give them [Syr. adds: into the hand of their enemies and] into the hand of those who seek their life and into the hand of Nebuchadrezzar the king of Babylon and into the hand of his servants" (cf. Jer. 19:7, 9; 21:7; 34:20–21; 44:30; 49:37). Redak interprets the final clause in

---

49. "The view that בו refers to Amon (Duhm, Volz) rather than Pharaoh should be discounted. However, those scholars who insinuate 'the Judaeans' into the thought of relying on Pharaoh (Cornill, Streane, Peake, Weiser) are not to be followed. The threat is uttered against Egypt and Egyptians and not against Judaeans in Egypt" (McKane, *Jeremiah XXVI–LII*, 1136).

MT 46:26b—"and afterwards she will dwell like days of old"—to mean that Egypt will no longer be a world power but a humble kingdom (see Ezek. 29:14–16).[50] Calvin, on the other hand, understands this to mean a return to former glory, and Keil reads it in light of Jeremiah 48:47; 49:6, 39, texts that speak of the restoration of the nations in the last days.[51] This agrees with Isaiah's view of Egypt's future: "In that day, Israel will be a third part to Egypt and Assyria, a blessing in the midst of the land, which the LORD of hosts has blessed, saying, 'Blessed be my people, Egypt, and the work of my hands, Assyria, and my inheritance, Israel'" (Isa. 19:24–25; see also Isa. 19:16–23).[52]

The text of Jeremiah 46:27–28 (LXX 26:27–28) has a close parallel in MT Jeremiah 30:10–11. While the Book of Comfort (Jer. 30–33) might seem to be a better context than the nations section for a passage about the deliverance of Israel, the text of MT Jeremiah 30:10–11 is not found in the Hebrew source behind Greek Jeremiah. Thus, it appears that Jeremiah 46:27–28 (LXX 26:27–28) is the primary context for this passage, which has been repeated secondarily in MT Jeremiah 30:10–11. There is no evidence that the Greek translator omitted these two verses from chapter 30 (LXX 37) simply because they appeared redundant after their first occurrence in 46:27–28 (LXX 26:27–28) according to the order of his source text.[53] The general faithfulness of the Greek translator to his source argues against such a conclusion. Much like Isaiah 14:1–3, which is embedded in an oracle about Babylon (Isa. 13–14) and speaks of the LORD's compassion for Israel, Jeremiah 46:27–28 reminds the reader of the LORD's plans for the true remnant of his people[54] and the relationship of those plans to his dealings with the nations (see also Jer. 50:4–7, 19–20; 51:5–6, 10, 35–36, 45–46, 50).

---

50. Rosenberg, trans., *Mikraoth Gedoloth: Volume Two*, 353.
51. Calvin, *Jeremiah*, 4:602. "From this it follows that, in the verse now before us also, it is not the future in general, but the last time, i.e., the Messianic future, that is pointed out" (Keil, *Jeremiah*, 378).
52. The land of the covenant extends from the Nile in Egypt to the Euphrates in Assyria (Gen. 15:18; see also Gen. 2:10–14).
53. It may be asked why 46:27–28 is not omitted for the same reason in the MT after the occurrence of these verses in 30:10–11. Furthermore, there are many doublets in the book of Jeremiah, and there is no evidence that a Hebrew scribe of the LXX *Vorlage* or the Greek translator himself systematically removed the second member of these doublets throughout the book.
54. Rashi: "The righteous men who were in Egypt, who were exiled there against their will" (Rosenberg, trans., *Mikraoth Gedoloth: Jeremiah Volume Two*, 353). See Jeremiah 43:1–7.

Jeremiah 46:27a (LXX 26:27a) revisits the language of the opening chapter of the book: "And as for you, do not fear, O my servant Jacob; and do not be dismayed/terrified [Syr., *Tg. Jon.*: and do not break], O Israel" (cf. Jer. 1:8, 17; see also Deut. 1:21; 31:8; Josh. 1:9; Jer. 17:18; 23:4; Ezek. 2:6; 3:9). Words once spoken to Jeremiah are now reapplied to the people represented by Jeremiah. This language is also common in Isaiah 40–55 (e.g., Isa. 40:9; 41:8, 10, 13, 14; 43:1, 5; 44:1, 2; 45:4; 48:20; 51:7; 54:4; see also Ps. 105:6). Jacob/Israel here is the eschatological reunited kingdom of Judah and Israel, including the believing Gentiles who join them (see Jer. 3:17–18). The reason that there is no need to fear or be dismayed is that the LORD is about to deliver them "from far away" (מרחוק) (see Jer. 5:15; cf. Zech. 6:15) and their "seed/offspring" (זרע) from the land of their captivity (cf. Isa. 6:13; 44:3; 45:25; 53:10; 61:9; 65:9; 66:22). Jacob will return and be quiet and at ease, and there will be no one to disturb him (Jer. 46:27b [LXX 26:27b]; cf. Lev. 26:6; Deut. 28:26; Ezek. 34:28; 39:26; Mic. 4:4; Zeph. 3:13).

Jeremiah 46:28a (LXX 26:28a) is similar to the opening line of 46:27a (LXX 26:27a) and thus also shares language with the opening chapter of the book: "As for you, do not fear, O my servant Jacob," the prophetic utterance of the LORD, "for with you am I" (cf. Jer. 1:8, 17, 19; 15:20b; see also Gen. 26:24).[55] Just as the LORD is present with his prophet, so is he present and active with his people. For he will make a complete destruction among all the nations where he has banished them, but he will not make a complete destruction of his people (Jer. 46:27b [LXX 26:27b]; cf. Jer. 4:27; 5:10, 18). This is not a contradiction of what is said about the restoration of the nations (Jer. 3:17; 12:14–17; 16:19; 46:26b [MT]; 48:47; 49:6 [MT], 39). The LORD will make a complete destruction "among" (ב) all the nations where he has banished them, not a complete destruction of all the nations. In other words, he will destroy the enemies of the people of God among the nations, but there will be a remnant of believing Gentiles who will join the people of God. Likewise, the LORD will discipline Jacob/Israel justly and by no means leave the guilty unpunished (cf. Exod. 20:7b; 34:7b; Num. 14:18b; Jer. 10:24; 31:18; Joel 4:21 [Eng., 3:21]; Nah. 1:3a). He will destroy unbelieving Israel, but he will preserve a remnant (i.e., believing Israel). Thus, what remains is the true people of God from Israel and all the nations.

---

55. A shorter version of this appears in MT Jeremiah 30:11.

BABYLON

(Jer. 50–51 [LXX 27–28])

50:1 (27:1) The word of the LORD *that he spoke concerning Babylon [MT: The word that the* LORD *spoke concerning Babylon, (mlt Mss add: and) concerning the land of the Chaldeans by the hand of Jeremiah the prophet]:*

50:2 (27:2) "Declare among the nations and proclaim and [MT adds: lift up a banner, proclaim] do not hide. Say, 'Babylon is captured; Bel [LXX adds: the fearless] is put to shame; [LXX adds: the delicate] Merodach is dismayed.[1] [MT adds: Her fashioned idols are put to shame; her dung idols are dismayed (Syr., Tg. Jon.: broken).]' 50:3 (27:3) For a nation from (the) north has come up against her. As for it [i.e., the nation from the north], it will make her land into a desolation [or, object of horror], and there will not be an inhabitant in her

---

1. The original Greek text is usually thought to be minus "Bel" and "Merodach is dismayed," leaving "the fearless" and "the delicate" as variant epithets of Babylon: "Babylon is captured; the fearless, the delicate is put to shame" (see Janzen, *Studies in the Text of Jeremiah*, 20; McKane, *Jeremiah XXVI–LII*, 1252; Sharp, "Take Another Scroll and Write," 496). The thinking is that the Greek text that actually appears in manuscript witnesses is a later correction toward the MT with the addition of "Bel" and "Merodach is dismayed": "Babylon is captured; [Bel] the fearless is put to shame; the delicate [Merodach is dismayed]." It may be asked, however, if the LXX is a correction toward the MT, why does it not include the MT's addition at the end of the verse? It seems more likely to be the case that the Hebrew source behind Greek Jeremiah read, "Babylon is captured; Bel is put to shame; Merodach is dismayed." The epithets "the fearless" and "the delicate" were added by the Greek translator to describe Bel and Merodach respectively.

from man to beast [MT: and there will not be an inhabitant in her. From man to beast they have fled, they have gone].[2] 50:4 (27:4) In those days and at that time," [MT, 4QJer[e] add: the prophetic utterance of the LORD], "the sons of Israel will come, they and the sons of Judah together; walking and weeping they will come, and the LORD their God they will seek.[3] 50:5 (27:5) Zion they will ask; a way, hither their faces [NETS: They shall ask the way to Sion, for here they will set their face]. And they will come and be joined to the LORD [LXX: and they will come and flee to the Lord God; MT: Come and be joined to the LORD]; [LXX adds: for] a perpetual covenant, it will not be forgotten.[4] 50:6 (27:6) Lost sheep are my people [see GKC §44m]. As for their shepherds, they have led them astray. On the mountains they have turned them away [Codex L kethiv: on the mountains turning away]. From mountain to hill they go. They have forgotten their resting place. 50:7 (27:7) All those who find them, they devour them. And their foes, they say, 'Let us not forgive them [cf. Syr.; MT: We are not guilty], because they have sinned against the LORD, a pasture of righteousness for the one who gathered their forefathers [MT: a pasture of righteousness and the hope of their forefathers is the LORD].' 50:8 (27:8) Flee from the midst of Babylon and from the land of the Chaldeans, and go forth [MT kethiv: יצאו] and be like he-goats [LXX: dragons; Tg. Jon.: leaders] before sheep [Tg. Jon.: the people]. 50:9 (27:9) For look, I am about to arouse [MT adds: and bring up] against Babylon an assembly of [MT adds: great] nations from (the) land of (the) north, and they will arrange for battle against her. From there she will be captured. Like an arrow of a skilled warrior, it [i.e., the assembly of nations] will not return empty-handed [MT: His arrows are like a bereaving (nonn Mss: skilled) warrior who does not return empty-handed]. 50:10 (27:10) And Chaldea [see BDB, 505; GKC §122i] will become plunder. All those who plunder her will be sated" [MT adds: the prophetic utterance of the LORD].

50:11 (27:11) "Because you rejoice and exult, O plunderers of my inheritance, because you skip like calves in the grass [MT: like a threshing heifer] and neigh [LXX: gore (from נגח?); Tg. Jon.: shout] like horses [lit.,

---

2. *BHS* arranges the clauses as follows: For a nation from the north has come up against her, it will make her land into a desolation; and there will not be an inhabitant in her, from man to beast they have fled, they have gone.

3. *Targum Jonathan* interprets this to be the return from weeping in exile.

4. REB: "Come let us join ourselves to the Lord in an everlasting covenant which will never be forgotten."

mighty ones; LXX: bulls; Tg. Jon.: warriors],[5] *50:12 (27:12) your mother [Tg. Jon.: your congregation] is very ashamed, a mother for good [MT: she who bore you feels shame; Tg. Jon.: your country is defeated], [MT adds: look,] end of nations, a wilderness [MT adds: dry land and desert plain]. 50:13 (27:13) Because of the wrath of the LORD she will not be inhabited, and she will be an appalling desolation, all of her. And [> MT] everyone who passes by [LXX: through] Babylon will be appalled [LXX: will be sad; Tg. Jon.: will shout] and hiss [Tg. Jon.: shake their head] because of all her wounds [LXX: her every wound]. 50:14 (27:14) Arrange for battle against Babylon all around, O archers! Shoot at her! Do not spare an arrow! [MT adds: For it is against the LORD that she has sinned.] 50:15 (27:15) And [> MT] shout against her [MT adds: all around]! Her hand is given [MT: She has given her hand]. Her bulwarks have fallen. Her city wall is torn down [MT: Her city walls are torn down]. For the vengeance of the LORD is what it is. Take vengeance against her. Just as she has done, do to her. 50:16 (27:16) Cut off seed [MT: sower; Tg. Jon.: the king] from Babylon and one who handles a sickle at harvest time [Tg. Jon.: at killing time]. Because of [lit., From before] a Greek sword [MT: a sword that oppresses; Tg. Jon.: the sword of the enemy, which is like wine that makes drunk], each to his people they will turn, and each to his land they will flee.*

50:17 (27:17) A scattered sheep is Israel. Lions, they have banished him [him > MT; Syr.: The shepherds have caused them to wander; Tg. Jon.: The kings have made them homeless]. The former, the king of Assyria devoured him [Tg. Jon.: ruled over him]. And this the latter, [MT adds: Nebuchadrezzar] the king of Babylon has gnawed / broken his bones [Syr.: has prevailed against him; Tg. Jon.: has brought him to an end; Vulg.: has taken out his bones; Luther: has overpowered him]. 50:18 (27:18) Therefore, thus says the LORD [MT adds: of hosts, the God of Israel]: Look, I am about to visit upon [i.e., punish] the king of Babylon and his land just as I visited upon [i.e., punished] the king of Assyria. 50:19 (27:19) And I will restore Israel to his pasture, and he will graze on Carmel [MT adds: and Bashan], and in the hill country of Ephraim and in Gilead [Tg. Jon.: and on the mountain of the house of Ephraim and the sanctuary (cf. Jer. 22:6)] his desire will be sated [NETS: and he shall feed on Carmel and Mount Ephraim and in Galaad, and his soul shall be satisfied (cf. Syr.)]. 50:20 (27:20) In those days and at that

---

5. The MT *kethiv* has second feminine singular verbs in this verse. The *qere* and the Hebrew source behind Greek Jeremiah have second masculine plural verbs.

time," [MT adds: the prophetic utterance of the Lord*], "they will seek the iniquity of Israel [MT: the iniquity of Israel will be sought], and there will be none, and the sins of Judah, and they will not be found. For I will forgive those who are left in the land [MT: For I will forgive whomever I leave],"*[6] *the prophetic utterance of the* Lord *[> MT].*

The oracle about Babylon (Jer. 50–51 [LXX 27–28]) is easily the longest of Jeremiah's oracles concerning the nations (cf. Isa. 13–14). In the MT, it is the conclusion to the book (just prior to the appendix in chapter 52) and the culmination of the book's prophecy about a historical enemy from the north and about a literal period of seventy years in captivity (MT Jer. 25:9, 11; 29:10). The instrument of judgment (MT Jer. 27:6) is now the object of judgment (MT Jer. 25:12, 13; see also Isa. 47:6; Zech. 1:15). On the other hand, the location of the oracle about Babylon in the Hebrew source behind Greek Jeremiah is significantly less prominent. The collection of oracles concerning the nations is in the middle of the book, and the oracle about Babylon is in the middle of the collection. Furthermore, Babylon is not the eschatological enemy from the north that the edition of the book behind Greek Jeremiah envisions (LXX Jer. 25:9, 11, 12), but the eschatological framework of the oracles concerning the nations provided by the first (Jer. 49:34–39) and last (Jer. 48) oracles, both of which conclude with the phrase "at the end of the days" (Jer. 49:39 and 48:47), enables the reader to see how the judgment of historical Babylon prefigures the eschatological enemy from the north.[7] This feature of the book has had a major influence on the book of Revelation, which casts the final enemy in the context of a new Babylon (Rev. 17–18). According to the index in the UBS Greek New Testament, there are more than twenty allusions to Jeremiah 50–51 in Revelation.[8]

Within the breadth of the biblical canon, Babylon represents worldly opposition to God and his people. The story of the tower of Babylon (Gen. 11:1–9), which appears after the list of seventy nations from the three sons of Noah (Gen. 10) and between the two genealogies of "Shem" (שם) (Gen. 10:21–31 and 11:10–26), is the story of humanity's attempt to make a "name" (שם) for itself. This is in stark contrast to the story of Abram/Abraham and his descendants, which is the story of a man called out of the context of Babylon to be the means of restoring

---

6.   See Sharp, "Take Another Scroll and Write," 501–2.
7.   The oracle about Babylon in Isaiah 13–14 is also illustrative of the eschatological Day of the Lord (see Childs, *Isaiah*, 122–28).
8.   See also Bullinger, *Figures of Speech*, 315.

the lost blessing to all the nations (Gen. 11:27–12:9). Babylon's role as a historical foe (2 Kgs. 25; Jer. 52; 2 Chr. 36) is thus refashioned by the Prophets as the prototype of eschatological opposition and as the context out of which the people of God will be delivered in the last days (see, e.g., Isa. 40–66; Zech. 1–6; see also Dan. 2; 7). Despite the return from Babylon in the latter part of the sixth century BC, the eschatological prophecies of deliverance from Babylon in the prophetic literature have yet to come to fruition in world history.

The heading for Jeremiah 50–51 in the Hebrew source behind Greek Jeremiah—"The word of the LORD that he spoke concerning Babylon"—has been expanded considerably in the MT: "The word that the LORD spoke concerning Babylon, [mlt Mss add: and] concerning the land of the Chaldeans by the hand of Jeremiah the prophet" (Jer. 50:1 [LXX 27:1]; cf. Jer. 46:13). The conclusion to the oracle about Babylon in Jeremiah 51:59–64 indicates that the words of this message were written in the fourth year of Zedekiah (see also Jer. 28:1). The plural imperatives in 50:2a (LXX 27:2a) to declare among the nations and proclaim without concealing anything are not directed to any group in particular (cf. Jer. 4:5; 46:14).[9] They serve a rhetorical purpose to announce the demise of Babylon and her so-called gods. The oracle about Babylon should not be received according to temporal categories either as an account of a past or present event or as a prediction of a future event but as a timeless textual image of the downfall of a great world power. "Babylon is captured; Bel is put to shame; Merodach is dismayed" (Jer. 50:2b [LXX 27:2b]; cf. Isa. 46:1–2; Jer. 51:44). "Bel" here is not the Canaanite storm/fertility god Baal but a title ("lord") for the chief god of Babylon whose name was "Merodach" or "Marduk."[10] The Greek translator describes "Bel" as "the fearless" and "Merodach" as "the delicate" (see note to translation above). The MT adds, "Her fashioned idols are put to shame; her dung idols are dismayed [Syr., *Tg. Jon.*: broken]" (cf. Isa. 46:1; Ezek. 20:7, 8, 18, 24, 39). This is essentially a clarification that the gods of Babylon are non-gods.

Jeremiah 50:3 (LXX 27:3) explains that a nation from the north has come up against Babylon. This nation will make the land of Babylon into a desolation (or, object of horror), "and there will not be an inhabitant in her from man to beast" (MT: "and there will not be an inhabitant in her. From man to beast they have fled, they have gone" [cf.

---

9. The addition in the MT ("lift up a banner, proclaim") recalls the language of Isaiah 13:2 and Jeremiah 4:6 (see also Jer. 51:27).

10. The term *bel* is the Akkadian equivalent of *baal*. "Bel" was also the title of the storm god Enlil, the chief god of Nippur.

Jer. 9:9b (Eng., 9:10b)]).[11] Such an explanation is problematic for MT Jeremiah, which has already identified Babylon as the enemy from the north (see MT Jer. 25:9). This issue does not arise in the Hebrew source behind Greek Jeremiah because it never identifies the enemy from the north as a historical enemy (see LXX Jer. 25:9). It would be very convenient for defenders of the MT to reapply this designation to Persia (Isa. 41:25), Media (Isa. 13:17), or both (e.g., Rashi), but such a reapplication does not fit the evidence. The peaceful takeover of Babylon by the Persians hardly matches what the reader finds in Jeremiah 50–51 (*ANET*, 315–16). The Medes are mentioned in Jeremiah 51:11, 28, but they are not explicitly identified as the enemy from the north. The enemy from the north in Jeremiah 50:3, 9, 41; 51:48 matches well the eschatological enemy from the north in Ezekiel 38:15–16. This enemy will use and abuse Babylon to accomplish his own purposes in the last days (see Rev. 17–18).

"In those days and at that time" (cf. MT Jer. 33:15), Israel and Judah will come together, "walking and weeping," and they will "seek" the Lord their God (Jer. 50:4 [LXX 27:4]; cf. Isa. 14:1–3). As noted in the commentary on Jeremiah 46:27–28, there are several references to the deliverance of the people of God throughout the oracle concerning Babylon (Jer. 50:4–7, 19–20; 51:5–6, 10, 35–36, 45–46, 50). This text envisions a reunited Israel and Judah (cf. Isa. 11:13; Jer. 3:17–18; 23:6; 30:3; 31:27, 31; 33:7; Ezek. 37:15–28; Zech. 9:13; 10:6). It is not clear whether the people are depicted here as weeping tears of contrition or joy, but the former seems more likely (see *Tg. Jon.*; BDB, 113; see also Jer. 31:9; 41:6; Pss. 30:6 [Eng., 30:5]; 126:5–6; cf. Judg. 2:4–5). Nevertheless, they will "seek" the Lord their God (cf. Jer. 29:13). This language is very similar to that of Hosea 3:5 and Zephaniah 2:3. The text of Hosea 3:5 comes from the postexilic composer of the Twelve and serves as the programmatic text for the entire composition: "Afterward, the sons of Israel will return and seek the Lord their God and David their king [*Tg. Jon.*: and they will listen to the Messiah, the son of David, their king] and fear to the Lord and to his goodness at the end of the days" (cf. Ezek. 34:23).[12] This text is a citation from Jeremiah 30:9: "And they will serve the Lord their God and David their king [*Tg. Jon.*: the Messiah, the son of David, their king] whom I will raise up for them" (cf. Jer. 23:5).

The syntax of Jeremiah 50:5a (LXX 27:5a) is somewhat halting according to the Masoretic accentuation: "Zion they will ask; a way, hither

---

11. Cf. Exodus 9:25; 12:12; Jeremiah 4:25, 29b; 49:18b, 33b; 51:62.

12. See Shepherd, *Commentary on the Book of the Twelve*, 23–25, 52–54.

their faces." The LXX smooths this out in order to give the sense: "They shall ask the way to Sion, for here they will set their face" (NETS). This anticipates the return from Babylon, not the returns under the leadership of Zerubbabel and Joshua, Ezra, or Nehemiah, but the eschatological return (see Isa. 66:20; Jer. 30:18; 31:6, 12, 21).[13] The Hebrew source behind Greek Jeremiah 50:5b (LXX 27:5b) says, "And they will come and be joined to the LORD" (LXX: "and they will come and flee to the Lord God"). The MT has imperatives: "Come and be joined to the LORD." Interpretation depends upon whether those who are to come and be joined to the LORD are the remnant of Israel and Judah (Jer. 50:4) or the people of the nations who will join the remnant of Israel and Judah (see Isa. 2:1–5; 14:1–3; 66:18–24; Jer. 3:17–18; 12:14–17; Amos 9:12; Mic. 4:1–5; Zech. 2:15 [Eng. 2:11]; 8:20–23). The verse concludes with reference to a "perpetual covenant" (ברית עולם) that will not be forgotten. All of the major divine-human covenants in the Bible are called ברית עולם: Noah (Gen. 9:16), Abraham (Gen. 17:7, 13, 19), Moses (Exod. 31:16), David (2 Sam. 23:5), and New (Isa. 55:3; 61:8; Jer. 32:40; Ezek. 16:60; 37:26). A conditional covenant like the Mosaic covenant is perpetual or indefinite only in the sense that the time of its breaking is unknown at its inception. Jeremiah 50:5b looks beyond the broken Mosaic covenant (Jer. 11:10) to the unconditional new covenant that will never be broken or forgotten (Jer. 31:31–34).

In Jeremiah 50:6a (LXX 27:6a), the LORD compares his people in their current state to lost sheep (cf. Num. 27:17; 1 Kgs. 22:17; Jer. 50:17; Ezek. 34:5; Zech. 10:2; Matt. 9:36; 10:6). This is because their shepherds (i.e., their kings) have led them astray (see Jer. 2:8; 10:21; 21:1–23:4). They have turned them away on the mountains. "From mountain to hill they go. They have forgotten their resting place" (Jer. 50:6b [LXX 27:6b]). This may mean nothing more than that they wander from place to place, but Rashi suggests that it speaks of how the kings of have led the people into idol worship at the alternative religious sites in the mountains and hills (see Jer. 2:20; 25:34–38; cf. Jer. 50:19).[14] What's more, "All those who find them, they devour them" (Jer. 50:7a [LXX 27:7a]). This is a rather deliberate reversal of the wording of Jeremiah 2:3: "Israel was holy [or, set apart] to the LORD, the first fruits of his produce. All who ate [or, devoured] him would be guilty; calamity would come to them" (cf. Jer. 30:16; see also Jer. 50:17; 51:34). According to the supposed Hebrew source behind Greek Jeremiah, their foes say, "Let us not forgive them" (לא נשאם). According to the MT,

---

13. See Rosenberg, trans., *Mikraoth Gedoloth: Jeremiah Volume Two*, 382.

14. See Rosenberg, trans., *Mikraoth Gedoloth: Jeremiah Volume Two*, 382.

they say, "We are not guilty" (לֹא נֶאְשָׁם) (cf. Jer. 2:3; 51:5; Zech. 11:5; see also Isa. 36:10). Redak, Holladay, and McKane all agree that the quotation of the foes stops here since it seems unlikely that such foes would provide the following rationale: "because they have sinned against the LORD" (Jer. 50:7b [LXX 27:7b]; cf. Jer. 3:25; 8:14; 14:7, 20; 16:10; 40:3; 44:23; 50:14b [MT]).[15] Yet there is evidence that the writer may have characterized their words in this sort of theological fashion (see Deut. 29:23–27 [Eng., 29:24–28]). The wording of the conclusion to Jeremiah 50:7b varies in the two Hebrew editions of the book. The Hebrew source behind Greek Jeremiah says: "a pasture of righteousness for the one who gathered (לְמַקְוֵה) their forefathers." According to this reading, the people are the "pasture of righteousness" (i.e., the righteous flock) for their shepherd the LORD who gathered their forefathers (cf. Ezek. 34:31; Pss. 74:1; 79:13; 95:7; 100:3; see also Jer. 31:23 [MT]; 33:12–13). The MT says: "a pasture of righteousness and the hope of (וּמִקְוֵה) their forefathers is the LORD."[16] According to this reading, the LORD is both "a pasture of righteousness" (cf. Jer. 50:19) and "the hope of their forefathers" (cf. Jer. 14:8; 17:13).

McKane raises the question whether Jeremiah 50:8 (LXX 27:8) belongs with 50:4–7 and concerns Israel's exodus from Babylon or whether it belongs with 50:9 and concerns the dispersion of Babylonians from their land after defeat:[17] "Flee from the midst of Babylon and from the land of the Chaldeans" (Jer. 50:8a).[18] The use of נוד ("flee") might suggest the latter option, but the consensus view sides with the former option due to the perceived dependence upon Isaiah 48:20: "Go forth from Babylon, flee from Chaldea" (see also Isa. 52:11; Jer. 50:16, 28; 51:6, 45). Even more instructive are the texts of Zechariah 2:10a (Eng., 2:6a) ("Ho, ho, and flee from the land of the north") and 2:11 (Eng., 2:7) ("Ho, Zion. Escape, inhabitant of daughter Babylon [or, Ho, escape to Zion, inhabitant of daughter Babylon]"). "The reality is that the people to whom Zechariah prophesied had already returned from Babylon, and there is no indication that this message was merely a call for more people to

---

15. See Rosenberg, trans., *Mikraoth Gedoloth: Jeremiah Volume Two*, 382; Holladay, *Jeremiah 2*, 416; McKane, *Jeremiah XXVI–LII*, 1256.

16. The proposal in the *BHS* apparatus suggests emendation of the MT's יהוה ("the LORD") at the end of 50:7 to הוי ("Ho"), which is then to be placed at the beginning of 50:8 (cf. Zech. 2:10, 11 [Eng., 2:6, 7]).

17. McKane, *Jeremiah XXVI–LII*, 1258.

18. The placement of the *athnach* in the MT requires the *kethiv* (יצאו) or the *qere* (צאו) to be read with 50:8a. The use of the conjunction in the Hebrew source behind Greek Jeremiah (וצאו) puts this word with 50:8b.

return from the land of Babylon under Persian rule. The language suggests that the land of the north here is the eschatological land of the north" (cf. Jer. 16:14–15; 23:7–8; see Rev. 18:4; see also 2 Cor. 6:17).[19] *Targum Jonathan* interprets "be like he-goats before sheep" (Jer. 50:8b) to mean "be like leaders before the people" (see BDB, 800). The LXX has "dragons" (δράκοντες) instead of "he-goats," but this is likely an inner-Greek corruption of "leaders" (ἄρχοντες) (cf. Isa. 14:9).

In Jeremiah 50:9a (LXX 27:9a), the Lord explains that he is about to arouse against Babylon "an assembly of nations" (קהל גוים) (cf. Gen. 35:11) from the land of the north that will arrange for battle against her (cf. Jer. 50:14, 41; 51:1), and from the land of Babylon she will be captured. As noted in the commentary on 50:3, this enemy from the north is not Persia or Media, despite texts elsewhere that speak of the Lord arousing either Cyrus (Isa. 41:2, 25; Ezra 1:1) or the Medes (Isa. 13:17; Jer. 51:11). The key phrase here is "an assembly of nations" (קהל גוים) from the land of the north (cf. Jer. 50:41). While the Medes are included in a group of nations summoned against historical Babylon in Jeremiah 51:27–28, this group is not designated an assembly of nations from the land of the north. The use of קהל ("assembly") for a military force is particularly well known from the book of Ezekiel (e.g., Ezek. 17:17; 23:24; 26:7; 32:3, 22, 23) where it occurs most prominently in Ezekiel 38:4, 7, 13, 15 to describe the horde of nations that will accompany Gog, the enemy from the north who will appear in the last days. Like an arrow of a skilled warrior, this eschatological enemy will not return empty-handed (MT: "His arrows are like a bereaving (מַשְׁכִּיל) [nonn Mss: skilled (מַשְׂכִּיל)] warrior who does not return empty-handed) (Jer. 50:9b [LXX 27:9b]). In other words, the assembly of nations will accomplish the purpose for which it is sent (cf. Isa. 55:11). Chaldea will become plunder, and all those who plunder her will be satisfied (Jer. 50:10 [LXX 27:10]; cf. Jer. 30:16; 49:32; Hab. 2:8).

Because the Babylonians rejoice and exult as the plunderers of the Lord's inheritance (Jer. 50:11a [LXX 27:11a]; cf. Isa. 19:25; Jer. 12:7, 8, 9) because they skip "like calves in the grass" (כְּעֶגְלֵי בַדֶּשָׁא)[20] and neigh like horses (Jer. 50:11b [LXX 27:11b]; cf. Jer. 8:16; 47:3), their "mother" is very ashamed (Jer. 50:12a [LXX 27:12a]). The mother here is the personified city or nation in an abstract sense (see *Tg. Jon.*, Rashi; cf. Isa. 50:1; Hos. 2:4 [Eng., 2:2]; 4:5). The children are the inhabitants of the city/nation. The Hebrew source behind Greek Jeremiah calls

---

19. Shepherd, *Commentary on the Book of the Twelve*, 404.
20. Cf. Malachi 3:20; MT: "like a threshing heifer" (כְּעֶגְלָה דָשָׁה) (cf. Deut. 25:4; Hos. 10:11).

Babylon "a mother for good" (אם על טובה). The MT has instead: "she who bore you feels shame" (חפרה יולדתכם). According to Sharp, "it is far more difficult to explain the MT and LXX versions of l 12 by derivation one from the other than to concede the possibility of two differing original *Vorlagen*."[21] Jeremiah 50:12b (LXX 27:12b) calls Babylon "end of nations" (אחרית גוים), "a wilderness" (MT adds: "dry land and desert plain" [cf. Jer. 51:43]). The phrase אחרית גוים ("end of nations") only occurs here in the Hebrew Bible, but the phrase ראשית גוים ("beginning of nations") occurs in Numbers 24:20. Keil comments, "'The last of the nations' is the antithesis of 'the first of the nations,' as Balaam calls Amalek, Num. 24:20, because they were the first heathen nation that began to fight against the people of Israel" (see Exod. 17:8).[22] Babylon is the last to do so, and its end will likewise be ruin.[23]

Due to the LORD's wrath, Babylon will not be inhabited; all of her will be an appalling desolation (Jer. 50:13a [LXX 27:13a]; cf. Jer. 6:8; 9:10 [Eng., 9:11]; 12:10–11; 34:22b; 44:6; 49:33). Everyone who passes by Babylon will be appalled and hiss because of all her wounds (Jer. 50:13b [LXX 27:13b]; cf. Jer. 18:16; 19:8; 49:17). In Jeremiah 50:14 (LXX 27:14), commands are given to the enemy archers who are to surround Babylon and arrange for battle (cf. Jer. 46:3, 9; 50:9, 29): "Shoot at her! Do not spare an arrow!" The MT adds a theological explanation at the end of the verse: "For it is against the LORD that she has sinned" (cf. Jer. 50:7b). This text is not in the Hebrew source behind Greek Jeremiah, but it does provide insight into how a former instrument of the LORD's judgment (Jer. 27:6; 51:7) has become the object of the LORD's wrath (see Isa. 47:6; Jer. 50:24b, 29b; Zech. 1:15).

The instruction in 50:15a (LXX 27:15a) to "shout" against Babylon (i.e., to give a battle cry in order to cause panic [see Redak]) is accompanied by the statement, "Her hand is given" (נִתְּנָה יָדָהּ) (MT: "She has given her hand" [נָתְנָה יָדָהּ]). This expression indicates submission (see 1 Chr. 29:24; 2 Chr. 30:8; BDB, 680). Babylon's bulwarks have fallen. Her city wall is torn down. 50:15b (LXX 27:15b) explains that this is "the vengeance of the LORD" (cf. Num. 31:3; Jer. 50:28; 51:11). The enemy is to take vengeance against Babylon and do to her as she has done (cf. Jer. 50:29; Obad. 15; see also Rev. 18:6). The final imperative

---

21. Sharp, "Take Another Scroll and Write," 498.
22. Keil, *Jeremiah*, 428.
23. The phrase ראשית הגוים occurs in Amos 6:1 where it describes Israel as "the best of the nations." It is possible then that אחרית גוים in Jeremiah 50:12b may describe Babylon as "least/worst of nations."

of the sequence occurs in 50:16a (LXX 27:16a): "Cut off[24] seed (זרע) [MT: sower (זורע); *Tg. Jon.*: the king] from Babylon and one who handles a sickle at harvest time [*Tg. Jon.*: at killing time]." *Targum Jonathan* understands this in a metaphorical sense (cf. Jer. 51:33; Hos. 6:11), but Redak interprets it to be the literal stoppage of sowing and harvesting due to the devastation of the land.[25] Jeremiah 50:16b (LXX 27:16b) adds, "Because of a Greek (יונייה) sword [MT: a sword that oppresses (היונה); *Tg. Jon.*: the sword of the enemy, which is like wine (חמר = Heb. יין) that makes drunk], each to his people they will turn, and each to his land they will flee" (cf. Isa. 13:14; Jer. 25:38; 46:16; 50:8, 16, 28).[26] This anticipates the flight of foreigners living in Babylon to their respective homelands (see Jer. 50:37).

In Jeremiah 50:17a (LXX 27:17a), the LORD calls Israel a scattered "sheep" (שה). This noun in Hebrew is not collective like the word צאן (cf. Jer. 50:6). Thus, the metaphor is that of a single sheep driven away and isolated from the flock by lions. Both the Syriac ("shepherds" and *Targum Jonathan* ("kings") understand the lions to be kings according to 50:17b (LXX 27:17b) (cf. Jer. 2:15; Nah. 2:12–14 [Eng., 2:11–13]). The former king, the king of Assyria, "devoured" Israel (cf. Jer. 50:7). This refers primarily to the exile of the northern kingdom of Israel (2 Kgs. 17), which also had negative consequences for Judah (see Isa. 7–8). The former king, the king of Babylon, "has gnawed broken his bones" (עצמו).[27] This refers to the Babylonian invasion and captivity of Judah (2 Kgs. 25; Jer. 39; 52; 2 Chr. 36).[28] Therefore, the LORD (MT: "the LORD of hosts, the God of Israel" [cf. Jer. 50:33]) says that he is about to "visit upon" or "punish" the king of Babylon and his land just as he

---

24. Based on usage, Rudolph suggests in the *BHS* apparatus that *hiphil* הכרתו has been corrupted to *qal* כרתו due to haplography (see לה at the end of 50:15), but see Jeremiah 11:19.
25. See Rosenberg, trans., *Mikraoth Gedoloth: Jeremiah Volume Two*, 385.
26. Parke-Taylor raises the question whether the rendering "Greek sword" comes from a translator thinking of the campaigns of Alexander the Great (*Formation of the Book of Jeremiah*, 169). On the other hand, it is possible that this reading was already present in the translator's *Vorlage* and referred not to an actual Greek invasion of Babylon but to an invasion characterized by the kind of warfare for which the Greeks were known.
27. NETS: "and this later one, king of Babylon, his bones (= עַצְמוֹ? or עַצְמוּ?)."
28. Kara: "The figure is a sheep that was torn by a wild beast, who devoured its flesh, leaving over only the bones. Another beast comes along, finding only dry bones, and breaks them to suck out the marrow. So was it with Nebuchadnezzar, he found only the remains of the tribes of Judah and Benjamin" (Rosenberg, trans., *Mikraoth Gedoloth: Jeremiah Volume Two*, 386).

punished the king of Assyria (Jer. 50:18 [LXX 27:18]; cf. Isa. 52:1–6; see comments on MT Jer. 50:14b). The divine judgment of Assyria is vividly depicted in the book of Nahum (see also Isa. 37:21–29), which provides a helpful analogy for the judgment of Babylon envisioned here. It is worth noting that the historical judgment of Nineveh/Assyria in the book of Nahum serves to illustrate the eschatological judgment anticipated in Nahum 1:2–8.[29]

After the announcement of judgment against Babylon, the text turns again to the restoration of Israel: "And I will restore Israel to his pasture, and he will graze on Carmel [MT adds: and Bashan], and in the hill country of Ephraim and in Gilead [*Tg. Jon.*: and on the mountain of the house of Ephraim and the sanctuary (cf. Jer. 22:6)] his desire will be sated [NETS: and he shall feed on Carmel and Mount Ephraim and in Galaad, and his soul shall be satisfied (cf. Syr.)]" (Jer. 50:19 [LXX 27:19]; cf. Jer. 50:4–7). In contrast to Jeremiah 50:6–7, where reference is made to the people as "lost sheep" (cf. Jer. 50:17a: "a scattered sheep") wandering "from mountain to hill" and being "devoured" (lit., eaten) by all who find them (cf. Jer. 50:17b), the present text speaks of Israel restored to its pasture (cf. Jer. 50:7b), grazing (i.e., eating) on Mount Carmel (MT adds "Bashan") and having its desire satisfied in the hill country of Ephraim and in Gilead (cf. Jer. 2:7a; 31:23 [MT]; 33:12–13; Ezek. 34:14; Mic. 7:14).[30] *Targum Jonathan* has "the sanctuary" in place of "Gilead," presumably because of the comparison made between the royal palace and both Gilead and Lebanon in Jeremiah 22:6 and similar description of the temple elsewhere (e.g., 1 Kgs. 5:19–20 [Eng., 5:5–6]).

"In those days and at that time" (Jer. 50:20a [LXX 27:20a]; cf. Jer. 50:4), the iniquity of the northern kingdom of Israel will be sought, but there will be none. The sins of the southern kingdom of Judah will be sought, but none will be found. Redak comments, "This could not possibly be referring to the time of the Second Temple, when the Jews committed many sins, as they do in this present exile."[31] Yet the reason provided in the text for the inability to find iniquity or sin is not the absence of sins committed but the forgiveness of sin: "For I will forgive those who are left

---

29. See Shepherd, *Commentary on the Book of the Twelve*, 285–309.
30. "Rudolph and Weiser discern a significance in the circumstance that these pastures are located in parts of the land alienated since Assyrian times. They are within the borders of the former northern kingdom which is, therefore, also embraced by the promise of return" (McKane, *Jeremiah XXVI–LII*, 1270). See Jeremiah 3:18; 50:4.
31. Rosenberg, trans., *Mikraoth Gedoloth: Jeremiah Volume Two*, 387.

in the land [MT: For I will forgive whomever I leave]" (Jer. 50:20b [LXX 27:20b]; see Jer. 31:34; 33:8; 36:3).[32] In other words, neither iniquity nor sin will be reckoned to the people; therefore, such things will not be found. Because this is a feature of the eschatological new covenant relationship, Keil rightly comments, "The deliverance of Israel from Babylon coincides with the view given of the regeneration of the people by the Messiah, just as we find throughout the second portion of Isaiah."[33]

50:21 (27:21) "Merathaim [LXX: Bitterly], go up against her [MT: Against the land,[34] Merathaim, go up against her; Tg. Jon.: Go up against the land of the rebellious people; Vulg.: Go up against the land of rulers], and against the inhabitants upon her, Pekod [LXX: take vengeance; MT: and against the inhabitants of Pekod], O sword [MT: attack], and exterminate [MT adds: after them (Tg. Jon.: their remnant)]," the prophetic utterance of the LORD, "and do according to all that I have commanded you. 50:22 (27:22) A sound of battle [MT adds: in the land] and great breaking in the land of the Chaldeans [in the land of the Chaldeans > MT]! 50:23 (27:23) How the hammer of all the earth [Tg. Jon.: the king who made all the earth shake] is cut down and broken! How Babylon has become a desolation [or, object of horror] among the nations! 50:24 (27:24) They lay snares for you [LXX: They will attack you; MT: I lay snares for you (or, You lay snares for yourself)], and also you are captured, O Babylon; and you, you do not know. You are found, and also you are caught [You are found, and also you are caught > Syr.], for it is with the LORD [Tg. Jon.: the people of the Lord] that you have engaged in strife [LXX: because you resisted the Lord]. 50:25 (27:25) The LORD has opened his storehouse and brought forth the vessels of his indignation [Tg. Jon.: vessels of a cup of curse before him], for the Lord GOD [MT adds: of hosts] has a work in the land of the Chaldeans. 50:26 (27:26) For her ends [LXX: times] have come [MT: Come to her from end]. Open her granaries [Syr., Tg. Jon.: gates], pile her up [LXX, Syr.: search her] like a cave [MT: like heaps; Syr.: as naked], and exterminate her [Tg. Jon.: destroy her possessions; like those who destroy a heap of grain, so destroy her]. Do not let her have a remnant. 50:27 (27:27) Attack [LXX: Dry up] all her fruit [MT: all her bulls (Tg. Jon.: warriors)], and [and > MT] let them go down to the slaughter. Woe to them, for their day has come, and [and > MT] the time of their visitation." 50:28 (27:28) A sound of people fleeing and escaping from the land of Babylon to declare

---

32. The MT has the phrase עַל הָאָרֶץ at the beginning of 50:21.
33. Keil, *Jeremiah*, 430.
34. The LXX reads the phrase עַל הָאָרֶץ with the end of 50:20 (LXX 27:20).

in Zion the vengeance of the LORD *our God [MT adds: the vengeance for his temple]. 50:29 (27:29) "Summon against Babylon many [cf. Syr., Tg. Jon., Vulg., Luther; or, shooters / archers], all archers [lit., all benders of a bow]. Encamp against her all around. Do not let her have an escaped remnant. Repay her according to her work. According to all that she has done, do to her. For it is against the* LORD *[Tg. Jon.: the people of the Lord] that she has acted presumptuously [LXX: she has resisted], against the Holy One of Israel. 50:30 (27:30) Therefore, her choice young men will fall in her squares, and all her fighting men will be thrown down [MT: will be silenced / destroyed in that day]," the prophetic utterance of the* LORD. *50:31 (27:31) "Look, I am against you, Zadon [Presumption; Tg. Jon.: wicked king]," the prophetic utterance of the* LORD *[MT: Lord* GOD *of hosts], "for your day has come and the time of your visitation [MT: the time that I visit you]. 50:32 (27:32) And your presumption [MT: Zadon / Presumption; Tg. Jon.: the wicked king] will stumble and fall and not have anyone raising up. And I will kindle a fire in its / his forest [MT: cities], and it will consume all its / his surroundings."*

50:33 (27:33) Thus says the LORD *[MT adds: of hosts], "The sons of Israel and the sons of Judah together are oppressed. All their captors, they have kept hold of them, for [for > MT] they have refused to send them away. 50:34 (27:34) But [> MT] their redeemer is strong. The* LORD *of hosts is his name. Contending [or, With contention] he will contend with those who contend with him [MT: he will contend their contention (or, plead their cause)] in order to give rest to the land [LXX: take away the land; Tg. Jon.: break the wicked of the earth] but cause disquiet for the inhabitants of Babylon. 50:35 (27:35) A sword [Tg. Jon.: Those who slay by the sword will come] against the [the > MT] Chaldeans," [MT adds: the prophetic utterance of the* LORD*], "and against the inhabitants of Babylon and against her leaders and against her wise men, 50:36 (27:36) [MT adds: a sword against the empty talkers (false prophets, diviners), and they will be shown to be fools], a sword against her mighty men, and they will be dismayed / terrified [LXX: paralyzed; Syr., Tg. Jon.: broken], 50:37 a sword against their [MT: his] horses and against their [MT: his] chariots,*[35] *(27:37) a sword against their mighty men [> MT] and against [MT adds: all] the mixed multitude [Tg. Jon.: troops] that is in her midst, and they will become women [LXX: and they will be as women], a sword against her treasures / treasuries, and they will*

---

35. The MT's "a sword against his horses and against his chariots" appears at the beginning of 50:37, but LXX 27:37 does not begin until after "a sword against their horses and against their chariots."

be scattered [MT: plundered], 50:38 (27:38) [MT adds: a drought (Syr.: a sword)] against her water(s), and they will be ashamed [MT: dry], for a land of carved/sculpted idols is she, and among the coastlands they boast [or, act madly; MT: and because of idols (lit., terrors) they act madly; Tg. Jon.: and in idols they boast]. 50:39 (27:39) Therefore, desert creatures will live with jackals/hyenas, and ostriches will live in her [NETS: Therefore phantoms shall live in the islands, and daughters of Sirens shall inhabit her]. She [MT: And she] will never again be inhabited forever [MT adds: and she will not be settled for generations to come]. 50:40 (27:40) Like God's overthrow of Sodom and Gomorrah and their neighbors [MT: her neighbors]," the prophetic utterance of the Lord, *"a man/person will not live there, and a human being will not sojourn in her [LXX: there]. 50:41 (27:41) Look, a people coming from north; and a great nation and many kings, they are aroused from earth's remote parts [LXX: from the end of the earth]. 50:42 (27:42) Bow and javelin/spear they grasp. He is cruel, and he does not have compassion [MT: They are cruel, and they do not have compassion]. Their sound, like the sea it roars, and upon horses they ride. He is arranged like a fire [MT: like a man] for battle against you, O daughter Babylon. 50:43 (27:43) The king of Babylon hears the report of them, and his hands go slack. Distress, it grips him, writhing like that of a woman in labor. 50:44 (27:44) Look, [Tg. Jon. adds: a king with his armies will go up against them] like a lion that goes up from the Jordan [MT: the pride/ majesty of the Jordan] to Ethan [MT: a perennial pasture], indeed I will suddenly cause them to run away from upon her, and every choice young man will I appoint against her [MT: and whomever is chosen will I appoint against/over her]. For who is like me? And who will summon/ arraign [LXX: oppose] me? And who is the shepherd [Tg. Jon.: king] who will stand before me? 50:45 (27:45) Therefore, hear the counsel of the* Lord *that he has made against Babylon and his thoughts that he has had against the inhabitants [Codex L: land] of the Chaldeans: The he-goats [LXX: lambs; MT: little ones; Tg. Jon.: strong] of the flock [Tg. Jon.: people] will surely be dragged away [LXX: destroyed; MT: they will surely drag them away], pasture [Syr., Tg. Jon., Vulg.: their pasture] will surely be desolated from upon them [MT: pasture will surely be appalled at them].*[36] *50:46 (27:46) For/Indeed [> MT] from/because of the sound that is made when Babylon is captured, the earth/ground is made to quake, and an outcry [Syr., Tg. Jon.: her outcry] among the nations is heard."*

---

36. Lit., "If the he-goats of the flock are not dragged away, if pasture is not desolated from upon them."

"Merathaim" and "Pekod" are place names in the Babylonian region (Jer. 50:21a [LXX: 27:21a]; see Ezek. 23:23), but they are chosen here as parts for the whole (synecdoche) because of their meanings "double rebellion" (מרתים) and "punishment" (פקוד).[37] Babylon has been doubly or fully rebellious (cf. Isa. 40:2; Jer. 16:18); therefore, divine visitation or punishment is due to it (see Jer. 50:18, 27b, 31b [LXX 27:18, 27b, 31b]). According to Greek Jeremiah, the commands to go up against Merathaim and Pekod and exterminate them are directed to a "sword" (חֶרֶב) (Jer. 50:21b [LXX 27:21b]; see Jer. 50:35–38 [LXX 27:35–38]). The enemy is to do according to all that the LORD commands. In the MT, however, the commands are directed to the unidentified enemy generally, and חרב is vocalized as חֲרֹב ("attack") (cf. Jer. 50:27). The MT also includes the phrase אחריהם ("after them") after the imperative "exterminate" (cf. Lev. 26:33). *Targum Jonathan* interprets this phrase as if it were אחריתם ("their remnant") (see Jer. 50:26; Amos 9:1).

Jeremiah 50:22 (LXX 27:22) highlights a "sound of battle" (MT adds: "in the land") and "great breaking (שבר גדול) in the land of the Chaldeans" ("in the land of the Chaldeans" > MT). This hearkens back to earlier descriptions of the coming of the enemy from the north (Jer. 4:6; 6:1; see also Jer. 14:17b; 48:3; 51:54; Zeph. 1:10). Thus, the exclamation, "How the hammer of all the earth [*Tg. Jon.*: the king who made all the earth shake] is cut down and broken (וישבר)" (Jer. 50:23a [LXX 27:23a]; see Jer. 51:8, 20–23; see also Jer. 23:29)! Just as Babylon has done, so is it done to Babylon (Jer. 50:15, 29; cf. Obad. 15). "How Babylon has become a desolation [or, object of horror] among the nations!" (Jer. 50:23b [LXX 27:23b]; cf. Jer. 51:41; Zeph. 2:15).

Greek Jeremiah 50:24a (LXX 27:24a) reflects יקשו לך ("They lay snares for you"). The MT has the verbal form יקשתי, which may be first common singular ("I lay snares for you") or second feminine singular ("You lay snares for yourself") (see GKC §44h). Babylon is captured yet unaware of it, which means that its downfall occurs suddenly and unexpectedly due to its pride and overconfidence (cf. Jer. 51:8). Babylon is found and caught because it is with the LORD (*Tg. Jon.*: "the people of the Lord") that it has engaged in strife (Jer. 50:24b [LXX 27:24b]). Babylon has overstepped its bounds as the LORD's instrument of judgment (Isa. 47:6; MT Jer. 50:14b, 29b; Zech. 1:15). The Syriac version reflects a Hebrew text that lacks the first part of 50:24b ("You are

---

37. The Greek πικρῶς ("bitterly") is based on interpretation of מרתים from מרר ("to be bitter") rather than מרה ("to be rebellious"). The Vulgate's "rulers" is apparently based on the Aramaic מרא ("lord").

found, and also you are caught"). This allows the statement at the end of 50:24a ("you do not know") to be read with the כִּי clause at the end of 50:24b as a content clause: "you do not know that it is with the LORD that you have engaged in strife." This reading suggests that Babylon has acted in ignorance of its offense against the LORD.

The image of Jeremiah 50:25a (LXX 27:25a) is that of the LORD opening his armory (lit., "his storehouse") and bringing forth his weapons (lit., "the vessels of his indignation") (cf. Isa. 13:5; see also Rom. 9:22). *Targum Jonathan* interprets "the vessels of his indignation" to be "vessels of a cup of curse before him" (see Jer. 25:15–26; cf. *Tg. Jon.* Jer. 8:14). The LORD himself is fighting against Babylon, albeit by means of the enemy from the north. Jeremiah 50:25b (LXX 27:25b) explains that the Lord GOD has a "work" to do in the land of the Chaldeans (cf. Jer. 51:10). The Hebrew source behind Greek Jeremiah 50:26a (LXX 27:26a) begins with a causal clause: "For her ends [LXX: times] have come" (כִּי בָאוּ קִצֶּיהָ). That is, the times of Babylon's reign of terror have come to an end. On the other hand, the MT has an imperative directed to the members of the attacking army: "Come to her from end" (בֹּאוּ לָהּ מִקֵּץ). This apparently means to attack from the remotest parts of the earth (see Vulg.). The following imperative, "Open her granaries," seems to command the enemy to hit Babylon's food supply (cf. Jer. 50:16), yet *Targum Jonathan* interprets this metaphorically: "Open her gates [cf. Syr.], destroy her possessions; like those who destroy a heap of grain, so destroy her." There may very well be some validity to this since it is Babylon that is piled up and not her grain (cf. Jer. 51:33). The imperative סלוה ("pile her up") is rendered by the LXX and Syriac as "search her." This is likely an accommodation to the following phrase in the perceived *Vorlage* of these versions. The LXX reflects כמערה or כמו מערה ("like a cave"), while the Syriac reflects כמו ערמה ("as naked/exposed/bare"). The MT has כמו ערמים ("like heaps"). The enemy is to exterminate Babylon and not leave her a remnant (Jer. 50:26b [LXX 27:26b]; cf. Jer. 50:21b, 29a; 51:3b; see also Jer. 11:23). Needless to say, this did not take place at the hands of the Medes or the Persians or any other historical nation. It anticipates an eschatological judgment of the wicked. The first part of 50:27a (LXX 27:27a) in Greek continues the metaphor from 50:26: "Dry up all her fruit (פִּרְיָהּ)." This interprets the imperative חרבו as if it were a *hiphil* of חָרֵב ("to be dry") rather than a *qal* of חָרַב ("to attack"). The MT says, "Attack all her bulls (פָּרֶיהָ)." This fits with the remainder of 50:27a: "let them go down to the slaughter." *Targum Jonathan* interprets the bulls to be warriors (cf. Isa. 34:7; Jer. 48:15; 51:40; Ezek. 39:18). "Woe to them," says Jeremiah 50:27b (LXX 27:27b), "for their day has come, and [and > MT] the time of their visitation" (cf. Jer. 46:21b; 49:8b; 50:18, 21a, 31b; 51:18; see also Jer. 8:12; 10:15).

In addition to the "sound of battle" referenced in 50:22 is the "sound of people fleeing and escaping from the land of Babylon" (Jer. 50:28a [LXX 27:28a]; cf. Jer. 51:6, 50). (Note also the "sound" of the army from the north in 50:42 and the "sound" of Babylon's outcry in 50:46.) These are people fleeing and escaping specifically "to declare in Zion the vengeance of the Lord our God" (Jer. 50:28b [LXX 27:28b]; cf. Jer. 50:8, 15b; 51:10; see also Jer. 46:10). The MT adds that this is "the vengeance for his temple" (see Jer. 51:11b, 51; see also 2 Kgs. 25:9; Jer. 39:8; 52:13; 2 Chr. 36:19). Jeremiah 50:29a (LXX 27:29a) begins, according to the early versions (Syr., *Tg. Jon.*, Vulg.; see also Luther), with a call to summon against Babylon "many" (רַבִּים). Modern versions tend to interpret this same word as "shooters/archers" (= רֹבִים) to provide a parallel for the following "all archers" (lit., "all benders of a bow") (cf. Jer. 50:14). These archers are to encamp against Babylon all around and are not to allow an escaped remnant (cf. Jer. 50:26b). Babylon is to be repaid according to what she has done (cf. Jer. 50:15; 51:6b, 24, 56; Obad. 15; Rev. 18:6). This *lex talionis* ("law of retaliation") is a prominent theme in the oracle concerning Babylon. Jeremiah 50:29b (LXX 27:29b) explains that it is against the Lord (*Tg. Jon.*: "the people of the Lord") that Babylon has acted presumptuously (cf. Jer. 50:14b, 24b, 31, 32; see again Isa. 47:6; Zech. 1:15; see also the description of the Egyptians' behavior in Exod. 18:11; Neh. 9:10). Babylon's presumption is against "the Holy One of Israel" (cf. MT Jer. 51:5b), a favorite title for the Lord in the book of Isaiah (Isa. 1:4; 5:19, 24; 10:20; 12:6; 17:7; 29:19; 30:11, 12, 15; 31:1; 37:23; 41:14, 16, 20; 43:3, 14; 45:11; 47:4; 48:17; 54:5; 60:9, 14).

The announcement of judgment in Jeremiah 50:30 (LXX 27:30) is virtually identical to Jeremiah 49:26 (see also Jer. 51:6a; 1 Macc. 2:9): "Therefore, her choice young men will fall in her squares, and all her fighting men will be thrown down [MT: will be silenced/destroyed in that day]," the prophetic utterance of the Lord. The Greek text of 50:30b (LXX 27:30b) has "will be thrown down" (= יֵרַמּוּ), whereas the Greek text of 49:26b (LXX 30:15b) has "will fall." The MT has "will be silenced/destroyed" (יִדַּמּוּ) in both texts. The phrase "in that day," which is present in both texts in the MT, does not appear in either text in the Hebrew source behind Greek Jeremiah. The addition of צבאות at the end of MT 49:26 is absent from LXX 30:15 and from MT 50:30 and LXX 27:30.

In Jeremiah 50:31a (LXX 27:31a), the Lord says, "Look, I am against you, Zadon" (cf. Jer. 21:13a). The name "Zadon" ("presumption"), which *Targum Jonathan* renders as "wicked king," is a name for Babylon much like "Merathaim" ("double rebellion") and "Pekod" ("punishment") in 50:21a. Babylon has acted presumptuously against the Lord and his people (see Jer. 50:29b; cf. Jer. 49:16). The Lord is now against Babylon because its day has come and the time of its visitation/punishment (Jer. 50:31b [LXX 27:31b]; cf. Jer. 46:21b; 49:8b; 50:27b; 51:18; see also Jer. 50:18). Babylon's presumption will fall and not have anyone to raise it up (Jer. 50:32a [LXX 27:32a]; cf. Isa. 24:20b; Jer. 25:27; Amos 5:2; 8:14b). According to the Hebrew source behind Greek Jeremiah 50:32b (LXX 27:32b), the Lord will kindle a fire "in its/his forest" (ביערו), which will consume all its/his surroundings.[38] This text is very close to that of Jeremiah 21:14b. On the other hand, the MT says that the Lord will kindle a fire "in its/his cities" (בעריו) (cf. Amos 1:14).

Jeremiah 50:33–34 (LXX 27:33–34) begins a new subsection with a clear indication that the Lord is acting on behalf of his people. Both the children of Israel and the children of Judah are oppressed (Jer. 50:33a), the former by the Assyrians and the latter by the Babylonians (see Jer. 50:17). All their captors have kept hold of them, refusing to send them away (Jer. 50:33b). This language is reminiscent of Pharaoh's refusal to dismiss the people of Israel at Moses' request (see Exod. 4:23; 5:1–2; 7:14, 27; 9:2). Nevertheless, there will be a future reunification of Israel and Judah (Jer. 3:18; 50:4; 51:5). Despite the fact that their captors "have kept hold of them" (החזיקו), their redeemer is "strong" (חזק), and the Lord of hosts/armies is his name (Jer. 50:34a; cf. Prov. 23:11a; Rev. 18:8; see also Amos 4:13b; 5:8b). It is not necessary to see in every occurrence of "redeemer" (גאל) an intentional reference to the instruction for kinsman-redeemers (see Lev. 25:25–55; see also Ruth). In this context, it is essentially a dead metaphor that falls within the same semantic field as "savior/deliverer" (מושיע) (see Isa. 49:26b; 60:16b; see also Isa. 41:14; 43:14; 44:6, 24; 47:4; 48:17; 49:7; 54:5, 8; 63:16; Jer. 31:11). The Hebrew source behind Greek Jeremiah says that the Lord will contend "with those who contend with him" (את רביו) (cf. Jer. 25:31). The MT says that he will contend "their contention" (את ריבם); that is, plead their cause (cf. Isa. 49:25b; Jer. 51:36; Prov. 23:11b; see also Jer. 5:28; 22:16; 30:13). This is "in order to give rest (הרגיע) to the land but cause disquiet (הרגיז) for the inhabitants of Babylon" (Jer. 50:34b; see Jer. 6:16).[39] Once again, the

---

38. The pronominal suffixes in the Hebrew text are masculine because they refer not to "Babylon" but to זדון ("presumption"). The Greek text uses feminine pronouns because the noun for "presumption" in Greek is feminine.

39. The MT's suffixed conjugation verbs in this last part of the verse should perhaps be vocalized as infinitives (see *BHS* apparatus). The "land" in the immediate context is likely the land of Israel, although it is certainly true that Babylon's reign of terror extended well beyond the borders of Israel.

tables are turned. As Babylon has done (disrupting the land for its own gain), so will it be done to Babylon (Jer. 50:15, 29).

Verses 35–38 are united by their repetition of the keyword חרב ("sword"), which *Targum Jonathan* takes to represent those who slay by the sword (cf. Jer. 46:10; 50:16). This sword will come "against the Chaldeans and against the inhabitants of Babylon and against her leaders and against her wise men" (Jer. 50:35 [LXX 27:35]; cf. Jer. 51:57). The wise men here may be of the same class as those encountered in Daniel 2:1–13 (cf. Isa. 19:11–12). MT 50:36a is absent from the Hebrew source behind Greek Jeremiah, and this causes a difference in versification in printed editions of the MT and the LXX. The absence of MT 50:36a in the Hebrew *Vorlage* of the LXX may be due to homoioarchton, but the presence of this text in the MT may be an added explication of the wise men based on wording from Isaiah 19:11–12 and 44:25: "a sword against the empty talkers [false prophets, diviners], and they will be shown to be fools." Those considered wise advisors of the Babylonian king, those who no doubt promised good things to come in an effort to win the king's favor, will be exposed as fools and frauds in the downfall of Babylon.[40] In addition to the general populace of Babylon and its leadership, there will also be a sword against her "mighty men" (i.e., warriors), and they will be "dismayed/terrified" (LXX: "paralyzed"; Syr., *Tg. Jon.*: "broken") (Jer. 50:36b [LXX 27:36a]). Indeed, the sword will be against all of Babylon's military forces: "a sword against their [MT: his] horses and against their [MT: his] chariots" (Jer. 50:37a [LXX 27:36b]). The Hebrew source behind Greek Jeremiah then adds, "a sword against their mighty men" (LXX 27:37a), a virtual repetition of 50:36b (LXX 27:36a) that is absent from the MT. This is followed by a reference to the "mixed multitude" (ערב): "and against [MT adds: all] the mixed multitude [*Tg. Jon.*: troops] that is in her midst, and they will become women [LXX: and they will be as women]." This mixed multitude presumably consists of foreign mercenaries who have come to aid Babylon against its enemies (cf. Jer. 46:9, 16; see also Exod. 12:38). They prove not to be strong and

---

40. The Talmud interprets הבדים ("the empty talkers") to be those who study the Torah "each by himself" (בדים) and not in groups (see Neusner, *Jeremiah in Talmud and Midrash*, 275–76, 296, 367). This refers to those who neglect the insights of others in the study of the Torah. Of course, Psalm 1 commends individual study of the Torah, and there are times when a person must sit alone with the Torah apart from others (see Jer. 15:17), but such individual study should be understood in conjunction with community study (Neh. 8–9).

courageous like mighty warriors but weak and fearful like women (cf. Jer. 48:41; 49:22; 51:30; Nah. 3:13). The attacking enemy will come against Babylon's "treasures/treasuries" (Jer. 50:37b [LXX 27:37b]), and, according to the Hebrew source behind Greek Jeremiah, they will be "scattered" (וּבֹזְרוּ). The MT says that they will be "plundered" (וּבֻזָּזוּ). The final verse of this unit begins in the Hebrew source behind Greek Jeremiah as follows: "against her water(s), and they will be ashamed (וְיֵבֹשׁוּ)" (Jer. 50:38a [LXX 27:38a]; see Jer. 51:13). This seems to imply that the sword of verses 35–37 will be against Babylon's water, which seems odd at first glance, but only if taken in an overly literal fashion. It is likely nothing more than a way to indicate devastation at the hands of the enemy army. The MT, however, says, "a drought (חֹרֶב) against her water(s), and they will be dry (וְיָבֵשׁוּ)" (cf. Jer. 51:36b; Rev. 16:12). This appears to be an adjustment in reaction to the initial oddness of the image of a sword against water. The Syriac, however, which follows the same consonantal Hebrew text here as that found in the MT, renders חרב not as "drought" (חֹרֶב) but as "sword" (חֶרֶב). Jeremiah 50:38b (LXX 27:38b) explains that the sword against Babylon in 50:35–38a is due to the fact that Babylon is "a land of carved/sculpted idols," "and among the coastlands (וּבָאִיִּים) they boast [or, act madly]" (cf. Ps. 97:7). For this last clause the MT has: "and because of idols (וּבָאֵימִים) they act madly" (*Tg. Jon.*: "and in idols they boast").[41] Thus, in addition to overstepping its bounds as the LORD's instrument of judgment (Isa. 47:6; Zech. 1:15), Babylon has sinned against the LORD in its worship of other gods (see Jer. 50:14b, 24b, 29b; see also Jer. 51:17, 47, 52).

The announcement of judgment in Jeremiah 50:39–40 (LXX 27:39–40) resembles Isaiah 13:19–22 very closely, and, according to Janzen, it constitutes deliberate "selection and reshaping of some of the Isa. material."[42] The great city of Babylon will ironically become a place inhabited by creatures that normally live in the desert and in other remote locations (Jer. 50:39a; cf. Isa. 13:21–22; see also Isa. 14:23; 34:10–15; Jer. 49:33a; 51:37; Lam. 4:3). That is, in the final judgment, Babylon itself and all that it represents as a world power in opposition to God and his people will be transformed into a distant wilderness (see Rev. 18:2). Babylon will never again be inhabited by people, "and," the MT adds, "she will not be settled for generations to come" (Jer.

---

41. It is not entirely clear why אֵימִים ("terrors") is used for idols, although it is usually suggested that the idols are the object of the people's fear. It is also possible that the term is intended to be derogatory in some way.

42. Janzen, *Studies in the Text of Jeremiah*, 60; see also Parke-Taylor, *Formation of the Book of Jeremiah*, 174.

50:39b; cf. Isa. 13:20a). Jeremiah 50:40a compares the desolation of Babylon to that of Sodom and Gomorrah and their neighbors (cf. Isa. 13:19b; see Gen. 19; see also Jude 7): "a man/person will not live there, and a human being will not sojourn in her [LXX: there]" (Jer. 50:40b; cf. Jer. 4:25a, 29b). The same text in a slightly different form appears in the oracle concerning Edom (Jer. 49:18).

Jeremiah 50:41–43 (LXX 27:41–43) adapts the threat of the enemy from the north, which was addressed to Judah and Jerusalem in 6:22–24, for the oracle concerning Babylon.[43] In order to maintain a consistent view of the enemy from the north throughout the book, this enemy cannot be Babylon in either passage (against MT Jer. 25:9). The view of the present commentary has been that the enemy from the north, especially in the first edition of the book represented by Greek Jeremiah, is an eschatological foe. The text at hand envisions a people (i.e., an army) coming from the north, "a great nation and many kings"; they are "aroused" from the remote parts of the earth (Jer. 50:41; cf. Jer. 6:22; see also Isa. 13:17; 14:13; Jer. 25:32; 31:8; 50:3, 9; 51:48; Ezek. 38:6, 15; 39:2). This enemy consists of a leader ("a great nation") and a horde of nations ("many kings") (see Jer. 1:15; Ezek. 38:1–9, 14–17). They take their bows and javelins/spears—an enemy cruel and without compassion (Jer. 50:42a; cf. Jer. 6:23a). Thus, just as Babylon has done (e.g., Isa. 47:6), so will it be done to Babylon (Jer. 50:15, 29). The sound of the enemy army roars like the sea, and upon horses they ride. According to the Hebrew source behind Greek Jeremiah, the enemy is arranged "like a fire" (כאש) for battle against Babylon (Jer. 50:42b; cf. Jer. 6:23b). According to the MT, however, he is arranged "like a man" (כאיש). As noted in the commentary on Jeremiah 6:23b, the strangeness of an enemy army arranging for battle "like a fire" has likely prompted the change to the more expected image of an army arranging for battle "like a man" (i.e., as a single man, unified). The king of Babylon hears the report of the enemy army, and his hands go slack in despair (Jer. 50:43a; cf. Jer. 6:24a; 51:31; see also Isa. 13:7; Ezek. 7:17). As noted in the commentary on Jeremiah 6:24b, just as the members of the enemy army "grasp" (hiphil of חזק) their bows and spears, so distress has "gripped" (hiphil of חזק) the king (Jer. 50:43b). Writhing grips him "like that of a woman in labor" (cf. Isa. 13:8; Jer. 4:31; 22:23; 49:24; Mic. 4:9).

Jeremiah 50:44–46 (LXX 27:44–46) and 49:19–21 form yet another doublet in the book of Jeremiah. These verses are employed in two separate oracles, one concerning Babylon and the other concerning Edom. It is neither possible nor necessary to determine which use

---

43. See Parke-Taylor, *Formation of the Book of Jeremiah*, 175–76.

came first, although it is often thought that the downfall of Babylon is the more likely of the two to be considered an earth-shaking event.[44] The text makes a comparison with a lion that goes up from the thicket of the Jordan (cf. Jer. 12:5) to "Ethan" (איתן) (MT: "a perennial pasture" [נוה איתן]) (Jer. 50:44a; cf. Jer. 49:19a). According to *Targum Jonathan*, this is an image of a king with his armies going up against the people of Babylon who are like a flock of defenseless small livestock. It is in this manner that the Lord will suddenly cause the people to run away from the land of Babylon (cf. Jer. 50:24a).[45] The Hebrew source behind Greek Jeremiah then says: "and every choice young man will I appoint against her" (וכל בחור אליה אפקד). This speaks of how every eligible member of the enemy army will be mustered for battle against Babylon. The MT, however, has: "and whomever is chosen will I appoint against/over her" (ומי בחור אליה אפקד). This could have the same sense as the Hebrew source behind Greek Jeremiah, but it could also mean that the Lord will appoint a chosen leader over the enemy army. For who is like the Lord (Jer. 50:44b; cf. Jer. 10:6 [MT]; 49:19b; see also Exod. 15:11; Isa. 44:7; 46:9; Pss. 35:10; 71:19; 89:9 [Eng., 89:8])? Who will arraign him? Who is the "shepherd" (*Tg. Jon.*: "king") who will stand before him? These rhetorical questions assume that there is no one like the Lord who can oppose him as he brings judgment against Babylon (cf. Job 9:19). Thus, the counsel of the Lord against Babylon stands (Jer. 50:45a; cf. Jer. 49:20a; see also Jer. 29:11; 49:30): "The he-goats (שעירי) [LXX: lambs; MT: little ones (צעירי); *Tg. Jon.*: strong] of the flock [*Tg. Jon.*: people] will surely be dragged away (יסחבו) [LXX: destroyed; MT: they will surely drag them away (יסחבום)]" (Jer. 50:45b; cf. Jer. 49:20b). The Hebrew text features a syntactical construction here designed to express certitude (see GKC §149). According to the Hebrew source behind Greek Jeremiah, the lion (i.e., the enemy) will drag away the "he-goats" (i.e., leaders) first. According to the MT, the "little ones" (i.e., the most vulnerable) will be dragged away. The Hebrew source behind Greek Jeremiah says that the "pasture [Syr., *Tg. Jon.*, Vulg.: their pasture] will surely be desolated from upon them" (אם לא ישם מעליהם נוה). The MT personifies the pasture: "pasture will surely be appalled at them" (אם לא ישים עליהם נוה). Due to the sound that is made when Babylon is captured, "the earth/ground is made to quake, and an outcry among the nations heard" (Jer. 50:46; cf. Jer.

---

44. Parke-Taylor, *Formation of the Book of Jeremiah*, 155–57.

45. The *kethiv* ארוצם and *qere* אריצם are usually thought to be the *qal* and the *hiphil* of רוץ ("run") respectively. It is possible, however, that the *kethiv* is the *qal* of רצץ ("crush").

49:21). There is some question here as to whether the outcry heard among the nations is the very sound that Babylon makes when it is captured, making the earth/ground to shake (see Syr., *Tg. Jon.*). The other option is to understand the earth-shaking sound to be that of the enemy army when it captures Babylon (see Jer. 50:42b). The outcry heard among the nations would then be that of the nations themselves in response to Babylon's downfall (see Rev. 18:9–10, 15–17, 19).

51:1 (28:1) Thus says the LORD *[Syr. adds: the strong God (= the God of hosts)], "Look, I am about to arouse against Babylon and against the inhabitants of Chaldea [MT:* לב קמי*]*[46] *a destructive east wind [LXX: a destructive scorching wind; MT: a destructive wind (or, a destroyer's spirit)], 51:2 (28:2) and I will send to/against Babylon presumptuous ones [MT: strangers/foreigners (or,* זרים*, winnowers)], and they will act presumptuously against her [MT: and they will scatter/winnow her] in order to make her land empty [LXX: mistreat her land; Syr.: trample her land; see GKC §107q]. Woe, Babylon [LXX: Woe to Babylon], from every side in the day of her calamity [MT: for/when they are (Syr.: and they will assemble) against her from every side in a day of calamity]. 51:3 (28:3) Let the one who bends his bow [i.e., the archer] bend [MT: Do not let the one who bends his bow bend],*[47] *and let him lift himself up in his armor [LXX: and let him who has his armor put it on; MT: and do not let him lift himself up in his armor]. Do not spare [MT: And do not spare] her choice young men, and [and > MT] exterminate the whole of her army. 51:4 (28:4) And they will*

---

46. לב קמי ("the heart of those who rise up against me"; see Vulg.) is *atbash* for כשדים ("Chaldeans" or "Chaldea") (see also MT Jer. 25:26; 51:41). *Targum Jonathan* interprets this phrase to describe those who are being brought against the Chaldeans: "peoples, murderers, whose heart is proud, and beautiful in stature; their spirit destroys." The last part of this rendering interprets the destructive "wind" (רוח) to be the destructive "spirit" of those who are being brought against the Chaldeans.

47. What appears to be a preposition אֶל ("to") in Codex L is likely a variant vocalization of אַל ("not"), which appears in multiple manuscripts. The vowel *seghol* is frequently a modification of the vowel *pathach* (see GKC §8a). It is unlikely that אֶל ("to") in Codex L was ever intended to be a preposition in front of a verb (cf. Deut. 2:9; Josh. 22:19; see also Prov. 12:28). This applies also to the occurrence in the following clause. It is possible, however, that there is an ellipsis of אשר after the preposition in both cases (cf. 1 Chr. 15:12). See also אֶל for אַל in Judges 19:23 of the Leningrad Codex.

fall slain in the land of the Chaldeans and pierced/wounded in her streets. 51:5 (28:5) For Israel and Judah are not forsaken by their [MT: his] God, by the Lord *of hosts, for/though their land is full of guilt against the holy things [MT: the Holy One] of Israel. 51:6 (28:6) Flee from the midst of Babylon, and save each his life, and [and > MT] and do not be thrown down [MT: silenced/destroyed] for/in her iniquity/punishment, for it is the* Lord's *time of her [her > MT] vengeance, recompense is he repaying to her. 51:7 (28:7) A cup of gold was Babylon in the* Lord's *hand, making drunk all the inhabited earth. Of her wine nations have drunk. Therefore, they [MT: nations] act madly [LXX: are shaken]. 51:8 (28:8) And suddenly [MT: Suddenly] Babylon fell and was broken. Wail for her! Take balm for her pain [LXX: ruin]. Perhaps she will be healed. 51:9 (28:9) [NET adds: Foreigners living there will say,] 'We tried to heal Babylon, but she was not healed. Leave her [LXX: Let us leave her (cf. Syr.)], that we may go each to his land [see GKC §108d]. For her judgment has reached to the sky, and it is lifted up to clouds [LXX: the stars; Tg. Jon.: the highest heavens].' 51:10 (28:10) [NET adds: The exiles from Judah will say,] 'The* Lord *has brought forth his righteousness [LXX: his judgment; MT: our righteous acts; Syr. = our righteousness/vindication]. Come, and let us recount in Zion the works [MT: work] of the* Lord *our God.'"*

51:11 (28:11) Polish [LXX: Prepare] the arrows! Fill the quivers! The Lord *has aroused the spirit of the king [MT: kings] of the Medes. For against Babylon is his indignation [MT: his plan] to destroy it, for the vengeance of the* Lord *is what it is—vengeance for his temple. 51:12 (28:12) To the city walls of Babylon lift up a banner! Strengthen the watch [LXX: Set up quivers]! Station guards! Prepare weapons [MT: the ambushes; Syr.: and sink her in water]! For the* Lord *has planned and will do [MT: has both planned and done] what he has spoken against the inhabitants of Babylon [cf. Syr.]. 51:13 (28:13) Dwelling [MT kethiv:* שכנתי; *qere:* שכנת*] by many waters and by the abundance of her treasures [MT: abundant in treasures]. Your end has come for sure in your inward parts [MT: Your end (Tg. Jon.: The day of your defeat) has come, the cubit/measure of your unjust gain (Syr.: your wound has prevailed; Tg. Jon.: the time of punishment for your evil)]. 51:14 (28:14) For the* Lord *swears by his arm [MT: The* Lord *of hosts swears by himself], "I have filled you with men like locusts [Tg. Jon.: armies of peoples who are as numerous as locusts; see GKC §163d], and those who come down will sing in victory against you [MT: and they will sing in victory against you with a shout (Syr.: and they will sing in victory against you and say, 'Alas! Alas!'; Tg. Jon.: and they will raise their voice against you)]."*

51:15 (28:15) He is the one who [Syr.: The Lord is the one who (cf. Tg. Jon.)] made land by his strength, established a world by his wisdom, [MT adds: and] by his understanding stretched out sky. 51:16 (28:16) At the sound of his giving a roar of water in the sky, he brought up clouds from the end of the land [MT: from land's end]. Lightning for the rain he made, and he brought forth light [MT: wind] from his storehouses.[48] *51:17 (28:17) Every man [or, All mankind; Tg. Jon.: All the peoples] is brutish [Ziegler: ἐματαιώθη; Rahlfs: ἐμωράνθη] without knowledge. Every refiner is put to shame by/because of [or, is ashamed of] his carved/sculpted images [MT: a carved/sculpted image]. For deception is what they pour out, no breath is in them [MT: For deception is his molten image, and no breath is in them]. 51:18 (28:18) Vanity are they, works [MT: work] of mockery. At the time of their visitation they will perish. 51:19 (28:19) Not like these is the portion of Jacob; for the fashioner of all, he is his inheritance [MT: for the fashioner of all is he, and Israel is (Israel is > Codex L, Syr.) the tribe of his inheritance], the LORD [MT adds: of hosts] is his name.*

This section begins in 51:1 (LXX 28:1) with the introductory formula כה אמר יהוה ("Thus says the LORD"). According to the Hebrew source behind Greek Jeremiah, the LORD says, "Look, I am about to arouse against Babylon and against the inhabitants of Chaldea (כשדים) a destructive east wind (רוח קדים משחית)" (cf. Jer. 18:17). According to the MT, however, he says, "Look, I am about to arouse against Babylon and against the inhabitants of the heart of those who rise up against me (לב קמי) a destructive wind (רוח משחית)." The phrase לב קמי ("the heart of those who rise up against me") is *atbash* for כשדים ("Chaldea"). *Atbash* (אתבש) is an exegetical technique whereby the first and last letters of the Hebrew alphabet can be substituted for one another (א and ת), the second and second to last (ב and ש), and so on.[49] This technique is also employed in MT Jeremiah 25:26; 51:41 (ששך for בבל). Richard Steiner suggests that while לב קמי likely began in popular usage as a code word for Chaldea out of fear of retaliation for any anti-Babylonian speech, it now appears in Jeremiah 51 alongside clear references to Babylon as a way of "flouting the taboo against anti-Babylonian agitation."[50] The MT's רוח משחית ("a destructive wind") can also be in-

---

48. See Sharp, "Take Another Scroll and Write," 504.

49. See Rashi in Rosenberg, trans., *Mikraoth Gedoloth: Jeremiah Volume One*, 394.

50. Richard C. Steiner, "The Two Sons of Neriah and the Two Editions of Jeremiah in the Light of Two *Atbash* Code-Words for Babylon," *VT* 46 (1996): 83.

terpreted as "a destroyer's spirit" (cf. *Tg. Jon.*). Keil notes that the *hiphil* of עור ("arouse") with the object רוח is normally for the arousal of a person's spirit (see Jer. 51:11; Hag. 1:14; Ezra 1:1; 1 Chr. 5:26; 2 Chr. 21:16; 36:22; see also Isa. 13:17; Jer. 50:9, 41).[51]

In the Hebrew source behind Greek Jeremiah 51:2a (LXX 28:2a), the LORD says that he will send to/against Babylon "presumptuous ones" (זדים), "and they will act presumptuously against her" (וזדוה) in order to make her land empty (cf. Jer. 50:29b, 31, 32; see also Isa. 24:1). In the MT, he says that he will send "strangers/foreigners" (זָרִים), "and they will scatter her" (וזרוה) (cf. Lev. 26:33; Jer. 49:32, 36; Ezek. 5:10; 12:15). Some prefer to re-vocalize the text so that it says the LORD will send "winnowers" (זֹרִים), "and they will winnow her" (וזרוה) (see *BHS* apparatus). The Hebrew source behind Greek Jeremiah 51:2b (LXX 28:2b) says, "Woe, Babylon (הוי בבל), from every side in the day of her calamity (מסביב ביום רעתה)." The MT has either a causal or a temporal clause: "for/when they are against her (כי היו עליה) from every side in a day of calamity (מסביב ביום רעה)" (cf. Jer. 17:17, 18).

The Hebrew source behind Greek Jeremiah 51:3a (LXX 28:3a) is fairly straightforward: "Let the one who bends his bow bend, and let him lift himself up in his armor" (cf. Jer. 50:29). According to this reading, the armed archers of the attacking enemy are to prepare their bows to shoot against Babylon. The textual history of the MT is considerably more complicated. There is first of all the issue of the two occurrences of אל (which are not present in the Hebrew source behind Greek Jeremiah), one at the beginning of each clause. The Leningrad Codex vocalizes these as prepositions (אֶל), in which case it is usually assumed that there is an ellipsis of something that should follow them (see Rashi), since prepositions normally do not govern finite verbs. On the other hand, a multiple of Masoretic manuscripts vocalizes these as negations (אַל), in which case the two clauses may be translated as follows: "Do not let the one who bends his bow bend, and do not let him lift himself up in his armor." The words would thus be a discouragement directed to the Babylonian archers. The Leningrad Codex has an added problem with its two occurrences of ידרך in the first clause: אֶל־יִדְרֹךְ ידרך. The second occurrence of ידרך does not appear in a multitude of Masoretic manuscripts. It occurs without vowel pointing in the Leningrad Codex because it is one of eight examples of words that are "written (*kethiv*) but not read (*qere*)" (see 2 Sam. 13:33; 15:21; 2 Kgs. 5:18; Jer. 38:16; 39:12; Ezek. 48:16; Ruth 3:12). Its presence in some witnesses is likely due to an instance of dittography, which was then copied and transmitted. The

---

51. Keil, *Jeremiah*, 436–37.

remainder of Jeremiah 51:3 calls for the members of the enemy army not to spare Babylon's choice young men but to exterminate the whole of its army (Jer. 51:3b [LXX 28:3b]; Jer. 50:21, 26). The end result of this is that the Babylonian soldiers will fall "slain" in their own land and "pierced/wounded" in their streets (Jer. 51:4 [LXX 28:4]). The above translation presupposes that the words "slain" and "pierced/wounded" function adverbially. It is also possible that they are subjects: "And (the) slain will fall in the land of the Chaldeans, and (the) pierced/wounded (will fall) in her streets" (cf. Jer. 51:49, 52).

Jeremiah 51:5 (LXX 28:5) explains that Israel and Judah are not "forsaken" (or, "widowed") by their God (see Isa. 54:4–8; see also Jer. 3:18; 50:4, 33–34), "for/though their land is full of guilt against the holy things [MT: the Holy One] of Israel." Interpretation of 51:5b largely depends upon whose land is "their land." If "their land" is Israel's land, then the clause must be concessive ("though"). That is, despite Israel's guilt against either "the holy things" (LXX) or "the Holy One" (MT) of Israel, the people are not forsaken by the Lord. If "their land" is Babylon's land, then the clause is causal ("for"). Babylon's claim to be guiltless (MT Jer. 50:7a) is false. They are indeed full of guilt against either "the holy things" (see MT Jer. 50:28b; 51:11b) or "the Holy One" (see Jer. 50:29b) of Israel. Thus, the Lord will hold the Babylonians accountable for their guilt, vindicating his people in the process (see Jer. 51:10).

If Jeremiah 51:6a (LXX 28:6a) is read as a continuation of 51:5, then the commands are specifically for the people of Israel to flee from the midst of Babylon and save themselves (cf. Jer. 50:8, 28; 51:10, 45; see also Isa. 48:20; Zech. 2:10–11 [Eng., 2:6–7]; Rev. 18:4). On the other hand, if it is read with what follows (see Jer. 51:7–9), it is possible that the commands are also for foreigners living in Babylon (cf. Jer. 50:16). In addition to the imperatives is the injunction, "and do not be thrown down (ואל תרמו)" either "for her iniquity" or "in her punishment" (בעונה). The MT has, "do not be silenced/destroyed (אל תדמו)" (cf. Jer. 49:26b; 50:30b). The reason for the flight from Babylon is that it is the Lord's time of vengeance to repay her according to what she has done (Jer. 51:6b [LXX 28:6b]; cf. Jer. 50:15, 28, 29; 51:11, 24, 36, 56).

Jeremiah 51:7 (LXX 28:7) says that Babylon was "a cup of gold" in the Lord's hand that made the inhabited earth drunk (see Rev. 14:8; 17:2, 4; 18:3; cf. 4Q386). The nations have drunk of her wine, and for this reason they act madly (cf. Hab. 2:15). Readers are not necessarily to think of a cup made of gold or a cup filled with golden-colored liquid. Rather, it is that Babylon was full of treasures (Jer. 51:13). The cup of judgment is a familiar metaphor in the book of Jeremiah. The prophet is instructed in 25:15–26 to take this cup from the Lord's hand in order to make the nations drink its wine so that they act madly (see also Jer. 49:12). Babylon was initially the LORD's instrument of judgment (Jer. 27:6), but she would also have to drink of the cup (Jer. 25:26b [MT]; 51:39, 57; cf. Hab. 2:16). Thus, Babylon fell "suddenly" from her privileged position and was broken (Jer. 51:8a [LXX 28:8a]; cf. Isa. 14:12; 21:9; Jer. 50:22–24; 51:44b; Rev. 14:8; 18:2). An unidentified group is called upon to wail for her and to take balm for her pain in hopes that she will be healed (Jer. 51:8b [LXX 28:8b]; cf. Jer. 8:22; 46:11; see also Rev. 18:9, 19). It becomes apparent from the following verse (Jer. 51:9 [LXX 28:9]) that this effort to heal Babylon is an openly disingenuous one designed to demonstrate that Babylon cannot be healed.

Jeremiah 51:9 (LXX 28:9) features the voice of foreigners living in Babylon (see NET): "We tried to heal Babylon, but she was not healed." The response to the call to take balm for Babylon's pain has been in vain (cf. MT Jer. 51:58b). Thus, the foreigners conclude that they should leave or forsake Babylon and go to their respective lands (cf. Jer. 50:16), for her judgment has reached to the sky and is lifted up to the clouds. To say that Babylon's judgment has reached to the sky may be a way to say either that her crimes to be judged are very great or that God's judgment of her is very great (cf. Ps. 36:6 [Eng., 36:5]). Another possibility is that it means the outcry against Babylon has reached God (cf. Gen. 18:21; Jon. 1:2). That is, it has come to God's attention that Babylon should be judged for her crimes. This appears to be the way this text has been received in Revelation 18:5: "because her sins have piled up all the way to the sky, and God has remembered her crimes." Following the voice of the foreigners in 51:9 is the voice of the exiles from Judah (see again NET) in 51:10 (LXX 28:10): "The LORD has brought forth his righteousness (צדקתו)." The LXX interprets this to mean that he has brought forth his judgment of Babylon, which works nicely with 51:9b. The MT says that the LORD has brought forth "our righteous acts" (צדקתינו), which Rashi interprets to be the merits of the forefathers.[52] The Syriac version reflects צדקתנו ("our righteousness"), which could be interpreted to mean "our vindication."[53] Because of this act of God, the Judean exiles can encourage one another to go recount in Zion what the LORD has done (cf. Jer. 50:25, 28).

It is not evident who the speaker is in Jeremiah 51:11 (LXX 28:11), but the plural imperatives are apparently directed to the archers of the invading army (cf. Jer. 50:29; 51:3): "Polish [LXX: Prepare] the arrows! Fill the quivers!" The LORD has aroused the spirit of the "king" (MT:

---

52. See Rosenberg, trans., *Mikraoth Gedoloth: Jeremiah Volume One*, 397.
53. See Calvin, *Jeremiah*, 5:210.

"kings") of the Medes (cf. Isa. 13:17; 41:25; Jer. 51:1, 28). It is important to note that neither here nor in verse 28 are the Medes identified as the enemy from the north who completely destroys Babylon (see Jer. 50:3, 9, 41; 51:48). The takeover of the Babylonian empire by the Medes and Persians was a relatively peaceful transaction (see Dan. 5:28–6:1 [Eng., 5:28–31]; *ANET*, 305–306). It is also worth noting that Persia is included among the horde of nations led by the eschatological enemy from the north named Gog (see Ezek. 38:5). Thus, the historical reality serves to prefigure the eschatological one. The LORD aroused the Medes because "his indignation" (זעמו) was against Babylon to destroy it. The MT says that "his plan" (מזמתו) was against Babylon to destroy it. This was the LORD's vengeance for what the Babylonians did to his temple (cf. Jer. 50:15b, 28b [MT]; see also 2 Kgs. 25:9; Jer. 39:8; 52:13; 2 Chr. 36:19).

Calvin interprets Jeremiah 51:12 (LXX 28:12) to be the prophet taunting the Babylonians in their efforts to defend their city.[54] Most commentators, however, see a continuation of the imperatives directed to the invaders in 51:11. They are to lift up a banner to the city walls of Babylon (cf. Jer. 4:6 [MT]; 51:27), thus giving the signal to attack. They are to strengthen the watch and station guards so that no one escapes the city during the invasion (cf. Jer. 52:7–8). According to the Hebrew source behind Greek Jeremiah, they are also to prepare "weapons" (נשק), whereas the MT says that they are to prepare "the ambushes" (הארבים). It may be that the MT represents an adjustment designed to match more closely the commands to strengthen the watch and to station the guards. All this must be done because "the LORD has planned and will do" (זמם יהוה ועשה) what he has spoken against the inhabitants of Babylon (cf. MT Jer. 51:11a). The MT says that "the LORD has both planned and done" (גם זמם יהוה גם עשה). This latter reading lends a sense of certitude to the accomplishment.

The Hebrew source behind Greek Jeremiah 51:13a (LXX 28:13a) describes Babylon as "Dwelling by many waters and by the abundance of her treasures" (שכנת על מים רבים ועל רבת אוצרתיה). The MT has "Dwelling by many waters, abundant in treasures" (שכנת[י] על מים רבים רבת אוצרת). The consonants for either the *kethiv* (שכנתי) or the *qere* (שכנת) can be interpreted and vocalized as a participle or as a second feminine singular suffixed conjugation verb (see GKC §44h, 90n). A second-person verb would work well with 51:13b. The Euphrates constitutes the many waters by which Babylon dwells (see Jer. 51:36, 63; Rev. 17:1; cf. Nah. 3:8; see also Jer. 51:42, 55). Yet, despite the presence of this great resource, the end has come for Babylon (Jer. 51:13b [LXX 28:13b]; cf. Amos 8:2).

---

54. Calvin, *Jeremiah*, 5:214.

The Hebrew source behind Greek Jeremiah says, "Your end has come for sure (אֱמֶת) in your inward parts (בְּמֵעָיִךְ)." The MT says, "Your end has come, the cubit/measure (אַמַּת) of your unjust gain (בִּצְעֵךְ)." This perhaps means that Babylon's allotted measure of wealth acquired unjustly has come to an end. It could also mean that Babylon will be judged according to the measure of its injustice (Jer. 50:15, 29). Bright, however, prefers the translation, "Your end has come, Your life's thread is cut." He explains, "The metaphor is taken from the weaving industry; the cutting of the web from the loom is a figure for death (cf. Isa xxxviii 12)."[55]

According to the Hebrew source behind Greek Jeremiah 51:14a (LXX 28:14a), the LORD swears or takes his oath "by his arm" (בזרועו), which is the symbol of his strength (cf. Isa. 62:8) and the assurance that he will do what he says (see Jer. 51:12b). The MT says that he swears "by himself" (בנפשו), for he has no one greater by whom to swear (see Heb. 6:13; cf. Isa. 45:23; Jer. 22:5; 44:26; 49:13; Amos 6:8). The content of the oath in 51:14b (LXX 28:14b) is introduced by כי אם, which, according to GKC §163d, appends an exception to a principal statement that must be supplied from the context ("I have done nothing else except that . . ."): "I have filled you with men like locusts, and those who come down (הירדים) will sing in victory against you." *Targum Jonathan* renders that these men are "armies of peoples who are as numerous as locusts" (cf. Jer. 51:27b; Joel 2:5). The MT has a slightly different text for the last clause: "and they will sing in victory against you with a shout (הידד)" (cf. Jer. 25:30; 48:33). Thus, the oath seems to be that the soldiers of the invading army who have filled Babylon like locusts will ultimately sing in victory. As McKane notes, however, the NEB translates this text so that it is a contrast between a once bustling city of Babylon (filled with men like locusts) and the present state of the city (defeated by its enemies who sing over it in victory).[56]

For Jeremiah 51:15–19 (LXX 28:15–19), see the commentary on Jeremiah 10:12–16. These two passages form one of the many doublets in the book of Jeremiah. While many commentators focus on the question of priority, it is also important to consider the role of each passage in its respective context within the final form of the book. The passage in chapter 10 is the conclusion to a sustained polemic against the worship of manmade idols, a polemic that contrasts the creator God with created gods. In chapter 51, the same text serves to show that God judges idol worshipers like the Babylonians (see Jer. 50:38) and vindicates those who are truly his.

---

55. Bright, *Jeremiah*, 356.
56. McKane, *Jeremiah XXVI–LII*, 1308.

51:20 (28:20) "A war club is what you are to me, vessel(s) of war [LXX: You scatter for me vessels of war; Syr.: Prepare for me vessels of war; Tg. Jon.: You scatter before me the fortified city in which are vessels of war], and I shatter [LXX, Syr., Tg. Jon.: scatter] with you nations, and I destroy with you kingdoms, 51:21 (28:21) and I shatter [LXX, Syr., Tg. Jon.: scatter] with you horses and their riders, (28:22) and I shatter [LXX, Syr., Tg. Jon.: scatter] with you chariots and their charioteers, 51:22 and I shatter [LXX, Syr., Tg. Jon.: scatter] with you choice young men and virgins, and I shatter [LXX, Syr., Tg. Jon.: scatter] with you men and women [MT: and I shatter with you men and women, and I shatter with you old men and young men, and I shatter with you choice young men and virgins],[57] 51:23 (28:23) and I shatter [LXX, Syr., Tg. Jon.: scatter] with you shepherds and their flocks, and I shatter [LXX, Syr., Tg. Jon.: scatter] with you farmers and their teams of oxen [LXX: farming/field], and I shatter [LXX, Syr., Tg. Jon.: scatter] with you governors and rulers. 51:24 (28:24) But I will repay Babylon and all the inhabitants of Chaldea all their evil that they have done in Zion before your eyes," the prophetic utterance of the LORD.

51:25 (28:25) "Look, I am against you, the corrupted mountain [or, O corrupted mountain] that corrupts/destroys all the inhabited earth [MT: Look, I am against you, a mountain (Tg. Jon.: fortified city) that destroys (or, O mountain of destruction)," the prophetic utterance of the LORD, *"which destroys all the inhabited earth], and I will stretch out my hand against you and roll you from the cliffs and make you into a burning mountain [lit., into a mountain of burning; LXX: as a burned-out mountain]. 51:26 (28:26) And they will not take from you a stone for a corner [Tg. Jon.: a king for a kingdom] or a stone for a foundation [MT: foundations; Tg. Jon.: a ruler for a dominion], for an everlasting desolation [MT: desolations] is what you will be," the prophetic utterance of the* LORD.

51:27 (28:27) Lift up a banner throughout the inhabited earth. Blast a shofar among the nations. Consecrate against her nations. Summon against her kingdoms—Ararat, Minni [Syr.: Armenia], and Ashkenaz [NETS: kingdoms of Araret, from me also the Aschanazeans]. Appoint against her an official scribe [NETS: set up siege engines against her].

---

57. "These verses [51:22, 57a] show both pluses in the MT (expansions of a series and a list) and differences in word order. The rationale motivating the changes in word order is not now apparent, but it is reasonable to assume that these changes were made by the MT editor when the pluses were added" (Sharp, "Take Another Scroll and Write," 499).

Bring up against her horses like locusts in number [MT: Bring up horses like bristling (Tg. Jon.: yellow) locusts]. 51:28 (28:28) Consecrate against her nations, the king [MT: kings] of the Medes and all the inhabited earth [LXX: and of all the earth; > MT], his [MT: her] governors and his [MT: her] rulers [MT adds: and all the land of his dominion]. 51:29 (28:29) And the land shook and writhed, for the thought [MT: thoughts] of the Lord stood [MT qere^{Or}: קָמוּ; but see GKC §145k] against Babylon to make the land of Babylon into a desolation [or, object of horror] without inhabitant. 51:30 (28:30) The mighty man [MT: men] of Babylon ceased to fight. They sit there in a stronghold [MT: They sat in the strongholds]. Their might was dry [or, failed]. They became women [LXX: They became like women]. Their dwellings were set on fire [MT: They set their dwellings on fire]. The bars of her city gates were broken. 51:31 (28:31) One runner runs to meet another, and one messenger to meet another, to declare to the king of Babylon that his city has been captured [MT includes at the end of this verse מִקָּצֶה (on all sides); LXX translates this at the beginning of the following verse as מִקָּצֶה (from / at [the] end of)]. 51:32 (28:32) "At the end of [see MT Jer. 51:31b] his fords [or, crossing places] they were seized [MT: And the fords were seized], and the reed marshes they burned with fire [or, in the fire]; and as for the men of battle [or, soldiers], they went [MT: they were terrified]."

51:33 (28:33) For thus says the Lord [MT adds: of hosts, the God of Israel], "The houses of the king of Babylon [MT: Daughter Babylon] will be like a threshing floor at the time of its leveling. Yet a little while, and the [MT adds: time of the] harvest will come for her [Tg. Jon.: and plunderers will come against her]. 51:34 (28:34) [Syr., Tg. Jon. add: Jerusalem said,] 'Nebuchadnezzar [MT: Nebuchadrezzar] the king of Babylon has devoured me [Codex L kethiv: us]; he has confused [LXX: divided] me [Codex L kethiv: us]; he has overtaken me [Codex L kethiv: us], a small [MT: an empty] vessel [MT: he has made me an empty vessel]; he has swallowed me [Codex L kethiv: us] like a sea creature [LXX: dragon]; he has filled his belly with my delicacies [MT includes at the end of this verse הדיחנו / הדיחני (he has rinsed me / us); LXX translates הֱדִיחַנִי at the beginning of the following verse]. 51:35 (28:35) My violence, and my breaking, has banished me [see MT Jer. 51:34b] to Babylon [MT: The violence done to me and my kinsmen (or, flesh) be upon Babylon],' says the inhabitant of Zion, 'and my blood be upon the inhabitants of Chaldea,' says Jerusalem."

51:36 (28:36) Therefore, thus says the Lord, "Look, I am about to contend with the one who contends with you [LXX: I am judging your adversary;

MT: I am about to contend your contention (or, plead your cause)], and I will take vengeance for you. And I will dry up her sea [Syr.: the sea of Babylon], and I will dry up her spring. 51:37 (28:37) And Babylon will become a desolation [or, object of horror] without inhabitant [MT: And Babylon will become heaps, a habitation for jackals, an object of horror and hissing without inhabitant]. 51:38 (28:38) Together [> Syr.] like young lions they are aroused, and like lions' cubs [MT: Together like young lions they roar, they growl like lions' cubs]. 51:39 (28:39) When they are hot [Syr.: In heat/anger], I will set their feast [LXX: I will give drink to them], and I will make them drunk in order that they swoon [MT: exult] and sleep a perpetual sleep and not wake up [Tg. Jon.: Bring distress upon them, and they will be like a drunkard so as not to be strong, and they will die the second death, and they will not live for the world to come]," the prophetic utterance of the LORD. 51:40 (28:40) "I will bring them down like lambs to the slaughter [MT: to slaughter], and [> MT] like rams with he-goats."

In Jeremiah 51:20 (LXX 28:20), the LORD calls Babylon his "war club" (מפץ) (cf. Ezek. 9:2; see also Isa. 10:5).[58] Babylon has already been called "the hammer of all the earth" (Jer. 50:23). The term מפץ comes from the root נפץ ("shatter"), which appears repeatedly in 51:20–23 in the form of a *piel weqatal* first common singular verb ("and I shatter"). The LXX, Syriac, and *Targum Jonathan* all translate this verb as if it were from the homonym נפץ ("scatter"), but this word only occurs in the *qal* stem ("be scattered") in the Hebrew Bible. Babylon has been the LORD's "vessel" (read כְּלִי) of war by means of which he has shattered nations and destroyed kingdoms (see Jer. 27:6–8)—an instrument of judgment by which he has brought justice to the inhabited world. Printed editions of the LXX and the MT differ in their versification of 51:21–22 (LXX 28:21–22) (see translation above). There are also differences in length and arrangement between the Hebrew source behind Greek Jeremiah and the MT. The LORD continues here to list those whom he has shattered by means of Babylon: "horses and their riders" (Jer. 51:21a [LXX 28:21]) and "chariots and their charioteers" (Jer. 51:21b [LXX 28:22a]). The remainder of the list in verse 22 appears in the following order in the Hebrew source behind Greek Jeremiah: "choice young men and virgins" and "men and women." The MT switches the order of these two groups and adds another group between them: "men and women," "old men and young men," and "choice

---

58. This term is also suggested in the *BHS* apparatus for Nahum 2:2 (Eng., 2:1) and Proverbs 25:18.

young men and virgins." The addition of "old men and young men" in the MT looks suspiciously like an uninformed attempt to make the list look even more indiscriminate in an effort to show the thoroughness of what the LORD did through Babylon. The problem with this addition is that it stands in contradiction to Isaiah 47:6, which says that Babylon's treatment of old men went beyond the LORD's intention (see also Zech. 1:15). It was precisely because of behavior like this that Babylon itself would face judgment, even though it had been the LORD's servant (cf. Isa. 10:5–19). The remainder of the list of those shattered occurs in verse 23: "shepherds and their flocks," "farmers and their teams of oxen," and "governors and rulers." The combination "shepherds and their flocks" may refer to kings and their armies (see Jer. 6:3). The combination of "governors" and "rulers" also occurs in 51:28. Despite its usefulness for the LORD's purposes, the LORD will "repay" Babylon in particular "all their evil that they have done in Zion" before those who witnessed it (Jer. 51:24 [LXX 28:24]; cf. Jer. 50:29; 51:6, 56). Here it is to be noted that whereas "you" (sg.) in 51:20 is Babylon, "your (pl.) eyes" in 51:24 is a reference to the eyes of the inhabitants of Zion.

The LORD addresses Babylon again in 51:25a (LXX 28:25a), indicating that he is against Babylon, "the corrupted mountain" (הָהָר הַמַּשְׁחָת) that corrupts or destroys all the inhabited earth. Here again the irony is that Babylon was to some extent intended to serve this very purpose by the LORD himself (Jer. 27:6–8; 50:23; 51:20). *Targum Jonathan* interprets "mountain" to be a figure of speech for the "fortified city" of Babylon. According to the MT, the LORD calls Babylon "a mountain that destroys" or "the mountain of destruction" (הַר הַמַּשְׁחִית). Holladay argues that the phrase "the mountain of destruction" (הַר הַמַּשְׁחִית) in 2 Kings 23:13 was originally "the mountain of anointing" (הַר הַמִּשְׁחָה), the old name for the Mount of Olives (see *Tg. Jon.* 2 Kgs. 23:13; see also 2 Sam. 15:30; Zech. 14:4; Matt. 26:30; Acts 1:12), which was subsequently changed to "the mountain of destruction" (הַר הַמַּשְׁחִית) due to the destruction of the olive trees when the Babylonians built siege-works against Jerusalem (2 Kgs. 25:1).[59] He further contends that "the mountain of anointing" (הַר הַמִּשְׁחָה) originally appeared in Jeremiah 51:25 to mock the Babylonians for supposedly thinking that their heaps and heaps of oil-producing sesame seeds in Babylon were superior to the olive trees that they encountered on the Mount of Olives outside of Jerusalem. Holladay thinks that an editor did not understand this sense of the phrase and thus changed it to "the mountain of destruction" (הַר הַמַּשְׁחִית). The LORD will stretch out his hand against this mountain and roll it down from the cliffs and

---

59. Holladay, *Jeremiah 2*, 425–26.

make it into a burning mountain (Jer. 51:25b [LXX 28:25b]). This is not a description of an erupting volcano. Rather, it is simply a way to say that the mountain will be reduced to smoldering rubble and ash (cf. Isa. 7:4; see also Jer. 51:30b, 32, 37). Holladay proposes that the word שרפה ("burning") is a link to Genesis 11:3, a text that speaks of the "burnt bricks" out of which the Tower of Babel (Babylon) was made. The end result of this is that there will not even be one decent stone left for use as a cornerstone or as a foundation. Babylon will be an everlasting desolation (Jer. 51:26 [LXX 28:26]).[60] Thus, there will be no rebuilding of the city, nor will there be anything left for any other sort of building project. *Targum Jonathan* understands the terms פנה ("corner") and מוסדה ("foundation") metaphorically (see Judg. 20:2; 1 Sam. 14:38; Isa. 19:13; 28:16; Zech. 10:4). There will be no king left for a kingdom or ruler for a dominion.

In Jeremiah 51:27 (LXX 28:27), the call goes out to the nations to come against the one who once came against them: "Lift up a banner throughout the inhabited earth. Blast a shofar among the nations. Consecrate against her nations." This kind of language has already been encountered earlier in the book of Jeremiah (see, e.g., Jer. 4:5–6; 6:1, 4; 50:2; 51:12). The three kingdoms to be summoned against Babylon—Ararat, Minni, and Ashkenaz—are said to have been located in or near Armenia (see Syr.; see also Gen. 8:4; 10:3; 2 Kgs. 19:37) and subjected to the Medes (see Jer. 51:28). (The LXX misreads the place name מני ["Minni"] as if it were the prepositional phrase "from me" [see BDB, 577].) An "official scribe" (טפסר), an Akkadian loanword for a high-ranking military officer, is to be appointed against Babylon (cf. Nah. 3:17). According to the Hebrew source behind Greek Jeremiah, horses are to be brought up against her like locusts in "number" (מספר) (cf. Jer. 51:14; Joel 2:4; Rev. 9:7). The MT, however, says that horses are to be brought up like "bristling" (סמר) locusts. The rarity of the term סמר ("bristling") and uncertainty about the imagery have historically given commentators pause about the exact meaning of the MT.[61] The Syriac version has no representation of either מספר ("number") or סמר ("bristling") in its translation. As in 51:11, the Medes are to lead the charge: "Consecrate against her nations, the king [MT: kings] of the Medes and all the inhabited earth [LXX: and of all the earth; > MT], his [MT: her] governors and his [MT: her] rulers [MT adds: and all the

---

60. Again, the expectation here is an eschatological one (Rev. 17–18). Nothing of the kind ever took place historically.

61. The explanation in BDB (702)—"perh. with allusion to horn-like sheaths enclosing wings of the pupa"—is pure speculation.

land of his dominion]" (Jer. 51:28 [LXX 28:28]; see Jer. 51:23b; see also 1 Kgs. 9:19b).

Jeremiah 51:29 (LXX 28:29) switches to narrative mode with its use of *wayyiqtol* forms: "And the land shook and writhed, for the thought [MT: thoughts] of the LORD stood against Babylon to make the land of Babylon into a desolation [or, object of horror] without inhabitant" (cf. Judg. 5:4; Jer. 29:11; 51:37, 41). This is not necessarily because the text is a description of a past event. Rather, it is simply the use of story to paint a textual portrait. The same Babylon that rendered Jerusalem a desolation/appalment without inhabitant (Isa. 6:11) will become so itself (Rev. 50:15, 29; Rev. 18:6). In this image of defeat, Babylon's warriors ceased to fight, hunkering down in their stronghold (Jer. 51:30a [LXX 28:30a]). Their strength failed, and they became weak like women (cf. Jer. 50:37; Nah. 3:13). Meanwhile, their dwellings were set on fire, and the bars of Babylon's city gates were broken (Jer. 51:30b [LXX 28:30b]; cf. Jer. 51:25b, 32; Lam. 2:9). Jeremiah 51:31 (LXX 28:31) describes one messenger running after another to declare to the king of Babylon that his city has been captured (cf. 2 Sam. 18:19–32; see also Jer. 50:43; 51:41). It is possible that this is a description of a kind of relay, but it is more likely that it indicates what McKane calls "a continuous traffic of dispatches" (cf. Job 1:13–22).[62] According to the MT, the report of the messengers is that the city has been captured "on all sides" (מִקָּצֶה) (cf. Jer. 50:26). The LXX translates these same consonants with the beginning of the following verse as if they were vocalized differently: "At the end of (מִקְצֵה) his fords [or, crossing places] they were seized [MT: And the fords were seized], and the reed marshes they burned with fire [or, in the fire]" (Jer. 51:32a [LXX 28:32a]; cf. Jer. 51:25b, 30b; see also Job 41:12 [Eng., 41:20]). The capture of those attempting to cross the fords (or the seizure of the fords themselves) along with the burning of the reed marshes prevented the escape of any who tried to flee the city (see Jer. 51:12a; cf. Judg. 12:5–6). The Hebrew source behind Greek Jeremiah simply says that the Babylonian soldiers "went" (הלכו), while the MT says that they "were terrified" (נבהלו) (Jer. 51:32b [LXX 28:32b]). 51:32 thus summarizes the report from the messengers to the king.

The conjunction כי at the beginning of 51:33 (LXX 28:33) introduces the following word of the LORD as an explanation of 51:27–32. According to the Hebrew source behind Greek Jeremiah, the LORD says, "The houses of the king of Babylon (בתי מלך בבל) will be like a threshing floor at the time of its leveling" (Jer. 51:33a). The MT has "Daughter Babylon" (בת בבל) instead of "The houses of the king of

---

62. McKane, *Jeremiah XXVI–LII*, 1320.

Babylon" (בתי מלך בבל). The third feminine singular pronominal suffix translated "its" may refer to "Babylon" rather than "threshing floor" (גרן), which is a masculine noun. The leveling of the threshing floor is its preparation for the coming harvest. Thus, Babylon will be made ready so to speak for its "harvest" (i.e., judgment), which is about to arrive shortly (Jer. 51:33b; cf. Jer. 50:16; Hos. 6:11; see also Isa. 10:25; 29:17). *Targum Jonathan* interprets this to mean that plunderers will come against her.

According to the Syriac and *Targum Jonathan*, Jeremiah 51:34–35 (LXX 28:34–35) is a quote of the people of Jerusalem (see Jer. 51:35; cf. Jer. 51:10, 51). The Hebrew source behind Greek Jeremiah, a few Masoretic manuscripts, and the *qere* of the Leningrad Codex feature first common singular object suffixes ("me") in 51:34, which is consistent with the use of first common singular pronominal suffixes ("my") in 51:35. The *kethiv* of the Leningrad Codex has first common plural object suffixes ("us") in 51:34. The complaint of 51:34 is that Nebuchadnezzar has "devoured" Jerusalem (cf. Jer. 2:3; 50:7, 17). He has "confused" (המם) the people, a term for throwing an enemy army into a state of confusion (cf. Exod. 14:24; 23:27; Josh. 10:10; Judg. 4:15; 1 Sam. 7:10; 2 Sam. 22:15; Ps. 144:6). The Hebrew source behind Greek Jeremiah says: "he has overtaken me (השיגני), a small vessel (כלי דק)." The MT says: "he has made me (הציגני) an empty vessel (כלי ריק)." Whether this is about reduction in size or removal of contents, the lament seems to be for the depopulation of Jerusalem. Nebuchadnezzar has swallowed the city like a sea creature (see Jer. 51:36b where the Euphrates is called Babylon's "sea"; see also Gen. 1:21; Isa. 27:1; 51:9; Ps. 74:13) and filled his belly with its delicacies, yet the LORD will make Babylon spit out what he has swallowed (see Jer. 51:44). The MT includes at the end of 51:34 הֱדִיחָנוּ/הֱדִיחָנִי ("he has rinsed me/us"). The LXX translates הִדִּיחַנִי ("has banished me") at the beginning of the following verse: "My violence, and my breaking (שברי), has driven me out to Babylon" (Jer. 51:35a [LXX 28:35a]). The MT says, "The violence done to me and my kinsmen (שארי) be upon Babylon." It is possible that שארי should be translated "my flesh." The language of this imprecation finds a parallel in 51:35b (LXX 28:35b): "and my blood be upon the inhabitants of Chaldea" (cf. Lev. 20:9, 11–13, 27).

The LORD responds in 51:36a (LXX 28:36a), "Look, I am about to contend with the one who contends with you (רבך) [MT: I am about to contend your contention (ריבך)], and I will take vengeance for you" (cf. Jer. 50:34; see also Jer. 50:15, 28; 51:6, 11). The LORD will dry up Babylon's "sea" (Jer. 51:36b [LXX 28:36b]; cf. Exod. 14:21; Jer. 50:38; 51:13; Rev. 16:12), which is the term used here for the Euphrates (see the use of this word for the Nile in Isa. 18:2; 19:5; Nah. 3:8), and he will dry up her spring. Babylon will become a "desolation" (or, "object of horror") without inhabitant (Jer. 51:37 [LXX 28:37]; cf. Jer. 51:29, 41). The MT has a longer text for 51:37 that features material from elsewhere in the book of Jeremiah: "And Babylon will become heaps, a habitation for jackals, an object of horror and hissing without inhabitant" (cf. Jer. 9:10 [Eng., 9:11]; 10:22; 19:8; 25:9, 11, 18; 29:18; 49:33; 50:39; see also Jer. 51:25). Once again, what Babylon has done to others will be done to Babylon (Jer. 50:15, 29).

The Hebrew source behind Greek Jeremiah 51:38 (LXX 28:38) compares the leaders of Babylon to young lions when they are aroused: "Together like young lions they are aroused (נֵעֹרוּ), and like lions' cubs" (cf. Jer. 2:15; Nah. 2:12–14 [Eng., 2:11–13]). The MT, however, says, "Together like young lions they roar (יִשְׁאָגוּ), they growl (נָעֲרוּ) like lions' cubs." This roaring suggests that they are aroused by their prey (see Amos 3:4; see also Isa. 31:4), which, according to 51:34–35, is Jerusalem. When they are hot (בְּחֻמָּם) for their prey,[63] the LORD will set their "feast" (מִשְׁתֶּה), which is primarily characterized by drinking (Jer. 51:39 [LXX 28:39]). Rashi comments that it was on the night of the feast that Belshazzar was killed and Darius the Mede received the kingdom (Dan. 5).[64] The LORD will make them drunk from the cup of judgment (Jer. 25:15–26; 51:7, 57) in order that they "swoon" (יֵעָלְפוּ; MT: "exult" [יַעֲלֹזוּ]) and sleep a perpetual sleep and not wake up (cf. MT Jer. 51:57; Ps. 13:4b [Eng., 13:3b]). *Targum Jonathan* interprets this to mean that they will die "the second death" and not live for the world to come (cf. Rev. 20:14).[65] The LORD will bring these lions down like lambs to the slaughter and like rams with he-goats (Jer. 51:40 [LXX 28:40]; cf. Isa. 34:6–8; Jer. 11:19; 46:10; 48:15; 50:27; Ezek. 39:18; Rev. 19:17–18).

51:41 (28:41) "How she [MT: Sheshach; Tg. Jon.: Babylon] was captured and seized, the praise of all the earth! How Babylon has become a desolation [or, object of horror] among the nations [MT: How she has become a desolation, Babylon among the nations]! 51:42 (28:42) The sea has come up over Babylon with the roar / multitude of its waves, and she has been covered [MT: The sea (Tg. Jon.: A king with his armies who are as numerous as the waters of the sea) has come up over Babylon, with the roar / multitude of its waves she has been covered]. 51:43 (28:43) Her

---

63. The Syriac ("In heat/anger") reflects בְּחֵמָה, which may be translated, "With poison" (cf. Deut. 32:24; Hab. 2:15).

64. Rosenberg, trans., *Mikraoth Gedoloth: Jeremiah Volume Two*, 405.

65. Cf. Neusner, *Jeremiah in Talmud and Midrash*, 64.

cities are a dry land and a desert plain [MT: Her cities have become a desolation (or, object of horror), a dry land and a desert plain]. No one will live in her, and nobody will pass through [LXX: lodge in] her [MT: a land in whose cities no one (כל > pc Mss) lives and through whose cities nobody passes]. 51:44 (28:44) And I will visit upon [or, punish] Babylon [MT: Bel in Babylon] and bring out what she [MT: he] has swallowed [Syr.: his cake; Tg. Jon.: his possessions] from her [MT: his] mouth, and nations will never again flow to her [MT: him].[66] *51:49b (28:49) Also / Indeed at Babylon the slain of all the land will fall [MT: and that for Babylon the slain of all the earth have fallen (see MT 51:49a)]. 51:50 (28:50) Fugitives of dry ground, go and do not remain [MT: Survivors of (the) sword, go, do not remain]! From far away remember the* Lord *[MT: Remember from far away the* Lord*], and let it be Jerusalem that goes up upon your heart / mind. 51:51 (28:51) [Syr. adds: Those of the house of Israel will say,] 'We are ashamed, for we have heard our reproach. Humiliation has covered our face. Strangers have entered [Tg. Jon. adds: and defiled] our sanctuaries, the house of the* Lord *[MT: the sanctuaries of the house of the* Lord*].' 51:52 (28:52) Therefore, look, days are coming," the prophetic utterance of the* Lord*, "and I will visit upon [or, punish] her carved / sculpted idols, and in all her land (the) slain [or, mortally wounded] will fall [MT: groan; cf. Syr., Tg. Jon.]. 51:53 (28:53) Even if Babylon goes up like the sky [MT: goes up to the sky; Tg. Jon.: builds buildings that are high up to the sky], and even if she fortifies the height of her strength [or, her strong elevated place], from me will come destroyers to her," the prophetic utterance of the* Lord*. 51:54 (28:54) "A sound of an outcry in [MT: from] Babylon and great breaking in [MT: from] the land of the Chaldeans! 51:55 (28:55) For the* Lord *has devastated [MT: is devastating] Babylon, and he has*

---

66. The text of MT 51:44b–49a does not appear in the LXX. A translation of the MT is provided here as follows: "'Also/Indeed the city wall of Babylon, it has fallen. Go forth from her midst, my people, and save each his life from the burning of the Lord's anger. And lest your heart be weak and you be afraid at the report that is heard in the land, and the report comes in the year, and after it in the year the report, and violence is in the land, and ruler against ruler. Therefore, look, days are coming, and I will visit upon [or, punish] the carved/sculpted idols of Babylon; and all her land, it will be ashamed [Syr.: perish; cf. *Tg. Jon.*]; and all her slain, they will fall in her midst. And sky and land and all that is in them will give a ringing cry over Babylon, for from (the) north the destroyers will come [pc Mss: יבאו; cf. Jer. 51:53b] to her,' the prophetic utterance of the Lord. 'It is both that Babylon is about to fall [see GKC §114i] for the slain of Israel [see MT 51:49b above].'"

destroyed [MT: will destroy] from her [Syr. adds: people and livestock] a great sound [Tg. Jon.: many armies] roaring like many waters [MT: and their waves will roar like many waters; Tg. Jon.: and armies of many peoples will be gathered against him]; he has made her sound a crash [MT: the crash of their sound is given; Tg. Jon.: and they will raise with noise their sound]. 51:56 (28:56) For devastation has come upon Babylon [MT: For a destroyer has come against her, against Babylon], and her mighty men have been captured [or, will be captured]; their bow has been broken [see BDB, 369, GKC §52k; LXX: their bow has been terrified; MT: she has shattered their bows (but see GKC §44m)]. For it is God who recompenses them [MT: For the Lord is a God of recompense, he will surely repay]. 51:57 (28:57) The Lord, he will surely repay [see MT 51:56b], and he will surely make drunk [MT: And I will make drunk] her officials and her wise men [MT adds: her governors] and her rulers [MT adds: and her mighty men, and they will sleep a perpetual sleep and not wake up (Tg. Jon.: and they will die the second death and not live for the world to come)]," the prophetic utterance of the king whose name is the Lord of hosts. 51:58 (28:58) Thus says the Lord [MT adds: of hosts], "As for the city wall of Babylon, (though) it was made broad, it will surely be leveled [MT: As for the broad city wall (Codex L: walls) of Babylon, it will surely be leveled], and her high gates will be set on fire. And peoples will not grow weary for nothing, and/ nor will nations in rule grow faint [MT: And peoples will grow weary for nothing; and nations for fire, they will grow faint]."

The exclamation in 51:41 (LXX 28:41) expresses astonishment at the demise of the once great Babylon: "How she [MT: Sheshach; *Tg. Jon.*: Babylon] was captured and seized, the praise of all the earth! How Babylon has become a desolation [or, object of horror] among the nations [MT: How she has become a desolation, Babylon among the nations]!" (cf. Isa. 14:12; Jer. 49:25; 50:23; Zeph. 2:15; see also Jer. 51:29, 32, 37). The name "Sheshach" (שׁשׁך), which appears in the MT but not in the Hebrew source behind Greek Jeremiah, is *atbash* for "Babylon" (בבל) as identified by *Targum Jonathan* (see Jer. 25:26; see also Jer. 51:1). As noted in the commentary on 51:1, *atbash* is a technique whereby the first and last letters of the Hebrew alphabet are substituted for one another (א and ת), the second and second to last (ב and שׁ), and so forth.[67]

The combination in 51:42 (LXX 28:42) and 51:43 (LXX 28:43) of the sea covering Babylon (51:42) and her cities being a dry land and

---

67. See the commentary on 51:1 for an explanation of the use of code names for Babylon.

a desert plain (51:43) initially appears to be a strange juxtaposition of images, but the "sea" in 51:42 is likely not a literal reference to the Euphrates as the sea (as in Jer. 51:36b; see also Jer. 51:13) flooding the land (cf. Nah. 2:7 [Eng., 2:6]). There may be an allusion here to the covering of the Egyptian army with the Sea of Reeds (see Exod. 14:28), but *Targum Jonathan* is likely correct to understand the sea covering the land as a metaphor for a "king with his armies who are as numerous as the waters of the sea" (cf. Isa. 8:7; Jer. 46:7; 47:2; 51:48, 55; Ezek. 26:19; see also Isa. 17:12; Ps. 65:8 [Eng., 65:7]; Luke 21:25). Thus, 51:42 is not a picture of a wet land followed by a picture of a dry land in 51:43. Rather, both verses speak of the desolation of the land. The description of the land in 51:43 is consistent with depictions of uninhabitable wilderness elsewhere (see Jer. 2:6; 4:29; 49:18; 50:12, 40). Since such desolation of Babylon never occurred historically, the reader is left to conclude either that 51:43 is extreme hyperbole or that it is a portrait of Babylon's eschatological fate (see again Jer. 51:36b; Rev. 16:12).

The two Hebrew versions of 51:44a (LXX 28:44a) give two very different senses. According to the Hebrew source behind Greek Jeremiah, the Lord will punish Babylon and bring out what she has swallowed from her mouth. This apparently refers to Israel, which the king of Babylon has swallowed (Jer. 51:34), and the redemption of Israel from Babylon. As a result of this punishment, nations will never again "flow" to Babylon either as captives or because of Babylon's status as the center of the Gentile world. Rather, they will "flow" to Mt. Zion in the last days (Isa. 2:2; Mic. 4:1). On the other hand, according to the MT, the Lord will punish Bel in Babylon (see Isa. 46:1; Jer. 50:2) and bring out what he has swallowed, and nations will never again flow to him. This potentially refers to food offerings thought to be swallowed by the Babylonian god Bel. By bringing out what Bel has supposedly swallowed (Syr.: "his cake"), the Lord will expose Bel as the false god that he is (see Bel and the Dragon),[68] and Bel will no longer have the allegiance of his worshipers among the nations.

The text of MT 51:44b–49a does not appear in the LXX. Rudolph suggests that this is due to homoioarchton (see *BHS* apparatus). That is, either the Hebrew scribe responsible for the source of the Greek translation or the Greek translator himself accidentally skipped from גם at the beginning of 51:44b to גם at the beginning of 51:49b, unwittingly

---

68. In the story of Bel and the Dragon, which is one of the additions to the book of Daniel in Greek translation tradition, Daniel exposes the fact that Bel does not eat the food that his worshipers put before him.

omitting the intervening text. But the matter is not quite so simple. Given the correspondences between 51:44b–49a and 51:49b–53 (v. 44b // v. 49b, v. 45 // v. 50, v. 46 // v. 51, v. 47 // v. 52, v. 48 // v. 53), Janzen may very well be correct to suppose that these two units are old variants now conflated in the MT.[69] If this is right, then the shorter version of the LXX likely represents a more original Hebrew text.

MT 51:44b states that the city wall of Babylon has fallen. Thus, the imperatives of 51:45 are given: "Go forth from her midst, my people, and save each his life from the burning of the Lord's anger" (cf. Isa. 48:20; 52:11; Jer. 50:8; 51:6, 50, 58; Zech. 2:10–11 [Eng., 2:6–7]; 2 Cor. 6:17; Rev. 18:4; see also Gen. 19:17). The combination of the two conjunctions וּפֶן ("And lest") at the beginning of 51:46 is unusual since it would normally only occur if a negative purpose clause were being coordinated with another, preceding negative purpose clause (see, e.g., Deut. 4:9, 16–19; 12:30). Perhaps there is an ellipsis of some kind in the present context. In any case, the negative purpose clause is given in conjunction with the imperatives in 51:45. God's people are to flee Babylon, which is the object of divine judgment, lest their hearts become weak and they fear the annual reports heard in the land (see Jer. 51:31)—reports of violence in the land and rulers engaging in warfare with one another. Jesus alludes to this text in response to his disciples' question about the sign of his coming and of the end of the age: "And you are about to hear of wars and reports of wars. See that you are not alarmed, for it is necessary for such things to happen, but it is not yet the end" (Matt. 24:6; cf. Mark 13:7; Luke 21:9; see also Ezek. 7:26). These things are the beginning of birth pains (Matt. 24:7; Mark 13:8). The people of God are not to be disheartened by such reports. Rather, they are to flee "Babylon" so to speak (i.e., flee the ways of the world) and prepare themselves for the imminent Day of the Lord and the sign of the coming of the Son of Man (Matt. 24:15–31; Mark 13:14–27; Luke 21:20–28).

The introduction to what appears to be an announcement of judgment at the beginning of 51:47 ("Therefore, look, days are coming") has a parallel in 51:52 (cf. Jer. 7:32; 19:6; 48:12; 49:2); but since neither text follows a formal accusation, it is likely that the announcement of Babylon's judgment is an announcement of eschatological salvation for the people of God referenced in 51:45–46 and 51:50–51 (cf. Jer. 16:14; 23:7). The Lord has already indicated that he will punish Babylon (Jer. 51:44; or, per the MT, Bel in Babylon). Now he says that he will punish the carved/sculpted idols of Babylon (Jer. 51:47, 52; cf. Jer. 50:38; see also Exod. 12:12; Isa. 44:9–20). It is not that these idols are real gods deserving of punishment.

---

69. Janzen, *Studies in the Text of Jeremiah*, 119.

Rather, God judges the human worship of such objects. The people of the land of Babylon will be ashamed of their worship of false gods, and all the slain of Babylon will fall in the midst of the land (cf. Jer. 51:49). All creation ("sky and land") will rejoice over the fall of Babylon (Jer. 51:48a; cf. Isa. 44:23; 49:13; Prov. 11:10; Rev. 18:20), for from the north the destroyers will come to her (Jer. 51:48b; cf. Jer. 51:53b; see commentary on Jer. 50:3, 9, 41 for discussion of this eschatological enemy from the north).

The text of MT 51:49 as it currently stands combines the two halves of the verse by means of a גַּם . . . גַּם ("both . . . and") construction: "It is both that Babylon is about to fall for the slain of Israel and that for Babylon the slain of all the earth have fallen (נָפְלוּ)" (cf. Jer. 51:47b, 52b; Rev. 18:24).[70] This translation assumes restoration of the prefixed preposition לְ ("for") to the phrase חַלְלֵי יִשְׂרָאֵל ("the slain of Israel") in 51:49a. The preposition was accidentally lost due to haplography (see the preceding לִנְפֹּל; see also the *BHS* apparatus). הָאָרֶץ at the end of 51:49b must mean "the earth" in the MT rather than "the land." On the other hand, the Hebrew source behind Greek Jeremiah only has 51:49b (LXX 28:49). This text does not feature the "both . . . and" construction, and הָאָרֶץ must mean "the land" (i.e., the land of Babylon): "Also/Indeed at Babylon the slain of all the land will fall (יִפְּלוּ)" (see Jer. 51:4).

The Hebrew source behind Greek Jeremiah 51:50a (LXX 28:50a) says, "Fugitives of dry ground, go and do not remain!" (פְּלֵטִים מֵחָרְבָה לְכוּ וְאַל תַּעֲמֹדוּ) (see *BHS* apparatus). This reading is attractive because it has the normal form for the masculine plural imperative of הלך (לְכוּ) rather than the unusual הִלְכוּ of the MT. Sharp, however, contends that the Greek translator would have used ξηρά rather than γῆ for חָרְבָה ("dry ground") (see MT and LXX Hag. 2:6).[71] MT 51:50a says, "Survivors of (the) sword, go, do not remain!" (פְּלֵטִים מֵחֶרֶב הִלְכוּ אַל תַּעֲמֹדוּ) (cf. Jer. 31:2–3; 44:28; Ezek. 6:8). The summons to flee Babylon is comparable to 51:45 (see also Isa. 48:20; 52:11; Jer. 50:8, 28; 51:6, 50, 58; Zech. 2:10–11 [Eng., 2:6–7]; Rev. 18:4). This is specifically for the remnant of the people of God who are to remember the LORD from far away (Jer. 51:50b), not in terms of time (as in the period of seventy years [Jer. 29:10]) but in terms of space. The city of Jerusalem is to be that which goes up upon their hearts and minds (cf. Deut. 30:1; 1 Kgs. 8:46–50; Jer. 31:21–22; 50:28; 51:10). If the hope expressed here is an eschatological one, then this is presumably the new Jerusalem (Isa. 65:17–18; Jer. 31:38–40; Zech 14:10; Rev. 21:9–22:5).

---

70. Some translators and commentators treat this as if it were a כַּאֲשֶׁר . . . כֵּן ("just as . . . so") construction (see, e.g., Keil, *Jeremiah,* 448, 450).

71. Sharp, "Take Another Scroll and Write," 504–5.

The Syriac version introduces 51:51 (LXX 28:51) as a quote from the house of Israel (cf. Jer. 51:34–35): "We are ashamed, for we have heard our reproach. Humiliation has covered our face. Strangers have entered [*Tg. Jon.* adds: and defiled] our sanctuaries, the house of the Lord [MT: the sanctuaries of the house of the Lord]." The expression of shame and humiliation is reminiscent of the ideal confession found in 3:25, but in that text the shame is due to sin (cf. Ezek. 33:10). Here the shame is due to the reproach that has come with the defiling of the temple's "sanctuaries" (Redak: the porch, the Temple, and the Holy of Holies) by foreigners (cf. Ps. 79:1; see Ps. 69:8 [Eng., 69:7]; Neh. 1:3; see also Ps. 68:36 [Eng., 68:35]). This initial objection to the call to remember the Lord from far away (Jer. 51:50b) does not take into account that the Lord intends to avenge the destruction of his temple (see Jer. 50:28; 51:11). Thus, the Lord declares in 51:52 (LXX 28:52) that days are coming when he will punish Babylon's idols and those who worship them (see commentary on MT Jer. 51:47; see also Jer. 50:38). The Hebrew source behind Greek Jeremiah 51:52b says: "and in all her land (the) slain will fall (יפל)." This reading is closer to MT 51:47 (see also Isa. 21:9; Jer. 51:4, 49). MT 51:52b has: "and in all her land (the) mortally wounded will groan (יאנק)" (cf. Ezek. 26:15).

Even if Babylon ascends as high as the sky and fortifies itself in an elevated place, the Lord will still be able to send destroyers to her (Jer. 51:53 [LXX 28:53]; cf. Jer. 51:48; see also Isa. 14:12). Rashi comments that this is because the Lord is in the heavens that are even higher than Babylon's height.[72] The thought of 51:53 is not unlike that of Jeremiah 49:16b (cf. Obad. 4), which addresses Edom's pride by saying that the Lord could bring Edom down even if it were to make its nest high like the eagle does. *Targum Jonathan* interprets Babylon's ascent to the sky to be the construction of buildings that are high up to the sky. This seems to hint at an allusion to the story of the Tower of Babylon (Gen. 11:1–9) in which the people attempt to make a name for themselves by building a city and a tower whose top reaches into the sky (Gen. 11:4).

The next subunit begins with the sound of an outcry in or from Babylon and great breaking in or from the land of the Chaldeans (Jer. 51:54 [LXX 28:54]; cf. Jer. 4:6; 6:1; 48:3; 50:22; Zeph. 1:10). This is the sound of the downfall of Babylon. "For the Lord has devastated [MT: is devastating] Babylon, and he has destroyed [MT: will destroy] from her [Syr. adds: people and livestock] a great sound [*Tg. Jon.*: many armies]" (Jer. 51:55a [LXX 28:55a]; cf. Jer. 51:48b, 53b). The Syriac's addition to 51:55a ("people and livestock") assumes that the great sound destroyed

---

72. Rosenberg, trans., *Mikraoth Gedoloth: Jeremiah Volume Two*, 409.

from Babylon is that of the bustling city itself (see commentary on Jer. 51:14). *Targum Jonathan*, on the other hand, understands the great sound to be that of Babylon's "many armies." The Hebrew source behind Greek Jeremiah 51:55b (LXX 28:55b) describes this sound as one "roaring like many waters" (cf. Jer. 51:13). The Lord has turned this great sound of the city into a "crash." The text of MT 51:55b, however, is open to a different interpretation: "and their waves will roar like many waters; the crash of their sound is given." These waves could be those of Babylon, but they could also be those of the enemy (see Jer. 51:42; Ezek. 26:19; see also Luke 21:25). *Targum Jonathan* interprets the text of the MT in the latter sense: "and armies of many peoples will be gathered against him; and they will raise with noise their sound."

The reason for the "crash" of Babylon is that "devastation" (שׁוד) has come upon the city (Jer. 51:56 [LXX 28:56]; MT: "For a destroyer [שׁודד] has come against her, against Babylon"; cf. Jer. 51:48b, 53b, 55a). Babylon's mighty men are captured, their bow is broken (cf. 1 Sam. 2:4). "For it is God who recompenses them." The MT concludes 51:56b as follows: "For the Lord is a God of recompense, he will surely repay" (cf. Jer. 50:29; 51:6, 24). The Hebrew source behind Greek Jeremiah has "the Lord" as the subject of "will repay" ("The Lord, he will surely repay"), and the versification in the Göttingen Septuagint places this at the beginning of 51:57 (LXX 28:57). The Lord will make drunk (MT: "And I will make drunk") Babylon's officials and her wise men (MT adds: "her governors") and her rulers (MT adds: "and her mighty men") (cf. Isa. 19:11; Jer. 50:35; 51:39; see Jer. 25:26 [MT]; 51:7; see also Jer. 51:23, 28). The MT, which has a longer text for 51:57, adds at the end of the verse: "and they will sleep a perpetual sleep and not wake up" (see commentary on Jer. 51:39). Translations of the MT normally understand 51:57 alone to be "the prophetic utterance of the king whose name is the Lord of hosts" (cf. Jer. 46:18a; 48:15b), since it is the only verse in 51:54–57 in which the Lord speaks in the first person. In the Hebrew source behind Greek Jeremiah 51:54–57 (LXX 28:54–57), the text refers to the Lord in the third person without exception. Thus, there is no reason why the entire unit cannot be the prophetic utterance of the Lord.

Jeremiah 51:58 (LXX 28:58) reintroduces the Lord as the speaker: "Thus says the Lord [MT adds: of hosts]." Despite the broadness of Babylon's city wall, it will indeed be razed: "As for the city wall of Babylon, (though) it was made broad (הָרְחָבָה), it will surely be leveled [MT: As for the broad (הָרְחָבָה) city wall (Codex L: walls) of Babylon, it will surely be leveled]" (cf. MT Jer. 51:44b). Babylon's high gates will be set on fire. The presumed Hebrew source behind Greek Jeremiah 51:58b differs slightly from the MT: "And peoples will not grow weary for nothing, and/nor will nations in rule (ברֹאשׁ) grow faint."[73] The MT has: "And peoples will grow weary for nothing; and nations for fire (בְּדֵי אֵשׁ), they will grow faint." Tov considers the presumed text behind the LXX to be an example of what he calls a "pseudo-variant."[74] That is, the reading בְרֹאשׁ ("in rule") did not actually appear in the Greek translator's *Vorlage*. It only existed in the translator's mind. It can be very difficult, however, to determine with any degree of certainty whether a variant is true or not. The text of MT 51:58b is cited in a slightly different form by the composer of the Twelve in Habakkuk 2:13: "Is it not, look, from the LORD of hosts that peoples grow weary for fire, and nations for emptiness grow faint?"[75] The international slave labor of the Babylonians has built the city in vain (cf. Isa. 33:12; 65:23; see also Jer. 51:9). The syntactical oddness of וְיָעֵפוּ (LXX = וְיָעֵפוּ) at the end of MT 51:58b and its reappearance at the end of MT 51:64a (> LXX) has prompted the following explanation by McKane: "The oracle ends at v. 58 and 'It is here that Jeremiah's words end' (v. 64) was originally associated with the end of v. 58 as a marginal gloss which ran, 'with respect to יָעֵפוּ (יָעֵפוּ, a *lemma*), it is here that Jeremiah's words end.' After vv. 59–64 were added, the gloss was transferred to the end of v. 64 and the text of v. 58b was corrupted (וְיָעֵפוּ) by the gloss."[76]

51:59 (28:59) The word that the LORD *commanded Jeremiah the prophet to speak to Seraiah [MT: The word that Jeremiah the prophet commanded Seraiah] the son of Neriah, the son of Mahseiah, when he came from Zedekiah [MT: with Zedekiah; Tg. Jon.: with the message / commission of Zedekiah] the king of Judah to Babylon in the fourth year of his reign. (And Seraiah was an official of gifts [MT: rest; Syr.: encampment; Tg. Jon.: gift; Vulg.: prophecy].) 51:60 (28:60) And Jeremiah wrote all the calamity that would come upon Babylon in a / one document, all these words that are written about Babylon. 51:61 (28:61) And Jeremiah said to Seraiah, "When you come [Codex L: As soon as you come] to Babylon, you will see and read publicly [or, see to it that you read publicly; Syr.: read and see] all these words. 51:62 (28:62) And you will say, 'LORD, LORD [> MT], you are the one who spoke against this place to cut it off and [and*

---

73. This apparently means that efforts against Babylon will prevail.
74. Tov, *Text-Critical Use of the Septuagint*, 178–81.
75. For a discussion of this citation from Jeremiah as part of the work of the composer of the Book of the Twelve, see Shepherd, *Commentary on the Book of the Twelve*, 21–36, 332–38. The citation from Jeremiah 51:58b in Habakkuk 2:13 interrupts the series of woe oracles in Habakkuk 2:5–20 and is paired with a citation from Isaiah 11:9 in Habakkuk 2:14.
76. McKane, *Jeremiah XXVI–LII*, 1349.

> *MT] so that there not be in it an inhabitant from human to animal, for a perpetual desolation [or, object of horror; MT: perpetual desolations] will she be.' 51:63 (28:63) And then, as soon as you finish reading this document publicly, you will bind on it a stone and cast it into the midst of the Euphrates. 51:64 (28:64) And you will say, 'Thus will Babylon sink and not rise up from before [or, because of] the Chaldeans [MT: the calamity] that I am bringing upon/against her.'" [MT adds: And with regard to* יעפו *(see 51:58b), up to here are the words of Jeremiah.]*

In the edition of the book of Jeremiah represented by the LXX, this passage (Jer. 51:59–64) serves to conclude the words about Babylon in chapters 50 and 51 (LXX 27 and 28). In the edition of the book represented by the MT, however, this same text concludes both the corpus of oracles about the nations as a whole and the entire composition of Jeremiah prior to the addition of the appendix in chapter 52. Alternatively, the text of Jeremiah 45, which likely served at one time to conclude the scroll of Jeremiah that was originally produced in 605 BC (see Jer. 36), now appears as the conclusion (prior to the appendix in Jer. 52) to the entire edition of the book of Jeremiah represented by the LXX. J. R. Lundbom has made the case that both Jeremiah 45 (which mentions Jeremiah's scribe Baruch) and Jeremiah 51:59–64 (which mentions Baruch's brother Seraiah) qualify as scribal colophons that have been repurposed to function as conclusions to the two editions of the book respectively.[77] Lundbom suggests that Baruch was responsible for the first edition, which is the Hebrew text behind LXX Jeremiah, concluding with his scribal colophon in chapter 45. Baruch went to Egypt (Jer. 43:1–7) and produced this edition of the book, which became the basis for the ancient Greek translation of the book made in Alexandria.[78] Thus, the material leading up to the colophon in chapter 45 primarily concerns the community's move to Egypt (Jer. 42–44). On the other hand, Seraiah was responsible for the second edition of the book, which is now represented by the MT. Seraiah went to Babylon (Jer. 51:59; cf. Bar. 1:1) and produced an edition of the book that concluded with the words about Babylon (Jer. 50–51).[79] Both colophons form an inclusio by incorporating words from the book's

---

77. J. R. Lundbom, "Baruch, Seraiah, and Expanded Colophons in the Book of Jeremiah," *JSOT* 36 (1986): 89–114.
78. See Aejmelaeus, "Jeremiah at the Turning Point of History," 460.
79. This became the dominant text form in the land of Israel, although evidence of the presence of a text form close to that of the LXX *Vorlage* was discovered at Qumran (4QJer[b, d]).

introduction. Jeremiah 45:4 features text from the programmatic Jeremiah 1:10, and MT Jeremiah 51:64b ("up to here are the words of Jeremiah") deliberately echoes MT Jeremiah 1:1a ("The words of Jeremiah") but not LXX 1:1a ("The word of God that came to Jeremiah").

The Hebrew source behind Greek Jeremiah 51:59 introduces the following (Jer. 51:61–64) as the message that the LORD commanded Jeremiah to speak to Seraiah. According to the MT, however, what follows is the word that Jeremiah commanded Seraiah. Seraiah is called "the son of Neriah, the son of Mahseiah," which makes him the brother of Baruch, Jeremiah's scribe (see Jer. 32:12). Scribal work was a family trade (see 1 Chr. 2:55), and this strongly suggests that Seraiah himself had scribal training, regardless of the exact nature of his position in the service of Zedekiah. It is likely that his skill and status as one of the scribal elite gave him his prominent role.[80] According to the Hebrew source behind Greek Jeremiah, Jeremiah spoke to Seraiah when he (Seraiah) came "from" (מאת) Zedekiah to Babylon in the fourth year of his reign (c. 594/93 BC; cf. Jer. 28:1). On the other hand, the MT says that Jeremiah commanded Seraiah when he (Seraiah) came "with" (את) Zedekiah to Babylon. *Targum Jonathan* interprets this to mean that Seraiah came "with the message/commission of Zedekiah." Thompson comments that Seraiah's trip to Babylon took place in the same year as the plot to rebel against Nebuchadnezzar recorded in Jeremiah 27.[81] Thus, there was a need to pledge loyalty to the Babylonian king once again. Thompson says that Jeremiah's letter in chapter 29 was sent earlier "to assure Nebuchadrezzar that the people of Judah were in no way implicated in the disturbances referred to in 29:21–23." It is difficult to determine with certainty what the exact relationship of 51:59 to chapters 27–29 might be.[82]

The Hebrew source behind Greek Jeremiah 51:59b provides the following parenthetical comment about Seraiah: "And Seraiah was an official of gifts (מנחות)." *Targum Jonathan* says that he was an official of "gift" (= מנחה). These witnesses seem to suggest that Seraiah was a royal official tasked with the responsibility of bearing tribute to the foreign king to whom the Judeans were subject. The MT, however, says that Seraiah was an official of "rest" (מנוחה), which the Syriac translates as an official of "encampment" (= מחנה?). English versions commonly

---

80. See Christopher A. Rollston, *Writing and Literacy in the World of Ancient Israel: Epigraphic Evidence from the Iron Age* (Atlanta: SBL, 2010), 85–90.
81. Thompson, *Book of Jeremiah*, 770–71.
82. See McKane, *Jeremiah XXVI–LII*, 1351.

take this to mean that Seraiah was quartermaster (e.g., ESV),[83] but the Latin Vulgate interprets the phrase to mean "an official of prophecy" (cf. Vulg. 1 Chr. 15:27). This may be based on the idea that the Spirit of prophecy "rests" upon true prophets (see, e.g., Isa. 11:2; cf. 42:1; 61:1; Mic. 3:8; see also Jer. 45:3). It may also be linked to Seraiah's role as a scribe and his association with his brother Baruch. The Talmud calls both Baruch and Seraiah "prophets" along with Jeremiah (*b. Meg.* 14b–15a). The biblical scribes/authors were exegetes of the book of the prophet Moses (see MT and LXX Prov. 29:18; see also Ezra 7:6, 10; Neh. 8–9) and thereby produced textual prophecy.[84] Jeremiah himself likely had scribal training as part of his priestly background (Jer. 1:1; see Jer. 30:2; 36:2; 51:60; cf. Isa. 8:1; 30:8; Ezek. 43:11; Hab. 2:2).

Jeremiah 51:60 (LXX 28:60) is inserted between the introduction to what Jeremiah said to Seraiah (Jer. 51:59) and the record of what he said (Jer. 51:61–64). It is something of a parenthetical indication of what Jeremiah wrote that supplies an antecedent for the phrase "all these words" in 51:61b: "And Jeremiah wrote all the calamity that would come upon Babylon in a/one document, all these words that are written about Babylon." This is a reference back to the words about Babylon's judgment now recorded in Jeremiah 50–51. It is not clear from this whether Jeremiah himself wrote these words (cf. Jer. 30:2) or whether he dictated the words to someone like Baruch (cf. Jer. 36:2, 4). The matter is not quite so simple as pointing out the fact that Jeremiah is the grammatical subject of the verb "wrote." For example, Solomon is the subject in the clause, "and he built the house of the LORD" (MT 1 Kgs. 6:1b), yet it is clear that Solomon himself did not build the temple. Rather, Solomon had the temple built. Likewise, where the instruction for the king in Deuteronomy 17:18b says, "and he will write" (וכתב) for himself a copy of the Torah, the Temple Scroll (11Q19 56:21) says, "and they will write"

---

83. McKane refers to Ehrlich's view based on 1 Kgs 8:56 (1 Chr 22:9) where the word for "rest" is an antonym of the word for "war": "Seraiah was an anti-war statesman opposed to Judah's rebellion against Babylon" (McKane, *Jeremiah XXVI–LII*, 1352). Less likely is the view of Calvin who says that "official of rest" describes Seraiah's placid disposition (*Jeremiah*, 5:287–88).

84. See Karel van der Toorn, *Scribal Culture and the Making of the Hebrew Bible* (Cambridge, MA: Harvard University Press, 2007), 107, 169. "It will not escape us that this identification of prophecy with scribal activity marks a shift from direct revelation through the person of the prophet to revelation accruing from the inspired interpretation of biblical texts. In other words, the exegete or theologian is now the prophet" (Joseph Blenkinsopp, *Prophecy and Canon: A Contribution to the Study of Jewish Origins* [Notre Dame, IN: University of Notre Dame Press, 1977], 129).

(וכתבו) for him. The Temple Scroll interprets the text to mean that the king will have the copy written for him. It is thus possible that Jeremiah had the words about Babylon written for him.

The difference between what Jeremiah said to Seraiah according to the Hebrew source behind Greek Jeremiah 51:61 (LXX 28:61) and a multitude of Masoretic manuscripts on the one hand, and the Leningrad Codex on the other hand, is very subtle: "And Jeremiah said to Seraiah, 'When you come (בבאך) [Codex L: As soon as you come (כבאך)] to Babylon, you will see and read publicly all these words.'"[85] The instruction to see and read publicly all the words that Jeremiah wrote about Babylon in a/one document (Jer. 50–51) is not an instruction to perform two separate actions, as if Seraiah were to see the words for the first time in Babylon and then read them publicly. Rather, the verb "see" is an auxiliary verb: "you will see to it that you read publicly all these words" (see ESV, NET). The verb קרא ("call") means to read the words aloud publicly (cf. Jer. 2 Kgs. 23:2b; 3:12), just as to "call in" (קרא ב) a scroll or a document means to give a public reading (see Jer. 36:6; Neh. 8:8). If the instruction had been to perform a private reading, then הגה ("murmur") or הגה ב ("murmur in") would have been used to indicate reading aloud quietly to oneself (see Josh. 1:8; Ps. 1:2). It is not clear what audience, if any, Seraiah would have had in Babylon. Nevertheless, the performance of the public reading, regardless of who might have heard it, was part and parcel of his assignment and a prerequisite for the symbolic sign act in Jeremiah 51:63.

The declaration that was to accompany Seraiah's public reading of the words about Babylon is essentially a concise summary of the document in chapters 50–51 addressed to the Lord himself: "And you will say, 'Lord, Lord [> MT], you are the one who spoke against this place to cut it off and [and > MT] so that there not be in it an inhabitant from human to animal, for a perpetual desolation [or, object of horror; MT: perpetual desolations] will she be'" (Jer. 51:62 [LXX 28:62]; cf. Jer. 50:3; 51:26). Upon completion of the public reading of the document, Seraiah was to bind a stone on it and cast it into the midst of the Euphrates (Jer. 51:63 [LXX 28:63]; cf. Jer. 36:23). This is a prophetic sign act comparable to other such symbolic actions in the book of Jeremiah (see Jer. 13:1–11; 16:1–9; 18:1–12; 19:1–13; 27–28; 32; 43:8–13). The explanation of the act was to follow it: "And you will say, 'Thus will Babylon sink and not rise up from before [or, because of] the Chaldeans [MT:

---

85. See Christo H. J. van der Merwe, Jackie A. Naudé, and Jan H. Kroeze, *A Biblical Hebrew Reference Grammar* (Sheffield: Sheffield Academic, 1999), 156–57.

the calamity] that I am bringing upon/against her'" (Jer. 51:64a [LXX 28:64]; see Jer. 51:13, 42). Just as Pharaoh and his army sank like a stone in the Sea of Reeds (Exod. 15:5), so would Babylon sink like the stone bound to Jeremiah's document and never recover again. John takes up this image in the description of his vision of the fall of eschatological Babylon: "And a mighty angel took up a stone like a great millstone and cast it into the sea, saying, 'Thus with violence Babylon the great city will be cast and never be found again'" (Rev. 18:21).[86]

The addition at the end of MT 51:64 ("And with regard to יעפו [see 51:58b], up to here are the words of Jeremiah") does not appear in the Hebrew source behind Greek Jeremiah.[87] The conjunction and verb ויעפו are not to be read as a *weqatal* form ("and they will grow weary") joined syntactically to the preceding text of 51:64a. Rather, this text earlier appeared after 51:58b to explain that the verb יעפו at the end of that verse was the last of Jeremiah's words prior to the addition of the appendix in chapter 52 (cf. MT Jer. 48:47b; see also Dan. 7:28a). Once the instructions to Seraiah were included in 51:59–64, this addition was moved to the end of verse 64 so that the book in its second edition (MT) began, "The words of Jeremiah" (MT Jer. 1:1a; cf. Jer. 36:10), and ended, "up to here are the words of Jeremiah" (MT Jer. 51:64b).[88] Since the Hebrew source behind Greek Jeremiah (the first edition of the book) begins, "The word of God that came to Jeremiah" (LXX Jer. 1:1a), and since it does not conclude with Jeremiah 50–51, no such concluding notice appears in its text at this point.

---

86. See Keil, *Jeremiah*, 455–56.

87. See Neusner, *Jeremiah in Talmud and Midrash*, 36, 62, 63, 168.

88. "We have said that the prophets, after having spoken in the Temple, or to the people, afterwards collected brief summaries, and that these contained the principal things: from these the prophetic books were made up. For Jeremiah did not write the volume as we have it at this day, except the chapters; and it appears evident that it was not written in the order in which he spoke. The order of time is not, then, everywhere observed; but the scribes were careful in this respect, that they collected the summaries affixed to the doors of the Temple; and so they added this conclusion, *Thus far the words of Jeremiah*. But this, in my view, is not to be confined to the prophecies respecting the fall of Babylon; for I doubt not but that the scribe who collected all his prophecies, added these words, that he had thus far transcribed the words of Jeremiah" (Calvin, *Jeremiah*, 5:293). Calvin goes on to say that chapter 52 was subsequently added in order to provide historical context for the prophecy of the book.

PHILISTIA

(Jer. 47 [LXX 29:1–7])

47:1 (29:1) Concerning the Philistines [LXX: foreigners; MT: That which was the word of the LORD to Jeremiah the prophet concerning the Philistines before Pharaoh struck Gaza (cf. 2QJer)]:

47:2 (29:2) Thus says the LORD, "Look, waters are rising from (the) north [Syr.: I am bringing youths from the north; Tg. Jon.: peoples are coming from the north], and they will become an overflowing torrent and overflow [Tg. Jon.: plunder] (the) land and its fullness, (the) city and (the) inhabitants therein, and the people will cry out, and all the inhabitants of the land [Codex L: and every inhabitant of the land] will wail. 47:3 (29:3) From the sound of his stamping, from the hooves of his mighty horses [MT: From the sound of the stamping of the hooves of his mighty horses], and [> MT] from the shaking of his chariots, the noise of his wheels, fathers do not turn to [cf. 2QJer; Tg. Jon.: to pity] their sons / children because of slackness of hands, 47:4 (29:4) upon the day that is coming to destroy [Tg. Jon.: plunder] all (the) Philistines [LXX: foreigners], and I will cut off [cf. 2QJer] Tyre and Sidon and all the survivors of their help [MT: to cut off for Tyre and for Sidon every helping survivor], for the LORD is destroying [Tg. Jon.: has plundered] the remnant of the coastlands [MT: the Philistines, the remnant of the island of Caphtor / Crete]. 47:5 (29:5) Baldness [Syr.: Wound / Blow; Tg. Jon.: Vengeance / Retribution] has come to Gaza. Ashkelon is cast away [MT: ruined / destroyed (or, silent)], and the remnant of (the) Anakim [MT: the remnant of their valley (Tg. Jon.: the remnant of their strength; Syr.: and all those who are left among their inhabitants)]. (29:6) How long will you cut yourself [2QJer: תתגוררי (cf. Hos.

7:14)]?[1] *47:6 'O sword of the* Lord *[MT: Woe / Ah, sword of the* Lord*!], how long will you not be quiet? Be gathered to your sheath! Rest and be lifted up [MT: be silent / still]!' 47:7 (29:7) How can it be quiet, and it is the* Lord *who has commanded it, against Ashkelon and against the seashore, a remnant, to be aroused? [MT: How can you be quiet, and it is the* Lord *who has commanded it? Against Ashkelon and against the seashore, there (2QJer:* שמה*) has he appointed it.]"*

The short heading אל פלשתים ("Concerning the Philistines"), which is found in the Hebrew source behind Greek Jeremiah, is the original text of Jeremiah 47:1 (LXX 29:1).[2] This heading is free of any historical moorings and lends itself to the eschatological context of the oracles concerning the nations set by the use of the phrase "at the end of the days" in the first (Jer. 49:39) and last (Jer. 48:47) oracles according to the arrangement of the Hebrew source behind Greek Jeremiah. The LXX translates "Philistines" as "foreigners," which reflects the view that the Philistines are outsiders living in the land of Israel (see Jer. 47:4b), but the oracle itself makes no reference to the historical relationship between the Philistines and Israel as presented elsewhere in the Bible. The expanded heading of the MT (see also 2QJer) has the original heading embedded within it: "That which was the word of the Lord to Jeremiah the prophet concerning the Philistines before Pharaoh struck Gaza" (cf. MT Jer. 14:1; 46:1; 49:34). This expanded version of 47:1 works well with the historicized second edition of the book represented by the MT.[3]

The Lord envisions waters rising from the north (Jer. 47:2 [LXX 29:2]; cf. Isa. 14:31b), which both the Syriac and *Targum Jonathan* interpret to be people coming from the north (cf. Isa. 8:7; 17:12; Jer.

---

1. NETS 29:6a: "How long will you cut, you dagger of the Lord? How long until you will be quiet?"
2. Other prophetic oracles about the Philistines include Isaiah 14:28–32; Ezekiel 25:15–17; Amos 1:6–8; Zephaniah 2:4–7; Zechariah 9:5–7.
3. There are several options for the time of Pharaoh's strike of Gaza referenced in MT 47:1. The first is 609 BC, when Pharaoh Necho went north to aid Assyria, killing King Josiah along the way at Megiddo (2 Kgs. 23:29; see McKane, *Jeremiah XXVI–LII*, 1143). The second is 605 BC, when Pharaoh Necho retreated from the north after the battle of Carchemish (Jer. 46:2; see Thompson, *Book of Jeremiah*, 696). The third option is during the reign of Zedekiah when Pharaoh Hophra's army withdrew from its attempt to help Jerusalem against the Babylonians (Jer. 37:5–8; see Rashi in Rosenberg, trans., *Mikraoth Gedoloth: Jeremiah Volume Two*, 354; Calvin, *Jeremiah*, 4:610; Keil, *Jeremiah*, 381–82).

46:7; 51:42, 55; Ps. 65:8 [Eng., 65:7]). These "waters" so to speak will become an overflowing torrent and overflow (*Tg. Jon.*: "plunder") the land and its fullness (i.e., the city [Gaza? Ashkelon?] and the inhabitants therein). The Philistines will cry out, and all the inhabitants of Philistia will wail (cf. Isa. 14:31a). In the first edition of the book represented by the LXX and 4QJer[b, d], the enemy from the north is an eschatological enemy (see commentary on Jer. 1:13–15 and 25:9). Thus, this enemy even comes against Babylon in the manner described here (see Jer. 51:42, 48, 53, 55). In the second edition of the book represented by the MT, the enemy from the north is normally understood to be Babylon (see MT Jer. 25:9; but see Jer. 50:3, 9, 41). It has been suggested, however, that in the present context of MT 47:1–7 the enemy from the north is Pharaoh Necho returning from the north after his efforts to help Assyria.[4] According to this view, Necho attacked not only Gaza but other Philistine cities as he moved south toward Egypt.

When the Philistine fathers hear the sound of stamping from the hooves of the enemy's mighty horses (cf. Jer. 8:16; 50:11; see also Isa. 5:28b) along with the shaking of his chariots (i.e., the noise of his wheels [cf. Isa. 5:28b; Nah. 3:2]), they do not even turn to help (*Tg. Jon.*: "pity") their own sons/children due to their "slackness of hands" (i.e., sense of helplessness) (Jer. 47:3 [LXX 49:3]; cf. Jer. 14:5; 46:5, 21). The thought of 47:3 then continues in 47:4 (LXX 29:4). The fathers do not turn to help their sons in the day that is coming to destroy all the Philistines. Both the LXX and 2QJer (והכרתי) attest to a following first singular finite verb: "and I will cut off Tyre and Sidon and all the survivors of their help (שרידי עזרם)." The MT has an infinitive: "to cut off (להכרית) for Tyre and for Sidon every helping survivor (שריד עזר)." It may seem strange for a reference to Tyre and Sidon in Phoenicia to appear here, but these two cities are mentioned in conjunction with Philistia in other prophetic oracles (see Ezek. 25:15–17; 26–28; Joel 4:4 [Eng., 3:4]; Amos 1:6–10; Zech. 9:2–7; see also Jer. 27:3; Ps. 83:8 [Eng., 83:7]). Philistia (south) and Phoenicia (north) are connected by virtue of their location along the Mediterranean coast. Rashi suggests that the "survivors of their help" (MT: "every helping survivor") are the Philistines who aided Tyre and Sidon.[5] Redak, however, says that Tyre and Sidon aided the Philistines. It is possible to read the text either way. The final clause of the Hebrew source behind Greek Jeremiah 47:4b explains that the Lord is destroying "the remnant of the coastlands" (שארית האיים) (cf. Isa. 14:30b; Amos 1:8b). The MT has expanded

---

4. See McKane, *Jeremiah XXVI–LII*, 1143.
5. Rosenberg, trans., *Mikraoth Gedoloth: Jeremiah Volume Two*, 355.

"the remnant of the coastlands" to "the Philistines, the remnant of the island of Caphtor/Crete" (את פלשתים שארית אי כפתור). This expansion has its basis in Amos 9:7 (see also Gen. 10:14; Deut. 2:23; Zeph. 2:5), which speaks of the island of Caphtor/Crete as the place of origin for the Philistines.

Baldness has come to Gaza (Jer. 47:5a [LXX 29:5a]). This refers to the forbidden pagan practice of shaving the head as a sign of mourning for the dead (see Lev. 21:5; Deut. 14:1; Isa. 3:24; 15:2; Jer. 48:37; Ezek. 7:18; 27:31; Mic. 1:16 [cf. Job 1:20]; Amos 8:10). Ashkelon is "cast away" (נרמתה) [MT: "ruined/destroyed/silent" (נדמתה)], and so is the entire remnant of the "Anakim" (ענקים) (LXX; see Num. 13:22, 33). According to Joshua 11:22, there were no Anakim left in the land of Israel when Joshua made his conquest; only in Gaza, Gath, and Ashdod (Philistine territory) did they remain. On the other hand, the MT has "the remnant of their valley (עמקם)." *Targum Jonathan* interprets this to mean "the remnant of their strength" (cf. Ugaritic; see also Syr.: "and all those who are left among their inhabitants"). The MT places the disjunctive *athnach* accent under עמקם ("their valley"), requiring the phrase "the remnant of their valley" to be read in apposition to "Ashkelon." It is possible, however, that this phrase should be read with what follows: "Remnant of their valley, how long will you cut yourself (תתגודדי)?" This is yet another pagan ritual for the dead (see Deut. 14:1; 1 Kgs. 18:28; Jer. 16:6; 41:5). The variant תתגוררי found in 2QJer is due to the common confusion of ד and ר. The same accidental error in transmission occurs in Hosea 7:14 where יתגוררו is written in the Leningrad Codex in place of the correct reading יתגודדו found in other Masoretic manuscripts. The LXX reads the question at the end of Jeremiah 47:5 as one addressed to the sword at the beginning of 47:6 so that it forms a parallel with the following question: "How long will you cut, you dagger of the Lord? How long until you will be quiet?" (NETS). The problem with this rendering is that it ignores the reflexive *hithpael* stem of the verb תתגודדי in the Hebrew *Vorlage*.

Jeremiah 47:6 (LXX 29:6) represents the hypothetical voice of the Philistines: "O sword of the Lord, how long will you not be quiet? Be gathered to your sheath! Rest and be lifted up (ורמי) [MT: and be silent/still (ודמי)]!" The MT's הוי ("Woe/Ah") at the beginning of 47:6 is not present in the Hebrew source behind Greek Jeremiah. This appeal to the sword of the Lord (see Isa. 34:6; Jer. 12:12; 46:10) acknowledges that the enemy from the north is the Lord's instrument of judgment. The response to the question about how long the sword of the Lord will not be quiet (i.e., cease from its activity) is yet another question: How can the sword be quiet when the Lord himself is the one who has commanded it against Ashkelon and against the seashore (Jer. 47:7 [LXX 29:7]; Ezek. 25:16b)?[6] This rhetorical question assumes that the instrument of judgment cannot relent once the Lord has decreed its mission. The Hebrew source behind Greek Jeremiah 47:7b calls Ashkelon and the seashore "a remnant" (שאר; cf. Jer. 47:4b, 5b) and indicates that the Lord has commanded his sword "to be aroused" (הער) against them. The MT, however, concludes 47:7b with a clause: "there has he appointed it" (שם יעדה). That is, the Lord has appointed his sword in Ashkelon and in Philistia by the sea.

---

6. The MT maintains the voice of the Philistines in 47:7: "How can you be quiet (תשקטי)?" The LXX has a third-person verb (= תשקט), likely indicating a shift back to the voice of the Lord.

EDOM

(Jer. 49:7–22 [LXX 29:8–23])

49:7 (29:8) Concerning Edom:

Thus says the LORD *[MT adds: of hosts], "There is no longer wisdom in Teman [MT: Is there no longer wisdom in Teman?].[1] Counsel has perished from those who have understanding [MT: Has counsel perished from those who have understanding (Tg. Jon.: from sons)?]. Their wisdom has gone free [MT: Has their wisdom gone free?]. 49:8 (29:9) Their face has been deceived [MT: Flee, turn back (see GKC §46a[2])]. Make deep to dwell [see GKC §63o], O inhabitants of Dedan, for a disaster [LXX: difficult things] he made. I bring upon him a time [LXX: in a time] when I visit/punish him [see GKC §130d; MT: for the disaster of Esau I bring upon him, a time when I visit/punish him]. 49:9 (29:10) If [LXX: Because] grape gatherers were to come [MT adds: to you], would they not leave gleanings? If [LXX: As] robbers (were to come) [cf. Obad. 5a] at night, they would stay their hand [MT: they would damage only what is enough for them]. 49:10 (29:11) Indeed, I, I have stripped [Syr.: searched (cf. Tg. Jon.)] Esau. I have uncovered his hiding places, they will not be able to hide [MT: and he will hide, he will not be able]. The arm/strength of his brother has been destroyed, and (of) his neighbor [MT: His offspring has been destroyed, and his*

---

1. "Perhaps οὐκ is rather a rendering of the interrogative particle ה, than οὐκ ἔστιν being a rendering of אֵין, since οὐκ taken as an interrogative particle is closer to the meaning of the Hebrew text than if οὐκ is taken as a negative, and thus the translator perhaps intended οὐκ to be taken as an interrogative particle as well" (Walser, *Jeremiah*, 367).

*brothers and his neighbors], and he is not. 49:11 (29:12) Your orphan /
fatherless is to be left in order that he might live [MT: Leave your orphans, I will be the one to keep (them) alive]; and as for your widows,
let it be in me that they trust [Tg. Jon.: As for you, house of Israel, you
will not be forsaken. As for your orphans, I will raise (them); and as for
your widows, in my word they can trust]." 49:12 (29:13) For thus says
the* Lord, *"Those whose custom it was not to drink the cup, they drank;
and as for you, you will certainly not go unpunished [MT: Look, those
whose custom it is not to drink the cup (Tg. Jon.: the cup of curse), they
will certainly drink; and as for you, will you indeed go unpunished?
You will not go unpunished, for you will certainly drink]. 49:13 (29:14)
For it is by myself that I swear," the prophetic utterance of the* Lord,
*"that an object of horror [or, desolation], an object of reproach [MT
adds: a waste], and an object of contempt [or, curse] you will become in
her midst [MT: Bozrah will become]; and as for all her cities, they will
become perpetual ruins." 49:14 (29:15) A report have I heard from the*
Lord, *and messengers among the nations has he sent [MT: and a messenger among the nations is sent]: "Gather together and come against
her, [MT adds: and] rise up for battle!" 49:15 (29:16) "Small have I
made you [MT: For look, small have I made you] among the nations,
despised among mankind. 49:16 (29:17) Your horror [GKC §147c], the
presumption of your heart has deceived you. He has dwelt in the clefts
of the rock, he has grasped a hill's height [MT: dwelling in the clefts
of the rock, grasping a hill's height]. If he makes his nest [MT: If you
make your nest] high like the eagle [cf. Obad. 4a; Syr.], from there I
will bring you down" [MT adds: the prophetic utterance of the* Lord].[2]
*49:17 (29:18) "And Edom will become an object of horror [or, desola-
tion]. Every one who passes by her will hiss [MT: be appalled and
hiss at all her wounds; cf. Jer. 19:8]. 49:18 (29:19) Like the overthrow
[Syr.: God's overthrow; cf. Jer. 50:40] of Sodom and Gomorrah and her
neighbors," says the* Lord *of hosts [of hosts > MT], "a man / person will
not live there, and a human being will not sojourn in her. 49:19 (29:20)
Look, [Tg. Jon. adds: a king with his armies will go up against them]
like a lion that goes up from the midst of [MT: from the pride / majesty
of] the Jordan to a perennial pasture [LXX: a place of Aithan], indeed
[LXX: because] I will suddenly cause them [MT: him] to run away
from upon her; and as for choice, young men, over / against her appoint (them) [MT: and whomever is chosen I will appoint over / against*

---

2.   LXX: "Your sporting laid hands on [= הׁשיעג?] you; recklessness of your heart
     broke up holes in rocks; it seized strength of a high hill. Because like an
     eagle he set his nest high, from there I will bring you down" (NETS).

her]. For who is like me? And who will summon/arraign [LXX: oppose] me? And who is the shepherd [Tg. Jon.: king] who will stand before me? 49:20 (29:21) Therefore, hear the counsel of the LORD that he has made against Edom and his thought [MT: thoughts] that he has had against the inhabitants of Teman: The little ones [LXX: least; Tg. Jon.: strong] of the flock [Tg. Jon.: people] will surely be dragged away [MT: they will surely drag them away], their pasture will surely be desolated upon them [MT: their pasture will surely be appalled at them].[3] 49:21 (29:22) For/Indeed [> MT] from/because of the sound of their fall, the earth/ground quakes, and [> MT] an outcry [Syr.: her outcry] at the Sea of Reeds is heard [Codex L: an outcry, at the Sea of Reeds her voice (mlt Mss: their voice) is heard]. 49:22 (29:23) Look, like the eagle he will see [MT: he will go up and fly swiftly] and spread his wings over her fortifications [MT: Bozrah],[4] and the heart of the mighty men of Edom in that day will be like (the) heart of a woman suffering birth pains."

The relationship between the nations of Israel and Edom in the Bible is a long and storied one that extends back to the relationship between the brothers Jacob and Esau (see Mal. 1:2–4).[5] Jeremiah 49:7–22 (LXX 29:8–23) is one of several prophetic oracles about Edom (see Num. 24:18; Isa. 21:11–12 [LXX]; 34; Jer. 25:21; Ezek. 25:12–14; Amos 1:11–12; 9:12; Obad. 1–21; Mal. 1:2–5). The similarity between אדום ("Edom") and אדם ("mankind") in the Hebrew language lends itself to the use of Edom in prophetic oracles to represent mankind (i.e., the nations) either in prophecies concerning worldwide, eschatological judgment of unbelieving Gentiles (see Isa. 34:1–4 and 34:5–17) or in prophecies about the inclusion of believing Gentiles in the eschatological kingdom of God (see Amos 9:12 [MT and LXX]; Obad. 19–21; Acts 15:17; see also MT Ezek. 34:31; 35; 36:37–38).[6] While the judgment of Edom was certainly a historical reality (as emphasized by the arrangement of oracles about the nations in MT Jer.), this historical judgment also serves to prefigure eschatological judgment

---

3. Lit., "If the little ones of the flock are not dragged away, if their pasture is not desolated upon them . . .".

4. *Tg. Jon.*: "Look, like an eagle that goes up and flies, so a king will come up with his armies and camp against Bozrah."

5. For an overview of this relationship, see Thompson, *Book of Jeremiah*, 720. It is noteworthy that Jeremiah 49:7–22 makes very little of this relationship as opposed to the book of Obadiah.

6. See Shepherd, *Commentary on the Book of the Twelve*, 200–205.

of mankind (as highlighted by the framing of the oracles about the nations in the Hebrew source behind Greek Jeremiah with references to the last days in Jer. 49:39 first and 48:47 last).[7]

The word of the LORD in the Hebrew source behind Greek Jeremiah 49:7 (LXX 29:8) is given as a series of statements (but see note to translation above): "There is no (אֵין) longer wisdom in Teman. Counsel has perished from those who have understanding. Their wisdom has gone free" (cf. Deut. 32:28; Isa. 29:14). The MT has this as a series of questions: "Is there no (הַאֵין) longer wisdom in Teman? Has counsel perished from those who have understanding? Has their wisdom gone free?" Teman, which is put here for Edom (see Gen. 36:11, 15, 42; Jer. 49:20; Amos 1:12; Obad. 9; Hab. 3:3), was well known for its wisdom as represented by Eliphaz in the book of Job (Job. 2:11), but this brand of wisdom boasted in itself and not in the LORD (see Jer. 9:22–23 [Eng., 9:23–24]). Obadiah 8 echoes the sentiment of Jeremiah 49:7: "Will it not be in that day," the prophetic utterance of the LORD, "and I will destroy wise men from Edom and understanding from the mountain of Esau?"

The Hebrew source behind Greek Jeremiah 49:8 (LXX 29:9) begins, "Their face has been deceived" (נִפְתּוּ פְּנֵיהֶם). The MT has, "Flee, turn back" (נֻסוּ הָפְנוּ) (cf. Jer. 49:30). The expression, "Make deep to dwell," means to hide (see BDB, 770; cf. Jer. 49:30). The inhabitants of Dedan are addressed because of their proximity to Edom (see Isa. 21:11, 13; Jer. 25:21, 23; Ezek. 25:13). They are to attempt to hide (albeit in vain) because "a disaster he made (עָשָׂה)." The text of the MT is perhaps preferable here: "for the disaster of Esau (עֵשָׂו) I bring upon him, a time when I visit/punish him" (cf. Jer. 46:21; 50:31).

The text of 49:9 (LXX 29:10) differs slightly between the LXX and the MT, especially at the end of the verse: "If [LXX: Because] grape gatherers were to come [MT adds: to you], would they not leave gleanings? If [LXX: As] robbers (were to come) [cf. Obad. 5a] at night, they would stay their hand (יַשִּׁיתוּ יָדָם) [MT: they would damage only what is enough for them (הִשְׁחִיתוּ דַיָּם)]."[8] The idea seems to be that, unlike grape gatherers and robbers, the LORD will leave no remnant of his enemies in Edom. The version of this text in Obadiah 5 uses הֲ interrogatives

---

7. Redak: "This prophecy is for the future, just as Isaiah, Obadiah, and Eze-kiel prophesied concerning Edom, and all their prophecies appear to be meant for the future" (Rosenberg, trans., *Mikraoth Gedoloth: Jeremiah Volume Two*, 371).
8. Walser (*Jeremiah*, 368) considers the LXX to be a misunderstanding of the MT rather than a witness to a different Hebrew text.

to make it explicit that these are questions rather than statements: "If robbers were to come to you, if nighttime despoilers (O how you are ruined!), would they not steal only what is enough for them? If grape gatherers were to come to you, would they not leave gleanings?" This version switches the order of the scenarios. According to R. Isaac, "The same message reaches many prophets, but no two prophets prophesy in the same wording" (*b. Sanh.* 89a). On the other hand, most modern scholars believe that there is textual dependence between Jeremiah and Obadiah, given the continued similarities between Jeremiah 49:14–16 and Obadiah 2–4. McKane comments, "There is wide agreement that v. 9 is secondary and has been inserted from Obad 5 (Giesebrecht, Duhm, Cornill, Rudolph, Weiser). The principal arguments are that the transition to second person shows v. 9 to be discontinuous with what precedes and that v. 8 is continuous with v. 10 ('Esau' in both verses)."[9] There is, however, a case to be made for the priority of the Jeremiah version.[10] Obadiah consistently has the longer version of the text and thus shows signs of expansion of the shorter version found in Jeremiah. Furthermore, the seams of the composition of the Book of the Twelve typically feature citation from Jeremiah.[11]

The LORD declares in 49:10a (LXX 29:11a) that he has stripped (Syr.: "searched") Esau. He has uncovered Edom's hiding places. Thus, despite the people's attempts to hide (see Jer. 49:8a, 16b), they will not be able to do so (read הֶחְבָּה or נֶחְבָּה). The language of this half verse is echoed in Obadiah 6: "How Esau is searched, his hidden treasures are searched out!" The Hebrew source behind Greek Jeremiah 49:10b (LXX 29:11b) appears to refer to Edom's brother Israel (cf. Amos 1:11; Obad. 10): "The arm/strength of his brother (זרוע אחיו) has been destroyed, and (of) his neighbor (ושכנו), and he is not" (cf. Jer. 31:15b; see also Jer. 49:12). The MT, however, seems only to refer to Edom and those around him: "His offspring (זרעו) has been destroyed, and his brothers (ואחיו) and his neighbors (ושכניו), and he is not."

The Hebrew source behind Greek Jeremiah 49:11 (LXX 29:12) translates, "Your orphan/fatherless is to be left (הֶעָזֵב) in order that he might live (למען יחיה), and as for your widows, let it be in me that they trust." The MT has an imperative in 49:11a: "Leave (עָזְבָה) your

<hr>

9. McKane, *Jeremiah XXVI–LII*, 1217.

10. See Julius A. Bewer, *A Critical and Exegetical Commentary on Obadiah and Joel*, ICC (New York: Charles Scribner's Sons, 1911), 33–37; Paul Raabe, *Obadiah: A New Translation with Introduction and Commentary*, AB 24D (New York: Doubleday, 1996), 108–12.

11. See Shepherd, *Commentary on the Book of the Twelve*, 23–36.

orphans, I will be the one to keep (them) alive (אני אחיה).” The NEB and REB translate both parts of the verse as rhetorical questions expecting the answer no: “Am I to keep alive your fatherless children? Are your widows to trust in me?” Others have suggested that 49:11 is “the quotation of the hypothetical helpful neighbor.”[12] *Targum Jonathan* interprets the verse as if it were addressed to Israel: “As for you, house of Israel, you will not be forsaken. As for your orphans, I will raise (them); and as for your widows, in my word they can trust.” It seems best, however, to take these words as bitter instruction directed to the men of Edom from the LORD. These are not words of consolation. Rather, they are an eerily matter-of-fact way to communicate that the LORD's enemies among the men of Edom will all be killed, leaving their children without fathers and their wives without husbands.

MT 49:12 (LXX 29:13) has expanded the shorter version of the text behind the LXX, but the thought essentially remains the same (cf. Jer. 25:29; Joel 4:21 [Eng., 3:21]). Interpretation of this verse largely turns on how the term משפט is understood. Keil, for example, takes it to mean “judgment” and thus concludes that those whose original “judgment” it was not to drink the cup were the people of Israel: “If, now, these are not left (spared such an affliction), still less can Edom, as a heathen nation, lay claim to exemption.”[13] But since there was never really a time when Israel was not subject to judgment (see Deut. 9:7, 24; Jer. 3:25; 7:25–26; 32:30), it is more likely that משפט has the sense “custom” here. That is, it had not been the custom in the recent history of the nations listed in Jeremiah 25:15–26 to drink the cup of God's judgment (cf. Jer. 48:11), but all would have to drink it (see Jer. 51:7). This included Edom. Therefore, there was no reason for Edom to think that it would be an exception.[14] The LORD gives his assurance of this by swearing by himself (cf. Isa. 45:23; Jer. 22:5; 44:26; 51:14 [MT]; Amos 6:8; Heb. 6:13) that “an object of horror [or, desolation], an object of reproach [MT adds: a waste], and an object of contempt [or, curse] you will become in her midst [MT: Bozrah will become]; and as for all

---

12. Holladay, *Jeremiah 2*, 376.

13. Keil, *Jeremiah*, 409.

14. “*Abarbanel* asserts that the prophecy until this point refers to the Edomite nation neighboring on the Holy Land, which fell to Nebuchadnezzar when all the other nations were vanquished by his hosts. From here on, God reveals to the prophet the downfall of the present-day Edom, settled in Italy. He sees Bozrah as Rome, which will be destroyed when the Messiah comes, never to be rebuilt” (Rosenberg, trans., *Mikraoth Gedoloth: Jeremiah Volume Two*, 372).

her cities, they will become perpetual ruins" (Jer. 49:13 [LXX 29:14]). This kind of language is found elsewhere in Jeremiah (e.g., Jer. 24:9; 25:9, 11). The addition of לחרב ("a waste") in the MT appears oddly out of place among the other terms in the list (cf. MT Jer. 25:11). The MT also has בצרה ("Bozrah") instead of בתוכה ("in her midst") in order to make the words specific to Edom (cf. MT Jer. 49:22). The meaning of the Hebrew text behind Greek Jeremiah is apparently that the people of Edom will become an object of horror, reproach, and contempt in the land of Edom, whose cities will be subject to destruction from which they will not recover.

The text of Jeremiah 49:14–16 (LXX 29:15–17) is cited and expanded in Obadiah 1–4.[15] In Jeremiah 49:14 the prophet indicates that he has heard a report from the LORD. It is a report that he has sent messengers among the nations to declare, summoning the nations to gather together and come against Edom for battle (cf. Jer. 10:22): "A report have I heard (שמעתי) from the LORD, and messengers (צירים) among the nations has he sent (שָׁלַח) [MT: and a messenger (ציר) among the nations is sent (שָׁלוּחַ)]: 'Gather together and come against her, [MT adds: and] rise up for battle (התקבצו ובאו עליה קומו)!'" Obadiah 1 says: "A report have we heard (שמענו) [LXX: I heard (= שמעתי)] from the LORD, and a messenger (ציר) among the nations has been sent (שָׁלָח): 'Arise so that we may rise up against her for battle (קומו ונקומה עליה למלחמה).'" Jeremiah 49:15 adds: "Small have I made you [MT: For look, small have I made you] among the nations, despised among mankind (באדם)." Obadiah 2 has: "Look, small have I made you among the nations, despised are you very much so (אתה מאד)."

Jeremiah 49:16a (LXX 29:17a) differs only slightly between the Hebrew source behind Greek Jeremiah and the MT: "Your horror, the presumption of your heart has deceived you. He has dwelt (שכן) in the clefts of the rock, he has grasped (תפש) a hill's height [MT: dwelling (שכני) in the clefts of the rock, grasping (תפשי) a hill's height]." This text speaks of Edom's pride and its false sense of security that a high dwelling place can escape judgment (see Jer. 49:8, 10; see also Jer. 22:23; 48:28; 51:53). The word תפלצת ("horror"), which only occurs here, may be related to מפלצת (see 1 Kgs. 15:13), which is some sort of object of idolatry. In any case, the feminine noun תפלצת cannot be the grammatical subject of the masculine verb השיא ("has deceived"). The masculine noun זדון ("presumption") is the subject. The noun תפלצת does not appear in Obadiah 3, but Obadiah 3 has the overall longer version of the text, including a quote of Edom's thought: "The presumption of

---

15. See Shepherd, *Commentary on the Book of the Twelve*, 207–10.

your heart is what has deceived you [note the fronting of the subject], dwelling in clefts of rock, the high place of his living, saying in his heart, 'Who will bring me down to ground?'" Edom's confidence, however, will prove to be ill-founded: "If he makes his nest [MT: If you make your nest] high like the eagle, from there I will bring you down" [MT adds: the prophetic utterance of the LORD] (Jer. 49:16b [LXX 29:17b]; cf. Num. 24:21; Jer. 50:31–32; Amos 9:2; Hab. 2:9). The version of this text in Obadiah 4 features an addition about the stars: "If you make high like the eagle, and if among stars your nest is set, from there I will bring you down," the prophetic utterance of the LORD.[16] This addition has made its way into the Syriac version of Jeremiah 49:16b.

The Hebrew source behind Greek Jeremiah 49:17 (LXX 29:18) has the shorter, more original version of the text: "And Edom will become an object of horror [or, desolation]. Every one who passes by her will hiss [MT: be appalled and hiss at all her wounds]." The language is close to that of Jeremiah 19:8 (see also Jer. 18:16; 50:13). Of course, the difference is that it is here applied to Edom rather than Judah. The language of 49:18 (LXX 29:19) is similar to that of 50:40 where the words apply to Babylon: "Like the overthrow [Syr.: God's overthrow] of Sodom and Gomorrah and her neighbors," says the LORD of hosts [of hosts > MT], "a man/person will not live there, and a human being will not sojourn in her" (cf. Deut. 29:22 [Eng., 29:23]; Isa. 13:19; Amos 4:11; see Gen. 19; see also Jer. 4:25, 29; 49:33; 51:43). The Syriac version of 49:18 has borrowed the phrase "God's overthrow" from 50:40.

The text of Jeremiah 49:19–21 (LXX 29:20–22) has already appeared in a slightly different form in 50:44–46 (LXX 27:44–46) (see commentary there). Only the most outstanding differences are discussed here. First, the references to Babylon and the Chaldeans in 50:45 have changed to references to Edom and the inhabitants of Teman in 49:20. Second, this change opens up the possibility for an emendation in 49:19b that would not have worked very well in 50:44b. The verb יעידני ("will summon/arraign me") could be adjusted to יעירני ("will arouse me") so that the question ("And who will arouse me?") alludes to the messianic lion king in Genesis 49:9b ("He bows down, he lies down like a lion, and like a lioness who will arouse him [יקימנו]?"). The attractiveness of this option increases when it is realized that the description of this king in Genesis 49:11–12 serves as the basis for the depiction of the blood-stained warrior who emerges from Edom in Isaiah 63:1–6

---

16. Note how Obadiah 4 interprets the כי at the beginning of Jeremiah 49:16b as אם ("If").

(see also Num. 24:7–9, 17–18; Rev. 14:20; 19:13). The third and final major difference between Jeremiah 49:19–21 and 50:44–46 comes at the very end of the unit where 49:21b has the phrase "at the Sea of Reeds" (בים סוף), indicating the place where the outcry is heard, rather than the phrase "among the nations" (בגוים) found in 50:46b. Redak considers this to be hyperbolic: "although there is a desert between them, the sound of the downfall of the land of Edom will be heard."[17]

The final verse of the oracle about Edom switches metaphors from that of a lion (Jer. 49:19) to that of an eagle to describe the invading king and his army (see *Tg. Jon.*): "Look, like the eagle he will see [MT: he will go up and fly] and spread his wings over her fortifications [MT: Bozrah], and the heart of the mighty men of Edom in that day will be like (the) heart of a woman suffering birth pains" (Jer. 49:22 [LXX 29:23]). Where the Hebrew source behind Greek Jeremiah has the verb יראה ("he will see"), the MT has יעלה וידאה ("he will go up and fly swiftly"). Where the Hebrew source behind Greek Jeremiah has מבצרה ("her fortifications"), the MT has בצרה ("Bozrah") (cf. Jer. 49:13). The text of Jeremiah 49:22 will reappear in a slightly different form in the oracle about Moab (Jer. 48:40–41).

---

17. Rosenberg, trans., *Mikraoth Gedoloth: Jeremiah Volume Two*, 376. "Malbim renders: a cry such as the one whose sound was heard in the Red Sea. I.e. such a cry was emitted by the Egyptians when they were over-whelmed at the Red Sea."

AMMON
(Jer. 49:1–5 [LXX 30:1–5])

49:1 (30:1) Concerning the sons of Ammon:

*Thus says the L*ORD*, "Does Israel have no sons? Does he have no heir?
Why has Milcom [MT: their king] taken possession of Gilead [MT: Gad],
and (why) does his [LXX: their] people live in his [LXX: their] cities?
49:2 (30:2) Therefore, look, days are coming," the prophetic utterance of
the L*ORD*, "and I will cause a shout of wars [MT: war] against Rabbah
[MT adds: of the sons of Ammon] to be heard, and they will become a
mound and a desolation [MT: and she will become a mound of desola-
tion], and her high places [LXX: altars; MT: daughters/villages] will
be burned with fire, and Israel will (dis)possess his inheritance [LXX:
his rule; MT: his (dis)possessors]" [MT adds: says the L*ORD*]. 49:3 (30:3)
"Wail, O Heshbon, for Ai is devastated. Cry out, O daughters [or, vil-
lages] of Rabbah. Gird on sackcloth and [and > MT] lament [MT adds:
and go to and fro among the walls/hedges (NET: covered with gashes;
cf. Jer. 48:37)]; for Milcom [MT: their king], into exile he will go, his
priests and his officials together" [Syr. adds: says the Lord]. 49:4 (30:4)
"Why do you boast [or, How you boast] in the valleys [Rahlfs adds: of
the Anakim (cf. Jer. 47:5 [LXX 29:5]); MT adds: your valley/strength
flows (cf. Tg. Jon.; see Jer. 47:5)], O apostate daughter [LXX: daughter
of arrogance (LXX*L239*: disgrace); Symm.: captive daughter; Syr.: beloved
daughter; Vulg.: delicate daughter] who trusts in her treasures/store-
houses [LXX, pc Mss, Syr., Tg. Jon., Vulg. add: who says], 'Who will
come against me?' 49:5 (30:5) Look, I am about to bring fear upon you
[MT: upon you fear]," the prophetic utterance of the L*ORD* [MT: the Lord
G*OD* of hosts], "from all those around you, and you will be banished [pc
Mss, Syr.: and I will banish them], each before him, and there will be no*

one gathering [MT adds: the fugitive]. [MT adds 49:6: And afterwards I will restore the fortunes (Vulg.: captives) of the sons of Ammon," the prophetic utterance of the LORD.]

The Ammonites (and Moabites) were born out of the incestuous relationship between Abraham's nephew Lot and his daughters (Gen. 19:29–38) in the wake of the destruction of Sodom and Gomorrah (Gen. 19:1–28). It is thus fitting that the oracle about Ammon follows the reference to Sodom and Gomorrah (Jer. 49:18 [LXX 29:19]) in the oracle about Edom according to the order of the oracles about the nations in the Hebrew source behind Greek Jeremiah (see also Zeph. 2:9). It is also fitting that the MT places the oracle about Moab (Jer. 48) and the one about Ammon (Jer. 49:1–5) back to back. The history of the relationship between Israel and Ammon is largely about land rights, particularly the rights to the land allotted to Reuben, Gad, and the half-tribe of Manasseh on the other side of the Jordan (Num. 32; Josh. 22), including the territory from the Arnon to the Jabbok that once belonged to Sihon the king of Amorites, which Israel acquired only because Sihon would not allow the people to pass by peacefully (Num. 21:21–31). Israel was not allowed to take land that rightfully belonged to Ammon (see Deut. 2:17–25).[1] Nevertheless, the Ammonites later claimed that Israel wrongfully took their land when they came out of Egypt, a claim to which Jephthah responded with the facts (Judg. 11:12–28). In the days of Samuel, the Ammonite king Nahash attempted to take Jabesh Gilead but was defeated by Saul (1 Sam. 11; see also 2 Sam. 10 [1 Chr. 19]; 12:26–31; 2 Chr. 20; 26:8; 27:5). The exile of Reuben, Gad, and the half-tribe of Manasseh to Assyria during the time of Tiglath-pileser (2 Kgs. 15:29; 1 Chr. 5:26) left their land exposed and open to seizure by the Ammonites. Other prophetic oracles about Ammon include Ezekiel 25:1–7; Amos 1:13–15; Zephaniah 2:8–11. While the Ezekiel and Zephaniah oracles focus on Ammon's response to the destruction of the temple in Jerusalem and the Babylonian exile of the Judeans, Amos mentions Ammon's violent efforts to expand their border (Amos 1:13).

The rhetorical questions in Jeremiah 49:1a (LXX 30:1a) imply that Ammon has acted as if there is no one from Israel to possess land that has historically belonged to Israel: "Does Israel have no sons? Does he have no heir?" (cf. Gen. 15:3). The questions in 49:1b (LXX 30:1b) are

---

1. This instruction was given despite the fact that Ammon did not meet Israel with food and water, a circumstance that led to the disallowance of Ammonites in the assembly of Israel (Deut. 23:4–5; Neh. 13:1–3).

somewhat more complicated from a text-critical standpoint: "Why has Milcom [MT: their king] taken possession of Gilead [MT: Gad], and (why) does his [LXX: their] people live in his [LXX: their] cities?" The consonantal text מלכם has been interpreted differently by the LXX and the MT. According to the former, it should be vocalized מִלְכֹּם ("Milcom") the name of the god of the Ammonites (1 Kgs. 11:5, 33; 2 Kgs. 23:13; Syr. Amos 1:15; LXX[L], Syr., Vulg. Zeph. 1:5), otherwise known as Molech (Lev. 18:21; 20:2–5; 1 Kgs. 11:7; 2 Kgs. 23:10; Jer. 32:35). The MT vocalizes the same text as מַלְכָּם ("their king") (cf. MT Amos 1:15; Zeph. 1:5). According to the Hebrew source behind Greek Jeremiah 49:1b (LXX 30:1b), the first question concerns the wrongful possession of "Gilead" (גלעד), a name used not only for the territory between the Arnon and the Jabbok but also for entire land occupied by Israel east of the Jordan (BDB, 166). The MT, however, has "Gad" (גד) instead of "Gilead." Gad, of course, was one of the two and a half tribes to whom this territory rightfully belonged. According to Deuteronomy 33:20, blessed is the messianic lion king who enlarges the territory of Gad (cf. Gen. 49:8–12; Num. 24:7–9). This land is not to be taken by Ammon, nor should the Ammonites be living in Israel's cities.[2]

The conjunction לכן ("Therefore") introduces the announcement of judgment for Ammon in Jeremiah 49:2 (LXX 30:2; cf. Jer. 7:32; 16:14; 19:6; 48:12; 51:47, 52). Redak interprets הנה ימים באים ("look, days are coming") as באחרית הימים ("at the end of the days") (Jer. 23:20; 30:24; 48:47; 49:39; cf. Jer. 23:5, 7; 30:3; 31:27, 31; 33:14).[3] The LORD will cause a battle cry against the Ammonite capital Rabbah to be heard (cf. Ezek. 25:5; Amos 1:14; 1 Macc. 5:6–8). The city will become a mound of ruins and a desolate place. According to the Hebrew source behind Greek Jeremiah, "her high places" (במותיה; LXX: βωμοὶ αὐτῆς ["her altars"]) will be burned with fire. The MT says that "her daughters/villages" (בנתיה) will be burned with fire. The former says that Israel will (dis)possess "his inheritance" (ירשתו; LXX: "his rule" [= ראשו?]) (cf. Zeph. 2:9). The latter says that Israel will (dis)possess "his (dis)possessors" (ירשיו).

The city of Heshbon, on the border between Moab and Ammon (Isa. 15:4; 16:8, 9; Jer. 48:2, 34, 45), is called upon to wail because Ai is devastated (Jer. 49:3 [LXX 30:3]; cf. Isa. 13:6; 14:31; 15:2; 16:7; 23:1, 6, 14). This is not the Canaanite city Ai southeast of Bethel but an otherwise unknown city of Ai in the land of Ammon. Perhaps the city of Rabbah is being characterized here as the old Canaanite city

---

2. If "his people" (עמו) refers to Milcom's people, there is a nice parallel in Jeremiah 48:46: "the people of Chemosh," Moab's god (1 Kgs. 11:7).

3. Rosenberg, trans., *Mikraoth Gedoloth: Jeremiah Volume Two*, 369.

of Ai because of the infamous destruction of that city: "And Joshua burned Ai and made it a perpetual mound (תל), a desolation (שממה), to this day" (Josh. 8:28; cf. Jer. 49:2). Thus, the call is given for the daughters (or, villages) of Rabbah to cry out. The imperatives to gird on sackcloth (BDB, 974) and lament are supplemented in the MT with an unusual expression: "and go to and fro among the walls/hedges" (והתשוטטנה בגדרות). The meaning of this expression is not entirely clear. *Targum Jonathan* renders גדרות as "bands, troops" (= גדדות?). This may be a clue that the MT should read גדדות ("cuts"). That is, the daughters or villages of Rabbah are to go about with cuts on themselves. Cutting is a well-known form of mourning (see Jer. 48:37). In any case, this addition is not part of the Hebrew source behind Greek Jeremiah. The daughters or villages of Rabbah are to lament because "Milcom [MT: their king], into exile he will go, his priests and his officials together" (cf. Jer. 48:7; 49:1; Amos 1:15).

Jeremiah 49:4 (LXX 30:4) is either a question ("Why do you boast in the valleys?") or an exclamation ("How you boast in the valleys!"). מה can be understood either as "Why?" or as "How!" The MT adds a comment to this: "your valley flows" (זב עמקך). This is likely a way to say that Ammon boasts in its valleys because its valleys are fertile (cf. the expression "a land flowing with milk and honey" [Exod. 3:17b]). Others interpret the noun עמק to mean "strength" rather than "valley" (see *Tg. Jon.* and the above commentary on Jer. 47:5): "Why do you brag about your great power? Your power is ebbing away" (NET).[4] The Lord addresses Ammon here as "apostate daughter," which some have thought should only apply to Israel (see Jer. 31:22), but McKane is right not to accept this limitation.[5] It should be kept in mind that Israel, like all nations, has never been faithful to the Lord (Deut. 9:7, 24; Jer. 3:25; 7:25–26; 32:30). All nations are accountable in one way or another for their rebellion against the Lord as part of fallen humanity (see, e.g., Amos 1–2). Ammon's trust in her treasures/storehouses has given her the false sense of security that no one will come against her (cf. Jer. 48:7).

The Lord is about to bring fear upon Ammon from all those who surround her (Jer. 49:5a [LXX 30:5a]; cf. Jer. 48:43), and Ammon will be banished (pc Mss, Syr.: "and I will banish them"), "each before

---

4. See Bright, *Jeremiah*, 325. See Lamentations 4:9. Rashi comments that Ammon is a land of valleys unaffected by lack of rainfall. Therefore, an overabundance of rain will come upon it until the water flows into the valley and inundates the grain (Rosenberg, trans., *Mikraoth Gedoloth: Jeremiah Volume Two*, 370).

5. McKane, *Jeremiah XXVI–LII*, 1210.

him" (cf. Amos 4:3), and there will be no one gathering (MT adds: "the fugitive") (Jer. 49:5b [LXX 30:5b]). The text of Jeremiah 49:6 ("And afterwards I will restore the fortunes of the sons of Ammon") is not in the Hebrew source behind Greek Jeremiah, and its addition in the MT is likely on the analogy of Jeremiah 48:47 and 49:39 (see also Jer. 12:15; 46:26). Since the subsequent history of the Ammonites does not feature such a restoration (see Neh. 2:10, 19; 4:1 [Eng., 4:7]; 1 Macc. 5:6–8), the added text likely envisions an eschatological restoration. Zephaniah 2:11 anticipates the conversion of some Ammonites in the wake of their judgment.[6]

6.　See Shepherd, *Commentary on the Book of the Twelve*, 364.

KEDAR

(Jer. 49:28–33 [LXX 30:6–11])

49:28 (30:6) Concerning Kedar, concerning (the) queen of (the) court [MT: and concerning the kingdoms of Hazor], which Nebuchadnezzar [MT: Nebuchadrezzar] the king of Babylon struck:

Thus says the LORD, *"Arise and go up [MT: Arise, go up] against Kedar and destroy [see BHS apparatus] the sons of the east. 49:29 (30:7) Their tents and their flocks they will take. Their curtains [LXX: clothes] and all their vessels and their camels they will take for themselves. And proclaim [MT: And they will proclaim] against them, 'Terror [LXX: Destruction] is on every side.' 49:30 (30:8) Flee greatly [MT: Flee, wander (Tg. Jon.: go into exile) greatly], make deep to dwell, O inhabitants of court [MT: Hazor]" [MT adds: the prophetic utterance of the* LORD*], "for [MT adds: Nebuchadrezzar] the king of Babylon has advised counsel against you and he has made a plan against you [MT kethiv: them]. 49:31 (30:9) Arise and go up [MT: Arise, go up] against a nation at ease, living in security" [MT adds: the prophetic utterance of the* LORD*]. "It has no doors, [MT adds: and] no bar(s) [LXX: no oak bars, no bars].*[1] *They live alone. 49:32 (30:10) And their camels will become plunder, and the multitude of their livestock will become spoil, and I will scatter them to every wind, cut off of side/corner [i.e., those with hair clipped on the temples; NETS: when they have been sheared before them]. From their every side [MT: And from all his sides] I will bring their distress/calamity," the prophetic utterance of the* LORD*. 49:33 (30:11) And the court [MT: Hazor] will become a habitation for jackals [LXX: a haunt of*

---

1. The Greek text has two translations for the same word here.

sparrows], a desolation perpetually. A person will not live there, and a human being will not sojourn in it [see BDB, 346]."

This oracle is about Kedar to the east (Jer. 49:28 [LXX 30:6]; see Gen. 25:13; Isa. 21:16–17; Jer. 2:10). According to the MT, it concerns "the kingdoms of Hazor" (ממלכות חצור). This is not the royal city of northern Canaan (Josh. 11:1), and there is no known city of Hazor or place by that name in the region of Kedar. The Hebrew source behind Greek Jeremiah has instead of "the kingdoms of Hazor" the phrase "(the) queen of (the) court" (מלכת חצר; LXX: τῇ βασιλίσσῃ τῆς αὐλῆς). This is somewhat of an ironic description for a nomadic people, but it may be a play on two different uses of חצר ("enclosure"). This term can be used of a court, such as that of a royal palace (e.g., 1 Kgs. 7:8, 9, 12), but it can also refer to an unwalled village (BDB, 346–47 lists these as homonyms rather than two uses of the same word). Thus, in Isaiah 42:11 the חצרים ("unwalled villages") are the modest settlements (so-called "cities") where the nomads of Kedar live in the desert. It is this Kedar that Nebuchadnezzar the king of Babylon struck at some unknown point in time. Since this Babylonian strike is given as a past event merely to describe Kedar for the reader, it should be apparent that what follows is not a description of a current or future Babylonian invasion of Kedar. Rather, the oracle's depiction of Kedar's future is given in fairly undefined terms (but see Jer. 49:30). The LORD's instructions (plural imperatives) to arise and go up against Kedar are not addressed to any one group in particular. No accusation or reason for judgment is provided for the command to destroy "the sons of the east" (בני קדם; see Gen. 29:1; Judg. 6:3, 33; Job 1:3), nor is there any indication of Kedar's relationship to Israel (but see Gen. 16:11–12; 25:13, 18).

The tents and flocks of the nomadic people of Kedar will be taken by unidentified invaders (Jer. 49:29a [LXX 30:7a]; see the phrase "the tents of Kedar" in Ps. 120:5; Song 1:5). These enemy invaders will carry off their tent curtains, all their vessels, and their camels for themselves. According to the Hebrew source behind Greek Jeremiah 49:29b (LXX 30:7b), the instructions from 49:28b continue: "And proclaim (וְקִרְאוּ) against them, 'Terror [LXX: Destruction] is on every side'" (cf. Jer. 6:25; 20:3, 10; 46:5). On the other hand, the MT maintains the account from 49:29a of what the invaders will do: "And they will proclaim (וְקָרְאוּ) against them, 'Terror is on every side.'" The inhabitants of "court/village" (חצר; MT: "Hazor" [חצור]) are advised, "Flee greatly" (נסו מאד; MT: "Flee, wander greatly" [נסו נדו מאד]) (Jer. 49:30a [LXX 30:8a]). They are to "make deep to dwell," which means they should hide (cf. Jer. 49:8). The invasion of Kedar appears designed not to annihilate its people but to scatter its people and to make the land void of people (see Jer. 49:32–33). The reason given for the flight and the hiding of the people of Kedar is the plan that the king of Babylon has made against them (Jer. 49:30b [LXX 30:8b]; cf. Jer. 18:11; 49:20). Since 49:28 describes Kedar as a place already stricken by Babylon, it is not clear what plan is in view here. It is possible that the mere threat of another Babylonian invasion (whether or not another invasion would actually occur) is enough to scatter the inhabitants of Kedar, while the attack envisioned in 49:28b, 29, 31, 32 will come at some undesignated time from an unnamed invader.

The directives from 49:28b to arise and go up against Kedar resume in 49:31 (LXX 30:9). This time the otherwise not very well-defined region and people of Kedar are called "a nation" (גוי), one that is "at ease, living in security." This means that the people lived with a false sense of security, unaware of how vulnerable they were to an attack (cf. Judg. 18:7; Ezek. 38:11a). The unwalled settlements of Kedar had no doors, no city gates with bars to serve as a defense (cf. Ezek. 38:11b). Furthermore, they lived alone (see again Judg. 18:7). This situation may have contributed to the feeling that no one would bother them, but it gave invaders the confidence that no one would come to the aid of the unprotected people. According to 49:32 (LXX 30:10), the camels of the inhabitants of Kedar will become plunder (cf. Jer. 49:29), and the multitude of their livestock will become spoil (cf. Jer. 50:10). The LORD himself will scatter the people to every wind (i.e., in every direction; cf. Jer. 49:36). It is possible that the Hebrew source behind Greek Jeremiah described these people as "the cut off of their face(s)" (קצוצי פניהם), but the MT has "cut off of side/corner" (קצוצי פאה). This expression likely refers to those with hair clipped on the temples, although some have understood the MT phrase to mean those cut off at the corner of the desert (e.g., Rashi). It is used of the Arabian tribes (Jer. 9:25 [Eng., 9:26]; 25:23). The LORD will bring the distress/calamity against Kedar from every side. "The court/village" (החצר; MT: "Hazor" [חצור]) will become a habitation for jackals, a perpetual desolation (Jer. 49:33a [LXX 30:11a]; cf. Jer. 9:10 [Eng., 9:11]; 10:22; 50:39; 51:37). No people will live there (Jer. 49:33b [LXX 30:11b]; cf. Jer. 49:18b; see also Jer. 4:25, 29b).

DAMASCUS
(Jer. 49:23–27 [LXX 30:12–16])

49:23 (30:12) Concerning Damascus:

"Hamath is ashamed, and Arpad, for a bad report have they heard. They melt away [LXX: They are astonished]. In the sea is anxiety [LXX: They are angered; see BHS apparatus], they are unable to be quiet [MT: it is unable to be quiet]. 49:24 (30:13) Damascus goes slack [i.e., loses heart]. She turns to flee, but trembling/panic grips her. [MT adds: Distress (and pains), it takes hold of her like a woman in labor.] 49:25 (30:14) How does she not forsake/fortify a city of praise [MT: How is a city of praise not (not > Vulg.) forsaken/fortified], the city of my joy [Syr., Tg. Jon., Vulg., Luther: city of joy]? 49:26 (30:15) Therefore, choice young men [MT: her choice young men] will fall in your squares [MT: her squares], and all the fighting men will be silenced/destroyed [LXX: will fall] [MT adds: in that day]," the prophetic utterance of the LORD [MT adds: of hosts]. 49:27 (30:16) "And I will set the city wall of Damascus on fire, and it will consume the prominent buildings of Ben Hadad."

The oracle concerning Damascus, the capital of Syria (Isa. 7:8), also mentions two other Aramean city-states—Hamath north of Damascus (see BDB, 333) and Arpad even further to the north (only mentioned in the Bible in conjunction with Hamath; see BDB, 75).[1] Since these three all fell to Tiglath-pileser in the eighth century BC (2 Kgs. 16:9; Isa.

---

1. "All three of these Aramean states, but especially Damascus, played their part in the history of the Syria-Palestine region during much of the period of the kings of Israel, and their kings Hazael, Ben-hadad, and Rezin feature in biblical history in wars that were waged over possession of the

10:9; 36:19; 37:13), it is assumed that they recovered to some extent after the demise of the Assyrian empire in 609 BC. The only biblical reference to Syria's involvement with Judah in the time of Jeremiah is Nebuchadnezzar's sending of Aramean troops against Judah in the narrative of 2 Kings 24:2. No reason is stated in the oracle of Jeremiah 49:23–27 (LXX 30:12–16) for the judgment of Damascus, but two other prophetic oracles about Damascus may provide a clue as to why such a passage would be included among Jeremiah's oracles about the nations. The oracle in Amos 1:3–5 announces judgment "for their threshing with the iron sledges Gilead" (Amos 1:3). Part of the judgment announced in this passage is the exile of the people of Syria to Kir from which they came (Amos 1:5; see Amos 9:7). This prophecy finds it fulfillment in the narrative of 2 Kings 16:9. Such information suggests that the historical judgment of Damascus has already occurred, leaving the inclusion of an oracle about Damascus in the book of Jeremiah only to signify an eschatological judgment. Likewise, the oracle about Damascus in Isaiah 17:1–3 sees the fate of Damascus wrapped up in that of the northern kingdom of Israel due to their shared involvement in the conflict narrated in Isaiah 7 (c. 735–732 BC; cf. 2 Kgs. 16; 2 Chr. 28), yet the oracles in Isaiah 17:4–6, 7–8, 9–11—each prefaced by the phrase "in that day"—appear to look beyond the past to eschatological realities.

In the Hebrew syntax of 49:23 (LXX 30:12), "Hamath" is given as the lead city (see Zech. 9:1–2), agreeing with the singular verb "is ashamed," and "Arpad" is added secondarily to form the compound subject.[2] These cities are ashamed because they have heard a "bad report" (cf. Jer. 49:14). Since Hamath and Arpad lie to the north of Damascus, it is unlikely that they have heard a bad report about the destruction of Damascus. Rather, the report is about the advancement of the enemy from the north (cf. Jer. 4:6, 15). This enemy will attack Hamath and Arpad before reaching Damascus. The report of coming invasion causes them to "melt away" (cf. Exod. 15:15; Josh. 2:9). According to the Masoretic accentuation (see the *athnach*), the verb נמגו ("melt away") belongs with what precedes it and not with what follows it. The suggestion in the *BHS* apparatus is to read this verb with what follows and then emend the text to read נמוג לבם מדאגה ("Their heart melts away because of anxiety"). This is an unnecessary maneuver that overlooks the similarity between Jeremiah 49:23b and Isaiah 57:20. The text of Isaiah 57:20 says, "And the wicked are like the sea (כים), which

---

northern parts of Transjordan (1 K. 20; 22; 2 K. 5; 9:14–15; 10:32–33; 12:17–18; 14:23–29; 16:5–9; etc.)" (Thompson, *Book of Jeremiah*, 724).

2. See Shepherd, "Compound Subject in Biblical Hebrew," 107–20.

is tossed, for it is unable to be quiet (הַשְׁקֵט לֹא יוּכָל), and its waters toss mire and mud." Jeremiah 49:23b says, "In the sea is anxiety (בַּיָּם דְּאָגָה), they are unable to be quiet (הַשְׁקֵט לֹא יוּכָלוּ)."[3] In other words, the anxiousness of Hamath and Arpad is compared to the restlessness of the sea (cf. Isa. 17:12–13).[4] Calvin suggests making this comparison explicit by altering בַּיָּם ("In the sea") to כַּיָּם ("Like the sea"),[5] but this is not a necessary move.

Damascus "goes slack" (i.e., loses heart) (Jer. 49:24a [LXX 30:13]; cf. Jer. 6:24a; 50:43a). This is presumably due to the same report that has given Hamath and Arpad such loss of hope (Jer. 49:23). The city turns to flee, but trembling/panic grips it. The "x + *qatal*" syntax of the clause וְרֶטֶט הֶחֱזִיקָה ("but trembling/panic grips it") suggests a contrast in the present context rather than mere addition of extra information.[6] That is, the people of the city want to flee, but they cannot because their trembling or panic has paralyzed them. This explains why the city is not forsaken (Jer. 49:25 [LXX 30:14]) and why the warriors will fall in the city squares (Jer. 49:26 [LXX 30:15]). The MT adds a second half to 49:24: "Distress (and pains), it takes hold of her like a woman in labor" (Jer. 49:24b; cf. Jer. 6:24b; 50:43b). This addition has apparently been made to conform 49:24 to 6:24 and 50:43, both of which put labor pains as a parallel to slack hands. The shorter text of the Hebrew source behind Greek Jeremiah 49:24 (LXX 30:13) is to be preferred as the more original reading.

The adverb אֵיךְ ("How") at the beginning of 49:25 (LXX 30:14) can introduce either a question or an exclamation. According to the LXX, it introduces a question with an active verb: "How does she not forsake/fortify (עָזְבָה) a city of praise, the city of my joy?" According to the MT, there is a passive verb: "How is a city of praise not forsaken/fortified (עֻזְּבָה), the city of my joy?" An understanding of this question (or exclamation) largely depends upon whether the main verb is from the common root עזב ("leave, forsake") or the homonym עזב ("restore, repair"; see Neh. 3:8). Rashi and Bullinger take it in the latter sense so that the verse is an expression of disbelief or lament that such a praiseworthy city could fail to fortify itself against an attack.[7] On the other hand, the former sense (with negation) in the MT ("not forsaken") is

---

3.   The MT has הַשְׁקֵט לֹא יוּכָל ("it [the sea] is unable to be quiet").
4.   See Rashi in Rosenberg, trans., *Mikraoth Gedoloth: Jeremiah Volume Two*, 376.
5.   Calvin, *Jeremiah*, 5:98.
6.   See Niccacci, *Syntax of the Verb*, 64.
7.   Rosenberg, trans., *Mikraoth Gedoloth: Jeremiah Volume Two*, 377; Bullinger, *Figures of Speech*, 1009.

thought to be unintelligible in the Latin Vulgate, resulting in the loss of the negation (see Isa. 17:9), but Keil explains why it is not necessary to drop the negation: "it is not the desolation of the city that is bewailed, but the fact that the inhabitants have not saved their lives by flight. The way is prepared for this thought by v. 24, where it is said that the inhabitants of Damascus wish to flee, but are seized with convulsive terror."[8] According to the Hebrew source behind Greek Jeremiah, the text laments that "she" (the city, i.e., the people of the city of Damascus) does not forsake/fortify a "city" (i.e., the place of the city of Damascus) of praise.[9] Some of the early versions (Syr., *Tg. Jon.*, Vulg.; see also Luther) render the phrase "the city of my joy" as "city of joy," apparently due to the thought that designation of Damascus as the city of the LORD's joy would not be suitable. McKane suggests that such a description is more appropriate for Jerusalem (see Isa. 32:13; 62:7; Zeph. 3:19, 20; Ps. 48:3 [Eng., 48:2]; Lam. 2:15), and he proposes the following translation: "Why did it (Damascus) not leave (unscathed) my celebrated and joyful city?"[10] But this overlooks the importance of Damascus in the LORD's plans (e.g., 1 Kgs. 19:15; see also Isa. 17:10) and the designation of other foreign cities as praiseworthy (e.g., Jer. 51:41; Ezek. 26:17).

The people of Damascus are paralyzed by panic (49:24) and thus do not flee the city (49:25). "Therefore" (לכן), the young men will fall in the city squares, and all the warriors will be silenced/destroyed (Jer. 49:26 [LXX 30:15]; cf. Jer. 50:30; see also Jer. 49:22; 1 Macc. 2:9). The LORD will set the city wall of Damascus on fire, and it (the fire) will consume the prominent buildings of Ben Hadad (Jer. 49:27 [LXX 30:16]; cf. Amos 1:4, 14; see also Jer. 17:27b). The name "Ben Hadad" here is likely not the name of a particular Syrian king as it is elsewhere (see BDB, 122), but, as Bright suggests, the name of "the dynasty that ruled Damascus in the ninth-eighth centuries" (cf. "Pharaoh," "Caesar").[11]

---

8. Keil, *Jeremiah*, 414–15.

9. Cf. Zechariah 12:6b: "And Jerusalem [i.e., the people of Jerusalem] will dwell again in its place, in Jerusalem [i.e., in the city of Jerusalem]."

10. McKane, *Jeremiah XXVI–LII*, 1234.

11. Bright, *Jeremiah*, 335.

MOAB

(Jer. 48 [LXX 31])

48:1 (31:1) Concerning Moab:

*Thus says the L*ord* [MT adds: of hosts, the God of Israel], "Woe to Nebo, for it is destroyed! Kiriathaim is captured [MT: Kiriathaim is put to shame, it is captured]. The secure height is put to shame and dismayed / shattered [NETS: Hamasagab was put to shame, and Hatath].*[1]* 48:2 (31:2) The healing [MT: praise] of Moab is no more. In Heshbon they plan against her disaster: 'Let us cut her off [MT: Come and let us cut her off] from being a nation.' Indeed, she will certainly be silent [MT: Also Madmen, you will be silent]. After you a sword will go. 48:3 (31:3) A sound of an outcry from Horonaim, 'Destruction and great breaking!'*[2]* 48:4 (31:4) Moab is broken. Proclaim to Zoar [Codex L: Her little ones have caused to hear an outcry; mlt Mss: Proclaim an outcry, her little ones (Tg. Jon.: their rulers)]. 48:5 (31:5) For Lahoth is full with weeping; weeping goes up [MT: For as for the ascent of Luhith (qere), it is with weeping that weeping goes up]. On the descent of Horonaim, an outcry of breaking have you heard [MT: For on the descent of Horonaim, foes of an outcry of breaking have they heard]. 48:6 (31:6) Flee, save yourselves! And you will be like a wild ass [MT: a shrub; Tg. Jon.: the tower of Aroer] in a [MT: the] wilderness. 48:7 (31:7) Because you have trusted in your*

---

1. The original text had the masculine noun המשגב ("the secure height") with the masculine verbs הביש ("is put to shame") and חת ("is dismayed/shattered"). When the noun was interpreted as a place name ("Misgab"), the verbs were adjusted to feminine forms (see MT). The LXX interpreted both המשגב ("Hamasagab") and חת ("Hatath") as place names.
2. The LXX adds a causal conjunction at the beginning of this verse.

strongholds [MT: For, because you have trusted in your works and in your treasures/storehouses], you [2QJer: אתה] too will be captured; and Chemosh will go out into exile, his priests and his officials together. 48:8 (31:8) And destruction [MT: a destroyer] will come to every city, it [MT: a city] will not escape; and the valley will perish, and the plain will be destroyed, just as [MT: which] the LORD has said. 48:9 (31:9) Give a signpost [or, monument, grave marker; MT: blossom/flower (see Vulg.), shining thing; Syr., Tg. Jon.: crown; BDB: wings] to Moab, for she will certainly fall in ruins [LXX: for she will be kindled with kindling (from יצת?); see Jer. 2:15; 9:9, 11 (Eng., 9:10, 12); 46:19; MT: for flying she will go out; Tg. Jon.: for she will certainly go into exile; Vulg.: for in its flower it will go out], and all her cities will become a desolation [or, object of horror] without inhabitant(s) in them [LXX: from where will she have an inhabitant?]. 48:10 (31:10) Cursed is one who does the works [MT: work] of the LORD negligently [Syr., Tg. Jon.: in deceit], withholding [MT: and cursed is one who withholds] his sword from blood. 48:11 (31:11) Moab has been at ease since youth [MT: his youth], and he is undisturbed on his lees [or, wine dregs, sediment; Tg. Jon.: possessions; LXX: and he was confident in his glory]. He [MT: And he] has not been emptied [LXX: has not poured] from vessel to vessel, and into exile he has not gone. Therefore, his taste has remained in him, and his scent has not changed [LXX: left]. 48:12 (31:12) Therefore, look, days are coming," the prophetic utterance of the LORD, "and I will send to him tippers [Syr., Tg. Jon.: plunderers], and they will tip him over [Syr., Tg. Jon.: plunder them], and his vessels [Tg. Jon.: possessions] they will crush [MT: empty], and his [MT: their] jars [Tg. Jon.: the good of their land; see BHS apparatus] they will shatter [Tg. Jon.: destroy]. 48:13 (31:13) And Moab will be ashamed of Chemosh just as the house of Israel was ashamed of Bethel, the object of their trust [or, the source of their confidence].

48:14 (31:14) How can you say, 'We are mighty men and men of strength [LXX: a strong man] for battle'? 48:15 (31:15) Moab is destroyed [Syr., Tg. Jon.: plundered]. As for his city and the choicest of his young men, they have gone down to the slaughter [MT: Moab is destroyed, and his cities has he gone up; and as for the choicest of his young men, they have gone down to the slaughter]" [MT adds: the prophetic utterance of the king whose name is the LORD of hosts]. 48:16 (31:16) "Near is the day [MT: disaster] of Moab to come, and his calamity, very quickly [MT: and as for his calamity, it hastens greatly]. 48:17 (31:17) Mourn for him, all those around him, [MT adds: and] all those who know his name. Say, 'How (the) staff of strength [or, strong staff; Tg. Jon.: harmful king] is broken, (the) rod of beauty [or, beautiful rod; Tg. Jon.: oppressive ruler]!'

48:18 (31:18) Come down from glory and sit in thirst [LXX: moisture; Syr.: shame], O inhabitant of Abaddon [MT: O inhabitant of daughter Dibon]. For Moab is destroyed; the destroyer of your fortifications [LXX: fortress] has come up against you [MT: For the destroyer of Moab has come up against you; he has destroyed your fortifications]. 48:19 (31:19) By a road stand and watch, O inhabitant of Aroer. Ask one fleeing and escaping and say [MT: Ask a man fleeing and a woman escaping, say], 'What has happened [or, What has been done]?' 48:20 (31:20) Moab is put to shame, for he [MT: she] is dismayed / shattered. Wail and cry out [f. sg.; Codex L qere, nonn Mss: m. pl.]! Declare [m. pl.] in Arnon that Moab is destroyed [Tg. Jon.: plundered]. 48:21 (31:21) And judgment is coming to the land of the plain [LXX: Misor], to Holon and to Jahzah [LXX: Rephas] and to Mophaath [qere: Mephaath] 48:22 (31:22) and to Dibon and to Nebo and to Beth Diblathaim [LXX: the house of Deblathaim] 48:23 (31:23) and to Kiriathaim and to Beth Gamul [LXX: the house of Gamol] and to Beth Meon [LXX: the house of Maon] 48:24 (31:24) and to Kerioth and to Bozrah and to all the cities of [MT adds: the land of] Moab, far and near. 48:25 (31:25) The horn [Tg. Jon.: kingdom] of Moab is cut off, and his arm is broken [Tg. Jon.: and their rulers are broken / defeated]" [2QJer, MT add: the prophetic utterance of the LORD].

The history of Moab's relationship with Israel is well known to readers of the Bible (Gen. 19:29–38; Num. 22–24; Deut. 2; Judg. 3; 2 Sam. 8:2; 2 Kgs. 1:1; 3; Ps. 83:6–9 [Eng., 83:5–8]; 2 Chr. 20). There are several prophetic oracles about Moab in addition to the one found here in Jeremiah (Isa. 15–16; Ezek. 25:8–11; Amos 2:1–3; Zeph. 2:8–11). Of these, Isaiah 15–16 bears the closest relationship to Jeremiah 48, a relationship to be discussed in the course of the following commentary. Jeremiah 48 begins like a woe oracle: "Woe [הוי = אוי] to Nebo, for it is destroyed! Kiriathaim is captured [MT: Kiriathaim is put to shame, it is captured]. The secure height is put to shame and dismayed/shattered" (Jer. 48:1 [LXX 31:1]; cf. Jer. 48:20). The MT has expanded the text of Jeremiah 48:1 both in its introduction and in its main text. Nebo and Kiriathaim were once assigned to the tribe of Reuben on the other side of the Jordan (Num. 32:3; Josh. 13:19), but they are here assumed to be Moabite cities (see *ANET*, 320; see also BDB, 612, 900). The first hint at an accusation against Moab in Jeremiah 48 appears in verse 7. The entire chapter is for the most part a depiction of Moab's judgment, but Jeremiah 48:12–13 is the only formally marked announcement of such.

The Hebrew source behind Greek Jeremiah 48:2 (LXX 31:2) says that the "healing" (תעלת) of Moab is no more, whereas the MT says that the "praise" (תהלת) of Moab is no more. There are then two wordplays in the Hebrew text of this verse (see Rashi). The first is as follows: "In Heshbon (חשבון) they plan (חשבו) against her disaster: 'Let us cut her off [MT: Come and let us cut her off] from being a nation'" (for "Heshbon," see Num. 21:25–30; 32:37; Josh. 13:17, 26; BDB, 363–64; see also Jer. 48:42). This apparently indicates that the enemy has taken control of the Moabite city of Heshbon and is planning an attack against the nation of Moab from that location. The second wordplay is in 48:2b: "Indeed, she will certainly be silent (דמום תדם) [MT: Also Madmen (מדמן), you will be silent (תדמי)]. After you a sword will go" (see Jer. 48:10). This wordplay differs between the Hebrew *Vorlage* of the LXX and the MT, but the sounds involved are the same. It has been suggested that the otherwise unknown "Madmen" of the MT may be the end result of a development from "Dibon" (Jer. 48:18, 22) to "Dimon" (Isa. 15:9) to "Madmen."[3]

Jeremiah 48:3 (LXX 31:3) cites the sound of an outcry from the Moabite city of Horonaim (see Isa. 15:5; Jer. 48:5, 34; *ANET*, 321): "Destruction and great breaking!" This is in response to the coming of the enemy from the north (see Jer. 4:6; 6:1; see also Jer. 50:22; 51:54; Zeph. 1:10).[4] The Hebrew source behind Greek Jeremiah 48:4 (LXX 31:4) says, "Moab is broken. Proclaim to Zoar (צערה)" (see Isa. 15:5; Jer. 48:34; see also BDB, 858). The Leningrad Codex, however, says, "Her little ones (*kethiv*: צעוריה; *qere*: צעיריה) have caused to hear (הִשְׁמִיעוּ) an outcry." A multitude of Masoretic manuscripts have an imperative: "Proclaim (הַשְׁמִיעוּ) an outcry, her little ones." BDB (859) interprets "little ones" here in terms of significance rather than age. *Targum Jonathan* renders "her little ones" as "their rulers."

It is generally held that Jeremiah 48:5 (LXX 31:5) is dependent upon Isaiah 15:5, although the two texts are by no means identical in every way.[5] The differences between the Hebrew source behind Greek Jeremiah and the MT, both of which depart from Isaiah 15:5 in their own ways, are as follows: "For Lahoth is full (מלאה) with weeping; weeping goes up [MT: For as for the ascent (מעלה) of Luhith (*qere*), it is with weeping that weeping goes up]. On the descent of Horonaim, an outcry of breaking have you heard (שמעתם) [MT: For on the descent of Horonaim, foes (צרי) of an outcry of breaking have they heard (שמעו)]." Isaiah 15:5 has בבכי יעלה בו ("it is with weeping that he goes up in

---

3. See McKane, *Jeremiah XXVI–LII*, 1157–58.

4. Note that the context for this language in Zephaniah 1:10 is the Day of the Lᴏʀᴅ (Zeph. 1:7, 14–16).

5. See Holladay, *Jeremiah 2*, 346; McKane, *Jeremiah XXVI–LII*, 1159; Parke-Taylor, *Formation of the Book of Jeremiah*, 128–31.

it") rather than בבכי יעלה בכי ("it is with weeping that weeping goes up"). Isaiah 15:5 also does not have צרי ("foes"), which is only in MT Jeremiah 48:5. The main thrust of this text is to show a correspondence between what goes up the ascent of Luhith ("weeping") and what goes down the descent of Horonaim ("an outcry").

The Moabites are encouraged to flee and to save themselves (Jer. 48:6a [LXX 31:6a]; cf. Jer. 51:6). Masculine plural imperatives are used, but then there is a shift to a second-person feminine plural verb, apparently with the cities (f.) of Moab in view: "And you will be like a wild ass (ערוד) [MT: a shrub (ערוער); *Tg. Jon.*: the tower of Aroer (see Jer. 48:19)] in a [MT: the] wilderness" (Jer. 48:6b [LXX 31:6b]).[6] According to the Hebrew source behind Greek Jeremiah, the people of Moab's cities will be like a "wild ass" wandering in the wilderness (see Job 39:5). The MT, however, says that they will be like a "shrub" in the wilderness (cf. Jer. 17:6). They are like those who trust in mankind and are comparable to a shrub in the desert plain (Jer. 17:5–6). On the other hand, those who trust in the Lord are like a tree planted by water (Jer. 17:7–8). This connection back to Jeremiah 17:5–8 makes for a nice segue to Jeremiah 48:7 (LXX 31:7), which speaks of Moab's misplaced trust.

The Hebrew source behind Greek Jeremiah 48:7 (LXX 31:7) gives the reason for the judgment of Moab as follows: "Because you have trusted in your strongholds (במצדותיך)." The MT has: "because you have trusted in your works and in your treasures/storehouses" (במעשיך ובאוצרותיך) (cf. Jer. 48:13; 49:4). Chemosh, the god of the Moabites (1 Kgs. 11:7), will go into exile, "his priests and his officials together" (cf. Jer. 49:3b; Amos 1:15; see also Jer. 48:13). Destruction (MT: "a destroyer") will come to every Moabite city, and not one of them will escape (Jer. 48:8 [LXX 31:8]). The valley will perish, and the plain will be destroyed. "City," "valley," and "plain" are of course metonymy for the inhabitants of the land of Moab.[7]

The original text of Jeremiah 48:9 (LXX 31:9) is reconstructed here as follows: "Give a signpost (ציון) to Moab, for she will certainly fall in ruins (נצה תצה), and all her cities will become a desolation [or, object of horror] without inhabitant(s) in them" (cf. Jer. 4:7). The signpost is a monument or grave marker that signifies the death of Moab (see 2 Kgs. 23:17). The MT gives a very different sense for 48:9a: "Give a blossom/ flower (ציץ) [or, shining thing; Syr., *Tg. Jon.*: crown] to Moab, for flying

---

6. Tov considers the presumed text behind the LXX (ערוד) to be an example of a "pseudo-variant" (*Text-Critical Use of the Septuagint,* 183).

7. Bullinger, *Figures of Speech,* 579.

she will go out (נצא תצא).” Rashi suggests that צִיץ here means כנף ("wing[s]"),[8] and this is indeed the sense that this word has in Aramaic (see BDB, 851). *Targum Jonathan* interprets this to mean that Moab will go into exile (cf. Jer. 48:7b). More recently, it has been suggested that this word means "salt-field" on the basis of Ugaritic evidence.[9] Thus, Moab is to be made a field sown with salt. It should be admitted, however, that Hebrew has its own terminology for this sort of expression (see Judg. 9:45; Jer. 17:6). The ruin of Moab is certain, and cursed is any instrument of God's judgment who is negligent, withholding his sword from blood (Jer. 48:10 [LXX 31:10]; cf. Jer. 46:10; 47:6; 48:2).

According to Jeremiah 48:11 (LXX 31:11), Moab has been at ease since its youth. He is undisturbed on his "lees" (or "wine dregs," "sediment"; cf. Isa. 25:6; Zeph. 1:12). *Targum Jonathan* interprets "lees" here to be symbolic of Moab's possessions. The LXX says that Moab was confident in its glory. The wine imagery is very appropriate for a place well known for its grapevines and wine (see Jer. 48:32–33). Moab has been like a wine allowed to age, not emptied from vessel to vessel. The text interprets this to mean not that Moab has never had trouble from foreign adversaries but that Moab has never gone into exile. It is in this sense that Moab has been left to settle in its place. Therefore, like a fine wine, Moab's "taste" has remained, and its "scent" has not changed. Such a contented state of being stands in stark contrast to what lies on the horizon for Moab (Jer. 48:7, 12–13; cf. Jer. 49:12).

"Therefore" (לכן), Jeremiah 48:12 (LXX 31:12) announces, "days are coming" (cf. Jer. 49:2; 51:47, 52) when the Lord will send to Moab "tippers" (Syr., *Tg. Jon.*: "plunderers"), and they will tip Moab over (i.e., pour him out like wine). They will "crush" (ידקו; MT: "empty" [יריקו]; cf. Jer. 48:11) his vessels and shatter his jars (cf. Jer. 13:12, 14). Moab will be ashamed of Chemosh just as the house of Israel was ashamed of Bethel, which was the object of their trust or their source of confidence (Jer. 48:13 [LXX 31:13]; see Jer. 48:7, 46; cf. Jer. 51:47). Bright thinks that "Bethel" here is a divine epithet rather than a place name (cf. Gen. 35:7),[10] but there is little evidence for this other than the parallel with "Chemosh." Rashi is likely more correct to say that "Bethel" represents the golden calf that was set up for worship at that location by Jeroboam (1 Kgs. 12:28–32).[11] Just as the golden calf went

---

8. Rosenberg, trans., *Mikraoth Gedoloth: Jeremiah Volume Two*, 359.

9. See Holladay, *Jeremiah 2*, 357.

10. Bright, *Jeremiah*, 320.

11. Rosenberg, trans., *Mikraoth Gedoloth: Jeremiah Volume Two*, 360. See also McKane, *Jeremiah XXVI–LII*, 1169.

into exile (Hos. 10:5), so Chemosh will go into exile (Jer. 48:7). Just as the northern kingdom of Israel went into exile (1 Kgs. 17; Jer. 7:12–15), so Moab will go into exile for the first time. The object of their trust will prove to be a source of shame (cf. 1QIsaᵃ 20:5).

In light of what lies ahead for Moab, how can the Moabites say, "We are mighty men and men of strength for battle" (Jer. 48:14 [LXX 31:14]; cf. Jer. 2:23; 8:8; see also 1Q33 6:13; 11Q19 57:9)? Theirs is a false sense of security for sure (Jer. 48:7, 13). "Moab is destroyed. As for his city and the choicest of his young men, they have gone down to the slaughter [MT: Moab is destroyed, and his cities has he gone up; and as for the choicest of his young men, they have gone down to the slaughter]" (Jer. 48:15 [LXX 31:15]). MT 48:15 contrasts the going up of the enemy against Moab's cities (cf. Jer. 48:18b) with the going down of Moab's young men to the slaughter (cf. Jer. 50:27; 51:40). (For the addition at the end of MT 48:15, see Jer. 46:18a; 51:57b.)

According to the Hebrew source behind Greek Jeremiah 48:16a (LXX 31:16a), the "day" (יום) of Moab is near to come. According to the MT, the "disaster" (איד) of Moab is near to come. Both of these words are found in the text upon which Jeremiah 48:16 depends, Deuteronomy 32:35b: "For near is the day of their disaster (יום אידם)" (note the Sodom and Gomorrah reference in Deut. 32:32 [see the origin of Moab in Gen. 19]). The Hebrew source behind Greek Jeremiah 48:16b (LXX 31:16b) is elliptical: "and his calamity, very quickly (מְהֵרָה)." The MT has: "and as for his calamity, it hastens (מִהֲרָה)." The call to all those around Moab (those who know his reputation) to mourn for him is somewhat ironic (Jer. 48:17a [31:17a]), but it is another way to sound the death knell. The lament takes the form of an expression of great loss: "How (the) staff of strength [or, strong staff] is broken, (the) rod of beauty [or, beautiful rod]" (Jer. 48:17b [LXX 31:17b]; cf. Jer. 50:23; 51:41)! *Targum Jonathan* interprets the staff of strength and the rod of beauty to stand for a harmful king and an oppressive ruler respectively.

In MT Jeremiah 48:18a (LXX 31:18a), the addressee is the "inhabitant of daughter Dibon" (ישבת בת דיבון). Dibon is a well-known Moabite city earlier occupied by the tribe of Gad (see BDB, 192; see also Jer. 48:22; *ANET*, 320). In the Hebrew source behind Greek Jeremiah (NETS: "seated she is being destroyed"), the addressee is the "inhabitant of Abaddon" (ישבת אבדון). The name "Abaddon" means "place of destruction" (see BDB, 2; see also Rev. 9:11). The addressee is told to come down from glory (cf. Jer. 48:17b) and sit "in thirst" (בצמא), which the Syriac interprets to mean sit "in shame." The parallel in Isaiah 47:1 suggests that this expression may be another way to say sit "in dust" after removal from the throne. Moab must do this because the destroyer of its fortifications has come up against it (Jer. 48:18b [LXX 31:18b]; cf. Jer. 48:15). The inhabitant of Aroer, another Moabite city (BDB, 792), is told to stand by a road and watch in order to ask one fleeing and escaping what has happened (Jer. 48:19 [LXX 31:19]; cf. Jer. 48:6; see also 1 Sam. 4:12–18). The MT coordinates masculine and feminine participles here ("a man fleeing and a woman escaping"), perhaps to indicate completeness (cf. Isa. 11:12; see GKC §122v). The conclusion is that Moab is put to shame, for he/she is dismayed/shattered (Jer. 48:20 [LXX 31:20]; cf. Jer. 48:1). There is nothing left to do except to wail and to cry out and to declare in Arnon that Moab is destroyed (see BDB, 75).

Judgment is coming to the land of the plain, that is, Moab (Jer. 48:21a [LXX 31:21a]; see Josh. 13:17). Jeremiah 48:21b–24a (LXX 31:21b–24a) lists the cities of Moab to which judgment is coming (see *ANET*, 320–21): Holon, Jahzah (Josh. 13:18),[12] Mophaath/Mephaath, Dibon (Josh. 13:17; Jer. 48:18), Nebo (Jer. 48:1), Beth Diblathaim (Num. 33:46–47), Kiriathaim (BDB, 900), Beth Gamul, Beth Meon (Josh. 13:17), Kerioth (Syr. Jer. 48:41; Amos 2:2), and Bozrah (BDB, 131). So as not to leave anyone out, Jeremiah 48:24b (LXX 31:24b) adds the following: "and to all the cities of [MT adds: the land of] Moab, far and near" (cf. Jer. 25:26). The "horn" (*Tg. Jon.*: "kingdom") of Moab is cut off, and his arm is broken (*Tg. Jon.*: "and their rulers are broken/ defeated") (Jer. 48:25 [LXX 31:25]). The horn and the arm are symbolic of Moab's strength.

48:26 (31:26) "Make him drunk [Syr.: Make him miserable; cf. Tg. Jon.], for it is against the Lord [Tg. Jon.: the people of the Lord] that he has magnified himself, and Moab will clap with his hand [MT: splash in his vomit], and he too will become a laughingstock. 48:27 (31:27) And was not Israel a laughingstock to you? Was he found among your thieves [LXX: among your thefts (cf. 2QJer); MT: among thieves], that against him you would fight [or, gather in troops (cf. Syr.); MT: that as often as your words (pc Mss: word) against him you would shake your head (cf. 2QJer)]? 48:28 (31:28) The inhabitants [2QJer: inhabitant] of Moab have forsaken cities [2QJer: your cities], and they live [2QJer: שכוני] in the rock(s) / cliff [MT: Forsake cities and live in the rock, O inhabitants of Moab]. They are like [MT: And be like] a dove that nests in rocks / cliffs [MT: sides] of a pit's mouth. 48:29 (31:29) I have heard

---

12. McKane suggests that יהצה ("Jahzah") is יהץ ("Jahaz") with He locale (cf. Deut. 2:32; see also MT Jer. 48:34), but he notes that such an ending would be redundant with the preposition אל (Jeremiah XXVI–LII, 1177).

[MT: We have heard; 2QJer: שמעו נא*] the pride of Moab, very proud, his pride and his arrogance [cf. 2QJer, Syr., Isa. 16:6; MT: his loftiness and his pride and his arrogance] and the haughtiness of his heart/mind [LXX: and his heart was lifted up]. 48:30 (31:30) As for me, I know," [MT adds: the prophetic utterance of the* Lord*], "his work [cf. Syr., Tg. Jon.; MT: his arrogance]. It is not enough for him [MT: And not right/so are his empty words (or, boasts)]. Not so has he done [2QJer:* עשתה*; MT: Not right/so have they done].*[13] *48:31 (31:31) Therefore, for Moab wail, all of him. Cry out for the men of Kir Hadas [2QJer:* חרשת*; cf. Isa. 16:7; LXX*[A]*: κιδαραϛ] with moaning [LXX: of drought]. [MT: Therefore, for Moab I will wail, and for Moab—all of him—I will cry out. For the men of Kir Heres he (Ms: I) will moan.] 48:32 (31:32) Like [MT: More than; Isa. 16:9: With] the weeping for Jazer will I weep for you, O grapevine of Sibmah [cf. 2QJer; MT: O grapevine, Sibmah]. As for your branches, they crossed over (the) sea. As for cities, Jazer they reached [Codex L: Up to the sea of (the sea of > 2 Mss, Isa. 16:8) Jazer they reached]. It is upon [2QJer: And it is upon] your summer fruit, upon [2QJer, MT: and upon] your grape gatherers [Codex L: your vintage; pc Mss, Isa. 16:9: your harvest] that destruction [MT: a destroyer; Isa. 16:9: a shout] has fallen. 48:33 (31:33) Rejoicing is gathered, and joy, from the land of Moab [MT: And rejoicing is gathered, and joy, from a fertile land and from the land of Moab]. And wine was in your wine vats [MT: And wine from wine vats I have stopped]. Early in the morning they do not tread [MT: He does not tread with a shout; cf. Cairo Genizah, Syr., Tg. Jon., Vulg.; see also Isa. 16:10]. Shout, shout, not a shout [LXX: they did not make a shout; MT: Shout, not a shout]. 48:34 (31:34) From the outcry of Heshbon to Elealeh, their cities [MT: as far as Jahaz] they give their voice, from Zoar as far as Horonaim and [and > MT] Eglath-shelishiyah. For also the waters of Nimrim will become desolations [LXX: because also the water of Nebrim will become a burning]. 48:35 (31:35) And I will stop in Moab," the prophetic utterance of the* Lord*, "a person going up [MT: sending up an offering] upon a high place and making sacrifice to his god(s). 48:36 (31:36) Therefore, my heart, it is for Moab that it murmurs like flutes. And as for my heart, it is for the men of Kir Hadas [MT: Kir Heres] that it murmurs like a flute [MT: like flutes]. Therefore, that which he has done perishes [LXX adds: from (a) man; MT: Therefore, as for the*

---

13. The placement of the *athnach* in the MT yields a different arrangement of the syntax: "As for me, I know," the prophetic utterance of the Lord, "his arrogance, and it is not right/so. As for his empty words, not right/so have they done."

abundance (Syr.: evil) of what he has done, those things perish]. 48:37 (31:37) Every head in every place is bald(ness) [LXX: Every head in every place they will shave; MT: For (pc Mss add: upon) every head is baldness], and every beard is diminished [LXX: will be shaved (cf. 2QJer); nonn Mss: is cut off], and all hands are cut [MT: upon all hands are cuts], and upon all [all > Codex L] loins is sackcloth, 48:38 (31:38) and [> MT] upon all the rooves of Moab and in her squares [MT adds: all of him wailing], for I have broken [MT adds: Moab]," [LXX source adds: the prophetic utterance of the LORD], "like a vessel in which there is no delight [or, like an undesirable vessel; LXX: like a vessel for which there is no use]," [MT adds: the prophetic utterance of the LORD]. 48:39 (31:39) "How he is dismayed / shattered, (how) he wails [LXX: How Hatat shouted; MT: How she is dismayed / shattered, (how) they wail]! How Moab has turned the back of his neck, (how) he is ashamed! And Moab will become [LXX: has become] a laughing-stock and an object of terror to all those around her [MT: him]."

48:40 (31:40) For thus says the LORD [MT adds: "Like an eagle he (Tg. Jon.: a king with his armies) will fly swiftly (Syr.: he will go up and fly; cf. Jer. 49:22) and spread his wings to / against Moab"], 48:41 (31:41) "Captured are the cities [Syr.: Kerioth], and the strongholds are seized [GKC §44m, 145k]. [MT adds: And the heart of the mighty men of Moab will be in that day like (the) heart of a woman suffering birth pains.] 48:42 (31:42) And Moab will be destroyed from being a people, for it is against the LORD [Tg. Jon.: the people of the LORD] that he has magnified himself. 48:43 (31:43) Trap and dread and pit [MT: Dread and pit and trap] are upon you, O inhabitant of Moab. 48:44 (31:44) The one who flees from / because of the dread [Syr., Isa. 24:18: the sound of dread] is the one who will fall into the pit, and the one who goes up from [nonn Mss, Syr., Tg. Jon., Isa. 24:18: from the midst of] the pit is the one who will be captured in the trap, for I will bring these things [MT: for I will bring to her] to Moab in the year of their visitation" [MT adds: the prophetic utterance of the LORD]. 48:45 "In the shadow of Heshbon fugitives stand without strength [Theod., Vulg.: from a trap; 48:45a > Syr.], for it was a fire that went forth from Heshbon, and a flame from between [pc Mss: from the house of; 2QJer, Theod., Syr., Num. 21:28: from the city of] Sihon, and it consumed the temples of Moab and the top of the head of [pc Mss, Num. 24:17: and he will tear down; see also Theod.] the sons of tumult [warriors? boasters?]. 48:46 Woe to you, Moab! The people of Chemosh have perished [Ms, Theod., Syr., Vulg., Num. 21:29: You have perished, O people of Chemosh]. For your sons have been taken into captivity, and your daughters into captivity. 48:47 But I will restore the fortunes [Tg. Jon.: exile(s); Vulg.: captivity] of Moab at the end of the days," the prophetic utterance of the LORD.[14]

[MT editorial addition: Up to here is the judgment of Moab.]

The command to make Moab drunk in 48:26a (LXX 31:26a) is tied to the metaphor of the cup of judgment (see Jer. 25:15–26). Moab is to be made to drink of this cup because he has magnified himself against the LORD (cf. Jer. 48:42). *Targum Jonathan* understands this to mean that Moab has magnified himself against the people of the LORD, and this is the wording of the text of MT Zephaniah 2:10b: "for they reproached and magnified themselves against the people of [the people of > LXX] the LORD of hosts." According to the Hebrew source behind Greek Jeremiah 48:26b (LXX 31:26b), Moab will "clap" (ספק) "with his hand" (בידו or בכפו), perhaps in anger (cf. Num. 24:10). The MT, however, says that Moab will "splash" (ספק) "in his vomit" (בקיאו), the result of his drunkenness (see BDB, 706). The end of the verse adds that "he too" (גם הוא) will become a laughingstock (cf. Jer. 48:39; see also Jer. 20:7). That is, just as Israel has been the object of Moab's reviling (see Zeph. 2:8), so also Moab will become an object of reproach. Thus, the rhetorical questions follow in 48:27 (LXX 31:27): "And was not Israel a laughingstock to you?[15] Was he found among your thieves [LXX: among your thefts; MT: among thieves], that against him you would fight (כי בו תתגודד) [MT: that as often as your words (pc Mss: word) against him you would shake your head (כי מדי דבריך בו תתנודד); cf. Jer. 31:20]?" To be considered a thief was to be held in contempt (see Job 30:5).

The Hebrew source behind Greek Jeremiah 48:28 (LXX 31:28) features a series of statements about the inhabitants of Moab: "The inhabitants of Moab have forsaken cities, and they live in the rock(s)/cliff. They are like a dove that nests in rocks/cliffs (בצורי) of a pit's mouth" (cf. Jer. 49:16). On the other hand, the MT has a series of imperatives: "Forsake cities and live in the rock, O inhabitants of Moab. And be like a dove that nests in sides (בעברי) of a pit's mouth." The main difference between these two texts (statements vs. commands) is primarily a difference in vocalization, not a difference in the consonantal text.

Jeremiah 48:29–38 (LXX 31:29–38) closely resembles material found in Isaiah 15–16. It is usually assumed that the Jeremiah passage

---

14. Jeremiah 48:45–47 does not appear in the LXX. The commentary will explain why 48:45–47a is still included in the main body of the text.

15. Or, "And surely Israel was a laughingstock to you" (see McKane, *Jeremiah XXVI–LII*, 1180).

is dependent upon the text of Isaiah, but this should not be taken for granted. The oracle about Moab in Jeremiah 48 is overall substantially larger than the one in Isaiah 15–16, and it is not immediately clear why Jeremiah 48 would feature such a selective and seemingly haphazard sampling of text from Isaiah 15–16: Isa. 15:5 (Jer. 48:4–5); Isa. 16:6–10 (Jer. 48:29–33); Isa. 15:4–6 (Jer. 48:34); Isa. 16:11 and 15:7 (Jer. 48:36); Isa. 15:2–3 (Jer. 48:38). For instance, why does Jeremiah 48 not include any material from Isaiah 16:1–5, especially since the messianic interests of Isaiah 16:5 (see *Tg. Jon.*) align so well with what the reader finds elsewhere in the book of Jeremiah (e.g., Jer. 23:5–6)? Of course, the possibility of a common source (or circulation of stock material about Moab) always lurks in the background, but such a scenario is impossible to prove without textual evidence. For the present commentary, the two texts will be compared without making a decision about direction of dependence. In any case, the task is not to reconstruct one text from the two sources but to appreciate the unique roles of both oracles in their respective contexts.

Witnesses to 48:29 (LXX 31:29) differ on the opening verb: LXX, "I have heard" (= שמעתי); MT (and Isa. 16:6), "We have heard" (שמענו); 2QJer, "Hear" (שמעו נא). Nevertheless, it is abundantly clear from the multiplication of synonyms that this verse is about the reputation of Moab's pride: "the pride of Moab, very proud, his pride and his arrogance [cf. 2QJer, Syr., Isa. 16:6; MT: his loftiness and his pride and his arrogance] and the haughtiness of his heart/mind [LXX: and his heart was lifted up]." In 48:30 (LXX 31:30), the LORD says that he knows "his work" (עבדתו) (MT: "his arrogance" [עברתו]). The Hebrew source behind Greek Jeremiah then says, "It is not enough for him (לא דיו). Not so (οὕτως) has he done (לא כן עשה)." This reading suggests that Moab wants more beyond his prideful work, but he has not really done anything to warrant this. The syntax of the MT can be understood in more than one way, depending upon whether the guidance of the *athnach* accent is heeded. The current placement of this accent suggests the following translation of 48:30: "As for me, I know," the prophetic utterance of the LORD, "his arrogance, and it is not right/so (ולא כן). As for his empty words, not right/so have they done (בדיו לא כן עשו)." On the other hand, a comparison with Isaiah 16:6b suggests the following arrangement: "As for me, I know," the prophetic utterance of the LORD, "his arrogance. And not right/so are his empty words (ולא כן בדיו). Not right/so have they done (לא כן עשו)." The Hebrew word כן can mean either "right" or "so." It is a question of whether Moab's words and actions are wrong or simply not as Moab has claimed.

The Hebrew source behind Greek Jeremiah 48:31 (LXX 31:31) features imperative forms: "Therefore, for Moab wail (הילילו), all of him.

Cry out (זעקו) for the men of Kir Hadas with moaning (הגה)." The MT, however, has first-person verbs: "Therefore, for Moab I will wail (איליל), and for Moab—all of him—I will cry out (אזעק). For the men of Kir Heres he [Ms: I] will moan (יהגה [Ms: אהגה])."[16] It may be asked why the LORD would wail for Moab. Is this an indication that he regrets his judgment of Moab? This issue also arises in 48:32, 36. Suffice it to say here that there is no remorse on the LORD's part for his own action. Rather, the wailing for Moab is an indication of the seriousness of Moab's judgment. The LXX has the name "Kir Hadas" ("new city/wall"), while the MT has "Kir Heres" ("city/wall of potsherds"). 2QJer (and Isa. 16:7) has "Kir Hareseth." It is also worth noting that Isaiah 16:7 has the phrase לאשישי קיר חרשת ("for the raisin cakes of Kir Hareseth") rather than אל אנשי קיר חרש ("for the men of Kir Hadas/Heres").

In 48:32a (LXX 31:32a), the grapevine of Sibmah is addressed as if it were a person.[17] Due to the severity of Moab's judgment, there is reason to weep for Sibmah. According to the Hebrew source behind Greek Jeremiah, this weeping is "like the weeping" (כבכי) for Jazer (MT: "more than the weeping" [מבכי]; Isa. 16:9: "with the weeping" [בבכי]). Rashi comments that Jazer, which was near Moab, had already been destroyed.[18] Sibmah was well known for its grapevines in Moab. Its production of fruit was so abundant that it could be said that its branches crossed over the sea (i.e., the Dead Sea). The Hebrew source behind Greek Jeremiah says, "As for cities, Jazer they reached" (ערים יעזר נגעו). That is, the branches of Sibmah's grapevines were so extensive that it could be said that they reached even to the city of Jazer. On the other hand, the Leningrad Codex says, "Up to the sea of [the sea of > 2 Mss, Isa. 16:8] Jazer they reached" (עד ים יעזר נגעו). This reading was likely generated when ערים was mistaken as עד ים. The textual witnesses to 48:32b (LXX 31:32b) differ considerably, and this can be illustrated as follows: "It is upon [2QJer: And it is upon] your summer fruit, upon [2QJer, MT: and upon] your grape gatherers (בצריך) [Codex L: your vintage (בצירך); pc Mss, Isa. 16:9: your harvest (קצירך)] that destruction (שד) [MT: a destroyer (שדד); Isa. 16:9: a shout (הידד)] has fallen." The destruction of Sibmah's once glorious grapevine is a stirring snapshot of the downfall of Moab. Rejoicing and joy are gathered "from the land of Moab" (MT: "from a

---

16. Isaiah 16:7 has two occurrences of the third-person verb ייליל. See also יהגו (Ms: תהגו).

17. 1QIsaᵃ skips from the first occurrence of גפן שבמה in Isaiah 16:8 to the second in Isaiah 16:9, accidentally omitting the intervening text.

18. Rosenberg, trans., *Mikraoth Gedoloth: Jeremiah Volume Two*, 364.

fertile land and from the land of Moab") (Jer. 48:33a [LXX 31:33a]; cf. Isa. 16:10a). The Hebrew source behind Greek Jeremiah 48:33b (LXX 31:33b) implies that wine was formerly in Moab's wine vats but is now no longer there: "And wine was in your wine vats" (ויין ביקביך). The MT makes this explicit: "And wine from wine vats I have stopped" (ויין מיקבים השבתי). The Hebrew source behind Greek Jeremiah has השכם ("early") instead of השבתי ("I have stopped") and puts it with what follows: "Early in the morning they do not tread" (השכם לא דרכו) (i.e., they do not stomp the grapes). The MT says, "He does not tread with a shout" (לא ידרך הידד). The above translation of the Hebrew source behind Greek Jeremiah puts the last word of this text ("shout") with what follows: "Shout, shout, not a shout" (הידד הידד לא הידד) (MT: "Shout, not a shout"). These witnesses to Jeremiah 48:33b may be compared to the text of MT Isaiah 16:10b: "Wine in the vats the one who treads does not tread (יין ביקבים לא ידרך הדרך); a shout I have stopped (הידד השבתי)." Keil comments on the repetition of הידד ("shout") in Jeremiah 48:33b, "This word generally signifies any loud shout, not merely the shout of the wine-pressers as they tread the grapes (see on 25:30), but also a battle-cry; cf. 51:14. Hence the meaning is, '*Hedad* is heard, but not a merry shout of the wine-pressers.'"[19]

The text of Jeremiah 48:34 (LXX 31:34), which features multiple place names, resembles material from several verses in Isaiah 15 (Isa. 15:4–6). The main difference between the Hebrew source behind Greek Jeremiah and MT Jeremiah occurs in the first half of the verse. The former says, "From the outcry of Heshbon to Elealeh, their cities (עריהם) they give their voice, from Zoar as far as Horonaim and [and > MT] Eglath-shelishiyah" (Jer. 48:34a [LXX 31:34a]). The MT has עד יהץ ("as far as Jahaz") instead of עריהם ("their cities") (cf. Isa. 15:4). The LXX rendering of 48:34b (LXX 31:34b) is interpretive and does not reflect a different Hebrew *Vorlage*: "For also the waters of Nimrim will become desolations [LXX: because also the water of Nebrim will become a burning]." The LORD says in 48:35 (LXX 31:35) that he will stop in Moab "a person going up" (עלה; MT: "a person sending up an offering" [מעלה]) upon a high place and making sacrifice to his god(s) (cf. Isa. 16:12b). This hearkens back to what has already been said about Moab's false sense of security in Chemosh (Jer. 48:7, 13).

"Therefore," the LORD's heart murmurs for Moab like flutes (Jer. 48:36a [LXX 31:36a]; cf. Isa. 16:11a; see also Matt. 9:23). It is for the men of "Kir Hadas" (MT: "Kir Heres") that it murmurs like a flute

---

19. Keil, *Jeremiah*, 399. See also Isaiah 16:10a2: "and in the vineyards they will not cry out, they will not shout."

(MT: "like flutes") (cf. Jer. 48:31–32). McKane's comment here is apropos: "Yahweh does not really bewail the ruin of Moab, since he purposes it and is Moab's judge. The style of the lament is subordinate to prediction and reflects the magnitude of the disaster involved in Moab's downfall rather than Yahweh's grief."[20] The Hebrew source behind Greek Jeremiah 48:36b (LXX 31:36b) concludes, "Therefore, that which he has done perishes" (על כן אשר עשה אבד). The phrase ἀπὸ ἀνθρώπου ("from [a] man") at the end of LXX 31:36b is an addition. MT 48:36b says, "Therefore, as for the abundance [Syr.: evil] of what he has done, those things perish" (על כן יתרת עשה אבדו) (cf. Isa. 15:7).

Jeremiah 48:37–38 (LXX 31:37–38) closely resembles Isaiah 15:2–3. Baldness (קרחה), cut hands, and sackcloth are all expressions of mourning for the dead (Jer. 48:37 [LXX 31:37]; see BDB, 151, 901, 974; see also Jer. 16:6; 47:5; Amos 8:10).[21] A diminished beard is a symbol of shame and disgrace (cf. 2 Sam. 10:4). Such outward displays are upon all the rooves of Moab and in her squares because the LORD has broken Moab like an unwanted vessel (Jer. 48:38 [LXX 31:38]; cf. Jer. 22:28; Hos. 8:8). "How he is dismayed/shattered, (how) he wails [LXX: How Hatat shouted; MT: How she is dismayed/shattered, (how) they wail]! How Moab has turned the back of his neck, (how) he is ashamed! And Moab will become [LXX: has become] a laughingstock and an object of terror to all those around her [MT: him]" (Jer. 48:39 [LXX 31:39]; cf. Jer. 48:1, 20, 26).

The Hebrew source behind Greek Jeremiah 48:40 (LXX 31:40) only has the introductory formula, "For thus says the LORD." The remainder of this verse in the MT is an addition from Jeremiah 49:22a: "Like an eagle he [*Tg. Jon.*: a king with his armies] will fly swiftly [Syr.: he will go up and fly] and spread his wings to/against Moab" (cf. Hab. 1:8). Likewise, the text of 48:41 (LXX 31:41) is substantially shorter in the Hebrew source behind Greek Jeremiah ("Captured are the cities, and the strongholds are seized"), and the addition in the MT comes from 49:22b: "And the heart of the mighty men of Moab will be in that day like (the) heart of a woman suffering birth pains." Jeremiah 48:42 (LXX 31:42) then reiterates the thoughts of 48:2, 26: "And Moab will be destroyed from being a people, for it is against the LORD [*Tg. Jon.*: the people of the LORD] that he has magnified himself" (see again Zeph. 2:10).

The text of Jeremiah 48:43–44 (LXX 31:43–44) is an adaptation of material from Isaiah 24:17–18. The eschatological context of the Isaiah passage could hardly have escaped the author's notice. Furthermore, a

---

20. McKane, *Jeremiah XXVI–LII*, 1190.

21. The phrase בכל מקום ("in every place") in the Hebrew source behind Greek Jeremiah 48:37 (LXX 31:37) does not appear in the MT.

comparable passage in Amos 5:18–20 describes a similar series of unfortunate events to occur in the judgment to come in the Day of the LORD (see also Eccl. 10:8). The Hebrew text of Jeremiah 48:43–44 features alliteration, although the order of words differs between the Hebrew source behind Greek Jeremiah 48:43 (LXX 31:43), פח ופחד ופחת ("Trap and dread and pit"), and the MT, פחד ופחת ופח ("Dread and pit and trap") (cf. Jer. 49:5; Lam. 3:47). It should be noted, however, that both witnesses to the sequence of events in 48:44 (LXX 31:44) presuppose the order of the words in MT 48:43. The one who flees from the dread will fall into the pit, and the one who goes up from the pit will be captured in the trap (Jer. 48:44a). There will be no escape from the coming judgment, for the LORD will bring "these things" (אֵלֶּה; MT: "to her" [אֵלֶיהָ]) to Moab in "the year of their visitation" (Jer. 48:44b; cf. Jer. 11:23; 23:12; 46:21).

It is usually assumed without further discussion that the absence of Jeremiah 48:45–47 in the LXX is an indication that these verses were not part of the original text and have been added secondarily in the MT.[22] The present commentary is somewhat unique in that it argues for the originality of 48:45–47a. It is believed that the omission of this text from the LXX is due to scribal or translator oversight. Either the scribe responsible for the translator's Hebrew *Vorlage* or the Greek translator himself accidentally skipped from נאם יהוה at the end of 48:44b to נאם יהוה at the end of 48:47a, unwittingly leaving out the intervening text (homoioteleuton). The formula נאם יהוה or its translation equivalent was subsequently dropped from the end of 48:44b altogether. As for 48:47b, it is an editorial addition in the MT (cf. MT Jer. 51:64b).[23]

Jeremiah 48:45–46 cites material from Numbers 21:28–29 and 24:17. Numbers 21:28–29 is itself part of a citation of proverbial material about king Sihon's conquest of Moab (see Num. 21:27), which was launched from Heshbon. Numbers 24:17 comes from Balaam's fourth oracle. Keil comments, "These insertions are made for the purpose of showing that, through this judgment which is now coming upon Moab, not only those ancient sayings, but also the prophecy of Balaam, will find their full accomplishment. Just as in the time of Moses, so now also there again proceeds from Heshbon the fire of war which will consume Moab."[24] Keil also notes the irony of fugitives from around Heshbon seeking refuge there only to find that it is from Heshbon that Moab's calamity comes

---

22. See Janzen, *Studies in the Text of Jeremiah*, 59; Parke-Taylor, *Formation of the Book of Jeremiah*, 143.

23. "An addition made by the editor, when the oracle was received into the collection of Jeremiah's prophecies" (Keil, *Jeremiah*, 403).

24. Keil, *Jeremiah*, 402.

(see Jer. 48:2, 45). The fire that went forth from Heshbon consumed "the temples of Moab and the top of the head of (וקדקד) the sons of tumult (בני שאון)." A few Masoretic manuscripts change וקדקד ("and the top of the head of") to וקרקר ("and he will tear down") in order to agree with MT Numbers 24:17, but this produces a lack of agreement with the feminine subject ("fire/flame"). In Numbers 24:17, the subject is the messianic king from Israel (see LXX, *Tg. Onk.*) who will strike the temples of Moab "and tear down (וקרקר; SP: וקדקד) all the sons of destruction (כל בני שת; cf. Lam. 3:47; or, all the sons of Seth)."

Thus, woe to Moab; the people of the false god Chemosh have perished (Jer. 48:46a; cf. Num. 21:29a; see also Jer. 48:1, 7, 13; 49:1b), for their sons and daughters have been taken into captivity (Jer. 48:46b; cf. Num. 21:29b). Nevertheless, the LORD will restore the "fortunes" (or, "captivity") of Moab "at the end of the days" (Jer. 48:47a). The fourth oracle of Balaam, which has already been cited in Jeremiah 48:45 (Num. 24:17), also anticipates what will befall Moab "at the end of the days" (Num. 24:14) in the messianic future (see Num. 24:7–9; cf. Gen. 49:1, 8–12; Isa. 2:1–5; Jer. 30:21–24; Hos. 3:5; Dan. 2:28; 10:14). Despite the devastating judgment of Moab, there will be a remnant of Moabites included among the people of God in the kingdom of God (see Isa. 16:14; Zeph. 2:11; Dan. 11:41 [> Old Greek]), and this idea is consistent with the view of the nations elsewhere in the book of Jeremiah (e.g., Jer. 1:10; 3:17; 4:2; 12:14–17; 16:19) and in Jeremiah's nations corpus (Jer. 49:39; see also MT Jer. 46:26b; 49:6). In the arrangement of the nations corpus found in the Hebrew source behind Greek Jeremiah, the first (Jer. 49:34–39) and last (Jer. 48) oracles both conclude with messages of eschatological restoration for the nations, and this hope for the future frames the entire collection.

APPLICATION OF THE NATIONS SECTION

Application of Jeremiah's oracles about the nations largely depends upon what edition of the book the reader is following. If the reader is following the second edition of the book represented by the MT, then application will require an additional step of updating and contextualization in order to make the nations corpus relevant to a contemporary audience. This is due to the fact that the second edition of the book has so historicized the nations section by its arrangement of the oracles and by its placement of them at the end of the book that the meaning of this collection is largely limited in its application to the events of the sixth century BC. What this means is that any attempt now to apply the nations section as it stands in this second edition is inevitably at odds with the meaning of the text. Modern interpreters typically ignore this difficulty and seek to navigate a two-stage process. The first stage is the establishment of the historical meaning, which is assumed to require reconstruction of historical context known to ancient readers but unknown to modern readers. The second stage is application, which is usually a rather forced and artificial attempt either to formulate universally applicable principles (i.e., what the interpreter already knows) or to find analogous people, places, or events in the modern world (the importance of which is dictated from outside the Bible by the news media). Suffice it so say that this second stage is in no way directly related to the first, nor can it lay any claim to authorial intent or biblical authority.

There is fortunately an alternative to the above scenario. If the reader is following the first edition of the book represented by the LXX, then the placement of the nations corpus in the middle of the book and the arrangement of the oracles with an eschatological framework signal the fact that the author has anticipated future readers who do not have knowledge of the ancient historical context. No such context is supplied by the author, indicating that it is unnecessary and beside the point. The composer has built and packaged his text in such a way that future generations of readers have everything that they need within the text itself. This means that the meaning of the text and the ongoing application of the text are inextricably bound together. The application of Jeremiah's nations corpus within the first edition of the book is not only the ultimate judgment of the nations but also the ultimate restoration of a remnant of Gentiles. Thus, there is future hope not only for believing Israel and Judah but also for the nations who join them. Nowhere is this application better illustrated than in John's allusions to Jeremiah 50–51 in Revelation 17–18. Furthermore, the inclusion of the nations within the people of God is everywhere a concern in biblical revelation (e.g., Amos 9:12; Acts 15:17).

Acceptance of this application requires contentment with the biblical text. Much of what passes for Christian application is not generated by the Bible at all. Rather, such application is reactionary, as if there were nothing to do with the Bible other than to respond to external stimuli apologetically or otherwise. The mindset seems to be that whatever we find worthwhile to do, the Bible must speak to it. But to go about the business of biblical interpretation for its own sake shows a watching world that preoccupation with the biblical text has value and merit in its own right. If we merely pursue the symptoms of a fallen world with theological sound bites, we will only appear to be driven by the world itself, chasing our tails and putting out brushfires. On the other hand, if we allow the biblical text to form its own coherent conception of the world, then the biblical revelation rather than the system of the world will determine for us what is most important and relevant.

JEREMIAH 25:15–38 (LXX 32:1–24)

25:15 (32:1) Thus [MT: For thus] says the LORD, the God of Israel [MT adds: to me], "Take this cup of wine [LXX: unmixed wine; MT: wine, that is, fury] from my hand and make all the nations to whom I am sending you drink [MT adds: it]. 25:16 (32:2) And they will vomit [4QJer^c, MT: And they will drink and stagger] and act madly because of the sword that I am sending among them." 25:17 (32:3) And I took the cup from the LORD's hand, and I made [MT adds: all] the nations to whom the LORD sent me drink: 25:18 (32:4) Jerusalem and the cities of Judah and its kings and [and > Codex L] its officials to make them into a ruin and [and > MT] an object of horror and [and > MT] an object of hissing [MT adds: and an object of contempt (or, and a curse) as this day], 25:19 (32:5) and [> MT] Pharaoh the king of Egypt and his servants and his officials (32:6) and all his people 25:20 and all the mixed multitude [MT adds: and all the kings of the land of Uz] and all the kings of the [MT adds: land of the] Philistines [LXX: foreigners], [MT adds: and] Ashkelon and Gaza and Ekron and the remnant of Ashdod, 25:21 (32:7) and Edom and Moab and the sons of Ammon, 25:22 (32:8) and [MT adds: all] the kings of Tyre and [MT adds: all] the kings of Sidon and kings [MT: the kings of the coastland] who are on the other side of the sea, 25:23 (32:9) and Dedan and Tema and Rosh [MT: Buz] and all those cut off of side / corner [i.e., those with hair clipped on the temples; or, those cut off to a side / corner], 25:24 (32:10) [MT adds: and all the kings of Arabia] and all [MT adds: the kings of] the mixed multitude, those who dwell in the wilderness, 25:25 (32:11) [MT adds: and all the kings of Zimri] and all the kings of Elam and all the kings of Persia [MT: Media], 25:26 (32:12) and *all the kings of the north [LXX: east], the far and the near [MT: the near and the far] one to another, and all the kingdoms [MT adds: the land/world] that are on the surface of the earth. [MT adds: And as for the king of Sheshach (Tg. Jon.: Babylon), he will drink after them.] 25:27 (32:13) "And you will say to them, 'Thus says the LORD of hosts [MT adds: the God of Israel], "Drink and be drunk and vomit and fall down and do not get up because of the sword that I am sending among you."' 25:28 (32:14) And then, when they refuse to take the cup from your hand to drink, you will say, 'Thus says the LORD [MT adds: of hosts], "You will indeed drink. 25:29 (32:15) For [MT adds: look] against the city upon which my name is called am I beginning to bring calamity; and you, you will by no means go unpunished [MT: and you, will you by any means go unpunished? You will not go unpunished]. For a sword am I summoning against [MT adds: all] the inhabitants of the earth," [MT adds: the prophetic utterance of the LORD of hosts].'*

25:30 (32:16) And as for you, you must prophesy to them [MT adds: all] these words and say [MT adds: to them], 'The LORD, from on high he roars [LXX: he will reveal], from his holy place [MT: and from his holy habitation] he gives his voice. He roars loudly against his pasture/habitation [LXX: He will reveal a word over his place], and [> MT] with a shout like those who tread [i.e., tread grapes] they answer/sing [MT: he answers/sings],[1] and [> MT] against the inhabitants of the earth tumult has come [MT joins "tumult has come" to the beginning of the next verse] 25:31 (32:17) to the end of the earth [MT: Tumult has come to the end of the earth]. For the LORD has a point of contention [or, lawsuit/case] against the nations. He is entering into judgment with all flesh. As for the wicked, they are given [MT: he has given them; Vulg.^{Mss}: I have given] to the sword,' the prophetic utterance of the LORD. 25:32 (32:18) Thus says the LORD [MT adds: of hosts; Syr. adds: of hosts, the God of Israel], 'Look, calamity is going forth from nation to nation, and a great tempest is being stirred up from earth's remote parts. 25:33 (32:19) And those slain by the LORD in the Day of the LORD [MT: in that day] will be from one end of the earth to the other. They will not be buried [MT: They will not be mourned, and they will not be gathered, and they will not be buried]. As dung on the surface of the ground will they be. 25:34 (32:20) Wail, O shepherds [Tg. Jon.: kings], and cry out; and roll in the dust, O leaders [LXX: rams] of the flock! For your days are fulfilled to slaughter [i.e., to be slaughtered], [MT adds: and your dispersions (Syr.: and you

---

1. The Hebrew words עָנָה ("answer") and עָנָה ("sing") are homonyms.

will be shattered; Tg. Jon.: and you will be scattered)] and you will fall like choice rams [MT: like a choice/desirable vessel]. 25:35 (32:21) And flight [Syr., Tg. Jon.: house/place of flight] will perish from the shepherds [Tg. Jon.: kings], and escape from the leaders [LXX: rams] of the flock. 25:36 (32:22) The sound of the outcry of the shepherds [Tg. Jon.: kings] and the wailing of the leaders [LXX: rams] of the flock, for the LORD has destroyed [MT: is destroying] their pasture [Tg. Jon.: people]. 25:37 (32:23) And the peaceful pastures will be silenced/destroyed [LXX: will cease] because of the burning of my anger [MT: the LORD's anger]. 25:38 (32:24) He has left like a young lion his lair [Tg. Jon.: A king has gone into exile from his fortified city], for their land has become a desolation [or, object of horror] because of the great sword [see LXX^{BS}; MT: because of the burning of the oppressor (nonn Mss: because of a sword that oppresses) and because of the burning of his anger].'"

This section serves as a conclusion to the nations corpus in the arrangement of the book according to the Hebrew source behind Greek Jeremiah. In the MT, where the nations corpus appears at the end of the book, this section is separated from the collection of oracles about the nations by a great distance. Nevertheless, as noted in the introduction to the commentary on the nations section, the sequence of the presentation of the nations in MT Jeremiah 25:19–26 has had an influence on the arrangement of the oracles in MT Jeremiah 46–51: Egypt (Jer. 25:19; 46), Philistia (Jer. 25:20; 47), Edom/Moab/Ammon (Jer. 25:21; 48:1–49:22 [Moab/Ammon/Edom]), Elam (Jer. 25:25; 49:34–39), and Babylon (Jer. 25:26; 50–51).[2] The conjunction כִּי ("For") has been added at the beginning of MT 25:15 in order to connect the following passage with MT 25:1–14, but since this passage does not follow 25:1–14 in the Hebrew source behind Greek Jeremiah, the presence of this conjunction is unnecessary.

In Jeremiah 25:15–17 (LXX 32:1–3), the prophet to the nations (Jer. 1:5, 10) receives instruction from the LORD to take a cup of wine and make the nations drink it. It is then narrated that Jeremiah followed this instruction. Since it is hardly realistic to imagine that Jeremiah received a literal cup of wine from the LORD and then marched around to all the nations to force them to drink it, some interpreters have

---

2. The only nations in Jeremiah 46–51 that do not appear in 25:19–26 are Damascus/Syria (Jer. 49:23–27) and Kedar (Jer. 49:28–33), although MT 25:23–24 mentions Dedan, Tema, and Arabia, with which Kedar is associated in Isaiah 21:13–17. MT Jeremiah 25:19–26 also mentions Tyre, Sidon, and Media (Jer. 25:22, 25), who do not have oracles in Jeremiah 46–51.

considered this account to be a prophetic vision (e.g., Redak, Calvin). It is more probable, however, that this is another example of a symbolic sign act (cf. Jer. 13:1–14; 16:1–9; 18:1–12; 19:1–13; 27–28; 32; 43:8–13; 51:59–64).[3] The LXX ("the cup of this unmixed wine") reflects כוס יין החמר הזאת (cf. Ps. 75:9 [Eng., 75:8]). The MT's כוס היין החמה הזאת ("this cup of wine, that is, fury") features החמה ("fury") as an explanatory gloss in apposition to היין ("wine").[4] The nations who must partake of the judgment symbolized by the wine will "vomit" (וקאו; cf. Jer. 25:27a; MT: "drink and stagger" [ושתו והתגעשו]) and act madly. Of course, this is a natural reaction to too much wine, but it is also symbolic of a violent reaction to invasion by the enemy who serves as the instrument of divine judgment. Thus, they will act this way, the LORD says, "because of the sword that I am sending among them" (cf. Jer. 25:27b).

The list of nations to whom Jeremiah is sent to give the cup of wine begins strangely enough with Jerusalem and the cities of Judah, along with its kings and officials (Jer. 25:18a [LXX 32:4a]; cf. *Pss. Sol.* 8:14). This is no doubt because Judah has become like the nations in its worship of other gods. The judgment will make them into a ruin, an object of horror, and an object of hissing (Jer. 25:18b [LXX 32:4b]; cf. Jer. 19:8; 25:9; 29:18; 42:18; see also 11Q19 59:4). The MT adds that they will be an object of contempt (cf. Jer. 24:9) "as this day." This last phrase ("as this day") betrays the fact that the MT's addition is a late one that presupposes rather than anticipates Judah's judgment (see Rashi). Such a presupposition is at odds with Jeremiah 25:29.

The list continues in Jeremiah 25:19 (LXX 32:5) with Pharoah the king of Egypt along with his servants, officials, and people (see Jer. 46; cf. Neh. 9:10). The "mixed multitude" (ערב) at the beginning of 25:20 (LXX 32:6) apparently refers to various foreigners, traders, and mercenaries living in the land of Egypt (see Exod. 12:38; Jer. 50:37; Neh. 13:3). The MT adds after this: "and all the kings of the land of Uz." The secondary

---

3. "The whole action is accordingly emblematical of a real work of God wrought on kings and peoples, and is performed by Jeremiah when he announces what he is commanded. And the announcement he accomplished not by travelling to each of the nations named, but by declaring to the king and his princes in Jerusalem the divine decree of judgment" (Keil, *Jeremiah*, 235).

4. For other examples of the cup metaphor, see Isaiah 51:17, 22; Jeremiah 49:12; 51:7; Ezekiel 23:31–33; Obadiah 16; Habakkuk 2:15–16; Zechariah 12:2; Psalms 11:6; 60:5 (Eng., 60:3); Lamentations 4:21; Matthew 20:22; Mark 10:38; Revelation 14:10; 15:7; 16:19; 17:4; 18:6. See also Numbers 5:16–28.

nature of this addition, which is not in the Hebrew source behind Greek Jeremiah, is evident from the fact that Uz is in the land of Edom (Lam. 4:21), yet Edom does not appear in the list until 25:21 (LXX 32:7). Next on the list are all the kings of Philistia—Ashkelon, Gaza, Ekron, and the remnant of Ashdod (see Jer. 47).[5] Of the five major Philistine cities (1 Sam. 6:17), only Gath is not mentioned (cf. Zech. 9:5–7).

Edom, Moab, and Ammon appear next in 25:21 (LXX 32:7) (see Jer. 48–49). Jeremiah 25:22 (LXX 32:8) then continues with the kings of Tyre and those of Sidon and the kings who are on the other side of the sea. The MT expands the description of this last group to "the kings of the coastland who are on the other side of the sea." Jeremiah 25:23–24 (LXX 32:9–10) features the desert peoples ("those who dwell in the wilderness" [Jer. 25:24b (LXX 32:10b)]): Dedan (BDB, 187), Tema (Isa. 21:14), Rosh (LXX; cf. Ezek. 38:2; MT: Buz [?]), and "all those cut off of side/corner" (i.e., those with hair clipped on the temples; or, those cut off to a side/corner; see Lev. 19:27; Jer. 9:25 [Eng., 9:26]; 49:32). According to the Hebrew source behind Greek Jeremiah 25:24 (LXX 32:10), the only remaining group of the desert peoples is the "mixed multitude" (עֶרֶב). The expanded text of the MT, however, forms a doublet: "all the kings of Arabia (עֲרָב) and all the kings of the mixed multitude (עֶרֶב)" (see Isa. 21:13).

The MT adds at the beginning of 25:25 (LXX 32:11) "and all the kings of Zimri." This text does not appear in the Hebrew source behind Greek Jeremiah. One suggestion is that the name "Zimri" is related to the name "Zimran" in Genesis 25:2 (see Dedan and Tema in Gen. 25:3, 15). Another proposal is that זמרי ("Zimri") should be emended to זמכי and considered *atbash* for עילם ("Elam") (see *BHS* apparatus). This latter option would thus essentially create a doublet with the following "and all the kings of Elam" (see Jer. 49:34–39). The Hebrew source behind Greek Jeremiah then concludes the verse with all the kings of "Persia," whereas the MT has "Media" (see Dan. 5:27; 8:3, 20).

McKane suggests that the phrase "all the kings of the north" in 25:26a (LXX 32:12) is a catchall for any nation not listed thus far;[6] but given the prominence of the enemy from the north up to this point in the book, it seems highly unlikely that this phrase would be used for such a general purpose. It is more likely that the following phrase "all the kingdoms [MT adds: the land/world] that are on the surface of the earth" is the one that serves to include all those not mentioned

---

5. "According to Herodotus (II, 157) Ashdod was taken and destroyed by Psammetichus I (663–609) of Egypt" (Bright, *Jeremiah*, 161).

6. McKane, *Jeremiah I–XXV*, 640.

by name in the preceding list. As for the kings of the north,[7] it has been discussed at length in the present commentary that the identity of the enemy from the north depends upon what edition of the book of Jeremiah is read. The first edition of the book, which is the Hebrew text behind Greek Jeremiah, leaves this enemy unidentified and open to the interpretation found in Ezekiel 38–39 where the enemy is an eschatological enemy. This enemy is a horde of nations from near and far (see Jer. 1:15; Ezek. 38; Rev. 16:14; cf. Jer. 48:24)—an enemy that will eventually be judged itself (Ezek. 39; Rev. 16:19). The second edition of the book, which is MT Jeremiah, identifies the enemy from the north as Babylon and the kings subjugated to it (MT Jer. 25:9; but see Jer. 50:3). This is why MT Jeremiah 25:26b adds, "And as for the king of Sheshach [*Tg. Jon.*: Babylon], he will drink after them."[8] This text does not appear in the Hebrew source behind Greek Jeremiah. According to the MT, the historical instrument of judgment (see Jer. 27:5–8; 51:7) will itself be judged.

The words that the LORD instructs Jeremiah to say to the nations in Jeremiah 25:27 (LXX: 32:13) are a reiteration of 25:16: "Drink and be drunk and vomit and fall down and do not get up because of the sword that I am sending among you" (cf. Jer. 8:4; Amos 5:2). Jeremiah 25:28 (LXX 32:14) anticipates that the nations will be resistant to the cup of judgment. When they refuse it, the prophet is to insist that they must drink (cf. Jer. 27:8). Calvin comments, "We hence see that we are not to take the words in their literal sense: for the Prophet did not speak to aliens, but what he had in view was the event itself, or rather the disposition of the people. These nations had indeed some power, and doubtless they strenuously defended their own safety; and this was the act of refusing intended by the Prophet."[9] If the city of Jerusalem, which bears the name of God,[10] is not spared the impending calamity, how can the heathen nations expect to go unpunished (Jer. 25:29 [LXX

---

7. The LXX translates צפון ("north") here as "east," presumably because the translator envisioned an enemy that would come from the east and then move south into the land of Israel from the north.

8. The name "Sheshach" is *atbash* for "Babylon." See commentary on Jeremiah 51:1, 41. The secondary nature of MT 25:26b is evident from the fact that it unwittingly separates Babylon from the kings of the north, which is contrary to its own purpose in adding Babylon to its text (cf. MT Jer. 25:9).

9. Calvin, *Jeremiah*, 3:284.

10. The designation "upon which my name is called" is usually reserved for the temple (Jer. 7:10, 11, 14, 30; 32:34; 34:15), but see Daniel 9:18 (see also Deut. 12:5; 1 Esd. 4:63).

32:15]; cf. Jer. 49:12 [MT]; Joel 4:21 [Eng., 3:21]; 1 Pet. 4:17; see Exod. 34:7; see also BDB, 667)? The sword or instrument of judgment that the LORD is summoning is for all the inhabitants of the earth (cf. Jer. 12:12; 1QM 16:1).

The next unit, Jeremiah 25:30–38 (LXX 32:16–24), which is bracketed by the lion imagery in verses 30 and 38, builds on the thought of 25:29 that the judgment of Jerusalem will be dealt to all the nations (cf. Rev. 10:11). The text of 25:30b (LXX 32:16b) has in the past been considered a citation of Joel 4:16 (Eng., 3:16) and Amos 1:2, but more recent research suggests that the Joel and Amos texts are citations from Jeremiah designed by the postexilic prophetic composer of the Twelve to form a compositional seam between the two books.[11] It is worthwhile to note that the end of Joel and the beginning of Amos also feature judgment of Judah/Israel and the nations (Joel 4:19 [Eng., 3:19]; Amos 1:3–2:16). The Jeremiah text says that the LORD roars like a lion (cf. Jer. 2:15; Hos. 11:10; Amos 3:4, 8) from "on high."[12] The Joel and Amos texts say that he does this from "Zion." Likewise, where the Jeremiah text says that the LORD gives his voice from "his holy place" (MT: "his holy habitation"), the Joel and Amos texts say that he does this from "Jerusalem."[13] Thus, those who think that the Jeremiah text is the dependent one conclude that the prophet has taken something local and made it universal.[14] No longer does the LORD roar or give his voice from Zion/Jerusalem. Rather, he does this from his heavenly abode (see BDB, 928; see also Deut. 26:15; Zech. 2:17 [Eng., 2:13]; Pss. 11:4; 68:6 [Eng., 68:5]; 2 Chr. 30:27). On the other hand, if the Joel and Amos texts are dependent, then they have interpreted the general expressions "on high" and "his holy place" (MT: "his holy habitation") to be specifically "Zion" (see Jer. 31:12) and "Jerusalem." The reading מקדשו ("from his holy place") in the Hebrew source behind Greek Jeremiah can refer to Jerusalem or the temple (see BDB, 871–72). The MT's וממעון קדשו ("and from his holy habitation") likely refers only to the LORD's heavenly habitation (see BDB, 732–33; but see Ps. 26:8; 2 Chr. 36:15; see also Exod. 15:13; 2 Sam. 15:25b).

The LORD roars loudly against "his pasture/habitation" (i.e., the land of the covenant and the people therein; see Jer. 10:25; 31:23;

---

11. See Shepherd, *Commentary on the Book of the Twelve*, 21–36, 142–52.
12. The LXX interprets this roar to be the roar of revelation.
13. This is comparable to Exodus 19s where God gives his "voice/sound" (קול) from Sinai (Exod. 19:16, 19; 20:18). See also 2 Samuel 22:14; Psalm 18:14 (Eng., 18:13).
14. See, e.g., Holladay, *Jeremiah 1*, 679–80.

cf. Jer. 49:19; 50:44). According to the Hebrew source behind Greek Jeremiah, "they" (i.e., the people of the land) will respond with a shout like those who tread grapes. The term הידד ("shout") can be the shout of harvest or the shout of a foe (see Jer. 48:33). Thus, the Hebrew text reflected by the LXX must mean that the response of the people is comparable to the shout of those who tread grapes but is in reality the shout of a foe who is defiant in his opposition to the LORD. According to the MT, "he" (i.e., the LORD) sings with a shout like those who tread grapes. If this reading is correct, then it is the LORD whose shout of a foe is comparable to that of those who tread grapes.[15] The latter part of Jeremiah 25:30 (LXX 32:16) and the first part of 25:31 (LXX 32:17) differ between the two main Hebrew witnesses in their syntactical arrangement. The Hebrew source behind Greek Jeremiah says, "He roars loudly against his pasture/habitation, and with a shout like those who tread they answer/sing, and against the inhabitants of the earth tumult has come to the end of the earth." According to this reading, the rest of the inhabitants of the earth are only brought in at the end of 25:30, and the focus remains on them into 25:31. The MT, however, says, "He roars loudly against his pasture/habitation, with a shout like those who tread he answers/sings against the inhabitants of the earth. Tumult has come to the end of the earth." According to this reading, it is already against the inhabitants of the earth that the LORD answers/sings with a shout (unless הארץ is to be rendered "the land" instead of "the earth"). Tumult has come to the end of the earth because the LORD has a lawsuit not only against his people but also against the nations (Jer. 25:31a; cf. Hos. 4:1; Mic. 6:2), and he is entering into judgment with all flesh (cf. 4Q266 2 I, 7). Jeremiah 25:31b clarifies that the wicked of all flesh are the ones who are given to the sword. The judgment does not apply to those who are righteous by faith.

The reported discourse of the LORD is reintroduced at the beginning of 25:32 (LXX 32:18). He points out that calamity is going forth from nation to nation. A great tempest is being stirred up from earth's remote parts. This is comparable to what is said in Jeremiah 6:22 about the enemy from the north (see also Jer. 23:19; 30:23). According to the Hebrew source behind Greek Jeremiah 25:33a (LXX 32:19a), those slain by the LORD "in the Day of the LORD" (ביום יהוה) will be from one end of the earth to the other (cf. Jer. 12:12). The MT uses the phrase

---

15. The image of enemies trampled like grapes and blood splattered like juice is known from Genesis 49:11–12 and Isaiah 63:1–6 (see also Rev. 14:19–20; 19:15). See Shepherd, *Text in the Middle*, 49. See also McKane, *Jeremiah I–XXV*, 649.

"in that day" (ביום ההוא) (cf. Jer. 30:7–8). This eschatological Day of the LORD is well known to readers of Isaiah (e.g., Isa. 13:6, 9) and the Twelve (e.g., Joel 1:15; Amos 5:18; Obad. 15; Zeph. 1:7; Zech. 14:1; Mal. 3:23 [Eng., 4:5]).[16] The corpses of the LORD's enemies will be strewn across the inhabited earth in that day of tribulation (cf. Rev. 6:8). They will not be buried;[17] they will be as dung on the surface of the ground (Jer. 25:33b [LXX 32:19b]; cf. Jer. 8:2; 9:21 [Eng., 9:22]; 16:4; see also Isa. 5:25; *Jub.* 23:23; *Pss. Sol.* 2:27).

The shepherds (i.e., the kings) of the nations are urged to wail and to cry out and to roll in the dust because the time has come for their flocks (i.e., their people) to be slaughtered (Jer. 25:34a [LXX 32:20a]; cf. Zech. 10:3; see Joel 1:13–14; Mic. 1:10; see also Jer. 11:19; 48:15; 50:27; 51:40; Jas. 5:5). In other words, their judgment is imminent. The MT adds וּתְפוֹצוֹתִיכֶם ("and your dispersions") at the beginning of 25:34b (LXX 32:20b), but this does not have any place in the syntax of the verse. The early versions translate it as a finite verb: Syriac, "and you will be shattered"; *Tg. Jon.*, "and you will be scattered." Modern scholars have suggested emendation to a *tiphil* verb וּתְפִיצוֹתִיכֶם ("and I will scatter you").[18] The conclusion to 25:34 (LXX 32:20) in the Hebrew source behind Greek Jeremiah says that the leaders will fall "like choice rams" (כאילי חמדה). The MT says that they will fall "like a choice/desirable vessel" (ככלי חמדה). The former reading is better suited to the context, but it is possible that the MT is a corruption of ככלי אין חפץ בו ("like a vessel in which there is no delight" or "like an undesirable vessel") (cf. Jer. 22:28; 48:38; Hos. 8:8).

In the end, flight will perish from the shepherds/kings of the nations, and there will be no escape for them (Jer. 25:35 [LXX 32:21]; cf. Amos 2:14). There will be only the sound of their outcry and that of their wailing, for the LORD has destroyed their pasture (Jer. 25:36 [LXX 32:22]; cf. Jer. 25:34; Zech. 11:3). The word "pasture" here is metonymy for the flock (i.e., the people; see *Tg. Jon.*). According to the Hebrew source behind Greek Jeremiah 25:37 (LXX 32:23), the LORD says that the once peaceful pastures of the nations will be silenced/destroyed because of the burning of "my anger" (אפי). The reading in the MT is a product of misreading אפי ("my anger") as an abbreviation for אף יהוה ("the LORD's anger"). While it is not impossible for the LORD to refer to

---

16. See Shepherd, *Commentary on the Book of the Twelve*, 120.
17. The MT has a longer text here: "They will not be mourned, and they will not be gathered, and they will not be buried."
18. See Keil, *Jeremiah*, 239.

himself in the third person, such a reading is not the most likely one in the present context.

The subject of the main verb עזב is not explicit in 25:38a (LXX 32:24a): "He has left like a young lion his lair." *Targum Jonathan* interprets this to mean that a king has gone into exile from his fortified city. This certainly fits with the remainder of the verse, which would then be an explanation of the king's departure, but it is not clear which king is in view. McKane suggests that the language of 25:38a revisits the description of the enemy from the north in 4:7, although he admits that such a reference to that enemy is somewhat abrupt at this point (but see Jer. 6:22 and 25:32).[19] Most commentators understand 25:38a to be a return to the lion metaphor of 25:30, in which case the Lord is the one who has left his lair like a young lion (cf. Hos. 5:14). Both Redak and Calvin interpret this to mean that the Lord has abandoned his temple because his people have not done his will; therefore, the people of Judah and Jerusalem cannot expect the Lord's protection simply because they have the temple (see Jer. 7:1–15; Ezek. 11:23).[20] Redak comments: "just as the lion abandons his den when he does not find food there, so did the Lord abandon the Temple when his will was not executed there, and since He abandoned it and hid His countenance from it, it was destroyed."[21] This is not, however, the only way that the Lord's activity has been understood here. Keil suggests that the Lord has left his heavenly habitation (cf. Mic. 1:3) not simply to judge Judah and Jerusalem but to judge all the nations.[22] According to both these views, the remainder of 25:38 is an explanation of why such a claim about the Lord's departure would be made: "for their land [i.e., the shepherds' land] has become a desolation [or, object of horror] because of the great sword (החרב הגדולה) [MT: because of the burning of the oppressor (חרון היונה) (nonn Mss: because of a sword that oppresses [חרב היונה]) and because of the burning of his anger]" (Jer. 25:38b [LXX 32:24b]; cf. Jer. 46:16; 50:16; see also Jer. 25:29b). In other words, this is the evidence that the Lord has left his lair.

---

19. McKane, *Jeremiah I–XXV*, 653–54.

20. See Calvin, *Jeremiah*, 3:302.

21. Rosenberg, trans., *Mikraoth Gedoloth: Jeremiah Volume One*, 210.

22. Keil, *Jeremiah*, 240. Keil follows MT 25:30 and thus interprets the Lord's "holy habitation" to be his heavenly habitation. See commentary on 25:30 above.

JEREMIAH 26 (LXX 32)

26:1 (33:1) In the beginning of the kingdom / reign of Jehoiakim the son of Josiah [MT adds: the king of Judah], this word came [Syr. adds: to Jeremiah] from the Lord, [MT adds: saying], 26:2 (33:2) "Thus says the Lord, 'Stand in the court of the house of the Lord and speak [LXX: reveal; Tg. Jon.: prophesy] to all the Judeans [MT: to all the cities of Judah] who are coming to worship in the house of the Lord all the words that I command you to speak [LXX: reveal; Tg. Jon.: prophesy] to them. Do not withhold a word. 26:3 (33:3) Perhaps they will listen and turn each from his evil way that I may relent concerning the calamity that I am planning to do to them because of the evil of their deeds. 26:4 (33:4) And you will say [MT adds: to them], "Thus says the Lord, 'If you do not listen to me to walk in my instructions [MT: instruction] that I have set before you, 26:5 (33:5) to listen to the words of my servants the prophets whom I am sending to you rising early and sending [i.e., urgently sending], and you have not listened, 26:6 (33:6) then I will make this house like Shiloh, and the city [MT: this city] I will make into an object of contempt [or, a curse] to all the nations of all [all > MT] the earth.'"'"

26:7 (33:7) And the priests and the prophets [LXX, Syr.: false prophets; Tg. Jon.: scribes] and all the people heard Jeremiah speaking these words in the house of the Lord. 26:8 (33:8) As soon as Jeremiah finished speaking all that the Lord commanded him [him > MT] to speak to all the people, the priests and the prophets [LXX, Syr.: false prophets; Tg. Jon.: scribes] and all the people grabbed him, saying, "You must certainly die! 26:9 (33:9) Why have you prophesied in the name of the Lord, saying, 'Like Shiloh will this house be, and this city will be desolate without inhabitant'?" And all the people assembled against Jeremiah in the house of the Lord. 26:10 (33:10) And the officials of Judah heard this word, and they went up from the house of the king to the house of the Lord and sat in the entrance of the new [Tg. Jon.: eastern] gate of the house [of the house > Codex L] of the Lord. 26:11 (33:11) And the priests and the prophets [LXX, Syr.: false prophets; Tg. Jon.: scribes] said to the officials and to all the people, [MT adds: saying], "Judgment of death to this man, for he has prophesied against this city just as you have heard with your ears."

26:12 (33:12) And Jeremiah said to [MT adds: all] the officials and to all the people, saying, "It was the Lord who sent me to prophesy against this house and against this city all the words that you have heard. 26:13 (33:13) And now, improve your ways and your deeds and obey the voice of the Lord that the Lord may relent concerning the calamity that he has spoken against you. 26:14 (33:14) And look, I [MT: And as for me, look, I] am in your hand. Do to me according to what is good and upright in your eyes. 26:15 (33:15) Only know for sure that if you kill me, you are putting innocent blood on yourselves and on this city and on its inhabitants, for in truth the Lord *sent me to you to speak in your ears all these words."*

26:16 (33:16) And the officials and all the people said to the priests and to the prophets [LXX, Syr.: false prophets; Tg. Jon.: scribes], "There is not to this man judgment of death, for it is in the name of the Lord *our God that he has spoken to us." 26:17 (33:17) And men from the elders of the land arose and said to all the assembly of the people, [MT adds: saying], 26:18 (33:18) "Micah the Morashtite, he came [MT: he was prophesying] in the days of Hezekiah the king of Judah and said to all the people of Judah, [MT adds: saying], 'Thus says the* Lord *[MT adds: of hosts], "Zion, like a field it will be plowed; and Jerusalem, ruins it will be, and the mountain of the house [i.e., the temple mount] will become high places of a forest."' 26:19 (33:19) Did Hezekiah and all Judah kill him?[1] Did they [MT: he] not fear the* Lord *and appease the* Lord*, and the* Lord *relented concerning the calamity that he spoke against them? Yet we are about to do great harm to ourselves."*

26:20 (33:20) And also a man, he was prophesying in the name of the Lord*, Uriah the son of Shemaiah from Kiriath Jearim, and he prophesied [MT adds: against this city and] against this land according to all the words of Jeremiah. 26:21 (33:21) And King Jehoiakim heard, [MT adds: and all his mighty men] and all the officials, all [> MT] his words, and they sought [MT: and the king sought] to kill him, and Uriah heard [MT adds: and was afraid and fled] and entered Egypt. 26:22 (33:22) And the king [MT: King Jehoiakim] sent men to Egypt [Syr.: sent an Egyptian man] [MT adds: Elnathan the son of Achbor and men with him to Egypt]. 26:23 (33:23) And they brought him out of there [MT: And they brought Uriah out of Egypt], and they brought him to the king [MT: King Jehoiakim], and he struck him with the sword, and he cast him [MT: his corpse] into the grave of the sons of his people [MT: into the graves of the sons of the people (i.e., the common people; Tg. Jon.: the exiles)].*

26:24 (33:24) Yet the hand of Ahikam the son of Shaphan, it was with Jeremiah not to give him into the hand of the people to kill him.

---

1. The LXX, Syriac, and Latin Vulgate have a singular verb here to indicate that Hezekiah is the lead member of the compound subject. The MT has a plural verb.

Jeremiah 26 (LXX 33) is Baruch's account of the situation surrounding Jeremiah's temple gate speech in Jeremiah 7:1–15. It may be asked why this account has been separated from the speech itself in the composition of the book, and the answer seems to be that this chapter also has an important role to play in the contrast between the true prophet Jeremiah and the false prophets mentioned in chapters 27–29. According to 26:1, the instruction from the Lord to give the speech came in the beginning of Jehoiakim's reign (בראשית ממלכת יהויקים). Bright comments that this expression "corresponds to Akk. *rēš šarrūti*, a technical term for the period between a king's accession and the following New Year, from which his first regnal year was counted: in this case between ca. September 609 and April 608."[2] It must be admitted, however, that the text of Jeremiah is Hebrew and not Akkadian. Usage of this phrase elsewhere in the book suggests that it is not so precise in its reference. For example, MT Jeremiah 28:1 employs the same phrase to refer to the fourth year of Zedekiah, nearly halfway through his reign, as the beginning of his reign (cf. MT Jer. 27:1; see also Jer. 25:1).

According to the Lord's instruction in 26:2a (LXX 33:2a), Jeremiah was to stand in the temple court and "speak" (LXX: "reveal"; *Tg. Jon.*: "prophesy") to all the Judeans (MT: "all the cities of Judah") coming to worship in the temple all the words commanded to him by the Lord (cf. Jer. 19:14).[3] This may be compared to MT Jeremiah 7:2 where Jeremiah is instructed to do this in the temple gate (> LXX Jer. 7:2). In anticipation of the negative response to these words and the temptation to mitigate them, the Lord adds, "Do not withhold a word" (Jer. 26:2b [LXX 33:2b]; cf. Jer. 38:14; 42:4; see also Deut. 4:2; 13:1 [Eng., 12:32]; 1 Sam. 3:17). "Perhaps," the Lord says, "they will listen and turn each from his evil way that I may relent concerning the calamity that I am planning to do to them because of the evil of their deeds" (Jer. 26:3 [LXX 33:3]; cf. Jer. 25:5; 36:3; see also Jer. 4:4; 26:13). The opportunity for repentance is built into the threat of judgment (cf. Jon. 3:4, 5–10).

---

2. Bright, *Jeremiah*, 169.

3. "There has been a claim since Duhm that v. 2 is best understood as a command to Jeremiah to make a public proclamation of collected oracles revealed over a period of time: 'all the words which I commanded you to speak, subtracting nothing.' . . . It was this perception of 26.2 which led Duhm to detect a parallelism between chapters 26 and 36. . . . This parallelism is drawn out by Holt, who says that chapter 26 sets in motion a trend which reaches completion in 36: the threat posed by Jehoiakim in 26 is fulfilled in 36 and, moreover, in both chapters Jeremiah depends for protection on the family of Shaphan" (McKane, *Jeremiah XXVI–LII*, 666).

The text of 26:4–6 (LXX 33:4–6) is a summary of Jeremiah's speech in 7:1–15. First is the condition: "If you do not listen to me to walk in my instructions [MT: instruction] that I have set before you, to listen to the words of my servants the prophets whom I am sending to you rising early and sending [i.e., urgently sending]" (Jer. 26:4–5 [LXX 33:4–5]; cf. Jer. 7:5–7; see 2 Kgs. 17:13–15; Jer. 9:12 [Eng., 9:13]; 32:23; 44:23; see also Jer. 7:13 [MT], 25; 11:7 [MT] 25:3, 4; 29:19 [MT]; 32:33; 35:14–15; 44:4).[4] The prophets are the bearers of the Torah, and the truth of their words is measured not only by the fulfillment of what they say but also by the consistency of their message with that of the Torah itself. Added somewhat parenthetically to this at the end of verse 5 is the comment: "and you have not listened" (cf. Jer. 25:7). That is, the people have already met the condition, and there is little indication that anything will change about this. Thus, if nothing does change, then the LORD will make the Jerusalem temple like the former tabernacle at Shiloh (Jer. 26:6a [LXX 33:6a]; see commentary on Jer. 7:12–15), and the city of Jerusalem itself will become an object of contempt to all the nations (Jer. 26:6b [LXX 33:6b]; see commentary on Jer. 24:9).

Jeremiah 26:7 (LXX 33:7) indicates that three different groups heard Jeremiah speaking these words in the temple: the priests, the prophets, and all the people (cf. 2 Kgs. 23:2; Jer. 28:1; 29:1; see also Jer. 20:1). The priests and the prophets are often mentioned together in the book of Jeremiah but not in a positive light (Jer. 2:8; 4:9; 5:31; 6:13; 14:18; 23:11; see also Isa. 28:7; Mic. 3:11). Jeremiah himself, however, is a prophet from a priestly family (Jer. 1:1–3; see also Jer. 11:18–23). The LXX and the Syriac designate the prophets here as false prophets (see Jer. 23:9–40) as opposed to true prophets like Jeremiah, Micah, and Uriah (Jer. 26:17–23).[5] In verses 7–9, "all the people" are joined with the priests and the prophets against Jeremiah. In verses 11–12 and 16, however, "all the people" are joined with the officials who

---

4. The LXX reflects בְּתוֹרֹתַי ("in my instructions"), while the MT has בְּתוֹרָתִי ("in my instruction"). The consonantal text is the same either way. This difference between plural (LXX) and singular (MT) of תורה without change in the consonantal text also occurs in Jeremiah 31:33. In Jeremiah 32:23, the variation between plural and singular exists among the Masoretic witnesses themselves. Sometimes the LXX has the singular, while the MT has the plural (see Isa. 24:5; Dan. 9:10).

5. *Targum Jonathan* calls them "scribes," which is consistent with the later conception of the new prophet as biblical scholar or exegete (see, e.g., LXX Prov. 29:18).

defend Jeremiah or at least his right to a fair trial. Thus, the phrase does not always refer to the same group.

As soon as Jeremiah finished delivering the message that he received from the LORD, the priests and the prophets and all the people grabbed him, saying, "You will certainly die" (Jer. 26:8 [LXX 33:8]; cf. 1 Kgs. 18:40; Jer. 38:4; Hos. 9:7–8; Acts 21:27; 22:22; see also Matt. 27:22–23)! Holladay suggests on the basis of 1 Samuel 14:44 and 1 Kings 2:37, 42 that this is "the formula by which a death sentence is pronounced against the accursed."[6] Because Jeremiah's audience trusted in the temple itself and believed that it could never be destroyed (see Jer. 7:4), any prophecy suggesting otherwise was automatically considered a false prophecy that warranted the death penalty (see Deut. 18:20–22; see also Lam. 2:20). Such opposition to Jeremiah was anticipated in Jeremiah 1:17–19, and the prophet's struggles with this kind of opposition are vividly portrayed in the confessions located in Jeremiah 11–20. When the people ask in Jeremiah 26:9a (LXX 33:9a) why Jeremiah has prophesied in the name of the LORD, they are not asking him for information (cf. Jer. 32:3). Since in their minds Jeremiah's message could not possibly be from the LORD, their question is a rhetorical one designed to accuse Jeremiah of falsely representing the LORD (cf. Jer. 23:21, 25; 36:29).[7] The people's paraphrase of Jeremiah's message omits the protasis of 26:4–5: "Like Shiloh will this house be, and this city will be desolate without inhabitant" (cf. Jer. 26:6). Their characterization of Jeremiah's words reveals that they selectively heard only an announcement of judgment, a prediction that the temple and the city of Jerusalem would be destroyed, without any opportunity for repentance to avoid disaster. Jeremiah 26:9b (LXX 33:9b) narrates that all the people assembled "to" or "against" Jeremiah in the temple. Keil believes that this group is distinct from the one in verse 8 since it is nonsensical to say that the same group grabbed him and then assembled against him.[8] Others prefer to delete the phrase "all the people" from verse 8b (see *BHS* apparatus). Narrative sequencing, however, is not always temporal sequencing, and it is not necessary to view the final clause of verse 9 as a separate event that follows all previously

---

6. Holladay, *Jeremiah 2*, 105.
7. Since the penalty for misusing the LORD's name was stoning (Lev. 24:10–23), and since the penalty for what those like Jeremiah did was execution by the sword (Jer. 26:23), it seems most probable that the primary charge against Jeremiah was not blasphemy but false prophecy. See also 2 Chronicles 24:20–22.
8. Keil, *Jeremiah*, 242.

narrated events in time. It is likely that verse 9b is a summary conclusion to 26:7–9 (see this use of *wayyiqtol* in GKC §111k). Bright considers this assemblage of the people to be an example of attempted mob violence (cf. Acts 7:54–60).[9]

The officials of Judah heard the threat to Jeremiah's life and went up from the royal palace to the temple and sat for judgment (cf. Dan. 7:10b) in the entrance of "the new gate," the precise location of which is not known (Jer. 26:10 [LXX 33:10]; but see *Tg. Jon.*: "the eastern gate"; see also *b. Sanh.* 88b). It is not clear how they heard the word, whether by the loudness of the commotion or by the report of a messenger (cf. Gen. 45:2, 16; Jer. 36:12–13). It is then narrated that the priests and the prophets minus "all the people" made their case against Jeremiah to these officials and another group known as "all the people": "Judgment of death to this man, for he has prophesied against this city just as you have heard with your ears" (Jer. 26:11 [LXX 33:11]; cf. Deut. 19:6; Lam. 4:13; Matt. 26:65–66; Acts 6:13; 21:28). This indicates that the officials have heard not only the threat against Jeremiah but also Jeremiah's prophecy against the city, either Jeremiah's own words or the people's paraphrase. McKane comments that the phrase מִשְׁפַּט מָוֶת ("judgment of death") can mean either "deserves the death penalty" or "should be tried on a capital charge,"[10] although it should be admitted that the former option fits better with 26:8b ("You must certainly die!").

Before the officials have a chance to respond to the priests and the prophets, Jeremiah offers his own defense of himself before all in 26:12–15 (LXX 33:12–15). Jeremiah appeals to the officials and all the people in particular (Jer. 26:12a [LXX 33:12a]) and says that it was the LORD who sent him to prophesy against the temple and against the city of Jerusalem using the very words that they have heard (Jer. 26:12b [LXX 33:12b]; note the fronting of יהוה in the syntax of the Hebrew text). Just like Moses (Exod. 3:10), Jeremiah has been sent by the LORD (Jer. 1:7); but also like Moses (Exod. 4), Jeremiah needs proof that this is so. According to the test in Deuteronomy 18:21–22, the "prophet" whose word spoken in the name of the LORD does not come to pass is a false prophet not sent by the LORD (see Jer. 23:21, 25; 28:9, 17). The problem

---

9. "One gains the impression that Jeremiah was about to be lynched, but that the clergy wished his execution to be given the form of legality" (Bright, *Jeremiah*, 170). McKane entertains the possibility that a crowd gathered around Jeremiah simply out of curiosity (*Jeremiah XXVI–LII*, 662). While verse 9b by itself may be understood this way, it can hardly work as such in context (see especially 26:8b).

10. McKane, *Jeremiah XXVI–LII*, 678.

is that Jeremiah's prophecy would not come to pass for another twenty years or so. Thus, a demonstrated fulfillment does him little good in the immediate circumstances. There is another way, however, to show that Jeremiah is a true prophet sent by the Lord and not merely someone acting on his own. A true prophet speaks in accordance with the words of Moses, and it was Moses who first anticipated destruction and exile as a consequence of the broken covenant relationship (see Deut. 28:58–68; 29:21–27 [Eng., 29:22–28]; 31:16–18, 29). Thus, the true prophet is the one who calls the people to repentance (Jer. 23:14, 22), and this is precisely what Jeremiah does in 26:13 (LXX 33:13): "And now, improve your ways and your deeds and obey the voice of the Lord that the Lord may relent concerning the calamity that he has spoken against you" (cf. Jer. 7:3, 5; 26:3; Jon. 3:8–10).

Jeremiah acknowledges in 26:14 (LXX 33:14) that the authorities have the power to do with him as they please: "And look, I [MT: And as for me, look, I] am in your hand. Do to me according to what is good and upright in your eyes" (cf. Josh. 9:25; Jer. 38:5). Nevertheless, he also recognizes that God is in control of the situation: "Only know for sure that if you kill me, you are putting innocent blood on yourselves and on this city and on its inhabitants, for in truth the Lord sent me to you to speak in your ears all these words" (Jer. 26:15 [LXX 33:15]; cf. 2 Kgs. 21:16; 24:4; Jer. 2:34; 7:6; 19:4; 22:3, 17). Jeremiah will be vindicated one way or another. Ultimately, it is the hand of Ahikam that delivers him from the hand of the people (Jer. 26:24 [LXX 33:24]).

After Jeremiah's defense, the officials and all the people respond to the priests and the prophets by saying that there should be no judgment of death for him, because he has spoken in the name of the Lord (Jer. 26:16 [LXX 33:16]; see Deut. 18:19; cf. Luke 23:4, 15, 22, 25). In other words, Jeremiah has claimed to be a prophet sent by the Lord. Therefore, according to the law, it is not enough to disagree with Jeremiah's message. In order to put him to death, it must be demonstrated either that he has represented other gods (Deut. 13) or that his prophecy has not come to pass, which will take time (Deut. 18:20–22).[11] Thus, the officials and all the people do not necessarily embrace Jeremiah and his message, but they are willing to grant him the benefit of the doubt and the right to due legal process (cf. the role of the officials in Jer. 36:19). As noted, the intervention of the influential

---

11. If the people repent, then Jeremiah's words will prove to be true when the city of Jerusalem and its temple avoid disaster. If the people do not repent, then his words will prove to be true when both the city and the temple are destroyed.

Ahikam will still be required for Jeremiah to avoid falling into the hands of the mob (Jer. 26:24; cf. Judg. 6:31–32).

Another group emerges in 26:17 (LXX 33:17): men from the elders of the land. These are apparently older, respected men of the community whose opinion on matters such as these is valued. They wisely appeal to a historical precedent for the assembly to consider (cf. Acts 5:33–42). The precedent is the reaction to the prophecy of the eighth-century prophet Micah the Morasthite (Mic. 1:1, 14) who prophesied in the days of Hezekiah to all the people of Judah (Jer. 26:18 [LXX 33:18]). Micah's prophecy, like Jeremiah's, was a prophecy of doom for the city of Jerusalem and the temple: "Zion, like a field it will be plowed; and Jerusalem, ruins it will be, and the mountain of the house [i.e., the temple mount] will become high places of a forest" (see Mic. 3:12; cf. 1 Kgs. 9:8; Ps. 79:1; 2 Chr. 7:21; 4Q371, 372).[12] Yet Hezekiah (and all Judah) did not kill Micah as the priests and prophets have proposed to do with Jeremiah (Jer. 26:19 [LXX 33:19]). Rather, Hezekiah (and all Judah) feared the LORD and appeased the LORD with the result that the LORD relented concerning the calamity that he spoke against them (cf. Jer. 26:3b, 13b).[13] The elders' use of rhetorical questions to

---

12. "The marginal note in the MT indicates that the announcement of judgment in Micah 3:12 is the middle verse of the Book of the Twelve (cf. 4Q371, 372). Jeremiah 26:18 is usually understood to be a citation of Micah 3:12, but the spelling of "ruins" (עיין) in Micah 3:12 suggests that the textual form of the prophecy in the book of Micah is actually later than the one in Jer. 26:18 (see GKC §87e; see also Mic. 1:6), even though the prophecy itself is attributed to Micah. Thus, what Jeremiah 26:18 cites is the oral prophecy of Micah. The composer of the Twelve, who consistently cites the book of Jeremiah in his work, quotes Jeremiah 26:18 in a deliberately later form to mark the middle of his composition. The connection to the Jeremiah context suggests a more positive reception of Micah than what he received according to Micah 2:6. Was Micah's prophecy not fulfilled simply because the Assyrians did not capture Jerusalem in the time of Hezekiah (Jer. 26:19)? This is apparently not the inner-biblical understanding of the prophecy. Hezekiah was able to avoid disaster (2 Kgs. 18–19), but the prophecy was ultimately about what would happen to Jerusalem in the hands of the Babylonians (2 Kgs. 20; Mic. 4:10; Ps. 79:1) in fulfillment of words once spoken to Solomon (1 Kgs. 9:8; 2 Chr. 7:21)" (Shepherd, *Commentary on the Book of the Twelve*, 252–53).
13. "Neither in the book of Micah, nor in the accounts of the book of Kings, nor in the chronicle of Hezekiah's reign are we told that, in consequence of that prophecy of Micah, Hezekiah entreated the Lord and so averted judgment from Jerusalem. There we find only that during the siege of Jerusalem

communicate this strongly suggests that they believe the example set by Hezekiah should be followed in the present instance, lest they be found guilty of persecuting a true prophet of the LORD. Their final comment contrasts this option with the alternative of putting Jeremiah to death: "Yet we are about to do great harm to ourselves." This echoes the warning of Jeremiah himself (Jer. 26:15). Of course, Jeremiah is ultimately not killed (Jer. 26:24); but because the people still refuse to repent, both the city and the temple do not avoid disaster.

There are at least three views on the inclusion of the story about Uriah in Jeremiah 26:20–23 (LXX 33:20–23). One says that it is the rebuttal of the wicked who argue that Jeremiah should be killed just as Uriah was killed.[14] The difficulty with this view is that there is no formal introduction of this group to distinguish them from the elders prior to the discourse. Another view says that the story is a continuation of the elders' discourse. According to this view, the story serves as a negative example to illustrate what should not be done with Jeremiah.[15] The problem is that there is no explicit indication that what was done with Uriah was a mistake not to be repeated. Indeed, it would be strange for the elders to speak so publicly and critically of a decision made by the currently reigning king (Jehoiakim). Still another view says that 26:20–23 is not the discourse of one of the parties in the account of 26:1–19 but a parenthesis added by Baruch to show the reader the gravity of Jeremiah's situation.[16] In other words, the addition indicates that, given the policy of Jehoiakim for dealing with Uriah, there is no reason to believe that Jeremiah would be treated any differently (see Jer. 36:26). Thus, despite the efforts of the officials and the elders, Jeremiah likely would have been killed if it were not for Ahikam (Jer. 26:24).

The word גַּם ("also") at the beginning of 26:20 (LXX 33:20) has been classified as both an adverb and a conjunction.[17] While it can denote addition of an entire clause, it typically denotes addition of the immediately following word (see BDB, 169). In the present instance, it functions as an inter-clausal conjunction that joins "a man" (i.e., Uriah)

---

by the Assyrians, Hezekiah besought the help of the Lord and protection from that mighty enemy. The elders have combined this fact with Micah's prophecy, and thence drawn the conclusion that the godly king succeeded by his prayer in averting the mischief" (Keil, *Jeremiah*, 244).

14. See Neusner, *Jeremiah in Talmud and Midrash*, 9, 18.

15. See Calvin, *Jeremiah*, 3:339.

16. See Kara and Malbim in Rosenberg, trans., *Mikraoth Gedoloth: Jeremiah Volume Two*, 216.

17. See the discussion in Andersen, *Sentence in Biblical Hebrew*, 154.

as an example in addition to Micah in 26:18. This man, Uriah the son of Shemaiah from Kiriath Jearim, was "prophesying" (מתנבא) in the name of the LORD (cf. Jer. 26:9, 16). Holladay suggests that the *hithpael* of נבא, as opposed to the *niphal*, indicates that Uriah was acting like a prophet or pretending to be a prophet: "If there is a distinction intended by the narrator, then Micah is presented as a true prophet by common consent, while Uriah, a contemporary of the narrator, made prophetic claims, and nothing at this point is implied about the rightness or wrongness of his message."[18] Normally, the use of the *hithpael* of נבא describes ecstatic behavior as opposed to prophetic discourse for which the *niphal* stem is usually employed (see BDB, 612). Elsewhere, however, the *hithpael* and *niphal* are used interchangeable for prophetic discourse, and that appears to be the usage in the present context. The very next clause uses the *niphal* to say that Uriah prophesied "against this land" (MT: "against this city and against this land") according to all the words of Jeremiah. Uriah, like Micah and Jeremiah, was a true prophet who prophesied similar words of judgment against the city of Jerusalem. Nothing more is known about this prophet outside the present passage.

When King Jehoiakim heard, "and all the officials" (MT: "and all his mighty men and all the officials"), Uriah's words, "they sought to kill him" (MT: "the king sought to kill him") (Jer. 26:21a [LXX 33:21a]). It is noteworthy then that Jehoiakim is not directly involved in Jeremiah's case (cf. Jer. 36:26). Furthermore, the officials from the king's house (Jer. 26:10) are the ones who say that there should be no judgment of death for Jeremiah (Jer. 26:16; cf. Jer. 36:11–19, 25). When Uriah "heard" that his life was in danger (MT adds: "and was afraid and fled"), he went to Egypt (Jer. 26:21b [LXX 33:21b]; cf. 1 Kgs. 11:17, 40; Jer. 36:19, 26; see also 1 Sam. 27). So, Jehoiakim sent men to Egypt to retrieve him (Jer. 26:22 [LXX 33:22]). The Hebrew source behind the Greek version of verse 22 is the shorter, more original text: "And the king sent men to Egypt." The MT has awkwardly added a longer substitute for "men to Egypt" but without removing "men to Egypt": "And King Jehoiakim sent men to Egypt, Elnathan the son of Achbor and men with him to Egypt." The Syriac attempts to resolve this problem by changing "men to Egypt" to "an Egyptian man": "And King Jehoiakim sent an Egyptian man, Elnathan the son of Achbor and men with him to Egypt." But Elnathan was not an Egyptian man, and the addition in the MT was likely intended to produce the following result: "And King Jehoiakim sent Elnathan the son of Achbor

---

18. Holladay, *Jeremiah 2*, 109.

and men with him to Egypt." The real difficulty with this addition is that Elnathan is known in Jeremiah 36 as someone who acts on behalf of Jeremiah (Jer. 36:12, 25; see 2 Kgs. 24:8; see also "Achbor" in 2 Kgs. 22:12, 14), making it unlikely that he would have led the effort to bring back a true prophet like Uriah for execution. Thus, the MT has added the name of one of Jehoiakim's officials here but has not taken into account his role elsewhere in the book.

The men sent by Jehoiakim brought Uriah out of Egypt and to the king who then struck him with the sword (i.e., he had him executed; Jer. 26:33a [LXX 33:23a]; cf. 1 Kgs. 18:4, 13; 19:10, 18; Jer. 2:30; Neh. 9:26; Acts 7:52). According to the Hebrew source behind Greek Jeremiah 26:23b (LXX 33:23b), Jehoiakim had Uriah cast into the grave of "the sons of his people" (בני עמו), that is, his family gravesite. According to the MT, Uriah's corpse was cast into the graves of "the sons of the people" (בני העם), that is, the graves of the common people (cf. 2 Kgs. 23:6; Jer. 17:19)—a disgrace for the prophet (cf. 1 Kgs. 13:22; see also Matt. 23:29–36). The later casting of Jehoiakim's corpse beyond the gate of Jerusalem (a donkey's burial), where it would be exposed to the elements, is retribution for the injustice done to Uriah (see Jer. 22:19; 36:30).

The parenthetical story about Uriah in Jeremiah 26:20–23 gives every indication that the reader should expect Jeremiah to be executed despite the appeal made by the officials and the elders. The use of אך ("Yet") at the beginning of the following verse, however, signals a contrast with this expectation (Jer. 26:24 [LXX 33:24]). The fronting of "the hand of Ahikam the son of Shaphan" in the Hebrew syntax also signals a contrast. Jeremiah acknowledged that he was in the "hand" or power of the officials (Jer. 26:14), but it was the "hand" of Ahikam that was with Jeremiah so that he was not delivered into the "hand" of the people to be killed. Ahikam had been an official during the reign of Jehoiakim's righteous father Josiah (2 Kgs. 22:12, 14; Jer. 22:15).[19] He was also the father of Gedaliah who later became governor of Judah (Jer. 39:14; 40:5). The fact that Ahikam was able to make the difference in Jeremiah's situation speaks volumes about the respect that he commanded. The text does not go into detail about how Ahikam was able to do this.

---

19. It is not clear whether Ahikam's father Shaphan was also the scribe by that name who served under Josiah (2 Kgs. 22:3, 8, 9, 10, 12, 14; see BDB, 1051; see also Jer. 29:3; 36:10, 11, 12). Jeremiah was closely associated with another family of scribes that included Baruch and Seraiah (Jer. 32:12; 51:59).

JEREMIAH 27 (LXX 34)

[MT adds 27:1: In the beginning of the kingdom / reign of Jehoiakim (pc Mss, Syr., Luther: Zedekiah) the son of Josiah, the king of Judah, this word came to Jeremiah from the LORD, saying,]

27:2 (34:1) "Thus the LORD said [4QJer^c, MT add: to me], 'Make [MT adds: for yourself] bonds and bars and put [MT adds: them] on your neck 27:3 (34:2) and send them [LXX^L: and send] to the king of Edom and to the king of Moab and to the king of the sons of Ammon and to the king of Tyre and to the king of Sidon by the hand of their [their > MT] messengers who are coming to meet them [to meet them > MT] in Jerusalem [MT: to Jerusalem], to Zedekiah the king of Judah, 27:4 (34:3) and charge them with a command to their masters, saying, "Thus says the LORD [MT adds: of hosts] the God of Israel, 'Thus you will say to your masters, 27:5 (34:4) "I am the one who made the earth [MT adds: the people and the animals that are on the surface of the earth] by my great strength and by my outstretched arm, and I will give it to whom it seems right in my eyes. 27:6 (34:5) [MT adds: And now I] I have given the earth [MT: all these lands] to [MT: into the hand of] Nebuchadnezzar the king of Babylon to serve him [MT: my servant; > Ms, LXX^S], and also the wild animals [MT adds: I have given to him] to serve him. [MT adds 27:7: And all the nations will serve him and his son and his grandson until the coming of the time of his land, even his (see GKC §135f), and many nations and great kings will serve by him.] 27:8 (34:6) And [MT: And it will be] the nation and / or the kingdom that do(es) not [MT adds: serve him, Nebuchadnezzar the king of Babylon, and that does not] put their neck [MT: his neck] in the yoke of the king of Babylon, with the sword and with the famine [MT adds: and with the plague] I will visit upon them [MT: that nation]," the prophetic utterance of the LORD, "until they are finished / destroyed in his hand [MT: until I finish / destroy them in his hand]. 27:9 (34:7) And you, do not listen to your prophets [LXX, Syr., Tg. Jon.: false prophets] and to your diviners and to your dreamers [MT: dreams] and to your soothsayers and to your sorcerers, saying [MT: who say to you, saying], 'You will not serve the king of Babylon.' 27:10 (34:8) For deception is what they are prophesying to you in order to move you far away from your land, [MT adds: and I will banish you (Vulg.: and banish you), and you will perish]. 27:11 (34:9) And the nation that brings its neck into the yoke of the king of Babylon and serves him, I will leave it on its land," [MT adds: the prophetic utterance of the LORD], "and he will serve him [MT: and he will work it] and live in it. 27:12 (34:10) And to Zedekiah the king of Judah I spoke according to all these words, saying, 'Bring your neck [MT: necks; MT adds: into the yoke of the king of Babylon] and serve [MT adds: him and his people and live. 27:13 Why should you die, you and your people, by the sword, by famine (nonn Mss: and by famine), and by plague, just as the LORD spoke to the nation that does not serve the king of Babylon? 27:14 And do not listen to the words of the prophets (Syr., Tg. Jon.: false prophets) who are saying to you, saying, "You will not serve] the king of Babylon, (34:11) for deception is what they are prophesying to you. 27:15 (34:12) For I have not sent them,' the prophetic utterance of the LORD, 'and they are prophesying in my name deceptively in order to banish you [MT: in order for me to banish you], and you and the prophets who are prophesying to you (deceptively) deception [(deceptively) deception > MT] will perish. 27:16 (34:13) To you and to all this people and to the priests [MT: And to the priests and to all this people] I spoke, saying, "Thus says the LORD, 'Do not listen to the words of the prophets [Tg. Jon.: false prophets] who prophesy to you, saying, "Look, the vessels of the house of the LORD are being returned from Babylon [MT adds: now quickly]," for deception is what they are prophesying to you. (34:14) I have not sent them [> MT]. [MT adds 27:17: Do not listen to them. Serve the king of Babylon and live [or, so that you may live]. Why should this city be a desolation (pc Mss: desolate)?] 27:18 (34:15) If [MT: And if] they are prophets, and if the word of the LORD is with them, let them entreat me [MT: the LORD of hosts] [MT adds: that the vessels that are left in the house of the LORD and in the house of the king of Judah and in Jerusalem may not enter Babylon].' 27:19 (34:16) For thus says the LORD, 'And concerning the rest of the vessels' [MT: For thus says the LORD of hosts concerning the pillars and concerning the sea and concerning the bases and concerning the rest of the vessels that are left in this city] 27:20 (34:17) 'that the king of Babylon did not take when he exiled Jeconiah from Jerusalem,' [MT: that Nebuchadnezzar the king of Babylon did not take when he exiled Jeconiah the son of Jehoiakim, the king of Judah, from Jerusalem to Babylon, and all the nobles of Judah and Jerusalem.] [MT adds 27:21: For thus says the LORD of hosts, the God of Israel, concerning the vessels that are left in the house of the LORD and in the house of the king of Judah and in Jerusalem,] 27:22 (34:18) 'To Babylon they will go,' the prophetic utterance of the LORD [MT: 'To Babylon they will be brought, and there they will be until the day I visit them,' the prophetic utterance of the LORD, 'and I will bring them up and restore them to this place'].""'""

Chapters 27–29 (LXX 34–36) are closely connected and serve to illustrate the difference between Jeremiah's message of judgment and the message of well-being (שלום) delivered by the false prophets (Jer. 6:13–15; 23:9–40).[1] Chapter 27 divides into three sections—vv. 1–11, vv. 12–15, and vv. 16–22—with messages to Zedekiah (vv. 12–15) and the priests (vv. 16–22) embedded within the message sent to the five kings (vv. 1–11). MT 27:1 is an addition not found in the Hebrew source behind Greek Jeremiah: "In the beginning of the kingdom/reign of Jehoiakim [pc Mss, Syr., Luther: Zedekiah] the son of Josiah, the king of Judah, this word came to Jeremiah from the LORD, saying" (cf. Jer. 26:1; 28:1). This addition contains an erroneous reference to the reign of Jehoiakim, which the Syriac and a few Masoretic manuscripts have attempted to rectify by changing it to a reference to the reign of Zedekiah (see Jer. 27:3, 12; see also MT 27:20). Both Rashi and Calvin attempt to alleviate the difficulty of MT 27:1 by suggesting that the message was revealed to Jeremiah in the beginning of Jehoiakim's reign but delivered only later during the reign of Zedekiah.[2] It is best, however, to follow the Hebrew source behind Greek Jeremiah, which generally has the shorter, more original text not only for chapter 27 but also for the whole book of Jeremiah.

The LORD instructs Jeremiah to make "bonds and bars" to put on his neck (Jer. 27:2 [LXX 34:1]; see Jer. 28:10, 12, 13; see also Lev. 26:13). It is usually thought that the words "bonds and bars" together denote one ox yoke,[3] but Holladay notes that the word על ("yoke") is not used here (see Jer. 27:8, 11, 12) and suggests that the instruction is for Jeremiah to wear a "collar" fit to bear a yoke.[4] This is a symbolic sign act designed to illustrate the message that Jeremiah is sent to deliver (cf. Jer. 13:1–14; 16:1–9; 18:1–12; 19:1–13; 32; 43:8–13; 51:59–64). According to most witnesses, Jeremiah is instructed to send "them" (m. pl.) to the five kings mentioned in 27:3 (LXX 34:2) by means of the messengers coming to Jerusalem to see Zedekiah.[5] This gives the

---

1. The names of Jeremiah and Nebuchadnezzar, which are normally spelled ירמיהו and נבוכדראצר ("Nebuchadrezzar") elsewhere in MT Jeremiah, are spelled ירמיה and נבוכדנאצר ("Nebuchadnezzar") in these three chapters with the exception of 29:21 (see Janzen, *Studies in the Text of Jeremiah*, 139–41, 145–48).

2. Rosenberg, trans., *Mikraoth Gedoloth: Jeremiah Volume Two*, 217; Calvin, *Jeremiah*, 3:348.

3. See, e.g., Keil, *Jeremiah*, 247. See also Jeremiah 2:20; 5:5.

4. Holladay, *Jeremiah 2*, 119–20.

5. The Hebrew source behind Greek Jeremiah says that the messengers are those who are coming "to meet them" (לקראתם) in Jerusalem. This

impression that Jeremiah is to send "bonds and bars" (f. pl.) to the five kings. The grammatical difficulty is that the Hebrew pronominal suffix translated "them" is masculine plural, while the nouns translated "bonds and bars" are feminine plural. Lucian's recension, however, reflects a Hebrew text without a pronominal suffix (ושלחת ["and send"]), in which case the implied object could be the message illustrated by the "bonds and bars." The text does not say why the messengers of the five kings are coming to see Zedekiah, but it is usually assumed from Jeremiah's exhortation to submit to Nebuchadnezzar that the kings have it in mind to form a coalition to rebel against Nebuchadnezzar.[6]

Jeremiah is to charge the messengers with a command to their masters from the LORD (Jer. 27:4 [LXX 34:3]). This command, which comes indirectly in the form of statements about how things will be one way or another, is prefaced by a claim: "I am the one who made the earth [MT adds: the people and the animals that are on the surface of the earth] by my great strength and by my outstretched arm, and I will give it to whom it seems right in my eyes" (Jer. 27:5 [LXX 34:4]; cf. Jer. 10:12; 32:17; 51:15; see also Jer. 21:5). Rudolph (*BHS* apparatus) suggests that the addition in the MT has dropped by accident (homoioteleuton) from the Old Greek either because the scribe responsible for

---

is likely a secondary addition. There is no antecedent for the pronoun "them."

6. "The meeting in Jerusalem of envoys from Edom, Moab, Ammon, Tyre, and Sidon to conspire with Zedekiah to revolt against Nebuchadnezzar is a direct consequence of a rebellion against the king in Babylon itself in December 595 and January 594. The rebellion is referred to in the Babylonian Chronicle: 'In the tenth year the king of Akkad was in his own land; from the month of Kislev to the month of Tebet there was rebellion in Akkad . . . with arms he slew many of his own army. His own hand captured his enemy'" (Holladay, *Jeremiah 2*, 118). See Jeremiah 25:15–26; 40:11. *Lamentations Rabbah* offers a different account of what happened (see Neusner, *Jeremiah in Talmud and Midrash*, 261–62). According to this account, Nebuchadnezzar appointed Zedekiah to rule over the five kings, and Zedekiah had freedom to come and go before Nebuchadnezzar (see Jer. 51:59). The five kings, who now resented Zedekiah's rulership over them, came to Zedekiah and belittled Nebuchadnezzar in his presence. They pretended that they thought dominion would be more fitting for Zedekiah. This gave Zedekiah a false sense of security, and he divulged to them a story about how he witnessed Nebuchadnezzar ripping the meat of a live hare and eating it. Zedekiah's story was subsequently reported to Nebuchadnezzar by the five kings, and Nebuchadnezzar charged Zedekiah with rebellion (see 2 Kgs. 24:20b).

its Hebrew source inadvertently skipped from the first instance of הארץ ("the earth") to the second, accidentally omitting the intervening text, or because the Greek translator himself did so. McKane, however, cautions against too much reliance upon this kind of explanation in chapter 27.[7] He considers it more probable that the longer text of the MT in this case is an exegetical expansion.[8] Whereas the Hebrew source behind Greek Jeremiah simply makes the claim that the LORD made the earth, the MT expands this to make explicit the implicit claim that he also made the humans and animals that inhabit the earth (see also Jer. 27:6). The claim to be the creator gives the LORD the authority to grant dominion to whom it seems right in his eyes (see Gen. 1:26–28). There is a clear echo of this in what is arguably the thesis of the book of Daniel: "the Most High is ruler over the kingdom of mankind, and to whomever he pleases he gives it" (Dan. 4:14 [Eng., 4:17]; cf. 2 Kgs. 19:15; Isa. 37:16).[9]

For the time being the LORD has elected to give the earth to Nebuchadnezzar the king of Babylon (Jer. 27:6 [LXX 34:5]; see Dan. 2:21, 37–38). Where the Hebrew source behind Greek Jeremiah has הארץ ("the earth"), the MT has כל הארצות האלה ("all these lands") (cf. Gen. 26:3). The reading הארץ does not mean "the planet earth" or "the globe," but "the immediately known inhabited earth." The MT's reading is likely an effort to refer more specifically to the lands of the five kings mentioned in 27:3.[10] According to the Hebrew source behind Greek Jeremiah, the earth has been given to Nebuchadnezzar "to serve him" (לעבדו). It is then added that the wild animals have also been given to him to do the same. In the MT, however, the LORD says that he has given all these lands to Nebuchadnezzar "my servant" (עבדי) (cf. MT Jer. 25:9; 43:10). This designation of Nebuchadnezzar as the LORD's servant, which occurs three times in MT Jeremiah but never in the Hebrew source behind Greek Jeremiah, is a secondary attempt to characterize the Babylonian king not as a willing servant but as an instrument of the LORD's will. It is possible that both readings, לעבדו ("to serve him") and עבדי ("my servant"), have been added secondarily. Neither one is represented in one Masoretic manuscript or in Codex

---

7. McKane, *Jeremiah XXVI–LII*, 686.

8. See also Emanuel Tov, "Exegetical Notes on the Hebrew *Vorlage* of the LXX of Jeremiah 27(34)," *ZAW* 91 (1979): 82.

9. See Shepherd, *Daniel in the Context of the Hebrew Bible*, 66, 79. The book of Daniel is known to be dependent upon the book of Jeremiah (see Dan. 9:2).

10. See the discussion in McKane, *Jeremiah XXVI–LII*, 687–88.

Sinaiticus. This would leave לעבדו ("to serve him") at the end of the verse to suffice.

MT Jeremiah 27:7 does not appear in the Hebrew source behind Greek Jeremiah. According to this text, all the nations will serve Nebuchadnezzar and his son and his grandson until the coming of the time of his own land, at which time many nations and great kings will serve by him (i.e., Babylon will be subjugated to them; cf. MT Jer. 25:14; 30:8).[11] The phrase "all the nations" need not refer to anything more than the many nations of the known inhabited earth conquered by the Babylonian empire. Keil suggests that the words "his son and his grandson" "simply express the long duration of the king of Babylon's power over them, without warranting us in concluding that he was succeeded on the throne by his son and his grandson."[12] The subjugation of Babylon to the many nations and great kings anticipates the fall of the Babylonian empire and of those who will conquer and rule over it. Holladay comments that the entire verse is a secondary expansion in the MT, "reflecting the interest of later generations in the reversal which will come when Babylon in turn will submit to surrounding nations."[13] The argument that the Greek translator deliberately omitted this verse due to perceived imprecision of detail in it is less convincing. Such a scenario would be inconsistent with the translator's faithfulness to his source text elsewhere in the book.

The nation that does not submit to Nebuchadnezzar and put its neck in his yoke will be punished with the sword and with the famine until it is finished/destroyed (Jer. 27:8 [LXX 34:6]; cf. Jer. 25:27–29; 27:12–13). MT 27:8 is an expanded version of the text. In particular, the addition of יעבדו אתו את נבוכדנאצר מלך בבל ואת אשר לא ("serve him, Nebuchadnezzar the king of Babylon, and that does not") creates subject-verb agreement issues (note that the following verb is singular). Thus, it will not suffice to say as Rudolph does in the *BHS* apparatus that the shorter text represented by Greek Jeremiah is due to homoioteleuton (skipping from לא to לא). The MT has also added ובדבר ("and with the plague") to complete the trio of sword, famine, and plague known from elsewhere (see Jer. 14:12; 21:7, 9; 24:10; 27:13; 29:18; 32:36). The grammar of the MT is problematic at the end of the verse where it has עד תמי אתם בידו ("until I finish/destroy them in his

---

11. The pronoun "him" does not refer to Nebuchadnezzar specifically but to the Babylonian king generally and to the Babylonian empire that he represents.
12. Keil, *Jeremiah*, 248.
13. Holladay, *Jeremiah 2*, 121.

hand"). The *qal* stem of תמם ("to be finished") is not normally transitive (see BDB, 1070). The reading of the Hebrew source behind Greek Jeremiah is preferable: עד תמם בידו ("until they are finished/destroyed in his hand") (cf. Jer. 14:15; 24:10).

The five kings are encouraged not to listen to their prophets (Jer. 27:9 [LXX 34:7]; cf. Jer. 27:14), whom the LXX, Syriac, and *Targum Jonathan* designate as "false prophets." The kings are also not to listen to their diviners, dreamers (MT: dreams), soothsayers, or sorcerers (see Lev. 19:26; Deut. 18:9–14; Jer. 23:25; 29:8). Each of these attempts to foretell the future by a variety of means. In this case, they predict, "You will not serve the king of Babylon," which is the exact opposite of Jeremiah's prophecy, but it is an attractive message because it promises well-being rather than servitude or doom. These false prophets must not be heeded, for they prophesy "deception" in order to remove those who listen to them far away from their land (Jer. 27:10 [LXX 34:8]; cf. Jer. 27:15; 29:9). Of course, they do not cause exile by design, but such is ironically the result of the reception of their false prophecy (see BDB, 775). The MT adds at the end of 27:10: "and I will banish you, and you will perish." This addition does not appear in the Hebrew source behind Greek Jeremiah. The MT has borrowed these words from 27:15b and added them to 27:10b.

As for the nation that brings its neck into the yoke of the king of Babylon and serves him, the LORD will leave that nation on its land and not send it into exile (Jer. 27:11 [LXX 34:9]; cf. Jer. 21:9). According to the Hebrew source behind Greek Jeremiah 27:11 (LXX 34:9), the verse concludes: "and he will serve him (ועבדו) and live in it." That is, the submissive nation will serve the king of Babylon and stay to live in its own land. According to the MT, the verse concludes: "and he will work it (ועבדה) and live in it." That is, the submissive nation will work its own land and live in it.

In Jeremiah 27:12–15 (LXX 34:10–12), Jeremiah reports to the messengers of the five kings that the LORD has already spoken to Zedekiah according to the above words. He has urged the king of Judah to bring his neck (MT adds: into the yoke of the king of Babylon) and serve (Jer. 27:12 [LXX 34:10]; cf. Sir. 51:26; Bar. 2:21; 4Q438).[14] In the Hebrew source behind Greek Jeremiah, the object of the imperative "serve" is found midway through 27:14: "the king of Babylon." This is then followed by the explanation: "for deception is what they are

---

14. Note that Jeremiah's report of the LORD's address to Zedekiah employs plural verbs and pronouns in the Hebrew text, indicating that the message is not only for Zedekiah but also for the people he represents.

prophesying to you" (LXX 34:11). Since this appears to be something of a non sequitur, it is usually assumed that the text from the end of MT 27:12 ("him and his people and live") to the middle of MT 27:14 has been omitted by accident (homoioteleuton; see *BHS* apparatus). The Hebrew scribe (or Greek translator) accidentally skipped from the object marker with pronominal suffix (אתו) at the end of 27:12 to the object marker (את) that precedes "the king of Babylon" in 27:14.

The content of MT 27:13–14a is very similar to that of 27:8–9 with a few key differences. Instead of predicting that the insubordinate nation will be punished with the sword, famine, and plague (> LXX 34:6) as in MT 27:8, Jeremiah indicates that the Lord has posed this to Zedekiah in the form of a rhetorical question: "Why should you die, you and your people, by the sword, by famine (nonn Mss: and by famine), and by plague, just as the Lord spoke to the nation that does not serve the king of Babylon" (Jer. 27:13; cf. MT Jer. 27:17b)?[15] Jeremiah also says that the Lord has warned Zedekiah about the false prophets (Jer. 27:14), but he gives no indication that Zedekiah has been warned about the diviners, dreamers (or dreams), soothsayers, and sorcerers listed in 27:9. Jeremiah 27:15 (LXX 34:12) adds to Jeremiah's report the Lord's further explanation that he has not sent the false prophets (cf. Jer. 14:14–15; 23:21, 32; see also Matt. 7:22). Such prophets prophesy in the Lord's name deceptively in order to banish the people into exile unwittingly (cf. Jer. 23:25; 27:10; 28:15). If Zedekiah and his people listen to the false prophets, they will perish along with those prophets (cf. Jer. 14:16; see Jer. 39; 52).[16]

The text of Jeremiah 27:16–22 (LXX 34:13–18) reports the Lord's address to the people and the priests, which differs considerably from the messages to the five kings and to Zedekiah. The messages to the five kings and to Zedekiah focus on the threat of exile, which the false prophets deny. The address to the people and the priests, however, focuses on the temple vessels and on what the false prophets are saying about them. The Hebrew source behind Greek Jeremiah 27:16 (LXX 34:13) appears to include Zedekiah and his associates along with all the people and the priests in the address ("To you [pl.] and to all this people and to the priests"). This is not a feature of the MT, which also has a different word order ("And to the priests and to all this people").

---

15. See Bullinger, *Figures of Speech*, 954.

16. Greek Jeremiah 27:15 (LXX 34:12) concludes with a conflated text not found in the MT: "(deceptively) deception." The text should say either "the prophets who are prophesying to you deceptively (= לשקר)" or "the prophets who are prophesying to you deception (= שקר)."

Such a change has likely been prompted by the thought that the priests in particular would be concerned about the fate of the temple vessels. In this address, the people and the priests are exhorted not to listen to the false prophets who say, "Look, the vessels of the house of the LORD are being returned from Babylon [MT adds: now quickly]" (for the deportation of the temple vessels, see 2 Kgs. 24:13; see also Ezek. 23:26; Dan. 1:2). The MT adds מהרה עתה ("now quickly") in order to clarify that what makes the prophecy deceptive is not the claim that the vessels will be returned at any point in the future (see Isa. 52:11; Jer. 27:22 [MT]; Ezra 1:7–11) but the claim that they will be returned very shortly (see Bar. 1:8; 4:25). Indeed, Hananiah prophesies that this will happen within two years (Jer. 28:3) as opposed to seventy years (Jer. 29:10). He is the representative of the false prophets mentioned here. The addition in LXX 34:14 ("I have not sent them") does not appear in the MT (cf. Jer. 27:15).

Jeremiah 27:17 is an addition in the MT that does not appear in the Hebrew source behind Greek Jeremiah. It reiterates the exhortation in 27:16 not to heed the voice of the false prophets. It also draws from MT 27:12b to urge the people and the priests to serve the king of Babylon and live. The rhetorical question in 27:17b ("Why should this city be a desolation [pc Mss: desolate]?") echoes that of 27:13 ("Why should you die, you and your people, by the sword, by famine [nonn Mss: and by famine], and by plague, just as the LORD spoke to the nation that does not serve the king of Babylon?"). Thus, the addition of 27:17 in the MT is essentially a patchwork of material from elsewhere in the chapter. It interrupts the flow of thought from 27:16 to 27:18–22, which is not primarily concerned with the destruction of Jerusalem but with the temple vessels.

Holladay states the key exegetical issue of 27:18 (LXX 34:15) very concisely: "Commentators and translations differ as to whether this verse is to be construed as a condition capable of fulfillment ('If they are prophets, and if the word of Yahweh is with them, then let them intercede . . .'), as the particle נָא with the verb of the apodosis implies, or whether it is to be construed as a contrary-to-fact condition ('If they were prophets . . .'), as the parallel in 23:22 and the general attitude of Jrm toward these prophets suggests" (see also Jer. 23:28).[17] Holladay prefers

---

17. Holladay, *Jeremiah 2*, 122–23. It is somewhat ironic that entreaty would be given here as a sign of a true prophet since Jeremiah himself has been told not to pray (Jer. 7:16; 11:14; 14:11). Of course, Jeremiah has continued to pray (e.g., Jer. 14:7–9, 19–22), and the prohibition not to pray has primarily served to indicate the LORD's resolve.

the latter option, but he concedes that there is also good reason to accept the former option. Malbim, who takes the former option, explains that if a message from the LORD about the remaining vessels being taken away is with these prophets privately, then they should entreat the LORD not to allow it.[18] If it were with them to publicize, then it would be for the people to repent and pray. The content of the entreaty is not part of the Hebrew source behind Greek Jeremiah. It is, however, added in the MT: "that the vessels that are left in the house of the LORD and in the house of the king of Judah and in Jerusalem may not enter Babylon."[19] This addition is based on an inference from 27:19–22.

The text of the Hebrew source behind Greek Jeremiah 27:19–22 (LXX 34:16–18) is considerably shorter than that of the MT. It reads as follows: "For thus says the LORD, 'And concerning the rest of the vessels that the king of Babylon did not take when he exiled Jeconiah from Jerusalem, To Babylon they will go,' the prophetic utterance of the LORD" (cf. Jer. 20:6).[20] According to this text, the remaining temple vessels will be taken to Babylon, and there is no indication that they will ever return. The MT has expanded this text so that it now reads in the following manner: "For thus says the LORD of hosts concerning the pillars and concerning the sea and concerning the bases and concerning the rest of the vessels that are left in this city that Nebuchadnezzar the king of Babylon did not take when he exiled Jeconiah the son of Jehoiakim, the king of Judah, from Jerusalem to Babylon, and all the nobles of Judah and Jerusalem. For thus says the LORD of hosts, the God of Israel, concerning the vessels that are left in the house of the LORD and in the house of the king of Judah and in Jerusalem, 'To Babylon they will be brought, and there they will be until the day I visit them,' the prophetic utterance of the LORD, 'and I will bring them up and restore them to this place.'" This version of the text contains two introductions to the LORD's discourse. The first in MT 27:19–20 is not followed by any discourse at all. Its expansion features material from Jeremiah 52:17 (see also 2 Kgs. 25:13–17; Jer. 52:18–23). The second introduction in MT 27:21 is somewhat redundant, but it does

---

18. Rosenberg, trans., *Mikraoth Gedoloth: Jeremiah Volume Two*, 222.

19. According to the apocryphal account in 2 Maccabees 2:4–8, Jeremiah went to the mountain from which Moses saw the land of the covenant. He found a cave dwelling into which he brought the tent, the ark, and the altar of incense. He also disallowed any marking of the way to this location, saying that God would disclose it at the appropriate time. See also *4 Baruch* 3:8.

20. For Jeconiah's (Jehoiachin's) exile, see 2 Kings 24:12–17; Jeremiah 22:24–30; 24:1; 28:4; 29:2.

add a reference to the vessels of the royal palace (cf. 2 Kgs. 24:13). The expansion of the discourse in MT 27:22 is what sets the MT apart the most. Whereas the Hebrew source behind Greek Jeremiah only says that the vessels will go to Babylon without any promise of return, the MT anticipates that the LORD will one day bring back the vessels and restore them to the temple in Jerusalem (see Jer. 29:10; Ezra 1).[21]

---

21. For the phrase הַמָּקוֹם הַזֶּה ("this place"), see the commentary on Jeremiah 7:1–15. See also Jeremiah 28:3.

JEREMIAH 28 (LXX 35)

28:1 (35:1) In the fourth year of Zedekiah the king of Judah, in the fifth month [MT: In that year, in the beginning of the kingdom / reign of Zedekiah the king of Judah, in the fourth year, in the fifth month], Hananiah the son of Azzur, the prophet [LXX, Syr., Tg. Jon.: false prophet] who was from Gibeon, said to me in the house of the Lord *before the eyes of the priests and all the people, saying, 28:2 (35:2) "Thus says the* Lord *[MT adds: of hosts, the God of Israel, saying], 'I have broken the yoke of the king of Babylon. 28:3 (35:3) Within two years I am restoring to this place [MT adds: all] the vessels of the house of the* Lord *[MT adds: that Nebuchadnezzar the king of Babylon took from this place and brought to Babylon] 28:4 (35:4) and Jeconiah and the exiles of Judah [MT: And Jeconiah the son of Jehoiakim, the king of Judah, and all the exiles of Judah who entered Babylon I am restoring to this place,' the prophetic utterance of the* Lord*], for I will break the yoke of the king of Babylon.'" 28:5 (35:5) And Jeremiah [MT adds: the prophet] said to Hananiah [MT adds: the prophet] before the eyes of all the people and before the eyes of the priests [MT: before the eyes of the priests and before the eyes of all the people] who were standing in the house of the* Lord*, 28:6 (35:6) and Jeremiah [MT adds: the prophet] said, "Amen. Thus may the* Lord *do. May he [MT: the* Lord*] make your word [Codex L: words] that you have prophesied happen by restoring the vessels of the house of the* Lord *and all the exiles from Babylon to this place. 28:7 (35:7) But hear the word of the* Lord *[MT: this word] that I am speaking in your ears and in the ears of all the people. 28:8 (35:8) The prophets who were before me and before you [pl.; MT: you (sg.)] long ago, they prophesied against many lands [LXX: much land]*[1] *and against great kingdoms about war [MT adds: and calamity (mlt Mss: famine) and plague]. 28:9 (35:9) As for the prophet who would prophesy about peace [or, well-being], it was in the coming of the word that they would recognize the prophet whom the* Lord *had truly sent [MT: it was in the coming of the word that the prophet whom the* Lord *had truly sent would be recognized]." 28:10 (35:10) And Hananiah [MT adds: the prophet] took before the eyes of all the people [before the eyes of all the people > MT] the bars [MT: the bar] from upon the neck of Jeremiah [MT adds: the prophet] and broke them [MT: it (m.)]. 28:11 (35:11) And Hananiah said before the eyes of [MT adds: all] the people,*

---

1.   See Henry St. John Thackeray, *A Grammar of the Old Testament in Greek According to the Septuagint*, vol. 1, *Introduction, Orthography, and Accidence* (Cambridge: Cambridge University Press, 1909), 143.

saying, "Thus says the LORD, 'Thus I will break the yoke of [MT adds: Nebuchadnezzar] the king of Babylon [MT adds: within two years] from upon the neck of all the nations.'" And Jeremiah [MT adds: the prophet] went on his way.

28:12 (35:12) And the word of the LORD came to Jeremiah [Syr. adds: the prophet] after Hananiah [MT adds: the prophet] broke the bars [MT: the bar] from upon his neck [MT: the neck of Jeremiah the prophet], saying, 28:13 (35:13) "Go and say to Hananiah, saying, 'Thus says the LORD, "Bars of wood you have broken, but I will make [MT: you will make] in their place bars of iron. 28:14 (35:14) For thus says the LORD [MT adds: of hosts, the God of Israel], 'A yoke of iron I have put upon the neck of all the nations [MT: all these nations] to serve [MT adds: Nebuchadnezzar] the king of Babylon [MT adds: and they will serve him, and also the wild animals I have given to him].'"" 28:15 (35:15) And Jeremiah [MT adds: the prophet] said to Hananiah [MT adds: the prophet], "[MT adds: Listen, Hananiah,] [t]he LORD has not sent you, and you have caused [MT: and you, you have caused] this people to trust in deception. 28:16 (35:16) Therefore, thus says the LORD, 'Look, I am about to send you away from the surface of the earth. In this year you are going to die [Tg. Jon. adds: and in another year you will be buried], [MT adds: for rebellion is what you have spoken against the LORD].'" 28:17 (35:17) And he died in the seventh month [MT: And Hananiah the prophet died in that year, in the seventh month (Tg. Jon.: and he was buried in the seventh month)].

The date formula at the beginning of the Hebrew source behind Greek Jeremiah 28:1 (LXX 35:1) puts the events of the narrative in this chapter in the fifth month of the fourth year of Zedekiah. This was ironically the same year that Jeremiah sent a message with Seraiah to Babylon concerning the judgment of Babylon (Jer. 51:59–64). The MT expands this date formula on the front end with two key phrases. The first is the phrase "In that year," which indicates that the events of chapter 28 took place in the same year as those of chapter 27. The second is the phrase "in the beginning of the kingdom/reign of Zedekiah" (cf. Jer. 26:1; 27:1).[2] According to MT Jeremiah 49:34–35, it was in the beginning of Zedekiah's reign that Jeremiah prophesied about the breaking

---

2.　The Hebrew word ראשית ("beginning") means "an initial indefinite period of time" and thus can refer to a period that is up to half of the total time for which it is the beginning (see, e.g., Job 8:7). It does not mean "starting point" (ראשון) or "first stage in a series of equal stages" (תחלה).

of the bow of Elam. Thus, the date formula provides some helpful context for Hananiah's words in Jeremiah 28:2–4 and the subsequent exchange with Jeremiah. Hananiah ("the Lord is gracious") is introduced as the son of Azzur, the prophet from Gibeon. The LXX, the Syriac, and *Targum Jonathan* designate Hananiah a "false prophet." He is thus a real flesh-and-blood example from the otherwise anonymous group of false prophets referenced in Jeremiah 27:9–10, 14–15, 16–18 (see also Jer. 6:13–15; 14:13; 23:9–40). Hananiah's discourse is introduced as that which he said "to me" (אלי). Since Jeremiah is referenced in the third person for the remainder of the chapter, Rudolph suggests that אלי is an abbreviation for אל ירמיה ("to Jeremiah") (see *BHS* apparatus). Hananiah spoke to Jeremiah in the temple in the presence of the priests and all the people. It is noteworthy that this was the same audience that threatened Jeremiah's life in Jeremiah 26:7–9.[3]

Hananiah prefaces his words with the typical introductory formula for a prophecy in the name of the Lord, as if he were sent by the Lord himself: "Thus says the Lord [MT adds: of hosts, the God of Israel, saying]" (Jer. 28:2a [LXX 35:2a]; see also Jer. 28:11). The opening claim that he attributes to the Lord is simple and straightforward: "I have broken the yoke of the king of Babylon" (Jer. 28:2b [LXX 35:2b]). This is a reference to the yoke symbolized by Jeremiah's collar in chapter 27 (see Jer. 27:2, 8, 12). For Hananiah, the end of the subjugation to Nebuchadnezzar is as good as done (cf. Jer. 28:3–4, 11). The Talmud suggests that Hananiah is making an argument a fortiori based on Jeremiah's prophecy in the beginning of Zedekiah's reign concerning the breaking of the bow of Elam (MT Jer. 49:34–35).[4] If the Lord says that he will break the bow of Elam, how much more can it be said that he will break the yoke of Babylon? It is also possible that Jeremiah's prophecy in the fourth year of Zedekiah about the fall of Babylon has given Hananiah the confidence to speak in this manner (Jer. 51:59–64). Of course, both Isaiah and Jeremiah speak of the removal or the breaking of an enemy's yoke (see Isa. 9:3 [Eng., 9:4]; 10:27; 14:3, 25; Jer. 30:8), but it is in the timing of such deliverance that they differ with prophets like Hananiah. For Jeremiah, the historical deliverance from Babylonian bondage will not take place for another seventy years (Jer. 29:10; cf. Isa. 14:3, 25). For both Isaiah and Jeremiah, the

---

3. Jeremiah was disallowed entry into the temple in the fourth year of Jehoiakim (Jer. 36:5) presumably because of his temple gate speech in the beginning of Jehoiakim's reign (Jer. 7:1–15; 26). Now, during the reign of Zedekiah, he apparently has access to the temple once again.

4. See Neusner, *Jeremiah in Talmud and Midrash*, 353.

ultimate restoration will take place in the messianic deliverance from a future and final enemy in the eschaton (see Isa. 9:3, 5–6 [Eng., 9:4, 6–7]; 10:20–27 [cf. Dan. 9:24–27]; 11–12; Jer. 30:8–9, 24 [cf. Hos. 3:5; Ezek. 34:23]). Hananiah's prophecy, on the other hand, essentially negates the possibility of any substantial subjection to the Babylonians and only promises a kind of status quo version of well-being.

Hananiah goes on to say on behalf of the Lord that the temple vessels will be restored to Jerusalem within two years (Jer. 28:3 [LXX 35:3]; cf. Jer. 27:16–22). The MT adds that these are the vessels that Nebuchadnezzar took from the temple in Jerusalem and brought to Babylon (see again 2 Kgs. 24:13; Dan. 1:2). Hananiah also says that Jeconiah (Jehoiachin) and the Judean exiles will be restored from Babylon to Jerusalem (Jer. 28:4 [LXX 35:4]; see 2 Kgs. 24:12–17; Jer. 22:24–30; 24:1; 29:2).[5] Calvin raises the question of whether such a return of Jehoiachin would mean the abdication of Zedekiah.[6] Of course, Jehoiachin never does return, and the book of Jeremiah concludes with Jehoiachin in the thirty-seventh year of his exile (561 BC) living out the rest of his days in Babylon (Jer. 52:31–34; cf. 2 Kgs. 25:27–30). As for the temple vessels, they do not return until the completion of seventy years (Jer. 29:10; Ezra 1).

The introduction to Jeremiah's response in 28:5 (LXX 35:5) features two key differences between the Hebrew source behind Greek Jeremiah and the MT. The first is the MT's addition of הנביא ("the prophet") as a designator for the names of Jeremiah and Hananiah. This happens throughout the chapter. Bright suggests that "the writer wished with the utmost emphasis—and irony—to point up the fact that prophet was contradicting prophet, and in the name of Yahweh."[7] This is not the first showdown between true and false prophets (see, e.g., 1 Kgs. 18:19–40). Perhaps the most comparable precedent is the story of Micaiah in 1 Kings 22 in which the true prophet prophesies death for Ahab in the upcoming battle against the Syrians, while the false prophets predict victory. The second difference between the two Hebrew versions of Jeremiah 28:5 is the word order. Where the Hebrew source behind Greek Jeremiah has "before the eyes of all the people and before the eyes of the priests," the MT has "before the eyes of the priests and before the eyes of all the people." McKane, following Duhm, notes the potential significance of the difference: "If the order of MT ('in the presence of the priests and all the people who were standing

---

5. The MT has an expanded version of this verse.
6. Calvin, *Jeremiah*, 3:389–90.
7. Bright, *Jeremiah*, 201.

in Yahweh's house') is followed, העמדים refers to both the priests and people and a particular sense of priestly service cannot be attached to it. This becomes a possibility with the word order of Sept. ('in the presence of all the people and the priests who were serving in Yahweh's house')."[8]

Jeremiah initially appears to affirm Hananiah's prophecy: "Amen. Thus may the Lord do. May he [MT: the Lord] make your word [Codex L: words] that you have prophesied happen by restoring the vessels of the house of the Lord and all the exiles from Babylon to this place" (Jer. 28:6 [LXX 35:6]).[9] A comparison with Micaiah's sarcastic repetition of the words of the false prophets (1 Kgs. 22:12b, 15b) might lead the reader to think that Jeremiah is somewhat disingenuous in his response, but it is preferable to assume that Jeremiah genuinely desires the speedy return of the vessels and the exiles, even if that return were to make him a false prophet for his preaching of the opposite.[10] He is nevertheless (אך) bound to proclaim the truth of the word of the Lord that he has received (Jer. 28:7 [LXX 35:7]).

Jeremiah appeals to the precedent of the former prophets who prophesied against many lands and against great kingdoms concerning war (Jer. 28:8 [LXX 35:8]; cf. Jer. 23:22).[11] This no doubt refers to the words of judgment associated with prophets such as Amos, Hosea, Isaiah, Micah, and Nahum in whose line Jeremiah now stands. Such words have never been popular (Isa. 6:9–10). Jeremiah's point is not that true prophets never proclaim well-being, nor is it that prophecies of judgment need not be fulfilled in order to be true.[12] Rather, it is that prophecies of well-being are normally for the future and not for the present.[13] Prophecies of judgment must be vindicated by their fulfillment (see Deut. 18:20–22), but they come with greater credibility precisely because there is no compelling reason for a false prophet to

---

8. McKane, *Jeremiah XXVI–LII*, 711.
9. The restart of the introduction ("and Jeremiah said") in 28:6 may be due to the length of 28:5.
10. See Calvin, *Jeremiah*, 3:391–94; Keil, *Jeremiah*, 251.
11. The MT adds: "and calamity (רעה) [mlt Mss: famine (רעב)] and plague" (cf. Jer. 27:8, 13).
12. Rashi suggests that the possibility of God relenting concerning a prophecy of judgment (e.g., Jon. 3) makes its fulfillment unnecessary in order for it to be true (Rosenberg, trans., *Mikraoth Gedoloth: Jeremiah Volume Two*, 225), but the opportunity for repentance is often a feature of the prophecy itself.
13. See Malbim in Rosenberg, trans., *Mikraoth Gedoloth: Jeremiah Volume Two*, 226.

fabricate such an unpopular message. On the other hand, any prophet of yesteryear who would prophesy about immediate peace or well-being could easily have been motivated by popularity or financial compensation (see, e.g., Mic. 3:5). It was thus only in the coming to pass of the prophecy that the people would acknowledge such a prophet as one who was truly sent by the Lord (Jer. 28:9 [LXX 35:9]).[14] This was the test that was to be applied to anyone who claimed to speak a word in the Lord's name (Deut. 18:20–22; see also Deut. 13:2–4 [Eng., 13:1–3]). Jeremiah's history lesson indirectly challenges the veracity of Hananiah's prophecy and claims credibility for his own.

Hananiah, undeterred by the implications of Jeremiah's reply, reacts by taking the bars from Jeremiah's neck and breaking them (Jer. 28:10 [LXX 35:10]). The Hebrew source behind Greek Jeremiah has a feminine plural noun מוֹטוֹת or מֹטוֹת ("bars") and a subsequent third feminine plural pronominal suffix on the verb to refer back to it (cf. Jer. 27:2; 28:13). The MT has a feminine singular noun מוֹטָה ("bar") and a following third masculine singular suffix on the verb (cf. Jer. 28:12). Hananiah's gesture takes Jeremiah's sign act (Jer. 27:2), which was symbolic of servitude to the king of Babylon, and transforms it into one of his own, which symbolizes liberation. Not only is Hananiah unswayed by Jeremiah's response to him, but also he raises the stakes of his own prophecy. In 28:2–4, he claimed that the Lord would bring back the temple vessels and the Judean exiles within two years. Now he claims that just as he has broken Jeremiah's bars so will the Lord break the yoke of the king of Babylon (MT adds: "within two years") not just from the neck of Judah but from the neck of all the nations as well (Jer. 28:11a [LXX 35:11a]). At this, Jeremiah goes on his way (Jer. 28:11b [LXX 35:11b]), which apparently means that he departs the scene (cf. Gen. 19:2; 1 Sam. 30:2),[15] although it is not clear to where

---

14. "His design was not to prove that all were true prophets who predicted something that was true, for this was not his subject; but he took up another point—that all who predicted this or that, which was afterwards found to be vain, were thus convicted of falsehood" (Calvin, *Jeremiah*, 3:398–99). In addition to the ability to create (see Jer. 10:11–15), the ability to announce future events is what sets the Lord apart from other so-called gods (see Isa. 44:7).

15. This is not necessarily an indication that Jeremiah is exasperated, nor does it automatically signal his restraint and his willingness to take the high road. It may only be that Jeremiah has already said what he needs to say in 28:6–9 until he receives another word from the Lord in 28:12.

he departs. In any case, he must be summoned to go to Hananiah in order to continue the conversation (see Jer. 28:13a [LXX 35:13a]).

It is not evident how much time transpires between Jeremiah's departure in 28:11b and his return to deliver the word of the LORD to Hananiah in 28:12–17. The text simply says that the word of the LORD came to Jeremiah after Hananiah broke his bars (Jer. 28:12 [LXX 35:12]). It is also not evident whether the encounter in 28:12–17 takes place in the temple in the presence of the priests and the people (cf. Jer. 28:1b). It is possible that the two prophets met alone at another location. Jeremiah is instructed to go to Hananiah and say on behalf of the LORD, "Bars of wood you have broken, but I will make [MT: you will make] in their place bars of iron" (Jer. 28:13 [LXX 35:13]; cf. Deut. 28:48). The difference between the Hebrew source behind Greek Jeremiah and the MT is the difference between ועשיתי ("but I will make") and ועשית ("but you will make"). Since it is not for Hananiah to perform a symbolic sign act in the manner of Jeremiah (Jer. 27:2), the former reading is preferable. Malbim suggests that the replacement of the broken bars of wood with bars of iron signifies that any attempt to rebel against Nebuchadnezzar will be met with even more severe subjugation.[16] Keil, on the other hand, comments that Hananiah's action does not alter the divine decree but serves to set up the explication of the fact that the yoke of the king of Babylon is not so easily broken.[17] The LORD explains, "A yoke of iron I have put upon the neck of all the nations [MT: all these nations] to serve [MT adds: Nebuchadnezzar] the king of Babylon [MT adds: and they will serve him, and also the wild animals I have given to him]" (Jer. 28:14 [LXX 35:14]). The MT's "all these nations" may be a reference to the nations in Jeremiah 27:3 (see "all these lands" in MT Jer. 27:6). The addition at the end of MT 28:14 ("and they will serve him, and also the wild animals I have given to him"), which is not in the Hebrew source behind Greek Jeremiah, comes from Jeremiah 27:6.

Jeremiah then speaks directly to Hananiah, and his tone is quite different from that which he took in 28:6–9: "The LORD has not sent you, and you have caused [MT: and you, you have caused] this people to trust in deception" (Jer. 28:15 [LXX 35:15]; cf. Jer. 14:14; 23:21, 32; 27:15; 29:9, 31). Now that Hananiah has shown his resistance to Jeremiah's diplomacy, Jeremiah no longer concedes that the fulfillment of Hananiah's false prophecy would be desirable, nor does he offer again the lesson from the past about the prophets of old (Jer. 28:6–9). Rather,

---

16. Rosenberg, trans., *Mikraoth Gedoloth: Jeremiah Volume Two*, 227. See also McKane, *Jeremiah XXVI–LII*, 713.

17. Keil, *Jeremiah*, 252.

he states bluntly that Hananiah has not been sent by the Lord at all. Hananiah has spoken falsely in the Lord's name, leading the people astray. It may be asked how Jeremiah can know this prior to the conclusion of the two years in Hananiah's prophecy (Jer. 28:3). Jeremiah appeals to the announcement of judgment against Hananiah from the Lord himself: "Look, I am about to send you away from the surface of the earth. In this year you are going to die [MT adds: for rebellion is what you have spoken against the Lord]" (Jer. 28:16 [LXX 35:16]). Hananiah has not been "sent" by the Lord, but the Lord is going to "send" him away from the earth's surface (cf. Gen. 6:7; Acts 22:22). Hananiah will die within the first year of his prophecy. The fulfillment test in Deuteronomy 18:20–22 for those who speak in the name of the Lord is for the people to determine whether they have heard true or false prophecy. It is not for the Lord. The Lord can determine whether a self-proclaimed prophet is false prior to the time when his prophecy is supposed to come to pass. He knows whether he has called and sent a prophet to speak a word in his name. The MT adds at the end of 28:16 an explanation for Hananiah's death penalty: "for rebellion is what you have spoken against the Lord." This comes from Deuteronomy 13:6 (Eng., 13:5; see also Jer. 29:32). It associates Hananiah with those who lead the people after "other gods" (see Deut. 13:2–4 [Eng., 13:1–3]; see also Deut. 18:20).[18] Misrepresentation of the Lord's name and voice is a form of idolatry (see Exod. 20:3–7; Deut. 5:7–11). Thus, Hananiah pays the penalty for false prophecy (Deut. 13:6 [Eng., 13:5]; 18:20) and dies in the seventh month (Jer. 28:17 [LXX 35:17]; cf. Ezek. 11:13), a mere two months after making his claim (Jer. 28:1). The precise nature of his death is not disclosed.

---

18. Such "prophets" may even be able to give a confirmatory sign or wonder (Deut. 13:2–3 [Eng., 13:1–2]), but the content of their message must be measured against true revelation already received (Deut. 13:5 [Eng., 13:4]; cf. Gal. 1:8).

JEREMIAH 29 (LXX 36)

29:1 (36:1) And these are the words of the document that Jeremiah [MT adds: the prophet] sent from Jerusalem to the [MT adds: rest of the] elders of the exiles and to the priests and to the prophets [LXX, Syr.: false prophets; Tg. Jon.: scribes], a letter to Babylon to the exiles [> MT], and to all the people [MT adds: whom Nebuchadnezzar exiled from Jerusalem to Babylon] 29:2 (36:2) after the departure of Jeconiah the king and the queen mother and the officials and every free person [MT: the officials of Judah and Jerusalem] and smiths [LXX: prisoner] and craftsmen [MT: and the craftsmen and the smiths (Tg. Jon.: gatekeepers)] from Jerusalem 29:3 (36:3) by the hand of Elasah the son of Shaphan and Gemariah the son of Hilkiah whom Zedekiah the king of Judah sent to [MT adds: Nebuchadnezzar] the king of Babylon, to Babylon, saying, 29:4 (36:4) "Thus says the Lord *[MT adds: of hosts] the God of Israel to the exiles whom I exiled [Syr.: who were exiled] from Jerusalem [MT adds: to Babylon], 29:5 (36:5) 'Build houses and settle; and plant gardens and eat their fruit; 29:6 (36:6) and [> MT] take wives and father sons and daughters; and take wives for your sons and give your daughters to men [MT adds: that they may bear sons and daughters]; and increase and do not decrease; 29:7 (36:7) and seek for the peace [or, well-being] of the land [MT: and seek the peace of the city] where I have exiled you and pray on their [MT: its] behalf to the* Lord, *for in their [MT: its] peace [or, well-being] you will have peace [or, well-being].' 29:8 (36:8) For thus says the* Lord *[MT adds: of hosts, the God of Israel], 'Do not let the prophets [LXX, Tg. Jon.: false prophets] who are in your midst deceive you, and do not let your diviners deceive you [MT: and your diviners], and do not listen to your dreams that you dream [MT: that you cause to dream], 29:9 (36:9) for deception is what they are prophesying [Codex L: for in deception they are prophesying] to you in my name, and [> MT] I did not send them,' [MT adds: the prophetic utterance of the* Lord]. *29:10 (36:10) For thus says the* Lord, *'When seventy years are fulfilled for Babylon, I will make my words concerning you happen [MT: I will make happen concerning you my good word] to restore you to this place. 29:11 (36:11) And I am making concerning you a plan for well-being and not harm to give to you these things [MT: For I, I know the plans that I am making concerning you,' the prophetic utterance of the* Lord, *'plans for well-being and not for harm, to give to you a future and a hope]. 29:12 (36:12) And you will pray to me, and I will listen to you [MT: And you will call me and you will go (and you will go > Syr.) and you will pray to me, and I will listen to you (and I will listen to you > Syr.)]. 29:13 (36:13) And you will seek me and you will find me, for you will seek me [me > MT] with all your heart [Syr.: And when you seek me with all your heart; cf. LXX[S]], 29:14 (36:14) and I will appear to you [MT: and I will be found by you,' the prophetic utterance of the* LORD, *'and I will restore your fortunes (or, captivity) and gather you from all the nations and from all the places where I banished you,' the prophetic utterance of the* LORD, *'and I will restore you to the place from which I exiled you].'*

29:15 (36:15) Because you have said, 'The LORD *has raised up for us prophets [Tg. Jon.: teachers] in Babylon,'[1] 29:21 (36:21) thus says the* LORD *[MT adds: of hosts, the God of Israel] concerning Ahab [MT adds: the son of Kolaiah] and concerning Zedekiah [MT adds: the son of Maaseiah who are prophesying to you in my name deception], 'Look, I am about to give them into the hand of [MT adds: Nebuchadnezzar] the king of Babylon, and he will strike them before your eyes. 29:22 (36:22) And they will receive from them a curse formula among all the exiles of Judah in Babylon [MT: And there will be taken from them (BDB, 544: derived from their case) a curse formula by all the exiles of Judah in Babylon], saying, "May the* LORD *make you like Zedekiah and like Ahab whom the king of Babylon roasted in the fire," 29:23 (36:23) because they did what was senseless [LXX: lawless] in Israel and committed adultery with the wives of their neighbors and spoke [NETS: gave as oracle] a word in my name [MT adds: deception] that I did not command them, and I am a witness [MT: and I am the one who knows and a witness],' the prophetic utterance of the* LORD.*"*

---

1. MT adds Jeremiah 29:16–20: "For thus says the LORD concerning the king who sits on the throne of David and concerning all the people who are living in this city, your brothers who did not go out with you into exile. Thus says the LORD of hosts, 'Look, I am about to send against them sword, famine [mlt Mss: and famine], and plague, and I will make them like disgusting figs that cannot be eaten because they are so bad. And I will pursue them with sword, famine [nonn Mss: and famine], and plague, and I will give them as an object of terror to all the kingdoms of the inhabited earth, an object of curse and horror and hissing [pc Mss: contempt] and reproach among all the nations where I banish them, because they have not listened to my words,' the prophetic utterance of the LORD, 'to whom I sent [nonn Mss: which I sent to you] my servants the prophets rising early and sending [i.e., urgently sending], and you did not listen [Syr.: and they did not listen],' the prophetic utterance of the LORD. And as for you, hear the word of the LORD, all you exiles whom I sent from Jerusalem to Babylon."

Jeremiah 29:1 (LXX 36:1) introduces what follows as the words of the "document" (ספר) that Jeremiah sent from Jerusalem to the elders of the exiles,[2] the priests, the prophets (LXX, Syr.: "false prophets"; *Tg. Jon.*: "scribes"), and to all the people (MT adds: "whom Nebuchadnezzar exiled from Jerusalem to Babylon"). The Hebrew source behind Greek Jeremiah adds that this document was more specifically "a letter (אגרת) to Babylon to the exiles" (> MT). According to Jeremiah 29:2 (LXX 36:2), the letter was sent at some point "after the departure of Jeconiah the king and the queen mother and the officials and every free person [MT: the officials of Judah and Jerusalem] and smiths [LXX: prisoner] and craftsmen [MT: and the craftsmen and the smiths (*Tg. Jon.*: gatekeepers)] from Jerusalem" (see 2 Kgs. 24:12–17; Jer. 13:18; 24:1; 28:4). The term סריסים can refer more specifically to "eunuchs" (e.g., Est. 1:10, 12, 15), but here it refers more generally to "officials," as clarified by the MT's "the officials (שרי) of Judah and Jerusalem." Greek Jeremiah reflects וכל חפשי ("and every free person"), which led the translator to render the following ומסגר ("and smiths") as "and prisoner." The MT has a different word order, putting the craftsmen before the smiths. This exile of 597 BC involved the royalty, royal officials, and artisans, leaving behind the poorest of the people of the land (2 Kgs. 24:14; cf. 2 Kgs. 25:12 [587 BC]; Dan. 1:1–5 [605 BC]). Jeremiah sent the letter by the hand of Elasah the son of Shaphan and Gemariah the son of Hilkiah whom Zedekiah sent to the king of Babylon (Jer. 29:3 [LXX 36:3]; cf. Jer. 51:59). Elasah may have been the brother of Ahikam (see Jer. 26:24), and Gemariah may have been the son of the high priest Hilkiah (see 2 Kgs. 22:4–14).

The letter begins with the typical prophetic introduction to divine discourse: "Thus says the LORD [MT adds: of hosts] the God of Israel" (Jer. 29:4a [LXX 36:4a]). This discourse is addressed "to the exiles whom I exiled (הִגְלֵיתִי) [Syr.: who were exiled (= הָגְלְתָה)] from Jerusalem [MT adds: to Babylon]" (Jer. 29:4b [LXX 36:4b]). This provides a theological interpretation of the exile (cf. MT Jer. 29:7, 14). The LORD instructs the exiles to build houses and settle down, to plant gardens and eat their fruit (Jer. 29:5 [LXX 36:5]; cf. Jer. 1:10; 29:28; see Deut. 6:11; see also 1 Thess. 4:11).[3] They are to marry and have children and take

---

2. The MT says "the rest (יתר) of the elders of the exiles," which is usually understood to refer to the surviving elders, but it is possible that this refers to a group of leading elders (i.e., the most superior of the elders; cf. Gen. 49:3). See McKane, *Jeremiah XXVI–LII*, 727–28.

3. The fact that these instructions appear elsewhere in prophecies about the New Jerusalem (Isa. 65:21; Amos 9:14) makes their application in Babylon difficult to swallow for the addressees of the letter (see also Jer. 31:5).

wives for their sons and give their daughters to men (MT adds: "that they may bear sons and daughters") so that they may increase and not decrease (Jer. 29:6 [LXX 36:6]; see Deut. 26:5; Jer. 10:24; 30:19; 44:28; Hos. 8:10; Bar. 2:13, 34). Adele Berlin has suggested that these instructions cite the activities listed in Deuteronomy 20:5–10 that provide exemption from military service, thus discouraging the exiles from revolt against the Babylonians.[4] The exiles are to seek the peace or well-being of the land (MT: "the city") where the LORD has exiled them and to pray on their (MT: "its") behalf, for it is in the peace of that land that they will have peace (Jer. 29:7 [LXX 36:7]; cf. 2 Kgs. 25:24; Jer. 40:9; Ps. 122:6; Bar. 1:11–12). Thus, the message is for the exiles to accept the consequences of their actions, to submit to the Babylonians (cf. MT Jer. 27:13–14), and to await the peace or well-being that the LORD will give them after the Babylonian exile (Jer. 29:10–11).

Rudolph suggests transposing Jeremiah 29:8–9 (LXX 36:8–9) after 29:15 (see *BHS* apparatus), but this is unnecessary, and there is no extant textual evidence to support such a move. The LORD warns the exiles not to allow the prophets (LXX, *Tg. Jon.*: "false prophets") or diviners among them to deceive them (Jer. 29:8a [LXX 36:8a]; see Jer. 29:1, 15, 21–23; cf. Jer. 5:31; 27:9–10, 14–15; 37:9), nor are they to listen to their dreams (Jer. 29:8b [LXX 36:8b]; cf. Jer. 23:25), for they are prophesying what is false in the LORD's name, and the LORD has not sent them (Jer. 29:9 [LXX 36:9]; cf. Jer. 14:14; 23:21, 32; 27:15; 28:15; 29:31). These prophets have apparently been prophesying a quick return from Babylon (cf. Jer. 28:3–4) contrary to the message of Jeremiah 29:10–11.

Only after seventy years in Babylon will the LORD restore the exiles to Jerusalem (Jer. 29:10 [LXX 36:10]; cf. Isa. 23:15; MT Jer. 25:11; 27:7, 22; 28:6; 29:32; Zech. 1:12; Ps. 90:10; Ep. Jer. 2; see also Num. 14:33).[5] Since this period concludes with the decree of Cyrus in 539 BC (Dan. 9:1–2; Ezra 1:1; 2 Chr. 36:21, 22 [Lev. 26:34–35]), the *terminus a quo* is the beginning Jehoiakim's reign in 609 BC. Jehoiakim became the first Judean king to be invaded by Nebuchadnezzar in 605 BC (2 Kgs. 24:1–4; Jer. 25:1; Dan. 1:1–2). Within the larger context of the book of Jeremiah, the historical prophecy of restoration from Babylon after a literal period of seventy years foreshadows the eschatological deliverance from a final enemy at the end of a complete, indefinite period of

---

4. Adele Berlin, "Jeremiah 29:5–7: A Deuteronomic Allusion," *HAR* 8 (1984): 3–11.

5. Thus, it is best to begin the seventy years as a young person in order to endure the hardship and to live to see the end of the exile (Lam. 3:27).

time represented by the number seventy (see commentary on LXX Jer. 25:9, 11; see also Dan. 9:24–27).

It is possible that the shorter text of the Hebrew source behind Greek Jeremiah 29:11 (LXX 36:11)—"And I am making concerning you a plan for well-being and not harm to give to you these things"—is due to an oversight (homoioteleuton) wherein a Hebrew scribe or the Greek translator accidentally skipped from the first occurrence of אנכי ("I") to the second and unwittingly omitted the intervening text (see *BHS* apparatus): "For I (אנכי), I know the plans that I (אנכי) am making concerning you,' the prophetic utterance of the Lᴏʀᴅ, 'plans for well-being and not for harm, to give to you a future and a hope" (MT). This does not, however, explain the absence of the MT's נאם יהוה ("the prophetic utterance of the Lᴏʀᴅ"). It also does not explain why the Hebrew source behind Greek Jeremiah has אלה ("these things") rather than the MT's אחרית ותקוה ("a future and a hope"). The demonstrative אלה ("these things") apparently refers back to the "words" (LXX) about restoration in 29:10 (LXX 36:10). McKane comments, "The longer Hebrew text in MT is markedly inferior to Sept. and probably arose from an unskilful expansion of the Hebrew, associated with a concern to emphasize Yahweh's foreknowledge."[6] The message of Jeremiah 29:11 is that the Lᴏʀᴅ ultimately has a plan for the well-being of his people, despite the wrong impression that the current judgment might give (see Jer. 18:11; 21:10; 36:3; 39:16; 44:11, 27 [these texts declare the opposite of Jer. 29:11 for the time being]; see also Isa. 45:7; Zech. 8:14–15). This plan involves not only the historical return from Babylon but also the final redemption of God's people in the eschaton (see Jer. 30:24; 31:17).[7]

---

6. McKane, *Jeremiah XXVI–LII*, 728.
7. Jeremiah 29:11 is one of the most misquoted and misapplied texts in all the Bible. It is frequently cited in isolation from its context as if it were a personalized promise about God's plans for the life of the individual believer concerning matters such as education, marriage and family, and employment. It is used to offset any personal problems that a believer may face with the reassurance that God has something good in store for his or her individual journey. Efforts to correct such a use of Jeremiah 29:11 are sometimes met with the rationalization that misunderstanding or misapplication of the text does not do any harm as long as it stays within the bounds of orthodoxy. This is reminiscent of the view expressed by Augustine toward the end of book one of *On Christian Doctrine* where he says that erroneous interpretation is not pernicious so long as it leads to the building up of love, yet even Augustine goes on to say that erroneous interpretation should be corrected in order to prevent further damage. The harm done with the common misuse of Jeremiah 29:11 is that it is a replacement of the book's intended

The shorter, more original text of the Hebrew source behind Greek Jeremiah 29:12 (LXX 36:12) ("And you will pray to me, and I will listen to you") has been expanded in the MT with an addition at the beginning of the verse ("And you will call me and you will go . . ."). The Syriac reflects a shortened version of the MT ("And you will call me and you will pray to me"). McKane suggests that the MT's addition of והלכתם ("and you will go") refers to the making of a pilgrimage to Jerusalem,[8] but it may simply be an introductory use of הלך ("and you will go and pray to me"; see BDB, 233–34). The anticipation of a time when the LORD will listen to the prayers of his people stands in stark contrast to his refusal to hear the people (Jer. 2:27–28; 11:11; MT Ezek. 8:18b). It also contrasts with his repeated instruction to Jeremiah not to pray on behalf of the people (Jer. 7:16; 11:14; 14:11). It presupposes a new covenant relationship (see Isa. 30:19; 58:9; 65:24; Jer. 31:31; 33:3; Zech. 13:9; Ps. 91:15). The people will seek the LORD and find him, for they will seek him with all their heart (Jer. 29:13 [LXX 36:13]; cf. Syr.: "And when you seek me with all your heart"). This presupposes a new, circumcised heart (see Deut. 4:29–30; 10:16; 30:6; Jer. 4:4; 31:33; Ezek. 11:19–20; 18:31; 36:26–27; Rom. 2:28–29; Col. 2:11 see also Hos. 3:5; Amos 5:4–6; 9:12 [LXX]; 1 Chr. 28:9; 2 Chr. 15:2; *Jub.* 1:15; Matt. 7:7), for without such a heart the people do not seek the LORD (see Deut. 29:3 [Eng., 29:4]; cf. Jer. 24:7). The short Hebrew text behind Greek Jeremiah 29:14 (LXX 36:14) concludes the sequence of *weqatal* forms in verses 12–14: "and I will appear to you" (see Gen. 22:14). MT 29:14 begins with a redundancy ("and I will be found by you") and then continues with a significant expansion based on Deuteronomy 30:3: "and I will be found by you," the prophetic utterance of the LORD, "and I will restore your fortunes (or, captivity) and gather you from all the nations and from all the places where I banished you," the prophetic utterance of the LORD, "and I will restore you to the place from which I exiled you" (cf. Jer. 23:3). This language anticipates

---

message, thus diminishing the sense of need for the Bible's unique voice. If the reader can simply substitute his or her own meaning for that of the biblical text, then there is really no need for the biblical text at all. In fact, such an exercise could be performed with any work of literature. Such a reader never sees or enters Jeremiah's grand vision of restoration for the people of God because he or she only sees the small world of his or her personal life to which the book of Jeremiah is made to speak. Rather than focusing on the biblical text to such an extent that the insignificant details of daily life fade away, readers of this kind have a tendency to make those insignificant details into the most important matters of all.

8. McKane, *Jeremiah XXVI–LII*, 729.

what the reader will find in the Book of Comfort (Jer. 30:3, 18; 31:23; 32:37, 44; 33:7, 11; see commentary there).

The dependent causal clause of Jeremiah 29:15 (LXX 36:15)—"Because you have said, 'The LORD has raised up for us prophets in Babylon'"—is immediately followed in the Hebrew source behind Greek Jeremiah by the main clause in 29:21a (LXX 36:21a): "thus says the LORD concerning Ahab and concerning Zedekiah." The connection between these two verses is very natural in terms of syntax and content. The MT, however, has interrupted this connection with its insertion of 29:16–20. While it is possible that a Hebrew scribe or the Greek translator accidentally omitted these verses by skipping from בבלה at the end of 29:15 to בבלה at the end of 29:20 (homoioteleuton), the awkwardness of the syntax and content of 29:16–20 makes it more likely that these verses have been added secondarily. With the addition, the dependent causal clause of 29:15 ("Because you have said . . .") is immediately followed by another causal clause at the beginning of 29:16 ("For thus says the LORD"). Efforts to alleviate this problem by rendering כי as "indeed" at the beginning of 29:16 appear forced.[9] Furthermore, whereas the text of 29:15, 21–23 focuses on the false prophets among the exiles, 29:16–20 has nothing to do with the false prophets. 29:16 ("For thus says the LORD") and 29:17 ("Thus says the LORD") feature a double introductory formula. The discourse is not about the exiles but concerning Zedekiah, the king who currently sits on the throne of David (cf. Jer. 22:2), and all the people still living in the city of Jerusalem, those ("your brothers") who did not go into exile (Jer. 29:16). According to Jeremiah 24, those who have already gone into exile are the "good figs" (Jer. 24:5–7), while those still in Jerusalem are the "bad figs" (Jer. 24:8–10). The LORD is about to send against those in Jerusalem sword, famine, and plague and make them like "disgusting figs" that cannot be eaten because they are so bad (Jer. 29:17; cf. Jer. 24:8, 10; see also Jer. 14:12; 27:8). He will pursue them with sword, famine, and plague and give them as an object of terror to all the kingdoms of the inhabited earth, an object of curse and horror and hissing (pc Mss: "contempt") and reproach among all the nations where he banishes them (Jer. 29:18; cf. Jer. 24:9; 25:9, 18; Bar. 2:4). This is all because they have not listened to the LORD's words (Jer. 29:19a; cf. Jer. 7:25–26; 25:5; 26:5; see also Jer. 7:13 [MT]; 11:7 [MT]; 25:3, 4; 32:33; 35:14–15; 44:4). The relative clause אשר שלחתי אליהם in 29:19b cannot refer back to "my words" ("which I sent to them"). It must refer to the subject of the verb "they have not listened" ("to whom

---

9. E.g., Keil, *Jeremiah*, 256.

I sent"). The LORD sent the prophets to them, but they did not listen.[10] Jeremiah 29:20 then attempts to make the transition back to where Jeremiah's letter to the exiles left off at the end of 29:15 in order to set up 29:21–23: "And as for you, hear the word of the LORD, all you exiles whom I sent from Jerusalem to Babylon."

The exiles have claimed that the LORD has raised up for them prophets in Babylon (Jer. 29:15 [LXX 36:15]; cf. Deut. 18:15, 18; see also Jer. 29:1), but these are the false prophets who promise a speedy return from Babylon (see Jer. 29:8–9). Therefore, because of this claim, the LORD speaks about two of these prophets, Ahab and Zedekiah (Jer. 29:21a [LXX 36:21a]). The MT adds that Ahab is the son of Kolaiah and that Zedekiah is the son of Maaseiah (see Jer. 29:25). Holladay notes that the name קוליה ("Kolaiah") may serve as the basis for a wordplay involving קללה ("curse") and אשר קלם ("whom he roasted") in 29:22 (LXX 36:22).[11] The MT also adds that Ahab and Zedekiah are those who are prophesying deception in the LORD's name (cf. Jer. 23:25). The LORD is about to give them into the hand of the king of Babylon (Jer. 29:21b [LXX 36:21b]). Of course, they have already gone into Babylonian exile, but what is meant here is that the king of Babylon will strike Ahab and Zedekiah in the presence of the other exiles. The result of this will be that their names will be used in a curse formula among/by all the Judean exiles in Babylon: "May the LORD make you like Zedekiah and like Ahab whom the king of Babylon roasted in the fire" (Jer. 29:22 [LXX 36:22]; cf. Jer. 26:6; see also Gen. 48:20; Isa. 65:15).[12] This presupposes an execution similar to the one found in the story of Daniel 3. According to Jeremiah 29:23a (LXX 36:23a), the judgment of Ahab and Zedekiah is due to the fact that they did "what was senseless" (נבלה) in Israel (cf. Gen. 34:7; Judg. 19:23–24; 20:6, 10; 2 Sam. 13:12). This is explained as the committing of adultery with the wives of their neighbors and the speaking of a word in the LORD's name that he did not command them (see Exod. 20:7, 14; Deut. 5:11, 18).[13] Such a combination of activities may seem strange at first glance, but it is to be remembered that false prophecy is closely linked to false worship (see

---

10. The MT has "and you did not listen," but the Syriac corrects this to "and they did not listen."

11. Holladay, *Jeremiah 2*, 143.

12. *Pesiqta de Rab Kahana* lists Jeremiah 29:22 among several passages from the book of Jeremiah that bestow the opposite of the priestly benediction from Numbers 6:25 (see Neusner, *Jeremiah in Talmud and Midrash*, 167). See also Fishbane, *Biblical Interpretation in Ancient Israel*, 333–34.

13. See Neusner, *Jeremiah in Talmud and Midrash*, 190–91.

Deut. 13:2–6 [Eng., 13:1–5; 18:20); and, according to Jeremiah 5:7–8, one of the symptoms of false worship (spiritual adultery) is literal adultery (see also Jer. 23:14). The LORD's discourse in the Hebrew source behind Greek Jeremiah 29:23b (LXX 36:23b) concludes: "and I am witness" (ואנכי עד). That is, the actions of Ahab and Zedekiah have not gone unnoticed by the LORD (cf. Mic. 1:2; Mal. 3:5). The MT says: "and I am the one who knows and a witness" (ואנכי היודע ועד).[14] This is likely a conflation of two synonymous variants: היודע and עד.[15]

29:24 (36:24) "And to Shemaiah the Nehelamite you will say [Syr.: And Shemaiah the Nehelamite said], [MT adds: saying,] 29:25 (36:25) [MT adds: 'Thus says the LORD of hosts, the God of Israel,] 'I did not send you in my name [MT: "Because you sent in your name (Syr.: And he sent in his name) a letter (GKC §124b[1]) to all the people who are in Jerusalem], and to Zephaniah the son of Maaseiah [MT adds: the priest and to all the priests], saying, 29:26 (36:26) "The LORD, he has appointed you priest in place of Jehoiada the priest to be overseer [MT: overseers] in the house of the LORD to every man prophesying [or, behaving ecstatically] and to every madman [MT: to every madman who prophesies (or, behaves ecstatically)], and you will put him in the stocks [LXX, Syr.: prison] and in the pillory [or, neck irons]. 29:27 (36:27) And now, why have you [pl.; MT: you (sg.)] not rebuked Jeremiah the Anathothite who is prophesying to you? 29:28 (36:28) For he has sent to us in Babylon, saying, 'It is long. Build houses and settle; and plant gardens and eat their fruit.'""[16]

29:29 (36:29) And Zephaniah [MT adds: the priest] read the letter [MT: this letter] in the ears of Jeremiah [MT adds: the prophet]. 29:30 (36:30) And the word of the LORD came to Jeremiah, saying, 29:31 (36:31) "Send to [Codex L adds: all] the exiles, saying, 'Thus says the LORD concerning Shemaiah the Nehelamite, "Because Shemaiah prophesied to you, and I did not send him, and he caused you to trust in deception, 29:32 (36:32) therefore," thus says the LORD, "Look, I am about to visit upon [or, punish] Shemaiah [MT adds: the Nehelamite] and his offspring, and [> MT] he will not have a man in your midst [MT: a man living in the midst of this people] to enjoy seeing [MT: and he will not enjoy seeing] the good that I am doing for you [MT: for my people,"] [MT adds: the prophetic utterance of the LORD, "for rebellion is what he has spoken against the LORD].'""

---

14. This follows the *qere*. For the *kethiv*, see the *BHS* apparatus.
15. See McKane, *Jeremiah XXVI–LII*, 731.
16. The LXX renders this verse as a question: "Has he not for this reason sent to us in Babylon, saying . . . ?"

This section is not a continuation of Jeremiah's letter in 29:4–23. Verses 24–28 give the LORD's response through Jeremiah (likely by letter) to a certain Shemaiah in Babylon who sent a letter to Jerusalem concerning Jeremiah's letter to the exiles in 29:4–23. (Verse 28 quotes directly from 29:5.) The piece of narrative in verse 29 is parenthetical and chronologically out of order. It recounts how Shemaiah's letter was read to Jeremiah, thus eliciting not only the response in 29:24–28 but also another letter to the exiles (see Jer. 29:30–32).

The Hebrew text of 29:24 (LXX 36:24) is the LORD's instruction to Jeremiah to say something to Shemaiah the Nehelamite ("And to Shemaiah the Nehelamite you will say"). The Syriac has adjusted this so that the text is an introduction to Shemaiah's discourse ("And Shemaiah the Nehelamite said"). Nothing more is known about this Shemaiah apart from what is found in the present passage. Redak suggests that he is called הנחלמי ("the Nehelamite") because he was חולם להם חלומות ("dreaming for them dreams") that the exiles would return to Jerusalem very soon (see Jer. 23:25; 27:9, 16; 28:3; 29:8), but, as Redak concedes, the term הנחלמי ("the Nehelamite") has a gentilic ending; furthermore, the root חלם ("dream") never occurs in the *niphal* stem.[17]

The MT prefaces 29:25 (LXX 36:25) with an introductory formula: "Thus says the LORD of hosts, the God of Israel." The Hebrew source behind Greek Jeremiah does not have this, and, despite the fact that Jeremiah is speaking on behalf of the LORD, its presence in the MT is secondary. The Hebrew text of this verse behind Greek Jeremiah simply says, "I did not send you in my name, and to Zephaniah the son of Maaseiah [I did not send you], saying" (cf. Jer. 28:15; 29:31). That is, the LORD did not commission Shemaiah to write the letter of 29:26–28 with divine authority. The MT's version is substantially different: "Because (יען אשר) you sent in your name a letter (ספרים)[18] to all the people who are in Jerusalem, and to Zephaniah the son of Maaseiah the priest and to all the priests, saying." The first difficulty with this version is that it establishes an accusation in a dependent causal clause (cf. Jer. 29:31) for a judgment that is never announced in a main clause (cf. Jer. 29:32). McKane comments, "If we search for a consequence corresponding to יען אשר, we shall not find it until the לכן of v. 32 is reached, but the grammar cannot sustain such a distance

---

17. See Rosenberg, trans., *Mikraoth Gedoloth: Jeremiah Volume Two*, 234. See also Bright, *Jeremiah*, 209.

18. GKC §124b[1] explains this not as a plural of extension but as a reference to "a sheet folded into several pages."

between the two."[19] The Syriac resolves this difficulty by altering the text to an independent clause: "And he sent in his name." According to the MT, the problem was not that Shemaiah sent a letter in the LORD's name falsely but that he sent one in his own name (i.e., by his own authority). The second difficulty with MT 29:25 is the expanded number of addressees for Shemaiah's letter. The content of the letter in 29:26–28 indicates that it was for Zephaniah. Thus, it seems unlikely that the letter was also for all the people in Jerusalem and for all the priests. Even the MT's designation of Zephaniah as הכהן ("the priest") in 29:25 and 29:29, which is not a feature of the Hebrew source behind Greek Jeremiah, is tenuous. Such a designation gives the impression that Zephaniah was the high priest when it is clear from 29:26 that he was not (but see Jer. 21:1; 37:3). MT Jeremiah 52:24 designates Zephaniah as the priest who was second in rank. The Greek text of this verse (52:24) does not mention Zephaniah's name, but both the MT and the LXX of the parallel text in 2 Kings 25:18 have Zephaniah's name.

In the letter, Shemaiah points out that the LORD has appointed Zephaniah priest in place of Jehoiada the priest to be "overseer" (פקיד) in the house of the LORD (Jer. 29:26 [36:26]). In other words, Zephaniah has a responsibility to fulfill. This is the same position once held by Pashhur (Jer. 20:1–6), the man who put Jeremiah in the stocks for his prophecy. Contrary to the MT, the LORD has not appointed Zephaniah high priest in order that there might be temple "overseers" (פקדים) (cf. the high priest Jehoiada who set up "overseers" [פקדות] in the temple during the time of Josiah [2 Kgs. 11:18]).[20] Shemaiah reminds Zephaniah that it is his duty to take every "madman" who prophesies (see Jer. 26:20; or, "behaves ecstatically" [see 1 Sam. 19:20–24]) and put him in the stocks and neck irons (see again the response to prophecy in the temple vicinity in Jer. 26). The word "madman" (משגע) is a dismissive and derogatory term used to describe true prophets by those who do not take them seriously as such (see 2 Kgs. 9:11; Hos. 9:7). Here Shemaiah has in mind Jeremiah in particular. Thus, he asks, "And now, why have you [pl.; MT: you (sg.)] not rebuked Jeremiah the Anathothite who is prophesying to you" (Jer. 29:27 [LXX 36:27]; see Jer. 1:1)? It is somewhat ironic that the Hebrew source behind Greek Jeremiah, which consistently portrays Zephaniah as the sole addressee of Shemaiah's letter, should have the plural verb גערתם, while the MT, which has expanded the number of addressees, has the singular verb גערת. The former should perhaps be corrected on the

---

19. McKane, *Jeremiah XXVI–LII*, 731.
20. The Jehoiada of Jeremiah 29:26 is unknown.

basis of the latter, unless the plural verb is intended to indicate that Zephaniah represents a larger group. Shemaiah concludes his letter with a sample of Jeremiah's prophecy to which he objects. It is a quote of 29:5 from Jeremiah's letter to the exiles in 29:4–23: "For he has sent to us in Babylon, saying, 'It is long.[21] Build houses and settle; and plant gardens and eat their fruit'" (Jer. 29:28 [LXX 36:28]).[22] Jeremiah has prophesied seventy years of exile (Jer. 29:10) rather than the two years prophesied by the false prophets (Jer. 28:3). He has encouraged the exiles to settle down and submit to Babylonian rule until the Lord sees fit to restore their fortunes. Furthermore, he has indicated that the worst is yet to come for those who still remain in Jerusalem (Jer. 24:8–10; MT Jer. 29:16–18). Shemaiah takes exception to Jeremiah's prophecy and wants Zephaniah to take action against him.

Jeremiah 29:29 (LXX 36:29) parenthetically provides the back-story for the response to Shemaiah's letter in 29:24–28. Zephaniah read the letter to Jeremiah. There is no indication that Zephaniah followed Shemaiah's instruction and put Jeremiah in the stocks. Indeed, it is not very clear at all what Zephaniah's relationship to Jeremiah was like. It is possible that he was sympathetic toward Jeremiah and simply wanted to inform him of Shemaiah's letter. It is also possible that Zephaniah was using the letter to warn Jeremiah not to prophesy anymore as before. In any case, the reading of Shemaiah's letter not only prompted the response to Shemaiah in 29:24–28 but also the word of the Lord that came to Jeremiah to send to the exiles concerning Shemaiah (Jer. 29:30–32 [LXX 36:30–32]). Thus, 29:31–32 provides the content of a second letter to the exiles in addition to the one recorded in 29:4–23. Whereas the first letter announced the judgment of the false prophets Ahab and Zedekiah (Jer. 29:21–23), this one announces the judgment of Shemaiah because he prophesied to the exiles without being sent by the Lord. He caused them to trust in a lie, that is, a short exile (Jer. 29:31 [LXX 36:31]; cf. Jer. 14:14; 23:21, 32; 27:15; 28:15; 29:9). The Lord is about to punish both Shemaiah and his offspring so that Shemaiah will not have a descendant who lives to enjoy the sight of the good that the Lord is going to do for his people (Jer.

---

21. I.e., the "exile" (גלות) is long (see Rashi).

22. The combination כי על כן sometimes appears to have the sense, "For for this reason . . ." (e.g., Gen. 18:5; 19:8; 33:10; Jer. 38:4). In other occurrences, it seems to be a pleonastic equivalent of כי (e.g., Gen. 38:26; Num. 10:31; 14:43; Judg. 6:22). McKane suggests the following paraphrase for Jeremiah 29:28: "for because you failed to keep him in check . . ." (McKane, *Jeremiah XXVI–LII*, 735).

29:32 [LXX 36:32]; cf. Jer. 17:6; 22:30; 28:16; 35:19; see also BDB, 908). In other words, neither Shemaiah nor his children will see the end of the seventy years and the restoration to follow (Jer. 29:10–14). The MT adds 29:32b: "for rebellion is what he has spoken against the LORD." This text comes from Deuteronomy 13:6. It is the same text that the MT added to Jeremiah 28:16b. False prophecy amounts to rebellion against the LORD.

APPLICATION OF JEREMIAH 25:15–29:32 (LXX 32:1–36:32)

Application of this section of the book lies in the continued development of the theme of opposition originally introduced in Jeremiah 1:17–19. The reader has already encountered significant development of this theme in the confessions of Jeremiah located in chapters 11–20. It was noted in the commentary on Jeremiah's confessions that the text deliberately depicts the prophet as a representative of the faithful remnant in order to make itself applicable for its readers. Those who follow in the footsteps of Jeremiah and devote themselves to the word of God by heeding its instruction can expect to face persecution (see Matt. 5:10–12; Acts 14:22; 2 Tim. 3:12; 1 Pet. 4:12–14).

The visceral response to Jeremiah's temple gate speech in chapter 26 and his uphill battle against the false prophets in chapters 27–29 illustrate well the struggle of those who hold fast to true prophecy in the here and now. Nevertheless, these chapters also serve to remind readers that the word of God will be vindicated, and thus all those who maintain fidelity to the word of God will ultimately see the light at the end of the tunnel—a light that shines very brightly in the following chapters of the Book of Comfort (Jer. 30–33). While false prophets and teachers may garner all the attention and popularity in the present, their time of judgment will come, and only the true word of God and its adherents will stand.

THE BOOK OF COMFORT

(Jer. 30–33 [LXX 37–40])

JEREMIAH 30:1–31:1 (LXX 37:1–38:1)

30:1 (37:1) The word that came to Jeremiah from the Lord, saying, 30:2 (37:2) "Thus says the Lord, the God of Israel, saying, 'Write all the words that I speak to you [NETS: that I gave you as oracles] in a document. 30:3 (37:3) For look, days are coming,' the prophetic utterance of the Lord, 'and I will restore the fortunes [LXX, Tg. Jon.: captivity] of my people Israel and Judah,' says the Lord, 'and I will restore them to the land that I gave to their forefathers [or, ancestors], and they will possess it.'"

30:4 (37:4) And these are the words that the Lord spoke concerning Israel and concerning Judah:

30:5 (37:5) "Thus says the Lord [MT: For thus says the Lord], 'A sound / voice of trembling / panic is what you hear [MT: we hear], "Dread!" and "There is no peace [or, well-being]!" 30:6 (37:6) Ask and see if a male gives birth, and concerning dread in which they grasp loins and deliverance [> MT]. Why do I see every man with his hands on his loins [MT adds: like a woman in labor]? Faces are turned, they have become pale / green [MT: And why have all faces turned pale / green?]. 30:7 (37:7) For that day is great [MT: Woe, for that day is great], and there is none like it [MT: without any like it (or, from where is any like it?)]; and it is a time of distress for Jacob, (37:8) but from it he will be delivered. 30:8 In that day,' the prophetic utterance of the Lord [MT adds: of hosts], 'I will break a yoke [MT: his yoke; Tg. Jon.: the yoke of the nations] from upon their neck [MT: your neck], and their bonds [MT: your bonds] I will tear *off, and they will never again serve strangers [MT: and strangers will never again serve by him]. 30:9 (37:9) And they will serve the L*ORD *their God and David their king [Tg. Jon.: the Messiah, the son of David, their king] [MT adds: whom] I will raise up for them.'*[1]

*30:12 (37:12) Thus says the L*ORD *[MT: For thus says the L*ORD*], 'I carry a fracture [MT: Your fracture is incurable], your wound is severe. 30:13 (37:13) There is no one pleading your cause, for a wound you are healed [NETS: you were doctored into pain],*[2] *there is no healing for you [MT: There is no one pleading your cause with regard to a wound, there are no medicines of healing for you].*[3] *30:14 (37:14) As for all your allies [or, friends / lovers], they have forgotten you; [MT adds: you] they do not seek. For with an enemy's wound I have stricken you, cruel discipline [MT: a cruel person's discipline], because of the abundance of your iniquity, [because] your sins are many.*[4] *30:16 (37:16) Therefore, all those who have devoured you, they will be devoured; and all your foes, each and every one of them will eat their flesh [MT: all of them (> Ms) into captivity they will go]. And those who have plundered you will become plunder, and all those who have despoiled you I will make into spoil. 30:17 (37:17) For I will bring up healing / restoration to / for you. From a severe wound [MT: and from your wounds] I will heal you,' the prophetic utterance of the L*ORD*. 'For "banished" is what they have called*

---

1. MT adds 30:10–11: '"And as for you, do not fear, O my servant Jacob; and do not be dismayed/terrified [Syr., *Tg. Jon.*: and do not break]. For look, I am about to deliver you from far away, and your seed/offspring [*Tg. Jon.*: your sons] from the land of their captivity. And Jacob will return and be quiet and at ease, and there will be no one causing trembling. For with you am I,' the prophetic utterance of the LORD, 'to deliver you, for I will make a complete destruction among all the nations where I have scattered you. But you I will not make a complete destruction, and I will discipline you justly [ESV: in just measure; *Tg. Jon.*: and I will bring against you sufferings to teach you but with judgment of restraint], and I will by no means leave you unpunished [*Tg. Jon.*: and I will not completely destroy you].'"

2. This presumably means that the healing received does no good. The people go from one wound to the next.

3. It is possible to divide the syntax of the MT differently: "There is no one pleading your cause, [there are no] medicines for a wound, there is no healing for you."

4. MT adds 30:15: "Why do you cry out about your fracture? Your pain is incurable. [Or, Why do you cry out about your fracture, that your pain is incurable?] Because of the abundance of your iniquity, [because] your sins are many, I have done these things to you."

you: "She is our food / prey [MT: It is Zion], for [> MT] there is no one seeking for her."'"

30:18 (37:18) Thus says the Lord, *'Look, I am about to restore the fortunes [LXX, Tg. Jon.: captivity; MT adds: of the tents] of Jacob, and on his captivity [MT: and on his dwelling places] I will have compassion, and a city [Tg. Jon. adds: Jerusalem] will be built on its mound, and a prominent building [LXX, Tg. Jon.: the temple] upon its rightful place [or, according to its plan] will sit. 30:19 (37:19) And thanksgiving [LXX: singers] and a sound of merrymakers will go forth from those places [lit., from them]; and I will increase them, and they will not decrease; [MT adds: and I will honor them, and they will not be insignificant]. 30:20 (37:20) And his [LXX: their] sons will come [MT: be] as before, and his [LXX: their] testimonies [cf. 4QJer^c: וְעֵדוֹתוֹ; MT: and his congregation] before me will be established, and I will visit upon [or, punish] his oppressors [LXX: those who oppress them]. 30:21 (37:21) And his majestic ones will be over them [MT: And his majestic one will be from him; Tg. Jon.: And their king will be anointed from them], and his ruler from him [MT: from his midst] will go forth [Tg. Jon.: and their Messiah from among them will be revealed]; and I will draw him near, and he will approach me [LXX: and I will gather them, and they will return to me]. For who is the one who would pledge his heart to draw near to me?' the prophetic utterance of the* Lord.[5] *30:23 (37:23) 'For the storm of the* Lord *[LXX: For the fierce wrath of the Lord has gone forth; MT: Look, the storm of the* Lord*], fury, it goes forth, a whirling [MT: sweeping] storm. Upon [MT adds: the head of] the wicked will it whirl. 30:24 (37:24) The burning of the anger of the* Lord *will not turn back until he accomplishes and until he makes happen the plan [LXX: undertaking; MT: plans] of his heart / mind. At the end of the days they [MT: you] will understand it [LXX: them (or, these things)]. 31:1 (38:1) At that time,' the prophetic utterance of the* Lord, *'I will become God to the family [4QJer^c, MT: to all the families] of Israel, and as for them, they will become my people.'"*

The text of Jeremiah 30:1–3 (LXX 37:1–3) serves as a heading for the next two chapters. Jeremiah 32 and 33 (LXX 39 and 40) have been appended to this section (see 32:1; 33:1) in order to form what is now known as the Book of Comfort within the larger composition of the book of Jeremiah. Thus far the edition of the book of Jeremiah that lies

---

5.   MT adds 30:22: "And you will become my people, and I will become your God."

behind its ancient Greek version has followed the pattern found also in the books of Isaiah and Ezekiel: judgment (Isa. 1–12; Jer. 1:1–25:13; Ezek. 1–24), nations (Isa. 13–23; LXX Jer. 25:14–31:44; Ezek. 25–32), and restoration (Isa. 40–55; Jer. 30–33 [LXX 37–40]; Ezek. 34–39). Now that the book has treated the "plucking up and tearing down" set forth in the program of Jeremiah 1:10, it is time to address the "building and planting."

The wording of 30:1 (LXX 37:1) is identical to what the reader finds in 7:1; 11:1; 18:1 (see also Jer. 21:1; 32:1; 34:1, 8; 35:1; 40:1). This time, however, the word of the LORD comes to Jeremiah not for proclamation but for writing: "Write all the words that I speak to you in a document" (Jer. 30:2b [LXX 37:2b]; cf. Exod. 17:14; Hab. 2:2). A comparison with Jeremiah 36:2, 4 suggests that Jeremiah may have dictated these words to his scribe Baruch (but see also Jer. 51:60). The explanation given in 30:3 (LXX 37:3) for this writing is essentially a summary of the message found in chapters 30–33 (LXX 37–40). Days are coming (cf. Jer. 23:7; 31:27, 31) when the LORD will restore or reverse the fortunes (see Vulg.: *convertam conversionem*) of his people "Israel and Judah." He will bring them back to the land that he gave to their forefathers so that they can possess it. The expression ושבתי את שבות עמי ("and I will restore the fortunes of my people"), which has already occurred in a slightly different form in MT 29:14 ("and I will restore their fortunes"),[6] depends upon Deuteronomy 30:3, which is part of a passage that looks beyond the broken Sinai covenant to the hope of a divinely initiated new covenant relationship (Deut. 28:69; 29:3 [Eng., 29:1, 4]; 30:6; cf. Jer. 4:4; 31:31–34).[7] The term שבות does not mean "captivity" (contra LXX, *Tg. Jon.*), as if it were from the root שבה ("take captive"). Rather, it comes from the root שוב ("turn, return") and thus is a cognate object of the main verb (see, e.g., Job 42:10; see also *TLOT* 3:1314–15).

The people whose fortunes the LORD will restore consists of "Israel and Judah." Rudolph proposes that "and Judah" has been added secondarily in both 30:3 and 30:4 (see *BHS* apparatus). This is not based on

---

6. See also Jeremiah 30:18; 31:23; 32:44; 33:7, 11. For occurrences outside the book of Jeremiah, see Ezekiel 16:53; 39:25; Hosea 6:11; Joel 4:1 [Eng., 31]; Amos 9:14; Zephaniah 2:7; 3:20; Psalms 14:7; 53:7 [Eng., 53:6]; 85:2 [Eng., 85:1]; 126:1, 4; Lamentations 2:14.

7. See Shepherd, *Text in the Middle*, 96–99. See also Amanda R. Morrow and John F. Quant, "Yet Another New Covenant: Jeremiah's Use of Deuteronomy and שוב שבות/שבית in the Book of Consolation," in *The Book of Jeremiah: Composition, Reception, and Interpretation*, eds. Jack R. Lundbom, Craig A. Evans, and Bradford A. Anderson (Leiden: Brill, 2018), 170–90.

textual evidence. It is based upon a tenuous hypothetical reconstruction of chapters 30–31 as a message of restoration for the northern kingdom of Israel from early in Jeremiah's career during the time of Josiah. According to Rudolph and others, it was only later that these chapters were updated with references to Judah.[8] Given the inherent problems of this proposal, it is best to deal with the text as it is in the extant textual witnesses. Jeremiah 3:14–18 has already provided a prophecy of the re-unification of the northern and southern kingdoms (see also Jer. 23:5–6), and it is to this reunification that Jeremiah 30:3 and the whole of the Book of Comfort look. The restoration will include believing Gentiles from among the nations in addition to the faithful remnant of Israel and Judah (Jer. 3:17–18). The Lord will restore to this people of God the lost blessing of life and dominion in the land of the covenant that was given to the forefathers for their possession (Gen. 1:26–28; 2:10–14; 15:18). According to Redak, this refers to the messianic era.[9]

Jeremiah 30:4 (LXX 37:4) gives a formal introduction to the words that Jeremiah was to write concerning Israel and Judah (cf. Jer. 30:2–3). The first subunit in 30:5–7 (LXX 37:5–7) offers a depiction of tribulation in the eschatological Day of the Lord (see Jer. 30:24). Both Rashi and Redak comment that the passage is about the war of Gog and Magog (Ezek. 38–39).[10] The Lord is the speaker ("Thus says the Lord");[11] therefore, the main verb in 30:5 (LXX 37:5) should be תשמעו ("you hear"), as in the Hebrew source behind Greek Jeremiah, rather than the MT's שמענו ("we hear"): "A sound/voice (קול) of trembling/panic is what you hear [MT: we hear]." According to Holladay, this introduces quoted material (cf. Jer. 4:15–16, 31): "Dread!" and "There is no peace [or, well-being]!" (cf. Jer. 6:14).[12] The directives in 30:6 (LXX 37:6) to ask and see if a male gives birth are clearly rhetorical. Everyone knows that a male does not give birth. Why then does every man have his hands on his loins (MT adds: "like a woman in labor")? Why have their faces turned pale (cf. Isa. 29:22)? The answer is that the day of distress (Jer. 30:7 [LXX 37:7]) has caused the men to behave like women giving birth (cf. Isa. 13:8; Jer. 4:31; 6:24; 13:21; 22:23). The Hebrew source

---

8. See Bright, *Jeremiah*, 284–87; Holladay, *Jeremiah 2*, 156–71.

9. "When the Jews returned from the Babylonian exile, only Judah and Benjamin, who were exiled there, returned" (Rosenberg, trans., *Mikraoth Gedoloth: Jeremiah Volume Two*, 237).

10. Rosenberg, trans., *Mikraoth Gedoloth: Jeremiah Volume Two*, 237–38.

11. MT 30:5 begins with the conjunction כי (> LXX), but this is not appropriate to the context (cf. Jer. 30:12).

12. Holladay, *Jeremiah 2*, 171.

behind Greek Jeremiah appears to have a double version for verse 6: (1) "and concerning dread in which they grasp loins and deliverance" (> MT); and (2) "Why do I see every man with his hands on his loins?" (cf. Jer. 46:5). At the beginning of 30:7 (LXX 37:7), the MT has the word הוי ("Woe"). The Hebrew source behind Greek Jeremiah has the form of a verb (היו) and includes it at the end of verse 6. Jeremiah 30:7 (LXX 37:7) says that the Day of the LORD is "great" (cf. Isa. 13:6, 9; Joel 2:11; 3:4 [Eng., 2:31]; Zeph. 1:14; Mal. 3:23 [Eng., 4:5]). There is none like it (cf. Joel 2:2; Dan. 12:1). It is a time of "distress" for Jacob/Israel (cf. Zeph. 1:15; Dan. 12:1; 1QM 1:11–12; 15:1), but he will be delivered from it (cf. Jer. 14:8; Joel 3:5 [Eng., 2:28]; Nah. 1:7; Dan. 12:1–2). This hope of deliverance is what makes the present passage so fitting for the Book of Comfort.

In that day of great tribulation, the LORD will break the yoke of servitude from upon the neck of his people and tear off their bonds (Jer. 30:8a [LXX 37:8a]). While this language is certainly reminiscent of Nebuchadnezzar's yoke (see Jer. 27:2, 11, 12; 28:2, 11, 12–14; cf. Isa. 14:25; Nah. 1:13), and while the MT's "his yoke" (cf. LXX: "a yoke") apparently refers to Nebuchadnezzar in a manner consistent with its historicizing tendencies elsewhere, it must be admitted that there is no explicit reference to Nebuchadnezzar in the present context.[13] Furthermore, it is apparent from what precedes and follows that an eschatological deliverance from a future and final enemy is in view (cf. Isa. 10:23, 27; Dan. 9:27; see also Isa. 9:3 [Eng., 9:4]; Ezek. 34:27). Thus, if anything, Nebuchadnezzar is prefigurative.[14] According to the Hebrew source behind Greek Jeremiah 30:8b (LXX 37:8b), the people of God will never again serve strangers (ולא יעבדו הם עוד זרים) (cf. Jer. 5:19b). According to the MT, strangers will never again serve by him/ Jacob (ולא יעבדו בו עוד זרים).[15] That is, foreigners will never again put the people of God in subjection to them. Rather, the people will serve the LORD their God and David their king (*Tg. Jon.*: "the Messiah, the son of David, their king") whom the LORD will raise up for them (Jer. 30:9 [LXX 37:9]; cf. Isa. 9:5–6 [Eng., 9:6–7]; Ezek. 34:23; 37:24; Hos. 3:5).[16] This is the language of the covenant with David (see 2 Sam.

---

13. See Keil, *Jeremiah*, 263.

14. See Jerome's comments in Wenthe, ed., *Jeremiah, Lamentations*, 203.

15. For this expression, see Leviticus 25:39, 46; Jeremiah 22:13; 25:14 (MT); 27:7; 34:9. Cf. Joel 4:17b (Eng., 3:17b): "and strangers, they will never again pass through it" (וזרים לא יעברו בה עוד).

16. The apparent lack of a relative אשר ("whom") in the LXX *Vorlage* allows either for a translation that supplies a relative ("And they will serve the

7:12; 23:1 [4QSam[a]]), and it expresses the great messianic hope of the book of Jeremiah and the Prophets (see Jer. 23:5–6; 30:21; Amos 9:11; see also *Pss. Sol.* 17:21).[17] Jeremiah 30:9 (LXX 37:9) is cited in Hosea 3:5 not by the eighth-century prophet Hosea but by the postexilic composer of the Twelve in order to set forth the program of the entire composition of Hosea through Malachi: "Afterward, the sons of Israel will return and seek the LORD their God and David their king [*Tg. Jon.*: and they will listen to the Messiah, the son of David, their king] and fear to the LORD and to his goodness at the end of the days" (cf. Jer. 29:13; 50:4; Amos 9:12).[18] The temporal context of the last days referenced in Hosea 3:5 likely comes from Jeremiah 30:24 (LXX 37:24).

MT 30:10–11 does not appear in the Hebrew source behind Greek Jeremiah. These verses have already occurred in a slightly different form in 46:27–28 (LXX 26:27–28). While they are undoubtedly well suited to the context of the Book of Comfort, making their addition in MT 30:10–11 understandable, the textual evidence strongly suggests that they are secondary. For further comment on the content of these verses, see the commentary on 46:27–28.

Jeremiah 30:12–17 (LXX 37:12–17) describes the current state of Judah as that of a battered and bruised body (cf. Isa. 1:5–6; see also Deut. 28:61; 29:21 [Eng., 29:22]). The LORD says, "I carry (נושא) a fracture [MT: Your fracture is incurable (אנוש)], your wound is severe" (Jer. 30:12 [LXX 37:12]; cf. Jer. 6:7; 8:21; 10:19; 14:17; 15:18; Mic. 1:9; Nah. 3:19).[19] 30:13a (LXX 37:13a) translates this metaphor: "There is no one pleading your cause" (cf. Jer. 5:28; 22:16). There is no healing (Jer. 30:13b [LXX 37:13b]; cf. Jer. 8:22; 46:11; Hos. 5:13). Judah's allies have all forgotten her (note the use of second feminine singular pronouns to refer to Judah throughout vv. 12–17); they do not seek or care for her (Jer. 30:14a [LXX 37:14a]; see Jer. 2:18; 4:30; Lam. 1:2). For it is with an enemy's wound that the LORD has stricken Judah, "cruel discipline" (MT: "a cruel person's discipline") (Jer. 30:14b [LXX 37:14b]; cf. Isa. 9:12 [Eng., 9:13]; 60:10; Jer. 31:18). This has been due to the

---

LORD their God and David their king whom I will raise up for them") or a translation like the one that appears in the LXX: "And they will work for the Lord their God, and David their king I will raise up for them." Cf. Hosea 3:5, which has "the LORD their God and David their king" as a coordinated double object.

17. See Calvin, *Jeremiah*, 4:15, 20.
18. See Shepherd, *Commentary on the Book of the Twelve*, 23–25, 52–54.
19. This apparently means that the LORD brings the fracture upon the people (see Jer. 30:14b).

abundance of Judah's iniquity, her many sins (cf. Jer. 5:6; 13:22; 14:7). The MT has added 30:15, a text that does not appear in the Hebrew source behind Greek Jeremiah. It asks Judah why she cries out about her fracture and incurable pain. It then repeats the thought of 30:14b to say that Judah has brought this situation on herself. It is no injustice on God's part to judge her in this way.

The inferential conjunction לכן ("Therefore") at the beginning of 30:16 (LXX 37:16) is often rendered as "But" or the like, but this is based on the assumption that 30:16 immediately follows 30:15. In the Hebrew source behind Greek Jeremiah, 30:16 follows 30:14, and 30:15 is absent from the text. Thus, the sense is that all of Judah's allies have forgotten her (30:14); therefore, it is left for the Lord to plead her cause and bring healing/restoration to her (30:16–17). All those who have devoured Judah will be devoured (Jer. 30:16a [LXX 37:16a]; cf. Jer. 2:3; 5:17; 8:16; 10:25; 50:7). Greek Jeremiah reflects the following Hebrew text: וכל צריך כלה בשרם יאכלו ("and all your foes, each and every one of them will eat their flesh") (cf. Deut. 28:53–57; 2 Kgs. 6:24–31; Isa. 9:19 [Eng., 9:20]; 49:26; Jer. 19:9; Ezek. 5:10; Zech. 11:9; Lam. 2:20; 4:10).[20] The MT, however, has a different text: וכל צריך כלם בשבי ילכו ("and all your foes, all of them [> Ms] into captivity they will go") (cf. Jer. 22:22). Those who have plundered Judah will become plunder, and the Lord will make all those who have despoiled Judah into spoil (Jer. 30:16b [LXX 37:16b]; cf. Jer. 50:10–11; Hab. 2:8; see also Jer. 2:14). For, as the Lord explains in 30:17a (LXX 37:17a), he will bring up "healing/restoration" (ארכה) for Judah and heal her "from a severe wound" (ממכה נחלה; MT: "and from your wounds" [וממכותיך]; cf. Jer. 33:6; see also Isa. 30:26b; 61:1; Ezek. 34:16; Hos. 14:5 [Eng., 14:4]; Mal. 3:20 [Eng., 4:2]). This is because Judah's enemies have called her "banished" (נדחה) (Jer. 30:17b [LXX 37:17b]). They have said, "She is our food/prey (צידנו) [MT: It is Zion (ציון)], for [> MT] there is no one seeking (דרש) for her" (cf.

---

20. See the discussion in Tov, *Text-Critical Use of the Septuagint*, 187. Tov suggests that one of the two words in the MT (בשבי ילכו) was read differently by the Greek translator or in his Hebrew *Vorlage*: "In the new context, the 'captivity' did not fit the 'eating,' or alternatively the 'flesh' did not fit the 'going' and the second word was therefore adapted to suit the new context (for 'eating,' see also the first part of the verse). Consequently, the translator either changed 'captivity' to 'flesh' or 'they shall go' to 'they shall eat.'" It must be admitted, however, that the same argument could be made starting with בשרם יאכלו as the original text, in which case those responsible for the MT read one of the two words differently and thus either changed "their flesh" to "captivity" or "they will eat" to "they will go."

Jer. 30:14, 16). According to Isaiah 62:4, Jerusalem will no longer be called "forsaken" (עזובה). Rather, she will be called "sought" (דרושה) (Isa. 62:12).

Jeremiah 30:18a (LXX 37:18a) articulates the core message of the Book of Comfort: "Look, I am about to restore the fortunes of Jacob,[21] and on his captivity (ושביתו) [MT: and on his dwelling places (ומשכנתיו)] I will have compassion" (see Jer. 30:3; 31:23; 32:44; 33:7, 11). A city will be built "on its mound" (על תלה), and "a prominent building" (ארמון) will sit "upon its rightful place" or "according to its plan" (על משפטו) (Jer. 30:18b [LXX 37:18b]; cf. Jer. 31:4; Amos 9:11; see also Jer. 1:10). *Targum Jonathan* interprets the city to be Jerusalem (see Jer. 31:38), but the lack of an article on the noun עיר ("city") may suggest that the referent is any Judean city to be rebuilt on the site of its ruins (תל).[22] Both the LXX and *Targum Jonathan* interpret ארמון ("prominent building") to be the temple, although it could refer to a palace or to a fortress of some sort. Again, the lack of an article may indicate that the noun refers to any prominent building in Judah that is to be restored to its rightful place.

Thanksgiving and a sound of merrymakers will go forth from the places mentioned in 30:18 (Jer. 30:19a [LXX 37:19a]; cf. Isa. 51:3). The Hebrew source behind Greek Jeremiah has a plural verb (ויצאו) to agree with the compound subject. The MT's masculine singular verb (ויצא) agrees neither with the feminine noun תודה ("thanksgiving") nor with the compound subject. The thanksgiving mentioned here receives further elaboration in Jeremiah 33:11. It is the sound of those saying, "Give thanks (הודו) to the LORD of hosts, for the LORD is good, for his covenant loyalty lasts forever." The people will bring "thanksgiving" (תודה) into the house of the LORD, for the LORD will restore the fortunes of the land as before. The sound of merrymakers is that of tambourines and dancing (MT) in response to the LORD rebuilding Israel (Jer. 31:4; cf. 2 Sam. 6:5).[23] The LORD will increase the people, and they will

---

21. The MT has אהלי יעקוב ("the tents of Jacob") (see Num. 24:5; Jer. 4:20; 10:20).

22. See Bright, *Jeremiah*, 279. Cf. Deuteronomy 13:17. See also Isaiah 44:26, 28; Daniel 9:25; Ezra 1:1–4. According to the instruction in Deuteronomy 13:17, a city reduced to ruins because of worship of other gods would never again be rebuilt under the old covenant, but Jeremiah 30:18 presupposes a new covenant relationship (Jer. 31:31–34; see also the commentary on Jer. 3:1–5). See also Deuteronomy 13:16 and Jeremiah 25:9.

23. This is obviously not the same kind of merrymakers as those mentioned in Jeremiah 15:17.

not decrease (Jer. 30:19b [LXX 37:19b]; cf. Deut. 26:5; Jer. 10:24; 29:6; 44:28; Hos. 8:10).[24] The MT adds an expansion to the end of verse 19b: "and I will honor them, and they will not be insignificant" (cf. Mic. 5:1 [Eng., 5:2]), possibly forming a doublet. Jacob's sons will come (LXX) or be (MT) as before (Jer. 30:20a [LXX 37:20a]). Calvin understands this to mean that the state of the people of God will be comparable to that of the former kingdom of David (see Isa. 1:26; Jer. 33:7, 11; Zech. 12:7).[25] The text goes on to say: "and his [LXX: their] testimonies [4QJer^c: ועדותו] before me will be established" (see Jer. 44:23; see also Ps. 78:5).[26] The MT says: "and his congregation (ועדתו) before me will be established" ("an assembly of nations"; see Gen. 28:3; 35:11; 48:4). The LORD will visit upon or punish Jacob's oppressors (Jer. 30:20b [LXX 37:20b]; cf. Jer. 25:12–13; 30:16).

Greek Jeremiah reflects a plural noun at the beginning of 30:21 (LXX 37:21): "And his majestic ones (אַדִּירָו) will be over them" (cf. Isa. 32:1; Jer. 3:15; 23:4; Mic. 5:4–5 [Eng., 5:5–6]). The MT, however, has a singular noun, "his majestic one" (אַדִּירוֹ), which *Targum Jonathan* interprets to be an anointed king from Jacob (see v. 18; cf. Num. 24:17).[27] This works well with the singular noun in the following clause: "and his ruler (משלו) from him [MT: from his midst] will go forth." *Targum Jonathan* says that this is the Messiah who will be revealed from among the people (cf. Jer. 30:9).[28] The language of this text perhaps depends upon Micah 5:1 (Eng., 5:2): "from you for me he will go forth [*Tg. Jon.*: before me the Messiah will go forth] to be a ruler (מושל) over Israel"

---

24. Ephrem the Syrian: "Like many other things in the Lord's divine plan predicted by the prophet and fulfilled by the redemption and restoration of the people of God, this passage also should not be simply understood in the sense of Israel but of people that the divine Paul calls the Israel of God who consisted of, and were gathered from, Jews and people of other nations. This passage is not simply about biological children of Abraham but about children of promise, and Paul teaches the same" (Wenthe, ed., *Jeremiah, Lamentations*, 204–5).

25. Calvin, *Jeremiah*, 4:40.

26. This presumably means that the people will keep the Torah (Jer. 31:33; Ezek. 11:19–20; Rom. 8:4).

27. "It was the same then as though Jeremiah had promised the Jews a resurrection, for they were in their exile as dead men, as their hope of public safety had vanished when their king was destroyed. Here, then, he bids them to entertain good hope, because the Lord was able to raise them from death to life" (Calvin, *Jeremiah*, 4:43).

28. See also b. Sanhedrin 98b; Redak in Rosenberg, trans., *Mikraoth Gedoloth: Jeremiah Volume Two*, 242.

(see also 2 Sam. 23:3; Isa. 11:1). The MT's מקרבו ("from his midst") echoes the thought of Deuteronomy 17:15b: "From the midst (מקרב) of your brothers you will set over you a king" (cf. Deut. 18:15, 18). The LXX interprets the remainder of verse Jeremiah 30:21 (LXX 37:21) to be about the LORD gathering the people so that they might return to him, but this apparently does not reflect a Hebrew text different from the one found in the MT. The translator has simply misunderstood and thus misrepresented his Hebrew source. Where the text says, "and I will draw him near (והקרבתיו), and he will approach me," there is a strong connection to the vision of the Son of Man in Daniel 7:13b (see Dan. 9:2): "and up to the Ancient of Days he came, and before him they drew him near (הקרבוהי)." The text goes on to ask who would pledge his heart to draw near to the LORD (Jer. 30:21b [LXX 37:21b]). That is, who would take his life into his own hands to enter the LORD's presence (cf. Pss. 15:1; 24:3)? The privilege of entering the LORD's presence is reserved for the priests (see Ezek. 44:13, 15; see also Exod. 28:35, 43). This calls to mind the story of Uzziah who overstepped his bounds as king and attempted to do what only the priests could do (2 Chr. 26:16–21). The difference with the Messiah, however, is that he will be both priest and king (Zech. 6:13; Ps. 110:4; Heb. 7).

MT Jeremiah 30:22 ("And you will become my people, and I will become your God") is not present in the Hebrew source behind Greek Jeremiah, but this covenant formula does occur in Jeremiah 31:1, 33; 32:38. Its presence in the context of the Book of Comfort presupposes a new covenant relationship (cf. Jer. 24:7; see also Jer. 7:23; 11:4). The text of Jeremiah 30:23–24 has already appeared in a slightly different form in Jeremiah 23:19–20 (see commentary there). As noted in the commentary on 23:19–20, these verses within the context of chapter 23 are concerned more specifically with the judgment of false prophets, whereas in the context of chapter 30 they speak more generally of the judgment of the wicked. Only in the last days will there be full comprehension of what these verses reveal. At that time every knee will bow, and every tongue will confess (Isa. 45:23; Php. 2:10–11). Also at that time (i.e., at the end of the days), the LORD will become God to the family (4QJer[c], MT: "to all the families") of Israel, and they will become his people (Jer. 31:1 [LXX 38:1]; cf. Jer. 30:22 [MT]; 31:33; 32:38).[29]

---

29. The Masoretic section division after 31:1 and the introduction of the LORD's discourse in 31:2 suggest that 31:1 belongs with the end of chapter 30.

JEREMIAH 31:2–40 (LXX 38:2–40)

31:2 (38:2) "Thus says the Lord, *'I found (him) hot in the wilderness with those slain by sword. Go, and do not disturb [LXX: destroy] Israel [MT: A people of survivors of sword found grace in the wilderness when I went to give him, Israel, rest].'[1] 31:3 (38:3) The* Lord *from far away [or, long ago] appeared to him [MT: 'From far away (or, Long ago) the* Lord *appeared to me'].[2] 'With [Codex L: And with] an everlasting devotion have I devoted myself to you. Therefore, I have drawn you with covenant loyalty [or, I have prolonged covenant loyalty to you (BDB, 604); LXX: I have drawn you into compassion].[3] 31:4 (38:4) Again I will build you, and you will be built, O virgin Israel. Again you will adorn yourself with tambourines, and you will go out with an assembly of merrymakers [MT: in a dance of merrymakers]. 31:5 (38:5) Again you will plant vineyards on the mountains of Samaria. Plant, and praise [MT: Planters will plant and enjoy the fruit]. 31:6 (38:6) For there is a day of watchmen calling [LXX: a day of calling of people who argue (= נִצִּים?);[4] MT: a day when watchmen call] in the mountains/hills of Ephraim [MT: in the hill country of Ephraim], "Arise, and let us go up [LXX: Arise and go up] to Zion, to the* Lord *our God.'"[5]*

31:7 (38:7) For thus says the Lord *to Jacob, 'Be glad and neigh over the head of the nations [MT: For thus says the* Lord, *'Give a ringing cry for Jacob with gladness and neigh over the head of the nations]. Proclaim and [and > MT] praise, [MT adds: and] say, "The* Lord *has delivered [cf. 4QJer*[c]*; MT: O* Lord, *deliver] his people [MT: your people], the remnant of Israel." 31:8 (38:8) Look, I am about to bring them out of the north [MT: the land of the north], and I will gather them from*

---

1. *Tg. Jon.*: "Thus says the Lord who gave compassion to the people whom he brought up out of Egypt. He supplied their needs in the wilderness when they were fleeing from those who killed with the sword. He guided Israel by his word to make him dwell in a place of rest."
2. *BHS* arranges the text so that the last clause of 31:2 and the first clause of 31:3 are parallel.
3. According to *Targum Jonathan*, Jerusalem is the speaker in 31:3a, and the prophet is the speaker in 31:3b.
4. See Exodus 2:13.
5. *Tg. Jon.*: "For there is length of days and much good that is about to come to the righteous who have kept my Torah since before. Their portion is in the land of Israel, because they have been longing for the years of comfort that are coming, saying, 'When will we arise and go up to Zion and appear before the Lord our God?'"

the remote parts of the earth [MT: from earth's remote parts] at the appointed time of Passover [MT: among them blind and lame], and you will give birth to a great assembly [MT: pregnant and giving birth together], and they will return hither [MT: a great assembly will return hither]. 31:9 (38:9) With weeping they went out [MT: With weeping they will come; Tg. Jon.: When they went into exile, when they were weeping, they went into exile], and with comfort [MT: supplications] I will lead them, making them lodge [MT: I will walk them] by streams of water in a straight path, and they will not stumble in it [cf. 4QJerᶜ; MT: in a straight path in which they will not stumble]. For I have become Israel's father, and Ephraim is my firstborn.' 31:10 (38:10) Hear the word of the LORD, O nations, and declare among the coastlands far away. Say [MT: And say], 'The one who scattered Israel is the one who will gather him and keep / watch / guard him like a shepherd does his flock.' 31:11 (38:11) For the LORD has ransomed Jacob, he has redeemed him from a hand / power too strong for him [or, stronger than he]. 31:12 (38:12) And they will come and give a ringing cry on Mount Zion [MT: on the height of Zion], and they will flow [or, shine] to [or, over; 4QJerᶜ: עַל] the goodness of the LORD, a land of [> MT] grain and new wine and fresh olive oil [LXX: fruit] and young large and small [MT: small and large] livestock, and their life will be like a fruitful tree [MT: like a watered garden], and they will never again be hungry [MT: languish]. 31:13 (38:13) 'At that time a virgin will be glad in an assembly of choice, young men, and old men will rejoice [MT: At that time a virgin will be glad in a dance, and choice, young men and old men together], and I will turn their mourning [4QJerᶜ: your mournings] into exultation, and I will make them glad [4QJerᶜ, MT: and I will comfort them and make them glad from their grief]. 31:14 (38:14) I will magnify [> 4QJerᶜ, MT] and saturate [LXX: intoxicate] the life / desire of the priests [4QJerᶜ, MT add: with fatness / abundance], the sons of Levi [> 4QJerᶜ, MT], and my people will be sated with my goodness' [4QJerᶜ, MT add: the prophetic utterance of the LORD].

31:15 (38:15) Thus says the LORD, 'A sound / voice in Ramah [Vulg.: in excelso] is heard, wailing and weeping and bitterness [MT: wailing, bitter weeping]. Rachel is weeping [MT adds: for her children]. She refuses to be comforted for her children, for they are not [MT: he is not].'[6] 31:16 (38:16) Thus says the LORD, 'Withhold your voice from weeping,

---

6.   *Tg. Jon.*: "Thus says the Lord, 'The voice in the height of the world is heard, the house of Israel who weep and groan after Jeremiah the prophet, when Nebuzaradan the chief executioner sent him from Ramah, lamentation,

and your eyes from tears, for there is a wage for your work [Tg. Jon.: the works of your righteous forefathers],' [MT adds: the prophetic utterance of the LORD], 'and they will return from enemy territory. 31:17 (38:17) There is hope [MT: And there is hope] for your posterity / future [LXX: There is permanence for your children],' [MT adds: the prophetic utterance of the LORD, 'and children will return to their border]. 31:18 (38:18) I have surely heard Ephraim grieving [Vulg.: wandering; Tg. Jon. adds: because they wandered], "You disciplined me [Tg. Jon.: You brought upon us sufferings], and I was disciplined [or, and I allowed myself to be disciplined (see GKC §51c); Tg. Jon.: but we did not learn], like an untrained calf [LXX: like a calf I was not trained]. Bring me back, and I will return [or, so that I may return], for you are the LORD my God. 31:19 (38:19) For after my captivity [MT: my turning] I repented [Tg. Jon.: For when we return to the Torah we receive compassion], and after I was instructed, I groaned about days of shame [MT: I slapped upon thigh, I was ashamed], and also I was humiliated [LXX: I yielded (or, showed) to you],⁷ for I bore the reproach of my youth." 31:20 (38:20) Ephraim is my precious / beloved son, a delightful child [MT: Is Ephraim my precious / beloved son, a delightful child?]. For as often as [LXX: since] my words are [MT: I speak] in / about / against him [Tg. Jon.: For when I put the words of my Torah on his heart / mind to do them], I surely remember him [MT adds: again]. Therefore, I hasten to him [MT: my bowels roar for him], I will surely have compassion on him,' the prophetic utterance of the LORD.

31:21 (38:21) Set up for yourself signposts [Rahlfs: Zion], make for yourself guideposts [or, bitterness; Rahlfs: punishment; Syr.: and live in the wilderness],⁸ put your heart / mind to the highway [LXX: to the shoulders], the road by which you went [see GKC §44h].⁹ Return, O virgin Israel, return to your cities mourning [MT: to these your cities].¹⁰ 31:22

---

and who weep for the bitterness of Jerusalem weeping for her children, refusing to be comforted for her children, for they have gone into exile.'"

7. See Walser, *Jeremiah*, 410.
8. Walser, *Jeremiah*, 411.
9. NETS: "Return by the road which you went, O virgin Israel. Return to your cities in mourning."
10. *Tg. Jon.*: "O congregation of Israel, remember the good works of your fathers. Pour out supplications with bitterness. Consider, understand the works that you did whether they were good, for thus you went into exile on a path far away. Now return, O congregation of Israel, to the Torah, and return to these your cities."

(38:22) How long will you turn this way and that [Bright: dilly-dally; Syr.: be divided; Tg. Jon.: restrain yourself from returning], O apostate daughter [LXX: dishonored daughter]? For the LORD has created salvation for a new planting in which men will go about in safety [MT: For the LORD has created something new in the land: a female will encompass/surround (Syr.: love) a man (Tg. Jon.: the people, the house of Israel, will eagerly follow the Torah)].'"[11]

According to the Hebrew source behind Greek Jeremiah 31:2 (LXX 38:2), the LORD says, "I found (him) hot in the wilderness with those slain by sword (מצאתי חם במדבר עם שדודי חרב). Go, and do not disturb [LXX: destroy] Israel (הלוך ואל תרגיעו ישראל)." This recalls the "discovery" of Israel in the wilderness under the hot sun (see Deut. 32:10; Hos. 9:10; 12:5b [Eng., 12:4b]; see also Isa. 4:5–6) when some of the people were slain by the sword (see Num. 14:39–45). The directives to go and not disturb Israel are apparently a characterization of the LORD's efforts to ward off enemy attack (cf. Jer. 2:2–3). In the MT, however, the LORD says, "A people of survivors of sword found grace in the wilderness (מצא חן במדבר עם שרידי חרב) when I went to give him, Israel, rest (הלוך להרגיעו ישראל)."[12] As indicated by *Targum Jonathan*, this alludes to Israel's escape from Pharaoh and his army (Exod. 14; 18:4) and the subsequent favor that Moses and the people found in the wilderness (see Exod. 33:12b, 13a, 16a, 17b; cf. Gen. 6:8) when the LORD went to deliver them from Egypt and to give them rest in the land of the covenant (see Exod. 33:14; 2 Sam. 7:23; see also Deut. 28:65; Jer. 6:16; 50:34). Such a reminiscence of the original exodus sets up the depiction of future deliverance in terms of a new exodus (cf. Num. 23:22; 24:8; Isa. 11:16; 43:16–21; 51:9–11; Jer. 16:14–15; 23:7–8; 51:50; Hos. 2:16–17 [Eng., 2:14–15]; 11:1, 5, 11; Mic. 7:15).[13]

The phrase מרחוק in 31:3a (LXX 38:3a) can mean "from far away" or "long ago." The clause in which this appears in the Hebrew source behind Greek Jeremiah has the LORD referring to himself in the third person,

---

11. See Walser, *Jeremiah*, 412.

12. Holladay (*Jeremiah 2*, 181) proposes to revocalize חֶרֶב ("sword") as חֹרֵב ("Horeb").

13. "A profitable doctrine may hence be gathered: Whenever despair presents itself to our eyes, or whenever our miseries tempt us to despair, let the benefits of God come to our minds, not only those which we ourselves have experienced, but also those which he has in all ages conferred on his Church" (Calvin, *Jeremiah*, 4:55). See Psalms 77–78. See also Keil, *Jeremiah*, 269.

assuming that he is still the speaker: "The LORD from far away [or, long ago] appeared to him (לוֹ)." This is perhaps a reference to the LORD's appearance at a distance (or, long ago) to the people at Sinai (see Exod. 20:18). On the other hand, the MT, which says, "From far away (or, Long ago) the LORD appeared to me (לִי)," seems to be a quote of what Moses was to say to the elders of Israel in Egypt: "The LORD, the God of your fathers, appeared to me" (Exod. 3:16a; see Exod. 3:2).[14] That is, the LORD appeared to Moses in a distant land (or, long ago). The LORD then says in 31:3b (LXX 38:3b), "With [Codex L: And with] an everlasting devotion have I devoted myself to you." The Hebrew term אהבה ("devotion") does not mean "love" in the typical English sense of a purely emotional attachment.[15] Rather, it is an act of commitment, which fits nicely with the noun in the following clause: חסד ("covenant loyalty"). There are two options for translation of the final clause in 31:3b: (1) "Therefore, I have drawn you with covenant loyalty" (cf. Hos. 11:4); or (2) "I have prolonged covenant loyalty to you" (cf. Pss. 36:11 (Eng., 36:10); 109:12; see BDB, 604).

Verses 4 and 5 take up the language of building and planting from the programmatic text of Jeremiah 1:10 (see also Ezek. 28:26). The LORD pledges that he will rebuild virgin Israel, and she will be built (Jer. 31:4a [LXX 38:4a]; cf. Jer. 30:18; 31:27–28, 38; Ps. 147:2).[16] According to Jeremiah 12:16, this rebuilding will include those from the nations who learn the way(s) of the people of God (see also Jer. 3:17). Israel will once again adorn herself with tambourines and go out "with an assembly (בקהל) of merrymakers" (MT: "in a dance [במחול] of merrymakers") (Jer. 31:4b [LXX 38:4b]; cf. Judg. 11:34; 1 Sam. 18:6–7; 2 Sam. 6:5; Isa. 30:32; Jer. 30:19; 31:8, 13; Pss. 68:26 [Eng., 68:25]; 149:3). This contributes to the new exodus imagery, for this is how Miriam and all the women celebrated in response to the original exodus (Exod. 15:20–21). Israel will again plant vineyards on the mountains of Samaria (Jer. 31:5a [LXX 38:5a]; cf. Jer. 32:15; Amos 9:14). Such a hope is not to be spiritualized but embraced as an important part of the earthiness of the new garden of Eden and New Jerusalem in the new creation (Isa. 51:3; 65:17–18; Jer. 31:12).[17] The references to

---

14. See Holladay, *Jeremiah 2*, 180.

15. See the discussion in Shepherd, *Textuality and the Bible*, 94–102.

16. Redak: "You will still be like a virgin never possessed by a man" (Rosenberg, trans., *Mikraoth Gedoloth: Jeremiah Volume Two*, 244). Cf. Jeremiah 3:1, where Israel was depicted as an unfaithful wife.

17. Rather than building houses and planting gardens in Babylon (Jer. 29:5), the people of God will do so in the land of the covenant when the lost blessing of life and dominion is restored (Gen. 1:26–28; 2:10–14; 15:18).

Samaria and Ephraim in verses 5 and 6 (see also vv. 9, 15, 18, 20) need not mean that the prophecy is only for the northern kingdom of Israel, nor is it necessary to interpret "Samaria" and "Ephraim" as code for "Judah." As McKane notes, the "Israel" (vv. 2, 4) of this passage is the Israel that came out of Egypt in the exodus.[18] Therefore, any reference to the north or the south in the Book of Comfort is to be seen as part of a reunited kingdom, which will also include those from the nations who join (Jer. 3:17–18; 30:3–4). The difference between the LXX and MT of 31:5b (LXX 38:5b) can be traced back to differences in textual witnesses to the Pentateuchal law on which the text is based.[19] The LXX reflects: נִטְעוּ וְהַלֵּלוּ ("Plant, and praise"). This agrees with the MT's version of the law in Leviticus 19:23–25, which says that the fruit of any tree planted in the land of Israel cannot be eaten for three years;[20] in the fourth year, the fruit will be holy, "praise offerings" (הלולים) to the LORD (cf. Deut. 20:6 [LXX]; Judg. 9:27; see also Jer. 31:7b); then, in the fifth year, the fruit may be eaten. The Samaritan Pentateuch, however, says that the fruit in the fourth year will be "profaned" (חלולים); that is, the fruit will be treated as common and ready to be enjoyed (cf. Deut. 20:6 [MT, SP]; 28:30; see also Isa. 65:22; Amos 5:11). This is reflected in the MT's version of Jeremiah 31:5b: נָטְעוּ נֹטְעִים וְחִלֵּלוּ ("Planters will plant and enjoy the fruit").

Jeremiah 31:6 (LXX 38:6) provides an explanation for the hope of building and planting in verses 4 and 5. There is coming a day when watchmen will call in the hill country of Ephraim, "Arise, and let us go up to Zion, to the LORD our God" (see Jer. 3:14).[21] According to *Targum Jonathan*, the "watchmen" (נצרים) are the righteous who have kept the Torah and whose portion is in the land of Israel (see Ps. 119:2, 22, 33, 34, 56, 69, 100, 115, 129, 145). They will have been longing for the years of comfort and thus will be prepared to see the signs of the times (see Tg. 1 Chr. 12:33 [Eng., 12:32]; see also Deut. 33:18–19).[22] According to Keil, however, נצרים "denotes the watchmen who were posted on the mountains, that they might observe and given [*sic*] notice of the first appearance of the crescent of the moon after new-moon, so that the festival of the new-moon and the feast connected with it might

---

18. McKane, *Jeremiah XXVI–LII*, 786.
19. See Geiger, *Urschrift und Uebersetzungen*, 181–84.
20. This language is applicable to a grapevine (Ezek. 15:2).
21. The time to which this day refers has already been established in Jeremiah 30:7, 24; 31:1.
22. Torah study prepares the reader for the last days (e.g., Gen. 49:1, 8–12; Num. 24:7–9, 14, 17).

be fixed."[23] The summons to go up to Zion, to the LORD, is remarkably similar to the eschatological invitation in Isaiah 2:3 (Mic. 4:2), which is to be spoken by many peoples: "Come, and let us go up to the mountain of the LORD, to the house of the God of Jacob" (see also Isa. 66:18–24; Zech. 8:20–23).[24] This is in expectation of messianic salvation through which justice and peace will be brought to the world (Isa. 2:4; 9:5–6 [Eng., 9:6–7]; 11:1–10; Jer. 23:5–6). Zion will once again be the central place of worship (Deut. 12:5), and the alternative worship of the old northern kingdom of Israel will be a thing of the past (1 Kgs. 12:25–33; see also 2 Chr. 30:1, 10–11).

Jeremiah 31:7 (LXX 38:7) begins a new subunit that extends through verse 14. The LXX's Hebrew *Vorlage* and the MT of verse 7a differ in their placement of ליעקב. The former says, "For thus says the LORD to Jacob (ליעקב), 'Be glad (שמחו) and neigh over the head of the nations'" (cf. Jer. 31:13). The latter says, "For thus says the LORD, 'Give a ringing cry (רנו) for Jacob (ליעקב) with gladness (שמחה) and neigh over the head of the nations.'" The LXX has no representation of the MT's רנו ("Give a ringing cry"). Shouting and rejoicing are elsewhere responses to the coming of the divine king in the flesh (Isa. 12:6; 49:13; Zeph. 3:14–15; Zech. 2:14 [Eng., 2:10]; 9:9–10; Matt. 21:5; John 12:15; see also Isa. 35:10). Thus, while most commentators consider the phrase "the head of the nations" to be a reference to Israel (cf. Amos 6:1; see also Prov. 1:20–21), this contextual clue may indicate that it refers to the new David (Jer. 30:9, 21) as the head of the nations (see 2 Sam. 22:44; Ps. 18:44 [Eng., 18:43]; see also Gen. 49:10; Isa. 11:10; 42:1, 4, 6; 49:6; 55:3–5; Jer. 10:7 [MT]; Ps. 22:29 [Eng., 22:28]). This observation also works well with verse 7b: "Proclaim and praise, say, 'The LORD has delivered (הושע) his people (עמו), the remnant of Israel.'" There is a clear echo of this language in the depiction of the triumphal entry of the king found within Psalm 118:24–26: "This is the day that the LORD has made, let us be glad and rejoice (ונשמחה) in it. Please, O LORD, deliver (הושיעה), please, O LORD, grant success. Blessed is the one who comes in the name of the LORD, we bless you from the house of the LORD" (see also Zeph. 3:14–15; Zech. 2:14 [Eng., 2:10]; 9:9–10; Ps. 24:7–10; Matt. 21:9; Mark 11:9–10; Luke 19:38; John 12:13).[25] Indeed, the MT's version of Jeremiah 31:7b seems to be designed to bring the

---

23. Keil, *Jeremiah*, 270. See also Isaiah 52:8; 62:6–7; Jeremiah 4:15–16.

24. It is an invitation to learn the Torah from God himself.

25. See Psalm 118:14 for the connection between this psalm and both the exodus (Exod. 15:2) and the new exodus (Isa. 11:16; 12:2) (Shepherd, *Text in the Middle*, 62–64).

text even closer to Psalm 118:25: "Proclaim, praise, and say, 'O LORD, deliver (הוֹשַׁע) your people (עמך), the remnant of Israel.'" The people of God here are called "the remnant of Israel." This remnant includes all the faithful from Israel, Judah, and the nations (see Isa. 2:1–5; 4:2–6; 10:20–23; 11:10–11; 35:10; 66:18–24; Jer. 1:10; 3:17–18; 12:14–17; 16:19; Amos 9:12; Mic. 2:12–13; 4:1–7; 5:6–7 [Eng., 5:7–8]; Zeph. 2:11; 3:13; Zech. 2:15 [Eng., 2:11]; 8:20–23).

In Jeremiah 31:8 (LXX 38:8), the LORD says that he is about to bring his people out of the north and gather them from the remote parts of the earth (cf. Deut. 30:3; Jer. 29:14 [MT]; Ezek. 11:17; 34:13; 36:24; see also Jer. 6:22; 25:32). If the reader is following MT Jeremiah (e.g., MT Jer. 25:9), then this text is about deliverance from Babylonian exile. If the reader is following the Hebrew source behind Greek Jeremiah (e.g., LXX Jer. 25:9), then this text is potentially about eschatological deliverance from a final enemy (see Ezek. 38–39).[26] Jeremiah 16:14–15 and 23:7–8 have already cast this deliverance in terms of a new exodus, and Jeremiah 30:5–7 has established that the context from which this deliverance will take place is that of eschatological tribulation. Also contributing to the new exodus theme, the LXX reflects a Hebrew text that says the deliverance will come "at the appointed time of Passover" (בְּמוֹעֵד פֶּסַח).[27] This text goes on to say: "and you will give birth (וְיָלַדְתְּ) to a great assembly, and they will return hither" (cf. Isa. 66:7–9; see also Gen. 28:3; 35:11; 48:4).[28] The MT, however, has: "among them blind and lame (בָּם עִוֵּר וּפִסֵּחַ), pregnant and giving birth together (הרה וְיֹלֶדֶת יחדו), a great assembly will return hither" (cf. Isa. 29:18; 33:23; 35:5–6; 42:7, 16, 18; 43:8; Mic. 4:6–7; Zeph. 3:19; see also Matt. 21:14). There may be an allusion in this text to the story of David's capture of Jerusalem wherein the Jebusites say that even the blind and the lame among them will turn back David and his men (2 Sam. 5:6). David

---

26. See Neusner, *Jeremiah in Talmud and Midrash*, 137, 210.

27. Tov assumes the originality of the MT for this verse (*Text-Critical Use of the Septuagint*, 185–86). He suggests that once the translator read בָּם עִוֵּר וּפִסֵּחַ ("among them blind and lame") as בְּמוֹעֵד פֶּסַח ("at the appointed time of Passover") subsequent adjustments had to be made to the text in order for it to make sense. It is entirely possible, however, to argue this the other way. Assuming the originality of a different Hebrew text behind the LXX, a change from the latter to the former reading led to subsequent adjustments in the text.

28. Use of the term הנה ("hither") reflects the perspective of someone in Israel. See Seeligmann, *Septuagint Version of Isaiah*, 79; McKane, *Jeremiah XXVI–LII*, 790.

subsequently refers to the Jebusites as the lame and the blind, and on this basis it is said, "The blind and the lame will not come into the house" (2 Sam. 5:8; cf. Lev. 21:18). Thus, the MT's version of Jeremiah 31:8 may indicate not only that strength will be given to the weak to return but also that those formerly forbidden to return may once again be allowed entry.

The Hebrew source behind Greek Jeremiah 31:9a (LXX 38:9a) says, "With weeping they went out (יָצְאוּ), and with comfort (ובתנחומים) I will lead them, making them lodge (מלין) by streams of water in a straight path, and they will not stumble in it." This text makes a contrast between the way the people went into exile and the way they will return (cf. *Tg. Jon.*)—a restoration that will take place fully only in the eschaton. Their sorrowful weeping will be transformed into comfort (cf. Jer. 31:13). They will be like trees by streams of water (see Num. 24:6; Jer. 17:7–8; 31:12; Pss. 1:1–3; 23:2),[29] and the LORD will lead them in a straight path free of stumbling blocks (see Isa. 35:8; 49:11; 57:14; 62:10; Pss. 23:3; 107:7). On the other hand, the MT says, "With weeping they will come (יבאו), and with supplications (ובתחנונים) I will lead them, I will walk them (אוליכם) by streams of water in a straight path in which they will not stumble." This text does not make a contrast between the way the people left and the way they will return. Rather, it only speaks of the way that they will come back—with weeping and supplications. Keil comments that these are tears of joy with contrition of heart over favor undeserved (cf. Jer. 3:21; 50:4; Ps. 126:6).[30] Verse 9b explains the LORD's care for his people with a variation of the covenant formula (cf. Jer. 30:22 [MT]; 31:1, 33b): "For I have become Israel's father, and Ephraim is my firstborn" (see Exod. 4:22; Deut. 32:6; Isa. 63:16; 64:7; Jer. 31:20; Hos. 11:1; 2 Cor. 6:18; Rev. 21:7; see also Jer. 2:27; 3:4, 19). This language may be compared first of all with Genesis 48:5 and its interpretation in 1 Chronicles 5:1–2. In Genesis 48:5, Jacob says that Joseph's two sons, Ephraim and Manasseh, will be like Reuben and Simeon, the first and second born (see Gen. 29:32–33), and, according to Genesis 48:14–20, Ephraim is treated as the firstborn of Joseph in place of his older brother Manasseh. Thus, due to an incident recorded

---

29. See also Isaiah 35:6; 41:17–20; 43:16–21; 44:3–4; 48:21 (cf. Exod. 17:1–7; Num. 20:1–13; Deut. 8:7).

30. Keil, *Jeremiah*, 271. "*Abarbanel* explains that they will weep because of the trials and tribulations they will have experienced during the time preceding the Messianic Era, known as the Birthpangs of the Messiah" (Rosenberg, trans., *Mikraoth Gedoloth: Jeremiah Volume Two*, 246). See Matthew 24:8 (see also Jer. 51:46 [MT]; Matt. 24:6).

in Genesis 35:22 (see also Gen. 49:3–4), 1 Chronicles 5:1–2 indicates that the firstborn Reuben has lost his birthright, and that right of the firstborn now belongs to the sons of Joseph and to Ephraim in particular. It is also to be noted that the men of the northern tribes of Israel refer to themselves as the "firstborn" (πρωτότοκος) over against Judah in LXX 2 Samuel 19:44 (cf. Ezek. 16:46; 23:4).

In Jeremiah 31:10 (LXX 38:10), the nations are called upon to hear the prophetic word of the Lord and to declare it among the coastlands far away. This is not merely for their information, nor is it merely for those from Israel who are scattered among the nations. These Gentile heralds are participating members of the people of God who not only bring back the righteous remnant of Israel but also declare the good news of God's glory to the nations themselves (see Isa. 41:1; 49:1, 6; 66:18–21; see again Jer. 3:17). They are to say, "The one who scattered Israel is the one who will gather him and keep/watch/guard him like a shepherd does his flock" (cf. Jer. 15:7; 31:8). The image of Israel as a scattered flock is a familiar one (see Num. 27:17b; 1 Kgs. 22:17; Jer. 50:6, 17; Ezek. 34:5; Zech. 10:2; Matt. 9:36; 10:6). The Davidic Messiah is the one who will gather and guard the people as the divine shepherd/ king in the flesh (see Jer. 23:1–6; Ezek. 34; John 10). "For," as 31:11 (LXX 38:11) explains, "the Lord has ransomed Jacob, he has redeemed him from a hand/power too strong for him [or, stronger than he]" (cf. Jer. 50:34; Ps. 35:10). Both פדה ("ransom") and גאל ("redeem") can be used for legal redemption of a person or property, redemption from Egypt, or redemption from exile (see BDB, 145, 804).

Jeremiah 31:12 (LXX 38:12) revisits the content from verses 5–7, 9. The people from verses 10 and 11 will come and give a ringing cry "on Mount Zion" (בהר ציון) (MT: "on the height of Zion" [במרום ציון]) (see again Isa. 2:1–5). They will either "flow" (I נהר; Isa. 2:2) or "shine" (II נהר; Isa. 60:5) to/over the goodness of the Lord (cf. Jer. 31:14; Hos. 3:5). This goodness is described in terms of the produce of the land to be enjoyed: "grain and new wine and fresh olive oil [LXX: fruit] and young large and small [MT: small and large] livestock" (cf. Hos. 2:10, 24 [Eng., 2:8, 22]; see also Jer. 31:23–26). According to the Hebrew source behind Greek Jeremiah 31:12b (LXX 38:12b), the life of the people will be "like a fruitful tree" (כעץ פרי) (cf. Gen. 1:11; Ps. 148:9; see also Num. 24:6; Isa. 61:3; 65:22; Jer. 17:7–8; 31:9; Ps. 1:1–3). The MT says that they will be "like a watered garden" (כגן רוה) (cf. Isa. 58:11). According to the former, they will never again be hungry (לרעבה); according to the latter, they will never again languish (לדאבה) (see Jer. 31:25; Bar. 2:18).[31]

---

31. See also Tov, *Text-Critical Use of the Septuagint*, 181–82.

The Hebrew source behind Greek Jeremiah 31:13a (LXX 38:13a) and the MT present two different versions: (1) "At that time a virgin will be glad in an assembly (בקהל) of choice, young men, and old men will rejoice (יַחְדוּ)" (cf. Jer. 31:4, 8b; see also Zech. 8:4–5); and (2) "At that time a virgin will be glad in a dance (במחול), and choice, young men and old men together (יַחְדָּו)" (cf. Jer. 31:4 [MT]).[32] The former has a virgin in an assembly of young men, but there is no dancing. The latter has a virgin in a dance, but the young men and the old men are kept separate from her. *Targum Jonathan* identifies the virgin as "the assembly of Israel" made up of young men and elders rejoicing in the dances. The LORD will turn their mourning into exultation, and he will make them glad (4QJer^c, MT: "and I will comfort them and make them glad from their grief") (cf. Isa. 61:3; Jer. 31:7, 9; Ps. 30:12 [Eng., 30:11]).

Rudolph proposes that the LXX reflects a double version at the beginning of 31:14 (LXX 38:14): רִבִּיתִי וְרִוֵּיתִי, "I will magnify [> 4QJer^c, MT] and saturate" (see *BHS* apparatus). The LORD will saturate the life/desire of the priests (cf. Jer. 31:25). 4QJer^c and the MT add דשן ("with fatness/abundance"). This addition is a term used for the ashes of sacrificial victims mixed with their fat (Lev. 1:16; 4:12; MT Jer. 31:40), but here it is parallel to "goodness," which, according to verse 12, refers to the produce of the land. The same term can also refer to spiritual blessings (e.g., Isa. 55:2; Ps. 36:9 [Eng., 36:8]). The Hebrew source behind Greek Jeremiah adds a description of the priests as "the sons of Levi," but this addition does not appear in 4QJer^c or the MT. It should be considered secondary (cf. MT Jer. 33:14–26). Here the saturated life of the priests is parallel to the people sated with the LORD's goodness. Thus, it is likely that two groups are not in view (the priests and the people) but one (the priestly people). This envisions a restoration of the ideal kingdom of priests wherein there is no separate mediating class of priests (see Exod. 19:6; Isa. 61:6; 66:21; 1 Pet. 2:9; Rev. 1:6; 5:10; 20:6).

Verse 15 begins a new subunit that continues through verse 20. The LORD says that a sound or voice ברמה is heard. The phrase ברמה is usually translated "in Ramah," and it is assumed that this is the Ramah in Benjamin on the border of Ephraim five miles north of Jerusalem (BDB, 928). The problem is that the place name "Ramah" normally has the article in Hebrew, yet it is not vocalized as arthrous in MT 31:15. Thus, the phrase ברמה may simply mean "on a height" (see *Tg. Jon.*: "in the height of the world"; Vulg.: *in excelso*). The sound or voice that is heard here is that of "wailing and weeping and bitterness" (MT: "wailing,

---

32. This is a reversal of Jeremiah 6:11.

bitter weeping").[33] It is the sound of Rachel weeping (MT adds: "for her children").[34] She refuses to be comforted for her children, for "they are not" (אינם) (MT: "he is not" [איננו]; *Tg. Jon.*: "they have gone into exile"; cf. Jer. 10:20; 49:10b; Mic. 1:16). Rachel is the mother of Joseph and the grandmother of Ephraim and Manasseh (Gen. 30:22–23).[35] *Genesis Rabbah* suggests that Jacob buried Rachel on the way to Ephrath (i.e., Bethlehem) because he foresaw that the exiles would pass by there (Gen. 35:16–21; 48:7).[36] It must be admitted, however, that Jeremiah 31:15 (LXX 38:15) makes no reference to Rachel's burial place.[37]

One of the most interesting features of verse 15 is the grammatical incongruence of איננו ("he is not") at the conclusion of the MT's version of the text. Nathan Mastnjak has shown that this likely bears an intertextual relationship to the story of Rachel's son Joseph in Genesis.[38] When Jacob hears the report of Joseph's death, he refuses to be comforted and weeps for Joseph (Gen. 37:34–35)—the very words used of Rachel in Jeremiah 31:15. Joseph's brothers repeatedly use איננו ("he is not") euphemistically for Joseph's death (Gen. 37:30; 42:13, 32; cf. Gen. 5:24), even though they know that Joseph has been sold into slavery, and this use of איננו subsequently occurs in the discourse of Jacob who is unaware of the true story about Joseph (Gen. 42:36). Of course, Joseph and his family are eventually reunited. Thus, Mastnjak summarizes, "By means of an allusion to Genesis 37, Jer. 31:15 makes a case both for the continued existence of the people of Israel and for the legitimacy of experiencing the exile as a metaphorical death."[39]

---

33. Cf. Isaiah 33:7; Jeremiah 3:21; 6:26; 8:23 (Eng., 9:1); 9:16–21 (Eng., 9:17–22).

34. According to *Targum Jonathan*, the house of Israel is weeping after Jeremiah the prophet whom Nebuzaradan the chief executioner sent from Ramah (Jer. 40:1) and for the bitterness of Jerusalem.

35. Once again, the northern kingdom of Israel is in focus, but, as noted in the commentary on 31:5, this is not to the exclusion of Judah or in place of Judah (i.e., as code for Judah). The remnant of the north is but one part of the people of God, which also includes the remnant of Judah and the believing Gentiles (Jer. 3:17–18).

36. See Neusner, *Jeremiah in Talmud and Midrash*, 125.

37. The precise location of Rachel's grave or tomb is not known. Genesis 35:16 only says that it was at some distance from Ephrath. First Samuel 10:2 refers to an unknown "Zelzah" somewhere along the border of Benjamin.

38. Sébastien Doane and Nathan Robert Mastnjak, "Echoes of Rachel's Weeping: Intertextuality and Trauma in Jer. 31:15," *BibInt* 27 (2019): 413–35.

39. Doane and Mastnjak, "Echoes of Rachel's Weeping," 413.

The citation of Jeremiah 31:15 in Matthew 2:17–18 occurs within a series of fulfillment quotations in Matthew 1–4 (Matt. 1:22–23; 2:5–6, 15, 23; 3:3; 4:14–16; see also Matt. 5:17–18). The specific form of the citation does not fit MT Jeremiah 31:15 or LXX Jeremiah 38:15 exactly. The principal difficulty with this citation is that Herod's slaughter of the infants is said to be the event that fulfilled what was spoken by Jeremiah (Matt. 2:17), as if Jeremiah 31:15 were merely a prediction of that moment in time. This differs from other introductory formulae that simply identify an event as a necessary occurrence for the fulfillment of a prophecy (e.g., Matt. 1:22; 2:15; 4:14). If Jeremiah 31:15 is only about the children of Israel in exile, then Matthew's citation has to be considered a serious misuse of the text. It must be remembered, however, that the tribulation of which the Book of Comfort speaks is not merely that of Assyrian captivity or Babylonian exile but that of the last days (see again Jer. 30:5–7, 24). Matthew's citation of Jeremiah is best understood as an example of the evangelist's inaugurated eschatology.[40] There is an accepted tension in Matthew's Gospel between the "already" and the "not yet." Matthew sees Herod's slaying of the infants as a manifestation of the eschatological tribulation envisioned in Jeremiah 30–31. Messianic salvation comes out of this context (Jer. 30:9). It is likely no coincidence that the account of Matthew 2:16–18 is a recapitulation of the story in Exodus 1:15–22, thus setting up the depiction of Jesus as a new Moses and a leader of a new exodus (see also Matt. 2:15). The present commentary has already established that the new exodus is a prominent theme in Jeremiah 31 (e.g., Jer. 31:2–4).

Jeremiah 31:16–17 (LXX 38:16–17) is the divine response to Rachel's weeping. The LORD tells Rachel to withhold her voice from weeping, and her eyes from tears (cf. Isa. 25:8; 65:19; Rev. 21:4), for there is a wage for her work (cf. 2 Chr. 15:7). This speaks of a reward for Israel's endurance of exile (cf. Isa. 40:1–2; see also Rev. 2:7, 11, 17, 26; 3:5, 12, 21), not only that of historical exile but also that of the perennial exile that lasts until the eschaton. Because the northern kingdom never returned from Assyrian captivity, and because Judah never experienced the fulfillment of prophecies such as those found in Isaiah 40–55 even after the return from Babylon, the assumption is that the people remain in exile in some sense until the last days (see Isa. 56–66; Zech. 1–6). The reward for the faithful remnant of the

---

40. See Craig L. Blomberg, *Matthew*, NAC 22 (Nashville: Broadman, 1992), 95; Charles Quarles, *Sermon on the Mount: Restoring Christ's Message to the Modern Church* (Nashville: B&H Academic, 2011), 10–11, 47–52, 62, 65, 75, 103–4, 170, 200, 281, 305, 332–33.

people of God that emerges from this is a return from enemy territory in a new exodus (Jer. 23:7–8; 30:3; 31:8). The shorter text of the Hebrew source behind Greek Jeremiah 31:17 (LXX 38:17) simply says, "There is hope for your posterity/future." The Hebrew word אחרית can mean "posterity" or "future" (cf. Jer. 29:11) in this context (see BDB, 31). The parallel addition in the MT seems to favor "posterity": "and children will return to their border" (cf. Isa. 49:17–23; 54:12–13; 62:5).

In Jeremiah 31:18–19 (LXX 38:18–19), the LORD cites the grieving of Ephraim that he has heard: "You disciplined me, and I was disciplined, like an untrained calf" (Jer. 31:18a; cf. Hos. 4:16; 10:10–11; see also Deut. 32:15; Isa. 1:3; Jer. 6:8; 7:28; 10:24; 30:11, 14; 46:28). Ephraim's prayer is that the LORD would bring him back so that he may return, for the LORD is his God (Jer. 31:18b; cf. Jer. 3:22b; Pss. 80:8 [Eng., 80:7]; 85:5 [Eng., 85:4]; Lam. 5:21; see also Jer. 15:19; Zech. 1:3; Mal. 3:7; 2 Chr. 30:6). Ephraim has learned his lesson and is now ready to be restored to the land of the covenant.[41] According to the Hebrew source behind Greek Jeremiah 31:19a (LXX 38:19a), Ephraim explains, "For after my captivity (שביי) I repented, and after I was instructed, I groaned about days of shame (אנקתי על ימי בשת)" (cf. Jer. 8:6). The phrase אחרי הודעי ("after I was instructed") may very well mean "after I was chastised" (cf. Judg. 8:16; Isa. 53:3),[42] which would make for a tighter parallel for "after my captivity." The MT has שובי ("my turning") instead of שביי ("my captivity"). *Targum Jonathan* interprets this to mean, "For when we return to the Torah we receive compassion." The meaning "after I was instructed" for the phrase אחרי הודעי works better as a parallel for the MT's "after my turning."[43] In place of אנקתי על ימי בשת ("I groaned about days of shame"), the MT has ספקתי על ירך בשתי ("I slapped upon thigh, I was ashamed"), a gesture of remorse (cf. Ezek. 21:17 [Eng., 21:12]). The verb בשתי ("I was ashamed") belongs with 31:19b according to the Masoretic accentuation (see the *athnach*). Ephraim says that he was humiliated because he bore the reproach of his youth (Jer. 31:19b), which is a reference to the consequence of sins committed since his youth (see Jer. 3:25; 32:30; cf. Ps. 25:7).

The Hebrew source behind Greek Jeremiah 31:20a (LXX 38:20a) opens with a statement: "Ephraim is my precious/beloved son, a delightful child." The MT puts this in the form of a question: "Is Ephraim my precious/beloved son, a delightful child?" Calvin asserts that this

---

41. See McKane, *Jeremiah XXVI–LII*, 800.

42. Barr, *Comparative Philology*, 19–21.

43. McKane: "after I had come to my senses" (*Jeremiah XXVI–LII*, 796). Luther: *und als ich zur Einsicht kam.*

question assumes a negative answer,[44] yet the LORD has already declared Ephraim to be his firstborn son in verse 9b.[45] The next part of the verse explains this status of Ephraim: "For as often as my words are (דְּבָרִי) [MT: I speak (דַבְּרִי)] in/about/against him, I surely remember him [MT adds: again]" (cf. Jer. 20:8a; 48:27b). *Targum Jonathan* interprets this to mean that the LORD remembers to do good to Ephraim when he puts the words of his Torah on Ephraim's heart/mind (cf. Jer. 31:33). Those who assume a negative answer for the preceding question in the MT translate that the LORD remembers Ephraim as often as he speaks "against" him, but it is preferable to translate the preposition בּ here more neutrally as "about." The language of remembering Ephraim recalls the remembrance of Ephraim's grandmother Rachel (Gen. 30:22). Ephraim is God's son to be remembered in a beneficial way at every mention of him. "Therefore," the LORD infers, "I hasten to him (מהרתי לו) [MT: "my bowels roar for him" (המו מעי לו)], I will surely have compassion on him" (Jer. 31:20b [LXX 38:20b]; cf. Isa. 16:11; Jer. 4:19; Hos. 11:8; see also 1 Kgs. 3:26).

The small subunit in 31:21–22 (LXX 38:21–22) begins in verse 21 with a series of feminine singular imperatives addressed to the people collectively. The first two are parallel: "Set up for yourself signposts (צינים), make for yourself guideposts (תמרורים)." The Old Greek transliterates these terms as σιωνιμ and τιμρωριμ (Ziegler). The Greek text found in Rahlf's edition represents a secondary development: Σιων ("Zion") and τιμωρίαν ("punishment"). The Hebrew word צינים ("signposts") is known from 2 Kings 23:17 and Ezekiel 39:15. The word תמרורים ("bitterness") from מרר occurs in 31:15, but this sense does not work very well in the parallelism of 31:21a where it must mean something like "guideposts" (but see *Tg. Jon.*: "Pour out supplications with bitterness"). Rashi suggests that it is a diminutive form of תמרים ("palm trees").[46] This instruction from the first part of 31:21a ironically assumes that the people are to mark the way from the land of Israel to the land of exile so that they will be able to remember the way back for the new exodus, yet the remainder of the verse presupposes

---

44. Calvin, *Jeremiah*, 4:105–6.

45. Holladay (*Jeremiah 2*, 191) refers to an article by Adriaan van Selms ("Motivated Interrogative Sentences in Biblical Hebrew," *Semitics* 2 [1972]: 148–49) who suggests that the question implies an unreality but is motivated by the reality of what is expressed in the following כִּי clause: "Is Ephraim my dear son?—of course not, but he could just as well be, given the fact that every time I speak of him."

46. Rosenberg, trans., *Mikraoth Gedoloth: Jeremiah Volume Two*, 251.

that they are already in exile and ready to return. McKane suggests the possibility that a party of pathfinders is to go ahead of the main body of returning exiles in order to mark the way for those who follow.[47] The people are to put their heart/mind to the highway, the road by which they went (cf. Isa. 11:16; 35:8; 49:11; 57:14; 62:10; Jer. 50:5; 51:50; Ps. 84:6 [Eng., 84:5]; *Tg. Jon.*: "Consider, understand the works that you did whether they were good, for thus you went into exile on a path far away").[48] The Hebrew source behind Greek Jeremiah 31:21b (LXX 38:21b) then says, "Return, O virgin Israel, return to your cities mourning (אל עריך אבלה)" (cf. Jer. 31:4, 9, 13b, 24). The MT says "to these your cities" (אל עריך אלה). *Targum Jonathan* interprets this to mean that Israel is to return to the Torah and to its cities.

In 31:22a (LXX 38:22a), the LORD laments the indecisiveness of Israel: "How long will you turn this way and that, O apostate daughter" (cf. Gen. 42:1; 1 Kgs. 18:21; see also Jer. 3:6, 8, 14, 22; 49:4)? Why should Israel hesitate when the LORD has created "salvation for a new planting in which men will go about in safety?" (ישועה לנטעה חדשה באשר ישועה יסובבו גברים) (Jer. 31:22b [LXX 38:22b]; cf. Isa. 60:21; Jer. 1:10; 24:6; 31:5, 28; 32:41). The MT has a substantially different text for 31:22b. It says that the LORD has created "something new in the land: a female will encompass/surround a man" (חדשה בארץ נקבה תסובב גבר).[49] Bright suggests that this is possibly "a proverbial saying indicating something that is surprising and difficult to believe, the force of which escapes us."[50] Early Christian interpreters (e.g., Jerome) understood this to mean that the Virgin Mary would carry Christ in her womb, but more recent commentators generally do not accept this understanding of the text.[51] Several interpreters take the saying to mean that Israel as a woman will in some way be transformed into a man. Rashi, for instance, cites Rabbi Judah and proposes that virgin daughter Israel will become like a son, a male, who inherits everything.[52] Calvin suggests that the Israelites, who are like

---

47. McKane, *Jeremiah XXVI–LII*, 804. On the other hand, *Targum Jonathan* considers the "signposts" to be a metaphor for the good works of the forefathers that Israel is to remember at this time.

48. Rashi makes an attempt to explain the *kethiv* הלכתי ("I went"): "everywhere that you went I went with you" (Rosenberg, trans., *Mikraoth Gedoloth: Jeremiah Volume Two*, 251).

49. The proposal in the *BHS* apparatus is the following emendation: נְקֵבָה תְּסוֹבֵב גְּבְרָה ("a cursed woman is changed into a lady").

50. Bright, *Jeremiah*, 282.

51. See Keil, *Jeremiah*, 276–77.

52. Rosenberg, trans., *Mikraoth Gedoloth: Jeremiah Volume Two*, 252.

women without strength, will become superior to their enemies.[53] The basic difficulty with any view that sees a female becoming a male is the simple fact that the meaning "turn into" is not a recognized one for the *poel* of סבב (see BDB, 686). One possible alternative is that a female will "protect" a man in the sense that life will be so peaceful in the messianic age that the women will be able to defend the men so that they need not concern themselves with warfare (see Isa. 2:4).[54]

Redak interprets 31:22b to mean that Israel will return to the LORD.[55] This has some support from the use of the *poel* of סבב in Psalm 7:8a (Eng., 7:7a): "And let the assembly of peoples gather around you (תסובבך)." There may be an intential play on words in Jeremiah 31:22 between השובבה ("the apostate") and תסובב ("encompass/surround"). The apostate wife will return to her faithful husband (see Jer. 3:1–4:4). *Targum Jonathan* understands 31:22 to say that the people of the house of Israel will eagerly follow the Torah. This exegesis has its basis in the statement that the LORD has "created" (ברא) "something new" (חדשה) (cf. Num. 16:30). These terms are used for the redemptive work of God in Isaiah (e.g., Isa. 4:5; 42:9; 45:8, 12; 48:6), including the new exodus (Isa. 43:19) and the new creation (Isa. 65:17; 66:22). In the context of Jeremiah 31, the "something new" (חדשה) is the "new covenant" (ברית חדשה) (Jer. 31:31). In this new covenant relationship, the Torah will be written on the heart/mind of the people (Jer. 31:33).

31:23 (38:23) "Thus says the LORD [MT adds: of hosts, the God of Israel], 'Again they will say this word in the land of Judah and in its cities when I restore its fortunes [LXX, Tg. Jon.: captivity], "Blessed be the LORD upon righteous, his holy mountain [MT: May the LORD bless you, O righteous habitation, O holy mountain]." 31:24 (38:24) And there will be those who live in the cities of Judah and in all its land together with a farmer, and he will be elevated with the flock [MT: And they will live in it, Judah and all its cities, together, farmers and those who travel with the flock (cf. Syr., Tg. Jon.)]. 31:25 (38:25) For I have saturated every thirsty [MT: faint] person, and every hungry [MT: languishing] person I have filled.' 31:26 (38:26) At this I awoke and saw; and as for my sleep,

---

53. Calvin, *Jeremiah*, 4:114. Likewise, Holladay sees a reversal in 31:22b of the depiction of the men as women from 30:6 (*Jeremiah 2*, 195). Holladay also proposes that the saying indicates that the female will be the initiator in sexual relations, but this seems to be without exegetical warrant and foreign to the context.

54. This is the view of Giesebrecht (see McKane, *Jeremiah XXVI–LII*, 807).

55. Rosenberg, trans., *Mikraoth Gedoloth: Jeremiah Volume Two*, 252.

it was sweet/pleasant to me [Tg. Jon. The prophet said, 'Because of this news about the days of comfort that are about to come,' said the prophet, 'I awoke and saw. I slept again, and my sleep was beneficial to me'].[56]

31:27 (38:27) 'Therefore [> MT], look, days are coming,' the prophetic utterance of the Lord, *'and I will sow [MT adds: the house of] Israel and [MT adds: the house of] Judah with human seed and animal seed [Tg. Jon.: I will increase them with people and make them prosperous with animals]. 31:28 (38:28) And so, just as I watched over them [MT adds: to pluck up and] to tear down [MT adds: and to throw down and to destroy] and to harm, so will I watch over them to build and to plant,' the prophetic utterance of the* Lord. *31:29 (38:29) 'In those days, they will never again say, "Fathers ate sour grapes, and the [the > MT] children's teeth are the ones that are blunt/dull/numb [Tg. Jon.: The fathers sin, and the children are punished]." 31:30 (38:30) But each for his iniquity will die; and the one [MT: every man] who eats the sour grapes, his teeth will be blunt/dull/numb [Tg. Jon.: every man who sins, he will die].*

31:31 (38:31) Look, days are coming,' the prophetic utterance of the Lord, *'and I will make with the house of Israel and with the house of Judah a new covenant,*[57] *31:32 (38:32) not like the covenant that I made with their forefathers when I took them by their hand to bring them out of the land of Egypt, who broke my covenant [or, my covenant that they broke; LXX: because they did not remain in my covenant],*[58] *and as for me, I loathed them [LXX: I neglected them; MT: I was husband/lord over them; Syr.: I despised them; Tg. Jon.: I was pleased with them],' the prophetic utterance of the* Lord. *31:33 (38:33) 'For this is the covenant that I will make with the house of Israel after these days,' the prophetic utterance of the* Lord: *'I will indeed put [*נתן אתן*; Codex L:* נתתי*; mlt Mss:* ונתתי*] my instructions [MT: my instruction (or, my Torah)] within them [LXX: in their mind], and on their heart/mind I will write them [MT: it], and I will become their God, and as for them, they will become my people. 31:34 (38:34) And they will never again teach each his neighbor and each his brother, saying, "Know the* Lord *[Tg. Jon.: Know to fear before the Lord]," for all of them will know me [Tg. Jon.: will learn to know the fear of me] from the least of them to the greatest of them [Syr.: from their youngest to their oldest; NET: from the least important to the*

---

56. TEV: "So then, people will say, 'I went to sleep and woke up refreshed.'"
57. See Walser, *Jeremiah*, 413–14.
58. See Holmstedt, *Relative Clause*, 172.

most important],' [MT adds: the prophetic utterance of the Lord*], 'for I will forgive their iniquity, and their sin I will never again remember.'*

31:37 (LXX 38:35) [MT adds: Thus says the Lord*,] 'If the sky could be raised on high [MT: If the sky above could be measured],' the prophetic utterance of the* Lord *[> MT], 'and if land's foundation [MT: foundations] below could be searched [LXX: be brought low], also/indeed I could not [not > MT] reject [MT adds: all] the seed of Israel,' the prophetic utterance of the* Lord *[> MT], 'for all that they have done,' [MT adds: the prophetic utterance of the* Lord*]. 31:35 (38:36) Thus says the* Lord *who provides the sun for light by day, [MT adds: the statutes of] the moon and the stars for light by night, and the raging [LXX: shout] of the sea [MT: who disturbs (Syr., Tg. Jon.: rebukes) the sea] so that its waves roar [Syr.: so that its waves cease/are silent], the* Lord *of hosts is his name, 31:36 (38:37) 'If these statutes depart [LXX: cease] from before me,' the prophetic utterance of the* Lord*, 'also the seed of Israel will cease to be a nation from before me all the days.*[59]

31:38 (38:38) Look, days are coming [are coming > Codex L kethiv],' the prophetic utterance of the Lord*, 'and the city will be built for the* Lord *[or, and the city of the* Lord *will be built] from the Tower of Hananel [Tg. Jon.: Piqqus] to the Corner Gate. 31:39 (38:39) And its measure will go out before them up to the hill of Gareb [MT: And the measuring line will go out still further to the hill of Gareb], and it will turn toward Goah [NETS: and it shall be encompassed all round with a circle of choice stones; Tg. Jon.: and it will turn toward the pool of the calf]. 31:40 (38:40) [MT adds: And all the valley (see GKC §127g) of corpses (Syr.: excrement) and the fatty ashes (Tg. Jon.: And all the valley, the place where the army of the Assyrians fell)] [a]nd all the fields [LXX: ασαρημωθ; Codex L kethiv:* השרמות*; Codex L qere, mlt Mss:* השדמות*; Tg. Jon.: brooks; Vulg.: region of death] up to the Kidron Valley, up to the corner of the Horse Gate eastward, will be a place set apart [lit., holiness] to the* Lord*. It will not be plucked up, and it will never again be thrown down forever.'"*

Jeremiah 31:23 (LXX 38:23) looks forward to a time when the Lord will restore the fortunes of his people (cf. Jer. 30:3, 18; 32:44; 33:7, 11). "It looks to a grander consummation when the diaspora *in toto* would be gathered; it is eschatological in its outreach, not bogged down in the

---

59. *Targum Jonathan* puts this in the negative. Just as it is impossible for these statutes to depart, so the seed of Israel cannot cease to be a nation.

stages of recovery but boldly discerning the goal and grasping the end of the process."[60] At that time, they will again say in the land of Judah and in the cities of Judah, "Blessed be the LORD upon righteous, his holy mountain" (ברוך יהוה על צדיק הר קדשו).[61] This version of the text anticipates the restoration of worship upon Mount Zion (cf. Isa. 2:1–5; Jer. 31:6, 12). The MT says, "May the LORD bless you, O righteous habitation, O holy mountain" (יברכך יהוה נוה צדק הר קדשו). This version expects restored prayer for the blessing of Zion and the temple (cf. Num. 6:24; Pss. 128:5; 134:3; see also Isa. 1:21, 26; Jer. 25:30; 50:7, 19; 33:12–13).

According to the Hebrew source behind Greek Jeremiah 31:24 (LXX 38:24), there will be those who live in the cities of Judah and in all his land together with a farmer, "and he will be elevated" (ונשא) with the flock. This apparently means that farmers and livestock will thrive due to the prosperity of the land (see Jer. 31:5, 12, 27). The MT has a different version of the text: "And they will live in it, Judah and all its cities, together, farmers and those who travel (ונסעו) with the flock." Even the lowly farmers and shepherds will inhabit Judah and all his cities (see Gen. 46:34; Jer. 39:10; cf. Zech. 12:7–8).[62] Jeremiah 31:25 (LXX 38:25) explains the indiscriminate way in which everyone will enjoy the good of the land: "For I have saturated every thirsty (צמאה) [MT: faint (עיפה)] person, and every hungry (רעבה) [MT: languishing (דאבה)] person I have filled" (cf. Jer. 31:12, 14; see also Matt. 5:6; 11:28; Luke 6:21).

Various interpretations of Jeremiah 31:26 (LXX 38:26) have been offered. For instance, the TEV translates the verse as if it contained the words of what people will say when they experience the restfulness of the future: "So then, people will say, 'I went to sleep and woke up refreshed'" (cf. Prov. 3:24; Eccl. 5:11 [Eng., 5:12]; see also *4 Bar.* 5). The most consistently held understanding of this verse throughout the history of interpretation is also the one that does the most justice to the form and content of the text. It is the view that the verse is the prophet's response to the vision of verses 23–25, which he has received in a dreamlike or sleeplike state: "At this I awoke and saw; and as for my sleep, it was sweet/pleasant to me" (cf. Gen. 15:12; 28:16; 1 Kgs. 3:15;

---

60. McKane, *Jeremiah XXVI–LII*, 808. See also Calvin, *Jeremiah*, 4:117.

61. LXX: "Blessed be the Lord upon a righteous mountain, his holy place."

62. '"In it' in v 24 refers to 'the land' (feminine in Hebrew); 'Judah and all its cities' is best taken as a gloss to explain 'in it' (see Text) rather than as the subject of 'shall dwell' as *RSV* and *NAB* have it: 'farmhands and those who journey with flocks' is the true subject of the verb" (Holladay, *Jeremiah 2*, 196). If "Judah and all its cities" is the subject, then it is possible that "in it" refers to the "city" (f.) of Jerusalem (see Jer. 31:6, 12, 38).

Jer. 23:28; Zech. 4:1; Job 33:15–16; Dan. 10:9). This interpretation is already present in *Targum Jonathan*: "The prophet said, 'Because of this news about the days of comfort that are about to come,' said the prophet, 'I awoke and saw. I slept again, and my sleep was beneficial to me.'"[63] It may seem to be a difficulty for this view that the prophet only "saw" something after he awoke,[64] but the sense of the verb ראה here is that the prophet "considered" or "reflected upon" what he saw in his sleep after he awoke (see BDB, 907). It was only then that it occurred to him how sweet or pleasant his sleep was to him because of the content of the vision.[65]

Days are coming when the LORD will "sow" both Israel and Judah with human seed and animal seed (Jer. 31:27 [LXX 38:27]; cf. Jer. 32:41; see also Isa. 60:21; 61:3b; Ezek. 34:29; 36:9–11, 36; Amos 9:15). Once again the text of the Book of Comfort envisions the reunification of the northern and southern kingdoms as forecasted already in Jeremiah 3:18 (see again Jer. 30:3). *Targum Jonathan* rightly interprets Jeremiah 31:27 to mean that the LORD will increase Israel and Judah with people and make them prosperous with animals, a reversal of the desolation depicted in Jeremiah 4:23–29. There is also an echo of Hosea 2:25 (Eng., 2:23) in this verse: "And I will sow her for myself in the land, and I will have compassion on Lo Ruhamah, and I will say to Lo Ammi, 'You are my people,' and as for him, he will say, 'My God'" (see also Zech. 10:9). The trajectory of Hosea 2:25 in the Book of the Twelve is such that it includes the Gentiles (see Hos. 2:1 [Eng., 1:10]; 3:5; Amos 9:12; Acts 15:17; Rom. 9:25–26; see also Jer. 3:17).[66] Jeremiah 31:28 (LXX 38:28) then revisits the programmatic language of Jeremiah 1:10, 12 to drive the point home: "And so, just as I watched over them [MT adds: to pluck up and] to tear down [MT adds: and to throw down and to destroy] and to harm, so will I watch over them to build and to plant" (cf. Jer. 24:6; 31:4–5; 42:10; see also Jer. 32:42; Zech. 8:13–15; Ps. 90:15). The longer text of the MT makes the connection to Jeremiah 1:10 even greater, but the link is evident even without the expansion. Just as the LORD is providentially faithful to oversee judgment, either in exile according to the terms of the old covenant (Deut. 28:63–68) or in the tribulation of the last days, so is he faithful to oversee restoration, not only in the return from exile but also in the

---

63. See also Keil, *Jeremiah*, 278; Holladay, *Jeremiah 2*, 196.

64. McKane, *Jeremiah XXVI–LII*, 810.

65. There is no indication in the text that this is merely someone "waking up" to the harsh realities of life after considering the dream of a better future.

66. Shepherd, *Commentary on the Book of the Twelve*, 42–43.

ultimate restoration of the eschaton. Never again will he pluck up or thrown down (Jer. 31:40b).

In the days referenced by verses 27–28, the people will never again say, "Fathers ate sour grapes, and the [the > MT] children's teeth are the ones that are blunt/dull/numb" (Jer. 31:29 [LXX 38:29]; cf. Ezek. 18:2–3). To state that they will one day never say this again presupposes that the proverb is in circulation for the time being (cf. Jer. 3:16; 7:32). This stands in contrast to 31:23, which states what the people will say again, assuming that what they will say is something that is not currently said. *Targum Jonathan* forgoes the metaphor of 31:29 and very plainly says, "The fathers sin, and the children are punished." This is essentially how 31:30 (LXX 38:30) translates the metaphor when it indicates the reversal of the proverb: "But each for his iniquity will die; and the one [MT: every man] who eats the sour grapes, his teeth will be blunt/dull/numb [*Tg. Jon.*: every man who sins, he will die]" (cf. Ezek. 18:4, 19–20). The exposition of this proverb in Ezekiel 18 is part of a series of responses to sayings that served as excuses not to heed the warnings of the prophet (see, e.g., Ezek. 12:22). The people have insisted that their fate is already sealed by the actions of their forefathers (cf. Isa. 14:21; Lam. 5:7).[67] Therefore, what use is their repentance? The LORD explains that each is personally responsible for his or her behavior regardless of family heritage. The wicked man who repents will be treated accordingly, and the righteous man who turns from his righteousness will be treated accordingly. The people have misunderstood the words of the Decalogue: "for I, the LORD your God, am a jealous God, visiting the iniquity of the fathers upon the sons to the third and fourth generations of those who reject me" (Exod. 20:5b).[68] This does not mean that God punishes future generations for the iniquity of previous generations.[69] Deuteronomy 24:16 clarifies this explicitly: "Fathers will not be put to death because of sons, and sons will not be put to death because of fathers; each for his sin will be put to death." Exodus 20:5b is clear that those who perpetuate the iniquity of the fathers ("those who reject me") are the ones who are punished (see also Lev. 26:39). It may very well be that the lack of this

---

67. Ezekiel 14:12–23 addresses the other side of this coin—the argument that the righteousness of a few can count for the many.

68. It is evident from Jeremiah 32:18 that Jeremiah knows this text.

69. Of course, it is possible for future generations to suffer the consequences of acts committed by previous generations (corporate solidarity [e.g., Num. 14:33]), but this is not the same as paying for the sins of previous generations (individual responsibility).

key feature of Exodus 20:5b in texts like Exodus 34:7b led to the misunderstanding. Jeremiah 31:29–30 looks forward to a time when such misunderstanding and excuse making will be eradicated. Since there is no one who is free of sin (1 Kgs. 8:46), the following new covenant passage takes up the question of how anyone can participate in the future restoration. While the wicked will die for their iniquity (Jer. 31:30), the iniquity of the new covenant community will be forgiven (Jer. 31:34).

Jeremiah 31:31 (LXX 38:31) begins the same way 31:27 began, "Look, days are coming." The passage highlights future realities that do not currently exist from the perspective of the author. Within the context of the Book of Comfort, the days referenced here must be considered the last days (see Jer. 30:24b). In these coming days, the LORD will make with the house of Israel and with the house of Judah a "new covenant" (ברית חדשה).[70] It is evident from the larger context of the book of Jeremiah that this new covenant relationship is not limited to ethnic Israel and ethnic Judah (see Jer. 3:17–18; see also Jer. 1:5, 10; 4:2; 12:14–17; 16:19; 46:26b [MT]; 48:47; 49:6 [MT], 39). This is the only place in the Hebrew Bible where the phrase ברית חדשה ("new covenant") is used, although other passages do refer to this same covenant using different terms (see, e.g., Deut. 28:69 [Eng., 29:1]; Isa.

---

70. A "covenant" is a self-binding obligation (see *TLOT* 1:256–66; see also Jer. 34:8–22). It is not a promise (see the discussion in Sailhamer, *Meaning of the Pentateuch*, 419–38). There are several divine-human covenants in the Bible (Noah, Abraham, Moses, David, and the new covenant). There is no covenant with Adam (see Shepherd, *Commentary on the Book of the Twelve*, 71–72), and the covenant with Aaron is included within the Mosaic covenant (Num. 18:19; 25:13). These are not different administrations of the same covenant, nor are they different covenants for different periods (note the textual variation between "covenant" and "covenants" in Rom. 9:4). Rather, they are coexisting covenants, each designed to contribute in its own unique way to the achievement of the same goal: restoration of the lost blessing of life and dominion in the land (Gen. 1:26–28). Of these covenants, the Mosaic covenant is the only conditional and thus temporal covenant (see Lev. 26; Deut. 28). The charge given to Abraham in Genesis 17:10–14 does not change the unconditional and unilateral manner in which the covenant was made in Genesis 15, and the text of 2 Samuel 7:14 does not put a condition on the covenant with David in the manner of the conditions put on the Mosaic covenant (see Shepherd, *Text in the Middle*, 122–29). Thus, while the Mosaic covenant is called a ברית עולם ("indefinite/perpetual covenant") like the others (see Exod. 31:16; cf. Gen. 9:16; 17:7; 2 Sam. 23:5; Jer. 32:40), it is only indefinite or perpetual in the sense that the time of its breaking is not known from the outset.

42:6; 49:8; 59:21; 61:8; Jer. 32:40; 50:5; Ezek. 34:25; 37:26; Hos. 2:20 [Eng., 2:18]; Bar. 2:35). The phrase ברית חדשה does not mean "renewed covenant," something that would require a *pual* participle from חדש to modify ברית.[71] The *piel* of חדש means "renew" (see, e.g., the renewal of the kingship in 1 Sam. 11:14), but it never has ברית ("covenant") for its object anywhere in the Hebrew Bible. The first time that this happens in Hebrew literature is among the Qumran sectarian documents (1Q28b 5:21; 1Q34 3 II, 6; see also CD-A 6:19; 8:21; CD-B 19:33–34; 20:12),[72] and this must be considered an innovation. The correct understanding of ברית חדשה in Jeremiah 31:31 is found in conjunction with the citation of Jeremiah 31:31–34 in Hebrews 8:8–12; 10:16–17. The new covenant does not renew the first covenant (i.e., the Mosaic covenant); rather, it makes the first covenant "obsolete" (Heb. 8:13).[73] This new covenant was made in the inaugural last days with the shedding of the blood of Jesus Christ (see Matt. 26:28; Luke 22:20; 1 Cor. 11:25; cf. Exod. 24:8), and it continues to have implications for the future consummation of all things.

The explication of the new covenant starts in 31:32 (LXX 38:32) with a clear indication of what the new covenant is not. It is not like the covenant that the Lord made with their forefathers when he took them by their hand to bring them out of the land of Egypt (cf. Deut. 29:24

---

71. Even after the initial breaking of the covenant in Exodus 32, there is no covenant renewal. Rather, there is a making of another covenant (Exod. 34:10) based on similar terms (Exod. 34:11–26; cf. Exod. 20–24)

72. The Qumran community believed that it was the new covenant community. For them, the new covenant was essentially a renewal of the old covenant.

73. See Craig A. Evans, "Jeremiah in Jesus and the New Testament," in *Jeremiah: Composition, Reception, and Interpretation*, eds. Jack R. Lundbom, Craig A. Evans, and Bradford A. Anderson (Leiden: Brill, 2018), 303–19. This does not mean that the Old Testament or Hebrew Bible is obsolete, only the old covenant made at Sinai. The New Testament authors appeal to the Hebrew Bible to explain what the new covenant is. Calvin says that the difference between the old and new covenants is one of form but not of substance (*Jeremiah*, 4:127), which seems to minimize the distinction, but Calvin goes on to clarify what he means by this. The continuity between the two is the fact that the Torah written on the tablets in the old covenant is the same Torah written on the heart in the new covenant (132). Calvin acknowledges the newness of the efficacious penetration of the heart in the new covenant and the fact that Jeremiah 31:32 says the new covenant is not like the old one (127–28). Readers can decide whether these are merely formal rather than substantive differences.

[Eng., 29:25]; 1 Kgs. 8:21; see also Isa. 41:13).[74] The LXX translates the following אשר at the beginning of verse 32b with the causal conjunction ὅτι ("because"): "because they did not remain in my covenant." In other words, the new covenant that the LORD will make is not like the old one because the people did not stay in the old one. Others translate the relative clause as a clarification of which covenant is meant: "my covenant that they broke" (see, e.g., ESV). This cannot be any covenant other than the uniquely conditional and temporal Mosaic covenant (see Jer. 11:10; Ezek. 17:19). The translation given above assumes that the relative refers back to "their forefathers" mentioned in the previous clause: "their forefathers . . . who broke my covenant."[75] The new covenant is not like the old one because, unlike the old covenant, the new covenant cannot be broken.[76] Thus, the new covenant is not merely more recent; it is fundamentally better.[77] The final clause of verse 32 differs considerably between the LXX and the MT. The LXX says: "and as for me, I neglected (ἠμέλησα) them" (cf. Syr.: "I despised them"; see also Heb. 8:9). This Greek verb reflects Hebrew גְעלתי ("I loathed"). That is, because the people broke the covenant, the LORD accordingly "loathed" them (see Lev. 26:30; Jer. 14:19 [MT]). On the other hand, the MT says: "and as for me, I was husband/lord (בעלתי) over them" (cf. *Tg.*

---

74. Deuteronomy 5:2–3 makes a similar differentiation between the Sinai covenant (i.e., the Mosaic covenant) and the covenant with the patriarchs (i.e., the Abrahamic covenant).

75. The apostle Paul reiterates that the failure of the old covenant relationship was not the LORD's but the people's (see Rom. 9:6, 31–32). The law itself is good, but because of sin it can only condemn (Rom. 7:10–13). Its offer of life is only a hypothetical one for sinners (Lev. 18:5; Ezek. 20:11, 13, 21, 25; see Shepherd, *Textual World of the Bible*, 38–40).

76. See Neusner, *Jeremiah in Talmud and Midrash*, 14. Leviticus 26:42 casts the new covenant hope in terms of a return of sorts to the unconditional relationship with the patriarchs. Thus, the covenant faithfulness referenced in Leviticus 26:44–45 does not indicate continuation of the Mosaic covenant but faithfulness to the covenant with the patriarchs (see the commentary on Jer. 7:21–28; 11:1–13). Note how Paul also sees the continuity between the Abrahamic covenant and the new covenant (see Rom. 4). For the continuity between the Noahic and Abrahamic covenants, see Sailhamer, *Pentateuch as Narrative*, 128. For the continuity between the Abrahamic and Davidic covenants, see Shepherd, *Text in the Middle*, 123.

77. This is generally the sense of חדש ("new") when the prophets speak of "new things" (Isa. 42:9; 48:6), such as the new exodus (Isa. 43:19) or the new creation (Isa. 65:17). The new thing is not only newer but also better in one way or another.

Jon.: "I was pleased with them"). This probably does not mean that, due to the broken covenant relationship, the Lord had to enforce his lordship over the people. Rather, as many English versions have it, the clause is concessive: "though I was their husband" (see, e.g., ESV). In spite of the fact that the Lord was a faithful husband to the people in the old covenant relationship (see Isa. 54:5; Jer. 3:14), they broke the covenant and did not remain faithful to him (see Jer. 3:1–13; see also Hos. 2:4, 18 [Eng., 2:2, 16]).

Jeremiah 31:33 (LXX 38:33) then states positively what the new covenant actually is that the Lord will make with "the house of Israel" (i.e., the faithful remnant of Israel and Judah and the Gentiles who join them [Jer. 3:17–18]) after these days:[78] "I will indeed put [נתן אתן; Codex L: נתתי; mlt Mss: ונתתי] my instructions [MT: my instruction (or, my Torah)] within them [LXX: in their mind], and on their heart/mind I will write them [MT: it], and I will become their God, and as for them, they will become my people." The Greek Διδοὺς δώσω reflects a Hebrew construction with an infinitive absolute followed by a finite verb from the same root (נתן אתן). MT witnesses have either the *qatal* verb נתתי (Codex L) or the *weqatal* verb ונתתי (mlt Mss). If the reading of the Leningrad Codex is correct, then temporal indicators in the context require that the *qatal* verb be translated into English with a future tense verb (cf. the use of the *qatal* verb in Gen. 15:18).[79] The plural νόμους μου ("my laws") in the Old Greek text reflects תּוֹרֹתַי (also Heb. 8:10; 10:16),[80] a different vocalization of תורתי from that found in the MT's תּוֹרָתִי ("my instruction" [or, "my Torah"]) (cf. Jer. 26:4 [LXX 33:4]; see also *kethiv-qere* Jer. 32:23 [LXX 39:23]). Since the difference between these two requires no change in the consonantal Hebrew text, it is not so much a matter of textual criticism as it is one of interpretation.[81] In the old

---

78. True Israel is believing Israel (see Rom. 4:11–12, 16; 9:7).

79. See Kugel (*Idea of Biblical Poetry*, 17) for *qatal-yiqtol* sequencing in parallel clauses. Adrian Schenker considers the MT's use of the *qatal* verb and the following singular "my instruction" (or, "my Torah") to be a deliberate reference back to the giving of the Torah at Sinai (*Das Neue am neuen Bund und das Alte am alten. Jer 31 in der hebräischen und griechischen Bibel*, FRLANT 212 [Göttingen: Vandenhoeck & Ruprecht, 2006]).

80. The original reading of Codex Sinaiticus has the singular "my law."

81. There are other examples where the Old Greek has the singular "law" where the MT has the plural "instructions" (e.g., Isa. 24:5; Dan. 9:10). See Seeligmann, *Septuagint Version of Isaiah*, 271–72. The use of Greek νόμος to translate Hebrew תורה, which has influenced the use of English "law" to translate this same Hebrew word, is one of the more unfortunate

covenant, God's instruction was simply set "before" the people (Deut. 4:8; 11:32; 1 Kgs. 9:6; Jer. 9:12 [Eng., 9:13]; 26:4; 44:10). In the new covenant, it will be put "within" the people (LXX: "in their mind"; cf. Ps. 40:9 [Eng., 40:8]). In the old covenant, God's instruction was written on tablets of stone (Exod. 24:12; 31:18; 32:15; 34:28–29; Deut. 4:13; 5:22; 9:11; 10:2, 4) but was ineffective to produce faith and obedience.[82] The law was added because of transgression to show the need for a new covenant relationship (Rom. 5:13, 20; 7:8; Gal. 3:19). In the new covenant, this instruction will be written on the heart/mind (see Isa. 51:7; Ps. 37:31; Rom. 2:15; 2 Cor. 3:3, 6). This does not merely mean that the instruction will be committed to memory. Rather, in comparison to other new covenant passages, it speaks of the transformation of the heart/mind (Deut. 10:16; 30:6; Jer. 4:4; 32:39; Ezek. 18:31; Rom. 2:28–29; Jas. 1:21; *L.A.E.* 13:5) and the enabling of faith and obedience by means of the Spirit of God (Ezek. 11:19–20; 36:26–27; Rom. 8:4).[83] Under the old covenant, the people did not yet have a heart/mind to know God (Deut 29:3 [Eng., 29:4]), and only their sin was written on the tablet of their heart/mind (MT Jer. 17:1), but in the new covenant they will no longer bound by sin. They will be free to do the will of God (see Jer. 24:7; Rom. 6).[84] The LORD will truly be the God of the new covenant people, and

---

occurrences in the translation history of the Bible. The Hebrew word תורה does not mean "law" but "instruction." Of course, it can refer to a law code as instruction, but it can also refer to things like parental instruction (e.g., Prov. 1:8) or the entire Pentateuch (e.g., Neh. 8:1; see also John 10:34; 15:25; Rom. 3:19 [where *nomos* is used more broadly for the Hebrew Bible in general]). In the LXX, the term νόμος is basically a symbol for תורה, so that readers of LXX-influenced literature like the Greek New Testament must learn to think of תורה when they see νόμος (see Tov, *Greek and Hebrew Bible*, 90).

82. The instruction written on the tablets of stone was the Decalogue, which represented the entire covenant (Deut. 4:13; 1 Kgs. 8:21).

83. See also Deuteronomy 6:5–6; 11:18; 30:14; Psalms 51:12 (Eng., 51:10); 119:11; Proverbs 3:3; 7:3. Study of the Torah is still necessary for the new covenant believer (Josh. 1:8; Ps. 1:2). Transformation of the heart/mind does not mean that members of the new covenant community will automatically know the Torah, only that they will be receptive to it and will be able to respond to it appropriately.

84. Thus, the instructions of the Pentateuch remain relevant for the new covenant believer to learn wisdom, which is the fear of the LORD (Deut. 4:6; 31:13; Jer. 32:39–40; Ps. 19:10 [Eng., 19:9]; Job 28:28; Prov. 1:9; 9:10). The laws must now be read according to their function within the composition of the Pentateuch (see Sailhamer, *Pentateuch as Narrative*; *Introduction to*

they will truly be his people (see Exod. 6:7; 29:45; Lev. 26:12; Jer. 7:23; 11:4; 24:7; 30:22 [MT]; 31:1; 32:38; Ezek. 11:20; 36:28; Hos. 2:25 [Eng., 2:23]; Zech. 13:9; Bar. 2:35; Rev. 21:3).

For the new covenant people of God, there will no longer be any need to teach one another to know the LORD (Jer. 31:34a [LXX 38:34a]).[85] Under the old covenant, it was possible for someone to be a member of the community by birth without any authentic knowledge of the LORD. In the new covenant community, knowing the LORD will be the requirement for membership. Thus, all members will already know the LORD (i.e., they will be taught by God; see Isa. 54:13; 1 Thess. 4:9; see also Isa. 2:3). There will be no such thing as a new covenant member who does not know the LORD, for all of them will know the LORD "from the least of them to the greatest of them" (Jer. 31:34b [LXX 38:34b]; see Jer. 24:7).[86] This does not mean that there will be no need for teaching of any kind in the new covenant community. The apostle John cites this text in 1 John 2:27 to reassure his readers that they know the LORD and are thus members of the new covenant community (see 1 John 5:13), but he is also teaching them many things throughout his epistle. According to the conclusion of the new covenant passage in Jeremiah 31:34b, it is the LORD's forgiveness of the people's iniquity and his perpetual forgetting of their sin that makes the new covenant relationship possible (see Isa. 43:25; 44:22; Jer. 5:7; 14:10; 33:8; Mic. 7:19; Ps. 103:12; Luke 24:44–47; Acts 10:43; Rom. 11:27). The blood of Jesus Christ, which was shed once for all, makes provision for this forgiveness by paying the penalty for sin, meeting God's just demands and thus satisfying him in his wrath (Isa. 53:4–6; Zech. 12:10; 13:1; Rom. 3:21–26; Heb. 9:22; 10:12).

The small unit in Jeremiah 31:35–37 (LXX 38:35–37) addresses the permanence of the new covenant relationship (see again Jer. 32:40).

Old Testament Theology; Meaning of the Pentateuch). New covenant readers of the Pentateuch are not ancient Israelites receiving the law on tablets of stone at Sinai for the terms of an old covenant relationship in which blessing depends upon a kind of obedience that cannot possibly be maintained.

85. Holladay contrasts this with what is said about the people in Jeremiah 9:4–5 (Eng., 9:5–6) (*Jeremiah 2*, 198). See also Jeremiah 2:8; 34:17. According to Jeremiah 9:23 (Eng., 9:24) and 22:15–16, to know the LORD is to do justice and righteousness. See also Hosea 6:6.

86. This could mean "from their youngest to their oldest," as the Syriac has it (cf. Jer. 6:11, 13; Joel 3:1–2 [Eng., 2:28–29]), or it could mean "from the least important to the most important," as the NET has it (cf. Jer. 5:4–5; 42:1; 44:12). The text may be intentionally ambiguous. See also Psalm 115:13.

The arrangement of these verses differs between the Hebrew source behind Greek Jeremiah and the MT. The last verse of the unit in the MT (31:37) is the first verse of the unit in the LXX (38:35). The MT has added an introduction ("Thus says the Lord") to 31:37 (LXX 38:35), perhaps due to its relocation of this verse to the end of the unit (cf. Jer. 31:35 [LXX 38:36]). This introduction does not appear in the Hebrew source behind Greek Jeremiah. The remainder of 31:37 (LXX 38:35) is fairly straightforward. If the sky could be "raised on high" (ירמו; MT: If the sky above could be "measured" [ימדו]), and if land's foundation (MT: foundations) below could be searched (LXX: brought low), even then, according to the Hebrew source behind Greek Jeremiah, the Lord could not (not > MT) reject the seed of Israel (MT: all the seed of Israel) for all that they have done. The MT does not have the negation in the apodosis, which gives the sense that the Lord could reject all the seed of Israel only if the impossibilities of measuring the sky and searching land's foundations could be accomplished. Either way, the point is clear. There is no way that the Lord could reject the seed of Israel (see Jer. 14:19; 31:27).[87]

The text of 31:35–36 (LXX 38:36–37) makes a similar argument. 31:35 (LXX 38:36) introduces the Lord as the one who provides the sun for light by day, the moon and the stars for light by night, and the "raging" (רגז; LXX: "shout") of the sea so that its waves roar (see Gen. 1:14–19; Isa. 51:15; Jer. 5:22; Amos 4:13; 5:8; 4Q392 1:6). The Lord of hosts is his name (cf. Jer. 10:16b; 32:18b [MT]; 46:18 [MT]; 48:15 [MT]; 50:34; 51:19, 57). The MT refers to the "statutes" or "ordinances" (חקת) of the moon and the stars (cf. Jer. 5:22; 31:36; 33:25; Ps. 148:6; Job 38:10; Prov. 8:27, 29). The MT also has a different reading for 31:35b (LXX 38:36b): "who disturbs (רגע) the sea" (cf. Isa. 51:15; Job 26:12). Both the Syriac and *Targum Jonathan* have "rebukes" (= נער?). According to 31:36 (LXX 38:37), if the statutes or ordinances of 31:35 (LXX 38:36) depart (LXX: cease) from before the Lord, then the seed of Israel will cease to be a nation from before him all the days (cf. Isa. 54:9–10; Jer. 33:19–26 [MT]; Pss. 72:5, 7; 89:37–38 [Eng., 89:36–37]; 93; Matt. 5:18). Since the Lord is the one who sustains creation (Gen. 8:22), the continuance of Israel is guaranteed.[88] This passage is not about the permanence of ethnic or political Israel but that of believing

---

87. The seed of Israel in Isaiah is the remnant of the people of God (Isa. 6:13; 44:3; 45:25; 53:10; 61:9; 65:9; 66:22; see also Ezra 9:2).

88. The present creation will pass away, but the new creation will last forever (Isa. 65:17; 66:22; Ps. 102:27–29 [Eng., 102:26–28]; 2 Pet. 3:1–13; Rev. 21:1–4; see also Isa. 60:19–20; Zech. 14:6–7; Rev. 21:22–22:5).

Israel as part of the new covenant people of God (see Rom. 9:6–7, 24–25; 10:12; 11:1–2, 25–27, 29).

The final subunit of chapter 31 (LXX 38) in verses 38–40 looks forward to the new Jerusalem to be enjoyed by the new covenant community when they return in the new exodus (cf. Isa. 65:18–25; Rev. 21:9–22:5; see also Isa. 51:3; Ezek. 36:35). Rashi comments, "Now this prophecy relates to the future, to the final redemption, since it did not take place in the time of the Second Temple."[89] Days are coming (cf. Jer. 31:27, 31) when the city will be built for thye LORD (or, the city of the LORD will be built) from the Tower of Hananel to the Corner Gate, from northeast to northwest (Jer. 31:38 [LXX 38:38]; see 2 Kgs. 14:13; Zech. 14:10; Neh. 3:1; 12:39; 2 Chr. 26:9; see also Jer. 30:18; 31:4). The city's measure (MT: measuring line) will extend to the hill of Gareb and then turn toward Goah (Jer. 31:39 [LXX 38:39]; cf. Zech. 2:6 [Eng., 2:2]). Gareb and Goah are otherwise unknown,[90] but the measurement here is perhaps from the southwest to the southeast.[91] The addition at the beginning of MT 31:40 does not appear in the Hebrew source behind Greek Jeremiah (LXX 38:40): "And all the valley of corpses and the fatty ashes." This is usually taken to be a reference to the valley of Ben Hinnom (see Jer. 7:31–8:3; 19:6–7).[92] The remainder of verse 40a says that all the fields up to the Kidron Valley (BDB, 871), up to the corner of the Horse Gate eastward (Neh. 3:28), will be a place set apart to the LORD (cf. Ezek. 45:1; Zech. 14:21). The word translated "the fields" appears transliterated in the LXX as ασαρημωθ, and it is spelled in the *kethiv* of the Leningrad Codex with a *resh*: השרמות. Keil follows this reading and explains it on the basis of an Arabic root meaning "to cut off" in the sense of "ravines, hollows" (cf. *Tg. Jon.*: "brooks").[93] On the other hand, the reading of the Leningrad Codex *qere* and a multitude of other Masoretic manuscripts spells this word with a *daleth*: השדמות

---

89. Rosenberg, trans., *Mikraoth Gedoloth: Jeremiah Volume Two*, 257. See also Calvin, *Jeremiah*, 4:150; Keil, *Jeremiah*, 287. The prophecy also presupposes a resurrection that will enable the people of God throughout the ages to participate (Dan. 12:2).

90. The LXX translator apparently did not know what to do with the latter part of verse 39 (NETS: "and it shall be encompassed all round with a circle of choice stones"; cf. Jer. 31:22 [MT]; Zech. 9:16). *Targum Jonathan* interprets גּעתה ("toward Goah") from the root גּעה ("to low") and thus translates "toward the pool of the calf."

91. See Bright, *Jeremiah*, 283; Holladay, *Jeremiah 2*, 199.

92. See Bright, *Jeremiah*, 283; but see also McKane, *Jeremiah XXVI–LII*, 834.

93. Keil, *Jeremiah*, 286.

("the fields"; see BDB, 995; see also 2 Kgs. 23:4).[94] Efforts to analyze this word on the basis of Ugaritic evidence as "the field of death" (cf. Vulg.) or "the field of Mot" (the Canaanite god of death) have not been met with widespread acceptance.[95] Jeremiah 31:40b (LXX 38:40b) concludes the chapter with a reiteration of 31:28 (also Jer. 24:6): "It will not be plucked up, and it will never again be thrown down forever." This is yet another part of the development of the program set forth in Jeremiah 1:10. It is not immediately evident what the grammatical subject of the masculine verbs in 31:40b might be. In the MT, it could be the word "valley" (עמק) at the beginning of the verse, but this word does not appear in the Hebrew source behind Greek Jeremiah. The noun קדש, which is typically translated here as an adjective ("holy"), should probably be understood in the sense "holy place." Thus, it is the place set apart to the LORD that will never be plucked up or thrown down (cf. Amos 9:15).

---

94. Holladay translates this word as "terraces" (*Jeremiah 2*, 200).

95. See Bright, *Jeremiah*, 283–84; Holladay, *Jeremiah 2*, 200; McKane, *Jeremiah XXVI–LII*, 833.

JEREMIAH 32 (LXX 39)

32:1 (39:1) The word that came from the LORD *to Jeremiah [MT: to Jeremiah from the* LORD*] in the tenth year of King Zedekiah [MT: of Zedekiah the king of Judah] (that is, the eighteenth year of Nebuchadnezzar [MT: Nebuchadrezzar] the king of Babylon):*

32:2 (39:2) (And [MT adds: at that time] the army of the king of Babylon was besieging Jerusalem, and Jeremiah [MT adds: the prophet] was confined in the court of the guard, which was in [or, attached to] the royal palace [MT adds: of Judah], 32:3 (39:3) whom King Zedekiah [MT: Zedekiah the king of Judah] confined [LXX: in which King Zedekiah confined him], saying, "Why are you prophesying, saying, 'Thus says the LORD*, "Look, I am about to give / deliver this city into the hand / power of the king of Babylon, and he will capture it; 32:4 (39:4) and as for Zedekiah [MT adds: the king of Judah], he will not escape from the hand / power of the Chaldeans, for he will surely be given / delivered into the hand / power of the king of Babylon, and his mouth will speak with his mouth, and his eyes will see his eyes, 32:5 (39:5) and to Babylon Zedekiah will go [MT: he will cause Zedekiah to go], and there he will be [LXXA: die; MT adds: until I visit him," the prophetic utterance of the* LORD*; "when / if you fight the Chaldeans, you will not succeed]'"?")*

32:6 (39:6) And the word of the LORD *came to Jeremiah, saying [MT: And Jeremiah said, "The word of the* LORD *came to me, saying"], 32:7 (39:7) "Look, Hanamel the son of Shallum your uncle is coming to you, saying, 'Purchase my field [LXX: the field],[1] which is in Anathoth [Syr. adds: which is in the land of Benjamin], for you have the right of redemption to purchase.'" 32:8 (39:8) And Hanamel the son of Shallum my uncle came to me [MT adds: according to the word of the* LORD*] in the court of the guard, and he said to me, "Purchase my field, which is in the land of Benjamin, the one that is in Anathoth [MT: which is in Anathoth, which is in the land of Benjamin], for you have the right of possession, and you are an elder [MT: and you have the redemption; purchase]." And I knew that it was the word of the* LORD*. 32:9 (39:9) And I purchased the field from Hanamel the son of my uncle [MT adds: which was in Anathoth], and I weighed to him [MT adds: the silver] seventeen shekels of silver. 32:10 (39:10) And*

---

1. The imperative is followed in the Hebrew text by the so-called *dativus ethicus*, which is normally untranslated (see *IBHS* 11.2.10d).

I wrote in the document and sealed (it), and I took witnesses; and I weighed the silver on scales. 32:11 (39:11) And I took the document of purchase, the sealed [MT adds: the command and the statutes] and the opened, 32:12 (39:12) and I gave it [MT: the document, the purchase; eastern qere: the document of purchase] to Baruch the son of Neriah, the son of Mahseiah in the presence of Hanamel the son of my uncle and in the presence of those standing and those writing [Codex L: in the presence of the witnesses who were writing (mlt Mss: written)] in the document of purchase and [and > Codex L] in the presence of [MT adds: all] the Judeans who were [MT adds: sitting] in the court of the guard. 32:13 (39:13) And I commanded Baruch in their presence, saying, 32:14 (39:14) "Thus says the LORD of hosts [MT adds: the God of Israel], 'Take [MT adds: these documents] this document of purchase [MT adds: both the sealed] and the [MT: this] opened document and put [MT adds: them] in an earthenware vessel in order that it [MT: they] may stand/remain for many days.' 32:15 (39:15) For thus says the LORD [MT adds: of hosts, the God of Israel], 'Again fields and houses [MT: houses and fields] and vineyards will be purchased in this land.'"

*32:16 (39:16) And I prayed to the LORD after I gave the document of purchase to Baruch the son of Neriah, saying, 32:17 (39:17) "Ah [LXX: The one who is], LORD [MT: Lord GOD]! You are the one who made the sky and the land by your great strength and by your outstretched [LXX: high] arm. Nothing is too difficult for you [LXX, Syr., Tg. Jon.: Nothing is hidden from you], 32:18 (39:18) performing covenant loyalty for thousands and repaying iniquity [LXX: sins] of fathers into the bosom/lap of their children after them, the great, the mighty God [MT adds: whose name is the LORD of hosts], 32:19 (39:19) the LORD [> MT; see v. 18b], the great of counsel [LXX: Lord of great counsel] and the great of deed [LXX: deeds], great God of hosts [LXX: the great God Almighty], LORD of great name [great God of hosts, LORD of great name > MT], your eyes are upon [MT: whose eyes are opened to all] the ways of people to give to each according to his way [MT adds: and according to the fruit of his deeds], 32:20 (39:20) who put signs and wonders in the land of Egypt until this day [LXX*L*: and until this day], and in Israel and among mankind [or, both in Israel and among mankind; Syr.: for Israel among mankind; Tg. Jon.: and for Israel you performed miracles in the midst of mankind], and made for yourself a name as this day 32:21 (39:21) and brought your people Israel out of the land of Egypt with signs and with wonders and with a strong hand and with an outstretched [LXX: high] arm and with* *great spectacle [MT: fear/awe]*[2] *32:22 (39:22) and gave to them this land, which you swore to their forefathers [MT adds: to give to them], a land flowing with milk and honey, 32:23 (39:23) and they came and possessed it, but they did not obey your voice, and in your instructions [Codex L qere, mlt Mss: your instruction] they did not walk, all that you commanded them [MT adds: to do] they did not do, and you caused all this calamity to befall them. 32:24 (39:24) Look, the mounds [LXX: a crowd],*[3] *they have come to the city to capture it, and the city has been given/delivered into the hand/power of the Chaldeans who are fighting against it because of the sword and the famine [MT adds: and the plague]. Just as you spoke, so it has happened [MT: And that which you spoke is what has happened]. [MT adds: And look, you are seeing.] 32:25 (39:25) And you, you have said to me [MT adds: O Lord* GOD], *'Purchase the field with silver.' And I wrote in the document and sealed and took witnesses [MT: 'Purchase the field with silver and take witnesses']; and the city, it has been given/delivered into the hand/ power of the Chaldeans."*

Jeremiah 32 and 33 (LXX 39 and 40) now form the second half of the Book of Comfort and thus contribute to the prophecy of future redemption for the people of God begun in chapters 30 and 31 (LXX 37 and 38). The heading that appears in 32:1a (LXX 39:1a)—"The word that came from the LORD to Jeremiah [MT: to Jeremiah from the LORD]"—appears throughout the book (Jer. 7:1; 11:1; 18:1; 21:1; 30:1; 34:1, 8; 35:1; 40:1). Jeremiah 33:1 (LXX 40:1) builds on the word from the LORD in chapter 32 (LXX 39) and introduces a second word of the LORD. The word from the LORD in chapter 32 came in the tenth year of Zedekiah, which is coordinated with the eighteenth year of Nebuchadnezzar (Jer. 32:1b [LXX 39:1b]; cf. Jer. 25:1; 52:12).[4]

Verses 2–5 provide parenthetical background information for the account of Jeremiah's purchase of his cousin's field in verses 6–15. Thus,

---

2. The Göttingen Septuagint (Ziegler) and the NETS put this phrase at the beginning of verse 22, but the MT and Rahlfs' edition of the LXX have it at the end of verse 21. See also Tov, *Text-Critical Use of the Septuagint*, 193.

3. LXX ὄχλος ("a crowd") is perhaps an inner-Greek corruption of ὁ χοῦς ("the earth/soil heaped up") (see *BHS* apparatus).

4. "The synchronism with Zedekiah's tenth year (588/7) is correct only if Nebuchadnezzar's reign is counted from his accession in the fall of 605 (cf. xxv 1; lii 12; II Kings xxv 8); counting from his first official regnal year (604/3), as in lii 29, 588/7 was his seventeenth year" (Bright, *Jeremiah*, 236). See also Jeremiah 39:1–2.

the word from the LORD introduced in verse 1 has to be reintroduced in verse 6 before it appears in verse 7. Nevertheless, the entire chapter is about this word from the LORD, including Jeremiah's prayer (vv. 16–25) and the word of the LORD that comes in response to Jeremiah's prayer (vv. 26–44). The background in verses 2–5 is connected to the narrative of Jeremiah 37–38. The Babylonian siege of Jerusalem began in the ninth year of Zedekiah (Jer. 39:1; 52:4). When the Babylonians heard that Pharaoh's army had departed from Egypt, the siege was temporarily lifted (Jer. 37:5, 11). During that time, Jeremiah departed Jerusalem to go to the land of Benjamin "to receive a portion" (לחלק; LXX: "to buy") from there in the midst of the people (Jer. 37:12). Bright comments on the transaction in Jeremiah 32:6–15, "Indeed, it is probable that Jeremiah had been trying to go to Anathoth to attend to this very matter, when he was arrested."[5] When Jeremiah attempted to go to the land of Benjamin, he was accused of desertion and thrown in prison (Jer. 37:13–16), but at Jeremiah's request Zedekiah had him relocated to "the court of the guard" (Jer. 37:20–21) where he stayed, with the exception of a brief time in the pit/cistern (Jer. 38:6–13), until Jerusalem was captured (Jer. 38:28). It was during the time of the Babylonian siege, when Jeremiah was confined in the court of the guard in or attached to the royal palace, that Hanamel came to him (Jer. 32:2, 8 [LXX 39:2, 8]; see also Jer. 33:1; 34:1).

When Zedekiah confined Jeremiah in the court of the guard, he questioned him about his prophecy: "Why are you prophesying, saying, 'Thus says the LORD, "Look, I am about to give/deliver this city into the hand/power of the king of Babylon, and he will capture it'"?" (Jer. 32:3 [LXX 39:3]; cf. Jer. 34:2, 22; 37:8). This is not an attempt to gather information from Jeremiah. Rather, it is a rhetorical question designed to express objection to Jeremiah's prophecy (cf. Jer. 26:9; 36:29). The remainder of Jeremiah's prophecy as quoted by Zedekiah focuses on Zedekiah himself (note the fronting of Zedekiah's name in the Hebrew syntax of Jer. 32:4a [LXX 39:4a]). Zedekiah will not escape from the Chaldeans. He will be delivered to the king of Babylon, "and his mouth will speak with his mouth, and his eyes will see his eyes" (Jer. 32:4b [LXX 39:4b]; cf. Jer. 21:7; 34:3; 39:7; 52:11; see also Isa. 52:8). The shorter text of the Hebrew source behind Greek Jeremiah 32:5 (LXX 39:5) says: "and to Babylon Zedekiah will go (ילך), and there he will be [LXX[A]: die]" (cf. Jer. 34:4–5; 39:7; 52:11; Ezek. 12:8–16; 17:16). The longer text of MT 32:5 says: "and to Babylon he will cause Zedekiah to go (יולך), and there he will be until I visit him," the prophetic utterance

5. Bright, *Jeremiah*, 239.

of the LORD, "when/if you fight the Chaldeans, you will not succeed." Rashi comments that the visitation here is that of Zedekiah's death (cf. Num. 16:29).[6]

After the parenthesis of verses 2–5, the word of the LORD introduced in verse 1 is reintroduced in verse 6: "And the word of the LORD came to Jeremiah, saying [MT: And Jeremiah said, 'The word of the LORD came to me, saying']."[7] This word of the LORD is essentially an announcement that Hanamel, the son of Jeremiah's uncle Shallum, is coming to the prophet to request that Jeremiah exercise his right of redemption to purchase Hanamel's field in Anathoth (Jer. 32:7 [LXX 39:7]).[8] It is known from Jeremiah 1:1 that the prophet came from a priestly family in Anathoth in the land of Benjamin. It is also known from the two confessions in 11:18–23 and 12:1–6 that Jeremiah faced bitter opposition from the people of Anathoth and from members of his own family. This background creates a fascinating dynamic for the account of Hanamel's request. The precise nature of Jeremiah's relationship with Hanamel is otherwise unknown. Hanamel's request appears to follow the law of land redemption in Leviticus 25:25–34.[9] It is not stated whether Jeremiah was Hanamel's nearest of kin or simply the only family member willing and able to fulfill the obligation.[10] The

---

6. Rosenberg, trans., *Mikraoth Gedoloth: Jeremiah Volume Two*, 259. "It, however, seems that some alleviation was promised, if indeed a certain kind of death may be deemed a favor" (Calvin, *Jeremiah*, 4:157).

7. "Let then this history be remembered, that though Jeremiah was a captive, yet his word was free and his tongue at liberty, as Paul also boasts, that though he was bound with chains, yet God's word was not bound" (Calvin, *Jeremiah*, 4:155). See Acts 28:16–31; 2 Timothy 2:9.

8. "It may now be asked, how could Hanameel, who was of the Levitical order, sell a field, for we know that fields did not belong to the Levites, and that they had tithes for their inheritance (Num. xviii. 21). But this is to be taken for a suburban field, for they had the suburbs, and each had a meadow" (Calvin, *Jeremiah*, 4:163).

9. "The right of redemption consisted in this, that if any one was forced through circumstances to sell his landed property, the nearest blood-relation had the right, or rather was obliged, to preserve the possession for the family, either through pre-emption, or redemption from the stranger who had bought it" (Keil, *Jeremiah*, 289). Ownership of the land subsequently reverted to the original owner in the year of Jubilee. Thompson speculates that Hanamel may have either fallen into debt or despaired of the future and decided to sell (*Book of Jeremiah*, 588).

10. Information about Jeremiah's source of income and economic status is not provided.

conclusion to Jeremiah's prayer in 32:25 (LXX 39:25) shows that the word of the LORD about Hanamel's request was received as a command from the LORD to purchase the field.

Jeremiah 32:8a (LXX 39:8a) narrates that Hanamel did in fact come to Jeremiah (MT adds: "according to the word of the LORD") in the court of the guard to request that the prophet purchase his field in Anathoth. The wording of Hanamel's request is slightly different from what was anticipated in verse 7. He uses the term "the right of possession" (משפט הירשה) as a substitute for "the right of redemption" (משפט הגאלה). Furthermore, according to the Hebrew source behind Greek Jeremiah, Hanamel explains that Jeremiah is an elder (ואתה זקן), whereas in the MT he simply adds that the redemption belongs to Jeremiah and then repeats his request that Jeremiah purchase the field ("and you have the redemption; purchase"). Jeremiah then says that he knew on the basis of this encounter that the word he received in verse 7 was truly a word from the LORD (Jer. 32:8b [LXX 39:8b]). According to Deuteronomy 18:22, only the word that comes to pass is the word of the LORD.[11]

According to the first-person narrative in 32:9 (LXX 39:9), Jeremiah purchased the field from Hanamel and weighed to him seventeen shekels of silver, which was presumably a fair price (cf. Gen. 23:15). He wrote in the document of purchase and sealed it and took witnesses; and he weighed the silver on scales (Jer. 32:10 [LXX 39:10]; cf. Isa. 8:2). Verse 10 appears to be a topical overview of the purchase narrated in verse 9. Holladay suggests that Jeremiah "wrote" in the document in the sense that he dictated to his scribe Baruch who is subsequently mentioned in verse 12 (cf. Jer. 36:2, 4, 32).[12] The sealing not only closed the document (cf. Isa. 8:16) but also attested Jeremiah's subscription to the transaction.[13] The taking of witnesses seems to be out of chronological order, but Holladay comments that "the evidence of deeds from Elephantine and the Judean desert indicates that witnesses signed the outside of the sealed section of the deed" (see also

---

11. "The Prophet therefore did not then for the first time learn that God had spoken, but as he was confirmed in the certainty of his faith, and in the thing itself, there is no inconsistency; for nothing is taken away from the credit and authority of God's word, when the reality and experience confirm us; and thus God often has a regard to the weakness of his people" (Calvin, *Jeremiah*, 4:162).

12. Holladay, *Jeremiah 2*, 214.

13. Holladay, *Jeremiah 2*, 214.

Jer. 32:44 [LXX 39:44]).[14] According to the Mishnah, an unfolded document has the signatures of witnesses at the bottom of the page, while a folded document has them behind each page (*m. B. Bat.* 10:1). Both an unfolded document with signatures on the back and a folded document with signatures on the inside are invalid. An unfolded document has two witnesses, and a folded document has three (*m. B. Bat.* 10:2; see also *b. B. Bat.* 160b and Deut. 17:6; 19:15).

The document of purchase is described in 32:11 (LXX 39:11) as "the sealed and the opened." The MT adds that "the sealed" contained "the command and the statutes" (> LXX) or "the order of transfer and the stipulations." Older commentators (e.g., Calvin) assumed that verse 11 referred to two separate versions of the document of purchase, but the more recent view, which is based on the discovery of ancient deeds at Elephantine and in the Judean desert, proposes that "the sealed and the opened" were two parts of the same document.[15] The top half of the document included the fine print of the contract and was rolled and sealed (possibly to protect it from alteration). The bottom half may have been an exact copy of the top, but the wording of the MT suggests that it was more of a summary, which was left open and available for reference (cf. Est. 3:14; 8:13). Jeremiah gave this document of purchase to his scribe Baruch (Jer. 32:12a [LXX 39:12a]). Baruch is mentioned here for the first time in the book of Jeremiah. He was the brother of Seraiah (Jer. 51:59). Both men are called "the son of Neriah, the son of Mahseiah." Jeremiah gave the document to Baruch in the presence of Hanamel and in the presence of the witnesses who signed the document. There were also onlooking Judeans who were present in the court of the guard when Jeremiah gave the document to Baruch (Jer. 32:12b [LXX 39:12b]).[16]

When Jeremiah gave the document of purchase to Baruch in the presence of all those listed in verse 12, he also gave him instructions (Jer. 32:13 [LXX 39:13]), which appear in verse 14 in the form of divine discourse: "Take [MT adds: these documents] this document of purchase [MT adds: both the sealed] and the [MT: this] opened document and put [MT adds: them] in an earthenware vessel in order that it [MT: they] may stand/remain for many days." The longer text of the MT provides some clarification of the shorter text behind Greek Jeremiah. Baruch was to take the two-part document of purchase ("the sealed and the opened") and deposit it in an earthenware vessel for

---

14. Holladay, *Jeremiah 2*, 214.
15. See Bright, *Jeremiah*, 238; Holladay, *Jeremiah 2*, 215.
16. See Holladay, *Jeremiah 2*, 216.

safekeeping (cf. Dan. 8:26b; 12:4). The successfulness of this method of preservation is attested by the modern discovery of jars containing ancient scrolls at Qumran.

Thus far the account of the transaction between Jeremiah and Hanamel, while interesting in its own right, appears to have little to do with the larger context of the Book of Comfort. It is the LORD's explanation of the purchase in 32:15 (LXX 39:15) that provides the first clear indication that the entire transaction is a prophetic sign act that symbolizes future redemption:[17] "Again fields and houses [MT: houses and fields] and vineyards will be purchased in this land" (cf. Jer. 31:5; 32:43–44). Land redemption would have seemed absurd at a time when the land was under siege from the Babylonians (Jer. 32:24–25). The land was about to fall into the hands of the Babylonians anyway, so what was the point of the transaction? Verse 15 shows that Jeremiah's purchase of Hanamel's field was much more than a futile attempt to keep property in the family. It illustrated the future restoration of all that would be lost in the coming judgment. Given the eschatological context set by the Book of Comfort (e.g., Jer. 30:5–7, 24b; 31:1, 27, 31, 38), this should not be understood merely as a reference to a revitalized economy when Judeans would begin to trickle back into the land in the postexilic period. Rather, as explained in 32:36–44, it looks forward to an eschatological gathering of the people of God and a new covenant relationship to be enjoyed in a final state of affairs in the land of the covenant. Elsewhere this new setting is variously known as the new creation (Isa. 65:17), the new garden of Eden (Isa. 51:3; Ezek. 36:35), the New Jerusalem (Isa. 65:18; Jer. 31:38–40), or the messianic kingdom.[18]

Jeremiah's relatively lengthy prayer in 32:16–25 (LXX 39:16–25) does not reach its main objective until the final two verses, where he points out the seemingly illogical relationship between the current Babylonian siege and the LORD's instruction to purchase Hanamel's field, which is essentially Jeremiah's way of requesting further explanation beyond what is provided in verse 15. Jeremiah builds up to this with an extensive affirmation of his theological conviction that has enabled him for the time being to follow the LORD's direction despite the

---

17. For other prophetic sign acts in the book, see Jeremiah 13:1–14; 16:1–9; 18:1–12; 19:1–13; 27–28; 43:8–13; 51:59–64.

18. According to Isaiah 61:1, the messianic servant of the LORD is sent to proclaim "liberty" (דרור) to captives (cf. Luke 4:16–30). This terminology comes from the instructions for the year of Jubilee (Lev. 25:10), the same year in which redeemed property was to revert to original ownership (Lev. 25:28).

fact that he has not fully grasped the meaning of that direction. This feature of Jeremiah's prayer, like the prayers in the book of Psalms, is exemplary. Indeed, the entire exchange between Jeremiah and the LORD in the second half of chapter 32 (LXX 39) is beneficial to the reader not only because of the model that Jeremiah's prayer provides but also because of the elaborated exposition of the prophetic sign act that comes in verses 26–44 as a result of Jeremiah's prayer.

According to 32:16 (LXX 39:16), Jeremiah did not begin to pray until after he gave the document of purchase to Baruch (see Jer. 32:12). The opening to Jeremiah's prayer ("Ah [LXX: The one who is], LORD [MT: Lord GOD]!") is similar to other alarmed or grieved responses in the book (see commentary on Jer. 1:6; 4:10; 14:13). In the present instance, Jeremiah is simply trying to work out his confusion. Jeremiah affirms that the LORD is the creator who made the sky and the land (a merism for the whole world) by his great strength and by his outstretched arm (Jer. 32:17a [LXX 39:17a]; see Gen. 1:1; Jer. 10:12; 27:5; 32:21). Nothing is too difficult for him (Jer. 32:17b [LXX 39:17b]; cf. Gen. 18:14; Zech. 8:6; Job 42:2; *1 En.* 84:3; Matt. 19:26; Luke 1:37)—a statement that the LORD himself reiterates from Jeremiah's prayer later in verse 27b. There is an implied argument from the greater to the lesser in this affirmation. If Jeremiah can believe that the LORD is the creator of the universe, then nothing else that the LORD says or does should be beyond the reach of Jeremiah's faith. Certainly the purchase of Hanamel's field and the restoration that it symbolizes should not be considered unreasonable, regardless of what the present circumstances of Babylon invasion are communicating. If the LORD created the world and prepared the land of the covenant, then he can recreate the world and prepare again the land of the covenant.

Jeremiah's description of the great and mighty God in 32:18a (LXX 39:18a; cf. Deut. 10:17; Neh. 9:32) as one who performs covenant loyalty for thousands and repays the iniquity of fathers into the bosom or lap of their children after them is based on texts like Exodus 20:5–6 (see also Exod. 34:7; Deut. 5:9–10; 7:9–10; Isa. 65:6–7). Jeremiah 31:29–30 has already clarified that these texts do not mean that innocent children pay for the sins of their guilty fathers (see commentary there; see also Deut. 24:16; Ezek. 18). Rather, children who commit the sins of their fathers and reject the LORD as their fathers did will be punished. In addition to creation, the LORD's revealed and demonstrated faithfulness and justice are also reasons to trust him despite the seemingly contradictory nature of Jeremiah's present situation. MT Jeremiah 32:18b concludes with יהוה צבאות שמו ("whose name is the LORD of hosts") (cf. Jer. 31:35b). In the Hebrew source behind Greek Jeremiah, the divine name יהוה appears at the beginning of the following verse (v. 19), and צבאות שמו is not found. Verse 19a goes on to describe the Lord as "the great of counsel" and "the great of deed." The LXX *Vorlage* adds "great God of hosts, Lord of great name," which does not appear in the MT. The text of verse 19b also varies between the LXX *Vorlage* and the MT: "your eyes are upon [MT: whose eyes are opened to all] the ways of people to give to each according to his way [MT adds: and according to the fruit of his deeds]" (cf. 1 Kgs. 8:29; Jer. 5:3; 16:17; 17:10; 21:14; Prov. 5:21). This is yet another affirmation of the Lord's equity.

There are at least two options for the interpretation of the Hebrew syntax in 32:20a (LXX 39:20a): (1) "who put signs and wonders in the land of Egypt until this day, and in Israel and among mankind"; or (2) "who put signs and wonders in the land of Egypt and until this day both in Israel and among mankind." The main difference in the second option is the addition of the conjunction "and" before the phrase "until this day" according to Lucian's recension of the LXX (cf. Jer. 7:25; 11:7). Since the signs and wonders in Egypt did not continue until Jeremiah's day, Redak and Calvin interpret the first option to mean that those signs and wonders were mentioned or remembered until the time of Jeremiah.[19] The text then adds that beyond Egypt the Lord has also put signs and wonders in Israel and among mankind. Keil, however, appears to follow the second option when he renders, "Thou hast done wonders in Egypt, *and hast still been doing them* until this day in Israel and among other men."[20] In performing such signs and wonders, the Lord made for himself a name or reputation "as this day" (Jer. 32:20b [LXX 39:20b]; cf. Isa. 63:12, 14; Dan. 9:15; Neh. 9:10; Bar. 2:11).[21] It was with these signs and wonders and "with a strong hand and with an outstretched arm and with great spectacle [MT: fear/awe]" that the Lord brought his people out of Egypt (Jer. 32:21 [LXX 39:21]; cf. Deut. 26:8; Jer. 32:17; see also Exod. 15:14–16).[22] The display of power in the original exodus should be enough to instill confidence that the symbolic act of purchasing Hanamel's field is not a waste of time or money (see Exod. 14:31). As envisioned by Jeremiah 31, the Lord will one day lead his people in a new exodus back into the land of the covenant (see, e.g., Jer. 31:2–6; cf. Ezek. 20:33).

---

19. Rosenberg, trans., *Mikraoth Gedoloth: Jeremiah Volume Two*, 263; Calvin, *Jeremiah*, 4:177.

20. Keil, *Jeremiah*, 292.

21. God made himself known and is acknowledged as יהוה, the God who is present with his people (see Exod. 3:12, 14–15; 7:3–5; 9:16).

22. The LXX reflects ובמראה גדול ("and with great spectacle"; cf. Syr., *Tg. Jon.*) where the MT has ובמורא גדול ("and with great fear/awe").

The Lord gave the people the land that he swore to their forefathers, "a land flowing with milk and honey" (TEV: "rich and fertile land") (Jer. 32:22 [LXX 39:22]; cf. Deut. 26:9; Jer. 2:7; 11:5). Thus, it stands to reason that he could give them the land again, even though now from Jeremiah's perspective all seems to be lost. The people have taken possession of the land, but they have not obeyed the Lord's voice, nor have they walked/lived in his instruction(s); they have not done what the Lord commanded them (Jer. 32:23a [LXX 39:23a]; cf. Jer. 7:28; 26:4). For this reason the present calamity of Babylonian invasion has befallen them by divine judgment (Jer. 32:23b [LXX 39:23b]). This biblical-theological overview (cf. Jer. 2:1–13) brings Jeremiah's prayer up to the current crisis and sets it within the larger framework of the biblical narrative, which is precisely the orientation that it needs.

Jeremiah points out that the siege mounds of the Babylonians have come to the city of Jerusalem to capture it (Jer. 32:24 [LXX 39:24]; cf. Jer. 32:2; 33:4). The city has been delivered into the power of the Chaldeans who are fighting against it (cf. Jer. 32:3, 28). This fall of Jerusalem is due to "the sword and the famine" (MT adds: "and the plague") (see Jer. 14:12; 32:36; et al.; see also 2 Kgs. 25:1–3; Jer. 52:4–6). Everything has happened just as the Lord said it would: "Just as you spoke, so it has happened [MT: And that which you spoke is what has happened]." The small addition at the end of MT 32:24 ("And look, you are seeing") highlights the fact that the Lord's instruction to purchase Hanamel's field has not been given in ignorance of the current circumstances. And so, Jeremiah says, "And you, you have said to me [MT adds: O Lord God], 'Purchase the field with silver.' And I wrote in the document and sealed and took witnesses [MT: 'Purchase the field with silver and take witnesses']; and/but the city, it has been given/delivered into the hand/power of the Chaldeans" (Jer. 32:25 [LXX 39:25]; cf. Jer. 32:6–15). The clear implication of the juxtaposition of verses 24 and 25 is that the concise explanation of the sign act in verse 15 has not sufficed for Jeremiah to make sense of the transaction in light of the loss of the land to the Babylonians, even though his theological conviction is sound.[23] Therefore, the Lord graciously condescends to him. He provides a broader context for the crisis at hand in verses 26–35, and he expands his explanation of the prophetic meaning of the transaction with Hanamel in verses 36–44.

---

23. This may be compared to Daniel 7:19–20 where, after a concise explanation of the vision from 7:1–14 in 7:17–18, Daniel desires more information about one particular aspect of the vision (the fourth beast), which is subsequently granted in 7:21–27.

32:26 (39:26) And the word of the LORD *came to me [MT: to Jeremiah], saying, 32:27 (39:27) "I [MT: Look, I] am the* LORD, *the God of all flesh. Is anything too difficult for me [LXX, Syr., Tg. Jon.: Is anything hidden from me]?" 32:28 (39:28) Therefore, thus says the* LORD, *"This city will surely been given/delivered [MT: Look, I am about to give/deliver this city] into the hand/power of [MT adds: the Chaldeans and into the hand/power of Nebuchadrezzar] the king of Babylon, and he will capture it. 32:29 (39:29) And the Chaldeans who are fighting against this city will come and set this city on fire [Syr.: and uproot this city] and burn the houses [MT: and burn it and the houses; Syr.: and burn it with fire and the houses] on whose rooves they have offered sacrifices to Baal and poured out drink offerings to other gods in order to provoke me. 32:30 (39:30) For the sons of Israel and the sons of Judah have only been doing evil in my sight since their youth. [MT adds: Indeed, the sons of Israel have only been provoking me with the work of their hands," the prophetic utterance of the* LORD.] *32:31 (39:31) For upon my anger and upon my fury has this city been [MT adds: to me; Tg. Jon.: For my anger and my fury have rested upon this city] since the day that they built it and until this day to remove it [Tg. Jon.: to exile it] from before me 32:32 (39:32) because of all the evil of the sons of Israel and the sons of Judah who have acted to provoke me, they and their kings and their officials and their priests and their prophets, the men of Judah and the inhabitants of Jerusalem [MT: they, their kings, their officials, their priests, and their prophets (Tg. Jon.: false prophets), and the men of Judah and the inhabitants of Jerusalem], 32:33 (39:33) and they turned to me neck [LXX: back] and not face, and I taught them [Tg. Jon.: and I sent to them all my servants the prophets] rising early and teaching [i.e., urgently teaching], but they were not listening to receive discipline/instruction, 32:34 (39:34) and they put their detested idols in the house upon which my name is called in their uncleannesses [MT: to make it unclean], 32:35 (39:35) and they built the high places of Baal [Syr. adds: at Topheth], which are in the valley of Ben Hinnom, to cause their sons and their daughters to pass [through the fire]*[24] *to the king [MT: to Molech], which I did not command them [Tg. Jon. adds: in my Torah], and it did not enter my mind to do this abomination in order to cause Judah to sin."*

32:36 (39:36) And now [MT adds: therefore], thus says the LORD, *the God of Israel, "Concerning this city about which you [sg.] are saying [MT: you (pl.) are saying], 'It is given/delivered into the hand/power of the king of Babylon by sword and by famine and by sending away*

---

24. Syr.: "to burn their sons and their daughters."

[MT: plague],' 32:37 (39:37) look, I am about to gather them from all the earth [MT: lands] where I have banished them in my anger and in my fury and in great wrath, and I will restore them to this place, and I will cause them to dwell in security, 32:38 (39:38) and they will become my people, and I will become their God. 32:39 (39:39) And I will give to them another way and another heart / mind [MT: one heart / mind and one way (Syr.: spirit)] to fear me all the days and [and > MT] for their good and for their children after them. 32:40 (39:40) And I will make with them a perpetual covenant, which I will not turn back from after them [MT: that I will not turn back from after them to do good to them], and the fear of me I will put in their heart / mind so as not to turn aside from me. 32:41 (39:41) And I will attend to [MT: rejoice over] them to do them good, and I will plant them in this land faithfully and [and > MT] with all [MT adds: my] heart / mind and with all [MT adds: my] self."

*32:42 (39:42) For thus says the L*ORD*, "Just as I have brought upon this people all this great calamity, so am I about to bring upon them all the good that I am speaking concerning them. 32:43 (39:43) And the field [LXX: fields] will be purchased again in the land [MT: this land] of which you [sg.] are saying [MT: you (pl.) are saying], 'It is a desolation without man or beast, and they are given / delivered [MT: it is given / delivered] into the hand / power of the Chaldeans.' 32:44 (39:44) And fields will they purchase with silver and write in the document and seal and take witnesses in the land of Benjamin and in the areas surrounding Jerusalem and in the cities of Judah and in the cities of the hill country and in the cities of the lowland and in the cities of the south country, for I will restore their fortunes [LXX, Tg. Jon., Vulg.: captivity]" [MT adds: the prophetic utterance of the L*ORD*].*

The Hebrew source behind Greek Jeremiah 32:26 (LXX 39:26) introduces the LORD's response to Jeremiah's prayer from the first-person perspective of Jeremiah: "And the word of the LORD came to me (אלי), saying." The tradition behind the MT interpreted אלי ("to me") to be an abbreviation for אל ירמיהו ("to Jeremiah"), which led to the change to a third-person perspective. The LORD begins his response by reiterating Jeremiah's theology: "I [MT: Look, I] am the LORD, the God of all flesh. Is anything too difficult for me [LXX, Syr., *Tg. Jon.*: Is anything hidden from me]" (Jer. 32:27 [LXX 39:27])? Jeremiah declared in verse 17 that the LORD is the creator for whom nothing is too difficult. Thus, the LORD affirms that as the creator he is not only "the God of Israel" (MT Jer. 32:14) but also "the God of all flesh" (cf. Num. 16:22; 27:16). He also takes Jeremiah's statement ("Nothing is too difficult for you.")

and communicates the same thought by converting it into a rhetorical question ("Is anything too difficult for me?") (see GKC §152b; cf. Gen. 18:14; Num. 11:23; Isa. 50:2; 59:1). This forces Jeremiah to think about how the answer to his implied question in verses 24–25 is already embedded within his prayer. If the LORD is the creator of the world and the God of all mankind, then nothing is impossible for him, including the restoration that the redemption of Hanamel's field symbolizes, regardless of the Babylonian invasion.

Nevertheless, the hope of restoration is not a denial of the judgment at hand. Therefore, the LORD says, "This city will surely been given/delivered [MT: Look, I am about to give/deliver this city] into the hand/power of [MT adds: the Chaldeans and into the hand/power of Nebuchadrezzar] the king of Babylon, and he will capture it" (Jer. 32:28 [LXX 39:28]; cf. Jer. 32:3, 24; 34:1–7; see also Jer. 39; 52). The Chaldeans who are fighting against this city will come and set the city of Jerusalem on fire and burn the houses on whose rooves the people have offered sacrifices to Baal and poured out drink offerings to other gods to provoke the LORD (Jer. 32:29 [LXX 39:29]; cf. Jer. 7:18–19; 19:13; 21:10; 37:8; 52:13; see also Zeph. 1:4).

In Jeremiah 32:30a (LXX 39:30), the LORD explains that both the sons of Israel and the sons of Judah have "only" (אַךְ) been doing evil in his sight since their youth (cf. Jer. 3:25; 31:19; 32:23).[25] The adverb אַךְ is translated above in a restrictive sense ("only"). It is possible that this word is asseverative ("surely"), but the context seems to indicate that the issue is not the certitude of the people's actions but the exclusive nature of their behavior throughout their history. The point, however, is not that no individual has ever done the will of God but that the nation as a whole has always been rebellious (see Deut. 9:7, 24). MT 32:30b, which does not appear in LXX 39:30, appears to be a variant version of MT 32:30a: "Indeed, the sons of Israel have only (אַךְ) been provoking me with the work of their hands." The phrase "the work of their hands" can refer generally to "the things they have done" (NET; see MT Jer. 25:14), but the context suggests a more specific reference to idols (see Jer. 32:29, 34, 35; see also Jer. 1:16; 10:3; 25:6, 7). Throughout

---

25. "The mention of the children of Israel in connection with the children of Judah is not to be understood as if the destruction of Jerusalem was partly owing to the former; but it is here made, to signify that Judah can expect no better fate that the Israelites, whose kingdom has been destroyed long before, and who have for a long time now been driven into exile" (Keil, *Jeremiah*, 293–94).

the book of Jeremiah, idolatry is the core sin problem or evil of which all other sins are symptoms (see, e.g., Jer. 5:7–8).

Jeremiah 32:31 (LXX 39:31) begins a more expansive explanation of the impending judgment. It continues unbroken through verse 35. The syntactical construction of verse 31 is somewhat puzzling: "For upon my anger and upon my fury has this city been [MT adds: to me] since the day that they built it and until this day to remove it from before me" (cf. 2 Kgs. 24:20; Jer. 52:3; see also Jer. 7:25; 11:7). *Targum Jonathan* interprets the first part of the verse to mean that the LORD's anger and fury have rested upon the city. Keil suggests that the construction refers to "the superincumbency of a duty or burden lying on one."[26] He translates, "This city became to me a burden on my wrath," that is, "an object which lay upon my wrath, called it forth." Both Rashi (because of Solomon's marriage to Pharaoh's daughter) and Redak (because of sacrifices on high places that began after Solomon built the temple) understand the third feminine singular pronominal suffix "it," which is the object of the verb "built" and the infinitive "to remove" in verse 31, to refer to the temple.[27] But since the words normally used for the temple in Hebrew are grammatically masculine (e.g., בית, היכל, מקדש), it is more likely that the city (f.) of Jerusalem is the antecedent (see 2 Kgs. 23:27). Verse 31 probably does not refer to unknown origins of the city of Jerusalem but to the time when David captured the city (2 Sam. 5:7, 9). Since that time, the anger of the LORD has been aroused in various ways to remove the inhabitants of the city (*Tg. Jon.*: "to exile it").

The LORD has been angry with the city of Jerusalem because of all the evil (i.e., idolatry) of the sons of Israel and the sons of Judah who have acted to provoke him (Jer. 32:32 [LXX 39:32]; see Jer. 7:12; 11:17). This includes the leadership—kings, officials, priests, and prophets (*Tg. Jon.*: "false prophets")—and the general populace of Judah and Jerusalem (cf. Jer. 1:18; 2:8, 26). These people have turned the back of their neck to the LORD in rebellion and have not faced him to receive his instruction (Jer. 32:33a [LXX 39:33a]; cf. Jer. 2:27; 7:24; see also Jer. 17:23; 19:15). The LORD taught them with a sense of urgency, but they would not listen (Jer. 32:33b [LXX 39:33b]; cf. Jer. 7:28). *Targum Jonathan* interprets this on the basis of similar texts elsewhere in the book to mean that the LORD sent to them his servants the prophets (see Jer. 7:25; 25:4; 26:5; 29:19 [MT]; 35:15; 44:4; see also Jer. 7:13 [MT]; 11:7 [MT]).

---

26. Keil, *Jeremiah*, 294.
27. See Rosenberg, trans., *Mikraoth Gedoloth: Jeremiah Volume Two*, 266. See also Neusner, *Jeremiah in Talmud and Midrash*, 142.

The people put their detested idols in the temple that bears the
LORD's name (Jer. 32:34 [LXX 39:34]; see 2 Kgs. 21:4–5; 23:4; Jer. 7:30;
23:11; Ezek. 8; *b. Sanh.* 103b). They built the high places of Baal (i.e.,
alternative places of worship) in the valley of Ben Hinnom to make
their children pass through the fire as sacrifices "to the king" (לַמֶּלֶךְ)
(Jer. 32:35 [LXX 39:35]; see commentary on Jer. 7:31; 19:5; see also
2 Kgs. 17:17; 21:6, 11, 16; *b. Sanh.* 64b; BDB, 718).[28] The MT vocalizes
למלך as לַמֹּלֶךְ ("to Molech") on the analogy of בֹּשֶׁת ("shame"), which is
elsewhere a substitute for "Baal" (e.g., Jer. 3:24; 11:13 [MT]).[29] Molech
was the god of the Ammonites (see 1 Kgs. 11:7; see also 2 Kgs. 23:10),
also known as "Milcom" (מִלְכֹּם) (1 Kgs. 11:5),[30] but here בעל ("Baal"), the
storm/fertility god of the Canaanites, and מלך ("king" or "Molech") appear to be interchangeable.[31] The abominable practice of child sacrifice
was not commanded by the LORD in the Torah. In fact, it was expressly
forbidden (Lev. 18:21; 20:2–4; Deut. 12:31; 18:10), but the people confused the law of the firstborn (Exod. 13:2; 22:28 [Eng., 22:29]; Neh.
10:37) with the religious practices of their Canaanite neighbors (see
Mic. 6:7b) and did not take into consideration the full instruction of the
Torah (Exod. 13:13; Num. 3:12–13, 41; 8:16–17; 18:15–16).[32]

ועתה ("And now") at the beginning of Jeremiah 32:36 (LXX 39:36)
marks a shift from the backdrop of judgment in verses 28–35 to the
hope of the future in verses 36–44. Redak suggests that verses 36–41
refer to future redemption, while verses 42–44 refer to the return from
Babylon,[33] but it remains to be seen whether verses 42–44 are in fact
limited in their scope to the postexilic period. It is in verses 36–44
that the LORD finally addresses the concern expressed by Jeremiah in
verses 24–25. Indeed, verse 36 opens with a quote from Jeremiah's
words in verse 24: "Concerning this city about which you [sg.] are
saying [MT: you (pl.) are saying], 'It is given/delivered into the hand/
power of the king of Babylon by sword and by famine and by sending
away [MT: plague]'" (cf. Jer. 32:43; 33:10). The LXX reflects אתה אמר
("you [i.e., Jeremiah] are saying"), while the MT has אתם אמרים ("you

---

28. See Mezudath David in Rosenberg, trans., *Mikraoth Gedoloth: Jeremiah
Volume Two*, 267; Bright, *Jeremiah*, 296.

29. Holladay, *Jeremiah 2*, 219–20.

30. The MT has מַלְכָּם ("their king") in Jeremiah 49:1, 3 where the LXX reflects מִלְכֹּם ("Milcom"). See also Zephaniah 1:5.

31. See McKane, *Jeremiah XXVI–LII*, 848. See also Zephaniah 1:4–5.

32. See Shepherd, *Text in the Middle*, 59.

33. Rosenberg, trans., *Mikraoth Gedoloth: Jeremiah Volume Two*, 268. See
also Calvin, *Jeremiah*, 4:207.

[i.e., Jeremiah and those whom he represents] are saying").[34] When Jeremiah said that Jerusalem was being delivered to the Babylonians, he implied that the purchase of Hanamel's field was thus nonsensical (v. 25). The LORD has affirmed the reality of the Babylonian invasion (vv. 28–29), and now he seeks to demonstrate that the hope of future restoration can coexist with that present reality.

The LORD says that he is about to gather his people from all the earth (MT: "lands") where he has banished them in his anger (cf. Deut. 29:27 [Eng., 29:28]; Dan. 9:7) and restore them to this place (i.e., the New Jerusalem) where he will cause them to dwell in security (Jer. 32:37 [LXX 39:37]; cf. Deut. 30:3; Jer. 23:3; 24:6; 27:22 [MT]; 29:14 [MT]; 30:3; 31:8; Ezek. 11:17; 34:13; 36:24; see also Jer. 23:6; Ezek. 28:26; 34:25, 27, 28). As noted repeatedly in the commentary on chapters 30–31, it is evident throughout the book of Jeremiah that this people will consist of not only the faithful remnant of Israel and Judah (Jer. 3:18) but also all those from the nations who join them (Jer. 1:5, 10; 3:17; 4:2; 12:14–17; 16:19; 46:26b [MT]; 48:47 [MT]; 49:6 [MT], 39). They will be the true, new covenant people of God (Jer. 32:38 [LXX 39:38]; cf. Jer. 24:7; 30:22 [MT]; 31:1, 33; Ezek. 11:20; 37:23; Zech. 8:8). It is apparent then that these verses look well beyond a mere return from Babylon in the latter part of the sixth century BC.

In the commentary on Jeremiah 31:33, it was noted that the writing of the Torah on the heart/mind in the new covenant is not simply a matter of memorization. Rather, it speaks of a transformation of the human heart/mind by the Spirit of God. This reading of 31:33 is confirmed by 32:39 (LXX 39:39). According to the Hebrew source behind Greek Jeremiah, the LORD says that he will give the people "another" (אחר) way and "another" (אחר) heart/mind, which refers to a replacement of their current way of living and thinking (cf. Rom. 12:2; see also Deut. 10:16; 29:3 [Eng., 29:4]; 30:6; Jer. 4:4; 24:7; Ezek. 11:19–20; 18:31; Rom. 2:28–29; Col. 2:11; 4Q434).[35] According to the MT, he says that he will give them "one" (אחד) heart/mind and "one" (אחד) way, which seems to refer to a unification of their thinking and living (cf. Ps. 86:11). The difference between אחר ("another") and אחד ("one") is the difference between ר and ד, two letters commonly confused in scribal transmission. The same interchange of letters occurs in Ezekiel 11:19 between the LXX (= לב אחר ["another heart/mind"]) and Codex L

---

34. Calvin takes the plural of the MT to refer only to the people (not Jeremiah), but he does not take into consideration verse 24 (*Jeremiah*, 4:205).

35. This change will turn the people to the way of the Torah that was once rejected (Jer. 6:16).

(לב אחד ["one heart/mind"]). A few Masoretic manuscripts and the Syriac of Ezekiel 11:19 have לב חדש ("a new heart/mind"). The LORD will give the people a new heart/mind and a new spirit by removing their unreceptive heart of stone and replacing it with a receptive, malleable heart of flesh in order that they might walk in his statutes, keep his judgments, and become the new covenant people of God (Ezek. 11:19–20; 18:31; 36:26 [> p967]). This will be accomplished by the placement of God's own Spirit within them (Ezek. 36:27 [> p967]). The purpose of this new heart is the perpetual fear of the LORD for the people's own good and for their children after them,[36] which is the same purpose given for the regular reading of the Torah (Deut. 31:13; see also Deut. 4:10; 5:29; 10:12, 16).[37] This fear of the LORD is wisdom for the people of God (Deut. 4:6; Ps. 19:10 [Eng., 19:9]; Job 28:28; Prov. 1:9; 9:10). It is not only a healthy fear or reverence for the LORD but also an expression of faith and dependence upon the LORD (see Exod. 14:31; Jon. 1:16; 3:5; Hab. 1:5; 2:4; 3:2; Prov. 3:5–7; see also *TLOT* 1:143).

Whereas Jeremiah 31:31 uses the term ברית חדשה ("new covenant"), 32:40 (LXX 39:40) has ברית עולם ("perpetual covenant") to describe the relationship that the LORD will make with the people beyond the old Sinai covenant that was broken (Jer. 11:10; 31:32). As noted in the commentary on Jeremiah 50:5, all the major divine-human covenants in the Bible are called ברית עולם (Gen. 9:16; 17:7, 13, 19; Exod. 31:16; Lev. 24:8; 2 Sam. 23:5; see also Isa. 24:5; Ps. 105:10; 1 Chr. 16:17). This phrase is used repeatedly of the new covenant (Isa. 55:3; 61:8; Jer. 32:40; 50:5; Ezek. 16:60; 37:26; Heb. 13:20). The precise nature of the word עולם ("indefiniteness") has to be defined according to context. If a covenant is unconditional like the covenants with Noah, Abraham, or David or the new covenant, then it can be rendered "everlasting" or "eternal" (see again the commentary on Jer. 31:31). If a covenant is conditional like the Mosaic covenant, then the perpetuity of the covenant depends upon the time of its breaking (Jer. 11:10). According to the Hebrew source behind Greek Jeremiah, the perpetual new covenant is one that the LORD will not turn back from after the people. On the other hand, the MT says that the obligation of this covenant is that the LORD himself will not turn back from after the people to do them good (cf. Exod. 14:19; Isa. 30:21). In either case, the image is that

---

36. *Targum Jonathan* has "a fearing heart and a fearing spirit" in Ezekiel 11:19; 18:31; 36:26.

37. Again, it should be remembered here that the Torah will be written on the heart/mind of the people in the new covenant (Jer. 31:33). See also Ephesians 5:18 and Colossians 3:16.

of the Lᴏʀᴅ's covenant faithfulness in pursuit of the people and their well-being (Ps. 23:6). The latter part of verse 40 reiterates the thought of verse 39: "and the fear of me I will put in their heart/mind so as not to turn aside from me" (cf. Exod. 20:20; Bar. 3:7). The Lᴏʀᴅ will enable the people to do his will so that they are no longer bound by their sin.[38]

In the Hebrew source behind Greek Jeremiah 32:41 (LXX 39:41), the Lᴏʀᴅ says that he will "attend to" the new covenant people to do them good (cf. Jer. 23:2). That is, he will providentially oversee their well-being (see Jer. 1:11–12; 31:28). In the MT, however, he says that he will "rejoice over" them to do them good (cf. Deut. 28:63; 30:9; Isa. 62:5; 65:19; Jer. 33:9; Zeph. 3:17).[39] The Lᴏʀᴅ will plant the people in the land of the covenant faithfully with all his heart/mind and with all his being (cf. Exod. 15:17; 2 Sam. 7:10; Isa. 61:3b; Jer. 1:10; 24:6; 31:5, 22 [LXX], 27–28; Ezek. 36:36; Hos. 2:25 [Eng., 2:23]; Amos 9:15; see also Isa. 27:2–6; John 15:1–10; Rom. 11:17–24). Normally, the language of devoting the whole self is found in texts that call upon the people to devote themselves to the Lᴏʀᴅ (see Deut. 6:5; 10:12; 13:4; 26:16; 30:6, 10; 1 Kgs. 2:4; 2 Kgs. 23:25), but here it is used to describe the Lᴏʀᴅ's faithful devotion to his people (cf. *Jub.* 1:16).

Just as the Lᴏʀᴅ has brought upon the people all the great calamity of judgment, so will he bring upon them all the good that he is speaking about them (Jer. 32:42 [LXX 39:42]; cf. Deut. 28:63; Josh. 23:15; Jer. 31:28; Zech. 8:13–15). This appears to be a reference to the Lᴏʀᴅ's words in verses 36–41, yet verses 43–44 simply speak of the purchase of fields, leading many to make a distinction between the future restoration envisioned in verses 36–41 and what is perceived to be the more immediate return from Babylon mentioned in verses 42–44. The thought seems to be that just as Jeremiah's purchase of Hanamel's field prefigures the return from Babylon (Jer. 32:15), so the return from Babylon prefigures eschatological restoration and confirms the hope of it. It is nevertheless problematic for this understanding of the text that verses 42–44 are given as an explanation of verses 36–41. It is entirely possible that Jeremiah's purchase of Hanamel's field already prefigures eschatological restoration. If this is correct, then verses 43–44 are a description of that future reality and not merely one of a rather modest historical return from Babylon. If the objection to this is that the purchase of fields is too understated to be a description of the messianic kingdom, it is to be remembered that most prophecies of future

---

38. See Abarbanel in Rosenberg, trans., *Mikraoth Gedoloth: Jeremiah Volume Two*, 268–69.
39. See Neusner, *Jeremiah in Talmud and Midrash*, 201.

restoration are very earthy (e.g., Amos 9:11–15). The purchase of fields is simply a recognizable way to depict a return to life in the land of the covenant. In general, the prophets are not primarily concerned with a mere return from Babylon but with the final state of affairs in the new creation (Isa. 40–66). Indeed, no return from Babylon is complete until such a final state is achieved.

השדה ("the field") in verse 43 is apparently collective (LXX: "fields"; cf. v. 44). Fields will once again be purchased in the land of the covenant. This is the land of which, according to the LXX, Jeremiah ("you" sg.) is saying (MT: "you [pl.] are saying"), "It is a desolation without man or beast, and they are given/delivered [MT: it is given/delivered] into the hand/power of the Chaldeans" (cf. Jer. 33:10; 36:29). Unlike verse 36, which is a quote of Jeremiah's words in verse 24, verse 43 does not appear to be quoting from anything in verses 16–25. Holladay suggests that it may be a citation of Jeremiah 4:23–28 (see 4:25, 27 in particular).[40] Just as in the transaction between Jeremiah and Hanamel, which took place in the midst of the desolation, so will fields be purchased with silver in the future (Jer. 32:44 [LXX 39:44]; cf. 32:9–15, 25). The purchases will be recorded in documents to be sealed and then signed by witnesses. This will happen "in the land of Benjamin [where Hanamel's field was located] and in the areas surrounding Jerusalem and in the cities of Judah and in the cities of the hill country and in the cities of the lowland and in the cities of the south country" (cf. Jer. 17:26; 33:13). Such a listing of the different regions of the land gives a sense of the whole. This will all be possible because the LORD himself, the creator of the world (Jer. 32:17, 27),[41] will "restore their fortunes."[42] This is the same expression used for eschatological restoration throughout the Book of Comfort (Jer. 30:3, 18; 31:23; 33:7, 11). Thus, Abarbanel understands Jeremiah 32:44 to be a reference to the Messianic Era.[43]

---

40. Holladay, *Jeremiah 2*, 218.

41. It is precisely because the LORD is the creator of the world that he has the right to give the land of the covenant to whomever he pleases (see Rashi's commentary on Gen. 1:1; see also Jer. 27:5; Dan. 4:14 [Eng., 4:17]).

42. There is apparently no difference in meaning between the *qal* and the *hiphil* of שוב in this expression (contra Keil, *Jeremiah*, 295; see BDB, 998–99).

43. Rosenberg, trans., *Mikraoth Gedoloth: Jeremiah Volume Two*, 269.

JEREMIAH 33 (LXX 40)

33:1 (40:1) And the word of the Lord *came to Jeremiah a second time, and he was still confined in the court of the guard, saying, 33:2 (40:2) "Thus says the* Lord *who made (the) land / earth [MT: it; Syr.: you (m. sg.)] and [> MT] formed it [Syr.: you (m. sg.)] to establish it [Syr.: and established you (m. sg.)], the* Lord *is his name, 33:3 (40:3) 'Call to me, and I will answer you [Tg. Jon.: and I will receive your prayer], and I will tell you great and fortified [pc Mss: guarded] things that [that > Codex L; mlt Mss: and] you do not know.'*[1]

33:4 (40:4) For thus says the Lord *[MT adds: the God of Israel] con·cerning the houses of this city and concerning the houses of the king [MT: kings] of Judah, which are torn down [NET adds: for defenses] against the mounds and against the rampart [MT: sword] 33:5 (40:5) [MT adds: coming (pl.)] to fight against [Codex L: אֵת] the Chaldeans and to fill it [MT: them] with the corpses of the men whom I strike in my anger and in my fury and from whom I hide my face [MT: and which I hide my face from this city] because of all their evil, 33:6 (40:6) 'Look, I am about to bring up to it [LXX*[A]*, Tg. Jon.: them] restoration and healing, and I will reveal to them and heal it and make for them peace / well-being and stability [MT: and I will heal them and reveal to them an abundance of (LXX*[-B 106]*: to hear; Syr.: paths of [cf. Tg. Jon., 4Q434 1 I, 9]) peace and stability], 33:7 (40:7) and I will restore the fortunes [LXX, Tg. Jon.: captivity] of Judah and the fortunes [LXX, Tg. Jon.: captivity] of Israel [LXX*[Mss]*: Jerusalem], and I will build them as before [Syr. adds: and I will be good to them as before], 33:8 (40:8) and I will cleanse them from all their iniquity that they have committed against me, and I will not remember their sin [MT: and I will forgive all their iniquities] that they have committed against me and whereby they have transgressed against me, 33:9 (40:9) and it will become rejoicing and praise and beauty to all the people of the earth [MT: and it will become a name of rejoicing, praise, and beauty to all the nations of the earth] who hear all the good that I am doing [Codex L adds: them], and they will be in awe and tremble at all the good and all the prosperity that I am making for them [Codex L: it].'*

33:10 (40:10) Thus says the Lord, *'Again will be heard in this place of which you are saying, "It is desolate without man and without beast," in the cities of Judah and in the streets of Jerusalem that are desolate*

---

1.   See GKC §108d.

*without man [MT adds: and without inhabitant] and without beast
33:11 (40:11) sound of rejoicing and sound of joy, sound of bridegroom
and sound of bride, sound of those saying, "Give thanks to the LORD of
hosts, for the LORD is good, for his covenant loyalty lasts forever," and
[> MT] bringing thanksgiving [LXX: gifts] to the house of the LORD, for
I will restore the fortunes [LXX, Tg. Jon.: captivity] of that land [MT: of
the land] as before,' says the LORD.*

*33:12 (40:12) Thus says the LORD [MT adds: of hosts], 'Again there will
be in this desolate place [MT adds: lacking from man to beast] and
in all its cities a pasture for shepherds making sheep lie down. 33:13
(40:13) In the cities of the hill country and [and > MT] in the cities of
the lowland and in the cities of the south country and in the land of
Benjamin and in the areas surrounding Jerusalem and in the cities of
Judah, again will the sheep pass according to the hands of one counting
[Tg. Jon.: again will the people follow the words of the Messiah],' says
the LORD."*

According to Jeremiah 33:1 (LXX 40:1), the word of the LORD came to
Jeremiah "a second time" (שנית) while he was still confined in the court of
the guard (cf. Jer. 1:13; 13:3; Hag. 2:20). This is in addition to the word of
the LORD that came to the prophet according to chapter 32 (Jer. 32:1, 6,
26) when he was confined in the court of the guard (Jer. 32:2). Thus, the
present chapter is a continuation of the message of hope beyond judgment begun in chapter 32. Abarbanel comments that if chapter 32 is
about redemption from Babylon, then chapter 33 is about "the second
redemption" or the redemption in messianic times.[2] It has been noted in
the present commentary, however, that chapter 32 itself already looks
beyond historical redemption to eschatological redemption.

The key exegetical issue in 33:2 (LXX 40:2) is the object of the two
participles and the one infinitive. The LXX reflects a Hebrew text that
supplies the feminine noun ארץ ("land/earth") as the object of the first
participle and as the antecedent of the subsequent third feminine singular pronominal suffixes: "Thus says the LORD who made (the) land/
earth (ארץ) and formed it (f. sg.) to establish it (f. sg.), the LORD is his
name." This fits well with the use of this language elsewhere in the book
to describe the LORD as the creator (see Jer. 10:12, 16; 27:5; 32:17; 51:15,
19; cf. Isa. 45:18). Indeed, following Jeremiah 32:17, 27, this would seem
to be an appropriate affirmation to serve as the basis for hope in the
restoration envisioned by 33:6–13. The MT, however, only has third

---

2. Rosenberg, trans., *Mikraoth Gedoloth: Jeremiah Volume Two*, 270.

feminine singular suffixes throughout the verse: "Thus says the LORD who made it (f. sg.), the LORD who formed it (f. sg.) to establish it (f. sg.), the LORD is his name." This opens up at least two more possibilities. Both Redak and Calvin assume the feminine noun עִיר ("city") or the proper noun "Jerusalem" to be the referent (see Jer. 32:44; 33:4). On the other hand, the NJPS and the NET understand the pronominal suffixes to refer more generally to the work or plan of the LORD described in the preceding and the following contexts (cf. 2 Kgs. 19:25; Isa. 22:11; 37:26; 44:7; see GKC §135p).[3] Last but not least, the Syriac has second masculine singular pronominal suffixes: "Thus says the LORD who made you (m. sg.) and formed you (m. sg.) and established you (m. sg.), the LORD is his name." This apparently has its basis in the text of Jeremiah 1:5a1: "Before I formed you in the belly I knew you." The last clause of Jeremiah 33:2 is somewhat parenthetical: "the LORD is his name" (cf. Jer. 10:16; 31:35; 32:18; 46:18; 48:15; 50:34; 51:19, 57; Amos 5:8; 9:6).

The LORD invites Jeremiah to call to him, and he will answer him (Jer. 33:3a [LXX 40:3a]). This is a reversal of the LORD's earlier instruction in the book not to pray to him and not to expect an answer (Jer. 7:16; 11:14; 14:11). It is evident from the use of second masculine singular pronominal suffixes in this verse that this is primarily for the prophet in the present context, but such a reversal has already been forecasted for the people in Jeremiah 29:12 (cf. Jer. 11:11; Ezek. 8:18b [MT]; Zech. 7:13; see also Isa. 30:19; 58:9; 65:24; Zech. 10:6b; 13:9; Ps. 91:15). When the LORD answers Jeremiah, he will tell him great and "fortified" things that he does not know (Jer. 33:3b [LXX 40:3b]). The word בְּצֻרוֹת ("fortified") normally describes cities (see BDB, 131), but here it refers to hidden things that need to be revealed (cf. Deut. 29:28 [Eng., 29:29]; Jer. 33:6).[4] A few Masoretic manuscripts have נְצֻרוֹת ("guarded") instead of בְּצֻרוֹת ("fortified") (cf. Isa. 48:6). Since the things that are revealed to Jeremiah in 33:6–13 are very similar to what has been revealed in chapters 30–32, Calvin wonders about the sense in which they are hidden: "We hence see that those things are often hidden to us which God has again and again made known to us; for either they do not immediately penetrate into our minds, or the memory of them is extinguished, or faith is not so vigorous in us as it ought to be, or we are disturbed and confounded by obstacles thrown in our way."[5] Keil, however, suggests that the LORD does not merely

---

3. See also Keil, *Jeremiah*, 296.
4. Rashi: "to inform you of future events" (Rosenberg, trans., *Mikraoth Gedoloth: Jeremiah Volume Two*, 270).
5. Calvin, *Jeremiah*, 4:231.

communicate knowledge but makes known by his deeds.[6] Both Calvin and Keil assume that nothing new is revealed in Jeremiah 33, but this is not a valid assumption. While it is true that verses 6–13 speak of the same restoration envisioned by chapters 30–32, the specific way in which these verses speak is not simply a repetition of previous material. There is some overlap in the language, but chapter 33 makes its own unique contribution.

The LORD prefaces his revelation of the future with a reference to the current situation concerning the houses of the city of Jerusalem and the royal houses of Judah, which are torn down for defenses against the mounds and "the rampart" (החל; MT: "the sword" [החרב]) set up by the Chaldeans for their siege (Jer. 33:4 [LXX 40:4]; cf. Isa. 22:10; see also Jer. 32:2, 24, 28–29, 36). The houses are torn down for now, but they will eventually be rebuilt as before (Jer. 33:7b) in accordance with the program of the book of Jeremiah (Jer. 1:10; 24:6; 31:4, 28). The MT adds the participle באים ("coming") at the beginning of 33:5 (LXX 40:5) to describe the Judeans coming to fight against the Chaldeans, but this interrupts the flow of the syntax from verse 4 to verse 5. According to the Hebrew source behind Greek Jeremiah, which does not have the participle at the beginning of verse 5, the infinitive להלחם ("to fight") gives the purpose for the tearing down of the houses in verse 4. Since the Judeans were instructed to submit to the Babylonians rather than to fight against them (Jer. 38:17–18), their fighting would only result in filling the city or the land with the corpses of the men stricken by the LORD in his anger and fury, men from whom the LORD hid his face because of all their evil.[7] The Hebrew source behind Greek Jeremiah has ולמלאה ("and to fill it"; i.e., to fill the city or the land). The MT has ולמלאם ("and to fill them"; i.e., to fill the torn down houses). The MT's ואשר הסתרתי פני מהעיר הזאת ("and which I hide my face from this city") is a corruption of והסתרתי פני מהם ("and from whom I hide my face"), which lies behind the LXX.

The LORD then points to what he will do beyond the devastation of the Babylonian invasion: "Look, I am about to bring up to it [LXX[A], *Tg. Jon.*: them] restoration and healing, and I will reveal to them and heal it and make (ועבדתי) for them peace/well-being and stability" (Jer. 33:6 [LXX 40:6]). This is essentially the same message as Jeremiah 30:17. The LORD will bring up to the city/land spiritual restoration (ארכה) and physical healing (מרפא). He will reveal those things to the people and heal the city/land and produce for them "peace/well-being

---

6.   Keil, *Jeremiah*, 297.

7.   See Rosenberg, trans., *Mikraoth Gedoloth: Jeremiah Volume Two*, 271. See also BDB, 711.

and stability" (שלום ואמת) (cf. Isa. 39:8; Jer. 14:13). The wording of the second half of this verse in the MT differs from the Hebrew source behind Greek Jeremiah: "and I will heal them and reveal to them an abundance of [עתרת; LXX[-B] [106]: to hear (= העתר); Syr.: paths of (= נתבת; cf. *Tg. Jon.*, 4Q434 1 I, 9)] peace and stability." The LORD will restore the fortunes of both Judah and Israel (Jer. 33:7a [LXX 40:7a]; cf. Jer. 30:3, 18; 31:23; 32:44; 33:11; see also Hos. 6:11b–7:1a1), including those of the nations who join them (Jer. 3:17–18), and he will build them as before (Jer. 33:7b [LXX 40:7b]; cf. Jer. 1:10; 24:6; 30:18; 31:4). The phrase "as before" (כראשנה) refers to the golden age of David and Solomon when Judah and Israel were united (cf. Isa. 1:26; Jer. 33:11b; LXX Zech. 12:7; see also Amos 9:11). The period of David and Solomon is often idealized in the prophetic literature as the standard for the kingdom of the Davidic Messiah (Jer. 23:5–6; 30:9).

The LORD adds in 33:8a (LXX 40:8a) that he will "cleanse" the people from all their iniquity that they have committed against him (cf. Ezek. 36:25; 11QPs[a] 19:13–14). The Hebrew source behind Greek Jeremiah then has "and I will not remember their sin," while the MT has, "and I will forgive all their iniquities." Both of these expressions are found in the description of the new covenant relationship in Jeremiah 31:34b (see also Jer. 50:20). This sin or these iniquities is/are what the people have committed against the LORD and that by which they have transgressed against him. No longer will their sin or their iniquities be held against them. The subject of the verb והיתה ("and it will be[come]") at the beginning of 33:9 (LXX 40:9) is not explicit, but it is possible that either the city/land or the general situation described in 33:6–8 is the subject. The city/land and/or its restoration will become to all the people of the earth a reason to rejoice and to praise and to ascribe beauty (MT: "and it will become a name of rejoicing, praise, and beauty to all the nations of the earth"). It is not that the city/land itself will be the object of praise but that the LORD's work of restoration will garner praise (cf. Deut. 10:21; 26:19; Isa. 43:21; 62:7; Jer. 13:11; 17:14; Zeph. 3:19–20; see also Deut. 28:63; 30:9; Isa. 62:5; 65:18–19; Jer. 32:41; Zeph. 3:17). This is because the nations will hear about all the good that the LORD is doing for his people, and they will be in awe and tremble at all the good and all the prosperity that he is producing for them. Calvin rightly comments that this speaks of the kingdom of Christ and the conversion of the Gentiles.[8]

The LORD's discourse is reintroduced in 33:10 (LXX 40:10). According to verses 10–11, the sounds of joy and weddings and worship

---

8. Calvin, *Jeremiah*, 4:239–40.

will be heard again in the place of which the people are saying that it is desolate without man and without beast (cf. Jer. 32:36, 43; see also Jer. 4:23–29; Rev. 19:7). This is a reference to the cities of Judah and the streets of Jerusalem that are desolate. The return of the sounds of daily life and well-being is a reversal of the earlier loss of such (see Jer. 7:34; 16:9; 25:10). A new feature added here is the sound of the liturgical formula, "Give thanks to the LORD of hosts, for the LORD is good, for his covenant loyalty lasts forever" (cf. Pss. 100:5; 106:1; 107:1; 118:1–4, 29; 136; Ezra 3:11; 1 Chr. 16:34, 41; 2 Chr. 5:13; 7:3, 6; 20:21). This is what the people will say as they bring their thanksgiving to the eschatological temple in the New Jerusalem (Isa. 51:3; Jer. 17:26; 30:19; Ezek. 40–48; Rev. 21:3, 22), for the LORD will restore the fortunes of the land as before (see again Jer. 33:7).[9]

Once more the LORD's discourse is reintroduced in 33:12 (LXX 40:13) to indicate what will be "again" (עוד) in the now desolate place of Judah and its cities (cf. Jer. 33:10). There will be "a pasture for shepherds making sheep lie down" (cf. Ezek. 34:15; Ps. 23:2). On the one hand, it is possible that this simply speaks of the restoration of pastoral life in the land. On the other hand, the use of the shepherd metaphor elsewhere in the book of Jeremiah strongly suggests in the present context that this is about the restoration of the king and his people, specifically the messianic king and those who reign with him (see Jer. 3:15; 23:4–6; Ezek. 34:11–31; see also Isa. 32:18; 33:20; Jer. 31:23 [MT]; 50:7, 19).[10] "In the cities of the hill country and [and > MT] in the cities of the lowland and in the cities of the south country and in the land of Benjamin and in the areas surrounding Jerusalem and in the cities of Judah, again will the sheep pass according to the hands of one counting" (Jer. 33:13 [LXX 40:13]; cf. Jer. 17:26; 32:44; see Lev. 27:32; Ezek. 20:37; see also BDB, 391).[11] *Targum Jonathan* interprets this in accordance with the book's messianic shepherd metaphor to mean "again will the people follow the words of the Messiah" (cf. John 10:27). Likewise, Rashi comments, "Israel will come and go under the hands of a king who walks at their head" (cf. Mic. 2:12–13).[12]

---

9. Keil notes that the use of the phrase "as before" in verses 7 and 11 renders the translation "restore the captivity" in appropriate because there was no previous restoration of captives insofar as the exodus from Egypt is never represented as a bringing back from captivity (Keil, *Jeremiah*, 301).

10. It is possible that the understanding of the shepherds in this verse as kings was part of what prompted the addition of Jeremiah 33:14–26 in the MT (see Jer. 33:15, 17, 21, 22, 26).

11. See Neusner, *Jeremiah in Talmud and Midrash*, 149.

12. Rosenberg, trans., *Mikraoth Gedoloth: Jeremiah Volume Two*, 273.

[MT adds: 33:14 "Look, days are coming," the prophetic utterance of the Lord, *"and I will raise up (or, make happen) the good word (Theod.: my good word) that I spoke concerning the house of Israel and concerning the house of Judah. 33:15 In those days and at that time, I will cause to sprout for David a branch of righteousness (pc Mss: a righteous Branch; Theod.: a righteous sunrise/dawn; Syr.: the radiance of righteousness; Tg. Jon.: a Messiah of righteousness; mlt Mss add: and a king will reign and act wisely), and he/it will do justice and righteousness in the land (or, and justice and righteousness will be done in the land). 33:16 In those days, Judah will be delivered, and Jerusalem will dwell in security. And this is what he will call it (or, And this is what it will be called; pc Mss, Syr.: And this is his name that they will call him): the* Lord *our righteousness." 33:17 For thus says the* Lord, *"There will not be cut off for David a man sitting on the throne of the house of Israel. 33:18 And for the priests, the Levites (LXX[62], Syr., Vulg.: the priests and the Levites), there will not be cut off a man from before me bringing up burnt offerings and burning grain offerings and making sacrifices all the days."*

33:19 And the word of the Lord *came to Jeremiah, saying, 33:20 "Thus says the* Lord, *'If you break my covenant (Lucian: If my covenant is broken) with the day and my covenant with the night so that (4QJer[c]: לֹ[ן]בלתי) day and night do not come at their time, 33:21 then also my covenant can be broken with David my servant so that he does not have a son reigning on his throne, and with the Levites, the priests, my ministers. 33:22 Just as the host of the sky cannot be counted, and the sand of the sea cannot be measured, so will I increase the seed of David my servant and the Levites who minister to me.'" 33:23 And the word of the* Lord *came to Jeremiah, saying, 33:24 "Have you not seen what this people has spoken, saying, 'The two families that the* Lord *chose, he rejected them (GKC §143d)'? And my people they spurn from being again a nation before them (Lucian, Theod., Syr.: before me). 33:25 Thus says the* Lord, *'If not my covenant with day and night, (if) statutes of sky and land I have not set, 33:26 then also the seed of Jacob and David my servant will I reject from taking from his seed rulers (Origen, Lucian, Theod., Syr.: a ruler) over the seed of Abraham, Isaac, and Jacob. For I will restore their fortunes (Tg. Jon.: captivity) and have compassion on them.'"]*

Jeremiah 33:14–26 is the longest continuous passage that appears in the MT (see also 4QJer[c]) but not in the Hebrew source behind Greek Jeremiah (cf. Jer. 39:4–13). There is no evidence of either accidental or deliberate omission of this text by the scribe(s) responsible for the Hebrew *Vorlage* of the LXX or by the Greek translator, and there is every reason to conclude that it was not present in the original edition of the book. It was appended to the Book of Comfort as part of the second edition of Jeremiah. The passage leverages the text of Jeremiah 23:5–6 (Jer. 33:14–16) to introduce a covenant with the Levites alongside the covenant with David. It is clear, however, that such an interest in the Levitical priesthood is foreign to the messianic and eschatological message of Jeremiah 23:5–6 and to the first edition of the book in general. Thus, the text of MT 33:14–26 provides some insight into those who produced the book's second edition in the postexilic period. They were Levites or scribes who sought to support the Levites for whatever reason, perhaps seeking to capitalize on what was perceived to be criticism of the Aaronic priesthood in particular elsewhere in the book (e.g., Jer. 2:8; 5:31). The rift between the Levitical priesthood and the Aaronic priesthood was indeed a longstanding one (see, e.g., Num. 16; Ezek. 44). This kind of preoccupation with the historical situation of the past is consistent with the outlook of the second edition of Jeremiah in general.

The opening words of 33:14 are identical to those of 23:5: '"Look, days are coming,' the prophetic utterance of the LORD, 'and I will raise up'" (הנה ימים באים נאם יהוה והקמתי). Citation of the remainder of 23:5 is delayed until 33:15. Meanwhile, the object of the main verb in 33:14 is "the good word that I spoke concerning the house of Israel and concerning the house of Judah." Despite the effort of Theodotion to connect this with "my good word" in Jeremiah 29:10, it is clear that the cited text of 23:5–6, which is for both Judah and Israel, is the good word in view here. According to 33:15a, the LORD will cause to sprout for David a branch of righteousness in the coming days. The choice of the verb אצמיח ("I will cause to sprout") in place of והקמתי ("I will raise up") is not only stylistically appropriate to avoid repetition from 33:14 but also fitting for the following object צמח ("branch"). The phrase צמח צדקה ("a branch of righteousness") differs from the messianic title צמח צדיק ("a righteous Branch") in 23:5a. Of course, צמח צדקה can be translated "a righteous Branch," but it is noteworthy that a few Masoretic manuscripts have changed צמח צדקה in 33:15 to צמח צדיק in order to align the text with 23:5a.[13] If the two expressions were understood to be identical, then there would be no need to make the adjustment. It is possible that "a branch of righteousness" in 33:15a is not a reference to a messianic figure at all but simply a reference to the emergence of righteousness itself in the city of David. This option becomes

---

13. The renderings of this phrase in 33:15 in Theodotion, the Syriac, and *Targum Jonathan* all harmonize with the corresponding renderings in 23:5.

increasingly likely when the content of 33:16 is taken into consideration. A multitude of Masoretic manuscripts add "and a king will reign and act wisely" after 33:15a, yet another harmonization with 23:5, but the Leningrad Codex represents the shorter, more original reading and makes no reference to this king. Thus, 33:15b is left without a subject: "and he/it will do justice and righteousness in the land." Such a verb with an indefinite subject may be rendered as a passive (see GKC §114d, k): "and justice and righteousness will be done in the land." Jeremiah 33:16 then continues with the repurposing of 23:6. Whereas 23:6a speaks of Judah's deliverance and Israel's dwelling in security in "his" days (i.e., in the days of the messianic king), the text of 33:16a speaks of Judah's deliverance and Jerusalem's dwelling in security in "those" days (cf. Zech. 14:11; see also 4Q522 9 II, 8). Whereas 23:6b focuses on the naming of the Messiah as "the Lord our righteousness" (note the use of the third masculine singular pronominal suffix on יקראו), the text of 33:16b focuses on the naming of the city of Jerusalem as "the Lord our righteousness" (note the use of the third feminine singular pronominal suffix on יקרא לה) (cf. MT Ezek. 48:35b).[14] Thus, 33:14–16 shifts the meaning of 23:5–6 from a prophecy about the righteous Messiah to a prophecy about the righteous city (cf. Isa. 1:26; Zech. 8:3). It is apparent from what follows that this is due not only to the fact that Jerusalem is the royal city but also to the fact that it is the city of the temple and its priests.[15]

Jeremiah 33:17 explains that there will not be cut off for David a man sitting on the throne of the whole house of Israel (cf. 1 Kgs. 2:4; 8:25; 9:5; 2 Chr. 6:16; 7:18; 4Q252 5:1–5; see also Jer. 22:30; 29:32; 35:19).[16] This is only tangentially related to the text of 23:5–6, which is concerned with the one Davidic king who will reign over an everlasting kingdom (2 Sam. 7:12–15; 1 Chr. 17:11–14), not with the Davidic

---

14. A few Masoretic manuscripts and the Syriac attempt to harmonize 33:16b with 23:6b.

15. "Both of these changes at v. 16 look like a deliberate promoting of Jerusalem over against 23:5f, and the first of them can be interpreted as a promotion of the priesthood at the expense of the Davidic king" (McKane, *Jeremiah XXVI–LII*, 861). On the other hand, Keil downplays the differences between 23:6 and 33:16 (Keil, *Jeremiah*, 302–3).

16. Rashi comments: "permanently, but if it is discontinued, it will ultimately be reinstated" (Rosenberg, trans., *Mikraoth Gedoloth: Jeremiah Volume Two*, 274). See also Keil, *Jeremiah*, 303. This may be the view of MT Jeremiah 33:17, but elsewhere the idea seems to be that the Davidic dynasty can end, but the hope of the Davidic Messiah remains. See Psalm 89:31–34 (Eng., 89:30–33).

dynasty (2 Sam. 7:11b, 16). Nevertheless, the reference to the ongoing succession of Davidic sons sets up the real interest of this passage: the continuation of the Levitical priesthood (Jer. 33:18). The language of verse 18 seems to come out of nowhere, especially since it has nothing to do with the cited text of 23:5–6,[17] yet those responsible for the inclusion of this passage wanted to draw an analogy between the Davidic dynasty and the Levitical priesthood. Here the Levitical priesthood is called "the priests, the Levites," which can refer to priests in general from the tribe of Levi (including the Aaronic priesthood and the Levitical priesthood) or to the Levitical priesthood in distinction from the Aaronic priesthood (see BDB, 463).[18] It does not mean "legitimate priests."[19] In the immediate context, the expression "the priests, the Levites" is interchangeable with "the Levites, the priests" (Jer. 33:21b) and "the Levites" (Jer. 33:22b), making it clear that the intended reference is to the Levites in particular to the exclusion of the Aaronic priesthood. This makes the language of verse 18 appear even stranger. The thought that there will not be a man cut off from before the LORD bringing up burnt offerings and burning grain offerings and making sacrifices seems to depend upon a special covenant relationship, which is referenced in 33:21, yet there is no separate covenant made with the Levites elsewhere in biblical literature. Furthermore, making offerings and sacrifices was not among the duties of the Levites (see Num. 3). That was the unique privilege of the Aaronic priesthood (see Ezek. 43:19; 44:15; 1 Chr. 6:33–34; 23:28; 2 Chr. 23:18; 29:34). Such disparity between the two groups led to the rebellion recorded in Numbers 16 and likely motivated the creation of Jeremiah 33:14–26. The present passage seeks to put the Levitical priesthood on equal footing with the Aaronic priesthood. It reflects a time in the postexilic period during the reorganization of temple worship when it was considered opportune to assert the equal status of the Levites.

---

17. Calvin thinks that 33:17–18 speaks of Christ performing the offices of priest and king (cf. Zech. 6:12–13; Ps. 110), but such an interpretation is foreign to the context (Calvin, *Jeremiah*, 4:257). Keil notes that the two pillars of the old covenant theocracy, the Davidic kingdom and the Levitical priesthood, were broken with the destruction of Jerusalem and the temple, and he admits that the present prophecy gives no indication of the manner of their reinstitution, although he assumes a renovation not of their form but of their essential features (Keil, *Jeremiah*, 303).

18. The combination "the priests and the Levites" would be a reference to the Aaronic priesthood and the Levitical priesthood together (BDB, 464).

19. Contra Bright, *Jeremiah*, 297.

The next two subunits in 33:19–22 and 33:23–26 are closely related and are presented as words from the LORD that came to Jeremiah (Jer. 33:19, 23; cf. Jer. 33:1). In the first of these two, it is said that if the LORD's covenant with the day and the night is broken, then his covenant with David and with the Levites can be broken. The seed of David and the Levites will increase like the stars in the sky and like the sand of the sea (cf. the Abrahamic covenant [Gen. 15:5; 22:17]).[20] A similar hypothetical scenario has already been given in Jeremiah 31:35–37 to declare the perpetuity of the new covenant (Jer. 31:31–34). The covenant with the day and the night is the covenant with Noah (Gen. 8:22; 9:11). Since it is not possible to break the covenant with Noah, the endurance of the covenant with David is assured (see Ps. 89:34–38 [Eng., 89:33–37]; see also 2 Sam. 23:4–5; Ps. 72:5, 17). The Levites are not part of the covenant with David. Thus, verse 21b must have a separate covenant with the Levites in view. The problem is that there is no such thing as a separate covenant with the Levites.[21] There is a covenant with the Aaronic priesthood (Lev. 2:13; Num. 18:19; 25:10–13; Mal. 2:4–5; Neh. 13:29),[22] but that covenant is discontinued with the breaking of the Sinai covenant (Jer. 11:10; Mal. 2:8). Thus, there is no biblical basis for any claim to an eternal covenant with the Levites. This betrays the secondary nature of Jeremiah 33:14–26. It is to be noted that the case made for a covenant with the Levites has thus far appealed to the unconditional covenants with David (Jer. 33:17, 21, 22), Noah (Jer. 33:20), and Abraham (Jer. 33:22) but not to the conditional covenant with Moses—the very covenant that stipulates a subordinate role for the Levites.

---

20. This does not mean that the sons of David and the Levites will outnumber the rest of the people, nor is it a reference to all the people as a kingdom of priests (Exod. 19:6; Isa. 61:6; 66:21). It is an affirmation that both the sons of David and the Levites will continue indefinitely, a sign of the well-being of the people in general.

21. Deuteronomy 33:9b does not speak of a covenant with the Levites. It is a reference to the fidelity of the Levites to the Sinai covenant in the story of Exodus 32:26–29.

22. The covenant in Malachi 2:4–5 is not a covenant with the Levites (contra the LXX) but a covenant with Levi, the father of the tribe from which the Aaronic priesthood comes. It is clear from Malachi 1:6–2:9 that the duties of the Aaronic priesthood are in view (see Shepherd, *Commentary on the Book of the Twelve*, 483–89). The text of Nehemiah 13:29 refers to the defilement of three separate entities: the priesthood, the covenant of the priesthood, and the Levites. It makes a careful distinction between the covenant of the priesthood (i.e., the Aaronic priesthood) and the Levites.

The second subunit (Jer. 33:23–26) begins with a rhetorical question posed to Jeremiah (cf. Jer. 3:6): "Have you not seen what this people has spoken, saying, 'The two families that the LORD chose, he rejected them'?" This is explained to mean that the people spurn themselves from being a nation in the presence of the two families once chosen but now rejected, although some textual witnesses have "before me" (i.e., in the presence of the LORD) rather than "before them." In other words, the people do not believe in the continued existence of the nation of Israel with a Davidic monarchy and a Levitical priesthood, thus requiring a reiteration of verses 17–22 in verses 25–26. There is a division of opinion in the history of interpretation as to the identity of the two families mentioned here. Rashi and Redak identify the two families to be the royalty (David) and the priesthood (Levi), which is consistent with the general content of the passage (cf. Zech. 12:12–13).[23] Calvin, Keil, and Bright understand the two families to be Israel and Judah (see Jer. 33:14).[24] Neither view receives explicit confirmation from the remainder of the passage, which speaks neither of David and Levi nor of Israel and Judah but of Jacob and David: "If not my covenant with day and night, (if) statutes of sky and land I have not set, then also the seed of Jacob and David my servant will I reject from taking from his seed rulers [Origen, Lucian, Theod., Syr.: a ruler] over the seed of Abraham, Isaac, and Jacob. For I will restore their fortunes and have compassion on them" (Jer. 33:25–26; cf. Jer. 31:35–37; 33:7, 11, 17, 20–22; see also *b. Sanh.* 99b). This affirms that the continuance of the nation of Jacob/Israel (i.e., Israel and Judah) and that of the Davidic monarchy is as sure as the rising and setting of the sun. Given the close association made between the Davidic covenant and the supposed covenant with the Levites earlier in this passage (Jer. 33:17–18, 20–22), the reader may assume that the continuance of the Levitical priesthood is implied here as well.[25]

APPLICATION OF JEREMIAH 30–33 (LXX 37–40)

As noted at the outset of the commentary on the Book of Comfort (Jer. 30–33 [LXX 37–40]), this section of the book of Jeremiah is devoted to the building and the planting portion of the book's program (Jer. 1:10; 24:6; 30:18; 31:4–5, 27; 32:41; 33:7). It is about the eschatological

---

23. Rosenberg, trans., *Mikraoth Gedoloth: Jeremiah Volume Two*, 275. See also Holladay, *Jeremiah 2*, 230–31.

24. Calvin, *Jeremiah*, 4:264; Keil, *Jeremiah*, 305; Bright, *Jeremiah*, 297.

25. See Redak in Rosenberg, trans., *Mikraoth Gedoloth: Jeremiah Volume Two*, 277.

restoration of the true people of God from Israel, Judah, and all the nations (Jer. 30:3, 18; 31:23; 32:44; 33:7, 9, 11; cf. Jer. 3:17–18). This restoration depends upon the coming of the Davidic Messiah (Jer. 30:9, 21) and the making of a new covenant relationship (Jer. 31:31–34; 32:38–40). The book of Jeremiah is thus not designed to turn the people back to the old covenant but to function as new covenant Scripture for its readers (see Heb. 8). Therefore, the applicability and relevance of the Book of Comfort is more immediately obvious. An understanding of the theological truth revealed here is essential to every believer's walk of faith.

The human faculty of imagination is part of reality, but what humans imagine is not necessarily part of the real world and is often nothing more than an escape from it. The prophetic imagination is unique because it is guided by the Holy Spirit (2 Pet. 1:19–21). What the biblical prophets imagine defines reality. Their revelatory vision of the future for the people of God includes redemption from a fallen world not as an imaginary coping mechanism but as part of the real world itself. It is into this reality rendered textually that the prophetic books invite their readers to enter. The distinctive contribution of the book of Jeremiah to the textual world of the Bible is fundamental to the hope of God's people. To the extent that the believing reader invests in its study, he or she becomes an active participant in the world as God designed it to be.

REALIZATION OF JEREMIAH'S HISTORICAL PROPHECY

(Jer. 34–44 [LXX 41:1–51:30])

JEREMIAH 34 (LXX 41)

34:1 (41:1) The word that came to Jeremiah from the LORD, and Nebuchadnezzar [MT: Nebuchadrezzar] the king of Babylon and all his army and all the land of his dominion [MT: and all the kingdoms of the land of the dominion of his power and all the peoples] were fighting against Jerusalem and against all the cities of Judah [MT: all its cities], saying, 34:2 (41:2) "Thus says the LORD [MT adds: the God of Israel], 'Go [MT: Go and say] to Zedekiah the king of Judah and say to him, "Thus says the LORD, 'This city will surely be given / delivered [MT: Look, I am about to give / deliver this city] into the hand / power of the king of Babylon, and he will capture it [> MT] and burn it with fire. 34:3 (41:3) And as for you, you will not escape from his hand / power, and [MT: for] you will surely be seized, and into his hand / power you will be given / delivered, and your eyes will see his eyes [MT: the eyes of the king of Babylon], [MT adds: and his mouth will speak with your mouth], and to Babylon you will go.' 34:4 (41:4) But hear the word of the LORD, O Zedekiah the king of Judah. Thus says the LORD [MT adds: concerning you], [MT adds: 'You will not die by the sword.'] 34:5 (41:5) 'In peace you will die, and like [mlt Mss: with] the burnings of your fathers [LXX: and like they wept for your fathers; Syr.: and like they danced / mourned for your fathers], the former kings who were before you [LXX: those who reigned (= הַמֹּלְכִים) before you], so they will burn [LXX: weep; Syr.: dance / mourn] for you. And "Ah, lord / master," will they mourn for you, for it is a word that I myself have spoken,' the prophetic utterance of the LORD.'"" 34:6 (41:6) And Jeremiah [MT adds: the prophet] spoke to King Zedekiah [MT: Zedekiah the king of Judah] all these words in Jerusalem. 34:7 (41:7) And the army of the king of Babylon was fighting against Jerusalem and against the cities of Judah [MT: all the cities of Judah that were left], against Lachish and against Azekah, for they were the ones that remained among the cities of Judah as fortified cities.

34:8 (41:8) The word that came to Jeremiah from the LORD after King Zedekiah made an agreement [or, covenant] with the people [MT: with all the people who were in Jerusalem] to proclaim [MT adds: to them] liberty, 34:9 (41:9) to send away each his servant and each his maidservant, the Hebrew man and the Hebrew woman, free, so that no one from Judah would serve [MT: so that no one would serve by them, by a Judean, his brother]. 34:10 (41:10) And all the officials and all the people who entered into the agreement [or, covenant] to send away each his servant and each his maidservant [MT adds: free so as not to serve by them again] reneged [MT: heeded] [MT adds: and they heeded and sent away.] 34:11 (41:11) [MT adds: And they reneged afterwards and brought back the servants and the maidservants whom they sent away free], and they subdued them as servants and maidservants. 34:12 (41:12) And the word of the LORD came to Jeremiah [MT adds: from the LORD], saying, 34:13 (41:13) "Thus says the LORD [MT adds: the God of Israel], 'As for me, I made a covenant with your forefathers when I brought them out of the land of Egypt from a place of servitude, saying, 34:14 (41:14) "At the end of six [MT: seven] years you [sg.] must send away your Hebrew brother [MT: you (pl.) must send away each his Hebrew brother] who is sold to you [or, who sells himself to you]. And he will serve you for six years, and you will send him away free [MT adds: from you]."[1] *But they [MT: your forefathers] did not listen to me, and they did not incline their ear. 34:15 (41:15) And they [MT: you (pl.)] returned today to do [MT: and you (pl.) did] what was right in my eyes by proclaiming liberty each to his neighbor, and they [MT: you (pl.)] made an agreement [or, covenant] before me in the house upon which my name is called. 34:16 (41:16) And you reneged and profaned my name by bringing back [MT: and brought back] each his servant and each his maidservant, whom you sent away free according to their desire, to you as servants and maidservants [MT: and you subdued them to become your servants and maidservants].' 34:17 (41:17) Therefore,*

---

1. The ESV follows the Masoretic accentuation for verse 14a: "At the end of seven years each of you must set free the fellow Hebrew who has been sold to you and has served you six years; you must set him free from your service."

thus says the Lord, *'As for you, you have not listened to me to proclaim liberty [MT adds: each to his brother and] each to his neighbor. Look, I am about to proclaim liberty to you [MT: to you liberty,' the prophetic utterance of the* Lord*] to the sword and to plague and to famine [Tg. Jon.: from the sword and from death and from famine], and I will make you into an object of terror [LXX: a dispersion] to all the kingdoms of the earth. 34:18 (41:18) And I will make the men who have transgressed my covenant who have not upheld my covenant [MT: the words of my covenant] that they made before me like the calf that they made to serve with it [MT: like the calf that they cut in two and passed between its pieces], 34:19 (41:19) the officials of Judah [MT adds: and the officials of Jerusalem] and [> MT] the court officials and the priests and the people [MT: all the people of the land, those who passed between the pieces of the calf], 34:20 (41:20) and I will give/deliver them to their enemies [MT: into the hand/power of their enemies and into the hand/ power of those who seek their life], and their corpse will become food for the flying creatures of the sky and for the large land animals. 34:21 (41:21) And Zedekiah the king of Judah and their [MT: his] officials I will give/deliver into the hand/power of their enemies [MT adds: and into the hand/power of those who seek their life], and the army of the king of Babylon is for those who are going up from upon them [MT: and into the hand/power of the army of the king of Babylon that is going up from upon them (i.e., withdrawing from them)]. 34:22 (41:22) Look, I am about to command,' the prophetic utterance of the* Lord, *'and I will bring them back to this land [MT: city], and they will fight against it and capture it and burn it with fire and the cities of Judah, and I will make a desolation without inhabitant [MT: and the cities of Judah I will make a desolation without inhabitant.]'"*

Chapter 34 (LXX 41) begins a relatively lengthy section of prose (Jer. 34–44) that includes Jeremiah's prophecy of the fall of Jerusalem to the Babylonians (Jer. 34:2), an account of the Babylonian invasion (Jer. 39), and a narrative of the aftermath (Jer. 40–44). The material in this section is not always arranged chronologically. For example, the word of the Lord that comes to Jeremiah in 34:1–7 is directed to Zedekiah, but the word that comes to Jeremiah in chapter 35 moves back in time to the days of Jehoiakim. This allows for a thematic contrast between the covenant infidelity of Zedekiah in 34:8–22 and the covenant faithfulness of the Rechabites in chapter 35. Chapter 34 divides into two distinct yet related subunits. The first (Jer. 34:1–7) announces the fate of Jerusalem and Zedekiah suffered at the hands of the Babylonians (cf. Jer. 21:1–10). The second (Jer. 34:8–22) gives an indication of why things will not turn out well for Jerusalem and Zedekiah. Their failure to sustain the release of Hebrew servants in accordance with the Mosaic law is symptomatic of a systemic failure to keep the terms of the old covenant.

According to the Hebrew source behind Greek Jeremiah 34:1 (LXX 41:1), the word of the LORD came to Jeremiah when Nebuchadnezzar and all his army and "all the land of his dominion" were fighting against Jerusalem and against "all the cities of Judah" (cf. Jer. 34:7). In place of "all the land of his dominion," the MT has "and all the kingdoms of the land of the dominion of his power and all the peoples." This presumably refers to "contingents from the various vassal states of the empire."[2] In place of "all the cities of Judah," the MT has "all its cities," which may refer to cities surrounding Jerusalem rather than Judean cities in general. No date is given for this word of the LORD.

Jeremiah is instructed to go to Zedekiah and say to him first of all that the city of Jerusalem will be delivered into the power of the king of Babylon who will capture it and burn it with fire (Jer. 34:2 [LXX 41:2]; cf. Jer. 21:10; 32:3, 28–29; 34:22; 37:8; 39:8 [MT]; 52:13). The MT puts this in the first person ("Look, I am about to deliver this city into the power of the king of Babylon")[3] and does not include the verb ולכדה ("and he will capture it"). Abarbanel notes the similarity of this prophecy to the one in 32:3 and suggests that the prophecy referenced there was given publicly while the present one was to be given privately.[4] Keil adds that the present prophecy is not a supplement to the one in 32:3–5, nor was it the reason for Jeremiah's imprisonment (see commentary on Jer. 32:2–5).[5]

Jeremiah is then to turn to Zedekiah himself ("And as for you") and declare to him that he will not escape from the king of Babylon (Jer. 34:3a [LXX 41:3a]; cf. Jer. 21:7; 32:4a; 37:17b). Rather, he will be seized and come face to face with Nebuchadnezzar ("and your eyes will see his eyes [MT: the eyes of the king of Babylon]") and go into exile in Babylon (Jer. 34:3b [LXX 41:3b]; cf. Jer. 32:4b, 5; see also Isa. 52:8). The MT adds "and his mouth will speak with your mouth" (cf. Jer. 32:4b). This anticipates the narrative of Jeremiah 39:5–7 (MT) and 52:8–11

---

2. Bright, *Jeremiah*, 215.
3. It is doubtful that the LXX translator deliberately changed this in order to avoid the statement that the LORD would deliver the city into the power of the king of Babylon (contra McKane, *Jeremiah XXVI–LII*, 867). See Jeremiah 32:3 (LXX 39:3).
4. Rosenberg, trans., *Mikraoth Gedoloth: Jeremiah Volume Two*, 277–78.
5. Keil, *Jeremiah*, 308.

(see also 2 Kgs. 25:5–7; Ezek. 12:8–16; 17:11–21) in which Zedekiah attempts to flee but is captured and brought to Nebuchadnezzar who speaks judgments with him and executes his two sons in front of him before he blinds him and takes him to Babylon.

The Hebrew word אַךְ at the beginning of 34:4 (LXX 41:4) can mean "but" (in contrast with what precedes) or "only" (in contrast with other ideas generally) (see BDB, 36). Some commentators understand 34:4–5 to place a condition on Zedekiah's fate: "If you will only heed the word of the LORD, then you will die in peace."[6] This view is largely based on a feeling that the harsh treatment suffered by Zedekiah at the hands of Nebuchadnezzar can hardly be characterized as dying in peace. The problem is that the syntactical construction of the Hebrew text does not fit the pattern of a protasis ("if") followed by an apodosis ("then") known from elsewhere in the book (see, e.g., Jer. 38:17–18; see also Jer. 21:9). Furthermore, no word of the LORD is given for Zedekiah to heed in the present context in order to avoid disaster. It is preferable to read verses 4–5 as a mitigation of verse 3—a consolation so to speak. These verses indicate what will happen to Zedekiah, not what will happen to him if he meets a condition.

The MT gets an early start on the word of the LORD that Zedekiah is to hear by adding a clause at the end of verse 4: "You will not die by the sword" (> LXX). Of course, this is true. Zedekiah is not executed by Nebuchadnezzar (Jer. 39:5–7 [MT]; 52:8–11). Verse 5 continues, "In peace you will die." It is a misunderstanding of this statement to say that it means Zedekiah will live out the rest of his days in Jerusalem unharmed. As Calvin observes, it means that he will die a natural, nonviolent death in Babylon.[7] The remainder of verse 5 focuses on the proper mourning that Zedekiah will receive after his death in contrast to Jehoiakim who was not mourned and whose body was not buried but was thrown to the elements like a donkey (Jer. 22:18–19): "and like [mlt Mss: with] the burnings of your fathers [LXX: and like they wept for your fathers; Syr.: and like they danced/mourned for your fathers], the former kings who were before you [LXX: those who reigned before you], so they will burn [LXX: weep; Syr.: dance/mourn] for you. And 'Ah, lord/master,' will they mourn for you, for it is a word that I myself have spoken" (cf. Jer. 22:18). If the MT is correct, then the text likely does not refer to the burning of corpses but to the burning of incense

---

6. See, e.g., Bright, *Jeremiah*, 216; Holladay, *Jeremiah 2*, 232–35. On the other hand, see Keil, *Jeremiah*, 308–9.
7. Calvin, *Jeremiah*, 4:274.

(cf. 2 Chr. 16:14; 21:19).[8] Rudolph (*BHS* apparatus) suggests that the Greek ὡς ἔκλαυσαν ("like they wept") is not an inner-Greek corruption of ὡς ἔκαυσαν ("like they burned") (see also κλαύσονται). It may be a characterization of the burnings as a mourning ritual, or, as McKane suggests, it may be an attempt to avoid the impression of cremation.[9] It is possible, however, that the Greek translation is based on a slightly different Hebrew *Vorlage*. In place of וכמשרפות אבותיך ("and like the burnings of your fathers"), the translator may have had וכמשפדי אבותיך ("and like the mournings for your fathers"), where וּכְמִשְׂפְּדֵי is equivalent to וּכְמִסְפְּדֵי; and in place of ישרפו לך ("they will burn for you"), the translator may have had ישפדו לך ("they will mourn for you"), where יִשְׂפְּדוּ is equivalent to יִסְפְּדוּ (note that LXX Jer. 22:18b uses κλαύσονται for יִסְפְּדוּ). Jeremiah's message to Zedekiah comes with the assurance that it is one that the LORD himself has spoken (Jer. 34:5b [LXX 41:5b]).

The narration of Jeremiah 34:6 (LXX 41:6) confirms that Jeremiah delivered the above words to Zedekiah in Jerusalem as instructed. Jeremiah 34:7 (LXX 41:7) forms an inclusio with verse 1 by repeating the circumstance of the Babylonian army fighting against Jerusalem and the cities of Judah (MT: "all the cities of Judah that were left"). The only remaining fortified cities among the cities of Judah were Lachish and Azekah southwest of Jerusalem. A message to the military commander at Lachish preserved on Lachish Ostracon 4 mentions both cities: "And let (my lord) know that we are watching for the signals of Lachish, according to all the indications which my lord hath given, for we cannot see Azekah" (*ANET*, 322). Holladay comments, "It is possible that Azekah was not visible from the location of the writer, but it is more likely that by the time the message was written, Azekah had fallen."[10]

Jeremiah 34:8 (LXX 41:8) introduces the word that came to Jeremiah from the LORD after Zedekiah made an "agreement" (ברית) with the people (MT: "all the people who were in Jerusalem").[11] Due to the extended description of the nature of this agreement and the subsequent failure to keep it in verses 9–11, the word of the LORD has to be reintroduced in verse 12 and does not begin until verse 13. The text of verse 8 initially describes this agreement very succinctly: "to proclaim [MT adds: to them (i.e., to the servants)] liberty" (cf. Lev. 25:10).

---

8. See Neusner, *Jeremiah in Talmud and Midrash*, 8, 94, 98; Rosenberg, trans., *Mikraoth Gedoloth: Jeremiah Volume Two*, 278; Calvin, *Jeremiah*, 4:276–77; Keil, *Jeremiah*, 309.

9. McKane, *Jeremiah XXVI–LII*, 869.

10. Holladay, *Jeremiah 2*, 235.

11. See Walser, *Jeremiah*, 429.

It becomes apparent from what follows that this was an agreement to keep the law of Exodus 21:1–6 and Deuteronomy 15:12–18 in accordance with the Sinai "covenant" (ברית). The people were to free their Hebrew servants and maidservants so that no one from Judah would be a servant (MT: "so that no one would serve by them, by a Judean, his brother") (Jer. 34:9 [LXX 41:9]; cf. Lev. 25:39–46).[12] While the general description of the release in verse 9 may give the impression that all Hebrew servants were to be freed, the later citation of the law in verse 14 suggests that only those who had served for six years were given their liberty.[13] The motivation for this agreement is not stated in the text, but given the widespread lack of regard for the law (Jer. 7:9), the question of why there would be such attention at this time to the instruction for manumission of servants naturally arises. Keil suggests the possibility that liberated servants would have provided more manpower in defense of the city against the Babylonians.[14] Thompson proposes that it may have been "a matter of convenience since slaves had to be fed and could no longer be used for work in the fields."[15] Whatever the case may have been, it is evident from the quick renege (Jer. 34:10–11, 16) that the agreement was disingenuous. It was perhaps an effort on the part of Zedekiah and the people to appease the LORD and to benefit themselves in some way at the same time.

The Hebrew source behind Greek Jeremiah and the MT differ considerably in verses 10 and 11. The former (LXX *Vorlage*) indicates already in verse 10 that all the officials and people who entered into the agreement "reneged" (וישובו) (cf. Jer. 34:16a). It then has a short text for verse 11: "and they subdued them as servants and maidservants" (cf. MT Jer. 34:16b). This version of verses 10 and 11 simply assumes that the people heeded the agreement at some point before they went back on their word (cf. Jer. 34:15). On the other hand, the latter (MT) makes

---

12. The terms עבד and שפחה present a difficult challenge for English translation. If they are translated as "servant" and "maidservant," there is a risk that the words will be misunderstood to refer to hired workers whose lives are still their own. On the other hand, if the terms are translated as "male slave" and "female slave," there is a risk that a foreign conception of slavery will be read into the text. It seems best to choose the more neutral of these options ("servant" and "maidservant") and allow the explanation of these terms in the text to speak for itself.

13. See Rosenberg, trans., *Mikraoth Gedoloth: Jeremiah Volume Two*, 279; Keil, *Jeremiah*, 310.

14. Keil, *Jeremiah*, 310.

15. Thompson, *Book of Jeremiah*, 610.

this explicit in verse 10a by saying that all those who entered into the agreement "heeded" (וישמעו). This is then reiterated in the MT's addition of verse 10b: "and they heeded and sent away." With this change to verse 10, an addition is required in verse 11a to include the renege: "And they reneged (וישובו) afterwards and brought back the servants and the maidservants whom they sent away free" (cf. Jer. 34:16). The MT's overall longer version of verses 10 and 11 appears to be a secondary expansion.[16] The reason for the reneging is not stated, but it becomes apparent that it is emblematic of the people's covenant infidelity in general. It is possible that the temporary withdrawal of the Babylonian army due to a report about Pharaoh's army coming to help Judah gave the people a false confidence that they could return to their former pattern of life without consequence (see Jer. 34:21b [MT]; 37:5, 7).

When the word of the LORD finally comes in the text (Jer. 34:8, 12 [LXX 41:8, 12]), the citation of the law of manumission in verse 14a is introduced as the "covenant" (ברית) that the LORD made with the forefathers when he brought them out of the land of Egypt "from a place of servitude" (Jer. 34:13 [LXX 41:13]; cf. Exod. 20:2; Deut. 5:6; Jer. 31:32). This is important for two reasons. First, the law of manumission is made to represent the whole of the Sinai covenant. Second, the "agreement" (ברית) that Zedekiah made with the people (Jer. 34:8b–9) is now equated with the "covenant" (ברית) that the LORD made with the forefathers. The description of Egypt as "a place of servitude" is not superfluous. It is written into the law of manumission itself as it appears in Deuteronomy 15:12–18: "And you will remember that you were a servant in the land of Egypt, and the LORD your God ransomed you; therefore, I am commanding you this word today" (Deut. 15:15; cf. Deut. 5:15; 16:12; 24:18, 22; see also Lev. 25:42). It is not that memory of servitude in Egypt motivates the keeping of the law. Rather, it is that the keeping of the law reminds the people of their servitude in Egypt and their deliverance from it. The law is designed to bring to mind the whole basis for the covenant relationship (Exod. 20:2; Deut. 5:6).[17]

---

16. Note how the addition at the end of verse 10a ("free so as not to serve by them") conforms to the MT's version of verse 9b.

17. See Childs' comments about Deuteronomy 5:15: "How does Israel's memory of her redemption from slavery relate to the sabbath command? The syntax of the sentence makes it clear that Israel's memory does not act as the motivation for allowing slaves to participate in the observance of the sabbath. In such a case one would have expected the sentence to read: Remember that you were a slave and keep the sabbath. But this frequent interpretation does not adequately explain the subsequent clause:

Jeremiah 34:14a (LXX 41:14a) is a citation of the law in Exodus 21:2 and Deuteronomy 15:1, 12.[18] According to the MT, Hebrew servants are to be released at the end of "seven" years (cf. Deut. 15:1; 31:10), yet the text goes on to say that the term of service is "six" years. The Hebrew source behind Greek Jeremiah appears to be an attempt to address this discrepancy. It says that Hebrew servants are to be released at the end of "six" years.[19] The MT preserves the more difficult and more original reading.[20] The sense of the text is that Hebrew servants are to serve a term of six years and then be released in the seventh year (Exod. 21:2; Deut. 15:12).[21] This is not exactly the same

---

'therefore he commanded you' of v. 15b. Memory does not serve to arouse a psychological reaction of sympathy for slaves, rather quite a different theology of memory is at work. Israel is commanded to observe the sabbath in order to remember its slavery and deliverance. This connection is even more explicit in Ex. 16.3. The festival arouses and excites the memory. The Deuteronomist's concern is not primarily humanitarian, but theological. He is basically concerned that 'all Israel' participate in the sabbath. This is only a reality when the slaves also share in its observance. Israel's memory functions to assure the proper celebration of the Sabbath by remembering the nature of the sabbath in Egypt at the time of the Exodus" (Brevard S. Childs, *The Book of Exodus: A Critical, Theological Commentary*, OTL [Louisville: Westminster John Knox, 1974], 417). But see also Exodus 22:20 (Eng., 22:21); 23:9; Leviticus 19:33–34; Deuteronomy 10:19.

18. The Hebrew source behind Greek Jeremiah uses a second-person singular verb (תשלח) and second-person singular pronominal suffixes in verse 14a. The MT uses a second-person plural verb (תשלחו) and second-person singular pronominal suffixes. Holladay suggests that the shift from the second-person plural forms of address elsewhere in verses 13–17 to second-person singular in verse 14a marks the citation of earlier material (Holladay, *Jeremiah 2*, 241).

19. This is reminiscent of the textual variation in Genesis 2:2. The MT says that God completed his work on the "seventh" day, which seems problematic because he rested on the seventh day. The Samaritan Pentateuch, LXX, and Syriac all say that he completed his work on the "sixth" day. This latter reading appears to be the result of an effort to rectify the reading found in the MT, which is an argument for the originality of the MT. The interpreter is forced to reckon with the sense of God completing his work on the seventh day.

20. On the other hand, the MT's addition of מעמך ("from you") at the end of the verse 14a may be a secondary attempt to make the text match Deuteronomy 15:12 more closely.

21. See Neusner, *Jeremiah in Talmud and Midrash*, 382; Keil, *Jeremiah*, 311; Calvin, *Jeremiah*, 4:286n1; Bright, *Jeremiah*, 222.

as the land Sabbath (Exod. 23:10–11; Lev. 25:3–7), which is a regular cycle ("every seven years").[22] Rather, it depends upon completion of a term of service, which begins when a fellow Hebrew sells himself out of necessity. The forefathers did not pay any attention to this instruction from the LORD (Jer. 34:14b [LXX 41:14b]; cf. Jer. 7:26; 25:4; 35:15b).

The Hebrew source behind Greek Jeremiah 34:15 (LXX 41:15) says, "And they returned today to do what was right in my eyes by proclaiming liberty each to his neighbor, and they made an agreement [or, covenant] before me in the house upon which my name is called." The use of third-person plural verbs makes it seem as though the forefathers are the subject, yet it is clear from the use of היום ("today") and the use of second-person plural verbs in verse 16 that the present generation is in view. Thus, the MT has changed the verbs in verse 15 to second-person plural. Nevertheless, the LXX represents the more original reading. This is yet another example where the past and present generations are spoken of interchangeably (see again Jer. 2:2). The forefathers did not listen to the LORD with regard to the law of manumission (Jer. 34:13–14). The present generation made an agreement to observe the law and did so temporarily, but they ultimately reneged and thus were no different than their forefathers (Jer. 34:8b–11, 15–16). The new element in verse 15b is the reference to the making of the agreement "before me [i.e., before the ark] in the house upon which my name is called [i.e., in the temple]" (cf. Exod. 16:34; Josh. 24:1, 25–26; see also Jer. 7:30; 32:34). This sets up the reference to the profanation of the LORD's name in verse 16. The people made an agreement in the temple that bore the LORD's name, an agreement that would have honored and set apart his name; but when they reneged by bringing back the servants and maidservants, they disrespected the LORD's name and made it seem common. Verse 16 contributes the phrase "according to their desire" (לנפשם), which does not appear earlier in the chapter, to describe the manner in which the servants were sent away. This indicates that these servants did not opt to devote themselves to their masters for life (as in Exod. 21:5–6; Deut. 15:16–17) but wished to be released on schedule. The conclusion to verse 16 differs between the LXX *Vorlage* and the MT due to an addition in the MT. According to the former, the phrase "to you as servants and maidservants" is the indirect object of "bringing back." The MT, however, adds "and you subdued them to become" from verse 11b at the beginning of verse 16b, which

---

22. Contra Bright, *Jeremiah*, 219; Thompson, *Book of Jeremiah*, 611–12. See McKane, *Jeremiah XXVI–LII*, 880.

results in the following combination: "and you subdued them to become your servants and maidservants."

לָכֵן ("Therefore") introduces the announcement of judgment for the people's covenant infidelity (Jer. 34:17 [LXX 41:17]). In a remarkable turn of phrase, the LORD says that just as the people have not listened to him "to proclaim liberty" to their Hebrew servants, so is he about "to proclaim liberty" to them, but this latter liberty is "to the sword and to plague and to famine" (cf. Jer. 14:12, et al.). He will make them into an "object of terror" to all the kingdoms of the earth (cf. Jer. 15:4; 24:9; 29:18). The LORD will judge the people justly in accordance with their own actions. It will be done to them as they have done to others. They have refused to grant freedom to those to whom it is due; so, their freedom will be taken from them.

According to the Hebrew source behind Greek Jeremiah 34:18 (LXX 41:18), the LORD will make the men who have transgressed his covenant like the calf that they "made to serve with it." Once again, it is important to recognize that the "agreement" between Zedekiah and the people is being equated with the Sinai "covenant" precisely because the particular Mosaic instruction that the people agreed to keep has been made to represent the entire covenant relationship with the LORD. The people's failure to keep the one law of manumission is symbolic of their breaking of the whole covenant (cf. Jas. 2:10). When the LXX *Vorlage* says that the transgressors will be made like the calf that they made, there appears to be an allusion to the golden calf episode (Exod. 32; Deut. 9).[23] If this is correct, then the point is that the people will suffer a fate analogous to that of the golden calf, which Moses burned and ground into powder and then scattered on the water for the people to drink (Exod. 32:20; Deut. 9:21). On the other hand, the MT says that the transgressors will be made like the calf that they "cut in two and passed between its pieces." This indicates that the covenant ceremony was similar to the one described in Genesis 15:9–10, 17–18.[24] Thompson comments, "The rite has its parallel in the covenant ceremonies of the ancient Near East in which a beast was cut in pieces to serve as a symbol of the judgment that would befall the covenant-breaker" (cf. 1 Sam. 11:7).[25] The extent of involvement in the transgression of the covenant is indicated by the list of transgressors in Jeremiah 34:19 (LXX 41:19): "the officials of Judah [MT adds: and the

---

23. See McKane, *Jeremiah XXVI–LII*, 873.
24. See Bright, *Jeremiah*, 222.
25. Thompson, *Book of Jeremiah*, 613. This may provide some insight into the Hebrew idiom כרת ברית (lit., "cut a covenant").

officials of Jerusalem] and [> MT] the court officials and the priests and the people [MT: all the people of the land, those who passed between the pieces of the calf]."

Of course, the people will not literally be burned and ground into powder like the golden calf or cut in two like the calf of the covenant ceremony. According to 34:20 (LXX 41:20), the LORD will deliver them to their enemies (MT: "into the hand/power of their enemies and into the hand/power of those who seek their life") (cf. Jer. 19:7a; 21:7; 44:30). Their corpses will become food for the flying creatures of the sky and for the large land animals (cf. Deut. 28:26; Jer. 7:33; 16:4; 19:7b; Ps. 79:2). As for Zedekiah and the officials, the LORD will also deliver them into the power of their enemies (MT adds: "and into the hand/power of those who seek their life") (Jer. 34:21a [LXX 41:21a]). The Hebrew source behind Greek Jeremiah 34:21b (LXX 41:21b) says: "and the army of the king of Babylon is for those who are going up from upon them." This appears to be a reference to the attempted flight of Zedekiah and his men from the Babylonian army (see Jer. 39:4–5 [MT]; 52:7–9). The MT, however, says: "and into the hand/power of the army of the king of Babylon that is going up from upon them." This is a reference to the temporary withdrawal of the Babylonian army when they heard of Pharaoh's army coming to help Judah (Jer. 37:5–11; see also Jer. 21:2). The LORD is about to issue a divine decree to bring the Babylonian army back to the "land" of Judah (MT: the "city" of Jerusalem) (Jer. 34:22 [LXX 41:22]). The Hebrew source behind Greek Jeremiah says that they will fight against "it" (i.e., the land of Judah) and capture it and burn it with fire along with the cities of Judah (cf. Jer. 34:1, 7) and make a general desolation without inhabitant. The MT says that they will fight against "it" (i.e., the city of Jerusalem) and capture it and burn it with fire (cf. Jer. 21:10; 34:2) and make the cities of Judah a desolation without inhabitant. There is a correspondence between the people's temporary release of their servants who were then brought back (Jer. 34:15–16) and the temporary withdrawal of the Babylonian soldiers who would subsequently be brought back (Jer. 34:21–22).[26]

---

26. See McKane, *Jeremiah XXVI–LII*, 874.

JEREMIAH 35 (LXX 42)

35:1 (42:1) The word that came to Jeremiah from the Lord *in the days of Jehoiakim [MT adds: the son of Josiah] the king of Judah, saying, 35:2 (42:2) "Go to the house of the Rechabites [LXX: the house of Archabin] [MT adds: and speak with them] and bring them to the house of the* Lord, *into one of the rooms [LXX: courts], and give them wine to drink." 35:3 (42:3) And I took Jaazaniah the son of Jeremiah [LXX: Jeremin; Syr.: Amariah] the son of Habazziniah and his brothers and [MT adds: all] his sons and all the house of the Rechabites. 35:4 (42:4) And I brought them to the house of the* Lord, *into the room of the sons of [Ms: the son of; > LXX^A] Hanan [Ms: יחנן] the son of Gedaliah [MT: Igdaliah], the man of God [Syr.: the prophet of God; Tg. Jon.: the prophet of the Lord], which was next to the room of the officials, which was above [LXX: who were over] the room of Maaseiah the son of Shallum, the keeper of the threshold [LXX: court]. 35:5 (42:5) And I set before them [MT: the sons of the house of the Rechabites] a bowl/goblet [LXX: jar] of wine [MT: bowls filled with wine] and cups, and I said [MT adds: to them], "Drink wine." 35:6 (42:6) And they said, "We will not drink wine, for Jonadab the son of Rechab, our father, he commanded us, saying, 'You must not drink wine, neither you nor your sons, forever. 35:7 (42:7) And a house you must not build, and seed you must not sow, and a vineyard [MT adds: you must not plant and] you must not have, for in tents you must dwell all your days in order that you may live for many days upon the land where you are sojourning.' 35:8 (42:8) And we obeyed the voice of Jonadab [MT: Jehonadab the son of Rechab] our father [MT adds: according to all that he commanded us] not to drink wine all our days, we and our wives and our sons and our daughters [MT: we, our wives, our sons, and our daughters], 35:9 (42:9) and not to build houses to dwell there [MT: for our dwelling], and a vineyard and a field and seed we did not have [MT: we do not have], 35:10 (42:10) and we dwelt in tents and obeyed and did according to all that Jonadab our father commanded us. 35:11 (42:11) And so, when Nebuchadnezzar [MT: Nebuchadrezzar the king of Babylon] came up against the land, we said, 'Come, and let us go to Jerusalem from before [or, because of] the army of the Chaldeans and from before [or, because of] the army of Assyria [LXX: the Assyrians; MT: Aram; Syr.: Edom].' And we dwelt in Jerusalem."*

35:12 (42:12) And the word of the Lord *came to me [MT: to Jeremiah], saying, 35:13 (42:13) "Thus says the* Lord *[MT adds: of hosts, the God of Israel], 'Go and say to the men of Judah and to the inhabitants of Jerusalem, "Will you not receive instruction by listening to my words?*

35:14 (42:14) The sons of Jonadab the son of Rechab have upheld the word that he commanded his sons [MT: The words of Jehonadab the son of Rechab that he commanded his sons have been upheld] not to drink wine, and they have not drunk [MT adds: until this day, for they have obeyed the command of their father]. Yet I, on the other hand, I have spoken to you rising early and speaking [i.e., urgently speaking], and you have not obeyed [MT: and you have not listened to me]. 35:15 (42:15) And I sent to you [MT adds: all] my servants the prophets [MT adds: rising early and sending], saying, 'Return, each from his evil way, and improve your ways, and do not go after other gods to serve/worship them, and dwell [or, that you may dwell (GKC §110i)] in the land that I gave to you and to your forefathers.' But you did not incline your ears, and you did not obey [MT: and you did not listen to me]. 35:16 (42:16) And [MT: Because; Syr.: Lo] the sons of Jonadab [MT: Jehonadab] the son of Rechab have upheld the command of their father [MT adds: that he commanded them]; but this people, they have not listened to me. 35:17 (42:17) Therefore, thus says the LORD [MT adds: the God of hosts, the God of Israel], 'Look, I am about to bring to Judah and to the inhabitants of Jerusalem all the calamity that I have spoken against them [MT adds: because I spoke to them (Tg. Jon.: because I sent to them all my servants the prophets), and they did not listen/obey, and I called to them (Tg. Jon.: and they prophesied to them), and they did not answer (Tg. Jon.: turn)].' 35:18 (42:18) [MT adds: And to the house of the Rechabites Jeremiah said,] Therefore [> MT], thus says the LORD [MT adds: of hosts, the God of Israel], 'Because the sons of Jonadab the son of Rechab obeyed the command of their father to do just as he commanded them [MT: Because you listened to the command of Jehonadab your father and kept all his commands and did according to all that he commanded you], 35:19 (42:19) [MT adds: therefore, thus says the LORD of hosts, the God of Israel,] a man will not be cut off of the sons of Jonadab [MT: for Jonadab] the son of Rechab standing [Tg. Jon.: ministering] before me all the days of the land/earth [of the land/earth > MT].'"""

Chapter 35 (LXX 42) is introduced as the word that came to Jeremiah from the LORD in the days of Jehoiakim (609–598 BC) (Jer. 35:1 [LXX 42:1]; see Jer. 22:13–23). The correspondence between 2 Kings 24:2 and Jeremiah 35:11 (LXX 42:11) suggests that this word came in the latter part of Jehoiakim's reign. As noted in the introduction to the commentary on Jeremiah 34, chapters 34 and 35 are not in chronological sequence. Chapter 34 presents words that came to Jeremiah during the reign of Zedekiah (597–587 BC). The juxtaposition of these two chapters is designed to highlight a contrast between the covenant infidelity of the

Judeans (Jer. 34) and the faithfulness of the Rechabites to their father Jonadab (Jer. 35; see in particular Jer. 35:14, 16).

Jeremiah is instructed to go to "the house of the Rechabites" and bring them to the temple, into one of the rooms, and give them wine to drink (Jer. 35:2 [LXX 42:2]). It is generally agreed that the phrase "the house of the Rechabites" does not refer to a dwelling place but to a family or a community,[1] although Holladay suggests that it refers to a dwelling place in verse 2 but to a family in verses 3, 5, and 18.[2] Very little is known about the Rechabites apart from what is found in the present chapter.[3] According to 1 Chronicles 2:55, the families of the scribes who lived in Jabez were Kenites who descended from Hammath, the father of "the house of Rechab." The Kenites are listed in Genesis 15:19 as inhabitants of the land given to Abram's seed. Moses' father-in-law is said to be a Kenite (Judg. 1:16; 4:11),[4] and the relationship between the Kenites and Israel is generally said to be a good one (see Judg. 4:17–21; 5:24–27; 1 Sam. 15:6). It is not clear why Jeremiah is to bring the Rechabites to the temple, although it may be surmised from what happens in the temple according to the accounts of Jeremiah 7 and 26 that the intent is to publish a message to the people of Judah. It is questionable whether the offer of wine to the Rechabites is a symbolic sign act or even a test as commonly suggested.[5] On the one hand, the action does not symbolize anything in the manner of other sign acts in the book, although it does serve to illustrate a point. On the other hand, the whole design of the offer seems to depend upon the guarantee of the outcome. Thus, it can hardly be characterized as a test.

Jeremiah follows orders and takes Jaazaniah along with his brothers and sons and all the family of the Rechabites and brings them to the temple (Jer. 35:3–4 [LXX 42:3–4]). Nothing else is known about Jaazaniah who is called here "the son of Jeremiah the son of Habazziniah," although it appears from this text that he was a leader among the Rechabites at this time. The family of the Rechabites must

---

1. See, e.g., Keil, *Jeremiah*, 313; Bright, *Jeremiah*, 189.
2. Holladay, *Jeremiah 2*, 247.
3. See Herbert B. Huffman, "The Rechabites in the Book of Jeremiah and Their Historical Roots in Israel," in *The Book of Jeremiah: Composition, Reception, and Interpretation*, eds. Jack R. Lundbom, Craig A. Evans, and Bradford A. Anderson (Leiden: Brill, 2018), 191–210. See also Nehemiah 3:14 and the *History of the Rechabites*.
4. According to *Sifre* to Numbers (Num. 10:29–32), Jethro and the Rechabites loved the Torah (Neusner, *Jeremiah in Talmud and Midrash*, 16).
5. See Holladay, *Jeremiah 2*, 246; McKane, *Jeremiah XXVI–LII*, 896.

have been relatively small in order for the entire community to follow Jeremiah to the temple. Upon arrival at the temple, Jeremiah brings the Rechabites into the room of the sons of Hanan the son of Gedaliah (MT: "Igdaliah"). No further information is provided about Hanan except for the designation "the man of God," which is normally reserved for prophets (see BDB, 36; Syr.: "the prophet of God"; *Tg. Jon.*: "the prophet of the Lord"). Thus, the phrase "the sons of Hanan" can refer either to a family of prophets or to a prophetic guild (cf. the phrase "the sons of the prophets," BDB, 611). The latter part of verse 4 locates the room of the sons of Hanan next to the room of the officials (unidentified), which was above the room of Maaseiah the son of Shallum, the keeper of the threshold (cf. 2 Kgs. 25:18; Jer. 52:24; see also Jer. 21:1; 29:25; 37:3). Jeremiah sets before the Rechabites a "bowl" (גביע) of wine (MT: "bowls filled with wine") and "cups" (כסות) and invites them to drink (Jer. 35:5 [LXX 42:5]). The term גביע ("bowl" or "goblet"; LXX: "jar") has a variety of uses, but here it seems to refer to a larger container from which smaller drinking cups were filled.

The Rechabites refuse Jeremiah's offer of wine, explaining that Jonadab the son of Rechab, their father, commanded them never to drink wine (Jer. 35:6 [LXX 42:6]; cf. 1 Kgs. 13:16). Jonadab was not their biological father but their ancestor who lived in the ninth century BC during the time of Jehu whose efforts to eradicate Baal worship were supported by Jonadab (see 2 Kgs. 10:15–17, 23).[6] Bright is one of a minority of commentators to suggest a connection between Jonadab's command and the well-known Nazirite vow (Num. 6:1–21), which not only forbids vine products but also razors and corpses (cf. Ezek. 44:20–21, 25).[7] This connection is usually dismissed due to the fact that the other components of the Nazirite vow are not mentioned in Jonadab's command. Nevertheless, Samson, who is explicitly called a Nazirite (Judg. 13:5), is never instructed to avoid corpses, which would have proved to be impossible for him. Rather, he is told (presumably by his parents) to avoid wine and strong drink, unclean food, and razors (Judg. 13:4–5, 14). It appears then that avoidance of unclean food has taken the place of avoidance of corpses. Likewise, Samuel, who is called a Nazirite in 4QSam[a] (1 Sam. 1:22) but not in the MT or LXX, is only under a vow to avoid the razor in the MT (1 Sam. 1:11; cf. Jer. 7:29; Acts 18:18; 21:24), to

---

6. There appears to be an intentional play on the name רכב ("Rechab") in 2 Kings 10:15–16 using several different words: ברך ("bless"), מרכבה ("chariot"), and רכב ("ride"). The "sons of Jonadab" are also mentioned in the superscription to LXX Psalm 70 (MT 71).

7. Bright, *Jeremiah*, 191.

which the LXX adds that he is to avoid wine and strong drink (cf. Luke 1:15), but there is no reference to avoidance of corpses (nor is there any substitute for it).[8] Furthermore, both Samson and Samuel were under their vows from birth and for life, which is not a feature of the instruction in Numbers 6. Thus, the lack of exact correspondence with the Nazirite vow as described in Numbers 6 is not necessarily an indication of a complete lack of connection (see also *b. Nazir*).

Jonadab's command includes other features, however, that seem to separate it even further from the Nazirite vow. The Rechabites are not to build houses or sow seed or own vineyards (Jer. 35:7a [LXX 42:7a]). The explanation given for this is that the Rechabites are to have a nomadic existence: "for in tents you must dwell all your days in order that you may live for many days upon the land where you are sojourning" (Jer. 35:7b [LXX 42:7b]). This information is not superfluous. Not only does it show that the refusal to drink wine is part of a larger pattern of life, but also it provides a link to the Decalogue that sets up the contrast with the infidelity of Judah in verses 14 and 16. The purpose clause ("in order that you may live for many days upon the land") comes from the command to honor parents in Exodus 20:12 and Deuteronomy 5:16 (see also Prov. 3:1–2). If the Rechabites keep Jonadab's command, then they will be honoring their "father," thus paving the way for a long life upon the land. The main difference in the wording is the description of the land as the place "where you are sojourning" (Jer. 35:7b) rather than the land "that the LORD your God is giving to you" (Exod. 20:12; Deut. 5:16). Rashi takes this to mean that the Rechabites had no rightful share in the land,[9] but that seems unlikely since it would make Jonadab's command to dwell in tents completely unnecessary. If they were unable to possess land, then they would have no choice in the matter. It appears more likely that the language of sojourning is in deference to Leviticus 25:23: "And as for the land, it must not be sold irrevocably, for the land is mine, for sojourners and settlers are you with me." That is, all the inhabitants of the land are in a sense "sojourners."[10]

---

8. See Matitiahu Tsevat, "Was Samuel a Nazirite?" in *"Sha'arei Talmon": Studies in the Bible, Qumran, and the Ancient Near East Presented to Shemaryahu Talmon*, eds. Michael Fishbane and Emanuel Tov (Winona Lake, IN: Eisenbrauns, 1992), 199–204; Anneli Aejmelaeus, "Was Samuel Meant to Be a Nazirite? The First Chapter of Samuel and the Paradigm Shift in Textual Study of the Hebrew Bible," *Textus* 28 (2019): 1–20.

9. Rosenberg, trans., *Mikraoth Gedoloth: Jeremiah Volume Two*, 285.

10. "The patriarchs had been sojourners in the land of Canaan; the Israelites had been sojourners in Egypt and were then given the land of Canaan for

The Rechabites' outline of their obedience in verses 8–10 reveals their interpretation of Jonadab's command. They have interpreted the prohibition not to drink wine "forever" (עד עולם) to mean not to drink wine "all our days" (כל ימינו) (Jer. 35:8 [LXX 42:8]). They have understood the pronoun "you" (m. pl.) from verse 6b to include not only the men but also their wives, and they have understood "your sons" from verse 6b to mean "your children," including sons and daughters. They have rearranged the list of things not to do from verse 7a (building houses, sowing seed, and owning vineyards) and have added owning a field: "and not to build houses to dwell there [MT: for our dwelling], and a vineyard and a field and seed we did not have [MT: we do not have]" (Jer. 35:9 [LXX 42:9]).[11] Not sowing seed has become not owning seed at all. The Rechabites say that they have dwelt in tents in accordance with Jonadab's command (Jer. 35:10 [LXX 42:10]), but they give no indication of the long life that they have enjoyed upon the land as a result (cf. Jer. 35:7b). Rather, they explain why they are currently living in a fortified city like Jerusalem in apparent contradiction to Jonadab's command (see Rashi). They have only done so because of the threat of Nebuchadnezzar and his army against the land (Jer. 35:11 [LXX 42:11]; see 2 Kgs. 24:2).[12] It was to be expected that people living in outlying regions would flee to the cities when a land was under attack (see Lev. 26:25; Jer. 4:5; 8:14). Therefore, the Rechabites have not violated the instruction of their forefather.

The Hebrew source behind Greek Jeremiah 35:12 (LXX 42:12) maintains the first-person perspective established by verses 3–5: "And the word of the Lord came to me (אלי)" (cf. Jer. 32:26; 36:1 [LXX 39:26; 43:1]). The MT is possibly the result of reading אלי ("to me") as an abbreviation for אל ירמיהו ("to Jeremiah"), which shifts the perspective to third person (see Jer. 35:1; see also MT Jer. 35:18). Jeremiah is now instructed to go to the men of Judah and the inhabitants of Jerusalem (cf. Jer. 35:2) and to urge them to learn the lesson provided by the Rechabites' example (Jer. 35:13 [LXX 42:13]): "Will you not receive instruction by listening to

---

their own possession. The Rechabites, on the other hand, continued to be sojourners on the land" (Holladay, *Jeremiah 2*, 248).

11. This relieves them of any concern about property (cf. Jer. 32:6–15, 25).

12. The Hebrew source behind Greek Jeremiah also mentions the army of "Assyria" (אשור). The MT has "Aram" (ארם), and the Syriac has "Edom" (אדם). Of these three readings, only "Aram" has support from 2 Kings 24:2. This was an army from a people conquered by Nebuchadnezzar and now in his service.

my words?"[13] It would have been a fairly easy move for Jeremiah to go from the room of the sons of Hanan (Jer. 35:4) out to the larger temple complex to find his audience (cf. Jer. 36:10).

The lesson that Jeremiah is to deliver is stated very succinctly in Jeremiah 35:14 (LXX 42:14). The Hebrew source behind Greek Jeremiah for verse 14a says, "The sons of Jonadab the son of Rechab have upheld the word that he commanded his sons (הקימו בני יונדב בן רכב את הדבר אשר צוה את בניו) not to drink wine, and they have not drunk" (cf. Jer. 35:16a). The MT arranges the syntax differently and has a substantially longer text: "The words of Jehonadab the son of Rechab that he commanded his sons have been upheld (הוקם את דברי יהונדב בן רכב אשר צוה את בניו) not to drink wine, and they have not drunk until this day, for they have obeyed the command of their father."[14] Only the faithfulness not to drink wine is mentioned here, not the nomadic lifestyle.[15] The obedience of the Rechabites to uphold their forefather's command stands in stark contrast to the infidelity of the people in Jeremiah 34:18 who have not "upheld" (הקימו) the words of their agreement/covenant. Thus, Jeremiah 35:14b says, "Yet I, on the other hand, I have spoken to you rising early and speaking [i.e., urgently speaking], and you have not obeyed [MT: and you have not listened to me]." The Rechabites have given their forefather Jonadab the honor due to him, but the Judeans have not given their father the LORD his respect (see Mal. 1:6).

The lesson of verse 14 is reiterated in verses 15 and 16. The LORD has sent to the people prophets like Jeremiah urging them to turn from their worship of other gods so that they might dwell in the land given to them and their forefathers, but they have not paid attention (Jer. 35:15 [LXX 42:15]; cf. Jer. 7:3–9, 13 [MT], 25; 11:7 [MT] 18:11; 25:4–7; 26:5; 29:19 [MT]; 32:33; 34:14b; 44:4). The Rechabites have upheld the command of their forefather in order to live for a long time on the land (Jer. 35:7; see again Exod. 20:12; Deut. 5:16), but the people of Judah and Jerusalem have not listened to their heavenly father (Jer. 35:16 [LXX 42:16]; see Jer. 3:19–20), which will result in their exile from

---

13. Cf. Deuteronomy 18:19. Holladay rightly notes that the rhetorical question in Jeremiah 35:13b is not an invitation to change but a chastisement (*Jeremiah 2*, 248).

14. The marker את can mark the grammatical subject of a passive verb, but in this case (הוקם את דברי) the plural subject does not agree with the singular verb.

15. It should be stressed that the intention here is not to commend the specifics of the Rechabites' lifestyle but to commend their obedience and fidelity.

the land (Jer. 35:17). The MT begins verse 16 with the conjunction כִּי. Since verse 16 is not properly an explanation of verse 15, commentators who nevertheless want to interpret this conjunction as causal propose that it introduces the reason for the judgment announced in verse 17.[16] Another option is to translate it as "Indeed." This conjunction does not appear in the Hebrew source behind Greek Jeremiah.

לָכֵן ("Therefore") introduces the announcement of judgment for Judah and Jerusalem (Jer. 35:17 [LXX 42:17]). The LORD is about to bring to them all the calamity that he has spoken against them (cf. Jer. 11:11; 36:30–31). The Hebrew source behind Greek Jeremiah for verse 17 is substantially shorter than the MT, which is consistent with the overall shorter text of the LXX *Vorlage* for the present chapter and for the book of Jeremiah as a whole. The MT adds verse 17b: "because I spoke to them (*Tg. Jon.*: because I sent to them all my servants the prophets), and they did not listen/obey, and I called to them (*Tg. Jon.*: and they prophesied to them), and they did not answer (*Tg. Jon.*: turn)]" (cf. Jer. 7:13; Zech. 7:13).

At the beginning of 35:18 (LXX 42:18), the MT adds, "And to the house of the Rechabites Jeremiah said." This text does not appear in the Hebrew source behind Greek Jeremiah. Rather, the LXX *Vorlage* begins with an introduction of the LORD's discourse: "Therefore [> MT], thus says the LORD [MT adds: of hosts, the God of Israel]." The remainder of verse 18 states the reason for the blessing of the sons of Jonadab in verse 19. Unlike the Judeans in relationship to the LORD, the sons of Jonadab have obeyed the command of their father (note the difference in wording between the LXX *Vorlage* and the MT in the translation of v. 18 above). The MT reintroduces the LORD's discourse in verse 19 ("therefore, thus says the LORD of hosts, the God of Israel"), but this addition is unnecessary and is not found in the Hebrew source behind Greek Jeremiah. The LORD says that "a man will not be cut off of the sons of Jonadab [MT: for Jonadab] the son of Rechab standing [*Tg. Jon.*: ministering] before me all the days of the land/earth [of the land/earth > MT]" (cf. 1 Kgs. 2:4b; Jer. 33:17–18 [MT]; note the contrast with Jehoiakim in Jer. 36:30 and Jehoiachin in Jer. 22:30; see also Jer. 29:32). Because the expression "standing before me" is sometimes used of priestly service (e.g., Deut. 10:8; cf. Jer. 33:18), some have supposed that the Rechabites' daughters married priests, and their grandsons offered sacrifices on the altar,[17] but the expression is not limited to priests (see, e.g., Deut. 4:10; 1 Kgs. 17:1; 18:15; 2 Kgs. 3:14; Jer.

---

16. See Rosenberg, trans., *Mikraoth Gedoloth: Jeremiah Volume Two*, 288.

17. Rosenberg, trans., *Mikraoth Gedoloth: Jeremiah Volume Two*, 288.

7:10; 15:1, 19; 18:20). It is possible that the service provided by the Rechabites is simply their ongoing example of fidelity. The Hebrew source behind Greek Jeremiah says that the sons of Jonadab will not lack a man serving the Lord "all the days of the land/earth" (the MT only has "all the days"). Those who understand this phrase to mean "all the days of the earth" draw a comparison with Genesis 8:22 and the assurance that the seasons of earth will not cease (see *BHS* apparatus). It is possible, however, that the phrase means "all the days of the land," in which case it would correspond to the expectation that the Rechabites will live for a long time in the land of the covenant because of their obedience to their father Jonadab (Jer. 35:7; see once again Exod. 20:12; Deut. 5:16).

JEREMIAH 36 (LXX 43)

36:1 (43:1) [MT adds: ויהי] In the fourth year of Jehoiakim the son of Josiah, the king of Judah, the word of the LORD came to me [MT: this word came to Jeremiah from the LORD], saying, 36:2 (43:2) "Take a scroll of a document and write on it all the words that I have spoken [LXX: revealed] to you concerning Jerusalem [MT: Israel] and concerning Judah and concerning all the nations since the day that I spoke to you, since the days of Josiah the king of Judah [the king of Judah > MT] until this day. 36:3 (43:3) Perhaps the house of Judah will hear all the calamity that I am planning to do to them in order that they may return from their [MT: his] evil way, and that I may forgive their iniquity and their sin." 36:4 (43:4) And Jeremiah called [pc Mss: called to] Baruch the son of Neriah, and he [MT: Baruch] wrote from the mouth of Jeremiah [ESV: at the dictation of Jeremiah] all the words of the LORD that he spoke [LXX: revealed] to him on a scroll of a document. 36:5 (43:5) And Jeremiah commanded Baruch, saying, "I am restrained [ESV: banned]. I am unable to enter the house of the LORD. 36:6 (43:6) And you must read aloud this scroll [MT: And you must go and read aloud in the scroll that you wrote from my mouth the words of the LORD] in the ears of the people in the house of the LORD on a day of fasting, and also in the ears of all Judah, those who are coming from their cities, you must read them [LXX: to them]. 36:7 (43:7) Perhaps their supplication will fall before the LORD, and they will turn from their evil way [MT: each from his evil way], for great is the anger and the fury of the LORD [of the LORD > MT] that he [MT: the LORD] has spoken against this people." 36:8 (43:8) And Baruch [MT adds: the son of Neriah] did according to all that Jeremiah [MT adds: the prophet] commanded him, reading aloud in the document the words of the LORD in the house of the LORD.

36:9 (43:9) And so, in the eighth [MT: fifth] year of King Jehoiakim [MT: Jehoiakim the son of Josiah, the king of Judah], in the ninth month, all the people in Jerusalem and the house of Judah [MT: and all the people who came from the cities of Judah into Jerusalem] called a fast before the LORD. 36:10 (43:10) And Baruch read aloud in the document the words of Jeremiah in the house of the LORD, in the room of Gemariah the son of Shaphan, the scribe, in the upper court, at the entrance of the new [Tg. Jon.: eastern] gate of the house of the LORD, in the ears of [MT adds: all] the people. 36:11 (43:11) And Micaiah the son of Gemariah the son of Shaphan heard all the words of the LORD from the document. 36:12 (43:12) And he went down to the house of the king, into the room of the scribe; and look, there all the officials were sitting: Elishama the scribe and Delaiah the son of Shelemiah [MT: Shemaiah; LXX^S: Zedekiah] *and Jonathan [MT: Elnathan] the son of Achbor and Gemariah the son of Shaphan and Zedekiah the son of Hananiah and all the officials. 36:13 (43:13) And Micaiah told them all the words that he heard when Baruch read aloud [MT adds: in the document] in the ears of the people.*

36:14 (43:14) And all the officials sent to Baruch the son of Neriah [the son of Neriah > MT] Jehudi [> LXX^BS] the son of Nethaniah the son of Shelemaiah the son of Cushi, saying, "The scroll in which you read aloud in the ears of the people, take it in your hand and come." And Baruch took the scroll [MT adds: in his hand] and went down [MT: and came] to them. 36:15 (43:15) And they said to him, "Read aloud again in our ears [MT: Sit and read it aloud in our ears]." And Baruch read aloud [MT adds: in their ears]. 36:16 (43:16) And then, as soon as they heard all the words, they advised one another [MT: they expressed dread to one another] and said [MT adds: to Baruch], "We must certainly tell the king all these words." 36:17 (43:17) And Baruch they asked, saying, "From where [LXX^B: Where; MT: Tell us, how] did you write all these words [MT adds: from his mouth]?"[1] 36:18 (43:18) And Baruch said [MT adds: to them], "From his mouth Jeremiah [MT: he] would dictate to me all these words, and I would write on a [MT: the] document [MT adds: in ink]." 36:19 (43:19) And they [MT: the officials] said to Baruch, "Go, hide, you and Jeremiah, [MT adds: and] let no one know where you are."

36:20 (43:20) And they came to the king courtward, and the scroll they had deposited in the room of Elishama [MT adds: the scribe], and they told the king [MT: in the ears of the king] all the words [mlt Mss, LXX^A, Syr.: all these words]. 36:21 (43:21) And the king sent Jehudi to take the scroll, and he took it from the room of Elishama [MT adds: the scribe]. And Jehudi read [MT adds: it] aloud in the ears of the king and in the ears of all the officials who were standing by the king. 36:22 (43:22) And the king was sitting in the winter house [MT adds: in the ninth month], and a pot of fire was before him [MT: and the firepot was burning before him (or, and the firepot before him was burning)]. 36:23 (43:23) And so it was that as soon as [eastern kethiv: when] Jehudi would read three or four columns, he would tear it with the scribe's knife and cast into the fire that was in the pot until all the scroll was consumed in the fire that was in the pot. 36:24 (43:24) And the king and [MT adds: all] his servants who were hearing all these words were not in dread and did not tear their garments. 36:25 (43:25) And [MT adds: also / even / though]

---

1. ESV: "Tell us, please, how did you write all these words? Was it at his dictation?"

Elnathan and Gedaliah [MT: Delaiah] and Gemariah, they entreated the king not [not > LXX^BS] to burn the scroll [MT adds: and he did not listen to them]. 36:26 (43:26) And the king commanded Jerahmeel the king's son [or, a member of the royal family] and Seraiah the son of Azriel [MT adds: and Shelemiah the son of Abdeel] to take Baruch [MT adds: the scribe] and Jeremiah [MT adds: the prophet], and they hid [MT: and the LORD hid them].*

36:27 (43:27) And the word of the LORD came to Jeremiah [Syr. adds: the prophet] after the king burned the scroll, all the words [or, with all the words; MT: and the words] that Baruch wrote from the mouth of [or, at the dictation of] Jeremiah, saying, 36:28 (43:28) "Take again another scroll and write [MT adds: on it] all the [MT adds: former] words that were on the [MT adds: former] scroll that King Jehoiakim [MT: Jehoiakim the king of Judah] burned. 36:29 (43:29) And [MT adds: to Jehoiakim the king of Judah] you will say, 'Thus says the LORD, "As for you, you burned this scroll, saying, 'Why did you write on it, saying, "The king of Babylon will surely come and destroy this land and exterminate from it man and beast"?'"

36:30 (43:30) Therefore, thus says the LORD concerning Jehoiakim the king of Judah, 'He will not have one sitting on the throne of David, and his corpse will be cast to the heat by day and to the frost by night. 36:31 (43:31) And I will visit upon him and upon his seed/offspring and upon his servants [MT adds: their iniquity], and I will bring upon/against them and upon/against the inhabitants of Jerusalem and upon/against the land [MT: men/people] of Judah all the calamity that I spoke to/against them, and they did not hear.'"

36:32 (43:32) And Baruch took another scroll [MT: And Jeremiah, he took another scroll and gave it to Baruch the son of Neriah, the scribe], and he wrote on it from the mouth of [or, at the dictation of] Jeremiah all the words of the document that Jehoiakim [MT adds: the king of Judah] burned [MT adds: in the fire], and still many words like these were added to them.

Chapter 36 (LXX 43) provides an invaluable account of the textualization of Jeremiah's prophecy. It gives insight into how the prophet and his message from God became a "book" (see LXX Jer. 1:1).[2] The

---

2. "The story is unique in the Old Testament, since its subject is neither a person, nor an act of Jahweh's providence or appointment, but a book. But

narrative moves further back in time (cf. Jer. 35:1, 11) to the fourth year (605 BC) of Jehoiakim (Jer. 36:1a [LXX 43:1a]). This is the same date given for Jeremiah 25:1–13 (Jer. 25:1), which concludes the "Book" of Jeremiah (Jer. 25:13). It is also the date provided for Baruch's scribal colophon in chapter 45 (Jer. 45:1), which originally stood at the end of Jeremiah 1:1–25:13 and then moved with the subsequent growth of the book (Jer. 36:32b) to its present position in the Hebrew source behind Greek Jeremiah just prior to the appendix in chapter 52. The MT has chapters 46–51 placed between chapters 45 and 52 so that 51:59–64 serves as the concluding colophon in that version of the book (see also Jer. 46:2). The first-person perspective of the Hebrew source behind Greek Jeremiah 36:1b (LXX 43:1b) ("the word of the LORD came to me [אלי]") appears to conflict with the third-person perspective of the remainder of the account (see, e.g., Jer. 36:4). It is possible that the Greek translator misinterpreted אלי, which was intended to be an abbreviation for אל ירמיהו ("to Jeremiah").

The instruction given to Jeremiah in 36:2 (LXX 43:2) is to take "a scroll of a document" (מגלת ספר) and write on it all the words that the LORD has spoken to him concerning Jerusalem (MT: "Israel") and Judah and all the nations since the days of Josiah (cf. Jer. 1:1–3; 25:3). A scroll of a document is perhaps "a scroll suitable for a document" (cf. Ezek. 2:9; Ps. 40:8 [Eng., 40:7]).[3] The exact content of the words to be written on this scroll is unknown, but there is general agreement that it corresponds in some measure to what now appears in Jeremiah 1:1–25:13.[4] At the very least, the scroll's message of judgment (Jer. 36:3, 29–31) corresponds to what the reader finds in 1:1–25:13 (e.g., Jer. 20:4–5; 22:18–19; 25:5). According to the LXX *Vorlage*, the words to be

---

the book's fortunes epitomize the fortunes of the message it contained. Once more the *motif* is that of the great failure, which Jeremiah plays with his own particular variations. We might therefore almost speak of a 'passion' undergone by the book as well as by its author" (Gerhard von Rad, *Old Testament Theology*, vol. 2, *The Theology of Israel's Prophetic Traditions*, trans. D. M. G. Stalker [New York: Harper & Row, 1965], 45).

3. "Further reference in the chapter is either to 'the scroll' (vv 4, 14 twice, 20, 21, 25, 27, 28 twice, 29, 32) or to 'the document' (vv 8, 10, 11, 13, 18, 32); there seems to be no pattern for the choice of terms" (Holladay, *Jeremiah 2*, 255).

4. According to traditional rabbinic interpretation, the scroll contained part of the book of Lamentations, to which the rest was subsequently added (Jer. 36:32b), but there is little evidence for this view. See Neusner, *Jeremiah in Talmud and Midrash*, 239, 263; Rosenberg, trans., *Mikraoth Gedoloth: Jeremiah Volume Two*, 289, 297.

written on the scroll are concerning "Jerusalem" and Judah and all the nations. Bright notes that the usual order is "Judah and Jerusalem" (but see Jer. 36:31).[5] Perhaps the MT, which has "Israel" in place of "Jerusalem," is to be preferred here.[6] The content of 1:1–25:13 is concerned not only with Judah and Jerusalem but also with Israel and the nations (see, e.g., Jer. 1:5, 10; 3:17–18; 12:14–17; 16:19). The length of the scroll had to be short enough to be read three times in one day (Jer. 36:10, 15, 21; see also Jer. 36:13, 20b; cf. Deut. 31:11; 2 Kgs. 23:2; Neh. 8:3, 8; 9:3) yet long enough to include all messages received over a period of more than twenty years (627–605 BC; see again Jer. 25:3).

It is perhaps too unrealistic to imagine that Jeremiah somehow preserved all of these messages word for word in his memory,[7] and there is no indication that the Lord spoke all of them to Jeremiah afresh in the fourth year of Jehoiakim. Rather, it is likely that some messages were kept by memory and others in various written documents. The task then was to combine all the messages on a single scroll according to some sort of meaningful scheme,[8] which, judging from the content of 1:1–25:13, was obviously not chronology.[9] Thus, Jeremiah's dictation from memory and from written sources largely determined the shape of the scroll's material (Jer. 36:4). The job of giving the prophecies their final written form was entrusted to Jeremiah's scribe Baruch (Jer. 36:4; cf. Jer. 32:12; Bar. 1:1),[10] despite the fact that Jeremiah himself was commanded to write, and despite the fact that Jeremiah, as a member of a priestly family, was likely capable of writing (cf. Jer. 32:10). Why were these words committed to writing? The simple answer from the immediate context is that Jeremiah was restrained from delivering the words in the temple himself (Jer. 36:5), and Baruch could not be expected to deliver them on his behalf extemporaneously. The

---

5. Bright, *Jeremiah*, 179.
6. McKane notes Volz's suggestion that there may have been an abbreviation ׳, which might have stood for ישראל ("Israel") or ירושלם ("Jerusalem") (McKane, *Jeremiah XXVI–LII*, 901).
7. Keil suggests that Jeremiah was simply to commit "the essential contents of all his discourses" to writing (Keil, *Jeremiah*, 318), but this hardly does justice to the phrase "all the words."
8. See McKane, *Jeremiah XXVI–LII*, 900. According to 2 Timothy 3:16 and 2 Peter 1:21, this compositional process was superintended by the Holy Spirit.
9. In its present form, Jeremiah 1 lays out the program of the book.
10. Baruch, along with his brother Seraiah (Jer. 51:59–64), thus becomes known as a prophet himself (see *b. Meg.* 14b, 15a).

text provided a written aid for the delivery of the words. The writing of the words also had the added benefit of preservation for posterity. Of course, there was always a concern about scribal tampering with written texts (Jer. 8:8), and such texts were no mere substitutes for the living voice of the teacher or prophet. Nevertheless, it was also true that the prophets did not live forever; only their written words remained (Zech. 1:5–6).[11]

Jeremiah 36:3 (LXX 43:3) expresses hope that through the writing and the public reading of the scroll the people of Judah might hear of their impending judgment and repent so that they may be forgiven: "Perhaps the house of Judah will hear all the calamity that I am planning to do to them in order that they may return from their [MT: his] evil way, and that I may forgive their iniquity and their sin" (cf. Jer. 26:3; 36:7; but see Jer. 35:17; 36:31). Yet the reader of the present book of Jeremiah knows that such forgiveness of iniquity and sin will only be a reality in the new covenant (Jer. 31:34; 33:8; 50:20). The people do not repent prior to the Babylonian invasion. Thus, the reading of the scroll only makes the people (and Jehoiakim in particular) accountable for their rejection of it and serves to demonstrate that the coming judgment of the people is a just one (Isa. 6:9–10; Ezek. 2:5).

According to Jeremiah 36:4 (LXX 43:4), Jeremiah called Baruch, and he (MT: "Baruch") wrote at Jeremiah's dictation all the words of the LORD that he (i.e., the LORD) spoke to him (i.e., Jeremiah) on a scroll suitable for a document.[12] This does not contradict verse 2, which suggests a collection (from memory and from various preserved written sources) of words spoken by the LORD to Jeremiah over a lengthy period of time. It only indicates that this combination of disparate material was dictated in full by Jeremiah to Baruch with the design to produce a coherent written composition. Jeremiah explained that the reason for this was that he was "restrained" (עָצוּר) and unable to enter the temple (Jer. 36:5 [LXX 43:5]). This does not mean that he was "confined" or "imprisoned" (as in Jer. 33:1; 39:15; see also Jer. 32:2). Verses 19 and 26 indicate that Jeremiah was able to move about freely enough to go into hiding from the authorities. What it means is that he had been banned from the temple and forbidden to enter it, probably due either to his

---

11. Calvin also notes the advantage that written texts provide their readers for long, leisurely reflection (Calvin, *Jeremiah*, 4:326).
12. The reference to Jeremiah's dictation in Ezra 1:1 and 2 Chronicles 36:21, 22 strongly suggests that the scroll included Jeremiah's prophecy of seventy years (see again the difference between LXX and MT Jer. 25:11; see also Jer. 29:10; Dan. 9:1–2, 24–27).

temple gate speech in Jeremiah 7:1–15 (see the reaction in Jer. 26) or to the incident recorded in Jeremiah 19:14–20:6. Therefore, if Jeremiah wanted to deliver messages to a large crowd of people from Judah and Jerusalem, a gathering that only the temple could provide, then he would have to send someone else with a written script. Jeremiah thus instructed Baruch to give a public reading of the scroll in the temple "on a day of fasting" (Jer. 36:6 [LXX 43:6]).[13] The use of the indefinite phrase צום ביום ("on a day of fasting") suggests that Jeremiah did not have a particular predetermined fast day in mind. He simply wanted Baruch to wait until the next called fast day because this would yield a larger audience in the temple.[14] Since fast days were special occasions called in times of crisis (cf. Jon. 3:5), Calvin comments that a fast day ought to have rendered the people more teachable.[15] Jeremiah expressed the same hope for repentance that the LORD expressed in verse 3, albeit with different wording: "Perhaps their supplication will fall before the LORD, and they will turn from their evil way [MT: each from his evil way], for great is the anger and the fury of the LORD [of the LORD > MT] that he [MT: the LORD] has spoken against this people" (Jer. 36:7 [LXX 43:7]; cf. Jer. 37:20; 42:2). The narration of Jeremiah 36:8 (LXX 43:8) provides a summary of Baruch's adherence to Jeremiah's instruction for which verses 9 and 10 give the details.

According to the Hebrew source behind Greek Jeremiah 36:9 (LXX 43:9), it was in the ninth month of the "eighth" year of Jehoiakim (i.e., the late fall or early winter of 601 BC) that a fast was called.[16] According to the MT, the fast was called in the ninth month of the "fifth" year of Jehoiakim (604 BC). Holladay prefers the reading "eighth" as the more difficult reading since "fifth" would be expected to follow "fourth"

---

13. In the Hebrew source behind Greek Jeremiah, the object of the verb "read aloud" is "this scroll." In the longer text of the MT, the object of the verb is "the words of the LORD." The instruction is to read aloud in the scroll written at Jeremiah's dictation the LORD's words (cf. Jer. 36:8). This provides an antecedent for the pronominal suffix on תקראם ("you must read them") at the end of the verse. The absence of "the words of the LORD" in the LXX *Vorlage* forced the Greek translator to render the suffix as an indirect object ("you must read to them").

14. See Bright, *Jeremiah*, 179–80.

15. Calvin, *Jeremiah*, 4:331.

16. Of course, the general populace of Judah and Jerusalem did not have the authority to call a fast officially (see McKane, *Jeremiah XXVI–LII*, 903; cf. Jon. 3:7). Rather, as Bright comments, the people "observed" the fast called by the authorities (Bright, *Jeremiah*, 180).

(Jer. 36:1).[17] He also comments that the Babylonian sack of Ashkelon in the "fifth" year, which is usually thought to be what prompted the fast,[18] threatened Judah and probably would have created an environment in which Jehoiakim would not have felt comfortable burning the scroll (Jer. 36:23, 29). Holladay goes on to say that a defeat dealt to the Babylonians by Egyptian forces in the "eighth" year led to a withdrawal that would have given Jehoiakim the boldness necessary to respond to the scroll the way that he did. Holladay proposes (following Rudolph) that the fast in the "eighth" year was prompted by the drought mentioned in Jeremiah 14:1. As Malbim notes, this event met the prerequisites set by Jeremiah in 36:6 for the reading of the scroll—a fast day for which large numbers of people from Judah and Jerusalem gathered to the temple.[19]

Baruch read aloud "the words of Jeremiah" (cf. MT Jer. 1:1; 51:64b) from the written document in the temple (Jer. 36:10a [LXX 43:10a]; cf. Bar. 1:3–5). More specifically, he read these words "in the room of Gemariah the son of Shaphan, the scribe, in the upper court, at the entrance of the new [*Tg. Jon.*: eastern] gate of the house of the LORD, in the ears of [MT adds: all] the people" (Jer. 36:10b [LXX 43:10b]; cf. Jer. 26:10). This room was apparently situated in such a way that Baruch could be in it and yet address his audience from it (cf. Jer. 35:2, 4, 13). Since Gemariah was absent from the reading (Jer. 36:2), Baruch must have had free access to the room to come and go as he pleased. This is understandable given the fact that Baruch was a member of the scribal elite, although evidently not in an official capacity like his brother Seraiah (Jer. 51:59). The scribe Shaphan had been a key member of Josiah's administration during the reforms made after the discovery of the book of the Torah (2 Kgs. 22:3, 8, 9, 10, 12, 14), an event that had a profound effect on Jeremiah (Jer. 15:16). Ahikam, who was very possibly the son of this Shaphan (2 Kgs. 22:12, 14), was the man who aided Jeremiah in the story of chapter 26 (Jer. 26:24; see also Elasah the son of Shaphan in Jer. 29:3). Furthermore, Gedaliah the son of Ahikam was sympathetic toward Jeremiah (Jer. 39:14; 40:6). The close relationship between Jeremiah and the scribal families of Shapan and the sons of Neriah (Baruch and Seraiah) sheds some light on how the textualization of biblical prophecy came to be.

---

17. Holladay, *Jeremiah 2*, 255–56.
18. See, e.g., Bright, *Jeremiah*, 182. On the other hand, Keil believes that the fast was held in remembrance of the siege mentioned in Daniel 1:1 (Keil, *Jeremiah*, 317).
19. Rosenberg, trans., *Mikraoth Gedoloth: Jeremiah Volume Two*, 291.

Gemariah was not present at Baruch's reading, but his son Micaiah was (Jer. 36:11 [LXX 43:11]). After hearing the reading of the scroll, Micaiah went down to the royal house, into "the room of the scribe" (cf. Jer. 36:20), where the officials were sitting, including Micaiah's father Gemariah (Jer. 36:12a [LXX 43:12a]). Listed among those sitting are "Elishama the scribe and Delaiah the son of Shelemiah [MT: Shemaiah; LXX[S]: Zedekiah] and Jonathan [MT: Elnathan] the son of Achbor and Gemariah the son of Shaphan and Zedekiah the son of Hananiah and all the officials" (Jer. 36:12b [LXX 43:12b]). Elishama the scribe is listed first, perhaps because the scribe's room belonged to him (see Jer. 36:20).[20] It is possible, however, that all of these men were scribes who functioned in an official capacity. Two of them, Elishama and Gemariah (Jer. 36:10), are explicitly designated as scribes. Delaiah is called "the son of Shelemiah" (cf. Jer. 36:14) in the LXX *Vorlage*, but the MT has "the son of Shemaiah" (see also "Delaiah" in MT Jer. 36:25). "Jonathan" (LXX *Vorlage*), also known as "Elnathan" (MT), the son of Achbor (see 2 Kgs. 22:12, 14) might seem strange as a supporter of Jeremiah (see Jer. 36:25) given his role in MT Jeremiah 26:22, but it should be remembered that his name does not appear in the LXX *Vorlage* of that text (LXX 33:22). Jonathan/Elnathan and Gemariah are mentioned again together in Jeremiah 36:25, and their fathers (Achbor and Shaphan) are mentioned together in the story of Josiah (2 Kgs. 22, 12, 14). The last man listed here is Zedekiah the son of Hananiah, but the text adds "and all the officials," indicating that the officials designated by name in this list were part of a larger group gathered in the scribe's room. Micaiah told these men all the words that he heard Baruch read publicly (Jer. 36:13 [LXX 43:13]). Since Micaiah did not have the scroll or a copy of the scroll, it is not clear how he was able to relay "all the words" (cf. Jer. 36:20b). It is possible that the request for Baruch to reread the scroll (Jer. 36:14–15) was not only to confirm Micaiah's report but also to ascertain the exact details of "all the words." Calvin observes that Micaiah's motives for reporting the reading are not stated.[21] Thus, it is not known whether his personal reaction to the reading was positive or negative. It is likely, however, that he was motivated at least in part by the great importance of the reading and wanted to work through the chain of command from the

---

20. Holladay notes that this may be the same Elishama as the grandfather of Ishmael the assassin of Gedaliah (2 Kgs. 25:25; Jer. 41:1) (Holladay, *Jeremiah 2*, 257). It should also be noted, however, that the Greek version of 41:1 (LXX 48:1) has "Eleasa" instead of "Elishama."

21. Calvin, *Jeremiah*, 4:337–38.

officials to the king. This was expedited by the fact that he was the son of one of the royal officials.

In response to Micaiah's report, the officials sent to Baruch a man named Jehudi (see also Jer. 36:21),[22] saying, "The scroll in which you read aloud in the ears of the people, take it in your hand and come" (Jer. 36:14a [LXX 43:14a]; cf. Ezra 7:14). Thus, Baruch took the scroll and went to them (Jer. 36:14b [LXX 43:14b]). Again, while Baruch was not himself a royal official, he was one of them in the sense that he was among the scribal elite like Gemariah and Elishamah. This explains in part the reception that the officials gave Baruch according to the subsequent narrative. According to the vocalization of the Hebrew text reflected in Greek Jeremiah 36:15 (LXX 43:15), the officials requested, "Read aloud again in our ears" (שֵׁב נָא וקרא באזנינו), and Baruch did so. According to the MT, however, they said, "Sit and read it aloud in our ears" (שֵׁב נָא וקראנה באזנינו).[23] Since the primary difference between these two readings is vocalization and not the consonantal text, it is more a matter of interpretation than one of textual variation.

The Hebrew source behind Greek Jeremiah 36:16 (LXX 43:16) recounts that the officials "advised" (נועצו) one another as soon as they heard the words read by Baruch,[24] "We must certainly tell the king all these words." The MT, however, says that they "expressed dread" (פחדו) to one another and said to Baruch that they had to tell the king (cf. Jer. 36:24). It is not immediately clear whether this means that they feared because of the coming judgment in the prophecy of the scroll or because of the reaction to the reading of the scroll that they anticipated from the king. There was little choice involved in making the decision to tell the king. The very public nature of Baruch's reading in the temple virtually guaranteed that word would get to the king one way or another.[25] Thus, the officials would have been liable for not reporting what they knew. Furthermore, they had an opportunity to shape the way that the king received the report so as to ensure the safety of Baruch and Jeremiah and to make an attempt to preserve the scroll (Jer. 36:19–20). Before they did so, they asked Baruch, "From where (מאין) did you write all these words" (Jer. 36:17 [LXX 43:17])? This was a question of source. Baruch's reply was very straightforward: "From his mouth Jeremiah would dictate to me all these words [or, From his mouth. Jeremiah

---

22. Jehudi is called "the son of Nethaniah the son of Shelemaiah the son of Cushi" (see Keil, *Jeremiah*, 319–20; Holladay, *Jeremiah 2*, 258).

23. The reading וקראנה may have arisen from וקרא נא.

24. See McKane, *Jeremiah XXVI–LII*, 904–5.

25. See Keil, *Jeremiah*, 320.

would dictate to me all these words], and I would write on a document" (Jer. 36:18 [LXX 43:18]).[26] According to the MT, however, the question was one of manner: "Tell us, how (אֵיךְ) did you write all these words? From his mouth?" Baruch replied, "From his mouth he would dictate to me all these words [or, From his mouth. He would dictate to me all these words], and I would write on the document in ink."[27] Either way, the officials wanted to confirm that they had their information about the scroll correct. Jeremiah was the source of the words, and he worked closely with Baruch to produce a written version of them.[28] Thus, the officials instructed Baruch, "Go, hide, you and Jeremiah, [MT adds: and] let no one know where you are" (Jer. 36:19 [LXX 43:19]). This effort to protect Baruch and Jeremiah reveals decisively that the royal scribes were sympathetic toward them (see also Jer. 36:25; cf. Jer. 26:16–19, 24). The need to go into hiding shows, much like the story in Jeremiah 26:20–23, that the threat from Jehoiakim to the lives of Baruch and Jeremiah was a very real one. According to the sequence of the narration, Baruch and Jeremiah did not go into hiding until after Jehoiakim's negative reaction to the reading of the scroll (Jer. 36:26b).

English versions of 36:20 (LXX 43:20) typically give the impression that the officials went to the king in the court (e.g., NIV), but חֲצֵרָה means "courtward." McKane comments, "The sense of the Hebrew is that they made their way to the king's quarters in the palace and only at v. 22 is information supplied about the precise location of the king."[29] Verse 20 also provides the background information ("x + *qatal*") that the officials had deposited the scroll in the room of Elishama (possibly but not necessarily identical to "the room of the scribe" in v. 12) for safekeeping. They then came to the king and told him "all the words." This is much like Micaiah's report to the officials of "all the words" without the aid of the scroll itself (Jer. 36:13); much like the officials (Jer. 36:14–15), the king subsequently requested a reading of the words from the actual scroll (Jer. 36:21).

The king sent Jehudi (see Jer. 36:14) to take the scroll, and he retrieved it from Elishama's room (Jer. 36:21a [LXX 43:21a]; see Jer.

---

26. See Neusner, *Jeremiah in Talmud and Midrash*, 80.
27. The absence of the phrase "in ink" in the LXX is not due to the translator's inability to recognize בַּדְּיוֹ, nor is it because the translator considered the phrase superfluous. The translator's general faithfulness to his source text argues against arbitrary omission of phrases. The more likely scenario is that this phrase was not present in the translator's Hebrew text.
28. See Keil, *Jeremiah*, 320.
29. McKane, *Jeremiah XXVI–LII*, 906.

36:12, 20). The king apparently knew that the scroll was in the possession of the officials, for he did not send for Baruch (or Jeremiah) to bring the scroll and read it (cf. Jer. 36:14). Jehudi read the scroll aloud in the hearing of the king and in the hearing of all the officials who were standing by him (Jer. 36:21b [LXX 43:21b]). It is evident from what follows that the king wanted to hear the words read from the scroll not only to determine what should be done with Baruch and Jeremiah (Jer. 36:26) but also to decide the fate of the scroll itself (Jer. 36:23). Verse 22 provides important background information that sets the context for the king's action in verse 23. The king was sitting in "the winter house," an area of the palace designed to retain heat, as opposed to the well-ventilated "summer house" (Amos 3:15).[30] The Hebrew source behind Greek Jeremiah says: "and a pot of fire was before him" (ואח אש לפניו). The MT says: "and the firepot was burning before him [or, and the firepot before him was burning]" (ואת האח לפניו מבערת).[31]

The manner in which the scroll was read and destroyed is given in detail in 36:23 (LXX 43:23). Jehudi would read three or four "columns" at a time. The term דלתות ("doors") does not refer to pages (as in a codex) or lines/verses but to columns of text.[32] Three or four columns would occupy a single section of a papyrus (or parchment) scroll. This section would then be pasted (or stitched) to another section of three or four columns, and so on. Thus, the scroll was torn along the seam after the reading of each section, and the sections were thrown into the fire one after the other until the entire scroll was destroyed (cf. *m. Shabb.* 16:1).[33] The entire scroll was read to the king, and at the regular intervals of each section division the decision was made to tear and burn it, showing that the content of every part of the scroll was unacceptable to the king. It is unlikely that the king himself handled the scribe's knife and then cast each section of the scroll into the pot of fire.[34] Jehudi is

---

30. The MT's addition of "in the ninth month" (late fall or early winter) is an unnecessary detail already known from verse 9.

31. The definite direct object marker can mark the grammatical subject when the predicate is passive because the grammatical subject of a passive predicate is also the object of the action.

32. See Rosenberg, trans., *Mikraoth Gedoloth: Jeremiah Volume Two*, 294–95. See also Neusner, *Jeremiah in Talmud and Midrash*, 81–82, 304.

33. See McKane, *Jeremiah XXVI–LII*, 919. The destruction of the scroll about Babylon (Jer. 51:63) is symbolic of the destruction of Babylon (Jer. 51:64). It is possible that the burning of the scroll about Judah and Jerusalem is unwittingly symbolic of the burning of Jerusalem (Jer. 39:8; 52:13).

34. See Holladay, *Jeremiah 2*, 259.

the default subject of יקרעה ("he would tear it"). It is true that the king was held responsible for the burning of the scroll (Jer. 36:27–29), but this was not because he performed the act with his own hands. It is more likely that he gave the order to Jehudi to tear each section and then cast it into the fire.[35]

Jeremiah 36:24 (LXX 43:24) says that the king and "his servants" (עבדיו) who were hearing the words of the scroll were not "in dread" (פחדו) and did not tear their garments. This stands in marked contrast to the reaction of the "officials" (שרים) who did "express dread" (פחדו) according to the MT's version of verse 16. Thus, the "servants" mentioned here were a group distinct from the "officials" (see also Jer. 36:31; cf. Jer. 37:2). While both groups were present at the reading, only the servants joined the king in his disdain for the content of the scroll. Instead of tearing his garments in response to the scroll's threat of judgment and call for repentance, the king tore the scroll itself. This is yet another indication of the vast difference between Jehoiakim and his father Josiah (Jer. 22:13–23). King Josiah tore his garments when he heard the words of the Torah (2 Kgs. 22:11; cf. Neh. 8:9). This tearing of garments was not one of outrage (as in Matt. 26:65) but one of distress and of recognition that an urgent and appropriate response was in order (see 2 Kgs. 22:13; cf. Joel 2:13; Ezra 9:3; see also BDB, 902). The implication is that Jehoiakim should have torn his garments in response to the words of a prophet like Moses (Jer. 1:4–10) just as his father tore his garments in response to the words of the prophet Moses himself.

The Hebrew source behind Greek Jeremiah 36:25 (LXX 43:25) names Elnathan, Gedaliah, and Gemariah as those who entreated the king not to burn the scroll. There is no one named Gedaliah in the list of officials in verse 12 (but see Jer. 39:14; 40:5, 7). MT 36:25 has Delaiah instead of Gedaliah. The MT also makes it explicit that the king did not listen to these men. The absence of any indication of this in Greek Jeremiah is intriguing when it is taken into account that Vaticanus and Sinaiticus also lack the negation of the infinitive "to

---

35. "It is possible, if the king suspected Jrm was a true prophet, that he wanted to rid the land of the power of the prophet's words [cf. Num. 5:23–24]. On the other hand, if the king is struck by the contrast between Jrm's description of the foe from the north and the setback dealt the Babylonian forces that same month, then he might well have judged the words to be worthless, or even destroyed the words of the false prophet in anticipation of destroying the false prophet himself (v 26; compare Deut 18:20)" (Holladay, *Jeremiah 2*, 260).

burn." In other words, these two witnesses depict the three officials as those who urged the king to burn the scroll. This would seem to run contrary to the way these officials were portrayed earlier in the narrative, but McKane prefers this reading and suggests that the servants in verses 24 and 31 are the same as the officials elsewhere in the chapter.[36] He considers the MT's version of verses 16 and 25 to be a secondary attempt to make the officials look sympathetic toward Baruch and Jeremiah in contrast to the king's servants. It remains problematic for McKane that his view has no satisfactory explanation for the action of the officials in verse 19 where they appear to have had the best interests of Baruch and Jeremiah in mind. Holladay reconstructs verse 25 so that there is division among the officials themselves: "Elnathan and Gedaliah had also urged the king to burn the scroll, but Delaiah and Gemariah urged him not to burn the scroll; he did not listen to them."[37] This reconstruction depends upon Elnathan's presence in the text of Jeremiah 26:22 as one who acted against true prophets on behalf of Jehoiakim, but he appears there only in the MT, not in the Hebrew source behind Greek Jeremiah. It also depends upon including both Gedaliah (LXX) and Delaiah (MT) in the same text, identifying this Gedaliah with the Gedaliah mentioned in Jeremiah 38:1–6 as an opponent of Jeremiah, an identification that is far from certain.

King Jehoiakim commanded Jerahmeel the king's son and Seraiah the son of Azriel (MT adds: "and Shelemiah the son of Abdeel") to arrest Baruch and Jeremiah (Jer. 36:26a [LXX 43:26a]). The designation of Jerahmeel as "the king's son" (בן המלך) may only mean that he was a member of the royal family generally or that he held an office of some sort in the king's court (cf. 1 Kgs. 22:26; Jer. 38:6), although it is not impossible that Jehoiakim had a son younger than Jehoiachin yet old enough to perform this duty.[38] According to the Hebrew source behind Greek Jeremiah 36:26b (LXX 43:26b), Baruch and Jeremiah hid at this point in accordance with the advice given to them by the officials in verse 19. It was clear now from the reaction of the king to the reading of the scroll that their lives were in danger (see again Jer. 26:20–23). The MT's version of verse 26b says that the LORD hid Baruch and Jeremiah (cf. 1 Kgs. 17:3), which is a decidedly theological interpretation of the story—one that highlights the role of divine

---

36. McKane, *Jeremiah XXVI–LII*, 907–9.

37. Holladay, *Jeremiah 2*, 252–53.

38. "Jehoiachin was born in 616 (2 Kgs 24:8); Jerahmeel, if he were the son of the king, might have been born soon thereafter and be fourteen or fifteen years old in 601" (Holladay, *Jeremiah 2*, 261).

providence. In other words, it was not merely a matter of Baruch and Jeremiah going into hiding as advised. It was the LORD's protection of those who had represented him well. The success of the hiding is reflected in the narrative itself, for the narrator does not even inform the reader of their whereabouts at this time. Bright comments, "How long Jeremiah remained in hiding, and what caused the king finally to drop the matter, we do not know; but Jeremiah was later able to move about freely" (see Jer. 35).[39]

Sometime after the king burned the scroll containing the words that Baruch wrote at Jeremiah's dictation, the word of the LORD came to Jeremiah again (Jer. 36:27 [LXX 43:27]; cf. Jer. 36:1–3). Jeremiah was to take yet another scroll and write all the words that were on the scroll burned by Jehoiakim (Jer. 36:28 [LXX 43:28]). The process for this reproduction was the same as that for the first scroll (see Jer. 36:4, 32). There is in this a reminiscence of the rewriting of the Decalogue on the two tablets of stone (Exod. 34:1, 28b; Deut. 10:1–5) after Moses smashed the original tablets in response to the golden calf incident (Exod. 32:19; Deut. 9:17). Jeremiah, a prophet like Moses, had to reproduce the scroll destroyed by the unrighteous King Jehoiakim.

Verse 29 gives the impression that Jeremiah was to speak to Jehoiakim directly: "And [MT adds: to Jehoiakim the king of Judah] you will say, 'Thus says the LORD, "As for you, you burned this scroll, saying, 'Why did you write on it, saying, "The king of Babylon will surely come and destroy this land and exterminate from it man and beast"?'"'" In light of the threat described in verse 26, this seems highly unlikely. Furthermore, the announcement of Jehoiakim's judgment in verses 30–31 for his negative reaction to the scroll referred to the king in the third person. At the very least, it must be said that there is no account of a direct encounter between Jeremiah and Jehoiakim concerning this matter. The scroll itself sufficed to communicate the coming judgment against the king. The accusation against Jehoiakim in verse 29 includes not only his burning of the scroll but also his accompanying words, which were not a feature of the account of the scroll's burning in verse 23. These words are quoted as if they were spoken directly to Jeremiah himself. The nature of the king's question is similar to that of the rhetorical questions in Jeremiah 26:9 and 32:3. Thus, when he asked Jeremiah why it was written on the scroll that the king of Babylon would come and destroy the land (cf. Jer. 20:4; 32:43; Ezek. 14:13, 17, 19, 21; see also Exod. 12:12), he was not looking for

---

39. Bright, *Jeremiah*, 181.

a response. Rather, he was making an accusation against Jeremiah.[40] Jehoiakim's accusation against Jeremiah ironically became the reason to accuse Jehoiakim.

The judgment announced for Jehoiakim in verse 30a is that he would not have a son to succeed him sitting on the throne of David. The very brief three-month reign of Jehoiakim's son Jehoiachin (2 Kgs. 24:8) apparently did not qualify as having one sitting on the throne of David.[41] Indeed, McKane comments that "a reign of three months could well be regarded as a fulfillment of what is predicted rather than a non-fulfillment."[42] Similar words are spoken about Jehoiachin's offspring in Jeremiah 22:30b: "for a man sitting on the throne of David [MT adds: and] ruling again over Judah will not prosper from his seed/offspring" (Jer. 22:30b; cf. Jer. 29:32). Thus, no one from the line of Jehoiakim would be king for any considerable amount of time. Jehoiakim's brother Zedekiah would be the last king of Judah (Jer. 37:1). As for Jehoiakim himself, "his corpse will be cast (מֻשְׁלֶכֶת) to the heat by day and to the frost by night" (Jer. 36:30b [LXX 43:30b]; cf. Bar. 2:25). This is comparable to what is said about Jehoiakim in Jeremiah 22:19: he will be given a donkey's burial, dragged and "cast" (הֻשְׁלֵךְ) beyond the gate (MT: "gates") of Jerusalem (cf. Jer. 26:23b). In the present context, this may be considered poetic justice for the manner in which Jehoiakim had the scroll torn and "cast" (הֻשְׁלַךְ) into the fire. Such treatment of Jehoiakim's corpse may appear to be at odds with the statement in 2 Kings 24:6a that Jehoiakim lay with his fathers. It may also seem to be contrary to what is said in 2 Chronicles 36:6 about how Nebuchadnezzar bound him in bronze fetters to take him away to Babylon. The statement in 2 Kings 24:6a need not mean anything more than that Jehoiakim died (see TEV). As for the exile in Babylon, the biblical authors do not explain the correlation between the ill-treatment of Jehoiakim's corpse and his removal to Babylon. Nevertheless, the two are not irreconcilable. It may very well have been the case that Jehoiakim's exile and death in Babylon were understood to be what it meant to be cast beyond the gate of Jerusalem and exposed to the elements. Thus, the LORD will "visit upon him and upon his seed/offspring and upon his servants [MT adds: their iniquity]" and bring against them and the inhabitants of Jerusalem and the land (MT: "men/people") of Judah all the calamity that he has spoken against them, which they have not heard

---

40. See Holladay, *Jeremiah 2*, 254.

41. See Redak in Rosenberg, trans., *Mikraoth Gedoloth: Jeremiah Volume Two*, 296; Keil, *Jeremiah*, 322.

42. McKane, *Jeremiah XXVI–LII*, 921.

(Jer. 36:31 [LXX 43:31]). The possibility of hearing the word of the LORD in order to avert disaster appears not to be a real one after all (see again Jer. 26:3; 36:3). The language of visiting the iniquity of the father (Jehoiakim) upon the son (Jehoiachin) comes from Exodus 20:5; 34:7. It is true that the consequences of Jehoiakim's actions would affect Jehoiachin, but it is also true that Jehoiachin followed in the footsteps of his father (2 Kgs. 24:9; Jer. 22:24–30) and was therefore accountable for his own sin. Jehoiachin did not pay for the sin of Jehoiakim (see again the commentary on Jer. 31:29; see also Deut. 24:16; Ezek. 18). The same may be said for Jehoiakim's servants (Jer. 36:24) and for the people of Judah and Jerusalem. They willingly followed in the pattern of rebellion set for them by their leaders.

According to the Hebrew source behind Greek Jeremiah 36:32a (LXX 43:32a), it was Baruch who took another scroll. The MT, which has an expanded version of this verse, has adjusted the text so that it conforms to verse 28a and says that it was Jeremiah who took another scroll and gave it to Baruch.[43] Baruch then wrote on the scroll all the words of the previous document that Jehoiakim burned. He did this at Jeremiah's dictation as before (cf. Jer. 36:2, 4). The difference, however, was that many words like the former ones were added to them (Jer. 36:32b [LXX 43:32b])—an extension of the process of composition described earlier. This is significant for several reasons. First, the undefined nature of the statement allows for the growth and development of the book of Jeremiah until it reached its final form in the LXX *Vorlage*. As discussed in the introduction to the present commentary, the book was subsequently made into a second edition as represented by the MT. Second, the statement of verse 32b indicates that the content of what was added to the book was consistent with what came before ("many words like these"). This is reflected in the present book of Jeremiah in which both halves speak of judgment and restoration, both historically and eschatologically. And third, the book of Jeremiah apparently did not have what might be called a "canonical" status until it was finished and stood at the beginning of its process of transmission in a recognizable form. It was normally forbidden to add words to books that had this kind of status (see, e.g., Deut. 4:2; Prov. 30:6; Rev. 22:18–19). Thus, while the earlier words of Jeremiah carried the weight and authority of the word of God in their various oral and written forms prior to the finished product of the book of Jeremiah, it was the book as it is now known that achieved the status of canonical Scripture.

---

43. See the discussion in McKane, *Jeremiah XXVI–LII*, 909–10.

JEREMIAH 37 (LXX 44)

37:1 (44:1) And Zedekiah [MT: King Zedekiah] the son of Josiah, whom Nebuchadnezzar [MT: Nebuchadrezzar the king of Babylon] made king in Judah [MT: in the land of Judah], reigned in place of [MT adds: Coniah the son of] Jehoiakim. 37:2 (44:2) And he did not listen, nor his servants nor the people of the land, to the words of the Lord that he spoke by the hand of [i.e., by the agency of] Jeremiah [MT adds: the prophet].

37:3 (44:3) And King Zedekiah sent Jehucal [Aq., Symm., Syr., Vulg.: Jucal] the son of Shelemiah and Zephaniah the son of Maaseiah, the priest, to Jeremiah [MT adds: the prophet], saying, "Pray on our behalf to the Lord [MT adds: our God]." 37:4 (44:4) (And as for Jeremiah, he came in and went out in the midst of the city [MT: And Jeremiah was coming in and going out in the midst of the people], and they had not put him in the house of confinement [i.e., prison]. 37:5 (44:5) And the army of Pharaoh, it had gone out from Egypt, and the Chaldeans [MT adds: who were besieging Jerusalem] heard the report about them, and they withdrew [MT: withdrew themselves] from Jerusalem.)

37:6 (44:6) And the word of the Lord came to Jeremiah [MT adds: the prophet], saying, 37:7 (44:7) "Thus says the Lord [MT adds: the God of Israel], 'Thus you [MT pl.] will say to the king of Judah who sent to you [MT: who sent you (pl.) to me] to seek me [i.e., to inquire of me or to seek help from me], "Look, the army of Pharaoh that went out to you for help, it is about to return to the land of Egypt [MT: to its land, Egypt]. 37:8 (44:8) And the Chaldeans will return and fight against this city, and they will capture it and burn it with fire. 37:9 (44:9) For thus says the Lord: Do not deceive yourselves, saying, 'The Chaldeans will surely go away from us,' for they will not go. 37:10 (44:10) And if [MT: For if] you were to strike all the army of the Chaldeans who are fighting with you, and there were left among them pierced men, each in his place [MT: each in his tent; Syr.: each from his tent], they would rise up and burn this city with fire."'"

37:11 (44:11) And so [LXX = ויהי; MT: והיה; see GKC §112uu], when the army of the Chaldeans withdrew from Jerusalem because of the army of Pharaoh,[1] 37:12 (44:12) Jeremiah went out from Jerusalem to go to

---

1.   The סתומא ("closed") paragraph division after this verse in the MT indicates that the text was read as the last part of the Lord's previous discourse: "And so will it be when the army of the Chaldeans withdraws from

the land of Benjamin to receive a portion [LXX: to buy] from there in the midst of the people. 37:13 (44:13) And he was in the gate of Benjamin, and there was his overseer [lit., the lord of his oversight; LXX: a man with whom he used to lodge; MT: an overseer (lit., a lord of oversight)], Seruiah [MT: and his name was Irijah (Syr.: Neriah)] the son of Shelemiah the son of Hananiah, and he seized/arrested Jeremiah [MT adds: the prophet], saying, "To the Chaldeans you are deserting/defecting!" 37:14 (44:14) And he [MT: Jeremiah] said, "That's a lie! I am not deserting/defecting to the Chaldeans." But he did not listen to him. And Seruiah [MT: Irijah; Syr.: Neriah] seized/arrested Jeremiah and brought him to the officials. 37:15 (44:15) And the officials were very mad at Jeremiah, and they struck [MT: והכו; Seb: ויכו] him and put [MT: ונתנו; Seb: ויתנו] him [MT adds: in prison] in the house of Jonathan [Jehonathan] the scribe, for it was what they made into the house of confinement. 37:16 (44:16) And Jeremiah came [MT: When Jeremiah came] to the dungeon and to the chereth [MT: the cells] and [MT adds: Jeremiah] sat/remained there for many days.

37:17 (44:17) And [MT adds: King] Zedekiah sent and summoned [MT: took/received] him, and the king asked him [MT adds: in his house/palace] in secret, saying [MT: and said], "Is there a word from the LORD?" And he [MT: Jeremiah] said, "There is." [MT adds: And he said,] "Into the hand/power of the king of Babylon you will be given/delivered." 37:18 (44:18) And Jeremiah said to the king [MT: to King Zedekiah], "How have I sinned against you and against your servants and against this people that you [MT pl.] have put me in the house of confinement? 37:19 (44:19) And where are your [pl.] prophets [Tg. Jon.: false prophets] who prophesied to you [pl.], saying, 'The king of Babylon will not come [MT adds: against you (pl.) and] against this land'? 37:20 (44:20) And now [MT adds: hear], my lord the king, let my supplication fall before you, and why should you return me to the house of Jonathan the scribe? And will I not die there? [MT: and do not return me to the house of Jonathan the scribe, lest I die there (see GKC §109g).]" 37:21 (44:21) And the king [MT: King Zedekiah] commanded, and they deposited him [MT: Jeremiah (Syr. adds: the prophet)] in the court of the guard and gave to him one loaf of bread per day from the bakers' street [LXX: from outside where they bake] until [MT adds: all] the bread of the city was finished. And Jeremiah sat/remained in the court of the guard.

Jerusalem because of the army of Pharaoh." This was likely prompted by the occurrence of והיה, which should probably be corrected to ויהי or read as a functional equivalent to ויהי.

Chapters 37–44 form a single unit for which 37:1–2 serves as a heading and as a transition from the account in chapter 36, which was set during the reign of Jehoiakim.[2] The relationship between Jeremiah 21:1–7 and 37:3–10 is such that 21:1–7 belongs to the time of the initial Babylonian siege of Jerusalem (Jer. 21:2), while 37:3–10 is associated with the temporary withdrawal of the Babylonians (Jer. 37:5; cf. MT Jer. 34:21b).[3] The harsh treatment of Jeremiah in 37:11–16 and his subsequent exchange with Zedekiah in 37:17–21 have close parallels in chapter 38.

The longer text of MT 37:1 (LXX 44:1) is mostly due to the MT's typical addition of titles ("Zedekiah" becomes "King Zedekiah," and "Nebuchadnezzar" becomes "Nebuchadrezzar the king of Babylon") and to the expansion of the phrase "in Judah" to "in the land of Judah." The most significant textual variation, however, is the MT's addition of the name "Coniah" (i.e., Jehoaichin). Whereas the Hebrew source behind Greek Jeremiah simply says that Zedekiah reigned in place of Jehoiakim, the MT says that he reigned in place of Coniah the son of Jehoiakim.[4] The former reading of the LXX *Vorlage* agrees with Jeremiah 36:30, which indicated that Coniah's (Jehoiachin's) three-month reign would not be substantial enough to count as Jehoiakim having one of his sons succeed him on the throne. The MT's addition of "Coniah" is a mere technicality. The "real" successor to Jehoiakim was his brother Zedekiah, another son of Josiah. This arrangement was made by Nebuchadnezzar who installed Zedekiah as king in Judah (see 2 Kgs. 24:17). The hallmark of Zedekiah's reign was that he did not listen, "nor his servants nor the people of the land," to the words of the LORD spoken by means of Jeremiah (Jer. 37:2 [LXX 44:2]; cf. Jer. 36:24, 31; see also Jer. 34:19; 37:18).[5] "And he did what was evil in the eyes of the LORD his God. He did not humble himself before Jeremiah the prophet from the mouth of the LORD" (2 Chr. 36:12).[6]

2. See Bright, *Jeremiah*, 222. "Most commentators have affirmed the traditional attribution of these chapters to Baruch" (Holladay, *Jeremiah 2*, 286).

3. See McKane, *Jeremiah XXVI–LII*, 940–41.

4. See Neusner, *Jeremiah in Talmud and Midrash*, 194.

5. Shelley Birdsong argues that the MT and the Old Greek of Jeremiah 37(44):1–40(47):6 present two different depictions of Zedekiah (*The Last King[s] of Judah: Zedekiah and Sedekias in the Hebrew and Greek Versions of Jeremiah 37[44]:1–40[47]:6* [Tübingen: Mohr Siebeck, 2017]). In the Old Greek he is "manipulative and mysterious," while in the MT he is "hesitant and kind," metaphorically mirroring the fall of Jerusalem. According to Birdsong, the MT's version is a later edited text.

6. This was not because Zedekiah rejected Jeremiah as a true prophet. See Jeremiah 37:17–21; 38:14–28. Second Chronicles 36:13 adds that Zedekiah

In the story of chapter 21, Zedekiah sent Pashhur and Zephaniah the priest to Jeremiah to request that he "seek" the LORD on their behalf concerning the Babylonian siege to find out if the LORD might act in such a way that would lead to the withdrawal of the Babylonians (Jer. 21:1–2). The answer that came through the prophet was that Zedekiah and the people of Jerusalem would be given into the hands of the Babylonians (Jer. 21:7). According to the narrative of chapter 37, Zedekiah sent Jehucal and Zephaniah the priest to Jeremiah to ask that he "pray" or intercede on their behalf to the LORD during the time of the temporary withdrawal of the Babylonians (Jer. 37:3, 5 [LXX 44:3, 5]; cf. Jer. 42:2).[7] This is characterized in verse 7 as "seeking" the LORD.[8] Thus, Zedekiah wanted to know if the withdrawal signaled a change in the forecasted fate of the city (cf. Isa. 37:4).[9] It becomes evident in the course of the narrative, however, that the answer to Zedekiah's inquiry remained the same (Jer. 37:6–8). For the reader of the book of Jeremiah, it is somewhat ironic at this juncture to hear a request for the prophet to pray on behalf of the people. The reader has already encountered several texts in which the LORD instructs Jeremiah not to pray for them because he is not listening (Jer. 7:16; 11:14; 14:11). Their fate was already sealed. Zedekiah, however, would not be satisfied with this response and would eventually send for Jeremiah himself to engage him in person (Jer. 37:17–21).

Verses 4 and 5 provide parenthetical background information for the story. According to verse 4, Jeremiah was free to go in and out of the city of Jerusalem at this time. He was not yet placed in the house of confinement (see Jer. 37:15–16; see also Jer. 52:31).[10] This explains

---

also rebelled against Nebuchadnezzar, who made him take an oath in God's name. The text does not go into detail about the precise nature of this oath.

7. Both Pashhur (Jer. 21:1) and Jehucal/Jucal (Jer. 37:3) are mentioned again in MT 38:1 (Pashhur > LXX). Zephaniah (Jer. 21:1; 37:3) is absent from 38:1. He is mentioned, however, in 29:25, 29.

8. "Zedekiah sought a prophetic interpretation of the raising of the siege. Victory was in the air and the king was uncertain what substance there was in this change of mood" (McKane, *Jeremiah XXVI–LII*, 942).

9. "Perhaps Zedekiah hoped almost beyond all hope that Yahweh would repeat the miracle of 701 B.C. when he removed the Assyrian armies from Jerusalem in the days of Hezekiah (2 K. 19:32–37). Jeremiah had already foretold the fate of Zedekiah and the city at the commencement of the siege (34:1–7)" (Thompson, *Book of Jeremiah*, 631).

10. "It must be stressed that imprisonment was not a legal punishment in Israel until the Persian period, so that prison (literally 'house of confinement')

why Jeremiah was able to attempt his departure from Jerusalem to go to the land of Benjamin (Jer. 37:12). Verse 5 adds that the army of Pharaoh had gone out from Egypt; and when the Chaldeans heard about it, they withdrew from Jerusalem (cf. Jer. 21:2; 34:21b [MT]; see also 2 Kgs. 24:7). This Pharaoh was Pharaoh Hophra (Jer. 44:30). It was a constant temptation for the people of Judah and Jerusalem to trust in Egypt's aid rather than to trust in the LORD (see Jer. 42–43), but this misplaced trust never worked out very well for them (see Isa. 30:1–5; 31:1–3; see also Isa. 36:6; Jer. 46; Ezek. 29:6–7).

The word of the LORD came to Jeremiah in response to Zedekiah's inquiry in verse 3 (Jer. 37:6 [LXX 44:6]). According to the Hebrew source behind Greek Jeremiah 37:7a [LXX 44:7a], the message was addressed to Jeremiah: "Thus you [sg.] will say to the king of Judah who sent you [sg.] to seek me." The MT, however, has it addressed to Jehucal and Zephaniah: "Thus you [pl.] will say to the king of Judah who sent you [pl.] to me to seek me." The message was that Pharaoh's army, which had left Egypt to help Jerusalem against the Babylonians, was about to return to its land (Jer. 37:7b [LXX 44:7b]; see Ezek. 17:7, 15). Furthermore, the Chaldeans would return and fight against Jerusalem; they would capture it and burn it with fire (Jer. 37:8 [LXX 44:8]; cf. Jer. 21:10; 34:22; see also Jer. 39:8; 52:13). This was, of course, not the news for which Zedekiah was hoping.

The continuation of the LORD's discourse in verse 9 indicates that Zedekiah and his servants were not to deceive themselves by thinking that the Chaldeans would simply go away (cf. Isa. 36:14; Jer. 29:8). This does not mean that the Chaldeans were still engaged in the siege against Jerusalem at this point. Rather, it is a reiteration of verse 8 that the withdrawal of the Chaldeans would not be permanent. Even if Zedekiah and his army were to strike the Chaldeans so that only pierced men were left among them, "each in his place (איש במקומו) [MT: each in his tent (איש באהלו); Syr.: each from his tent (= איש מאהלו)]," they would still rise up and burn the city of Jerusalem with fire (Jer. 37:10 [LXX 44:10]).[11] This only added to the sense of utter hopelessness about the situation.

The appearance of והיה at the beginning of 37:11 (LXX 44:11) in the text received by the Masoretes led to the assumption that this verse was the last part of the LORD's discourse: "And so will it be when the army of the Chaldeans withdraws from Jerusalem because of the army

---

was simply a place of detention, under guard, until clarification of a case" (Holladay, *Jeremiah 2*, 287).

11. See the discussion of the syntax in McKane, *Jeremiah XXVI–LII*, 925.

of Pharaoh." This is why a section division appears after this verse in the MT. There are several passages, however, where והיה appears to be equivalent to ויהי (e.g., 1 Sam. 1:12; 17:48; 25:20; 2 Sam. 6:16 [4QSamᵃ: ויהי; cf. 1 Chr. 15:29]; Jer. 3:9; 38:28b [pc Mss: ויהי]; 40:3b; see GKC §112uu). The LXX translator (καὶ ἐγένετο) either had ויהי in his *Vorlage* or understood והיה to be equivalent to ויהי. In this occurrence, ויהי is not a regular finite verb but a macrosyntactic marker. The resultant translation is a dependent, temporal clause that introduces the main clause in the following verse: "And so (ויהי), when the army of the Chaldeans withdrew from Jerusalem because of the army of Pharaoh" (cf. Jer. 37:5).

When the Chaldean army withdrew temporarily from Jerusalem, Jeremiah went out from Jerusalem to go to the land of Benjamin "to receive a portion" (לחלק) from there in the midst of the people (Jer. 37:12 [LXX 44:12]; see again Jer. 37:4–5). Since Jerusalem was already in the land of Benjamin (Josh. 18:28), the most likely scenario is that Jeremiah departed the city to go to his hometown of Anathoth in the land of Benjamin (Jer. 1:1). The meaning of the infinitive לחלק has remained a problem with many different solutions throughout the history of interpretation. According to the LXX, Jeremiah went "to buy" something. Some witnesses add that he went "to buy bread/food" (see Jer. 37:21). Rabbi Benjamin ben Levi suggests that Jeremiah went "to divide up prophecies," appealing to the plural "The words of Jeremiah" in MT Jeremiah 1:1.[12] Both Redak and Calvin think that he went "to separate himself" from the city of Jerusalem.[13] The most straightforward explanation within the larger context of the book may very well be that of Bright, Holladay, and others who suggest that Jeremiah was on his way to exercise his right of redemption by purchasing the field of his cousin Hanamel in Anathoth.[14] Since Jeremiah was arrested in his efforts to do so and subsequently placed in "the court of the guard" (Jer. 37:13–16, 21; see also Jer. 32:2; cf. Hos. 9:7–8), Hanamel had to come to Jeremiah to complete the transaction (Jer. 32:6–15).

Jeremiah was in the north gate of Benjamin (Jer. 37:13 [LXX 44:13]; see Jer. 38:7; Zech. 14:10; see also 2 Kgs. 14:13; Neh. 8:16), and there according to the LXX was "a man with whom he used to lodge," which perhaps reflects the following Hebrew *Vorlage*: בעל פקדתו ("the lord of his oversight" or "his overseer"). If this is correct, then this man had the responsibility to make sure that Jeremiah in particular did not

---

12. Neusner, *Jeremiah in Talmud and Midrash*, 159.
13. Rosenberg, trans., *Mikraoth Gedoloth: Jeremiah Volume Two*, 300; Calvin, *Jeremiah*, 4:373.
14. Bright, *Jeremiah*, 229; Holladay, *Jeremiah 2*, 287.

desert to the Chaldeans. Thus, even though Jeremiah was free to leave the city at this time (Jer. 37:4), he was being closely watched. The MT, however, has בעל פקדת ("a lord of oversight" or "an overseer"), a guard or sentinel whose duty it was to keep anyone from deserting to the Chaldeans. According to the Hebrew source behind Greek Jeremiah, the man's name was Seruiah; but according to the MT it was Irijah. The Syriac strangely enough has "Neriah," the name of the father of Baruch and Seraiah (Jer. 32:12; 51:59). This man was the son of Shelemaiah the son of Hananiah (not the Hananiah of Jer. 28). He seized Jeremiah and accused him of deserting or defecting to the Chaldeans (cf. Jer. 38:19; 52:15; see also Jer. 21:9; 38:2).

Jeremiah responded to Seruiah's/Irijah's charge by saying that it was a "lie" (שקר) (Jer. 37:14 [LXX 44:14]; 2 Kgs. 9:12). The reader already knows from verse 12 that Jeremiah was in fact not deserting or defecting to the Chaldeans but on his way "to receive a portion" (לחלק) in the land of Benjamin. It is possible that Jeremiah is the subject of "he did not listen to him" in verse 14, which would indicate that he simply ignored Seruiah/Irijah after his initial response to him, but most translations and commentaries understand Seruiah/Irijah to be the subject of this clause; that is, Seruiah/Irijah disregarded Jeremiah's claim of innocence. Seruiah/Irijah then seized/arrested Jeremiah and brought him to the officials. When Seruiah/Irijah "seized" Jeremiah in verse 13b, he did so in order to engage the prophet. After their exchange, Seruiah/Irijah made the official arrest.

When Jeremiah was brought to the officials (obviously not the same officials from Jer. 36), they were very mad at him, presumably because they believed Seruiah's/Irijah's accusation against him (Jer. 37:15 [LXX 44:15]). The MT has suffixed conjugation verbs in verse 15 that appear to be oddly out of place: "and they struck (והכו) him and put (ונתנו) him."[15] The *Sebirin* ("supposed") or scribal suggestions for this verse are the *wayyiqtol* forms ויכו and ויתנו, which seem to be the forms that lay behind the Greek translation. The officials put Jeremiah "[MT adds: in prison] in the house of Jonathan [Jehonathan] the scribe, for it was what they made into the house of confinement" (see Heb. 11:36). This arrangement is further explained in verse 16: "And Jeremiah came (ויבא ירמיהו) to the dungeon (בית הבור) and to the chereth (החרת)

---

15. "They no doubt ordered their servants to smite him; for it would have been more than strange, had the princes themselves risen up to strike the Prophet with their fists, or to smite him with their hands. It is then probable that he was smitten by their orders and at their bidding" (Calvin, *Jeremiah*, 4:375). See also Jeremiah 18:18; 20:2.

and sat/remained there for many days" (cf. Gen. 37:24, 28; 39:20; 41:14; Exod. 12:29; Isa. 24:22; Jer. 38:6, 13; Lam. 3:53, 55; Dan. 6:17, 24). It is not clear what the Greek transliteration χερεθ is intended to represent. The MT of verse 16 is often interpreted as a temporal protasis to the main clause in verse 17: "When Jeremiah came (כי בא ירמיהו) to the dungeon and to the cells (החניות) and Jeremiah sat/remained there for many days." The open paragraph division after verse 16 in the MT argues against such an understanding. The MT should probably be rendered, "When Jeremiah came to the dungeon and to the cells, Jeremiah sat/remained there for many days." The MT's version of this verse pictures a dungeon with multiple holding cells. The specific duration of Jeremiah's confinement is not indicated, but the "many days" must have been substantial enough for Jeremiah to fear that a longer stay would threaten his life (Jer. 37:20). It is possible that verse 20 is only a request that he not live out his days in the dungeon, but the relocation to another place of confinement in verse 21 suggests that conditions in the dungeon were harsh.

After the "many days" passed, Zedekiah "sent and summoned him (ויקראהו) [MT: sent and took/received him (ויקחהו)]" (Jer. 37:17a [LXX 44:17a]).[16] There is no indication of the person(s) whom the king sent to bring Jeremiah. There is also no indication that this summoning of Jeremiah was done secretly. It was the conversation between the two that took place "in secret" (cf. MT Jer. 38:16). If Jeremiah 38:24–26 is any clue, Zedekiah wanted to keep the nature of their conversation private, even though the meeting itself was known to have happened. The desire for privacy was due to the fear of repercussions for Jeremiah (and perhaps also for Zedekiah) from the officials who opposed the prophet. It would not have been good for them to find out that the king was listening to Jeremiah's prophecy. The officials believed that the city would not fall to the king of Babylon, and they objected to desertion to the Babylonians (Jer. 21:9; 37:13–16; 38:1–6, 17–18). Zedekiah asked Jeremiah, "Is there a word from the LORD" (cf. Jer. 23:37)? This was in spite of the fact that a word from the LORD about the situation had already been received much earlier (Jer. 37:3, 6–10). McKane comments, "It has been conjectured that in the interval the Babylonians resumed

---

16. "He wished then for some new message, and to hear something respecting the future deliverance of the city: for he was no doubt persuaded that Jeremiah had been hitherto discharging the office of a Prophet, as it became him; for he did not ask him as a common man, nor did he regard him as an impostor, but inquired whether there was a word from God" (Calvin, *Jeremiah*, 4:378).

the siege and that it was this change in historical circumstances which moved Zedekiah to ask Jeremiah again for a word from Yahweh. Verse 19 may be pressed into service in this connection: this would have been an appropriate taunt for Jeremiah to offer only if the siege had been resumed and predictions of *Heil* arising from the raising of the siege had been falsified."[17] Jeremiah's response remained the same because the word of the LORD remained the same: "There is. Into the hand/ power of the king of Babylon you will be given/delivered" (Jer. 37:17b [LXX 44:17b]; cf. Jer. 21:7; 32:3–4; 34:3, 21). The MT adds ויאמר ("And he said") between Jeremiah's initial positive reply ("There is") and his full response. This kind of reintroduction of discourse without a change of speaker often indicates a pause.[18] Jeremiah was faithful to the word of the LORD even when abandonment of his prophetic calling would surely have guaranteed him the relief from his circumstances that he so desired (see Jer. 37:20).

After a pause (ויאמר), Jeremiah asked the king, "How have I sinned against you and against your servants and against this people that you [MT pl.] have put me in the house of confinement" (Jer. 37:18 [LXX 44:18]; cf. Dan. 6:23 [Eng., 6:22])? Of course, Jeremiah had not sinned against anyone to deserve such treatment, but he was looking for an admission of this from the king. According to the Hebrew source behind Greek Jeremiah, Jeremiah pointed to Zedekiah in particular as the one who put him in the house of confinement ("you [sg.] have put me in the house of confinement"). According to the MT, he highlighted Zedekiah and his servants and the officials as the ones who did this ("you [pl.] have put me in the house of confinement"; see Jer. 37:2, 15–16). Jeremiah then asked, "And where are your [pl.] prophets [*Tg. Jon.*: false prophets] who prophesied to you [pl.], saying, 'The king of Babylon will not come [MT adds: against you (pl.) and] against this land' (Jer. 37:19 [LXX 44:19]; see Jer. 6:14 et al.)? BDB notes that the interrogative איה ("where?") is often in poetic or elevated style, where the answer "nowhere" is expected (BDB, 32). The return of the Babylonians showed that the punished prophet (Jeremiah) was true and that the rewarded prophets of peace were false. Thus, Zedekiah and his men had egg on their face, and Jeremiah took the opportunity to make sure that they knew it.

ועתה ("And now") at the beginning of 37:20 (LXX 44:20) introduces a logical conclusion based on the preceding discourse of Jeremiah in verses 17b–19; the MT adds the imperative שמע נא ("hear") to this:

---

17. McKane, *Jeremiah XXVI–LII*, 939.
18. See Shimon Bar-Efrat, *Narrative Art in the Bible* (Sheffield: Sheffield Academic, 1989; repr., London: T&T Clark, 2004), 43.

"And now [MT adds: hear], my lord the king, let my supplication fall before you" (cf. Jer. 36:7; 38:26; 42:2). The Hebrew source behind Greek Jeremiah gives Jeremiah's request in the form of rhetorical questions: "and why should you return me to the house of Jonathan the scribe? And will I not die there?" The MT converts these into a plea: "and do not return me to the house of Jonathan the scribe, lest I die there" (cf. Jer. 38:26; see GKC §109g). Jeremiah feared that a return to the conditions described in verses 15–16 would threaten his life (cf. Jer. 38:9).

Zedekiah obliged Jeremiah and gave the order to have him relocated to "the court of the guard" (Jer. 37:21 [LXX 44:21]; see Jer. 32:2; 38:6, 13). Jeremiah was given one "loaf" or "disk" (ככר) of bread per day from the bakers' street until the bread of the city was finished (see Jer. 38:9; 52:6; see also Lev. 26:26; cf. 1 Kgs. 22:27), and he remained in the court of the guard.[19] The phrase מחוץ האפים ("from the bakers' street) is translated by the LXX as "from outside where they bake." This reflects a view that Jeremiah was given bread of a lesser quality sold outside the bakers' shops.[20] Such a view does not fit very well with Zedekiah's sympathetic attitude toward Jeremiah in the present context. The word חוץ here does not mean "outside" the place of business. Rather, it is a reference to the bazaar itself (see the usage in 1 Kgs. 20:34; see also Num. 22:39).

---

19. Rudolph (*BHS* apparatus) proposes transposition of Jeremiah 38:24–28a to the end of 37:21, but McKane advises against this: "There is a legitimate fear that this kind of operation may amount to a doctoring of the problem rather than a method for achieving its solution" (McKane, *Jeremiah XXVI–LII*, 933).

20. See Neusner, *Jeremiah in Talmud and Midrash*, 207.

JEREMIAH 38 (LXX 45)

38:1 (45:1) And Shephatiah the son of Mattan heard, and Gedaliah the son of Pashhur and Jucal the son of Shelemiah [MT adds: and Pashhur the son of Malkijah], the words that Jeremiah was speaking to [MT adds: all] the people, saying, 38:2 (45:2) "Thus says the LORD, 'The one who stays in this city, he will die by the sword or by famine [MT: by the sword, by famine, or by plague], but the one who goes out to the Chaldeans, he will live, and his life will be [MT: and he will have his life] as plunder [LXX: windfall], and he will live.' 38:3 (45:3) For [> MT] thus says the LORD, 'This city will surely be given / delivered into the hand / power of the army of the king of Babylon, and he will capture it.'" 38:4 (45:4) And [MT adds: the officials] said to the king, "This man must be put to death, for he is making the hands of the warriors who are left in the city [MT: in this city] and the hands of all the people go slack [see GKC §75rr] by speaking to them according to these words, for this man is not seeking peace [or, well-being] for this people but harm." 38:5 (45:5) And the king [MT: King Zedekiah] said, "Look, he is in your hand," for the king was powerless against them [MT: "Look, he is in your hand, for the king is not able to do a thing against you"]. 38:6 (45:6) [MT adds: And they took Jeremiah] [a]nd they cast him into the pit / cistern [see GKC §127f] of Malkijah the son of the king [or, member of the royal family], which was in the court of the guard, and they sent him into the pit / cistern [MT: and they sent Jeremiah with ropes]. And in the pit / cistern there was no water, only mud, and he was [MT: and he sank] in the mud.

38:7 (45:7) And Ebed Melech the Cushite / Ethiopian [MT adds: an official / eunuch] heard [Tg. Jon.: And the servant of King Zedekiah, a great man, heard], and he was in the king's house [or, royal palace], that they put Jeremiah in the pit / cistern, and the king was sitting [NET: holding court] in the gate of Benjamin. 38:8 (45:8) And he [MT: Ebed Melech] went out to him [MT: went out from the king's house (or, royal palace)] and spoke to the king and said [MT: saying], 38:9 (45:9) "You have acted badly in what you have done to kill this man from before the famine [MT: My lord the king, these men have acted badly in all that they have done to Jeremiah the prophet in that they cast him into the pit / cistern so that he will die (see GKC §111l) in his place because of the famine], for there is no longer any bread in the city." 38:10 (45:10) And the king commanded Ebed Melech [MT adds: the Cushite], saying, "Take with you [lit., in your hand] from here thirty [Ms: three] men and bring him [MT: Jeremiah the prophet] up from the pit / cistern lest he die [MT: before he dies]." 38:11 (45:11) And Ebed Melech took the men [MT adds: with him] and entered the king's house to a place underground [MT: to a place under the treasury] and took from there worn out clothes and worn out rags [LXX: ropes; see GKC §132c] and sent them to Jeremiah in the pit / cistern [MT adds: with ropes]. 38:12 (45:12) And he said [MT: And Ebed Melech the Cushite said to Jeremiah], "Put these under the ropes [MT: Put the worn out clothes and rags under your armpits beneath the ropes]." And Jeremiah did so. 38:13 (45:13) And they pulled him [MT: Jeremiah] with the ropes and brought him up from the pit / cistern. And Jeremiah remained in the court of the guard.

38:14 (45:14) And the king sent and summoned him to him [MT: And King Zedekiah sent and took Jeremiah the prophet to him] at the third entrance [see GKC §126w; LXX: at the house of Aselisel], which was in the house of the LORD. And the king said to him [MT: Jeremiah], "I am asking you something, and [> MT] do not hide a word / thing from me." 38:15 (45:15) And Jeremiah said to the king [MT: to Zedekiah], "If I tell you, will you not surely kill me? And if I advise you, you will not listen to me." 38:16 (45:16) And the king swore to him [MT: And King Zedekiah swore to Jeremiah in secret], saying, "As the LORD lives [or, By the life of the LORD] who made for us this life, I will not kill you [lit., if I kill you] and I will not give / deliver you [lit., and if I give you; see GKC §149b] into the hand / power of these men [MT adds: who are seeking your life]." 38:17 (45:17) And Jeremiah said to him [MT: Zedekiah], "Thus says the LORD [MT adds: the God (> Cairo Geniza) of hosts, the God of Israel], 'If indeed you go out to the officials of the king of Babylon, you will live, and this city will not be burned with fire; and you will live, and your household. 38:18 (45:18) And if you do not go out [MT adds: to the officials of (officials of > Cairo Geniza) the king of Babylon], this city will be given / delivered into the hand / power of the Chaldeans, and they will burn it with fire; and as for you, you will not escape [MT adds: from their hand / power].'" 38:19 (45:19) And the king [MT: King Zedekiah] said to Jeremiah, "I am anxious [LXX: I have a word / concern] about the Judeans who have deserted / defected to the Chaldeans, lest they give / deliver me into their hand / power and they deal severely with me." 38:20 (45:20) And Jeremiah said, "They will not give / deliver [LXX adds: you]. Obey the word [MT: voice] of the LORD that [MT: with regard to what] I am speaking to you, and it will be good for you, and you will live. 38:21 (45:21) And if you refuse to go out, this is the word that the LORD has shown me: 38:22 (45:22) And look, all the women who are left in the house of the king of Judah are being brought out to the officials of the king of Babylon, and they are saying, 'The men *of your friendship incited you and prevailed over you, and they sank in the mire your feet [MT: and your feet were sunk in the mire (Tg. Jon.: in shame)]; they turned back [LXX add: from you].' 38:23 (45:23) And [MT adds: all] your wives and your sons/children they are bringing out to the Chaldeans; and as for you, you will not escape [MT adds: from their hand], for by the hand of the king of Babylon you will be seized; and as for this city, it will be burned [Codex L: and as for this city, it will burn (pc Mss: be burned) with fire (or, and this city you will burn with fire)]." 38:24 (45:24) And the king [MT: Zedekiah] said to him [MT: Jeremiah], "Do not let anyone know about these words, lest you die. 38:25 (45:25) And if/when the officials hear that I have spoken with you and come to you and say to you, 'Tell us what the king spoke to you [MT: Tell us what you spoke to the king (Syr. transposes here: and what the king spoke to you)]. Do not hide from us, lest we kill you. And what did the king speak to you?' 38:26 (45:26) then you will say to them, 'I was casting my supplication before the king not to return me to the house of Jonathan to die there.'" 38:27 (45:27) And all the officials came to Jeremiah, and they asked him, and he told them according to all these words that the king commanded him [him > Codex L]. And they were silent [MT adds: from him], for the word of the LORD was not heard [MT: for the word was not heard]. 38:28 (45:28) And Jeremiah remained in the court of the guard until (the) day that Jerusalem was captured. [MT adds: When Jerusalem was captured]*

The story of Jeremiah 38 (LXX 45) is best understood as a continuation of the one in chapter 37 (LXX 44) and not as an alternative, parallel account of the same narrative found in Jeremiah 37. Shephatiah the son of Mattan, a man not mentioned elsewhere, is listed first in 38:1 (LXX 45:1) as the lead figure of a group of men who heard the words that Jeremiah was speaking to the people (note the agreement in the Hebrew text between the singular verb and the first member of the compound subject). Listed with Shephatiah are Gedaliah the son of Pashhur (see Jer. 20:1–6) and Jucal (Jehucal) the son of Shelemiah (see Jer. 37:3). The MT adds a fourth name, "Pashhur the son of Malkijah" (see Jer. 21:1), which does not appear in the LXX *Vorlage*. It is usually assumed that Jeremiah was somehow able to speak to the people while confined to the court of the guard (see Jer. 37:21; cf. Jer. 32:6–15). Others have felt that this would have been an unlikely scenario and have suggested that Jeremiah must have been free to be among the people at this time.[1] There is, however, a third, unexplored option to

---

1. See the discussion in McKane, *Jeremiah XXVI–LII*, 962–63.

consider. The words that these men are said to have heard Jeremiah speaking to the people, which appear in verses 2 and 3, are essentially the same words that Jeremiah had been speaking publicly long before his confinement. Thus, it is perhaps the case that the objection of these men in verse 4 was not to the continued preaching of Jeremiah but to the relocation of the prophet from the dungeon in 37:16 to the court of the guard in 37:21. Since Jeremiah was no longer condemned to die under harsh conditions as a false prophet, the relocation gave new life to what he had already preached to the people for some time.

The words that the men heard Jeremiah speaking to the people in the name of the LORD are quoted in 38:2–3 (LXX 45:2–3). They are basically the same words that the reader has previously encountered in Jeremiah 21:9–10 (see also Jer. 34:2, 17, 22; 38:17–18; 39:18). Their message essentially encouraged desertion. Since the city of Jerusalem would definitely be delivered into the power of the king of Babylon and captured, the only way to survive was to surrender. The men (MT: "the officials") insisted to the king that Jeremiah must be put to death because he was making the hands of the warriors left in the city and those of all the people go slack by speaking to them according to these words (Jer. 38:4a [LXX 45:4a]; cf. Jer. 26:8; Ezra 4:4; see also BDB, 475; *ANET*, 322). For them, the continued existence of the prophet meant that his message would be perpetuated in the city one way or another. They preferred to move him to a place not only where he would be silenced but also where his death would be imminent, yet they were not so rash as to demand his immediate execution. These men were not interested in the truth of Jeremiah's message. Their only concern was the demoralizing effect that they perceived his message to have had on the people, which was contrary to their desire. They viewed Jeremiah as a troublemaker who did not seek the well-being of the people (Jer. 38:4b [LXX 45:4b]; cf. Jer. 6:14). The irony was that the harm or judgment of the people had to come before the peace or well-being of restoration (Jer. 21:10; 29:11). Jeremiah did not preach judgment because he liked it. He did so because he was compelled by the word of the LORD (Jer. 20:9). Disobedience to the terms of the old covenant demanded that the people face the consequences before there could be any way forward.

The king's response to the men in 38:5 (LXX 45:5) differs between the Hebrew source behind Greek Jeremiah and the MT. According to the former (LXX *Vorlage*), the king granted the men permission, which is then explained by the narrator as his powerlessness against them: '"Look, he is in your hand,' for the king was powerless against them" (cf. Jer. 26:14). Thus, despite the fact that the men had to come to the king before they acted, Zedekiah was powerless against them as

Nebuchadnezzar's puppet king (2 Kgs. 24:17). According to the latter (MT), the king granted the men permission and then explained that he was unable to do anything against them: "Look, he is in your hand, for the king is not able to do a thing against you." This would have been a startling admission on the king's part but one that is consistent with what is later reported about his uneasy relationship with his officials (Jer. 38:24–26). The balance of power between Zedekiah and his officials was complex to say the least. On the one hand, Zedekiah gave Jeremiah over to these men knowing that they wanted to put him to death. On the other hand, he was eventually persuaded by the Cushite to have Jeremiah delivered from the very place where the men put him (Jer. 38:7–13)—something that the reader has seen Zedekiah do before (Jer. 37:15–16, 21). Zedekiah subsequently had a private conversation with Jeremiah, which was deliberately kept from the officials (Jer. 38:14–28; cf. Jer. 37:17–21).

The beginning of MT 38:6 (LXX 45:6) adds that the officials "took" Jeremiah, whereas the LXX *Vorlage* simply begins by saying that they cast Jeremiah into the "pit/cistern" (בור) of Malkijah the son of the king, which was in the court of the guard (cf. 1 Kgs. 22:26; Lam. 3:53). The phrase בן המלך ("the son of the king") has been encountered in Jeremiah 36:26. It is possible that Zedekiah had a young teenage son (see 2 Kgs. 24:18), but it is also possible that the phrase merely designates a member of the royal family or court. If this Malkijah was the king's son, then he would not have been old enough to be the father of the Pashhur mentioned in MT 38:1. Thus, either two different individuals named Malkijah are in view, or there was one Malkijah who was not literally the king's son. The clause "and they sent him into the pit/cistern" appears redundant in the Hebrew source behind Greek Jeremiah. The MT has "and they sent Jeremiah with ropes," which is either a contradiction of the casting of Jeremiah into the pit/cistern or an explication of it. The "pit/cistern" (בור) mentioned here is not the same as "the house of the pit" (בית הבור), which was a multi-celled dungeon in the house of Jonathan (Jer. 37:16). The pit/cistern of 38:6 was in the court of the guard, and, contrary to expectation, did not have any water in it, only mud. Thus, Jeremiah was in the mud (MT: "and he sank in the mud"). This detailed description of the pit/cistern appears to be deliberately reminiscent of the story of Joseph who was treated unjustly by his own brothers and cast into an empty "pit/cistern" (בור) without any water (Gen. 37:22, 24; see also Jer. 18:20, 22 [MT]; 41:7–10; Ps. 69:16 [Eng., 69:15]).

Jeremiah 38:7 (LXX 45:7) introduces the reader to a new character, "Ebed Melech the Cushite/Ethiopian" (cf. Num. 12:1), who will appear again in Jeremiah 39:15–18. The Hebrew עבד מלך is best understood as a name ("Ebed Melech") rather than a description ("a royal servant"), although this has not always been the understanding in the history of interpretation. *Targum Jonathan* refers to this individual as "the servant of King Zedekiah, a great man." The rabbinic literature bases its understanding of this man as a servant of the king on the reference to Cushite skin color in Jeremiah 13:23. *Sifre* to Numbers says, "The meaning is that just as a Kushite has skin different from others, so Baruch b. Neriah was distinguished in his deeds among all the members of the king's establishment."[2] The Talmud says, "Was his name not Zedekiah? But just as a Kushite [Ethiopian] has a skin that is different, so Zedekiah did deeds that were distinguished?"[3] The MT adds that Ebed Melech was איש סריס, a designation that does not appear in the Hebrew source behind Greek Jeremiah. This does not necessarily mean that Ebed Melech was specifically a "eunuch." It may simply indicate that he was a court official (see Jer. 29:2; cf. 2 Kgs. 20:18). Ebed Melech was in the royal palace when he heard that they put Jeremiah in the pit/cistern. The king, on the other hand, was "sitting" in the gate of Benjamin (Jer. 20:2; 37:13), which probably means that he was "holding court" (NET; cf. Jer. 26:10). Thus, Ebed Melech had to depart the palace and go to the king in order to speak to him about Jeremiah (Jer. 38:8 [LXX 45:8]). The background of Ebed Melech, including his relationship to others involved in the story, seems to be of little interest to the narrator and should therefore be of little interest to the reader. In any case, no such information is available.

The Hebrew source behind Greek Jeremiah 38:9 (LXX 45:9) presents Ebed Melech's words to the king as a direct accusation against the king himself: "You have acted badly in what you have done to kill this man from before the famine, for there is no longer any bread in the city." The reference to the lack of bread is somewhat premature (Jer. 37:21; 52:6; see Lev. 26:26), but the intended implication is probably that Jeremiah would die in the pit/cistern if the conditions of the city of Jerusalem were to continue on the same trajectory. Such a bold confrontation with the king might not seem to be a wise tactic, but the LXX *Vorlage* depicts it as a successful one. Zedekiah tacitly conceded his wrongdoing and gave the order to retrieve Jeremiah (Jer. 38:10 [LXX 45:10]). On the other hand, the MT presents Ebed Melech's words as an appeal to the king to rescue Jeremiah from the men who cast Jeremiah into the pit/cistern: "My lord the king, these men have acted badly in all that they have done

---

2.   See Neusner, *Jeremiah in Talmud and Midrash*, 19.

3.   Neusner, *Jeremiah in Talmud and Midrash*, 303.

to Jeremiah the prophet in that they cast him into the pit/cistern so that he will die [see GKC §111l] in his place because of the famine, for there is no longer any bread in the city." The king then apparently regretted his decision to give Jeremiah over to these men (Jer. 38:5) and had mercy on the prophet. According to most witnesses, Zedekiah instructed Ebed Melech to take "thirty" (שלשים) men to bring up Jeremiah from the pit/cistern "lest he die" (MT: "before he dies") (Jer. 38:10 [LXX 45:10]). One Masoretic manuscript says that he was to take "three" (שלשה) men. This is likely an attempt to "correct" the larger number with the thought that such a large number of men would not be required to pull Jeremiah from the pit/cistern. Keil comments, "Ebedmelech was to take thirty men, not because they would all be required for drawing out the prophet, but for making surer work in effecting the deliverance of the prophet, against all possible attempts on the part of the princes or of the populace to prevent them."[4]

Ebed Melech took the men and entered the king's house "to a place underground" (אל תחת הארץ) from which he took worn out clothes and worn out rags that he sent to Jeremiah in the pit/cistern (Jer. 38:11 [LXX 45:1]). The MT says that he entered the king's house "to a place under the treasury" (אל תחת האוצר). Rudolph (*BHS* apparatus) suggests reading "to the wardrobe of the treasury/storehouse" (אל מלתחת האוצר) (cf. 2 Kgs. 10:22). The LXX translates מלחים ("rags") as "ropes" and thus does not include "with ropes" at the end of the verse as in the MT. The inclusion of "with ropes" in the MT is obviously in anticipation of verse 12, which presupposes that ropes were sent to Jeremiah. Ebed Melech told Jeremiah to put the "these" (i.e., the worn out clothes and rags) under the ropes (Jer. 38:12 [LXX 45:12]). The MT more explicitly says that Jeremiah was to put the worn out clothes and rags under his "armpits" (Holladay: "elbows") beneath the ropes in order to avoid having the ropes cut into his flesh when they pulled him out of the pit/cistern. Jeremiah followed the instruction, and they pulled him with the ropes and brought him up from the pit/cistern (Jer. 38:13a [LXX 45:13a]). Jeremiah then remained in the court of the guard once again (Jer. 38:13b [LXX 45:13b]; cf. Jer. 37:21b). Just as Joseph was delivered, so to speak, from a waterless pit/cistern by foreigners (Gen. 37:24, 28), so the foreigner Ebed Melech the Cushite delivered Jeremiah from the mud of the waterless pit/cistern (Jer. 38:6, 13; see Zech. 9:11; Ps. 40:3 [Eng., 40:2]).

The textual variation at the beginning of 38:14 (LXX 45:14) is similar to that of 37:17. According to the Hebrew source behind Greek Jeremiah, the king "sent and summoned" Jeremiah. According to the

---

4. Keil, *Jeremiah*, 328.

MT, he "sent and took" him (cf. MT 38:6). This time Jeremiah was not summoned or taken to the royal palace. Rather, the meeting took place "at the third entrance, which was in the house of the LORD." The precise location of this entrance is unknown. The LXX renders the phrase אל מבוא שלישי ("at the third entrance") as if it were אל בית שלישי ("at the house of Aselisel"), transliterating שלישי as a name. Zedekiah told Jeremiah at this entrance that he had something to ask him, and he insisted that Jeremiah not hide a word/thing from him (cf. 1 Sam. 3:17; Jer. 26:2; 38:25; 42:4). Jeremiah's initial response shows that he had little patience for the king at this point: "If I tell you, will you not surely kill me? And if I advise you, you will not listen to me" (Jer. 38:15 [LXX 45:15]). There is a distinct echo of this language in the words of Jesus' reply to the question of the chief priests and the scribes about whether he was the Christ: "If I tell you, you will not believe" (Luke 22:67). The king, however, swore an oath to Jeremiah that by the life of the LORD,[5] the very giver of life, he would not kill him or give him over to those who sought to kill him (Jer. 38:16 [LXX 45:16]). The MT adds that this was done "in secret" in order to match the description of the meeting in 37:17. The MT's addition of "who are seeking your life" (cf. Jer. 19:7, 9; 21:7; 34:20, 21; 44:30; Pss. 38:13 [Eng., 38:12]; 40:15 [Eng., 40:14]; 70:3 [Eng., 70:2]) to describe the men into whose hand the king would not deliver Jeremiah may be an intentional attempt to continue the depiction of Jeremiah as a prophet like Moses (Jer. 1:5–9). When the LORD called Moses to return to Egypt, he explained, "For all the men who were seeking your life have died" (Exod. 4:19; see also Elijah in 1 Kgs. 19:10).

Jeremiah then replied to Zedekiah with a reiteration of his previous message. If Zedekiah would only go out to the Babylonian officials, he would live, and the city of Jerusalem would not be burned (Jer. 38:17 [LXX 45:17]; cf. Jer. 21:9; 38:2; see also 2 Kgs. 18:31; 24:12). Zedekiah and his household would survive. On the other hand, if the king refused to go out, then the city would be delivered to the Chaldeans who would burn it; and Zedekiah himself would not escape (Jer. 38:18 [LXX 45:18]; cf. Jer. 21:10; 32:4; 34:2–3; 38:23). It is interesting to note that the fate of the city depended upon the decision of one man in this moment, despite all the earlier prophecy of impending judgment for all of

---

5. It is possible that the unvocalized את following יהוה in the Leningrad Codex is a designation of the LORD as the Aleph (Alpha) and the Taw (Omega), the beginning and the end (see Isa. 41:4; 44:6; Rev. 1:8; 22:13). For other examples of this, see the rendering of Amos 9:12 in Codex Alexandrinus (also Acts 15:17); see also Zechariah 12:10. For discussion of these texts, see Shepherd, *Commentary on the Book of the Twelve*, 200, 463–64.

Judah and Jerusalem.[6] Of course, the surrender of Zedekiah remained only a hypothetical possibility that was never realized, and the people of Judah and Jerusalem continued on the trajectory toward judgment for their covenant infidelity.

The king's response to Jeremiah reveals his lack of trust in the Lord: "I am anxious (דאג) about the Judeans who have deserted/defected to the Chaldeans, lest they give/deliver me into their hand/power and they deal severely with me" (Jer. 38:19 [LXX 45:19]; cf. 1 Sam. 31:4). The man who trusts in the Lord, however, is like a tree planted by water, which is not "anxious" (ידאג) in a year of drought (Jer. 17:7–8). The subjects of the verbs יתנו ("give/deliver") and והתעללו ("deal severely") are not explicit in the Hebrew text of verse 19, although most commentators assume that the Chaldeans would be the ones to deliver the king to the Judeans who would then deal severely with him. Rashi characterizes Zedekiah's words as follows: "Lest the Chaldeans deliver me into the hands of the Jews, saying, 'Your king shall be your slave since you have made peace with us first.'"[7] A. B. Ehrlich, however, has suggested that the Judeans would be the ones to deliver Zedekiah to the Chaldeans for maltreatment.[8] Jeremiah gave his word to the king that they (whoever "they" may be) would not hand him over to be mistreated (Jer. 38:20a [LXX 45:20a]). If Zedekiah would only obey the word (MT: "voice") of the Lord that he heard from Jeremiah, it would be good for him, and he would live (Jer. 38:20b [LXX 45:20b]; see again Jer. 21:9; 38:2, 17; see also BDB, 405).

Jeremiah then reported to Zedekiah what would happen if he refused to go out (Jer. 38:21a [LXX 45:21a]). He presented the "word" that the Lord had "shown" him in a vision (Jer. 38:21b [LXX 45:21b]; cf. Jer. 1:11, 13). Thus, the depiction in verse 22 is not an indication of what had already occurred or what was currently taking place, nor is it a mere prediction of what would happen. Rather, it is a word picture without time reference. It was given for Zedekiah's consideration in the moment. The vision to which Jeremiah directed Zedekiah's attention ("And look") was that of all the women left in the royal palace of Judah

---

6. A similar scenario appears in 1 Samuel 13:13 where Samuel tells Saul that the Lord would have established Saul's kingdom over Israel forever if he had only obeyed. One can only imagine how the history would have unfolded differently if Saul or Zedekiah had chosen to follow the words of the prophets who guided them.

7. Rosenberg, trans., *Mikraoth Gedoloth: Jeremiah Volume Two*, 308.

8. A. B. Ehrlich, *Randglossen zur Hebräischen Bibel. Textkritisches, Sprachliches und Sachliches*, vol. 4, *Jesaiah, Jeremia* (Leipzig, 1912), 341.

being brought out to the Babylonian officials and saying, "The men of your friendship incited you and prevailed over you, and they sank in the mire your feet [MT: and your feet were sunk in the mire (*Tg. Jon.*: in shame)]; they turned back [LXX add: from you]" (Jer. 38:22 [LXX 45:22]).[9] This appears to be a deliberate reversal of the image of women coming out to sing with tambourines and dances in celebration of military victory (see Exod. 15:20–21; Judg. 11:34; 1 Sam. 18:6–7; Jer. 31:4). Verse 23 interprets verse 22 to be the bringing out of Zedekiah's wives and children to the Chaldeans (cf. 2 Sam. 15:16); Zedekiah himself would not escape, and the city of Jerusalem would be burned (cf. Jer. 38:18).[10] The phrase אנשי שלמך ("the men of your friendship") in verse 22 refers either to the false prophets (Rashi) or to the king's advisors/officials or to both (cf. Jer. 20:10; Ps. 41:10 [Eng., 41:9]). Zedekiah should have been able to count on those closest to him to counsel him to do the right thing, but these men incited him and prevailed upon him to do the opposite. They sank his feet in the mire and turned back. Thus, Zedekiah found himself metaphorically in the same position as Jeremiah did literally in verse 6.

The king forbade Jeremiah to let anyone know about their conversation, lest he (Jeremiah) die (Jer. 38:24 [LXX 45:24]). This was not a threat. Zedekiah did not intend to kill Jeremiah (Jer. 38:16), but he feared those who already wanted to kill him (Jer. 38:4). Furthermore, Zedekiah likely feared the repercussions for himself if word of their exchange were to become known (see again Jer. 38:5, 19). While the nature of their conversation was private, the knowledge of their meeting was apparently public (cf. Jer. 37:17). Thus, Zedekiah instructed Jeremiah in anticipation of his inevitable encounter with the officials who would inquire about what was said between the two (Jer. 38:25–26 [LXX 45:25–26]). There are three different versions of the text of verse 25. According to the Hebrew source behind Greek Jeremiah, the king

---

9. "Targ. assumes logically that since רגלך is the subject of the passive הטבעו, it is also the subject of נסגו, and so it renders נסגו with a third feminine plural (אשתקעא). The point is not that the friends (אנשי שלמך) desert the king, but rather that Zedekiah's feet are unable to extricate him from the mud or to secure for him a firm footing in it" (McKane, *Jeremiah XXVI–LII*, 960).

10. The end of verse 23 in the Leningrad Codex can be translated: "and this city you will burn with fire." Rashi comments, "It is as though you are burning it with your hands for you are causing it" (Rosenberg, trans., *Mikraoth Gedoloth: Jeremiah Volume Two*, 309). See also Bullinger, *Figures of Speech*, 571.

expected the officials to say, "Tell us what the king spoke to you. Do not hide from us, lest we kill you. And what did the king speak to you?" According to the MT, they would say, "Tell us what you spoke to the king. Do not hide from us, lest we kill you. And what did the king speak to you?" Lastly, the Syriac says, "Tell us what you spoke to the king and what the king spoke to you. Do not hide from us, lest we kill you." McKane suggests that ומה דבר אליך המלך ("and what the king spoke to you") at the end of the verse in the LXX *Vorlage* and the MT is a misplaced doublet of מה דבר אליך המלך earlier in the verse in the LXX *Vorlage*. The first occurrence of the doublet was altered in the MT to מה דברת אל המלך ("what you spoke to the king"). The Syriac then rearranged the word order to combine the two: "Tell us what you spoke to the king and what the king spoke to you." Thus, the original text without the doublet is translated, "Tell us what the king spoke to you. Do not hide from us, lest we kill you" (cf. Jer. 38:14). The officials would have been primarily interested in what the king said, since Jeremiah's message to the king was already public knowledge. The king had already delivered Jeremiah from the dungeon and the pit/cistern (Jer. 37:15–21; 38:6–13). Therefore, they wanted to know how deep his sympathy toward Jeremiah and his message ran, especially since they believed that Jeremiah's words were contrary to the best interests of the city (Jer. 38:4). Such a threat from the officials would put Jeremiah between a rock and a hard place. If he were to tell what the king said, then he would potentially die (v. 24). If he did not tell what the king said, he would be killed (v. 25). Zedekiah advised Jeremiah to say that he was casting his supplication before the king not to be returned to the house of Jonathan to die there (Jer. 38:26 [LXX 45:26]). This was, of course, the subject of their previous conversation (Jer. 37:20).[11] Some commentators have called into question the morality or ethics of such a seemingly dishonest reply, but it is not the place of the exegete to offer an independent evaluation of characters in the biblical narrative.[12]

---

11. Malbim: "This was indeed what the king said to him, viz. that he should give this as the answer to the officers' question" (Rosenberg, trans., *Mikraoth Gedoloth: Jeremiah Volume Two*, 310).
12. It is to be noted that the sort of righteous "deception" or "lie" involved here is never explicitly forbidden in Scripture. In fact, it is sometimes celebrated as an act of faith (see Exod. 1:15–22; Josh. 2:1–7; Heb. 11:31; Jas. 2:25). Prohibitions against lying in the Bible are never general. They are always specific prohibitions against things such as false accusation in a court of law (e.g., Exod. 20:16: Deut. 5:20) or false prophecy (e.g., Deut. 13:2–6 [Eng., 13:1–6]).

Such evaluation is often provided by the narrator (e.g., 2 Sam. 11:27b). It is the task of the exegete to explain what is present in the text, not what is absent from it. The biblical authors must be allowed to select what they include or omit without their interpreters taking it upon themselves to delete from their work or to add to it. Thus, if the text does not offer an evaluation of a character's words or actions, the decision not to do so must be respected.

The officials came to Jeremiah and interrogated him as anticipated by Zedekiah (Jer. 38:27 [LXX 45:27]). He told them "according to all these words" that the king instructed him to say. This response apparently satisfied the officials, for they were silent. The Hebrew source behind Greek Jeremiah explains that they were silent because the word of the LORD was not heard. This is presumably a reference to the word of the LORD spoken by Jeremiah in his conversation with Zedekiah (Jer. 38:17–18, 21–23). The MT, however, says that the officials were silent because the word was not heard, which is more of a general reference to the conversation between Jeremiah and Zedekiah, including the words of both. Jeremiah remained in the court of the guard until the day that Jerusalem was captured (Jer. 38:28 [LXX 45:28]; see Jer. 37:21; 38:13; 39:14). The MT adds "When Jerusalem was captured" (> LXX *Vorlage*) at the end of verse 28. This appears to be a superfluous introduction to the following chapter. The TEV and NRSV, however, move these words to the beginning of 39:3.

JEREMIAH 39 (LXX 46)

39:1 (46:1) And then [> MT], in the ninth year [LXX[BS]: in the ninth month] of Zedekiah the king of Judah, in the tenth month [> LXX[BS]], Nebuchadnezzar [MT: Nebuchadrezzar] the king of Babylon came, and all his army, to / against Jerusalem, and they laid siege to it. 39:2 (46:2) And in the eleventh year of Zedekiah, in the fourth month [pc Mss, Syr.: in the fifth month], on day nine of the month [Vulg.: on the fifth of the month], the city was breached. 39:3 (46:3) And all the officials of the king of Babylon came and sat in the Middle Gate: Nergalsarezer, Samgar, Nebusarsechim, Nebusaris, Nergalsarezer, Rabmag [NET: Nergal Sharezer of Samgar, Nebo Sarsekim (who was a chief officer), Nergal Sharezer (who was a high official)], and all the rest of the officials of the king of Babylon.[1] 39:14 (46:14) And they sent and took Jeremiah from the court of the guard, and they gave him to Gedaliah

---

1. MT adds 39:4–13: "And so, when Zedekiah the king of Judah, and all the soldiers, saw them, they fled and went out by night from the city the way of the king's garden through a gate between the two city walls, and he [nonn Mss: they] went out the way of the Arabah [or, plain]. And the army of the Chaldeans pursued after them, and they overtook Zedekiah in the plains of Jericho [pc Mss, Syr. add: and as for all his army, they were scattered from him], and they took him and brought him up to Nebuchadrezzar the king of Babylon at Riblah in the land of Hamath; and he spoke judgments with him. And the king of Babylon slaughtered the sons of Zedekiah at Riblah before his eyes, and all the nobles of Judah the king of Babylon slaughtered. And the eyes of Zedekiah he blinded, and he bound him in bronze shackles to bring him to Babylon [Theod. adds: and to put him in a mill house]. And the house of the king and the house [Syr.: houses] of the people the Chaldeans burned with fire, and the city walls of Jerusalem they tore down [Syr.: the Chaldeans burned with fire, and the wall of Jerusalem; when it surrounded, they fled]. And the rest of the people who were left in the city and the deserters/defectors who deserted/defected to him and the rest of the people who were left Nebuzaradan the captain of the guard took into exile to Babylon. And some of the poor people who did not have anything Nebuzaradan the captain of the guard left in the land of Judah, and he gave to them vineyards and fields [Syr.: trade/service; Theod., Vulg.: cisterns] in that day. And Nebuchadrezzar the king of Babylon commanded concerning Jeremiah by the hand of [or, through the agency of; > Syr., Vulg.] Nebuzaradan the captain of the guard, saying, 'Take him and set your eyes upon him, and do not do to him anything bad; but just as he speaks to you, so do with him.' And Nebuzaradan the captain of the guard sent, and Nebushazban a chief official and Nergal Sarezer a chief official and all the chiefs of the king of Babylon."

the son of Ahikam, the son of Shaphan, and he brought him out [MT: to bring him out to the house]; and he lived in the midst of the people.

39:15 (46:15) And to Jeremiah the word of the LORD came [MT adds: when he was confined] in the court of the guard, saying, 39:16 (46:16) "Go and say to Ebed Melech the Cushite [MT adds: saying], 'Thus says the LORD [MT adds: of hosts] the God of Israel, "Look, I am about to bring my words against this city for harm / calamity and not for good [MT adds: and they will happen before you in that day]. 39:17 (46:17) But I will rescue you in that day," [MT adds: the prophetic utterance of the LORD], "and I will not give / deliver you [MT: and you will not be given / delivered] into the hand / power of the men before whom [or, because of whom] you are fearing. 39:18 (46:18) For I will surely deliver you, and by the sword you will not fall; and your life will become plunder [LXX: and your life will be for windfall; MT: and you will have your life as plunder], for you have trusted in me," the prophetic utterance of the LORD.'"

The shorter version of chapter 39 (LXX 46) found in the LXX and its *Vorlage* does not have verses 4–13.[2] In this version, the siege and breach of Jerusalem are in the background (Jer. 39:1–3), and the focus is on the fate of Jeremiah (Jer. 39:14) and the word of the LORD concerning Ebed Melech (Jer. 39:15–18). The longer version, which appears in the MT, incorporates material from Jeremiah 52:7–11, 13–16 (Jer. 39:4–10) and devotes more attention to the fate of Zedekiah and the city of Jerusalem. Both versions show the fulfillment of Jeremiah's prophecy (e.g., Jer. 32:28) about Babylonian invasion and thus vindicate Jeremiah as a true prophet.[3]

According to 39:1 (LXX 46:1), Nebuchadnezzar came with all his army to or against Jerusalem in the tenth month of the ninth year of Zedekiah and laid siege to it. Vaticanus and Sinaiticus refer to the ninth month without mention of the year. Both 2 Kings 25:1 (MT) and Jeremiah 52:4 add more precisely that Nebuchadnezzar and his army came on day ten of the tenth month of Zedekiah's ninth year (cf. Ezek. 24:1). They camped against the city and built a siege wall around it. It was on day nine (Vulg.: "on the fifth of the month") of the fourth month (pc Mss, Syr.: "in the fifth month") of Zedekiah's eleventh year that the city of Jerusalem was

---

2. It should also be noted here that the first two verses of this chapter are absent from the Old Latin Wirceburgensis palimpsest codex (fifth century CE). These verses are also marked with an asterisk in Origen's Greek text. This evidence may indicate that these two verses are not part of the Old Greek.

3. See Calvin, *Jeremiah*, 4:421.

breached (Jer. 39:2 [LXX 46:2]; cf. 2 Kgs. 25:8; Jer. 1:3; 52:12; see also Jer. 32:1; Zech. 7:3, 5; 8:19). Second Kings 25:2–4 and Jeremiah 52:5–7 indicate that there was a famine in the city at this time.[4]

Jeremiah 39:3 (LXX 46:3) says that all the officials of the king of Babylon came and "sat" (NET: "set up quarters") in the Middle Gate, the precise location of which is unknown. The versions both ancient and modern disagree about what to do with the following list of officials. One option is to render it as a list of names without titles: "Nergalsarezer, Samgar, Nebusarsechim, Nebusaris, Nergalsarezer, Rabmag" (cf. LXX, Vulg.). The NET has three names, the first with a place name, and the second and third with titles: "Nergal Sharezer of Samgar, Nebo Sarsekim (who was a chief officer), Nergal Sharezer (who was a high official)" (cf. Rudolph's proposal in the *BHS* apparatus), although it is possible that סמגר is also a title.[5] The name "Nergalsharezer" ("May Nergal protect the king") only appears once in MT 39:13, but Thompson comments that "the name was a common one and it is possible that there were two men of this name among Nebuchadrezzar's officials."[6] Rudolph (*BHS* apparatus) suggests the name "Nebushazban" ("May Nabu save me") in place of Nebo Sarsekim (see MT Jer. 39:13). However this list is rendered, it is clear that those mentioned here were lead officials distinguished from "all the rest of the officials of the king of Babylon."

According to the LXX, the text moves directly from verse 3 to verse 14 so that those listed in verse 3 are the ones who sent and took Jeremiah from the court of the guard (see Jer. 38:28) and gave him to Gedaliah. The MT, however, includes verses 4–13. Rudolph (*BHS* apparatus) says that verses 4–10 have been added from Jeremiah 52:7–11, 13–16, and that verses 11–12 ought to be transposed before 40:1. He also says that verse 13 has been added. Nevertheless, despite the secondary nature of these verses, Rudolph says that the absence of these verses in Greek Jeremiah (or in its Hebrew *Vorlage*) is due to translator (or scribal) oversight (homoioteleuton) whereby the eye of the responsible individual accidentally skipped from "Babylon" at the end of verse 3 to "Babylon" at the end of verse 13 and continued without knowing that

---

4. "At this period years were counted from the Babylonian New Year in the spring (March/April). The siege of Jerusalem thus began in January 588 and lasted until July 587 (with a brief interlude, probably in the summer of 588)" (Bright, *Jeremiah*, 242).

5. McKane, *Jeremiah XXVI–LII*, 974–75. See also 2 Kings 18:17; Zechariah 7:2.

6. Thompson, *Book of Jeremiah*, 644n1.

the intervening text had been omitted. McKane summarizes this odd conclusion of critical scholarship: "The coincidence between the text of Sept. and what are judged, in the light of higher-critical criteria, to be original constituents of chapter 39 is entirely fortuitous: text-critical error (haplography) created a text which miraculously reproduced the text which is reached by higher-critical arguments."[7] McKane adds, "It is difficult to discern why there should have been such a resistance to the simplicity and economy of the hypothesis that the Hebrew *Vorlage* of Sept. was not defective, but preserved a Hebrew text shorter and earlier than MT."[8] Homoioteleuton is not uncommon within and between verses, but it is somewhat less realistic to expect it to happen over a large piece of text. Furthermore, the fact that "Babylon" appears at the end of verses 3, 6, 9, and 13 makes it likely that the correspondence between verses 3 and 13 is mere coincidence.

The added material begins in MT 39:4 with the attempted flight of Zedekiah and his soldiers (cf. 2 Kgs. 25:4; Jer. 52:7). When Zedekiah saw the officials mentioned in verse 3, he and all the soldiers fled the city by night.[9] They went the way of the king's garden through a gate between the two city walls (see Neh. 3:15; Isa. 22:11; 2 Chr. 32:5), and "he" (nonn Mss: "they") went out the way of the Arabah. Holladay assumes that Zedekiah was trying to cross the Jordan, perhaps in an effort to find protection from the king of Ammon (see Jer. 40:14; 41:15; see also LXX Jer. 52:8).[10] The attempt to flee, however, was in vain (see Jer. 25:35; Lam. 4:20). The Chaldean army pursued Zedekiah and his soldiers, and they overtook Zedekiah in the plains of Jericho (Jer. 39:5; cf. 2 Kgs. 25:5a; Jer. 52:8a). A few Masoretic manuscripts and the Syriac add: "and as for all his army, they were scattered from him." This reference to the scattering of Zedekiah's army is also found in 2 Kings 25:5b and Jeremiah 52:8b. The Chaldean army took Zedekiah and brought him up to Nebuchadrezzar at Riblah in the land of Hamath (cf. 2 Kgs. 25:6a; Jer. 52:9a; see also 2 Kgs. 23:33). Thus, Nebuchadnezzar came to Jerusalem in the ninth year of Zedekiah (Jer. 39:1), but he was not present there in the eleventh year when his officials set up quarters in the Middle Gate (Jer. 39:2–3). When Zedekiah was brought to Nebuchadnezzar, the Babylonian king spoke "judgments" (cf. pc Mss,

---

7. McKane, *Jeremiah XXVI–LII*, 977.

8. McKane, *Jeremiah XXVI–LII*, 977.

9. In the Hebrew construction, Zedekiah is the lead member of a compound subject. Thus, the first verb is singular, and the subsequent verbs are plural (see Shepherd, "Compound Subject in Biblical Hebrew").

10. Holladay, *Jeremiah 2*, 292.

Tg. Jon. 2 Kgs. 25:6b; MT Jer. 52:9b; "judgment" [2 Kgs. 25:6b; LXX, Syr. Jer. 52:9b]) with him, which is usually understood to mean that he "passed sentence on him" (NET; cf. Jer. 1:16; 2 Chr. 24:24).

The king of Babylon slaughtered the sons of Zedekiah "before his eyes" (לעיניו), and he also slaughtered all the nobles of Judah (Jer. 39:6; cf. 2 Kgs. 25:7; Jer. 52:10; see also Jer. 21:7). As for the "eyes" (עיני) of Zedekiah, Nebuchadnezzar blinded them (or, had them blinded), although there is no indication as to how this was done (Jer. 39:7a; cf. 2 Kgs. 25:7; Jer. 52:11a; see also Ezek. 12:12–13). Jeremiah 34:3 stressed that Zedekiah's "eyes" would see Nebuchadnezzar's "eyes" (also Jer. 32:4). The text of Jeremiah 39:6–7 sets up this encounter to highlight the fact that the last thing that Zedekiah saw with his eyes before his eyes were blinded was the slaughter of his own sons (see also Deut. 28:32). There would thus be no continuation of Zedekiah's line. Nebuchadnezzar bound Zedekiah (or, had him bound) in bronze shackles to bring him to Babylon (Jer. 39:7b; cf. 2 Kgs. 25:7; Jer. 34:4–5; see Ezek. 17:20; see also 2 Kgs. 23:34). Theodotion adds that this was also "to put him in a mill house," which is similar to the LXX rendering of the last clause of Jeremiah 52:11: "and he put him in a mill house until the day that he died." MT Jeremiah 52:11 says: "and he put him in prison until the day of his death."

MT 39:8a says that the Chaldeans burned the house of the king (or, the royal palace) and "the house of the people" (בית העם) (see Jer. 22:6–7). Since the phrase בית העם ("the house of the people") has no clear referent, it is possible that this text is the result of an accidental corruption of בתי העם ("the houses of the people"), which is reflected in the Syriac translation. 2 Kings 25:9 and Jeremiah 52:13 say that Nebuzaradan burned the house of the Lord (i.e., the temple) and the house of the king (i.e., the royal palace) and all the houses of Jerusalem, including every large house (see Lam. 2:6–7; Bar. 1). MT Jeremiah 39:8b adds that the Chaldeans tore down the city walls of Jerusalem (cf. 2 Kgs. 25:10; Jer. 52:14). The Syriac, however, arranges the syntax of 39:8 differently: "And the house of the king and the houses of the people the Chaldeans burned with fire, and the wall of Jerusalem; when it [i.e., the fire] surrounded, they [i.e., the people] fled." According to this reading, the city wall was burned along with the houses; and the people fled once they were surrounded by the fire (cf. Jer. 17:27).

Jeremiah 39:9 appears to be redundant: "And the rest of the people who were left (ואת יתר העם הנשארים) in the city and the deserters/defectors who deserted/defected to him and the rest of the people who were left (ואת יתר העם הנשארים) Nebuzaradan the captain of the guard took into exile to Babylon" (see Jer. 21:9; 37:13–14; 38:19; see also

MT Jer. 52:28–30).[11] Jeremiah 52:15 has ואת יתר האמון ("and the rest of the craftsmen") in place of the second occurrence of ואת יתר העם הנשארים ("and the rest of the people who were left") (cf. 2 Kgs. 24:14). Second Kings 25:11 has ואת יתר ההמון ("and the rest of the multitude"). Nebuzaradan left some of the poor people in the land of Judah and gave them "vineyards and fields" (כְּרָמִים וִיגֵבִים) (Jer. 39:10; cf. 2 Kgs. 24:14; see also Jer. 40:7). This might give the impression that the poor became landowners, but 2 Kings 25:12 and Jeremiah 52:16 clarify that Nebuzaradan left these people "as vinedressers and plowmen" (לְכֹרְמִים וּלְיֹגְבִים) to work the land that now belonged to the Babylonians.[12]

Nebuchadrezzar gave specific instructions regarding Jeremiah through Nebuzaradan (Jer. 39:11). Thompson suggests that Jeremiah became known to the Babylonian authorities through the Judean deserters whom they pressed for information.[13] Because of his insistence upon the inevitable fall of Jerusalem to the Babylonians, Jeremiah must have appeared to some as a supporter of the Babylonians (see, e.g., Jer. 37:13; 38:4).[14] Of course, the reality was that Jeremiah believed Nebuchadnezzar to be a temporary instrument in the hand of God to serve the purpose of divine judgment (see, e.g., Jer. 27:5–8; 40:2–3). This meant that surrender and submission to the Babylonians had to be the policy for the time being until God saw fit to restore his people (see Jer. 21:9; 29:4–14; 38:17–18). The instruction concerning Jeremiah was to take him and set eyes on him (Jer. 39:12). To set eyes on someone is a Hebrew idiom for taking care of a person (BDB, 963; see Gen. 44:21; Jer. 24:6; 40:4; see also, in a negative sense, Amos 9:4). Nothing bad was to be done to Jeremiah. Whatever Jeremiah spoke, so was it to be done with him.[15] Thus, Nebuzaradan sent, along with

---

11. "Nebuzaradan" ("Nabu has given offspring") was Nebuchadnezzar's רב טבחים ("chief butcher"), a title that apparently came to mean "chief of bodyguard" (BDB, 371) or "provost marshal" (see Holladay, *Jeremiah 2*, 292–93) (cf. Gen. 37:36; 39:1; 40:3, 4; 41:10, 12; see also Dan. 2:14).

12. See McKane, *Jeremiah XXVI–LII*, 979.

13. Thompson, *Book of Jeremiah*, 648n2. See also Eupolemus Fragment 4.

14. See Holladay, *Jeremiah 2*, 293.

15. Contrary to all expectation, Nebuchadnezzar comes across as extraordinarily magnanimous in his treatment of Jeremiah. This is comparable to his behavior toward Daniel and his three friends (Dan. 2:46–49; 3:28–30). Theodoret of Cyr: "Both Nebuchadnezzar the king and Ebedmelech the Ethiopian increased the condemnation of the Jews. Although they were foreigners, they respected the prophet, but the Jews (who had been raised on the words of the prophets) did not want to pay attention to the divine

Nebushazban and Nergal Sarezer and all the chiefs of Babylon (Jer. 39:13; cf. Jer. 39:3),[16] and they took Jeremiah (Jer. 39:14).

In the MT, verse 14 is a continuation of verse 13 with its list of officials, whereas in the LXX *Vorlage* it is a continuation of verse 3 with its list of officials. Jeremiah was taken from the court of the guard (Jer. 38:28) and given to Gedaliah the son of Ahikam, the son of Shaphan (see commentary on Jer. 26:24), who was appointed governor of Judah by the king of Babylon (Jer. 40:5). According to the Hebrew source behind Greek Jeremiah, Gedaliah brought Jeremiah out, and Jeremiah lived in the midst of the people. The MT says that Jeremiah was given to Gedaliah "to bring him out to the house," but this presents an unnecessary problem with Jeremiah 40:1–6, which presupposes that Jeremiah was not in Gedaliah's house but in the midst of the people. Keil attempts to resolve the discrepancy between MT 39:11–13 and 40:1–6 by suggesting that it is due to the brevity of the narrative. When Nebuzaradan came to Jerusalem to carry out the king's instruction concerning Jeremiah, he had to take him from the crowd of those who had already been carried away to Ramah.[17] More recent commentators resolve this issue differently. Jeremiah was initially released into the general populace (Jer. 39:14) but then was erroneously rearrested, thus requiring his second release (Jer. 40:1–6).[18] The problem is that MT 39:14 does not say that Jeremiah was released into the general populace. It says that he was to be brought to the house of Gedaliah where he would live in the midst of the people. Thus, Holladay's contrast between "gave him to Gedaliah" in verse 14 and "return to Gedaliah" in 40:5 carries no force.[19] 40:5 says nothing about the house of Gedaliah. A far simpler solution to the problem at hand is to recognize that Jeremiah 39:4–13 is not part of the original text of the chapter, for which LXX Jeremiah is the primary witness. The difficulty of the two accounts in 39:11–13 and 40:1–6 does not exist in the Hebrew source behind Greek Jeremiah. Jeremiah was released from the court of the guard to Gedaliah who brought him out to live in the

---

words, but they subjected the prophets to punishment of every kind" (Wenthe, ed., *Jeremiah and Lamentations*, 237).

16. "Nebuzaradan did not reach Jerusalem (52.12; 2 Kgs 25.8) until a month after its capture and falls out of the chronological framework constructed (vv. 1–2, 4–10) for Jeremiah's release in chapter 39" (McKane, *Jeremiah XXVI–LII*, 981).
17. Keil, *Jeremiah*, 335.
18. See McKane, *Jeremiah XXVI–LII*, 985.
19. Holladay, *Jeremiah 2*, 293.

midst of the people, and in it was in the midst of the people at Ramah that Jeremiah found himself about to be taken into exile to Babylon (Jer. 40:1). From there Jeremiah was given the option to go to Babylon or to stay in the midst of the people under the governorship of Gedaliah in Judah (Jer. 40:2–6). The MT has created an unnecessary difficulty with its addition of 39:4–13.

The unit found in Jeremiah 39:15–18 (LXX 46:15–18) initially appears to be out of order. Its content suggests that it belongs after the story in 38:7–13 where Ebed Melech advocated for the retrieval of Jeremiah from the pit/cistern. Nevertheless, the present placement of the unit is probably intentional, since it speaks of the deliverance of Ebed Melech from the very attack against Jerusalem narrated in 39:1–3. In the MT, this attack is recounted in much greater detail in 39:4–10, and there is a notable contrast between the fate of Zedekiah (Jer. 39:4–7) and that of both Jeremiah (Jer. 39:11–14) and Ebed Melech (Jer. 39:15–18).

The word of the LORD came to Jeremiah not when he was taken from the court of the guard (Jer. 39:14) but when he was still in the court of the guard (Jer. 39:15 [LXX 46:15]; see Jer. 37:13; 38:28). Thus, Jeremiah was not in a position to "go and say" anything to anyone in the sense of departing the court of the guard to do so (Jer. 39:16 [LXX 46:16]). Rather, Ebed Melech had to come to him before he could perform this task (cf. Jer. 32:8). Jeremiah was to say to Ebed Melech on behalf of the LORD that he (the LORD) was about to bring his words against the city of Jerusalem for harm/calamity and not for good (cf. Jer. 18:11; 21:10; 36:3; 44:11, 27). The MT adds: "and they [i.e., the words] will happen before you in that day."

Despite the fact that Ebed Melech would witness the destruction of Jerusalem, the LORD would rescue him in that day and not give him into the hand of the men whom he feared (Jer. 39:17 [LXX 46:17]; cf. Jer. 22:25; see also *4 Bar.* 3:12–14, 21–22). Rashi understands "the men" here to be the Chaldeans, which would fit the immediate context well.[20] On the other hand, Malbim suggests that "the men" were the officials (see Jer. 38:1–6) who opposed Ebed Melech for his efforts to save Jeremiah from the pit/cistern, which would fit the context of Jeremiah 38:7–13.[21] When both contexts are taken into consideration, it seems best to interpret "the men" to be the Chaldeans, since deliverance from the officials would have meant very little if there were no subsequent deliverance from the Chaldeans. Furthermore, the language of 39:18

---

20. Rosenberg, trans., *Mikraoth Gedoloth: Jeremiah Volume Two*, 315.
21. Rosenberg, trans., *Mikraoth Gedoloth: Jeremiah Volume Two*, 315.

(LXX 46:18) strongly suggests deliverance from enemy invasion. Ebed Melech would not fall "by the sword" (cf. Jer. 20:4; 21:9; 27:8, 13; 38:2; but see also Jer. 26:23; 41:2). Because he trusted in the LORD, his life would become plunder (LXX: "and your life will be for windfall"; MT: "and you will have your life as plunder"). Blessed is the man who trusts in the LORD (Jer. 17:7). Earlier in the book, the language of having one's life as plunder referred to mere survival of the Babylonian invasion (Jer. 21:9; 38:2), but now in the case of Ebed Melech and later in the case of Baruch (Jer. 45:5) this expression takes on a different connotation. These men were members of the believing people of God who could expect to participate in the restoration envisioned in Jeremiah 30–33. Of course, this would not happen in their lifetime, but the prophecy of the future for the people of God in the Book of Comfort presupposes a hope in the resurrection (Dan. 12:1–2). It is worth noting that the two individuals of whom this is said, Ebed Melech and Baruch, were a foreigner and a native respectively, reiterating that the book's message of salvation is not only for believers from Judah and Israel but also for those from the nations (Jer. 1:5, 10; 3:17–18; 12:14–17; 16:19; 46:26 [MT]; 48:47; 49:6 [MT], 39).

APPLICATION OF JEREMIAH 34–39 (LXX 41–46)

These chapters provide readers with a contrast between covenant infidelity and covenant faithfulness (Jer. 34–35), a guide to the making of the book of Jeremiah (Jer. 36), and a picture of a persecuted yet vindicated prophet (Jer. 37–39). The interpreter's job is not to reenact the events of the narrative or to evaluate the characters independently but to follow the unique literary presentation of the stories. A conscious effort must be made not to replace the distinctive and revelatory message of the book of Jeremiah with generic lessons or principles common to world literature. Chapter 36 is a reminder in the midst of this section that the reader is not witnessing the uninterpreted events themselves but a God-given textual depiction deliberately selected and arranged for theological purposes.

Chapters 34–35 continue the development of the book's theme of covenant infidelity originally introduced in Jeremiah 1:16. The Rechabites appear as an unexpected example of faithfulness to be followed. Jeremiah's enduring faithfulness in the midst of persecution has also been a key part of the book thus far (Jer. 1:17–19; 11–20; 26), but here his persecution for the prophecy about Babylonian invasion (Jer. 37–38) is set over against his vindication in the fulfillment of the prophecy (Jer. 39). This shows the reader that God is indeed watching over his word to do it (Jer. 1:11–12), and that he is present with his prophet (Jer. 1:8, 19) and his people (Jer. 30:10–11 [MT]; 46:27–28). Those like Jeremiah who endure and remain faithful despite persecution will find that there is in fact a light at the end of the tunnel. The presence of Baruch (Jer. 36) and Ebed Melech (Jer. 38:7–13; 39:15–18) in this context is a reminder that Jeremiah represents a remnant of believers of whom the faithful readership of the book of Jeremiah now forms a part. Readers of the book can find great comfort in the fulfillment of Jeremiah's historical prophecy. It serves as a down payment on the eschatological prophecies (e.g., Jer. 30–33) and thus encourages readers to believe that Jeremiah's prophecies about the future will come to pass just as his prophecies about the past did.

JEREMIAH 40 (LXX 47)

*40:1 (47:1) The word that came from the L*ORD* to Jeremiah [MT: to Jeremiah from the L*ORD*] after Nebuzaradan the captain of the guard sent him from Damah [MT: Ramah] when he took him in manacles [MT: when he took him, and he was bound in manacles] in the midst of [MT adds: all] the exiles of Judah [MT: Jerusalem and Judah] who were being exiled to Babylon. 40:2 (47:2) And the captain of the guard took him [MT: Jeremiah; see GKC §117n] and said to him, "It was the L*ORD* your God who spoke this calamity against this place. 40:3 (47:3) And the L*ORD* did [MT: And he brought, and the L*ORD* did just as he spoke], for you [pl.] sinned against him [MT: the L*ORD*], and you [pl.] did not obey his voice, [MT adds: and this thing happened to you (pl.); see GKC §112qq]. 40:4 (47:4) Look [MT: And now, look], I have released you from the manacles that were on your hands. If it is good in your eyes to come with me to Babylon, come, and I will set my eyes [MT: eye] on you. [MT adds: And if it is bad in your eyes to come with me to Babylon, forbear. See, all the land is before you. To where it is good and upright in your eyes to go, go.] 40:5 (47:5) But if not, return and [MT: But before he could return/reply (or, But still he would not return/reply); Tg. Jon.: And if you do not want to reply] go back to Gedaliah the son of Ahikam, the son of Shaphan, whom the king of Babylon appointed over the land [MT: the cities] of Judah and live/stay with him in the midst of the people in the land of Judah [in the land of Judah > MT]. To all the good [MT: Or to all the upright] in your eyes to go, go." And the captain of the guard gave to him a portion/present [LXX: gifts; MT: a meal allowance and a portion/present; Syr.: gifts for the road] and sent him away. 40:6 (47:6) And he [MT: Jeremiah] came to Gedaliah [MT adds: the son of Ahikam] at Mizpah and lived/stayed [MT adds: with him] in the midst of the people who were left in the land.*

40:7 (47:7) And all the army officials who were in the country heard, they and their men, that the king of Babylon appointed Gedaliah [MT adds: the son of Ahikam] over the land and that he appointed with him men and their wives whom he had not exiled to Babylon [MT: men and women and children and some of the poor of the land of those who had not been exiled to Babyon]. 40:8 (47:8) And Ishmael the son of Nethaniah came to Gedaliah at Mizpah [MT: And they came to Gedaliah at Mizpah, and (or, that is,) Ishmael the son of Nethaniah], and Johanan the son of Kareah [Codex L: and Johanan and Jonathan the sons of Kareah] and Seraiah the son of Tanhumeth and the sons of Opheh [MT kethiv: Ophai; qere: Ephai] the Netophathite and Jezaniah [pc Mss: Jaazaniah] the son of the Maacathite, they and their men. 40:9 (47:9) And Gedaliah [MT adds: the son of Ahikam, the son of Shaphan,] swore to them and to their men, saying, "Do not be afraid of the servants of the Chaldeans [MT: Do not be afraid of serving the Chaldeans]. Live / Stay in the land and serve the king of Babylon, and it will be good for you. 40:10 (47:10) And as for me, look, I am living / staying before you [before you > MT] at Mizpah to stand before the Chaldeans who will come to us. And as for you, gather wine and summer fruit [Luther: figs] and olive oil and put them in your vessels and live / stay in the cities [MT: in your cities] that you have seized." 40:11 (47:11) And [MT: And also] all the Judeans who were in Moab and among the sons of Ammon and in Edom and those who were in all the land [MT: lands], they heard that the king of Babylon gave a remnant to Judah and that he appointed over them Gedaliah the son of Ahikam [MT adds: the son of Shaphan], 40:12 (47:12) [MT adds: and all the Judeans returned from all the places where they had been banished] and they came to Gedaliah in the land of Judah [MT: and they came to the land of Judah to Gedaliah] at Mizpah, and they gathered wine and very much summer fruit.

40:13 (47:13) And Johanan the son of Kareah and all the army officials who were in the country, they came to Gedaliah at Mizpah. 40:14 (47:14) And they said to him, "Do you indeed know that Baalis the king of the sons of Ammon, he sent to you Ishmael [MT adds: the son of Nethaniah] to strike you mortally?" But Gedaliah [MT adds: the son of Ahikam] did not believe them. 40:15 (47:15) And Johanan [MT adds: the son of Kareah], he said to Gedaliah in secret at Mizpah, [MT adds: saying], "Let me go and strike Ishmael [MT adds: the son of Nethaniah], and no one will know. Why should he strike you mortally [LXX: lest he strike your life], and all Judah, those gathered to you, be scattered [LXX has a sg. verb], and the remnant of Judah perish?" 40:16 (47:16) And Gedaliah [MT adds: the son of Ahikam] said to Johanan [MT adds: the son of Kareah], "Do not do this thing, for deception is what you are speaking about Ishmael."

Jeremiah 40:1 (LXX 47:1) introduces what follows as the word that came from the LORD to Jeremiah (cf. Jer. 7:1; 11:1; 18:1; 30:1; 34:1; 35:1), yet commentators have long noted that what follows does not appear to be a word from the LORD at all. *Pesiqta de Rab Kahana* suggests that this word was the instruction in verse 5 to go back to Gedaliah, without which Jeremiah would not return,[1] but there is no clear indication of

---

1. See Neusner, *Jeremiah in Talmud and Midrash*, 164; see also *Lamentations Rabbah* (Neusner, *Jeremiah in Talmud and Midrash*, 243).

this. Rashi proposes that the word from the LORD mentioned in 40:1 is the one that comes later in 42:7,[2] but it must be admitted that this is too far removed from the present context. Keil argues that just as 1:2 forms the heading for all of Jeremiah's prophecies from the thirteenth year of Josiah until the destruction of Jerusalem, so 40:1 is the superscription for his prophecies after the destruction in chapters 40–45.[3] The difficulty with this view is the fact that Jeremiah 1:1–3 is the superscription for the whole book, while 40:1 is more comparable to the many subheadings distributed throughout the book. Perhaps the most plausible suggestion is that the word from the LORD is hiding in plain sight in 40:2–3.[4] According to these verses, Jeremiah received confirmation that his prophecy of the destruction of Jerusalem had been fulfilled, but this confirmation came through an unlikely source—Nebuzaradan the captain of the guard. Contrary to Calvin's view, this does not make Nebuzaradan a prophet.[5] Rather, it makes him an unwitting vehicle of the word of the LORD to Jeremiah. The remainder of 40:1 indicates that this word from the LORD came after Nebuzaradan sent Jeremiah from "Damah" (הדמה; MT: "Ramah" [הרמה]) when he took him in manacles in the midst of the exiles of Judah who were being exiled to Babylon (see 4Q385b).[6] The following text of 40:2–5 clarifies that this means the word of the LORD came to Jeremiah after Nebuzaradan released him from the manacles.

When Nebuzaradan took Jeremiah,[7] he said to him that it was the LORD who spoke the calamity against "this place" (Jer. 40:2 [LXX 47:2]). It is not clear if "this place" refers to the temple, Jerusalem, the land of Judah, or all of the above (see the usage in Jer. 7:1–15). Of course, it was through Jeremiah that the LORD spoke the calamity (e.g., Jer. 21:10), and Nebuzaradan was likely made aware of this somehow.

---

2.   Rosenberg, trans., *Mikraoth Gedoloth: Jeremiah Volume Two*, 316.

3.   Keil, *Jeremiah*, 336.

4.   See Bright, *Jeremiah*, 244, Holladay, *Jeremiah 2*, 294.

5.   Calvin, *Jeremiah*, 4:443.

6.   Ramah in Benjamin north of Jerusalem was "a staging area for those to be exiled to Babylon" (Holladay, *Jeremiah 2*, 293–94). For the relationship of 40:1 to MT 39:11–14 (or the lack thereof), see the above commentary.

7.   The LXX *Vorlage* proposed here is ויקח אתו ("and he took him"), although it could be ויקחהו ("and he took him"). The MT ויקח . . . לירמיהו ("and he took Jeremiah") reflects the usage of ל in Aramaic and later biblical Hebrew to mark the direct object (see GKC §117n). On the other hand, it is possible that the LXX *Vorlage* had ויקח . . . לו ("and he took him"), and the MT is the result of misreading לו as לי, an abbreviation for לירמיהו.

Nebuzaradan added that the LORD "did" (MT: "And he brought, and the LORD did just as he spoke"), "for you [pl.] sinned against him [MT: the LORD], and you [pl.] did not obey his voice, [MT adds: and this thing happened to you (pl.)]" (Jer. 40:3 [LXX 47:3]; cf. Jer. 50:7).[8] This confirmed that the word of the LORD that came to Jeremiah concerning the coming calamity had come to pass. It is important to note the use of the second person plural in Nebuzaradan's discourse. Jeremiah was not personally responsible for what happened. Rather, the people of Judah and Jerusalem in general sinned against the LORD and brought judgment on themselves. At first glance this seems like an incredible expression of piety on Nebuzaradan's part to acknowledge that what has transpired has happened by the LORD's will in fulfillment of prophecy, but it is not necessary or even plausible to understand his words in this way. His words are comparable to what the Rabshakeh said to Hezekiah's officials on behalf of the king of Assyria: "And now, is it apart from the LORD that I have come up against this land to destroy it? It was the LORD who said to me, 'Go up against this land and destroy it'" (Isa. 36:10). This was a way to dishearten the people by claiming that their God had conceded victory to their enemy. While this was not true in the case of the Rabshakeh, it was in the case of Nebuzaradan insofar as the king of Babylon was the LORD's instrument to execute judgment (Jer. 27:5–8). Of course, Nebuzaradan did not look at it this way. He simply wanted to point out that it appeared as if the calamity was the will of the God of the defeated people, and his knowledge of Jeremiah's prophecy (however little he understood it) provided a convenient way to express this. Thus, Nebuzaradan spoke better than he knew (cf. John 11:49–53).

In Jeremiah 40:4–5 (LXX 47:4–5), Nebuzaradan points out to Jeremiah that he is free to go where he chooses now that he has been released from the manacles: "If it is good in your eyes to come with me to Babylon, come, and I will set my eyes [MT: eye] on you" (Jer. 40:4a; cf. MT Jer. 39:12; see also *2 Bar.* 85:3; *4 Bar.* 3:15). Some of the people would go into exile, while others would stay in the land, but Jeremiah was somewhat unique in that he was given the option to choose his fate. If he chose to go to Babylon, he had the official guarantee that he would be treated well. This must have been something of a temptation for the prophet. The remainder of verse 4 in the MT is a lengthy addition based on material in verse 5: "And if it is bad in your eyes to come with me to Babylon, forbear. See, all the land is before you. To where

---

8. The MT has obviously expanded this verse, and it reflects Aramaic influence again (see GKC §112qq).

it is good and upright in your eyes to go, go" (cf. Gen. 13:9; 20:15; 47:6; see also Josh. 24:15). The combination of אל טוב ("to good") and אל הישר ("to the upright") is a conflation of variant readings from verse 5 where the LXX *Vorlage* has אל כל הטוב ("to all the good"), and the MT has אל כל הישר ("to all the upright").[9]

The Hebrew source behind Greek Jeremiah 40:5a (LXX 47:5a), since it follows the shorter text of verse 4, simply gives the alternative to going to Babylon with Nebuzaradan: "But if not, return and go back (ואם לא שוב ושבה) to Gedaliah the son of Ahikam, the son of Shaphan, whom the king of Babylon appointed over the land [MT: cities] of Judah and live/ stay with him in the midst of the people in the land of Judah [in the land of Judah > MT]." Jeremiah could go back to Gedaliah, someone who was likely a supporter of the prophet as was his father Ahikam (see Jer. 26:24). Gedaliah had been appointed over Judah by the king of Babylon (see also 2 Kgs. 25:22; Jer. 40:7, 11). This does not mean that Jeremiah would go back to live in Gedaliah's house (contra MT Jer. 39:14). Rather, it means that he could live in the midst of the people in the land of Judah under Gedaliah's leadership. The MT, however, has at the beginning of 40:5 what appears to be a parenthetical interruption of Nebuzaradan's discourse: ועודנו לא ישוב ("But before he could return/reply"). Of course, this follows the longer text of MT 40:4 where the alternative to return to Judah has already been given. Thus, it gives the impression that Jeremiah did not have a chance to return or reply before Nebuzaradan urged him to go back to Gedaliah. Nevertheless, Nebuzaradan added, "To all the good [MT: Or to all the upright] in your eyes to go, go." He then gave to Jeremiah "a portion/present" (משאת) (Jer. 40:5b [LXX 47:5b]; cf. Gen. 43:34; Est. 2:18; Dan. 2:46; 5:17). It is not clear what the exact nature of this gift was. The MT says that Neubzaradan gave Jeremiah "a meal allowance and a portion/present" (ארחה ומשאת) (see Jer. 37:21; cf. 2 Kgs. 25:30; Jer. 52:34). McKane suggests that the MT is a conflation of two synonymous readings, which are represented separately in different Greek witnesses.[10]

Jeremiah opted to go to Gedaliah at Mizpah and stay in the midst of the people who were left in the land (Jer. 40:6 [LXX 47:6]). The text does not say why he made this choice. Mizpah was located in the land of Benjamin, which was considered part of the land of Judah (Jerusalem, the capital of Judah, was also in the land of Benjamin), not far from Ramah (Jer. 40:1).[11] Gedaliah's residence could not have

---

9. See McKane, *Jeremiah XXVI–LII*, 999.

10. McKane, *Jeremiah XXVI–LII*, 1000.

11. See Holladay, *Jeremiah 2*, 294–95.

been in Jerusalem, since the city was destroyed, and Mizpah was likely chosen because it was the most strategically located of the cities not completely devastated by the Babylonians (see Neh. 3:7).[12]

The text of Jeremiah 40:7–9 (LXX 47:7–9) is parallel to 2 Kings 25:23–24. McKane suggests that the witnesses to these two passages testify to three stages.[13] MT 2 Kings 25:23–24 has the shortest text and represents the earliest stage. The LXX *Vorlage* of Jeremiah 40:7–9 shows some expansion and thus occupies an intermediate position. MT Jeremiah 40:7–9 has the longest text and so represents the third and final stage.[14] According to Jeremiah 40:7 (LXX 47:7), all the army officials who were in the country with their men heard that the king of Babylon had appointed Gedaliah over the land (cf. 2 Kgs. 25:22–23; Jer. 40:5, 11). These were the men who scattered after Zedekiah was caught when they fled the city of Jerusalem with him (2 Kgs. 25:4–5; Jer. 39:4–5; 52:7–8). The Hebrew source behind Greek Jeremiah says that they heard that the king of Babylon had appointed with Gedaliah "men and their wives whom he had not exiled to Babylon" (cf. 2 Kgs. 25:22). The MT expands this: "men and women and children and some of the poor of the land of those who had not been exiled to Babylon" (cf. 2 Kgs. 25:12; Jer. 39:10; 52:15). Bright translates this as an appositive: "men, women, and children of the very poorest of the people."[15]

Jeremiah 40:8 (LXX 47:8) provides a list of army officials who came along with their men to Gedaliah at Mizpah (cf. 2 Kgs. 25:23; Jer. 40:13). The Hebrew source behind Greek Jeremiah presents Ishmael the son of Nethaniah as the lead figure in this list: "And Ishmael the son of Nethaniah came (ויבא) to Gedaliah at Mizpah" (cf. MT: "And they came [ויבאו] to Gedaliah at Mizpah, and [or, that is,] Ishmael the son of Nethaniah"). It is noted in Jeremiah 41:1 that Ishmael was "of the royal seed," and this may in part explain his opposition to Gedaliah (Jer. 40:13–41:3). Next in the list is Johanan the son of Kareah who plays a prominent role in the following narrative of Jeremiah 40:13–43:7. The Leningrad Codex has "Johanan and Jonathan the sons of Kareah," which Janzen explains as a conflation of variants caused by

---

12. See Thompson, *Book of Jeremiah*, 653.

13. McKane, *Jeremiah XXVI–LII*, 996.

14. On the other hand, 2 Kings 25:22–26 appears to be an abbreviation or summary of what is found in Jeremiah 40–43. It does not appear in LXX or MT Jeremiah 52. The LXX for the most part represents the original text of Jeremiah 52, which was expanded differently by 2 Kings 25 (e.g., 2 Kgs. 25:22–26) and MT Jeremiah 52 (e.g., MT Jer. 52:28–30 > LXX Jer. 52).

15. Bright, *Jeremiah*, 253.

corruption of "Johanan" to "Jonathan."[16] After Johanan is Seraiah the son of Tanhumeth. In 2 Kings 25:23, the name is "Seraiah the son of Tanhumeth the Netophathite" (see Ezra 2:22; Neh. 7:26), but witnesses to Jeremiah 40:8 interrupt the connection between "Seraiah the son of Tanhumeth" and "the Netophathite" with the insertion of the nameless "sons of Opheh/Ophai/Ephai." This insertion should probably be dropped to restore the original reading. The last man in the list is Jezaniah (pc Mss: Jaazaniah) the son of the Maacathite (see Deut. 3:14; Josh. 12:5).

When the army officials came to Gedaliah, he took an oath to represent them well before the Chaldeans (Jer. 40:9–10 [LXX 47:9–10]; cf. 2 Kgs. 25:24). Gedaliah prefaced this oath by urging the army officials to submit to Babylonian rule: "Do not be afraid of the servants (מֵעַבְדֵי) of the Chaldeans [MT: Do not be afraid of serving (מֵעֲבוֹד) the Chaldeans]. Live/Stay in the land and serve the king of Babylon, and it will be good for you" (Jer. 40:9; see BDB, 405). According to Gedaliah, the officials did not need to fear retaliation from the Chaldeans. Things would go well for them if only they would be content to stay in the land and not rebel against the king of Babylon. This advice is reminiscent of Jeremiah's words to the Babylonian exiles to accept the fate that they had brought upon themselves and to wait upon what the LORD had in store for the future (Jer. 29:4–7, 10–14). It also anticipates Jeremiah's counsel to the army officials in response to their inquiry about leaving the land of Judah (and Babylonian rule) to go to Egypt (Jer. 42:10).

For Gedaliah's part, he would stay at Mizpah to mediate between the Chaldeans and the army officials: "to stand before the Chaldeans who will come to us" (Jer. 40:10a).[17] As for the officials, they were encouraged to gather wine and summer fruit (i.e., figs and dates) and olive oil and put them in their vessels (Jer. 40:10b). McKane notes that this refers not to harvesting but to expropriation of produce already harvested.[18] That is, the officials were to take stores abandoned by those who had been displaced. These would come from cities depopulated due to the Babylonian invasion and since seized by the Judean army officials, cities in which the officials and their men were now to stay and take up residence.

In addition to the army officials, the Judeans who were in Moab and among the sons of Ammon and in Edom and those who were in all

---

16. Janzen, *Studies in the Text of Jeremiah*, 17.
17. Greek witnesses have ὑμᾶς ("you") instead of ἡμᾶς ("us") as in Ziegler's text, but this may only be the result of itacism (i.e., the ancient pronunciation of the initial letters of both words as iota).
18. McKane, *Jeremiah XXVI–LII*, 1002.

the land (MT: "lands") heard that the king of Babylon had given a remnant to Judah and had appointed Gedaliah over them (Jer. 40:11 [LXX 47:11]; cf. Jer. 40:5, 7). These were Judeans who fled east of the Jordan and elsewhere when the Babylonians invaded (see Jer. 27:3; 40:15; 41:10, 15; 43:5; 48–49). Now it seemed safe for them to return. The MT adds at the beginning of 40:12 (LXX 47:12) that all the Judeans returned from all the places where they had been banished (cf. Deut. 30:4; Neh. 1:9). The LXX *Vorlage* simply begins this verse by narrating that those Judeans mentioned in verse 11 came to Gedaliah in the land of Judah at Mizpah (MT: "and they came to the land of Judah to Gedaliah at Mizpah"). When they arrived, they gathered wine and very much summer fruit (Jer. 40:12b). The instruction to do so was originally given to the army officials and their men (Jer. 40:10), but the Judeans apparently joined them in their efforts.

At first glance, Jeremiah 40:13 (LXX 47:13) may appear in English translation to be a repetition of 40:8, but 40:13 does not continue the sequence of narration from 40:7–12. Whereas 40:8 has a *wayyiqtol* verbal form (LXX *Vorlage*: "And Ishmael the son of Nethaniah came [ויבא] to Gedaliah at Mizpah"; MT: "And they came [ויבאו] to Gedaliah at Mizpah, and [or, that is,] Ishmael the son of Nethaniah"), the text of 40:13 has an "x + *qatal*" clause with a fronted subject: "And Johanan the son of Kareah and all the army officials who were in the country, they came (באו) to Gedaliah at Mizpah." Thus, 40:13 backtracks to a previous point in the narration (40:8) where the officials came to Gedaliah at Mizpah. This time, however, Johanan rather than Ishmael appears as the lead figure, and it becomes apparent from the following verses why this is so.

Johanan and the other officials asked Gedaliah, "Do you indeed know that Baalis the king of the sons of Ammon, he sent to you Ishmael [MT adds: the son of Nethaniah] to strike you mortally" (Jer. 40:14a [LXX 47:14a])? Keil comments that Baalis' motive in this cannot be determined with any degree of certainty, but he speculates that it may have been hostility toward Gedaliah or the hope of destroying any remaining support for the Judeans with a view toward obtaining possession of the country for the Ammonites.[19] He adds that the choice of Ishmael may have been due to his connection to the royal family (Jer. 41:1). Ishmael may have resented the fact that Gedaliah was appointed to be his leader. As a member of the royal family, he likely resisted subordination to someone else. He may also have disagreed with Gedaliah's policy of submission to the Babylonians. Ishmael eventually

---

19. Keil, *Jeremiah*, 339.

fled to Ammon and thus lived "opposite" his brethren (Jer. 41:10, 15; cf. Gen. 16:11–12). Gedaliah, however, did not believe what Johanan and the others were telling him about Ishmael (Jer. 40:14b [LXX 47:14b]). It is not clear whether this was because such a heinous act committed by a fellow Judean was inconceivable to Gedaliah or because Gedaliah was the type of person who gave everyone the benefit of the doubt. It is also possible that Gedaliah suspected that there was jealousy toward Ishmael due to his unique status as a member of the royal family.

Jeremiah 40:15 (LXX 47:15) does not continue the sequence of narration from verse 14 with a *wayyiqtol* verbal form. It begins with an inverted "x + *qatal*" clause with a fronted subject: "And Johanan [MT adds: the son of Kareah], he said to Gedaliah in secret at Mizpah, [MT adds: saying]" (cf. Jer. 37:17; 38:16). This provides background information to what is narrated in verse 14. Whereas Johanan came with other officials to inform Gedaliah of what Baalis sent Ishmael to do (Jer. 40:14), he met with Gedaliah privately to propose a solution to the problem: "Let me go and strike Ishmael [MT adds: the son of Nethaniah], and no one will know" (Jer. 40:15a). Johanan would strike Ishmael before Ishmael could strike Gedaliah, and he would do it in such way that the act could not be traced back to Gedaliah.[20] Johanan added that this was not merely for Gedaliah's sake but for the sake of all the remnant of Judah: "Why should he strike you mortally [LXX: lest he strike your life], and all Judah, those gathered to you, be scattered [LXX has a sg. verb], and the remnant of Judah perish" (Jer. 40:15b; see again Jer. 40:11)? The survival of the fledgling remnant of Judah depended upon the stability of Gedaliah's leadership for the time being. Assassination of a Babylonian appointed leader would presumably be received as rebellion against Babylonian rule. This would lead to panic among the Judeans, and indeed the subsequent chapters of the book of Jeremiah reveal that the community sought to flee to Egypt. Thus, there was a great deal more at stake than Gedaliah may have considered, and Johanan made a convincing case for his proposed course of action. Nevertheless, Gedaliah forbade Johanan to do this thing and insisted that what he was saying about Ishmael was not true (Jer. 40:16 [LXX 47:16]). Jeremiah 40–44 consistently shows that not all was well in Judah despite the fact that the Babylonian invasion was in the rearview mirror. The fulfillment of Jeremiah's prophecy of judgment did little to change the hearts of the people, showing the need for the transformation envisioned in Jeremiah 30–33.

---

20. The irony is that Ishmael would kill Gedaliah without anyone knowing at first (Jer. 41:4).

JEREMIAH 41 (LXX 48)

*41:1 (48:1) And then, in the seventh month, Ishmael the son of Nethaniah, the son of Eleasa [MT: Elishama], from the royal seed [MT adds: and the chief officers of the king], came, and ten men with him, to Gedaliah [MT adds: the son of Ahikam] at Mizpah, and they ate there bread together [MT adds: at Mizpah]. 41:2 (48:2) And Ishmael [MT adds: the son of Nethaniah] arose, and the ten men who were with him, and they struck Gedaliah [MT adds: the son of Ahikam, the son of Shaphan, with the sword, and he (Syr., Vulg.: they) killed him], whom the king of Babylon appointed over the land, 41:3 (48:3) and all the Judeans who were with him [MT adds: with Gedaliah] at Mizpah and all [all > MT] the Chaldeans who were found there. [MT adds: The soldiers (nonn Mss: And the soldiers) Ishmael struck.] 41:4 (48:4) And then, on the second day of killing Gedaliah, and no one knew [> Syr.], 41:5 (48:5) men came from Shechem and from Salem [MT: from Shiloh] and from Samaria, eighty men, with beards shaved and clothes torn and flesh cut, and a grain offering and frankincense were in their hand to bring to the house of the L*ORD*. *41:6 (48:6) And Ishmael [MT adds: the son of Nethaniah] went out to meet them [MT adds: from Mizpah]. They were weeping as they went [MT: He was weeping as he went]. And he said to them [MT: As soon as he met them, he said to them], "Come in to Gedaliah [MT adds: the son of Ahikam]." 41:7 (48:7) And then, as soon as they came into the midst of the city, he [MT: Ishmael the son of Nethaniah] slaughtered them [Syr. adds: and cast them] into [MT adds: the midst of] the pit / cistern, [MT adds: he and the men who were with him]. 41:8 (48:8) And there were ten men found there [MT: among them] who said to Ishmael, "Do not kill us, for we have hidden stores in the field: wheat and barley, honey and olive oil [MT: and olive oil and honey]." And he forbore and did not kill them in the midst of their brothers / fellows. 41:9 (48:9) And the pit / cistern where Ishmael cast all those he struck was a large pit / cistern that King Asa made because of Baasha the king of Israel [MT: And the pit / cistern where Ishmael cast all the corpses of the men whom he struck beside Gedaliah, it was the one that King Asa made because of Baasha the king of Israel]. That is what Ishmael [MT adds: the son of Nethaniah] filled with slain men. 41:10 (48:10) And Ishmael turned away [MT: took captive] all the people who were left [MT: all the remnant of the people who were] in Mizpah and [and > Codex L] the royal daughters [(and) the royal daughters > Syr.; MT adds: and all the people who were left in Mizpah (> Syr.)] whom [MT adds: Nebuzaradan] the captain of the guard appointed Gedaliah the son of Ahikam. [MT adds: And Ishmael the son of Nethaniah took them* *captive (pc Mss, LXX*[OL]*: arose early).] And he went to the region beyond [MT: to cross over to] the sons of Ammon.*

41:11 (48:11) And Johanan the son of Kareah heard, and all the army officials who were with him, all the evil that Ishmael [MT adds: the son of Nethaniah] did [Syr.: all the captivity that Ishmael the son of Nethaniah took]. 41:12 (48:12) And they took all their army [MT: all the men] and went to fight with him [MT: Ishmael the son of Nethaniah], and they found him by the great waters [Tg. Jon.: by the pool of great waters] at Gibeon [MT: that were at Gibeon]. 41:13 (48:13) And then, as soon as all the people who were with Ishmael saw Johanan [MT adds: the son of Kareah] and [MT adds: all] the army officials who were with him, [MT adds: they rejoiced,] 41:14 (48:14) [MT adds: and all the people whom Ishmael took captive from Mizpah turned and] they returned [MT adds: and went] to Johanan [MT adds: the son of Kareah]. 41:15 (48:15) And as for Ishmael [MT adds: the son of Nethaniah], he escaped with eight men from Johanan, and he went to the sons of Ammon. 41:16 (48:16) And Johanan [MT adds: the son of Kareah] took, and all the army officials who were with him, all the rest of the people whom he brought back from Ishmael [MT adds: the son of Nethaniah from Mizpah after he struck Gedaliah the son of Ahikam]—mighty men [Codex L: men], the soldiers, and women and children [LXX: the rest] and officials [LXX: eunuchs] whom he brought back from Gibeon. 41:17 (48:17) And they went and stayed at Gabberoth Kimham [MT: at Geruth Kimham; Syr.: at the threshing floor of Bimham; Tg. Jon.: at Geruth, which David gave to Kimham the son of Barzillai the Gileadite; Vulg.: as sojourners in Kimham; Luther: at the lodge of Kimham], which was near Bethlehem, to go to Egypt [MT: to go to enter Egypt] 41:18 (48:18) because of the Chaldeans, for they were afraid of them, for Ishmael [MT adds: the son of Nethaniah] struck Gedaliah [MT adds: the son of Ahikam] whom the king of Babylon appointed over the land.

Chapter 41 (LXX 48) is a continuation of the narrative in chapter 40 (LXX 47). There is thus no reason to assume that a large period of time has transpired in the illusion of a gap created by the artificial chapter division. Textual witnesses vary as to whether Jeremiah 39:2 refers to the fourth or fifth month of Zedekiah's eleventh year (cf. 2 Kgs. 25:8; Jer. 1:3; 52:12; Zech. 8:19), but the most natural reading of 41:1 is that it refers to the seventh month of that same year. The lack of an explicit year in 41:1 is not an invitation to supply one in an exegetical free for all (e.g., Jer. 52:30). Rather, the reason that the year is not given is because it remains the same and does not need to be repeated. Two or three months would have been sufficient time for the events narrated in chapters 39 and 40 to occur. The very concise version of the story of Jeremiah 41 found in 2 Kings 25:25–26 seems also to presuppose that the seventh month was that of the same year (2 Kgs. 25:8). This month was eventually commemorated with fasting (Zech. 7:5; 8:19).

Ishmael is identified here not only as the son of Nethaniah (as in Jer. 40:8) but also as the grandson of Eleasa (MT: Elishama) from the royal seed. According to Redak, the rabbis say that this is the Elishama mentioned in 1 Chronicles 2:41.[1] Keil, on the other hand, suggests that this Elishama was either the secretary of state mentioned in Jeremiah 36:12 or the son of David by that name (2 Sam. 5:16; 1 Chr. 3:8; 14:7).[2] Both "Ishmael" and "Elishama" mean "God hears." The LXX, however, has "Eleasa" ("God makes") instead of "Elishama." This Eleasa could either have been the descendant of Judah mentioned in 1 Chronicles 2:39, 40 or the son of Shaphan mentioned in Jeremiah 29:3. The royal lineage of Ishmael likely provides some insight into why he agreed to be sent by the Ammonite king Baalis to assassinate Gedaliah (Jer. 40:14).[3] He may have taken exception to being passed over by the Babylonian authorities in favor of Gedaliah. This may have in turn led to a lack of regard for Babylonian rule. While Baalis and Ishmael may not have had the same intentions or goals, the assassination of Gedaliah was apparently thought to serve both their interests.

The addition of "and the chief officers of the king" in the MT is very awkward, and its intended role in the syntax of verse 1 is not clear. This text does not appear in the LXX *Vorlage* or in 2 Kings 25:25. English translations typically interpret the addition as if it were "and from the chief officers of the king" so that Ishmael is said to be from the royal family and one of the royal officers, but the present state of the

---

1. "In verse 26, it is mentioned that Jerachmeel, the first-born of Hezron, married a woman named Atarah, a gentile woman whom he took 'to crown himself with.' Hence the name Atarah, a *crown*. She was of a royal family, into which Jerachmeel married to gain prestige. She was a forebear of Ishmael. Thus, he was descended from proselytes" (Rosenberg, trans., *Mikraoth Gedoloth: Jeremiah Volume Two*, 321). Redak also notes that an emancipated Egyptian slave is found among Ishmael's forebears (1 Chr. 2:34–35; cf. Gen. 16:1).

2. Keil, *Jeremiah*, 339.

3. The voice of the speaker in Psalm 89:39–52 (Eng., 89:38–51) reflects a fundamental misunderstanding of how the terms of the covenant with David applied to the sons of David (see Calvin, *Jeremiah*, 4:460; Shepherd, *Text in the Middle*, 122–29). Ishmael presumably had a similar mindset about his royal privileges.

MT gives the impression that the chief officers of the king are a distinct group compounded with Ishmael (the leader) and the ten men who were with him. The problem is that this group of officers is not mentioned again in the subsequent narrative. Another option is that the addition in the MT is either a variant of "from the royal seed" or a variant of "and ten men with him."[4] Ishmael came with his ten men to Gedaliah at Mizpah, and they all ate bread together there. Gedaliah welcomed Ishmael and his men as his guests despite Johanan's previous warning about Ishmael (Jer. 40:14). Ishmael was able to take advantage of this lack of suspicion and preparedness, which created a situation wherein he could slaughter his victims and take a large group of people hostage fairly easily and with a relatively small number of men.

Ishmael and the ten men who were with him arose and struck Gedaliah (Jer. 41:2 [LXX 48:2]; cf. 2 Kgs. 25:25).[5] The MT adds that Gedaliah was "the son of Ahikam, the son of Shaphan" and that it was with the sword that they struck him (> LXX and 2 Kgs. 25:25). The last clause of the addition says that "he" (Syr., Vulg.: "they") killed him (וַיְמֶת אֹתוֹ), stressing that it was Ishmael in particular who killed Gedaliah. The text of 2 Kings 25:25, however, has וַיָּמֹת ("and he died"). The designation of Gedaliah as the one "whom the king of Babylon appointed over the land" (cf. Jer. 40:5, 7, 11) is repeated at the end of the chapter (Jer. 41:18) to explain why the Judeans feared the Chaldeans in the wake of Gedaliah's assassination and thus sought to flee to Egypt.

Verse 3 indicates that Ishmael and his men also struck "all the Judeans who were with him" (MT adds: "with Gedaliah") at Mizpah (cf. 2 Kgs. 25:25b). This cannot mean all the Judeans in Mizpah (see Jer. 41:10). It may refer only to the Judeans who were present with Gedaliah at the meal in Mizpah. The text of verse 3 also says that Ishmael and his men struck "all [all > MT] the Chaldeans who were found there" (cf. 2 Kgs. 25:25b). Bright suggests that these Chaldeans were either the ones stationed at Mizpah or those who happened to be present at the meal.[6] The addition at the end of MT 41:3 ("The soldiers [nonn Mss: And the soldiers] Ishmael struck"), which does not

---

4. See the discussion in McKane, *Jeremiah XXVI–LII*, 1013–14. McKane also mentions and rejects Barthélemy's view that "from the royal seed" and "and the chief officers of the king" describe Elishama rather than Ishmael.
5. See Shepherd, "Compound Subject in Biblical Hebrew." LXX 2 Kings 25:25 reflects וַיַּךְ ("and he struck") rather than ויכו ("and they struck").
6. Bright adds, "But Ishmael would certainly have had to dispose of all Chaldean troops in the town. Presumably the detachment was small and could be taken by surprise" (Bright, *Jeremiah*, 254).

appear in the LXX *Vorlage* or in 2 Kings 25:25b, is usually worked into the syntax of English versions in such a way that it refers only to the Chaldeans as soldiers. It is possible, however, that this addition was designed to clarify in light of verse 10 that both the Judeans and the Chaldeans struck by Ishmael and his men were soldiers and not members of the general populace (see also the commentary on Jer. 41:16b).[7]

The phrase "on the second day of killing Gedaliah" in 41:4 (LXX 48:4) likely means "the day after the murder of Gedaliah" rather than "two days after the murder of Gedaliah." At this early moment after the event, no one outside of Mizpah knew about Ishmael's assassination of Gedaliah ("and no one knew" > Syr.). Of course, Johanan had anticipated that something like this would happen (Jer. 40:14) and had suggested a preemptive strike of Ishmael that no one would know about (Jer. 40:15). Gedaliah did not believe Johanan or allow him to do what he proposed (Jer. 40:14b, 16) and thus ironically became the victim (at the hands of Ishmael) of the very act that he forbade Johanan to commit against Ishmael. Ishmael struck Gedaliah without anyone knowing about it (at least initially).

It was on the day after the murder of Gedaliah when no one outside of Mizpah yet knew about it that eighty men came from Shechem, Salem (MT: Shiloh), and Samaria (Jer. 41:5 [LXX 48:5]). Since "Salem" is short for "Jerusalem" (see Ps. 76:3 [Eng., 76:2]), it is likely that ומשלם ("and from Salem") in the Hebrew source behind Greek Jeremiah is a corruption of the more original reading משלו ("from Shiloh") found in the MT. Otherwise, men came from Jerusalem to go to Jerusalem, which is nonsensical. Shechem, Shiloh, and Samaria had each been prominent cities in the north both religiously and politically. People living in these locations had participated in the reforms of Hezekiah (2 Chr. 30:1, 11) and Josiah (2 Kgs. 23:15, 19–20; 2 Chr. 34:6, 9) and presumably continued to celebrate Passover in the first month and Tabernacles in the seventh month (see Jer. 41:1) with trips to Jerusalem (see Deut. 16:16–17). The men in Jeremiah 41:5, however, did not come prepared for festivities but "with beards shaved and clothes torn and flesh cut." Shaved heads and torn clothes were common outward expressions of mourning (see Mic. 1:16; Job 1:20; Est. 4:1; Ezra 9:3; but see Lev. 19:27; see also the rule for priests in Lev. 21:5), but cutting the flesh was considered a pagan practice and was forbidden by the law (Deut. 14:1; 1 Kgs. 18:28; Jer. 16:6). It is possible that these men were simply ignorant of the prohibition. They very likely intended to mourn the devastation of Jerusalem (see Zech. 7:1–5; 8:18–19). There is no

---

7. See McKane, *Jeremiah XXVI–LII*, 1017–18.

indication that they intended to stop at Mizpah to see Gedaliah. In all likelihood, they were merely passing by or through Mizpah on their way to Jerusalem when Ishmael stopped them. They wanted to bring an offering "to the house of the LORD" not because they were unaware that the temple had been destroyed but because they still had regard for the former site of the temple (cf. Dan. 6:11 [Eng., 6:10]).[8] Their offering consisted of "a grain offering and frankincense" (מנחה ולבונה), two words frequently combined in the Hebrew Bible (see Lev. 2:1, 2, 15, 16; 6:8; Isa. 43:23; 66:3; Jer. 17:26; Neh. 13:5, 9).

According to 41:6 (LXX 48:6), Ishmael went out to meet the eighty pilgrims (MT adds: "from Mizpah"). There is no explanation of Ishmael's motive in taking this course of action. Perhaps Ishmael thought that these men were coming to see Gedaliah and thus concluded that he must dispose of them before his assassination of Gedaliah became known. The problem is that there is no evidence from the text that the eighty men ever wanted to enter the city of Mizpah on their way to Jerusalem. Readers of this narrative might expect Ishmael to flee unnoticed to Ammonite territory at this point in the story after accomplishing his mission (Jer. 40:14a; 41:10b, 15b). The text does not explain Ishmael's strange behavior. It only narrates his actions. According to the Hebrew source behind Greek Jeremiah, the pilgrims were weeping as they went (cf. 2 Sam. 3:16; Jer. 50:4). The MT, however, says that Ishmael was weeping as he went to meet them. This depicts Ishmael attempting to deceive the pilgrims by feigning empathy. His invitation to come into the city to see Gedaliah thus appeared to come from someone who understood them and supported them on behalf of their newly appointed leader Gedaliah.

As soon as the men entered the city, Ishmael slaughtered them (Jer. 41:7 [LXX 48:7]). The addition at the end of verse 7 in the MT clarifies that Ishmael did not do this alone. He and the ten men who were with him slaughtered the pilgrims. Verse 8 further clarifies that they only slaughtered seventy of the eighty men. Ten men were spared. It must be kept in mind that Ishmael and his men had the element of surprise on their side, and that the pilgrims were unarmed and unprepared to defend themselves against such an attack. Both the LXX *Vorlage* and the MT say that Ishmael slaughtered the men "into [MT adds: the midst of] the pit/cistern." While it is possible that the slaughter took place inside the pit/cistern itself (cf. 2 Sam. 23:20; 1 Chr. 11:22), a comparison with verse 9 suggests that there is an ellipsis in

---

8. See the discussion in Rosenberg, trans., *Mikraoth Gedoloth: Jeremiah Volume Two*, 322; Calvin, *Jeremiah*, 4:463; Keil, *Jeremiah*, 340.

verse 7. The Syriac supplies this missing information when it says that Ishmael slaughtered them "and cast them" into the pit/cistern. This must have been a rather large pit/cistern (cf. Jer. 37:16; 38:6; see also Jer. 41:9 [LXX 48:9]). Ten of the eighty men pleaded with Ishmael not to kill them and explained that they had hidden stores of "wheat and barley, honey and olive oil [MT: and olive oil and honey]" (Jer. 41:8a [LXX 48:8a]; cf. Jer. 40:10b, 12b). This persuaded Ishmael to spare their lives, and he did not kill them along with their fellow pilgrims (Jer. 41:8b [LXX 48:8b]). It is not clear, however, why Ishmael would have had an interest in such hidden stores. Did he plan to take them with him to Ammonite territory (Jer. 40:14a; 41:10b, 15b)?

Jeremiah 41:9 (LXX 48:9) provides background information regarding the pit/cistern into which Ishmael cast the bodies of the seventy men whom he struck. The text of the first half of this verse differs between the Hebrew source behind Greek Jeremiah and the MT. According to the former, it says, "And the pit/cistern where Ishmael cast all those he struck (כל אשר הכה) was a large pit/cistern (בור גדול הוא) that King Asa made because of Baasha the king of Israel." This version explains how Ishmael was able to deposit such a large number of bodies in the pit/cistern. It was "a large pit/cistern" (בור גדול). In the MT, however, the text says, "And the pit/cistern where Ishmael cast all the corpses of the men whom he struck (כל פגרי האנשים אשר הכה) beside Gedaliah (ביד גדליהו), it (הוא) was the one that King Asa made because of Baasha the king of Israel." This version does not make reference to "a large pit/cistern" (בור גדול) but refers to the corpses of the men whom Ishmael struck "beside Gedaliah" (ביד גדליהו). The Talmud explains this phrase to mean "through the agency of Gedaliah" (b. Nid. 61a). That is, because Gedaliah ignored Johanan's warning about Ishmael (Jer. 40:14–16), it was as if he had been responsible for the deaths of the pilgrims. It is more likely, however, that the phrase either indicates that the seventy men were slaughtered "along with Gedaliah" or that their bodies were cast "alongside Gedaliah."[9] Up to this point in the narrative, there has been no reference to where Ishmael deposited the body of Gedaliah or the bodies of the Judeans and Chaldeans whom he killed (Jer. 41:2–3).

The significance of the pit/cistern being the one that King Asa made because of Baasha king of Israel is not immediately evident. The inclusion of this information may be for no other reason than to provide a point of reference: "That is what Ishmael [MT adds: the son of

---

9. For the former view, see Redak in Rosenberg, trans., *Mikraoth Gedoloth: Jeremiah Volume Two*, 323; for the latter, see Keil, *Jeremiah*, 342.

Nethaniah] filled with slain men" (Jer. 41:9b [LXX 48:9b]). The biblical narrative about King Asa's relationship to Baasha does not mention such a pit/cistern (1 Kgs. 15:16–22; cf. 2 Chr. 16:1–16). It recounts how Baasha built or fortified Ramah to prevent "going out and coming in" to Asa when he and Asa were at war with one another (1 Kgs. 15:16–17). Asa then bribed the king of Syria to break his treaty with Baasha, which led to the cessation of Baasha's efforts to build or fortify Ramah (1 Kgs. 15:18–21). Asa subsequently used the stones and wood that Baasha had used to build Ramah in order to build Geba and Mizpah (1 Kgs. 15:22). It was perhaps during this building of Mizpah that the large pit/cistern was made.[10]

The beginning of 41:10a (LXX 48:10a) in the Hebrew source behind Greek Jeremiah says, "And Ishmael turned away (וַיָּשָׁב) all the people who were left (כל העם הנשארים) in Mizpah." The MT says, "And Ishmael took captive (וַיִּשְׁבְּ) all the remnant of the people who were (כל שארית העם אשר) in Mizpah" (cf. Jer. 40:11; 41:16). The MT later adds superfluously "and all the people who were left (כל העם הנשארים) in Mizpah" (> LXX, Syr.). It is evident that "all the remnant of the people" (כל שארית העם) and "all the people who were left" (כל העם הנשארים) were variant readings that have been preserved in the conflated text of the MT.[11] The people who were left in Mizpah consisted of men, women, and children and some of the poor of the land (see Jer. 39:10; 40:7). Also included in this group were the royal daughters (see also Jer. 43:6; cf. Jer. 39:6). The Syriac does not include the royal daughters in its translation of verse 10a, and there is some question as to why the royal daughters would have been left with the poor. Calvin comments, "But it is probable that some of the king's daughters had escaped when the city was besieged; for Ishmael himself was of the royal seed, but he had escaped before the city

---

10. Malbim offers a different explanation: "*Malbim* explains that Baasa built Ramah to prevent his people from performing the three pilgrimages to the Temple. The route to Jerusalem was through Mizpah, where Asa stationed his army to protect the pilgrims and to battle against Baasa's troops. He dug a pit to supply his army with water. Now, that very pit that had been used to benefit the pilgrims going to the house of the Lord, was now used to cast into it the corpses of those going to the house of the Lord" (Rosenberg, trans., *Mikraoth Gedoloth: Jeremiah Volume Two*, 323).

11. "It is to be noted that 𝔊 translates the *second* of the two variants, but in the place occupied by the *first*, agreeing with the first variant on the proper place of the clause" (Janzen, *Studies in the Text of Jeremiah*, 17). Janzen argues that the first variant in the MT is the original text, but McKane contends that the LXX *Vorlage* is more original (McKane, *Jeremiah XXVI–LII*, 1015).

was taken."[12] It is not clear whose daughters they were, but they were members of the royal family. These were the people whom the captain of the guard appointed Gedaliah (see Jer. 40:11). Bright suggests that Jeremiah was likely present among this group of people since he was with them near Bethlehem after their rescue (Jer. 42:2).[13] It is possible that Baruch was with them as well (see Jer. 43:6).

The MT adds in 41:10b (LXX 48:10b), "And Ishmael the son of Nethaniah took them captive (וישבם) [pc Mss, LXX[OL]: arose early (וישכם)]." This is an unnecessary repetition of the first part of the verse in the MT unless the reading וישכם ("arose early") is followed. The Hebrew source behind Greek Jeremiah concludes verse 10 by saying that Ishmael went "to the region beyond the sons of Ammon" (לְעֵבֶר בני עמון), which suggests that Ammonite territory was not his final destination, whereas the MT says that he went "to cross over to the sons of Ammon" (לְעֲבֹר אל בני עמון) (see Jer. 40:11, 14; 41:15). Ishmael sought to return to the Ammonite king Baalis who sent him to assassinate Gedaliah (Jer. 40:14). It is somewhat of a mystery why Ishmael would want to burden himself with hostages and take them to the land of Ammon. Perhaps he did not want to leave any witnesses, but it was inevitable that what had happened in Mizpah would eventually become known (see Jer. 41:11). It may very well be that it is an intentional feature of this narrative to depict Ishmael in such a way that his actions do not make sense. In other words, the reader is supposed to conclude that Ishmael's behavior was irrational.

Johanan, and all the army officials who were with him, heard about all the evil that Ishmael committed (Syr.: "all the captivity that Ishmael the son of Nethaniah took") (Jer. 41:11 [LXX 48:11]). The text does not say how this report reached them. Johanan and the other army officials were the ones who first suspected that Ishmael might do something like this (Jer. 40:13–16). Thus, they may have required only a few details and were then able to fill in the rest of the story based on what they had anticipated would happen all along. They took their army (MT: "all the men") and went to fight with Ishmael, and they found him by the great waters (*Tg. Jon.*: "by the pool of great waters") at Gibeon (Jer. 41:12 [LXX 48:12]). *Targum Jonathan* apparently derives its rendering from the reference to the pool of Gibeon in 2 Samuel 2:13. It has been noted that Ishmael's movement from Mizpah to Gibeon was rather circuitous for someone who was en route to Ammonite territory. Bright suggests that this was either "to throw

---

12. Calvin, *Jeremiah*, 4:470.
13. Bright, *Jeremiah*, 255.

off pursuit, or for other reasons unknown to us."[14] Again, it is possible that commentators have given Ishmael too much credit. The depiction of his character thus far in the narrative strongly implies that he was not thinking too well at all at this point.

The Hebrew source behind Greek Jeremiah has a considerably shorter version of verses 13 and 14: "And then, as soon as all the people who were with Ishmael saw Johanan and the army officials who were with him, they returned to Johanan." The MT not only adds "the son of Kareah" with both occurrences of the name "Johanan" and the qualifier "all" with "the army officials" but also adds "they rejoiced" at the end of verse 13 and a lengthy, redundant repetition of the subject at the beginning of verse 14 ("and all the people whom Ishmael took captive from Mizpah turned"). The MT also expands "they returned to Johanan" in verse 14 to "they returned and went to Johanan." These additions in the MT are all quite superfluous and unnecessary. Only the indication of the people's emotional reaction ("they rejoiced") adds anything of substance to the narrative.

Jeremiah 41:15 (LXX 48:15) is the last of what the reader sees of Ishmael in the story: "And as for Ishmael [MT adds: the son of Nethaniah], he escaped with eight men from Johanan, and he went to the sons of Ammon." The narrative does not go into detail about how Ishmael managed to escape. The fact that he escaped with only eight men rather than the original ten (Jer. 41:1) may indicate that two of the men either abandoned Ishmael or were killed in the fighting (Jer. 41:12), although the narrative does not specify that any fighting actually took place. Ishmael fled to take refuge in Ammonite territory, having accomplished the mission for which he was sent (i.e., the assassination of Gedaliah) by the Ammonite king Baalis (Jer. 40:14; 41:10b). Much like Ishmael the son of Abram by Hagar, this Ishmael the son of Nethaniah would have to live out the rest of his days "opposite" his brethren (see Gen. 16:11–12).[15]

Johanan, along with all the army officials who were with him, took "all the rest of the people whom he brought back from Ishmael"

---

14. Bright, *Jeremiah*, 255.

15. Calvin answers the question of why Ishmael was allowed to escape with an appeal to Psalm 59:12 (Eng., 59:11): "The Psalmist there asks God not to destroy immediately the wicked; for an oblivion of a remarkable punishment might easily creep in, if God executed it suddenly and instantly. But when God impresses a mark of his curse on the impious and the wicked, and prolongs their life, it is the same as though he placed them in a theatre to be looked on leisurely and for a long time" (Calvin, *Jeremiah*, 473).

(Jer. 41:16a [LXX 48:16a]; cf. Jer. 40:11; 41:10). The MT adds to this that Johanan took the people whom he brought back from Ishmael "the son of Nethaniah from Mizpah after he struck Gedaliah the son of Ahikam." This insertion is somewhat awkward because it gives the surface impression that Johanan took the people back to Mizpah after he rescued them at Gibeon and then departed from there (i.e., Mizpah). It is likely, however, that it was meant to say that this group of people originated at Mizpah. In other words, Johanan took the people whom he brought back from Ishmael who took the people from Mizpah after he struck Gedaliah.[16]

The people brought back by Johanan are listed as follows: "mighty men (הַגִּבּוֹרִים) [Codex L: men (הַגְּבָרִים)], the soldiers, and women and children [LXX: the rest] and officials [LXX: eunuchs] whom he brought back from Gibeon" (Jer. 41:16b [LXX 48:16b]). Rudolph (*BHS* apparatus) suggests that אנשי המלחמה ("the soldiers") is a gloss for גברים, indicating that it should be read as גִּבֹּרִים or גִּבּוֹרִים ("mighty men") rather than גְּבָרִים ("men"). If, however, verse 3 indicates that Ishmael killed the Judean soldiers at Mizpah (see above), then this gloss cannot be correct. גברים should be interpreted as "men," and the gloss should be removed.[17] Thus, the people consisted of "men and women and children" (cf. Jer. 40:7; 43:6; 44:20). The LXX renders טף ("children") as "the rest" (cf. Jer. 43:6). The list does not mention "the royal daughters" (Jer. 41:10; 43:6), but it does have "officials" (סרסים). The LXX translates this term as "eunuchs," and it has been suggested that these eunuchs had the responsibility to protect the royal daughters.[18]

The people went and stayed at a location near Bethlehem with the intent to go to Egypt (Jer. 41:17 [LXX 48:17]). According to the LXX *Vorlage*, the name of this otherwise unknown place was "Gabberoth Kimham" (גברות כמהם). The MT, however, has it as "Geruth Kimham" (גרות כמהם), which the versions have understood in a variety of ways. The Syriac interprets it to mean "the threshing floor of Bimham," as if the Hebrew original were גרן במהם. *Targum Jonathan* provides the most interpretive rendering: "Geruth, which David gave to Kimham the son of Barzillai the Gileadite." This refers to the account of David's return to Jerusalem after the death of Absalom in 2 Samuel 19. Barzillai had taken care of the king while he was at Mahanaim, and he crossed the Jordan with the king to send him on his way from there (2 Sam. 19:32–33 [Eng., 19:31–32]). David pledged to take care

---

16. See the discussion in McKane, *Jeremiah XXVI–LII*, 1021.

17. McKane, *Jeremiah XXVI–LII*, 1016.

18. See Holladay, *Jeremiah 2*, 298.

of Barzillai, but Barzillai insisted that he was too old and burdensome and should return to his city to be near the grave of his parents (2 Sam. 19:34–38a [Eng., 19:33–37a]). Barzillai then commended to the king "your servant Kimham" to cross over with him instead (2 Sam. 19:38b [Eng., 19:37b]). David obliged Barzillai and took Kimham with him, and Barzillai returned to his place (2 Sam. 19:39–41 [Eng., 19:38–40]). David later gave instructions to Solomon to be loyal to the sons of Barzillai and to allow them to be among those who ate at his table (1 Kgs. 2:7; cf. 2 Sam. 9:13). Albrecht Alt proposed that the "Geruth Kimham" in Jeremiah 41:17 was a kind of fief—a grant of land for services rendered to the king.[19] On the other hand, Luther simply translates גרות כמהם as "the lodge of Kimham." The Latin Vulgate interprets גרות to indicate how the people stayed in a place called Kimham: "they went and stayed as sojourners in Kimham."

The people wanted to flee to Egypt because they feared retaliation from the Chaldeans for the murder of Gedaliah whom the king of Babylon appointed over the land (Jer. 41:18 [LXX 48:18]; cf. 2 Kgs. 25:26). The assassination of Gedaliah, not to mention the Chaldean soldiers (Jer. 41:2–3), surely would have been perceived as an act of rebellion against Babylonian authority, regardless of who was responsible for it.[20] This was at the very least what the people seemed to think. Gedaliah had given the people reason not to fear the Chaldeans as he acted on their behalf (Jer. 40:9–10), but now that protection was gone. Since chapters 42–44 focus on deliberation about a flight to Egypt (Jer. 42) and on the account of the eventual migration there (Jer. 43–44), it becomes apparent from 41:17–18 that the entire purpose of chapters 40 and 41, and chapter 41 in particular, has been to provide background for what the reader finds in the subsequent chapters.

---

19. Albrecht Alt, "Der Anteil des Königtum an der sozialen Entwicklung in der Reichen Israel and Judah," *KS* 3 (1959): 358–59. See the discussion of this proposal in Thompson, *Book of Jeremiah*, 662; McKane, *Jeremiah XXVI–LII*, 1022.
20. The later exile mentioned in MT Jeremiah 52:30 may very well have been a belated part of the Babylonian reaction.

JEREMIAH 42 (LXX 49)

42:1 (49:1) And all the army officials and Johanan [MT adds: the son of Kareah] and Azariah the son of Maaseiah [MT: Jezaniah the son of Hoshaiah] and all the people from small to great [i.e., from insignificant to important] drew near 42:2 (49:2) [MT adds: and said] to Jeremiah the prophet, and they said to him [> MT], "Let our supplication fall before you, and pray [MT adds: on our behalf] to the LORD your God on behalf of all this remnant [on behalf of all this remnant > Syr.], for we are left few from many just as your eyes see [MT adds: us]. 42:3 (49:3) And let the LORD your God [pc Mss: our God] tell us the way in which we should go and the word/thing that we should do." 42:4 (49:4) And Jeremiah [MT adds: the prophet] said to them, "I have heard. Look, I am about to pray to the LORD your God [LXX: our God] according to your words; and it will be, the word [MT: every word] that the LORD answers [MT adds: you] is what I will declare to you. I will not withhold from you a word." 42:5 (49:5) And as for them, they said to Jeremiah, "May the LORD become against us a true and faithful witness if not according to all the word that the LORD [MT adds: your God] sends you to us thus we do. 42:6 (49:6) And [> MT] whether good or bad, it is the voice of the LORD our God to whom we are sending you that we will obey in order that it may go well for us when we obey the voice of the LORD our God."

42:7 (49:7) And then, after ten days, the word of the LORD came to Jeremiah. 42:8 (49:8) And he summoned Johanan [MT adds: the son of Kareah] and the army officials [MT adds: who were with him] and all the people from small to great [i.e., from insignificant to important]. 42:9 (49:9) And he said to them, "Thus says the LORD [MT adds: the God of Israel to whom you sent me to cause your supplication to fall before him], 42:10 (49:10) 'If you will only [MT, Tg. Jon.: returning (GKC §19i); Vulg.: resting] stay in this land, I will build you and not throw down, and I will plant you and not pluck up, for I have relented concerning the calamity that I have done to you. 42:11 (49:11) Do not be afraid of the king of Babylon of whom you are afraid. Do not be afraid [MT adds: of him],' the prophetic utterance of the LORD, 'for I am with you to deliver you and to rescue you from his hand/power. 42:12 (49:12) And I will give to you compassion, and I [MT: he] will have compassion on you, and I [MT: he] will restore you to your land [Aq., Syr., Vulg.: cause/allow you to live/stay in your land]. 42:13 (49:13) And if you say, "We will not stay in this land," so as not to obey the voice of the LORD [MT adds: your God], 42:14 (49:14) [MT adds: saying], "for [MT: No, for] the land of Egypt we will enter, and we will not see war [MT: where we will not see war], and a sound of a *shofar we will not hear, and for bread/food we will not hunger, and there we will live," 42:15 (49:15) therefore [MT: and now, therefore], hear the word of the L*ORD *[MT adds: O remnant of Judah]. Thus says the L*ORD *[MT adds: of hosts the God of Israel], "If you set your faces to Egypt [MT: If you do indeed set your faces to enter Egypt] and enter there to sojourn, 42:16 (49:16) then the sword of which you are afraid will overtake you in [MT adds: the land of] Egypt, and the famine about which you are anxious will follow closely after you in Egypt, and there you will die, 42:17 (49:17) and all the people and all the strangers/foreigners [and all the strangers/foreigners > MT] who set their faces to the land of Egypt [MT: to enter Egypt] to sojourn there will die by sword and by famine [MT: by sword, by famine, and by plague], and they will not have [MT adds: a survivor or] one who escapes from the calamity that I am bringing upon them."[1] 42:18 (49:18) For thus says the L*ORD *[MT adds: of hosts the God of Israel], "Just as my fury [MT: my anger and my fury] was poured out upon the inhabitants of Jerusalem, so will my fury pour out upon you when you enter Egypt, and you will become [MT adds: an object of a curse and] an object of horror [LXX: desolate], and you will be in subjection [> MT], and you will become an object of contempt and reproach, and you will never again see this place.'" 42:19 (49:19) This is what [> MT] the L*ORD *has spoken to you [Vulg.: The word of the Lord to you (cf. Tg. Jon.)], O remnant of Judah: 'Do not enter Egypt.' And now [> MT], you must acknowledge [MT adds: that I have warned you today] 42:20 (49:20) that you have acted wickedly [MT: you have erred] at the cost of your lives. You sent me [MT: For you were the ones who sent me to the L*ORD *your God], saying, 'Pray on our behalf to the L*ORD *[MT adds: our God], and according to all that the L*ORD *says to you we will do [MT: and according to all that the L*ORD *our God says to you, thus tell us, and we will do].' 42:21 (49:21) And you have not obeyed the voice of the L*ORD *who sent me to you [MT: And I told you today, and you have not obeyed the voice of the L*ORD *your God and (and > Ms, LXX*[L]*, Tg. Jon.*[Ms]*, Vulg.) concerning all that he sent me to you]. 42:22 (49:22) And now, [MT adds: you must acknowledge that] by sword and by famine [MT adds: and by plague] you will die in the place where you desire to enter to sojourn."*

Jeremiah 42 (LXX 49) is a continuation of the narrative in chapter 41. According to the Hebrew source behind Greek Jeremiah 42:1–2 (LXX 49:1–2), all the army officials and Johanan and "Azariah the son of Maaseiah" and all the people from the least to the greatest drew near to Jeremiah who was apparently present for the whole ordeal narrated

---

1. See GKC §112y.

in chapter 41. While Johanan has played an important role in the story thus far,[2] this is the first mention of Azariah the son of Maaseiah. The MT does not have "Azariah the son of Maaseiah" but "Jezaniah the son of Hoshaiah." Jeremiah 40:8 mentions a "Jezaniah [pc Mss: Jaazaniah] the son of the Maacathite." MT Jeremiah 43:2 (LXX 50:2) has "Azariah the son of Hoshaiah" (listed before Johanan), but the LXX *Vorlage* has "Azariah the son of Maaseiah." It is likely that "Azariah the son of Maaseiah" should be read in both 42:1 and 43:2. Keil prefers to read "Jezaniah the son of Hoshaiah" in 42:1 and 43:2 and to identify this Jezaniah with the one in 40:8,[3] but the problem is that no textual witness has "Jezaniah the son of Hoshaiah" for 43:2.

The people said to Jeremiah, "Let our supplication fall before you, and pray [MT adds: on our behalf] to the LORD your God on behalf of all this remnant [on behalf of all this remnant > Syr.], for we are left few from many just as your eyes see [MT adds: us]" (Jer. 42:2 [LXX 49:2]; cf. Jer. 36:7; 37:3, 20; 38:26; 42:9, 20; see also 4Q385b).[4] This was an appeal to Jeremiah to function in his role as an intercessor prophet like Moses (see Jer. 15:1; see also Gen. 20:7; 1 Sam. 7:5; 12:19, 23; 1 Kgs. 13:6). Prior to the Babylonian invasion, the LORD had indicated to Jeremiah that he would not hear the prophet's prayer on behalf of the people to avert the disaster (Jer. 7:16; 11:14; 14:11); but once the judgment passed, there was an opportunity to hear from the LORD afresh concerning the next course of action. The basis for the people's request

---

2. It is worth noting that apart from Jeremiah 40:8 Johanan's name has preceded mention of the other army officials up to this point (Jer. 40:13; 41:11, 16), whereas here the other officials are mentioned first.

3. Keil, *Jeremiah*, 345.

4. Holladay notes the use of "your [sg.] God" in verses 2–3, the use of "your [pl.] God" in verse 4, and the use of "our God" in verse 6: "These shifts are not accidental; each side is making points. The group says in effect to Jrm, 'Deal with Yahweh: that is your specialty.' Jrm says to the group, 'I shall deal with Yahweh, but it is you who are obligated by the transaction.' The group senses that Jrm has made his point, so it says, in effect, 'We accept our obligation'" (*Jeremiah 2*, 298–99; cf. Isa. 7:11, 13). Calvin, however, suggests that the people called the LORD Jeremiah's God to acknowledge the prophet as true, and that Jeremiah called him the people's God to urge them to devote themselves to the LORD (*Jeremiah*, 4:479, 481). It is also possible that Jeremiah was correcting the people's "your God" (vv. 2–3) so that it would become "our God" (v. 6). On the other hand, Bright does not think that there is any significance to the use of the pronouns here (*Jeremiah*, 255).

was their status as a small remnant (cf. Jer. 40:11; 41:10; see also Jer. 42:15 [MT], 19), which Calvin says was added "to produce pity."[5]

The people concluded their request by expressing their desire that the LORD tell them the way in which they should go and the thing that they should do (Jer. 42:3 [LXX 49:3]). By coming to the prophet in this way and subsequently binding themselves to whatever the LORD's reply might be (Jer. 42:5–6), the people made themselves accountable in a manner that they would not have been if they had simply departed for Egypt. Their initial exchange with Jeremiah appears sincere enough, but it is evident from Jeremiah 41:17–18 that their intent all along was to go to Egypt. Thus, they wanted confirmation of their chosen course of action from a true prophet; but if they did not receive such confirmation, they would accuse Jeremiah of deception (Jer. 43:2–3).[6] Malbim even suggests that the people were not asking whether they should go to Egypt.[7] Rather, they were asking which way they should go to Egypt. It is certainly ironic that the people would seek to return to the place of their historical servitude from which God had delivered them (Jer. 2:6, 16, 18), but it was a constant temptation to seek refuge in Egypt (see Isa. 30:1–5; 31:1–3). The whole account in Jeremiah 42–43 of the people's insistence upon a return to Egypt against the counsel of their prophet like Moses is reminiscent of the story in Numbers 14 in which the people sought to replace Moses with a new leader and return to Egypt (Num. 14:4).

Jeremiah indicated that he heard the people's request and that he would pray to the LORD in accordance with their words (Jer. 42:4a [LXX 49:4a]).[8] He was very clear, however, that he would declare to them only the message of the LORD's reply and that he would not withhold from them a word (Jer. 42:4b [LXX 49:4b]; cf. 1 Sam. 3:17; Jer.

---

5. Calvin, *Jeremiah*, 4:480.

6. "He who asks counsel, ought first to see that he bring no prejudice, but be free and honest: but it is, however, a fault too common, that men deliberate and ask counsel, when they have already settled what to do; nay, nothing is more common than this; for those who consult do not, for the most part, wish to learn what is right, but that others should fall in with their own inclinations. He who has resolved on this or that point, pretends that he is in doubt, and held in suspense; he asks what ought to be done: if the answer be according to his wishes, he embraces what is said; but if he who is consulted, disapproves of what he has already resolved to do, he rejects the counsel given" (Calvin, *Jeremiah*, 4:478).

7. Rosenberg, trans., *Mikraoth Gedoloth: Jeremiah Volume Two*, 326.

8. Calvin suspects that Jeremiah regarded the people with suspicion (*Jeremiah*, 4:481).

26:2; 38:14; Tob. 12:11). This meant that there would be no adjustment of the answer to conform to the people's expectation. Such a forewarning on Jeremiah's part brings to mind the words of Micaiah: "By the life of the LORD, what the LORD says to me, that is what I will speak" (1 Kgs. 22:14; cf. 2 Chr. 18:13; see also Num. 22:18, 38). The context of these words has several points of contact with Jeremiah's situation. Ahab only reluctantly summoned Micaiah at Jehoshaphat's request, for Micaiah was known not to prophesy "good" (what Ahab wanted to hear) concerning Ahab, only "bad" (what Ahab did not want to hear) (1 Kgs. 22:8; cf. 2 Chr. 18:7; see Jer. 42:6). Micaiah was urged to speak "good" (what Ahab wanted to hear) and thus to conform to what the false prophets were saying (1 Kgs. 22:13; cf. 2 Chr. 18:12). Micaiah's prophecy would be accepted only if it matched the prescribed response. Thus, both Micaiah and Jeremiah were under pressure from their audiences to reply in a certain way, yet they were both faithful to deliver only what they heard from the LORD no matter how unpopular it was.

The people's response to Jeremiah in 42:5 (LXX 49:5) gives every indication that they thought they would receive the answer that they desired from the LORD through the prophet: "May the LORD become against us a true and faithful witness if not according to all the word that the LORD [MT adds: your God] sends you to us thus we do."[9] Keil comments, "God is to be a faithful witness, not in regard to the truth of what they say, but as regards the fulfillment of their promise, so that, if they would not obey His word, He might come forward to punish them."[10] The people insisted that it was the voice of the LORD that they wanted to obey, "whether good or bad," in order that things might go well for them (Jer. 42:6 [LXX 49:6]; see BDB, 405). This would seem to give the impression that the people believed that the LORD's will was what was best for them regardless of how it aligned with their plans. This was easy for the people to say at a time when they wholeheartedly anticipated the LORD's answer to be "good." The expression "whether good or bad" has been understood in various ways. Calvin takes it to mean "whether joyful or sad."[11] Keil, however, interprets it in light of Ecclesiastes 12:14 to mean "whether it announces good or evil to

---

9. This recalls the confident yet premature and naïve response of the people to Moses in Exodus 19:8: "All that the LORD has spoken we will do."

10. Keil, *Jeremiah*, 346. "Jeremiah did not in express words require them to make an oath; they yet did make an oath; and then in various ways still more bound themselves over to punishment, if they became perjurers" (Calvin, *Jeremiah*, 4:484).

11. Calvin, *Jeremiah*, 4:483.

come."[12] Thompson understands the expression to be a common idiom: "We will obey his word whatever it is" (cf. Gen. 24:50; 31:24, 42; Num. 24:13; Deut. 1:39; 2 Sam. 13:22).[13] Given the similarity of the present context to 1 Kings 22 (see above), it may be best to interpret "whether good or bad" to mean "whether it is what we want to hear or not" (see again 1 Kgs. 22:8).

Much has been made of the fact that the word of the Lord came to Jeremiah after ten days (Jer. 42:7 [LXX 49:7]). Abarbanel offers a scenario in which the answer came only a day or two after Jeremiah's prayer.[14] Calvin suggests that God intentionally delayed the response in order to lend more weight to the prophecy.[15] Keil believes that the reason was a disciplinary one to give the people time to consider the situation so that they might be more receptive to the word of the Lord.[16] If either Calvin or Keil is correct, then it must be said from what follows that the period of ten days did not achieve its purpose. Bright proposes that the delay is "evidence of Jeremiah's unwillingness to speak in the name of Yahweh until sure that he had in fact received Yahweh's word," not unlike the delay in Jeremiah's response to Hananiah (Jer. 28:11–12).[17] It is possible, however, that ten days is simply a nice round number that designates a suitable period of time (see the usage in 1 Sam. 25:38; Dan. 1:12; Rev. 2:10; cf. Gen. 31:7, 41; Num. 14:22; Neh. 4:6 [Eng., 4:12]; Job 19:3). When Jeremiah received the word of the Lord, he summoned Johanan, the army officials, and all the people from the least to the greatest (Jer. 42:8 [LXX 49:8]).[18]

Jeremiah's introduction to his report of the Lord's discourse in 42:9 (LXX 49:9) is significantly longer in the MT than it is in the Hebrew

---

12. Keil, *Jeremiah*, 346.

13. Thompson, *Book of Jeremiah*, 664.

14. "As stated above, the assassination of Gedaliah transpired on Rosh Hashanah, the first of Tishri, or, as he asserts, on the second day of Tishri. Immediately, Johanan the son of Kareah pursued Ishmael and rescued the captives. Then they appealed to Jeremiah to pray to God for His word whether they should flee to Egypt to avoid the wrath of Nebuchadnezzar. At the end of the ten day period, i.e. on Yom Kippur, the last of the Ten Days of Penitence, God gave him His answer. This was but one or two days after his prayer" (Rosenberg, trans., *Mikraoth Gedoloth: Jeremiah Volume Two*, 327).

15. Calvin, *Jeremiah*, 4:486.

16. Keil, *Jeremiah*, 346.

17. Bright, *Jeremiah*, 203, 255.

18. Note that Johanan is restored here to his place at the head of the list (see Jer. 40:13; 41:11, 16; cf. Jer. 40:8; 42:1). Note also that Azariah (MT: Jezaniah) is not mentioned here (cf. Jer. 42:1; 43:2; see also Jer. 40:8).

source behind Greek Jeremiah: "Thus says the LORD [MT adds: the God of Israel to whom you sent me to cause your supplication to fall before him]" (cf. Jer. 42:2, 20, 21; 43:1). The addition in the MT stresses that the people were the ones who sent Jeremiah to the LORD and had made themselves accountable to obey the LORD's voice that came through the prophet (Jer. 42:1–6). The word of the LORD begins with a condition: "If you will only stay (אם ישוב תשבו) in this land" (Jer. 42:10a [LXX 49:10a]). The MT says, "If returning you stay (אם שוב תשבו) in this land," which GKC §19i says is an example of aphaeresis of a weak consonant with a full vowel, in which case the reading is equivalent to the one in the LXX *Vorlage* (אם ישוב תשבו). On the other hand, the sense of the MT may be that the people must repent of their intended departure for Egypt (Jer. 41:17–18) and return to the land in order to stay in it (cf. Jer. 42:12). If this is correct, then שוב in the MT is truly an infinitive absolute of שוב ("return") and not an abbreviated infinitive absolute of ישב ("stay"). Gedaliah had earlier advised the people to stay in the land and submit to the Babylonians (Jer. 40:9). This was not unlike Jeremiah's letter to the Babylonian exiles in which he urged them to accept the consequences of their actions and to wait upon the future work of God (Jer. 29:4–7, 10–14).

If the people would only stay in the land, then the LORD would build them and not throw them down; he would plant them and not pluck them up (Jer. 42:10a [LXX 49:10a]; cf. Gen. 26:2–4). This incorporates the distinctive language of the programmatic text of the book in Jeremiah 1:10, which has been developed throughout the book in various ways.[19] A decision to stay in the land would essentially be equivalent to an expression of faith in what the LORD has in store for the future of his people, and a comparison with the usage of the language of building and planting elsewhere in the book strongly suggests that something more than a mere return of Babylonian exiles is in view (see in particular Jer. 12:14–17; 24:6–7; 31:4–5, 28, 31–34; 32:37–41). The text looks forward to a new covenant people of God made up of believers from all the nations who will inhabit the messianic kingdom (Jer. 3:14–18; 23:5–6; 30:8–9, 24b). It is only in the resurrection that Jeremiah's immediate

---

19. "At 1.10 the destructive processes are envisaged as a necessary preparation for rebuilding and new growth, but at 42.10 the building and the planting are incorporated in a promise which excludes demolition and uprooting. The constructive and destructive terms are set against each other as mutually exclusive" (McKane, *Jeremiah XXVI–LII*, 1033). This is likely because the prerequisite throwing down and plucking up are now considered to be in the past (see Jer. 42:10b [LXX 49:10b]).

audience could take part in this. On the other hand, a decision not to stay in the land would be equivalent to a rejection of God's plan for his people and a deliberate choice of another path (Jer. 6:16). The LORD indicates that the way is now clear for building and planting because he has "relented" concerning the calamity that he has done to the people (Jer. 42:10b [LXX 49:10b]; cf. Jon. 3:9–10). Bright rightly notes that the *niphal* of נחם here does not mean "repent" but "relent": "Jeremiah does not mean that Yahweh realizes that he has made a mistake and is sorry for it. . . . Yahweh is appeased by what he has done, remits further punishment, and promises better things in the future."[20]

In Jeremiah 42:11 (LXX 49:11), the LORD encourages the people not to be afraid of the king of Babylon anymore. Their desire to flee to Egypt was driven by fear of retaliation from the Chaldeans for Ishmael's assassination of Gedaliah whom the king of Babylon appointed over the land (Jer. 41:17–18). Gedaliah had been the one who gave the people reason not to fear the Chaldeans (Jer. 40:9–10). It is not clear how the people could avoid repercussion for what had happened by staying in the land, but the LORD reassured them that he was present with them: "for I am with you to deliver you and to rescue you from his hand/power." These are the same words that the LORD used when he called Jeremiah to be his prophet and to face the difficulties that would come with that responsibility (Jer. 1:8, 17 [LXX], 19; 15:20–21). Such words have been reapplied to the people of God elsewhere in the book (Jer. 30:11 [MT]; 46:28), indicating that Jeremiah is depicted as their representative by design.

The Hebrew source behind Greek Jeremiah 42:12 (LXX 49:12) maintains first-person verbs throughout the verse: "And I will give to you compassion, and I will have compassion (ורחמתי) on you, and I will restore (והשיבותי) you to your land." The MT, however, switches from first person to third person: "And I will give to you compassion, and he will have compassion (ורחם) on you, and he will restore (והשיב) you to your land." It has been suggested that the forms רחם and השיב were originally infinitives absolute, which were variously interpreted as equivalent to first-person (LXX) or third-person (MT) verbs.[21] The difficulty with this view is that the *hiphil* infinitive absolute of שוב would normally be spelled השב, not השיב. The third-person verbs in the MT apparently assume Nebuchadnezzar to be the subject. That is, the LORD would have compassion on the people, and Nebuchadnezzar would likewise have compassion on them and restore them to their land. Some of the early versions (Aq., Syr., Vulg.) had difficulty with

---

20. Bright, *Jeremiah*, 255–56. See also Calvin, *Jeremiah*, 4:489.
21. See McKane, *Jeremiah XXVI–LII*, 1034.

the thought that the people, who had not yet departed from the land, would be restored to the land. These versions have first-person verbs and interpret the last verb to be from the root יָשַׁב ("live/stay") rather than the root שׁוּב ("return/restore"): "and I will cause/allow you to live/stay in your land" (cf. Jer. 42:10). This change, however, is unnecessary. The movement in Jeremiah 41:17–18 shows that the people were in a sense already on their way to Egypt. Thus, they were between Judah and Egypt so to speak, and it could be said that they had a choice either to continue to Egypt or to return to Judah.

Verse 13 provides the antithesis to the protasis in verse 10: "And if you say, 'We will not stay in this land.'" This choice is cast not merely as a refusal to heed the advice of the prophet but as disobedience to the voice of the LORD himself. The anticipated rationale for this potential decision is given in verse 14: "for the land of Egypt we will enter, and we will not see war, and a sound of a shofar we will not hear, and for bread/food we will not hunger, and there we will live" (cf. Jer. 4:5, 19, 21; 6:1; 40:10, 12; 52:6; see also Gen. 26:1–2). The MT explicitly reintroduces the quoted discourse in verse 14 ("saying") and adds the negation לֹא ("No, for the land of Egypt we will enter"). The MT also features description of Egypt as the place where war will not be seen ("where we will not see war"). Of course, this idealistic view of Egypt was exactly the thought process of the people whose shortsightedness prevented them from considering the possibility that they would not be immune to disaster there (see Jer. 43:8–13; 46). Their only concern was the belief that calamity was sure to reach them in Judah, despite what the LORD said to them. Thus, their inclination was to trust in Egypt rather than the LORD.

Jeremiah 42:15 (LXX 49:15) introduces the announcement of judgment for the inevitable decision of the people to go to Egypt. In the longer text of the MT, this is addressed to the "remnant of Judah" (cf. Jer. 42:2, 19). If the people set their faces to Egypt to live as resident aliens there, then they must consider themselves warned about what they will encounter there (cf. Jer. 44:12). That is, if they are determined and resolved to go to Egypt contrary to the LORD's will, then they must at least hear that what they expect to happen will in fact not be the reality of the situation. The sword (i.e., warfare) that they needlessly fear in the land of Judah and that they seek to avoid in Egypt will overtake them in the very place where they hope to take refuge (Jer. 42:16a [LXX 49:16a]; cf. Jer. 42:14a; see also Jer. 24:8–10).[22] The famine about which they unnecessarily worry in Judah will follow closely after them

---

22. See Neusner, *Jeremiah in Talmud and Midrash*, 45, 73, 193.

in Egypt where they assume that they will be free of such trouble (Jer. 42:16b [LXX 49:16b]; cf. Jer. 42:14b; see again Jer. 24:8–10). The small community of Judeans will die in the land of Egypt.[23] In other words, Egypt will not be a temporary shelter from which they will eventually return to their land.

The Hebrew source behind Greek Jeremiah 42:17a (LXX 49:17a) says that "all the people and all the strangers/foreigners" (כל האנשים וכל הזרים) who set their faces to the land of Egypt to sojourn there will die by sword and famine (cf. Jer. 42:22; 44:12). The term זרים ("strangers/foreigners") likely does not refer to foreigners who will join the Judeans to flee to Egypt. Rather, it refers to the new status that the Judeans will have in a foreign land. Another possibility is that it describes the Judeans as those who are estranged from the LORD (cf. MT Isa. 1:4). The MT, however, does not have "and all the strangers/ foreigners." Furthermore, MT Jeremiah 43:2 (LXX 50:2) has "and all the presumptuous people" (וכל האנשים הזדים), leading some to believe that הזדים ("the presumptuous") rather than הזרים ("the strangers/for-eigners") belongs in 42:17a, yet the Greek text of 43:2 (LXX 50:2) rep-resents neither הזדים nor הזרים.[24] MT 42:17a converts "by sword and by famine" into the triad "by sword, by famine, and by plague" (cf. Jer. 24:8b, 10; 42:22; 43:11; 44:13), but this is inconsistent with the wording of 42:14, 16, unless "plague" is considered a substitute for the death mentioned at the end of verse 16 (cf. Jer. 15:2; but see also Jer. 44:12). The people will not have "one who escapes" (פליט) from the calamity that the LORD is bringing upon them (Jer. 42:17b [LXX 49:17b]). The MT's "a survivor or one who escapes" (שריד ופליט) may very well be a conflate text (cf. Jer. 44:14).

The LORD adds the explanation in 42:18a (LXX 49:18a) that he will pour out his fury on the people when they enter Egypt just as it was poured out upon the inhabitants of Jerusalem (cf. Jer. 44:6, 13). The people will become "[MT adds: an object of a curse and] an object of horror [LXX: desolate]" (Jer. 42:18b [LXX 49:18b]; cf. Jer. 24:8b–9; 44:8, 12). The LXX adds that the people will be "in subjection," which does not appear in the MT. They will become "an object of contempt and reproach," and they will never again see "this place." The phrase "this place" may refer to the land of Judah,[25] but the reference to Jerusalem

---

23. The phrasing of ושם תמתו ("and there you will die") in verse 16b deliber-ately contradicts that of ושם נשב ("and there we will live") in verse 14b.
24. See the discussion in McKane, *Jeremiah XXVI–LII*, 1036–37.
25. See Calvin, *Jeremiah*, 4:499.

earlier in the verse suggests that the city may be in view.[26] Rudolph (*BHS* apparatus) proposes that 43:1–3 (the response of the people to Jeremiah) should be transposed between 42:18 and 42:19 due to the fact that 42:19–22 presupposes that the people have not heeded the voice of the Lord. This proposal has no warrant from any extant textual witness. Furthermore, it is unnecessary, for the problem that it seeks to solve does not really exist. The text of Jeremiah 41:17–18 has already made it clear that the people decided to go to Egypt before they ever consulted Jeremiah. Their expected rejection of any word from the Lord that might be contrary to their decision is latent throughout chapter 42. Thus, their narrated response in 43:1–3 comes not as a surprise but as something that has been a foregone conclusion in the preceding narrative.

In Jeremiah 42:19a (LXX 49:19a), Jeremiah gives a very clear and succinct summary of the Lord's response to his prayer on behalf of the "remnant of Judah" (cf. Jer. 42:2, 15 [MT]): "Do not enter Egypt" (cf. Deut. 17:16). English versions normally render the remainder of this verse to say that the people are to know something for sure (cf. MT Jer. 42:22), but it seems more fitting in context to understand Jeremiah's words to mean that the people must acknowledge or recognize that a prophet has delivered the word of the Lord to them, whether or not they choose to obey that word (cf. Ezek. 2:5). The Hebrew source behind Greek Jeremiah 42:19b (LXX 49:19b) says, "And now, you must acknowledge" (ועתה ידע תדעו), whereas in verse 22 it simply says, "And now" (ועתה). MT 42:19b has, "You must acknowledge" (ידע תדעו), and in verse 22 it has, "And now, you must acknowledge that" (ועתה ידע תדעו כי). The LXX *Vorlage* has no object clause at the end of verse 19, only at the beginning of verse 20. The MT has an object clause at the end of verse 19 ("that I have warned you today") followed by another at the beginning of verse 20. It is possible that the scribe responsible for the LXX *Vorlage* or the Greek translator himself accidentally skipped from the first כי ("that") to the second and thus unwittingly omitted the first object clause at the end of verse 19 (homoioarchton).

The object clause at the beginning of 42:20 (LXX 49:20) in the LXX *Vorlage* is as follows: "that you have acted wickedly (הרעתם) at the cost of your lives" (see BDB, 659). The MT *qere*, however, has the following: "that you have erred (התעתם) at the cost of your lives" (the *kethiv* התעתים is erroneous). Commentators have assumed the MT verb to be transitive and have thus understood it to mean either that the people

---

26. See Abarbanel in Rosenberg, trans., *Mikraoth Gedoloth: Jeremiah Volume Two*, 330. See also the use of "this place" (המקום הזה) in Jeremiah 7:1–15.

have deceived the LORD or that the leaders have led the people astray,[27] but it is likely that the verb is intransitive (see BDB, 1073). Jeremiah explains how the people have behaved. They were the ones who sent him to the LORD to pray on their behalf (Jer. 42:2, 9).[28] They were the ones who said that they would do according to all that the LORD might say to Jeremiah (Jer. 42:5), but they said this disingenuously (see Jer. 41:17–18; 42:21–22).[29]

According to the shorter text of 42:21 (LXX 49:21) in the Hebrew source behind Greek Jeremiah, the prophet says that the people have not obeyed the voice of the LORD who sent him to them (cf. Jer. 43:4). Once again, critical scholars wonder how something like this could be said prior to the response of the people narrated in 43:1–3. It has been noted above, however, that the people's decision to disobey what has now been revealed to Jeremiah was already made in Jeremiah 41:17–18.[30] The longer text of MT 42:21 is as follows: "And I told you today [cf. MT Jer. 42:20b], and you have not obeyed the voice of the LORD your God and [and > Ms, LXX[L], Tg. Jon.[Ms], Vulg.] concerning all that he sent me to you." Thus, Jeremiah concludes, "And now, [MT adds: you must acknowledge that] by sword and by famine [MT adds: and by plague] you will die in the place where you desire to enter to sojourn" (Jer. 42:22 [LXX 49:22]; cf. Jer. 42:17, 19b; see also Gen. 15:13). Their decision to disregard the very word for which they sent Jeremiah to the LORD would indeed be at the cost of their lives (see again Jer. 42:16).

---

27. See McKane, *Jeremiah XXVI–LII*, 1038; Holladay, *Jeremiah 2*, 301.

28. "*Abarbanel*, followed by *Mezudath David*, renders: 'You have erred with your souls, for you have sent me, etc. Had you not sent me to pray to God on your behalf and to ask Him whether you should flee to Egypt, you would have been unintentional sinners. Now, however, since you have sent me to inquire of God and you refuse to obey, you are intentional sinners'" (Rosenberg, trans., *Mikraoth Gedoloth: Jeremiah Volume Two*, 330).

29. The MT's additional כן הגד לנו ("thus tell us"), which does not appear in the LXX *Vorlage*, is presupposed at the beginning of MT 42:21 ("And I told you today" [ואגד לכם היום]), but not at the beginning of verse 21 in the LXX *Vorlage*.

30. Redak: "Although he had not yet completed his words, and they had not yet responded, he recognized that they intended to go to Egypt in any case" (Rosenberg, trans., *Mikraoth Gedoloth: Jeremiah Volume Two*, 331).

JEREMIAH 43 (LXX 50)

43:1 (50:1) As soon as Jeremiah finished speaking to [MT adds: all] the people all the words of the Lord *[MT adds: their God] that the* Lord *[MT adds: their God] sent him [Syr. adds: to say] to them, all these words, 43:2 (50:2) Azariah [Syr.: Jezaniah] the son of Maaseiah [MT: Hoshaiah] said, and Johanan the son of Kareah and all the [MT adds: presumptuous] people who were saying to Jeremiah, saying [> MT], "Deception [MT adds: you are speaking]. The* Lord *has not sent you to us [MT: The* Lord *our God has not sent you] to say, 'You must not enter Egypt to sojourn there.' 43:3 (50:3) For [LXX: But] Baruch the son of Neriah [the son of Neriah > 4QJer^d] is inciting you against us in order to give / deliver us into the hand / power of the Chaldeans to kill us or to take us into exile in Babylon." 43:4 (50:4) And Johanan [MT adds: the son of Kareah (> 4QJer^d)] did not obey, and all the army officials and all the people, the voice of the* Lord *to stay in the land of Judah. 43:5 (50:5) And Johanan [MT adds: the son of Kareah (> 4QJer^d)] took, and all the army officials, all the remnant of Judah who returned [MT adds: from all the nations where they were banished (cf. 4QJer^d)] to sojourn in the land [MT adds: of Judah],[1] 43:6 (50:6) the mighty men [MT: the men] and the women and the children [LXX: the rest] and the royal daughters and [MT adds: all] the people whom Nebuzaradan [MT adds: the captain of the guard] left Gedaliah the son of Ahikam [MT adds: the son of Shaphan (> 4QJer^d)] and Jeremiah the prophet and Baruch the son of Neriah, 43:7 (50:7) and they entered [MT, 4QJer^d add: the land of] Egypt, for they did not obey the voice of the* Lord, *and they entered [MT: they came as far as] Tahpanhes [LXX: Taphnas; 4QJer^d:* תחפסם; *Syr.:* תחפיס; *cf. Jer. 2:16; 43:8, 9; 44:1; 46:14; 4Q385b].[2]*

43:8 (50:8) And the word of the Lord *came to Jeremiah at Tahpanhes, saying, 43:9 (50:9) "Take for yourself [4QJer^d, MT: in your hand (cf. Jer. 38:10)] large stones and hide them [MT adds: in the mortar[3] in the brick kiln / terrace that is] at the entrance of the house of Pharaoh*

---

1. Syr.: "And Johanan the son of Kareah took all the army officials and all the rest of those who were left from the house of Judah."

2. The LXX uses καὶ εἰσήλθοσαν εἰς for both occurrences of ויבאו in this verse. Thus, the preposition εἰς is not necessarily a representation of the MT's עד following the second occurrence. Note that עד is absent in 4QJer^d. Furthermore, ἕως is normally the translation of עד in LXX Jeremiah.

3. Aquila, Symmachus, Theodotion, and the Latin Vulgate all reflect בלט ("in secrecy") rather than במלט ("in the mortar").

in Tahpanhes in the sight of the people of Judah [2QJer, 4QJer[d], MT: Judean people] 43:10 (50:10) and say [MT adds: to them], 'Thus says the LORD [MT adds: of hosts the God of Israel], 'Look, I am about to send and bring [MT: take] Nebuchadnezzar [MT: Nebuchadrezzar] the king of Babylon [MT adds: my servant], and he [MT: I; Syr. = LXX] will put his throne above these stones that you [MT: I; Syr. = LXX] have hidden, and he will lift up his armor/weapons against them [MT: and he will stretch out his canopy (Tg. Jon.: seat/pedestal;[4] cf. Vulg.) over them], 43:11 (50:11) and he will come and strike the land of Egypt [MT kethiv: and it will come, and he will strike the land of Egypt]—whoever to death, to death; and whoever to captivity, to captivity; and whoever to the sword, to the sword—43:12 (50:12) and he [MT: I; Syr., Vulg. = LXX] will kindle a fire in the houses/temples of their gods [MT: the gods of Egypt] and burn them and take them captive, and he will delouse [or, wrap himself in; or, grasp] the land of Egypt just as a shepherd delouses [or, wraps himself in; or, grasps] his garment, and he will go out in peace, 43:13 (50:13) and he will shatter the pillars/obelisks of the city of the sun [LXX: Heliopolis; MT: the house/temple of the sun], which are in On [MT: which is in the land of Egypt], and their houses/temples [MT: the houses/temples of the gods of Egypt] will he burn with fire.'"

As soon as Jeremiah finished speaking to the people all the words that the LORD sent him to say to them (Jer. 43:1 [LXX 50:1]; cf. Jer. 42:21),[5] they accused him of false prophecy (Jer. 43:2 [LXX 50:2]; cf. Jer. 44:16). According to the Hebrew source behind Greek Jeremiah, the leader of this response was "Azariah the son of Maaseiah" (see commentary on Jer. 42:1 [LXX 49:1]), followed by Johanan and all the people. The MT has "Azariah the son of Hoshaiah," and the Syriac has "Jezaniah the son of Hoshaiah" (cf. Jer. 40:8; 42:1). Whoever this individual was, he does not appear again in the narrative, and Johanan resumes his role as the leading figure of the Judean remnant in verses 4 and 5. The MT designates the people here as "the presumptuous people" (האנשים הזדים), which is not a feature of the LXX *Vorlage* (see commentary on Jer. 42:17 [LXX 49:17]). When they did not hear what they wanted to hear from Jeremiah, they accused him of "deception" (שקר) and claimed that the LORD did not send him to them (cf. Jer. 23:21, 25, 32).[6] This is a decidedly different attitude from the

---

4. Some witnesses to *Targum Jonathan* have "palace."
5. The phrase "all these words" refers back to Jeremiah 42:9–22.
6. The LXX *Vorlage* says, "The LORD has not sent you to us (אלינו)," whereas the MT says, "The LORD our God (אלהינו) has not sent you." The MT likely

open-mindedness that the people claimed to have in Jeremiah 42:5–6. Rather than accepting the LORD's will for them, the people insisted on their own plans and released themselves from any obligation to the word of the LORD by pretending that the word from Jeremiah was that of a false prophet.[7] It is evident from what follows in the narrative that they did not really believe this about Jeremiah, for he did not receive the death penalty that would have been due a false prophet (Deut. 13:6 [Eng., 13:5]; 18:20; Jer. 26:8; 28:15–17), and they took Jeremiah with them to Egypt (Jer. 43:5–7). Indeed, their rejection of Jeremiah's message is predicated upon a misrepresentation of the prophet's words: "You must not (לא) enter Egypt to sojourn there" (see commentary on Jer. 26:9).[8] This would essentially have meant that the people were never to go to Egypt in an absolute sense (see GKC §107o, 152b); but Jeremiah actually said, "Do not (אל) enter Egypt" (Jer. 42:19). That is, the response to the people's specific request at that time was that they were not to go to Egypt. Thus, the people made Jeremiah's message into something that it was not and then accused him of not delivering the word of the LORD. They in effect transformed what Jeremiah said into something harsher and even less desirable (cf. Gen. 2:16–17; 3:1–3; Exod. 19:10–11, 14–15).

The people, however, did not lay the blame entirely at Jeremiah's feet for his supposed deception. They falsely accused his scribe, Baruch, of inciting him against them in order to deliver them into the power of the Chaldeans to kill them or to take them into exile in Babylon (Jer. 43:3 [LXX 50:3]; see Jer. 8:8). This once again reflects the belief of the people that they had reason to fear the Chaldeans if they stayed in the land of Judah (Jer. 41:17–18; but see again Jer. 42:11). Up to this point in the book, the references to Baruch have not given the reader any indication that he would have influenced Jeremiah in this way (Jer. 32:12, 13, 16; 36:4–32). Abarbanel suggests that Baruch aspired to be a prophet himself and believed that this could only be fulfilled in Judah.[9]

---

represents a deliberate change designed to highlight a difference in the way the people referred to the LORD. In Jeremiah 42:2, they called the LORD Jeremiah's God ("your God"), but now that they do not accept Jeremiah's prophecy, the LORD is their God ("our God").

7.   Despite suffering the consequences of their previous refusal to heed the word of the LORD that came through Jeremiah (see Jer. 42:18), the people failed to learn their lesson and continued to reject the prophetic word (see Zech. 1:4–6).

8.   See also Holladay, *Jeremiah 2*, 300.

9.   Rosenberg, trans., *Mikraoth Gedoloth: Jeremiah Volume Two*, 332.

Thus, he had to avoid migration to Egypt even at the cost of the lives of the Judean remnant. The problem with this suggestion is that it gives too much credit to the people's accusation and has no evidence in the text to support it. Likewise, the thought that Jeremiah and Baruch were somehow advocating to stay in Judah at the expense of the people because they believed that they personally would be protected there (but not in Egypt) by the Babylonian authorities (Jer. 39:11–12 [MT]) has little, if any, foundation in the text.[10] The fact that the people eventually took Baruch with them to Egypt reveals that they did not really view him as their adversary (Jer. 43:5–7). They simply needed a scapegoat to excuse themselves from obedience to the voice of the LORD. This brief account of the persecution of Baruch gives a glimpse of what he suffered due to his association with Jeremiah whose sufferings are much more well documented in the book (see also Jer. 36:26). It also prepares the reader for the otherwise somewhat unexpected reference to Baruch's struggles in the scribal colophon of chapter 45.

Led by Johanan, the army officials and the people did not obey the voice of the LORD to stay in the land of Judah (Jer. 43:4 [LXX 50:4]; see Jer. 42:10–12). This course of action was already anticipated in Jeremiah's words (Jer. 42:21) based on his knowledge of what the people had previously decided to do (Jer. 41:17–18). Verses 5 and 6 provide a list of those taken by Johanan (and the army officials) to go to Egypt. All indications are that the decision to go to Egypt was not one left for the individual Judean man or woman to make. Whatever the leadership decided to do, that was what everyone would do. Either everyone would stay in the land, or everyone would go to Egypt. There would be no such thing as some staying and some going. Since Johanan and the army officials had made up their minds to go to Egypt, there was simply no other option for any dissenting members of the community, including Jeremiah and Baruch.

Verse 5 begins with a general description of the Judean remnant. The Syriac preserves the shortest version of this text: "And Johanan the son of Kareah took all the army officials and all the rest of those who were left from the house of Judah." The LXX *Vorlage* features slightly

---

10. "The narrator implies, according to Carroll, that Jeremiah has nothing to fear from Nebuchadrezzar, whereas Johanan and his group would risk their skins by remaining in Judah—it is all very well for him to canvass such a policy. The intention of vv. 1–7 could hardly be further removed from this. It is to represent that those who emigrated to Egypt rejected the word of Yahweh spoken by his prophet and sought to justify themselves by asserting that he was a false prophet" (McKane, *Jeremiah XXVI–LII*, 1052).

different syntax and a slightly longer text: "And Johanan took, and all the army officials, all the remnant of Judah who returned to sojourn in the land." This describes the remnant as those who came back to live as resident aliens in their own land. The longest version of this text is found in the MT: "And Johanan the son of Kareah took, and all the army officials, all the remnant of Judah who returned from all the nations where they were banished to sojourn in the land of Judah." This refers specifically to the Judeans mentioned in Jeremiah 40:11–12.

Verse 6a offers a more specific breakdown of the makeup of the Judean remnant taken to Egypt by Johanan and the army officials: "the mighty men (הַגִּבֹּרִים or הַגִּבּוֹרִים) [MT: the men (הַגְּבָרִים)][11] and the women and the children [LXX: the rest] and the royal daughters and [MT adds: all] the people whom Nebuzaradan [MT adds: the captain of the guard] left Gedaliah the son of Ahikam [MT adds: the son of Shaphan (> 4QJerᵈ)]" (see Jer. 40:7; 41:10, 16; 44:20). Verse 6b then mentions that Jeremiah and Baruch were among those taken, presumably against their will. This is the final irony of Jeremiah's tenure as a kind of bizarro prophet like Moses (see Jer. 1:4–10; 7:16; 11:14; 14:11; 15:1). Whereas Moses led the people out of Egypt, Jeremiah was taken to Egypt by the people. The people entered Egypt because of their disobedience to the LORD's voice and came to the city of Tahpanhes in northeastern Egypt (Jer. 43:7 [LXX 50:7]; see Deut. 28:68; Hos. 8:13; 9:3; 11:5).

The word of the LORD that came to Jeremiah at Tahpanhes (Jer. 43:8 [LXX 50:8]) instructed the prophet to perform a symbolic action in full view of the people of Judah who were there (Jer. 43:9 [LXX 50:9]). This is not unlike the prophetic sign acts that the reader has encountered thus far in the book (Jer. 13:1–11; 16:1–9; 18:1–12; 19:1–13; 27–28; 32; 51:59–64). Jeremiah was to take large stones and hide them at the entrance of the house of Pharaoh in Tahpanhes (cf. Jer. 13:4). This house of Pharaoh at a frontier city such as Tahpanhes was likely not the royal palace but a government building of some sort that was used by Pharaoh when he visited the city.[12] The MT has an addition to verse

---

11. See commentary on Jeremiah 41:16. "את הגברים (v. 6) is rendered by τοὺς δυνατοὺς ἄνδρας (Sept.ᴼᴸ τοὺς ἄνδρας is an equalization with MT). τοὺς δυνατούς arises from the pointing of הגברים as הַגִּבֹּרִים as at 41.16 and ἄνδρας, which Ziegler deletes from his critical text, represents הַגְּבָרִים. Hence Sept. is conflated" (McKane, *Jeremiah XXVI–LII*, 1053).

12. See Bright, *Jeremiah*, 263; McKane, *Jeremiah XXVI–LII*, 1055. See also A. Cowley, *Aramaic Papyri of the Fifth Century B.C.* (Oxford: Clarendon, 1923), 4–6.

9 that is not likely part of the original text but has nevertheless been the subject of much discussion.[13] According to this reading, Jeremiah was to take large stones and hide them "in the mortar in the brick kiln/terrace that is" (במלט במלבן אשר) at the entrance of the house of Pharaoh. The rare phrase במלט was interpreted by several early versions—Aquila, Symmachus, Theodotion, and the Latin Vulgate—as if it were בלט ("in secrecy").[14] Since the act was to be performed in the sight of the people of Judah, this would have to mean that the stones were to be hidden in such a way that they were inconspicuous. It could not mean that Jeremiah was to hide the stones without anyone knowing or seeing the act of hiding itself. On the other hand, it has been suggested that במלבן ("in the brick kiln/terrace") is a gloss for במלט ("in the mortar"), or that the two phrases are variants.[15] Keil interprets מלבן to mean "brick kiln" (see BDB, 527) and comments that the mortar and the brick kiln were present at the sight temporarily while construction on the building was still underway.[16] Jeremiah was to embed the stones in the mortar so that they could not be easily perceived. The stones would thus form the base for Nebuchadnezzar's throne and make a firmer foundation than the brick used in the construction of Pharaoh's house.[17] More recent commentators have opted for the meaning "brick terrace" for מלבן.[18] According to this view, Jeremiah was somehow to hide the stones within the mortar of the terrace's brickwork.

Verses 10–13 explain the meaning of the sign act. The LORD is about to send and bring (MT: take) Nebuchadnezzar the king of Babylon whom the LORD calls "my servant" in the MT but not in the LXX *Vorlage* (Jer. 43:10a [LXX 50:10a]; cf. MT Jer. 25:9; 27:6; see also Jer. 46:2, 13, 26). The remainder of verse 10a in the Hebrew source behind Greek Jeremiah is as follows: "and he (i.e., Nebuchadnezzar) will put (ושם את) his throne above these stones that you (i.e., Jeremiah) have hidden (טמנת)" (cf. Jer. 1:15).[19] McKane contends that the second-person

---

13. See McKane, *Jeremiah XXVI–LII*, 1054.

14. The other possibility is that מלט was interpreted to be a mem-preformative derivative from the noun לט ("secrecy") (Holladay, *Jeremiah 2*, 301). See also Rashi in Rosenberg, trans., *Mikraoth Gedoloth: Jeremiah Volume Two*, 333.

15. See Bright, *Jeremiah*, 263; Holladay, *Jeremiah 2*, 301.

16. Keil, *Jeremiah*, 350.

17. See also McKane, *Jeremiah XXVI–LII*, 1055; Holladay, *Jeremiah 2*, 302.

18. See Bright, *Jeremiah*, 263; Holladay, *Jeremiah 2*, 302.

19. The stones were hidden perhaps because the time for building the throne had not yet arrived (see Calvin, *Jeremiah*, 4:513).

verb טמנת ("you have hidden") is inappropriate to the context because Jeremiah was to address these words of the LORD "to them" (אליהם),[20] but he fails to note that this phrase is absent from the LXX *Vorlage*. The MT has the text as follows: "and I (i.e., the LORD) will put (ושמתי) his throne above these stones that I (i.e., the LORD) have hidden (טמנתי)" (cf. Jer. 49:38). According to this reading, the LORD himself will put (via his servant Nebuchadrezzar) the throne of the king of Babylon above the stones that he has hidden via his prophet Jeremiah. Verse 10b in the LXX *Vorlage* adds: "and he will lift up his armor/weapons against them" (ונשא סריונו עליהם) (cf. Jer. 51:3 [LXX 28:3]). The MT, however, has a different reading: "and he will stretch out his canopy over them" (ונטה את שפרירו עליהם). Some witnesses to *Targum Jonathan* have אודניה ("his seat/pedestal") for שפרירו (cf. Vulg.), while other witnesses have אפדניה ("his palace"). The term in the MT likely refers to a canopy in which a throne would be set up (cf. Dan. 11:45).

Nebuchadnezzar will come and strike the land of Egypt—"whoever to death, to death; and whoever to captivity, to captivity; and whoever to the sword, to the sword" (Jer. 43:11 [LXX 50:11]). The language of verse 11b is very close to that of Jeremiah 15:2 (see also Jer. 42:17; 46:10, 14, 19, 25; cf. Exod. 12:12; Rev. 13:10). The term "death" (מות) is in lieu of the term "plague" (דבר). McKane argues that this threat is only for the land of Egypt and not for Judeans living in the land of Egypt, despite the use of the same language in Jeremiah 42:17.[21] In order to make his case for this, McKane deliberately isolates 43:8–13 from its context and willfully ignores the placement of the unit between 42:1–43:7 and chapter 44. Such a disregard for composition is surely untenable. It is unquestionably the purpose of this unit's inclusion at the present juncture to show that Egypt would not be the place of refuge from Nebuchadnezzar that the Judean remnant thought it would be. The fate of the land of Egypt would be the fate of all those living there, including the Judeans. How could the Judeans or anyone else living in the land of Egypt expect to escape such devastation? McKane offers no explanation of how a Babylonian strike against Egypt would somehow leave the Judean remnant there unaffected.

The verb varies again between third person and first person at the beginning of verse 12a (cf. v. 10). The LXX *Vorlage* says: "and he (i.e., Nebuchadnezzar) will kindle (והצית) a fire in the houses/temples of their gods and burn them and take them captive." The MT says: "and I (i.e., the LORD via his servant Nebuchadrezzar) will kindle (והצתי) a

---

20. McKane, *Jeremiah XXVI–LII*, 1056.
21. McKane, *Jeremiah XXVI–LII*, 1058.

fire in the houses/temples of the gods of Egypt, and he will burn them and take them captive" (see also Isa. 19:1). The verbs "burn" and "take captive" both have third-person plural object suffixes ("them") in the Hebrew text, but these suffixes apparently do not have the same antecedent. The king of Babylon will burn the houses/temples of the gods (see Jer. 43:13b) and take the gods (i.e., idols) captive (cf. Isa. 46:1–2).[22]

The verb עטה in verse 12b normally means "wrap oneself" in biblical Hebrew, and there is possibly a homonym that means "grasp" (see BDB, 741–42): "and he will wrap himself in [or, grasp] the land of Egypt just as a shepherd wraps himself in [or, grasps] his garment." Rashi interprets this to mean that Nebuchadnezzar will wrap up all of Egypt's plunder and leave, "as a shepherd wraps up and rolls his garment and casts it over his shoulder when he leads his flock before him."[23] Keil, however, cites Ewald and says that the point of the comparison is "the easiness of the action."[24] The LXX translator was apparently aware of a homonym עטה that meant "delouse" (see *HALOT* 1:814):[25] "and he will delouse the land of Egypt just as a shepherd delouses his garment." Holladay believes that the use of עטה in this verse "involves a witty double meaning."[26] Nebuchadnezzar will enwrap himself with Egypt and delouse the land of Egypt in the sense that he will pillage it and walk away with its riches. According to the conclusion of verse 12b, Nebuchadnezzar will go out "in peace" (בשלום); that is, he will depart the land of Egypt unscathed.

The Hebrew source behind Greek Jeremiah 43:13 (LXX 50:13) says that the king of Babylon will shatter the pillars/obelisks of "the city of the sun" (עיר השמש; LXX: Heliopolis), which are in On, and their houses/temples will he burn with fire (cf. Jer. 43:12a). The word מצבות

---

22. See Keil, *Jeremiah*, 351; McKane, *Jeremiah XXVI–LII*, 1059. The other option is to understand the gods to be the antecedent for both suffixes, which would require the following rendering: "and burn them or take them captive." It is also possible that the text is intended to say that Nebuchadnezzar will burn the houses/temples of the gods and take the people captive (cf. v. 11), but the people are not immediately available in the syntax of verse 12 to serve as an antecedent.

23. Rosenberg, trans., *Mikraoth Gedoloth: Jeremiah Volume Two*, 334.

24. Ewald: "As easily as any shepherd in the open field wraps himself in his cloak, so will he take the whole of Egypt in his hand, and be able to throw it round him like a light garment, that he may then, thus dressed as it were with booty, leave the land in peace, without a foe—a complete victor" (Keil, *Jeremiah*, 351).

25. See also McKane, *Jeremiah XXVI–LII*, 1059–60.

26. Holladay, *Jeremiah 2*, 302.

is commonly translated "pillars," but it means "standing objects" and thus can refer to "obelisks." The "city of the sun," Heliopolis, was also known as On (see MT, LXX Gen. 41:45, 50; 46:20; LXX Exod. 1:11; LXX Ezek. 30:17; see also LXX, Syr. Hos. 4:15; 5:8; 10:5, 8). It was devoted to the worship of the Egyptian sun god Amun-Ra (Amon-Re). MT Isaiah 19:18 refers to this city as "the city of destruction" (עיר החרס; cf. Judg. 2:9), but 1QIsa[a] and some Masoretic manuscripts have "the city of the sun" (עיר החרס; cf. *Tg. Jon.*, Vulg.). LXX Isaiah 19:18 reflects עיר הצדק ("the city of righteousness"; cf. Isa. 1:26).[27] On the other hand, MT Jeremiah 43:13 says that the king of Babylon will shatter the pillars/obelisks of "the house/temple of the sun" or "Beth Shemesh" (בית שמש), which is in the land of Egypt, and the houses/temples of the gods of Egypt will he burn with fire. The relative clause, "which is in the land of Egypt," is probably intended to distinguish this "Beth Shemesh" from the one in the land of Judah.[28]

It is generally agreed that the fulfillment of the prophecy in Jeremiah 43:8–13 took place in some sense circa 568 BC (see Ezek. 29:17–21; see also *ANET*, 308).[29] It must be kept in mind, however, that the ultimate judgment of Egypt will take place in the eschatological Day of the LORD (see commentary on Jer. 46:10).

---

27. See Seeligmann, *Septuagint Version of Isaiah*, 220; McKane, *Jeremiah XXVI–LII*, 1061.

28. See Bright, *Jeremiah*, 263.

29. Keil, *Jeremiah*, 351–54; Thompson, *Book of Jeremiah*, 671–72; Holladay, *Jeremiah 2*, 302.

JEREMIAH 44 (LXX 51)

44:1 (51:1) The word that came to Jeremiah for all the Judeans who were living in [MT adds: the land of] Egypt and / even [and / even > MT; cf. Syr.] those who were living in Migdol and in Tahpanhes [MT adds: and in Noph / Memphis] and in the land of Pathros, saying, 44:2 (51:2) "Thus says the LORD *[MT adds: of hosts] the God of Israel, 'You [pl.], you saw all the calamity that I brought upon / against Jerusalem and upon / against [MT adds: all] the cities of Judah; and look, they are a ruin [2QJer, MT add: this day] without inhabitant [MT: and there is not in them an inhabitant; > 2QJer] 44:3 (51:3) because of their evil that they committed to provoke me by going to send sacrifices up in smoke [MT adds: to serve / worship] to other gods that you did not know [MT: that they did not know, you and your forefathers], 44:4 (51:4) and I sent to you [MT adds: all] my servants the prophets rising early and sending [i.e., urgently sending], saying, "Do not do the thing of [the thing of > Syr.] this abomination that I hate," 44:5 (51:5) but they did not listen and they did not incline their ear to turn from their evil not to send sacrifices up in smoke to other gods, 44:6 (51:6) and my fury poured out, and my anger, and it burned in the cities of Judah and in the streets of Jerusalem, and they became a ruin and [and > Codex L] a desolation [or, an object of horror] as this day.'*

44:7 (51:7) And now, thus says the LORD *[MT adds: the God] of hosts [MT adds: the God of Israel], 'Why are you doing this great harm to yourselves, to cut off of you man and woman, infant and nursing baby, from the midst of Judah so as not to leave for yourselves a remnant, 44:8 (51:8) by provoking me with the works [Cairo Geniza, mlt Mss, Syr.: work] of your hands by sending sacrifices up in smoke to other gods in the land of Egypt where you are entering to sojourn in order to cut off of you [or, in order to cut yourselves off; Syr.: in order that I might destroy you] and in order to become an object of contempt and an object of reproach among all [pc Mss: to all] the nations of the earth? 44:9 (51:9) Have you forgotten the evils of your forefathers and the evils of the kings of Judah and the evils of your officials [MT: his wives; Syr.: their wives] [MT adds: and your evils (> LXX, Syr.)] and the evils of your wives [> Syr.] that they committed in the land of Judah and in the streets of Jerusalem? 44:10 (51:10) And [> MT] they have not restrained themselves [or, they have not been restrained; LXX, Tg. Jon.: they have not ceased; MT: they have not been made contrite; Aq., Symm., Syr., Vulg.: they have not been made pure] to this day, [MT adds: and they have not feared] and they have not walked [MT adds: in my instruction and] in my statutes that I set [MT adds: before you and] before their forefathers [MT: before your forefathers].'*

44:11 (51:11) Therefore, thus says the LORD [MT adds: of hosts the God of Israel], 'Look, I am about to set my face [MT adds: against you for calamity and/even to cut off all Judah] 44:12 (51:12) to cut off [MT: and I will take] all the remnant that is in Egypt [MT: the remnant of Judah who set their face to enter the land of Egypt to sojourn there, and all will be finished], and they will fall, by the sword and by famine they will be finished from small to great [MT: in the land of Egypt they will fall, by the sword (mlt Mss add: and) by famine they will be finished, from small to great by the sword and by famine they will die], and they will become [MT adds: an object of a curse] an object of reproach and an object of horror and an object of contempt [MT: an object of horror and an object of contempt and an object of reproach], 44:13 (51:13) and I will visit upon [i.e., punish] those living in Egypt [MT: in the land of Egypt] just as I visited upon [i.e., punished] Jerusalem by the sword and by famine [MT: by the sword (2QJer, Mss add: and) by famine and by plague], 44:14 (51:14) and there will not be one who escapes [MT adds: or a survivor] of the remnant of Judah, those who are sojourning in the land of Egypt [MT: those who are entering to sojourn there in the land of Egypt], to return [MT: and to return] to the land of Judah where they long to return [MT adds: to live (> Syr.)]; [MT adds: for] they will not return, except those who escape [Syr.: except a few].'"

44:15 (51:15) And all the men who knew that their wives were sending sacrifices up in smoke to other gods and all the wives [MT adds: who were standing], a great assembly, and all the people who were living in the land of Egypt, in Pathros [Syr., Luther: and in Pathros] answered Jeremiah, saying, 44:16 (51:16) "As for the word that you have spoken to us in the name of the LORD, we are not listening to you. 44:17 (51:17) For we will certainly do every word/thing that goes forth from our mouth to send sacrifices up in smoke to the queen of the sky [MT: the work of the sky; Tg. Jon.: the star(s) of the sky] and to pour out to her drink offerings just as we and our fathers and our kings and our officials did in the cities of Judah and in the streets of Jerusalem and were satisfied with bread/food and were well off and did not see calamity [lit., and as for calamity, we did not see (it)]. 44:18 (51:18) But from the time that we stopped sending sacrifices up in smoke to the queen of the sky [MT: the work of the sky; Tg. Jon.: the star(s) of the sky] [MT adds: and pouring out to her drink offerings] we have lacked everything, and by the sword and by famine we have been finished. 44:19 (51:19) [LXX^L adds: And the women said (cf. Syr.)] And when we were sending sacrifices up in smoke [see GKC §145u] to the queen of the sky [MT: the work of the sky; Tg. Jon.: the star(s) of the sky] and pouring out to her drink offerings, was it apart from our husbands that we made for her sacrificial cakes [MT adds: to fashion her (see BDB, 781; GKC §58g); Tg. Jon.: tunics for the idols] and poured out to her drink offerings?"

44:20 (51:20) And Jeremiah said to all the people, to the mighty men [MT: to the men] and to the women and to all the people who were answering him words [MT: a word; Syr.: these words], saying, 44:21 (51:21) "Were not the sacrifices that you and your fathers and [and > MT] your kings and your officials and the people of the land sent up in smoke, [MT adds: them] what the LORD *remembered, and it came to his mind? 44:22 (51:22) And the* LORD *was no longer able to bear [Syr., Tg. Jon.: forgive] because of the evil of your deeds, because of the abominations that you committed, and your land became a ruin and a desolation [or, object of horror] and an object of contempt [MT adds: without inhabitant] as this day. 44:23 (51:23) Because you sent sacrifices up in smoke and because you sinned against the* LORD *and did not obey the voice of the* LORD *and in his statutes and in his instruction and in his testimonies [MT: and in his instruction and in his statutes and in his testimonies] did not walk, [MT adds: therefore] this calamity befell you [MT adds: as this day]."*

44:24 (51:24) And Jeremiah said to [MT adds: all] the people and to [MT adds: all] the women, "Hear the word of the LORD *[MT adds: all you of Judah who are in the land of Egypt]. 44:25 (51:25) Thus says the* LORD *[MT adds: of hosts] the God of Israel [MT adds: saying], 'You women, with your mouth you have spoken [MT: You (m. pl.) and your (m. pl.) wives, you (f. pl.) spoke with your (m. pl.) mouth] and with your [MT m. pl.] hands you [MT m. pl.] have fulfilled, saying, "We will certainly perform our vows that we made to send sacrifices up in smoke to the queen of the sky [MT: the work of the sky; Tg. Jon.: the star(s) of the sky] and to pour out to her drink offerings." You must indeed carry out your [MT m. pl.] vows and perform [MT adds: your (m. pl.) vows (pc Mss: your drink offerings)]!' 44:26 (51:26) Therefore, hear the word of the* LORD *all you of Judah who are living in the land of Egypt, 'Look, I swear by my great name,' says the* LORD*, 'My name will never again be [MT adds: called] in the mouth of all Judah [MT: all the people of Judah (or, any person of Judah)],*[1] *saying, "As the*

---

1.   See GKC §149b.

*L*ORD *lives [or, By the life of the* L*ORD*; *MT: As the Lord* G*OD* *lives (or,
By the life of the Lord* G*OD*)*]," in all the land of Egypt. 44:27 (51:27)
For [> MT] look, I am watching over them for harm and not for good
[LXX: to harm them and not to do good], and all those of Judah [MT:
all the people of Judah] who are living [living > MT] in the land of
Egypt will be finished by the sword or by famine until they come to an
end. 44:28 (51:28) And as for those who escape from the sword, they
will return [MT adds: from the land of Egypt] to the land of Judah few
in number, and [MT adds: all] the remnant of Judah, those entering
the land of Egypt to sojourn there, will know whose word stands [MT
adds: mine or theirs]. 44:29 (51:29) And this to you will be the sign,'
the prophetic utterance of the* L*ORD, 'that I am watching over you for
harm [MT: that I am visiting upon (i.e., punishing) you in this place in
order that you may know that my words against you will surely stand
for harm]': 44:30 (51:30) Thus says the* L*ORD, 'Look, I am about to
give/deliver Hophra [MT: Pharaoh Hophra; Syr.: Pharaoh the lame;
Tg. Jon.: Pharaoh the broken] the king of Egypt into the hand/power
of his enemy and into the hand/power of those who seek his life just
as I gave/delivered Zedekiah the king of Judah into the hand/power
of Nebuchadnezzar [MT: Nebuchadrezzar] the king of Babylon, his
enemy and the one who sought his life.'"*

Jeremiah 44:1a (LXX 51:1a) introduces the chapter as "The word
that came to Jeremiah for all the Judeans who were living in Egypt"
(cf. Jer. 7:1; 11:1; 18:1; 21:1; 30:1; 32:1; 34:1, 8; 35:1; 40:1). The remainder of this opening verse further indicates that the Judeans at
this time were not only in Tahpanhes (Jer. 43:7–9) but also in Migdol
near Tahpanhes (see Exod. 14:2; Num. 33:7; Jer. 46:14; Ezek. 29:10;
30:6) and in the land of Pathros in the south (see Isa. 11:11; Jer. 44:15;
Ezek. 29:14; 30:14).[2] An addition in the MT (> LXX *Vorlage*) includes
Noph (Memphis) near Cairo as another location where Judeans settled (see Isa. 19:13; Jer. 2:16; 46:14, 19; Ezek. 30:13). This raises the
question of how Jeremiah could have delivered his message for such a
large and dispersed group. Verse 15 provides a clue that there was at
Pathros a great assembly of representatives from these various locations to whom Jeremiah spoke.

---

2. "It is now known that a sizeable Jewish community was established at
    Elephantine, an island on the Nile in southern Egypt, during the fifth
    century B.C." (Thompson, *Book of Jeremiah*, 675). See Cowley, *Aramaic
    Papyri of the Fifth Century B.C.* It is not known what relationship, if any,
    this community may have had to the one mentioned in Jeremiah 44.

The LORD reminds the community of Judeans living in Egypt of the calamity that they witnessed when he brought judgment upon Jerusalem and the cities of Judah (Jer. 44:2a [LXX 51:2a]). How easy it was for them to forget! He thus highlights the evidence for them: "and look, they are a ruin [2QJer, MT add: this day] without inhabitant [MT: and there is not in them an inhabitant; > 2QJer]" (Jer. 44:2b [LXX 51:2b]). The LXX reflects the original reading מאין יושב ("without inhabitant"; cf. MT Jer. 44:22b), whereas the text has been corrupted to ואין בהם יושב ("and there is not in them an inhabitant") in the MT. This latter reading cannot be original because the third masculine plural pronominal suffix ("them") does not agree with the antecedent "cities" (f. pl.) (cf. Jer. 4:29b).[3] The "calamity" (רעה) was due to the people's "evil" (רעה) that they committed as if to provoke the LORD (cf. Jer. 7:18b; 11:17; 32:29) by going to send their sacrifices up in smoke to other gods that they did not know (Jer. 44:2 [LXX 51:3]; cf. 2 Kgs. 22:17; Jer. 1:16; 19:4; see also Deut. 13:3, 7, 14 [Eng., 13:2, 6, 13]). The infinitive לקטר ("to send sacrifices up in smoke") is often translated "to burn incense," but it seems best in context to see a reference to the burning of sacrifices.[4] McKane suggests that the MT's addition of לעבד ("to serve/worship" [> LXX *Vorlage*]) is either a doublet or a supplementation.[5] The sudden switch to second person in the LXX's description of the other gods or idols as those "that you did not know" has been considered awkward, but it must be kept in mind that the people addressed in the second person in verse 2 were those who saw the calamity for themselves. There is likely a deliberate effort here to demonstrate solidarity between generations past and present (cf. Jer. 2:1–13). This is made explicit in the MT's version of the text: "that they did not know, you and your forefathers."

The prohibition against idolatry has been central to the program of the book of Jeremiah because idolatry is viewed as the core sin problem of which all other sins are symptoms (Jer. 1:16; 5:7–8; 10:1–16). The LORD recalls for the people how he sent them his servants the prophets urgently, saying, "Do not do the thing of this abomination that I hate" (Jer. 44:4 [LXX 51:4]; cf. Jer. 7:13 [MT], 25; 11:7 [MT]; 25:4; 26:5; 29:19 [MT]; 32:33; 35:15a); but they did not listen, nor did they pay attention to turn from their evil so as not to burn sacrifices to other gods (Jer. 44:5 [LXX 51:5]; cf. Jer. 7:26; 25:4; 26:5; 35:15b). Thus, the LORD's fury poured out, along with his anger, and it burned in the cities of Judah

---

3. See the discussion in McKane, *Jeremiah XXVI–LII*, 1070.
4. See Bright, *Jeremiah*, 264.
5. McKane, *Jeremiah XXVI–LII*, 1070.

and in the streets of Jerusalem with the result that they became a ruin and a desolation (or, object of horror) "as this day" (Jer. 44:6 [LXX 51:6]; cf. Jer. 42:18; 44:22b, 23b). The cities of Judah and the streets of Jerusalem were the very places where the people practiced their idolatry (Jer. 7:17; 44:9, 17).

Given the above lesson that the people should have learned from their recent past, the Lord now asks, "Why are you doing this great harm to yourselves, to cut off of you man and woman, infant and nursing baby, from the midst of Judah so as not to leave for yourselves a remnant" (Jer. 44:7 [LXX 51:7]; cf. Jer. 3:24; 44:11)?[6] That is, why do they insist on perpetuating their former sins, for which they were judged so severely, by provoking the Lord with the works of their hands (i.e., their idols) by burning sacrifices to other gods in the land of Egypt where they have only recently entered to sojourn (Jer. 44:8a [LXX 51:8a])? They will only succeed in cutting themselves off and becoming an object of contempt and reproach among all the nations (Jer. 44:8b [LXX 51:8b]; cf. Jer. 42:18; 44:12, 22). As indicated in Jeremiah 7:19, the people were not primarily provoking or harming the Lord with actions such as these. Rather, they were "provoking" (i.e., harming) themselves. They should have been an example among the nations of a people made wise by the Torah (Deut. 4:6–7), but instead they became quite the opposite (Jer. 4:22).

Thus, the Lord inquires, "Have you forgotten the evils of your forefathers and the evils of the kings of Judah and the evils of your officials [MT: his wives; Syr.: their wives] [MT adds: and your evils; > LXX, Syr.] and the evils of your wives [> Syr.] that they committed in the land of Judah and in the streets of Jerusalem" (Jer. 44:9 [LXX 51:9]; cf. Jer. 44:17)? The Hebrew source behind Greek Jeremiah has שריכם ("your officials") where the MT has נשיו ("his wives"; Syr.: "their wives" [= נשיהם]).[7] The MT anticipates verse 10 and adds "and your evils" (> LXX, Syr.) to ensure that the present generation is included with the forefathers (cf. Jer. 2:5, 9). Both the LXX and the MT then include "and the evils of your wives," which is absent from the Syriac. This latter addition is likely in anticipation of the key role that the wives play later in the chapter (see Jer. 44:15, 19, 20, 24, 25).

The people have not "restrained themselves" (נכלאו; or, "they have not been restrained"; LXX, *Tg. Jon.*: "they have not ceased") even to

---

6. Holladay interprets להכרית לכם ("to cut off of you") as a "dative of disadvantage" ("to cut off for yourselves") (*Jeremiah 2*, 303).

7. McKane (*Jeremiah XXVI–LII*, 1072) refers to the view of Barthélemy who suggests that the MT's נשיו ("his wives") is a reference to Solomon's wives (see 1 Kgs. 11:3, 4, 8).

the present day (Jer. 44:10a [LXX 51:10a]). The MT says that they have not "been made contrite" (דכאו) (cf. Isa. 19:10; 57:15; 66:2; Ps. 51:19 [Eng., 51:17]).[8] Aquila, Symmachus, the Syriac, and the Latin Vulgate interpret this same verb in its Aramaic sense: "they have not been made pure" (cf. LXX Isa. 53:10). The MT adds the gloss: "and they have not feared" (> LXX *Vorlage*). The Hebrew source behind Greek Jeremiah 44:10b says that the people "have not walked in my statutes that I set before their forefathers." The MT expands and alters this to include second-person references: "and they have not walked in my instruction [or, Torah] and in my statutes that I set before you and before your forefathers" (cf. Jer. 26:4; 32:23; 44:23).

The conjunction לכן ("Therefore") at the beginning of Jeremiah 44:11 (LXX 51:11) introduces the announcement of judgment against the community of Judeans living in Egypt (Jer. 44:11–14) after the accusation made against them in verses 7–10. In the Hebrew source behind the Greek version of verse 11, the LORD simply says, "Look, I am about to set my face," and the thought continues in verse 12: "to cut off all the remnant that is in Egypt" (cf. Jer. 44:7–8). The MT, however, has a longer text for verse 11: "Look, I am about to set my face against you for calamity and/even to cut off all Judah" (cf. Jer. 3:12; 21:10). Both versions of the text express the LORD's resolve to judge the people.

Whereas the LXX *Vorlage* of verse 12 completes the thought of verse 11 ("to cut off all the remnant that is in Egypt"), the MT begins a new clause and expands the text: "and I will take the remnant of Judah who set their face to enter the land of Egypt to sojourn there, and all will be finished" (cf. Jer. 42:15–17). This establishes a correspondence between the setting of the remnant's face to enter Egypt (Jer. 44:12) and the setting of LORD's face to judge them (Jer. 44:11). Both have determined their course of action, and neither will relent. Verse 12 in the LXX *Vorlage* resumes: "and they will fall, by the sword and by famine they will be finished from small to great" (cf. Jer. 42:17, 22; 43:11; 44:13, 27). The MT once again expands the text: "in the land of Egypt they will fall, by the sword [mlt Mss add: and] by famine they will be finished, from small to great by the sword and by famine they will die." Verse 12 in the LXX *Vorlage* then concludes: "and they will become an object of reproach and an object of horror and an object of contempt" (cf. Jer. 44:6, 8, 22). The MT expands and rearranges this: "and they will become an object of a curse [NET: an example of those who have been

---

8. Rudolph (*BHS* apparatus) proposes reading נכאו ("disheartened") from כאה (Ps. 109:16; Dan. 11:30), but there is no textual evidence for this.

cursed and that people use in pronouncing a curse], an object of horror and an object of contempt and an object of reproach." The language of verse 12 is quite common in the book of Jeremiah.[9] The judgment that was once announced for the people living in Judah who were idolatrous and thus disobedient to the terms of the covenant is now announced for the Judeans living in Egypt who have perpetuated the idolatry of their forefathers (see again Jer. 42:18; 44:2–6, 13).

The LORD will punish those living in Egypt just as he did Jerusalem "by the sword and by famine" (MT: "by the sword [2QJer, Mss add: and] by famine and by plague") (Jer. 44:13 [LXX 51:13]; cf. Jer. 14:12; 42:17–18, 22; 43:11; 44:12, 27). There will not be one person who escapes (MT adds: "or a survivor") of the remnant of Judah sojourning in the land of Egypt (Jer. 44:14a [LXX 51:14a]; cf. Jer. 42:17). Not one of them will return to the land of Judah where they long to be (Jer. 44:14b [LXX 51:14b]; cf. Jer. 22:27; 42:16). The wording of this suggests that the people believed their sojourn in Egypt to be providential and temporary, perhaps thinking of the LORD's words to Jacob to whom he said not to fear going down to Egypt where he would become a great nation and where the LORD would be present with him and from which he would bring him back up again (Gen. 46:3–4). On the contrary, the people of Jeremiah's day would have been in a position not to fear only if they had stayed in the land of Judah (Jer. 42:10–12). The people will not return, "except those who escape." Rashi interprets this to be a reference to Jeremiah and Baruch who were taken to Egypt against their will,[10] although there is no indication in the text that they ever returned to the land of Judah from Egypt. Calvin suggests that "those who escape" refers to those who would eventually return from Babylonian exile after the decree of Cyrus,[11] but this seems unlikely in the present context.[12] The Syriac version interprets "except those who escape" to mean "except a few." On the surface, this seems like a contradiction of the earlier part of the verse, but it is consistent with what is said later in verse 28. Only a very few would escape the sword and return to Judah, so few in fact that there would appear to be none at all to return (cf. Hos. 9:6).

---

9. See Parke-Taylor, *Formation of the Book of Jeremiah*, 21–23, 113, 201–4, 243–44.

10. Rosenberg, trans., *Mikraoth Gedoloth: Jeremiah Volume Two*, 338.

11. Calvin, *Jeremiah*, 4:539.

12. An editorial footnote to Calvin's commentary suggests that "those who escape" would have been those who escaped to the land of Judah in the meantime prior to Nebuchadnezzar's invasion.

Jeremiah 44:15–19 (LXX 51:15–19) is the reply of the people to the word of the LORD that came to Jeremiah for them. Those who answered Jeremiah are divided into two groups in verse 15. First of all there were all the men who had knowledge of the fact that their wives were guilty of burning sacrifices to other gods. They and all the wives formed one group, which is designated "a great assembly." Along with this specifically identified primary group was a more general assemblage of Judeans who were living in the land of Egypt. Keil rightly notes that the phrase "in Pathros" is not in apposition to "in the land of Egypt," as if only those living in Pathros were present.[13] Rather, Pathros was the place where the people from the various places mentioned in verse 1 answered Jeremiah when they gathered at Pathros.

The opening statement of the people's reply indicates very clearly that they had no intention of paying attention to the prophet's message: "As for the word that you have spoken to us in the name of the LORD, we are not listening to you" (Jer. 44:16 [LXX 51:16]; see Jer. 44:1). This response may be compared to the one in Jeremiah 43:1–7. There the people accused Jeremiah of "deception" (שֶׁקֶר) and said that the LORD did not send him to advise against going to Egypt (Jer. 43:2). This amounted to an accusation of false prophecy (Jer. 23:21, 25, 32). Thus, they refused to listen to him (Jer. 43:4, 7), but they did not give him the death penalty. In the present context, the people have said that they are not listening to the word that the prophet has spoken to them in the name of the LORD. This is in direct violation of the given instruction for how to respond to a prophet like Moses (Deut. 18:15, 18–19). It is thus to be concluded that the people were insinuating that Jeremiah was speaking in the name of the LORD falsely (Deut. 18:20; Jer. 23:25), yet they did not have him executed in accordance with the law (see again Jer. 1:8, 17–19; 15:20–21).

Not only did the people reject "the word" (הדבר) that Jeremiah spoke in the LORD's name, but also they insisted that they would do "every word/thing that goes forth from our mouth" (כל הדבר אשר יצא מפינו) (Jer. 44:17 [LXX 51:17]), an expression that refers to religious vows that the people made (see Num. 30:3; Deut. 23:22–24 [Eng., 23:21–23]; Jer. 44:25). The specific wording of this seems designed to contradict that of Deuteronomy 8:3b2: "but by all that goes forth from the mouth of the LORD does man live" (see also Jer. 36:4). The description of the word/thing that went forth from the people's mouth matches that of the pagan religious practice described in Jeremiah 7:18 (see commentary there). The people were intent on burning sacrifices to

---

13. Keil, *Jeremiah*, 358.

"the queen of the sky" (MT: "the work of the sky"; *Tg. Jon.*: "the star(s) of the sky; see Deut. 4:19) and pouring out drink offerings to her just as they and their fathers and their kings and their officials did in the cities of Judah and in the streets of Jerusalem (see Jer. 7:17; 44:6, 9). Such an appeal to the widespread nature of the practice from the family to the royalty no doubt made it seem legitimate in the minds of the people. Furthermore, they saw a correspondence between their worship of the queen of the sky during the reign of Manasseh (2 Kgs. 21:5) and the prosperity that they enjoyed during that same period when they "were satisfied with bread/food and were well off and did not see calamity" (cf. Num. 11:5–6; see Jer. 12:1; see also Jer. 42:14b). They forgot that the religious practices established during the time of Manasseh were ultimately the cause of the Babylonian exile (2 Kgs. 21:10–16; Jer. 15:4).

The argument of Jeremiah 44:18 (LXX 51:18) is that ever since the stoppage of burning sacrifices to the queen of the sky that took place with the official reforms of Josiah (2 Kgs. 22–23) the people have lacked everything. In the minds of the people, the reforms of Josiah marked the beginning of the end for them. They saw a correspondence between those reforms and their demise by the sword and by famine. Of course, the pagan religious practices of the people did not stop completely after the reforms of Josiah (see again Jer. 7:18). It was only in an official sense that they were brought to an end. Nevertheless, the people blamed their problems on their inability to fulfill their vows to the queen of the sky openly due to the official restrictions placed upon them.[14]

Both the Lucianic recension and the Syriac introduce Jeremiah 44:19 (LXX 51:19) as that which the women (i.e., the wives) said, which, despite the presence of the following masculine plural participle (see GKC §145u), is consistent with the remainder of the verse where the speakers refer to "our husbands." The women claimed that the vows they made to burn sacrifices and to pour out drink offerings to the queen of the sky (Jer. 44:25) were made in accordance with the instruction for the making of vows in Numbers 30:7–16, which required husbands to grant approval of vows made by wives. This claim was made emphatically by means of a rhetorical question: "was it apart from our husbands that we made for her sacrificial cakes and poured out to her drink offerings?" According to Jeremiah 7:18, the making of these cakes was a family affair, but the emphasis in the present context is clearly upon the husbands. Such a focus on the role of the husbands

---

14. See Redak in Rosenberg, trans., *Mikraoth Gedoloth: Jeremiah Volume Two*, 339.

in this matter recalls the failure of Adam in the garden of Eden (Gen. 2:17; 3:6). The MT adds that the women made cakes "to fashion her" (להעצבה).[15] That is, they made idolatrous images of her (see BDB, 781), perhaps in the shape of stars.[16]

Jeremiah, unfazed by the people's line of argumentation, doubled down on his earlier accusation against them (Jer. 44:20–23 [LXX 51:20–23]).[17] Using the people's own words against them (see Jer. 44:17), he asked rhetorically whether the sacrifices that they and their fathers and their kings and their officials and the people of the land sent up in smoke were not what the Lord remembered (Jer. 44:21 [LXX 51:21]). Did they really think that such action never came to the Lord's mind simply because there was an official sanction against it in the reforms of Josiah? The argument of the people was pure nonsense. There was absolutely no correlation between their worship of the queen of the sky and the good times that they enjoyed during the reign of Manasseh, nor was there any correlation between the reforms of Josiah and the subsequent fall of Judah to Babylon. Judah fell because the people insisted on perpetuating the pagan religious practices from the time of Manasseh despite the official reforms of Josiah. That attitude of the people continued into the time of their sojourn in Egypt.

The Lord was no longer able to bear (Syr., *Tg. Jon.*: "forgive") because of the evil of the people's deeds, because of the abominations (i.e., acts of idolatry) that they committed (Jer. 44:22a [LXX 51:22a]). Thus, their land became "a ruin and a desolation [or, object of horror] and an object of contempt [MT adds: without inhabitant] as this day" (Jer. 44:22b [LXX 51:22b]; see again Jer. 44:2, 6, 8, 12). It was precisely because they burned sacrifices to other gods that the calamity befell them (Jer. 44:23 [LXX 51:23]). It had nothing to do with the fact that the reforms of Josiah hindered their ability to fulfill vows made to the queen of the sky. It was because they sinned against the Lord and did not obey his voice. It was because they did not walk in his statutes and in his instruction and in his testimonies revealed in his Torah and communicated to them by the prophets (see again Jer. 44:10).

---

15. This infinitive should probably not be understood from the homonymous root עצב ("pain"), which, in the *hiphil* stem would mean "to cause pain" (see Keil, *Jeremiah*, 358), unless the pronominal suffix is reanalyzed as third masculine singular so that it would mean "to cause him [i.e., the Lord] pain" (see McKane, *Jeremiah XXVI–LII*, 1077).

16. See McKane, *Jeremiah XXVI–LII*, 1077.

17. For the difference between "mighty men" (LXX) and "men" (MT) in verse 20, see the commentary on Jeremiah 41:16 and 43:6.

The reintroduction of Jeremiah's discourse in 44:24 (LXX 51:24) suggests a pause between the content of verses 20–23 and that of verses 24–30. In contrast to verses 20–23, which consisted of Jeremiah's own reiteration of the word from the LORD (Jer. 44:1–14) in response to the people (Jer. 44:15–19), the remainder of the chapter features fresh delivery of the word of the LORD (see Jer. 44:25, 26, 30). The expansion of verse 24b in the MT is based on material found in verse 26a. According to the Hebrew source behind Greek Jeremiah 44:25 (LXX 51:25), the message from the LORD was specifically for the women, even though Jeremiah addressed it to the people more generally in verse 24: "You women, with your mouth you have spoken and with your hands you have fulfilled, saying, 'We will certainly perform our vows that we made to send sacrifices up in smoke to the queen of the sky and to pour out to her drink offerings.' You must indeed carry out your vows and perform" (cf. Jer. 44:17–19)! The MT, however, has a potentially confusing mixture of masculine plural and feminine plural forms: "You [m. pl.] and your [m. pl.] wives, you [f. pl.] spoke with your [m. pl.] mouth and with your [m. pl.] hands you [m. pl.] have fulfilled, saying, 'We will certainly perform our vows that we made to send sacrifices up in smoke to the work of the sky [*Tg. Jon.*: the star(s) of the sky] and to pour out to her drink offerings.' You must indeed carry out [f. pl.] your [m. pl.] vows and perform [f. pl.] your [m. pl.] vows [pc Mss: drink offerings]!" Such a mixture is only intelligible with an understanding that the husbands were responsible for the vows made by their wives (Num. 30:7–16; Jer. 44:19). The appeal of the wives to their husbands' approval of their vows did not legitimate those vows. It only made their husbands complicit. The sarcastic exhortation to fulfill such vows is comparable to Jeremiah 7:21 (see commentary there; see also Isa. 29:1; Ezek. 20:39; Amos 4:4–5). On the one hand, the Mosaic law instructed those who made vows to make sure that they fulfilled them (Num. 30:3; Deut. 23:22 [Eng., 23:21]; Eccl. 5:3–4 [Eng., 5:4–5]). On the other hand, if a vow involved a violation of the Mosaic law, such as worship of other gods (Exod. 20:3–6; Deut. 5:7–10) or child sacrifice (Deut. 12:31; Jer. 7:31), it was not to be fulfilled but renounced. For instance, the rendering of Judges 11:39 in *Targum Jonathan* suggests that Jephthah should not have fulfilled his foolish vow, which involved child sacrifice. Rather, he should have consulted the priest and redeemed his daughter in accordance with Exodus 13:13; 34:20; Numbers 18:15–17 (see also Lev. 5:4).

The Judeans living in the land of Egypt were committed to their worship of the queen of the sky. Therefore, the LORD announced his judgment of them once again (Jer. 44:26 [LXX 51:26]; cf. Jer. 44:11). He swore by his great name because there was no greater name by which he could swear in order to communicate the certitude of what would happen (see Heb. 6:13; cf. Isa. 45:23; Jer. 22:5; 49:13; 51:14 [MT]; Amos 6:8). His words in the Hebrew text take the typical form of an oath with an elided self-imprecation (see GKC §149b). According to this oath, his name (i.e., Yahweh [the LORD]) would never again be used in the mouth of all Judah to introduce an oath with the words, "As the LORD lives," in all the land of Egypt.[18] This refers to the inappropriate use of the name of God to swear falsely or disingenuously (see Jer. 5:2, 7; 12:16; 7:9; see also Exod. 20:7, 16; Deut. 5:11, 20). There was likely such a misuse of God's name in the vows that went forth from the people's mouth to worship the queen of the sky (see Jer. 44:17, 25). The coming judgment of the community of Judeans in Egypt would eradicate this kind of swearing in the name of the LORD. This would be part of paving the way to form a community of true believers who would swear in the LORD's name faithfully (see commentary on Jer. 4:2).

According to Jeremiah 44:27 (LXX 51:27), the LORD was watching over the Judeans living in Egypt for harm and not for good so that they would be finished by the sword or by famine until they came to an end (cf. Jer. 44:12–13; see also Bar. 2:9). This language runs contrary to the words of hope given to the faithful remnant of the people of God (Jer. 29:11; 31:28). The LORD was providentially overseeing his words of judgment against the Judeans in Egypt to ensure that those words would come to pass (see Jer. 1:11–12). As for those who might escape from the sword, they would return to the land of Judah "few in number" (מתי מספר) (Jer. 44:28a [LXX 51:28a]; cf. Jer. 44:14; 51:50; Ezek. 6:8; 12:16; see also Deut. 4:27; 28:62). This would mark a reversal of fortune from the time when the family of Jacob, which was relatively "few in number," grew into a mighty nation in the land of Egypt (see Deut. 26:5; Ps. 105:12; see also Jer. 10:24; 29:6; 30:19; Hos. 8:10; Bar. 2:13, 34). The remnant of Judah, which McKane identifies as the remnant in Judah (i.e., those who were in Egypt but managed to escape back to Judah),[19] would then have to recognize whose word, the LORD's or theirs, had stood the test (Jer. 44:28b [LXX 51:28b]; cf. Num. 11:23). Kara and Abarbanel disagree over which word is in view here.[20] According to Kara, the people would know whether they were right that their worship of the queen of the sky brought them prosperity and

---

18. The consonantal text of the MT includes the written *qere* אדני ("Lord") alongside the name יהוה, which forced the Masoretes to supply the name with the vowels of אלהים ("God").
19. McKane, *Jeremiah XXVI–LII*, 1081.
20. Rosenberg, trans., *Mikraoth Gedoloth: Jeremiah Volume Two*, 343.

that their neglect thereof brought them ruin, or the Lord was right that such worship would bring ruin upon them (Jer. 44:15–19). Abarbanel, however, contends, that the reference is to the prophecy that the people would perish in Egypt, which they denied (Jer. 43:2).

Verse 29 in the LXX *Vorlage* introduces verse 30 as the confirmatory sign that the Lord was watching over the people (פקד אני עליכם) "for harm," which echoes the language of verse 27a. On the other hand, the MT's verse 29 incorporates the language of verse 28b to introduce verse 30 as the sign that the Lord was visiting upon or punishing the people (פקד אני עליכם) "in this place" (i.e., Egypt) in order that they may know that his words against them would surely stand for harm. Calvin comments that the sign given in verse 30 would not provide assurance of something that was yet to come, as in the case of the sign given to Gideon (Judg. 6:17); rather, it would confirm something that had already occurred, as with the sign given to Moses: "and this to you will be the sign that I am the one who has sent you: when you bring the people out of Egypt, you [pl.] will serve/worship the one true God at/on this mountain" (Exod. 3:12).[21] Of course, a sign of the demise of Egypt had already been provided by the prophet in the form a symbolic action (Jer. 43:8–13).[22]

The Lord pointed to the fate of Pharaoh Hophra as the sign that would come (Jer. 44:30 [LXX 51:30; see Jer. 37:5, 7 for this Pharaoh's earlier involvement in the narrative; see also Ezek. 17:7, 15). Hophra, also known as Apries, was the fourth king of the twenty-sixth dynasty. He reigned alone in Egypt from 589 to 570 BC (and then with Amasis from 570 to 564 BC according to BDB, 344).[23] He is called "Pharaoh the lame" by the Syriac and "Pharaoh the broken" by *Targum Jonathan* (cf. the description of Pharaoh Necho as "Pharaoh the lame" in Syr., *Tg. Jon.* Jer. 46:2). According to Rashi, the rendering in *Targum Jonathan*

---

21. Calvin, *Jeremiah*, 4:561–62. On the other hand, Keil comments, "If no definite time be fixed for the occurrence of this sign, then it may not appear till a considerable time afterwards, and yet be a pledge for the occurrence of what was predicted for a still later period" (Keil, *Jeremiah*, 361). Likewise, McKane says, "The sign that judgement will fall on the Judaeans in Egypt is the fall of Hophra, and this means that the fall of Hophra precedes the judgement which Yahweh is to inflict on the Judaeans in Egypt" (McKane, *Jeremiah XXVI–LII*, 1081).

22. Nevertheless, as the prophecy in Isaiah 19 indicates, there was not only judgment in store for Egypt (Isa. 19:1–15) but also salvation (Isa. 19:16–25).

23. But see Bright (*Jeremiah*, 264) who says that Hophra died in the rebellion of 570 BC.

is based on reading the name חפרע ("Hophra") as the *hophal qatal* third masculine singular verb הפרע from the root פרע, which involves taking the word פרעה ("Pharaoh") and making its last letter first.[24] The LORD would deliver Hophra into the power of his enemy and into the power of those who sought his life just as he delivered Zedekiah into the power of his enemy Nebuchadnezzar who sought his life (see Jer. 21:7). McKane comments that Nebuchadnezzar is mentioned here only for the sake of comparison.[25] Nebuchadnezzar was not necessarily the enemy who sought Hophra's life (cf. Jer. 46:26). According to Herodotus, it was Amasis who led a revolt against Hophra that resulted in his capture and dethronement in 570 BC.

Keil discusses how the extermination of Judeans in Egypt (Jer. 44:27–28) can be squared with the presence of a thriving Jewish community in Egypt centuries later:[26] "But as little can we find any proofs that Alexander the Great found so many Jews in Egypt that he could, to a large extent, people with them the city he had founded. It is merely testified by Josephus . . . that Alexander had Jewish soldiers in his army." Keil goes on to say that Alexander's newly founded city attracted an ever increasing number of Jewish immigrants (see *Letter of Aristeas*) so that the inhabitants of Egypt in that time need not be regarded as descendants of those who once moved there with Jeremiah. The Elephantine papyri do provide evidence of a Jewish community in southern Egypt in the fifth century BC (see above note to commentary on Jer. 44:1). Nevertheless, there is nothing to contradict the prophecy of Jeremiah 44, which does not preclude the possibility of the formation of communities in Egypt at a later time.

Jeremiah 44 (LXX 51) is the last narrative of the book in which the prophet Jeremiah appears. All indications are that he lived his last days in Egypt and never returned to the land of Judah (but see *4 Bar.* 4:6; 6:19; 8; 9:7, 14, 31–32). According to an ancient extrabiblical work entitled *Lives of the Prophets* (ch. 2), Jeremiah died in Tahpanhes (Jer. 43:7, 8; 44:1) when he was stoned to death by the Jews (cf. Matt. 23:31; Acts 7:52).[27] He was buried in the place where Pharaoh's house stood (Jer. 43:9; but cf. Deut. 34:6). The sojourn of Jeremiah in Egypt likely

---

24. "According to this interpretation, Hophra is not a proper name, but a pejorative, given this Pharaoh as a portent of his impending downfall" (Rosenberg, trans., *Mikraoth Gedoloth: Jeremiah Volume Two*, 343).
25. McKane, *Jeremiah XXVI–LII*, 1082.
26. Keil, *Jeremiah*, 362–63.
27. *Lives of the Prophets* chapter 2 also compares Jeremiah to Moses as one who helped people with their snake bites (see Num. 21:4–9; Jer. 8:17).

has implications for the history of the text of Jeremiah's book: "the text form represented by the Septuagint, which is about 14% shorter than the MT, is an earlier edition of the book, which was expanded and placed in a new order by later editors. The existence of two so different editions of the text side by side may be explained by the fact that the *Vorlage* of the Septuagint (i.e., the Hebrew source text of the translation), having been brought to Alexandria, remained there in geographical isolation and was largely untouched by the final Palestinian edition."[28] The earlier Hebrew edition of the book was translated into Greek in the second half of the second century BC. "By this time the text had probably undergone changes in Palestine and possibly reached the form we know from the MT, but this second, augmented edition of the book never became popular in Egypt."[29]

APPLICATION OF JEREMIAH 40–44 (LXX 47:1–51:30)

This section of the book of Jeremiah brings together for the reader several of the themes introduced in chapter 1 that have been developed in the book thus far. There is the depiction of Jeremiah as a prophet like Moses (Jer. 1:4–9; 42:1–6), which receives yet another twist in Jeremiah 43:1–7. There is also the further development of the language of the book's programmatic text (Jer. 1:10) in Jeremiah 42:10–11. The LORD appears once again in this section as the God who watches over his word to do it (Jer. 1:11–12; 44:27). Jeremiah continues to play the role of the persecuted prophet whose God is with him to rescue him (Jer. 1:8, 17–19), especially in chapters 43 and 44. The problem of idolatry (Jer. 1:16), which is so prominent throughout the book, continues to manifest itself among the people even after the Babylonian invasion (Jer. 44).

There is perhaps no greater illustration for the reader of the need for the new covenant (Jer. 31:31–34) than what is found in these chapters. It can hardly be a coincidence that these chapters form the conclusion to a larger section (Jer. 34–44) that follows the Book of Comfort (Jer. 30–33). The initial clue is the unsettled nature of the community that the reader encounters in Jeremiah 40–41 after the account of the Babylonian invasion in chapter 39. It becomes clearer when Jeremiah, already vindicated as a true prophet by the fulfillment of his prophecy about the Babylonians, is accused of false prophecy (Jer. 43:2) when he does not give the people the answer they want concerning the

---

28. Aejmelaeus, "Jeremiah at the Turning Point of History," 460. See commentary on Jeremiah 51:59–64 for the initial formation of the second edition in Babylon.
29. Aejmelaeus, "Jeremiah at the Turning Point of History," 460.

possibility of a sojourn in Egypt (Jer. 42). Finally, the people's illogical defense of their idolatrous religious practices (Jer. 44:15–19) leaves no doubt that no amount of persuasion from prophecy or experience will ever change their hearts and minds. Only the transformation of their hearts and minds in the new covenant (Jer. 4:4; 31:31–34; 32:39–40) will make them receptive to the will of God.

While points of application will be part of the commentary on the remaining chapters 45 and 52, the present section is the last one in this volume specifically devoted to application of the text. Thus, it seems appropriate to offer a few concluding thoughts in general about the application, preaching, and teaching of the book of Jeremiah. Perhaps the most important thing to remember about application is that it is not a free for all. Application must be exegetically demonstrable.[30] Since application is part of the intended meaning of the text, the task is to explain that meaning—not to add to it. Students often ask me how to preach and teach large prophetic books like the book of Jeremiah. The first thing that I tell them is that this is not the primary question to ask. If they try to answer this question before they do the long and hard work of learning the text of the book, then it will only be an exercise in frustration. On the other hand, if they do the necessary work in all the details of the text, then the question of how to preach and teach the text in a variety of settings will answer itself. In other words, they will know that their familiarity with the text of Jeremiah is sufficient when the manner in which the book should be preached and taught becomes obvious to them. The second thing that I tell them is that preaching and teaching are often done in different communication situations. Preaching is typically one-way communication, which requires the preacher to maintain a general audience's attention with big ideas (outlines, themes, etc.). Teaching, however, can occur in smaller, more interactive settings that allow for more attention to detail. It is important to allow for both of these modes.

---

30. This requires attention to the words (textual criticism, grammar, syntax, semantics, composition, intertextuality), not merely discussion of ideas or theological concepts to which the words refer.

SCRIBAL COLOPHON

(Jer. 45 [LXX 51:31–35])

45:1 (51:31) The word that Jeremiah the prophet spoke to Baruch the son of Neriah when he wrote these words on a document from the mouth of Jeremiah [ESV: at the dictation of Jeremiah] in the fourth year of Jehoiakim the son of Josiah, the king of Judah [MT adds: saying]: 45:2 (51:32) "Thus says the LORD [MT adds: the God of Israel] to / concerning you, Baruch, 45:3 (51:33) 'Because [> MT] you have said, "Woe to me! Woe to me![1] *For the LORD has added grief to my pain. I am weary [LXX: I sleep]*[2] *with groanings [MT: with my groaning]; and as for rest [Tg. Jon.: prophecy], I have not found it." 45:4 (51:34) Say to him [MT: Thus you will say to him], "Thus says the LORD, 'Look, that which I have built I am throwing down, and that which I have planted I am plucking up [MT adds: and all that land (or, and all the land / earth, that is; pc Mss: and all the land, it is mine; Syr.: and all the land I am destroying; Tg. Jon.: and all the land of Israel, which is mine)]. 45:5 (51:35) And as for you, do you seek for yourself great things? Do not seek. For look, I am*

---

1. The MT only has one occurrence of this expression. It is possible that the double occurrence in the LXX is due to dittography on the part of the scribe of the LXX *Vorlage* or on the part of the Greek translator. The Greek οἴμμοι does not consistently translate anything in particular. It is sometimes doubled where there is no doubling in the source text being translated. On the other hand, the MT could be the result of haplography.
2. The Greek ἐκοιμήθην ("I sleep") probably does not represent a Hebrew variant. It is likely an inner-Greek corruption of ἐκοπώθην ("I am wearied" = MT יגעתי) (see Rudolph, *BHS* apparatus).

*about to bring calamity upon / against all flesh,' the prophetic utterance
of the* LORD, *'and I will give [MT adds: to you] your life as plunder [LXX:
windfall] in every place [or, in all the places][3] where you go.'"'"*

Jeremiah 45 (LXX 51:31–35) is the scribal colophon that concludes
the LXX *Vorlage* of Jeremiah prior to the appendix added in chapter 52.[4]
It provides details about the scribe who produced the book of Jeremiah,
namely, Baruch. Verse 1 introduces the colophon as the word that
Jeremiah spoke to Baruch when he (Baruch) wrote "these words" on a
document at Jeremiah's dictation in the fourth year of Jehoiakim (605
BC) (see CD-A 8:20; cf. Bar. 1:1; *2 Bar.* 1:1). The phrase "these words"
refers to the words Jeremiah dictated to Baruch in the fourth year of
Jehoiakim according to the narrative in Jeremiah 36:1–8, which provides an account of the making of a scroll that concluded with Jeremiah
25:1–13—a passage dated in the fourth year of Jehoiakim (Jer. 25:1; see
also Jer. 46:2). Thus, the colophon of chapter 45 once stood after 25:1–13,
but the story of Jeremiah 36 indicates that the scroll was later not only
rewritten after its destruction but also expanded (Jer. 36:32). The unal-
tered scribal colophon maintained its position at the end of the book as
the book grew into the form that Baruch left it in Egypt (Jer. 43–44),[5]
the form that became the basis for the Greek translation of the book. The
book was subsequently reworked in Babylon into the proto-MT, which
became the dominant text form in Palestine. This second edition of the
book concluded (prior to the appendix in Jer. 52) with its own separate
scribal colophon (Jer. 51:59–64), which names Baruch's brother Seraiah
(see commentary on Jer. 51:59–64).

There is an often overlooked ambiguity in Jeremiah 45:2 (LXX
51:32) that serves well to set up the remainder of the colophon and to
mitigate the force of some of the perceived problems therein. The preposition עַל can be translated "to" or "concerning." If verse 2 is translated,
"Thus says the LORD [MT adds: the God of Israel] to you, Baruch," then
it fits best with verse 3, which addresses Baruch directly. If the verse is
translated, "Thus says the LORD [MT add: the God of Israel] concerning
you, Baruch," then it works better with verses 4–5, which begin with
direct address to Jeremiah and third-person reference to Baruch.

---

3. Holladay (*Jeremiah 2*, 307) suggests כל מקום for the LXX *Vorlage* rather
    than כל המקמות (cf. Deut. 12:2; 1 Sam. 7:16; 30:31; Ezra 1:4; Neh. 4:6; but
    see Jer. 8:3; 24:9; Ezek. 34:12).
4. See Lundbom, "Baruch, Seraiah, and Expanded Colophons in the Book of
    Jeremiah."
5. See Holladay, *Jeremiah 2*, 308.

In Jeremiah 45:3 (LXX 51:33), the LORD quotes Baruch's own words back to him. The expression, "Woe to me," echoes Jeremiah's words at the beginning of his third confession in Jeremiah 15:10–14 (see also Isa. 6:5; Jer. 4:31b). This strongly suggests that Baruch's lament was not due to the impending doom of the people but to his own suffering as one who had elected to cast his lot with the persecuted prophet Jeremiah (see Jer. 36:19, 26; see also Jer. 43:3). The explanation follows: "For the LORD has added grief (יגון) to my pain (מכאבי). I am weary (יגעתי) with groanings (באנחת) [MT: with my groaning (באנחתי)]." Such an accusatory tone from Baruch toward the LORD is also reminiscent of Jeremiah's words (Jer. 20:7–9). Jeremiah cursed the day of his birth (Jer. 20:14) and wondered why he ever came forth from the womb only to see toil and "grief" (יגון) (Jer. 20:18; see also Jer. 8:18). According to Keil, Baruch's "pain" (מכאב) was "pain of soul, at the moral corruption of the people, their impenitence and obduracy in sin and vice, just like the prophet himself, 15:18,"[6] but the "pain" (כאב) of Jeremiah in 15:18 is not that of one who was lamenting the corruption of the people. It is the pain of one who had to sit alone because of his unique devotion to the Torah (Jer. 15:15–17). Keil also notes that the language of weariness with groaning and of lack of rest finds parallels in Psalm 6:7 (Eng., 6:6) (יגעתי באנחתי) and Lamentations 5:5 (see also Deut. 28:65). The contexts of both of these texts speak of persecution (see Ps. 6:9–11 [Eng., 6:8–10]; Lam. 5:5). *Targum Jonathan* interprets the "rest" (מנוחה) that Baruch had not found to be the gift of prophecy. This interpretation is based on the fact that the Spirit of prophecy is often said to "rest" (נוח) upon true prophets (e.g., Num. 11:25–26; 2 Kgs. 2:15; Isa. 11:2; see also Jer. 51:59b). Thus, according to this view, which is articulated more fully in the Mekhilta, Baruch complained that the Spirit of prophecy had not rested upon him after serving Jeremiah the way that it did for Joshua after serving Moses or for Elisha after serving Elijah.[7] Another suggestion has been that מנוחה in Jeremiah 45:3 means "resting place" rather than "rest." It is more likely, however, that the sense of the text is that Baruch had no relief from his grief and pain because he was struggling in his faith. He was "weary" (יגע) because he had failed to

---

6. Keil, *Jeremiah*, 364.
7. See Neusner, *Jeremiah in Talmud and Midrash*, 40. According to another tradition, however, Baruch was indeed a prophet (see *b. Meg.* 14b; see also Bar. 1:1; *2 Bar.* 1:1; 25:1; 29:3; 30:1), perhaps not a prophet of oral proclamation like Jeremiah, but one in the sense of a scribe and exegete of prophetic texts (see LXX Prov. 29:18; van der Toorn, *Scribal Culture*, 107).

wait on the LORD (see Isa. 40:31). Only with trust in the LORD to walk the path set for him would he find rest for himself (Jer. 6:16).

Jeremiah was to say to Baruch on behalf of the LORD, "Look, that which I have built I am throwing down, and that which I have planted I am plucking up" (Jer. 45:4 [LXX 51:34]).[8] This is the final iteration of the book's programmatic text in Jeremiah 1:10. From the perspective of the fourth year of Jehoiakim (Jer. 45:1), these words anticipated the Babylonian invasion of Judah and Jerusalem and the destruction of the temple.[9] On the other hand, from the perspective of the end of the book of Jeremiah for which Jeremiah 45 serves as the colophon, these words stand in expectation of a final tribulation (Jer. 4–6) from which the people of God will be delivered in order to be rebuilt and replanted (see again Jer. 24:6; 31:28; 32:41). As will be seen in the commentary on verse 5, this puts Baruch's desire for "great things" in the proper light. It was necessary for Baruch to be reoriented to the greater work of God.

The MT has an addition at the end of verse 4 that does not appear in the LXX *Vorlage*: ואת כל הארץ היא. This is best understood as a secondary interpolation.[10] It may be interpreted to mean "and all that land," since the demonstrative is inherently definite and need not have the article in order to agree with a definite noun as an attributive. On the other hand, the addition may be translated "and all the land, that is." In other words, what is said in the previous part of the verse applies to all the land. The Syriac version supplies a participle for which "all the land" is the object: "and all the land I am destroying." A few Masoretic manuscripts have a slightly different text (cf. *Tg. Jon.*): ואת כל הארץ לי היא ("and all the land, it is mine"). This would amount to an assertion that the LORD has the right to do what he wants with what belongs to him (cf. Jer. 27:5; Dan. 4:14 [Eng., 4:17]). A key issue in the interpretation of

---

8. "It is an insoluble question whether the occurrences of אֲשֶׁר refer to persons or things—'those whom I have built up I am overturning, and those whom I have planted I am uprooting' (so *G, V*) or 'what I have built up I am overturning, and what I have planted I am uprooting' (so Luther, Calvin, *KJV*, and all recent commentaries and translations); the Hebrew text covers both, and Cornill nicely covers both: 'My own building I myself must destroy, and my own planting I myself must uproot'" (Holladay, *Jeremiah 2*, 310).

9. Abarbanel suggests that the throwing down of what was built refers to the temple, while the plucking up of what was planted refers to the cessation of prophecy (Lam. 2:9) (Rosenberg, trans., *Mikraoth Gedoloth: Jeremiah Volume Two*, 344–45).

10. See McKane, *Jeremiah XXVI–LII*, 1096–97.

this addition is whether הָאָרֶץ means "the land" or "the earth" (i.e., "the inhabited earth"). *Targum Jonathan* renders "and all the land of Israel, which is mine." Keil, however, insists that the meaning must be "all the earth" due to the parallel "all flesh" (כל בשר) in verse 5 (cf. Jer. 25:31, 33).[11] Nevertheless, it is the land of the covenant that has been the focus of the book's prophecy (and indeed throughout the Bible it is the focus). Furthermore, an understanding of הָאָרֶץ as "the land" does not preclude implications of the prophecy for humanity in general (e.g., Jer. 25:15–26; 46–51; see also Jer. 12:14–17). Israel's loss of the land of the covenant (Gen. 15:18) was a reminder of what all humanity lost (Gen. 2:10–14; 3:24). The restoration of the lost blessing of life and dominion in the land (Gen. 1:26–28) to all the nations will come by means of Israel (Gen. 12:1–3), primarily through the coming of Israel's Messiah (Gen. 22:18; see commentary on Jer. 4:2; 23:5–6; 30:9).

Since the first clause of Jeremiah 45:5 (LXX 51:35) is not formally marked as a question, it may be taken as a statement ("And as for you, you seek for yourself great things.") or as a question ("And as for you, do you seek for yourself great things?"). Either way, Baruch was urged not to seek "great things" (גדלות) for himself, but what were the great things that he sought? The Mekhilta suggests, based on the occurrences of גדלות ("great things") in 2 Kings 8:4 and Jeremiah 33:3, that Baruch sought prophecies.[12] According to this view, Baruch was denied such prophecies not because he was unfit to be a prophet but because of the failure of Israel and the subsequent removal of prophecy.[13] Others have suggested that Baruch sought that the Lord would relent and not bring calamity.[14] When this did not happen, he was greatly disappointed, and the Lord had to rebuke him for being contrary to his purposes. The specific wording of verse 5, however, suggests something more personal: Baruch sought great things for himself. Lundbom rightly notes, "We know from certain Egyptian documents that scribes had high aspirations within their profession, which was due no doubt,

---

11. Keil, *Jeremiah*, 364.
12. See Neusner, *Jeremiah in Talmud and Midrash*, 40. Cf. the Levites who "sought" the priesthood (Num. 16:10).
13. See Rashi and Abarbanel in Rosenberg, trans., *Mikraoth Gedoloth: Jeremiah Volume Two*, 345.
14. See the discussion in McKane, *Jeremiah XXVI–LII*, 1098–99. Calvin seems to think that Baruch sought his own life: "Baruch thought that he should perish while the people were safe and secure; but God declares that none of the people would be safe, and that he would be safely preserved while all the rest were perishing" (*Jeremiah*, 4:571).

at least in part, to the fact that they came from noble families."[15] Baruch was a member of the scribal elite,[16] and many of those who belonged to this exclusive club had an official status (see, e.g., Jer. 29:3; 36:12; 51:59; see also 2 Chr. 34:8).[17] His standing in society demanded respect, yet, because of his association with Jeremiah, his life was threatened (Jer. 36:26), and he was later falsely accused of inciting Jeremiah to deceive the people (Jer. 43:2–3). It would be easy to despise Baruch for seeking great things for himself, but the reality was that he did not receive the treatment that he deserved. Nevertheless, he had to learn that he could not put his hope in any recognition that he might receive from others (see Luke 17:10). Such recognition would have been fickle at best. This text is a sobering reminder that the path of faithfulness is the path of suffering (2 Tim. 3:12; see also Mark 9:33–37; 10:29–30, 35–45), yet it is a path that leads to things much greater than what the world can offer (2 Cor. 4:17; Php. 3:7–11).

According to the explanation offered in verse 5, this was not the time to seek personal greatness (cf. 2 Kgs. 5:26; see also Jer. 12:5; 32:23b–25): "For look, I am about to bring calamity upon/against all flesh." From the perspective of the fourth year of Jehoiakim (Jer. 45:1), this would have anticipated the calamity of 587 BC (Jer. 11:11; 39; 52) and the related historical judgments of the nations (Jer. 25:15–26); but from the perspective of the end of the book of Jeremiah, it looks ahead to a worldwide judgment against "all flesh" (Jer. 25:31, 33) in the last days, beginning with Israel and the land of the covenant (Jer. 25:1–13; 46–51; see also Ezek. 38–39; Joel 4 [Eng., 3]; Zech. 12–14; Luke 21:20; Rev. 16; 20). Both perspectives must be taken into account for a proper understanding of the words of deliverance spoken to Baruch: "and I will give [MT adds: to you] your life as plunder in every place where you go (תלך)." These words are an echo of words originally spoken to Jeremiah—"For to all that I send you, you will go (תלך). . . . Do not be afraid because of them, for with you am I to rescue you" (Jer. 1:7–8; also Jer. 1:17–19; 15:20–21)—and subsequently reapplied to the people of God (Jer. 30:10–11 [MT]; 46:27–28). From the perspective of the fourth year of Jehoiakim, the gift of Baruch's life as plunder meant that he would survive the warfare of the Babylonian invasion (cf. Jer.

---

15. Lundbom, "Baruch, Seraiah, and Expanded Colophons in the Book of Jeremiah," 101. See the misguided aspirations of Shebna the scribe (Isa. 36:3) in Isaiah 22:15–19.
16. See Rollston, *Writing and Literacy in the World of Ancient Israel*, 133.
17. See Bright, *Jeremiah*, 185.

21:9; 38:2).[18] From the perspective of the conclusion to Jeremiah's book, the gift of life means so much more (see Luke 21:19). The building and planting (after the throwing down and plucking up [Jer. 45:4]) will take place for the new covenant community in the eschaton (Jer. 24:6; 31:28; 32:41). In order for Baruch to participate in this, he must have a hope in the resurrection (Dan. 12:1–3; see commentary on Ebed Melech in Jer. 39:18).[19] Thus, the LORD recalibrated Baruch's mind to think not of the great things that he might have expected to receive in his lifetime but of the greater things (indeed the greatest things) that he would enjoy as a member of the believing remnant of the people of God.

It is to be noted that Baruch himself preserved the text of Jeremiah 45 to function as a colophon despite the rather unflattering depiction of him that it contains. This suggests that Baruch embraced the word of the LORD that was delivered to him by Jeremiah. Furthermore, the above exposition indicates that Jeremiah 45 is more than a record of what was said to Baruch. It is a conclusion to the book of Jeremiah for the reader of the book. Baruch, much like Jeremiah throughout the book, serves as a representative of the faithful remnant. Any reader who puts his/her faith in the future revealed for the people of God (Jer. 30–33) will find that he/she is "blessed" (ברוך) like Baruch despite any lack of great things in this world.

---

18. Eissfeldt suggests that chapter 45 owes its present placement after chapter 44 to the desire to show that the calamity prophesied against the community of Judeans living in Egypt did not overtake Baruch (*Old Testament*, 354).

19. Eichrodt, *Theology of the Old Testament*, 2:514–15.

APPENDIX

(Jer. 52)

52:1 Zedekiah was twenty-one years old when he became king, and for eleven years he reigned in Jerusalem, and the name of his mother was Hamital [MT qere: Hamutal] the daughter of Jeremiah, from Libnah.[1] 52:4 In the ninth year of his reign, in the tenth month [LXX^BS: in the ninth month; LXX^A: in the seventh month], on day ten of the month, Nebuchadnezzar [MT: Nebuchadrezzar] the king of Babylon came, and all his army [MT: he and all his army], against Jerusalem, and they camped against it, and they built against it a siege wall [LXX: four-footed] all around. 52:5 And the city entered the siege until the eleventh year of King Zedekiah. 52:6 [MT adds: In the fourth month (Syr.: In the seventh month)], on day nine of the month, the famine was severe in the city, and there was no bread/food for the people of the land. 52:7 And the city was breached; and all the soldiers, they went out [MT: they fled and went out from the city] by night by way of a gate between the two walls [LXX: between the wall and the outer wall], which was along the king's garden, (and the Chaldeans were against the city all around), and they went the way of the Arabah [or, the plain]. 52:8 And the army of the Chaldeans pursued after the king, and they overtook him [MT: Zedekiah; Syr.: him, Zedekiah] across from Jericho [MT: in the plains of Jericho]; and as for all his servants [MT: all his army], they were

---

1. MT adds: 52:2 And he did what was evil in the eyes of the Lord according to all that Jehoiakim did. 52:3 For because of the Lord's anger it happened in Jerusalem and Judah [mlt Mss: and in Judah] until he cast them from before him, and Zedekiah rebelled against the king of Babylon.

scattered from him. 52:9 And they seized the king, and they brought him up to the king of Babylon at Diblah [MT: Riblah in the land of Hamath], and he spoke with him judgment [MT: judgments]. 52:10 And the king of Babylon slaughtered the sons of Zedekiah before his eyes, and [MT: and also] all the officials [Syr., Tg. Jon.: nobles] of Judah he slaughtered at Diblah [MT: Riblah]. 52:11 And the eyes of Zedekiah he blinded, and he bound him in bronze shackles, and the king of Babylon brought him to Babylon, and he put him in a mill house [MT: the house of oversight (= prison); Syr.: the house of custody (= prison); Tg. Jon.: a house of prisoners] until the day of his death [LXX: until the day that he died].

52:12 And in the fifth month, on day ten of the month [MT adds: that is, the nineteenth year of King Nebuchadrezzar the king of Babylon], Nebuzaradan, the captain of the guard who stood before the king of Babylon, entered Jerusalem 52:13 and burned the house of the LORD [i.e., the temple] and the house of the king [i.e., the royal palace] and all the houses of the city [MT: Jerusalem], and every great house he burned with fire. 52:14 And as for all the city walls [LXX: every city wall] of Jerusalem all around, [MT adds: all] the army of the Chaldeans that was with the captain of the guard tore them down.[2] 52:16 And the rest of the people [MT: some of the poor of the land] [MT adds: Nebuzardan] the captain of the guard left as vinedressers and plowmen.

52:17 And the bronze pillars that were in [Codex L: for] the house of the LORD [that were in / for the house of the LORD > Syr.] and the bases and the bronze sea that was in the house of the LORD the Chaldeans shattered, and they took away [MT adds: all] their bronze and brought it [cf. Syr.; and brought it > MT] to Babylon, 52:18 and the rim and the bowls for tossing liquid and the shovels [LXX: meat hooks] [MT: and the pots and the shovels and the trimming shears (Vulg.: psalteria) and the bowls for tossing liquid and the pans] and all the bronze vessels with which they would minister [MT adds: they took], 52:19 and the basins [MT: and the basins and the censers] and the trimming shears [MT: bowls for tossing liquid] and the pots and the lampstands and the censers [MT: pans] and the sacrificial bowls, which were gold, gold, and which were silver, silver, the captain of the guard took away. 52:20 And as for the two pillars and the one sea and the twelve bronze bulls under the sea [MT: the bases],

---

2. MT adds 52:15: And some of the poor of the people and the rest of the people who remained in the city and the deserters/defectors who deserted/defected to the king of Babylon and the rest of the craftsmen [Syr.: people; *Tg. Jon.*, Vulg.: multitude] Nebuzaradan the captain of the guard took into exile.

which King Solomon made for the house of the LORD, *there was no weight to their bronze [MT adds: all these vessels]. 52:21 And as for the pillars, the height of each pillar was thirty-five [MT: eighteen] cubits, and a cord / line of twelve cubits would surround each one, and the thickness of each was four fingers all around [MT: hollow], 52:22 and a capital upon them [MT: upon each one] was bronze, and the height of each capital was five cubits [LXX adds: in length], and latticework and pomegranates were on the capital all around; the whole was bronze; and like these for the second pillar [Syr.: another pillar], eight pomegranates [MT: and pomegranates] to the cubit for twelve cubits [> MT]. 52:23 And there were ninety-six pomegranates on the sides [on the sides > Syr.], and [and > MT] all the pomegranates were one hundred upon the latticework all around.*

52:24 And the captain of the guard took [MT adds: Seraiah] the chief priest and [MT adds: Zephaniah] the second priest and the three keepers of the threshold [LXX: the way],[3] *52:25 and [MT adds: from the city he took] one official who was overseer over the soldiers and seven men of name in the king's presence [MT: seven men of those who saw the king's face] who were found [Syr.: left] in the city and the army scribe [MT: the scribe of the army official; Syr.: the scribe and the army official; LXX*[OL]*, Tg. Jon., Vulg.: the scribe, the army official] who mustered the people of the land [Syr.: of the people of the land] and sixty men / people from the people of the land who were found in the midst of the city. 52:26 And Nebuzaradan the captain of the guard took them and brought them to the king of Babylon at Diblah [MT: Riblah]. 52:27 And the king of Babylon struck them [MT adds: and killed them] at Diblah [MT: Riblah] in the land of Hamath, [MT adds: and Judah went into exile away from its land].*[4]

52:31 In the thirty-seventh year of the exile of Jehoiachin [LXX: Jehoiakim][5] *the king of Judah, in the twelfth month, on the twenty-fourth [MT: twenty-fifth] day of the month, Evil Merodach the king of*

---

3. The Greek τὴν ὁδόν ("the way") may have originally been τὸν ὁδόν, an alternative spelling of τὸν οὐδόν ("the threshold") (see Walser, *Jeremiah*, 474).

4. MT adds 52:28–30: "This is the number of people whom Nebuchadrezzar took into exile: in year seven [Syr. adds: of his kingdom], 3,023 Judeans; in the eighteenth year of Nebuchadrezzar, [nonn Mss, Syr. add: he took into exile] from Jerusalem 832 lives; in the twenty-third year of Nebuchadrezzar, Nebuzaradan the captain of the guard took into exile 745 Judean lives; altogether 4,600 lives."

5. The LXX normally transliterates the name Jehoiachin as Ιωακιμ, which is the same way that it transliterates the name of his father Jehoiakim, even

Babylon lifted up the head of Jehoiachin [LXX: Jehoiakim] the king of Judah in the first year of his reign [MT: his kingdom], [LXX[B] adds: and he shaved him (or, and he shaved himself)], and he brought him out of the house of confinement [LXX: the house where he was kept]. 52:32 And he spoke with him good things, and he put his seat/throne above the seats/thrones [MT: seat/throne] of the kings [Codex L kethiv: of kings] who were with him in Babylon. 52:33 And he changed the clothes [LXX: robe] of his confinement and ate bread/food continually before him [MT: before him continually] all the days of his life [LXX: all the days that he lived]. 52:34 And his allowance of food to him was given continually [MT: And as for his allowance of food, a continual allowance was given to him] from the king of Babylon [NET: by the king of Babylon] daily until the day of his death [LXX: until the day that he died] [MT adds: all the days of his life].

Jeremiah 52 is clearly marked as an appendix in both the Hebrew source behind Greek Jeremiah and the MT. In the former, it follows the scribal colophon of Jeremiah 45, which concludes the book. In the latter, there is the preceding notice in Jeremiah 51:64b: "up to here are the words of Jeremiah" (cf. MT Jer. 1:1). It has already been noted in the present commentary that the addition of verses 4–13 in MT Jeremiah 39 draws heavily upon material found in the text of Jeremiah 52 (see Jer. 39:4–10; 52:7–11, 13–16). Thus, MT Jeremiah essentially has two accounts of the Babylonian invasion.[6] This is not the case in the LXX *Vorlage*, which does not have Jeremiah 39:4–13. The presence of Jeremiah 52 raises the question of why it has been added to the end of the book. It will become apparent in the course of the following commentary that the answer to this question is related to the role that the parallel passage in 2 Kings 25 plays as the conclusion to its respective composition.

There are four versions of the narrative found in Jeremiah 52, not counting Jeremiah 39 and 2 Chronicles 36: (1) LXX Jeremiah 52 and its *Vorlage*, (2) MT Jeremiah 52, (3) LXX 2 Kings 25 and its *Vorlage*, and (4) MT 2 Kings 25.[7] The LXX *Vorlage* of Jeremiah 52 appears to

---

in texts where the two are clearly distinguished from one another (2 Kgs. 24:6, 8, 12, 15, 27; but see 2 Chr. 36:8, 9).

6. One of the most important differences between the two MT accounts is the absence of any reference to the temple in Jeremiah 39 in contrast to the presence of such in Jeremiah 52.

7. Keil, who only compares MT Jeremiah 52 and MT 2 Kings 25, suggests a common source to explain their relationship (Keil, *Jeremiah*, 457–58).

be the shortest and earliest version of the story overall. For example, it does not include the material found in MT Jeremiah 52:28–30. Of course, this material is also absent from LXX and MT 2 Kings, but LXX and MT 2 Kings feature material not found in LXX or MT Jeremiah 52 (e.g., 2 Kgs. 25:22–26; cf. Jer. 40–41). Raymond Person makes several observations from his detailed analysis of these witnesses.[8] First, LXX 2 Kings 25 and MT Jeremiah 52 never agree against a common reading in MT 2 Kings 25 and LXX Jeremiah 52, suggesting that LXX Jeremiah 52 is based on a shorter and earlier *Vorlage* that best preserves the original.[9] This does not mean, however, that LXX Jeremiah 52 always

---

8. Raymond F. Person Jr., *The Kings-Isaiah and Kings-Jeremiah Recensions*, BZAW 252 (Berlin: Walter de Gruyter, 1997), 95–99.

9. Person does not think that LXX Jeremiah 52 is the result of abridgement, either in its Hebrew source text or by the Greek translator. "For the material JG preserves, there is general agreement among the four texts, excluding the cases where JH and JG agree against KH and KG" (*Kings-Isaiah and Kings-Jeremiah Recensions*, 99). "In some cases, JG appears to preserve a variant tradition from KH and KG, which the possibility of these variants occurring during the tradition's reapplication to Jeremiah does not adequately explain" (99). P.-M. Bogaert considers the still shorter Old Latin of Jeremiah 52 to be a closer witness to the original ("Les trois formes de Jérémie 52 [MT, LXX, OL]," in *Tradition of the Text*, eds. G. J. Norton, S. Pisano, OBO 109 [1991]: 1–17). Georg Fischer, however, argues that Greek Jeremiah 52 is "an abbreviated and occasionally modified translation" of MT Jeremiah 52 ("Jeremiah 52: A Test Case for Jer LXX," in *X Congress of the International Organization for Septuagint and Cognate Studies Oslo, 1998*, ed. Bernard A. Taylor [Atlanta: SBL, 2001], 38–48). Fischer is generally dismissive of evidence for a Hebrew text similar to Greek Jeremiah such as 4QJer[b] and considers the differences between MT Jeremiah and Greek Jeremiah to be due to the work of the Greek translator despite the typically faithful translation technique displayed throughout the book. Thus, for Fischer, what he sees in Greek Jeremiah 52 is a microcosm of what he sees elsewhere in the book, although he cites no precedent or parallel for such extensive reworking by a translator and does not take into account the fact that extensive reworking of Hebrew texts by Hebrew scribes, such as what appears in MT Jeremiah, is well known (see, e.g., Ulrich, *Dead Sea Scrolls*). Fischer appeals to the work of Alexander Rofé who points out the absence of references to the exile (Jer. 52:15, 27b, 28–30) in Greek Jeremiah 52 ("Not Exile but Annihilation for Zedekiah's People. The Purport of Jeremiah 52 in the Septuagint," SCS 41 [Atlanta: SBL, 1995], 165–70). Fischer believes that such omission "fundamentally changes the character of the text," but it does not occur to him that this is an argument in favor of the priority of LXX Jeremiah 52. Unless Fischer wants to argue that omission happened

preserves the best reading in each instance. Second, LXX Jeremiah 52 was not directly influenced by LXX 2 Kings 25. Third, the difference between MT Jeremiah 52 and LXX Jeremiah 52 is greater in degree than that between MT 2 Kings 25 and LXX 2 Kings 25 (LXX 2 Kgs. 25 represents a somewhat shorter and more original text than MT 2 Kgs. 25). MT Jeremiah 52 preserves the greatest amount of material and appears to be the latest of the four texts, having been "corrected" by the tradition behind MT 2 Kings 25 and LXX 2 Kings 25. This does not fully explain, however, why MT Jeremiah 52 has unique readings (e.g., Jer. 52:28–30) not found in any of the other texts.

Keeping in mind that the Hebrew source text of Greek Jeremiah 52 was originally independent of the book of Jeremiah prior to its inclusion as an appendix, it appears that this source text was expanded and modified in different ways by both 2 Kings 25 (LXX *Vorlage* and MT) and MT Jeremiah 52. The LXX *Vorlage* of 2 Kings 25 was the first to expand and modify the Hebrew source behind Greek Jeremiah 52, and this work was continued by MT 2 Kings 25. MT Jeremiah 52 subsequently expanded and modified the Hebrew source behind Greek Jeremiah 52 on the basis of knowledge of MT 2 Kings 25 while also making its own unique contribution.

The narrative of Jeremiah 52 begins with an introduction to the account of Zedekiah's reign. Such introductions to the accounts of Judean kings in the book of Kings typically follow the same pattern: age at time of accession, length of reign, ancestry through mother, and evaluation. Zedekiah was twenty-one years old when he became king, and he reigned in Jerusalem for eleven years from 597 to 587 BC (Jer. 52:1a; cf. 2 Kgs. 24:18a; 2 Chr. 36:11; but see also 2 Kgs. 23:31; 1 Chr. 3:15; 2 Chr. 36:2). His mother's name was Hamital (or, Hamutal) the daughter of Jeremiah, from Libnah (Jer. 52:1b; cf. 2 Kgs. 24:18b; see also 2 Kgs. 23:31). The phrase "from Libnah" is absent from LXX 2 Kings 24:18b.

The evaluation of Zedekiah's reign in verses 2–3 does not appear in the Hebrew source behind Greek Jeremiah. It has been added in the MT in accordance with 2 Kings 24:19–20. As indicated already in Jeremiah 21:1–23:4 (see also Jer. 34), Zedekiah and his brothers did

---

accidentally in LXX Jeremiah 52, which he does not, then he would have to say that LXX Jeremiah 52 inexplicably removed things on purpose that would have been expected and required. It seems rather more likely that the MT expanded the text and sought to make the appendix into a more fitting conclusion for the book. See also James Frohlich, *The Relationship between MT and LXX in Jeremiah 39(46):1–41(48):3 and 52*, FAT II 133 (Tübingen: Mohr Siebeck, 2022).

not live up to the standard of righteousness set by their father Josiah who did what was upright in the eyes of the LORD and walked in all the way of David (2 Kgs. 22:2). Zedekiah did what was evil in the eyes of the LORD according to all that Jehoiakim did (Jer. 52:2; cf. 2 Kgs. 24:19). The Chronicler characterizes this evil in terms of Zedekiah's refusal to humble himself before the prophet Jeremiah (2 Chr. 36:12). The syntax of Jeremiah 52:3a has been compared to that of Jeremiah 32:31, although the constructions are not identical. The text appears to say that Zedekiah did evil in the eyes of the LORD because of the LORD's anger: "For because of the LORD's anger it happened in Jerusalem and Judah [mlt Mss: and in Judah] until he cast them from before him" (cf. Jer. 7:15).[10] Zedekiah's evil was part of a larger divine plan to bring judgment upon Judah and Jerusalem because of what Manasseh did long before (see Jer. 15:4). Jeremiah 52:3b ("And Zedekiah rebelled against the king of Babylon") is commonly detached from the first half of the verse (cf. 2 Kgs. 24:20b), although it ought to be noticed that this clause employs a *wayyiqtol* verbal form to continue the sequence of the narration (see KJV). Second Chronicles 36:13a provides some insight into the nature of Zedekiah's rebellion: "And also against King Nebuchadnezzar he rebelled, who made him swear by God."

Jeremiah 52:4 refers to the ninth year of Zedekiah's reign, in the tenth month, on day ten of the month, when Nebuchadnezzar came against Jerusalem with all his army (cf. 2 Kgs. 25:1; Jer. 39:1; Ezek.

---

10. The subject of the feminine verb in this clause is the situation described in verse 2 (GKC §135p). Rashi explains the parallel text in 2 Kings 24:20a as follows: "Therefore, Zedekiah rebelled against the king of Babylonia. The Holy One, blessed, gave the desire into his heart to rebel against him in order that he should be exiled" (Rosenberg, trans., *Mikraoth Gedoloth: Jeremiah Volume Two*, 412). Redak: "Since the remnant in Jerusalem and in Judah was contrary to the Lord's will, i.e. because of their evil deeds and abominable acts, the Lord inspired Zedekiah to rebel against Nebuchadnezzar and bring about the destruction" (412). Bright considers it unlikely that the situation in Judah was occasioned by the LORD's anger, although he does not say why (Bright, *Jeremiah*, 366; see also Holladay, *Jeremiah 2*, 440). It is certainly impossible to convert the text to say Jerusalem and Judah caused the LORD's anger, even if this sort of thing is said elsewhere. McKane seems to interpret the text in a proleptic sense (i.e., in anticipation of the following narrative) rather than in reference to the preceding verse: "What happened in Jerusalem and Judah was a consequence of Yahweh's anger" (McKane, *Jeremiah XXVI–LII*, 1360–62; cf. NET). The difficulty with this interpretation is that it overlooks the conjunction כִּי at the beginning of verse 3. This conjunction appears to introduce an explanation of verse 2.

24:1).[11] Codices Vaticanus and Sinaiticus have this in the ninth month. Codex Alexandrinus has it in the seventh month.[12] Jeremiah 39:1 and the Old Greek of 2 Kings 25:1 do not include reference to the day. The Babylonian army camped against Jerusalem and built a siege wall around the city from which to make their attack (see Ezek. 4:1–3). The city entered the siege until the eleventh year (587 BC) of King Zedekiah (Jer. 52:5; cf. 2 Kgs. 25:2).

LXX Jeremiah 52:6 and 2 Kings 25:3 simply refer to day nine of the month without indicating what month of the eleventh year it was. MT Jeremiah 52:6 and Jeremiah 39:2 indicate that it was the fourth month (July 587). A few Masoretic manuscripts and the Syriac have it as the fifth month in Jeremiah 39:2 (see Jer. 52:12; see also Jer. 1:3). The Syriac has it as the seventh month for Jeremiah 52:6.[13] At this time the famine was severe in the city (see Lev. 26:26; Deut. 28:53–57; Jer. 19:9). There was no food for the people (cf. Jer. 37:21; 38:9; see also Lam. 1:19; 2:11–12, 20; 4:4–5, 8–10). Also at this time the city was breached, and all the soldiers went out (MT: "fled and went out from the city") by night by way of a gate between "the two walls" (see Isa. 22:11; 2 Chr. 32:5), which was along the king's garden (see Neh. 3:15); they did this even though the Chaldeans had the city surrounded, and they went the way of the Arabah/plain (Jer. 52:7; cf. 2 Kgs. 25:4). Jeremiah 39:4 indicates that this attempt to flee the city included Zedekiah. That this detail is presupposed in Jeremiah 52:7 is confirmed by the presence of the king in the narrative of Jeremiah 52:8–11.

The Chaldean army pursued the king in particular, and they overtook "him" (MT: "Zedekiah"; Syr.: "him, Zedekiah") "across from Jericho" (בעבר ירחו; MT: "in the plains of Jericho" [בערבת ירחו]) (Jer. 52:8a; cf. 2 Kgs. 25:5a; Jer. 39:5a; see also Lam. 4:19–20).[14] As for all "his servants" (עבדיו; MT: "his army" [חילו]), they were scattered from him (Jer. 52:8b; cf. 2 Kgs. 25:5b). The Chaldeans seized the king and brought him up to the king of Babylon at "Diblah" (MT: "Riblah in the land of Hamath"), and the Babylonian king spoke with him "judgment"

---

11. This was January 588 (see Bright, *Jeremiah*, 366).

12. Note also the variation for the month and day in Greek witnesses to 2 Kings 25:1.

13. The *BHS* apparatus shows that the Syriac has it as the fifth month for Jeremiah 52:6, but this should be corrected to the seventh month.

14. McKane understands the LXX *Vorlage* to mean "the eastern side of the Jordan" (McKane, *Jeremiah XXVI–LII*, 1364). It is possible, however, that "on the other side of Jericho" only indicates the trajectory of Zedekiah's flight (see Jer. 40:14; 41:15).

(MT: "judgments") (Jer. 52:9; cf. 2 Kgs. 25:6; Jer. 39:5; Ezek. 16:41; see also Jer. 52:26–27). That is, Nebuchadnezzar "passed sentence on him" (NET; cf. Jer. 1:16; 2 Chr. 24:24).

Zedekiah came face to face with the king of Babylon (see Jer. 32:4; 34:3), and the Babylonian king had Zedekiah's sons slaughtered before the eyes of their father (Jer. 52:10a; cf. 2 Kgs. 25:7a; Jer. 39:6a; see also Deut. 28:32). Nebuchadnezzar also executed all "the officials of Judah" (שרי יהודה) who were held prisoner at Diblah/Riblah (Jer. 52:10b; cf. Jer. 39:6b; > 2 Kgs. 25). Jeremiah 39:6b refers to these officials as "the nobles of Judah" (חרי יהודה), which is what the Syriac and *Targum Jonathan* have for Jeremiah 52:10b. Nebuchadnezzar made sure that the last thing Zedekiah saw with his own eyes was the death of his sons. He then blinded Zedekiah's eyes (see Ezek. 12:8–16) and bound him in bronze shackles and brought him to Babylon where, according to the LXX *Vorlage*, he put him "in a mill house" (בבית רחים) until the day of his death (LXX: "until the day that he died") (Jer. 52:11; cf. 2 Kgs. 23:33–34). The MT says that he put him "in the house of oversight" (בבית הפקדת; Syr.: "the house of custody"; *Tg. Jon.*: "a house of prisoners"). 2 Kings 25:7 and Jeremiah 39:7 have neither of these readings, but Theodotion's version of Jeremiah 39:7 does add that Nebuchadnezzar brought Zedekiah to Babylon "to put him in a mill house" (see also MT Jer. 25:10b). As a blinded man, Zedekiah was consigned to the work of grinding in a mill until his death, not unlike the fate of Samson (Judg. 16:21; see also Isa. 47:2).[15] Samson was also bound in "bronze shackles," and he became a grinder "in the house of prisoners" (בבית האסירים). It is not clear whether the phrase "until the day of his death" in Jeremiah 52:11b refers to the day of Zedekiah's death or the day of Nebuchadnezzar's death (cf. Jer. 52:34), although it is usually understood in the former sense (see Jer. 32:5; 34:4–5). If it is meant in the latter sense, then it would indicate that Zedekiah was released at a later time.

Jeremiah 52:12 refers to the fifth month (Jer. 1:3) and day "ten" of the month (MT adds: "that is, the nineteenth year of King Nebuchadrezzar the king of Babylon"; cf. Jer. 25:1b; 32:1b; 52:29; see also Bar. 1:2). The parallel text in 2 Kings 25:8 has day "seven" rather than day "ten." The Tosefta harmonizes the accounts: "But on the seventh of the month the gentiles conquered the Temple and took the pillars, the sea, and the stalls. So they were demolishing it on the

---

15. See Holladay, *Jeremiah 2*, 441.

seventh, eighth, and ninth, until sunset."[16] The MT puts this in the nineteenth year of Nebuchadrezzar (August 587), counting from the year of his accession to power (605 BC), whereas Jeremiah 52:29 has it as his eighteenth year, which counts from the first full year of his reign (see also Jer. 32:1b). Nebuzaradan, the captain of the guard, entered Jerusalem at this time (see Jer. 39:10–14; 40:1–6). MT 2 Kings 25:8 describes Nebuzaradan as the "servant" (עבד) of the king of Babylon, whereas MT Jeremiah 52:12 describes him as one who "stood" (עָמַד) before the king of Babylon. LXX 2 Kings 25:8 and LXX Jeremiah 52:12 reflect a Hebrew text that could be vocalized either as עָמַד ("stood") or עֹמֵד ("was standing"). Since Nebuchadnezzar was apparently not present in Jerusalem at this time (see Jer. 52:9–11),[17] the description of Nebuzaradan as one who stood before the king of Babylon should probably be understood to mean that he stood in the service of the king (see BDB, 764).[18] In other words, it is more or less equivalent to calling him Nebuchadnezzar's servant.

Nebuzaradan had the temple and the royal palace burned along with all the houses of Jerusalem (Jer. 52:13; cf. 2 Kgs. 25:9; Jer. 39:8; 2 Chr. 36:19; see also Jer. 21:10; 22:6–7; 34:22; 37:8; Ezek. 16:41; 23:47; Ps. 79:1; Jdt. 5:18). The last clause of verse 13 in the Hebrew source behind Greek Jeremiah appears to say that he also had "every great house" (כל בֵּית גדול) burned with fire, which is the consonantal text found in most Masoretic manuscripts of 2 Kings 25:9, although בית is vocalized there in the construct state (בֵּית). The chief difficulty with this reading is that the phrase is indefinite, yet it is preceded by a definite direct object marker (את). If this reading is correct, then it would seem to say that every prominent house in Jerusalem was burned in addition to all the houses of the city in general (see Isa. 5:9; Jer. 17:27; Amos 3:15; 6:11; 2 Chr. 36:19). MT Jeremiah 52:13, however, along

---

16. Neusner, *Jeremiah in Talmud and Midrash*, 10. See also *b. Ta'anit* 29a, which says that the temple was ignited on the evening of the ninth day and continued to burn through the tenth day.

17. It is possible, however, to translate the verse in such a way as to indicate that Nebuchadnezzar was in Jerusalem: "Nebuzaradan the captain of the guard came. He stood before the king of Babylon who was in Jerusalem" (see also Mezudath David in Rosenberg, trans., *Mikraoth Gedoloth: Jeremiah Volume Two*, 414).

18. *B. Sanhedrin* 96b offers two creative interpretations of this expression. One is that Nebuzaradan stood before an image of Nebuchadnezzar that he had engraved on his chariot. The other is that Nebuzardan was so in awe of Nebuchadnezzar that it was as if he were standing before him.

with a few Masoretic witnesses to 2 Kings 25:9, has the article on the last word of the construct chain: כל בית הגדול. Gesenius considers this an example of an idiomatic usage of adjectives "added in the genitive, like substantives, rather than as attributes in the same state, gender, and number as the noun which they qualify" (GKC §128w). Rashi comments that the phrase could refer to important buildings such as synagogues or study halls,[19] but this is surely anachronistic. Bright, on the other hand, translates the phrase as "the house of every important person."[20] Likewise, McKane translates it as "all the houses of the grandees."[21] Nevertheless, it should be noted, as McKane does, that Lucian's recension of 2 Kings 25:9 has no representation of גדול or הגדול. In addition to the burning of these buildings mentioned in verse 13, the Chaldean army that accompanied Nebuzaradan "tore down" the walls that surrounded the city of Jerusalem (Jer. 52:14; cf. 2 Kgs. 25:10; Jer. 39:8b; 2 Chr. 36:19; see Jer. 1:10; see also Deut. 28:52).

The text of Jeremiah 52:15 does not appear in the LXX *Vorlage* as it does in the MT. This text does appear, minus the opening phrase ("And some of the poor of the people"), in 2 Kings 25:11 and Jeremiah 39:9 (see 2 Kgs. 25:12a; Jer. 39:10a; 52:16a).[22] Despite the fact that all the references to exile are absent from LXX Jeremiah 52 (Jer. 52:15, 27b, 28–30), it is unlikely that the Greek translator deliberately omitted them in order to make the case that Zedekiah's people were annihilated rather than exiled. Such an effort would have been obviously futile. It is more likely that the MT added these references to provide further closure (i.e., in addition to Jer. 39–44) to the book's prophecy about the fate of the people in the hands of the Babylonians (see Jer. 1:3; 13:19; 20:4). It is possible that Jeremiah 52:15 was accidentally omitted by a Hebrew scribe or the Greek translator due to homoioteleuton, given the fact that both verse 14 and verse 15 end with רב טבחים ("the captain of the guard"), but it should be noted that LXX 52:16 and MT 52:16 do not begin the same way. If verses 15 and 16 are read together in the MT, then there is redundant reference to the poor. If verse 15 is included with LXX 52:16, then there is redundant reference to "the rest of the people" (cf. Jer. 39:9). Thus, verse 15 is a problem either way. It appears to be

---

19. Rosenberg, trans., *Mikraoth Gedoloth: Jeremiah Volume Two*, 415.
20. Bright, *Jeremiah*, 367.
21. McKane, *Jeremiah XXVI–LII*, 1366–67.
22. See the discussion in Leeor Gottlieb, "Repetition Due to Detected Omission," *Textus* 27 (2018): 39–40.

an awkward, secondary insertion based on 2 Kings 25:11.[23] According to
this addition, there were four groups taken into exile by Nebuzaradan:
(1) some of the poor of the people (cf. 2 Kgs. 24:14; but see Jer. 40:7;
see also Jer. 5:4), (2) the rest of the people who remained in the city, (3)
the deserters/defectors who deserted/defected to the king of Babylon (see
Jer. 21:9; 37:13–14; 38:19), and (4) the rest of "the craftsmen" (האמון) (cf.
2 Kgs. 24:14; Syr.: "the people" [העם]; cf. Jer. 39:9; *Tg. Jon.*, Vulg.: "the
multitude" [ההמון]; cf. 2 Kgs. 25:11). 2 Chronicles 36:17, 20 says that
the king of the Chaldeans slaughtered both young and old (cf. Isa. 47:6)
and took the rest into exile to be his servants. According to the Hebrew
source behind Jeremiah 52:16, which immediately follows the reference
to the tearing down of the city walls in verse 14, the captain of the guard
left the rest of the people as vinedressers and plowmen (cf. 2 Kgs. 25:12;
Jer. 39:10). This presupposes that the others were either slaughtered or
taken into exile. MT Jeremiah 52:16, however, following its own addition
of verse 15, makes a redundant reference to the poor of the land as those
whom Nebuzaradan left as vinedressers and plowmen to tend the land.

The list of looted temple articles in Jeremiah 52:17–23 varies considerably between the LXX and the MT, as can be seen in the above
translation. There is also variation between this list and the description of the original temple vessels in 1 Kings 7. Thompson comments
that this should not be surprising, given that the intent was not to
provide a detailed account of these items but to offer a summary for the
sake of the larger narrative (cf. 2 Chr. 36:18).[24] It is to be remembered
that the Babylonians had taken items from the Jerusalem temple on
at least two prior occasions in 605 and 597 (see 2 Kgs. 24:13; Jer. 27:16;
Dan. 1:2; 5:3; 2 Chr. 36:7). Thus, some of vessels taken in 587 were
likely replacements. Jeremiah had indicated very clearly that the articles remaining after 597 would eventually be taken to Babylon (Jer.
27:19–22).[25]

---

23. The text was also included in MT Jeremiah 39:9 as part of a larger addition to that chapter in verses 4–13. Jeremiah 39:4–13 does not appear in
the Hebrew source behind Greek Jeremiah.
24. Thompson, *Book of Jeremiah*, 781. Note that there is no reference to key
items such as the ark of the covenant.
25. See also 2 Maccabees 2:4–8: "It was also in the document that the prophet,
having received an oracle, ordered that the tent and the ark should follow
with him and that he went out to the mountain where Moyses had gone
up and had seen the inheritance of God. Jeremias came and found a cave
dwelling, and he brought there the tent and the ark and the altar of incense; then he sealed up the entrance. Some of those who followed him

Jeremiah 52:17 lists the bronze pillars ("Jachin" and "Boaz"; see 1 Kgs. 7:15–22), the bases (1 Kgs. 7:27–37), and the bronze sea (1 Kgs. 7:23–26). The Chaldeans shattered these items and took away their bronze to Babylon. Also listed as vessels taken by the captain of the guard are "the rim and the bowls for tossing liquid and the shovels [LXX: meat hooks] [MT: and the pots and the shovels and the trimming shears (Vulg.: psalteria) and the bowls for tossing liquid and the pans] and all the bronze vessels with which they would minister [MT adds: they took], and the basins[26] [MT: and the basins and the censers] and the trimming shears [MT: bowls for tossing liquid] and the pots and the lampstands and the censers [MT: pans] and the sacrificial bowls" (Jer. 52:18–19; cf. 1 Kgs. 7:40–45; 2 Kgs. 25:14–15). 2 Kings 25:14–15 and LXX Jeremiah 52:18–19 have shorter, more original versions of this list than the one found in MT Jeremiah 52:18–19. The expression אשר זהב זהב ואשר כסף כסף ("which were gold, gold, and which were silver, silver") in verse 19 apparently means that some of the articles were made of silver and others were made of gold (contra GKC §123e),[27] although the original versions of these items were likely all gold (see Exod. 25:29; 1 Kgs. 7:49–50; 2 Kgs. 24:13; but see Exod. 27:3; 1 Kgs. 7:51; Dan. 5:2; see also Hag. 2:8; Ezra 1:4).

Jeremiah 52:20 returns to the two pillars and the "sea" mentioned in verse 17. This time the twelve bronze bulls are included (see 1 Kgs. 7:25). According to the Hebrew source behind Greek Jeremiah, these twelve bronze bulls were "under the sea" (תחת הים), which is in accordance with the description provided in 1 Kings 7:25. The MT, however, says that the bulls were "under the bases" (תחת המכנות), which makes little sense.[28] The text of 2 Kings 25:16 makes no reference

---

came up intending to mark the way but could not find it. When Jeremias learned of it, he rebuked them and declared, 'The place shall remain unknown until God gathers his people together again and shows his mercy. Then the Lord will disclose these things, and the glory of the Lord will appear, and the cloud, as it showed itself to Moyses, and as Salomon prayed that the place be specially sanctified'" (NETS). Cf. *Lives of the Prophets* 2:9–15. See also Eupolemus Fragment 4; *Jewish Antiquities* 18:85–87; *2 Baruch* 6:1–9; *4 Baruch* 3:9–11, 18–19.

26. See BDB, 706.

27. See Bright, *Jeremiah*, 367–68; Holladay, *Jeremiah 2*, 442.

28. Rashi is aware of the problem and suggests altering the meaning to "beside the bases" (Rosenberg, trans., *Mikraoth Gedoloth: Jeremiah Volume Two*, 417), but this is not really a possible rendering of the Hebrew phrase. Mezudath David offers a different proposal: "when Ahaz removed the sea from the oxen and placed it on the floor, and removed the bases from the

to the twelve bronze bulls (cf. MT Jer. 27:19), and this is sometimes thought to be a superior reading given the fact that Ahaz supposedly sent the bulls to Tiglath-pileser as tribute long before (2 Kgs. 16:8, 17). On closer examination, however, it appears that Ahaz only sent silver and gold from the temple and the royal treasury (2 Kgs. 16:8). The text of 2 Kings 16:17 says that Ahaz had the sea taken down from the bronze bulls, but it does not say that he did anything else with these items (cf. 2 Kgs. 18:16). Even if he did send them to Assyria, replicas could have been made at a later time. Yet the wording of Jeremiah 52:20 ("which King Solomon made for the house of the Lord") seems to suggest that these items taken by the Babylonians were originals. According to the end of verse 20, "there was no weight to their bronze." This does not mean that the objects were incredibly light. Rather, it means that their weight was so great that it could not be weighed (see BDB, 1054). The MT's addition of the appositional phrase "all these vessels" is secondary (see GKC §128d; cf. 2 Kgs. 25:16b).

According to the Hebrew source behind Greek Jeremiah 52:21, the height of each pillar was "thirty-five" cubits. According to 2 Kings 25:17 and MT Jeremiah 52:21, the height of each pillar was "eighteen" cubits (see also 1 Kgs. 7:15). Since the temple was "thirty" cubits high (MT 1 Kgs. 6:2; LXX: "twenty-five"), each pillar could not have been thirty-five cubits. 2 Chronicles 3:15 provides some insight into the nature of this alleged discrepancy. There the text seems to indicate that the combined length of the pillars would be approximately "thirty-five" cubits (see NET). Thus, the height of each individual pillar would have been about "eighteen" cubits. The circumference of each pillar was twelve cubits (lit., "a cord/line of twelve cubits would surround [יסבנו] each one"). The text of 2 Kings 25:17 has no representation of this detail (but see 1 Kgs. 7:15) or the remainder of Jeremiah 52:21. The LXX *Vorlage* says at the conclusion of Jeremiah 52:21 that the thickness of each pillar was four fingers "all around" (סביב). On the other hand, the MT says that the thickness of each pillar was four fingers, "hollow" (נבוב). Tov explains, "The translator of Jeremiah 52, apparently ignorant of this root [נבב], represented נבוב as סבוב (an interchange of *nun/samekh* and *yod/waw*), probably under the influence of יסבנו in the immediate context."[29] This is admittedly a subjective judgment.[30]

---

lavers, he placed the lavers on the oxen, and they stood that way until the destruction of the Temple. Hence, we render: which were instead of the bases. I.e. which were instead of the bases supporting the lavers" (417).

29. Tov, *Text-Critical Use of the Septuagint*, 182.

30. See Tov, *Textual Criticism of the Hebrew Bible*, 22.

Each pillar had a bronze capital (Jer. 52:22). The text of Jeremiah says that the height of each capital was "five" cubits. Second Kings 25:17 says that the height was "three" cubits (cf. 1 Kgs. 7:16). Rashi explains that "the bottom two cubits of the capital were the same as the pillar because there were no designs on them. The upper three cubits, which were extended beyond the pillars, were surrounded with designs."[31] Latticework and pomegranates surrounded each capital. The whole was made of bronze. The conclusion to verse 22 varies considerably among the witnesses. After וכאלה לעמוד השני ("and like these for the second pillar"), 2 Kings 25:17 simply has על השבכה ("with the latticework"). MT Jeremiah 52:22 has ורמונים ("and pomegranates"). LXX Jeremiah 52:22 reflects שמנה רמונים לאמה לשתים עשרה אמה ("eight pomegranates to the cubit for twelve cubits"). This latter reading is clearly the longest of the three. McKane suggests that it may have been a marginal comment designed to explain how the figure of ninety-six in verse 23 was reached: "There were eight pomegranates to a cubit and the circumference of the pillar was twelve cubits."[32] According to Jeremiah 52:23, there were ninety-six pomegranates "on the sides" (רוחה; > Syr.), yet the total number of pomegranates on the latticework was one hundred. This text does not appear in 2 Kings 25 at all. Rashi points to the text of 1 Kings 7:20, 42: "You may deduce from here that there were four hundred for the two nets on the two pillars, two rows for each net, and each row was one hundred."[33] As for the discrepancy between the numbers ninety-six and one hundred, Rashi understands רוחה to mean "to the outside" and thus interprets the text to say that four pomegranates of each row were concealed, while ninety-six were visible to the outside.[34]

The captain of the guard (Nebuzaradan) took the chief priest and the "second" priest (NET: "the priest who was second in rank") and the three keepers of the threshold (Jer. 52:24; cf. 2 Kgs. 23:4; see also Jer. 35:4b).[35] 2 Kings 25:18 and MT Jeremiah 52:24 add names for the chief priest and the second priest: Seraiah (see 1 Chr. 5:40) and Zephaniah (see Jer. 21:1; 29:25–29; 37:3). At the beginning of Jeremiah 52:25, the MT adds

---

31. Rosenberg, trans., *Mikraoth Gedoloth: Jeremiah Volume Two*, 417.

32. McKane, *Jeremiah XXVI–LII*, 1375–76.

33. "That means two hundred for two rows around one pillar, and so for the second one, thus totaling four hundred" (Rosenberg, trans., *Mikraoth Gedoloth: Jeremiah Volume Two*, 418).

34. Rosenberg, trans., *Mikraoth Gedoloth: Jeremiah Volume Two*, 418. See also Neusner, *Jeremiah in Talmud and Midrash*, 7.

35. For the translation of "the threshold" as "the way" in the LXX, see note to translation above.

"from the city he took," which comes from 2 Kings 25:19. This addition, which does not appear in LXX Jeremiah 52:25, is unnecessary. Verse 25 is a continuation of the list of those taken from the city by Nebuzaradan in verse 24 where the verb "took" has already been introduced. It is possible that the addition was made to help readers follow the continuity of thought. Nebuzaradan took one official who was overseer over the soldiers "and seven men of name in the king's presence" (ושבעה אנשי שם פני המלך) who were found (Syr.: "left") in the city.[36] The seven men were apparently men of great reputation who served as close advisors to the king (cf. Gen. 6:4b; 1 Chr. 5:24; 12:30 [Eng., 12:30]). MT Jeremiah 52:25 has a slightly different reading: "and seven men of those who saw the king's face" (ושבעה אנשים מראי פני המלך). There is a comparable expression in Esther 1:14, which again suggests that these men were part of the king's inner circle, yet they did not attempt to flee the city with the king. The reading in 2 Kings 25:19 is similar to that of MT Jeremiah 52:25, but it has the number "five" instead of the number "seven." Rabbinic interpretation surmises that two of the seven men were scribes who aided the other five.[37] Also listed in Jeremiah 52:25 as one of those taken by Nebuzaradan is "the army scribe" (ספר הצבא) who mustered the people of the land (Syr.: "of the people of the land"). The MT (also LXX 2 Kgs. 25:19) describes this person as "the scribe of the army official" (ספר שר הצבא). Origen, Lucian, *Targum Jonathan*, the Latin Vulgate, and MT 2 Kings 25:19 have "the scribe" and "the army official" in an appositional relationship: "the scribe, the army official" (הספר שר הצבא). The Syriac version of Jeremiah 52:25 distinguishes two individuals: "the scribe and the army official" (= הספר ושר הצבא). Jeremiah 52:25 concludes its list with sixty men/people from the general populace ("the people of the land") who were found in the midst of the city. Nebuzardan took all the people listed in verses 24 and 25 and brought them to the king of Babylon at Diblah/Riblah (2 Kgs. 25:20; Jer. 52:26; cf. Jer. 52:9–11) in the land of Hamath where the king had them executed (2 Kgs. 25:21a; Jer. 52:27a). The LXX *Vorlage* of Jeremiah 52:27a simply says, "And the king of Babylon struck them (ויך אותם מלך בבל) at Diblah in the land of Hamath." Second Kings 25:21a and MT Jeremiah 52:27a appear to have a conflation of two interchangeable readings: "And the king of Babylon struck them and killed them (ויך [ויכה] אותם מלך בבל וימתם) at Riblah in the land of Hamath."[38]

---

36. The סריס in this verse is not specifically a "eunuch" (as in Est. 1:10), but, as elsewhere in Jeremiah (Jer. 29:2; 34:19; 38:7; 39:3, 13; 41:16), an "official."

37. See Neusner, *Jeremiah in Talmud in Midrash*, 94, 208.

38. Second Chronicles 36:17 indicates that the Babylonian king had no mercy on male or female, young or old (see Isa. 47:6).

Second Kings 25:21b and MT Jeremiah 52:27b add a clause to the end of their respective verses, a clause that does not appear in the Hebrew source behind Greek Jeremiah 52:27: "and Judah went into exile away from its land" (see commentary on MT Jer. 52:15). This added text does not fit the immediate context of the execution narrated in Jeremiah 52:24–27a (2 Kgs. 25:18–21a), but it does set up two very different additions of considerable length in 2 Kings 25:22–26 and MT Jeremiah 52:28–30, neither of which appear in LXX Jeremiah 52. Second Kings 25:22–26 provides a concise account of what happened to those left in the land of Judah after the others went away into exile. It is a short version of the brief governorship of Gedaliah, his assassination, and the flight of the Judeans to Egypt (cf. Jer. 40–43). This text does not appear in MT or LXX Jeremiah 52. On the other hand, MT Jeremiah 52:28–30 provides a breakdown and tally of those who were taken into exile in 597, 587, and 582. This text does not appear in 2 Kings 25 or LXX Jeremiah 52. Thus, 2 Kings 25 and MT Jeremiah 52 both expand upon the shorter, more original text behind LXX Jeremiah 52 in different directions.

MT Jeremiah 52:28 gives the number of people whom Nebuchadrezzar took into exile in year seven of his reign (597 BC) as 3,023 Judeans.[39] This is an oddly precise figure, but it seems at first glance to be low. According to 2 Kings 24:14, the Babylonian king took into exile in that year the people of Jerusalem and all the officials and the soldiers, 10,000. It is not clear if the craftsmen and smiths mentioned next in 2 Kings 24:14 are to be included in that number (see 2 Kgs. 24:16). According to 2 Kings 24:16, 7,000 soldiers (or, men of substance) were taken into exile along with 1,000 craftsmen and smiths. Rashi harmonizes by suggesting that Jeremiah 52:28 indicates that 3,000 out of the 10,000 were Judeans, while the remaining 7,000 were from other tribes.[40] Jeremiah 52:29 then gives the number of people taken into exile in the eighteenth year of Nebuchadrezzar (587

---

39. This counts from the first full year of Nebuchadnezzar's reign. Second Kings 24:12 has this as the eighth year of his reign, counting from his accession year. See the reference to the Babylonian Chronicle in McKane, *Jeremiah XXVI–LII*, 1381. For the argument that Jeremiah 52:28 should say "in the seventeenth year," see Keil, *Jeremiah*, 461. There is no reference here to the exile of 605 BC (see Dan. 1).

40. Rosenberg, trans., *Mikraoth Gedoloth: Jeremiah Volume Two*, 419. Others have suggested that the lower number in Jeremiah 52:28 only gives the number of adult males, or that there were two deportations in 597, or that the numbers in 2 Kings are exaggerations (see Holladay, *Jeremiah 2*, 443),

BC): 832 people from Jerusalem.[41] This figure is also remarkable for its precision. Lastly, in the twenty-third year of Nebuchadrezzar (582 BC), Nebuzaradan took into exile 745 Judeans (Jer. 52:30a). There is no other reference to this last exile in the Bible, and it is not known exactly who these Judeans were or how/where they were in the land or why they were taken into exile (but see Jer. 41:17–18). The total number of people listed in MT Jeremiah 52:28–30 equals 4,600 (Jer. 52:30b).[42]

The final unit of chapter 52 takes the reader down to the year 561 BC (Jer. 52:31–34). This very brief account shows Jehoiachin still alive in Babylonian exile. According to the Hebrew source behind Greek Jeremiah 52:31, Evil Merodach ("man of Marduk"),[43] the son of Nebuchadnezzar who was by then the new king of Babylon (561–560 BC), "lifted up the head" of Jehoiachin in the first year of his reign, which was the thirty-seventh year of Jehoaichin's exile, in the twelfth month, on the twenty-fourth day of the month. The MT says that this happened on the twenty-fifth day of the month, while 2 Kings 25:27 puts it on the twenty-seventh of the month.[44] The expression "lifted up the head" may be compared to its usage in the story of Genesis 40 where Pharaoh lifts up the head of the chief cupbearer in accordance with Joseph's interpretation of his dream (Gen. 40:13, 20). It was a gesture of favor. This link to the Joseph story may have prompted the addition "and he shaved him" (or, "and he shaved himself") in Codex Vaticanus' text of Jeremiah 52:31. The addition is reminiscent of what is said in Genesis 41:14 about Joseph who was brought out of the pit and prepared to come before Pharaoh (see also Jer. 52:33a). Evil

---

but it must be admitted that we do not really know the exact relationship of these numbers to one another.

41. This counts from the first full year of Nebuchadnezzar's reign, whereas MT Jeremiah 52:12 counts from his accession year and calls 587 BC the nineteenth year of his reign.

42. For a discussion of how such a larger number of people, 42,360 (Ezra 2:64), could have later returned to Jerusalem and Judah under the leadership of Zerubbabel, see Keil, *Jeremiah*, 462.

43. It has been suggested that the particular Hebrew spelling of this name (אֱוִיל מְרֹדַךְ) is meant to imply the meaning "fool of Marduk" (Bright, *Jeremiah*, 369).

44. Rashi: "Rather, on the twenty-fifth day, Nebuchadnezzar, his adversary, died, and on the twenty-sixth day he was interred and Evil-merodach removed him from his grave, and on the twenty-seventh he reigned and lifted up Jehoiachin's head" (Rosenberg, trans., *Mikraoth Gedoloth: Jeremiah Volume Two*, 420).

Merodach brought Jehoiachin out of his place of confinement, but he did not release him or send him home.

Evil Merodach spoke with Jehoiachin "good things" (Jer. 52:32a; cf. 2 Kgs. 25:28a) in contrast to the words of judgment that Nebuchadnezzar spoke with Zedekiah (Jer. 52:9b). Evil Merodach also put Jehoiachin's seat or throne above those of the other kings who were with him in Babylon (Jer. 52:32b; cf. 2 Kgs. 25:28b; see also Est. 3:1). The other kings mentioned here were presumably other conquered and exiled rulers like Jehoiachin, although it is not entirely out of the question that they could have been distinguished guests. McKane suggests that the higher seat granted to Jehoiachin refers to the seating arrangements at the king's table (cf. Gen. 43:33–34).[45] While this interpretation might initially appear to receive confirmation in verse 33, verse 34 seems to speak of daily rations for Jehoiachin in his own quarters. Of course, it is possible that verses 32 and 33 only have in view meals with the king on special occasions or in some other limited sense. On the other hand, the Hebrew word כסא in verse 32 may not refer to a "seat" at the king's table. It may refer to a "throne" set up in the midst of other thrones arranged for a formal assembly in the presence of Evil Merodach. In this situation, Jehoiachin's throne would have been positioned in such a way as to indicate the priority given to him in relation to the other kings. Yet another option is that the expression is simply an indication of higher status or position (cf. Est. 3:1). The text does not state why Jehoiachin was the object of such favor from Evil Merodach, and the reader is left to wonder if such accommodations were providential (cf. Dan. 1:9).

Jehoiachin no longer had to wear his prison clothes (Jer. 52:33a; cf. 2 Kgs. 25:29a; see also Gen. 41:14b),[46] and he ate bread/food continually before the king of Babylon all the days of his life (Jer. 52:33b; cf. 2 Kgs. 25:29b; see also 2 Sam. 9:10, 11, 13; 1 Kgs. 2:7; 18:19). Again, it is not clear how regularly Jehoiachin ate in the king's presence. The text simply indicates that eating in the king's presence was an ongoing privilege of his. The phrases "all the days of his life" (v. 33b) and "until the day of his death" (v. 34) do not refer to the days of Evil

---

45. McKane, *Jeremiah XXVI–LII*, 1386–87.
46. The possible allusion to the Joseph story here recalls the allusion in Jeremiah 31:15 (see commentary there) where, just as Joseph was once thought to be no more yet was seen again, so the people of God only appear to be no more. Likewise, the account of the Babylonian invasion in Jeremiah 52 marks the end of the Davidic dynasty. Nevertheless, a Davidic king resurfaces in the final verses of the chapter, rekindling hope in the future.

Merodach's life or the day of his death.[47] Rather, they refer to the days of Jehoiachin's life and the day of his death (cf. Jer. 52:11b). This means that Jehoiachin most likely enjoyed his special privileges beyond the time period of Evil Merodach's relatively short reign. Jehoiachin's allowance of food was given to him continually from the king of Babylon on a daily basis until the day of his death (MT adds redundantly: "all the days of his life") (Jer. 52:34; cf. 2 Kgs. 25:30; see also Jer. 40:5; Dan. 1:5). The syntax of the MT indicates that this allowance was separate from the continual eating of food in the king's presence: "And as for his allowance of food, a continual allowance was given to him." All indications are that Jehoiachin lived quite well in Babylonian exile from this point to the end of his life (see 2 Kgs. 20:18; Isa. 39:7).[48]

The parallel passage in 2 Kings 25:27–30 concludes not only the book of Kings or Samuel-Kings but also the entire literary complex of the Former Prophets, Joshua-Judges-Samuel-Kings.[49] The debate about the role of this passage in the composition of the Former Prophets concerns whether the image of Jehoiachin in Babylonian exile is a fundamentally negative one or a positive one.[50] On the one hand, to conclude the work with an account of the Babylonian invasion, the destruction of the temple, and a picture of the last surviving king who sat on the throne of David living in exile does not promote tremendous confidence in the future for the people of God. It is a depiction of the consequences of the broken covenant relationship as anticipated already by Moses (Deut. 28). The great expectations generated by the covenant with David (2 Sam. 7) have not come to fruition. Despite the initial promise shown by kings like Solomon, Hezekiah, and Josiah in their respective narratives, the reader comes to the end of the book still awaiting the king who will build a temple and reign over an everlasting kingdom (2 Sam. 7:12–16; Ezek. 40–48; Zech. 6:12–13; Rev. 21:22).[51] On the other hand, Moses himself prophesied about a restoration of the people of God—a new covenant relationship—beyond the expected consequences of the broken covenant (Deut. 30). This suggests

---

47. See Holladay, *Jeremiah 2*, 443; McKane, *Jeremiah XXVI–LII*, 1387.
48. It is not known what relationship Jehoiachin might have had to others like Daniel and his three friends who held prominent positions in the Babylonian royal court.
49. See Shepherd, *Textual World of the Bible*, 18–23.
50. See Marvin A. Sweeney, *I & II Kings: A Commentary*, OTL (Louisville: Westminster John Knox, 2007), 464–65.
51. For inner-biblical interpretation of the covenant with David, see Shepherd, *Text in the Middle*, 122–29.

to the reader of 2 Kings 25:27–30 that while the Babylonian invasion certainly marked the end of the old covenant relationship and the Davidic monarchy as it was known, it also signaled the beginning of hope—looking forward to what God had in store for his people. Thus, the favor shown to Jehoiachin in exile, while modest in comparison to expectation for the Davidic Messiah, provides a flickering reminder that the line of David continues (see 1 Chr. 3; Matt. 1:1–17). Indeed, the ideal Davidic king has not arrived. Therefore, he is still to come. Rather than disappointment in a lack of fulfillment, the end of Kings produces anticipation of what the future holds.

The conclusion to the book of Jeremiah has a similar function, yet one that is appropriate to its own context. Bright comments that the motive for this conclusion may have been the thought "that an account of the fall of Jerusalem, the event that brought vindication to Jeremiah's lifelong announcement of the divine judgment, would furnish a fitting conclusion to the book because it would allow history itself to give its silent witness to the truth of the prophetic word."[52] Jeremiah, a prophet like Moses, has prepared the reader for such an ending, yet Bright adds with reference to Jeremiah 52:31–34 that the text seems also to hint at the future that Jeremiah envisioned (Jer. 30–33): "In its present context the chapter seems to say: the divine word both has been fulfilled—and will be fulfilled!"[53] The demonstrated truth of Jeremiah's prophecy about what is now past is a guarantee of the truth of his prophecy about the future. Like Moses, Jeremiah looked forward to a new covenant relationship. Furthermore, the final image of the Davidic king in Jeremiah 52:31–34 leads the reader to recall the hope of the Davidic Messiah earlier in the book (Jer. 4:2; 23:5–6; 30:9, 21).[54] This hope is cast in terms of the covenant with David in 2 Samuel 7:12–16 (Jer. 23:5–6; Zech. 6:12–13), the same text upon which 2 Kings 25:27–30 depends for its trajectory. The relevance of such a message for today's reader can hardly be overstated as the community of believers awaits the coming of their king to establish his kingdom on earth.

---

52. Bright, *Jeremiah*, 370.
53. Bright, *Jeremiah*, 370.
54. See McKane, *Jeremiah XXVI–LII*, 1388. See also *4 Baruch* 9.

THE HEBREW SOURCE BEHIND THE OLD GREEK

JEREMIAH 1

‪¹ דבר אלהים אשר היה אל ירמיהו בן חלקיהו מן הכהנים אשר בענתות בארץ בנימן‬
‪² אשר היה דבר אלהים אליו בימי יאשיהו בן אמוס מלך יהודה בשלש עשרה שנה‬
‪למלכו ³ ויהי בימי יהויקים בן יאשיהו מלך יהודה עד אשתי עשרה שנה לצדקיהו בן‬
‪יאשיהו מלך יהודה עד גלות ירושלם בחדש החמישי ⁴ ויהי דבר יהוה אליו ⁵ בטרם‬
‪אצרך בבטן ידעתיך ובטרם תצא מרחם הקדשתיך נביא לגוים נתתיך ⁶ ואמר אהה‬
‪אדני יהוה הנה לא ידעתי דבר כי נער אנכי ⁷ ויאמר יהוה אלי אל תאמר כי נער‬
‪אנכי כי על כל אשר אשלחך תלך ואת כל אשר אצוך תדבר ⁸ אל תירא מפניהם כי‬
‪אתך אני להצלך נאם יהוה ⁹ וישלח יהוה את ידו אלי ויגע על פי ויאמר יהוה אלי‬
‪הנה נתתי דברי בפיך ¹⁰ ראה הפקדתיך היום הזה על הגוים ועל הממלכות לנתוש‬
‪ולנתוץ ולהאביד ולבנות ולנטוע ¹¹ ויהי דבר יהוה לאמר מה אתה ראה ואמר מקל‬
‪שקד ¹² ויאמר יהוה אלי היטבת לראות כי שקד אני על דברי לעשתם ¹³ ויהי דבר‬
‪יהוה אלי שנית לאמר מה אתה ראה ואמר סיר נפוח ופניו מפני צפונה ¹⁴ ויאמר יהוה‬
‪אלי מצפון תפתח הרעה על כל ישבי הארץ ¹⁵ כי הנני קרא לכל ממלכות צפונה‬
‪נאם יהוה ובאו ונתנו איש כסאו פתח שערי ירושלם ועל כל חומתיה סביב ועל כל‬
‪ערי יהודה ¹⁶ ודברתי אתם משפט על כל רעתם אשר עזבוני ויקטרו לאלהים אחרים‬
‪וישתחוו למעשי ידיהם ¹⁷ ואתה תאזר מתניך וקמת ודברת את כל אשר אצוך אל‬
‪תירא מפניהם ואל תחת לפניהם כי אתך אני להצלך נאם יהוה ¹⁸ הנה נתתיך היום‬
‪לעיר מבצר ולחומת נחשת מבצר על כל מלכי יהודה ולשריו ולעם הארץ ¹⁹ ונלחמו‬
‪אליך ולא יוכלו לך כי אתך אני להצילך נאם יהוה‬

JEREMIAH 2

2 ויאמר כה אמר יהוה זכרתי חסד נעוריך ואהבת כלולתיך לכתך אחרי קדוש
ישראל נאם יהוה 3 קדש ישראל ליהוה ראשית תבואתו כל אכליו יאשמו רעה תבא
אליהם נאם יהוה 4 שמעו דבר יהוה בית יעקב וכל משפחות בית ישראל 5 כה אמר
יהוה מה מצאו אבותיכם בי עול כי רחקו מעלי וילכו אחרי ההבל ויהבלו 6 ולא
אמרו איה יהוה המעלה אתנו מארץ מצרים המוליך אתנו במדבר בארץ ערבה
ושוחה בארץ ציה וצלמודה בארץ לא עבר בה איש ולא ישב אדם שם 7 ואביא אתכם
אל הכרמל לאכל פריה וטובה ותבאו ותטמאו את ארצי ונחלתי שמתם לתועבה 8
הכהנים לא אמרו איה יהוה ותפשי התורה לא ידעוני והרעים פשעו בי והנביאים
נבאו בבעל ואחרי לא יועלו הלכו 9 לכן עד אריב אתכם נאם יהוה ואת בני בניכם
אריב 10 כי עברו איי כתיים וראו וקדר שלחו והתבוננו מאד וראו הן היתה כזאת 11
ההימירו גוים אלהיהם והמה לא אלהים ועמי המיר כבודו בלוא יועילו 12 שמו שמים
על זאת ושערו הרבה מאד נאם יהוה 13 כי שתים רעות עשה עמי אתי עזבו מקור
מים חיים לחצב להם בארות נשברים אשר לא יכלו המים 14 העבד ישראל אם יליד
בית הוא מדוע היה היה לבז 15 עליו ישאגו כפרים ונתנו קולם ישיתו ארצו לשמה ועריו
נתצו מבלי ישב 16 גם בני נף ותחפנס ידעוך וקלסוך הלוא זאת עשה לך עזבך אתי
17 נאם יהוה אלהיך 18 ועתה מה לך ולדרך מצרים לשתות מי גיחון ומה לך ולדרך
אשור לשתות מי נהר 19 תיסרך רעתך ומשבותיך תוכחך ודעי וראי כי מר לך שזבך
אתי נאם יהוה אלהיך ולא חפצתי בך נאם יהוה אלהיך 20 כי מעולם שברת עלך
נתקת מוסרתיך ותאמרי לא אעבד והלכתי על כל גבעה גבהה ותחת כל עץ רענן
שם אני צעה בזנותי 21 ואנכי נטעתיך שרק כלה זרע אמת איך נהפכת למרה הגפן
הנכריה 22 כי אם תכבסי בנתר ותרבי לך ברית נכתם עונתיך לפני נאם יהוה 23 איך
תאמרי לא נטמאתי ואחרי הבעל לא הלכתי ראי דרכיך בגיא ודעי מה עשית בערב
קלה היליל 24 דרכיה פרצה למי מדבר באות נפשה שאפה רוח נתנה מי ישיבנה כל
מבקשיה לא ייעפו בענתה ימצאונה 25 מנעי רגלך מרכס וגרונך מצמאה ותאמר נואש
אני כי אהבה זרים ואחריהם תלך 26 כבשת גנב כי ימצא כן הבישו בני ישראל המה
ומלכיהם ושריהם וכהניהם ונביאיהם 27 לעץ אמרו אבי אתה ולאבן את ילדתני ויפנו
אלי ערף ולא פניהם ובעת רעתם יאמרו קומה והושיענו 28 ואיה אלהיך אשר עשית
לך אם יקומו ויושיעוך בעת רעתך כי מספר עריך היו אלהיך יהודה ומספר חצות
ירושלם קטרו לבעל 29 למה תדברו אלי כלכם פשעתם וכלכם פשעתם בי נאם יהוה
30 לשוא הכיתי את בניכם מוסר לא לקחתם אכלה חרב נביאיכם כאריה משחית ולא
יראתם 31 שמעו דבר יהוה כה אמר יהוה המדבר הייתי לישראל אם ארץ מאפליה
מדוע אמרו עמי לא נרדו ולא נבוא עוד אליך 32 התשכח כלה עדיה ובתולה קשריה
ועמי שכחוני ימים אין מספר 33 מה תיטבי דרכיך לבקש אהבה לא כן גם את הרעות
לטמא את דרכיך 34 גם בכפיך נמצאו דמי נפשות נקיות לא במחתרת מצאתים כי
על כל אלה 35 ותאמרי כי נקיתי אך ישב אפו ממני הנני נשפט אתך על אמרך לא
חטאתי 36 מה תזלי מאד לשנות את דרכיך גם ממצרים תבושי כאשר בשת מאשור
37 כי גם מאת זה תצאי וידיך על ראשך כי מאס יהוה במבטחך ולא תצליחי בו

JEREMIAH 3

1 הן ישלח איש את אשתו והלכה מאתו והיתה לאיש אחר הישוב תשוב אליו עוד
הלוא חנוף תחנף הארץ ההיא ואת זנית רעים רבים ושוב אלי נאם יהוה 2 שאי על

מישרים עיניך וראי איפה לא שגלת על הדרכים ישבת להם כערב במדבר ותחניפי
ארץ בזנותיך וברעותיך ³ ויהיו לך רעים רבים למוקש לך מצח זונה היה לך מאנת
הכלם לכל ⁴ הלוא מענה קראת אתי ואב ואלוף נעריך ⁵ הינטר לעולם אם ישמר
לנצח הנה דברת ותעשי הרעות ותוכל ⁶ ויאמר יהוה אלי בימי יאשיהו המלך הראית
אשר עשתה משבה ישראל הלכו על כל הר גבה ואל תחת כל עץ רענן ויזנו שם
⁷ ואמר אחר עשותה את כל אלה אלי תשוב ולא שבה ותרא בגודה אחותה יהודה
⁸ וארא כי על כל אדות אשר נאפה משבה ישראל שלחתיה ואתן אליה את ספר
כריתת ולא יראה בגדה יהודה ותלך ותזן גם היא ⁹ ויהי לכל זנותה ותנאף את העץ
ואת האבן ¹⁰ וגם בכל זאת לא שבה אלי בגודה יהודה בכל לבה כי אם בשקר ¹¹
ויאמר יהוה אלי צדק נפשו ישראל מבגדה יהודה ¹² הלך וקראת את הדברים האלה
צפונה ואמרת שובה משבה ישראל נאם יהוה ולוא אפיל פני בכם כי חסיד אני נאם
יהוה ולא אטור לעולם ¹³ אך דעי עונך כי ביהוה אלהיך פשעת ותפזרי את דרכיך
לזרים תחת כל עץ רענן ובקולי לא שמעתם נאם יהוה ¹⁴ שובו בנים שובבים נאם יהוה
כי אנכי בעלתי בכם ולקחתי אתכם אחד מעיר ושנים ממשפחה והבאתי אתכם ציון
¹⁵ ונתתי לכם רעים כלבי ורעו אתכם רעה והשכיל ¹⁶ והיה כי תפרו ורביתם בארץ
בימים ההמה נאם יהוה לא יאמרו עוד ארון ברית קדוש ישראל לא יעלה על לב
לא יזכרו בו ולא יפקדו ולא יעשה עוד ¹⁷ בימים ההמה ובעת ההיא יקראו לירושלם
כסא יהוה ונקוו אליה כל הגוים ולא ילכו עוד אחרי שררות לבם הרע ¹⁸ בימים
ההמה ילכו בית יהודה על בית ישראל ויבאו יחדו מארץ צפון ומכל הארצות על
הארץ אשר הנחלתי את אבותיהם ¹⁹ ואנכי אמרתי אמן יהוה כי אשיתך בבנים ואתן
לך ארץ חמדה נחלת אלהי צבאות גוים ואמר אב תקראו לי ומאחרי לא תשובו ²⁰
אך כבגד אשה מרעה כן בגד בי בית ישראל נאם יהוה ²¹ קול על שפתים נשמע בכי
ותחנוני בני ישראל כי העוו את דרכיהם שכחו אלהים קדושם ²² שובו בנים שובבים
וארפא שבריכם הנה אנחנו לך כי אתה יהוה אלהינו ²³ אכן לשקר הגבעות והמון
הרים אכן ביהוה אלהינו תשועת ישראל ²⁴ והבשת אכלה את יגיע אבותינו מנעורינו
את צאנם ואת בקרם ואת בניהם ואת בנותיהם ²⁵ נשכבה בבשתנו ותכסנו כלמתנו כי
לאלהנו חטאנו אנחנו ואבותינו מנעורינו ועד היום הזה ולא שמענו בקול יהוה אלהינו

JEREMIAH 4

¹ אם ישוב ישראל נאם יהוה אלי ישוב אם יסיר שקוציו מפיו ומפני לא ינוד ² ונשבע
חי יהוה באמת במשפט ובצדקה והתברכו בו גוים ובו יתהללו אלהים בירושלם ³
כי כה אמר יהוה לאיש יהודה ולישבי ירושלם נירו לכם ניר ולא תזרעו אל קוצים
⁴ המלו לאלהיכם והסרו ערלת לבבכם איש יהודה וישבי ירושלם פן תצא כאש
חמתי ובערה ואין מכבה מפני רע מעלליכם ⁵ הגידו ביהודה ובירושלם השמיעו
אמרו תקעו בארץ שופר וקראו מלאו אמרו האספו ונבואה אל ערי המבצר ⁶ שאו
נס ציונה העיזו אל תעמדו כי רעה אנכי מביא מצפון ושבר גדול ⁷ עלה אריה
מסבכו משחית גוים נסע ויצא ממקמו לשום הארץ לשמה וערים תצינה מאין יושב
⁸ על זאת חגרו שקים וספדו והילילו כי לא שב אף יהוה ממנו ⁹ והיה ביום ההוא
נאם יהוה יאבד לב המלך ולב השרים ונשמו הכהנים והנביאים יתמהו ¹⁰ ואמר
אהה אדני יהוה אכן השא השאת לעם הזה ולירושלם לאמר שלום יהיה והנה נגעה
חרב עד נפשם ¹¹ בעת ההיא יאמרו לעם הזה ולירושלם רוח צעים במדבר דרך
בת עמי לוא לזרות ולוא להבר ¹² רוח מלא יבוא לי עתה גם אני אדבר משפטים

אתם 13 הנה כענן יעלה וכסופה מרכבותיו קלו מנשרים סוסיו אוי לנו כי שדדנו
14 כבסי מרעה לבך ירושלם למען תושעי עד מתי תלין בקרבך מחשבות אונך 15
כי קול מגיד מדן יבוא ונשמע און מהר אפרים 16 הזכירו לגוים הנה באו השמיעו
על ירושלם צרים באים מארץ מרחק ויתנו על ערי יהודה קולם 17 כשמרי שדי
היו עליה מסביב כי אתי מרתה נאם יהוה 18 דרכיך ומעלליך עשו אלה לך זאת
רעתך כי מר כי נגע עד לבך 19 מעי מעי אחולה וקירות לבי המה לי נפשי המה
לי לבי לא אחריש כי קול שופר שמעה נפשי תרועת מלחמה 20 ושד על שבר
נקרא כי שדדה כל הארץ פתאם שדד האהל נתקו יריעתי 21 עד מתי אראה נס
שמע קול שופר 22 כי אילי עמי אותי לא ידעו בנים סכלים המה ולא נבונים המה
חכמים המה להרע ולהיטיב לא ידעו 23 ראיתי את הארץ והנה תהו ובהו ואל
השמים ואין אורם 24 ראיתי ההרים ורעשים וכל הגבעות התקלקלו 25 ראיתי והנה
אין האדם וכל עוף השמים נדדו 26 ראיתי והנה הכרמל מדבר וכל הערים נצתו
מפני יהוה ומפני חרון אפו נשמו 27 כה אמר יהוה שממה תהיה כל הארץ וכלה
לא אעשה 28 על זאת תאבל הארץ וקדרו השמים ממעל על כן דברתי ולא נחמתי
זמתי ולא אשוב ממנה 29 מקול פרש ודרכת קשת ברחת כל הארץ באו במערות
ויחבאו בעבים ובכפים עלו כל עיר עזובה ואין יושב בהן איש 30 ואת מה תעשי
כי תלבשי שני ותעדי עדי זהב כי תקרעי בפוך עיניך לשוא תתיפי מאסו בך
עגבים נפשך יבקשו 31 כי קול כחולה שמעתי צרתך כמבכירה קול בת ציון
תתיפח ותפרש כפיה אוי נא לי כי עיפה נפשי להרגים

JEREMIAH 5

1 שוטטו בחוצות ירושלם וראו נא ודעו ובקשו ברחובותיה אם תמצאו איש אם יש
עשה משפט ומבקש אמונה ואסלח לה נאם יהוה 2 חי יהוה יאמרו לכן לשקר ישבעו
3 יהוה עיניך הלוא לאמונה הכיתה אתם ולא חלו כליתם ומאנו קחת מוסר חזקו
פניהם מסלע ומאנו לשוב 4 ואני אמרתי אך דלים הם נואלו כי לא ידעו דרך יהוה
משפט אלהים 5 אלכה אל הגדלים ואדברה אתם כי המה ידעו דרך יהוה ומשפט
אלהים והנה יחדו שברו על נתקו מוסרות 6 על כן הכם אריה מיער וזאב עד
בית ישדדם ונמר שקד על עריהם כל היוצא מהנה יטרף כי רבו פשעיהם עצמו
משבותיהם 7 אי לזאת אסלח לך בניך עזבוני וישבעו בלא אלהים ואשבע אותם
וינאפו ובית זונה יתגוררו 8 סוסים משכים היו איש אל אשת רעהו יצהלו 9 העל
אלה לוא אפקד נאם יהוה ואם בגוי אשר כזה לא תתנקם נפשי 10 עלו בשרותיה
ושחתו וכלה אל תעשו אל התירו נטישותיה כי ליהוה המה 11 כי בגוד בגדו בי בית
ישראל ובית יהודה 12 כחשו ביהוה ויאמרו לא הוא לא תבוא עלינו רעה וחרב
ורעה לא נראה 13 נביאינו היו לרוח ודבר יהוה אין בהם כה יהיה להם 14 לכן כה
אמר יהוה צבאות יען דברכם את הדבר הזה הנני נתן דברי בפיך לאש והעם הזה
לעצים ואכלתם 15 הנני מביא עליכם גוי ממרחק בית ישראל נאם יהוה גוי אשר
לא תשמע לשונו 16 כלם גבורים ואכלו קצירכם 17 ולחמכם ואכלו בניכם ובנותיכם
אכלו צאנכם ובקרכם ואכלו גפנכם ותאנתכם וזיתכם ורששו ערי מבצריכם אשר
אתם בטחתם בהנה בחרב 18 והיה בימים ההמה נאם יהוה אלהיך לא אעשה אתכם
כלה 19 והיה כי תאמרו תחת מה עשה יהוה אלהינו לנו את כל אלה ואמרת אליהם
כאשר עבדתם אלהי נכר בארצכם כן תעבדו זרים בארץ לא לכם 20 הגידו זאת
בבית יעקב והשמיעוה ביהודה 21 שמעו נא זאת עם סכל ואין לב עינים להם ולא

 יראו אזנים להם ולא ישמעו 22 האותי לא תיראו נאם יהוה אם מפני לא תחילו
אשר שמתי חול גבול לים חק עולם ולא יעברנהו ויתגעש ולא יוכל והמו גליו ולא
יעברנהו 23 ולעם הזה היה לב סורר ומורה סרו וילכו 24 ולא אמרו בלבבם נירא
נא את יהוה אלהינו הנתן לנו גשם יורה ומלקוש בעתו שבעת חקת קציר וישמר לנו 25
עונותיכם הטו אלה וחטאותיכם מנעו הטוב מכם 26 כי נמצאו בעמי רשעים ומוקשים
הציבו השחית אנשים ולכדו 27 ככלוב מלא עוף כן בתיהם מלאים מרמה על כן
גדלו ויעשירו 28 גם עברו דין לא דנו דין יתום ומשפט אלמנה לא שפטו 29 העל אלה
לא אפקד נאם יהוה אם בגוי אשר כזה לא תתנקם נפשי 30 שמה ושערורה נהיתה
בארץ 31 הנביאים נבאו בשקר והכהנים ירדו על ידיהם ועמי אהבו כן ומה תעשו
לאחריתה

JEREMIAH 6

1 העזו בני בנימן מקרב ירושלם ובתקוע תקעו שופר ועל בית הכרם שאו משאת
כי רעה נשקפה מצפון ושבר גדול 2 וקומתך נדמתה בת ציון 3 אליה יבאו רעים
ועדריהם ותקעו עליה אהלים סביב ורעו איש את ידו 4 קדשו עליה מלחמה קומו
ונעלה בצהרים אוי לנו כי פנה היום כי ינטו צללי ערב 5 קומו ונעלה בלילה
ונשחיתה ארמנותיה 6 כי כה אמר יהוה כרתו עצה שפחו על ירושלם סללה הוי
עיר השקר כל עשק בקרבה 7 כהקיר בור מים כן הקרה רעתה חמס ושד ישמע
בה על פניה תמיד חלי ומכה 8 תוסרי ירושלם פן תקע נפשי ממך פן אשימך
שממה ארץ לוא נושבה 9 כי כה אמר יהוה עולל יעוללו כגפן שארית ישראל השב
כבוצר על סלסלותיו 10 על מי אדברה ואעידה וישמע הנה ערלה אזנם ולא יוכלו
להקשיב הנה דבר יהוה היה להם לחרפה לא יחפצו בו 11 ואת חמת י מלאתי
ונלאיתי ולא כליתים אשפך על עולל בחוץ ועל סוד בחורים יחדו כי גם איש גם
אשה ילכדו זקן עם מלא ימים 12 ונסבו בתיהם לאחרים שדות ונשיהם יחדו כי
אטה את ידי על ישבי הארץ הזאת נאם יהוה 13 כי מקטנם ועד גדולם כלו בוצע
בצע מכהן ועד נביא כלו עשה שקר 14 וירפאו את שבר עמי על נקלה לאמר שלום
שלום ואיה שלום 15 הבישו כי עזבו גם בוש לא יבבושו והכלם לא ידעו לכן יפלו
בנפלם בעת פקדתם יכשלו אמר יהוה 16 כה אמר יהוה עמדו על דרכים וראו
ושאלו לנתבות עולם יהוה וראו מה הדרך הטובה ולכו בה ומצאו מרגוע לנפשכם
ויאמרו לא נלך 17 הקמתי עליכם צפים הקשיבו לקול שופר ויאמרו לא נקשיב 18
לכן שמעו הגוים והרעים את עדריהם 19 שמעו הארץ הנה אנכי מביא אל העם הזה
רעה פרי משובתם כי על דברי לא הקשיבו ותורתי מאסו 20 למה זה לי לבונה
משבא תביאו וקנמון מארץ מרחק עולותיכם לא לרצון וזבחיכם לא ערבו לי 21
לכן כה אמר יהוה הנני נתן אל העם הזה מכשול וכשלו בו אבות ובנים יחדו שכן
ורעו יאבדו 22 כה אמר יהוה הנה עם בא מצפון וגוים יעורו מירכתי ארץ 23 קשת
וכידון יחזיקו אכזרי הוא ולא ירחם קולו כים יהמה על סוסים ורכב ערוך כאש
למלחמה עליך בת ציון 24 שמענו את שמעם רפו ידינו צרה החזיקתנו חיל כיולדה
25 אל תצאו השדה ובדרכים אל תלכו כי חרב לאיבים גרה מסביב 26 בת עמי
חגרי שק והתפלשי באפר אבל יחיד עשי לך מספד תמרורים כי פתאם יבא השד
עלינו 27 בחון נתתיך בעמי מבצר ותדע ובחנתי את דרכם 28 כלם סוררים הולכי
רכיל נחשת וברזל כלם משחיתים המה 29 נחר מפח מאש תם עפרת לשוא צרף
צרוף רעתם לא נתקה 30 כסף נמאס קראו להם כי מאס יהוה בהם

JEREMIAH 7

שמעו דבר יהוה כל יהודה [3] כה אמר יהוה אלהי ישראל היטיבו דרכיכם ומעלליכם [2]
ואשכנה אתכם במקום הזה [4] אל תבטחו לכם אל דברי השקר כי הועל לא יועילו לכם
לאמר היכל יהוה היכל יהוה [5] כי אם היטיב תיטיבו את דרכיכם ואת מעלליכם ועשו
תעשו משפט בין איש ובין רעהו [6] וגר יתום ואלמנה לא תעשקו ודם נקי לא תשפכו
במקום הזה ואחרי אלהים אחרים לא תלכו לרע לכם [7] ושכנתי אתכם במקום הזה
בארץ אשר נתתי לאבותיכם למן עולם ועד עולם [8] הן אתם בטחים לכם על דברי
השקר לבלתי הועיל [9] הרצח ונאף וגנב והשבע לשקר וקטר לבעל והלך אחרי אלהים
אחרים אשר לא ידעתם [10] ובאתם ועמדתם לפני בבית אשר נקרא שמי עליו
ואמרתם נצלנו למען עשות את כל התועבות האלה [11] המערת פרצים היה ביתי אשר
נקרא שמי עליו שם בעיניכם גם אנכי הנה ראיתי נאם יהוה [12] כי לכו נא אל מקומי
אשר בשילו אשר שכנתי שמי שם בראשונה וראו את אשר עשיתי לו מפני רעת עמי
ישראל [13] ועתה יען עשותכם את כל המעשים האלה ואדבר אליכם ולא שמעתם אלי
ואקרא אתכם ולא עניתם [14] ועשיתי לבית אשר נקרא שמי עליו אשר אתם בטחים בו
ולמקום אשר נתתי לכם ולאבותיכם כאשר עשיתי לשלו [15] והשלכתי אתכם מעל פני
כאשר השלכתי את אחיכם את כל זרע אפרים [16] ואתה אל תתפלל בעד העם הזה
ואל תשא בעדם רנה ותפלה ואל תפגע בי בעדם כי אינני שמע [17] האינך ראה מה המה
עשים בערי יהודה ובחצות ירושלם [18] הבנים מלקטים עצים ואבותם מבערים את האש
והנשים לשות בצק לעשות כונים לצבא השמים והסך נסכים לאלהים אחרים למען
הכעסני [19] האתי הם מכעסים נאם יהוה הלוא אתם למען בשת פניהם [20] לכן כה אמר
אדני יהוה הנה אפי וחמתי נתכת אל המקום הזה ועל האדם ועל הבהמה ועל כל עץ השדה
ועל פרי האדמה ובערה ולא תכבה [21] כה אמר יהוה צבאות עלותיכם ספו על זבחיכם ואכלו
בשר [22] כי לא דברתי את אבותיכם ולא צויתים ביום הוציאי אותם מארץ מצרים על
דברי עולה וזבח [23] כי אם את הדבר הזה צויתי אותם לאמר שמעו בקולי והייתי לכם
לאלהים ואתם תהיו לי לעם והלכתם בכל דרכי אשר אצוה אתכם למען ייטב לכם [24]
ולא שמעו אלי ולא הטו את אזנם וילכו בשררות לבם הרע ויהיו לאחור ולא לפנים
למן היום אשר יצאו אבותיהם מארץ מצרים ועד היום הזה ואשלח אליכם את כל [25]
עבדי הנביאים יום והשכם ושלח [26] ולא שמעו אלי ולא הטו אזנם ויקשו את ערפם
מאבותם [28] ודברת אליהם את הדבר הזה זה הגוי אשר לוא שמעו בקול יהוה ולא
לקחו מוסר אבדה האמונה מפיהם [29] גזי נזרך והשליכי ושאי על שפתים קינה כי מאס
יהוה ויטש את דור עברתו [30] כי עשו בני יהודה הרע בעיני נאם יהוה שמו שקוציהם
בבית אשר נקרא שמי עליו לטמאו [31] ובנו במת התפת אשר בגיא בן הנם לשרף את
בניהם ואת בנותיהם באש אשר לא צויתים ולא עלתה על לבי [32] לכן הנה ימים באים
נאם יהוה ולא יאמרו עוד במת התפת וגיא בן הנם כי אם גיא ההרגה וקברו בתפת
מאין מקום [33] והיתה נבלת העם הזה למאכל לעוף השמים ולבהמת הארץ ואין מחריד
והשבתי מערי יהודה ומחצות ירושלם קול ששון וקול שמחה קול חתן וקול כלה כי [34]
לחרבה תהיה כל הארץ

JEREMIAH 8

בעת ההיא נאם יהוה יציאו את עצמות מלכי יהודה ואת עצמות שריו ואת עצמות [1]
הכהנים ואת עצמות הנביאים ואת עצמות יושבי ירושלם מקבריהם [2] ושטחים לשמש
ולירח ולכל הכוכבים ולכל צבא השמים אשר אהבום ואשר עבדום ואשר הלכו

878

אחריהם ואשר דרשום ואשר השתחוו להם לא יספדו ולא יקברו והיו לדמין על
פני האדמה [3] כי בחרו מות מחיים ולכל השארית הנשארים מן המשפחה הזאת בכל
המקמות אשר הדחתים שם [4] כי כה אמר יהוה היפל ולא יקום אם ישוב ולא ישוב [5]
מדוע שובב עמי משבה נצחת והחזיקו בתרמיתם ומאנו לשוב [6] הקשיבו ושמעו לוא
כן ידברו אין איש נחם על רעתו לאמר מה עשיתי כלה שב ממרצתו כסוס שוטף
במצהלותיו [7] גם חסידה בשמים ידעה מועדה תר וסוס עגור שמרו את עת באנה
ועמי לא ידעו משפטי יהוה [8] איכה תאמרו חכמים אנחנו ותורת יהוה אתנו לשקר
היה עט שקר ספרים [9] הבישו חכמים וחתו וילכדו כי בדבר יהוה מאסו וחכמת מה
להם [10] לכן אתן את נשיהם לאחרים ושדותיהם ליורשים [13] ואסף אסיפם נאם יהוה
אין ענבים בגפן ואין תאנים בתאנה והעלה נבל [14] על מה אנחנו ישבים האספו ונבוא
אל ערי המבצר ונרמה כי האלהים הרמנו וישקנו מי ראש כי חטאנו לו [15] קוה שלום
ואין טוב לעת מרפא והנה בעתה [16] מדן נשמע נחרת סוסיו מקול מצהלות אביריו
רעשה כל הארץ ויבוא ויאכל ארץ ומלואה עיר וישבי בה [17] כי הנני משלח בכם
נחשים צפענים אשר אין להם לחש ונשכו אתכם [18] מבלי גהת עם יגון לבכם דוי [19]
הנה קול בת עמי מארץ מרחקים היהוה אין בציון אם מלך אין שם מדוע הכעסוני
בפסליהם ובהבלי נכר [20] עבר קציר כלה קיץ ואנחנו לוא נושענו [21] על שבר בת
עמי קדרתי שמה החזקתני חיל כיולדה [22] הצרי אין בגלעד אם רפא אין שם מדוע
לא עלתה ארכת בת עמי

JEREMIAH 9

[1] מי יתן ראשי מים ועיני מקור דמעה ואבכה עמי יומם ולילה את חללי בת עמי [2]
מי יתנני במדבר מלון ארחון ואעזבה את עמי ואלכה מאתם כי כלם מנאפים עצרת
בגדים [3] וידרכו את לשונם כקשת שקר ולא אמונה גברה בארץ כי מרעה אל רעה
יצאו ואתי לא ידעו [4] איש מרעהו השמרו ועל כל אח אל תבטחו כי כל אח עקוב
יעקב וכל רע רכיל יהלך [5] איש ברעהו יהתלו אמת לא ידברו למד לשונם דבר
שקר העוו ונלאו שב [6] תך בתוך מרמה במרמה מאנו דעת אותי [7] לכן כה אמר
יהוה הנני צורפם ובחנתים כי איכה אעשה מפני רעת בת עמי [8] חץ שוחט לשונם מרמה
דברי פיהם שלום את רעהו ידבר ובקרבו ישים איבה [9] העל אלה לא אפקד נאם
יהוה אם בגוי אשר כזה לא תתנקם נפשי [10] על ההרים שאו בכי ועל נאות מדבר
קינה כי נצתו מבלי איש לא שמעו קול מקנה מעוף השמים ועד בהמה נדדו הלכו
[11] ונתתי את ירושלם לגלות ולמעון תנים ואת ערי יהודה אתן שממה מבלי יושב [12]
מי האיש החכם ויבן את זאת ואשר דבר פי יהוה אליו ויגדה על מה אבדה הארץ
נצתה כמדבר מבלי עבר [13] ויאמר יהוה אלי על עזבם את תורתי אשר נתתי לפניהם
ולא שמעו בקולי [14] וילכו אחרי שררות לבם הרע ואחרי הבעלים אשר למדום
אבותם [15] לכן כה אמר יהוה אלהי ישראל הנני מאכילם לענה והשקיתים מי ראש [16]
והפצותם בגוים אשר לא ידעום המה ואבותם ושלחתי אחריהם את החרב עד כלותי
אותם בה [17] אמר יהוה קראו למקוננות ותבואינה ואל החכמות שלחו ותדברנה [18]
ותשנה עלינו נהי ותרדנה עינינו דמעה ועפעפינו יזלו מים [19] כי קול נהי נשמע בציון
איך שדדנו בשנו מאד כי עזבנו הארץ כי השליכנו משכנותינו [20] שמענה נשים דבר
אלהים ותקח אזנכם דברי פיו ולמדנה בנותיכם נהי ואשה רעותה קינה [21] כי עלה
מות בחלונינו בא בארמנתנו להכרית עולל מחוץ ובחורים מרחבות [22] והיו נבלת
האדם כדמין על פני האדמה וכעמיר מאחרי הקצר ואין מאסף [23] כה אמר יהוה אל

יתהלל חכם בחכמתו ואל יתהלל הגבור בגבורתו ואל יתהלל עשיר בעשרו 24 כי אם
בזאת יתהלל המתהלל השכל וידע כי אני יהוה עשה חסד ומשפט וצדקה בארץ כי
באלה חפצי נאם יהוה 25 הנה ימים באים נאם יהוה ופקדתי על כל מול בערלה 26
על מצרים ועל יהודה ועל אדום ועל בני עמון ועל מואב ועל כל קצוצי פאה
הישבים במדבר כי כל הגוים ערלים ובשר וכל בית ישראל ערלים בלבם

JEREMIAH 10

1 שמעו דבר יהוה אשר דבר עליכם בית ישראל 2 כה אמר יהוה אל דרכי הגוים
אל תלמדו ומאתות השמים אל תחתו כי יחתו לפניהם 3 כי חקות העמים הבל הוא
עץ מיער כרות מעשה חרש ומסכה 4 בכסף ובזהב ייפהו במקבות ובמסמרות יחזקום
ולוא יפיקו 5א כתם מקשה הוא לא ידברו 9 כסף מרקע מתרשיש יבוא זהב מאופז
ויד צורף מעשי חכמים כלם תכלת וארגמן ילבישום 5ב נשוא ינשאו כי לא יצעדו
אל תיראו מהם כי לא ירעו וגם היטיב אין אתם 11 כדנה תאמרון להום אלהיא די
שמיא וארקא לא עבדו יאבדו מארעא ומן תחות שמיא אלה 12 יהוה עשה ארץ בכחו
מכין תבל בחכמתו ובתבונתו נטה שמים 13 והמון מים בשמים ויעלה נשאים מקצה
הארץ ברקים למטר עשה ויוצא אור מאצרתיו 14 נבער כל אדם מדעת הביש כל
צורף מפסליו כי שקר נסכו לא רוח בם 15 הבל המה מעשי תעתעים בעת פקדתם
יאבדו 16 לא כאלה חלק יעקב כי יוצר הכל הוא נחלתו יהוה שמו 17 אספי מחוץ
כנעתך ישבת במבחר 18 כי כה אמר יהוה הנני קולע את יושבי הארץ הזאת בצרה
למען תמצא מכתך 19 אוי על שברך נחלה מכתך ואני אמרתי אך זה חליי ואשאני 20
אהלי שדד וכל מיתרי נתקו בני וצאני אינם אין עוד מקום אהלי מקום יריעותי 21
כי נבערו הרעים ואת יהוה לא דרשו על כן לא השכילה כל מרעית ונפוצו 22 קול
שמועה הנה באה ורעש גדול מארץ צפון לשום את ערי יהודה שממה ומעון תנים
23 ידעתי יהוה כי לא לאדם דרכו ולא איש הלך והכין את צעדו 24 יסרנו יהוה אך
במשפט ואל באף פן תמעטנו 25 שפך חמתך על גוים אשר לא ידעוך ועל משפחות
אשר בשמך לא קראו כי אכלו את יעקב ויכלהו ואת נוהו השמו

JEREMIAH 11

1 הדבר אשר היה מאת יהוה אל ירמיהו לאמר 2 שמעו את דברי הברית הזאת
ודברת אל איש יהודה ואל ישבי ירושלם 3 ואמרת אליהם כה אמר יהוה אלהי
ישראל ארור האיש אשר לא ישמע את דברי הברית הזאת 4 אשר צויתי את אבותיכם
ביום הוציאי אותם מארץ מצרים מכור הברזל לאמר שמעו בקולי ועשיתם כל אשר
אצוה אתכם והייתם לי לעם ואנכי אהיה לכם לאלהים 5 למען הקים את שבועתי
אשר נשבעתי לאבותיכם לתת להם ארץ זבת חלב ודבש כיום הזה ואען ואמר אמן
יהוה 6 ויאמר יהוה אלי קרא את הדברים האלה בערי יהודה ובחצות ירושלם לאמר
שמעו את דברי הברית הזאת ועשיתם אותם 8 ולא עשו 9 ויאמר יהוה אלי נמצא קשר
באיש יהודה ובישבי ירושלם 10 שבו על עונת אבותם הראשנים אשר מאנו לשמוע את
דברי והנה המה הלכו אחרי אלהים אחרים לעבדם והפרו בית ישראל ובית יהודה
את בריתי אשר כרתי את אבותם 11 לכן כה אמר יהוה הנני מביא על העם הזה רעה
אשר לא יוכלו לצאת ממנה וזעקו אלי ולא אשמע אליהם 12 והלכו ערי יהודה וישבי
ירושלם וזעקו אל האלהים אשר הם מקטרים להם לא יושיעו להם בעת רעתם 13 כי
מספר עריך היו אלהיך יהודה ומספר חצות ירושלם שמתם מזבחות לקטר לבעל

‫ואתה אל תתפלל בעד העם הזה ואל תשא בעדם רנה ותפלה כי אינני שמע בעת‬ 14
‫קראם אלי בעת רעתם‬ 15 ‫מה הידידה בביתי עשתה המזמתה הנדרים ובשר קדש‬
‫יעברו מעליך רעתכי או זאת התחזכי‬ 16 ‫זית רענן יפה תאר קרא יהוה שמך לקול‬
‫מולתו גדלה הצרה עליך ורעו דליותיו‬ 17 ‫ויהוה הנוטע אותך דבר עליך רעה בגלל‬
‫רעת בית ישראל ובית יהודה אשר עשו להם להכעסני לקטר לבעל‬ 18 ‫יהוה הודיעני‬
‫ואדעה אז ראיתי מעלליהם‬ 19 ‫ואני ככבש אלוף יובל לטבוח לא ידעתי עלי חשבו‬
‫מחשבות נשליכה עץ בלחמו ונכרתנו מארץ חיים ושמו לא יזכר עוד‬ 20 ‫יהוה שפט‬
‫צדק בחן כליות ולב אראה נקמתך מהם כי אליך גליתי את ריבי‬ 21 ‫לכן כה אמר‬
‫יהוה על אנשי ענתות המבקשים את נפשי לאמר לא תנבא בשם יהוה ואם לא תמות‬
‫בידנו‬ 22 ‫הנני פקד עליהם הבחורים ימתו בחרב ובניהם ובנותיהם ימתו ברעב‬ 23
‫ושארית לא תהיה להם כי אביא רעה אל אנשי ענתות שנת פקדתם‬

JEREMIAH 12

1 ‫צדיק אתה יהוה כי אריב אליך אך משפטים אדבר אתך מדוע דרך רשעים צלחה‬
‫שלו כל בגדי בגד‬ 2 ‫נטעתם גם שרשו ילדו גם עשו פרי קרוב אתה בפיהם ורחוק‬
‫מכליותיהם‬ 3 ‫ואתה יהוה ידעתני בחנת לבי אתך הקדשם ליום הרגם‬ 4 ‫עד מתי תאבל‬
‫הארץ ועשב כל השדה ייבש מרעת ישבי בה ספתה בהמה ועוף כי אמרו לא יראה‬
‫את ארחותינו‬ 5 ‫את רגליך רצתה וילאוך איך תתחרה את הסוסים ובארץ שלום אתה‬
‫בוטח איך תעשה בגאון הירדן‬ 6 ‫כי גם אחיך ובית אביך גם המה בגדו בך גם המה‬
‫קראו אחריך מלאו אל תאמן בם כי ידברו אליך טובות‬ 7 ‫עזבתי את ביתי נטשתי את‬
‫נחלתי נתתי את ידדות נפשי בכף איביה‬ 8 ‫היתה לי נחלתי כאריה ביער נתנה עלי‬
‫בקולה על כן שנאתיה‬ 9 ‫העיט צבוע נחלתי לי העיט סביב עליה לכו אספו כל חית‬
‫השדה והתיו לאכלה‬ 10 ‫רעים רבים שחתו כרמי בססו את חלקתי נתנו את חלקת‬
‫חמדתי למדבר שממה‬ 11 ‫שמה לשממה אבדה עלי שממה נשמה כל הארץ כי אין‬
‫איש שם על לב‬ 12 ‫על כל שפים במדבר באו שדדים כי חרב ליהוה אכלה מקצה‬
‫ארץ ועד קצה ארץ אין שלום לכל בשר‬ 13 ‫זרעו חטים וקצים קצרו נחלתיהם לא‬
‫יועלום בשו מתפארתכם מחרפה לאפי יהוה‬ 14 ‫כי כה אמר יהוה על כל השכנים‬
‫הרעים הנגעים בנחלתי אשר הנחלתי את עמי את ישראל הנני נתשם מעל אדמתם‬
‫ואת יהודה אתוש מתוכם‬ 15 ‫והיה אחרי נתשי אותם אשוב ורחמתים והשבתים איש‬
‫לנחלתו ואיש לארצו‬ 16 ‫והיה אם למד ילמדו את דרך עמי להשבע בשמי חי יהוה‬
‫כאשר למדו את עמי להשבע בבעל ונבנו בתוך עמי‬ 17 ‫ואם לא ישובו ונתשתי את‬
‫הגוי ההוא נתוש ואבד‬

JEREMIAH 13

1 ‫כה אמר יהוה הלוך וקנית לך אזור פשתים ושמתו על מתניך ובמים לא תבאהו‬ 2
‫ואקנה את האזור כדבר יהוה ואשם על מתני‬ 3 ‫ויהי דבר יהוה אלי לאמר‬ 4 ‫קח את‬
‫האזור אשר על מתניך וקום לך פרתה וטמנהו שם בנקיק הסלע‬ 5 ‫ואטמנהו בפרת‬
‫כאשר צוה יהוה אותי‬ 6 ‫ויהי מקץ ימים רבים ויאמר יהוה אלי קום לך פרתה וקח‬
‫משם את האזור אשר צויתיך לטמנו שם‬ 7 ‫ואלך פרתה ואחפר ואקח את האזור מן‬
‫המקום אשר טמנתיו שמה והנה נשחת האזור לא יצלח לכל‬ 8 ‫ויהי דבר יהוה אלי‬
‫לאמר כה אמר יהוה‬ 9 ‫ככה אשחית את גאון יהודה ואת גאון ירושלם‬ 10 ‫הרב הזה‬
‫המאנים לשמוע את דברי וילכו אחרי אלהים אחרים לעבדם ולהשתחות להם והיו‬

כאזור הזה אשר לא יצלח לכל 11 כי כאשר ידבק האזור מתני איש כן הדבקתי אלי
את בית ישראל ואת כל בית יהודה להיות לי לעם ולשם ולתהלה ולתפארת ולא
שמעו אלי 12 ואמרת אל העם הזה כל נבל ימלא יין והיה אם יאמרו אליך הידע
לא נדע כי כל נבל ימלא יין 13 ואמרת אליהם כה אמר יהוה הנני ממלא את ישבי
הארץ הזאת ואת מלכיהם הישבים בנים לדוד על כסאם ואת הכהנים ואת הנביאים
ואת יהודה ואת כל ישבי ירושלם שכרון 14 ונפצתים איש ואחיו ואבותם ובניהם יחדו
לא אחמול נאם יהוה ולא אחוס ולא ארחם מהשחיתם 15 שמעו והאזינו ואל תגבהו
כי יהוה דבר 16 תנו ליהוה אלהיכם כבוד בטרם יחשך ובטרם יתנגפו רגליכם על
הרי נשף וקויתם לאור ושם צלמות ושית לערפל 17 אם לא תשמעו במסתרים תבכה
נפשכם מפני גוה ודמע תדמע עיניכם ותרד עיני דמעה כי נשבה עדר יהוה 18 אמרו למלך ולגבורים
השפילו ושבו כי ירד מראשכם עטרת תפארתכם 19 ערי הנגב סגרו ואין פתח הגלת
יהודה כלה גלות שלמה 20 שאי עיניך ירושלם וראי הבאים מצפון איה העדר נתן
לך צאן תפארתך 21 מה תאמרי כי יפקד עליך ואת למדת אתם עליך אלפים לראש
הלוא חבלים יאחזוך כמו אשת לדה 22 וכי תאמרי בלבבך מדוע קראני אלה ברב
עונך נגלו שוליך נחמסו עקביך 23 היהפך כושי עורו ונמר חברברתיו גם אתם תוכלו
להיטיב למדי הרע 24 ואפיצם כקש עובר לרוח מדבר 25 זה גורלך ומנת מדיך מאתי
נאם יהוה אשר שכחת אותי ותבטחי בשקר 26 וגם אני חשפתי שוליך על פניך ונראה
קלונך 27 ונאפיך ומצהלותיך וזמת זנותך על גבעות ובשדה ראיתי שקוציך אוי לך
ירושלם כי לא תטהרי אחרי עד מתי עד

JEREMIAH 14

1 ויהי דבר יהוה אל ירמיהו על הבצרה 2 אבלה יהודה ושעריה אמללו וקדרו לארץ
וצוחת ירושלם עלתה 3 ואדיריה שלחו צעיריהם למים באו על גבים ולא מצאו מים
ושבו כליהם ריקם 4 ועבור האדמה חתה כי לא היה גשם בשו אכרים חפו ראשם 5
גם אילת בשדה ילדה ועזוב כי לא היה דשא 6 ופראים עמדו על שפים שאפו רוח
כלו עיניהם כי אין עשב 7 אם עונינו ענו בנו יהוה עשה למען שמך כי רבו משובתינו
לך חטאנו 8 מקוה ישראל יהוה ומושיע בעת צרה למה תהיה כגר בארץ וכאזרח
נטה ללון 9 לא תהיה כאיש נרדם כגבר לא יוכל להושיע ואתה בקרבנו יהוה ושמך
עלינו נקרא אל תנחנו 10 כה אמר יהוה לעם הזה אהבו לנוע רגליהם ולא חשכו
ויהוה לא רצם עתה יזכר עונם 11 ויאמר יהוה אלי אל תתפלל בעד העם הזה לטובה
12 כי יצמו אינני שמע אל רנתם וכי יעלו עלה ומנחה אינני רצם כי בחרב וברעב
ובדבר אנכי מכלה אותם 13 ואמר אהה יהוה הנה נבאיהם נבאים ואמרים לא תראו
חרב ורעב לא יהיה לכם כי אמת ושלום אתן על הארץ ובמקום הזה 14 ויאמר יהוה
אלי שקר הנבאים נבאים בשמי לא שלחתים ולא צויתים ולא דברתי אליהם כי
חזון שקר וקסם ואליל ותרמית לבם המה מתנבאים לכם 15 לכן כה אמר יהוה על
הנבאים הנבאים בשמי שקר ואני לא שלחתים האמרים חרב ורעב לא יהיה בארץ
הזאת ממותי תחלאים ימתו וברעב יתמו הנבאים 16 והעם אשר המה נבאים להם
יהיו משלכים בחצות ירושלם מפני החרב והרעב ואין מקבר להמה ונשיהם ובניהם
ובנתיהם ושפכתי עליהם את רעתם 17 ואמרת אליהם את הדבר הזה תרדנה עיניכם
דמעה יומם ולילה ואל תדמינה כי שבר נשברה בת עמי ומכה נחלה מאד 18 אם
יצאתי השדה והנה חללי חרב ואם באתי העיר והנה תחלואי רעב כי כהן ונביא
סחרו אל ארץ לא ידעו 19 המאס מאסת את יהודה ומציון גהלה נפשך מדוע הכיתנו

ואין לנו מרפא קוה לשלום ואין טוב לעת מרפא והנה בעתה [20] ידענו יהוה רשענו
עון אבותינו כי חטאנו לך [21] חדל נא למען שמך אל תנבל כסא כבודך זכר אל
תפר בריתך אתנו [22] היש בהבלי הגוים מגשמים ואם השמים יתנו רבבים הלא אתה
הוא ונקוה לך כי אתה עשית את כל אלה

JEREMIAH 15

[1] ויאמר יהוה אלי אם יעמד משה ושמואל לפני אין נפשי אל העם הזה שלח אליהם
ויצאו [2] והיה כי יאמרו אליך אנה נצא ואמרת אליהם כה אמר יהוה אשר למות
למות ואשר לחרב לחרב ואשר לרעב לרעב ואשר לשבי לשבי [3] ופקדתי עליהם
ארבע משפחות נאם יהוה את החרב להרג ואת הכלבים לסחב ואת בהמת הארץ
ואת עוף השמים לאכל ולהשחית [4] ונתתים לזועה לכל ממלכות הארץ בגלל מנשה
בן יחזקיהו מלך יהודה על כל אשר עשה בירושלם [5] מי יחמל עליך ירושלם ומי
ינוד לך ומי יסור לשלם לך [6] את נטשת אתי נאם יהוה אחור תלכי ואט את ידי
ואשחיתך ולא אנחם [7] ואזרם במזרה בשערי עמי שכלתי אבדתי את עמי מרעתם [8]
עצמו אלמנתם מחול הים הבאתי להם על אם בחור שד בצהרים הפלתי עליה פתאם
עיר ובהלות [9] אמללה ילדת השבעה נפחה נפשה בא שמשה בעד יומם בושה וחפרה
ושאריתם לחרב אתן לפני איביהם [10] אוי לי אמי כי ילדתני איש ריב ומדון לכל
הארץ לא נשיתי ולא נשו בי כחי כלה מקלליני [11] אמן יהוה באשרם אם לוא הפגעתי
בך בעת רעתם ובעת צרתם לטוב את האיב [12] היודע ברזל ומצפון נחשת חילך [13]
ואוצרותיך לבז אתן במחיר בכל חטאותיך ובכל גבוליך [14] והעבדתיך מסביב את
איביך בארץ אשר לא ידעת כי אש קדחה באפי עליכם תוקד [15] יהוה זכרני ופקדני
והנקם לי מרדפי אל לארך אפים דע שאתי עליך חרפה [16] מנאצי דבריך כלם ויהי
דברך לי לששון ולשמחת לבבי כי נקרא שמך עלי יהוה צבאות [17] לא ישבתי בסוד
משחקים ואעלז מפני ידך בדד ישבתי כי זעם מלאתי [18] למה המכאבי ינצחוני מכתי
אנושה מאין ארפא היו תהיה לי כמו אכזב מים לא נאמנו [19] לכן כה אמר יהוה אם
תשוב ואשיבך ולפני תעמד ואם תוצא יקר מזולל כפי תהיה ושבו המה אליך ואתה
לא תשוב אליהם [20] ונתתיך לעם הזה לחומת נחשת בצורה ונלחמו אליך ולא יוכלו
לך כי אתך אני להושיעך [21] והצלתיך מיד רעים ומכף עריצים

JEREMIAH 16

[1] ואתה לא תקח לך אשה אמר יהוה אלהי ישראל [2] ולא יהיה לך בן ובת במקום הזה
[3] כי כה אמר יהוה על הבנים ועל הבנות הילודים במקום הזה ועל אמתם הילדות
אותם ועל אבותם המולדים אותם בארץ הזאת [4] ממותי תחלאים ימתו לא יספדו ולא
יקברו לדמן על פני האדמה יהיו ולבהמת הארץ ולעוף השמים יפלו וברעב
יכלו [5] כה אמר יהוה אל תבוא בית מרזח ואל תלך לספוד ואל תנד להם כי אספתי
את שלומי מאת העם הזה [6] לא יספדו להם ולא יתגדדו ולא יקרחו [7] ולא יפרס להם
על אבל לנחם על מת ולא ישקו אותו כוס תנחומים על אביו ועל אמו [8] ובית משתה
לא תבוא לשבת אתם לאכל ולשתות [9] כי כה אמר יהוה אלהי ישראל הנני משבית
מן המקום הזה לעיניכם ובימיכם קול ששון וקול שמחה קול חתן וקול כלה [10] והיה
כי תגיד לעם הזה את כל הדברים האלה ואמרו אליך על מה דבר יהוה עלינו את כל
הרעה הגדולה הזאת ומה עוננו ומה חטאתנו אשר חטאנו ליהוה אלהינו [11] ואמרת אליהם על
אשר עזבו אבותיכם אותי נאם יהוה וילכו אחרי אלהים אחרים ויעבדום וישתחוו

לחם ואתי עזבו ואת תורתי לא שמרו ¹² ואתם הרעתם מאבותיכם והנכם הלכים איש
אחרי שררות לבו הרע לבלתי שמע אלי ¹³ והטלתי אתכם מעל הארץ הזאת על
הארץ אשר לא ידעתם אתם ואבותיכם ועבדתם שם את אלהים אחרים אשר לא יתנו
לכם חנינה ¹⁴ לכן הנה ימים באים נאם יהוה ולא יאמרו עוד חי יהוה אשר העלה
את בני ישראל מארץ מצרים ¹⁵ כי אם חי יהוה אשר העלה את בית ישראל מארץ
צפון ומכל הארצות אשר הדיחם שמה והשבתים על אדמתם אשר נתתי לאבותם
¹⁶ הנני שלח לדוגים רבים נאם יהוה ודיגום ואחרי כן אשלח לרבים צידים
וצדום מעל כל הר ומעל כל גבעה ומנקיקי הסלעים ¹⁷ כי עיני על כל דרכיהם
ולא נצפן עונם מנגד עיני ¹⁸ ושלמתי משנה עונם וחטאתם על חללם את ארצי
בנבלת שקוציהם ותועבותיהם מלאו את נחלתי ¹⁹ יהוה עזי ומעזי ומנוסי ביום צרה
אליך גוים יבאו מאפסי ארץ ויאמרו איך שקר נחלו אבותנו הבל ואין בם מועיל
²⁰ היעשה לו אדם אלהים והמה לא אלהים ²¹ לכן הנני מודיעם בפעם הזאת
את ידי ואודיעם את גבורתי וידעו כי שמי יהוה

JEREMIAH 17

⁵ ארור הגבר אשר יבטח באדם ושם בשר זרעו עליו ומן יהוה יסור לבו ⁶ והיה
כערער בערבה לא יראה כי יבוא טוב ושכן חררים במדבר ארץ מלחא ולא
תשב ⁷ וברוך הגבר אשר יבטח ביהוה והיה יהוה מבטחו ⁸ והיה כעץ שתול על
מים ועל יובל ישלח שרשיו ולא ירא כי יבא חם והיה עלהו רענן בשנת בצרת
לא ידאג ולא ימיש מעשות פרי ⁹ עמק הלב מכל ואנש הוא ומי ידענו ¹⁰ אני יהוה
חקר לב ובחן כליות לתת לאיש כדרכיו וכפרי מעלליו ¹¹ קרא דגר ולא ילד
עשה עשרו לא במשפט בחצי ימיו יעזבנו ובאחריתו יהיה נבל ¹² כסא כבוד
מורם מקדשנו ¹³ מקוה ישראל יהוה כל עזביך יבשו סרים בארץ יכתבו כי עזבו
מקור מים חיים את יהוה ¹⁴ רפאני יהוה וארפא הושיעני ואושעה כי תהלתי אתה
¹⁵ הנה המה אמרים אלי איה דבר יהוה יבוא נא ¹⁶ ואני לא אצתי מרעה אחריך
ויום אנוש לא התאויתי אתה ידעת מוצא שפתי נכח פניך היה ¹⁷ אל תהיה לי
למחתה מחסי ביום רעה ¹⁸ יבשו רדפי ואל אבשה אני יחתו המה ואל אחתה
אני הביא עליהם יום רעה ומשנה שברון שברם ¹⁹ כה אמר יהוה הלך ועמדת
בשערי בני עמך אשר יבאו בם מלכי יהודה ואשר יצאו בם ובכל שערי ירושלם
²⁰ ואמרת אליהם שמעו דבר יהוה מלכי יהודה וכל יהודה וכל ירושלם הבאים
בשערים האלה ²¹ כה אמר יהוה השמרו בנפשותיכם ואל תשאו משא ביום השבת
והבאתם בשערי ירושלם ²² ולא תוציאו משא מבתיכם ביום השבת וכל מלאכה
לא תעשו וקדשתם את יום השבת כאשר צויתי את אבותיכם ולא שמעו ולא הטו
את אזנם ²³ ויקשו את ערפם מאבותם לבלתי שמוע אלי ולבלתי קחת מוסר ²⁴
והיה אם שמע תשמעון אלי נאם יהוה לבלתי הביא משא בשערי העיר הזאת ביום
השבת ולקדש את יום השבת לבלתי עשות כל מלאכה ²⁵ ובאו בשערי העיר הזאת
מלכים ושרים ישבים על כסא דוד ורכבים ברכב ובסוסים המה ושריהם איש
יהודה וישבי ירושלם וישבה העיר הזאת לעולם ²⁶ ובאו מערי יהודה ומסביבות
ירושלם ומארץ בנימן ומן השפלה ומן ההר ומן הנגב מבאים עולה וזבח ומנחה
ולבונה מבאי תודה בית יהוה ²⁷ והיה אם לא תשמעו אלי לקדש את יום השבת
לבלתי שאת משא ובא בשערי ירושלם ביום השבת והצתי אש בשעריה ואכלה
ארמנות ירושלם ולא תכבה

JEREMIAH 18

הדבר אשר היה מאת יהוה אל ירמיהו לאמר ² קום וירדת בית היוצר ושמה תשמע ¹
את דברי ³ וארד בית היוצר והנהו עשה מלאכה על האבנים ⁴ ונשחת הכלי אשר הוא
עשה בידיו ושב ויעשהו כלי אחר כאשר ישר בעיניו לעשות ⁵ ויהי דבר יהוה אלי
לאמר ⁶ הכיוצר הזה לא אוכל לעשות לכם בית ישראל הנה כחמר ביד היוצר אתם בידי
רגע אדבר על גוי ועל ממלכה לנתוש אתם ולהאביד ⁸ ושב הגוי ההוא מרעתם ⁷
ונחמתי על הרעה אשר חשבתי לעשות להם ⁹ ורגע אדבר על גוי ועל ממלכה לבנת
ולנטע ¹⁰ ועשו הרעה בעיני לבלתי שמע בקולי ונחמתי על הטובה אשר אמרתי
להיטיב אותם ¹¹ ועתה אמר נא אל איש יהודה ועל יושבי ירושלם הנה אנכי יוצר
עליכם רעה וחשב עליכם מחשבה שובו נא איש מדרכו הרעה והיטיבו מעלליכם
ויאמרו נואש כי אחרי מחשבותינו נלך ואיש שררות לבו הרע נעשה ¹³ לכן כה ¹²
אמר יהוה שאלו נא בגוים מי שמע כאלה שערת עשתה מאד בתולת ישראל ¹⁴
היעזבו מצור שדים שלג לבנון אם ינתשו מים זדים קדים נוזלים ¹⁵ כי שכחני עמי
לשוא יקטרו ויכשלו בדרכיהם שבילי עולם ללכת נתיבות דרך לא סלולה ¹⁶ לשום
ארצם לשמה ושרוקת עולם כל עוברי עליה ישמו וינידו בראשם ¹⁷ כרוח קדים
אפיצם לפני אויביהם אראם ביום אידם ¹⁸ ויאמרו לכו ונחשבה על ירמיהו מחשבה
כי לא תאבד תורה מכהן ועצה מחכם ודבר מנביא לכו ונכהו בלשון ונקשיבה אל
כל דבריו ¹⁹ הקשיבה אלי יהוה ושמע לקול ריבי ²⁰ הישלם תחת טובה רעה כי
דברו שיחה לנפשי ומכשולם טמנו לי זכר עמדי לפניך לדבר עליהם טובה להשיב
את חמתך מהם ²¹ לכן תן את בניהם לרעב והגרם על ידי חרב תהינה נשיהם שכלות
ואלמנות ואנשיהם יהיו הרגי מות ובחוריהם מכי חרב במלחמה ²² תשמע זעקה
בבתיהם תביא עליהם גדוד פתאם כי כרו שיחה ללכדני ופחים טמנו לי ²³ ואתה
יהוה ידעת את כל עצתם עלי למות אל תכפר על עונם וחטאתם מלפניך אל תמח
יהי מכשולם לפניך בעת אפך עשה בהם

JEREMIAH 19

אז אמר יהוה אלי הלוך וקנית בקבק יצור חרש ולקחת מזקני העם ומהכהנים ¹
ויצאת אל גיא בן בניהם אשר פתח שער החרסית וקראת שם את כל הדברים ²
אשר אדבר אליך ³ ואמרת שמעו דבר יהוה מלכי יהודה ואיש יהודה וישבי ירושלם
והבאים בשערים האלה כה אמר יהוה אלהי ישראל הנני מביא על המקום הזה רעה
אשר כל שמעה תצלנה אזניו ⁴ יען אשר עזבני וינכרו את המקום הזה ויקטרו בו
לאלהים אחרים אשר לא ידעום המה ואבותיהם ומלכי יהודה מלאו את המקום הזה
דם נקים ⁵ ובנו את במות הבעל לשרף את בניהם באש אשר לא צויתי ולא עלתה
על לבי ⁶ לכן הנה ימים באים נאם יהוה ולא יקרא למקום הזה עוד התפת וגיא
בן הנם כי אם גיא ההרנה ⁷ ובקתי את עצת יהודה ואת עצת ירושלם במקום הזה
והפלתים בחרב לפני איביהם וביד מבקשי נפשם ונתתי את נבלתם למאכל לעוף
השמים ולבהמת הארץ ⁸ ושמתי את העיר הזאת לשמה ולשרקה כל עבר עליה ישם
וישרק על כל מכתה ⁹ ואכלו את בשר בניהם ואת בשר בנתיהם ואיש בשר רעהו
יאכלו במצור ובמצוק אשר יציקו להם איביהם ¹⁰ ושברת הבקבק לעיני האנשים
ההלכים אתך ¹¹ ואמרת כה אמר יהוה ככה אשבר את העם הזה ואת העיר הזאת
כאשר ישבר כלי חרש אשר לא יוכל להרפא עוד ¹² כן אעשה נאם יהוה למקום הזה
וליושביו לתת את העיר הזאת כתפת ¹³ והיו בתי ירושלם ובתי מלכי יהודה כמקום

תפת הטמאים לכל הבתים אשר קטרו על גגתיהם לכל צבא השמים והסך נסכים
לאלהים אחרים [14] ויבא ירמיהו מהתפת אשר שלחו יהוה שם להנבא ויעמד בחצר
בית יהוה ויאמר אל כל העם [15] כה אמר יהוה הנני מביא אל העיר הזאת ועל עריה
את כל הרעה אשר דברתי עליה כי הקשו את ערפם לבלתי שמוע את דברי

JEREMIAH 20

[1] וישמע פשחור בן אמר הכהן והוא פקיד נגיד בבית יהוה את ירמיהו נבא את
הדברים האלה [2] ויכהו ויתן אתו על המהפכת אשר בשער בית העליון אשר
בבית יהוה [3] ויצא פשחור את ירמיהו מן המהפכת ויאמר אליו ירמיהו לא פשחור
קרא יהוה שמך כי אם גר [4] כי כה אמר יהוה הנני נתנך למגור לכל אהביך ונפלו
בחרב איביהם ועיניך ראות ואתך ואת כל יהודה אתן ביד מלך בבל והגלם והכם
בחרב [5] ונתתי את כל חסן העיר הזאת ואת כל יגיעה ואת כל אוצרות מלך יהודה
ביד איביו והביאום בבלה [6] ואתה וכל ישבי ביתך תלכו בשבי ובבל תמות ושם
תקבר אתה וכל אהביך אשר נבאת להם בשקר [7] פתיתני יהוה ואפת חזקתני ותוכל
הייתי לשחוק כל היום כלה לעג לי [8] כי מר דברי אצחק חמס ושד אקרא כי היה
דבר יהוה לחרפה לי ולקלס כל יומי [9] ואמרתי לא אזכר שם יהוה ולא אדבר עוד
בשמו והיה כאש בערת להטת בעצמתי ונלאיתי כלה ולא אוכל [10] כי שמעתי דבת
רבים גורים מסביב התגדדו ונתגדדו כל אנוש שלומיו שמרו יצרו ונוכלה לו ונקחה
נקמתנו ממנו [11] ויהוה אתי כגבור עריץ על כן רדפו והשכל לא יכלו בשו מאד
כי לא השכילו כלמתם עולם לא תשכח [12] יהוה בחן צדיק ראה כליות ולב אראה
נקמתך בהם כי אליך גליתי את ריבי [13] שירו ליהוה הללוהו כי הציל את נפש אביון
מיד מרעים [14] ארור היום אשר ילדתי בו היום אשר ילדתני אמי אל יהי ברוך [15]
ארור האיש אשר בשר את אבי לאמר ילד לך זכר שמח [16] יהי האיש ההוא כערים
אשר הפך יהוה באף ולא נחם ישמע זעקה בבקר ותרועה בעת צהרים [17] אשר לא
מותתני ברחם ותהי לי אמי קברי ורחמה הרת עולם [18] למה זה יצאתי מרחם לראות
עמל ויגון ויכלו בבשת ימי

JEREMIAH 21

[1] הדבר אשר היה מאת יהוה אל ירמיהו בשלח אליו המלך צדקיהו את פשחור בן
מלכיה ואת צפניה בן מעשיה הכהן לאמר [2] דרש נא בעדנו את יהוה כי מלך בבל
נלחם עלינו אולי יעשה יהוה כ ככל נפלאתיו ויעלה מעלינו [3] ויאמר אליהם ירמיהו
כה תאמרן אל צדקיהו מלך יהודה [4] כה אמר יהוה הנני מסב את כלי המלחמה
אשר אתם נלחמים בם א את הכשדים הצרים עליכם מחוץ לחומה אל תוך העיר הזאת
[5] ונלחמתי אני אתכם ביד נטויה ובזרוע חזקה בחמה ובקצף גדול [6] והכיתי את כל
יושבי בעיר הזאת את האדם ואת הבהמה בדבר גדול ומתו [7] ואחרי כן נאם יהוה אתן
את צדקיהו מלך יהודה ואת עבדיו ואת העם הנשארים בעיר הזאת מן הדבר ומן
הרעב ומן החרב ביד איביהם ביד מבקשי נפשם והכם לפי חרב לא אחוס עליהם ולא
ארחמם [8] ואל העם הזה תאמר כה אמר יהוה הנני נתן לפניכם את דרך החיים ואת
דרך המות [9] הישב בעיר הזאת ימות בחרב וברעב ובדבר והיוצא ונפל על הכשדים הצרים
עליכם יחיה והיתה נפשו לשלל וחי [10] כי שמתי פני בעיר הזאת לרעה ולא לטובה
ביד מלך בבל תנתן ושרפה באש [11] בית מלך יהודה שמעו דבר יהוה [12] בית דוד

כה אמר יהוה דינו לבקר משפט והצילו גזול מיד עשקו פן תצא כאש חמתי ובערה
ואין מכבה ‏13 הנני אליך ישבת עמק צור המישר האמרים מי יחת עלינו ומי יבוא
במעונותינו ‏14 והצתי אש ביערה ואכלה כל סביביה

JEREMIAH 22

‏1 כה אמר יהוה הלוך ורד בית מלך יהודה ודברת שם את הדבר הזה ‏2 ואמרת
שמע דבר יהוה מלך יהודה הישב על כסא דוד אתה ועבדיך ועמך והבאים בשערים
האלה ‏3 כה אמר יהוה עשו משפט וצדקה והצילו גזול מיד עשקו וגר ויתום ואלמנה
אל תנו ואל תחמסו ודם נקי אל תשפכו במקום הזה ‏4 כי אם עשו תעשו את הדבר
הזה ובאו בשערי הבית הזה מלכים ישבים על כסא דוד ורכבים ברכב ובסוסים
המה ועבדיהם ועמם ‏5 ואם לא תעשו את הדברים האלה בי נשבעתי נאם יהוה כי
לחרבה יהיה הבית הזה ‏6 כי כה אמר יהוה על בית מלך יהודה גלעד אתה לי ראש
הלבנון אם לא אשיתך מדבר ערים לא נושבו ‏7 וקדשתי עליך משחתים איש וכליו
וכרתו מבחר ארזיך והפילו על האש ‏8 ועברו גוים על העיר הזאת ואמרו איש אל
רעהו על מה עשה יהוה ככה לעיר הגדולה הזאת ‏9 ואמרו על אשר עזבו את ברית
יהוה אלהיהם וישתחוו לאלהים אחרים ויעבדום ‏10 אל תבכו למת ואל תנדו לו בכו
בכו להלך כי לא ישוב עוד וראה את ארץ מולדתו ‏11 כי כה אמר יהוה אל שלם בן
יאשיהו המלך תחת יאשיהו אביו אשר יצא מן המקום הזה לא ישוב שם עוד ‏12 כי
אם במקום אשר הגליתי אתו שם ימות ואת הארץ הזאת לא יראה עוד ‏13 הוי בנה
ביתו בלא צדק ועליותיו בלא משפט ברעהו יעבד חנם ופעלו לא יתן לו ‏14 בנית
לך בית מדות עליות מרוחים קרוע חלון וספון בארז ומשוח בששר ‏15 התמלך כי
אתה מתחרה בארז אביך הלוא אכלו ושתו לך טוב משפט וצדקה ‏16 לא ידעו
לא דנו דין עני ואביון הלוא היא הדעת אתי נאם יהוה ‏17 הנה אין עיניך ולבך כי
אם על בצעך ועל דם הנקי לשפוך ועל העשק ועל המרוצה לעשות ‏18 לכן כה אמר
יהוה אל יהויקים בן יאשיהו מלך יהודה הוי על האיש הזה לא יספדו לו הוי אח
לא יספדו לו הוי אדון ‏19 קבורת חמור יקבר סחוב והשלך מהלאה לשער ירושלם
‏20 עלי הלבנון וצעקי ובבשן תני קולך וצעקי מעבר ים כי נשברו כל מאהביך ‏21
דברתי אליך בשלותך ואמרת לא אשמע זה דרכך מנעוריך לא שמעת בקולי ‏22
כל רעיך תרעה רוח ומאהביך בשבי ילכו כי אז תבשי ונכלמת מכל רעיך ‏23 ישבת
בלבנון מקננת בארזים ננחת בבא לך חבלים חיל כילדה ‏24 חי אני נאם יהוה כי אם
היה יהיה יכניהו בן יהויקים מלך יהודה חותם על יד ימיני משם אתקנך ‏25 ונתתיך
ביד מבקשי נפשך אשר אתה יגור מפניהם ביד הכשדים ‏26 והטלתי אתך ואת אמך
אשר ילדתך על ארץ אשר לא ילדת שם ושם תמותו ‏27 על הארץ אשר הם מנשאים
את נפשם לא ישובו ‏28 נבזה יכניהו ככלי אין חפץ בו מדוע הוטל והשלך על ארץ
אשר לא ידע ‏29 ארץ ארץ ארץ שמעי דבר יהוה ‏30 כתבו את האיש הזה ערירי כי לא
יצלח מזרעו איש ישב על כסא דוד משל עוד ביהודה

JEREMIAH 23

‏1 הוי רעים מאבדים ומפצים את צאן מרעיתם ‏2 לכן כה אמר יהוה על הרעים את
עמי אתם הפצתם את צאני ותדחום ולא פקדתם אתם הנני פקד עליכם את רע
מעלליכם ‏3 ואני אקבץ את שארית עמי מכל הארץ אשר הדחתי אתם שם והשבתי
אתם נוהם ופרו ורבו ‏4 והקמתי עליהם רעים ורעום ולא ייראו עוד ולא יחתו נאם

יהוה ⁵ הנה ימים באים נאם יהוה והקמתי לדוד צמח צדיק ומלך מלך והשכיל
ועשה משפט וצדקה בארץ ⁶ בימיו תושע יהודה וישראל ישכן לבטח וזה השם אשר
יקראו יהוה יהוצדק בנבאים ⁹ נשבר לבי בקרבי רחפו כל עצמותי הייתי כאיש
שבור וכגבר עברו יין מפני יהוה ומפני הדר כבודו ¹⁰ כי מפני אלה אבלה הארץ
יבשו נאות מדבר ותהי מרוצתם רעה וגבורתם לא כן ¹¹ כי גם כהן גם נביא חנפו גם
בביתי מצאתי רעתם ¹² לכן יהיה דרכם להם כחלקלקות באפלה ידחו ונפלו בה כי
אביא עליהם רעה שנת פקדתם ¹³ ובנביאי שמרון ראיתי תפלה הנבאו בבעל ויתעו
את עמי את ישראל ¹⁴ ובנבאי ירושלם ראיתי שערורה נאוף והלך בשקר וחזקו ידי
מרעים לבלתי שוב איש מרעתו הרעה היו לי כלם כסדם וישביה כעמרה ¹⁵ לכן כה
אמר יהוה הנני מאכיל אותם לענה והשקתים מי ראש כי מאת נביאי ירושלם יצאה
חנפה לכל הארץ ¹⁶ כה אמר יהוה צבאות אל תשמעו על דברי הנבאים כי מהבלים
המה חזון מלבם ידברו ולא מפי יהוה ¹⁷ אמרים למנאצי דבר יהוה שלום יהיה לכם
ולכל הלכים אחרי מחשבותיהם לכל הלך בשררות לבו אמרו לא תבוא עליכם
רעה ¹⁸ כי מי עמד בסוד יהוה וירא את דברו מי הקשיב וישמע ¹⁹ הנה סערת יהוה
וחמה יצאה סער מתחולל על ראש רשעים יחול ²⁰ ולא ישוב אף יהוה עד עשתו
ועד הקימו מזמת לבו באחרית הימים יתבוננו בה ²¹ לא שלחתי את הנבאים והם רצו
לא דברתי אליהם והם נבאו ²² ואם עמדו בסודי וישמעו דברי ואת עמי השבום מרע
מעלליהם ²³ אלהי מקרב אני נאם יהוה ולא אלהי מרחק ²⁴ אם יסתר איש במסתרים
ואני לא אראנו הלוא את השמים ואת הארץ אני מלא נאם יהוה ²⁵ שמעתי את אשר
אמרו הנבאים הנבאים בשמי שקר לאמר חלמתי חלום ²⁶ עד מתי יש בלב הנבאים
נבאי השקר ובהנבאם תרמת לבם ²⁷ החשבים להשכיח שמי בחלומתם אשר יספרו איש
לרעהו כאשר שכחו אבותם את שמי בבעל ²⁸ הנביא אשר אתו חלום יספר חלום
ואשר דברי אתו ידבר דברי אמת מה לתבן את הבר ²⁹ הלוא דברי כאש נאם יהוה וכפטיש
יפצץ סלע ³⁰ לכן הנני על הנבאים נאם יהוה מגנבי דברי איש מאת רעהו ³¹
הנני על הנבאים הלקחים לשונם וינאמו נום ³² הנני על הנביאים הנבאים חלמות שקר
ויספרום ויתעו את עמי בשקריהם ובפחזותם ואנכי לא שלחתים ולא צויתים והועל
לא יועילו לעם הזה ³³ וכי ישאלך העם הזה או כהן או נביא מה משא יהוה ואמרת
אליהם אתם המשא ונטשתי אתכם נאם יהוה ³⁴ והנביא והכהן והעם אשר יאמרו
משא יהוה ופקדתי על האיש ההוא ועל ביתו ³⁵ כה תאמרו איש אל רעהו ואיש אל
אחיו מה ענה יהוה ומה דבר יהוה ³⁶ ומשא יהוה לא תזכרו עוד כי המשא יהיה
לאיש הדבר ³⁷ ומה דבר יהוה אלהינו ³⁸ לכן כה אמר יהוה אלהים יען אמרכם את
הדבר הזה משא יהוה ואשלח אליכם לאמר לא תאמרו משא יהוה ³⁹ לכן הנני נשא
ונטשתי אתכם ואת העיר אשר נתתי לכם ולאבותיכם ⁴⁰ ונתתי עליכם חרפת עולם
וכלמות עולם אשר לא תשכח ⁷ לכן הנה ימים באים נאם יהוה ולא יאמרו עוד חי
יהוה אשר העלה את בית ישראל מארץ מצרים ⁸ כי אם חי יהוה אשר הביא את
כל זרע ישראל מארץ צפונה ומכל הארצות אשר הדיחם שם וישבם על אדמתם

JEREMIAH 24

¹ הראני יהוה שני דודאי תאנים מועדים לפני היכל יהוה אחרי הגלות נבוכדנאצר מלך
בבל את יכניהו בן יהויקים מלך יהודה ואת השרים ואת החרש ואת המסגר ואת העשיר
מירושלם ויבאם בבל ² הדוד אחד תאנים טבות מאד כתאני הבכרות והדוד אחד תאנים
רעות מאד אשר לא תאכלנה מרע ³ ויאמר יהוה אלי מה אתה ראה ירמיהו ואמר תאנים

הטבות טבות מאד והרעות רעות מאד אשר לא תאכלנה מרע ⁴ ויהי דבר יהוה אלי
לאמר ⁵ כה אמר יהוה אלהי ישראל כתאנים הטבות האלה כן אכיר את גלות יהודה
אשר שלחתי מן המקום הזה ארץ כשדים לטובה ⁶ ושמתי עיני עליהם לטובה והשבתים
על הארץ הזאת ובניתים ולא אהרס ונטעתים ולא אתוש ⁷ ונתתי להם לב לדעת אתי
כי אני יהוה והיו לי לעם ואנכי אהיה להם לאלהים כי ישבו אלי בכל לבם ⁸ וכתאנים
הרעות אשר לא תאכלנה מרע כה אמר יהוה כן אתן את צדקיהו מלך יהודה ואת שריו
ואת שארית ירושלם הנשארים בארץ הזאת והישבים במצרים ⁹ ונתתים לזועה לכל
ממלכות הארץ ולחרפה ולמשל ולשנאה ולקללה בכל המקמות אשר אדיחם שם ¹⁰
ושלחתי בם את הרעב ואת הדבר ואת החרב עד תמם מעל האדמה אשר נתתי להם

JEREMIAH 25:1–13

¹ הדבר אשר היה אל ירמיהו על כל עם יהודה בשנה הרביעית ליהויקים בן יאשיהו
מלך יהודה ² אשר דבר על כל עם יהודה ואל ישבי ירושלם לאמר ³ בשלש עשרה
שנה ליאשיהו בן אמוס מלך יהודה ועד היום הזה שלש ועשרים שנה ואדבר אליכם
השכם ודבר ⁴ ואשלח אליכם את עבדי הנבאים השכם ושלח ולא שמעתם ולא
הטיתם אזנכם ⁵ לאמר שובו נא איש מדרכו הרעה ומרע מעלליכם ושבו על האדמה
אשר נתתי לכם ולאבותיכם למן עולם ועד עולם ⁶ אל תלכו אחרי אלהים אחרים
לעבדם ולהשתחות להם ולא תכעיסו אותי במעשי ידיכם להרע לכם ⁷ ולא שמעתם
אלי ⁸ לכן כה אמר יהוה יען אשר לא האמנתם בדברי ⁹ הנני שלח ולקחתי משפחה
מצפון והבאתים על הארץ הזאת ועל ישביה ועל כל הגוים סביב והחרמתים ושמתים
לשמה ולשרקה ולחרפת עולם ¹⁰ והאבדתי מהם קול ששון וקול שמחה קול חתן
וקול כלה ריח מור ואור נר ¹¹ והיתה כל הארץ לשמה ועבדו בגוים שבעים
שנה ¹² ובמלאות שבעים שנה אפקד על הגוי ההוא ושמתי אתם לשממות עולם ¹³
והבאתי על הארץ ההיא את כל דברי אשר דברתי עליה את כל הכתוב בספר הזה

JEREMIAH 25:13b2; 49:34–39; 46:1 (= LXX 25:14–19; 26:1)[1]

13 ⁽¹⁴⁾ אשר נבא ירמיהו על הגוים ³⁴ אל עילם ⁽¹⁵⁾ ³⁵ כה אמר יהוה שבר את קשת עילם
ראשית גבורתם ³⁶ ⁽¹⁶⁾ והבאתי אל עילם ארבע רוחות מארבע קצות השמים וזרתים לכל
הרחות האלה ולא יהיה גוי אשר לא יבוא שם נדחי עילם ³⁷ ⁽¹⁷⁾ והחתתי אתם לפני איביהם
מבקשי נפשם והבאתי עליהם רעה את חרון אפי ושלחתי אחריהם את חרבי עד כלותי
אותם ³⁸ ⁽¹⁸⁾ ושמתי כסאי בעילם ושלחתי משם מלך ושרים ³⁹ ⁽¹⁹⁾ והיה באחרית הימים
אשוב את שבות עילם נאם יהוה ¹ בראשית ממלכת צדקיה המלך היה הדבר הזה על עילם

---

1. The Göttingen Septuagint and the NETS make the last verse of this unit
   the first verse of chapter 26 (= MT chapter 46), even though this verse
   clearly belongs with what precedes it rather than with what follows it. It
   is not equivalent to MT Jeremiah 46:1. Rahlfs more appropriately makes
   this verse the last verse of LXX chapter 25 (i.e., verse 20) and leaves LXX
   chapter 26 without a verse 1. The verse has no exact equivalent in the MT
   (but see MT 49:34). It is counted here as 46:1 only because of the arrangement in the Göttingen Septuagint and the NETS and because there is no
   way to indicate equivalent versification in the MT.

JEREMIAH 46:2–28 (= LXX 26:2–28)

² למצרים על חיל פרעה נכו מלך מצרים אשר היה על נהר פרת בכרכמש אשר
הכה נבוכדנאצר מלך בבל בשנת הרביעית ליהויקים מלך יהודה ³ ערכו מגן וצנה
וגשו למלחמה ⁴ אסרו הסוסים עלו הפרשים והתיצבו בכובעיכם רמו הרמחים ולבשו
הסרינת ⁵ מדוע המה חתים ונסגים אחור כי גבוריהם יכתו מנוס נסו ולא הפנו מגור
מסביב נאם יהוה ⁶ אל ינוס הקל ואל ימלט הגבור צפונה על יד נהר פרת כשלו נפלו
⁷ מי זה כיאר יעלה וכנהרות יתגעשו מים ⁸ מימי מצרים כיאר יעלה ויאמר אעלה
ואכסה ארץ ואבידה ישבי בה ⁹ עלו על הסוסים התהללו הרכב צאו הגבורים כוש
ופוט תפשי מגן ולודים תפשו דרכו קשת ¹⁰ והיום ההוא ליהוה אלהינו יום נקמה
להנקם מצריו ואכלה חרב ליהוה ושבעה ורותה מדמם כי זבח ליהוה מארץ צפון
אל נהר פרת ¹¹ עלי גלעד וקחי צרי בתולת בת מצרים לשוא הרבית רפאתיך תעלה
אין לך ¹² שמעו גוים קולך וצוחתך מלאה הארץ כי גבור בגבור כשלו יחדיו נפלו
שניהם ¹³ אשר דבר יהוה ביד ירמיהו לבוא מלך בבל להכות את ארץ מצרים ¹⁴
הגידו במגדול והשמיעו בנף אמרו התיצב והכן כי אכלה חרב סביבך ¹⁵ מדוע נס
חף אבירך לא עמד כי יהוה הדפו ¹⁶ והמונך כשל גם נפל ואיש אל רעהו יאמרו
קומו ונשבה אל עמנו אל ארץ מולדתנו מפני חרב יוניה ¹⁷ קראו שם פרעה נכו מלך
מצרים שאון עזבי המועד ¹⁸ חי אני נאם יהוה אלהים כי כתבור בהרים וככרמל בים
יבוא ¹⁹ כלי גולה עשי לך יושבת בת מצרים כי נף לשמה תהיה ונצתה מאין יושב
בה ²⁰ עגלה יפיפיה מצרים קרץ מצפון בא בה ²¹ גם שכריה בקרבה כעגלי מרבק
כי גם המה הפנו ונסו יחדיו לא עמדו כי יום אידם בא עליהם ועת פקדתם ²² קול
כנחש ילך כי בחול ילכו ובקרדמות באו לה כחטבי עצים ²³ כרתו יערה נאם יהוה
כי לא יחקר כי רבו מארבה ואין להם מספר ²⁴ הבישה בת מצרים נתנה ביד עם
צפון ²⁵ הנני פוקד אל אמון בנה על פרעה ועל הבטחים בו ²⁷ ואתה אל תירא עבדי
יעקב ואל תחת ישראל כי הנני מושעך מרחוק ואת זרעך מארץ שבים ושב יעקוב
ושקט ושאנן ואין מחריד ²⁸ אתה אל תירא עבדי יעקוב נאם יהוה כי אתך אני כי
אעשה כלה בכל הגוים אשר הדחתיך שמה ואתך לא אעשה כלה ויסרתיך למשפט
ונקה לא אנקך

JEREMIAH 50 (= LXX 27)

¹ דבר יהוה אשר דבר אל בבל ² הגידו בגוים והשמיעו ואל תכחדו אמרו נלכדה
בבל הביש בל חת מרדך ³ כי עלה עליה גוי מצפון הוא ישית ארצה לשמה ולא
יהיה יושב בה מאדם ועד בהמה ⁴ בימים ההמה ובעת ההיא יבאו בני ישראל המה
ובני יהודה יחדו הלוך ובכו ילכו ואת יהוה אלהיהם יבקשו ⁵ ציון ישאלו דרך הנה
פניהם ובאו ונלוו אל יהוה ברית עולם לא תשכח ⁶ צאן אבדות היה עמי רעיהם
התעום הרים שובבום מהר אל גבעה הלכו שכחו רבצם ⁷ כל מוצאיהם אכלום
וצריהם אמרו לא נשאם תחת אשר חטאו ליהוה נוה צדק למקוה אבותיהם ⁸ נדו
מתוך בבל ומארץ כשדים וצאו והיו כעתודים לפני צאן ⁹ כי הנה אנכי מעיר על
בבל קהל גוים מארץ צפון וערכו לה משם תלכד כחץ גבור משכיל לא ישוב ריקם
¹⁰ והיתה כשדים לשלל כל שלליה ישבעו ¹¹ כי תשמחו ותעלזו שסי נחלתי כי תפושו
כעגלי בדשא ותצהלו כאברים ¹² בושה אמכם מאד אם על טובה אחרית גוים מדבר
¹³ מקצף יהוה לא תשב והיתה שממה כלה וכל עבר על בבל ישם וישרק על כל
מכותיה ¹⁴ ערכו על בבל סביב כל דרכי קשת ירו אליה אל תחמלו אל חץ ¹⁵

והריעו עליה נתנה ידה נפלו אשיותיה נהרסה חומתה כי נקמת יהוה היא הנקמו בה
כאשר עשתה עשו לה 16 כרתו זרע מבבל ותפש מגל בעת קציר מפני חרב יוניה
איש אל עמו יפנו ואיש אל ארצו ינסו 17 שה פזורה ישראל אריות הדיחוהו הראשון
אכלו מלך אשור וזה האחרון עצמו מלך בבל 18 לכן כה אמר יהוה הנני פקד אל
מלך בבל ואל ארצו כאשר פקדתי אל מלך אשור 19 ושבבתי את ישראל אל נוהו
ורעה הכרמל ובשן ובהר אפרים והגלעד תשבע נפשו 20 בימים ההם ובעת ההיא יבקשו
את עון ישראל ואיננו ואת חטאת יהודה ולא תמצאנה כי אסלח לנשארי על הארץ
נאם יהוה 21 מרתים עלה עליה ואל יושבי פקוד חרב והחרם נאם יהוה ועשה
ככל אשר צויתיך 22 קול מלחמה ושבר גדול בארץ כשדים 23 איך נגדע וישבר פטיש
כל הארץ איך היתה לשמה בבל בגוים 24 יקשו לך וגם נלכדת בבל ואת לא ידעת
נמצאת וגם נתפשת כי ביהוה התגרית 25 פתח יהוה את אוצרו ויוצא את כלי זעמו
כי מלאכה לאדני יהוה בארץ כשדים 26 כי באו קציה פתחו מאבסיה סלוה כמערה
והחרימוה אל תהי לה שארית 27 חרבו כל פריה וירדו לטבח הוי עליהם כי בא יומם
ועת פקדתם 28 קול נסים ופלטים מארץ בבל להגיד בציון את נקמת יהוה אלהינו 29
השמיעו אל בבל רבים כל דרכי קשת חנו עליה סביב אל יהי לה פלטה שלמו לה
כפעלה ככל אשר עשתה עשו לה כי אל יהוה זדה אל קדוש ישראל 30 לכן יפלו
בחוריה ברחבתיה וכל אנשי מלחמתה ירמו נאם יהוה 31 הנני אליך זדון נאם יהוה
כי בא יומך ועת פקדתיך 32 וכשל זדון ונפל ואין לו מקים והצתי אש בעריו ואכלה
כל סביביו 33 כה אמר יהוה עשוקים בני ישראל ובני יהודה יחדו כל שביהם החזיקו
בם כי מאנו שלחם 34 וגאלם חזק יהוה צבאות שמו ריב יריב את רביו למען הרגיע
את הארץ והרגיז לישבי בבל 35 חרב על הכשדים ואל ישבי בבל ואל שריה ואל
חכמיה 36 חרב אל גבוריה וחתו חרב אל סוסיהם ואל רכבם 37 חרב אל גבוריהם
ואל הערב אשר בתוכה והיו לנשים חרב אל אוצרתיה ובזזו 38 אל מימיה ויבשו כי
ארץ פסלים היא ובאיים יתהללו 39 לכן ישבו ציים את איים וישבו בה בנות יענה
לא תשב עוד לנצח ולא תשכון עד דור ודור 40 כמהפכת אלהים את סדם ואת עמרה ואת שכניהן נאם יהוה
לא ישב שם איש ולא יגור בה בן אדם 41 הנה עם בא מצפון וגוי גדול ומלכים רבים
יערו מירכתי ארץ 42 קשת וכידון יחזיקו אכזרי הוא ולא ירחם קולם כים יהמה
על סוסים ירכבו ערוך כאש למלחמה עליך בת בבל 43 שמע מלך בבל את שמעם
ורפו ידיו צרה החזיקתהו חיל כיולדה 44 הנה כאריה יעלה מן הירדן אל איתן כי
ארגעה אריצם מעליה ומי בחור אליה אפקד כי מי כמוני ומי יועדני ומי זה רעה
אשר יעמד לפני 45 לכן שמעו עצת יהוה אשר יעץ אל בבל ומחשבותיו אשר חשב
אל יושבי כשדים אם לא יסחבו שעירי הצאן אם לא ישם נוה עליהם 46 כי מקול
נתפשה בבל נרעשה הארץ וזעקה בגוים נשמע

JEREMIAH 51 (= LXX 28)

1 כה אמר יהוה הנני מעיר על בבל ועל ישבי כשדים רוח קדים משחית 2 ושלחתי
לבבל זדים וזדוה ויבקקו את ארצה הוי בבל מסביב ביום רעתה 3 ידרך הדרך
קשתו ויתעל בסרינו אל תחמלו אל בחריה והחרימו כל צבאה 4 ונפלו חללים
בארץ כשדים ומדקרים בחוצותיה 5 כי לא אלמן ישראל ויהודה מאלהיהם מיהוה
צבאות כי ארצם מלאה אשם מקדושי ישראל 6 נסו מתוך בבל ומלטו איש נפשו ואל
תרמו בעונה כי עת נקמתה היא ליהוה גמול הוא משלם לה 7 כוס זהב בבל ביד
יהוה משכרת כל הארץ מיינה שתו גוים על כן יתהללו גוים 8 ופתאם נפלה בבל ותשבר

הילילו עליה קחו צרי למכאובה אולי תרפא ⁹ רפאנו את בבל ולא נרפתה עזבוה
ונלך איש לארצו כי נגע אל השמים משפטה ונשא עד שחקים ¹⁰ הוציא יהוה צדקתו
באו ונספרה בציון את מעשי יהוה אלהינו ¹¹ הברו החצים מלאו השלטים העיר יהוה
את רוח מלך מדי כי על בבל זממו להשחיתה כי נקמת יהוה היא נקמת היכלו ¹²
אל חומת בבל שאו נס החזיקו המשמר הקימו שמרים הכינו נשק כי זמם יהוה ועשה
את אשר דבר אל ישבי בבל ¹³ שכנת על מים רבים ועל רבת אוצרתיה בא קצך
אמת במעיך ¹⁴ כי נשבע יהוה בזרועו כי אם מלאתיך אדם כילק וענו עליך הירדים
¹⁵ עשה ארץ בכחו מכין תבל בחכמתו ובתבונתו נטה שמים ¹⁶ לקול תתו המון מים
בשמים ויעל נשאים מקצה הארץ ברקים למטר עשה ויצא אור מאצרתיו ¹⁷ נבער
כל אדם מדעת הביש כל צרף מפסליו כי שקר נסכו לא רוח בם ¹⁸ הבל המה מעשי
תעתעים בעת פקדתם יאבדו ¹⁹ לא כאלה חלק יעקוב כי יוצר הכל הוא נחלתו יהוה
שמו ²⁰ מפץ אתה לי כלי מלחמה ונפצתי בך גוים והשחתי בך ממלכות ²¹ ונפצתי
בך סוס ורכבו ²² ונפצתי בך רכב ורכבו ונפצתי בך בחור ובתולה ונפצתי בך איש
ואשה ²³ ונפצתי בך רעה ועדרו ונפצתי בך אכר וצמדו ונפצתי בך פחות וסגנים ²⁴
ושלמתי לבבל ולכל יושבי כשדים את כל רעתם אשר עשו בציון לעיניכם נאם יהוה
²⁵ הנני אליך ההר המשחית את כל הארץ ונטיתי את ידי עליך וגלגלתיך מן
הסלעים ונתתיך להר שרפה ²⁶ ולא יקחו ממך אבן לפנה ואבן למוסדה כי שממה
עולם תהיה נאם יהוה ²⁷ שאו נס בארץ תקעו שופר בגוים קדשו עליה גוים השמיעו
עליה ממלכות אררט מני ואשכנז פקדו עליה טפסר העלו סוס כילק מספר ²⁸
קדשו עליה גוים את מלך מדי וכל הארץ את פחותיו ואת כל סגניו ²⁹ ותרעש הארץ
ותחל כי קמה על בבל מחשבת יהוה לשום את ארץ בבל לשמה מאין יושב ³⁰ חדל
גבור בבל להלחם ישבו שם במצדה נשתה גבורתם היו לנשים נצתו משכנתיה נשברו
בריחיה ³¹ רץ לקראת רץ ירוץ ומגיד לקראת מגיד להגיד למלך בבל כי נלכדה
עירו ³² מקצה מעברותיו נתפשו ואת האגמים שרפו באש ואנשי המלחמה הלכו ³³
כי כה אמר יהוה בתי מלך בבל כגרן עת הדריכה עוד מעט ובאה הקציר לה ³⁴
אכלני הממני השיגני כלי דק נבוכדנאצר מלך בבל בלעני כתנין מלא כרשו מעדני
הדיחני חמסי ושברי על בבל תאמר ישבת ציון ודמי אל ישבי כשדים תאמר ירושלם
³⁶ לכן כה אמר יהוה הנני רב את רבך ונקמתי את נקמתך והחרבתי ימה והבשתי
את מקורה ³⁷ והיתה בבל לשמה מאין יושב ³⁸ יחדו ככפרים נערו וכגורי אריות ³⁹
בחמם אשית את משתיהם והשכרתים למען יעלפו וישנו שנת עולם ולא יקיצו נאם
יהוה ⁴⁰ אורידם ככרים לטבח וכאילים עם עתודים ⁴¹ איך נלכדה ותתפש תהלת כל
הארץ איך היתה בבל לשמה בגוים ⁴² עלה על בבל הים בהמון גליו ונכסתה ⁴³ היו
עריה ארץ ציה וערבה לא ישב בה כל איש ולא יעבר בה בן אדם ⁴⁴ ופקדתי על
בבל והצאתי את בלעה מפיה ולא ינהרו אליה עוד גוים ⁴⁹ גם לבבל יפלו חללי כל
הארץ ⁵⁰ פלטים מחרבה לכו ואל תעמדו מרחוק זכרו את יהוה וירושלם תעלה על
לבבכם ⁵¹ בשנו כי שמענו חרפתנו כסתה כלמה פנינו כי באו זרים על מקדשינו בית
יהוה ⁵² לכן הנה ימים באים נאם יהוה ופקדתי על פסיליה ובכל ארצה יפל חלל
⁵³ כי תעלה בבל כשמים וכי תבצר מרום עזה מאתי יבאו שדדים לה נאם יהוה ⁵⁴
קול זעקה בבבל ושבר גדול בארץ כשדים ⁵⁵ כי שדד יהוה את בבל ואבד ממנה
קול גדול והומה כמים רבים נתן שאון קולם ⁵⁶ כי בא על בבל שוד ונלכדו גבוריה
חתתה קשתם כי אל גמלות יהוה שלם ישלם ⁵⁷ יהוה שלם ישלם והשכר ישכיר שריה וחכמיה וסגניה
נאם המלך יהוה צבאות שמו ⁵⁸ כה אמר יהוה חומת בבל הרחבה ערער תתערער

ושריה הגבהים באש יצתו ולא יגעו עמים בדי ריק ולאמים בראש ייעפו 59 הדבר
אשר צוה יהוה ירמיהו הנביא לדבר אל שריה בן נריה בן מחסיה בלכתו מאת
צדקיהו מלך יהודה בבל בשנת הרבעית למלכו ושריהו שר מנחות 60 ויכתב ירמיהו
את כל הרעה אשר תבוא אל בבל אל ספר אחד את כל הדברים האלה הכתבים
אל בבל 61 ויאמר ירמיהו אל שריה בבאך בבל וראית וקראת את כל הדברים
האלה 62 ואמרת יהוה יהוה אתה דברת אל המקום הזה להכריתו ולבלתי היות בו
יושב למאדם ועד בהמה כי שממה עולם תהיה 63 והיה ככלתך לקרא את הספר
הזה וקשרת עליו אבן והשלכתו אל תוך פרת 64 ואמרת ככה תשקע בבל ולא תקום
מפני כשדים אשר אנכי מביא עליה

JEREMIAH 47 (= LXX 29:1–7)

אל פלשתים 1 כה אמר יהוה הנה מים עלים מצפון והיו לנחל שוטף וישטפו 2
ארץ ומלואה עיר וישבי בה וזעקו האדם והיללו כל ישבי הארץ 3 מקול שעטת
מפרסות אביריו ומרעש לרכבו המון גלגליו לא הפנו אבות על בניהם מרפיון
ידים 4 על היום הבא לשדוד את כל פלשתים והכרתי צר וצידון וכל שרידי
עזרם כי שדד יהוה שארית האיים 5 באה קרחה אל עזה נרמתה אשקלון ושארית
ענקים 6 עד מתי תתגודדי חרב ליהוה עד אנה לא תשקטי האספי אל תערך
הרגעי ורמי 7 איך תשקט ויהוה צוה לה אל אשקלון ואל חוף הים שאר הער

JEREMIAH 49:7–22 (= LXX 29:8–23)

(8) 7 לאדום כה אמר יהוה אין עוד חכמה בתימן אבדה עצה מבנים נסרחה חכמתם 8
(9) נפתו פניהם העמיקו לשבת ישבי דדן כי איד עשו הבאתי עליו עת פקדתיו 9 (10) אם
בצרים באו לא ישארו עוללות אם גנבים בלילה ישחתו ידם 10 (11) כי אני חשפתי את עשו
גליתי את מסתריו החבה לא יוכלו שדד זרוע אחיו ושכנו ואיננו 11 (12) העזב יתמך למען
יחיה ואלמנתיך עלי תבטחנה 12 (13) כי כה אמר יהוה אשר אין משפטם לשתות הכוס
שתו ואתה נקה לא תנקה 13 (14) כי בי נשבעתי נאם יהוה כי לשמה ולחרפה ולקללה
תהיה בתוכה וכל עריה תהיינה לחרבות עולם 14 (15) שמועה שמעתי מאת יהוה וצירים
בגוים שלח התקבצו ובאו עליה קומו למלחמה 15 (16) קטן נתתיך בגוים בזוי באדם 16
(17) תפלצתך השיא אתך זדון לבך שכן בחגוי הסלע תפש מרום גבעה כי תגביה כנשר
קנך משם אורידך 17 (18) והיתה אדום לשמה כל עבר עליה ישרק 18 (19) כמהפכת סדם
ועמרה ושכניה אמר יהוה לא ישב שם איש ולא יגור בה בן אדם 19 (20) הנה
כאריה יעלה מגוא הירדן אל נוה איתן כי ארגיעה אריצם מעליה ובחורים אליה פקדו
כי מי כמוני ומי יעידני ומי זה רעה אשר יעמד לפני 20 (21) לכן שמעו עצת יהוה אשר
יעץ אל אדום ומחשבתו אשר חשב אל ישבי תימן אם לא יסחבו צעירי הצאן אם לא
ישם עליה נוהם 21 (22) כי מקול נפלם רעשה הארץ וצעקה בים סוף נשמע 22 (23) הנה
כנשר יראה ויפרש כנפיו על מבצריה והיה לב גבורי אדום ביום ההוא כלב אשה מצרה

JEREMIAH 49:1–5 (= LXX 30:1–5)

לבני עמון כה אמר יהוה הבנים אין לישראל אם יורש אין לו מדוע ירש מלכם את 1
גלעד ועמו בעריו ישב 2 לכן הנה ימים באים נאם יהוה והשמעתי אל רבה תרועת
מלחמת והיו לתל ולשממה ובנתיה באש תצתנה וירש ישראל את ירשיו הילילי 3
חשבון כי שדדה עי צעקנה בנות רבה חגרנה שקים וספדנה כי מלכם בגולה ילך

כהניו ושריו יחדיו ⁴ מה תתהללי בעמקים הבת השובבה הבטחה באצרתיה מי יבוא
אלי ⁵ הנני מביא פחד עליך נאם יהוה מכל סביביך ונדחתם איש לפניו ואין מקבץ

JEREMIAH 49:28–33 (= LXX 30:6–11)

²⁸ ⁽⁶⁾ לקדר ולמלכת חצר אשר הכה נבוכדנאצר מלך בבל כה אמר יהוה קומו ועלו
אל קדר ושדדו את בני קדם ²⁹ ⁽⁷⁾ אהליהם וצאנם יקחו יריעותיהם וכל כליהם
וגמליהם ישאו להם וקראו עליהם מגור מסביב ³⁰ ⁽⁸⁾ נסו מאד העמיקו לשבת ישבי
חצר כי יעץ עליכם מלך בבל עצה וחשב עליכם מחשבה ³¹ ⁽⁹⁾ קומו ועלו אל גוי
שליו יושב לבטח לא דלתים לא בריח לו בדד ישכנו ³² ⁽¹⁰⁾ והיו גמליהם לבז והמון
מקניהם לשלל וזרתים לכל רוח קצוצי פאה ומכל עבריו אביא את אידם נאם יהוה ³³
⁽¹¹⁾ והיה החצר למעון תנים ושממה עד עולם לא ישב שם איש ולא יגור בה בן אדם

JEREMIAH 49:23–27 (= LXX 30:12–16)

²³ ⁽¹²⁾ לדמשק בושה חמת וארפד כי שמעה רעה שמעו נמגו בים דאגה השקט לא
יוכלו ²⁴ ⁽¹³⁾ רפתה דמשק הפנתה לנוס רטט החזיקה ²⁵ ⁽¹⁴⁾ איך לא עזבה עיר תהלה
קרית משושי ²⁶ ⁽¹⁵⁾ לכן יפלו בחוריה ברחבתיה וכל אנשי המלחמה ידמו נאם יהוה
²⁷ ⁽¹⁶⁾ והצתי אש בחומת דמשק ואכלה ארמנות בן הדד

JEREMIAH 48 (= LXX 31)

¹ למואב כה אמר יהוה הוי אל נבו כי שדדה נלכדה קריתים הביש המשגב וחת ²
אין עוד תהלת מואב בחשבון חשבו עליה רעה נכריתנה מגוי גם דמם תדם אחריך
תלך חרב ³ קול צעקה מחרונים שד ושבר גדול ⁴ נשברה מואב השמיעו צערה ⁵
כי מלאה הלחות בבכי יעלה בכי במורד חורנים צעקת שבר שמעתם ⁶ נסו מלטו
נפשכם ותהיינה כערוד במדבר ⁷ יען בטחך במצדותיך גם את תלכדי ויצא כמוש
בגולה כהניו ושריו יחד ⁸ ויבא שד אל כל עיר לא תמלט ואבד העמק ונשמד המישר
כאשר אמר יהוה ⁹ תנו ציון למואב כי נצא תצא וכל עריה לשמה תהיינה מאין יושב
בהן ¹⁰ ארור עשה מלאכת יהוה רמיה וארור מנע חרבו מדם ¹¹ שאנן מואב מנעוריו ושקט
הוא אל שמריו לא הורק מכלי אל כלי ובגולה לא הלך על כן עמד טעמו בו וריחו
לא נמר ¹² לכן הנה ימים באים נאם יהוה ושלחתי לו צעים וצעהו וכליו יריקו ונבליו
ינפצו ¹³ ובש מואב מכמוש כאשר בשו בית ישראל מבית אל מבטחם ¹⁴ איך תאמרו
גבורים אנחנו ואנשי חיל למלחמה ¹⁵ שדד מואב עירו ומבחר בחוריו ירדו לטבח ¹⁶
קרוב יום מואב לבוא ורעתו מהרה מאד ¹⁷ נדו לו כל סביביו וכל ידעי שמו אמרו
איכה נשבר מטה עז מקל תפארה ¹⁸ רדי מכבוד ושבי בצמא ישבת אבדון כי שדד
מואב עלה בך משחית מבצריך ¹⁹ אל דרך עמדי וצפי יושבת ערוער שאלי נס ונמלט
ואמרי מה נהיתה ²⁰ הביש מואב כי חת הילילי וזעקי הגידי בארנון כי שדד מואב ²¹
ומשפט בא אל ארץ המישר אל חלון ואל יהצה ועל מופעת ²² ועל דיבון ועל נבו
ועל בית דבלתים ²³ ועל קריתים ועל בית גמול ועל בית מעון ²⁴ ועל קריות ועל
בצרה ועל כל ערי מואב הרחקות והקרבות ²⁵ נגדעה קרן מואב וזרעו נשברה ²⁶
השכירהו כי על יהוה הגדיל וספק מואב בידו והיה לשחק גם הוא ²⁷ ואם לוא השחק
היה לך ישראל אם בגנבים נמצא כי בו תתגודד ²⁸ עזבו ערים ושכנו בסלע ישבי
מואב היו כיונה תקנן בצורי פי פחת ²⁹ שמעתי גאון מואב גאה מאד גאונו וגאותו
ורם לבו ³⁰ אני ידעתי עברתו לא דיו לא כן עשה ³¹ על כן על מואב היליל וכלה

זעקו אל אנשי קיר חדש הגה 32 כבכי יעזר אבכה לך גפן שבמה נטישתיך עברו ים
ערים יעזר נגעו על קיצך על בצריך שד נפל 33 נאספה שמחה וגיל מארץ מואב
ויין ביקביך השבם לא דרכו הידד הידד לא היידד 34 מזעקת חשבון עד אלעלה
עריהם נתנו קולם מצער עד חרנים ועגלת שלשיה כי גם מי נמרים למשמות יהיו
35 והשבתי למואב נאם יהוה עלה על במה ומקטיר לאלהיו 36 על כן לבי למואב
כחלילים יהמה ולבי אל אנשי קיר חדש כחליל יהמה על כן אשר עשה אבד 37 כל
ראש בכל מקום קרחה וכל זקן גרעה וכל ידים גדדת ועל כל מתנים שק 38 ועל כל
גגות מואב וברחבתיה כי שברתי את מואב ככלי אין חפץ בו נאם יהוה 39 איך חת היליל איך
הפנה ערף מואב בוש והיה מואב לשחק ולמחתה לכל סביביה 40 כי כה אמר יהוה
41 נלכדה הקריות והמצדות נתפשה 42 ונשמד מואב מעם כי על יהוה הגדיל 43 פח
ופחד ופחת עליך יושב מואב 44 הנס מפני הפחד יפל אל הפחת והעלה מן הפחת
ילכד בפח כי אביא אלה אל מואב שנת פקדתם

JEREMIAH 25:15–38 (= LXX 32:1–24)

15 (1) כה אמר יהוה אלהי ישראל קח את כוס יין החמר הזאת מידי והשקיתה את כל
הגוים אשר אנכי שלח אותך אליהם 16 (2) ושתו והתגעשו והתהללו מפני החרב אשר אנכי שלח
ביניתם 17 (3) ואקח את הכוס מיד יהוה ואשקה את הגוים אשר שלחני יהוה אליהם
18 (4) את ירושלם ואת ערי יהודה ואת מלכיו ואת שריו לתת אתן לחרבה ולשמה
ולשרקה 19 (5) ואת פרעה מלך מצרים ואת עבדיו ואת שריו (6) ואת כל עמו 20 ואת
כל הערב ואת כל מלכי פלשתים את אשקלון ואת עזה ואת עקרון ואת שארית
אשדוד 21 (7) ואת אדום ואת מואב ואת בני עמון 22 (8) ואת מלכי צר ואת מלכי צידון
ואת מלכים אשר בעבר הים 23 (9) ואת דדן ואת תימא ואת ראש ואת כל קצוצי פאה
24 (10) ואת כל הערב השכנים במדבר 25 (11) ואת כל מלכי עילם ואת כל מלכי פרס
26 (12) ואת כל מלכי הצפון הרחקים והקרבים איש אל אחיו ואת כל הממלכות אשר
על פני האדמה 27 (13) ואמרת אליהם כה אמר יהוה צבאות שתו ושכרו וקיאו ונפלו
ולא תקומו מפני החרב אשר אנכי שלח ביניכם 28 (14) והיה כי ימאנו לקחת הכוס
מידך לשתות ואמרת אליהם כה אמר יהוה שתו תשתו 29 (15) כי בעיר אשר נקרא שמי עליה
אנכי מחל להרע ואתם הנקה לא תנקו כי חרב אני קרא על ישבי הארץ 30 (16) ואתה
תנבא אליהם את הדברים האלה ואמרת אליהם יהוה ממרום ישאג מקדשו יתן קולו שאג
ישאג על נוהו והידד כדרכים יענו ואל ישבי הארץ בא שאון 31 (17) עד קצה הארץ כי
ריב ליהוה בגוים נשפט הוא לכל בשר הרשעים נתנו לחרב נאם יהוה 32 (18) כה אמר
יהוה הנה רעה יצאת מגוי אל גוי וסער גדול יעור מירכתי ארץ 33 (19) והיו חללי
יהוה ביום יהוה מקצה הארץ ועד קצה הארץ לא יקברו לדמן על פני האדמה יהיו
34 (20) הילילו הרעים וזעקו והתפלשו אדירי הצאן כי מלאו ימיכם לטבוח ונפלתם
כאלי חמדה 35 (21) ואבד מנוס מן הרעים ופליטה מאדירי הצאן 36 (22) קול צעקת
הרעים ויללת אדירי הצאן כי שדד יהוה את מרעיתם 37 (23) ונדמו נאות השלום מפני
חרון אפי 38 (24) עזב ככפיר סכו כי היתה ארצם לשמה מפני החרב הגדולה

JEREMIAH 26 (= LXX 33)

1 בראשית ממלכות יהויקים בן יאשיהו היה הדבר הזה מאת יהוה 2 כה אמר יהוה
עמד בחצר בית יהוה ודברת על כל היהודים הבאים להשתחות בית יהוה את כל
הדברים אשר צויתיך לדבר אליהם אל תגרע דבר 3 אולי ישמעו וישבו איש מדרכו

הרעה ונחמתי אל הרעה אשר אנכי חשב לעשות להם מפני רע מעלליהם 4 ואמרת
כה אמר יהוה אם לא תשמעו אלי ללכת בתורתי אשר נתתי לפניכם 5 לשמע על
דברי עבדי הנבאים אשר אנכי שלח אליכם השכם ושלח ולא שמעתם 6 ונתתי את
הבית הזה כשלה ואת העיר אתן לקללה לכל גויי כל הארץ 7 וישמעו הכהנים
והנבאים וכל העם את ירמיהו מדבר את הדברים האלה בבית יהוה 8 ויהי ככלות
ירמיהו לדבר את כל אשר צוהו יהוה לדבר אל כל העם ויתפשו אתו הכהנים
והנבאים וכל העם לאמר מות תמות 9 מדוע נבאת בשם יהוה לאמר כשלו יהיה הבית
הזה והעיר הזאת תחרב מאין יושב ויקהל כל העם אל ירמיהו בבית יהוה 10 וישמעו
שרי יהודה את הדבר הזה ויעלו מבית המלך בית יהוה וישבו בפתח שער בית
יהוה החדש 11 ויאמרו הכהנים והנבאים אל השרים ואל כל העם משפט מות לאיש
הזה כי נבא אל העיר הזאת כאשר שמעתם באזניכם 12 ויאמר ירמיהו אל השרים
ואל כל העם לאמר יהוה שלחני להנבא אל הבית הזה ואל העיר הזאת את כל
הדברים אשר שמעתם 13 ועתה היטיבו דרכיכם ומעלליכם ושמעו בקול יהוה וינחם
יהוה אל הרעה אשר דבר עליכם 14 והנני בידכם עשו לי כטוב וכישר בעיניכם 15
אך ידע תדעו כי אם ממתים אתם אתי כי דם נקי נתנים אתם עליכם ואל העיר הזאת
ואל ישביה כי באמת שלחני יהוה עליכם לדבר באזניכם את כל הדברים האלה
16 ויאמרו השרים וכל העם אל הכהנים ואל הנביאים אין לאיש הזה משפט מות כי
בשם יהוה אלהינו דבר אלינו 17 ויקמו אנשים מזקני הארץ ויאמר אל כל קהל העם
18 מיכיה המורשתי היה בימי חזקיהו מלך יהודה ויאמר אל כל עם יהודה כה אמר
יהוה ציון שדה תחרש וירושלים עיים תהיה והר הבית לבמות יער 19 ההמת המתהו
חזקיהו וכל יהודה הלא ירא את יהוה ויחלו את פני יהוה וינחם יהוה אל הרעה
אשר דבר עליהם ואנחנו עשים רעה גדולה על נפשותינו 20 וגם איש היה מתנבא בשם
יהוה אוריהו בן שמעיהו מקרית היערים וינבא על הארץ הזאת ככל דברי ירמיהו
21 וישמע המלך יהויקים וכל השרים את כל דבריו ויבקשו המית וישמע אוריהו
ויבא מצרים 22 וישלח המלך אנשים מצרים 23 ויוציאו אתו משם ויבאהו אל המלך
ויכהו בחרב וישלך אתו אל קבר בני עמו 24 אך יד אחיקם בן שפן היתה את ירמיהו
לבלתי תת אתו ביד העם להמיתו

JEREMIAH 27:2–22 (= LXX 34:1–18)

2 (1) כה אמר יהוה עשה לך מוסרות ומטות ונתת על צוארך 3 (2) ושלחתם אל מלך אדום
ואל מלך מואב ואל מלך בני עמון ואל מלך צר ואל מלך צידון ביד מלאכיהם
הבאים לקראתם ירושלם אל צדקיהו מלך יהודה 4 (3) וצוית אתם אל אדניהם לאמר
כה אמר יהוה אלהי ישראל כה תאמרו אל אדניכם 5 (4) אנכי עשיתי את הארץ בכחי
הגדול ובזרועי הנטויה ונתתיה לאשר ישר בעיני 6 (5) נתתי את הארץ לנבוכדנאצר
מלך בבל לעבדו וגם את חית השדה לעבדו 8 (6) והגוי והממלכה אשר לא יתן
צוארם בעל מלך בבל ובחרב וברעב אפקד עליהם נאם יהוה עד תמם בידו 9 (7)
ואתם אל תשמעו אל נביאיכם ואל קסמיכם ואל חלמיכם ואל ענניכם ואל כשפיכם
אמרים לא תעבדו את מלך בבל 10 (8) כי שקר הם נבאים לכם למען הרחיק אתכם
מעל אדמתכם 11 (9) והגוי אשר יביא את צוארו בעל מלך בבל ועבדו והנחתיו על
אדמתו ועבדו וישב בה 12 (10) ואל צדקיה מלך יהודה דברתי ככל הדברים האלה
לאמר הביאו את צואריכם ועבדו 14 (11) את מלך בבל 15 (12) כי שקר הם נבאים לכם
כי לא שלחתים נאם יהוה והם נבאים בשמי לשקר למען הדיח אתכם ואבדתם אתם

והנבאים הנבאים לכם [לשקר] שקר 16 (13) אליכם ואל כל העם הזה ואל הכהנים
דברתי לאמר כה אמר יהוה אל תשמעו אל דברי הנבאים הנבאים לכם לאמר הנה
כלי בית יהוה מושבים מבבלה כי שקר המה נבאים לכם (14) 18 לא שלחתים (15) אם
נבאים הם ואם יש דבר יהוה אתם יפגעו נא בי (16) 19 כי כה אמר יהוה ועל יתר
הכלים 20 (17) אשר לא לקחם מלך בבל בגלותו יכניה מירושלם 22 (18) בבלה יבואו
נאם יהוה

JEREMIAH 28 (= LXX 35)

1 ויהי בשנה הרבעית לצדקיה מלך יהודה בחדש החמישי אמר אלי חנניה בן עזור
הנביא אשר מגבעון בבית יהוה לעיני הכהנים וכל העם לאמר 2 כה אמר יהוה
שברתי את על מלך בבל 3 בעוד שנתים ימים אני משיב אל המקום הזה את כלי
בית יהוה 4 ואת יכניה ואת גלות יהודה כי אשבר את על מלך בבל 5 ויאמר ירמיה
אל חנניה לעיני כל העם ולעיני הכהנים העמדים בבית יהוה 6 ויאמר ירמיה אמן
כן יעשה יהוה יקם את דברך אשר נבאת להשיב כלי בית יהוה וכל הגולה מבבל
אל המקום הזה 7 אך שמעו דבר יהוה אשר אנכי דבר באזניכם ובאזני כל העם 8
הנביאים אשר היו לפני ולפניכם מן העולם וינבאו אל ארצות רבות ועל ממלכות
גדלות למלחמה 9 הנביא אשר ינבא לשלום בבא הדבר ידעו הנביא אשר שלחו יהוה
באמת 10 ויקח חנניה לעיני כל העם את המוטת מעל צואר ירמיה וישברהן 11 ויאמר
חנניה לעיני העם לאמר כה אמר יהוה ככה אשבר את על מלך בבל מעל צואר
כל הגוים בעוד שנתים ימים וילך ירמיה לדרכו 12 ויהי דבר יהוה אל ירמיה אחרי שבור חנניה את
המוטת מעל צוארו לאמר 13 הלוך ואמרת אל חנניה לאמר כה אמר יהוה מוטת עץ
שברת ועשית תחתיהן מטות ברזל 14 כי כה אמר יהוה על ברזל נתתי על צואר כל
הגוים לעבד את מלך בבל 15 ויאמר ירמיה אל חנניה לא שלחך יהוה והבטחת את
העם הזה על שקר 16 לכן כה אמר יהוה הנני משלחך מעל פני האדמה השנה אתה
מת 17 וימת בחדש השביעי

JEREMIAH 29 (= LXX 36)

1 ואלה דברי הספר אשר שלח ירמיה מירושלם אל זקני הגולה ואל הכהנים ואל
הנביאים אגרת בבבל אל הגולה ואל כל העם 2 אחרי צאת יכניה המלך והגבירה
והסריסים וכל חפשי ומסגר וחרש מירושלם 3 ביד אלעשה בן שפן וגמריה בן
חלקיה אשר שלח צדקיה מלך יהודה אל מלך בבל בבלה לאמר 4 כה אמר
יהוה אלהי ישראל לגולה אשר הגליתי מירושלם 5 בנו בתים ושבו ונטעו גנות
ואכלו את פרין 6 וקחו נשים והולידו בנים ובנות וקחו לבניכם נשים ואת בנותיכם
לאנשים תנו ורבו ואל תמעטו 7 ודרשו לשלום הארץ אשר הגליתי אתכם שמה
והתפללו בעדם אל יהוה כי בשלומם יהיה לכם שלום 8 כי כה אמר יהוה אל
ישיאו לכם הנביאים אשר בקרבכם ואל ישיאו לכם קסמיכם ואל תשמעו אל
חלמתיכם אשר אתם מחלמים 9 כי שקר הם נבאים לכם בשמי ולא שלחתים 10 כי
כה אמר יהוה כי לפי מלאת לבבל שבעים שנה אפקד אתכם והקמתי את דברי
עליכם להשיב עמכם אל המקום הזה 11 ואנכי חשב עליכם מחשבת שלום ולא
רעה לתת לכם אלה 12 והתפללתם אלי ושמעתי אליכם 13 ובקשתם ומצאתם
אתי כי תדרשני בכל לבבכם 14 ונראתי לכם 15 כי אמרתם הקים לנו יהוה נבאים
בבלה 21 כה אמר יהוה אל אחאב ואל צדקיהו הנני נתן אתם ביד מלך בבל והכם

לעיניכם 22 ולקחו מהם קללה בכל גלות יהודה כצדקיהו וכאחאב אשר קלם
מלך בבל באש 23 יען אשר עשו נבלה בישראל וינאפו את נשי רעיהם וידברו
דבר בשמי אשר לוא צויתם ואנכי עד נאם יהוה 24 ואל שמעיהו הנחלמי תאמר
25 לא שלחתיך בשמי ואל צפניה בן מעשיה הכהן לאמר 26 יהוה נתנך כהן תחת
יהוידע הכהן להיות פקיד בבית יהוה לכל איש מתנבא ולכל איש משגע ונתתה
אתו אל המהפכת ואל הצינק 27 ועתה למה לא גערתם בירמיהו הענתתי המתנבא
לכם 28 כי על כן שלח אלינו בבל לאמר ארכה היא בנו בתים ושבו ונטעו גנות
ואכלו את פריהן 29 ויקרא צפניה את הספר באזני ירמיהו 30 ויהי דבר יהוה אל
ירמיהו לאמר 31 שלח על הגולה לאמר כה אמר יהוה אל שמעיה הנחלמי יען
אשר נבא לכם שמעיה ואני לא שלחתיו ויבטח אתכם על שקר 32 לכן כה אמר
יהוה הנני פקד על שמעיה ועל זרעו ולא יהיה לו איש בתוככם לראות בטוב
אשר אני עשה לכם

JEREMIAH 30 (= LXX 37)

1 הדבר אשר היה אל ירמיהו מאת יהוה לאמר 2 כה אמר יהוה אלהי ישראל לאמר
כתב לך את כל הדברים אשר דברתי אליך אל ספר 3 כי הנה ימים באים נאם
יהוה ושבתי את שבות עמי ישראל ויהודה אמר יהוה והשבתים אל הארץ אשר נתתי
לאבותם וירשוה 4 ואלה הדברים אשר דבר יהוה אל ישראל ואל יהודה 5 כה אמר
יהוה קול חרדה תשמעו פחד ואין שלום 6 שאלו נא וראו אם ילד זכר ועל פחד
באשר יאחזו חלצים ותשועה מדוע ראיתי כל גבר וידיו על חלציו נהפכו פנים
לירקון היו 7 כי גדול היום ההוא ואין כמהו ועת צרה היא ליעקב (8) וממנה יושע 8
ביום ההוא נאם יהוה אשבר על מעל צוארם ומוסרותיהם אנתק ולא יעבדו בם עוד
זרים 9 ועבדו את יהוה אלהיהם ואת דוד מלכם אקים להם 12 כה אמר יהוה נושא
שבר נחלה מכתך 13 אין דן דינך למזור נרפאת תעלה אין לך 14 כל מאהביך שכחוך
לא ידרשו כי מכת אויב הכיתיך מוסר אכזרי על רב עונך עצמו חטאתיך 16 לכן
כל אכליך יאכלו וכל צריך כלה בשרם יאכלו והיו שסיך למשסה וכל בזזיך אתן
לבז 17 כי אעלה ארכה לך ממכה נחלה ארפאך נאם יהוה כי נדחה קראו לך צידנו
היא כי דרש אין לה 18 כה אמר יהוה הנני שב שבות יעקוב ומשכנתיו ארחם ונבנתה
עיר על תלה וארמון על משפטו ישב 19 ויצאו מהם תודה וקול משחקים והרבתים
ולא ימעטו 20 ובאו בניו כקדם ועדותו לפני תכון ופקדתי על לחציו 21 והיו אדירו
בם ומשלו ממנו יצא והקרבתיו ונגש אלי כי מי הוא זה ערב את לבו לנגשת אלי נאם
יהוה 23 כי סערת יהוה חמה יצאה סער מתחולל על רשעים יחול 24 לא ישוב חרון
אף יהוה עד עשתו ועד הקימו מזמת לבו באחרית הימים תתבוננו בה

JEREMIAH 31 (= LXX 38)

1 בעת ההיא נאם יהוה אהיה לאלהים למשפחת ישראל והמה יהיו לי לעם 2 כה אמר
יהוה מצאתי חם במדבר עם שדודי חרב הלוך ואל תרגיעו ישראל 3 יהוה מרחוק
נראה לו אהבת עולם אהבתיך על כן משכתיך חסד 4 עוד אבנך ונבנית בתולת
ישראל עוד תעדי עוד תפיך ויצאת בקהל משחקים 5 עוד תטעי כרמים בהרי שמרון
נטעו והללו 6 כי יש יום קרא נצרים בהרי אפרים קומו ונעלה ציון אל יהוה אלהינו
7 כי כה אמר יהוה ליעקוב שמחו וצהלו בראש הגוים השמיעו והללו אמרו הושע
יהוה את עמו את שארית ישראל 8 הנני מביא אותם מצפון וקבצתים מירכתי הארץ

במועד פסח וילדת קהל גדול ושבו הנה 9 בבכי יצאו ובתנחומים אובילם מלין אל
נחלי מים בדרך ישר ולא יכשלו בה כי הייתי לישראל לאב ואפרים בכרי הוא 10
שמעו דבר יהוה גוים והגידו באיים ממרחק אמרו מזרה ישראל יקבצנו ושמרו כרעה
עדרו 11 כי פדה יהוה את יעקב גאלו מיד חזק ממנו 12 ובאו ורננו בהר ציון ונהרו
אל טוב יהוה על ארץ דגן ועל תירש ועל יצהר ועל בני בקר וצאן והיתה נפשם כען
פרי ולא יוסיפו לרעבה עוד 13 אז תשמח בתולה בקהל בחרים וזקנים יחדו והפכתי
אבלם לששון ושמחתים 14 רביתי ורויתי נפש הכהנים בני לוי ועמי את טובי ישבעו
15 כה אמר יהוה קול ברמה נשמע נהי ובכי ותמרורים רחל מבכה מאנה להנחם על
בניה כי אינם 16 כה אמר יהוה מנעי קולך מבכי ועיניך מדמעה כי יש שכר לפעלתך
ושבו מארץ אויב 17 תקוה לאחריתך 18 שמוע שמעתי אפרים מתנודד יסרתני ואוסר
כעגל לא למד השיבני ואשובה כי אתה יהוה אלהי 19 כי אחרי שבי נחמתי ואחרי
הודעי אנקתי על ימי בשת וגם נכלמתי כי נשאתי חרפת נעורי 20 בן יקיר לי אפרים
ילד שעשעים כי מדי דברי בו זכר אזכרנו על כן מהרתי לו רחם ארחמנו נאם יהוה
21 הציבי לך צינים שמי לך תמרורים שתי לבך למסלה דרך הלכת שובי בתולת
ישראל שבי אל עריך אבלה 22 עד מתי תתחמקין הבת השובבה כי ברא יהוה ישועה
לנטעה חדשה באשר ישועה יסובבו גברים 23 כה אמר יהוה עוד יאמרו את הדבר
הזה בארץ יהודה ובעריו בשובי את שבותו ברוך יהוה על צדיק הר קדשו 24 וישבי
בערי יהודה ובכל ארצו יחדו אכר ונשא בעדר 25 כי הרויתי כל נפש צמאה וכל
נפש רעבה מלאתי 26 על זאת הקיצתי ואראה ושנתי ערבה לי 27 לכן הנה ימים
באים נאם יהוה וזרעתי את ישראל ואת יהודה זרע אדם וזרע בהמה 28 והיה כאשר
שקדתי עליהם לנתוץ ולהרע כן אשקד עליהם לבנות ולנטוע נאם יהוה 29 בימים
ההם לא יאמרו עוד אבות אכלו בסר ושני הבנים תקהינה 30 כי אם איש בעונו ימות
והאכל הבסר תקהינה שניו 31 הנה ימים באים נאם יהוה וכרתי את בית ישראל ואת
בית יהודה ברית חדשה 32 לא כברית אשר כרתי את אבותם ביום החזיקי בידם
להוציאם מארץ מצרים אשר המה הפרו את בריתי ואנכי געלתי בם נאם יהוה 33 כי
זאת הברית אשר אכרת את בית ישראל אחרי הימים ההם נאם יהוה נתן נתן אתן תורתי
בקרבם ועל לבם אכתבן והייתי להם לאלהים והמה יהיו לי לעם 34 ולא ילמדו עוד
איש את רעהו ואיש את אחיו לאמר דע את יהוה כי כולם ידעו אותי למקטנם ועד
גדולם כי אסלח לעונם ולחטאתם לא אזכר עוד 37 (35) אם ירמו שמים מלמעלה
נאם יהוה ויחקר מוסד ארץ למטה גם אני לא אמאס בזרע ישראל נאם יהוה על
כל אשר עשו 35 (36) כה אמר יהוה נתן שמש לאור יומם ירח וכוכבים לאור לילה
ורגז הים ויהמו גליו יהוה צבאות שמו 36 (37) אם ימשו החקים האלה מלפני נאם
יהוה גם זרע ישראל ישבתו מהיות גוי לפני כל הימים 38 הנה ימים באים נאם יהוה
ונבנתה העיר ליהוה ממגדל חננאל לשער הפנה 39 ויצאה מדתה נגדם עד גבעת
גרב ונסבה געתה 40 וכל השרמות עד נחל קדרון עד פנת שער הסוסים מזרחה
קדש ליהוה ולא ינתש ולא יהרס עוד לעולם

JEREMIAH 32 (= LXX 39)

1 הדבר אשר היה מאת יהוה אל ירמיהו בשנה העשרית למלך צדקיהו היא שנה
שמנה עשרה לנבוכדנאצר מלך בבל 2 וחיל מלך בבל צר על ירושלם וירמיהו היה
כלוא בחצר המטרה אשר בית מלך 3 אשר כלאו המלך צדקיהו לאמר מדוע אתה
נבא לאמר כה אמר יהוה הנני נתן את העיר הזאת ביד מלך בבל ולכדה 4 וצדקיהו

לא ימלט מיד הכשדים כי הנתן ינתן ביד מלך בבל ודבר פיו עם פיו ועיניו את
עיניו תראינה 5 ובבל ילך צדקיהו ושם יהיה 6 ויהי דבר יהוה אל ירמיהו לאמר 7
הנה חנמאל בן שלם דדך בא אליך לאמר קנה לך את שדי אשר בענתות כי לך
משפט הגאלה לקנות 8 ויבא אלי חנמאל בן שלם דדי אל חצר המטרה ויאמר אלי
קנה נא את שדי אשר בארץ בנימין אשר בענתות כי לך משפט הירשה ואתה זקן
ואדע כי דבר יהוה הוא 9 ואקנה את השדה מאת חנמאל בן דדי ואשקלה לו שבעה
שקלים ועשרה הכסף 10 ואכתב בספר ואחתם ואעד עדים ואשקל הכסף במאזנים
11 ואקח את ספר המקנה את החתום ואת הגלוי 12 ואתן אתו אל ברוך בן נריה בן
מחסיה לעיני חנמאל בן דדי ולעיני העמדים והכתבים בספר המקנה ולעיני היהודים
בחצר המטרה 13 ואצוה את ברוך לעיניהם לאמר 14 כה אמר יהוה צבאות לקוח
את ספר המקנה הזה ואת הספר הגלוי ונתת בכלי חרש למען יעמד ימים רבים 15
כי כה אמר יהוה עוד יקנו שדות ובתים וכרמים בארץ הזאת 16 ואתפלל אל יהוה
אחרי תתי את ספר המקנה אל ברוך בן נריה לאמר 17 אהה יהוה אתה עשית את
השמים ואת הארץ בכחך הגדול ובזרעך הנטויה לא יפלא ממך כל דבר 18 עשה
חסד לאלפים ומשלם עון אבות אל חיק בניהם אחריהם האל הגדול הגבור 19 יהוה
גדל העצה ורב העליליה אלהי צבאות גדול יהוה שם גדול עיניך על דרכי בני אדם
לתת לאיש כדרכו 20 אשר שמת אתות ומפתים בארץ מצרים עד היום הזה ובישראל
ובאדם ותעשה לך שם כיום הזה 21 ותצא את עמך את ישראל מארץ מצרים באתות
ובופתים וביד חזקה ובאזרוע נטויה 22 ובמראה גדול ותתן להם את הארץ הזאת
אשר נשבעת לאבותם ארץ זבת חלב ודבש 23 ויבאו וירשו אתה ולא שמעו בקולך
ובתורותך לא הלכו את כל אשר צויתה להם לא עשו ותקרא אתם את כל הרעה
הזאת 24 הנה הסללות באו העיר ללכדה והעיר נתנה ביד הכשדים הנלחמים עליה
מפני החרב והרעב כאשר דברת כן היה 25 ואתה אמרת אלי קנה לך השדה בכסף
ואכתב בספר ואחתם ואעד עדים והעיר נתנה ביד הכשדים 26 ויהי דבר יהוה אלי
לאמר 27 אני יהוה אלהי כל בשר הממני יפלא כל דבר 28 לכן כה אמר יהוה הנני נתן
תנתן העיר הזאת ביד מלך בבל ולכדה 29 ובאו הכשדים הנלחמים על העיר הזאת
והציתו את העיר הזאת באש ושרפו את הבתים אשר קטרו על גגותיהם לבעל והסכו
נסכים לאלהים אחרים למען הכעסני 30 כי היו בני ישראל ובני יהודה אך עשים
הרע בעיני מנערתיהם 31 כי על אפי ועל חמתי היתה העיר הזאת למן היום אשר בנו
אותה ועד היום הזה להסירה מעל פני 32 על כל רעת בני ישראל ובני יהודה אשר
עשו להכעסני המה ומלכיהם ושריהם וכהניהם ונביאיהם איש יהודה וישבי ירושלם
33 ויפנו אלי ערף ולא פנים ולמד אתם השכם ולמד ואינם שמעים לקחת מוסר 34
וישימו שקוציהם בבית אשר נקרא שמי עליו בטמאתם 35 ויבנו את במות הבעל אשר
בגיא בן הנם להעביר את בניהם ואת בנותיהם למלך אשר לא צויתים ולא עלתה
על לבי לעשות התועבה הזאת למען החטיא את יהודה 36 ועתה כה אמר יהוה אלהי
ישראל אל העיר אשר אתה אמר נתנה ביד מלך בבל בחרב וברעב ובשלוחים 37
הנני מקבצם מכל הארץ אשר הדחתים שם באפי ובחמתי ובקצף גדול והשבתים אל
המקום הזה והשבתים לבטח 38 והיו לי לעם ואני אהיה להם לאלהים 39 ונתתי להם
דרך אחר ולב אחר ליראה אותי כל הימים ולטוב להם ולבניהם אחריהם 40 וכרתי
להם ברית עולם אשר לא אשיב מאחריהם ואת יראתי אתן בלבבם לבלתי סור מעלי
41 ופקדתי אתם להטיב אותם ונטעתים בארץ הזאת באמת ובכל לב ובכל נפש 42
כי כה אמר יהוה כאשר הבאתי אל העם הזה את כל הרעה הגדולה הזאת כן אנכי

מביא עליהם את כל הטובה אשר אנכי דבר עליהם ⁴³ ונקנה עוד השדה בארץ אשר
אתה אמר שממה היא מאין אדם ובהמה ונתנו ביד הכשדים ⁴⁴ ושדות בכסף יקנו
וכתוב בספר וחתום והעד עדים בארץ בנימן ובסביבי ירושלם ובערי יהודה ובערי
ההר ובערי השפלה ובערי הנגב כי אשיב את שבותם

JEREMIAH 33 (= LXX 40)

¹ ויהי דבר יהוה אל ירמיהו שנית והוא עודנו עצור בחצר המטרה לאמר ² כה אמר
יהוה עשה ארץ ויוצר אותה להכינה יהוה שמו ³ קרא אלי ואענך ואגידה לך גדלות
ובצרות אשר לא ידעתם ⁴ כי כה אמר יהוה על בתי העיר הזאת ועל בתי מלך
יהודה הנתצים אל הסללות ואל החל ⁵ להלחם אל הכשדים ולמלאה את פגרי האדם
אשר הכיתי באפי ובחמתי ואשר הסתרתי פני מהם על כל רעתם ⁶ הנני מעלה לה ארכה
ומרפא וגליתי להם ורפאתים ועבדתי להם שלום ואמת ⁷ והשבתי את שבות יהודה
ואת שבות ישראל ובנתים כבראשנה ⁸ וטהרתים מכל עונם אשר חטאו לי ולא אזכר
לחטאתם אשר חטאו לי ואשר פשעו בי ⁹ והיתה לי לששון ולתהלה ולתפארת לכל עם
הארץ אשר ישמעו את כל הטובה אשר אנכי עשה אתם ופחדו ורגזו על כל הטובה ועל
כל השלום אשר אנכי עשה להם ¹⁰ כה אמר יהוה עוד ישמע במקום הזה אשר אתם
אמרים חרב הוא מאין אדם ומאין בהמה בערי יהודה ובחצות ירושלם הנשמות מאין
אדם ומאין בהמה ¹¹ קול ששון וקול שמחה קול חתן וקול כלה קול אמרים הודו
את יהוה צבאות כי טוב יהוה כי לעולם חסדו ומבאים תודה בית יהוה כי אשיב את
שבות הארץ ההוא כבראשנה אמר יהוה ¹² כה אמר יהוה עוד יהיה במקום הזה
החרב ובכל עריו נוה רעים מרבצים צאן ¹³ בערי ההר ובערי השפלה ובערי
הנגב ובארץ בנימן ובסביבי ירושלם ובערי יהודה עד תעברנה הצאן על ידי
מונה אמר יהוה

JEREMIAH 34 (= LXX 41)

¹ הדבר אשר היה אל ירמיהו מאת יהוה ונבוכדנאצר מלך בבל וכל חילו וכל ארץ
ממשלתו נלחמים על ירושלם ועל כל ערי יהודה לאמר ² כה אמר יהוה הלך אל
צדקיהו מלך יהודה ואמרת אליו כה אמר יהוה הנתן הנתן תנתן העיר הזאת ביד מלך
בבל ולכדה ושרפה באש ³ ואתה לא תמלט מידו ותפש תתפש ובידו תנתן ועיניך את
עיניו תראינה ובבל תבוא ⁴ אך שמע דבר יהוה צדקיהו מלך יהודה כה אמר יהוה
⁵ בשלום תמות וכמשרפות אבותיך המלכים הראשנים אשר היו לפניך כן ישרפו
לך והוי אדון יספדו לך כי דבר אני דברתי נאם יהוה ⁶ וידבר ירמיהו אל המלך
צדקיהו את כל הדברים האלה בירושלם ⁷ וחיל מלך בבל נלחמים על ירושלם ועל
ערי יהודה אל לכיש ואל עזקה כי הנה נשארו בערי יהודה ערי מבצר ⁸ הדבר אשר
היה אל ירמיהו מאת יהוה אחרי כרת המלך צדקיהו ברית את העם לקרא דרור
⁹ לשלח איש את עבדו ואיש את שפחתו העברי והעבריה חפשים לבלתי עבד איש
מיהודה ¹⁰ וישובו כל השרים וכל העם אשר באו בברית לשלח איש את עבדו ואיש
את שפחתו ¹¹ ויכבשום לעבדים ולשפחות ¹² ויהי דבר יהוה אל ירמיהו לאמר ¹³
כה אמר יהוה אנכי כרתי ברית את אבותיכם ביום הוצאי אותם מארץ מצרים מבית
עבדים לאמר ¹⁴ מקץ שש שנים תשלח את אחיך העברי אשר ימכר לך ועבדך שש
שנים ושלחתו חפשי ולא שמעו אלי ולא הטו את אזנם ¹⁵ וישבו היום לעשות את הישר
בעיני לקרא דרור איש לרעהו ויכרתו ברית לפני בבית אשר נקרא שמי עליו ¹⁶

ותשבו ותחללו את שמי להשיב איש את עבדו ואיש את שפחתו אשר שלחתם חפשים
לנפשם לכם לעבדים ולשפחות ¹⁷ לכן כה אמר יהוה אתם לא שמעתם אלי לקרא
דרור איש לרעהו הנני קרא דרור לכם אל החרב ואל הדבר ואל הרעב ונתתי
אתכם לזועה לכל ממלכות הארץ ¹⁸ ונתתי את האנשים העברים את ברתי אשר לא
הקימו את ברתי אשר כרתו לפני העגל אשר עשו לעבדו ¹⁹ שרי יהודה והסרסים
והכהנים והעם ²⁰ ונתתי אותם לאיביהם והיתה נבלתם למאכל לעוף השמים ולבהמת
הארץ ²¹ ואת צדקיהו מלך יהודה ואת שריהם אתן ביד איביהם וחיל מלך בבל
להעלים מעליהם ²² הנני מצוה נאם יהוה והשבתים אל הארץ הזאת ונלחמו עליה
ולכדוה ושרפה באש ואת ערי יהודה ונתתי שממה מאין ישב

JEREMIAH 35 (LXX 42)

¹ הדבר אשר היה אל ירמיהו מאת יהוה בימי יהויקים מלך יהודה לאמר ² הלוך
אל בית הרכבים והבאותם בית יהוה אל אחת הלשכות והשקית אותם יין ³ ואקח את
יאזניה בן ירמיהו בן חבצניה ואת אחיו ואת בניו ואת כל בית הרכבים ⁴ ואבא אתם
בית יהוה אל לשכת בני חנן בן גדליה איש האלהים אשר אצל לשכת השרים אשר
ממעל ללשכת מעשיהו בן שלם שמר הסף ⁵ ואתן לפניהם גביע יין וכסות ואמר שתו
יין ⁶ ויאמרו לא נשתה יין כי יונדב בן רכב אבינו צוה עלינו לאמר לא תשתו יין אתם
ובניהם עד עולם ⁷ ובית לא תבנו וזרע לא תזרעו וכרם לא יהיה לכם כי באהלים
תשבו כל ימיכם למען תחיו ימים רבים על האדמה אשר אתם גרים שם ⁸ ונשמע
בקול יונדב אבינו לבלתי שתות יין כל ימינו אנחנו ונשינו ובנינו ובנתינו ⁹ ולבלתי
בנות בתים לשבת שם וכרם ושדה וזרע לא היה לנו ¹⁰ ונשב באהלים ונשמע ונעש
ככל אשר צונו יונדב אבינו ¹¹ ויהי בעלות נבוכדנאצר על הארץ ונאמר באו ונבוא
ירושלם מפני חיל הכשדים ומפני חיל אשור ונשב שם ¹² ויהי דבר יהוה אלי לאמר
¹³ כה אמר יהוה הלך ואמרת לאיש יהודה וליושבי ירושלם הלוא תקחו מוסר לשמע
אל דברי ¹⁴ הקימו בני יונדב בן רכב את הדבר אשר צוה את בניו לבלתי שתות
יין ולא שתו ואנכי דברתי אליכם השכם ודבר ולא שמעתם ¹⁵ ואשלח אליכם את
עבדי הנבאים לאמר שבו נא איש מדרכו הרעה והיטיבו מעלליכם ואל תלכו אחרי
אלהים אחרים לעבדם ושבו אל האדמה אשר נתתי לכם ולאבותיכם ולא הטיתם
את אזניכם ולא שמעתם ¹⁶ והקימו בני יונדב בן רכב את מצות אביהם והעם הזה
לא שמעו אלי ¹⁷ לכן כה אמר יהוה הנני מביא אל יהודה ואל יושבי ירושלם את
כל הרעה אשר דברתי עליהם ¹⁸ לכן כה אמר יהוה יען אשר שמעו בני יונדב בן
רכב את מצות אביהם לעשות כאשר צום אביהם ¹⁹ לא יכרת איש לבני יונדב בן
רכב עמד לפני כל ימי הארץ

JEREMIAH 36 (= LXX 43)

¹ בשנה הרביעית ליהויקים בן יאשיהו מלך יהודה היה הדבר הזה אל ירמיהו מאת יהוה לאמר ² קח
לך מגלת ספר וכתבת אליה את כל הדברים אשר דברתי אליך על ירושלם ועל
יהודה ועל כל הגוים מיום דברתי אליך מימי יאשיהו מלך יהודה ועד היום הזה
³ אולי ישמעו בית יהודה את כל הרעה אשר אנכי חשב לעשות להם למען ישובו
מדרכם הרעה וסלחתי לעונם ולחטאתם ⁴ ויקרא ירמיהו את ברוך בן נריה ויכתב
מפי ירמיהו את כל דברי יהוה אשר דבר אליו על מגלת ספר ⁵ ויצוה ירמיהו את
ברוך לאמר אני עצור לא אוכל לבוא בית יהוה ⁶ וקראת במגלה הזאת באזני העם

בית יהוה ביום צום וגם באזני כל יהודה הבאים מעריהם תקראם [7] אולי תפל תחנתם
לפני יהוה וישבו מדרכם הרעה כי גדול האף וחמת יהוה אשר דבר אל העם הזה [8]
ויעש ברוך ככל אשר צוהו ירמיהו לקרא בספר דברי יהוה בית יהוה [9] ויהי בשנה
השמנית למלך יהויקים בחדש התשעי קראו צום לפני יהוה כל העם בירושלם ובית
יהודה [10] ויקרא ברוך בספר את דברי ירמיהו בית יהוה בלשכת גמריהו בן שפן
הספר בחצר העליון פתח שער בית יהוה החדש באזני כל העם [11] וישמע מכיהו בן
גמריהו בן שפן את כל דברי יהוה מעל הספר [12] וירד בית המלך על לשכת הספר
והנה שם כל השרים יושבים אלישמע הספר ודליהו בן שמעיהו ויונתן בן עכבור
וגמריהו בן שפן וצדקיהו בן חנניהו וכל השרים [13] ויגד להם מכיהו את כל הדברים
אשר שמע בקרא ברוך באזני העם [14] וישלחו כל השרים אל ברוך בן נריה את
יהודי בן נתניהו בן שלמיהו בן כושי לאמר המגלה אשר קראת בה באזני העם קחנה
בידך ולך ויקח ברוך את המגלה וירד אליהם [15] ויאמרו אליו שב נא וקרא באזנינו
ויקרא ברוך [16] ויהי כשמעם את כל הדברים נועצו איש אל רעהו ויאמרו הגיד נגיד
למלך את כל הדברים האלה [17] ואת ברוך שאלו לאמר מאין כתבת את כל הדברים
האלה [18] ויאמר ברוך מפיו יקרא אלי ירמיהו את כל הדברים האלה ואני כתב על
ספר [19] ויאמרו אל ברוך לך הסתר אתה וירמיהו איש אל ידע איפה אתם [20] ויבאו
אל המלך חצרה ואת המגלה הפקדו בלשכת אלישמע ויגידו למלך את כל הדברים
[21] וישלח המלך את יהודי לקחת את המגלה ויקחה מלשכת אלישמע ויקרא יהודי
באזני המלך ובאזני כל השרים העמדים על המלך [22] והמלך יושב בית החרף ואח
אש לפניו [23] ויהי כקרוא יהודי שלש דלתות וארבעה יקרעה בתער הספר והשלך
אל האש אשר אל האח עד תם כל המגלה על האש אשר על האח [24] ולא פחדו ולא
קרעו את בגדיהם המלך ועבדיו השמעים את כל הדברים האלה [25] וגם אלנתן וגדליהו
וגמריהו הפגעו במלך לבלתי שרף את המגלה [26] ויצוה המלך את ירחמאל בן המלך
ואת שריהו בן עזריאל לקחת את ברוך ואת ירמיהו ויסתרו [27] ויהי דבר יהוה אל
ירמיהו אחרי שרף המלך את המגלה ואת כל הדברים אשר כתב ברוך מפי ירמיהו
לאמר [28] שוב קח מגלה אחרת וכתב את כל הדברים אשר היו על המגלה הזאת אשר שרף
המלך יהויקים [29] ותאמר כה אמר יהוה אתה שרפת את המגלה הזאת לאמר מדוע
כתבת עליה לאמר בא יבוא מלך בבל והשחית את הארץ הזאת והשבית ממנה אדם
ובהמה [30] לכן כה אמר יהוה על יהויקים מלך יהודה לא יהיה לו יושב על כסא
דוד ונבלתו תהיה משלכת לחרב ביום ולקרח בלילה [31] ופקדתי עליו ועל זרעו ועל
עבדיו והבאתי עליהם ועל ישבי ירושלם ואל ארץ יהודה את כל הרעה אשר דברתי
אליהם ולא שמעו [32] ויקח ברוך מגלה אחרת ויכתב עליה מפי ירמיהו את כל דברי
הספר אשר שרף יהויקים ועוד נוסף עליהם דברים רבים כהמה

JEREMIAH 37 (= LXX 44)

[1] וימלך צדקיהו בן יאשיהו תחת יהויכים אשר המליך נבוכדנאצר ביהודה [2] ולא
שמע הוא ועבדיו ועם הארץ אל דברי יהוה אשר דבר ביד ירמיהו [3] וישלח המלך
צדקיהו את יהוכל בן שלמיה ואת צפניהו בן מעשיה הכהן אל ירמיהו לאמר התפלל
נא בעדנו אל יהוה [4] וירמיהו בא ויצא בתוך העיר ולא נתנו אתו בית הכלוא [5] וחיל
פרעה יצא ממצרים וישמעו הכשדים את שמעם ויעלו מעל ירושלם [6] ויהי דבר יהוה
אל ירמיהו לאמר [7] כה אמר יהוה כה תאמר אל מלך יהודה השלח אליך לדרשני
הנה חיל פרעה היצא לכם לעזרה שב לארץ מצרים [8] ושבו הכשדים ונלחמו על

העיר הזאת ולכדה ושרפה באש 9 כי כה אמר יהוה אל תשאו נפשתיכם לאמר הלך
ילכו מעלינו הכשדים כי לא ילכו 10 ואם הכיתם כל חיל כשדים הנלחמים אתכם
ונשארו בם אנשים מדקרים איש במקומו יקומו ושרפו את העיר הזאת באש 11 ויהי
בהעלות חיל הכשדים מעל ירושלם מפני חיל פרעה 12 ויצא ירמיהו מירושלם
ללכת אל ארץ בנימן לחלק משם בתוך העם 13 ויהי הוא בשער בנימן ושם בעל
פקדתו שריה בן שלמיה בן חנניה ויתפש את ירמיהו לאמר אל הכשדים אתה נפל
14 ויאמר שקר אינני נפל על הכשדים ולא שמע אליו ויתפש שריה בירמיהו ויבאהו
אל השרים 15 ויקצפו השרים על ירמיהו והכו אתו ויתנו אותו בית יהונתן הספר כי
אתו עשו לבית הכלא 16 ויבא ירמיהו אל בית הבור ואל החרת וישב שם ימים רבים
17 וישלח צדקיהו ויקראהו וישאלהו המלך בסתר לאמר היש דבר מאת יהוה ויאמר
יש ביד מלך בבל תנתן 18 ויאמר ירמיהו אל המלך מה חטאתי לך ולעבדיך ולעם
הזה כי נתת אותי אל בית הכלא 19 ואיה נביאיכם אשר נבאו לכם לאמר לא יבא
מלך בבל על הארץ הזאת 20 ועתה אדני המלך תפל נא תחנתי לפניך ומה תשבני
בית יהונתן הספר ולא אמות שם 21 ויצוה המלך ויפקדו אתו בחצר המטרה ונתן לו
ככר לחם ליום מחוץ האפים עד תם הלחם מן העיר וישב ירמיהו בחצר המטרה

JEREMIAH 38 (= LXX 45)

1 וישמע שפטיה בן מתן וגדליהו בן פשחור ויוכל בן שלמיהו את הדברים אשר
ירמיהו מדבר אל העם לאמר 2 כה אמר יהוה הישב בעיר הזאת ימות בחרב וברעב
ובדבר והיצא אל הכשדים יחיה והיתה נפשו לשלל וחי 3 כי כה אמר יהוה הנתן תנתן העיר
הזאת ביד חיל מלך בבל ולכדה 4 ויאמרו אל המלך יומת נא את האיש הזה כי
הוא מרפא את ידי אנשי המלחמה הנשארים בעיר ואת ידי כל העם לדבר אליהם
כדברים האלה כי האיש הזה איננו דרש לשלום לעם הזה כי אם לרעה 5 ויאמר
המלך הנה הוא בידכם כי אין המלך יכול להם 6 וישלכו אתו אל בור מלכיהו בן
המלך אשר בחצר המטרה וישלחו אתו אל הבור ובבור אין מים כי אם טיט ויטבע
בטיט 7 וישמע עבד מלך הכושי והוא בבית המלך כי נתנו את ירמיהו אל הבור
והמלך יושב בשער בנימן 8 ויצא אליו וידבר אל המלך ויאמר 9 הרעות אשר עשית
להמית את האיש הזה מפני הרעב כי אין עוד הלחם בעיר 10 ויצוה המלך את עבד
מלך לאמר קח בידך מזה שלשים אנשים והעלית אתו מן הבור פן ימות 11 ויקח
עבד מלך את האנשים ויבא בית המלך אל תחת האוצר ויקח משם בלוי סחבות
ובלוי מלחים וישלחם אל ירמיהו אל הבור 12 ויאמר אלה שים נא מתחת לחבלים
ויעש ירמיהו כן 13 וימשכו אתו בחבלים ויעלו אתו מן הבור וישב ירמיהו בחצר
המטרה 14 וישלח המלך ויקראהו אליו אל מבוא השלישי אשר בבית יהוה ויאמר
המלך אליו שאל אני אתך דבר ואל תכחד ממני דבר 15 ויאמר ירמיהו אל המלך
כי אגיד לך הלוא המת תמיתני וכי איעצך לא תשמע אלי 16 וישבע המלך אליו
לאמר חי יהוה אשר עשה לנו את הנפש הזאת אם אמיתך ואם אתנך ביד האנשים
האלה 17 ויאמר ירמיהו אליו כה אמר יהוה אם יצא תצא אל שרי מלך בבל וחיתה
נפשך והעיר הזאת לא תשרף באש וחיתה אתה וביתך 18 ואם לא תצא ונתנה העיר
הזאת ביד הכשדים ושרפוה באש ואתה לא תמלט 19 ויאמר המלך אל ירמיהו אני
דאג את היהודים אשר נפלו אל הכשדים פן יתנו אתי בידם והתעללו בי 20 ויאמר
ירמיהו לא יתנו שמע נא בקול יהוה אשר אני דבר אליך וייטב לך ותחי נפשך 21 ואם
מאן אתה לצאת זה הדבר אשר הראני יהוה 22 והנה כל הנשים אשר נשארו בבית

מלך יהודה מוצאות אל שרי מלך בבל והנה אמרות הסיתוך ויכלו לך אנשי שלמך
והטבעו בבץ רגליך נסגו אחור ²³ ואת נשיך ואת בניך מוצאים אל הכשדים ואתה לא
תמלט כי ביד מלך בבל תתפש ואת העיר הזאת תשרף ²⁴ ויאמר אליו המלך איש
אל ידע בדברים האלה ולא תמות ²⁵ וכי ישמעו השרים כי דברתי אתך ובאו אליך
ואמרו אליך הגידה נא לנו מה דבר אליך המלך אל תכחד ממנו ולא נמיתך ומה
דבר אליך המלך ²⁶ ואמרת אליהם מפיל אני תחנתי לעיני המלך לבלתי השיבני
בית יהונתן למות שם ²⁷ ויבאו כל השרים אל ירמיהו וישאלו אתו ויגד להם ככל
הדברים האלה אשר צוהו המלך ויחרשו כי לא נשמע דבר יהוה ²⁸ וישב ירמיהו
בחצר המטרה עד יום אשר נלכדה ירושלם

JEREMIAH 39 (= LXX 46)

¹ ויהי בשנה התשעית לצדקיהו מלך יהודה בחדש העשרי בא נבוכדנאצר מלך
בבל וכל חילו אל ירושלם ויצרו עליה ² ובעשתי עשרה שנה לצדקיהו בחדש
הרביעי בתשעה לחדש הבקעה העיר ³ ויבאו כל שרי מלך בבל וישבו בשער התוך
נרגלשראצר סמגר נבושרסכים נבוסריס נרגלשראצר רבמג וכל שארית שרי מלך
בבל ¹⁴ וישלחו ויקחו את ירמיהו מחצר המטרה ויתנו אתו אל גדליהו בן אחיקם בן
שפן ויוצאהו וישב בתוך העם ¹⁵ ואל ירמיהו היה דבר יהוה בחצר המטרה לאמר
¹⁶ הלוך ואמרת לעבד מלך הכושי כה אמר יהוה אלהי ישראל הנני מביא את דברי
אל העיר הזאת לרעה ולא לטובה ¹⁷ והצלתיך ביום ההוא ולא אתנך ביד האנשים
אשר אתה יגור מפניהם ¹⁸ כי מלט אמלטך ובחרב לא תפל והיתה נפשך לשלל כי
בטחת בי נאם יהוה

JEREMIAH 40 (= LXX 47)

¹ הדבר אשר היה מאת יהוה אל ירמיהו אחר שלח אתו נבוזראדן רב טבחים מן
הרמה בקחתו אתו באזקים בתוך גלות יהודה המגלים בבלה ² ויקח אתו רב טבחים
ויאמר אליו יהוה אלהיך דבר את הרעה הזאת אל המקום הזה ³ ויעש יהוה כי
חטאתם לו ולא שמעתם בקולו ⁴ הנה פתחתיך מן האזקים אשר על ידיך אם טוב
בעיניך לבוא אתי בבל בא ואשים עיני עליך ⁵ ואם לא שוב ושבה אל גדליה בן
אחיקם בן שפן אשר הפקיד מלך בבל בארץ יהודה ושב אתו בתוך העם בארץ
יהודה אל כל הטוב בעיניך ללכת לך ויתן לו רב טבחים משאת וישלחהו ⁶ ויבא
אל גדליה המצפתה וישב בתוך העם הנשארים בארץ ⁷ וישמעו כל שרי החילים
אשר בשדה המה ואנשיהם כי הפקיד מלך בבל את גדליהו בארץ וכי הפקיד אתו
אנשים ונשיהם אשר לא הגלה בבלה ⁸ ויבא אל גדליהו המצפתה ישמעאל בן נתניהו
ויוחנן בן קרח ושריה בן תנחמת ובני עופי הנטפתי ויזניהו בן המעכתי המה ואנשיהם
⁹ וישבע להם גדליהו ולאנשיהם לאמר אל תיראו מעבדי הכשדים שבו בארץ ועבדו
את מלך בבל וייטב לכם ¹⁰ ואני הנני ישב לפניכם במצפה לעמד לפני הכשדים אשר
יבאו אלינו ואתם אספו יין וקיץ ושמן ושמו בכליכם ושבו בערים אשר תפשתם ¹¹
וכל היהודים אשר במואב ובבני עמון ובאדום ואשר בכל הארץ שמעו כי נתן מלך
בבל שארית ליהודה וכי הפקיד עליהם את גדליהו בן אחיקם ¹² ויבאו אל גדליהו
ארץ יהודה המצפתה ויאספו יין וקיץ הרבה מאד ¹³ ויוחנן בן קרח וכל שרי החילים
אשר בשדת באו אל גדליהו המצפתה ¹⁴ ויאמרו אליו הידע תדע כי בעליס מלך בני
עמון שלח אליך את ישמעאל את להכתך נפש ולא האמן להם גדליהו ¹⁵ ויוחנן אמר אל

גדליהו בסתר במצפה אלכה נא ואכה את ישמעאל ואיש לא ידע למה יככה נפש
ונפוץ כל יהודה הנקבצים אליך ואבדה שארית יהודה 16 ויאמר גדליהו אל יוחנן אל
תעש את הדבר הזה כי שקר אתה דבר אל ישמעאל

JEREMIAH 41 (= LXX 48)

1 ויהי בחדש השביעי בא ישמעאל בן נתניה בן אלעשה מזרע המלוכה ועשרה אנשים
אתו אל גדליהו המצפתה ויאכלו שם לחם יחדו 2 ויקם ישמעאל ועשרת האנשים
אשר היו אתו ויכו את גדליהו אשר הפקיד מלך בבל בארץ 3 ואת כל היהודים
אשר היו אתו במצפה ואת כל הכשדים אשר נמצאו שם 4 ויהי ביום השני להמית
את גדליהו ואיש לא ידע 5 ויבאו אנשים משכם ומשלם ומשמרון שמנים איש מגלחי
זקן וקרעי בגדים ומתגדדים ומנחה ולבונה בידם להביא בית יהוה 6 ויצא לקראתם
ישמעאל המה הלך ובכה ויאמר באו אל גדליהו 7 ויהי כבואם אל תוך העיר וישחטם
אל הבור 8 ועשרה אנשים נמצאו שם ויאמרו אל ישמעאל אל תמתנו כי יש לנו
מטמנים בשדה חטים ושערים דבש ושמן ויחדל ולא המיתם בתוך אחיהם 9 והבור
אשר השליך שם ישמעאל את כל אשר הכה בור גדול הוא אשר עשה המלך אסא
מפני בעשא מלך ישראל אתו מלא ישמעאל חללים 10 וישב ישמעאל את כל העם
הנשארים במצפה ואת בנות המלך אשר הפקיד רב טבחים את גדליהו בן אחיקם
וילך לעבר בני עמון 11 וישמע יוחנן בן קרח וכל שרי החילים אשר אתו את כל
הרעה אשר עשה ישמעאל 12 ויקחו את כל חילם וילכו להלחם עמו וימצאו אתו
אל מים רבים בגבעון 13 ויהי כראות כל העם אשר את ישמעאל את יוחנן ואת שרי
החילים אשר אתו 14 וישבו אל יוחנן 15 וישמעאל נמלט בשמנה אנשים וילך אל בני
עמון 16 ויקח יוחנן וכל שרי החילים אשר אתו את כל שארית העם אשר השיב מאת
ישמעאל גברים אנשי המלחמה ונשים וטף וסרסים אשר השיב מגבעון 17 וילכו וישבו
בגברות כמהם אשר אצל בית לחם ללכת למצרים 18 מפני הכשדים כי יראו מפניהם
כי הכה ישמעאל את גדליהו אשר הפקיד מלך בבל בארץ

JEREMIAH 42 (= LXX 49)

1 ויגשו כל שרי החילים ויוחנן ועזריה בן מעשיה וכל העם מקטן ועד גדול 2 אל ירמיהו
הנביא ויאמרו אליו תפל נא תחנתנו לפניך והתפלל אל יהוה אלהיך בעד כל השארית
הזאת כי נשארנו מעט מהרבה כאשר עיניך ראות 3 ויגד לנו יהוה אלהיך את הדרך
אשר נלך בה ואת הדבר אשר נעשה 4 ויאמר אליהם ירמיהו שמעתי הנני מתפלל אל
יהוה אלהיכם כדבריכם והיה הדבר אשר יענה יהוה אתכם אגיד לכם לא אמנע מכם דבר 5
והמה אמרו אל ירמיהו יהי יהוה בנו לעד אמת ונאמן אם לא ככל הדבר אשר ישלחך
יהוה אלינו כן נעשה 6 ואם טוב ואם רע בקול יהוה אלהינו אשר אנו שלחים אתך אליו
נשמע למען אשר ייטב לנו כי נשמע בקול יהוה אלהינו 7 ויהי מקץ עשרת ימים ויהי
דבר יהוה אל ירמיהו 8 ויקרא אל יוחנן ואל שרי החילים ולכל העם למקטן ועד גדול
9 ויאמר אליהם כה אמר יהוה 10 אם ישוב תשבו בארץ הזאת ובניתי אתכם ולא אהרס
ונטעתי אתכם ולא אתוש כי נחמתי אל הרעה אשר עשיתי לכם 11 אל תיראו מפני מלך
בבל אשר אתם יראים מפניו אל תיראו נאם יהוה כי אתכם אני להושיע אתכם ולהציל
אתכם מידו 12 ואתן לכם רחמים ורחמתי אתכם והשיבותי אתכם אל אדמתכם 13 ואם
אמרים אתם לא נשב בארץ הזאת לבלתי שמע בקול יהוה 14 כי ארץ מצרים נבוא
ולא נראה מלחמה וקול שופר לא נשמע וללחם לא נרעב ושם נשב 15 לכן שמעו דבר

יהוה כה אמר יהוה אם אתם תשמון פניכם למצרים ובאתם שם לגור 16 והיה החרב
אשר יראים ממנה תשיג אתכם במצרים והרעב אשר אתם דאגים ממנו ידבק אחריכם
במצרים ושם תמתו 17 ויהיו כל האנשים וכל הזרים אשר שמו את פניהם לארץ מצרים
לגור שם ימותו בחרב וברעב ולא יהיה להם פליט מפני הרעה אשר אני מביא עליהם
18 כי כה אמר יהוה כאשר נתך חמתי על ישבי ירושלם כן תתך חמתי עליכם בבאכם
מצרים והייתם לשמה ולקללה ולחרפה ולא תראו עוד את המקום הזה 19 אשר
דבר יהוה עליכם שארית יהודה אל תבאו מצרים ועתה ידע תדעו 20 כי הרעתם
בנפשותיכם שלחתם אתי לאמר התפלל בעדנו אל יהוה וככל אשר יאמר יהוה אליך
ועשינו 21 ולא שמעתם בקול יהוה אשר שלחני אליכם 22 ועתה בחרב וברעב תמותו
במקום אשר חפצתם לבוא לגור שם

JEREMIAH 43 (= LXX 50)

1 ויהי ככלות ירמיהו לדבר אל העם את כל דברי יהוה אשר שלחו יהוה אליהם את
כל הדברים האלה 2 ויאמר עזריה בן מעשיה ויוחנן בן קרח וכל האנשים האמרים
אל ירמיהו לאמר שקר לא שלחך יהוה אלינו לאמר לא תבאו מצרים לגור שם 3
כי ברוך בן נריה מסית אתך בנו למען תת אתנו ביד הכשדים להמית אתנו ולהגלות
אתנו בבל 4 ולא שמע יוחנן וכל שרי החילים וכל העם בקול יהוה לשבת בארץ
יהודה 5 ויקח יוחנן וכל שרי החילים את כל שארית יהודה אשר שבו לגור בארץ 6
את הגברים ואת הנשים ואת הטף ואת בנות המלך ואת הנפש אשר הניח נבוזראדן
את גדליהו בן אחיקם ואת ירמיהו הנביא ואת ברוך בן נריהו 7 ויבאו מצרים כי
לא שמעו בקול יהוה ויבאו תחפנחס 8 ויהי דבר יהוה אל ירמיהו בתחפנחס לאמר
9 קח לך אבנים גדלות וטמנתם בפתח בית פרעה בתחפנחס לעיני אנשי אנשי יהודה 10
ואמרת כה אמר יהוה הנני שלח ולקחתי את נבוכדנאצר מלך בבל ושם את כסאו
ממעל לאבנים האלה אשר טמנת ונשא שריונו עליהם 11 ובא והכה את ארץ מצרים
אשר למות למות ואשר לשבי לשבי ואשר לחרב לחרב 12 והצית אש בבתי אלהיהם
ושרפם ושבם ועטה את ארץ מצרים כאשר יעטה רעה את בגדו ויצא בשלום 13 ושבר
את מצבות עיר השמש אשר בארץ ואת בתיהם ישרף באש

JEREMIAH 44 (= LXX 51)

1 הדבר אשר היה אל ירמיהו אל כל היהודים הישבים במצרים והישבים במגדל
ובתחפנחס ובארץ פתרוס לאמר 2 כה אמר יהוה אלהי ישראל אתם ראיתם את כל
הרעה אשר הבאתי על ירושלם ועל ערי יהודה והנם חרבה מאין יושב 3 מפני רעתם
אשר עשו להכעסני ללכת לקטר לאלהים אחרים אשר לא ידעתם 4 ואשלח אליכם
את עבדי הנביאים השכים ושלח לאמר אל נא תעשו את דבר התעבה הזאת אשר
שנאתי 5 ולא שמעו ולא הטו את אזנם לשוב מרעתם לבלתי קטר לאלהים אחרים
6 ותתך חמתי ואפי ותבער בערי יהודה ובחצות ירושלם ותהיינה לחרבה ולשממה
כיום הזה 7 ועתה כה אמר יהוה צבאות למה אתם עשים רעה גדולה אל נפשתכם
להכרית לכם איש ואשה עולל ויונק מתוך יהודה לבלתי הותיר לכם שארית 8
להכעסני במעשי ידיכם לקטר לאלהים אחרים בארץ מצרים אשר אתם באים לגור
שם למען הכרית לכם ולמען היותכם לקללה ולחרפה בגויי הארץ 9 השכחתם את
רעות אבותיכם ואת רעות מלכי יהודה ואת רעות שריכם ואת רעת נשיכם אשר עשו
בארץ יהודה ובחצות ירושלם 10 ולא נכלאו עד היום הזה ולא הלכו בתקתי אשר

נתתי לפני אבותיהם ¹¹ לכן כה אמר יהוה הנני שם פני ¹² להכרית את כל השארית
אשר במצרים ונפלו בחרב וברעב יתמו מקטן ועד גדול והיו לחרפה ולשמה
ולקללה ¹³ ופקדתי על היושבים במצרים כאשר פקדתי על ירושלם בחרב וברעב
¹⁴ ולא יהיה פליט לשארית יהודה הגרים בארץ מצרים לשוב ארץ יהודה אשר
המה מנשאים את נפשם לשוב שם לא ישובו כי אם פלטים ¹⁵ ויענו את ירמיהו כל
האנשים הידעים כי מקטרות נשיהם לאלהים אחרים וכל הנשים קהל גדול וכל העם
הישבים בארץ מצרים בפתרוס לאמר ¹⁶ הדבר אשר דברת אלינו בשם יהוה איננו
שמעים אליך ¹⁷ כי עשה נעשה את כל הדבר אשר יצא מפינו לקטר למלכת השמים
ולהסיך לה נסכים כאשר עשינו אנחנו ואבתינו ומלכינו ושרינו בערי יהודה ובחצות
ירושלם ונשבע לחם ונהיה טובים ורעה לא ראינו ¹⁸ ומן אז חדלנו לקטר למלכת
השמים חסרנו כל ובחרב וברעב תמנו ¹⁹ וכי אנחנו מקטרים למלכת השמים ולהסך
לה נסכים המבלעדי אנשינו עשינו לה כונים והסך לה נסכים ²⁰ ויאמר ירמיהו אל
כל העם על הגברים ועל הנשים ועל כל העם הענים אתו דברים לאמר ²¹ הלוא
את הקטר אשר קטרתם בערי יהודה ובחצות ירושלם אתם ואבותיכם ומלכיכם
ושריכם ועם הארץ זכר יהוה ותעלה על לבו ²² ולא יוכל יהוה עוד לשאת מפני רע
מעלליכם מפני התועבת אשר עשיתם ותהי ארצכם לחרבה ולשמה ולקללה כהיום
הזה ²³ מפני אשר קטרתם ואשר חטאתם ליהוה ולא שמעתם בקול יהוה ובחקתיו
ובתרתו ובעדותיו לא הלכתם ותקרא אתכם הרעה הזאת ²⁴ ויאמר ירמיהו אל העם
ואל הנשים שמעו דבר יהוה ²⁵ כה אמר יהוה אלהי ישראל אתנה הנשים בפיכן
דברתן ובידיכן מלאתן לאמר עשה נעשה את נדרינו אשר נדרנו לקטר למלכת
השמים ולהסך לה נסכים הקים תקימנה את נדריכן ועשה תעשינה ²⁶ לכן שמעו דבר
יהוה כל יהודה הישבים בארץ מצרים הנני נשבעתי בשמי הגדול אמר יהוה אם יהיה
עוד שמי בפי כל יהודה אמר חי יהוה בכל ארץ מצרים ²⁷ כי הנני שקד עליהם
לרעה ולא לטובה ותמו כל יהודה הישבים בארץ מצרים בחרב וברעב עד כלותם
²⁸ ופליטי חרב ישבון ארץ יהודה מתי מספר וידעו שארית יהודה הבאים לארץ
מצרים לגור שם דבר מי יקום ²⁹ וזאת לכם האות כי פקד אני עליכם לרעה ³⁰ כה
אמר יהוה הנני נתן חפרע מלך מצרים ביד איבו וביד מבקשי נפשו כאשר נתתי את
צדקיהו מלך יהודה ביד נבוכדנאצר מלך בבל איבו ומבקש נפשו

JEREMIAH 45:1–5 (= LXX 51:31–35)

^{1 (31)} הדבר אשר דבר ירמיהו הנביא אל ברוך בן נריה בכתבו את הדברים האלה
על ספר מפי ירמיהו בשנה הרבעית ליהויקים בן יאשיהו מלך יהודה ^{2 (32)} כה אמר
יהוה עליך ברוך ^{3 (33)} כי אמרת אוי לי אוי לי כי יסף יהוה יגון על מכאבי יגעתי
באנחת מנוחה לא מצאתי ^{4 (34)} אמר אליו כה אמר יהוה הנה אשר בניתי אני הרס
ואת אשר נטעתי אני נתש ^{5 (35)} ואתה תבקש לך גדלות אל תבקש כי הנני מביא
רעה על כל בשר נאם יהוה ונתתי את נפשך לשלל על כל המקמות אשר תלך שם

JEREMIAH 52

¹ בן עשרים ואחת שנה צדקיהו במלכו ואחת עשרה שנה מלך בירושלם ושם אמו
חמיטל בת ירמיהו מלבנה ⁴ ויהי בשנה התשיעית למלכו בחדש העשירי בעשור
לחדש בא נבוכדנאצר מלך בבל וכל חילו על ירושלם ויחנו עליה ויבנו עליה דיק
סביב ⁵ ותבא העיר במצור עד עשתי עשרה שנה למלך צדקיהו ⁶ בתשעה לחדש

ויחזק הרעב בעיר ולא היה לחם לעם הארץ ⁷ ותבקע העיר וכל אנשי המלחמה
יצאו לילה דרך שער בין החמתים אשר על גן המלך והכשדים על העיר סביב
וילכו דרך הערבה ⁸ וירדפו חיל הכשדים אחרי המלך וישיגו אתו בעבר ירחו וכל
עבדיו נפצו מעליו ⁹ ויתפשו את המלך ויעלו אתו אל מלך בבל דבלתה וידבר אתו
משפט ¹⁰ וישחט מלך בבל את בני צדקיהו לעיניו ואת כל שרי יהודה שחט בדבלתה
¹¹ ואת עיני צדקיהו עור ויאסרהו בנחשתים ויבאהו מלך בבל בבלה ויתנהו בבית
רחים עד יום מותו ¹² ובחדש החמישי בעשור לחדש בא נבוזראדן רב טבחים עמד
לפני מלך בבל בירושלם ¹³ וישרף את בית יהוה ואת בית המלך ואת כל בתי העיר
ואת כל בית גדול שרף באש ¹⁴ ואת כל חמות ירושלם סביב נתצו חיל הכשדים
אשר את רב טבחים ¹⁶ ואת יתר העם השאיר רב טבחים לכרמים וליגבים ¹⁷ ואת
עמודי הנחשת אשר בבית יהוה ואת המכנות ואת ים הנחשת אשר בבית יהוה שברו
הכשדים וישאו את נחשתם ויביאו בבלה ¹⁸ ואת המסגרת ואת המזרקת ואת היעים
ואת כל כלי הנחשת אשר ישרתו בהם ¹⁹ ואת הספות ואת המזמרות ואת הסירות
ואת המנרות ואת המחתות ואת המנקיות אשר זהב זהב ואשר כסף כסף לקח רב
טבחים ²⁰ והעמודים שנים והים אחד והבקר שנים עשר נחשת תחת הים אשר עשה
המלך שלמה לבית יהוה לא היה משקל לנחשתם ²¹ והעמודים שלשים וחמש אמה
קומת העמד האחד וחוט שתים עשרה אמה יסבנו ועביו ארבע אצבעות סביב ²²
וכתרת עליהם נחשת וקומת הכתרת האחת חמש אמות ושבכה ורמונים על הכותרת
סביב הכל נחשת וכאלה לעמוד השני שמנה רמונים לאמה לשתים עשרה אמה ²³
ויהיו הרמנים תשעים וששה רוחה וכל הרמונים מאה על השבכה סביב ²⁴ ויקח רב
טבחים את כהן הראש ואת כהן המשנה ואת שלשת שמרי הסף ²⁵ וסריס אחד אשר
היה פקיד על אנשי המלחמה ושבעה אנשי שם פני המלך אשר נמצאו בעיר ואת ספר
הצבא המצבא את עם הארץ וששים איש מעם הארץ הנמצאים בתוך העיר ²⁶ ויקח
אותם נבוזראדן רב טבחים וילך אותם אל מלך בבל דבלתה ²⁷ ויך אותם מלך בבל
בדבלה בארץ חמת ³¹ ויהי בשלשים ושבע שנה לגלות יהויכן מלך יהודה בשנים
עשר חדש בעשרים וארבעה לחדש נשא אויל מרדך מלך בבל בשנת מלכו את ראש
יהויכין מלך יהודה ויצא אותו מבית הכלוא ³² וידבר אתו טבות ויתן את כסאו ממעל
לכסא(ות) המלכים אשר אתו בבבל ³³ ושנה את בגדי כלאו ואכל לחם תמיד לפניו
כל ימי חייו ³⁴ וארחתו לו נתנה תמיד מאת מלך בבל דבר יום ביומו עד יום מותו

BIBLIOGRAPHY

Abegg, Martin, Jr., Peter Flint, and Eugene Ulrich. *The Dead Sea Scrolls Bible*. San Francisco: HarperSanFrancisco, 1999.

Aejmelaeus, Anneli. "Jeremiah at the Turning Point of History: The Function of Jer. XXV 1–14 in the Book of Jeremiah." *Vetus Testamentum* 52 (2002): 459–82.

______. "Was Samuel Meant to Be a Nazirite? The First Chapter of Samuel and the Paradigm Shift in Textual Study of the Hebrew Bible." *Textus* 28 (2019): 1–20.

Allen, Leslie C. *Jeremiah: A Commentary*. Old Testament Library. Louisville: Westminster John Knox, 2008.

Alt, Albrecht. "Der Anteil des Königtum an der sozialen Entwicklung in der Reichen Israel and Judah." *Kirjath-Sepher* 3 (1959): 349–72.

Auerbach, Erich. *Mimesis: The Representation of Reality in Western Literature*. Translated by Willard R. Trask. 50th anniv. ed. Princeton, NJ: Princeton University Press, 2003.

Bacher, Wilhelm. *Die exegetische Terminologie der jüdischen Traditionsliteratur*. Hildesheim: Georg Olms, 1965.

BIBLIOGRAPHY

Bailey, Randall C. "Jeremiah: Fortified City, Bronze Walls, and Iron Pillar against the Whole Land." *Hebrew Studies* 57 (2016): 117–38.

Bar-Efrat, Shimon. *Narrative Art in the Bible*. Sheffield: Sheffield Academic, 1989. Reprint, London: T&T Clark, 2004.

Barr, James. *Comparative Philology and the Text of the Old Testament*. Oxford: Oxford University Press, 1968. Reprint, Winona Lake, IN: Eisenbrauns, 1987.

Bauer, Hans, and Pontus Leander. *Grammatik des Biblisch-Aramäischen*. Halle: Niemeyer, 1927. Reprint, Hildesheim: Georg Olms, 1995.

Baumgartner, Walter. *Die Klagegedichte des Jeremia*. Beihefte zur Zeitschrift für die alttestamentliche Wissenschaft 32. Giessen: Töppelmann, 1917.

Beckwith, Roger T. "Formation of the Hebrew Bible." In *Mikra: Text, Translation, Reading, and Interpretation of the Hebrew Bible in Ancient Judaism and Early Christianity*, eds. Martin Jan Mulder and Harry Sysling, 39–86. Philadelphia: Fortress, 1988. Reprint, Peabody, MA: Hendrickson, 2004.

Berlin, Adele. "Jeremiah 29:5–7: A Deuteronomic Allusion." *Hebrew Annual Review* 8 (1984): 3–11.

Bewer, Julius A. *A Critical and Exegetical Commentary on Obadiah and Joel*. International Critical Commentary. New York: Charles Scribner's Sons, 1911.

Bezzel, Hannes. "The Suffering of the Elect. Variations on a Theological Problem in Jer 15, 10–21." In *Prophecy in the Book of Jeremiah*, eds. Hans M. Barstad and Reinhard G. Kratz, 48–73. Beihefte zur Zeitschrift für die alttestamentliche Wissenschaft 288. Berlin: de Gruyter, 2009.

Birdsong, Shelley L. *The Last King(s) of Judah: Zedekiah and Sedekias in the Hebrew and Greek Versions of Jeremiah 37(44):1–40(47):6*. Tübingen: Mohr Siebeck, 2017.

Blenkinsopp, Joseph. *Prophecy and Canon: A Contribution to the Study of Jewish Origins*. Notre Dame, IN: University of Notre Dame Press, 1977.

Block, Daniel I. *The Book of Ezekiel: Chapters 25–48*. New International Commentary on the Old Testament. Grand Rapids: Eerdmans, 1997.

Blomberg, Craig L. *Matthew*. New American Commentary 22. Nashville: Broadman, 1992.

______. *Judges, Ruth*. New American Commentary 6. Nashville: Broadman & Holman, 1999.

Bodner, Keith. *After the Invasion: A Reading of Jeremiah 40–44*. Oxford: Oxford University Press, 2015.

Bogaert, P.-M. "Les trois forms de Jérémie 52 (MT, LXX, OL)." In *Tradition of the Text*, ed. G. J. Norton, S. Pisano, 1–17. Orbis biblicus et orientalis 109 (1991).

Bordreuil, Pierre, and Dennis Pardee. *A Manual of Ugaritic*. Linguistic Studies in Ancient West Semitic 3. Winona Lake, IN: Eisenbrauns, 2009.

Boyarin, Daniel. *Intertextuality and the Reading of Midrash*. Bloomington: Indiana University Press, 1990.

Bright, John. *Jeremiah*. Anchor Bible. Garden City, NY: Doubleday, 1965.

Brueggemann, Walter. *A Commentary on Jeremiah: Exile and Homecoming*. Grand Rapids: Eerdmans, 1998.

Bruns, Gerald. "Midrash and Allegory." In *The Literary Guide to the Bible*, eds. Frank Kermode and Robert Alter, 626–27. Cambridge, MA: Belknap, 1987.

Bullinger, E. W. *Figures of Speech Used in the Bible*. London: Eyre and Spottiswoode, 1898. Reprint, Grand Rapids: Baker, 1968.

Calvin, John. *Commentaries on the Book of the Prophet Jeremiah and the Lamentations*. Vols. 1–5. Translated by John Owen. Calvin's Commentaries IX–XI. Grand Rapids: Baker, 2005.

Carroll, Robert P. *Jeremiah: A Commentary*. Old Testament Library. Philadelphia: Westminster, 1986.

Chapman, Stephen B. *The Law and the Prophets: A Study in Old Testament Canon Formation*. Forschungen zum Alten Testament 27. Tübingen: Mohr Siebeck, 2000.

Childs, Brevard S. *The Book of Exodus: A Critical, Theological Commentary*. Old Testament Library. Louisville: Westminster John Knox, 1974.

______. *Introduction to the Old Testament as Scripture*. Philadelphia: Fortress, 1979.

______. *Isaiah: A Commentary*. Old Testament Library. Louisville: Westminster John Knox, 2000.

Clements, Ronald E. *Jeremiah*. Interpretation. Atlanta: John Knox, 1988.

Cowley, A. *Aramaic Papyri of the Fifth Century B.C.* Oxford: Clarendon, 1923.

DeRouchie, Jason S. "YHWH's Future Ingathering in Zephaniah 1:2." *Hebrew Studies* 59 (2018): 173–91.

Diamond, A. R. *The Confessions of Jeremiah in Context: Scenes of Prophetic Drama*. Journal for the Study of the Old Testament: Supplement Series 45. Sheffield: Sheffield Academic, 1987.

Doane, Sébastien, and Nathan Robert Mastnjak. "Echoes of Rachel's Weeping: Intertextuality and Trauma in Jer. 31:15." *Biblical Interpretation* 27 (2019): 413–35.

Driver, G. R. "Linguistic and Textual Problems: Jeremiah." *Jewish Quarterly Review* 28 (1938): 97–129.

Driver, S. R. *An Introduction to the Literature of the Old Testament*. New York: Charles Scribner's Sons, 1891.

______. *Notes on the Hebrew Text and the Topography of the Books of Samuel*. 2nd ed. Oxford: Oxford University Press, 1912. Reprint, Eugene, OR: Wipf & Stock, 2004.

Duhm, Bernhard. *Das Buch Jeremia*. Kurzer Hand-Commentar zum Alten Testament 11. Tübingen: Mohr Siebeck, 1901.

Eggleston, Chad L. *See and Read All These Words: The Concept of the Written in the Book of Jeremiah*. Siphrut: Literature and Theology of the Hebrew Scriptures 18. Winona Lake, IN: Eisenbrauns, 2016.

Ehrlich, A. B. *Randglossen zur Hebräischen Bibel. Textkritisches, Sprachliches und Sachliches*. Vol. 4, *Jesaiah, Jeremia*. Leipzig, 1912.

Eichrodt, Walther. *Theology of the Old Testament*. Vol. 2. Translated by J. A. Baker. Philadelphia: Westminster, 1967.

Eissfeldt, Otto. *The Old Testament: An Introduction*. Translated by Peter R. Ackroyd. New York: Harper and Row, 1965.

Elitzur, Yoel. "The Interface Between Language and Realia in the Preexilic Books of the Bible." *Hebrew Studies* 59 (2018): 129–47.

Ellis, E. Earle. "The Old Testament Canon in the Early Church." In *Mikra: Text, Translation, Reading, and Interpretation of the Hebrew Bible in Ancient Judaism and Early Christianity*, eds. Martin Jan Mulder and Harry Sysling, 653–90. Philadelphia: Fortress, 1988. Reprint, Peabody, MA: Hendrickson, 2004.

Emerton, J. A. "A Problem in the Hebrew Text of Jeremiah vi. 23 and l. 42." *Journal of Theological Studies* NS 23 (1972): 106–13.

Eppstein, Victor. "The Day of Yahweh in Jer 4:23–28." *Journal of Biblical Literature* 87 (1968): 93–97.

Evans, Craig A. "Jeremiah in Jesus and the New Testament." In *Jeremiah: Composition, Reception, and Interpretation*, eds. Jack R. Lundbom, Craig A. Evans, and Bradford A. Anderson, 303–19. Leiden: Brill, 2018.

Fettke, Tom, ed. *The Hymnal for Worship and Celebration*. Waco, TX: Word, 1986.

Fischer, Georg. "Jeremiah 52: A Test Case for Jer LXX." In *X Congress of the International Organization for Septuagint and Cognate Studies Oslo, 1998*, ed. Bernard A. Taylor, 38–48. Atlanta: SBL, 2001.

______. *Jeremiah Studies: From Text and Contexts to Theology.* Forschungen zum Alten Testament 139. Tübingen: Mohr Siebeck, 2020.

Fishbane, Michael. *Biblical Interpretation in Ancient Israel.* Oxford: Clarendon, 1985.

______. "The Well of Living Water: A Biblical Motif and Its Ancient Transformations." In *"Sha'arei Talmon": Studies in the Bible, Qumran, and the Ancient Near East Presented to Shemaryahu Talmon*, eds. Michael Fishbane and Emanuel Tov, 3–16. Winona Lake, IN: Eisenbrauns, 1992.

Floyd, Michael H. "New Form Criticism and Beyond: The Historicity of Prophetic Literature Revisited." In *The Book of the Twelve and the New Form Criticism*, eds. Mark J. Boda, Michael H. Floyd, and Colin M. Toffelmire, 17–36. Atlanta: SBL, 2015.

Frei, Hans. *The Eclipse of Biblical Narrative: A Study in Eighteenth and Nineteenth Century Hermeneutics.* New Haven, CT: Yale University Press, 1974.

Frohlich, James. *The Relationship between MT and LXX in Jeremiah 39(46):1–41(48):3 and 52.* Forschungen zum Alten Testament II 133. Tübingen: Mohr Siebeck, 2022.

Geiger, Abraham. *Urschrift und Uebersetzungen der Bibel in ihrer Abhängigkeit von der inner Entwickelung des Judenthums.* Breslau: Hainauer, 1857.

Ghormley, Justus Theodore. "Scribal Revision. A Post-Qumran Perspective on the Formation of Jeremiah." *Textus* 27 (2018): 161–86.

Goldingay, John. *The Theology of Jeremiah: The Book, the Man, the Message.* Downers Grove, IL: InterVarsity, 2021.

______. *The Book of Jeremiah.* New International Commentary on the Old Testament. Grand Rapids: Eerdmans, 2021.

Goren, Yuval, and Eran Arie, "The Authenticity of the Bullae of Berekhyahu Son of Neriyahu the Scribe." *Bulletin of the American Schools of Oriental Research* 372 (2014): 147–58.

Gottlieb, Leeor. "Repetition due to Detected Omission." *Textus* 27 (2018): 22–43.

Greenberg, Gillian. "Jeremiah in the Peshitta." In *The Book of Jeremiah: Composition, Reception, and Interpretation*, eds. Jack R. Lundbom, Craig A. Evans, and Bradford A. Anderson, 340–58. Leiden: Brill, 2018.

Grudem, Wayne. *Systematic Theology: An Introduction to Biblical Doctrine*. Grand Rapids: Zondervan, 1994.

Hayward, Robert. *The Targum of Jeremiah: Translation, with a Critical Introduction, Apparatus and Notes*. The Aramaic Bible 12. Collegeville, MN: Liturgical, 1990.

Hirsch, E. D., Jr. *Validity in Interpretation*. New Haven, CT: Yale University Press, 1967.

Holladay, William L. *Jeremiah 1: A Commentary on the Book of the Prophet Jeremiah Chapters 1–25*. Hermeneia. Philadelphia: Fortress, 1986.

______. *Jeremiah 2: A Commentary on the Book of the Prophet Jeremiah Chapters 26–52*. Hermeneia. Minneapolis: Fortress, 1989.

Holmstedt, Robert D. *The Relative Clause in Biblical Hebrew*. Linguistic Studies in Ancient West Semitic 10. Winona Lake, IN: Eisenbrauns, 2016.

Holmstedt, Robert D., and Andrew R. Jones. "The Pronoun in Tripartite Verbless Clauses in Biblical Hebrew: Resumption for Left-dislocation or Pronominal Copula?" *Journal of Semitic Studies* 59 (2014): 53–89.

Horbury, William. *Jewish Messianism and the Cult of Christ*. London: SCM, 1998.

Huffman, Herbert B. "The Rechabites in the Book of Jeremiah and Their Historical Roots in Israel." In *The Book of Jeremiah: Composition, Reception, and Interpretation*, eds. Jack R. Lundbom, Craig A. Evans, and Bradford A. Anderson, 191–210. Leiden: Brill, 2018.

Janzen, J. Gerald. *Studies in the Text of Jeremiah*. Harvard Semitic Monographs 6. Cambridge, MA: Harvard University Press, 1973.

Jastrow, Marcus. *A Dictionary of the Targumim, the Talmud Babli and Yerushalmi, and the Midrashic Literature*. 2nd ed. New York: Judaica, 1996.

Kaiser, Walter C., Jr. *Walking the Ancient Paths: A Commentary on Jeremiah*. Bellingham, WA: Lexham, 2019.

Keil, C. F. *The Prophecies of Jeremiah*. Translated by David Patrick and James Kennedy. Keil & Delitzsch Commentary on the Old Testament 8. Edinburgh: T&T Clark, 1866–1891. Reprint: Peabody, MA: Hendrickson, 2001.

Kessler, Martin, ed. *Reading the Book of Jeremiah: A Search for Coherence*. Winona Lake, IN: Eisenbrauns, 2004.

Koorevar, Hendrik J. "Chronicles as the Intended Conclusion to the Old Testament Canon." In *The Shape of the Writings*, eds. Julius Steinberg and Timothy J. Stone, 207–35. Siphrut: Literature and Theology of the Hebrew Scriptures 16. Winona Lake, IN: Eisenbrauns, 2015.

Kreuzer, Siegfried. *The Bible in Greek: Translation, Transmission, and Theology of the Septuagint*. Septuagint and Cognate Studies 63. Atlanta: SBL, 2015.

Kugel, James L. *The Idea of Biblical Poetry: Parallelism and Its History*. New Haven, CT: Yale University Press, 1981. Reprint, Baltimore: The Johns Hopkins University Press, 1998.

______. "Two Introductions to Midrash." In *Midrash and Literature*, ed. Geoffrey H. Hartman and Sanford Budick, 77–105. New Haven, CT: Yale University Press, 1986.

Kumaki, F. Kenro. "A New Look at Jer 4,19–22 and 10,19–21." *Annual of the Japanese Biblical Institute* 8 (1982): 113–22.

Kynes, Will. "Reading Job Following the Psalms." In *The Shape of the Writings*, eds. Julius Steinberg and Timothy J. Stone, 131–45. Siphrut: Literature and Theology of the Hebrew Scriptures 16. Winona Lake, IN: Eisenbrauns, 2015.

Lange, Armin. "The Book of Jeremiah in the Hebrew and Greek Texts of Ben Sira." In *Making the Biblical Text: Textual Studies in the Hebrew and Greek Bible*, ed. Innocent Himbaza, 118–61. Göttingen: Vandenhoeck & Ruprecht, 2015.

______. "Texts of Jeremiah in the Qumran Library." In *The Book of Jeremiah: Composition, Reception, and Interpretation*, eds. Jack R. Lundbom, Craig A. Evans, and Bradford A. Anderson, Supplements to Vetus Testamentum 178, 280–302. Leiden: Brill, 2018.

Lewis, C. S. *The Weight of Glory: And Other Addresses*. New York: HarperOne, 2000.

Lindbeck, George A. *The Nature of Doctrine: Religion and Theology in a Postliberal Age*. Philadelphia: Westminster, 1984.

Lindblom, Johannes. "Der Kessel in Jeremiah 1:13f." *Zeitschrift für die alttestamentliche Wissenschaft* 68 (1956): 223–24.

Longman, Tremper, III. *Proverbs*. Baker Commentary on the Old Testament. Grand Rapids: Baker, 2006.

Lundbom, J. R. "Baruch, Seraiah, and Expanded Colophons in the Book of Jeremiah." *Journal for the Study of the Old Testament* 36 (1986): 89–114.

______. *Jeremiah 1–20*. Anchor Bible 21A. New York: Doubleday, 1999.

______. *Jeremiah 21–36*. Anchor Bible 21B. New York: Doubleday, 2004.

______. *Jeremiah 37–52*. Anchor Bible 21C. New York: Doubleday, 2004.

Lyons, Michael A. *From Law to Prophecy: Ezekiel's Use of the Holiness Code*. Library of Hebrew Bible/Old Testament Studies 507. London: T. & T. Clark, 2009.

Martin, Gary D. *Multiple Originals: New Approaches to Hebrew Bible Textual Criticism*. Atlanta: SBL, 2010.

Mastnjak, Nathan. "Jeremiah as Collection: Scrolls, Sheets, and the Problem of Textual Arrangement." *Catholic Biblical Quarterly* 80 (2018): 25–44.

BIBLIOGRAPHY

McCarter, P. Kyle, Jr. *1 Samuel: A New Translation with Introduction and Commentary*. The Anchor Yale Bible 8. New Haven, CT: Yale University Press, 1980.

McKane, William. *A Critical and Exegetical Commentary on Jeremiah*. Vol. 1, *Introduction and Commentary on Jeremiah I–XXV*. International Critical Commentary. London: Bloomsbury T&T Clark, 1986.

______. *A Critical and Exegetical Commentary on Jeremiah*. Vol. 2, *Introduction and Commentary on Jeremiah XXVI–LII*. International Critical Commentary. London: Bloomsbury T&T Clark, 1996.

Miller-Naudé, Cynthia L. "Mismatches of Definiteness within Appositional Expressions Used as Vocatives in Biblical Hebrew." *Journal of Northwest Semitic Languages* 40, no. 2 (2014): 97–111.

Mizrahi, Noam. *Witnessing a Prophetic Text in the Making: The Literary, Textual, and Linguistic Development of Jeremiah 10:1–16*. Beihefte zur Zeitschrift für die alttestamentliche Wissenschaft 502. Berlin: de Gruyter, 2017.

Morrow, Amanda R., and John F. Quant. "Yet Another New Covenant: Jeremiah's Use of Deuteronomy and שוב שבות/שבית in the Book of Consolation." In *The Book of Jeremiah: Composition, Reception, and Interpretation*, eds. Jack R. Lundbom, Craig A. Evans, and Bradford A. Anderson, 170–90. Leiden: Brill, 2018.

Moshavi, Adina. *Word Order in the Biblical Hebrew Finite Clause: A Syntactic and Pragmatic Analysis of Preposing*. Linguistic Studies in Ancient West Semitic 4. Winona Lake, IN: Eisenbrauns, 2010.

Mowinckel, Sigmund. *Zur Komposition des Buches Jeremia*. Kristiana: Dybwad, 1914.

Muraoka, Takamitsu. *A Greek-English Lexicon of the Septuagint*. Leuven: Peeters, 2009.

Najman, Hindy, and Konrad Schmid, eds. *Jeremiah's Scriptures: Production, Reception, Interaction, and Transformation*. Supplements to the Journal for the Study of Judaism 173. Leiden: Brill, 2016.

BIBLIOGRAPHY

Neusner, Jacob. *The Babylonian Talmud: A Translation and Commentary*. Vol. 15, Tractate *Baba Batra*. Peabody, MA: Hendrickson, 2005.

______. *Jeremiah in Talmud and Midrash: A Source Book*. Studies in Judaism. Lanham, MD: University Press of America, 2006.

Niccacci, Alviero. *Syntax of the Verb in Classical Hebrew Prose*. Translated by W. G. E. Watson. Journal for the Study of the Old Testament: Supplement Series 86. Sheffield: JSOT, 1990.

Noonan, Benjamin J. "Abraham, Blessing, and the Nations." *Hebrew Studies* 51 (2010): 73–93.

Noth, Martin. *The Deuteronomistic History*. Journal for the Study of the Old Testament Supplement Series 15. Sheffield: JSOT, 1981.

O'Connor, Kathleen M. *The Confessions of Jeremiah: Their Interpretation and Role in Chapters 1–25*. Society of Biblical Literature Dissertation Series 94. Atlanta: Scholars, 1988.

Parke-Taylor, Geoffrey H. *The Formation of the Book of Jeremiah: Doublets and Recurring Phrases*. Atlanta: SBL, 2000.

Person, Raymond F., Jr., *The Kings-Isaiah and Kings-Jeremiah Recensions*. Beihefte zur Zeitschrift für die alttestamentliche Wissenschaft 252. Berlin: Walter de Gruyter, 1997.

Pietersma, Albert, and Benjamin G. Wright, eds. *A New English Translation of the Septuagint*. Oxford: Oxford University Press, 2007.

Pritchard, James B., ed. *Ancient Near Eastern Texts Relating to the Old Testament*. 3rd ed. Princeton, NJ: Princeton University Press, 1969.

Quarles, Charles. *Sermon on the Mount: Restoring Christ's Message to the Modern Church*. Nashville: B&H Academic, 2011.

Raabe, Paul. *Obadiah: A New Translation with Introduction and Commentary*. Anchor Bible 24D. New York: Doubleday, 1996.

______. "What Is Israel's God Up to Among the Nations? Jeremiah 46, 48, and 49." In *The Book of Jeremiah: Composition, Reception, and Interpretation*, eds. Jack R. Lundbom, Craig A. Evans, and Bradford A. Anderson, 230–52. Leiden: Brill, 2018.

Rendtorff, Rolf. *The Canonical Hebrew Bible: A Theology of the Old Testament*. Translated by David E. Orton. Leiden: Deo, 2005.

Rofé, Alexander. "The Arrangement of the Book of Jeremiah." *Zeitschrift für die alttestamentliche Wissenschaft* 101 (1989): 390–98.

______. "Not Exile but Annihilation for Zedekiah's People: The Purport of Jeremiah 52 in the Septuagint." Septuagint and Cognate Studies 41. Atlanta: SBL, 1995.

Rollston, Christopher A. *Writing and Literacy in the World of Ancient Israel: Epigraphic Evidence from the Iron Age*. Atlanta: SBL, 2010.

Rosenberg, A. J., trans. *Mikraoth Gedoloth: Jeremiah Volume One*. Brooklyn: Judaica, 1985.

______. *Mikraoth Gedoloth: Jeremiah Volume Two*. Brooklyn: Judaica, 1989.

Rudolph, Wilhelm. *Jeremia*. 3rd ed. Handbuch zum Alten Testament 1/12. Tübingen: Mohr Siebeck, 1968.

Sailhamer, John H. *The Pentateuch as Narrative: A Biblical-Theological Commentary*. Grand Rapids: Zondervan, 1992.

______. *Introduction to Old Testament Theology: A Canonical Approach*. Grand Rapids: Zondervan, 1995.

______. *Genesis Unbound*. Sisters, OR: Multnomah, 1996.

______. "Biblical Theology and the Composition of the Hebrew Bible." In *Biblical Theology: Retrospect and Prospect*, ed. Scott J. Hafemann, 25–37. Downers Grove, IL: InterVarsity, 2002.

______. *The Meaning of the Pentateuch: Revelation, Composition, and Interpretation*. Downers Grove, IL: InterVarsity, 2009.

Schenker, Adrian. *Das Neue am neuen Bund und das Alte am alten. Jer 31 in der hebräischen und griechischen Bibel*. Forschungen zur Religion und Literatur des Alten und Neuen Testaments 212. Göttingen: Vandenhoeck & Ruprecht, 2006.

Schultz, Richard L. *The Search for Quotation: Verbal Parallels in the Prophets*. Journal for the Study of the Old Testament Supplement Series 180. Sheffield: Sheffield Academic, 1999.

Schniedewind, William M. *How the Bible Became a Book: The Textualization of Ancient Israel*. Cambridge: Cambridge University Press, 2004.

Screnock, John. "A New Approach to Using the Old Greek in Hebrew Bible Textual Criticism." *Textus* 27 (2018): 229–57.

Seeligmann, Isac Leo. *The Septuagint Version of Isaiah and Cognate Studies*. Edited by Robert Hanhart and Hermann Spieckermann. Forschungen zum Alten Testament 40. Tübingen: Mohr Siebeck, 2004.

______. *Gesammelte Studien zur Hebräischen Bibel*. Forschungen zum Alten Testament 41. Tübingen: Mohr Siebeck, 2004.

Seitz, Christopher R. "The Prophet Moses and the Canonical Shape of Jeremiah." *Zeitschrift für die alttestamentliche Wissenschaft* 101 (1989): 3–27.

______. *The Goodly Fellowship of the Prophets: The Achievement of Association in Canon Formation*. Grand Rapids: Baker, 2009.

Sharp, Carolyn J. "'Take Another Scroll and Write': A Study of the LXX and the MT of Jeremiah's Oracles against Egypt and Babylon." *Vetus Testamentum* 47 (1997): 487–516.

Shead, Andrew G. "The Text of Jeremiah (MT and LXX)." In *The Book of Jeremiah: Composition, Reception, and Interpretation*, eds. Jack R. Lundbom, Craig A. Evans, and Bradford A. Anderson, Supplements to Vetus Testamentum 178, 255–79. Leiden: Brill, 2018.

Shepherd, Michael B. *The Verbal System of Biblical Aramaic: A Distributional Approach*. Studies in Biblical Literature 116. New York: Lang, 2008.

______. *Daniel in the Context of the Hebrew Bible*. Studies in Biblical Literature 123. New York: Lang, 2009.

______. "The Compound Subject in Biblical Hebrew." *Hebrew Studies* 52 (2011): 107–20.

______. "So-called Emphasis and the Lack Thereof in Biblical Hebrew." *Maarav* 19 (2012): 181–95.

______. *The Textual World of the Bible*. Studies in Biblical Literature 156. New York: Lang, 2013.

______. *The Text in the Middle*. Studies in Biblical Literature 162. New York: Lang, 2014.

______. *Textuality and the Bible*. Eugene, OR: Wipf & Stock, 2016.

______. "The New Exodus in the Composition of the Twelve." In *Text and Canon: Essays in Honor of John H. Sailhamer*, eds. Robert L. Cole and Paul J. Kissling, 120–36. Eugene, OR: Pickwick, 2017.

______. *A Commentary on the Book of the Twelve: The Minor Prophets*. Kregel Exegetical Library. Grand Rapids: Kregel Academic, 2018.

Smith, Mark S. *The Laments of Jeremiah and Their Contexts*. Society of Biblical Literature Monograph Series. Atlanta; Scholars, 1990.

Soderlund, Sven. *The Greek Text of Jeremiah: A Revised Hypothesis*. Sheffield: JSOT, 1985.

Sommer, Benjamin D. *A Prophet Reads Scripture: Allusion in Isaiah 40–66*. Stanford, CA: Stanford University Press, 1998.

Steck, Odil Hannes. *The Prophetic Books and Their Theological Witness*. Translated by James D. Nogalski. St. Louis: Chalice, 2000.

Steinberg, Julius, and Timothy J. Stone. "The Historical Formation of the Writings in Antiquity." In *The Shape of the Writings*, eds. Julius Steinberg and Timothy J. Stone, 1–58. Siphrut: Literature and Theology of the Hebrew Scriptures 16. Winona Lake, IN: Eisenbrauns, 2015.

Steiner, Richard C. "The Two Sons of Neriah and the Two Editions of Jeremiah in the Light of Two *Atbash* Code-Words for Babylon." *Vetus Testamentum* 46 (1996): 74–84.

Steins, Georg. "Torah-Binding and Canon Closure: On the Origin and Canonical Function of the Book of Chronicles." In *The Shape of the Writings*, eds. Julius Steinberg and Timothy J. Stone, 237–80. Siphrut: Literature and Theology of the Hebrew Scriptures 16. Winona Lake, IN: Eisenbrauns, 2015.

Stipp, Hermann-Josef. *Das masoretische und alexandrische Sondergut des Jeremiasbuches*. Orbis biblicus et orientalis 136. Fribourg: Universitätsverlag, 1994.

______. *Studien zum Jeremiabuch: Text und Redaktion*. Forschungen zum Alten Testament 96. Tübingen: Mohr Siebeck, 2015.

Stulman, Louis. *The Other Text of Jeremiah: A Reconstruction of the Hebrew Text Underlying the Greek Version of the Prose Sections of Jeremiah with English Translation*. Lanham, MD: University Press of America, 1986.

______. *Jeremiah*. Abingdon Old Testament Commentaries. Nashville: Abingdon, 2005.

Sweeney, Marvin A. *I & II Kings: A Commentary*. Old Testament Library. Louisville: Westminster John Knox, 2007.

Sze Wing So, Catherine. "Structure in the Confessions of Jeremiah." In *The Book of Jeremiah: Composition, Reception, and Interpretation*, eds. Jack R. Lundbom, Craig A. Evans, and Bradford A. Anderson, 126–48. Leiden: Brill, 2018.

BIBLIOGRAPHY

Talmon, Shemaryahu. *Text and Canon of the Hebrew Bible: Collected Studies*. Winona Lake, IN: Eisenbrauns, 2010.

Thackeray, Henry St. John. *A Grammar of the Old Testament in Greek According to the Septuagint*. Vol. 1, *Introduction, Orthography, and Accidence*. Cambridge: Cambridge University Press, 1909.

Thomas, D. Winton. "*ml'w* in Jeremiah 4:5: A Military Term." *Journal of Jewish Studies* 3 (1952): 47–52.

______. "*Ṣalmāwet* in the OT." *Journal of Semitic Studies* 7 (1962): 191–200.

Thompson, J. A. *The Book of Jeremiah*. New International Commentary on the Old Testament. Grand Rapids: Eerdmans, 1980.

Tigay, Jeffrey H. *The Evolution of the Gilgamesh Epic*. Philadelphia: University of Pennsylvania Press, 1982. Reprint, Wauconda, IL: Bolchazy-Carducci, 2002.

Toorn, Karel van der. *Scribal Culture and the Making of the Hebrew Bible*. Cambridge, MA: Harvard University Press, 2007.

Tov, Emanuel. "Exegetical Notes on the Hebrew *Vorlage* of the LXX of Jeremiah 27(34)." *Zeitschrift für die alttestamentliche Wissenschaft* 91 (1979): 73–93.

______. *The Greek and Hebrew Bible: Collected Essays on the Septuagint*. Atlanta: SBL, 2006.

______. *Textual Criticism of the Hebrew Bible*. 3rd ed. Minneapolis: Fortress, 2012.

______. "The Septuagint." In *Outside the Bible: Ancient Jewish Writings Related to Scripture*, eds. Louis H. Feldman, James L. Kugel, and Lawrence H. Schiffman, 1:1–6. Philadelphia: The Jewish Publication Society, 2013.

______. *The Text-Critical Use of the Septuagint in Biblical Research*. 3rd ed. Winona Lake, IN: Eisenbrauns, 2015.

Tsevat, Matitiahu. "Was Samuel a Nazirite?" In *"Sha'arei Talmon": Studies in the Bible, Qumran, and the Ancient Near East Presented to Shemaryahu Talmon*, eds. Michael Fishbane and Emanuel Tov, 199–204. Winona Lake, IN: Eisenbrauns, 1992.

Ulrich, Eugene. *The Dead Sea Scrolls and the Origins of the Bible*. Grand Rapids: Eerdmans, 1999.

______, ed. *The Biblical Qumran Scrolls: Transcriptions and Textual Variants*. Leiden: Brill, 2010.

Van der Merwe, Christo H. J., Jackie A. Naudé, and Jan H. Kroeze. *A Biblical Hebrew Reference Grammar*. Sheffield: Sheffield Academic, 1999.

van Selms, Adriaan. "Motivated Interrogative Sentences in Biblical Hebrew." *Semitics* 2 (1972): 143–49.

Van Seters, John. *The Edited Bible: The Curious History of the "Editor" in Biblical Criticism*. Winona Lake, IN: Eisenbrauns, 2006.

von Rad, Gerhard. *Old Testament Theology*. Vol. 1, *The Theology of Israel's Historical Traditions*. Translated by D. M. G. Stalker. San Francisco: HarperSanFrancisco, 1962. Reprint, Louisville: Westminster John Knox, 2001.

______. *Old Testament Theology*. Vol. 2, *The Theology of Israel's Prophetic Traditions*. Translated by D. M. G. Stalker. New York: Harper & Row, 1965.

Walser, Georg. *Jeremiah: A Commentary Based on Ieremias in Codex Vaticanus*. Leiden: Brill, 2012.

Waltke, Bruce K., and M. O'Connor. *An Introduction to Biblical Hebrew Syntax*. Winona Lake, IN: Eisenbrauns, 1990.

Wanke, Gunther. *Jeremia*. 2 vols. Zürcher Bibelkommentare: AT 20. Zurich: Theologischer Verlag, 1995.

Watts, J. W. "Text and Redaction in Jeremiah's Oracles against the Nations." *Catholic Biblical Quarterly* 54 (1992): 432–47.

Wenthe, Dean O., ed. *Jeremiah, Lamentations*. Ancient Christian Commentary on Scripture XII. Downers Grove, IL: InterVarsity, 2008.

Westermann, Claus. *Basic Forms of Prophetic Speech*. Translated by Hugh Clayton White. Philadelphia: Westminster, 1967. Reprint, Louisville: Westminster John Knox, 1991.

Wilson, Robert R. "An Interpretation of Ezekiel's Dumbness." *Vetus Testamentum* 22 (1972): 91–104.

Ziegler, Joseph, ed. *Jeremias, Baruch, Threni, Epistula Jeremiae*. 3rd. ed. Septuaginta XV. Göttingen: Vandenhoeck & Ruprecht, 2006.